CW00927579

DAVID LYNCH

Beautiful Dark

Greg Olson

Filmmakers, No. 126

THE SCARECROW PRESS, INC.
Lanham • Toronto • Plymouth, UK

Published by Scarecrow Press, Inc.
A wholly owned subsidiary of
The Rowman & Littlefield Publishing Group, Inc.
4501 Forbes Boulevard, Suite 200, Lanham, Maryland 20706
http://www.scarecrowpress.com

Estover Road, Plymouth PL6 7PY, United Kingdom

First paperback edition 2011

British Library Cataloguing in Publication Information Available

Library of Congress Cataloging-in-Publication Data

The hardback edition of this book was previously cataloged by the Library of Congress as follows:

Olson, Greg, 1945–
David Lynch : beautiful dark / Greg Olson.
p. cm. — (Filmmakers ; 126)
Includes bibliographical references and index.
eISBN-13: 978-0-8108-6371-2
1. Lynch, David, 1946– 2. Motion picture producers and directors—United States—Biography. I. Title.
PN1998.3.L96O47 2008
791.43023'3092—dc22
[B] 2008009141

ISBN 978-0-8108-8184-6 (pbk. : alk. paper)

∞™ The paper used in this publication meets the minimum requirements of American National Standard for Information Sciences—Permanence of Paper for Printed Library Materials, ANSI/NISO Z39.48-1992.

Printed in the United States of America

CONTENTS

Acknowledgments and Photograph Credits v

Introduction viii

Chapter 1: Fearfully and Wonderfully Made, 1946–1970 1
(*The Alphabet, The Grandmother*)

Chapter 2: Factory Child, 1970–1976 53
(*Eraserhead*)

Chapter 3: Burden of Flesh, 1976–1980 99
(*The Elephant Man*)

Chapter 4: Golden Sands, Heavy Heart, 1980–1984 143
(*Dune*)

Chapter 5: Night Town, 1984–1986 203
(*Blue Velvet*)

Chapter 6: Buzz Saw, 1986–1990 249
(*Twin Peaks, Season 1*)

Chapter 7: Burning Love, 1990 303
(*Wild at Heart*)

Chapter 8: Our Schoolgirl of the Sorrows, 1990–1992 341
(*Twin Peaks*, Season 2 and *Twin Peaks: Fire Walk With Me*)
Chapter 9: Head Like a House on Fire, 1992–1997 395
(*Lost Highway*)
Chapter 10: An Autumn Afternoon, 1997–2000 457
(*The Straight Story*)
Chapter 11: Road to Dreamsville, 2000–2001 515
(*Mulholland Drive*)
Chapter 12: Man of the World, 2001–2007 585
(*DavidLynch.com, INLAND EMPIRE*)
Notes 681
Bibliography 707
Index 715
About the Author 733

ACKNOWLEDGMENTS

For Launching the Project: Anna Cottle and Mary Alice Keir of Cine/Lit Representation, and Anthony Slide and Stephen Ryan of Scarecrow Press.

From Another Place (interviews and conversations): David Lynch, Catherine Coulson, Peggy Reavey, Gaye Pope, Mary Sweeney, Toby Keeler, Bushnell Keeler, Jennifer Lynch, Donald and Sunny Lynch, John Lynch, Martha Lynch Levacy, Austin Lynch, Mark Frost, Jack Fisk, Sissy Spacek, Julie Duvic, Jack Nance, Naomi Watts, Richard Green, Isabella Rossellini, Julee Cruise, Richard Beymer, Michael J. Anderson, Sheryll Lee, Ray Wise, Al Strobel, Moira Kelley, Charlotte Stewart, Don Davis, Grace Zabriskie, Frank Silva, Dana Ashbrook, Gary Bullock, Tina Rathborne, Barry Gifford, Russel Baker, Tad Friend, Peter Langs, Harry Knowles, Craig Miller, John Thorne, Brett Wood, Josh Eisenstadt, Susan and David Eisenstadt, John Mitchell, Adam Stevenson, Jay Aaseng, Eric Crary, Donna Dubain, Kelly and Jordan Chambers, Pat and Don Shook, Vicki Curnutt, Eric Thomas, Martha Nochimson, John Pierce, Paul M. Sammon, Bruce Phillips, Tim Rooney and Tandem Press, Paul Collum, Neil Edelstein, Mark Steensland, Eddie Muller, Trevor Fairbrother, William K. Everson, Thelma Schoonmaker, Brian Kursar, John Kirk and MGM, Paramount Pictures, New Line Cinema, Focus Features, and UCLA Film and Television Archive.

From the Neighborhood (Northwest help and conversations): Will Anderson, Sean Axmaker, Jan Baross, Charlotte Brame, Robert Cumbow, R. C. Dale, Tom Douglass, Janice Findley, Bill Foster, Michelle Gallagher,

Paul Hansen, Norm Hill, Robert Horton, Tore Hoven, Richard T. Jameson, Tom Keogh, Willis Konick, Karl Krogstad, George Latsios, Rebecca Latsios Soriano, Steve Les, Matt Marshall, Chris Mathews, Patrick Mathewes, Kathleen Murphy, Don Myrhe, Stephanie Ogle, Melinda Olson, Sue Purton, Jill Rullkoetter, Jeff Shannon, Kevin Shannon, Bob Suh, Mark Steiner, and Lea Thompson.

And Linda Bowers for insights, support, and sharing the adventure.

PHOTOGRAPH CREDITS

Cover photo courtesy of Richard Beymer

1. Author's collection
2. Courtesy of Toby Keeler and the Jack Fisk collection
3. Courtesy of the Josh Eisenstadt collection
4. Courtesy of Tandem Press
5. Courtesy of Peggy Reavey
6. Author's collection
7. Author's collection
8. Author's collection
9. Courtesy of Tim Curtis (Page xvi)
10. Courtesy of Peggy Reavey (Page 25)
11. Courtesy of Peggy Reavey (Page 28)
12. Courtesy of Tandem Press (Page 58)
13. Courtesy of Peggy Reavey (Page 224)
14. Courtesy of Catherine Coulson (Page 433)
15. Courtesy of Matt Marshall (Page 504)
16. Courtesy of Matt Marshall (Page 599)

One who, preferring light,
Prefers darkness also
Is in himself an image of the world
And, being an image of the world,
Is continuously, endlessly
The dwelling of creation.

Lao Tzu, *The Way of Life*

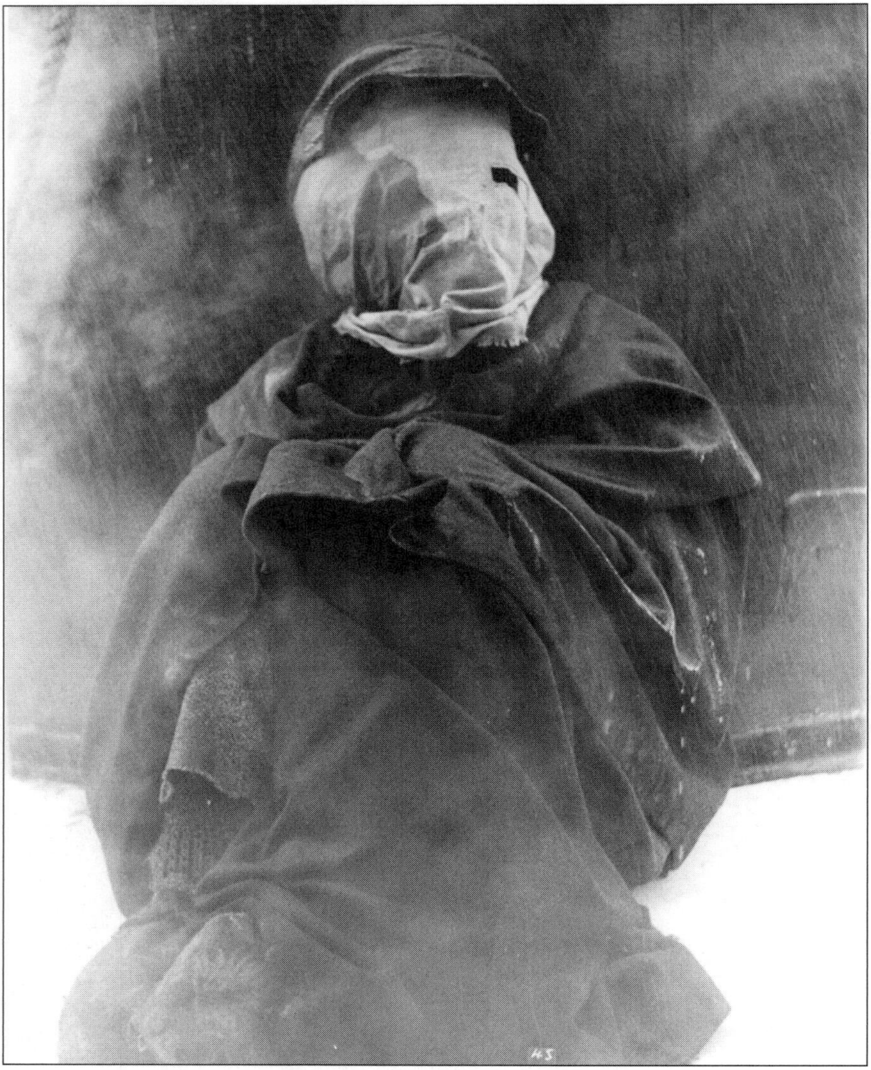

We'll go beneath the surface

To the source:

The man,

And his inner self.

We'll live the Hollywood life,

Meet monsters,

And angels,

And discover our strange world.

Light and dark, the house and the trees: the Lynch family's 1950s summer place.

I

FEARFULLY AND WONDERFULLY MADE

1946–1970
(*The Alphabet, The Grandmother*)

It's the early 1950s, in the woods outside of Idaho City, Idaho, where families of National Forest Service employees are vacationing in simple little white houses among the trees. The Curtises have invited the Lynches over for dinner, and as dusk begins to chill the air, the parents fire up the barbecue and sip cocktails, while nearby their children yell and cavort in the twilight. They play Red Rover and seven-year-old David Lynch, spotting the weakest link in the opposing line of kids, breaks through their defenses where a little girl stands.

Out of nowhere, a sound silences the buzz of the grown-ups' chitchat and the kids' playful taunts and shouts. Unlike Douglas fir trees in the western region of the Northwest, which grow close together and interweave their branches into a solid visual mass, the eastern Northwest's pines grow with airy spaces in between, so that you can see deep into the woods between their trunks. Parents and children, straining their eyes in the dim light, can make out nothing but the endless repetitions of dark vertical pine tree shapes. Yet there it is again—an eerie low moan that isn't all human or all animal. In the hushed, shivery air, David Lynch's mother, Sunny, nervously makes a joke: "I hope those are friendly sounds."[1]

A child of Big Sky Country, David Keith Lynch entered the world on January 20, 1946, in Missoula, the Garden City of Montana, which nestles between Mount Sentinel and Mount Jumbo. Aside from having twin peaks, Missoula possessed other characteristics that resonate with David Lynch's legend. The town grew up around a lumber mill, as have a number of the settlements in Lynch's fictions. And with its dusty streets, weathered two-story brick buildings, and rodeos, and with its site at the convergence of the Blackfoot and Bitterroot rivers and proximity to Rattlesnake Creek, the Deer Lodge and Pioneer mountains, grazing buffalo, and ghost towns, it evokes the Western American spirit Lynch loves. And as is common in Lynch's art works, the town had a double life, for beneath the surface streets was a netherworld of steam-heat tunnels, where Chinese laborers used to huddle on cold nights, and others, leading a secret life of drink, drugs, and worse, would lurk. Missoula was the perfect birthplace for Lynch, who sees the world as a flow of wonder and mystery, for the Salish Indian name for the city is "In-mis-sou-let-ka": "river of awe."[2]

His father, Donald Lynch, grew up on a Montana farm during the Great Depression, but financial hardship didn't hinder him from pursuing the life he wanted. Donald earned a master's degree in forestry at Duke and studied engineering at the Annapolis Naval Academy before being stationed as an officer on a South Pacific battleship during World War II. He was in Cuba with the Navy when the United States dropped the atom bombs on Japan, ending the war.

Western and Eastern America merged when Donald married Brooklyn-born Edwina (Sunny) Sundholm, who he met on a nature hike in North Carolina, and who also served in the Navy during the war. After the war, Donald returned to his roots in Montana, which he calls "the garden spot of the whole world."[3] He and Sunny settled in Missoula, where, as Donald says, they "eagerly got back into regular life and wanted to do the normal human things: build a home and raise children. Living a good, healthy, happy home life"[4] was important to Donald, but he also had a deep personal need to "advance my knowledge and ability, to do good work in the forest. I felt my life had a dual purpose."[5] While Donald was in the woods employing the scientific method to combat "insect problems, root rots, and contagious diseases, and striving to grow healthy trees,"[6] Sunny, who had a degree in English and foreign languages, was busy tutoring English and being a housewife.

Donald's research-scientist job kept the family—which, in addition to David, included his younger brother, John, and sister, Martha—moving around the lush, green Pacific Northwest landscape, from Sandpoint, Idaho, to Spokane, Washington, to Boise, Idaho. David attended elementary and junior high school in Boise and finished his high school career in Alexandria, Virginia.

Lynch's earliest memory is of himself and a friend sitting in a mud puddle, "kind of working the mud."[7] How appropriate a core self-image for an artist who today plunges into the messy stuff of life and shapes it to the contours of his unique vision. The adult Lynch is still moved by the elemental "idea of man and earth together."[8] As a boy growing up in the 1950s Northwest, Lynch and his native earth maintained an idyllic balance—with a twist. He calls his childhood "'Good Times On Our Street.' It was 'See Spot Run.' It was beautiful old houses, tree-lined streets, the milkman, building forts, lots and lots of friends. It was a dream world, those droning airplanes, blue skies, picket fences, green grass, cherry trees. Middle America as it was supposed to be. But then on the cherry tree would be this pitch oozing out, some of it black, some of it yellow, and there were millions and millions of red ants racing all over the sticky pitch, all over the tree. So you see, there's this beautiful world and you just look a little bit closer and it's all red ants."[9]

These few sentences conjure up the universe of Lynch's films. The sense of a dreamy, yet familiar world; the small-town landscape; the vivid, saturated hues of his cinematography; the droning sounds, usually of electricity and industry, that he melds with his images; the detailed, close-up fascination with textures. Most fundamental is the thrust of the wounded, ant-swarmed tree into a picture of an American paradise. A feeling of apprehensive alertness to an intriguing, yet threatening otherness within a realm of everyday safety. Even as a boy, Lynch had an extraordinary ability to sense the hum of malevolent, invisible energies at work in the world, a poetic gift he shared with two artistic giants he would someday idolize: Czechoslovakian writer Franz Kafka (1883–1924) and English painter Francis Bacon (1909–1992). French critic Gilles Deleuze speaks of Kafka and Bacon's ability to detect "the diabolic powers of the future knocking at the door."[10] Lynch, as well as the Diane Selwyn character he created for his film *Mulholland Drive* (2001), can also hear that monstrous pounding at the door.

The young Lynch was sensitive to the mysterious strangeness of life, and he lingered at the point where reality becomes surreal. When his father took him into the woods where Donald probed beneath tree bark for hidden pockets of disease, David saw sections of the living forest in which everything was labeled—and a furnished office among the trees, whose walls were covered with mounted and catalogued insects. In 1993, Lynch appeared on *The Tonight Show with Jay Leno*, sporting his typical black suit, white, top-buttoned shirt, and tall topknot of graying sandy hair. Projecting a wry, polite, laconic manner, he showed Leno his *Bee Board*, a collage from his current art exhibit. Lynch had mounted symmetrically spaced dead bees on a white background and attached little white nametags ("DON," "BING," "PHIL") below each one. Lynch's show-and-tell displayed the reflexive sequence-building tendency of a born director. Lynch had arranged for (1) Leno to show a close-up of the bees; (2) Bandleader Branford Marsalis to play "Flight of the Bumble Bees"; with the result that, (3) the audience laughed. More importantly, the linkage between the young Lynch's observance of labeled trees and insects and the bemused adult Lynch's *Bee Board* showed the creative interplay between his life experiences and what he calls his "Art Life."[11] In 1992, Lynch said that "a lot of my art work comes from memories of Boise, Idaho, and Spokane, Washington."[12]

Frightful sights also riveted the boy's attention and he learned that fearsome forces can invade a seemingly secure environment. At the age of six, Lynch saw Henry King's 1952 film *Wait 'Til the Sun Shines, Nellie* with his parents at a drive-in theater. "I remember this scene where a guy was machine-gunned while relaxing in a barber chair, and a scene where a little girl is playing with a button and suddenly her parents realize she's gotten it caught in her throat. I remember feeling a real sense of horror."[13] As a boy, Lynch "had a touch of that disease where you are afraid to go out of the house."[14] This fear, which he came to realize was agoraphobia (a panic that grips the sufferer when they venture outside self-defined "safe" precincts), persisted into adulthood. Speaking of a period when he consistently wore three neckties, he said, "That's the sign of a person who's very insecure and needs protection. I would have worn three coats if it wasn't so warm. I felt vulnerable, I had things I wanted to do outside, but I didn't like being out in the world. I liked being inside. There are many things to deal with outside the house; bad things can happen. Why bother with that? Why not stay inside and do your work?"[15]

Traveling with his parents from the "perfect world"[16] of his safe, sylvan home to his grandparents' house in Brooklyn "scared the hell"[17] out of him. "Going into the subway, I felt I was really going down into hell. As I went down the steps, going deeper into it, I realized it was almost as difficult to go back up and get out of it than to go through with this ride. It was the total fear of the unknown. I could feel this wind coming from the train down the tunnel. First the wind and then a smell and then a sound. I had lots of tiny tastes of horror every time I went to New York."[18]

Characteristically, Lynch, though apprehensive, went through with his subway ride and, years later, profited artistically from this intense, formative experience. For those spooky subway winds have become the soul-chilling, almost subliminal air currents that course through Lynch's filmscapes like the underworld's dark breath. As he matured, Lynch intuitively grasped the saving grace of transmuting his chaotic fears and unruly emotions into art: "the gift of feeling that you're in control, even if it's an illusion."[19] As he says,

"It's too frightening to really go certain places, so we can only go there in the movies."[20] Control is a key concept in Lynch's psychology. The process of his life organizes the chaotic fragments of existence into artistic forms, thus dealing with explosive, threatening actions and emotions in a manageable way. An abstract, invasive force of irrational, haphazard disorder is out beyond his carefully structured zone of safety, hungry to harm him and everything he loves. As he says, "the world outside, it's too random. I lose a bit of control thinking of the word 'outside.'"[21] In 2004, Jennifer Lynch, his daughter, adds that "he's afraid of things coming at him."[22] Because Lynch is so sensitive to the menace of uncontrollable randomness, he's able to portray it artistically with stunning, harrowing power, and the dynamic interplay between this threat and the haven of well-organized security drives his work. It's vitally important for Lynch to control his little portion of the world, the home base that generates his sacred creative ideas, so the worst thing this abstract force of randomness could do is to break in and control *him*, thus destroying the purity of his art. Lynch's house and head are well-guarded fortresses.

Lynch's youthful perception of the threatening big city did not formulate a simplistic "cities are bad, small towns are good" equation in his mind. Lynch feels that films should "obey certain rules, and one of the main ones is contrast,"[23]—for "when the contrast is great, the elements stand out."[24] His movies are driven by the charged, high-definition opposition of light and darkness, good and evil, innocence and knowledge, exhilaration and terror. But his sense of human complexity knows that beneath the surface of one side of a duality can flow symbiotic undercurrents of its opposite. In *Blue Velvet*, upright Jeffrey Beaumont can develop a taste for his loathsome nemesis Frank Booth's style of sadistic sexuality. Dr. Treves, savior of the monstrously deformed, sweet-souled *Elephant Man*, can fear that he is also that creature's exploiter. And *Wild at Heart's* Lula, feeling alienated from her good, loving Sailor, can have an against-her-will orgasm while being held in the assaultive grip of leering Bobby Peru. Reviewing his childhood homescape through bipolar glasses, Lynch said, "There is a goodness like those blue skies and flowers and stuff, but there is always a force, a sort of wild pain and decay, accompanying everything."[25]

In his art career, Lynch will give form to this malevolent force in paintings (*Shadow of a Twisted Hand Across My House*), photographs (the shadow of an unseen hand taints a lovely woman's face), films (a shadowy figure stains the window shade of a sunny suburban house; a dusky shape "who's causing all the fear" haunts Hollywood), and soundtracks (disturbing tones invade hypnotically beautiful melodies). As a boy, the world struck

Lynch as being a composition in primal Light and Darkness, and, like William Blake, he grew to become an artist who expresses his perceptions and intuitions of elemental energies through his own unique myth systems. It takes the powers of Hell *and* Heaven to make powerful, resonant art, and Lynch would certainly agree with Blake's declaration that "Fear and hope are—vision."[26]

Young Lynch may have sensed the presence of this dark, hidden force but he couldn't find any evidence of it under his own roof. He likens his memory of home life to archetypal 1950s advertising images: "a well-dressed woman bringing a pie out of an oven—with a certain smile on her face—or a couple smiling, walking together up to their house with a picket fence. Those smiles were pretty much all I saw."[27] He remembers, "My parents didn't drink. They didn't smoke, they never argued. And I wanted them to smoke, I wanted them to drink, I wanted them to argue, but they never did."[28]

Like many children of the 1950s, Lynch was raised in a church-going household. Donald Lynch was a Christian who believed that "God created the universe and all of us,"[29] and that even a lowly kangaroo rat was "part of God's world."[30] But he was also a scientist who knew that creation did not happen in a week. "He, or It, made everything through the process of evolution over a span of millions of years. You don't have to leave God out of the picture if you don't believe in instant creation."[31] David's family practiced the Presbyterian faith, which he calls "a perfect Northwest sort of religion,"[32] relating it in his mind to the 1950s and woodsy small towns. It's not surprising that a boy who sensed invisible forces in his backyard would be interested in spiritual matters, and as a youngster Lynch crafted striking *Crucifixion* and *Resurrection* pictures that hang in his parents' house to this day. As he entered adulthood, Lynch turned toward Asia and embraced Hindu beliefs and practices, but a number of films he has made since then exhibit Christian themes and motifs, and certain precepts of Presbyterianism are central to his artistic and personal worldview.

The concept of inspiration, a quickening surge of thought and feeling, is vital to Lynch, and as American theologian John S. Bonnell says, Presbyterians "believe in the 'inspiration' of the Scriptures: that God spoke through men whose minds and hearts He had touched. They therefore emphasize inspired men, not inspired words."[33] Presbyterians' conviction that "we are living in a moral universe where sin carries its own appropriate penalty and righteousness its own reward"[34] is in harmony with both Lynch's fictional universe and his adult belief in karmic justice. For Presbyterians, a vision of the Divine is the highest reward of virtuousness and, in Lynch's films, seemingly fallen souls are sometimes allowed to behold entities of heavenly grace. Lynch's artistic urge to make "abstractions"[35] of thought and feeling visible, and to expressionistically represent them in the material world, is congruent with the Presbyterian belief that, as Bonnell says, Heaven and Hell are "states of mind and character."[36]

Lynch's reflexive way of seeing the world in dualistic and moralistic terms was reinforced by Presbyterianism, which is based on the principles of Protestant reformer John Calvin (1509–1564), who believed humanity was divided into absolutist categories of good and evil, the righteous and the depraved, those worthy and unworthy of salvation. But Calvin, like Lynch, also had a subtler, paradoxical train of thought. As Oxford theologian and Calvin's biographer, Alister E. McGrath, says, "Calvin displays a pervasive tendency to distinguish radically between the human and the Divine realms—yet insists upon their union."

Calvin taught that, due to Adam and Eve's fall from Eden, "natural human gifts and faculties have been radically impaired,"[37] as McGrath says. This thought echoes in Lynch's fictional portrayal of special people having extrasensory visionary abilities. And Lynch, who certainly subscribes to Presbyterianism's emphasis on self-education and individual improvement, may feel he's metaphorically glimpsing Eden while meditating. Often unhappy in conventional schools, Lynch has been homeschooling himself at his own Institute of Ideas for decades.

Presbyterianism and Lynch were right on the same page in holding the individual as sacred, with inviolable rights and privileges. Bonnell adds, "The Presbyterian Church does not legislate for its people on personal moral issues."[38]

Like the patriotic Lynch's beloved America, the Presbyterian Church government was a representative democracy, and Presbyterians reflexively acted against forces of oppression, being seminal participants in the Revolutionary War and architects and signers of the United States Constitution. For young Lynch, Presbyterians made God and country inseparable—why even Dwight D. Eisenhower, the president of David's favorite decade, was practicing the Lynch family religion.

In spite of the comforting familiarity of Lynch's wholesomely "square" household, "I was ashamed of my parents for being the way they were. I longed for something out of the ordinary to happen in my life, something strange. I *knew* nothing was as it seemed, not anywhere, but I could never really find proof of it. It was just a feeling."[39]

As Lynch matured, his youthful yearning for something extraordinary to galvanize his life would be realized in his growing artistic ability to create strikingly personal worlds of unique form and substance. Rather than go through life like a passive movie watcher to whom "something happens," he would make every effort to become the show's director. In the meantime, the early teenaged Lynch fed his imagination and taste for the *beyond* at Boise's Vista Theatre, where he saw *The Fly* and *The Creature From the Black Lagoon*, and thrilled to a character's final admonishment in *The Thing* (from another world): "Keep watching the skies, we must keep watching the skies!" As an adult artist, Lynch, and his fictional characters, "long to see" other worlds beyond mundane reality, and in his film and TV stories many heads, in an attitude of mysterious anticipation, tip back to look upward.

Young David was proud to look up to the American flag. The cherished fact of being an American is a primal aspect of Lynch's self-image. When he accepted the 1990 Cannes Film Festival's highest honor, the Palme d'Or, for his flaming sex-and-violence road trip *Wild at Heart*, his biographical statement simply said: "Born in Missoula, Montana; Eagle Scout."[40] Lynch admires Ronald Reagan for being "a cowboy and a brush-clearer."[41] And in *Twin Peaks*, the character Lynch plays, FBI Chief Gordon Cole, and the character of the director's screen alter-ego, Special Agent Dale Cooper (Kyle MacLachlan), are bracingly patriotic and arrow-straight. Lynch isn't the first grown-up baby boomer to find himself championing attitudes and values that were uncool and irritating when his parents broadcasted them day and night around the house.

Today, Lynch's fondest memory of his father is of Donald Lynch donning his Forest Service suit and big ten-gallon cowboy hat and walking several miles to work across Alexandria's George Washington Bridge after the family's move from Idaho to Virginia. But young David was deeply embarrassed by this public spectacle ("He wouldn't go in a car or a bus").[42] To Lynch, it made no difference if his father stuck out like a sore thumb one minute or, with his mother, was "too conventional"[43] the next: The teenager had started to rebel "against those near and dear"[44] before they left Boise. But it was defiance devoid of confrontational histrionics. Lynch, who's known as a peacemaker among his friends and collaborators, will only say that he started doing "many things that I figured my parents would not enjoy knowing about."[45] Aiming his angst out into the world, Lynch began his adolescent process of independent self-definition by "getting into a few dangerous things that I don't talk about."[46] One of those dangers, however, is recorded on the Boise police blotter.

Lynch started playing with fire, despite having witnessed a horrific cautionary incident. One day, one of Lynch's young friends was using a metal rod to pack match heads into the shaft of a homemade rocket. As Lynch and the boy's pregnant mother watched, "the rocket went off, and these match heads had such a force that they drove the rocket right through his ankle and it blew fire and burnt match heads all over the porch. He fell down because he couldn't stand up. His foot was almost severed from his ankle, and he was in a pool of blood with dim little burned match heads and smoke all around. When his mother saw that, she almost lost the baby. But they took my friend to the hospital and sewed his foot back on, and he was OK after that."[47] Lynch and his friends kept advancing into the realm of deadly hazard. They started making pipe bombs that would explode "about eye level with such a force that the pipe would turn completely inside out, and shrapnel would fly."[48] In order to contain the blast of "a big bomb,"[49] they tossed it into the South Lake Junior High swimming pool one Saturday morning. The explosion shook houses for blocks, Lynch was arrested, and the incident was splashed across the Idaho and Salt Lake City newspapers.

Lynch stopped building literal bombs as his explosive creative fires found more potent and far-reaching expression in his Art Life, which would launch him to world-renowned status as a popular culture icon. He had been drawing "since I was very small."[50] And, though he may have been deeply frustrated by his parents' unwavering normalcy, he gives them much credit for encouraging his talents. "They were very supportive of my early art interest. My mother probably saved me: she refused to give me coloring books. Which is pretty interesting, because there was lots of school pressure to color—and once you have that coloring book the whole idea is to stay between the lines. So I didn't have the restriction of the lines. My imagination was never ruined, never limited by preconception. I could just go free. And my father would bring home paper that was blank on one side, so I was able to draw whatever I wanted all the time."[51]

Donald Lynch recalls that "David drew lots of airplanes and pistols and machine guns—I don't know why."[52] Lynch's adult art concerns the shifting balance of power between people, and senses the flow and accumulation of forces within objects and atmospheres. Planes and pistols vibrate with latent and active energy, and both will adorn Lynch's mature paintings, films, and a stage performance piece, often as agents of death. Donald also remembers that his son was not the sort of creator who eschews the commercial potential of art-making, for young David used colored felt-tip markers to draw the extreme facial expressions of wild and crazy *Mad* magazine characters on white sweat shirts, then sold each one for five big 1950s dollars.

Childhood drawing and dreaming is one thing, but the only Boise adults Lynch saw applying color with a brush for a living were house painters. It took having his girlfriend stolen to expand his artistic horizon. Lynch believes in fate, the way that events can coalesce in the time stream, forming a meaningful pathway into the future. After the Lynches moved to Alexandria, Virginia, fifteen-year-old David was standing with his girl, Linda Styles, in her snowy front yard when same-aged, tow-headed Toby Keeler sauntered up, became Lynch's fast friend, and stole Linda's heart. Still, knowing Toby brought David a priceless treasure: the certainty of what he was going to do for the rest of his life. One day, after school, Toby took Lynch to meet his father. For Lynch, stepping into the studio of professional artist Bushnell Keeler "thrilled my soul."[53] This event "completely changed my life,"[54] for David realized that he too could devote himself to art. Keeler (b. 1925) was one of those rare American men who followed a nonconformist path after World War II. An economics graduate from Dartmouth, he "got my ass way up the ladder too soon"[55] and dropped out of a management-level position at a big Cleveland bearing-manufacturing plant when "I thought I had the call to become an Episcopalian minister."[56] Keeler realized that seminary studies were not for him when an intuitive "little lightbulb went off"[57] and he decided to "go into art,"[58] a pursuit he had loved as a teenager. In his mid-thirties, Keeler sampled both the world of commercial art and illustration and the fine arts courses at Virginia's American University. The university's philosophical approach of relating the acts of seeing, feeling, and painting to the primal nature of being, the fundamental first principles of existence, excited Keeler's spiritual self and he emerged from his schooling as a full-time painter with his own studio and gallery. Keeler's almost religious zeal for the poetics of art-making was reinforced by Robert Henri's book *The Art Spirit*. And, in turn, when Lynch met Keeler, he was inspired by "the miracle"[59] of the man's lifestyle and the book that the painter urged him to read.

Henri (1865–1929) was a leader of New York's Ash Can School of urban realist painters and was a beloved art teacher and philosopher. *The Art Spirit* proclaimed his deepest convictions and the book became Lynch's "bible."[60] Lynch has said that a stimulating, metaphorical "jolt of electricity"[61] is good for the mind. We can imagine the high voltage that surged through his cranium when he read words that validated his dreamy childhood sense of mysteries hidden beneath the surfaces of life, and which today crystallize his credo. "There is an undercurrent, the real life, beneath all appearances everywhere. I do not say that any master has fully comprehended it at anytime, but the value of his work is that he has sensed it and his work reports the measure of his experience."[62]

Henri admonished artists to retain a child's innocent eye and sense of wonder at the world, and today Lynch, now in his sixties, still says, "I feel like I'm between six and seventeen."[63] Like an awestruck child, pondering a world in which not all forces and feelings have names yet, Lynch conveys the humming charge of power barely contained within the shapes of people and things. *Blue Velvet*'s almost supernatural first image, looking up at red flowers, white picket fence, and blue sky is, in Lynch's eye, "a kid's view."[64] The characters in his films, like adults looming over a child, spew out volcanic emotions in a visual vocabulary of intensified gestures and facial expressions. One of Lynch's 1988 canvases, peopled with a rudimentary stick figure a child might paint and title, is called *Oww, God, Mom, the Dog He Bited Me.* Henri's reference to the inability of any single artist to fully comprehend the universe's mysteries is central to Lynch's vision. Truth-seekers pursuing secrets keep Lynch's world spinning. His actual and metaphorical detectives read clues and make connections, but they are never able to expose all of the universe's dark hiding places to the harsh, reasoned light of absolute comprehension. And Lynch's sense of aesthetic and metaphysical proportion shapes his creative process: He likes to "float into strange intuitions and inspirations"[65] that he cannot explain to himself, nor to his audience.

Nor to his parents. Lynch's teenage "rebellion"[66] sharpened its obsessive focus: "I just didn't want anything to do with anything except painting, and living the Art Life."[67] In *The Art Spirit*, Robert Henri encouraged the artist to seek a state of consciousness in which he has "a grip on the fundamentals of nature, the spirit of life, the constructive force, the secret of growth, an understanding of the relative importance of things, order, balance."[68] This mandate set Lynch on a straightforward path: "The art comes first. In the Art Life, you don't get married and you don't have families. You have studios and models, and you drink a lot of coffee and you smoke cigarettes and you work mostly at night. Your place smells like oil paint, and you think beneath the surface of things and you live a fantastic life of ideas. And create stuff."[69] Lynch's inclusion of smoking in his creed was a palpable stroke of differentiation from his nicotine-spurning parents. (Lynch stopped smoking for many years, but took it up again as a mature adult, a fact that he confessed to his parents in a letter; these days family members assume he wears a nicotine patch when he attends Lynch family gatherings). Inhaling cigarette smoke and puffing it out was a gesture of behavioral and spiritual kinship with the family maverick, Grandfather Austin Lynch.

Along with Bushnell Keeler and Robert Henri, Lynch's paternal grandfather was one of the grown-ups that the youth wanted to be like. "He was a tremendous influence. I thought he was one of the coolest guys. He always drove these big black cars and he'd wear these thin leather driving gloves, and real, real good suits and engraved cowboy boots. He was fantastic."[70] As an adult, Lynch brought his detailed sensitivity to his grandfather's sartorial image to the careful creation of his own generic look. He typically wears a simply tailored black suit and a white shirt with the collar buttoned up ("I feel protective of my sternum"),[71] sometimes accompanied by a black tie. This black-and-white uniform so bespeaks Lynch that he has clothed his cinematic alter-egos in it for decades. Also, Grandfather Lynch's love of cars lives on in David, who casts vehicles in his films as precisely as he does actors. In *Twin Peaks*, Laura Palmer's outwardly wholesome, yet evil-possessed, incest-committing, child-murdering father, Leland, drives a dark convertible (two forms in one) whose Washington State license plate screams EAK. Driving around at night later than his parents wanted him to was one way Lynch expressed his youthful sense of independence, and when his freedom flights were threatened with grounding, he kept their duration secret. His parents went to bed early, so Lynch mastered the art of turning off the family car's motor as he approached home and silently coasting into the garage, then slowly turning all of the doorknobs he encountered inside the sleeping house, and softly creeping into his bed.

In the 1950s and early 1960s, America's homogenized self-image started to split into squares and hipsters. Squares were conforming upholders of the traditional status quo. Cleanliness, Judeo-Christian godliness, law and order, marriage-sanctioned sexuality, tame music, and station wagons were cardinal virtues. Hipsters questioned everything that squares solemnly stood for, opening themselves to idiosyncratic promptings of desire and soul-quest. They embraced earthiness, follow-your-bliss pantheism, situational ethics, sexual experimentation, the wild "jungle music" of jazz and rock and roll, and racy cars. Along with most children of America's postwar baby boom, David Lynch was a mixture of hip and square. Like a character in the 1950s family-values TV show *Father Knows Best*, he cheerfully ran for high school treasurer ("Save With Dave"),[72] and cheerfully lost. He and his sweetheart, photographed on a bicycle-built-for-two, were chosen his class's "Cutest Couple."[73] And, just like Jimmy Stewart in *It's a Wonderful Life*, he worked behind the soda fountain counter at the corner drugstore. But winds that would steer Lynch away from the mainstream were stirring, and Grandfather Lynch was one cool breeze. The article accompanying Lynch's October 1, 1990, *Time* magazine cover appearance finishes with the director enthusing over rejuvenation techniques that could someday make it possible for a "ninety-five-year-old mind"[74] to enjoy a body reconditioned to twenty-five-year-old spryness. With a seeming nod of affection to his unconventional forefather, Lynch concludes: "Granddad would start breaking into liquor stores and staying out late."[75]

Elvis Presley was a powerhouse of raw sexual energy who shivered and shook the teenaged Lynch's generation and American culture at large. The church-going Tupelo truck driver who became the king of rock and roll was the perfect amalgamation of hip and square. A devotee of both heavenly gospel music and down-and-dirty blues tunes, the sneering singer with the anarchic, thrusting pelvis was the same kid who worshipped his mother and responded to interviewers with a polite, soft-spoken humility. Along with 1950s sci-fi monsters, young Lynch watched Elvis on the silver screen. He loved Elvis's performing persona and music and would incorporate both into his cinematic reshaping (1990) of Barry Gifford's novel *Wild at Heart*. Lynch's most potent screen evildoers, with their violent, insatiable hungers of body and soul, are perfect personifications of Elvis's lyrics: "If you're looking for trouble, just look right in my face."[76]

As a teenager, Lynch had a hard time getting his parents to understand and sympathize with his immersion in the Art Life. Lynch habitually describes his youthful home life in rosy terms and speaks of his parents being "supportive"[77] of his artistic endeavors. But Bushnell Keeler remembers Lynch as "a young fellow with a battle going on inside him"[78] because of family tension over his art-making obsession. Lynch's home was, as he would as an adult say of households in his fictions, "a place where things can go wrong."[79]

While still in high school, Lynch was already spending some time away from the family hearth, painting in the room he and his same-age friend and fellow artist Jack Fisk rented from Bushnell Keeler, but relations in the Lynch house became so strained that David asked if he could move in with the Keelers for a while. He ended up staying for most of the school year.

Keeler recalls that "David didn't want to be with his family, because they were upset with him. They felt that art was something you do after you get your work done, and David's first order of business should be to do well in school. They thought he just wasn't producing at the academic level he ought to be. David was getting Cs on his report card, and he was having to compete against his extremely brilliant brother and sister."[80] His parents' dissatisfaction with his school performance only served to energize Lynch's desire to devote himself to painting, so he moved into the Keelers' home.

The elder artist immediately became aware of how much stress Lynch was feeling, for "every morning, as soon as David would wake up, he'd get sick."[81] Keeler decided he should talk to Lynch's father about the situation, so he and Donald met. David had told Keeler about his father living for two years in an Oregon Forest Service observation tower and "letting his beard grow down to his knees."[82] So Keeler reminded Donald of this wild-bearded mountain-man period of his life and averred that, just as with David, "there was something in him that was rather nonconformist."[83] Donald, who retired early (in 1975) from the "the rat race of bureaucratic administration,"[84] smiled and nodded, and listened to Bushnell Keeler make his case "as nicely as I could."[85] Keeler told David's father that "Your son is trying to maintain a vocation as a painter, and at the same time meet the standards laid down by the high school, and he *is* meeting them, he's doing his obligation there. At the same time, he's doubling in brass in terms of being a *real* painter, not a dilettante. He's trying to carry two vocations, and you're not helping him. He's got more talent in his little finger than I'll ever have, and he needs encouragement, not discouragement."[86] Donald silently absorbed what Keeler had told him, thanked him for speaking his mind, and, according to Keeler, "seemed to feel better after our conversation."[87] Donald remembers that as they parted, Keeler asked him, "if it was okay for David to take part in drawing sessions which included nude models. What could I say but yes?"[88] Thirty-four years later, David Lynch made a TV commercial for the Honda CR-V sport utility vehicle that shows a corporate man in a business suit transforming into a woodsman-costumed fellow with a supernaturally fast-growing beard after he gazes at the adventurous CR-V in a showroom window, clearly a loving homage to his father's independent spirit and bearded-frontiersman days.

Lynch credits his father with instilling in him the methodical work habits that have furthered his career and provided a soothing psychological refuge from emotional pain and a sometimes fearsome outside world. "My father taught me that if you want to do something, first you sit down and make a plan. Then you pull together the materials and tools you'll need, and go to work. This process applies to anything you want to do."[89] Like his father, Lynch became a woodworker at a young age, and once, to aggravate his mother, he drew up plans for a "Bird-Killing Machine."[90]

Over the years, Donald and Sunny Lynch clearly came to terms with their son's dedication to art, and they proudly displayed a range of his paintings, drawings, and prints in their suburban ranch house that's a five-freeway drive east of Los Angeles. The teenage Lynch's flair for realistic, representational work is evident in a carefully shaded graphite drawing of a New England wharf and sailboat, his easily readable signature merging with a sketched paintbrush and palette in a touching youthful declaration of his self-image as an artist. The Eagle Scout proclaims his love of America in a small rendering of the Washington, D.C. Capitol dome that appears to be skillfully composed of a single black ink line that intricately scrambles and tangles itself to form the familiar breastlike dome shape. Another Washington monument is the *Friendship Fire Department Founded in 1774 by George Washington*, which Lynch renders as a spatially flat, black-and-white structure with small, washed touches of mauve and blue. A building that houses men who battle chaotic flames should be a comforting place, and the worlds "Friendship" and "George Washington" are reassuring. But Lynch gives the image an eerie, haunted air, as though the malevolent forces he sensed but couldn't see in his own neighborhood lurked in the firehouse's dark abysslike windows and the twisted black, barren trees that will appear in artworks to come over the years.

As he matured, Lynch embraced eastern religious philosophies and practices, but he was raised in a Christian household (there was a copy of *The Living Bible* on a family room table when I visited his parents) and as a young artist he did a striking interpretation of the *Crucifixion* and the *Resurrection*, each in moderated shadings of black, white, and gray, and segmented in a tripartite icon-like fashion. These two works, which hang prominently in Donald and Sunny's living room, show Lynch's gift for abstraction, as he presents the archetypical images of Christ on the cross and rising from the cave of the dead as an organic melding of transforming flesh and spirit that feels like it's in motion—no wonder he made the natural next step to animate his drawings. *Crucifixion* and *Resurrection* also introduce motifs that will grace many future Lynch works: parting stage curtains, luminous spirit-light, a lone, simple peak-roofed house form, and star fields. Lynch's fascination for that unadorned house form may have originated on the plains of eastern Montana, for to the left of Donald and Sunny's star-motif quilt-covered bed hangs David's graphite drawing of the ranch house where his father grew up (yes, there are twin mountain peaks in the far horizon, and a welcoming, stairway-to-heaven sky occupies more than half of the image). Hanging beneath this picture of his father's origins is a companion drawing of the Brooklyn rowhouse street where Sunny was raised, and which was the Lynch family's destination when young David had his urban-fright, down-into-the-dark-subway-tunnel panic experience. Both of these parent-honoring drawings are superbly detailed: They look like slightly softened photo-realist works, and you expect the fulsome trees—blurred as though in motion and arching over the parked Model A Fords on Edwina's New York street—to gently sway and sigh as they will in *Blue Velvet*, *Twin Peaks*, and *The Straight Story*. The tangible tracings of love between two parents and their son that adorn Donald and Sunny's home (David signed some of the works as birthday and Christmas presents) culminate in a black-and-white photograph of mature film director David Lynch sitting with a big 35mm movie camera and grinning like he did as a five-year-old towhead. On the photo, Lynch has written in large letters, "To the Best Mom and Dad in the World." Lynch, who in the public world cares passionately about every small detail of the way his work is presented, loves his parents so much that he lets them hang a relatively recent $4,000 abstract painting *upside down* over their living room sofa because "that's the way we like it."[91]

Ninety-five percent of Lynch's early artwork hanging in his parents' house is monochromatic or a subdued shade of blue. Only one piece screams with vibrant color: a self-portrait of an unsmiling young man looking straight at us, sporting Beatle-style hair covering his forehead and wearing a top-buttoned shirt and suit coat. For decades, the world has known Lynch to present himself in clothing shades of black, white, and khaki. However, in a family photo, the teenaged Lynch sports a lilac-pink shirt, and his portrait shows him in a red shirt, canary-yellow sweater vest, and a peacock blue-green jacket, and behind him, a bright orange color field. The contrast in Lynch's early artwork between a dark palette and a light-splashed one reflects his lifelong sense that the realms of phenomena and emotions balance shadowy and radiant elements and forces, but his color-burst of a self-image may have an art historical motivation. Three of the fundamental hues of his self-portrait (red, orange, blue-green) are the primary color areas of Vincent Van Gogh's self-portrait from 1889, one year before the agonized artistic genius shot himself to death. In Van Gogh's picture there's a white bandage over the left side of his face, covering the wound where he razored off his lower ear in a rage of self-loathing. In Lynch's portrait, his right ear is prominent, but his left one, hidden by his longish hair, doesn't seem to be there. In Lynch's film *Blue Velvet*, a character's left ear is cut off by a mentally anguished man, himself a kind of tortured artist, who verbally refers to Van Gogh. Lynch the young art student and self-portraitist was certainly aware of Van Gogh's body of work, and says he was influenced by the work of others before he "got my own original thoughts."[92] Given the preoccupations of Lynch's later career, it's natural that as a young artist he would respond to Van Gogh's agitated, emotion-wracked visual language, and empathize with the Dutch master's mystical fire of ferocious creativity, his sorrowful yearning to share his soul with his fellow human beings.

Keeler was amazed at David's dedication to his artistic calling. "I never knew a kid that age who was so productive. He had creativity coming out of his ears, and he was willing to sacrifice everything for the opportunity to paint. I had a rule in the studio he rented from me: No partying. I knew he would never break it, and he never did."[93]

While the serious-minded Lynch was digging deep into the essentials of art and life, his friend Toby Keeler was "busy being a teenager"[94] and recalls that "there was always a tension"[95] between David's need to be both a solitary and social being. "When he was painting and thinking he didn't want someone hanging around trying to talk to him."[96] Still, Lynch took time to be a member of the high school fraternity Alpha Omega Upsilon with Toby, and loved the fact that he and his brothers used a secret motto and handshake. (Perhaps the fraternity's shrouded signs and signals combined with the do-gooder ethos of Lynch's Boy Scout career to spawn *Twin Peaks'* clandestine all-male Book House Boys group.) Wearing a typical college boy's button-down Oxford shirt and tweed jacket, David would accompany Toby to a nightclub in the Georgetown district of Washington, D.C., that bore the evocative Lynchian name of The Shadows. In the dim, smoky light, the two friends would sip beer and enjoy such fledgling mainstream acts as Bill Cosby and The Mugwumps (soon to become The Mamas and The Papas), and one night they watched with members of The Kingston Trio as David and Toby's pals, the folk music duo Ron and Buzz, won a chance to meet the Beatles.

Toby recalls that Lynch, along with Jack Fisk, also gravitated toward the cooler edges of fringe culture, where the Beat poets and artists and progressive jazz grooved. (A wild surge of Beat dancing and music vivifies an unbroadcast episode of Lynch's TV series *On the Air*, and his early 1960s love of the Dave Brubeck Quartet's *Take Five* manifests itself on the soundtrack of his *Mulholland Drive* pilot episode [2000–2001] and on his phone answering machine.) Keeler notes that Lynch, "who can flutter his hands at a phenomenal rate of speed,"[97] became an accomplished player of the beatnik's instrument of choice, the bongo drums. Lynch's smoking drum rhythms, which echoed off the walls of staid suburban living rooms at high school parties, earned him the esteemed nickname of Bongo Dave.

The hipster who produced the far-out bongo sounds also swore allegiance to God and country as a member of the Boy Scouts, earning the highest rank of Eagle Scout, which only 1 percent of members attain. On his fourteenth birthday, January 20, 1961, he got a major patriotic thrill when, resplendent in his Eagle Scout uniform, Lynch had the honor of helping seat dignitaries at John F. Kennedy's inauguration at the White House, and in the space of a few seconds saw Kennedy, Dwight Eisenhower, Lyndon Johnson, and Richard Nixon pass within touching distance.

Like everyone else in the country, Lynch was devastated when Kennedy was assassinated on November 23, 1963, and recalls that his Catholic girlfriend, Judy Westerman, was so grief-stricken that she stayed in her darkened bedroom for four days. Lynch coped by immersing himself in painting, but Toby Keeler came by and suggested that they go and pay their respects to the fallen president by viewing his body, which was lying in state in the Capitol rotunda. Promising Donald Lynch that he'd return the family car by an appointed hour, David steered the nondescript 1958 Chevrolet through the virtually empty streets of Alexandria, picked up Toby and some beer, and headed for D.C. The car looked like a sleepy family sedan but, as is often the case in Lynchland, a surging hidden power throbbed beneath its sedate exterior, for Donald had selected the big V-8 engine. Toby says David loved to shock other drivers by mashing his foot to the floor and leaving them behind in a cloud of tire smoke.

Once they got to D.C., they had a hard time finding a parking place, and were amazed to see that the ten-abreast line of people waiting to view Kennedy seemed to stretch on and on forever. David and Toby had thought that the whole process would take a couple of hours at most, but they ended up standing in line all night and never even got near the inner rotunda. David had promised his father to get the car back on time so, good Scout that he was, he and Toby relinquished their place in line and, frustrated and sad, headed back home. It had gotten cold during the night, and someone had given the two young men a blanket each, which they wore American Indian style, draped over their shoulders and hanging down to the ground. Before they had abandoned their vigil, an elderly woman had asked them, "Are you two brothers?"[98] Lynch had grinned and said, "We're in the same tribe."[99]

While still in high school, Lynch and his art-minded buddy, Jack Fisk, started staying up late painting in their Georgetown studio. Artists and scientists often share a free-thinking, imaginative, methodical mindset, and Donald Lynch thought enough of his son's venture to help pay the rent on his studio, which had recently been vacated by the California-bound Bushnell Keeler. David visited museums and galleries in Washington and New York and, at age eighteen, was struck by the paintings of British artist Francis Bacon. Many aspects of Bacon's work would come to inform Lynch's own aesthetic. Lynch noticed the intense sense of presence that emanated from Bacon's images of mundane objects like cigarettes and butcher's meat. He admired the textural thickness and beauty of the paint and Bacon's asymmetrical balancing of strongly contrasting elements. Bacon's canvasses emitted an alluring, ominous atmosphere that would also blanket the world of Lynch's art. There were figures with unspecified physical and psychic wounds, quivering with the doubled violence of victim and perpetrator. Naturalistic settings in which bodies distort in a flux of smeared faces slipping into atavistic contours, the human becoming nonhuman. People projected a dual aspect, coming face-to-face with their own ghosts. Earlier in the twentieth century, French Surrealist pioneer Andre Breton spoke for both Bacon and Lynch when he declared that "Beauty will be convulsive, or not at all."[100]

Bacon, as Lynch will come to do with film, established a one-to-one congruity between his nervous system, subconscious, and the paint he was applying to canvas. Both men speak of gleaning images from "waking dreams"[101] and of seeking to bypass logic and speech in communicating with their viewers. Lynch's films are alive with ebbs and flows of emotion, which the viewer can comprehend through what Lynch calls "inner knowing."[102] Furthermore, Bacon says the artist should "unlock the valves of feeling and therefore return the onlooker to life."[103]

The Surrealists, Bacon, and Lynch transport us to the realm of the sublime, as described by English writer Edmund Burke (1729–1797): "Whatever excites pain and danger, whatever is in any sort terrible, or is conversant about terrible objects, or operates in a manner analogous to terror is a source of the Sublime; it is productive of the strongest emotions which the mind is capable of feeling."[104] And the aesthetic qualities that arouse the sublime are attributes that will characterize decades of Lynch's artistic expressions: "terror, obscurity, power, vastness, infinity, difficulty, magnificence, and darkness."[105] Always, for Lynch, darkness.

After graduating from Hammond High School, Alexandria, Virginia, in 1964, Lynch attended the Corcoran School of Art in Washington, D.C., and the Boston Museum School. One day, back in Alexandria, Bushnell Keeler, who knew Lynch was happily studying art and painting all day long up in Boston, answered the doorbell and found the young man standing on his doorstep. As Lynch sipped a mug of Keeler's industrial-strength coffee he declared, "I'm through with that damned school,"[106] and recounted a tale of woe that Keeler (speaking in 2004) feels illustrates "an endearing side of David that worked to his detriment then, but now may be one of his greatest assets."[107]

At the Boston Museum School, Lynch had a sculpture instructor who, as Keeler says, "took to him right away and became his mentor."[108] The teacher was in the process of getting divorced from his wife and he asked if he and his girlfriend could use David's off-campus sleeping room for a rendezvous some time. The "way too accommodating"[109] young man said "Sure"[110] and, for night after night, had to sleep on the floor while his teacher and the man's paramour enjoyed the bed. As Keeler says, Lynch's "gentleness, his tendency to avoid confrontations,"[111] kept him from asserting his displeasure with this sleeping arrangement, so he concluded that the only way out of this messy situation was to quit school, which he did.

In Lynch's film fictions, characters sometimes stand and battle their demons face to face but more often they respond to threatening, stifling, intolerable predicaments by seeking an escape route. The young Lynch who bailed out of rough situations at home and in Boston is, as a grown-up, fully able to directly state his needs and wishes, and his gentle, harmony-seeking demeanor serves him well in contrast to an industry town full of aggressive predators and double-talking pretenders. However, if he had taken more of a fighting-tiger, territory-defending stance, *Dune* and parts of TV's *Twin Peaks* might have been less compromised projects.

In 1965, after completing his freshman year, Lynch and Jack Fisk set off for Europe to be schooled by Viennese Expressionist master Oskar Kokoschka (1869–1980). "I went to study under one of my least favorite painters, I really don't know why."[112] Ironically, today Kokoschka is one of the painters Lynch is "wild about"[113] and it's easy to see why: As a mature artist, he would view the Viennese creator of expressionistic portraits, figure studies, and cityscapes as a kindred spirit. Like Lynch, Kokoschka believed in the primal power of the penetrating eye wedded to the imagination, and declared that "the awareness of visions is life itself"[114] and that art is "a pointer, a bridge to a realm beyond the senses."[115] Kokoschka, who was called "the slicer-open of souls,"[116] infuses the personal space of his subjects with tension, and felt that the artist should "build houses outward from within,"[117] evoking Lynch's gift for portraying houses as psychic, emotion-manifesting spaces. Lynch planned to stay in Europe for three years. He lasted fifteen days.

Lynch and Fisk arrived in Salzburg at night, checked into a boarding house, and because their biological clocks were still running on American time, found themselves wide awake and starving at three in the morning. Their plan to hit the town for some food was stopped cold when they discovered the front door of their quarters was locked, so they made a meager meal of the few airline crackers still in their pockets from their flight. Lynch likes to look for signs and meaning and patterns in the flow of his life, and if he hadn't already learned the lesson that things often don't go the way you expect them to, this trip would hammer it into his brain.

The next morning the two eager art students hiked up to the hillside castle that housed Kokoschka's school—and were dumbfounded to learn that classes didn't start for ten weeks. Spontaneous, white-hot inspiration had motivated Lynch and Fisk's trip, so they hadn't considered the possibility that Kokoschka might schedule a summer break. In 2002, Fisk, with a sheepish chuckle, admits that "Kokoschka didn't actually know we were coming."[118]

Agreeing to pool their cash, they came up with $250, but arriving at a consensus about what to do next took some doing. Fisk was bent on seeing

Portugal, but Lynch wanted to go to Greece, for personal reasons more than cultural enrichment. Nancy Briggs, Lynch's stateside girlfriend (who, with her long, center-parted hair, Fisk feels is the archetype "for the imagery of The Blonde in David's artwork")[119] was staying with her parents in Athens. Fisk finally yielded to his romantic pal and they headed southeast toward Greece, traveling for three days in style on the legendary Orient Express train.

Trying to convince their fellow passengers that they were European, Fisk asked Lynch, "Vas is dat?"[120] But the best Lynch could come up with was, "Dat is mein arm."[121] Doing some sketching, Lynch drew a geometric pattern, to which an interested foreign passenger responded, "Looks like a labyrinth."[122] Lynch puzzled over this comment for a second and responded with a classic Lynchian non sequitur, "Sorry, I don't speak German."[123] The young men hadn't brought any food with them on the train and once again were going hungry, but found fellow travelers to be generous with their provisions. Ever sensitive to mysteries, Lynch became intrigued by whatever the heck it was that a Russian man they'd befriended was keeping inside a box he kept next to him on the bench seat. Finally, the fellow slid the lid aside to reveal what Fisk calls "a huge cigar like a cartoon: fat in the middle and tapered at both ends."[124] As a gesture of Cold War détente, the Russian insisted that his American comrades share his smoke, so all three took many puffs—but Fisk and Lynch got sick.

The next day, as the train chugged toward Athens, Fisk snoozed while Lynch chose to get away from everyone by standing on a small open-air platform and watching tens of centuries of civilized landscape roll by. When he rejoined Fisk, he couldn't understand why his buddy got a shocked look on his face and then started laughing uncontrollably. Unbeknownst to Lynch, the coal-fired locomotive's smoke had stained his face charcoal color, and refuse water tossed overboard had spattered little white dots on the shadow of Lynch's puzzled expression. Even before being conscious of doing so, Lynch was presenting a black-and-white image of himself to the world.

Ever the romantic, young Lynch knew that true love was worth suffering any hardship, but when he and Fisk reached Athens and searched out the house where his Nancy and her parents were staying for the summer, they discovered that the Briggs clan had just headed back to the states. Any lingering hint of Nancy's scent had been burned out of the one-hundred-five-degree air and Lynch was crestfallen.

He and Fisk holed up in a cheap hotel, hiding from the sun and sipping ouzo. They still had some American change in their pockets, and Fisk remembers that the money seemed "unreal and foreign, like you couldn't buy anything with it in the world we were in. We both suddenly felt very American, and David said, 'I want some J.C. Penney's khakis and blue work shirts.' In less than two weeks we'd reached the point where we wanted nothing more than to come home."[125]

Fisk recalls that "we were both in a lousy mood; nothing had worked out on this European trip. And we were kind of estranged from each other. David craved Marlboro cigarettes, which were $1 a pack, and Coca Colas, which were $1 each, so I saw what little money we had going up in smoke. From my point of view, it had been a big mistake to pool our money. We may have wanted to go home, but we couldn't afford it."[126]

Lynch knew that his parents, who had helped fund what was supposed to be their son's European art education, would be disappointed that he'd spent their money joyriding around the continent. Putting off the inevitable confrontation with his folks, he wisely contacted his grandparents to secure funds for a ticket home, while Fisk got a long-distance loan from his sister, Mary.

Not only was Lynch's romantic quest fruitless but he found that Europe didn't fire up his creative urges. There's a symbolic connection between Lynch's life and his art: He needs to have places and experiences that move him feed his work. The region around Kokoschka's school was "too clean. So wholesome and sterile. This is where I was going to be painting. And there was no inspiration for the kind of work I wanted to do. I knew that I was American and I wanted to be there."[127]

Back in the United States, Lynch returned to his parents' home in Alexandria. They were happy to see him but they dealt firmly with this young man who had abandoned his European study plan. "My parents disinherited me, sort of. They said, 'Okay, you're not going to school, you're not taking things seriously, so we're not giving you any more money. You'll have to go out and find a job.'"[128] Lynch performed a number of menial, 29-cents-an-hour tasks for bosses who eventually grew impatient with the artist-laborer's inability to get up early in the morning. When his parents relocated to California, Lynch moved into an apartment above an art-frame shop owned by a man named Michelangelo (Mike) Aloca, a fellow who, with his (as Bushnell Keeler says) "head of hair like the mane of a lion, huge shoulders like that wrestler who's a governor, Jesse Ventura, and two tiny legs he would kind of tie in a knot—he always had to be in a wheelchair,"[129] was the kind of unique person who fascinates Lynch. Keeler, Aloca's longtime friend, adds with a chuckle that "Mike had the most beautiful Italian wife you ever saw; she was like a young version of the actress Anna Magnani. I don't know how that happened."[130] Aloca had previously fired Lynch when he scratched a frame but he rehired him to be the janitor, and installed a bell to roust David out of bed for work. Subsisting on peanut butter, bread, and milk, Lynch remained optimistic and philosophical about the ups and downs of his lowly career. "Each time I was fired, it led me to somewhere else where I had a new experience. I could see that it all had a rhyme and a reason. Each time I was fired from a job, I was ecstatic."[131] Still, having to clean a stopped-up toilet that no one else would touch, and having Aloca threaten him with a gun, caused Lynch to question his employment status quo.

The specter of being drafted into the Army and sent to the killing fields of Vietnam haunted millions of young American men in the mid-1960s. Those who fought received physical wounds and psychic traumas, while those who stayed home were scarred with survivor's guilt. Lynch was living happily in his little apartment with orange drapes when he got a notice to report for the Army physical exam that would determine if he would be inducted into service and sent to Vietnam. Lynch's summons ordered him to report at five in the morning, and his pal Jack Fisk, who had the same report time, had to start trying to wake sleepy-head David at four in order to make their date. Fisk recalls that Lynch was classified 4-F, unfit for military service, because of "some health problems that David never enumerated."[132]

Lynch was greatly disturbed by the Vietnam conflict, and he told friends about a weapon he devised in a make-love-not-war spirit. It was a lightweight device that could be thrown at the Viet Cong fighters and, rather than exploding in lethal flames, it would blast out Vietnamese rock and roll music. Lynch's belief in the power of art is touching: He could picture U.S. soldiers and their enemies dropping their rifles and having a rockin' party.

By choice and necessity, Lynch, whose same-age friends had left to attend college, spent a lot of time with Bushnell Keeler, his architect brother, and other men who were more than twice his age. As Keeler says, "David built himself a nice compact little world for himself,"[133] something Lynch tries to do whenever he settles on a sympathetic place to live. The young man went to work as an architectural draftsman with Keeler's brother, was thrilled to see his paintings exhibited in Bushnell's gallery, and sat in on Keeler's life-drawing classes, where Lynch's mentor "had never seen anyone use a model the way he did."[134] Usually the person drawing the stationary, posing model sits working in one spot for the whole session. Lynch, who wouldn't become a filmmaker for a few more years, was already intrigued by multiple points of view and had a polymorphous way of looking at reality. "Lynch was all over the place when he was drawing. He'd get within two feet of the model, then go way back to the corner of the room, then come in and lie on his back looking up at her. He produced a fantastic abstraction that segmented the body and broke it apart: one leg was over here, another was up in the corner."[135] Over the years, Lynch would manifest his artistic impulse to fragment the human and animal form in his *Fish Kit* (1979) and *Chicken Kit* (1980), and *Lost Highway*'s (1997) severed body of the Renee Madison character. "David's approach was very creative, very interesting. I was tickled to be working with a young guy who was so talented, so dedicated; it made me feel kind of important."[136]

Bushnell Keeler deserves the gratitude of anyone who appreciates the art of David Lynch. Not only did he serve as a catalytic inspiration and a lifelong professional-artist role model for Lynch, and an encouraging, supportive teacher and friend, but he made some strategic moves that helped the young man begin the upward climb into his brilliant career: What better way to help Lynch than to reject him?

Lynch thought that he had a perfect setup, making enough money to eat, painting all the time, showing his work in a gallery, spending time with Bushnell and the small circle of other oldsters who appreciated his gifts—but Keeler saw it differently. "I thought he was going to bury himself here: he should be out there involved with people of his generation in the arts, instead of with us old fogeys. One night my brother and I and the rest of the older group, including Mike Aloca, drank and talked about 'the boy wonder,' and decided to get David to move on by giving him the cold shoulder. From now on life wasn't going to be so much fun with us."[137] So when Lynch stopped by for coffee with the group, Keeler says "we wouldn't say much to him, and his face became puzzled. We just kept up the cold treatment, not saying anything and acting estranged from him."[138]

Keeler knew that Lynch had been hearing about the fulfilling Art Life that David's pal Fisk was leading as a student at the Pennsylvania Academy of Arts in Philadelphia (whose grey stone steps Sylvester Stallone exultantly climbed in the American Bicentennial year's *Rocky*). Keeler figured that if he and his fellow co-conspirators kept freezing Lynch out, the young man himself would get the idea to join Fisk in Philly without Bushnell having to tell David that's what he thought he should do.

One day, Keeler answered the knock on his studio door and there stood Lynch, but for once he didn't enter when invited.

His face was set in a grim expression and he said with a loud voice, "I'm going to get the hell out of here and go up to Philadelphia and study with Jack Fisk."[139]

Keeler said, "Can you get in?"[140]

"I don't know, but I'll go up there and find out."[141]

Characteristically, Lynch had a chosen course of action, and nothing was going to deter his forward progress. Keeler noticed that Lynch had his packed bags with him; this was his last stop before catching the bus north. Bushnell gave Lynch a warm goodbye and reflected that his strategy to get David out of town had worked. He thought, "Gee, this is great, now how do we get him into the Pennsylvania Academy?"[142]

Just as when Keeler championed David's right to be an artist while still attending high school in a conversation with Lynch's father, Bushnell again took direct action on David's behalf and called the director of the Pennsylvania Academy. "This kid's loaded with talent and needs to be there. Can you possibly take him in?"[143] Keeler recalls the administrator saying that theoretically admissions were already closed for the semester, but added, "We'll wait for him. Don't worry, we'll fit him in."[144]

Arriving in Philadelphia by bus, Lynch turned in his portfolio to the Academy's entrance board, and was thrilled when "they accepted me."[145] The academic quarter would begin in early January 1966 and on New Year's Eve, Lynch and Fisk were carrying their belongings to a rental unit in a wheelbarrow. "A man stopped us. He said, 'You're moving—moving on New Year's

Mr. Lynch's neighborhood.

Eve! You need money!' And he began to put his hand in his pocket. And I said, 'Oh, no. Thanks, but we're rich.' And we didn't have any money at all. Isn't that strange—I always felt like I was rich. The strangest thing."[146]

Like many of his baby boom generation, who grew up with a bountiful national economy and an openness to new ways of being, Lynch had the luxury of following the imperatives of his mind, emotions, and talent. As Robert Henri counseled from an earlier generation in *The Art Spirit*, the artist's riches are counted not in money but in "moments of the purest freedom."[147] As an adult in the 2000s, Lynch still has a fear of being restricted, of not "being able to do what I want to do."[148] He feels that the increasing financial rewards that he now enjoys are primarily valuable as a means of expanding the expression of his Art Life. He stresses that even big bucks "won't help you if you desperately want to go to Mars."[149] As poetic fantasist Ray Bradbury showed in *The Martian Chronicles*, the best way to get to Mars is to launch the rocket of your imagination. For Lynch, Philadelphia was like a planet of monstrous, alien wonders. He has called the City of Brotherly Love "a very sick, degenerate, decaying, fear-ridden place where things are totally absurd and confusing. I saw horrible things, horrible, horrible things while I was there"[150]—things like flaming black–white racial hatred, a sidewalk murder, his house twice being broken into while Lynch was home, his car being stolen, a little girl pleading with her drunken father to get up out of the gutter and come home, and "guys ripping another guy out of a car while it's moving."[151] The landmarks of Lynch's neighborhood were seedy bars that opened early in the day, a prison, a morgue. An atmosphere of anxiety and dread, that had once inspired Edgar Allen Poe, who had lived nearby, gripped Lynch's soul. The protective walls of Lynch's house were brick, but to him they were "like paper."[152] Philadelphia was a "cocoon" of fear and he "thought I'd never get out of there, ever."[153]

Always stimulated by paradox, Lynch started to realize that Philadelphia's crucible of menacing tension was where he needed to be. Salzburg had been "too clean,"[154] too much like his Northwest years to be inspiring. But, breathing in the sooty air of the city's industrial zone, "only living at night"[155] and "never aware of anything normal,"[156] Lynch began to have the "first original, thrilling thoughts"[157] of his life. He actually began to experience the central conceptual metaphor of his worldview. "For the first time I really lived beneath the surface. I was only aware of this world of fear and art."[158] Lynch's sensory impressions took on a gritty lyricism. It wasn't just that a teenage boy had been shot to death in front of his house, it was the way the kid's white chalk outline haunted the sidewalk for days afterward. Lynch lived in a realm of "factories, smoke, railroads, diners, true factory people—you could see strange stories in their faces. You could see plastic curtains and windows held together with bandaids, oily rags stuck into holes in windows."[159] The black body bags hung out to dry in curved shapes at the morgue across from Lynch's first apartment became "the smiling bags of death,"[160] and showed up in *Twin Peaks* twenty years later. And, with an anticipatory nod to Lynch's penchant for humorously surrealistic juxtapositions, verbal and visual non sequiturs, he recalls his neighbors' dog. "They fed it so much it looked like a water balloon with little legs that stuck out. Almost couldn't walk, this dog. Had a little bitty head. It was like a Mexican Chihuahua with a watermelon in the middle. And there were lots of little bowls of candies in the room. This sort of thing stuck with me."[161]

The powerful industrial-zone impressions percolated to the core of Lynch's being, arousing his spiritual, as well as his aesthetic, nature. "Factories are what's beneath the surface, they are the unconscious, in a way. Factories get me in my soul. I feel the universe in them. They have all my favorite textures."[162] Lynch often expresses himself verbally in painterly terms: "texture, contrast, mood, atmosphere" show up again and again. Along with factories, another major textural discovery for the teenaged Lynch was sex. Toby Keeler recalls that Lynch lost his virginity near the end of his high school years on a summer excursion to Virginia Beach. "David and his girlfriend locked themselves in the bedroom for three days and only came out for meals."[163] For the sensitive, thoughtful Lynch, sex wasn't just an ecstatic physical sensation: "It was like a world that was so mysterious to me that I really couldn't believe that there was this fantastic texture to life that I was getting to do. I could see a world opening—this sexual dream. It was another indication that life was great and worth living. And it kept expanding, because I saw that the vast realm of sex has many different levels, from lust and fearful, violent sex, to the real spiritual thing at the other end. It's the key to some fantastic mystery of life."[164] In 1967, the young man who lived to lose himself in the convolutions of his inner consciousness and to record his solitary journeys on canvas, who felt that "women were a danger to the Art Life,"[165] got married. Paradox, biology, and love rule.

Peggy Lentz, of Chestnut Hill, Philadelphia, had first glimpsed Lynch in the Academy cafeteria and thought he was "a very beautiful, romantic looking boy who seemed vulnerable, sweet, and angelic. He looked like he needed you, and that's trouble for a sensitive young girl."[166] For Lynch, the lovely, blonde, bright, humorous, and artistically gifted Peggy was a wonderful mate. On top of her many charms and talents, "she had a beautiful singing voice"[167]: Perhaps Lynch's memories of newlywed love's domestic melodies prompted him, twenty-three years later in *Twin Peaks*, to refer

to a blissful realm where "there's always music in the air." Peggy already had a boyfriend but she and Lynch started to talk about art over lunch, and "we really connected immediately."[168] As Peggy puts it, this was the "preverbal"[169] stage of Lynch's life, in which he would have a hard time putting a few words together to explain what he meant to an average group of his fellow Americans—but she was right on his wavelength. She intuitively understood his "visceral-sensory"[170] way of perceiving the world, of dwelling on the physical and emotional "feel"[171] of things and being sensitive to the "intensities"[172] of occurrences and the balance between "contrasting"[173] forces and polarities. When Lynch described a painting with a whooshing wind sound, Peggy could see it. She also saw herself through his eyes as he described her face as "slow,"[174] meaning "simple and visually uncomplicated,"[175] but then "when you laugh it gets very fast."[176] And he spoke about the value of accident and happenstance in art, of how "too much perfection suffocates the life out of a painting."[177] Just as Lynch and his best friend, Jack Fisk, used to do, David and Peggy stayed up late painting. Lynch's Art Life now not only included a woman but musical accompaniment as well. Peggy liked to hum and she remembers that they'd work with the radio on and were always happy when Beatles songs played. And Lynch "was obsessed with '96 Tears' by ? and the Mysterians,"[178] a tune with a narrative that prefigured the emotional extremity of Lynch's films, in which a man relishes knowing that he's going to make a woman cry.[179]

Peggy was stirred by the vibrant pulse of life in Lynch, and soon they were sharing lunch, dinner, and breakfast, and had signed their names to a marriage license. They gamely moved into a huge, dilapidated house in the rundown old Brewery Town neighborhood, where they made art and love, and Lynch, already a creature of ritualistic habits, consumed nothing but baloney and tuna sandwiches, Coca-Cola, coffee, cigarettes, and "chocolate milk after sex."[180]

The couple was surprised to learn that Peggy was pregnant, and, in 1968, she gave birth to their daughter, Jennifer. Though Lynch was, according to the adult Jennifer, "panicked"[181] by the responsibility of becoming a father, he got directly involved in seeing his offspring into the world. In the 1960s it was highly unusual for expectant fathers to witness births but Lynch convinced the doctor that he "could handle it,"[182] and had an experience in which "it's not so much what you see as an abstraction you feel."[183] For Lynch "the idea of birth was a mysterious and fantastic thing involving, like sex, just pure meat and blood and hair. And at the same time, this feeling of life and spirit."[184] Jennifer's joyous birth was also a troubled one. She entered the world with severely clubbed feet, and had to endure surgeries and having both legs encased in waist-high casts. Lynch "felt close"[185] to Jennifer from the moment he laid eyes on her. He read that "putting moving colorful objects near infants' eyes stimulates their brains."[186] Far from being able to afford fancy toys, Lynch carefully "glued all these things onto a matchbook and bent little red match sticks out and had a little thread, and I'd dangle this thing in front of her."[187]

The murder that Lynch witnessed on the sidewalk in front of their house occurred in terrible proximity to his wife and dear young daughter. Peggy was taking Jennifer out for a ride in their "Cadillac of a perambulator"[188] that they'd bought cheap at the Goodwill store. Lynch's little brood shared the street that day with "a large family that was going to a christening of this small baby."[189] Suddenly a "teenage gang came swooping down"[190] and attacked the group. The family's "teenage son tried to defend the whole bunch, but the gang beat him down and shot him in the back of the head."[191] Aside from stunningly reinforcing the dark side of Lynch's best-of-times/worst-of-times view of Philadelphia, this incident would have a resounding effect on his future artwork. Physical and emotional violence would become a major motif. And in his films, iconographic human heads would be both targets for mayhem and passageways to paradise.

The fear Lynch felt in the gritty Philadelphia air crept into Peggy's life as well not long after they brought Jennifer home. She was up late feeding the baby after Lynch had dozed off when she heard rough male voices downstairs outside the front door—and then the sound of splintering wood as the men crashed through the door and entered the dark lower-floor hallway. Carefully putting down Jennifer, Peggy woke Lynch, which can be hard to do, and whispered, "There are people in the house!"[192] Lynch, petrified and "white as a sheet,"[193] got up and grabbed the military sword the Peggy's father had given them as a fireplace decoration.

Trying to hold in his panic as tightly as he gripped the sword, Lynch walked to the head of the stairs and yelled down, "Get the hell out of here—I have a sword!"[194] as he waved the blade in the air. The house invaders had thought the structure was vacant and had come in to drink and sleep. Surprised that the house was occupied, they quickly left. Once again, as when he'd been scared of the New York subway as a boy, yet continued down into the dark to ride, Lynch faced his fear and forged ahead. Of course the sight of a pale, bare-chested guy waving a sword, and wearing his hastily-pulled-on underpants backwards, might have been equally scary to some guys just looking for a place to get drunk and snooze.

On another night, Peggy was sitting with Jennifer on her lap next to the bedroom window. This peaceful, homey scene was disturbed by Peggy's feeling that behind the window's black glass, someone was watching her. Sure enough, she heard a person jump out of the tree outside the window and land on the ground. She hadn't seen anyone but was sickened by the certainty that someone had seen her and Jennifer. The police came, looked around, told her and Lynch to stay alert and be careful, and left.

Later that night, the Lynches heard someone stirring in the basement and again called the police, who found a shattered window where the invader had broken his way out of the cellar and fled onto the sidewalk. This time Lynch left the sword in its sheath and borrowed a loaded rifle from a friend. For many nights after the break-in, he sat up all night on the sofa with the rifle in his lap, in case the marauder came back. He never did.

Perhaps, as Lynch sat on the couch, he thought about how, when someone breaks into your house, fear invades your head. It's not surprising that home invasions, whether by overt or covert forces, would become a key dynamic of his fictions: The idea of an unwanted, anonymous person coming in and secretly watching the occupants of a house, and the police investigating and leaving, would echo in *Lost Highway* thirty years later.

In the beginning of his Philadelphia days, Lynch's canvases portrayed naturalistic street scenes. He progressed to mosaiclike drawings of geometric shapes that he called "industrial symphonies,"[195] the title he would give to his 1990 stage performance piece. In 1946, the year of Lynch's birth, the term *abstract expressionism* was coined to characterize a type of painting that can be seen as the free, democratic world's reaction against totalitarian Nazi and Stalinist strictures, which enforced strict realism as the only moral and permissible form of artistic endeavor. Lynch particularly admired the 1950s Abstract Expressionists and action painters Jackson Pollock, Franz Kline, and Jack Tworkov. These artists expressed their deepest feelings and thoughts in bold fields of color, slashing brushstrokes, and ejaculations of paint flung or dripped. The randomness and correctness of accident informed their technique and they seemed able to capture cosmic light and raw, dancing energy on their canvases. Lynch, who would make evocative use of dark tonalities in his films and paintings, must have been especially impressed with Kline's famous black-on-black images, which emitted a mysterious, poetic resonance. And it is fitting that Lynch, who was bored with his pre–art school classrooms and spent time figuring out "how to break their rules,"[196] would identify with the very painters who threw the established, traditional precepts of picture-making right out the window.

In the 1960s, many young people were tired of the old ways of doing things and eager to explore new ones. Painters and sculptors became interested in filmmaking and a flood of 8mm and 16mm experimental works gushed forth from art schools and neighborhood basements. A visionary experience injected the idea of making films into Lynch's brain. In 1967, at the Philadelphia Academy, he was quietly working on a canvas in his painting cubicle. Standing back from his easel, he looked intently at the image of dark green garden foliage emerging from blackness. Out of nowhere, "I heard a wind, and saw the plants move a little."[197] Lynch realized that he could "expand the mood of a painting through film by making it move. It could be so strange, so beautiful, like if the Mona Lisa opened her mouth and turned, and there would be a wind, and then she'd turn back and smile."[198] Lynch's belief that "sound is at least fifty percent of the film experience"[199] was born early on, as was his idea that wind is the air of mystery.

In May 1967, Lynch won the Pennsylvania Academy's Dr. William S. Biddle Cadwalader Memorial Prize of $250 for a multimedia piece that incorporated his first film and was his premiere portrayal of human beings trapped in unending agony. Lynch had sculpted a white "screen" with three gape-mouthed heads, cast from his own cranium, emerging from its surface. Onto this irregular plane was projected a continuously repeating loop of 8mm animation (*Six Figures Getting Sick*, 1967) that is a harbinger of themes and motifs that will preoccupy Lynch throughout his career. The process of gaining knowledge by paying close attention is central to his ethos, and the piece begins with an animated numerical countdown accompanied by the insistent word "LOOK." (Lynch will often add words to his images on canvas in years to come, perhaps as an outgrowth of having seen labels attached to trees and insect displays in his father's experimental forest.) With the three sculpted heads on the left, the number "1" of the countdown fills the right side of the screen, then vanishes as two animated male heads appear. A singleness that is actually double; two that are actually "one and the same"; this paradoxical phenomenological and philosophical equation will form the tantalizing core of many of Lynch's best future works. Also central to Lynch's vision is the idea of the dialectic between two polar elements yielding a synthesizing third term, and we see an elongated fluid form from each of the two heads flow out toward the other and join to form a central third head.

Lynch's future films will probe the deepest inner workings of the human psyche but his first movie manifests his urge to explore beneath the surface of things by revealing the interior physical plumbing of his six men (they're titled *Figures*, but the six human forms, being modeled on Lynch's head, read as men). Lynch knows that Heaven and Hell emanate from inside us, and as elongated esophageal shafts and stomachs appear beneath the six heads, we note that one fellow has a heavenly star field of white dots against a black background within the chamber of his chest. The stars will become an often-repeated Lynchian representation of the sublime *beyond*, but the artist's six men are fated to endure a hellish here and now.

Lynch loves the look of black-and-white imagery (as well as the metaphysical resonance of darkness and light); to this point, his *Six Figures Getting Sick* tableau has been a composition in charcoal and snowy hues. We've seen a black spiral, an ancient symbol signifying "sinking into the waters of death,"[200] invade five of the stomachs, and a plague of black has risen up to the men's chins, throwing their inner organs into vivid, white-toned contrasting relief. Then color assaults Lynch's composition as the spirals are obliterated by a virulent bright red. Just like the dark force that Lynch had sensed in his idyllic boyhood neighborhood, and the disease-spreading red ants that swarmed on his beautiful backyard cherry tree, a malevolent contagion is feeding on the artist's six men. In Lynch's world, evil has the power to transgress the physical, psychological, and social barriers that men and women erect for self-protection. After turning red, the five stomachs secrete a pale liquid beyond the perimeter of the stomachs' walls, poisoning more and more of the men's systemic territory. One man serenely still has only a star field inside him, rather than a death-spiraled red stomach. But Lynch knows that the darkest energies can be invisible, and he momentarily twins the word "SICK" next to the man's innards before all six men's mouths spew white vomit streaked with red blood like there's no tomorrow.

We all know that expelling toxins from our bodies by throwing up can make us feel cleansed, purified, healed, but Lynch's men only have a second's respite before they immediately start feeling queasy again and again, for as long as Lynch wants to project his film loop. It will be five years before the artist embraces Hindu spirituality and ponders the concept of karma, but in *Six Figures Getting Sick*, the idea of human beings enduring a repetitive round of suffering is clearly on his mind. And since the sculpted screen figures are casts of his own head, the sick men can be seen as successive agonized incarnations of the artist himself. Lynch's fascination for the cyclic nature of phenomena may have been sown in the deep woods, where, on excursions with his father, the boy experienced the birth and death of seasons, plants, and animals. The six endlessly stricken men are harbingers of characters who will be trapped in vortexes of hellish repetition in *Twin Peaks* and *Twin Peaks: Fire Walk With Me* (1989–1992) and *Lost Highway* (1997). The candles that burn at the bottom of the *Six Figures Getting Sick* composition as the men's stomachs turn red are the first flames of the many fires that will ignite Lynch's future works.

With its nauseating subject matter and loud-siren and rattling-squeaking (industrial) sound accompaniment, *Six Figures Getting Sick* was an assaultive experience for spectators. This would not be the last time that Lynch was rewarded for shocking and disturbing an audience. As Robert Henri said, "The artist goes to the market place, the exhibition place, wherever he can reach the people, to lay before them his new angle on life. He creates a disturbance and wins attention from those who have in them his kind of blood."[201]

Two of those who had seen and heard Lynch's prize-winning piece were truly moved: one offered the young artist a job, the other an art commission. So David started running off etchings at Roger La Pelle's printing press, and planning a second "moving painting" sculpture-film combination for young millionaire H. Barton Wasserman, who would pay him $1,000 for the unique living-room attraction.

Lynch, like his father, has always believed that it is important to have the right tools for the job at hand. He had shot *Six Figures Getting Sick* with a borrowed camera, but he'd become so "fixated"[202] on the joy of making films that he wanted a camera of his own—a good one, that cost a lot of money. "In the window of the Fotorama store I saw the Bolex of my dreams."[203] With his discerning eye for quality, Lynch had chosen the camera that set the standard of excellence for 16mm filmmaking, an instrument comparable to today's high-end video cameras. The Bolex was used, but in "mint condition,"[204] and cost a whopping $478.28 in late 1960s' currency.

Lynch had no down payment to offer, so he begged the store manager to set the camera aside for him, but was told that Fotorama had to sell the Bolex to any paying customer who might walk in the door. Lynch knew he had to be ready with the money when the store opened the next morning at eight. But since "I couldn't wake up early in those days, I stayed up all night,"[205] got a money advance from Wasserman, and bought the key to his artistic future in Philadelphia's cold morning light. To this day, Lynch treasures his Bolex as a sacred relic, nestling the gleaming machine in its original leather case lined with plush ruddy fabric the color of *Twin Peaks*' Red Room and the ubiquitous red curtains in his work.

So now Lynch had his camera and a subject to put on film (his wife, Peggy) but it would take some doing to transpose the concept taking shape in his head into three-dimensional reality. Peggy remembers David waking her late one night, his voice full of urgency: "I've got to get some rubber hosing and an old shower head and some clamps and plumbing fittings and. . . ." "Okay, we'll go look first thing in the morning." "No, I need them *now*." "But David, it's dark out, it's almost three o'clock in the morning!"[206] Still, Lynch braved the dreaded Philadelphia darkness, scrounging in back alleys and garbage cans, and finding almost everything he needed. (This example of his intense desire to pursue and complete a creative mission, no matter what anyone else says and what the obstacles may be, clearly means a lot to Lynch; in fact, one day in 2004 when he knew I was going to be talking to Peggy, he phoned her and said, "Be sure to tell Greg about the time. . . .")[207]

After assembling the bits and pieces of hardware he'd gathered, Lynch had an apparatus that would look like a normal bathroom shower fixture. He wanted to create the effect of a woman (Peggy) taking a shower and getting doused with colored liquid, rather than the expected clear water. Being painters, David and his wife had plenty of acrylic pigments on hand, and for the sake of her husband's art, Peggy let herself be color-coated like the woman in *Goldfinger*. Today, she laughs and winces over her and David's lack of concern about the toxic or corrosive effects the paints might have had on her skin.

Peggy was fated to be the first human being in a David Lynch film but not on this particular project. After toiling for two months to produce two-and-a-half minutes of film, model and artist were joined by their friend, sound designer Alan Splet, to view the processed product. Lynch held the celluloid strip up to the light, his eyes desperately searching for something recognizable—but the camera shutter had malfunctioned, the film was a blurred blank. All their work had added up to nothing. Lynch recalls that this setback didn't seem like a catastrophe: "I was almost kind of happy; I didn't know why."[208] Peggy has a more concrete memory: "David was shattered, devastated; he was in tears for a minute. But then he slammed his fist down on the table and said, 'Well fuck it! I'm going to paint the room black and do another film.'"[209] Just like he and his dad used to do, Lynch was moving right on to the next project.

The understanding Wasserman told Lynch to film whatever he wanted with what was left of the $1,000. Lynch's father chipped in some additional dollars, and David crafted four minutes of film that would put him in the running for an American Film Institute grant.

The artist's first autonomous film (not linked to a sculpted construction) was generated by a dream. Peggy told David about watching her young niece being gripped by a nightmare. The girl twitched with fearful agitation and kept reciting the alphabet. Lynch responded to this anecdote as though it was a secret message meant just for him. In *The Alphabet* (1968), the artist directed Peggy in "a little nightmare about the fear connected with learning."[210] Lynch has said that we live in a "learning world"[211] and that, as individuals, we have our unique problems to solve at various levels of the stairway to enlightenment. The expansive, self-taught school of life is one thing but the restrictive rote-learning of regimented classrooms is another. Lynch would passionately second the words of his mentor Robert Henri regarding a "fear of schools"[212] in which "teachers stand in the way"[213] of students and the learners are "possessed by the school."[214] In *The Alphabet*, Lynch is also metaphorically commenting on the psychic wrenching that accompanies a loss of primal innocence, the assigning of reductive, limiting names and sterile categories to the preliterate child's free-flowing "fancy of man and things,"[215] as Henri puts it. Lynch isn't saying that we shouldn't learn the alphabet; he wouldn't be where he is today without it. But it makes sense that this man who works hard at maintaining his childlike sense of wonder and who "didn't really learn to talk, to communicate with words, until I was twenty"[216] would, in *The Alphabet*, present the learning of letters as a symbolic plague upon a young girl.

For Lynch, childhood is a sacred, deep inner source of creative energy that he has kept alive and vital throughout his life. To the child, and the artist with an innocent eye and mind, each day is full of momentous discoveries and possible new beginnings. Certainly, the child within Lynch uses language but he has a poignant attraction to the pre-literate state in which magic and mystery abound, a state like Eden before the Fall. Now almost sixty years old, Lynch still instinctively avoids eating too much fruit from the Tree of Knowledge, and for decades has erased language from his mind twice daily while meditating. Over the span of his career, Lynch's childlike view will create films that, like fairy tales, are full of portents, transformations, ogres, talismans, and doppelgangers. Stories, like *The Alphabet*, are driven by a dark dynamic: the metaphorical eating of children by parent figures or the adult world.

Lynch's decades-long fascination with the interpenetration of dream state and waking reality begins with the simple image of a Girl asleep in bed. Her face pale, she lies prone under white sheets, the vertical iron bars of her headboard sharply outlined against the absolutely black background. Insistent, threatening children's voices chant, "A-B-C, A-B-C, A-B-C" as we see what fills the Girl's dreaming consciousness. In an animated landscape reminiscent of a Saul Steinberg blacklines-on-white-background *New Yorker* cover, a golden sun orb glows on high while alphabet letters sprout on stems, shoot from a long phallic shape, appear inside cartoon-dialogue-balloon shapes attached to the earth with umbilical cords, are enclosed inside a line of circles advancing left to right, and shine inside polyp-like fungus forms: This is a world imprinted with the building blocks of language. Accompanying this strange garden that melds botanical, zoological, and factory assembly-line forms and rhythms, is an opera tenor voice singing a simple rhyme. "The alphabet you can bet is fun. All the letters in a row, in the sun. And you'll know that you're the one. The alphabet is surely fun." The absurd contrast between the tony opera voice and the childish ditty provides the first passage of Lynchian screen humor. But at the same serious moment, it is the voice of the adult world manipulating the child to learn by promising her aggrandizing, egocentric self-knowledge ("you'll know that you're the one"). As a transition to his next animated tableau, Lynch inserts a live-action close-up of a tongue licking across teeth and red-lipsticked lips as a visual equivalent of an adult promising, "Kid, with an appetite for learning like that, the world will be your oyster."

Next, a capital letter "A" with organic cords extending down into the earth to tap subterranean waters sprouts a white phallic polyp through a black hairy opening and, with a few drops of blood, the polyp gives birth to two wailing small "aa"s. The crying sounds continue as one of the little "a"s becomes the head of a torso-form with organic shapes hanging beneath it. The "a" head becomes a phallic shape, which turns into a Picasso-like cubist head with a single breast beneath it. (Cubism gives visible form to Einstein's relativity-theory idea that perceptions of the world are determined by the position of the viewer, with cubist images combining multiple points of view of a subject in a single picture. Even as a beginning filmmaker, Lynch gravitates to modes of expression that reveal the multiform nature of seemingly single realities. He said of *Lost Highway* (1997), "time and space are relative: the film moves forwards and backwards, but it also stands still."[217]) A red, heart-shaped vagina with little hairs and an umbilical cord to the earth spurts "a b c d" into the cubist head. This injection of knowledge causes the head to gasp—and Lynch does a fast shock-cut and zoom-in to a close-up of the face of the Girl we first saw in bed. She also is gasping, while looking in a mirror, hand to her open mouth, indicating that Lynch's animations are portraying the Girl's interior psychological processes. Lynch cuts back to the animated cubist head, which spurts red blood from its eyes, then head. He then dissolves to a second live-action transition insert close-up of a red-lipped face saying, "Please remember, you are dealing with the human form." Yes, we are, but humorously and with confusion about the nature of truth and illusion, for Lynch has filmed this face topsy-turvy, with a putty nose sculpted onto his actor's chin at the top of the frame and the upside-down mouth below. Even at this early stage in his film career, Lynch is fascinated by the idea that the essential truth of an image can be the opposite of what it first appears to be, that the human form can have many dimensions of reality. The history of this shot, along with the way Lynch based his film on the inspiration of Peggy's niece's alphabet-nightmare dream, shows his openness to sympathetic collaboration and sudden creative connections. For, in a flash, Lynch's brain linked two separate elements: Peggy's recounted girlhood memory of the way her father's face took on a disturbing Otherness when she viewed it upside-down, and Peggy's grown-up complaint ("Please remember, you are dealing with the human form") when Lynch was positioning her body for an earlier *Alphabet* shot.

Lynch dissolves through an animated field of white flecks on black to the live-action image of the Girl sleeping on her white sheets. The animation of her dreams breaks the boundary between interior and exterior, spilling over onto her live-action bed and speckling the white sheets with black spots. Still dreaming, her live-action form strains to grab alphabet letters that are tied to her with umbilical cords. The letters are just out of reach. As she desperately reaches for them, we hear her voice singing the ABCs. In the middle of this letter-grasping sequence, Lynch shock-cuts to an arresting image of the Girl's whitened face silently screaming for a split second, a black strand of hair across her nose and mouth. She finally seizes the last few letters and concludes her song with the request "Tell me what you think of me." This appeal suggests the pride of accomplishment of a youngster who has done what the powerful grown-ups wanted her to do. But Lynch shows us the image of an immobile, entrapped victim, snared in a delicate web of the letters' umbilical cords, the bars of her headboard imprisoning her right arm. In a direct cut to a closer view of the pale Girl on her white bed, Lynch wakes his dreamer. The umbilical web is gone, her arm is free. She may be full of new knowledge, but she's also brimming with fear and revulsion. In slow motion, she spews red blood from her mouth, speckling the sheets as Lynch fades to black.

Though Lynch was untutored in filmmaking, saw few movies, and read little fiction, *The Alphabet* exhibits his intuitive understanding of cinematic and narrative structure. He has begun with a simple, neutral image (the Girl), then floated his camera inside it to reveal complex symbolic workings, and finished with the initial image altered to its sickened state. He has employed a cinematic vocabulary consistent thematically (fertilization, birth, transformation), visually (alphabet, sexual, zoological, botanical imagery), and aurally (alphabet recitations, human cries, and the rising and falling wind sounds—the first of the many invisible currents of air that will shiver through his films). He has built tension (forced learning) and evoked lighthearted, menacing, and serious moods, often simultaneously. He has shown his mastery of the principle of cinematic linkage in joining an extremely short shot of the anxious live-action Girl's face with a shot of the blood-spurting animated cubist head in her dream. This foreshadowing forms an almost subliminal gestalt of anticipation in the viewer's mind that is played out at the end as the live-action Girl spews blood. And Lynch has continued to integrate the abstractions and the actualities of his life with his art, for, in addition to Peggy's contributions, the crying little "aa"s are Jennifer.

Before trying filmmaking, Lynch had experienced and embraced a paradigm shift in the art world from the traditional narrative representation of reality to freeform abstraction and action painting: Old, established truths were replaced by fresh beliefs. Lynch says, "composition is so abstract. It's so powerful, where you place things and the relationships. But you don't work with any kind of intellectual thing. You just act and react. It's all intuition. It must obey rules, but these rules are not in a book."[218] *The Alphabet* shows Lynch approaching film as he does a painting, following his moment-to-moment sense of what feels right and balanced, using images and sounds like brushstrokes, building moods and emotions into a composition that exists as a metamorphosing sequence of time, rather than as a canvas hanging on a wall. The urge to express himself with abstractions runs deep in Lynch, and over his decades-long film career his most abstract works will be called the most primally Lynchian. In applying a painterly, this-move-suggests-that-move method to filmmaking, Lynch crafts works that don't behave like most other movies, and can best be appreciated by following a chaos-theory approach. Lynch presents us with cinematic experiences that lack the stable, orderly readability of most of what we are accustomed to seeing on the screen. His films can seem unpredictable, unstable, and chaotic, but they are composed of elements interacting in a dynamic process that conveys often sublingual sensory-emotional meanings. Certain thoughts and feelings and ideas will preoccupy Lynch throughout his career. With a nod to his beloved detective metaphor, we would do well to take in Lynch's works with a receptive, open mind, on alert for the hidden patterns, the internal logic, of the unique shapes he creates.

The Alphabet taught Lynch that film could do a lot more than just make his paintings move. And the strangely unruffled way he had responded to that botched initial two minutes of animation he had done for the Wasserman commission turned out to be prescient. For he realized that if that animation had been showable, its need to relate conceptually to the sculpted elements of the commission project would have weakened its ability to stand alone and prove that he was worthy of an American Film Institute grant. *The Alphabet* had the self-contained integrity of a pure film and Lynch submitted it for the Institute's consideration.

The twenty-two-year-old Lynch had fallen in love with this new artistic medium that could express so much of his inner life. But he still calls this "one of the bleakest periods of my entire existence."[219] He was depressed by the routine of his days and nights, watching soap operas (*Another World*) while printing at La Pelle's, coming home after dark with barely enough money to feed his family. When he saw the first-round list of Film Institute grant applicants, Lynch was "so embarrassed that I even applied,"[220] for the hopefuls were all older, established filmmakers—and even they were getting turned down. "I felt like a fool. I knew I didn't have one single chance."[221] The AFI director, George Stevens Jr., recalls that the grant-applications committee kept stacking the submitted films into categorical piles, and that when they had finished, there was one that didn't fit: *The Alphabet*.

Lynch recalls that "one morning it was raining in Philadelphia, and as I left the house I was standing in the rain, and I said to Peggy, 'Call me if anything exciting happens.' This was like a joke—as if anything big really could happen. She said the same to me, and I drove over to La Pelle's Printing in Germantown. I was working away when I heard the phone ring far away in another room. Roger La Pelle came to me and said I was going to get a call, like he knew something. The phone rang, and that call changed my life completely."[222] On the line from sunny Beverly Hills was the AFI director, asking if Lynch could make the $7,118-budgeted film he had proposed for $5,000. Lynch replied with lightning speed: "You got it."[223]

With characteristic enthusiasm, Lynch plunged into a project that was far more ambitious than *The Alphabet.* Eight times longer than the earlier film, the thirty-four-minute *The Grandmother* (1970, 16mm) required Lynch to shoot for nine weeks, direct four actors, construct sets and massive props, and spend 567 hours creating sound effects. *The Alphabet*, with its theme of a child's forced learning, obliquely touches on the idea of child abuse. *The Grandmother* viscerally explores the permutations of injurious family life and presents what would be a key dynamic in many of Lynch's subsequent art forms: the family home as "a place where things can go wrong."[224]

Even in his earliest works, Lynch's instincts lead him beneath the outer shell of surface reality, to sites where primal energies stir. He begins *The Grandmother* deep below the surface of the earth with an animated view of subterranean water and biomorphic tubes and tendrils. The artist's vision is so potent that it seems perfectly natural that inorganic rocks and organic tissue and fluids should be melded in some physical process we've never seen before. Two underground vertical shafts are fertilized with liquid and send a male form, and then a female form, toward the surface on columns of surging white foam. Lynch cuts to a magical live-action effect as a man (Robert Chadwick) and a woman (Virginia Maitland) break through a carpet of autumn leaves and sprout up from the ground like mushrooms.

In animation, the two put their arms around each other with an agitated twitching, scratching motion as a star field blossoms in the background sky, as though their "lovemaking" is part of a grand cosmic design. (This is the second of many star fields to appear in Lynch's work.) Back below ground, a red droplet from the man's birth shaft and a white one from the woman's combine in a third shaft and launch the couple's son up through the leaves. The slovenly live-action man wears an untucked T-shirt, the woman a cheap flower-print dress, while their boy sports an immaculate black tuxedo, white shirt, and black bow tie. The couple seems shocked by the arrival of their offspring, as if they didn't understand the connection between him and their "copulatory" motions. The heavy-set man is instantly hostile to his son and, on all fours, looms over the Boy barking gruffly like a dog, while the woman yips and whines as she thrashes on the ground in agitation. In animation, the man pounds on the Boy, who emits two red clouds of pain and two high, birdlike cries from his mouth. To escape, the Boy soars up into the sky. His Father tries to catch him, but falls back to the earth.

Born to be one step ahead of his parents (like youngsters in future Lynch projects), the live-action Boy (Richard White) emerges in his simple room with its white bed and chest of drawers standing against a black background. Lynch cuts back to the befuddled, still-barking parents, who don't know where their son has gone. They then appear in their room, which is the kind of overly full, visually disorderly space Lynch shuns in real life: a mess of cluttered tables with a clothesline of drying underwear vertically bisecting the black background. Lynch shows an animated tableau of a golden sun rising into a blue sky, accompanied by the sound of flowing water. The stream sound carries over to the live-action Boy sitting up in bed and looking under the bedcovers toward his private parts. As the Boy dresses in his tuxedo we see a large sunlike golden stain of urine on his sheets. Later the Father violently carries his son back to the Boy's room and repeatedly rubs the thrashing child's face in the yellow stain. The parents and their child don't talk to each other but the father screams "Mott!, Mott!" at the Boy. This appellation, which sometimes sounds like "Mutt! Mutt!," is appropriate to the parents' animalistic approach to life. Back in the "family room," the Mother, her hair in giant curlers, roughly attempts to kiss her son as Lynch, for the first time, shows a power figure trying to force intimacy on an unwilling participant. As he resists, she has a fit in which she grimaces grotesquely, puts her up-pointing fingers over her face and rubs them up and down violently, whining and shaking the Boy with her other hand.

Feeling alienated from the only other people in his world, the Boy sits dejectedly on his bed. Out of nowhere, Lynch shows us a dark shot of a staircase leading upward and we hear the call of a night bird. This sudden, anticipatory introduction of unexplained elements (the dark stairs, the bird sound) into an established context (the family's two rooms) is one of Lynch's ways of creating the mysterious atmosphere that he loves, of making us ponder the meaning of what he's just shown us, and it shows the importance of sound in his design strategy. Ascending the stairs to what will be a new stage of his life, the Boy follows the calling notes to a simple room like his own. A bed with a red iron frame and white sheets and a white bag labeled "SEEDS" fill the black space. In this realm of his birth colors (the red and white droplets that formed him), the Boy pulls out five seeds and discards them. The sixth one gives the familiar birdlike whistle. Mounding a circle of earth on the sheets (like the golden circle on his own bed), the Boy plants the seed and, accompanied by the elemental-power sound of thunder and a downpour of rain, sprinkles it with a galvanized watering can. An organic sound pulses from the mound at the rate of a human heart. The mound sprouts a fungus-like form whose shape is similar to the head of Steven Spielberg's title creature in *E. T. The Extra-Terrestrial* (1982), and, more pointedly, the iconographic mutant baby of Lynch's *Eraserhead*, which impressed moviegoers five years before Spielberg's creation.

The fungal sprout grows up into a seven-foot-tall, phallic-shaped pod that glistens like a mucous membrane and has a vagina-like circular opening at its base, and a barren tree branch appendage. (Denuded trees will show up in *Eraserhead*, *Twin Peaks*, and Lynch's Michael Jackson record commercial.) The Boy waters the pod's birth opening and lovingly strokes its outer lips. After another punishment session with his Father (face rubbed in yellow-stained sheets), the Boy, now alone, hears a liquid sound of straining mass. With a look of wonderment and his first big smile of the film, he delivers his Grandmother (Dorothy McGinnis) into the world. Amidst a rhythmic squishing and a viscous discharge, she slithers out head-first. Feeling that he has a true home at last, the Boy rests his head on this large, fleshy woman's shoulder and sweetly looks up at her consoling face.

Lynch presents episodes that reinforce the noxious-parents/nurturing-Grandmother theme. The director shows his early mastery of the vocabulary of screen violence in an eating scene at the slovenly family table. Like animals, the parents gorge on repulsive-looking food, while the Boy just stares at his plate for a long time. At last, he slowly reaches out for a bottle of ketchup—and Lynch does split-second close-up cuts to the Father screaming "Mott!," the ketchup bottle, and, in a wider table view, the Father's massive arm shooting across the frame to grab and shake the Boy as we hear the crash of spilled tableware: a couple of seconds that push you back in your seat.

That night, the Boy is awakened by his Grandmother's birdlike call. As he climbs the stairs to see her, his assaultive parents burst upon him ("Mott, Mott!") and try to drag him down to their level. To this point in the film, the Boy has enjoyed his communion with his Grandmother unimpeded but now his parents have discovered his secret, double life. Lynch has just launched a major theme of his fictions. His former wife (now Peggy Reavey) recalls that "from as far back as high school, the issue of cheating on a relationship has been central to David's life."[225] The situation of maneuvering around a socially sanctioned romantic partner or authority figure to pursue one's heart's desire stirs something deep in the artist's psyche. "He loves the secrecy of it, the sneaking away; he's utterly seduced by that."[226] The Boy's parents are unable to follow him as he ascends the stairs. Lynch expresses his animosity toward those who would curtail his freedom, as the Boy has an animated fantasy in which he pulls two strings, thus beheading Father and squashing Mother with a round weight. (Lynch's old friend Jack Fisk says that "If David didn't have his art somebody would probably be dead by now."[227]) The Boy performs these executions on a curtained stage, a setting that will figure prominently in a number of Lynch's productions, including *Eraserhead*, *The Elephant Man*, and *Twin Peaks*. In the midst of this animated death-dealing, Lynch inserts a momentary shot of the Boy's bed which spurts an orange-red liquid and an erect, phallic pod like the one that delivered Grandmother. Lynch has previously linked the sun's orb and the Boy's urine circles in a golden life-force amalgam. He adds the symbolic red of the parents' death to yield the orange pod that is a fleeting harbinger of the Boy's next onward-and-upward step.

Though this fantasy passage seems liberating, Lynch stresses the child's entrapment and sadness. In the film's most moving passage, the Boy seeks solace up in his Grandmother's room. Lynch beautifully orchestrates alternating close-ups of the two as warm looks and smiles banish melancholy. The Grandmother's mouth moves and the Boy answers in a silent language only they can hear. In an earlier, wrenching episode, the parents had thrust their accusatory pointing fingers at their son like knife blades. Lynch converts this dark gesture to gold as the beaming Grandmother and Boy face each other and gently use their index fingers to trade touches on shoulders, arms, and faces. With this simple gesture, Lynch sings out a playful, yet profound message: "You are here; I am so glad." He ends the sequence on a freeze frame of the two softly kissing on the lips, and before the shot fades, a sporelike dot appears within the white perimeter of the Boy's pale face. Scholars say that the practice of kissing originated with parents chewing food and passing it to their young children mouth-to-mouth, and the Boy's Grandmother has planted a seed within him that will nourish his evolution.

In a symbolic animation sequence, we see the Grandmother prepare a hole in the earth in which the Boy plants himself. A tall plant with a searchlight top sprouts up. After various fertilizings take place, the Boy, on black wings, flies out of the light and away into the sky. Then we see a large, dark tree form, reminiscent of the Grandmother's birth pod, pierced by the sudden thrust of a white, tendril-like shaft. The "Grandmother Tree" then sprouts a white, sickly branch. Lynch cuts directly to the live-action, stricken Grandmother. Trembling and shuddering, with her hands clasping her throat, she manages to emit a whistle for the Boy, who wakes and joins her. As though filled with a pent-up force that needs to get out of her body, she starts whistling a single note like a steaming teakettle. This sharp, loud sound goes on for an eternity-seeming two and a half minutes, and is the first outstanding example of Lynch's eccentric, elongated sense of screen timing. As the noise continues, the Boy runs downstairs to enlist his parents' help, but Father stares at him with dumb-ox eyes and Mother collapses in laughter. As both adults mock the Boy's panic, we see pixilated images of the whistling grandmother skittering and crashing around her room as though propelled by the violent air stream escaping from her pursed lips. The Boy runs up to show us a full-face close-up at his Grandmother's threshold, and Lynch shows his mastery of sonic drama as we hear her whistle stop and her heavy body hit the floor.

For the first time in this film of black-backgrounded images, we are in bright daylight, seeing a dry-grass field from a walking person's point of view. Lynch films the Boy from the back as he stops to contemplate the pale grass before him in a shot that anticipates by sixteen years actor Kyle MacLachlan pausing in the same body position to look at a fateful golden grass field in *Blue Velvet*. The Boy finds his Grandmother sitting in a chair in the tall grass, just as in Lynch's 1990 *Twin Peaks* MacLachlan's character will find his tale's Significant Woman sitting in a chair after death in an otherworldly zone of time and space that is metaphysically and aesthetically different from the rest of the film. Lynch invests the Boy and his Grandmother's encounter with a disturbing sense of distance and dislocation. In this post-death limbo, the Boy looks directly at her, but she peers from side to side without seeing him (a parent-and-child-not-seeing-each-other interaction appears in Lynch's 1997 *Lost Highway* screenplay, but not in the film). She opens her mouth and tips back her head into a frozen position, and the Boy screams a high organ-chord sound and falls to the earth with the weight of his loss.

Back in his room, the Boy lies down on his bed and Lynch watches his face in quiet close-up. Suddenly, in close-up, the Boy's head thrashes and rolls violently out of the frame. Lynch cuts to a wide-view image of profound mystery. We see the Boy's unmoving form lying on his bed, an erect, reddish, three-foot phallic podlike growth having sprouted in place of his head. Lynch holds the shot for only a few seconds, and we see white animated roots or branches growing in from the frame edges as the scene fades to black.

Ever sensitive to duality and paradox, Lynch first shows us the sickening terrors of a child's learning process in *The Alphabet*, and then the joy and survival value of acquiring knowledge in *The Grandmother*. *The Alphabet*'s knowledge is imposed from above by the hostile-seeming adult world. *The Grandmother*'s Boy climbs up from the debased, assaultive, downstairs level of his parents' existence to learn life lessons in the higher realm of intuition, loving emotion, and cosmic connection. This child of the universe shows his true life-force colors in his golden-sun sheet stains. Always ready to ascend, he is open to that first night-call that leads him up the staircase. The nighttime of free-flowing consciousness is his classroom. He first reads the "SEEDS" sign on the bag, and then goes deeper, applying his gift for sub-literal cognition by knowing what to do with *the* particular right seed and just how to bring his loving companion into the world. And by following the path of love, the Boy is equipped to survive her loss, and to make the next spiritual-evolutionary growth spurt that gathers force just beyond Lynch's final film frame.

Lynch's parents were "very upset"[228] when he showed them *The Grandmother*: They "wondered where all this stuff came from,"[229] and they knew how he worshiped his own grandmother. The film's antagonistic storm of alienation between parents and child was certainly not a realistic Lynch family snapshot. But David of the happy childhood, through his symbolic art language, could still give form to his need to escape the homefront "claustrophobia"[230] and differentiate himself from his mother and father. And Lynch's choice of the grandparent as the agent of release from parental oppression echoes his own adolescent lionization of his "racy"[231] grandfather as contrasted with his staid parents. The bond of harmonious intercourse between the Boy and his Grandmother is so strong and exclusive that it's impossible to imagine her being related to the two loathsome adults downstairs. Symbolically, the child has given birth to her, and she returns the favor, passing him, in a loving kiss, the seed of his future development.

The Grandmother's parent figures, beyond being effective dark narrative elements that allow the film's luminous goodness to shine all the brighter in contrast, are Lynch's first cinematic human figures to be inhabited by a disturbing otherness. In 1987, the director observed, "Something that looks human, but isn't, is frightening."[232] Twenty years earlier, he intuitively understood that the most dangerous and soul-chilling beasts are the ones that walk like men and women (Adolf Hitler was said to be thrilled that his first name meant "wolf.") Any other director might have been content to portray the villainous parents as hostile, assaultive, uncaring slobs. But Lynch stains them with a taint of evolutionary slippage. At one point, the mother crawls under the family dinner table and scratches the dust with a clawlike hand. She and her husband are all untrammeled impulse and appetite, unchecked by civilized refinement. These noxious parents and their unkempt lair are shadow-zone reflections of the warm, nurturing, well-ordered, and archetypally 1950s household that Lynch both enjoyed and rebelled against. In *The Grandmother*, Lynch begins a decades-long artistic wrestling match with that hellish, threatening, hidden "force"[233] that as a child he sensed pulsing behind the serene facade of his small-town life. The image of the father's distorted face screaming and growling above his cowering, supine son will be joined by Lynch's later, searing portraits of animalistic predators crouching over or pouncing on their helpless victims: *Dune*'s (1984) Baron Harkonen, *Blue Velvet*'s (1986) Frank Booth (Dennis Hopper), and *Twin Peaks*' (1990–1991) BOB (Frank Silva). (Following the reasoning of Jennifer Lynch, who wrote *The Secret Diary of Laura Palmer* in 1990, this book will refer to *Twin Peaks*' evil entity as BOB, not Bob. As Jennifer says, "Using all capital letters made him Other and gave him a different personality on the page. It made him not one of the normal people and gave him a louder voice. He was so much more frightening. Those three letters were like a code telling us to beware."[234])

Death is the human psyche's most primal fear, but its close cousin is the terror of depersonalization—the breathless, runaway panic as you feel your thoughts, emotions, and memory slipping away; your familiar sense of self invaded and displaced by alien energies; your horrified realization that the perpetrator of unspeakable perversions and violence is staring at you from the nearest mirror. Author Carlos Clarens posits that the idea of people being occupied by invasive entities/forces is an ancient one. He cites examples such as Zeus assuming human forms, Vishnu's many avatars, the Christian Mystery of the Incarnation, and Hebraic and medieval demonic possessions and dybbuks. And we can't forget tales like *Dr. Jekyll and Mr. Hyde* and films such as *Invasion of the Body Snatchers*, *Donovan's Brain*, and *The Exorcist*. Freud believed that monsters and doppelgangers are projected embodiments of our subconscious fears and unacceptable desires: dark psychic material that Jung called the shadow, which we are loath to call our own. Lynch will explore the horror of possession and depersonalization at length over the course of his career, and his approach will be very much in the spirit of Patricia Highsmith's 1981 story *The Terrors of Basket-Weaving*, in which a sophisticated Manhattan advertising executive finds an old broken basket on a country weekend. Aghast, she realizes that something inside her knows how to restore the basket by weaving twigs and tying knots, and she completes the job in just a few minutes. Rather than being pleased with herself, she has the horrifying sense of "a great many people"[235] from the ancient past being "in her brain and mind."[236] There's an atavistic, "prehistoric"[237] presence within her: "I feel lost in a strange way—*Identity*, I mean."[238] In Lynch's work, the humanity-displacing force will frequently be animalistic, and the early nerve-twitch of this brutal energy ripples through *The Grandmother*. For the Boy's worst nightmare would be to find himself starting to behave monstrously "like father, like son." No wonder he seeks refuge in some alternate, hybridized ecosystem of Lynch's imagination, in which human and plant gene pools are intermixed.

The director clearly identifies and sympathizes with his creative young gardening protagonist; the autobiographical fact of he and Peggy being surprised by pregnancy is echoed in the film's parents' shocked reaction to their son popping up into their lives. And the father figure's hostility toward his offspring could be Lynch's way of cathartically expressing, even subconsciously, any negative feelings about his own unplanned parenthood. Both the film's hellish father and innocent child are embodiments of Lynch's psychic energy.

It is telling that Donald and Sunny Lynch did not see the film's Boy character as some universalized allegorical figure, but as their David. In virtually every Lynch film, there appears a character who espouses the director's philosophies and sentiments. And that character, like the writer-director, commonly wears a black suit and white shirt. Watching the pale-faced, black-haired young Richard White sensitively portray the tuxedo-clad Boy, one easily pictures Kyle MacLachlan in *Dune*, *Blue Velvet*, and *Twin Peaks*, who in turn mirrors Lynch. Those who write about *The Grandmother*, and the body of Lynch's work, discuss its bizarre, surrealistic stylization and stress its physical and emotional violence. But certainly the young artist who could feel the universe vibrating in an industrial wasteland, and today matter-of-factly says "I still love everyone I ever loved,"[239] has a more fully rounded, humanly balanced sensibility. In *The Grandmother*, Lynch, through his surrogate black-suited Boy, shows his capacity for venturing into the unknown, creating a safe haven from a threatening environment, enjoying playfulness, and above all, venerating and loving women and yearning for transcendent transformations and a spiritual connection with the cosmos.

The Grandmother is Lynch's first film world to integrate emotional, metaphysical, and stylistic elements into a seamless whole. As though entering a dream, with its own system of signs and meanings, Lynch gently glides us into a place we've never been before, but that is also strangely familiar. The director grounds his imaginary world in a recognizable botanical-zoological matrix. Huge, grandmother-incubating pods with mucous membranes and barren tree limbs don't grow in our attic bedrooms. But Lynch establishes such visual elements with striking textural detail, and interrelates them with an unwavering dream-logic consistency that obliterates our disbelief—this is, simply, the way things are here. The film is like an answer to Thoreau's declaration: "Convince me that you have a seed there, and I will expect wonders."[240] Lynch reinforces the film's awestruck tone by melding the Boy's nocturnal explorations and discoveries with vibrant, droning organ notes that seem to suspend time as they hypnotically arc out and float in the night air. And, working for the first time with sound-design wizard Alan Splet, Lynch provides a rich, poetic aural background (humming insects, crickets, thunder and pouring rain) for the boy's grandma-growing gardening ritual. (In *The Grandmother*, Lynch, through the Boy's actions, presents a growth process and a progression of its component elements [earth on the bed, water, sprouting plant pod, Grandmother] that bear a striking resemblance to the ancient *Chandogya Upanishad* of the Hindu faith that Lynch will discover and embrace in the years following *The Grandmother*: "The essence of all beings is earth./ The essence of all earth is water./ The essence of all water is plants./ The essence of all plants is people."[241])

The integrity and force of Lynch's images has grown in the two years since he made *The Alphabet*. The first film's animated alphabet garden and cubist head-figure are certainly the work of an accomplished artist, but their motion is rudimentary and stilted; it is hard to forget that one is watching moving drawings and paintings. Whereas *The Grandmother*'s animated figures and plant kingdom pulse with a vibrant, independent life, and Lynch explores their realm with a smoothly free-flowing camera eye. The film's animated characters are convincingly stylized versions of its live actors. *The Grandmother*'s economy of form and motion shows that Lynch has the aesthetic gift of being able to stop short of doing too much, except when he wants to for the counterbalancing effect of exaggeration. As when, to emphasize the Boy's helpless, panicky, horror-struck reaction to his Grandmother's fatal seizure, Lynch extends the alarm of her protracted death throes into a single, endless-seeming whistle note that is a sad, darkened echo of the first birdlike call which drew the boy into her realm. We cannot escape the piercing duration of her and the Boy's distress. This unprecedented cinematic death scene shows Lynch's ability to convey strong emotions in absolutely unique forms, as when he stages the warmly affecting scene of loving communion between the Boy and his Grandmother that consists of tenderly traded finger-to-body touches.

Like the early-twentieth-century German Expressionist and French Surrealist filmmakers, Lynch is fascinated by the dreamlike quality of streaming cinematic images and sounds, and their ability to present intangible inner states of being as palpable audio-visual experiences for the audience.

He wants to suspend the viewer's eye and imagination in a trance of sensory impressions and psychological associations. Sometimes Lynch uses dreams and vision as formal, discrete plot elements (*The Alphabet*, *Dune*, *Blue Velvet*, *Twin Peaks*, *Wild at Heart*). Often, he blends his narratives' dream and nondream states so that the points of transition between various realities are tantalizingly obscure (*The Grandmother*, *Eraserhead*, *Blue Velvet*, *Twin Peaks*, *Lost Highway*, *Mulholland Drive*).

In *The Alphabet*, Lynch presents views of a normal, live-action sleeping Girl as a framing device for her fantastic animated dreams—whereas dreaminess suffuses every minute of *The Grandmother*. The film's live-action people and their habitat are as strange and stylized as their animated counterparts are. In this film, Lynch uses animation to facilitate large-scale, omniscient point-of-view sequences like the parents' underground birthing episode, which would cost a Spielbergian fortune to film with actual stage sets and human beings. Later, animation delineates the Boy's symbolic view of the grown-ups in his life, as when he slays his parents and is planted by his Grandmother and flies into the sky from the tip of a towering leafy growth. In conventional films, the line separating omniscient and interior-consciousness narrative elements is sharply drawn. But for Lynch, the barrier between internal and external, dream and reality, death and new life, is a permeable membrane.

In Robert Wiene's seminal 1920 German Expressionist film *The Cabinet of Dr. Caligari*, a fairground showman entices some students into a nightmarish realm of distorted physical reality and sleepwalking murder with the words "The real show is on the inside,"[242] a phrase that sums up Lynch's view of the world. In *Caligari*, to *come inside* means to penetrate the carnival's outer layers and approach its central, secret mystery, but it also signifies the drama being played out in someone's imagination, for as the film ends we realize that the bizarre doings and images we've experienced have been the inner, psychological scenario of a madman confined to an asylum. Lynch, like the makers of *Caligari*, is fascinated by the symbiotic relationship between fantasy and reality. But unlike the *Caligari* crew, he likes to erase the narrative line that separates dream and waking states of mind. Lynch wants to portray the interplay between powerful emotions and abstract forces, and he has the artistic ambition and skill to make these elements vivid, visceral, and intense whether a character encounters them in the street or in his head. The director strives to communicate a character's psychological reality which, sleeping or awake, is always with him or her.

German Gothic Revival writer E. T. A. Hoffmann (1776–1822) is credited with being the first to compose tales in which the inner and outer lives of characters were not separated. Figures of fantasy stepped into real life and, in an eerie, disturbing way, the supernatural and the psychological were one. Freud the scientist felt that he and Hoffmann the artist were tapping a common wellspring of psychoanalytic truth. One of Hoffmann's tales, with a storyline in which pages were purposefully missing, prefigured the narrative ambiguity of many Lynch films, which some viewers think need more gap-bridging explanatory scenes.

Wanting viewers to have their own inner experience of his work, Lynch doesn't come out and say, "This part is real, and then here's where the dream starts," or "The whole thing was a fantasy." As his career advanced beyond *The Grandmother*, Lynch had to learn to cope with an army of people focused on ferreting out the core of personal intent hidden within his often mystifying narrative and aesthetic modus operandi. He developed the technique of devising a pat phrase to characterize his latest project, which he would repeat verbatim to any journalist, talk show host, or fan who asked, like a prisoner of war divulging only his name, rank, and serial number. These formulaic verbalizations were designed to hide as much as they revealed: His still-unproduced *Ronnie Rocket* was to be "about the absurd mystery of the strange forces of existence."[243] It was as though Lynch made a sacred pact with himself to never expose his own conceptions of the meaning of his work in a clear, straightforward declaration of intent. But in order to enter the 1970 Bellevue Film Festival competition near Seattle, Lynch had to submit just such a statement with his film *The Grandmother*. And in just nine words he gave us the key to the kingdom of his imagination: For him the film is "a journey into the mind of a lonely boy."[244] Lynch understands that just as we move through the world, so the world moves through us; that we experience external phenomena as internal events and live our lives inside our heads, and over the years, this realization has shaped the many intriguing forms of his art. Lynch's youthful sense of human consciousness being one with what it observes was echoed by Henri in *The Art Spirit*, where a landscape is "like something thought, something remembered,"[245] and reinforced in coming decades by Lynch's practice of Transcendental Meditation and studies of Hindu philosophy. He discovered a kindred spirit in the English visionary poet and artist William Blake (1757–1827), who wrote that "For in the Brain of Man we live,"[246] and "To Me This World is all One continued Vision of Fancy or Imagination."[247] Thirty years after Lynch made *The Grandmother*, I noticed that one of the few books visible in his house was a volume on Blake.

Aside from its thematic richness, *The Grandmother* showcases Lynch's elegant design sense, as in his use of all-black rooms for his live-action tableaus. Furniture and figures stand out dramatically against the dark background. In some rooms, Lynch paints a white line where the invisible black wall meets the invisible black floor, giving a ghostly definition of spatial depth to a scene. So when the Boy follows that initial night-call up the stairs, and first approaches the doorway of what will be his Grandmother's room, he sees just a fine tracing of white lines and a white doorknob circle eerily delineating the portal of his heart's dream.

The Grandmother's excellence was recognized wherever it was shown. The picture screened in Europe and on TV in Boston, and won prizes at film festivals in Atlanta, San Francisco, and Bellevue. The Bellevue Film Festival juror Sheldon Renan noted that at a time when most young filmmakers were crafting cinematic protests against the Vietnam War and launching attacks against the establishment, Lynch was addressing universal human themes: "the experiences of growing up and needing love that are common to us all."[248] Renan found certain scenes, such as the Grandmother's birth, "truly amazing," and lauded the "great skill and taste with which the film has been executed."[249]

Lynch's five years in Philadelphia, a locus of "violence, hate, and filth,"[250] were days and nights of "extreme danger and intense fear."[251] But they were also times of red-hot creative inspiration that stimulated artistic experimentation and growth. Infernal Philadelphia joined with Lynch's idyllic small-town Pacific Northwest to indelibly imprint the artist with a bipolar, heaven-and-hell vision of America, and his urban adventure deepened his experience and understanding of human nature. The City of Brotherly Love immersed Lynch in the Art Life he so passionately craved, as well as delivering him a wife and young daughter and a minuscule bank balance.

Later in 1970, Tony Vellani, director of the American Film Institute's newly formed Center for Advanced Film Studies, invited Lynch to come and practice his singular art at the Center's lavish Beverly Hills–estate headquarters. So Lynch, this western-born visionary, and his extended family (Peggy, Jennifer, friend Jack Fisk, soundman Alan Splet) made the archetypal American journey from the east to the western edge of the country he so loved.

Lynch felt Philadelphia's oppressive fear evaporate in the California sunshine. But a growing strain between his Art Life and his family life could not be denied. And Lynch found that all those disturbing Philadelphia scenes "sank down inside of me."[252] Something was stirring in his subconscious, "a dream of dark and troubling things."[253] A cinematic shape unlike anything the world had ever seen before: *Eraserhead*.

2

FACTORY CHILD

1970–1976
(*Eraserhead*)

The City of Angels, home of the industry that sets the world to dreaming, was itself a dream place for brand-new resident David Lynch. Though "not a film buff,"[1] Lynch loved Billy Wilder's classic film noir *Sunset Boulevard* (1950). The twenty-four-year-old artist spent days driving through tony residential neighborhoods searching for a certain familiar break in the tall hedgerows. The vegetation-shrouded driveway into which William Holden's Joe Gillis, due to a tire blowout, accidentally pulls his car and begins an entrapping, spirit-killing visit to the haunted house of moldering Old Hollywood. Inside, forgotten screen queen Norma Desmond (Gloria Swanson) enwraps Joe in an unholy embrace, feeds on his youth and, hissing a vampire's lullaby, nods him off into the big sleep that lasts forever.

Unable to find the come-hither curve of concrete where Los Angeles's streets dissolved into Wilder's movie dream, Lynch expanded the range of his exploratory car trips beyond the unsolved mystery of Norma Desmond's driveway. He admired the elegant beige-and-cream geometry of the city's art deco municipal architecture and the sleek, flat-roofed simplicity of Richard Neutra's 1950s-modern residences, but he was most excited by the merging of industrial machinery and agricultural fields that skirted the Los Angeles River. Lynch's Philadelphia-spawned factory love sparked like an arc welder's torch; he was happy that his new West Coast home could provide "my favorite things: glass with wire in it, soot, steel, cement, fire, tremendously powerful sounds and images."[2]

But the school bell was ringing, and Lynch had to leave behind the dusty factory parking lots to tread the emerald-velvet lawns of Beverly Hills' Greystone Mansion estate, which housed the American Film Institute's Center for Advanced Film Studies. Lynch may not have been able to locate the *Sunset Boulevard* mansion but the big, grand Greystone house was an echo of Norma Desmond's manse: Its multicar garage building even looked like the one into which William Holden drove his ailing car. Under the guidance of Frank Daniel, founder of the Czechoslovakian Film School, Lynch analyzed the particular contributions of camera placement, acting, sound and music design, editing, and art direction to the narrative flow of a feature film story. It was Daniel who taught the methodical young man an amusingly concise formula for building a movie: "Frank said you need enough ideas for seventy scenes. Put them on three-by-five cards. As soon as you have seventy, you have a feature film."[3]

In addition to watching movies and learning how to build a film, Lynch did some reading in his American Film Institute days. Franz Kafka's *Metamorphosis* fascinated the young man with its surrealistic, quantum-leap transformation of a man into an insect, its lurking dread, black humor, and its expression of psychological states in physical forms. Another tale, *The Nose* by Nikolai Gogol, furthered Lynch's appreciation of the offbeat Eastern European sensibility and had a formative effect on him in his pre-*Eraserhead* days. The Russian Gogol (1809–1852), civil servant, history professor, and writer, spun stories that, as do Kafka's and Lynch's works, "penetrate into the hidden places of the human mind and reveal the most secret stirrings of the human heart,"[4] as Gogol scholar David Magarshack says. Kafka and Gogol were motivated to satirize their respective societies, which Lynch is not; however, even though *The Nose* pokes fun at the particular pretensions of Russia's civil-servant culture in great detail, it's easy to see why Lynch embraced the tale.

Lynch is a master at illuminating extraordinary happenings and images within a context of mundane, familiar, everyday reality, a modus operandi that Kafka and Gogol practice with ease. In *The Nose*, Ivan, a nineteenth-century St. Petersburg barber, wakes up, chats with his shrewish wife, and sits down at the breakfast table, like he does every morning. But on this day, digging his fingers into a soft chunk of bread, he "pulled out—a nose!"[5] Lynch, whose surreal imagination was capable of combining the unrelated terms "eraser" and "head," no doubt thrilled to Gogol's linkage of "bread" and "nose." And Lynch noted the dry humor in the author's matter-of-fact presentation of an uncanny occurrence. As often happens in a Lynch fiction, something strange gets stranger still, for Ivan recognizes the nose as that of pompous Major Kovalykov, who Ivan routinely shaves. Like a foreshadowing of Lynch's 1997 *Lost Highway*, in which a man wonders if he blanked out and killed his wife, Ivan is tortured by the thought that he may have done something horrible with his razor while drunk, something he doesn't remember. So, by only the second page of *The Nose*, we have the sort of situation Lynch cherishes: an engaging, highly unusual mystery.

Ivan takes the nose to a bridge and throws it into the river. He's observed by a policeman who doesn't see precisely what Ivan is doing but is suspicious. At this point Gogol shows his artistic kinship with Lynch by making the way he presents his narrative, as well as the doings of his characters, mysterious: "Ivan Yakovlevich turned pale. . . . But here the incident is completely shrouded in a fog and absolutely nothing is known of what happened next."[6]

Now we are with Major Kovalykov as he wakes, goes to the mirror, and sees smooth, flat flesh where his nose should be. (The lack of expected blood and gore adds to the tale's delicious absurdity.) Obsessed with impressing people and climbing socially, Kovalykov is driven to despair because he now is without a presentable face. Ivan finding the nose was Gogol's first touch of strangeness, Kovalykov losing it the second, and now the author delivers his masterstroke of humorous grotesquerie. Kovalykov sees "a gentleman in uniform"[7] jump out of a carriage and rush up some steps, and the Major "recognized that his was his own nose!"[8] Yes, wearing a dazzling suit, a sword at his side, and a plumed hat topping all, is Kovalykov's nose. Like Lynch, who leaves the interpretation of his work up to the individual who experiences it, Gogol cannily does not say anything about what size the nose is, so we can imagine any scale from a few inches to six feet (Lynch made a drawing of the nose that showed he pictured it as man-sized). Gogol makes it seem perfectly normal that the nose should go and pray in a church and chat amiably with its fellow citizens, hence increasing Kovalykov's sense of alienation, anger, and horror: No one else understands that the nose is *his* property, and not some autonomous gentleman with a higher social rank than his own. Kafka's *Metamorphosis* showed Lynch that a person could acquire a bizarre, monstrous form and still be himself (like John Merrick in *The Elephant Man*), while *The Nose* emphasized the idea of a person's identity having two forms.

Like an engaging storyteller should, Gogol throws a reversal at us: The tide turns for Kovalykov—or does it? A policeman comes to Kovalykov's apartment and gives him back his nose. It was "intercepted just before leaving town,"[9] and, mysteriously, "the chief accomplice in this affair is that scoundrel of a barber,"[10] Ivan. All seems well, but Kovalykov's travails are not over, for the nose (which we now perceive as normal-sized), won't adhere to Kovalykov's face, and keeps slipping off. How can Kovalykov ever accomplish a proper marriage and keep climbing the ladder of social advancement now? Again, Gogol does a Lynch-like narrative shift: That "thick fog"[11] again descends "on the incident, and what happened afterwards is completely unknown."[12] But, also as Lynch commonly does, Gogol creates a veil of enigma only to penetrate it and tell us more story, a narrative device that compels our avid interest.

Kovalykov wakes one morning, walks past a mirror, and sees that his nose is back where it should be. He's overjoyed, of course, and when Ivan shaves him, and sees that the nose has returned, he too is relieved and happy. Gogol has crafted a tale with two morals: If you drink too much like Ivan, you can lose consciousness of your behavior and destroy your peace of mind, and Kovalykov's obsessive concern for physical vanity and social pretension leads to a shallow, frivolous life.

As Lynch finished *The Nose*, he reflected on a sentence that reinforced a central attitude of his own sensibility: "The world is full of all sorts of absurdities."[13] Like Gogol does in *The Nose*, Lynch spends his life presenting strange, incongruous juxtapositions and scary-funny dislocations to the world. In the last lines of *The Nose*, Gogol injects the voice of a narrator to comment like an audience on this odd, marvelous tale, and it sounds like the passionate, divided response Lynch's work stirs up. It's "incomprehensible"[14] that "authors should choose such subjects. I confess that it is entirely beyond my comprehension. . . . I simply don't understand it . . . there's no benefit whatever. I simply don't know what to make of it. . . ."[15] This is followed by "there really is something in it. Say what you like, but such things do happen—not often, but they do happen."[16] As Lynch loves to do, Gogol leaves the window open at the end, primed for a flight of fancy.

Peggy Reavey, Lynch's wife at the time he fell in love with *The Nose*, feels that since Lynch read the story in translated form, he experienced it in a simplified way that left "white space"[17] into which he could project his own thoughts, feelings, and imagination. Over the years, Lynch has often said that in his work he strives to "give you room to dream."[18]

Film Center students were expected to produce a film and Lynch spent most of 1970 developing a script called *Gardenback*, which evolved from his painting of what Peggy called "a stooped figure with green things growing out of its back."[19] Like *The Grandmother* and many of Lynch's works to come, *Gardenback* portrays the family home as "a place where things can go wrong."[20] Henry and Mary (Lynch's first painting studio was on Henry Street) live happily in their house. One day, Henry "looks at a girl, and something crosses from her to him. That something is an insect which grows in Henry's attic, which is like his mind. The house is like his head. And the thing grows and metamorphoses into this monster that overtakes him. He doesn't become it, but he has to deal with it, and it drives him to completely ruin his home."[21]

This abstract meditation on "the theme of adultery"[22] adds definition to what will become characteristic Lynchian motifs. Throughout cultural history, writers and artists, philosophers, and healers of the psyche have represented the human head with the image of a house. Henry, with a malevolent insect in his attic, is the first of many Lynchian characters to have a monster in his head. The seventeenth-century Dutch philosopher Spinoza tells us that "Will and Intellect are one and the same"[23] and in Lynch's fictions, bad thoughts from inside the head often try to grasp and control the external world by means of malevolent physical acts. Lynch's choice of an insect to symbolize the agent of Henry's betrayal of Mary parallels twentieth-century Spanish writers Lorca's, Damasco's, and Alonso's use of the insect to represent unbalanced mental states of anxiety, desire, and terror. French literary avant-gardist Antonin Artaud felt that flies were evil thoughts sent by people far away to harm us. Though, even later in life, Lynch remains a stranger to the vast majority of the world's literature, his love of Kafka's *Metamorphosis* has remained strong. In 1992, Lynch first spoke of his desire to film the famous tale of Gregor Samsa's horrendously matter-of-fact transformation into a man-sized cockroach, so his use of the word "metamorphoses"[24] in regard to *Gardenback*'s invasively growing insect probably shows Kafka's influence. The great Spanish surrealist director Luis Buñuel inserted insect images into some of his films, though none were empowered with as much narrative thrust as Lynch's eight-legged house-destroyer. Lynch had not yet viewed any of Buñuel's work in the *Gardenback* period; his disruptive insect is more in the vein of *The Fly* (1958), a movie that the twelve-year-old Lynch had seen in Idaho. In that film, an experiment-gone-wrong leaves a scientist with the head and arm of a fly. As murderous bestial impulses infect what's left of the researcher's human personality, he attacks his fiancée and destroys his laboratory "home." Lynch was certainly familiar with a sexually perturbed Elvis Presley singing, "My friends say I'm acting wild as a bug; I'm in love, I'm all shook up."[25] Sixteen years later, in Lynch's masterwork *Blue Velvet* (1986), an innocent youth, who one character calls "the bug man," is gripped by an out-of-control, punishing sexual passion as the surface crust of his secure small-town world is gnawed from below by insects churning in darkness. And Lynch's 1998 print *Untitled (ant in house)* shows a gigantic insect invader barely contained by four domestic walls.

The bug realm aside, *Gardenback* is about a man betraying his mate and wrecking their communal world. Lynch discussed his ideas for the *Gardenback* film with Peggy Reavey, and thirty years later, she told me that his romantic nature is so strong that he firmly believes in "the Elevator Experience, where two strangers, each with their own mates, can lock eyes in an elevator and be jolted by the power of instant love."[26]

Lynch once said of *Gardenback*, "I always hide all my fears, and sometimes my films hide them too, only in different ways."[27] The films can also express his desires. Reavey says that the storyline of the potential film had a problem, in that David wasn't able to see the big bad monster of adultery as being evil, and so he couldn't kill it off in proper dramatic fashion. She adds that "as long as he and I were *talking* about these things I didn't think anything would actually be acted out. When we were in Philadelphia he used to say that 'Peggy is the only person in the world who understands me,' but in Los Angeles there was a line of people who said they understood him, and some of them were mighty good-looking. I didn't know that if you loved someone you could cheat on them."[28] And Lynch seemed so emotionally dependent on Peggy. Feeling he didn't have a body worthy of displaying on California beaches, Lynch would stay home while Peggy played at the seashore with friends. When she returned, she found that he'd pulled his chair up to the front door, waiting for her to open it and come back inside. Within a few years of Lynch's adultery fiction, he and his wife Peggy would separate and divorce.

The *Gardenback* screenplay was a pollen drift of emotion and event that Lynch wanted to realize as a forty-five-minute film, but his Film Center advisers would not accept the script in its present amorphous form. They pressured him to add a more "realistic" linear storyline and dialogue and to expand the project to feature length. These attempts to alter his vision sapped Lynch's enthusiasm for the film, but the deathblow was delivered by the mass-market commercial cinema. The artistically proud Lynch loves to burst upon the scene with images and ideas previously unseen and unheard of, so when Walon Green's slightly fictionalized documentary (*The Hellstrom Chronicle*, 1971) about insects eventually taking over the world came out, Lynch was "completely thrown off because someone else was working with bugs."[29] Depressed, Lynch "cried over some coffee."[30] He was also feeling dejected and aggravated because, even though he was a second-year student, he'd been assigned to take first-year classes, so he thought he might have flunked, which didn't square with his sense of how he'd been performing. Just as, a few years earlier, high school had become an impediment to the blossoming of Lynch's deep need to express and honor his true self, the AFI was now an oppressively negative force in his life. So he quit. The wise and understanding Frank Daniel gave Lynch some time away from school to absorb the emotional consequences of his decision to leave. Then he said to him, "David, if you're upset, then we're doing something wrong. Tell me what you *really* want to do."[31] Lynch responded to Daniel's nurturing sincerity, and the assurance that he'd been placed in first-year classes by mistake, by describing an idea that had burst into his brain with a single unprecedented image: "A man's head bouncing on the ground, being picked up by a boy and taken to a pencil factory. I don't know where it came from."[32]

Lynch recalls that Daniel didn't care too much for his sketchy *Eraserhead* script but felt strongly that David should make the film he wanted to make. Daniel died the late 1990s and, at the funeral, his son told Lynch just how much of a champion Frank had been for David's project. Back in 1971, a powerful AFI board member told Daniel that *Eraserhead* was not the sort of film the school should be making. Daniel retorted that it was most certainly a project they should endorse and support, and turned in his resignation to back up his strong stand on Lynch's behalf. Daniel knew the AFI top brass would realize that his resignation letter was a gesture rather than a statement of serious intent. But they took it at face value, and Daniel, who Lynch calls "the greatest film teacher who ever lived,"[33] left the AFI.

The Film Center told Lynch that he could film his twenty-two-page story of a man whose head gets converted into nullifying nibs for the ends of pencils as a twenty-one-minute movie. The making of *Eraserhead* sharpened Lynch's connoisseurship of life's absurd surprises to a cutting edge. For the 1971 project, which was slated to take weeks, expanded out over five years and finally premiered as an eighty-nine-minute feature film in 1977. Growing with a life of its own, the *Eraserhead* production became an endless stretch of financial sacrifice for Lynch and his family, and swallowed up countless hours of his uncommonly dedicated cast's and crew's lives. As Lynch says today, "We bit off quite a chunk of time."[34]

For Lynch the marathon production was a "wonderful long journey"[35] that completed his artistic progression from childhood drawing to youthful painting to short animated film (*The Alphabet*), to longer animated/live-action film (*The Grandmother*), to full-length live-action film. And *Eraserhead* stimulated Lynch's personal, as well as artistic, growth. Instead of spending much of the filmmaking process by himself drawing on celluloid, the sometimes socially uncomfortable and nonverbal artist was able to successfully communicate his vision to a large group of collaborators and financial backers: "The outside world sort of disappeared as we all tuned in to the inner world we were creating."[36] Directing and coordinating every aspect of the production, from the iconographic mushroom-cloud hairdo of his hero, Henry, to the hand-built architecture of Henry's world, Lynch crafted a real movie outside the Hollywood studio system, a feat that was 99 percent more unusual, courageous, and audacious in the early 1970s than it would be today.

Over the span of decades since Lynch shot *Eraserhead*, the artist has uttered but a handful of sentences about the one creation of his many works that he still considers "my favorite."[37] For Lynch the film is both "the *real* Philadelphia story"[38] and "a dream of dark and troubling things"[39]—it is a distillation of the artist's oppressive urban terrors and soot-stained Philly milieu, and a revealing cellar-to-attic tour of the house in his head.

In *Eraserhead*, Lynch composed the exterior views of his benighted cityscape out of actual bits and pieces of early 1970s Los Angeles, yet the resulting vision of an inhospitable urban wasteland is as meticulously detailed and stylized as the drawn landscapes and self-built environments he created for *The Alphabet* and *The Grandmother*. The artist's inspired eye can construct a fantasy out of real-world materials as easily as he can sketch or paint one.

Looking directly at us in a huge close-up, his brow furrowed with worry and confusion, Henry Spencer (Jack Nance) glances over his shoulder as though something scary is coming up on him from behind his back (Lynch instinctively knows what psychologists' research shows, that human beings find unanticipated approaches from the rear to be primally threatening). Clutching a paper sack to his black-suited-white-shirted chest, Henry proceeds through a black-and-white cityscape devoid of sunshine, cars, or other people. A tiny figure in the flat, gray light, he recedes into a gigantic black hole in a building-sized concrete wall, threads his way between sooty metal factory tanks and chemical puddles of unnaturally luminous liquid, and troops over mounds of ashen, toxic earth in which no seed could grow.

Home in his apartment at last, the glum Henry sits on his couch—the bed—and contemplates the blank brick wall outside his window, the nuclear-blast mushroom cloud photo on his wall, the scraggy, barren tree branch sprouting from an earth mound on his nightstand, and the hairy, oil-glistening tangles of unclassifiable matter that cling to his floor and dresser top like oversized, mutated dust balls.

Summoned to the home of his estranged girlfriend, Mary X (Charlotte Stewart), for family dinner, Henry traverses a derelict nightscape that's pierced by the scary sound of angry dogs barking and glass breaking somewhere in the dark. The "sidewalk" to Mary's house is a stretch of grimy factory railroad tracks, and as Henry approaches her dimly lit porch, ghostly clouds of machine-belched steam intrude into the frame. The sound of Henry's world is an industrial din. A hissing and whistling, a roaring and rumbling of unseen masses and forces shifting for unknown purposes. An infernal chugging that dwarfs and mocks Henry's organic human heartbeat.

With a few deft strokes, Lynch has conjured up a unique cinematic world and imbued it with a pernicious surface texture that reflects his nightmarish Philadelphia milieu. Now he is ready to plunge beneath its surface into characteristic realms of sexuality and birth, fear and family conflict, violent death, dream life, and spiritual transcendence. This thematic constellation illuminates almost every one of Lynch's fictions, yet it is never more intimately linked to its creator's actual life experience than in *Eraserhead*. As Lynch once said, "There are scenes in the movie that feel like they're more inside my head than on the screen."[40] When the artist began to write the *Eraserhead* screenplay, his subconscious spontaneously offered up Henry's visit to Mary X's house, scenes that are classic Lynch.

Henry Spencer is the film character that Lynch most identifies with. In his black suit and look of deep befuddlement, Henry is a modern Everyman who, according to his creator, "is puzzled by many things. He spends a lot of time trying to understand everything, but it just doesn't all add up."[41] Lynch has said that we live "in a learning world."[42] And the director's protagonists, from *The Alphabet*'s Girl tortured by her letters to *Twin Peaks*' FBI Special Agent Dale Cooper pondering the slippery interface between death and life, are all trying to make sense of a series of strange clues. If Henry's last name evokes civilized philosophers (Herbert Spencer) and poets (Edmund Spencer), the Xs are the uncharted, dangerous unknown.

When Henry's night journey brings him to the Xs' house, he finds it half-obscured by a factory steam cloud. In a beautiful passage, Lynch rhymes the white cloud surging into his dark frame with a cut to the dark window in the Xs' front door, a black aperture into which Mary X's pale, floating face glides forward to the steam-misted glass. (Throughout Lynch's career, faces will glide toward us out of the darkness of obscurity.) Just as *The Grandmother*'s Boy had severe trouble communicating with his parents, Henry gropes for understanding at the Xs' abode of warped domesticity.

There's been a rift between Henry and Mary. Her pictorially disembodied head floating behind the door glass mirrors the torn, head-only photograph of Mary that Henry clutches in his hand. There are no warm greetings between the couple. Calling through the separating glass door, Henry wonders if Mary "wanted me to come or not. Where have you been? You never come around any more." She stares at him in silence for awkward moments and, finally opening the door, promisingly offers that "Dinner's almost ready" with a hopeful voice. Standing together for the first time in the same frame, their faces blank, they look at each other without touching or speaking, the number "2416" prominent on the doorframe behind, and visually between them. The note of positive anticipation slips from Mary's voice, as she says "Come on in" with glum resignation and steps inside. The couple's exchanges have been halting and full of pauses, and Henry maintains this hesitant rhythm by stopping for a second to look at the portentous-seeming "2416" before following Mary across the threshold. Henry is an early member of the Lynchian cluster of characters who are searching for meaning in an inhospitable, chaotic universe. The seriousness and intensity with which these characters pay attention to what seem on the surface to be mundane details of their world invests the regarded objects with an almost metaphysical gravity and presence. In his own life, magical-thinking Lynch is always on the look out for mysterious signposts, portents, and synchronicities. If *Eraserhead*'s "2416" isn't a cosmic Lynch pin, maybe the talismanic number can at least help Henry focus the strength he'll need to get through the next hour of his life. But, of course, 2 and 4 and 1 and 6 add up to unlucky 13. (In Philadelphia, Lynch and Peggy lived at 13th and Maplewood.)

The stilted speaking rhythms and disconnected communications that Henry and Mary exhibited at the Xs' doorstep pervade the family's sparsely furnished living room. *Eraserhead* is the first film in which Lynch works with the aesthetic element of human speech, and he pares down his dialogue to theater-of-the-absurd perfection. The director creates domestic tableaus that are the alienated shadow-side of the idealized, cozy, and nurturing 1950s home life that he himself had enjoyed. And he further develops the eccentric, stretched-out sense of screen time that he showed in the prolonged whistling death of *The Grandmother*'s title character.

Edgy with nervousness over meeting Mary's parents for the first time, Henry enters a space that is lit more like the scene of a film noir shootout than a warm family evening. Harshly commanded to "Sit down" by Mrs. X (Jeanne Bates), Henry wades through the pools of shadow and the harsh light bulb glare that splashes onto a barren wall, and positions himself at the far end of the couch, well away from mother and daughter. A full thirty seconds after Mrs. X's "Sit down," she adds, "It's Henry isn't it?" In making the verbal-emotional gap between people so palpable and excruciating, Lynch obliterates the convention of screen dialogue rhythm that celebrates rapid-fire repartee. And this painter who had a hard time making himself understood with words fills the X family's chilly silences with a weird, sourceless whimpering-sucking sound. Lynch's narratives yield mysteries large and small, and he tweaks our curiosity about this strange noise just as he made us ponder the significance of an out-of-context shot of a staircase in *The Grandmother*. Moments later the stairs became a fitting, explainable part of *The Grandmother*'s storyline. In *Eraserhead*, as Henry squirms in an awkward pause between utterances, we see that the whimperers are a bunch of puppies vigorously suckling on a large dog.

Lynch's solving of the small mystery of the phantom sounds with this doggy image brings a chuckle to the viewer. The pure, flowing straightforwardness of the animals' instinctive behavior subtly mocks the human beings' stilted, half-frozen interactions. And the image's biological-procreational essence sets up a prefigurative link with the real reason Henry has been brought to the Xs' house this night.

With a deadpan stare, Mrs. X interrogates her houseguest: "It's Henry, isn't it?" It takes Henry some time to muster, "Yes, it is." His hesitancy bespeaks Henry's wariness of Mrs. X's aggressive-toned inquisition. More profoundly, it shows a stirring of doubt about Henry's sense of himself, an impulse that will bring him to the wrenching question of just who, or what, is running the show in his cranium and the universe beyond. Or are his head and the heavens the same place?

Lynch puts Henry in the same position relative to the X family that *The Grandmother*'s Boy was to his noxious, abusive parents: belonging to either clan is hell-on-earth. Mother and daughter X are subject to fits. As Mrs. X continues to quiz Henry, Mary starts to scratch her knee with a convulsive fury and deliver a series of guttural cries. She can only be calmed by regressing to a childhood behavioral pattern: letting her mother brush her long, blonde hair. At the dinner table, when Henry is asked to carve the chicken, the cooked carcass starts twitching its drumsticks and oozing thick blood. Mrs. X, in an orgasmic seizure, tips her head far back and emits gargling sounds with a fluttering tongue. Her crescendo of ever-louder cries climaxes in a final spewing ululation that catapults her away from the dinner table. These X family women exhibit paroxysms of violent physicality, whereas Grandmother X (Jean Lange), who's kept out of Henry's sight in the kitchen, is virtually comatose. She sits unmoving in a chair as Mrs. X places a mixing bowl of salad on her lap. Mrs. X, like a puppetmaster, then stirs the old woman's hands in a salad-tossing motion and rewards the crone with a cigarette. Whether the smoke rising from the cigarette placed between Granny's frozen lips is a result of her inhalation or of the unaugmented burning of tobacco remains one of Lynch's unsolved mysteries.

The director doesn't just make the X women vessels of strangeness: Mr. X (Allen Joseph) also has a high, disturbing oddness quotient. Upon meeting Henry, Mr. X launches into a manic, scattershot tirade: "Plumbing's my business. I've seen this neighborhood change from pastures to the hellhole it is now. People think pipes grow in their homes. Well, they don't—look at my knees, look at my knees!" Lynch heightens the violence of Mr. X's outburst with a cinematic crescendo in which the crazed patriarch's womenfolk try to quiet him—"Bill!," "Dad"—as the nursing dog barks loudly and a train roars by outside. At the dinner table, Mr. X matter-of-factly declares, "My arm's all numb," and socks his forearm hard. After Mrs. X has finished her orgasmic fit over the oozing chicken and fled to the kitchen, followed by Mary, Mr. X jovially says to Henry, "Well, what do you know?" and freezes his face in a toothy idiot's grin. Mr. X's rambunctious non sequiturs, his dissociation from what's actually going on in the room, are both funny and fearsome.

(Over the years since *Eraserhead*, Lynch has often used Mr. X's term *hellhole* to characterize a toxic physical, emotion, or social climate. The film's hellhole is certainly Lynch's dark impression of Philadelphia but it's also a reflection of the wrenching turmoil the artist's beloved America was suffering in the early 1970s: Generations and races were battling each other, college kids protesting the Vietnam War were shot by U.S. Army soldiers, the peace-and-love hippie dream was swallowed by the nightmare of longhaired druggie Charles Manson's murder cult and the killing of a fan at a Rolling Stones concert. Richard Nixon's presidency was disintegrating, Vietnam vets with wounded bodies and minds haunted the street, and Pope Paul VI proclaimed that ancient demonic forces were wreaking havoc in the late twentieth century.[43])

With a haunted-house door creak, Mrs. X emerges from the kitchen and sternly tells Henry that she wants to speak with him alone. She moves out of the frame and the director holds on an archetypal Lynchian image: Large in the foreground is Mr. X's face in its rictus of superficial jocularity, while behind him, his daughter's sobbing face and panicky hand-to-her-mouth gesture signal hidden depths of glossed-over X family dis-ease. It's not a family portrait that Henry would be eager to join but we get the uneasy feeling that mother and daughter X have already been cooking his goose in their kitchen.

While the X family violates the bounds of social propriety and rational discourse, Lynch breaks down the traditional narrative separation between his characters' inner psychic states and their physical surroundings. As the concerned-looking Henry gets up from the dinner table to follow Mrs. X's bidding, his rising panic and the overflowing tension in the room galvanize a table lamp, which, with an electrical buzzing-crackling, glows white-hot and blows out, creating a dark chamber for Henry's inquisition.

The contrast and interplay between light and shadow are central to Lynch's visual and metaphorical aesthetic, extending even to his meticulously controlled black-and-white self-adornment. Henry's fraught moment of sudden, awaiting darkness, which remains one of Lynch's favorite *Eraserhead* images, could be subtitled, "Now it's dark." Henry—like the young, small-town Lynch descending into the scary black hole of a New York subway tunnel for the first time—must face unknown terrors in the dark. The pictorial look and intangible metaphysics of Henry's darkened state, its "feeling"[44] as Lynch puts it, will resonate throughout the director's later work with growing complexity. In *Blue Velvet* (1986), the menacing Frank Booth (Dennis Hopper) utters the words "Now it's dark"[45] as both a proclamation of nocturnal solace found and an invocation to the ravenous, animalistic demons eager to spring forth from his twisted psyche. And in Lynch's lyrics for Julee Cruise's song *Into the Night*, "Now it's dark" launches a woman mourning a lost love on a nightly sea of tears. For Lynch the dark is a place of evil, fear, sadness, and pain, but it is also the imagination's fertile ground, a realm of creative self-discovery and cosmic soul-voyaging. Lynch knows that you need a very black sky to better see the stars.

However, poor Henry can't even see the sky and perdition is his future. Pulling him into the shadows, their faces inches apart, Mrs. X raises her stern voice, "Did you and Mary have sexual intercourse?" Lynch shockingly cuts right to the blood and bone of the situation, voicing the unspoken question that has hovered over countless mannerly parents-meet-daughter's-boyfriend movie scenes. Literally backed against the wall, Henry, his voice aquiver, tries to defy Mrs. X's accusatory assault: "I don't think that's any of your business." But his nervous defensiveness answers her query. Mrs. X holds the power in the room, and she adds a threat, "You're in big trouble if you don't cooperate" as, vampire-like, she jams her nose and mouth against Henry's neck in a nuzzling fit of wanton sexual indulgence.

This scene illustrates Lynch's razor-sharp instinct for stunning visual tableaus and dramatic situations of the most psychologically disturbing nature. Here the familiar boundaries that protect our bodies, thoughts, and feelings from dark, chaotic forces do not hold. Lynch will amplify this theme of a mother acting out her sexual hunger for her daughter's lover in *Wild at Heart* (1990), in which he violates a further social boundary by having Mom (Diane Ladd) aggressively come on to Sailor (Nicolas Cage) while he's urinating in the sanctum sanctorum of a marble-walled public men's room. In the thirty-three hours of *Twin Peaks* (1990–1991) that played on TV and movie screens, Lynch transgresses the ultimate laws of God and man by presenting a spirit-possessed father who has regularly ejaculated into, and then stabbed to death, his beloved teenage daughter. Again and again, beginning with *The Alphabet* (1968) and *The Grandmother* (1970), Lynch returns to the archetypal situation of power-wielding parents, and parent-surrogate figures like Henry's Mrs. X, having their way with their youngsters. Now, what variations on this theme will emerge when the youngsters have children of their own?

Staged as the antithesis of a joyful announcement, the horrified Henry is told by the accusatory Mrs. X that "There's a baby," and her sobbing daughter chillingly adds, "They're still not sure it *is* a baby!" In blunt, commanding tones, Mrs. X gives Henry and Mary their orders: they will get married and pick up their baby at the hospital. The stricken Henry's life has irrevocably changed with the shocking suddenness of that living room light blowing out. Beginning with *The Alphabet*'s Girl's blood-spewing mouth and *The Grandmother*'s Boy's wetting of his bed, many of Lynch's characters exhibit a physical manifestation of a psychic, emotional wound. Now Henry, freshly traumatized by the entrapping, domestic assault on his future as a free man, trickles blood from his nostrils. Is there no way to escape this loathsome turn of events? The turmoils of Henry's mind are the core of *Eraserhead*, and Lynch moves in for a huge close-up as Henry tips his head back to stop his vital blood from leaking out. His head is immobile in the frame, the spark of freedom-loving life in his eyes is prominent, and his eyes turn to the side, looking for a way out of this mess and attracted by a mewling, whimpering sound that foreshadows Henry's baby. In a beautiful subjective point-of-view shot, Lynch swoops his camera over the living room landscape of Henry's downfall. Over the whimpering dog overwhelmed and entrapped by her suckling brood, past the blown-out light fixture, up to and into the black aperture of the front window, Henry's mind races, trying in vain to catch the unseen roar of a passing, outbound train. This fleeing cinematic summation of Henry's psychic plight is what Lynch calls "an abstraction,"[46] a visual-aural rendering of an intangible state.

To firmly dash Henry's hope of escape, Lynch cuts directly to the imposed new members of Henry's household. The cheery refrain "Just Molly and me, and baby makes three, we're happy in my blue heaven"[47] does not quite apply. In Henry's shadowy one-room apartment, with its view of a brick wall, Mary tries to force food into the slit-like mouth of their nameless infant, which lies on its back atop a table, its head resting on a pillow. Like a living wound, the appendageless, pear-shaped body of this pitiful creature is swaddled in white gauze bandages. Its little eyes, positioned on either side of a bulbous, animal-like feeding-and-breathing snout, roll helplessly; its smooth, glistening skin is semi-transparent like a fetus's, showing cloudy veins beneath its surface. Monstrous and intensely pathetic, this mutant, "premature" offspring is a horrific melding of Henry's and Mary's gene pools, the perverse product of their joy of sex. And if for Lynch the world is a factory, then this travesty of a child is the perfectly natural spawn of Mr. X's "hellhole" of a town, this cauldron of industrial toxins. And, recalling the mushroom cloud photo on Henry's wall, we can perhaps add the invasive mutagenic agents of post-nuclear-holocaust fallout to the swirling mix of manmade poisons that have formed his child.

As Lynch did with the grotesque, violent family-eating episode in *The Grandmother* and Henry's dinner at the Xs', he makes Henry's homecoming scene a dark reflection of the idealized 1950s homelife that the director enjoyed as a child. Since the Spencers live in one cramped room, the head of the house doesn't have to call out, "Honey, I'm home" when he enters. This patriarch with the often-deadpan expression releases a couple of limp smiles as he regards mother and gurgling, food-spitting child. Confused and benumbed by life, Henry reflexively holds back, remains tentative, while he figures out what he thinks and feels about everything. Muddling through, he has no neat, absolute conclusions. Henry has said that he loves Mary and doesn't mind having to marry her, but his words seem half-hearted, a politeness born of their unexpected parenthood, rather than a blood passion. He still hasn't found a primal, deeply felt organizing principle to guide his life course; any bliss he might eagerly pursue remains undefined.

Henry is on vacation from La Pelle's printing factory (Lynch's former Philadelphia employer) but his days and nights are far from carefree. Henry feels he should stay home with Mary and their ghastly, miserable baby, who cries day and night. And in the couple's only refuge, under the bedcovers, Mary is cold with child-tending anger and fear of further baby-making, and shrugs away Henry's tentative sexual advances. If Henry's life is a question, his wife and child don't seem to be the answer.

Henry begins to perceive intimations of an alternative life. In his eternally shadowy, unattended apartment lobby, he finds a small package in his mail slot. With delicate care, Henry unwraps a little crescent-shaped seed or cocoon, which he doesn't show to Mary. And, staring into the vertical steel bars of his hissing radiator, he sees a light go on within its depths, where an anticipatory spotlight circle falls on an empty, awaiting theater stage with backdrop curtains. That night, while Mary sleeps, Henry places the little crescent seed inside a wall cabinet whose empty floor and curving scrollwork pediment echo the radiator theater stage with its over-arching, swooping-curtain curves. And when the sobbing Mary leaves for her parents' house one night to get some sleep uninterrupted by the baby's cries, Lynch immediately shows Henry's beautiful neighbor woman from across the hall strolling in a seductive, black, plunging-necklined party dress. The expansive stirrings of other ways of being are attracting Henry's attention. A faint ray of light is penetrating *Eraserhead*'s perpetual gloom.

In Lynch's original conception, the film's "dream of dark and troubling things"[48] was meant to be an unremitting nightmare, with no solace or hope of escape for Henry. And Henry's distress reflected Lynch's own deep existential pain. In 1973, "there was mostly this emptiness in me."[49] He was smoking heavily, guzzling coffee nonstop, and waking up in a sour mood that wouldn't lift. "I was supposedly doing what I wanted to do more than anything else: making films. I practically had my own little studio, and we were busy working, but I just wasn't happy."[50] If Henry now sleeps alone in his dreary apartment, so does his creator. Separated from his wife, Lynch became so immersed in Henry's dark world that, defying the Film Center's strict regulations, he secretly snuck onto the AFI grounds at night and slept within the visual-emotional tableaus he was committing to film. For almost eight months, Lynch lay back on Henry's musty pillow, the bedstand mound of earth with its barren, gnarled little tree near his dreaming head. Actor Jack Nance, who plays Henry, describes Lynch's tortured state of mind as a full-blown "spiritual crisis."[51]

Lynch was raised as a Presbyterian and his parents had expected him to go to Sunday school and church. He went, but, ever sensitive to people living double lives, he perceived that churchgoers "lived one way on Sunday and a different way the rest of the week."[52] Lynch wasn't getting what he needed in church and his understanding father told him he could stop going. But a spiritual hunger that even art-making couldn't satisfy continued to gnaw at him.

Unlike many of his baby-boomer generation, Lynch did not seek escape, or enlightenment, in psychedelic drugs. Peggy Reavey recalls, "David thought that whole scene was just a waste of time and energy that could be spent working on his art."[53] To attack his problem, Lynch simply followed the lead of John, Paul, George, and Ringo. When the Beatles' manager and dear friend Brian Epstein died of an apparent overdose of sleeping pills in 1967, the shattered pop music megastars retreated to Wales and spent some healing time with the Hindu sage the Maharishi Mahesh Yogi. The snowy bearded old guru taught the four men a simple technique that eased their suffering, a method that the Maharishi's followers introduced to America in 1968, and which Lynch first heard about from his sister, Martha.

Martha was riding on the Sun Valley chairlift with her ski instructor when she asked him a question that had been on her mind for days. The young man "always seemed so calm and happy, and he said that it was because of Transcendental Meditation."[54] He told Martha about the meditation technique, which centers on a repeated mantra, and when she repeated this information to her brother David, he said, "I want a mantra; I want a mantra."[55] (Martha became a TM devotee, and eventually, an instructor, in addition to being a financial planner.) Lynch "knew TM was for me"[56] but, at the same time, Catherine Coulson (Jack Nance's wife and *Eraserhead* crew member), who became interested in TM when Lynch did, remembers that he was characteristically leery of brainwashing and regimentation: "Cath, if they make us put on uniforms and do maneuvers, let's run."[57]

Lynch contacted a local TM teacher and brought along the requisite, consequential initiatory fee, a handful of flowers and fruit, and a white handkerchief. The TM ethos requires that the aspirant sacrifice money and time in his learning commitment. Lynch witnessed his personal teacher go through an incense-scented, Hindu-derived ritual using the offerings he had brought. Then the teacher gave him his own mantra, a Sanskrit sound attuned only to the vibrations of David Lynch's being, never to be revealed to anyone else (secrets aren't just part of his fictional world). In the following weeks, Lynch devoted his time to learning the TM technique, sitting quietly for twenty minutes twice a day with his eyes closed, repeating his mantra again and again with his inner voice.

Becoming one with the endless wave cycle of this resonant inner rhythm, the meditator enters a state of deep stillness and physical relaxation. Over the years, numerous scientific studies have shown that TM practitioners enjoy the energy conservation effect of a lowered rate of metabolism, breathing, and heartbeat. With this physical restfulness comes a psychic alertness. TM is a nonrepressive technique, with the meditator maintaining a convivial attitude toward thoughts that enter his head while he sits. The meditator does not waste energy trying to push thoughts out of his mind; a blank inner screen is not his goal. Stressful and painful images and memories will naturally arise but, in his state of physical serenity, the meditator learns to regard them with a distancing dispassion, not letting the stressors grip his being with anxiety. Over time, the meditator's knots of psychic tension loosen, and the ego's need to process, cope with, and heal its daily temporal problems lessens. Now that the mental-emotional housecleaning is done, the transcendental party can begin.

The Maharishi teaches that the mind-body being has a natural tendency to pay attention to what makes it happy, to proceed from pleasure to greater pleasure. The guru likens human consciousness to an ocean, a metaphor that visionary American poet Walt Whitman and pioneering Viennese psychoanalyst Sigmund Freud both used in their writings. Maharishi states that the hubbub of our crisp, focused everyday thoughts is on the surface of the consciousness sea, where our attention busily bobs from wave to wave. Yet when the mind concentrates on its repeating mantra, attention remains active and alert but pleasantly undirected. Seeking ever-greater satisfaction in the quiet depths, the mind's attention settles down, sinking beneath and transcending thought altogether. Consciousness is immersed in an undifferentiated field of pure being beyond the habitual din of named categories and opposing dualities. From at least the time of Siddhartha the Buddha (sixth century B.C.), human beings have sought to experience this universal ground of being, this limitless bond with the universe. Whitman, Freud, Ralph Waldo Emerson, and Carl Jung understood our capacity for this blissful experience. Robert Henri, Lynch's first spiritual guide, counseled that "He who has contemplated, has met with himself, is in a state to see into the realities beyond the surface."[58]

By the time Lynch took up meditation at the age of twenty-seven, he was already a contemplative, seasoned traveler on his own psychic journey. As a boy he had stared, transfixed, at the red ants swarming over the sticky pitch oozing from his family's wounded backyard cherry tree. And, sitting in the deep Northwest forest while his father worked, his acute senses had registered the murmuring, shadowy gloom, and thrilled at the sudden flash of sunlight glancing from the glistening flank of a stream-leaping rainbow trout. As a young man, Lynch "followed his bliss," in mythologist Joseph Campbell's phrase, and became a painter. Standing in front of his canvas, the artist would lose track of time and humdrum daily concerns. Beneath the level of verbal language, his hand, eye, mind, spirit, and subconscious would flow in a unified gesture, expressing elements that "all have their balance, their way of being."[59] As in the process of meditation, Lynch's consciousness bypassed his ego to plumb deeper realities: "I try to let nature paint more than me; I just try to stay out of the way."[60] For Lynch, art-making transcended the concrete physical realm of brushstrokes on canvas, oil paint fumes, pigment and stained hands: "You could paint forever and never paint the perfect painting and fall in love with a new thing every week and there's no end to it, your painting is never going to die."[61] Lynch's expansive, ecstatic sense of being part of humankind's unbroken, forward-moving creative continuum also sent him into the past. In the time before *Eraserhead*, and before Lynch's spiritual crisis and his split from his wife, an exhibit of ancient East Indian carved sandstone sculptures drew him, Peggy, and little Jennifer to the Los Angeles County Museum of Art. Near closing time in the museum hallways, Lynch wandered off and got separated from his family. "There was nobody around, just these carvings and it was really quiet. I rounded a corner and my eyes went down the corridor and there was a pedestal at the very end. My eyes went up the pedestal and at the top was this head of Buddha. When I looked at the head, white light shot out of it into my eyes and it was like—boom!—I was full of bliss."[62]

This fleeting, yet profound, solitary museum experience, was a metaphor for the divergence of Lynch's art life from his family life, and an example of his penchant for enjoying a secret existence, for Peggy Reavey first learned of this incident when I told her of it in the year 2000. The Buddha's light gave Lynch an image of deliverance and redemption that would illuminate his film work for decades to come. The artist remains acutely sensitive to the shadow side of life, as he said in the early 1990s: "The darkness is realizations about the world and human nature and my own nature, all combined into one ball of sludge."[63] But a moment later his inner sense of psychic balance exerts itself: "The more darkness you can gather up, the more light you can see. To me, love is like light."[64] So, twenty years before, in the universe of *Eraserhead*, how did Lynch's museum "boom!" of spirit light come to flood the benighted, despairing chamber of Henry Spencer's soul?

Whether it's the result of a visionary gift, a hyperactive imagination, or an upswelling subconscious that he can't shut off, Lynch can see things that other people cannot. When *Eraserhead* assistant and actress Catherine Coulson came into a room one day and put on her glasses, the prescient Lynch said that he saw her standing there, cradling a log in her arms. In 1989, Lynch phoned Coulson: "Cath, I'm ready for you to play that woman with the log,"[65] and soon the Log Lady was a beloved member of the *Twin Peaks* pantheon. Receptive to mysterious inspirations and obscure sign-posts, Lynch was sketching on the *Eraserhead* set one day when "I just drew this little lady, and little fetuses were falling out of her."[66] And in the director's agile mind, this arresting, fantastical image had a clear purpose: "I thought she would live in the radiator, where it's nice and warm, and this would be a real comfort for Henry."[67]

The Lady in the Radiator brought solace to Henry at the time when Transcendental Meditation brightened Lynch's life. Even though Lynch had been unfaithful to Peggy, and they split up, he still, touchingly, saw her as his significant other and wanted her to share his galvanizing TM experience: "Peg, I need you to be excited about this too."[68] Lynch was irritated when Peggy said she wasn't interested in pursing TM, and an echo of this emotional dynamic shows up in *Blue Velvet* fifteen years later when Sandy balks at sharing Jeffrey's Mystery-obsession, and Jeffrey says, "San-dy, don't take that attitude." Peggy recalls that "David was like a TM fundamentalist, and he embraced all this philosophical structure that was alarmingly detailed, like the Mormon religion. Where you go after death, what happens in heaven, the idea that suicide receives a horrifying punishment in the next world."[69] At the time, Peggy wrote in her journal that what David wanted more than anything else in life was "inner peace,"[70] and in order to help achieve it, he went to work on his outer, physical being. What Peggy calls "the era of the Pure David"[71] was born. "He became a vegetarian, he quit drinking, though previously he never used to have more than a little wine, and he quit smoking."[72] With a laugh, she adds that "there was plenty of sex, I'm sure, but everything else was out the window."[73]

For a man with hearty oral appetites (except for copious talking), Lynch was indeed making some sacrifices, and Peggy hypothesizes that he was trying to exorcise the guilt he felt for his part in fracturing their marriage. She feels she also contributed to the sundering of their union: "We both caused each other pain; he didn't want to be married and I didn't want to be married,"[74] yet, to this day, there's a warmth of mutual respect and affection between the two: "He could always make me laugh, even when I was mad at him."[75] Decades after the fact, Peggy feels that their friend sound designer Alan Splet "was right when he had said David and I were both being self-indulgent in not fighting to keep our marriage together, but at the time it just seemed easier to get divorced."[76] So while Peggy embraced the burgeoning sociopolitical movement for women's rights and "tried to figure out what I wanted in *this* life,"[77] Lynch was forging a spiritual path that stretched from here to eternity.

Having hand-built the spaces his *Eraserhead* characters will occupy by following the blueprints of his inner eye, Lynch felt "these interiors carry way more than what you see. Something about the light and the molding on the wall and the proportions indicates the mood outside. It seemed to me that there were factories, industrial buildings, and neighborhoods dark and forlorn tucked in somewhere, sort of like you can't get there from here. They're sort of lost in another kind of place. This comes from Philadelphia, and this is the world of *Eraserhead*."[78] Lynch spoke these words thirty years after making *Eraserhead*, and they evocatively sum up his ability to make interiors imply the world outside, the outside the inside, and to conjure realms, from *The Elephant Man*'s London to *Twin Peaks*' lumber town to *Mulholland Drive*'s Hollywood, that are, all at once, intimately familiar and accessible, and beautifully, poetically, "lost in another kind of place."

Once Lynch establishes the physical, emotional, and spiritual parameters of Henry's world, the director is now poised to dive into dreamland. In *The Grandmother*, Lynch initiated the narrative mode of interweaving passages of dream life and symbolic reality with the baseline naturalistic, albeit stylized, reality that his characters were living. The hero's states of mind became physical aspects of the story. In *Eraserhead*, Lynch carries this time and space-bending, story-weaving technique to the nth degree. The film's audacious, nonlinear style of exposition has challenged viewers over for decades. *Eraserhead* has been called "the strangest film ever made," "the ultimate cinematic mystery," and has been deemed to be "critic-proof." Even today's college film students, raised on the dizzying fast-cutting and fragmented storylines of music videos, are "driven crazy" by *Eraserhead*; they can't figure out "how real it is—or isn't."

Lynch's art addresses the primal mysteries of sex, birth, death, damnation, and salvation, but his deepest, unspoken concern is the nature of reality itself. Along with Walt Whitman, he wonders, "Whether that which appears to be is so, or is it all flashes and specks?"[79] And, beyond the question of whether the perceived universe is concrete or illusory, just who is running the show? The first image that Lynch shows us in *Eraserhead* can be seen as Henry's subjective dream or an objective, omniscient perspective on the way things are. But either way, Henry's world is out of his control: unwilled forces are pulling his strings. Free of the earth's gravity, Henry's pale face floats in dark space, the black reaches punctuated by two tiny, glowing stars. As though lying down, his head is in a horizontal position, mouth on the left, eyes on the right. Consternation furrows his brow and a rough-surfaced, brain-sized planet floats near his hairline. Henry's image is half-transparent, so as his head gently bobs up in the frame, we see the planet-brain positioned in Henry's cranial region.

It is Lynch's habit to delve beneath the surface of any situation, so as Henry floats out of frame, the director's camera-eye approaches and penetrates the planet. A man with scorched skin sits looking out a shattered six-pane window at the dark sky. If this is the window of Henry's soul, it is certainly the worse for wear. The Man in the Planet's (Lynch's friend Jack Fisk) hand trembles and twitches forward to pull a lever and, as Henry's mouth opens in a silent scream, an elongated, sperm-like fetus emerges from his lips and floats in front of his face. The Man in the Planet pulls another lever and the fetus shoots out of Henry's frame, splashing into an underground amniotic gestation pool that recalls *The Grandmother*'s birthing netherworld. Then, in an abstracted, baby's viewpoint of the birth act, Lynch's camera travels through an "inside" black space toward a white-light hole that grows ever larger. The camera dives into the white light, past a few stylized pubic hairs, and emerges "outside," as Lynch cuts to that archetypal close-up of the worried Henry looking over his shoulder at whatever it is that's gaining on him as he heads home to the waiting X family dinner invitation, and its attendant entrapment in marriage and fatherhood.

For the viewer, these opening floating head/planet-brain/procreational images are confounding. They are suspended beyond any contextual meaning, yet in a poetic-logic, almost subliminal way, they telegraph what the film will be about. Because of the contrast between the floating head's misty transparentness and the sharp-focus concreteness of Henry's worried close-up and walk home, it's easiest to read the opening passage as Henry's dream or parenthood-presaging vision. Our minds grasp at a comfort zone of comprehension by defining the floating imagery as subjective reality and Henry's domestic life and evening at the Xs' house as objective reality.

But Lynch is a quantum leap ahead of us and he ambushes our complacent "understanding" without mercy. For after we've become familiar with the status quo of Henry's industrial zone doings, Lynch starts mixing dream with reality, the concrete with the cosmic, the physical with the metaphysical, until we're as mystified and as needy of an escape route as Henry. Lynch's films challenge the viewer with a cerebral and emotional confrontation, and some just aren't up to the experience. The director's detractors accuse him of cynically dabbling in obscurity for its own sake, of exploitively sowing darkness and confusion without offering a counterbalancing enlightenment. His films, especially *Eraserhead*, are labeled "illegible," his attitude is deemed "self-indulgent and disrespectful of his audience."

But Lynch doesn't sit around casually wondering, "What can I put on the screen that viewers won't understand, that will frustrate them completely?" Lynch is the polar opposite of a shallow put-on artist or calculating poseur; he's a deeply personal creator committed to communicating the promptings of his inner being. His description of how he opens himself to a new artistic inspiration can stand as a roadmap for experiencing *Eraserhead*. "If you start worrying right away about the meaning of everything, chances are your poor intellect is only going to glean a little portion of it. If it stays abstract, if it feels truthful, and it hooks you in the right way, and thrills you as it moves to the next idea, and it moves with some intuitive sense, that is a real good guideline. There's a certain logic and truth and right workings that you have to trust. That's all you have to go by."[80] Lynch wants his art to be as rich, complex, and multifarious as life itself. And, ever the true-blue American, he democratically wants his work to have "some truth in it for everybody."[81] Lynch is happy if some elements in his art "mean the same thing to a large number of people, just so there's not one message spoon-fed."[82] Lynch achieves a tone of evocative suggestiveness that recalls Walt Whitman's artistic ideal: "Human thought, poetry, or melody, must leave dim escapes and outlets—must possess a certain fluid, aerial character, akin to space itself, obscure to those of little or no imagination, but indispensable to the highest purposes."[83]

Henry's only, dirt-level, purpose seems to be to endure the unshakable, low-grade fever of his life. Whether the power-wielding Man in the Planet with his fetus-launching levers is a figment of Henry's dream life, is God himself, a guiding and controlling *spiritus rector*, or Walt Whitman's universal "procreant urge,"[84] Henry has had fatherhood thrust upon him. As a reflection of Henry's knotted, confused, and directionless consciousness—and his infernal industrial-wasteland environment—the disharmonious, polluted surge of his life force has spawned an achingly sad and hideous child. And now that Mary has retreated to her parents' house, Henry is alone with the malformed embodiment of his genetic code. Then things get worse.

Lynch is about to plunge into *Eraserhead*'s celebrated thirty-seven-minute flow of mind-bending visionary imagery, and he gives us a reality-disrupting prelude. The baby is crying as usual and Henry takes its temperature: a normal reading. Then, in the split-second it takes to cut to the next shot, the infant is, preternaturally, somehow engulfed in disease. Its face is pricked with angry boils; discharge and dribble encrust its sorry eyes and mouth. Henry is shocked by this sudden intrusion of sickness, but he copes with it. Touching his child for the first time, Henry consolingly pats its head, sets up a little steaming vaporizer, and keeps it company. If Henry's offspring won't be quiet, neither will the silent cry of his own starving soul. Henry remembers his secret little mail-delivered seed-cocoon in the wall cabinet on *his* side of the bed. He rises to go down to the lobby and check for any further deliveries, but when he tries to leave the room, his child's pathetic wailing pierces his heart, so he stays. Torn between his responsibility to be a nurturing parent and his need to transcend his hellish life, Henry is trapped by contradictory impulses.

To fly from his cage, the passive Henry must let his psyche assume the active voice. Lying in bed alone at night, he regards the steel bars of the radiator, his own private dream factory. Before, when Henry saw the theater stage inside the radiator, Lynch presented it in a static tableau shot. Now, reflecting Henry's more energized approach, Lynch travels his camera up to the bars and penetrates them, then sweeps his camera across the entire stage from left to right. It's time for that comforting "little lady" that Lynch spontaneously sketched to make her appearance on film.

The introduction of a supernatural/otherworldly, often-angelic being into an established, mundane reality is a key Lynchian theme, which he initiated with *The Grandmother*'s Grandmother and expresses in many of his works. It is interesting to note that over the years Peggy Reavey has painted many versions of the biblical Annunciation, in which an angel enters the Virgin Mary's everyday reality to tell her she will give birth to Christ's incarnation. Looking back from the vantage point of 2004, Peggy says she and Lynch "navigate"[85] similar artistic territory: the unconscious, humor, mystery, dreams, emotion-charged man–woman relationships, the border between life and death. The second of Lynch's cinematic angels in white, the Lady in the Radiator (Laurel Near, sister of singer-songwriter Holly Near) stands facing us in her snowy, high-necklined party dress. Hands chastely clasped across her bosom, platinum puff of hair framing mounded, globular, Kewpie Doll cheeks and wholesome grin, she launches a little side-step routine across the black-and-white checked stage floor: Lynch's eternal dance of darkness and light. The Lady in the Radiator's bond with Henry is immediate and strong. She moves to Henry's theme song, a jaunty Fats Waller tune played on a warm-toned theater organ, and as she dances, she squishes the elongated fetuses that are plopping onto the floor from somewhere above. The shocking surprise of these unwanted drop-ins parallels the unexpected intrusion of Henry's fetus-child into his life. As a thick, milky liquid pops from beneath the Radiator Lady's stomping foot, her shoulders hunch up and her smiling face dips with a naughty-little-girl thrill.

Clearly, this is the woman for Henry. Lynch underscores the point by returning wife Mary to Henry's bed for contrast. Mary's somnambulant twitching and stirring wake Henry and almost push him off his side of the bed. As Mary shudders and makes a mouth-clacking sound that recalls her fit in the X family's living room, Henry reaches toward his wife under the covers and pulls out one of the attenuated fetuses. His face twisted with revulsion, he pulls more fetuses from Mary and, no longer a slave to the procreational mandate, vigorously splatters them against the wall, just as the Radiator Lady squashed them underfoot.

Lynch charts the further strengthening and growth of Henry's independent selfhood by having him sow some wild oats not linked to babymaking. As Carl Jung has said, the holding of a treasured secret empowers an individual's unique sense of being. Henry's secret is the little seed-like worm shape that he has kept in the wall cabinet on his side of the bed, the cabinet whose curtain-like scrollwork links it to the psychic locus of Henry's private curtained stage within the radiator. Previously inert, the worm, by means of Lynch's clay animation, now scoots around the surface of the Man in the Planet's brain-shaped world. Evincing Lynch's interest in permeability and interpenetration, we see that the planet's shell, rather than being solidly armor-like, is pierced by fissures and holes. The aroused worm, growing ever larger, cavorts in and out of the holes, finally bursting up through the planet's surface toward the camera, opening its mouth to trumpet a triumphant phallic cry right in our faces, and to eerily prefigure the image of the gigantic, power-charged sandworm in Lynch's *Dune* (1984).

Spirit inhabits flesh in Lynch's universe, and if Henry's soul is now rousing and advancing toward fulfillment, so is his body. Lynch has defined Henry's wife by her procreational function and preoccupation, her convulsive irritability, sexually rejecting behavior, and absence from her husband's bed. Whereas the Beautiful Girl Across the Hall (Judith Ann Roberts, wife of *Bonanza*'s Pernell Roberts) has perfumed the air between herself and Henry with her darkly exotic sexual presence, her lingering, "I'm available" way of relaying a mundane phone message to him. In the words of Lynch's *Gardenback* script, when Henry looks at her, "something crosses from her to you."[86] The director visualizes the physical consummation of this unseen link between Henry and the Beautiful Girl in an exquisite, unprecedented cinematic image. Henry's bed has become a dark, earthen cavity filled with a milky white liquid that recalls the fetal birthing pond of Henry's film-beginning dream and the white juice that spurts from various squashed fetuses, and also suggests semen. Naked and lost in an endless kissing embrace, Henry and the Beautiful Girl slowly sink into the white liquid until only her black hair floats on the pale surface. But even Henry's sexual exaltation is poisoned by his monstrous child, for as the lovers deliquesce the Beautiful Girl's eyes are fearful as she notices the babbling, malformed baby lying on the corner table.

If Henry was experiencing ripples of conflicting impulse before his erotic merging with the Beautiful Girl, his head now swirls in a maelstrom of confusion. Henry's consciousness-vision now contains the Beautiful Girl's baby-frightened visage, the all-witnessing Man in the Planet, and the Lady in the Radiator. As Lynch will do in *Blue Velvet*, he's giving his hero a choice between a raven-haired woman offering darkly sexual, earthy pleasures, and a chaste blonde who offers celestial, redemptive dreams. The Beautiful Girl gives Henry sex without babies, but the Radiator Lady speaks the language of Henry's deepest need: the transcendence of desire and the fleshy offspring of desire. Previously joined to Henry by the gesture of fetus-smashing, the Radiator Lady now sings the sweetest declaration: "In Heaven, everything is fine; you've got your good things, and you've got mine." She holds the promise of eternal bliss beyond the earthly plague of emotional tribulation and the messy oppression of procreation. For the first time, Henry and the Radiator Lady occupy the same frame of film, but when he tries to reach her, a blinding white light stops him, and she vanishes. As Henry looks in bereft bewilderment at the empty space where his dream girl just stood, Lynch intercuts a quick shot of the Man in the Planet and then back to Henry. In Lynch's cosmology, the chastely asexual, fetus-stomping Radiator Lady is like an anti-Christ to the Planet Man's Universal Procreational Lever-Puller in the sky. The momentary shot of the Planet Man's visage seems to admonish Henry: "Thou shalt not have her; get thee home to thy child."

Just as Lynch diverged from his parents' Presbyterian faith to pursue his own path into Hindu spirituallity, so Henry is discovering a uniquely personal route to salvation. His consciousness is making organic evolutionary choices, not following scriptural doctrines. Henry isn't on the Radiator Lady's level yet. He's got some more growing to do, and he must face the most hideous of all monsters: himself.

Lynch's inspired image of a man's head being made into pencil erasers is the catalyst that launched the *Eraserhead* project, and the director integrates this vision into his film in a passage of rich symbolic resonance. Standing in the center of the Radiator Lady's stage with its framing curtains, Henry hears a fierce, constant wind. Through the curtains, on squeaky little wheels, comes a man-sized denuded tree on a rock base that's like Henry's bedstand still-life decoration grown dream-sized large. This gnarled-limbed form stands center stage, and Henry retreats to the side, twitching his hands and watching the tree with nervous apprehension. In a sudden movement of raw shock and surprise, Henry's head pops off of his shoulders, launched by the penislike thrust of his pale, phallic-shaped neck stem. Dark blood flows from the rock at the twisted tree's base, streaming out across the stage and providing a dark background on which Henry's white, disembodied head floats, island-like, in profile. Back at Henry's torso, his "penis-head" neck stem is replaced by the result of the penis's pleasure: the squalling little head of Henry's mutant infant. The parenthood-entrapped Henry feels that his identity has been supplanted by his offspring. But as Lynch holds on the uncanny tableau of stage, tree, tree's blood stream with Henry's floating head, Henry's body with his baby's head, we hear *two* entwined infant voices wailing on the soundtrack.

There's the sense that, in his spiritual progression toward the Radiator Lady, Henry is being reborn, and that his own fledgling voice is crying in counterpoint to his offspring's. Henry's sexual immersion in the bed pool with the Beautiful Girl links up with the film's beginning images of the fetus splashing into the underground pond of birthing fluid. Lynch's visual poetry echoes Walt Whitman's phrase "the bath of birth."[87] The mysteries of generation that Lynch contemplates are akin to Whitman's "after the child is born of woman, the man is born of woman."[88] No sooner do we grasp one of Lynch's evocative metaphoric motifs, than he plunges us into the begetting of his film's namesake.

Henry's disembodied head experiences a birth, passing through the gnarled tree's stage-floor blood flow and dropping onto a daylight industrial-zone street. A young boy picks up the head and scurries to a storefront pencil factory. Like David Lynch's father taking a core sample of an evergreen tree, a factory worker extracts some of Henry's gray matter and processes it thorough the pencil-making machine. In another birth image, the pencil with some of Henry's head for an eraser emerges from the machine. The worker makes a single mark on white paper with the lead end of the pencil and erases his stroke with the other. Nodding "Okay," the worker brushes the erasure fragments into the air, where they float and expand in darkness like cosmic dust.

Henry is an eraserhead in more ways than one. He's rubbing out his former self as he becomes a newborn being. And, viewing the pencil as a metaphor for Henry's body, his penile pencil-point stroke has made a mark on the universal ledger of babies born: a black mark that his being is striving to somehow wipe out.

Henry wakes in bed, his head firmly on his shoulders, alone. In Lynch's world, Henry and the viewer don't have the luxury of being able to say with certainty, "Ah, it was only a dream," and to calmly resume their safe-and-sane waking reality. For a time it feels like we've firmly closed the door on dreamland, though we may actually have already opened another visionary portal and walked halfway down the hall. Whether waking or sleeping or traveling on some astral plane, we are experiencing Henry's state of mind and living the visceral reality of his moment-to-moment existential truth.

All dressed up in his black suit, Henry has nowhere to go. His baby holds all the power in the room. Henry, like a subservient child tiptoeing around a disapproving, dictatorial parent, keeps glancing at his for-once-quiet child before furtively opening his apartment door. The Beautiful Girl isn't home and as Henry closes the door with a dejected expression on his face, the baby responds with a spiteful-seeming chuckling sound. Henry lies on his bed, but there are no consoling dreamy visitations from the dark and blonde women in his life. As Henry's minutes pass like a silent, pounding headache, the baby continues to chuckle.

Henry hears the Beautiful Girl entering her apartment, but when he opens the door she's standing on the threshold of a dalliance with another man. Lynch underscores Henry's horror of having his identity subsumed by his twisted child with a quick shot of the Beautiful Girl's point of view. She, as in Henry's earlier head-loss vision of himself, now sees him as a black suit with a pathetic, monstrous, little baby head. Henry closes his door, squats down, and, through his keyhole, peeps at the Beautiful Girl as she takes her man friend into her room.

The despairing Henry is as low as he can get. Sitting on the floor, his point-of-view glance brushes past his beloved radiator. An impulse makes him rise and go to his bureau drawer. The dreamlike associations of Lynch's dark poetry echo and re-echo. Henry has, within his psyche, experienced the raw separation of his head from his body, and now he rummages in the drawer where he had previously found the two halves of Mary's photograph, the image whose head he had torn from its shoulders. At some earlier point in Henry's relationship with Mary, ripping her image had represented his doubts about the future of their union ("Where have you been"; "You never come around anymore"). Now Henry takes a pair of scissors from the drawer and approaches the living, breathing, wailing manifestation of the couple's bond.

With the care of an examining physician, Henry cuts open his baby's bandages. Aghast, we see that the white wrappings were the infant's only skin, and his glistening, absolutely real-looking viscera are exposed to the air. Henry's approach with the scissors has been hesitant and gentle, but now he plunges aggressively. The two lung sacs beneath the baby's elongated, phallic head resemble testicles, and Henry jabs the scissors into one of them. In attacking an image of genitalia, he is destroying their product: his child. But it's a child grown monstrous and freedom-stifling, and Henry must become a monster for a few seconds to erase it. Throughout the film Henry has been our Everyman hero, trying to cope with the frustrations of forced fatherhood in a benumbed, yet nurturing way. His child-killing stroke comes as a deeply disturbing shock.

For Lynch, violence is never casual. It is fraught with *gravitas* and triggers profound consequences. Henry, as though he's been gripped by a dark, murderous force and then released, recoils in terror and guilt from his deed and its aftermath (a behavioral-emotional sequence Lynch will repeat with daughter-killing Leland Palmer in *Twin Peaks*). His close-up face a chiaroscuro fear mask worthy of the German Expressionist cinema, Henry cringes against the wall as his child's life seeps away. The baby's head twitches and vibrates, recalling the X mother and daughter's dinner-hour sexual fits. And like the chicken that shook and spewed out blood when Henry tried to carve it, the baby hurls forth a nightmarishly exaggerated quantity of bodily fluids. First, a spray of blood, then torn-organ secretions, and a final flood of a viscous, porridge-like substance that is out of any sane proportion to the baby's small body.

The dying child, Henry's tortured mind, the electricity in his room, and the cosmos that interweaves all, pulse with the galvanized energy of an imminent culmination.

The rational laws that bind together our familiar physical world no longer hold. Henry sees horrifying things: his baby's blood-spraying head suspended out on the end of a sperm-like 4-foot neck cord, the shooting blood rhyming with the sparks flowing from the electrical wall outlet. Then, as Henry's torchiere-style floor lamp flashes on and off, the baby's head assumes shifting positions in the room's alternating light and shadow, finally becoming gigantic and suffocating the whole room. Just as *The Grandmother*'s Boy had his face mashed into his urine-wetted bed sheets as punishment, the agonized Henry is having his face rubbed in his crime. The light blows out, and the huge menacing head, grown monstrous to mirror Henry's monstrosity, looms menacingly toward his father in the darkness.

Earlier in the film, the light blowing out in the Xs' living room had marked the end of Henry's innocent freedom as a mobile single person and heralded the start of his trials with entrapping marriage, fatherhood, adultery, and child murder. By yearning for the chaste, anti-sexual Lady in the Radiator and destroying his own child, Henry has defied the prime mover of the universal life force, the Man in the Planet. Henry has committed the most heinous of sins, so he appropriately begins the third stage of his evolution in the shadows.

How dark is Henry's soul? Is he an evil man? Lynch presents his hero as an ordinary fellow trying to cope with that which life throws at him, which is always more than he bargained for. Eschewing the guidance of any formulaic behavioral or spiritual codes, Henry has followed the promptings of his yearning soul. In symbolic terms, Henry *is* his own offspring: the deformed, wailing baby represents Henry's repressed raw cry for nurturing and love. He can't find the primal emotional shelter he craves in his inhospitable industrial environment, or at the X family dinner table, or in his own room with Mary and their child. He just wants to go home, but he can't find it anywhere. Henry projects the open wound of his unmet needs onto his child and sees it as living outside himself, as the Other. An Other that can be erased, and with it, his pain.

In the darkness that follows Henry's killing stroke, Lynch shows us mirroring, confrontational close-ups of the monster baby's face and his father's face; Henry must look away. Then, as the overridden and vanquished Man in the Planet's sphere starts to crumble, we see the iconic *Eraserhead* image of Henry as wire-haired illuminata. His eyes wide with wonder, his brow finally unfurrowed, his tall hair a penumbra of radiance that melds with the sparkling particles of cosmic erasure dust that expand in a cloud behind and around him. With Henry's billowing gray-matter dust, Lynch poeticizes the scientific fact that we have as many brain cells in our heads as there are stars in the heavens. The Planet Man pushes his sparking levers with his last gasp of strength, but there's no stopping Henry now.

A blinding white light fills the screen and the Lady in the Radiator comes forward. In the next shot, Henry is alone in the light but his sub-verbal link with her is so strong that he knows to turn around, and there she is. They embrace, heads nuzzling each other's shoulders in a perfect fit. The globe of his face balanced by the round blonde back of her head, Henry is in ecstasy, his eyes closed. The sound of many voices singing a single harmonious note, rather than a pounding industrial din, now accompanies Henry's image. Lynch maximizes the emotional power of Henry's bliss by holding it for only a few moments, then cutting abruptly to black.

The circle of Henry's journey has closed. His torturous quest for a home that will shelter and inspire his emotions and spirit has been fulfilled. His love for the Lady in the Radiator has stirred him from benumbed confusion and despair to action. In terms of Lynch's all-time favorite film, *The Wizard of Oz*, Henry has made it "over the rainbow." He's only had to kill his child to get there.

Has Henry earned his heavenly reward? Or is Lynch portraying a value-free dream realm in which conventional morality doesn't apply?

Lynch presents Henry as a decent average Joe muddling through each day trying not to harm himself or others. But life sends Henry lots of puzzling messages and makes him a continual victim of circumstances. Rather than acting, he is acted upon: Mary tells him to come over for dinner, Mrs. X attacks him sexually, he's forced to accept the roles of husband and father, his child is a deformed mutant who cuts off his freedom, Mary leaves him, and, above all, the Man in the Planet keeps pulling the levers in Henry's head. But Henry meets life's assaults with an innate decency and good manners, and he's a more nurturing parent than Mary to their pathetic baby. So he meets his social obligations, but what of his higher calling, his Art Life? The idiosyncratic brand of freedom and love that Henry needs stands in opposition to the socially sanctioned family life, just as in Lynch's *Eraserhead*-era conception of the Art Life "the art comes first; you don't get married and have families."[89]

Henry doesn't paint paintings, but he's a sensitive soul who expresses his deepest feelings in his visionary inner life. He's Pygmalion to the Lady in the Radiator's Galatea, finding happiness with his personal image of the ideal woman. But how does Henry finally reach her? Does he know that killing his child will win him his prize, or is the murder unpremeditated and his blissful transport to the Lady in the Radiator an unanticipated result?

In symbolic terms, Lynch presents his hero with the notion of blood sacrifice in Henry's vision of losing his head on the Lady in the Radiator's theatrical stage. Before his head pops off, Henry sees a gnarled, barren tree fill the stage. The tree links Henry's vision with his room, where a denuded branch decorates his bedstand. And the copious stream of blood that flows from the tree prefigures the upswelling of bodily fluids that will surge from Henry's stabbed child. The twisted tree and Henry's twisted baby are also linked in being the biological issue of the industrially poisoned, socially debased world that Henry lives in. The positioning of Henry's stage tree on a raised, rocky mound recalls the cross of Christ's crucifixion, with its connotations of self-sacrifice, absolution of sin, and reborn life. And the tree form itself signifies branching evolutionary growth and the Adam and Eve–tempting biblical tree of the knowledge of good and evil. In Henry's vision, his head flies from his shoulders as he contemplates the blood-flowing tree, lands on the dark stream and submerges into it, and is transformed into a beautiful cloud of erasure dust at the pencil factory. And later, after Henry has made his child's blood flow, his head is engulfed in a cloud of the cosmic dust that is the primal stuff of the eternal creation-dissolution-creation cycle. Since Lynch has established the invasive horror of Henry's identification with his repugnant, ever-needy offspring, there's the sense that Henry's erasure of his nemesis has erased him too. Lynch doesn't blatantly tell Henry, "Kill the kid and you'll get the heavenly girl." But he lays out a whispering path of almost subconscious signifiers that lead his hero from the Lady in the Radiator's bloody stage and tree back to the treelike branch in his room, a view of the radiator, the monstrous baby, the scissors and a plunging blade, and a final dissolution and rebirth.

Henry's morality is that of the artist operating outside the accepted norms of religion and society. Indeed, Henry's stance as an alienated spiritual-emotional seeker bears a striking parallel with the early heretical Christian sect of Gnosticism. In her book, *Mystery Religions of the Ancient World*, author Jocelyn Godwin notes the Gnostic belief that "the world is a stupendous mistake, created by a foolish or vicious creator-god, a Demiurge of a very low grade on the celestial hierarchy who thinks he is supreme."[90] This dictatorial Demiurge enforces the material world's mundane brand of reality upon the population. The Gnostics felt that these benighted human beings are actually children of light who eschew the life of the body and seek the secret knowledge that will reveal their higher destiny. The Demiurge tries to hide from himself and his subjects the fact that there exists a transcendent, true, universal God, who is beneficently waiting for his duped and befuddled children to find their way to their true spiritual home. The Man in the Planet as the Lady in the Radiator–denying, procreation-enforcing Demiurge, and Henry as the light-seeking prisoner of his body and the mundane, world fit perfectly into the Gnostic philosophical system. There's even a correspondence between the re-birthing bed pool that Henry and the Beautiful Girl sink into as Henry has his vision of the beckoning Lady in the Radiator ("In Heaven, everything is fine") and the Gnostic's "Krater,"[91] a uterus-like vessel in which those seeking spiritual renewal and higher consciousness bathed.

Gnostic thought, and Lynch's films, are driven by the dynamic opposition of good and evil. For the Gnostics, the innocent truth-seekers were simply up against the wicked, manipulative Demiurge. But Lynch manifests both sun and shadow in a single figure. He knows that the repugnant, reviled parts of our psyche, that we see outside ourselves as the Other, need to be acknowledged and reintegrated for deep psychic growth to occur. *The Grandmother*'s victimized Boy has an animated fantasy of killing his abusive parents, long-suffering Henry kills his child-oppressor, and both protagonists attain the grace of transformation. Lynch believes that there is "a mysterious door right at the balance point between extreme evil and violence, and goodness and peace."[92] In expressing both the light and dark aspects of his psyche, the questing Henry has found that door and stepped through it.

By many interpretive measures, including Lynch's own, *Eraserhead* has a "happy" ending. The viewer celebrates the circle-closure of Henry's long-sought homecoming and is released from the confounding shifting realities of Lynch's dream labyrinth. However, we remain haunted by Henry's, and perhaps our own, revealed capacity for violence. There are grown men, fathers of young children, who cannot bear to stay in the theater with Henry's baby's final cries.

It's interesting to see how Jennifer Lynch, from the vantage point of a thirty-six-year-old woman, feels about Henry's final solution for his problem child, a child who can readily be seen as a metaphor for her own deformed state as a baby.

> Jack Nance named the baby Spike, and I could talk to Spike and play with him as long as I didn't touch him. This was when I was 3, 4, 5 years old. Having seen the film many times over the years, I think Henry has pity for himself *and* the baby. He's curious—is there freedom under those bandages? If I do this with such an innocent mind, can I be blamed? It's not a malicious act so much; it's done more in desperation. He doesn't know how to fix the baby and he doesn't know how to get out from under it."[93]

Jennifer thinks that, because of the dreams and fantasies Henry had experienced, "he has an inkling that the act will get him out. Every man is a boy when he has a child, and even if it just passes as a whim, it's easy to have the thought, 'If this baby would disappear or die, I wouldn't be in this situation anymore; it would be quiet; I would be free.' I don't fault Henry or the baby . . . or my father."[94]

Eraserhead's concluding white-on-black credits show the depth of Lynch's immersion in his first feature film: "Written, Produced, and Directed; Editing; Sound Effects; Production Design by David Lynch." And the words tell us that wife Peggy and daughter Jennifer acted minor roles, that brother John worked on the production, and there are special thanks to Lynch's mother and father and Peggy's parents. Never again would Lynch have the inclination to devote years of effort to dramatizing his inner life for public consumption. The director calls *Eraserhead* "the *real* Philadelphia story,"[95] referring to his anxiety-ridden years in the blighted, ominous industrial zone of the City of Brotherly Love. But, more than being a masterful stylized rendering of Philadelphian textures, the film is a symbolic story of his deepest psychic and autobiographical turmoil.

Aside from his personal commitment to be a freethinking and acting artist, Lynch came of age in times when liberty was a burning cultural, social, and political issue. The heroes of 1960s teen films had a brazen rejoinder for parents and authority figures: "Don't tell *me* what to do!" Elvis Presley sang, "I want to be free, like the bird in a tree,"[96] while Fabian growled to be turned loose[97] to any woman who might attempt to domesticate him. Individual African Americans, then thousands of like-minded multiracial protestors, attacked the ghosts of slavery and fought for equitable civil rights laws. Young men who accused the American government of prosecuting an undeclared, imperialistic, genocidal war in Southeast Asia burned their draft cards. Young women who defied centuries of exploitive, economically and sexually soul-stifling patriarchal authority burned their brassieres. American astronauts outran the law of gravity and played golf on the moon. Andy Warhol said that the image of a Campbell's soup can was art. The British rock group The Who said that smashing up their instruments on stage was art. Boldly experimental clothing styles for both sexes, and longhaired males, were everywhere. Polymorphous sexuality, psychedelic ("mind-manifesting") drugs, and esoteric forms of spirituality were explored and embraced. The stolid and stern military-industrial-corporate complex was out; playful "do your own thing" personal expression and anti-Puritan-heritage hedonism was in. While the last lumbering dinosaurs of the traditional Hollywood studio system sank deeper into the tar pits, industry-outcast actor-director Dennis Hopper shot the youth culture ode *Easy Rider* for $350,000 and made millions and millions of good old American dollars.

Young David Lynch's contribution to this progressive, newborn spirit of libertarian free expression was to choose to be an artist. Dedicated to crafting a tangible record of his unique, subterranean inner journey, Lynch assumed that this would be a solitary trip. But, in time, he welcomed Peggy Reavey as a beloved, understanding fellow-traveler on his voyage. Then, in this era of free love—and thanks to the birth control pill—sex liberated from pregnancy, Peggy discovered that she was going to have a baby. Today, Lynch doesn't elaborate on how the inescapable fact of becoming a father shook him to his core, and that his daughter, Jennifer, was born with two severely clubbed feet and had to undergo surgery and wear massive waist-high casts. Jennifer, who calls her father "my best friend in the whole world,"[98] does speak of these matters. "I came along as a surprise, and David, full of panic and fear, said, 'oh my God, a baby!'"[99] (she thumps her chest to mimic a racing heartbeat). So now Lynch, with his innate fear of feeling constrained, was a starving artist who had to somehow provide for a wife, and a daughter who didn't move across a room in the same way that other human beings did. Jennifer feels that the situation of her father and mother "having a surprise child"[100] and "the way I was born"[101] form the heart of *Eraserhead*. A linkage in Lynch's sensitive mind between a possible glitch in his genetic code and his daughter's birth deformity, or the thrilling act of sex with its aftermath of pain for a newborn girl and her parents, are certainly enough to inspire *Eraserhead*'s fear and queasy presentation of all things procreational. Today, Lynch says that the film "is so beneath the surface that I didn't understand it while I was making it."[102] Throughout his career Lynch will emphasize that when he's gripped by creative inspiration he just does "what feels correct,"[103] without analyzing the source or meaning of his artistic building blocks. When Lynch looked back at *Eraserhead*, "I learned so much about myself."[104] Exploring the film's deepest layers "scared the hell out of me, because it's so much a thing that's personal to me."[105] As Jennifer says,

> When a guy that age is going to have a child, he's still really a boy. The suddenness and surprise of it all really hit them. Even though they have nine months to think about it, it's more nine months of terror. Not only are they boys who don't know how to respond, or how to do what needs to be done, but they feel like they've had something vital taken from them. They have to share so much of themselves that they didn't expect to have to share, so they feel guilty for not wanting to participate fully, and being made to feel guilty really pisses boys off.[106]

Aside from mirroring Lynch's fear of parenthood and his anguish over Jennifer's deformity, the film traces his spiritual journey from anger and depression to an accepting equanimity. The expansion of Henry's consciousness, his progression through worldly darkness into cosmic light, is a resonant metaphor for Lynch's process of growth-through-meditation.

I told Lynch that *Eraserhead* is the only one of his films in which a person who kills a fellow human being gets what he wants out of life, but of course Henry rubs out his own life in the process of gaining his heavenly reward. Lynch chuckled and let this paradox hang in the air before adding, "*Eraserhead* is my most spiritual film and, uhm, so, that's all I'm going to say."[107]

In a conversation a year earlier, he had said more. He was fervently talking about how meditation helps one draw ever nearer to a state of enlightenment, a realm he called "the big home of everything."[108] Spontaneously, I asked, "Is that where Henry is?" Without hesitation Lynch said, "You bet."[109]

Henry's loss of his life is a metaphor for the meditator's loss of ego consciousness, his embrace of the Lady in the Radiator is an abstraction of his love for the Maharishi. Peggy Reavey says that the Radiator Lady came into *Eraserhead* at the time Lynch was discovering his new devotional path. And Jennifer Lynch adds, "I think the conclusion of *Eraserhead* is very much about Henry's third eye"[110] (referencing the Hindu symbol for expanded spiritual understanding).

In addition to reflecting Lynch's feelings about meditation and Hindu philosophy, *Eraserhead*, as do almost every one of his moving-image works, stresses his reverence for dream life by showing a main character lying in bed. The director's horizontal figures, like those painted by eighteenth-century English visionary William Blake, can more easily float into blissful reveries—and nightmares. And Lynch's prone people experiencing their inner states of consciousness remind us of the Asian reclining Buddhas immersed in their spirit journeys.

Chatting about *Eraserhead* with Lynch in 2004, he said, "There's a way out: you can choose to stay in the darkness and think that's all there is, or you can step onto the path and start coming out."[111] This describes the arc of Henry's journey and that of many Lynchian characters, and is the trajectory of Lynch's own life path. Before Transcendental Meditation and Hindu spirituality brightened Lynch's outlook, *Eraserhead* was to end very much like his unproduced pre-*Eraserhead Gardenback* script did, in which a character named Henry causes a dark creature to grow in his house, a "monster that overtakes him."[112] In the only existing script of *Eraserhead*, which Lynch wrote before he dreamed up Henry's delivering-angel Lady in the Radiator and a "happy" ending, the baby's head would grow monstrously large and devour Henry: we would see Henry's feet disappearing into the creature's gaping mouth. There would also be a difference in Henry's attitude as he approached the baby, scissors in hand. In the script, Henry would be motivated by curiosity about just what is beneath the baby's gauze bandages, and when he accidentally snipped the child's flesh, he would say, "God, I'm sorry."[113] Also in the script before Henry approaches the baby with the scissors, the child expresses its hostility by snapping at the air. In the film, Lynch indicates the baby's animus by having him chortle at Henry, and the director makes Henry's action with the scissors more purposeful, less accidental. And in the film Jack Nance's expressive body language communicates Henry's "I'm sorry"[114] emotion without words, heightening the I-did/I-did-not-want-this-to-happen ambiguity of his behavior.

Lynch's original *Eraserhead* script, which had no redeeming Lady in the Radiator for Henry, shows that the director first conceived the project as closer in letter and spirit to the unproduced *Gardenback* screenplay he wrote before *Eraserhead*. *Gardenback*, which also featured a Henry and Mary, was Lynch's abstract meditation on "the theme of adultery,"[115] in which Henry "looks at a girl, and something crosses from her to him."[116] This "thing grows and metamorphoses into this monster that overtakes him."[117] The "thing"[118] that catches and plagues Henry is his extramarital desire and secret cheating behavior, which, as Peggy Reavey says, Lynch acted out in their own marriage. In Lynch's film version of *Eraserhead*, Henry's night of love with the Beautiful Girl Across the Hall is a declaration of his independent spirit, which yearns to be free from the prison of marriage and his wailing baby. But in Lynch's initial *Eraserhead* script conception, the Beautiful Girl Across the Hall is also a dark force: the first femme fatale to appear in a Lynch fiction.

In the film version, the little wriggling bit of animal tissue that Henry gets in the mail and keeps secret from Mary is like an anonymous gift from the universe, a catalyst that stimulates Henry to explore the nature of his deepest self and nurture it into full expression. In Lynch's script version, the piece of organic matter also arouses growth, but of a destructive kind. In the film the Henry-galvanizing lump of tissue looks like a worm, but in his script Lynch calls it a piece of flesh and has Henry receive more chunks of it in the mail. As in the film, he keeps these secret, defining a separate zone of selfhood within the context of his married life. In the script, one day a black bone arrives, which Henry places with the flesh: we get the feeling that Henry is being sent the raw materials for something waiting to be born. Soon the parts meld, as the flesh becomes the animating energy within the bone and the bone gains "a jagged, open mouth,"[119] the archetype of the hungry hole that will haunt Lynchland, from *Dune*'s (1984) gaping sandworm maws to Jeffrey's creepy rubber mask in *Blue Velvet* (1986), to faces in Lynch's early-twenty-first-century prints.

In the script, the dark bone with its saw-toothed mouth is scary and threatening, and Lynch visually links it with the episode in which Henry and the Beautiful Girl Across the Hall kiss and slowly sink into the white liquid pool on Henry's bed. In the film version, Henry's extramarital tryst is a pivotal passage in the narrative, spotlighting the major choice Henry is faced with. Does he want to be with the smothering Mary and Baby, the sexy Beautiful Girl Across the Hall, or the chaste and spiritual Lady in the Radiator? Since there's no Lady in the Radiator in Lynch's script version, Henry faces two negative choices, for not only is the Beautiful Girl Across the Hall associated visually with the dark bone when she and Henry make love, but he discovers that she's the one who's been sending him the organic building materials in the mail. (Henry sneaks into her apartment when she's not there, a scene that's the progenitor of *Blue Velvet*'s Jeffrey slinking into Dorothy's apartment, and the first cinematic acting-out of one of Lynch's personal fantasies.)

The script Beautiful Girl is the agent of, and is conflated with, the malevolent flesh and bone, suggesting that she is a shadow reflection of the biblical Eve. When Henry is devoured by the giant baby head, the head becomes the dark bone for a moment, thus completing the linkage (Henry's adultery with an alluring woman, the woman is the agent of a devouring monster's growth) between the scripts for *Gardenback* and *Eraserhead* (you cheat on your mate, a monster grows, you are destroyed). Lynch always says how much he identifies with Henry, and clearly Henry unexpectedly becoming a father is an autobiographical portrait of Lynch. So perhaps the dark Beautiful Girl and her devouring black bone monster dispatching Henry in the early, scripted version of *Eraserhead* shows Lynch punishing himself for cheating on Peggy. By the time he shot the film version, he had psychologically come to terms with his unfaithfulness and was enjoying the life-and-art-changing benefits of Transcendental Meditation, which prompted him to have an agent of spiritual deliverance (the Lady in the Radiator) on his, and Henry's, mind.

Eraserhead's six-year-marathon production put a severe strain on Lynch's family. The director ran out of filming money countless times, and borrowed from many sympathetic souls, including his parents and his friend Jack Fisk (the Man in the Planet) and Fisk's wife, budding actress Sissy Spacek. To put food on Peggy and Jennifer's table, Lynch even took a paper route, driving through ritzy neighborhoods delivering the *Wall Street*

Journal for $48 a week. From early in her relationship with David, Peggy knew that he believed "An artist's life is very selfish; you can't have a lot of obligations."[120] Lynch realized that devoting his time and resources to his muse could hurt other people, but being held back from making his art hurt *him*. Unable to integrate creative and family needs in harmony, the couple agreed to an amicable divorce in 1974, with Peggy having custody of six-year-old Jennifer. Decades later, Lynch and Peggy, who has remarried and works as a teacher, writer, and artist, remain good friends and are very proud of their daughter. In 1990, the independent-minded, imaginative, humorous, and beautiful Jennifer published *The Secret Diary of Laura Palmer*, a fictional exploration of the dark themes Lynch and *Twin Peaks* co-creator Mark Frost had recently launched in their sensational TV series. The book was critically praised for its literary style and its insight into teenage female angst, and spent some time on the *New York Times* bestseller list. At the premiere of Jennifer's feature-film directing debut, the less-well-received *Boxing Helena* (1993), David and Peggy warmly embraced their daughter, and Lynch, commenting to his old friend, Catherine Coulson, gave his daughter an artist's ultimate compliment: "Cath, she's as round as a ball."[121]

Because he had a hard time getting up early in the morning, Lynch had often been late for his odd jobs in Philadelphia. So, naturally, as a beginning student at the Film Center, Lynch rarely attended the post-breakfast-hour workshop, How to Direct Actors, conducted by husband and wife thespians Jack Nance and Catherine Coulson. But the three shared enough contact during Lynch's Film Institute years for Nance to become the hero of the director's first feature film, and for Coulson to assume the protean role of *Eraserhead* actress, camera assistant, fundraiser, and maintainer of the iconic Henry Spencer high hairdo. Nance and Coulson gave up sleep to work with Lynch, let their living-room furniture be trucked off for use in the film, and, at a time when even American corporate men sported longish, flowing locks, Jack endured being a freakish public spectacle for *years* with his shave-sided head and tall, electrified zap of hair on top. Despite the travails of production, Nance and Coulson became Lynch's close friends. The couple's marriage didn't endure, but Lynch's appreciation of Nance's brilliant acting did, and he resolved to use the now-normal-haired actor in future projects.

Coulson, of course, became *Twin Peaks'* oracular Log Lady, but she appeared in a Lynch production even before *Eraserhead* was finished. In 1974, before the revolutionary Japanese video camera/video cassette recorder wave washed over the globe, Sony Corporation gave the American Film Institute some videotape to test. *Eraserhead* cinematographer Fred Elmes was to shoot some geometric color patterns for the Film Center brass to scrutinize. Lynch heard about Elmes' task, called in Coulson, and dreamed up a little theater-of-the-absurd piece called *The Amputee*, which presents a single, unedited five-minute scene in a doctor's examining room. Wearing a physician's white coat, Lynch sits in the foreground before Coulson, a woman with amputated legs who's nestled in a big easy chair. She smokes and writes a letter as Dr. Lynch, his back to the camera, tends to one of her white-bandaged thigh stumps. Without showing even a hint of blood, Lynch pushes the viewer well past his or her comfort zone as the doctor removes the bandage from Coulson's stumps, probes the exposed flesh with surgical pliers, and blots it with chunks of cotton. Then he makes a grotesque sexual reference by pushing the rubber bulb syringe with which he's been dribbling water onto the stumps into the vertical slit in the thigh's open end. How typical of Lynch that for his first turn in front of the camera he would engineer a scene that disturbingly mixes light and dark emotions. His doctor is a figure of healing consolation, yet we're instantly, squeamishly on edge anticipating the pain he may inflict on his patient. And, with deft humor, Lynch plays the moment-to-moment potential for violence and hurt against Coulson's casual, unconcerned smoking and writing.

We hear Coulson's voice speaking the words she's writing, as Lynch characteristically emphasizes her inner life (and prefigures the spoken-thoughts technique he'll employ eleven years later in *Dune*). Writing to a woman friend, Coulson speaks about the charged emotional interrelationship of people we don't know (Jim, Joanne, Paul, Helen, Harry), evoking the eternal continuum of human conflicts, jealousies, and suspicions. We may not be familiar with the specific players in Coulson's drama, but we recognize some typical Lynchian themes and motifs. There's a stress on intuition ("I knew, even if he didn't say it, that it was true"), the power of destructive flames ("Harry turned on all the stove burners in the cabin—he wanted to set fire to the whole row of houses"), and a lingering mystery that projects out beyond the final image of Lynch's fiction, with Coulson wondering, "Where were you when Paul got home at three in the morning?" as *The Amputee* ends with a black screen. Aside from these Lynchian preoccupations, it's intriguing to note that the writer-director-actor cast himself as a man of science, a figure who combats forces of chaos and disintegration as he investigates the enigmas of nature, just as Lynch's father does in his forests, and the writer-director-actor and his surrogate detective personas will do in many films to come.

After shooting this short scene, in which Lynch's face is never seen, Fred Elmes took the tape to the Film Center directors for viewing. Expecting to see test patterns, the executives were aghast. But one of them knew a distinctive style when he saw it and wondered in a scolding tone, "Did Lynch have something to do with this?"[122]

In the days of the *Eraserhead* production, Lynch and Coulson were involved in real-life medical drama. After the director and his wife, Peggy, split up, Lynch stayed with Nance and Coulson for a time. In addition to Lynch with his paper route, Coulson took up waitressing to help purchase film stock or otherwise bolster the production's finances. One winter morning she left Nance asleep in bed, put on her striped waitress's dress, and chatted with Lynch in the kitchen before heading to work. Her morning routine was disrupted by a sharp, queasy feeling in her stomach, and she told Lynch, "I feel really weird."[123] Thinking she just needed some nourishment, he urged her to drink some orange juice, which she began to vomit up.

The two friends realized that this was more than just an upset stomach as Coulson was wracked by a convulsive seizure. Dropping to the floor, she began to regurgitate her stomach lining and lose consciousness. Lynch sprang to the phone and called an ambulance, then returned to Coulson. Cradling her head, and terrified that she was ebbing away, he tried to keep her in this world by saying, "Keep repeating your mantra," and "Don't go to sleep."[124]

The ambulance raced Coulson, Lynch, and Nance to the hospital. Coulson had been taking a lot of aspirin for flu symptoms, and the pain-reliever's salicylic acid had eroded her stomach lining, causing internal bleeding which drained the blood from her brain and sent her into seizure. As if this wasn't enough of an assault on her system, she went into cardiac arrest in the hospital—but the medics were able to stabilize her condition. The doctors credited Lynch's fast action with saving Coulson's life and, to this day, every February on the anniversary of her ordeal, she makes a phone call to Lynch and thanks him for the greatest gift one friend could give another.

Coulson's medical emergency has had no lasting effect on her body, but it moved her abiding soul. As the seizure's surging waves engulfed her, she was bathed in golden light and felt a profound sense of peace. "It was like a tropical vacation, and it made me realize that if this is death, then everything's going to be okay: I can always go to that place again."[125]

Coulson's firsthand perception of death being a pathway to a realm of beneficent light reinforced Lynch's own sense of spiritual cosmology, and many times over the years a flood of loving light would banish the suffering of his fictional characters. Coulson's artistic friend was also struck by a stunning, raw image he had witnessed the morning of her seizure: her stomach lining, which Lynch said "looked like a big red fish,"[126] glistening down the front of her striped dress. Like an involuntary reflex of his sensibility, Lynch is drawn to the mystery of something normally hidden inside appearing in the outer world. And, almost twenty years after he'd watched Coulson's consciousness drift from this world into spaces defined by her own inner dimensions, he told actress Sherilyn Fenn of his and Coulson's experience when Fenn was preparing to play a traumatized car-crash victim in *Wild at Heart* (1990): a young woman who's dissociated from her stricken body and is living her last moments inside her head.

In the mid-1990s, Mark Frost, the co-creator of *Twin Peaks* and Lynch's short-lived ABC comedy series *On the Air*, called his collaborator "solitary and inaccessible."[127] But this introspective artist has a real gift for making lasting friendships. After *Eraserhead*, the director remained close to Coulson and Nance, Jack Fisk (the Man in the Planet and his old painting buddy from high school), sound design genius Alan Splet, and cinematographer Fred Elmes, who chuckles when he recalls Lynch's obsession with conjuring a shadowy mood: "Fred, it's not quite dark enough, I can still see something."[128] Jack and Lynch became family legally when the director married Jack's sister Mary in 1977. The solidarity of Lynch's extended family, which Charlotte Stewart (Mary X) says is like "a secret society,"[129] can be measured by the fact that, remaining true to the director's wishes, no one who knows how Lynch created *Eraserhead*'s biologically convincing baby has ever revealed it.

Having spent years shooting *Eraserhead*, it seemed only right that Lynch and Alan Splet should take another twelve months to edit picture and sound into flowing sequences. During this period Lynch tried, and failed, to get a rough cut of the film shown at the Cannes and New York film festivals. As the entry deadline for Los Angeles's Filmex exposition fast approached, the dejected Lynch thought, "There's no way I'm even going to get into festivals with this."[130] But wife Mary applied some pressure: "We're going to get in the car and drive over there, and you're going to turn it in; you've got to give it a try."[131] Expecting another rejection, Lynch even informed the Filmex committee of *Eraserhead*'s strikeout history as he handed it over. But, as at other turning points in Lynch's career (winning the sculpture prize at the Pennsylvania Academy of the Fine Arts, getting the American Film Institute grant), the uniqueness of his work was recognized and made available to an ever-wider audience. Filmex would show *Eraserhead*.

First, though, Lynch staged a private premiere of the film at the American Film Institute screening room. True to the shoestring-budget spirit of the production, the director offered crackers, canned fruit juice, and tap water to his guests before they filed into the auditorium. Lynch's parents, his present and former wives, his daughter, the cast and crew, assorted friends, those who had donated money to the production, and the Film Center directors took their seats as the lights dimmed. Lynch was nervous during the screening and depressed afterward, for as the lights came up no one clapped or even spoke. Fred Elmes recalls that "The film was really a shock; it does take your breath away, and it's hard to know how to respond to it, which disturbed David because he was expecting some response."[132] Lynch's parents had been troubled by *The Grandmother*'s dysfunctional child-parent relationship and wondered if it was their son's view of his home life ("Where did all this come from?").[133] With a smile, Catherine Coulson recalls that after the *Eraserhead* screening Sunny Lynch said to her son, "Oh God, honey, what have I done?"[134]

The film's first audience watched a full hour more of Henry's wrenching emotional travails than we see today (89 minutes), and a 142-minute version is the one that Lynch showed at Filmex. Jack Nance has a fond memory of the evening: "At the end there was a complete, dead silence, and I knew that the film worked. I said to Lynch, 'You see, I told you that it would turn them into zombies.' People were stunned, and there was this long, shocked silence. Then, a huge burst of applause. It was beautiful. I'd been waiting five years for that applause."[135] Lynch was glad that Nance had received his just reward, and that the crowed was happy and zombified. But the director, having experienced *Eraserhead* with just two audiences, exercised his sound creative judgment and decided to shorten his pet picture. He loved every scene in the film, and its deliberate, slow pacing, but the audience had too many spare moments to drift out of his dream, so he compressed it into its present 89 intense minutes.

Lynch may not yet have gotten the moment-to-moment response he hoped for as audiences watched his film, but soon Ben Barenholtz, New York's king of midnight movie exhibition, was ringing his telephone. Barenholtz had a stable of films that were too specialized for the mainstream commercial market, such as John Water's *Pink Flamingos*, Alexander Jodorowsky's *El Topo*, and Peter Henzell's *The Harder They Come*, which he played to growing late-night cult audiences in Gotham.

Barenholtz flew to Los Angeles and, true to Lynch's love of Old Hollywood, the fledgling director and the seasoned entrepreneur sat down to talk business in the fabled Schwabs drugstore, a location featured in Lynch's cherished *Sunset Boulevard* where, in real life, countless Hollywood insiders had gossiped and tried to reconcile their dreams with the cold, hard realities of the commercial marketplace. Lynch, to his amazement, didn't have to say much. Recognizing a unique vision when he saw it, Barenholtz bought *Eraserhead*, affixed his logo Libra Films to its opening credits, and showed it to only twenty-five paying customers the first night in New York, and fewer the second. But, thanks to the relatively low maintenance costs of Barenholtz's operation, he was able to stick with the film until it found its audience. The showman's persistence was rewarded, for *Eraserhead* became a staple of American midnight shows and repertory theaters well into the 1980s. The film's success grew to encompass a dozen countries, from Europe to Australia to Mexico, with the most fervent responses being scored in France and Japan, a pattern that persists with Lynch's work to this day. Consistent with Lynch's sense of personal loyalty, everyone who was part of the *Eraserhead* production family is still receiving exhibition revenue from the film.

The director's cinematic abstraction of his urban Philadelphian anxieties, his daughter's unplanned and deformed birth, his panic at becoming a father, the shattering of his marriage, and his growth of consciousness through meditation have tantalized, mystified, unsettled, and haunted viewers around the world. Over the years, filmmakers from John Waters (*Female Trouble*) to William Friedkin (*The French Connection*) to Stanley Kubrick (*2001: A Space Odyssey*) have declared their admiration for *Eraserhead*'s technical, thematic, and stylistic achievement. At a time when talented fellow members of Lynch's film-school generation were gaining fame and fortune in the mainstream major-studio marketplace (Francis Ford Coppola,: *The Godfather Part II*; Brian De Palma, *Carrie*; George Lucas, *Star Wars*; Martin Scorsese, *Taxi Driver*; Steven Spielberg, *Jaws*), Lynch was working in his own intimate, personal-scale mode contemplating the recesses of his soul and intuitively shaping the heaven and hell he found there into a ribbon of celluloid dreams. The image of Henry, with his glowing high hair and surrounding dust cloud, has become part of the culture. A recent *New Yorker* cartoon compared Lyle Lovett's *arriviste* tall hair with Henry's classic original. A young woman on a TV dating game show says her previous swain "looked like Eraserhead."

Lynch, who was frustrated because the first audiences for his film didn't audibly respond to it, has been getting an earful over the years. *Eraserhead* has been interpreted upside-down and backwards, from being the story of an infantile fellow trying to crawl back into the womb, to the tale of a nerd's psychotic breakdown, to a plea for abortion rights. Lynch is gratified that viewers bring so much of themselves to what they see in his film, and that today they catch the absurdist humor that attends some of Henry's predicaments, such as his disastrous social evening at the Xs' house.

In the early 1990s, Lynch was able to buy back the rights to *Eraserhead* and he now distributes the film himself. Before putting it back in exhibition, Lynch and Fred Elmes and Alan Splet took pains to refurbish the picture and sound to the highest technical standards, and, in a truly Lynchian image, the director proudly declared, "We printed the movie on film stock so tough you couldn't even tear it with your teeth."[136]

Eraserhead, in which a man engulfed in his fears discovers how to transcend them, remains a touchstone for Lynch. In 1995, he said, "I still feel like the same person who made that film."[137] The emblematic, twisted, barren tree branch that decorated Henry's bedside resides on Lynch's nightstand to this day. In 1990, Sherilyn Fenn, the actress who played mischievous high school temptress Audrey Horne on *Twin Peaks*, told Lynch that she really wanted to get married and have a child. He responded with a grin, "Go take a look at *Eraserhead* first."[138]

Fenn watched the film as the director suggested and saw what he meant. But then, as did Lynch and his second wife in 1982, she went ahead and brought a baby into the world anyway.

3

BURDEN OF FLESH

1976–1980
(*The Elephant Man*)

If *Eraserhead*'s Henry had finally achieved paradise, so had Lynch. "I was in heaven. I only had to work at my paper route one hour a day. Then at 2:30 in the afternoon I'd go to Bob's Big Boy and have a chocolate shake and coffee. That's when I discovered that sugar made me happy and gave me ideas. Sugar for me is granulated happiness. I'd sit and think at Bob's and get so inspired and so wound up that when I got home I'd be raring to go!"[1]

This testimonial bespeaks Lynch's love of diners and all-American comfort foods, which will enhance the texture and narrative of *Blue Velvet* and, especially, *Twin Peaks*. It shows his abiding fascination with altered states of awareness and consciousness, the heightened reality of dream states, creative impulses, obsessive sexual passions, drug trances, and evil possessions. Knowing his own, and hence the world's, capacity for panicky fear and core disintegration, Lynch has always sought the stability of small, simple habits that he can control and depend on: his uniform-like black-and-white attire, top-buttoned shirt, Henry-like haircut, and cycle of repeated food choices (Lynch maintained his daily Bob's Big Boy habit for years). Following nineteenth-century French author Honoré de Balzac's dictum that the artist needs to maintain order in his life so that he can go crazy in his work, Lynch can best launch his wild and free-ranging imagination from a base of secure, structured daily life. For Lynch, bright and shiny Bob's Big Boy was a Hemingwayesque clean, well-lit place, a safe base camp for the artist's disturbing psychic expeditions. There were no shadowy corners in

Bob's Big Boy, but even with a sugar-blissed grin on his face, Lynch often journeyed to the dark side of his own mind.

But the artist's demons were held at bay as he breezed through his *Wall Street Journal* delivery route. Spotting intriguing shapes of roadside wood as he drove, Lynch would stop and load these serendipitous treasures onto his Volkswagen bug's handmade wooden roof rack. The little boy who had loved to "work"[2] the mud in an Idaho puddle had grown into a man who always had to be making something. Back at his and wife Mary's abode, a garage with an attached apartment, the proud Lynch amazed his wife by building L-shaped, gable-roofed, and Egyptian-styled additions out of his collected, irregular raw materials.

Lynch's best friend, Jack Fisk, had been best man at Lynch's wedding to Peggy Lentz in 1967 and again at his buddy's second wedding in 1977, three years after Lynch and Peggy's divorce. By way of contrast, Lynch learned about Jack and Sissy Spacek's spur-of-the-moment decision to get married when they drove by him honking and smiling as he walked to meditation class in the *Eraserhead*-production days. Lynch's second bride was Jack's sister, Mary, who had been part of Lynch's life for years and had helped raise funds to complete *Eraserhead*. When she finally saw the finished film, Mary felt that "some of the images were really disconcerting. I mean, I just couldn't look at some of them, and sometimes that bothered me so much that I didn't actually see what was going on."[3] More viewings increased her appreciation of Lynch's effort, and she concluded that "there's a little *Eraserhead* in everybody."[4] Perhaps she was referring to Lynch's alter ego, Henry, married to a light-haired woman (as Peggy was) being tempted by the dark-haired Beautiful Girl Across the Hall (Mary was raven-tressed). As Peggy says, during the *Eraserhead* production years, Mary, then a Pan Am stewardess, would flirt with a responsive Lynch. When Peggy called them on it, they said, "Whaaat? Come on, we're not doing anything wrong."[5]

In David and Mary's wedding picture, the bride and groom and Jack and Sissy stand in the dark interior of a church, stained-glass windows glowing behind them like the ones that background Laura Dern's *Blue Velvet* recounting of her dream of light and love illuminating a shadowed world. Sissy stands in front of Jack, leaning into his chest, his hands encircling her tummy from behind. Both in white, they're like a single visual unit with two heads, one atop the other. Mary and David stand erect in a more formal side-by-side pose, his hand resting atop her shoulder. Mary's smile is smaller than those of the other three. A wedding-reception shot shows a homey domestic interior with an antique chandelier, flower painting, and bouquet of roses. Mary and David are frozen in a cutting-the-cake pose. Each has a hand on the big knife. Lynch grins and casts his shadow on the wall. Mary's expression is unsmiling and unreadable. Does she have a premonition about the viability of her union with this man who's so deeply committed to art-making?

Looking back from 2004, Jennifer Lynch remembers Mary and her father

> being very playful together when things were at their best. She represented where he thought he should be at the time. I don't think he was wrong for that, but there's a part of him that feels a marriage is a dangerous place for him to be. He's an incredibly powerful partner and mate to anyone who isn't going to make him say out loud, "You're it—forever." He needs to retain the illusion, or the semblance, of freedom, the idea that it's his choice, day-to-day: "If I wanted to I could just walk out that door, but I don't want to."[6]

Jennifer's mother, Lynch's first wife, Peggy, had found a loving relationship that had no need of an exit door. In 1977, she married Tom Reavey, former advertising man turned construction worker, then building contractor with his own business, who credits David Lynch's passion for mid-twentieth-century architecture for inspiring Tom to specialize in modernist projects. Jennifer lived with her mother and Tom, and he was a gentle, caring, supportive second father to her. Lynch got along amicably with the Reavey household and would routinely pick up Jennifer there. Lynch liked to take his daughter along when he visited his parents northeast of L.A., and one time he came and got her while Tom and Peggy were out. In his work, Lynch often portrays domestic tableaus invaded by a disturbing strangeness. One day, when Tom returned home and opened the front door, something sitting on the living room floor in the dim light caught his eye: an abstract David Lynch sculptural composition in white and red—tampons and catsup.

Lynch sketched and painted, and worked on a screenplay called *Ronnie Rocket*, a tale about "a little guy with red hair and sixty-cycle, alternating-current electricity,"[7] a dwarf idiot savant who becomes a rock and roll star. With his painter's sense of the balance between compositional elements, the interplay of negative and positive space, inert passivity and thrusting activity, Lynch was fascinated by the concept of power. He speaks of the power of factories and unexplained mysteries, of love and evil. Like a child or a native living on the land, he feels the pulse of manna in nature and people and manmade objects. Lynch often expresses his power buzz through the motif of electricity. People don't get shocked or electrocuted in his work; it's as though the mysterious flowing of electrons ("It's like humor, I don't know how it works" [8]) that surrounds us day and night is registering the pulsing of still more powerful and ineffable forces. Sparking wall sockets and disruptive on-and-off flashing lights illuminate moments of heightened apprehension, sadness, and violence. The ominous rotation of a domestic ceiling fan and eerie twittering of telephone lines let murderous, soul-snatching impulses seep into a sunny small-town afternoon. *Twin Peaks'* nocturnal traffic light burns an unchanging blood red to signal a permanent danger zone. In a stroke of unconscious poetry, Lynch made *Eraserhead's* hero his first electrical man, for in scientific nomenclature the term *henry*[9] is a unit of measure for a circuit with one volt of electromotive force. Maybe the jolt of creative electricity Lynch got from his chocolate shake and coffees made *him* feel like Ronnie Rocket.

With the memory of *Eraserhead's* grueling marathon production fresh in his head, Lynch was not eager to pull together another grassroots campaign to get *Ronnie Rocket* on the screen. His first feature film's level of modest market success got Lynch through the front door of some of the major studios, but none of them thought his story of the little charged-up rock and roller was a worthy commercial venture. Wanting to get busy learning more about telling stories on film, Lynch was getting desperate and depressed; then *Eraserhead* helped save the day.

Producer Stuart Cornfield had viewed Lynch's feature and thought it was "the best, most unique film I'd ever seen."[10] He and the artist became friends, and one day Lynch said he'd even consider directing someone else's script. Cornfield had just read an evocative screenplay by Christopher De Vore and Eric Bergren, which he mentioned to Lynch. The artist recalls that as soon as Cornfield said "elephant" and "man," the words "made a little noise in my head, and I knew I was going to do it."[11]

Instinctively responding to a poetic juxtaposition of unrelated terms, Lynch had no idea why the two words were linked in a single phrase, so he was fascinated to learn about the real-life Elephant Man of late nineteenth-century London. John Merrick, born in 1862, was afflicted with neurofibromatosis, a rare, incurable skeletal and skin disease, at the age of twenty-one months. Merrick's father, an engine driver who was not married to the boy's mother, Mary Jane, shirked his responsibilities and abandoned his woman and son. John's mother was a Baptist schoolteacher who had received a traumatic fright while pregnant when she was knocked down by some circus elephants. She was a loving parent to her pitiful son, and died of pneumonia when John was twelve. As John grew into young adulthood, he suffered from numerous ailments and hideous deformities. His misshapen skull, swollen to a circumference of thirty-six inches, made his forehead jut out in two huge, bulbous mounds that almost closed one eye. From the back of his hairless head hung a benignly tumorous bag of spongy skin resembling brown cauliflower. A mass of upper jawbone protruded a pink stump from his mouth and turned his upper lip inside out, making speech difficult and almost unintelligible. His nose was an ill-defined lump of flesh. Great sacks of the cauliflower skin also sprouted from his chest and from his back down to the middle of his thighs. John's right arm was grotesquely elongated and twice the normal thickness, his right hand a barely differentiated pad of flesh. His legs and feet were similarly giganticized tissue clumps.

Cross-cultural studies show that throughout history human beings around the globe have valued similar traits of physical beauty and symmetry. In any language, John Merrick was a walking nightmare. Or, rather, a bent and hobbling one, for, in addition to his appearance and unwashed stench that caused people to shun and torment him, John had a painful hip disease that made his cane-assisted locomotion slow and tortuous. With no one to call family or friend, outcast and penniless, John Merrick, shrouded in a hood and cloak, was shunted back and forth between brief hospital stays and poorhouse lodgings. But a certain class of debased entrepreneurs saw this monstrous pariah as a valuable commodity. An anonymous exhibitor of freaks, inspired by John's tusk-like mouth protrusion, named him the Elephant Man and charged Londoners two pence to gawk in wonder and disgust. But one man paid his viewing fee and looked upon Merrick with the compassion and scientific curiosity of a healer.

Dr. Frederick Treves, lecturer on anatomy at the London Medical College, brought Merrick to his examining room, analyzed and notated his condition, and published his findings in the *British Medical Journal*. Treves concluded that scientific techniques could not eradicate or even mitigate Merrick's maladies and, looking into a face incapable of any expression and listening to vocal sounds devoid of meaning, he assumed that Merrick was, in the terminology of the day, "imbecile."[12] Indeed, Treves hoped that John's mind and emotions were blank and unaware of the horror of his situation. The doctor gave Merrick his card and returned him to his showman-keeper. The next day, Treves noticed that the Elephant Man exhibition had left town.

Merrick's exploitative impresario was always on the move trying to stay ahead of the police, who would close down his inhumane show on sight. Finally, after being hounded by the authorities in Belgium, the showman gave up on his Elephant Man venture. Stealing Merrick's paltry percentage of the profits, he put his former meal ticket on a train for London and went his way. Arriving in the dank, autumnal city, Merrick had nowhere to turn. Taunted by a hostile crowd, he tried to hide in the darkest corner of the Liverpool Street Station. A policeman was called, and John, unable to explain himself, held out Treves' card to the officer. As if by magic, this gesture changed his life.

Dr. Frederick Treves, now chief surgeon of London Hospital, reversed the tide of social rejection and squalid degradation that had washed over John Merrick since early childhood. Treves, his colleague Dr. Carr Gomm, and wealthy benefactors in the community made it possible for Merrick to live out his remaining days in his own apartment within the hospital. Treves learned to understand John's speech, and was awestruck to realize that a gentle, intelligent, and romantic sensibility burned within the husk of shunned, misshapen flesh. For the first time in his life, Merrick was sheltered in a safe and secure home, but, due to the always-on-the-move nature of his previous life, it took him a while to rest assured that he wasn't going to have to leave it. Through his previous reading of books, Merrick had a sense of how "normal"[13] people lived and interacted, and Treves gently broke down John's conditioned fear of being stared at by bringing him visitors. John carried in his hand a miniature portrait of his beautiful mother, and in his heart, an idealized image of her nurturing love for him. Knowing that John venerated women and had amorous feelings for them, and that they had been the ones most likely to run screaming from his presence, Treves began John's social education with the celebrated actress Madge Kendal. Merrick was so stricken with joy after his first meeting with Mrs. Kendal, which she concluded by shaking his hand, that he wept after she left his room.

Merrick's case became known throughout London, and he welcomed many visitors, including Queen Alexandra, who often stopped in to chat and sent John her signed photograph, which he treasured. Treves was moved by the humility and dignity with which Merrick embraced the many kindnesses he received. The doctor understood John's fantasy wish to charm and love women just like any normal dashing young man, and gave him a silver-fitted dressing kit with which Merrick, in his mirrorless room, could make himself up to match some ideal vision of his inner eye. After grooming himself to perfection, Merrick enjoyed the fulfillment of his most cherished desire: He attended a musical pantomime play at the Drury Lane Theatre. Thanks to the efforts of Treves and Mrs. Kendal, Merrick watched the adventures of kings and princesses and fairies unnoticed by the crowd in a shadowed, private box. The play's magic exceeded even John's sky-high expectations, and he absorbed the thrilling proceedings with the wonderstruck awe of a child.

Many times Merrick told Treves "I am happy every day,"[14] yet he spoke with a wistful voice of the possibility of a blind woman falling in love with him. Even the resourceful doctor couldn't grant this wish, though he did transport Merrick to a long-dreamed-of sojourn in the English countryside. Staying in a cottage on the estate of Lady Knightley, John wrote Treves glowing letters of his momentous encounters with a hare and a fierce dog, and sun-drenched days picking wildflowers. Looking over the pressed blooms John had sent with the letter, Treves realized that what Merrick saw as rare specimens were trivial field weeds to the run of men.

The doctor had mapped every inch of Merrick's encumbered body, and now even a casual glance told him that his friend's condition was growing worse. In 1890, six months after he had returned from the country, the twenty-six-year-old Merrick was found dead in bed. John had often told Treves that he wished that he could lie down and stretch out fully and sleep "like other people,"[15] but the size and weight of his head prevented it. Every night previous to his last one, John had slept sitting up, his back propped against the corner juncture of two walls, his head tipped forward against his drawn-up knees. He was found lying prone, his head resting on a down pillow, his neck dislocated from the unnatural strain put upon it. There were no signs of any struggle; the coverlet Merrick had pulled up over his legs and chest was smooth and undisturbed.

Treves concludes his account of his six-year encounter with John Merrick, which provided the source material for De Vore and Bergren's screenplay, on a note of Christian spirituality. Merrick's flesh may have been "ignoble and repulsive,"[16] but his spirit was like "an upstanding and heroic man, smooth browed and clean of limb, and with eyes that flashed undaunted courage."[17] On his torturous journey through life, Merrick, like Christ, "had borne on his back a burden almost too grievous to bear."[18] Though he'd been "ill-treated and reviled and bespattered with the mud of Disdain,"[19] Merrick "had escaped the clutches of the Giant Despair, and at last reached the Place of Deliverance,"[20] where "his burden loosed from off his shoulders and fell from his back, so that he saw it no more."[21]

After a harmonious, enthusiastic meeting between Lynch, Stuart Cornfield, and producer Jonathan Sanger at Bob's Big Boy one afternoon, the trio was eager to make an Elephant Man film. But the major studios saw no commercial potential in the project, and then, as if to permanently squelch their little independent venture, the three saw Bernard Pomerance's play *The Elephant Man* become a Tony Award–winning Broadway sensation ("A giant of a play!"—Clive Barnes).[22] Still, a most unlikely benefactor was waiting in the wings, and once again it was *Eraserhead* that introduced the players to each other.

Manic comic madman-director Mel Brooks, who convulsed 1970s audiences with his films *Blazing Saddles* and *Young Frankenstein*, was busy preparing his latest genre burlesque, *History of the World—Part I*, and he also wanted to start producing independent projects for his new company, Brooksfilm. Brooks knew that Cornfield and Sanger were established in the film industry—but who was this Lynch character? Tense with nervous anticipation, Lynch paced outside the screening room while Cornfield showed *Eraserhead* to Brooks. "Short and sweet" is a dictum of comic timing, and Brooks didn't keep Lynch waiting. He burst from the auditorium yelling, "You're a madman, I love you, you're in!"[23] A brash farceur with hidden depths of sensibility, Brooks later elaborated: "I was flabbergasted by *Eraserhead.* It's very clear. It's beautiful. It's like Beckett, it's like Ionesco. And it's very moving."[24] The comic summed up Lynch's small-town Main Street charm and far-out imagination in the famous appellation, "Jimmy Stewart from Mars,"[25] and hired him to direct *The Elephant Man*. As Jennifer Lynch says, "God bless the eyes of Mel Brooks. People who knew David were certain he could handle *The Elephant Man*, but for a stranger, a comedic man, to have been so affected by *Eraserhead*. God, he really watched it, he understood—what a gift for my father."[26]

In a twinkling, Lynch had graduated from the level of shoestring independent filmmaking to the heady heights of full-blown Hollywood production, with all the financial backing and technical facilities he could ever hope for at his disposal. But, before he could start committing his vision of John Merrick's life to film, he would have to do something new to his singly focused Art Life: collaborate with other writers on his screenplay. Thankfully, Lynch and Chris De Vore and Eric Bergren "got along real well,"[27] wrote "a good script,"[28] and became friends in the process.

De Vore and Bergren's original script, which they wrote before Bernard Pomerance's play came out, was based on *The Elephant Man and Other Reminiscences* by Sir Frederick Treves and *The Elephant Man: A Study in Human Dignity* by anthropologist Ashley Montagu, which are the sole script sources listed in the film's credits. Yet the motion picture makes use of elements that are central to the play's dynamic, such as Merrick's painstaking, one-handed construction of a beautiful model of St. Philip's Church, which parallels his spiritual ascendance; and the haunting question of whether Treves and his genteel medical-social circle are, in their charitable way, exploiting John just like his lowlife freak-show impresarios had.

Upon arriving in London in the fall of 1979, Lynch's first concerns were aesthetic, rather than thematic. For fifteen years, one of the commandments of the mainstream film business had been that "movies are shot in color; that's what people want to see." But Lynch had a passionate vision of *The Elephant Man* in black and white. "It just had to be that way. Black and white is a magical thing; it instantly removes you one step from reality and lets you drift back in time. So many photographs from the past are in black and white. You feel things more; it has a purity."[29] Producer Jonathan Sanger and Mel Brooks saw the light Lynch's way, and hired on sterling British cinematographer Freddie Francis to work his monochromatic magic.

The last time that Lynch had left America for foreign shores to pursue artistic endeavors, he was to spend three years studying painting with Viennese expressionist Oscar Kokoschka beginning in 1965. But the picturesque, storybook quality of Austria was uninspiring: "too clean, wholesome, and sterile."[30] Pining for the land that spoke to his sensibilities, he returned to the United States in fifteen days. Now, fifteen years later, the still all-American film director found his now-more-expansive imagination on fire seven thousand miles away from home in London, England. Doing a crash course on the nineteenth-century Industrial Revolution era, Lynch's imagination heard the clip-clop of horses' hooves on fog-glistening cobblestones, saw elegant ladies and gentlemen cheek-by-jowl with sooty, squalid street urchins, heard the pounding and hissing of William Blake's "Dark, Satanic Mills"[31] as the Thames's murky mirror reflected gray skies and poisonous black clouds of smoke.

Lynch's sensitivity to atmospheric intuitions served him well when he went looking for a location to double as Dr. Treves' London Hospital. The young director was given access to a number of healing institutions that had been shut down for years. Most of the structures were empty, echoey shells. But one hospital "still had beds in it, and beautiful wards and walls, and all the original gas lights. Walking around in that place, the feeling of the past just came over me and from then on I knew exactly what it was. So many things came into me from that one place." (As he says this, Lynch flutters his hands together as he moves them in toward his chest.[32])

As Lynch became immersed in what would be the home ground of his Elephant Man project, he had a beloved young companion by his side: his twelve-year-old daughter, Jennifer, who, before shooting started, went back to mom and home and the start of school classes in the states. Jennifer was six when her parents divorced, and she was "already used to my father sleeping somewhere else,"[33] referring to *Eraserhead* Henry's room in the AFI stables, where Lynch bedded down for almost three years. She already saw her parents "more as best friends than husband and wife,"[34] yet it was still absolutely, totally effecting. Time with them became separate, so defined and circumscribed: it didn't just flow. I had to get used to being dropped off, to one of them not being around. No longer was it, "Your dad's called you from the living room," or "Go ask your mom about that." When there's a divorce the kid feels guilt, or like they're being punished. "Did I somehow cause this? If I was better my parents wouldn't have split up." You can intellectualize those thoughts away, but your heart still feels them.[35]

After the divorce mom and dad had to redefine what they were to each other. They were apart, but they made me feel like we were all still in the same environment. The situation was made so much more tolerable, and magical, by the fact that they were able to overcome their own issues on my behalf. They didn't cloud the importance of being my parents with negativity. They could be loving with each other over the fact that they had made a kid, and there was no shame in that, nothing to be upset about. [36]

Though they didn't live together anymore, Lynch the visionary artist had a loving concern for Jennifer's imagination.

I was having my ninth or tenth birthday party in a park, and my dad came by to give me my present. It was a set of headphones and a car stereo—just raw and disconnected from anything else. I had gotten all these other gifts, but his was the one I loved most. I could barely stand how excited I was. God, what a great thing, and I knew he had sat, and thought, and put it together for me. It was so full of imagination and potential: I could be anyone working with this contraption, anything from a pilot to a phone operator. I used to fantasize about being an operator. What a great job, sitting there pushing buttons and plugging stuff in all day.

(Twenty-four years later Lynch enabled his daughter to realize her fantasy with her call-in radio show, *Oddio*, on his website.)

My dad's approach to the world showed me that everything was neat, everything had something fantastic about it. I loved machines and factories. After *Eraserhead* was done, he'd take me back to what Jack Nance called "Lynch's Park," the abandoned industrial area where he'd filmed the scenes of Henry walking. This was across from Cedars-Sinai Hospital, where Beverly center now sits. We would stare at these giant black oil tanks, the ladders going up their sides, the gleaming rivets—just the sound in between those tanks, and the way your shoes felt, sort of sinking into the spongy ground, but not quite. We would collect these black, shiny rocks that were smooth like glass, and take them back to his house, where he'd put them in a yellow ceramic bowl. [37]

Jennifer's sense of wonder was further stimulated when she and her father explored the Elephant Man's London. "We got to visit John Merrick's room: this little tiny dark room with water dripping in it. You felt horrified for his life but inside you just felt prayer and hope. You could tell that every time light came into that room he was so grateful."[38] Jennifer's reverent sensitivity is moving, and it seems natural that she would feel a kinship with an afflicted London outcast of the nineteenth century. In 2004, after taking a deep breath, she said, "Because I was born with club feet and had to have surgery and be put in casts, and had to wear orthopedic shoes until I was thirteen, there was a whole sense to me that the scars on my legs and my shoes and all this made me freakish. There's something really touched by me in John Merrick's story."[39]

So Lynch now had his black-and-white aesthetic in place, the location for most of the film's action chosen, a soulful sense of his story's place and time, and some of the greatest actors in the world to work with: Anthony Hopkins as Dr. Treves, John Hurt as John Merrick, John Gielgud as Carr Gomm, Anne Bancroft as Mrs. Kendal, and Wendy Hiller as Mothershead. But, with only ten days to the start of shooting, John Merrick's Elephant Man makeup was still on the drawing board. Since boyhood, Lynch had thought of himself as an artist, and he knew himself to be an accomplished painter, sculptor, and the kind of hands-on filmmaker who creates everything but the acting. Since the film, at its heart, would be his vision, he felt that he should design the makeup. After all, he had given birth to *Eraserhead*'s mutant baby and its horrific, swollen manifestation that menaces Henry at the film's climax.

When Lynch proudly spread out his blueprint for Merrick's makeup, the director's English production colleagues were, with as much tact as possible, aghast. Production supervisor Tony Clegg recalls that Lynch's design "wouldn't have passed muster at a children's concert. It was rather like someone wearing a pair of long-johns covered in latex rubber—an utter disaster."[40] With *The Elephant Man*, Lynch was making a sometimes painful transition from a lifetime of creating art for the joy of personal expression to a new state of expanding collaboration in which he had to consider, and even acquiesce to, the needs and wishes of accountants, time-keepers, and fellow artists. Listening to his colleagues, the young director understood that his design just wasn't good enough, and he manfully turned the project over to makeup technician Christopher Tucker. As time pressures bore down on the crew, Lynch applied his talent for friendship to speed along the team effort. In the pre-production weeks, the director had developed an affinity for Mr. Nunn, an old gentleman who presided over the collection of John Merrick artifacts at the London Hospital. Now, in the midst of the makeup crisis, Lynch went to Nunn and was thrilled when the curator let him take the plaster cast of Merrick's misshapen head and shoulders back to Christopher Tucker. The artist was able to study the three-dimensional actuality of Merrick's features and design what Lynch calls "a beautiful thing."[41] Lynch had helped save the day; he'd responded to a dicey situation like a mature, true professional. But his humiliation burned deep: Seventeen years later he still felt that he "failed very miserably"[42] on the makeup project and called it "the worst time of my life."[43]

Now that all the inanimate details of Lynch's first big-studio production were worked out, the kid from Montana who'd previously crafted home movies with his family and friends had to start giving orders to a renowned pantheon of actors. Lynch had great visual and intuitive gifts, but he was also rather nonverbal. "When I was just coming out of painting, I really couldn't talk. I had a very bad time communicating with people, but actors are really great because everybody's sort of the same. You can communicate using only four or five words because pretty soon the words stop mattering. You get into a thing where you know you're getting something across and they're nodding their heads like you're nodding your head, and you do the next thing and you talk about that, and little by little the thing takes shape."[44]

Still, the prospect of trying to establish this free-flowing meeting of minds with John Gielgud was daunting. "If I'd started thinking about it the night before, I don't think I could have slept. In the morning I said, 'Here I am putting on my underwear and I'm going off to direct maybe the top guy in the world.' And I was thinking what a joke it was, that he was going to listen to me."[45] But Lynch mustered his courage and natural politeness, and found that the few words he was saying to Gielgud were the right ones: "He was super, very agreeable. If I ever needed to adjust what he was doing in a scene, I'd give a small indication, and he'd quickly say, 'I've got it,' and away we'd go."[46]

Lynch's minimalist method may have worked well for fine-tuning gestures and line readings, but it left Gielgud unsatisfied as to the director's opinion of his total performance. A shocked Lynch learned a lesson in human nature when he received a letter from Gielgud after the shooting was completed. "He said, 'David, you never told me what you thought about my performance. I hope you think that it was satisfactory for you and I hope that you feel that I did a good enough job.' So I quickly wrote him back and told him how great I thought he was. But it just goes to show you, no matter how big you get, you want that feedback. You're only big in other people's eyes."[47]

It was certainly important that Gielgud's portrayal of Mr. Carr Gomm, Dr. Treves' acerbic superior who comes to champion the Elephant Man's cause, deliver what Lynch needed. But it was absolutely vital that John Hurt's Merrick and Anthony Hopkins' Treves be right on the mark.

The archetypal mask of ancient Greek drama facilitates the magic of transformation, helping the actor manifest a persona that is not inherently his or her own. For each day of shooting, John Hurt sat for seven hours while Christopher Tucker encased him in John Merrick's burden of monstrous flesh. During these sessions, Hurt's actor's imagination contemplated Merrick's essence. He concluded that Merrick was a saint-like being with malice toward no one, so he developed a sweet, high, refined voice that was a stunning contrast to Merrick's monstrous physical image. Hurt knew he had to get the audience to love the Elephant Man.

Hurt's conception was right in sync with Lynch's master plan. "The point is that you could have someone who was so horrible on the outside, yet his spirit was so, so beautiful. And the more you get to know him, the more the outside disappears, the more the spirit shines through. No matter what he looked like, people fell in love with him. That's the story."[48] Just as Merrick's sweet soul dwelt within his misshapen flesh, so did John Hurt's creative spark vivify the twisted prosthetics he wore. Lynch was deeply moved by the tender voice that Hurt created for Merrick, and awestruck by the way the actor gave up his own personality and became someone else. This transformative act stimulated Lynch's fascination for human identity in flux, and he found Hurt's process monumental, metaphysical, and frightening. Also affected by Hurt's Merrick was Mr. Nunn, keeper of the Elephant Man's remains. When the old gentleman first glimpsed Hurt fully costumed, made up, and in character, he burst into tears.

For Lynch, Gielgud and Hurt were soothing balms of creative harmony, while Anthony Hopkins was a prickly contrarian. Hopkins, the only one of the actors who had read Treves' Elephant Man memoirs, came to the set with some definite ideas about the way his character should look and behave. Though in real life Treves wore only a mustache, Hopkins reported for work sporting an immaculately trimmed beard, which was the style preferred by many distinguished Victorian gentlemen. Lynch was not impressed with Hopkins' initiative. When he first set eyes on his leading man's face, his response was unequivocal: "I want the beard off."[49] The director was afraid that the expressiveness of Hopkins' face would be obscured, but the actor refused to shave. Lynch asked again and Hopkins stood his ground. The beard stayed on.

Hopkins was used to working with seasoned directors like Laurence Olivier, Tony Richardson, Bryan Forbes, Richard Lester, Robert Wise, and

Richard Attenborough, and he was put off by this upstart Lynch's penchant for wearing a big brown trilby hat, a long black cloak, and white tennis shoes. For Lynch, the three-cornered hat and the cloak that resembled the one John Merrick wore were instruments of sympathetic magic, a means of evoking the spirit of London's past and the Elephant Man who hobbled through it. Lynch is not an athletic man, but he habitually chose rubber-soled sports shoes, with their powers of fleetness and agility, for his filmmaking footwear. Hopkins complained to producer Jonathan Sanger: "Why doesn't he get that fucking hat off and stop playing at being a director and damn well *direct*!"[50]

For Hopkins, Lynch's eccentric attire was a minor irritation compared to the director's introspective presence and miserly communication style, which the actor took as a personal affront, a willful act of arrogance. Hopkins was accustomed to getting more guidance from his director and he angrily concluded, "This guy's not going to help me in any way."[51] And what Lynch *did* say, Hopkins didn't agree with. "He suggested that because I *care* about the Elephant Man I must give soft-eyed warm acting all the time. But life's not like that. I think there are moments when Treves actually hates Merrick. Treves is a victim, too."[52]

But Hopkins' and Lynch's dialogues of opposition stimulated the actor's creative growth. "It's a fascinating piece, one of the best experiences I've ever had and one in which I'm learning a lot about myself. I've found out how to be as simple as possible. Just actually speak the lines. Play the situation as simply and honestly as one can and get the balance right."[53] Having determined to make the filming process "a very private trip"[54] for himself, Hopkins had attained a sense of equanimity, but was "the balance right"[55] for Lynch? Could the two men follow their diverging approaches to *The Elephant Man* and still manage to synthesize some truth and beauty out of the damp fall air?

The just-beginning production was already behind schedule and over budget because everyone had to wait for Christopher Tucker to design the elaborate makeup that Lynch wasn't able to create. A vital element, John Hurt in character as John Merrick, wasn't available for filming. The stakes were already high, but Lynch and Hopkins chose to up the ante. They decided to film a crucial scene, the moment when Treves first sets eyes on Merrick, without Merrick.

On the dimly lit set that represented the squalid hovel where Bytes, the Elephant Man's sideshow keeper, houses his "treasure," Lynch set up a precise, delicate camera move. As Hopkins' face registers the terrible spectacle, Lynch would, with the utmost subtlety, float his camera forward until the actor's visage, pale against the background gloom, filled the screen. A stand-in would substitute for Merrick. The camera rolled on take one, and

Hopkins, keeping to his less-is-more philosophy, didn't grimace or gasp. Holding his mouth slightly open, the actor let the audience's sense of awe and horror and sadness play across Treves' witnessing gaze. And right at the moment when Lynch's camera glide stopped to contemplate Hopkins' larger-than-life face, a single, unscripted, tear fell from his eye. Lynch, looking back from 1995 with a sense of pride in his own, and Hopkins', and their technical team's mutual accomplishment, emphasizes, "We did it in one take; it was perfect."[56] Lynch and Hopkins had learned that they could transmute their creative tensions into beautiful, emotionally resonant film footage, and the actor soon came to characterize his sparring partner as "one of the most pleasant directors I've worked with."[57]

Lynch is both a savvy adult and a wonderstruck kid; he's the kind of protean artist who can strategize a career move and pursue a creative mission while spelunking deep within the caverns of his subconscious. He saw *The Elephant Man* as the perfect vehicle to "take me from surreal obscurity into the mainstream, and at the same time not compromise. I was worried about that. I want to make art popular. I want to make good films that I can really get into and love doing, and yet that people will like. I just worry whether that is possible."[58]

Dr. Treves' historical record, and screenwriters De Vore and Bergren, had provided Lynch with "a real solid story"[59] base from which he could launch his personal approach to the Elephant Man and his times, and conjure up some of his beloved "abstractions."[60] For Lynch this seminal term signifies those cinematic passages that intermix dream and reality, the concrete exterior world with the inner cosmos of fluid thoughts and feelings. This flow of imaginative, mysterious interconnection is the sea that Lynch naturally swims in, and it saturates *The Alphabet*, *The Grandmother*, and *Eraserhead*. With *The Elephant Man*, film industry powerhouse Mel Brooks was expecting Lynch to craft a commercially viable film, not a midnight-show art piece. Still, this director who sees the human path through life as a continuum of evolutionary steps feels that "There's a lot of *The Grandmother* in *Eraserhead*, and *Eraserhead* in *The Elephant Man*."[61] Indeed, the film shimmers into being with an opening passage that is akin to *Eraserhead*'s abstract first moments, in which we met Henry's horizontally floating head, the planet-brain, the Man in the Planet, and the sperm-fetus form and subterranean amniotic pool that would give birth to Henry's oncoming bad dream.

Lynch opens his second feature film with a huge pair of feminine eyes looking into our own. Then he pans down a graceful nose to a tender mouth, and pulls back to show the woman's face to be a photo in an oval Victorian frame. As the face loses the protective boundary of this frame, Lynch moves in on the woman's intelligent, sensitive eyes, and the music, like a child's tinkling music box with a melancholy three-quarter-time tinge, becomes a low, ominous vibration counterpointed by the pounding strokes of a heavy steam-piston-driven machine. Elephants, ponderous and slow-moving, trudging left-to-right across the film frame, are superimposed over the woman's face; her eyes look upward in awe and fear. The elephants advance toward the camera; the eye of one glints in the dim light as it draws way too near for comfort.

To the distorted sound of muffled trumpeting, the elephant raises its trunk high and snakes it forward, knocking the woman to the ground. Her white dress and pale face standing out from the dark ground, the woman thrashes her head from side to side in slow motion, her mouth open in a silent scream, as the trumpeting-roaring sound enwraps her plight. Lynch alternates close-ups of the screaming woman with medium shots of the agitated beast shaking its knobby head and flapping its ears. The woman and the molesting elephant fade to an empty black frame, into which, from the bottom upward, spreads a billowing white cloud of smoke. As the white half-circle of smoke fills the frame, we hear a cosmic wind and the cry of a baby.

At the time of John Merrick's birth, some Victorians believed in a concept of magical thinking called "maternal impressions,"[62] which posited that external factors in a pregnant woman's environment could influence the physique, and even the psyche, of her unborn baby. A strawberry placed on a belly swelling with child could yield a newborn's pleasing strawberry birthmark on delivery day. The fact of Mrs. Merrick's having been scared by a circus elephant, linked with the fact of her child's monstrous countenance and assumed-to-be subhuman consciousness, created the Elephant Man myth that John Merrick had to carry through life, the pseudo-scientific/mystical story that "explained" his grotesqueness to sideshow gawkers. In a hyper-condensed, shorthand form, Lynch's opening melds Mrs. Merrick's elephant fright with a vaporous image-and-sound evocation of Merrick's birth, but it also flirts with one of society's darkest taboos.

In earlier decades less scientifically educated than our own, freak show attractions like Jo-Jo the Dog-Faced Boy, the Alligator Man, and Percilla the Monkey Girl were suspected to be the spawn of unholy sexual couplings between male animals and human women. Most 1980 viewers watching Lynch's film would not know the historical fact of Mrs. Merrick's elephant trauma, a narrative detail that the director doesn't introduce until ten minutes after his opening woman-elephant-birth abstraction. Seeing this prologue for the first time, we perceive a kind of rape. As the woman falls back onto the ground, her waist-banded dress gives no indication that she's already pregnant, as Mrs. Merrick was. The swarthy beast advances toward her supine form, and their mutual head thrashings—hers in terror, the elephant's thrusting and aggressive—form a sensual, almost erotic synchrony. A moment later, a baby cries in an expanding cloud of white smoke.

Lynch crafts some of the cinema's most beautiful and thematically deft scene transitions. The airy white cloud is followed by another primary element, a burst of flame. Then we see spinning white circle forms with black spiral patterns on them sparking and smoking on a black background. The field of darkness isn't outer space and the gyres aren't galaxies. From his beginning abstraction of generation and birth, Lynch has bridged us from the ineffable, floating cosmos to the manmade, gravity-bound attractions of a carnival, with its show-business flame bursts and black wall of twirling, eye-teasing whirligigs.

With the back of his head toward us, in the same posture that *The Grandmother*'s Boy contemplated a grass field with searching wonder (as Jeffrey Beaumont will in *Blue Velvet*), Dr. Frederick Treves stands gazing at the swirling pattern field before him. Again and again, Lynch returns to the archetype of the watchful seeker standing like a painter before an empty canvas, looking for signs of the unknown, and himself, in the visual landscape.

Treves is prowling the sideshow hoping to catch a glimpse of this Elephant Man he's heard of and, three minutes after Lynch's elephant-assault prologue, the director subtly reinforces his rape theme when the doctor views an Elephant Man poster. Milling people obscure part of the sign, so we only see the painted representations of the woman (in her prologue-like oval frame) on the left and, on the right, a wild elephant head with a forty-five-degree phallic trunk erection. Then, as the crowd shifts, we see the full poster image that shows the product of the woman's and the beast's encounter: a monstrous hybrid creature with the aroused-trunk elephant head, two elephant legs, and a human torso with two human legs.

Along with detectives tracking mysteries, Lynch's universe is driven by the shifting balance of physical, emotional, and metaphysical power. And, from *The Grandmother*'s and *Eraserhead*'s unwanted advances of adults upon children to *The Elephant Man*'s hint of rape, the director often portrays the power that one being has over another through the motif of transgressive sexual behavior. Another of Lynch's abiding fears and fascinations is the terror of depersonalization, a theme he also links to the woman in his prologue.

Lynch first shows us the innocent woman, and then the ominous elephants, as separate images. But, just before the passage in which one of the beasts knocks her down and terrorizes her, Lynch freezes a frame in which the woman's frontal wide-eyed face and the brutish, massive shapes of elephant profiles are superimposed together. This short-duration image certainly connotes a grotesque physical merging of human being and beast. More disturbingly, it signifies the raping and rending of her psychic core, for there's a pale space between two of the dark animal forms that are melded with her features, so that her God-given singleness of self appears to be torn in two. Horribly split, her head is occupied by brutal invaders. How can this Elephant Woman help but spawn an Elephant Man?

The torture of Merrick's life, the prison that he's trapped in, is the unenlightened, general-public assumption that he *is*, blasphemously, part animal. Gawkers burn their unrelenting gaze into his flesh as though he was a zoo creature with no human dignity. At one point, he is caged, with fierce monkeys on either side of his bars. (The monkeys thrust their screaming faces at Merrick between the bars, just as, ten years later, teenage boys gripped by an animalistic bloodlust will do in *Twin Peaks*.) In a stunning sequence, the hooded Merrick, penniless and lost and ill in a crowded train station, knocks down a little girl by accident (we recall the elephant knocking down Merrick's mother—now Merrick is in the aggressor-brute position). An angry mob chases Merrick, who gasps for breath as he painfully tries to flee. His protective hood having fallen off, Merrick is cornered where he can run no further, in the men's lavatory. In this enclosed space where men leave their stinking "calling cards" like beasts, Merrick faces his tormentors and declares, "I am not an animal; I am a human being!" Lynch often equates animalistic behavior with evil, and as the Londoners surround Merrick like a pack of wolves, we see another example of civilized people giving free reign to feral impulses. *The Elephant Man* script had Merrick deliver his passionate declaration to those monkeys in Bytes' cage, but Lynch makes the speech more resonant by having it reflect on the debased morality of Merrick's human pursuers. Merrick speaks these simple words, which defy and rebuke a lifelong parade of those who have stared at him, with passionate courage. But earlier in the film, we didn't even know that the Elephant Man had a voice. He found it in the house of science where, just as in the sideshow or a common lane, people couldn't stop looking at him.

Compared to most directors, Lynch takes a supreme degree of care with the nature and placement of sound in his films. But, he was weaned as a painter and is a painter still; he's primarily a visual artist who uses his unique skills to show us the way his mind's eye reads the world. We look at the product of his interior and exterior looking.

Beyond the truism that, in their essence, *seeing* is what movies are, Lynch often focuses on characters who are keeping their eyes peeled. Gazing into his radiator, *Eraserhead*'s Henry finds a gateway to heaven. In the *Gardenback* script, the look a woman gives a man plunges his life into chaos. The *Ronnie Rocket* script's Detective character's credo is "Stay Alert."[63] *Blue Velvet* finds a young man secretly hiding in a strange woman's closet, peering out and witnessing a dark coupling of sex and violence that he will soon be participating in. The survival of two lovers on the run in *Wild at Heart* hinges on just what the man did or did not see on a night of fiery murder. And Special Agent Dale Cooper, his back straight as a fir tree, his eyes like a hunting eagle's registering every rustle of the undergrowth, scans the trees, the forest, and invisible dimensions for *Twin Peaks* clues.

Like Cooper (and Lynch's tree-scientist father), Dr. Treves is a professional watcher and investigator. Carefully and dispassionately, he looks at the troubled bodies of his fellow human beings, reads the signs of their disease, and uses his scientific knowledge to eradicate or ease their suffering. In Lynch's world of darkness and light, Treves, in contrast to the Elephant Man's carnival exploiters and gawkers, is a benign seer. When he first regards the wonder that is John Merrick, his unblinking eye sheds a tear, as though he has glimpsed one of William Blake's "portions of eternity too great for the eye of man."[64] Treves' moist, emotion-smitten eye forges a link with the film's first image: the huge, misty eyes of John Merrick's mother. In ancient symbology, the eye was a primal image of God before he was represented in human form, and Renaissance artists positioned an eye within a triangle to signify the Holy Trinity. In Lynch's film, Mary Merrick's noncorporeal, spiritual presence and the kindly Treves are, respectively, literal and figurative parents to the third part of the Trinity: misshapen young John.

Like a concerned father who knows that his son must perform or be ejected from the hospital, Treves tries not to let his fervor of concern and impatience show as he tries to get Merrick to utter a word: "We've got to show them that you're not a brick wall; I've got to understand how you say things, what you're feeling and thinking." And like a child taking one step at a time, Merrick progresses from a nod of comprehension, to "Hello," to a slurred, yet ringing rendition of the Psalm 23: "I shall dwell in the house of the Lord forever." Chance or fate or providence has delivered Merrick into Treves' care, and the doctor takes on this man's nurturance and growth as a sacred trust. Merrick, with his body of crude earth, has developed a sacerdotal and romantic soul. A worshipper of the Eternal Feminine, Merrick weeps and sobs incoherently when Treves takes him home for tea and he first sees the doctor's lovely wife, Anne (Hannah Gordon).

The scenes in Treves' house resonate with a sense of familial bonding. Merrick is fascinated by the photographs of his host and hostess's children and parents. And Merrick, with reverent delicacy, shows the Treveses his mother's image and says, "I must have been a great disappointment to her" (with her handsomeness and his ugliness in mind)—"perhaps now she could love me as I am; I've tried so hard to be good." Anne Treves, as moved by Merrick's sentiments as he was by beholding her beauty, answers her guest's tears with her own. The world views Merrick as a monster, but he sees himself as a refined gentleman, and in a delicious touch he lovingly consoles Anne ("oh please, please") and, with his good hand, reaches into his custom-tailored suit and offers his hostess his perfectly folded handkerchief.

Lynch poses the Treveses and their guest like a seated family portrait, with John sheltered between Anne and Treves, and a significant window behind him. Lynch, the ladder-climbing spiritual evolutionist, positioned *The Grandmother*'s and *Eraserhead*'s seekers of eternal bliss in the upper stories of their abodes. Merrick's hospital room is in the attic, and when he and Treves first grope toward a verbal understanding, there's a small, square, white-lit window like a little smidgen of heaven between them. In a subliminal way, this aperture subtly mirrors the introductory prologue picture frame in which Merrick's mother's image floats, and in turn is mirrored by the Treveses' window before which Merrick sits. The reverent, ritualistic passing of three families' pictures from hand to hand and the evocation of Merrick's exalted mother generates a sense of John being watched over by an extended, amalgamated family, both in the flesh and unseen. Within this multifamily image we note a small cruciform shape silhouetted against the Treveses' white-curtained window. Lynch, as he did with *Eraserhead* Henry's progression from his bedside radiator, to head loss, to sacrificial blood, to heavenly embrace, is laying down a pathway of signifiers that will lead Merrick home. A path that will, in the film's conclusion, progress from Merrick's dying head, past Mother Merrick's photo and a crucifix-embossed hymnal, to the "house of the Lord" cathedral model Merrick built with his one usable hand and his life, through the white-curtained window and into an eternal merging with white clouds, starry sky, and the loving eyes of his beautiful mother.

Merrick knows that if he tries to sleep horizontally, he will suffocate and die. It is the decision of his individuated consciousness to end the life he's lived in London, England, and flow forth into the eternal stream of universal being. Merrick doesn't choose to leave this world at a time when it is treating him most wretchedly, but rather at a point where he is most loved and celebrated by his fellows. Like *Eraserhead*'s protagonist, the Elephant Man has experienced hell on earth, but unlike the trapped and confused Henry, Merrick has found a heaven on the street where he lives. Henry had to slough off his temporal body to find a nurturing home in the cosmos. But Merrick, thanks to Treves, has what he wants in the here and now. He is surrounded by people who appreciate his splendidly attired body, refined mind, and gentle manner; Treves' friend, Mrs. Kendall (Anne Bancroft), a socially prominent and lovely woman, kisses his face; he's reduced to breathless wonder by the first theatrical performance he's ever seen, receives a standing ovation (led by Mrs. Kendall) from the audience, and is promised many more theater evenings. Merrick chooses to leave on this happiest of nights, and there's the sense that Treves, his protector and guide, has helped him grow up to the rich promise of his next evolutionary step. (A decade later, in *Twin Peaks*, another black-suited authority figure like Treves, Special Agent Dale Cooper, will help guide Leland Palmer, a dying man who has endured grievous suffering, into the Beyond.)

If at times Treves has been like a parent to Merrick, then the child has also been father to the man. Before the doctor ever sees the Elephant Man, he refers to the fabled sideshow attraction as "it." Trained by his profession to dispassionately objectify the human form, Treves' first response upon seeing the pathetic and wondrous creature is nonetheless a deeply human one: a tear. When the Elephant Man is brought to Treves' office for examination, the "it" has become a "he," though the doctor assumes that the sorry fellow's mental capacity is as blank as his flesh is grotesquely eruptive. Treves, like Lynch, is prone to wonder about states of mind, and he declares, "I pray to God that he's an idiot," and is thus oblivious to his squalid life and pariah social status. Lynch stresses Treves' high-minded approach to this medical phenomenon by contrasting the doctor's courteous "I'd like to examine you; would that be all right?" with Treves' colleague's rough knock on the door (which frightens the Elephant Man) and opportunistic, "You must have quite a find in there." For Treves, the sideshow monster has become a person named John Merrick.

When Treves exhibits the specifics of Merrick's condition to a meeting of the London Pathological Society, Lynch nonexploitively shows *us* only Merrick's silhouette projected onto a scrim-like curtain. Unlike the carnival gawkers who viewed the Elephant Man with panicked eyes, cries of dread and hate, and a rush for the exit door, the doctors regard Merrick with unemotional faces and silent, rapt attention. Certainly, these medical men, beneath the surface of their well-mannered composure, view Merrick with the same primal human curiosity about one of their species who is different from themselves to such a fantastic degree. But, following Treves' lead, their raw emotional response is tempered and modulated by a civilized sense of empathy, compassion, and a will to help. They see humanity within Merrick's Otherness, not a soulless animal or a stigmatized figure of god-forsaken evil (Jack the Ripper was at work in the historical John Merrick's neighborhood, and some actually suspected the dark-cloaked Elephant Man of committing crimes more horrific than his ugliness).

Treves' exhibition of Merrick parallels Bytes' (Freddie Jones) sideshow presentations, yet his motivation is altruistic. Beyond his desire to show his peers an unprecedented scientific phenomenon, Treves knows that his hospital does not house incurables, so he must make the healing community aware of the raw reality of Merrick's sorry life in order to secure his welfare.

Later in the film, after Merrick has become a widely appreciated permanent hospital resident, Treves stage-manages another mass viewing of him. Treves and Mrs. Kendall make Merrick's fond wish for a night at the theater come true. After the fairytale-like performance, which has enchanted Merrick, Mrs. Kendall takes the stage and dedicates the evening to John who, with Dr. and Mrs. Treves and Princess Alexandra, looks down from a box seat. By now, all of London knows Merrick's story, and the assembled crowd, resplendent in evening clothes, applauds, rises to its feet, and turns to face the seated honoree. Treves, who has guided Merrick beyond his fears and into ever-richer realms of new experiences, urges him on: "It's all right; stand up, they want to see you."

Lynch, who's so fond of doubling and duality, has given us a double whammy in this ovation scene, which is not part of the historical Dr. Treves' narrative. Not only is this the second time that Treves has publicly displayed Merrick (first as a medical specimen, now as a sentient crowd favorite), but the episode parallels Merrick's other big crowd scene in the train station men's room, where he stood up to his hostile pursuers. Then, he had bravely spoken to their mute fear and anger: "I am not an animal; I am a human being." Now, as London's best and brightest applaud Merrick for the simple truth of just being his own humble and heroic self, he is silent as the crowd speaks: "Bravo."

Like a good father, Treves had fed and clothed and sheltered his child, helped develop his communication skills, given him expensive presents (a mahogany and silver gentleman's dressing kit), and helped him to find his way into the social world. And Treves has grown from seeing the Elephant

Man as an examining-room specimen whom he treats with institutional *politesse* to a deep feeling that John Merrick is a dear friend of surpassing sensitivity and sensibility whom he hugs warmly after they've been parted. Lynch reinforces the image of Treves as a parent figure by having Merrick/ John Hurt project the awestruck sense of wonder of a child first discovering the world. After his big night at the theater, where the play was a musical pantomime fairy story, Merrick speaks to Treves in a fervor of earnestness: "I really did believe that the ogre would never get out of the dungeon." And in one of the film's most luminous moments, Treves gives his friend the dressing kit and—as the doctor, Carr Gomm (Gielgud), and Chief Nurse Mothershead (Wendy Hiller) look on—Merrick is transported into an ecstasy of delight and gratitude. His slurping voice is a stream of bubbling joy: "Oh, oh, oh, thank you, oh thank you, oh my friends [laughs for the first and only time in the film], oh, oh, oh, my friends, oh, thank you." The words that Lynch and his screenwriters have Merrick speak are simpler and less grown-up-sounding than the more formal and erudite speeches the character delivers in Pomerance's stage play version.

With Merrick's touching and delightful display of childlike ecstasy, Lynch introduces what will become a signature motif that reveals a primal facet of his own personality. In *Eraserhead*, Henry had to depart our temporal world to get a taste of heaven, but beginning with Merrick's blissed-out gift receiving, Lynch grants his characters heightened moments of transcendent rapture that are triggered by aspects of everyday physical reality that most people would call mundane and unremarkable. Lynch, with his artist's perceptiveness, sensitivity, and imagination, and his sense that emotionally he is still "between age nine and seventeen most of the time, and sometimes around six,"[65] can still feel that the world is "totally fantastic like when I was little."[66] Later, in *The Elephant Man*, we see a dwarf man and woman, costumed like children playing prince and princess. Between them is a box that looks like a miniature house and a vast grouping of small animal figures. As the prince carefully puts the creatures back in their box, the princess exclaims, "Look at all these beautiful animals! What a lot you have!" In *Wild at Heart*, when Sailor gets out of prison, his love Lula hands him a piece of clothing, and he exults, "Oh wow, baby, my snakeskin jacket!" Over the thirty hours of *Twin Peaks*, Special Agent Dale Cooper recites a veritable litany of celebration: "What are these fantastic trees you have around here?," "That's damn fine coffee, and hot!," "This must be where pies go when they die" (sitting in his favorite roadside cafe). Cooper functions as the alter ego of the diner-loving, coffee-guzzling, and pie-savoring David Lynch. When

Lynch himself, playing Coop's FBI boss Gordon Cole, comes on the scene, he manages to up the ante of elation: "Get me some paper; I want to write an epic poem about that cherry pie!" Even when playing a character, Lynch remains the artist, first having an intense emotional experience and then wanting to use his hands to record it and make it last forever.

But heavenly pie and coffee, and a misshapen Victorian child-man's triumphant night at the theater, are only half the story. For, as Lynch is always reminding us, "We live in a world of opposites."[67] If Treves is Merrick's good father figure, then the Elephant Man's sideshow keeper, Bytes, is the bad. Bytes houses Merrick in darkness and filth, beats him with a stick, and displays him like a zoo animal to paying customers whose most debased emotions are aroused by the sight. Such is the historical record, but Lynch gives a perverse twist to Bytes' relationship to his human commodity. There's a charge of dark eroticism in the way Bytes delicately touches Merrick's hair and, in an unclean whisper, calls Merrick "my treasure," and, confronting Treves in the hospital, entreats, "I want my man back; I want my man." When Treves first views the Elephant Man and pays Bytes a small fee so that he can take him to the hospital for examination, Bytes grabs the doctor's shoulder and pulls him close, as though he's forging a bond of transgressive conspiracy. Bytes thinks he's found a kindred spirit in Treves, someone who appreciates Merrick in a certain special, taboo way, and there's a kinky subtext to his words: "We have a deal, an understanding; we understand each other completely; more than money has changed hands." Homosexuality is one of the dark forces that seek to invade Lynch's heterosexual heroes, and the director will explore this theme more fully in *Blue Velvet* and *Twin Peaks*.

Lynch, with the action of Bytes grabbing hold of Treves and pulling him so close that their eyes and breath meet, initiates a significant gestural motif that he'll repeat throughout his career. In most films when good and evil agents confront each other (and before the shooting starts), they stand a few paces apart and exchange dialogue, or they dispense with talk, throw punches, and rearrange the furniture as they wrestle around the room. In the mid-1990s, Lynch said that "the body's most important function seems to be carrying the mind from one place to another."[68] With his reverence for imagination, dream, and consciousness, Lynch knows that heaven and hell are in the mind, and that the head is the mind's vessel. So when he places two heads in intimate opposition, the moment is charged with deep resonance: *when worlds collide*. The mind of shadow and the mind of light don't physically meet, but there's a real danger that they will meld. For in Lynch's world a contagion is in the air, a pulsing in the electrical wires, a look in another person's eyes that can pierce your defenses and reshape your soul into everything that you hate and fear. With the fluid, shivery ease of thought, darkness can slip inside you. The poetics of Lynch's imagination, like those of the early twentieth-century European surrealists, combines elements that don't normally go together (eraser + head = eraserhead); he melts the concrete boundaries of consensus and status quo reality. In his prologue to *The Elephant Man*, Lynch merges menacing elephant forms with Mary Jane Merrick's innocent, delicate face. And the director sees Merrick's misshapen body as being "like a product of the Industrial Revolution's smoke and fire."[69] For Lynch there is "a connection between the slow-motion curls of smoke of Mount St. Helens erupting and the growths on the Elephant Man's body; tumors are like slow-motion explosions."[70] So, in Lynch's realm, where chugging, polluting machines can figuratively touch and malform a human being, Treves had best beware Bytes' vile grip on his shoulder and the sideshow man's insinuation of their psychic kinship.

Merrick, of course, is the person in the film who most people look at, be it in a benign and empathetic or an exploitive and rejecting way. Treves, being Merrick's figurative father, is also looked at, and the good doctor is deeply disturbed when, in his repugnant clinch with Bytes, he sees himself reflected in the carney man's eyes. Bytes implies that Merrick will be providing some kind of voyeuristic sexual thrill for Treves, and that, in general, the doctor, like the sideshow man, will *use* the Elephant Man to gain some sort of personal profit. Treves averts his eyes from Bytes' gaze and pulls away from his complicitous words ("We understand each other completely").

Their second clinch occurs when Bytes invades the pure-white fortress that confers Treves high, and still rising, social status—London Hospital. When Bytes clutches Treves' lapel and says, "You think you're better than me?," the doctor again averts his eyes and shakes his head, as if to say, "No." Bytes' accusations are like stinging blows that Treves must pull himself back and away from: "You wanted the freak to show your doctor chums so you could make a name for yourself." Treves regains his emotional balance and counters with an accusation: "You do not own this man; you want him back so you can beat him and starve him." This is the voice of Treves the healer and protector, the man we want him to be and that he wants to be. But some hidden part of Treves has been recognized by Bytes' feverish eyes and wounded by his words.

In Lynch's world, self-doubt, guilt, and fear are dangerous emotions—the delicious food that *Twin Peaks*' evil extra-dimensional entity BOB feeds on as an appetizer before gulping down human souls whole. BOB inhabits a human host and makes his animal appetite for sex and murder their own: When a BOB-invaded person looks in the mirror, he's likely to see a face terrifyingly Other than the one he were born with. Another of Lynch's malevolent cinematic forces is *Blue Velvet*'s Frank Booth, a mortal man who nonetheless shares BOB's craving for punishing sex and torturous death. Frank doesn't literally inhabit wholesome young Jeffrey Beaumont, who's becoming fascinated by the bad man's netherworld. But when Frank gets Jeffrey in one of those violent-and-intimate clinches and hisses, "You're just like me," Jeffrey starts to realize that there's an aroused hunger for darkness within him.

Limited by the historical parameters of Treves' Elephant Man memoir, Lynch makes this film's Evil Twin character dynamic less intense than in his later, wholly fictional works. Still, Treves is truly disturbed by Bytes' insinuations of their kinship, especially when Head Nurse Mothershead accuses the doctor of putting Merrick in a position where "he's being stared at all over again." Of course, the lookers she refers to are the London gentlemen and ladies who visit Merrick and give him the genteel social interaction which he thrives on. But Treves also knows that Merrick's presence at the hospital has increased his own professional prestige and his, and the hospital's, bank balance. Late at night, Treves, his eyes as wide and unblinking as when he first saw Merrick, looks inside himself and asks a primal Lynchian question: "Am I a good man, or am I a bad man?" In *The Elephant Man* script, Treves' loving wife answers this question, reassuring him of his benevolent virtuousness. But while filming, Lynch realized that the scene's dramatic force would be increased by having the doctor remain haunted by his brooding query.

In the morning light, Treves' crisis of conscience, which is a fictional or at least not-historically revealed conceit, still clouds his face, so Lynch and his screenwriters devise a scene in which the hospital governors debate whether it's proper that Merrick should remain within their walls. Carr Gomm, who has engineered the event, notes Treves' emotionally shaken demeanor and briskly tells him, "Steady on." One governor adamantly argues against Merrick's further tenure and decries, "This competitive freak-hunting by young doctors" (as in Frederick Treves) "trying to make names for themselves. We have a sacred duty to cure the sick, not care for circus animals." At a prearranged moment, Carr Gomm has Princess Alexandra regally stroll into the room and read a message from Queen Victoria that thanks the hospital for "providing one of England's most unfortunate sons with a safe and tranquil harbor." As the governors prepare to vote on Merrick's fate, Alexandra adds, "I'm sure I can count on you gentlemen to do the Christian thing."

With this invocation of Queen, Empire, and God above all, the only possible vote can be to grant Merrick a permanent hospital home. And in the next scene, where Treves, Carr Gomm, and Mothershead tell Merrick the happy news and receive his delirious gratitude over their words and dressing-kit gift, Treves is affirmed as the good shepherd who has made this all possible. Still, the questions that Lynch asks his characters and the universe are lingering, haunting ones: Was *Eraserhead's* child-killing, heaven-attaining Henry a good or a bad man? Like many of Lynch's people, Treves is a seeker of self-awareness, and the complex, thoughtful shadings of Anthony Hopkins' performance convince us that Treves' self-questioning doesn't stop with Merrick's housewarming party.

If Treves is Merrick's symbolic father, then the hospital's Night Porter (Michael Elphick) is Bytes' brother in tormenting and exploiting the Elephant Man. Early in the film Lynch sets up an opposition between the *empathetic world* of Treves, Merrick, his hospital home, and extended family of sympathizers and the *netherworld* of Bytes, the Night Porter, and those who pay to ogle Merrick the Other, the zoo animal. Lynch deftly stresses this contrast by having both worlds react to the same *London Times* story about the Elephant Man. As though Merrick is a mirror reflecting the highs and lows of human nature, Mrs. Kendall, in her temple of art, the theater, reads of his superior intellect and gentle, refined mind. While in the smoky underworld of a pub, the Night Porter reads about Merrick's deformity and that "persons fly in terror at the sight of him." Mrs. Kendall sees past Merrick's body and wants to encounter his mind: "I should very much like to *meet* this gentleman." Whereas the Night Porter sees only Merrick's body and its commercial prospects as he delivers a pitch to the pub-crawlers: "For the right price you'll see something you'll never see again in your life." The film's script contains a scene in which the Night Porter forces himself sexually on a young woman patient who's immobilized with her limbs in traction, but when filming, Lynch eliminated the episode so that the brute's malevolence can be exclusively focused on poor Merrick.[71]

The contrary ways that Mrs. Kendall and the Night Porter view Merrick, aside from setting up the plot dynamics of the story at hand, state the oppositional dynamic of art and commerce, creativity and business, and the ideal and the material, a seemingly self-contradictory balancing act that young artists like Lynch and his screenwriters could feel in their bones. And the sequence underscores Lynch the daily meditator's tendency to most value what's going on inside one's head. As he said in 1992, "I'm not into exercise, so I worry about keeping my body in good enough shape to carry my mind around."[72]

Much of *The Elephant Man* is about the effect Merrick has on other people, the way he brings out their best or worst selves. But what goes on inside his own gigantic, knobby head? Like *The Alphabet*'s Girl, *The Grandmother*'s Boy, and *Eraserhead*'s Henry, Merrick is trapped in, and abused by, a hellish world. Yet since he, like the Boy and Henry, is a pure-souled seeker of light, his inner being offers him a means of escape. Merrick is the ultimate outsider, a man who would treasure more than anything just to be able to live like other men do, but who must endure the certainty that this will never happen. Yet, like magic, Treves makes it happen. And like a prodigious child growing up in supernaturally accelerated time, Merrick progresses from a seemingly mute pariah to an elegant, opinionated gentleman who socializes with royalty. And with a child's sense of innocence and wonder, he radiates and expresses the joyful gratitude that he brings to each new day and experience. Having been an icon of suffering for most of his life (like many Lynchian characters), Merrick is sensitive to others' capacity to be hurt and scared. When a socially prominent gentleman and his wife have tea with Merrick in his hospital apartment, the woman twitters with nervousness and seems ready to bolt from the room. Without seeming to notice, Merrick the perfect host gently says, "People are afraid of what they don't understand. It *is* hard to understand, even for me, because my mother was so very beautiful." And again, in adoring close-up, Lynch shows us the handsome photograph of Mary Jane Merrick with which he began the film.

In the years that Treves was caring for John Merrick, Dr. Sigmund Freud of Vienna was generating ideas that would radically change the way that human beings thought about themselves, ideas that arose from a mystery. Freud was confronted by patients who exhibited anxiety, obsessional thought, compulsive behavior, and physical maladies, and yet showed no objective causal evidence of disease. Extrapolating from his own self-analysis and work with patients, Freud concluded that past traumas and maladjusted emotions were causing behavioral and physical disorders. And that these thwarted emotions were hidden beneath the sufferer's awareness, in the vast, uncharted sea of the subconscious mind. Using free association exercises, hypnosis, and dreams as points of access, Freud analyzed the patient's conflicted urges of sexuality and aggression, and helped him or her recognize and resolve them in the present tense of daily life.

In the nineteenth century, good Bible-believing Christian folk read tales like Mary Shelley's *Frankenstein*, Bram Stoker's *Dracula*, and Robert Louis Stevenson's *Dr. Jekyll and Mr. Hyde*, which blurred the distinction between human beings and monsters to a disturbing degree. They were told by Charles Darwin that their ancestors were protozoa and proboscis monkeys. And then Freud said that, as infants, they had all passionately wished to obliterate their same-sex parent so they could enjoy an uninterrupted, lustful love life with Mama or Papa. Freud's insistence on sexuality, both infant and adult, as the primary definer of personality was a consciousness-transforming idea. As the French philosopher Michel Foucault (1928–1984) put it, *the* characteristic equation of the nineteenth century was (and today remains), "Tell me your desires, I'll tell you who you are."[73]

John Merrick's needs and wishes for shelter, social intercourse, and the accoutrements of a gentleman's lifestyle have been met. But what forces drive the hidden, deep-churning factory of his erotic desires? In the historical Treves' account of Merrick's life, he notes that John "cherished an emotional regard for women,"[74] and the doctor surmises that he was amorous, he "would like to have been a lover."[75] Bernard Pomerance's *Elephant Man* play makes Merrick's eroticism overt: John tells Treves that he would like to have a mistress—an impossible request. The refined-gentleman aspect of Merrick's self-image tries to keep his sexual desire in check, but his passion is unruly: "I put these things out of my mind, but they reappear—snap."[76] In the play, Mrs. Kendall intuitively understands John's unquenched need and for a moment exposes her naked body to him: "For a moment, Paradise."[77]

As the *Eraserhead* scene in which Henry and the Beautiful Girl deliquesce into the sex pool of Henry's bed shows, Lynch is not queasy about portraying on-screen eroticism. But the director chooses to keep Mrs. Kendall's clothes on and sublimate Merrick's libidinous urges into the couple's shared love of the theater and the cultured, soulful worship of Romantic feelings. At their first meeting, Mrs. Kendall and Merrick trade speeches from *Romeo and Juliet*. Sweetly kissing him on the cheek, she declares, "Oh, Mr. Merrick, you are not an Elephant Man, you are Romeo." Merrick could not have prayed for a more transformative verbal blessing. Mrs. Kendall gives Merrick her framed photograph, which he places next to his mother's, and we see a juxtaposition of his personal hierarchy of deification: that of an earthly goddess in relation to his heavenly mother. Freud would say that Merrick, being unable to go through the developmental psychosexual stages of a normal boy and young man, was fixated on an idealized image of his mother, imbuing her with a magnetic attractiveness and authoritative emotional power ("Do you think she could love me as I am now? I've tried so hard to be good").

Upon viewing *Blue Velvet*, the president of the Seattle Association of Psychiatrists said, "David Lynch has an intuitive understanding of human psychology that's at the genius level." A valid assessment, but Lynch is the antithesis of a reductionistic headshrinker. A Freudian reading of *The Elephant Man*'s mother-son dynamic, or those who conclude that *The Grandmother*'s, *Eraserhead*'s, and *The Elephant Man*'s protagonists are acting out the promptings of a back-to-the womb death wish, sell short the poetic depth and spiritual richness of Lynch's sensibility. His expansive cosmos cannot be contained within a psychoanalytic grid pattern. The director once visited a psychiatrist about a "disturbing habit I had."[78] He asked the doctor if a full program of analysis might somehow endanger his creativity. The psychiatrist said yes, and Lynch never came back.

Having lived within the fears, desires, and visions of *The Grandmother*'s Boy and *Eraserhead*'s Henry, we know that Lynch likes to make us feel at home, if not at ease, within his characters' heads. But, unlike his previous two films, which could slip into dreamy, visionary realms at any moment, *The Elephant Man* contains only three, short "abstract"[79] passages. Perhaps because on this film Lynch was collaborating with the world of commercial Hollywood filmmaking, these passages follow a more conventional storyline and are schematically positioned at the beginning, middle, and end; they don't spontaneously erupt into the film.

Still, Lynch imbues these short mini-movies with his characteristic sense of mystery. As previously noted, there's a time lag between the opening sequence of the anonymous, fearful woman, terrorizing elephants, clouds, and birth and our understanding that this passage was a mythic point of view. Then, in the film's center, Merrick has a dream. Up to a certain point in the film, Lynch follows a pattern in which good things happen to Merrick in daylight (his learning sessions with Treves, his romantic tête-a-tête with Mrs. Kendall, being told that he now has a permanent home) and bad things at night (the Night Porter displays him to drunken, lascivious low-lifes, Bytes kidnaps him back into sideshow slavery). One evening, sitting at his dark window, Merrick works on his cathedral model, a symbol of the much-desired "normal" life he is building, and of his spiritual ascendancy. Suddenly, the Night Porter raps on the glass, gives Merrick a menacing grin, and passes out of the window frame. Merrick contemplates the blackness outside and, with a shudder, whispers, "Night-time." Like Henry standing in the X family's living room after the light has blown out, and various Lynchian characters declaring "Now it's dark," Merrick's phrase is a resonant prelude to oncoming drama, a point of demarcation from waking consciousness.

As we know by now, Lynch likes to penetrate the surface of reality and delve into hidden secrets and inner workings. In *The Grandmother*, the director's camera dove deep underground to view the conception and birth of the Boy and his parents. In *Eraserhead*, we had a baby's-eye view of being expelled through the birth canal and swam in the cerebral fluid of Henry's psyche. Now, as John Merrick sleeps sitting up so that he won't choke off his breath, Lynch's camera finds the cloth hood that Merrick wears in public. Cut into the fabric is a single rectangular aperture through which Merrick views the world. Lynch dives through this black opening and into the dark flow of Merrick's dream.

Lynch's own head enjoys melding the organic with the inorganic, and the first thing we see inside Merrick's tender gray matter are dripping steel factory pipes accompanied by a steamy pounding sound. The director's camera travels through shadowy underground passageways that recall his fascination with interior birthing channels and the dark corridor Treves first traversed to get to Bytes' hovel, where the Elephant Man was born to him and us, as a living image. The womblike "inner chamber" feeling of these passageways, combined with industrial pumping sounds, reinforces Lynch's metaphorical notion that the deformed Merrick is the twisted spawn of the machine age. Merrick's dream proceeds to a row of men grasping levers and pumping their arms. The levers are attached to a steel shaft up in the steam that hangs above the workers, and the image raises the oppressive question, Are the men running the machine or is the machine working its slave laborers? Merrick no longer slaves to fatten Bytes' wallet, and his days are filled with the activities (albeit housebound) of a popular Victorian gentleman. Yet the fearsome shadow of his unerasable abnormality haunts his dreams. Some street toughs show Merrick his hideous face in a mirror. Lynch gives us Merrick's view of one of the tormentors kicking his boot in Merrick's (our) face. Merrick's facade of normality has been stripped from him, and he's left with the inescapable pain of his Elephant Man selfhood. His sad, sad cries blend with bestial trumpetings as Lynch shows us huge close-ups of Merrick's civilized, horrified eyes intercut with savage elephant orbs of brutal, aggressive impulse.

Merrick's mid-film nightmare of elephant-engulfment reflects the terrorization of his mother in the film's first minutes. Lynch, aside from linking son and mother in a mutual sense of animal-violated personhood, uses the elephant passage of Merrick's dream to change our perception of where the opening prologue came from. For a second or two in Merrick's dream, we see the prologue image of his elephant-savaged mother thrashing her head from side to side. The double use of this single image in an instant of revelation shows us that the opening abstraction of Mary Jane's trauma and Merrick's birth is not an omniscient, introductory overview, but the core story about his mother and his generation that Merrick tells himself in his own mind. Lynch further links the prologue and Merrick's dream by closing each with clouds: white and softly expanding in the opening birthing sequence, dark and violently roiling in Merrick's nightmare.

Lynch will employ dreams of portent and prophesy in *Dune*, *Blue Velvet*, *Twin Peaks*, and *Lost Highway*. Merrick's nightmare begins the lineage when a drunken group of pub-crawlers who've paid the Night Porter for an intimate look at the Elephant Man invade his waking-life hospital sanctuary and show him his screaming face in a mirror. Lynch, running on parallel tracks as usual, presents the scene as a benighted travesty of Merrick's previous, glorious hosting of Mrs. Kendall in his chambers. Lynch plays up the contrast by showing Merrick enjoying a most private romantic reverie with Mrs. Kendall's photograph at the moment the Night Porter and his marauders barge in. Lynch, as he will so often do, makes us feel the horror of a person being inundated and overwhelmed by invading forces. Like *Twin Peaks*'s evil entity BOB, who will take over Leland Palmer's wholesome mind and body and move him in a foul dance of incest and child murder, the Night Porter and his crew animate Merrick in a mocking violation of the civilized refinement he aspires to. Jamming themselves into Merrick's room, they pick him up and wave his arms like a puppet's, tear him from his moorings by spinning him round and round, and force liquor down his throat. And if in daylight he had enjoyed Mrs. Kendall's kiss on his cheek to climax their *Romeo and Juliet* communion, this night Merrick is virtually raped when a screaming woman's lips are mashed against his own and held there.

As chaos swirls in Merrick's room, Lynch once again shows us a seemingly safe and secure house in which "things can go wrong."[80] And much of the wild energy flowing in the room is sexual. Earlier in the film, Lynch flirted with the erotic thrill that some physically normal people get from interacting with living lumps of Otherness: Bytes' cruel, yet tender "ownership" of Merrick is charged with a master-slave eroticism, and the sideshow man thinks he recognizes something similar in Dr. Treves. In Merrick's room, these previously veiled urges are acted out. One man, inflamed with the thrill of invading the Elephant Man's lair, and the fear shown by his two female companions, wantonly kisses them both on the mouth. After forcing one woman to kiss Merrick, he pushes both women and Merrick onto the bed for a "foursome" close-up that suggests an imminent orgy.

Lynch shows his unique gift for inventing disturbing behavioral detail when the man kisses one of the women. As their joined heads tip back and away from the camera, the man throws open his jaws, covering her lower face, including her chin. Like a beast feeding or a demon sucking out her breath, the man fastens onto her. Remembering the bestial actions of the Boy's abusive parents in *The Grandmother* (Father growled and barked, Mother got down on all fours and scratched the floor), we note that Lynch often sees such regressive, devolutionary behavior as a manifestation of evil. In Lynch's world, the biological drives and appetites that drive the body's factory can be dangerous. The urge to merge gave *Eraserhead*'s poor Henry a monstrous baby, and *Twin Peaks'* ghoulish entity BOB, who feeds on human sadness and fear and would swallow the world, has an anguished hunger that is never satisfied. In *Twin Peaks: Fire Walk With Me* Lynch shows us the bottomless depth of BOB's appetite by plunging his camera into the monster's roaring mouth and throat, a shot the director prefigures in *The Elephant Man* when he puts his camera inside the gaping, bellowing maw of an elephant in Merrick's nightmare.

The dynamic dialectic between the drive for free expression and the need for control is central to Lynch's characters, as well as to their creator's own life drama. In *Twin Peaks*, there's a quantitative and qualitative difference between the lawmen's ecstatic love of restaurant pie and coffee, and BOB's eternal hunger to swallow everything that lives. Lynch's rule is: As with the mind, so with the body. It's the nature of the consciousness that moves within the body that makes behavior heavenly or hellish. Sailor and Lula's bouts of rough sex in *Wild at Heart* are couplings of righteous, loving communion. Whereas Jeffrey Beaumont's aggressive sex with Dorothy Vallens in *Blue Velvet*, accompanied by the sound of roaring beasts, arouses the youth's hidden capacity for shadowy thoughts and violent deeds. To taste and acknowledge the darkness makes us fully human, but we must not succumb. If we fall, we may fall forever, with no angels to catch us.

Merrick's invasive visitors thrust a mirror into his face, cruelly showing him that beneath his pretensions to normalcy, he is still the Elephant Man. (This intense mirror episode, not in the script, was added by Lynch.) But the invaders' behavior has shown them to be the only animals in the room. Bestial forces have pierced the secure armor with which Treves and other compassionate guardians have surrounded Merrick, and Bytes, who feels he holds ultimate dominion over his "treasure," slips through the breach and kidnaps him back into slavery. (Lynch omits further dialogue that was in his script so that this scene ends on the words "my treasure" and the creepy image of Bytes asserting his sexually perverse ownership of Merrick by caressing his head with his hand.) In Merrick's now-uninhabited room, Lynch pans his camera along the dismembered pieces of Merrick's cathedral model, the splashes of liquor and crushed flowers that are the sad detritus of Merrick's malevolent "house party." Ten years later in *Twin Peaks: Fire Walk With Me*, Lynch will move his camera along a similar, eloquent series of objects at the end of one of Laura Palmer's debauched nights: a path of empty beer bottles and smoldering cigarette butts that goes on forever.

In real life, Merrick's sideshow keeper didn't kidnap him back into Belgian servitude. This fictional screen event allows Lynch to heighten the drama by first having Merrick revel in his new hospital home, then be snatched from it in a pathetic, weakened condition by his bad father figure, Bytes, and later be welcomed back by his loving father figure, Treves. During Merrick's continental nightmare of beatings and sideshow oglings, Lynch develops his characteristic feeling of kinship for physical and social outsiders. As the child in the sunny Norman Rockwell neighborhood and the adult who makes his living with his vaulting imagination, Lynch has always been pulled by wayward currents that flow away from the mainstream. The director says that he identifies with *Eraserhead*'s "strange-looking"[81] Henry Spencer and with John Merrick. He refers to people "living in the fringe lands, they're the people I really love."[82] Actor Wendy Robie, who wears a black eye patch as *Twin Peaks*' Nadine, says that Lynch is drawn to "broken beauty."[83] The man whose daughter was born clubfooted plays *Twin Peaks*' FBI Chief Gordon Cole as a severely deaf man who needs two hearing aids. In our politically correct society, in which the thought police can brand you as a "lookist" just for casting an appreciative glance at a fellow human being, Lynch has been castigated as an exploiter of the physically challenged and the socially disenfranchised simply because he puts them on the screen. But the director's attitude is respectful and humble; he acknowledges and honors marginalized people in his film images because he's often felt that way himself. Henry Spencer's mutant offspring is no picture-perfect Ivory Snow baby, but it's a fantastic *fictional* creature; Lynch's naturalistic portrayal of those who are deformed and disabled begins with *The Elephant Man*.

The director, thinking in doubles as usual, gives Merrick two surrogate families: Treves and his benevolent hospital circle, on the one hand, and the dwarves, giant, female Siamese twins, and assorted physical curiosities who, with Merrick, comprise Bytes' Belgian sideshow, on the other. When Merrick's health deteriorates to the point where he can no longer stand up to be exhibited, the enraged Bytes locks him in a cage next to a terrifying bunch of screaming monkeys. As noted earlier, Merrick is most frequently abused at night. Lynch, with his belief in transformation and duality, shows for the first time in *The Elephant Man* that the night can have a positive charge, as well.

Merrick, in his caged misery, looks up to see his family of fellow "freaks" with the key to his prison. They release him, escort him to a sailing port, pay for his passage back to England, and send him off with a benediction of kinship: "Who needs good luck more than we?" When Lynch came to Austria to paint many years before, he found that no European muse would speak to him, so he returned early to America. But now, back on foreign soil as Merrick's sideshow family steals him into the night, Lynch is inspired to craft one of his most mysteriously beautiful images. Dressed in costumes from far places and ancient times, a procession of tiny and huge and misshapen people moves horizontally through dark woods left to right across the frame, their progress reflected upside down in a black mirror of water at the bottom of the frame. At once humane and emotionally touching, yet otherworldly, the image crystallizes the "fairy-tale quality"[84] Lynch saw in John Merrick's story. Back in London after Merrick stands up to his train station lavatory tormentors ("I am not an animal; I am a human being"), he shows the police Treves' business card, which, like a magical storybook key, readmits him to his hospital sanctuary and the literal embrace of his Good Father.

How appropriate that Lynch perceived Merrick's Victorian-era saga in a fairy-tale light, for one of history's most socially and morally repressive societies produced an unprecedented counterbalancing flow of fanciful children's literature. In proper Victorian parlors, families were covering immodest table legs with fabric skirts and reading their Bibles, while the likes of Charles Kingsley, Edward Lear, William Makepeace Thackeray, George MacDonald, Charles Dickens, J. M. Barrie, John Ruskin, Christina Rossetti, and Lewis Carroll were talking the pre-Christian language of stars and trees, and shape-shifting the sublime into the demonic with the winking of a wizard's eye. All of Lynch's work is touched by his childlike sense of awe at the universe's visible and invisible forces, but this aura of fresh discovery is especially fitting for John Merrick, with his large head like a child's and his innocence of the broad spectrum of worldly experience.

With his monstrous body and tender, yearning heart, Merrick reminds us of *Beauty and the Beast*'s hero. And when this storybook-like creature attends the theater with Treves and Princess Alexandra, he is himself engulfed in a fairy tale. As Merrick is spellbound by the musical play of *Puss in Boots*, Lynch once again stresses the primacy of the head and what goes on within it. In counterpoint to the ominous way the director superimposed elephant forms and urges on Mary Jane Merrick's head in the prologue, Lynch now melds an onstage fairy woman with a wand and Merrick's raptly attentive head into a single image. Merrick blessedly loses his self-consciousness in the spectacle before his eyes as Lynch crafts a montage of fleeting impressions: stagecraft horses prancing, a cat dancing, swimming swans wearing crowns, an ogre in a dungeon, sudden explosions of white smoke, and a Peaceable Kingdom finale in which a fairy arcs above humankind and nature, and unites all with a sprinkling of sparkling dust. Then, for a fairy tale ending to his evening, Merrick's attention shifts back inside his own skin as Mrs. Kendall and the assembled gentlefolk applaud him for the simple, extraordinary fact of his being. He's the hero of the night, yet this night he will choose to leave his friends and appreciators forever.

The historical Dr. Treves' record simply says that Merrick "was found dead in bed,"[85] having choked while trying to lie flat and sleep "like other people."[86] Bernard Pomerance's play has Merrick sleep in his usual, safe sitting position, but then he's visited by some fellow freaks in a dream. Two pinheads straighten him into a flat position, and as he dies, they sing "Sleep like others you learn to admire / Be like your mother, be like your sire."[87] Merrick's wish to sleep like others is certainly part of Lynch's *Elephant Man* conclusion. But Lynch, who sees Merrick's story as a fairy tale, wants an ending with more psychological and spiritual depth, more magic.

In poet-fantasist William Blake's *The Marriage of Heaven and Hell*, the tale's protagonist is trapped in an abyss, menaced by fire, giant spiders, and monsters—then suddenly he finds himself "sitting on a pleasant bank beside a river by moonlight,"[88] hearing a harp player sing a beautiful song. According to scholar and fantasy master J. R. R. Tolkien (*The Hobbit*, *Lord of the Rings*), the "highest function"[89] of the fairy tale is to provide "the Consolation of the Happy Ending."[90] The opposite of a sudden narrative descent into catastrophic tragedy, the "eucatastrophe"[91] is an equally abrupt turn into happiness. "It does not deny the existence of catastrophe, of sorrow and failure: the possibility of these is necessary to the joy of deliverance; the *eucatastrophe* denies (in the face of much evidence) universal final defeat and insofar is *evangelium*, giving a fleeting glimpse of Joy, Joy beyond the walls of the world, poignant as grief."[92]

Tolkien's words, along with Robert Henri's declaration about "an undercurrent, the true life, that pulses beneath all appearances everywhere,"[93] are like pages from David Lynch's brain. Both men's statements encapsulate Lynch's intuitions about the way the world works and the universe's sense of moral balance: They are keys to his art.

Returning to John Merrick on his triumphant theater night: Where do we find, in Tolkien's sense, the "sorrow and failure"[94] from which he needs to be delivered? For surely Merrick, nestled in the nurturing security that Treves has provided, is living in a heaven on earth. Still, despite Merrick's self-proclaimed happiness and his loving surrogate family, he is not yet truly home, for home is where Mother is.

Merrick has said that he will "dwell in the house of the Lord forever," and his cathedral-building and linkage to a cruciform in Treves' house certainly positions him within a Christian context, as does the historical Treves' memoir comparison of Merrick's suffering to Christ's. But it is Merrick's Mother Goddess who visits his dreams and in them suffers to bring him into the world. She is the Higher Purpose to which Merrick devotedly consecrates his actions ("I've tried so hard to be good; If she could see me now, perhaps she could love me as I am"), her beauty the touchstone that he works into so many conversations. Like *Eraserhead*'s Henry with his chaste, delivering radiator angel whom he doesn't know how to reach, Merrick is separated from his eternal love by a dimensional gulf. But, again like Henry and *The Grandmother*'s Boy, Merrick is an artist who uses his spirit and creative consciousness to craft his own salvation. Mary Jane Merrick is the muse who inspires her son's cathedral model-building. Merrick can actually see only the spire of the real building outside his window, and he tells Mrs. Kendall, "I have to rely on my imagination for what I can't really see." As Lynch will show us throughout his career, our dreams can get us where we want to go—and the dreams Lynch builds are palpable realities.

Unlike the Grandmother, whose last, long exhalation of breath propelled her around the room, Merrick exhales into serenity, sleeping "normally," prone like the picture of a child at rest hanging on the wall above his bed. And just as the dynamic of Merrick's bond with his mother cannot be contained within Freudian parameters, Lynch's Hindu-inspired metaphors expand beyond the bounds of Christianity. Lynch pans his camera from Merrick's resting head, past his mother's picture and a crucifix-embossed Bible to the cross-crowned steeple of Merrick's model cathedral. Lynch pauses on the cathedral's phallic spire and the swaying white window curtains next to it, which part slightly to form a vulval opening to the night sky beyond. This momentary image certainly supports a Freudian reading of Merrick as a man-child stuck in the Oedipal stage, who's built an erection-cathedral to his mother-in-the-sky. But the film as a whole shows Merrick's deepest instinctual drive to embody Jung's sweeping "passion for the spiritual."[95] The earthly phallic cathedral and vulval skygate curtain can also be seen in terms of Indian Tantra, a philosophical system more ancient than hundreds of generations of Freud's ancestors. In Tantra, the human body and the cosmos vibrate with spiritual-erotic energy, and the mating of male and female, earth and sky, produces the blissful hum of universal being.

Lynch's final "abstract"[96] passage, which is akin to the film's prologue and Merrick's nightmare, shows Merrick's consciousness departing the temporal world and being reborn in the spirit. Since we know that these sequences are not omniscient overviews, but Merrick's inner visions, his finale harmonizes with the words of Sri Krishna in the Hindu gospel, the *Bhagavad Gita*: "Whatever a man remembers at the last, when he is leaving the body, will be realized by him in the hereafter; because that will be what his mind has most constantly dwelt on, during his life."[97] And Merrick's last journey echoes William Blake's understanding that "This world of Imagination is the World of Eternity; it is the divine bosom into which we shall go after the death of the Vegetated body."[98]

A lifelong believer in the mind's power to make its own world, Lynch follows Merrick's final vision through the window curtains and into the black, starry sky. The stars rush past as Merrick's consciousness thrusts ever deeper into the cosmos, and he hears the consoling maternal voice that he cherishes more than any other: "Never, oh never; nothing will die. The stream flows, the wind blows, the cloud fleets, the heart beats." Mary Jane Merrick's pale face emerges toward us from the dark sky and looks into our eyes as she floats among the stars, surrounded by a glowing white circle of light, a symbol of universal wholeness. The image of Mrs. Merrick is the one from her photograph and the prologue, but now, for the first time, her eyes move: She is alive. To illustrate the eternal, alternating-current cycle of birth-life-death-rebirth, she vanishes, and we see the billowing white clouds of Merrick's prologue birth folding back inward as they reverse the life-force flow. But then, duplicating the narrative rhythm in which Merrick gained a home with Treves, lost it when Bytes kidnapped him, and then regained it, Mary Jane Merrick's face reappears in the stars. She soothes and reassures her son: "Nothing dies," as Lynch moves his camera in on the face that began his film, and fades out on her luminous white brow and all-regarding eyes. (Lynch typically identifies the cosmos and the Beyond with women and a feminine force, but the specific image of Merrick's loving, protective, consoling mother floating in the stars may have been inspired by Charles Laughton's *The Night of the Hunter* [1955]. In this masterpiece, the only film that actor Laughton ever directed, the cinema's archetypal muse-matriarch, Lilian Gish, symbolically speaks comforting words to her brood from a starfield.)

Like the Hindu Mother Goddess Kali, who dances the endless round of creation and destruction, Mary Jane Merrick presides over the cycle of life born and extinguished and reborn. And her words, which interweave streams, winds, clouds, and beating hearts, convey the Hindu sense of

World Soul present in all manifest phenomena. There is a remarkable correspondence between Merrick's mother's poem and the coda of Jean Renoir's 1951 film *The River*, which tells a timeless tale of Indian life and death along the sacred Ganges River: "The river runs, / The round world spins; / Dawn and lamplight, / Midnight noon. / Sun follows day, / Night, stars and moon. / The day ends, / The end begins."

Lynch graces many of his films with the possibility of endings becoming new beginnings. Even his 1989 song lyrics for *The World Spins*, in which a sad woman grieves for a lost love, project the consoling spirit of ever-flowing and renewing cycles: "The sun comes up and down each day, / The river flows out to the sea; / For ever and ever, / The world spins."[99] And Lynch's song itself may be part of a continuum in which one artist inspires another: *The River*, *The Elephant Man*, *The World Spins*.

Lynch, though he was working with collaborators and a factual story, nonetheless made the world of *The Elephant Man* spin his way. His familiar interest in the processes of birth and alienated life was again central to a film's vision. With the authority of a seasoned spiritual traveler, he was able to "unite the here and the hereafter"[100] (Walt Whitman) for another of his life-abused protagonists. For in being creative like artists, in using their minds and imaginations and sense of cosmic connectedness, Lynch's tormented characters have flown from their entrapments and demons. And, as in his previous two films, Lynch's ultimate agent of solace and deliverance has been a woman.

In *The Elephant Man*, Lynch's sense of mystery, a prime mover of his art, is limited to a few minutes of dreamy, abstract imagery and the director's tastefully slow, suspenseful approach to finally letting us cast our gaze on Merrick's flesh. And in the minds of Merrick's contemporaries, who don't understand the biology of his condition, there's the mystery of how such a creature could come to be, a question that haunts Merrick's own unscientific, childlike fancies, and that echoes an earlier unverbalized Lynchian question: How is it possible to grow a Grandmother from a seed?

In Lynch's 1994 book, *Images*, in which he chooses representative selections from his various modes of self-expression, he displays an evocative shot from *The Elephant Man*. As Treves penetrates deeper into the sideshow, before he sees Merrick, he passes a still-life tableau that includes a painting of Eve reaching for the apple, a jar in which floats a stillborn baby and an apple with a bite taken from it, and a sign that says "The fruit of the Original Sin." What can a detective make of these clues? Lynch's characters often feel that they have been expelled from, or excluded from,

Paradise; that they are toiling in a fallen state, in a world where deformities of mind and body are commonplace. Though they may munch pie and donuts instead of a single apple, they gain a deep knowledge of good and evil—and in the end, though their sins may be grave, they receive the grace of redemption, the actuality or hope of Paradise regained. This "Original Sin" image symbolically sets up the triangle of Treves, Mary Jane Merrick, and John Merrick, with Treves as surrogate father. And it establishes this Victorian tale's Christian context and the sense that Mrs. Merrick and her son have, in the eyes of God-fearing people, somehow done something to deserve his pariah status. Such conclusions are drawn from contemplating the still image for minutes on end; the moving shot is only onscreen but a few seconds. *The Elephant Man*, being Lynch's most collaborative and history-based project to date, has fleeting glimmers of mystery, while the moment-to-moment experience of his more personally generated films is mysterious from start to finish.

Critics reflexively say that there's no humor to be found in *The Elephant Man*. True, there's nothing resembling the comedy of Jerry Lewis or Mel Brooks, Noel Coward or Neil Simon. But the humor of David Lynch is clearly apparent. In Lynch's world, outrageous happenings erupt through the surface of our familiar, safe-and-sane sense of reality. And one of the ways we cope with, or defend ourselves against, the disturbing truths he slaps in our faces is by laughing, if not moaning or sobbing or screaming. While watching *The Grandmother* some of the audience always laughs when the Boy's cherished nurturing protector begins to die by flitting around the room while whistling like a teakettle. And if death can be funny, so can sex. While the cameras were rolling on a *Blue Velvet* scene in which Dennis Hopper calls Isabella Rossellini "Mommy," says "Baby wants to fuck," and enacts a bizarre perversion upon her body, the director, way over in the corner of the room, could only cope with the scandalous tableau he had created by laughing (which he stifled for the sake of his actors). In 1991, Lynch said that he's "really interested in embarrassing moments on film,"[101] and spoke of the point at which "the temperature of the audience's body rises and sweat comes out of their foreheads and they make small giggling sounds."[102] Just as Lynch's films reflect his own fears and loves, so they project his capacity for social discomfort and embarrassment, such as the time he froze up during an on-camera interview and was "unable to speak."[103]

As with the element of mystery, the humor in *The Elephant Man* is held in check by the commercial and reality-based dictates of the project, and its properly dominant mood of pathos and wonder. The film displays nothing comparable to the excruciating, protracted trial of social awkwardness that *Eraserhead*'s Henry endures at the X family's hellish house. But there's an echo of Henry's plight in the discomfort that some of Merrick's smart-set hospital visitors try in vain to mask with their proper Victorian manners: Tumors with tea? Well, really! And we chuckle in appreciation of Carr Gomm's wiles as he has Princess Alexandra deflate the opposition and promenade in to sway the vote at a dicey moment in the board meeting deciding Merrick's hospital-residency fate.

In Lynch's world, dogs are often agents of humor. We recall his description of a Philadelphia neighbor's dog as "a water balloon with a little bitty head and small legs that stick out; like a Mexican Chihuahua with a watermelon in the middle."[104] Isabella Rossellini has spoken of Lynch smiling "at the way dogs sit and look at you when you're eating."[105] The director began his cinematic parade of dogs in *Eraserhead* with the Great Dane and her noisily nursing pups that were an absurdly prominent feature of the X family's living room, and an amusing preview of parenthood to come for Henry. The dog in *The Elephant Man* doesn't have the narrative heft of his *Eraserhead* counterpart, but he's a heavyweight in his own right. In the sequence where Treves traverses atmospheric London streets on his way to see the Elephant Man for the first time, Lynch opens a shot on a pot-bellied runt of a dog like the one he knew in Philadelphia. The camera's motion is pulled around a corner and down a street by the waddling pooch with its stiff spike of a tail, and then the moving point of view stops to watch Treves coming toward us from the opposite direction. Doctor and dog pass each other separated by the wide avenue, but Treves, who's trained to spot physical anomalies, can't help but glance over at the stubby canine in what is Lynch's most subtly droll moment of doggy humor.

It is said that social class is the underlying subtext of all English drama. Lynch most certainly sets up a dynamic dichotomy between a day world of upper class, educated, compassionate people who help to elevate John Merrick, and a night world of working-class, pub-crawling, malevolent denizens who debase the Elephant Man. But the director is interested in the full spectrum of human complexity. So he gives some of Treves's colleagues mean-spirited, venal motivations, and haunts Treves with the thought that he's exploitive kin to Bytes. Also, the director portrays the transformation of the boy sideshow assistant, who is learning to mimic Bytes's nefarious ways, yet later helps Merrick's freakshow kin uncage him and speed his escape from Bytes, consequences be damned.

The consequences of Lynch's first foray into the realm of commercial filmmaking came swiftly; he didn't have to wait and wonder what viewers thought as he did when people first saw *Eraserhead*. Critics and audiences around the world were moved to tears by Merrick's story, and mesmerized by *The Elephant Man*'s dark beauty. All aspects of the production received high praise, and the film was nominated for eight Academy Awards: best film, director, screenplay, actor (John Hurt), editing, art direction, music, and costume design. While the film was breaking attendance records from Japan to New York City, Ben Barenholtz, who had launched *Eraserhead* with a series of Big Apple midnight screenings, decided to try an experiment. He played Lynch's first feature film for a normal week's run right next door to where the director's second feature was showing. Voting with their wallets, moviegoers kept flocking to Lynch's mainstream *Elephant Man*, while few chose to descend into his deeply personal *Eraserhead* netherworld.

As the Academy Awards ceremony at the end of March 1981 approached, Lynch marveled at his improving fortunes. The painter and underground filmmaker—who for years had to scrounge money to put food on his family's table and complete *Eraserhead*—was going to be honored by the cream of the world's film industry, who considered Lynch, along with Robert Redford (*Ordinary People*), Roman Polanski (*Tess*), and Martin Scorsese (*Raging Bull*) to be the best directors of the year. Vast audiences understood and were moved by what he was communicating with film, and they would no doubt continue to be—tomorrow and the next day and the next. Lynch's progression from small-town outsider to Hollywood insider was chugging forward with the steady thrust of a factory assembly line.

On March 30, in Washington, D.C., John W. Hinckley Jr., a young movie fan hoping to impress actress Jodie Foster, stepped forward and shot newly elected President Ronald Reagan in the chest, and for the first time ever, the Academy Awards ceremony was not held on its appointed day. The shooting of the former actor stunned the nation and the film community, and especially disturbed the usually apolitical Lynch. Reagan is the only politician that the director had spoken of voting for, saying that he responded to the former Warner Brothers contract player's "wind of old Hollywood that he carried, of a cowboy and a brush-clearer."[106] Lynch, who delves beneath shallow surface realities in his art, seems to have primarily warmed to the comforting and nation-unifying Reagan image, rather than the less-than-admirable policies that were implemented on the Gipper's watch. Most hip and sophisticated Lynch appreciators assume that he must be mocking and ironically subverting the wholesome small-town values and naive gushes of emotion that he portrays in his celluloid America: Dave's too cool to really belief that square stuff! But Lynch *is* a believer, and it's easy to see him standing up to salute Reagan's Morning in America vision of wheat farmers and office workers, moms and dads, brothers and sisters, and all races, colors, and creeds uniting to pursue happiness, reap prosperity, worship God, and guard the sovereignty of the most powerful nation on earth. Reagan was on guard against the machinations of evil empires, and Jennifer Lynch has said that her father "has strong feelings about the enemies of our country."[107] As an Eagle Scout in 1960, Lynch had participated in John F. Kennedy's inauguration in the nation's capital, only to see him gunned down three years later. Now, from out of nowhere, an icy finger of mortality had pierced the California-tanned skin of Lynch's president. Those dark forces that Lynch had sensed, but not seen, in his Northwest boyhood were indeed starting to creep into the world.

The Academy Awards were held twenty-four hours later than planned, on March 31, 1981. Lynch, looking like a character from one of his films, in his black suit and tieless buttoned white shirt, made his way along the red carpet leading into the Dorothy Chandler Pavilion, his face unrecognized by the crowds cheering for Goldie Hawn, Jack Lemmon, Robert Duvall, Jason Robards, Peter O'Toole, and Mary Tyler Moore.

The evening's host, Johnny Carson, began the proceedings by running a taped introduction that President Reagan had recorded a week before his shooting. From his Oval Office desk, Reagan told the film community that they lived in a country where one of their own, a former president of the Screen Actors Guild, could ascend to the chair of America's highest power. Carson and the applauding audience sent a sober get-well message to the president, but the witty king of late-night TV couldn't resist throwing in a good-natured barb about the chief executive's demand for cuts in humanities funding: "It's Reagan's strongest attack on the arts since he signed with Warner Brothers."[108]

As the ceremonies wore on, a pained Lynch noted an emerging pattern of *The Elephant Man* losing every category for which it was nominated. In John Hurt's Best Actor contest, Robert De Niro won for Martin Scorsese's *Raging Bull*. Scorsese's *Taxi Driver* (1976), starring Jodie Foster as a teenage prostitute and De Niro as the gun-crazed psychotic who massacres her corrupters, was the film that had inspired John Hinckley's Reagan assassination attempt. This dark linkage between art and life began America's serious debate about the actual or illusory dangers of violence in the movies, and so disturbed Foster and De Niro that they didn't venture before the cameras for many months.

Lynch was thrilled when Sissy Spacek won the Best Actress award for her inspired emoting-and-singing portrayal of country music legend Loretta

Lynn in *Coal Miner's Daughter*. Spacek was married to Jack Fisk, his old painting pal who was now a gifted art director (*Days of Heaven*, 1978), and who was also now his brother-in-law. And Spacek had been quick to help when Lynch needed extra money to complete *Eraserhead*. A few minutes after Spacek received her Oscar, Lynch smiled gamely as Robert Redford bounded to the stage to claim his golden statue for being Best Director of the year. So the *Elephant Man* contingent went home empty-handed this night, but they were soon rewarded when the British Film Academy recognized the film as the Best Picture, with the Best Production Design and Best Actor (John Hurt).

Ronald Reagan had been shot. *The Elephant Man* was shut out of the winner's circle. But David Lynch's world kept on spinning. The soft warm air outside the Dorothy Chandler Pavilion was scented with early springtime. Everyone who loved him four hours ago loved him still. One painting finished always led to a new one begun, the present completed film to the one just starting to percolate in his teeming brain. Tomorrow he could go to Bob's Big Boy in the middle of the hot afternoon, get wired in with a chocolate shake and cups of coffee, think about *The Elephant Man* fading out on Mary Jane Merrick's eyes in space, and keep his ears pricked, for the future was calling. Could another woman be whispering the first words of a new dream tale while she floated in the stars? In good time, Lynch saw that she was.

4

GOLDEN SANDS, HEAVY HEART

1980–1984
(*Dune*)

David Lynch was really on the ladder now. No, he wasn't up putting the finishing touches on a shed roof during another unemployed-filmmaker fallow period like the one he endured after *Eraserhead*. This time he was climbing the Ladder of Fortune like the young man in the nineteenth-century Currier and Ives lithograph ascending the rungs of Industry, Integrity, Courage, and Perseverance to pluck the apples of Riches and Success. Lynch's sister, Martha, was a financial planner, and he finally had some money to give her to build investment strategies. Lynch could afford food and clothing and art supplies, and he and Mary started thinking about having a child.

Lynch's climb up the ladder also brought him the golden apple of Esteem: the good wishes and artistic respect of empire-building visionary filmmaker-entrepreneurs like Francis Ford Coppola (*The Godfather*, 1972; *The Godfather, Part II*, 1974; *Apocalypse Now*, 1979) and George Lucas (*Star Wars*, 1977; *The Empire Strikes Back*, 1980). Lucas had so much confidence in Lynch's abilities that he asked him to direct the third *Star Wars* installment, *Return of the Jedi*. Lynch was flattered, but he made the sound judgment that he didn't want to be a journeyman worker within a minutely detailed imaginative universe of established characters and situations that another artist had dreamed up. Lynch's projects needed narrative space into which his own creative consciousness could expand. Coppola, who was putting together an independent production company, Zoetrope Studios, was interested in Lynch's long-cherished script *Ronnie Rocket*, "an absurd mystery about the strange forces of existence"[1] in which a 3-foot-tall man zapped by electricity becomes a rock star. When Lynch visited Coppola's Napa Valley home to talk about *Ronnie Rocket*, he met a real-life rock and roller, the charismatic Sting, who was lead singer for the group Police and a fledgling film actor (*Brimstone and Treacle*, 1982). Lynch patiently waited while Coppola read *Ronnie* three times, but balked when his potential producer wanted to lie down on a couch, close his eyes, and have Lynch read it to him one more time. The massive financial failure of Coppola's *One From the Heart* (1982) plunged the would-be mogul into bankruptcy, ended his Zoetrope dream, and wiped out his ability to help Lynch launch *Ronnie Rocket*. It was a heady feeling, being up on the Ladder of Fortune, but Lynch saw in Coppola's example that the higher you climbed, the farther you could fall.

Lynch's unproduced script for *Ronnie Rocket*, which he began after completing *Eraserhead* in the mid-1970s, showed that the director was capable of writing a story for way more than his usual handful of characters and deploying these people in a wide range of locales, as opposed to the four or five settings each of *The Grandmother* and *Eraserhead*. These earlier works were small-neighborhood films, but in *Ronnie Rocket* Lynch had no trouble envisioning a tale that would encompass a whole city—and an imaginary city at that, which would require many pre-computer-graphics era special effects and massive set-building in order to live on film. Not only the scale of the production would be mammoth, but the story was, by mainstream standards, bizarre and disturbing: Lynch's big-city tale lacked the broad appeal of a *Manhattan Melodrama* or a *West Side Story*.

The movie would cost a small fortune to make and the chances of big profits were slim, so it's not surprising that producers weren't lining up to back Lynch's *Ronnie Rocket* project. In the early 1990s, thanks to Lynch's three-picture deal with French funder CiBy 2000, it looked like the movie might finally get off the ground, but after the commercial failure of his first CiBy-backed film (*Twin Peaks: Fire Walk With Me*), Lynch's *Ronnie Rocket* enthusiasm evaporated. Since his dedication to pursue a certain artistic path depends on the ebb and flow of his intuitive desire, Lynch today feels the project would have been realized if he'd gotten the necessary money right after he had first completed the script, when he was in the hot grip of his initial inspiration.

Written without collaborators, *Ronnie Rocket* is one of Lynch's most personal and abstract scenarios, and I planned to write about it in terms of what it reveals about its author, and how he has incorporated some of the script's atmospheres, themes, and motifs into projects that he *has* gotten to make. But recently Jennifer Lynch told me, "The other day Dad looked at me with a gleam in his eye and said, 'Jen, do you think this might be the time for *Ronnie Rocket*?,'"[2] so maybe the film isn't dead and buried after all. Knowing Lynch's passion for keeping the details of his work private until he feels it is ready to meet the public eye, I asked him if there was still a chance he would make *Ronnie Rocket*. His reply: "You probably shouldn't write anything about it."[3] But he did give me the okay to say a few things.

In *Eraserhead*, Lynch condensed his visceral feelings about Philadelphia being a threatening, toxic, twisted environment into images of Henry's apartment, Mary X's house, and a few shots of Henry walking through a bleak urban landscape. The director did a masterful job of *suggesting* the massive presence of a menacing cityscape out beyond the edges of the frames he showed us. In *Ronnie Rocket*, he would enable us to directly experience a vast urban milieu along with his characters. And, since we're in Lynch's world, this would be a factory town, the broadest-ever envisioning of the oil-slick, smokestack, steel-steam-soot, fire-sparks and electrical-arcs realm that Lynch loves. This is the place that constitutes the always-the-same background of his *The Angriest Dog in the World* cartoon panels, and which he, to a degree, puts on film in *The Elephant Man* and the Giedi Prime planet of *Dune* (in addition to the planet's general industrial trappings, Baron Harkonen's laboratory-like main chamber is the same shade of green Lynch had in mind for a *Ronnie Rocket* laboratory). Ace cinematographer Frederick Elmes (*Eraserhead, Blue Velvet, Wild at Heart*) heard a lot about *Ronnie Rocket* in the *Eraserhead* era, and it's tempting to see an image Elmes shot for Ang Lee's 1997 *The Ice Storm* as a shot from *Ronnie Rocket*: at night a train car, darkly glistening like it's coated with oil, stalls on its tracks, and the black steel cylinder is illuminated by the flashing arc of a shorted-out power line. In *Ronnie Rocket*'s city, the electricity is on, but that's not a good thing.

Following his penchant for exploring the negative potential of something normally seen as positive (learning the ABCs, living with parents, being a father, going on a joyride with a neighbor, coming to Hollywood with stars in your eyes), Lynch shows us the dark side of electrical power. Ever since, as a child, Lynch sensed that invisible "force of wild pain and decay"[4] in his backyard, he's been sensitive to currents of good and bad energy. Beginning in the early 1970s of *Eraserhead*, Lynch began to practice Transcendental Meditation and to study Hindu spirituality, which reinforced the idea that factors beyond our conscious will (our unconscious fears and desires, inherited karma from past lives) can influence our thoughts and behavior. In *Ronnie Rocket*'s city, the story's villain spews out unseen waves of Bad

Electricity that confuse people's minds, gives them fits and skin diseases, makes them mutilate themselves, and saps their freedom of will. One of the pictures in which Lynch did get to explore his Bad Electricity concept was *Twin Peaks: Fire Walk With Me*, in which BOB's dark impulses flow in telephone wires, hissing TV snow, and that iconic rotating ceiling fan.

Lynch is fascinated by the idea that our bodies are electromagnetic power plants, that the electrons that flow within us are the same as the ones that hum in rocks and chocolate bunnies and mallard ducks and star clusters. In *Ronnie Rocket*, Lynch, like Mary Shelley in *Frankenstein*, plays with the idea of extra-large amounts of electricity energizing the human system, specifically that of the Ronnie Rocket character, who was to be portrayed by Michael J. Anderson. For Lynch, electricity is a powerful, invisible, mysterious force and its bifurcation into positive and negative polarities reinforces his tendency to perceive dualistic oppositions. Electrical circuits can be open or closed and in *Ronnie Rocket* Lynch applies this principle to energies of good and evil, the two polarities most fundamental to his narratives: Bad circuits must be broken for virtue to prevail. Electrical terminology is common currency in Lynch's mind; even in his early days as a painter, he spoke of an energy circuit being established between an artwork and the person contemplating it.

Ronnie Rocket's city is a characteristically Lynchian "hellhole,"[5] a place where bewilderment, disorientation, fear, and pain have control. Again typical for a Lynch work, a detective figure with a questing intelligence will strive to restore an illuminating order to a shadow zone of chaos. Like Lynch and many of his characters, *Ronnie Rocket*'s detective crosses barriers and boundaries to penetrate into realms of hidden knowledge, and he has to pay close attention to learn the new rules that help decipher the new places he's exploring, and he receives guidance in his investigations.

Ronnie Rocket would, as many of Lynch's works do, use out-of-control animalism and the loss of personal freedom and identity to threaten goodness, focus on the archetypal relationship of parents to children, revel in wacky/absurdist humor, and reveal a deeper, metaphysical story hiding within the surface tale we're watching.

Something new to Lynch's cinematic aesthetic would be *Ronnie Rocket*'s color palette, which would be darker than ever and monochromatic, using brighter hues for precisely controlled points of emphasis. This sparing, minimalist deployment of color would be congruent with many of Lynch's paintings, as well as the Jacques Tati films he loves.

As the 1980s began, Lynch was moving within the circles of Hollywood power, but he couldn't quite believe his ears when he got a call from international mega-producer Dino De Laurentiis, who had worked with the likes of Roberto Rossellini, Federico Fellini, Vittorio De Sica, King Vidor, John Huston, Robert Altman, and Ingmar Bergman. Following a now-familiar pattern, a viewer (De Laurentiis' daughter, Raffaella) had been deeply moved by Lynch's current work (*The Elephant Man*) and was stimulated to employ the artist's unique talents. De Laurentiis enthusiastically told Lynch that he wanted him to direct a film of author Frank Herbert's monumentally popular space-epic novel *Dune.* Herbert's complex, mystical saga of a young superhero, consciousness-expanding drugs, ecological awareness, feminist religion, and interplanetary intrigue became a popular culture touchstone after its 1965 publication, yet infrequent-reader Lynch had never heard of it. Like one of the director's own characters caught in a moment of muddled communication, Lynch thought that De Laurentiis had said he wanted to make a film called *June.*

Lynch the former underground filmmaker had an inherent skepticism about big, "creative," hands-on producers, who could meddle with an artist's work and misshape it according to their own wrong-headed whims.

> When Dino offered me *Dune,* I went to see him more out of curiosity than anything else. I thought I would meet a man with whom I wouldn't want to spend more than a few minutes. But I discovered that Dino really *loves* movies. He's a lot more sensitive guy than you would think, and he throws out so many ideas that you can't help but get excited about them. Sure, he's a strong person, and sometimes his approach may be wrong, but he's a man who tries to move things forward, not destroy them.[6]

Two months after Academy Awards night, Lynch was under contract to Dino De Laurentiis and working on the screenplay for *Dune.* Like some evolutionary process of nature, the artist's career was expanding into ever-larger projects and, with a budget of $40 million (in early 1980s dollars), *Dune* would be one of the most expensive films ever made.

The fictional universe of *Dune* may have been new to Lynch, but it had put a gleam in the eye of many a filmmaker over the years. In the late 1960s, producer Arthur P. Jacobs of *Planet of the Apes* (1968) fame optioned Frank Herbert's novel, but a sudden heart attack took his life and returned the property to the open market. In the mid-1970s, Alejandro Jodorowsky, the Chilean-Mexican surrealist whose "religious western" *El Topo* (1971) was a sacramental experience for a cult of midnight moviegoers, teamed with wealthy Parisian Michael Seydoux to put a fourteen-hour version of *Dune* on the screen. Jodorowsky assembled a remarkable group of collaborators: French illustrator Jean "Moebius" Giraud; H. R. Giger, who would design the space nightmare *Alien*; and surrealist master Salvador Dali, who would not only contribute visual ideas, but act in the film along with Orson Welles and Gloria Swanson. With script and visual design completed, *Dune* was ready to roll, but the budget was mushrooming out of control, so forward momentum slowed as the filmmakers sought added production funds in Los Angeles. Creative differences flared up, no U.S. money was forthcoming, and the French abruptly withdrew their support. Jodorowsky turned the project loose and, three years later in 1978, Dino De Laurentiis grabbed it up. The Italian risk-taker passionately wanted to honor the evocative spirit of the book he loved, so he went straight to the source for a screenplay: Frank Herbert, the literary magus of Washington State.

Herbert, who was born in Tacoma, Washington, in 1920, worked as a photographer, oyster diver, and jungle-survival instructor before settling into years of newspaper journalism. He had long believed that "superheroes are disasters for humankind, that even if we find a real hero (whatever that may be), eventually fallible mortals take over the power structure around a leader. What better way to destroy civilization?"[7] No matter how charismatic a leader may be, from Jesus to John F. Kennedy, Herbert warned, "Don't give over all your critical faculties to people in power, no matter how admirable those people may appear."[8] While doing research for an article on the Department of Agriculture's project to control sand dunes on the Oregon coast near Florence, Herbert took a plane ride. Looking down on the vast expanse of sand, Herbert pondered the idea that barren landscapes have historically given rise to messiahs, and he envisioned an epic tale about a desert planet, Arrakis, also called Dune. The resulting novel's skepticism about leaders and authority figures, sense of ecological balance, interest in mystical, sometimes drug-induced states of consciousness, and glimmers of esoteric wisdom, endeared it to the late-1960s counterculture and endowed Herbert with the unsought status of guru.

The book, aside from Herbert's compelling musings on political power shifts and the human need for spiritual belief, showed a real flair for visual scene-setting, and the author, at De Laurentiis' behest, confidently began to translate his written pages into cinematic terms. But Herbert was so in love with his book's every little subplot that his scenario weighed in at an unworkable 175 pages.

De Laurentiis, with his best manners, told Herbert he just couldn't use his screenplay. Then the producer read the novel three more times and moved on to a new strategy. He decided that he should first engage a director with a strong pictorial gift and then bring in a seasoned screenwriter. De Laurentiis chose Ridley Scott, who was fresh from piloting *The Duellists*

(1978) and *Alien* (1979), and Rudolph Wurlitzer, who had scripted *Two-Lane Blacktop* (1971) and *Pat Garrett & Billy the Kid* (1973). Wurlitzer audaciously injected a theme into his script that wasn't in the book. Herbert was outraged to hear that the screenwriter had created an incestuous lovemaking scene between his young hero, Paul Atreides, and Lady Jessica, his mother. This conceit was immediately dropped, but director Scott's proposed budget was running rampant, so De Laurentiis sadly aborted his third attempt to film *Dune*. Then Dino's daughter wept while watching another movie, and salvation arrived.

"There's so much *heart* in *The Elephant Man*. I'm tough. I haven't cried in a movie in years. But I had tears in my eyes several times during the film. After I saw it, I had to talk to the director,"[9] says Raffaella. From daughter's lips to father's ear, and it was now David Lynch's turn to wrestle with the monster of complexity that is *Dune*. Reading Herbert's book, Lynch "was just knocked out. And not just by its adventurous aspects. In a lot of ways, this novel is the antithesis of the usual raygun and spaceship science fiction I'm used to seeing. *Dune* has believable characters and a lot of depth, a lot of resonance. It's not all surface flash. In many ways, Herbert created an *internal* adventure, one with a lot of emotional and physical textures. And I love textures."[10] Textures and inner space were Lynch's home turf, but he saw *Dune* as "a giant project, and I couldn't write the script on my own."[11]

The director called in his screenwriter friends Christian De Vore and Eric Bergren, with whom he had collaborated so successfully on *The Elephant Man*'s Oscar-nominated script. The trio came up with a lengthy screenplay that "just wasn't happening"[12] for Lynch. "Chris and Eric wanted to go in a different direction than I was intending, so we parted company. I told Dino I wanted to take a crack at it myself. He wasn't too sure about that, but he told me to go ahead and start and we'd see how it went."[13]

Before beginning, Lynch spent some time with Frank Herbert on his farm near Port Townsend, Washington. Leaving behind the blazing blue skies and palm trees of Southern California for the moody, leaden cloudscapes and dripping evergreens of the Northwest region where he had spent his boyhood, Lynch stepped into Herbert's six-acre experiment in technology and ecology. The director was fascinated by the master-of-*Dune*'s windmill power, an early application of home computers, and a duck pond for climate regulation.

The bearded and barrel-chested sixty-one-year-old Herbert was an affable, welcoming host to the returning Northwest native, and the two formed a warm, immediate bond of mutual admiration. Herbert, like Lynch, was a man who trusted his intuition as well as his intellect, and when he saw

The Elephant Man, he had "a funny, gut sensation that we have the guy who could do *Dune*, we've got him."[14] This fictioneer who revered the written word was struck by the rich "visual metaphors"[15] of Lynch's cinematic language and the "subtlety and beauty"[16] with which the director communicated emotions and moods that were "felt but not seen, sensed without being observed directly."[17] And Lynch respected Herbert's ability to "capture fantastic ideas"[18] and the way his book purposefully "leaves a lot to the reader's imagination; he gives you a feeling and your mind takes over from there."[19] Each man could be describing his own work in these statements. These two conjurers of imaginary worlds felt a kinship of what Lynch calls "friendship and support,"[20] and Herbert recalled that over an association of years "the only thing we disagreed about was where to eat dinner."[21]

While Lynch was staying with Herbert, the neighborhood kids were all abuzz, having mistakenly gotten the idea that *Stars Wars* creator George Lucas, now a pop-culture icon, was in their midst. For Herbert, this community misconception dripped with irony, for the author had been angered by sixteen points of "absolute identity"[22] between his *Dune* book and Lucas's *Star Wars*. Among them, as Herbert's son, Brian, recalls, were "an evil galactic empire, a desolate desert planet, hooded natives, strong religious elements, and a messianic hero with an aged mentor."[23] There were also "spice mines and a Dune Sea."[24] Herbert and other science fiction authors who felt Lucas had used their ideas to make his film called themselves the "We're Too Big to Sue George Lucas Society."[25] Herbert was, of course, thrilled with Lynch's commitment to having as many points of absolute identity between the *Dune* book and film as possible. He liked the idea that Lynch was a painter and would bring a strong visual sense to his conception of the project. Herbert generously told Lynch "anything and everything he wanted to know"[26] about the world of *Dune*, and the director headed back to Los Angeles full of confidence and excitement, his screenwriting pen at the ready.

Lynch wrote seventeen pages and took them over to De Laurentiis' Beverly Hills house. The producer read them and joyfully announced that they were the best seventeen pages of all the *Dune* scripts that he had seen over the years. Even the sky wasn't the limit any more. *Dune* was finally ready to blast off, with Lynch at the controls. And with a woman as co-pilot.

Dino De Laurentiis had always "wanted to have a strong hand"[27] in the making of *Dune* ("I had to be able to call the shots"),[28] yet he was giving the producer's job, which would oversee every aspect of one of the biggest, most labyrinthine films ever made, to his twenty-seven-year-old daughter, Raffaella. The second of De Laurentiis' and actress Silvana Mangano's (*Bitter*

Rice, 1949) four children, Raffaella had already worked many hours on the art direction and costume design of her father's pictures, and shared production duties on *Beyond the Reef* (1979) and *Conan the Barbarian* (1981). With her trim figure, long honey-colored hair, and wide-eyed beauty, some felt that her natural place was in front of the camera. But Dino was well aware of Raffaella's unaggressively commanding manner (dubbed "blonde steel"[29] by writer Ed Naha), and her dedication to Frank Herbert's book, and certainly she was in a position to listen to any suggestions Papa might care to offer. Yes, it would be the producer's chair for Raffaella, and father and daughter could even talk Mama Silvana into acting a small role in the film. So how would David Lynch fit into this family affair? Would he be seen as the De Laurentiises' simpatico kin or their hired artist?

Lynch's boyish sense of wonder and mature dedication to his craft, his serious yet bemused outlook on life, and his gift for relating to people on *their* level naturally make people want to be his friend, and his employers were no exception. In the months ahead, Dino would pat Lynch's cheek with affection, and Raffaella would say that David had become part of her life, "like your brother or sister."[30] Father and daughter cared so deeply for *Dune* that, like Frank Herbert, they reflexively bonded with the man who was capable of delivering it to the screen. For Raffaella, "the biggest challenge was to turn that book into a movie and keep all that's in the book in the movie; David's the first to capture the essence of the book in one, tight script."[31]

So what was this tale that readers guarded with such protectionistic zeal, this story that, with its four sequels, had sold more than thirteen million copies by the early 1980s? In the far future, there is a fiefdom among the stars, in which noble families own planets as well as castles. The benevolent Duke Leto Atreides, his consort, Lady Jessica, and their son, Paul, reside on the water-blessed, verdant world of Caladan. Following the orders of the Emperor of the Known Universe, Shaddam IV, the Atreides and their extended clan, which includes armies, are sent to the parched sandscape of planet Arrakis, called Dune, where water is valued in proportion to its severe scarcity. Moisture may be rare on Dune but its sands yield the cinnamon-scented spice, which expands the perceptions and extends the life of those who ingest it, and allows the Spacing Guild Navigators to fold space and control travel between planets. The House of Atreides will now be in charge of spice production on Dune, taking over from the evil Baron Harkonnen and his clan, who live on the industrialized world of Giedi Prime. Dune would seem to be a wealth-expanding plum for the Atreides, but it is actually a trap.

Carrying out the Emperor's orders, the Harkonnens, with the aide of Duke Leto's traitorous advisor, Dr. Yueh, attack and kill the Duke. Paul and Lady Jessica escape into the desert, where they are befriended by the sand-dwelling natives, the Fremen. The ancient prophesies of Dune have foretold the coming of a messiah who will make the desert bloom and initiate a reign of goodness throughout the universe. The Fremen believe that Paul is the chosen one, and the young man, after fighting side by side with his desert brethren and experiencing mystical states of spice awareness, discovers his true destiny.

Rousing physical action, political intrigue, a youth coming of age—the onrushing surface of Herbert's narrative compels our involvement. But what really grabbed Lynch were the rich layers of embellishment that support the saga of Paul's heroism. Details such as the Bene Gesserit sisterhood, a secretive group who have developed their innate intuitive skills to an almost telepathic level and can masterfully control their physical and emotional responses to the world. Through vocal modulation, they can use The Voice to overpower the most formidable of male opponents. And in a manipulative intergalactic example of self-fulfilling prophecy, they have spread myths and superstitions about a coming messiah throughout distant worlds, and then engineered a system of controlled breeding to bring this savior into being. According to the Bene Gesserit plan, Lady Jessica was supposed to bear only daughters. But, full of love for Duke Leto and knowing his desire for a male heir, she sires her son, Paul. Jessica's action may have ruined the Bene Gesserit design, or Paul may actually be the chosen one, born prematurely out of sequence and hence not the malleable puppet the sisters wanted to produce. The unexpected interjection of this male into the sisterhood's plan allowed Herbert to address issues of sexual politics, the element of gender in human nature, and androgyny, which were part of the late-1960s and 1970s women's movement's cultural dialogue. Paul Atreides emerged as an archetype of positive integration: a "masculine" warrior and leader who relies on his "feminine" intuition and the wisdom of the sisterhood.

The magical spell of Herbert's book was also maintained by the monstrous 1,500-foot-long sandworms that swim beneath the desert planet's dunes, and which can rise up and swallow a spaceship-sized spice-mining machine and its screaming crew in one terrible, sucking gulp. Herbert goes on to intriguingly link the threat of great danger with the promise of supreme reward by eventually revealing that the fearsome worms biologically produce the treasured spice. Though Lynch was not one to ingest illicit psychoactive chemicals, he was familiar with meditative and visionary states of consciousness, and hence fascinated by the spice that facilitated space travel and enabled Paul to, as Herbert writes, "sense the available paths, the winds of the future, the winds of the past."[32] Herbert wafted breezes and hints about what was to come to Paul, but he wasn't handing him stone tablets on which the future was immutably etched. Within his own individual mind, Paul sought to discern the shape of the Universal Mind. Reading clues and dreams, relating concrete reality to cosmic designs, Paul is—like Henry Spencer (*Eraserhead*), Jeffrey Beaumont (*Blue Velvet*), and Dale Cooper (*Twin Peaks*)—the archetypal Lynchian hero: a metaphysical detective. Indeed, Herbert's approach to all of *Dune*'s people was right on Lynch's wavelength. For the author not only stressed Paul's grapplings with existential mysteries, he emphasized the mental life, the inner voices of a planet-sized cast of characters, which he indicated with italicized passages. As when Hawat, one of the Atreides' advisors, tells Paul of the harsh conditions they will encounter on Dune and thinks, "*Perhaps I'm doing it, getting across to him the importance of this planet as an enemy. It's madness to go in there without caution in our minds.*"[33] Lynch immediately decided to incorporate Herbert's inner-voice literary technique into his screenplay by having the actors' voices speak their hidden thoughts throughout the film. Herbert's concepts harmonized with many aspects of Lynch's personal and artistic sensibility. Lynch, and a number of his characters, see the world as a strange place that has to be figured out as you progress through it, which is Paul's position in *Dune*. As Lynch often says, "It's a learning world"[34] or "a lesson world."[35] And in Herbert's book, Paul "knew that any experience carries its lesson."[36]

One of Lynch's mottoes has always been "It's important to pay close attention,"[37] which becomes a key attitude of many of his fictional people, especially *Blue Velvet*'s Jeffrey Beaumont and *Twin Peaks*' Agent Cooper, both of whom are played by Kyle MacLachlan, *Dune*'s Paul Atreides. The two characters are similar: Herbert's descriptions of Paul fit Cooper perfectly. Paul "studied the room with a searching intensity,"[38] exhibiting "a poised assurance, as though he saw and heard things all around him that were not visible to others."[39] Paul, like Cooper, uses "questions and hyperawareness"[40] to "register"[41] a person, as when Cooper accurately discovers people's secret relationships by reading their manner and body language. Lynch didn't studiously take notes on *Dune*, thinking that someday he'd create a detective character with these traits. Lynch lives out a romantic, mystical, spiritual idea of the creative process, enjoying the way the moment-to-moment promptings of his subconscious steer him in the "correct"[42] direction that the work wants to go. The work "talks to me"[43] and tells him how to proceed. In Lynch's psyche, there's an uncatalogued swirl of things he loves and hates, fragments of situations and images that touch, anger, excite, disgust, and amuse him; bits of books, films, music, landscapes, and people that he's drawn to. The "talking" that his art-in-the-making does to him is an unwilled focusing, a subconscious selecting of elements that feed the still-forming shape of this particular painting, film, song, or piece of furniture. Lynch wants the process to be spontaneous and emotional, not cerebral and pre-planned. He's often said that "ninety percent of the time I don't know why I'm doing what I'm doing,"[44] and stressed that "Greg, you would see things in my work that I wouldn't know are there when I'm doing them; sometimes I see them later."[45] Years after *Dune*, during the production of *Twin Peaks*, the presence of Kyle MacLachlan may have triggered Lynch's mind to echo a passage in *Dune*. For Gordon Cole, the character Lynch plays in *Twin Peaks*, perceives Agent Cooper (MacLachlan) approaching before he can see him, just as *Dune*'s Paul (MacLachlan) "senses"[46] his comrades drawing near before they're in his sight.

Other correspondences between Herbert's words and Lynch's philosophy, themes, and aesthetics abound. Both men lovingly and repeatedly work coffee into their fictions, and *Dune*'s room in which "the dark stone walls swallowed the light"[47] is the sort of space that has haunted Lynch's paintings and films since the 1960s. Herbert and Lynch are both fascinated by the dark capacities of the human psyche, and *Dune*'s infectious "wild race consciousness that was moving the human universe toward chaos"[48] burns feverishly in many Lynch films (especially *Wild at Heart*) and sometimes in Lynch's own troubled thoughts. In *Dune*, Paul speaks of a "magnetic and terrifying trembling awareness,"[49] a shivering state that grips Cooper in *Twin Peaks* and Betty in *Mulholland Drive* as they're poised on the brink of a momentous hidden knowledge. Lynch and Herbert share a fundamental belief that there's a doubleness to existence—another, mysterious, realm beyond our normal perception. As Paul in *Dune* says, quoting the *Orange Catholic Bible*, "What senses do we lack that we cannot see or hear another world all around us?"[50] Whether there's some other realm coexisting with the one we're perceiving, both Lynch and Herbert also see this world we're in through a bifurcated lens. Lynch energizes his fictions with the dynamic contrast between opposing forces and qualities: in *Blue Velvet*, Jeffrey learns that being a detective can be both "wonderful" and "horrible," and in *Dune*'s pages, Duke Leto views Arrakis as a potential "good home"[51] and a "hideous place."[52] Throughout the ages, wise people have striven to reconcile opposites, to combine them in a third truth, and Lynch speaks of "a mysterious door at the balancing point"[53] between polarities, just as

Herbert writes of Paul being "at the fulcrum"[54] between the will to give and to take. A beaming Herbert stressed "how delighted I am with what David Lynch has done"[55] in adapting his book for the screen: "I hear my dialogue all the way through the script."[56] And the author respected the way "David has taken my original projections and has expanded on them with his own concepts; now he has to take it and carry it to some kind of ultimate artistic extreme, so that it's fixed in the mind of the viewer—because this is it!"[57]

Lynch saw himself as the refining "filter"[58] through which all the raw materials of the production would pass before flowing across the screen in a parade of stately, entrancing, mammoth-scaled images. But on a film that more than dwarfed *The Elephant Man*, the director needed plenty of help from his friends. Lynch assembled a technical team composed of old cohorts and new collaborators. British cinematographer Freddie Francis, who shot *The Elephant Man* for Lynch, felt that the relatively inexperienced American visionary was "the most unorthodox director in the world. He gets an idea in his head that may be impractical technically but he likes it."[59] It was then Francis's task "to make his vision a reality. I like that."[60] The lensmaster eagerly joined Lynch's outer-space mission. As did the director's Philadelphia-era friend Alan Splet, the phenomenal sound designer who had enhanced the dreamy atmosphere of *The Grandmother* and *Eraserhead* and won a 1979 Academy Award for his work on *The Black Stallion*. Most prominent of the fresh faces would be British production designer Tony Masters, who had lent his impeccable pictorial sense to *Lawrence of Arabia* and *2001: A Space Odyssey*, and who, after Frank Herbert and Lynch, would be most responsible for the look of *Dune*. As Masters and Lynch began to plan the spaces that the film's myriad characters would occupy, the production designer found his director "completely approachable at all times, always interested and full of ideas."[61] At first blush, Masters felt that some of Lynch's notions "are crazy ideas that you don't think will ever work, until you actually try them out—and then they're not so crazy."[62] Both men adhered to a primal operating principle: "If it's been done or seen before, throw it out!"[63] Lynch didn't want "high-tech sci fi, like most of the outer space stuff you see"[64]; he wanted "everything to look old, like it's been around for awhile."[65] Lynch figured that although *Dune*'s characters live on various planets in a far-flung galaxy, their ancestors came from Earth, so Masters worked in references to the Victorian, Assyrian, Mayan, and Egyptian artistic traditions. All-American Lynch was becoming a seasoned world traveler susceptible to foreign influences. He was not only choosing French Comme des Garcons white shirts as his standard model, but he returned from a trip to Venice glowing with admiration for Renaissance decor. Masters duly added Venetian elements to his aesthetic mix, and acted on the director's enthusiastic declaration that it would be "neat and strange"[66] to find filigreed tile mosaics adorning the underground hewn-rock halls of the outwardly barren and primitive desert planet. And thus another example of a core element of Lynch's sensibility: surprises are hidden within the interior. Back on the surface of things, Masters added some final embellishments to his designs in the form of the zigzags, triangles, and small circles from which Lynch had composed his early art school drawings.

Two more additions to Lynch's technical team were special effects artist Kit West, who had won an Oscar for his work on Steven Spielberg's *Raiders of the Lost Ark* (1981), and creature-maker Carlo Rambaldi, who crafted the beloved otherwordly lost child for Spielberg's *E.T.: The Extra-Terrestrial* (1982), an alien who looks rather like Lynch's *Eraserhead* baby.

Raffaella De Laurentiis had scoured the globe searching for a location that would meet all the needs of her gargantuan, elaborate production. She finally settled on the Churubusco Studio complex in Mexico City, which could provide eight large sound stages and was just two hours away from the picturesque golden dunes of the Samalayuca Desert.

So Lynch had a polished script that Frank Herbert had blessed, a cameraman, and a place to shoot. Now all he needed was someone to portray the hero of the piece, Paul Atreides. Returning to origins, we have a source novelist and a film director who lived early years in Washington. Would the gods of cinema not smile upon a Pacific Northwest trinity?

Most Americans think of Washington State as a land of leaping salmon, dense evergreen forests, and eternally gloomy, raining skies. But the eastern half of the territory looks like cowboy country: golden-tan plains the color of a lion's flank, deep rock canyons, coyotes, sagebrush, and tumbleweeds. The town of Yakima lies roughly in the state's center, with Frank Herbert's youthful home (Tacoma) to the far west and David Lynch's (Spokane) to the far east. In the hot, dry Yakima summer of 1971, a fourteen-year-old named Kyle MacLachlan read and fell in love with *Dune*. MacLachlan's early teen years were a time when he was "going through all these little changes"[67] and "looking for a direction."[68] Paul Atreides, with his superb physical and mental conditioning, was "a hero figure, a real role model"[69] for the Yakima youth, and *Dune*, which he continued to read yearly, "almost became my Bible."[70] One of the book's compelling themes is the Fremen's dream of painstakingly transforming some of Dune's sandscapes into green oases of cultivation. So in the sunstruck Yakima Valley, which, over the last hundred years, had been partly converted from desert to agricultural wonderland,

Kyle MacLachlan could smell the acres of hops and mint around him and fully imagine himself at home in Herbert's fiction.

Over the next few years, MacLachlan began behaving as though he were a member of Shakespeare's and Moss Hart's and Edward Albee's literary worlds, for the handsome youth with the chiseled chin and jet-black hair had a gift for acting. At Seattle's University of Washington, he graduated from the prestigious Professional Actor Training Program, where a "Hollywood casting lady"[71] saw MacLachlan on stage in a Seattle production of *Tartuffe*, and she immediately set up a Los Angeles plane flight so he could go audition for the lead role in *Dune*. Paul Atreides! MacLachlan could only conclude that he was living a charmed life as the possibility of portraying his very own personal hero in a gigantic motion picture suddenly opened before him.

Never having been in L.A. nor seen any of Lynch's films, MacLachlan was on edge with nervous anticipation as he sat in the Universal Pictures reception room waiting to meet the director. The actor's Seattle friends had said that *Eraserhead* "was the weirdest thing they'd seen in their lives,"[72] so MacLachlan "was expecting someone pretty strange."[73] He was surprised when "the most normal-looking guy I'd ever seen"[74] stepped forward, shook his hand warmly, and ushered him past the receptionist into the halls of Hollywood power.

Lynch's low-key style of interviewing actors would become legendary, and even back in 1982, there was something about the director's uncluttered office with its six prominent toy figures of Woody Woodpecker (whose erect topknot mimics *Eraserhead* Henry's and Lynch's own hair) that put MacLachlan at ease. Both men were pleased to discover their mutual Northwest roots, and reminisced about each having enjoyed idyllic childhood visits to Idaho's Lake Coeur d'Alene. Then the topic shifted to their shared love of red wine, and talk of favorite brands and vintages and places where a certain bottle had been savored flowed freely. MacLachlan was amazed at how quickly their meeting time was up, and Lynch hadn't even asked him to read a *Dune* scene or said anything about the movie. "He was just getting to know who I was, and on my way out he said, 'Here's a script. Look at these scenes, come back in a few days, and we'll do a screen test.'"[75]

MacLachlan returned to Seattle, prepared the scenes Lynch had given him, flew back to L.A., suited up in Paul Atreides' formal court uniform, and stepped in front of the cameras. Lynch was impressed with the actor's youthful, yet mature manner; the agile intelligence at work behind dark, questing eyes; and his self-contained, serious-minded bearing. He didn't show too much or smile too often. Though Kyle was accustomed to standing on stage and projecting his performance to the back row seats, he seemed to intuitively grasp the film-acting secret of holding his emotions in check so that the audience, curious and intrigued, would come forward to meet him half way. On a snippet of video tape shot just after MacLachlan's screen test, Lynch shows his enthusiasm and, with stammering emotion, communicates the fact that the final casting choice is not his alone to make: "What was so surprising is that every doggone thing he's supposed to have is there. Now if he doesn't get it we're-we're-we're-we're crazy."[76] When MacLachlan, tired and excited after his big audition, returned to his hotel room, there was a bottle of Lynch's favorite red wine waiting for him. The young actor would never forget where and when he had sipped *this* particular vintage, and he had no doubt about which way the director had voted. MacLachlan learned that over the past year, hundreds of actors (including Brad Pitt) had been interviewed for the male lead, and that two men besides himself were being considered by the De Laurentiis faction. Called to Mexico for a second screen test, MacLachlan did his best and stayed in town for five days until the phone rang. Raffaella and Dino had voted with Lynch: He *would* be Paul Atreides.

A cast of international notables would back him up: Jose Ferrer, Max von Sydow (star of a number of the Ingmar Bergman films Lynch loved), Francesca Annis, Silvana Mangano, Sian Phillips, Jurgen Prochnow from *Das Boot*, quirky cult favorite Brad Dourif (*Wise Blood*, a movie Lynch revered), Patrick Stewart before he joined *Star Trek: The Next Generation*, and the powerfully diminutive Linda Hunt (*The Year of Living Dangerously*). The evil House of Harkonnen would be ably represented by Kenneth McMillan, Paul Smith, and the hot rock star Sting, whose acting in *Brimstone and Treacle* had caught Lynch's eye. Everett McGill would play the Fremen leader and, in the early 1990s, would be a regular resident of *Twin Peaks*. Lynch's established artistic family would be present in the formidable form of Jack Nance (Henry of *Eraserhead*) and Freddie Jones (*The Elephant Man*'s nasty sideshow keeper). The enticing Sean Young would be Paul Atreides' Fremen lover, and five-year-old Alicia Rosanne Witt, who would play a grown-up role in Lynch's *Hotel Room* (1993) and who portrayed Cybil Shepard's TV daughter on *Cybil* (1995), would be Paul's little sister. As an adult, 1940s child star Dean Stockwell (*The Boy With Green Hair*, *The Secret Garden*) had limited success in films, and spent years away from the screen selling real estate in New Mexico. Vacationing with his wife in Mexico City, he heard about the big *Dune* production that was setting up and, on a whim, paid a visit to the administrative offices. When he walked into Lynch's quarters, the director said, "I thought you were dead,"[77] and promptly gave him the tasty role of the man who betrays House Atreides. Stockwell's *Dune* work brought him the attention of filmmakers worldwide and his career was off and running again.

For a stretch of many months, the actors would be pretending to cope with life on a harsh, hostile desert planet, and the conditions in Mexico City certainly put them in the proper beleaguered mood. As Sting put it, "The smog and the altitude and the food all conspire against you."[78] Located 7,200 feet above sea level, Mexico City's thin air made the physical exertions of the huge film production doubly hard. And despite all the precautions about carefully selecting food and drink, at least 15 percent of the cast and crew were wracked with gastrointestinal distress at any given time. Raffaella De Laurentiis wasn't sure if she was "running a movie or a hospital."[79] Services taken for granted in the United States, like dependable telephones and electrical sockets that always had power in them, proved to be maddeningly unreliable south of the border. And the Mexican customs officials seemed as villainous as the Harkonnens, ripping Raffaella's time-is-money schedule to shreds by randomly halting the flow of production necessities like costumes and film stock.

Lynch, like his co-workers, was "confronted with these absolutely screwy things every day,"[80] but his overriding sense of wonder helped him keep things in perspective. To him, "Mexico is magic. Just take Mexican art. I never liked it until I came down here. Now it strikes me as being fantastic. It comes from this place. It comes from being here and breathing this air and feeling these vibes."[81] Lynch's sensitivity to his environment, developed in his Northwest childhood and forcefully expressed in reference to Philadelphia (*Eraserhead*) and London (*The Elephant Man*), was again working overtime. "There are so many ideas floating around this land and so many triggers for these ideas that, if it got any more intense, it would drive you crazy. There is just so much stimulation to be gotten from this environment. Really, it's magic."[82]

Just before shooting began, Lynch got a brainwave, remembering how impressed Jack Nance has been when he screened *The Grandmother* for him before they'd started to make *Eraserhead*. Since many of the people he would be sweating and slaving with for many months to come were not familiar with his artistic sensibility, he decided to give them a sample. He would show them one of his films. Feeling then, as he does now, that *Eraserhead* was his most intimately personal work, he called his pal Catherine Coulson in Los Angeles and had her fly in with a print.

After the screening, Lynch received a number of respectful, appreciative comments, especially from Sting. But many of the native crew members just nodded with blank looks on their faces: "Gracias, señor."[83] Remembering her hands-across-the-border cultural mission, Coulson chuckles, "I'm sure they all thought they'd signed on to work with a madman."[84] In a country that worships the Madonna and Child, Lynch's twisted family tale of a man who attains heaven by murdering his child certainly didn't jibe with Catholic orthodoxy.

Anyone Lynch may have alienated with his *Eraserhead* visions were won back with his behavior during the making of *Dune*. Sting noted that "the set was always relaxed. That comes from David. Nothing seems to faze him or upset him."[85] Max von Sydow found him "very likeable as a person and also as a director. He seems to know what he wants. He doesn't say too much to the actors. He seems to trust his actors. That's very nice, too."[86] (Anthony Hopkins, who had a conniption over Lynch's less-is-more directing style on *The Elephant Man*, would certainly have debated von Sydow's positive assessment of the director's methods.)

Patrick Stewart had some astute observations about the relationship between the way the director handled his actors and his general plan for the film. "I think David as a director has been influenced by David as an art student. I always have the feeling that, in his frames, nothing is there by chance. Nothing is accidental. Nothing is arbitrary. Everything is important. Everything has its proper place. It's nice to feel yourself part of something which is exquisite."[87]

Although Raffaella kept myriad production details organized and Lynch presided over a happy set, deep down both producer and director harbored a gnawing worry. "We're still nervous about the script,"[88] admitted Raffaella. "I think we've been faithful to the book, but I'm sure that of the millions of *Dune* readers there will be some who say, 'That's not the way I think it should have been filmed.'"[89] This uncertainty was "really difficult"[90] for Lynch to cope with: "You can't help wondering if the people who loved the book will love your script."[91] Lynch knew that there were legions of "real *Dune* freaks"[92] and also millions of people who, like himself, had never heard of the book. "That frightens me. It's not like this movie is a sure thing."[93]

Producer and director were allied in their focused concern about being judged by both fans and nonfans of the book (in other words, all possible moviegoers), but Lynch felt he and his partner were poles apart in their general approach to life. "How I got together with Raffaella, when she is rational, so logical, the common sense is so strong, and *I* love mysteries and dreams and ambiguities and absurdities . . . it's not a good complement."[94] While Lynch envisioned *Dune* as a grand "dark poem"[95] with a majestic slowness and pauses filled with silence, Raffaella needed to turn out a product with a running time that synchronized with the needs of the world's theatrical marketers. Lynch fretted, "It's going to be really hard for me to get the movie I really see there into two and a half hours,"[96] let alone a shorter running time. "I don't know what parts of the script we're going to lose and what parts we're going to keep."[97] Lynch faced a daunting, three-fold task. He was making a picture that had to be a Frank Herbert book, a De Laurentiis production, and a David Lynch film. So just what did he end up with?

Lynch's muse, the Woman Who Floats in Space, was waiting for him on the first page of *Dune*. In the form of John Merrick's mother, she had begun and ended *The Elephant Man*, and she would reappear to waft through *Industrial Symphony Number One*, *Wild at Heart*, and *Twin Peaks: Fire Walk With Me*. Suspended in space, she encompasses space within her. She can be full of secrets or, through the gestation of a child, can forge a generational link with the future, the certainty of genetic immortality, worlds within worlds. The first words of Herbert's book are written by Princess Irulan about Muad'Dib (the Fremen's name for Paul Atreides) and stress his ties to the desert planet. Lynch not surprisingly chooses to show us the Princess, and opens his first color film with her green eyes and golden face floating in a black void dotted with white stars, accompanied by the faint wind sound the director often uses to waft us into realms of mystery and wonder.

But the Princess is full of facts, rather than poetry, and begins the massive exposition of background details and Herbert-coined terms for which Lynch's film has been criticized. Scientists who study human cognition tell us that the average person can absorb and retain about seven bits of unfamiliar, new data at a sitting. Most of those who saw the film, including the reviewers and critics who wrote about it, had not read the book. So within the film's first ten minutes, while their eyes were feasting on Lynch's alluring visuals, their brains were trying to keep straight a barrage of details and concepts: Shaddam IV, spice melange, Spacing Guild, folding of space, the Fremen, Arrakis, Caladan, Giedi Prime, Kaitain, House Atreides, House Harkonnen, Third Stage Guild Navigator, Bene Gesserit, Lansraad, Sardaukar, Paul Atreides, Duke Leto. Five more minutes of screen time would add Kwisatz Haderach, Lady Jessica, programmed breeding, Mentat, red-stained lips, the giant worms of Dune, the Ducal signet ring, Thufir, Dr. Yueh, Gurney, shield practice, the slow blade penetrates the shield, Arakeen, blue-within-blue eyes, CHOAM Company contract, the weirding module.

This mountain of information is certainly in Herbert's book, but it builds at a rate that the reader can assimilate, and the author provides a twenty-two-page glossary of terminology that the reader can refer to at leisure. This glossary bears the prefacing phrase "To increase understanding is a laudable goal."[98] Herbert's data coalesces to form what many critics and readers call the most successful example of a science fiction myth system in literature, while Lynch is accused of creating an irritating, frustrating quagmire that bogs down the viewer's ability to enjoy the film as a unified, flowing experience. Lynch's love for Herbert's world causes him to be a too-faithful and literal adaptor of it, and the "understanding"[99] that Herbert prizes eludes many who see the film. Even Kyle MacLachlan, who worshipped the *Dune* book, felt he and his fellow actors were speaking masses of dialogue that they didn't understand.

The director's most successful films start with simple details that lead to metaphysical mysteries. For many *Dune* viewers, a complicated setup leads only to mystification and fatigue, consequently, a lessening of the film's emotional power, a dulling of the story's high points. In *Eraserhead*, Lynch contemplated the twists and turns of still-unsolved human and cosmic mysteries that we can feel in our own nervous systems. In *Dune*, the organic pathway to the depths is strewn with an obstacle course of trivia, rather than resonant, meaningful signposts. Lynch urges us to be detectives as we experience art and life, but this film reduces us to being collectors of inconsequential minutiae. He wanted "everything in *Dune* to seem foreign and alien."[100] Lynch is a master at making something we think we know, like a blue sky, red roses, and a sharp picket fence, seem strange, like an evocative memory we've somehow never seen before. But too many *Dune* viewers were blitzed by its 100 percent foreignness, the moment-to-moment need to learn so many new terms, characters, and story convolutions. Even a simultaneous translation in an earphone wouldn't have solved the problem: The movie was just too much *work*.

Even we purist film buffs, who argue for the sovereign right of a book-derived film to stand alone as a work of cinematic art and be judged on its own merits, have felt twinges of pain and outrage over what some film director has made of one of our own favorite tomes. Lynch was well aware that his film would not coincide with the *Dune* movie that the book-lovers already carried in their heads. And sure enough, the book club felt Lynch ventured too deeply into realms of grotesque physicality, gave short shrift to the feminine-religion aspects of the story, and left out all their own personal-favorite scenes. But some rare souls who venerated the book thought that Lynch did just fine. Cranky and hard-to-please science fiction author and critic Harlan

Ellison (*A Boy and His Dog*) raved, "*Dune* is a complex symphony of mystic grandeur."[101] He found it "filled with magic! And like an encounter with a wizard, the film stuns normal perceptions, demanding a sense of wonder and close attention."[102] These are two qualities that Lynch and his heroes live by, so let's use them to glide past the film's sensory-overload problems and take the full measure of what the writer-director has given us.

Returning to the floating woman who begins the film's glut of expository information, we note that, like the image of Merrick's mother at the end of *The Elephant Man*, her visage fades away, then reappears. In both films, we still hear the woman's voice though we don't see her: Lynch knows that the invisible can speak to us. The cyclic fading and returning also mirrors natural and cosmic rhythms of change, extinguishment, and rebirth, and prefigures Paul Atreides' metamorphosis from the green planet Caladan's young Ducal heir to the desert planet Dune's timeless messianic warrior. The viewer receives Princess Irulan's wavering image like an ebbing and flowing transmission from the far future, prefiguring the way that Paul will experience "atmospheric disturbance"[103] when trying to divine the shape of things to come.

The going away and coming back of the Princess (Virginia Madsen) certainly fits with Lynch's artistic sensibility, but for years there's been a rumor that the effect was a technical necessity that covers a glitch in the synchronization of Madsen's lips and dialogue. This would have been an amazingly symmetrical mistake, for the Princess's two fades are located precisely equidistant from the beginning and ending of her scene. Or the snafu could have happened once, with Lynch then choosing to add a balancing second fade: twin peaks of invisibility.

Lynch begins his film on the same first page as Frank Herbert, with Princess Irulan's introductory remarks, but then he shows us something that isn't in the book. With his fascination for physical and psychological transformation and the potential Otherness of flesh, Lynch is compelled to visualize a Third Stage Guild Navigator, who is coming to ask the wary Emperor of the Known Universe, Shaddam IV (Jose Ferrer), some pointed questions. The Emperor's burnished gilt-and-emerald Grand Hall is penetrated by a glistening black locomotive-sized oblong box that's flanked on either side by a number of pale-faced bald men wearing head-to-foot black leather greatcoats. Once again, Lynch shows us the surface, then goes inside. The sides of the huge box slide back, revealing a glass tank filled with orange fog. Then, just as characters step forward out of the night in *Eraserhead* and *Blue Velvet*, a creature glides out of the mist and up to the camera. A giant peach-colored head with a massive cranial dome, cauliflower-textured face with a small, vulva-shaped vertical mouth, pale, wide-spaced eyes almost on the sides of the head, spindly arms and hands, and a long, insect-pupa-like body tapering back into the fog.

The image of a creature with a large head topping an elongated neck or body reminds us of the alien visitor from *E.T. The Extraterrestrial* (1982), which Carlo Rambaldi also designed, and the deformed baby of Henry Spencer and Mary X in *Eraserhead* (1977) with which Lynch began the lineage. Incredibly, *Dune*'s Guild Navigator, like Henry's child, was born of a normal human woman. Starting life as a physically average man, the Guild Navigator trainee, over an extended period of genetic manipulation and copious spice use, passed through stages of transformation. His final form was the long-bodied, large-headed being whose extended lifespan, prescient vision, and ability to bend space and facilitate intergalactic travel gave him massive political power.

The bald men who accompany the Third Stage Navigator to the Emperor's court are in the early stages of transformation. One of them displays eruptive red skull cracks from which protrudes a black tube that curves down into his left nostril, a sheen of mucous highlighting the point where the tube enters his nose. This character is primally Lynchian in the abnormal, tortured look of his physiognomy and the prominence of his head. Lynch loves organic textures, and he makes the Navigator's black traveling vehicle remind us of a big black slug as it slides out of the Grand Hall, leaving a slimy liquid trail on the Emperor's pristine floor—evidence of another Lynchian home invasion.

As we've noted all along, Lynch, who personally relies upon imagination and the life of the mind, visually stresses the human head and the worlds that spin within it. In *Dune* he gives us the head-as-character Spacing Guild Third Stage Navigator, the Guild with their pale heads prominently floating atop black costumes, the telepathic Bene Gesserit sisterhood, also draped in black with conspicuous shaved domes (a Lynchian detail not in the book), and the blue-upon-blue eyes of the soulful, far-sighted Fremen who scan the desert horizon for signs of their prophesied messiah. Each of Lynch's major films from *The Grandmother* on presents a character's dreams and visions, and in *Dune* he naturally emphasizes Paul Atreides' head as the young man sees figments of his own future coalescing into an image of destiny. And when the Bene Gesserit Reverend Mother Gaius Helen Mohiam telepathically "listens in" on the meeting between the Emperor and the Third Stage Navigator from another room, Lynch moves in close to her headress-accentuated bald dome and her eyes-closed face turning slightly so her ear can catch the flow of invisible conversation.

Another example of Lynch's head-emphasis that doesn't appear in Herbert's story is the director's visualization of the evil Baron Harkonnen. In the book, the Baron is a grossly obese man whose "baby-fat hands"[104] like to wander over the bodies of captive slave boys while he plots his vendetta against the good and popular Duke Leto's House of Atreides. Lynch brings all of this baronial detail to his film, but he adds a riveting head-accentuation by covering much of the villain's ruddy face with angry pustules and boils, as though the man's malevolent thoughts and hidden scarlet urges were erupting on his countenance for all to see. As with the early-stage Space Guildsman with his cracked skull and its protruding black tube, the Baron's evil face shows Lynch's interest in externalizing the internal. The director can see both sides of this equation, of course, for his key theme in *The Elephant Man* was that a man who looked like a malefic monster could house a hidden, saintly soul. But in the world of *Dune*, the Baron looks dangerous, and he is. And the monstrous Guild Navigator, who resembles Henry's *Eraserhead* baby who tried to suffocate the freedom-loving life out of his father, wants to eradicate *Dune*'s hero, Paul Atreides. The creature floating in his spice gas–filled glass enclosure can see beyond the veil of tomorrow, and knows that the youth will someday threaten the production of vital spice on the desert planet. The conclusion is elementary: "Paul Atreides must be killed." Here, at the beginning of his story, Paul has not yet realized and assumed the intergalactic power he was born to. But the attentive viewer-detective can already put alpha and omega together. Princess Irulan has told us that a man, a messiah, will come to Dune to lead the Fremen to freedom. The Spacing Guild is alarmed about a plot that could jeopardize spice production on Dune. They tell the Emperor that it isn't Duke Leto they're worried about, it's his *son*. Hearing this, the Reverend Mother and her Bene Gesserit sisters, who have been manipulating bloodlines for generations hoping to produce the Kwisatz Haderach, a "Super Being," hastily rocket over to Caladan to check out this Paul Atreides. After testing Paul, the Reverend Mother wonders, "Could he be the one?," and fifty-seven minutes into the film, Paul asks himself, "Am I the one?" But just ten minutes into this 137-minute film, the viewer can empirically and intuitively assume that Paul *is* the messiah.

This early correct deduction can lessen the audience's enjoyment of the proceedings. Though, for the viewer drowning in a sea of expositional detail and strange-sounding words and names, the sense of having figured out a key plot dynamic ahead of some of the "heady" types on the screen is an empowering sensation. Alfred Hitchcock, a lifelong practitioner and philosopher of suspense, stressed that true suspense, as opposed to sudden surprise, depends upon the audience "being perfectly aware of all the facts involved."[105] If some characters are sitting around a table and a bomb that we didn't know about unexpectedly explodes in their faces, we jump. But if we know ahead of time that there's a bomb hidden beneath the table, and then sit helplessly for five minutes watching the characters talk about their lives or play cards, many more of our emotions than momentary surprise are involved. Knowing in advance that Paul will be the one to battle forces of chaotic darkness does not dim our interest in the playing out of his story, though it's impossible to believe that he'll ever be in real danger of losing his life or not emerge as a victorious winner. In terms of Hitchcock's example, there just isn't a bomb under Paul's table, or if there is, he'll surely defuse it in time.

Although Paul's story is set in the future, his saga is as primal as the tales told around ancient campfires, the flame-conjured dramas that, as French filmmaker and Hitchcock admirer François Truffaut once said, were the progenitors of this century's moving pictures. Paul's adventures trace the patterns of the archetypal questing-hero legend that resonates throughout all the world's cultures. A core human story that mythologist Joseph Campbell spent his lifetime studying in all its many manifestations: A story of one who ventures forth from his familiar world into a realm of fear and wonder, where he battles and defeats deadly supernatural forces. The hero's journey concludes when he returns from his mysterious adventure with the power to bestow benefits and blessings on his home community. And thus does Paul Atreides, a young man trained in the arts of fighting and thinking, journey forth from his familiar home world of Caladan to the harsh wilderness world of Dune. There, after his father has been killed by their family's sworn enemies, the Harkonnens, Paul ventures into the unknown desert reaches, where he is initiated into the ways of this sandy region by the native Fremen. Paul confronts a physical monster, one of the gigantic sandworms, and triumphantly rides on its back. He faces his inner fears by ingesting the poisonous Water of Life and not only survives the experience, but emerges with a vision of his own and the planet's future. He discovers romantic and sexual love with a Fremen woman. Now mature in body, mind, and spirit, Paul returns to Dune's capital city, where he leads his father's army and the Fremen warriors in a battle against Baron Harkonnen's and Emperor Shaddam's evil forces. Having avenged his father's death, Paul proclaims his stunning victory and begins to bring about the greening of Dune. Paul fulfills the role of mythic hero for the viewer in the present tense, and, thanks to the Bene Gesserit's prophetic preparations, he is doubly heroic to the characters in the film by becoming and living out the legend that thousands of lips have repeated for generations. Paul is a hero who discovers and enacts his story. Unlike *Eraserhead*, *Blue Velvet*, and *Twin Peaks*, in which we viewers have to *be* detectives to keep our bearings in a maelstrom of dreams and puzzling story clues in order to find a pathway to final truth, *Dune* has a sense of foregone conclusion about it. This tale will follow the time-honored hero's journey trajectory, so our role is to *watch* Paul be a detective as he figures out where *we* know he's going.

The first indication that Paul is "the special one" comes when the Reverend Mother Mohiam, the Emperor's Truthsayer, visits House Atreides on Caladan. Eschewing social pleasantries, she chastises Jessica for having borne a son to Duke Leto in defiance of the grand Bene Gesserit breeding plan. This strategy would have produced a super-gifted man whom the sisters could program to deal directly with the male bastions of galactic political power, thus ending the centuries-old need for the Bene Gesserits to make only indirect, behind-the-scenes political moves. Jessica has grievously disrupted the plan, and the Reverend Mother calls the woman who was once her greatest student "my greatest disappointment." The women are speaking above Paul's sleeping form, but he's actually awake and hearing everything they say. Both he and Jessica are shocked when the prescient Reverend Mother proclaims words that sound like a foretelling of certain death: "For the father, nothing." Duke Leto, Jessica, and Paul are the most closely knit, loving family that Lynch has so far portrayed in his work, and the Reverend Mother's threatening tone toward them fosters an adversarial dynamic between she and Paul. This formidable, almost supernaturally knowing woman ("He is awake and listening to us") orders Paul to get dressed and report for a test so dreaded that it causes Jessica to agonize with her inner voice: "I may lose my son tonight."

Lynch plays up a battle-of-the-sexes element in his film, stressing the generalized confrontation between Duke Leto the Just's benign patriarchy and the Reverend Mother Mohiam's scheming matriarchy. The film's first on-screen reference to Mohiam comes when a Space Guildsman calls her a "Bene Gesserit witch." In the book, after Mohiam and Jessica have exchanged strong words about the latter's son-bearing, the Reverend Mother's manner softens. She tells Jessica that she's "as dear to me as one of my own daughters,"[106] and that she will treat her with "kindness."[107] Lynch leaves out these conciliatory sentiments and emphasizes Jessica and Paul's feelings of fear and antagonism as Paul is summoned to the test of The Box. Mohaim certainly sounds like a witch as, thanks to Alan Splet's sound wizardry, she commands Paul using The Voice like a blast of wind from the graveyard:

"Now, *you* come here." Paul's mind resists but his body obeys her guttural, sound-warped, echoey order. In the book, Paul stood during his ordeal; Lynch heightens Paul's humiliation by having Mohaim force the youth to kneel in front of her.

The box is designed to separate the "human beings" from the "animals," a resonant dichotomy for Lynch, who commonly demonizes animalistic behavior on the part of Homo sapiens, and makes a dramatic high point of John Merrick's *Elephant Man* declaration: "I am not an animal; I am a human being." Pressing a poison-tipped gom jabbar needle "that kills only animals" against Paul's neck, the Reverend Mother makes him put his right hand into the box's frontal opening. Telling Paul that "Your awareness may be strong enough to control your instinct to withdraw your hand; if you try to remove it, you die by my needle," Mohiam begins the ordeal. Through a technique of nerve induction, Paul is made to feel an itching, a rising heat, and a fiery burning. Mohaim amplifies his anguish with her whispered litany: "You feel your flesh crisping; you feel flesh dropping off." Lynch seeks intimacy with crises of the body as well as the mind, and he takes us inside Paul's pain, showing us the youth's mental image of his hand smoking and bubbling beneath a throbbing overlay of writhing flames. The director stages this scene in his two-character-clinch mode, in which two people (generally representing the forces of good and evil), their heads almost touching, their emotions seething with almost unbearable intensity, confront one another. As Mohaim weaves her searing spell, Paul has but one defense. With his inner voice, he recites a catechism of courage. "I must not fear. Fear is the mind-killer. Fear is the little death that brings total obliteration. I will face my fear. I will permit it to pass over me and through me." For an artist like Lynch, whose work and life are about wrestling with fears and transcending them, these are potent words. This passage could just as rightly have been spoken by Kyle MacLachlan's Cooper character in *Twin Peaks*, for his nemesis, the evil entity BOB, creeps into our world feeding on veins of human fear.

Locked in their torture-box embrace, Paul and Mohaim interweave their simultaneous chants ("I must not fear"; "You feel heat upon *heat*") until, in a paroxysm of agony that's like a sexual climax, he cries out, "The pain!" and she answers, "Ohh! Enough!" The eroticization of violence, which brought a shudder of sexual violation to the clinch between *Eraserhead*'s Mrs. X and Henry, and *The Elephant Man*'s Bytes and Dr. Treves, remains a major theme in Lynch's film work. In the book of *Dune*, Herbert says that a few men other than Paul had taken the Box test, whereas Lynch's screenplay magnifies the sexual politics-battle aspect of his film by having Paul be the only male to have ever been tested.

Later, while Paul and his combined Fremen and Atreides forces engage in their climactic battles with the Harkonnen warriors and the Emperor's Sardaukar "terror troops," Paul's five-year-old sister, Alia, pays a visit to the Emperor's command post. The last child of Jessica and the assassinated Duke Leto, Alia was still in her mother's womb when Jessica swallowed the lethal Water of Life. Jessica had the spiritual strength to neutralize the poison, and the experience expanded her consciousness. But the toxin was still a shock to her system, a jolt which caused Alia to be born with a preternaturally grown-up mind that has the collected strength and wisdom of a Reverend Mother, and then some. The Emperor believes that Paul was reduced to worm food long ago, so he's thunderstruck when Alia says that her brother not only lives, but is Muad'Dib, the fierce, legendary desert warrior-commander. Having put the Emperor of the Known Universe on the defensive with her coy, little-girl manner and stunning revelation about Paul Muad'Dib, Alia does invisible violence to the Emperor's Truthsayer, the Reverend Mother Mohiam. The old woman recoils as though being struck by the thin air and hisses, "Get out of my mind!" Having one's inner self invaded by alien forces is a primal fear in Lynch's work, and this is the only film in which we side with the predatory cortex. Mohiam admonishes the Emperor to "Kill this child; she's an abomination," but it's too late: Alia and Paul and Jessica and the Fremen are already masters of Dune, and their winds of war will sweep across the galaxies.

Paul and Mohiam have a final confrontation in the Great Hall of Dune's capital, Arakeen, as the victors face the vanquished. He recalls to her the Box-test ordeal she put him through, with her gom jabbar needle at his neck. "I remember your gom jabbar, now you remember mine: I can kill with a word." This is literally true. In book and film, the Bene Gesserits have the ability to control others with their Voice. Lynch, the man who for much of his early life felt ill-equipped to express himself in words, gives the House of Atreides some vocal help that they don't have in the novel. The Weirding Module is a small machine that straps to the throat, and amplifies the vibration of a certain chanted word. This resonance then activates a handheld laser gun, which shoots at the enemy. In some other director's movie, those who are shot would simply fall down dead. But Lynch wants his violence to shake us, so Weirding Module victims experience tissue pulverization and spontaneous combustion. Paul and the Fremen discovered that his Fremen tribal name, Muad'Dib, could activate the device, so chants of "Muad'Dib!" have accompanied every battle since. Like his mother, Paul has taken the Water of Life, but he has gone where no female Bene Gesserit can—in "the direction that is dark." There, floating through concentric rings of light, he has learned the secret that he holds the power of all worlds, and can control the worms, the spice, and the Spacing Guild Navigators. The Water of Life hasn't just given Paul strategic political might, it has graced him with spiritual ascendancy. In the temporal realm of physical battles, Paul's name is a killing word. And in the realm of spirit, he can speak with righteous authority: "One cannot go against the word of God." Hearing his rebuking declaration, the Reverend Mother Mohiam averts her once-commanding eyes. Paul has shattered the Spacing Guild's domination of space travel and obliterated the Bene Gesserits' control of the future.

The Reverend Mother's sin, as a representative of her sisterhood, has been that of hubris, of assuming that her group's personal, selfish needs are those of humanity at large. Like Nazis trying to breed a lock-stepping master race, the Bene Gesserits have manipulated the childbearing function of human beings, thus offending the laws of science (natural evolutionary genetic selection) and God. Seeking to bend an entire galaxy to their will, the Bene Gesserits have violated countless human freedoms and souls. There is great irony in Paul's ascendancy, of course, for he is a product of the Bene Gesserit breeding program and, through his mother's teachings, their mental training program. But, like Jessica, he is his own person. The Bene Gesserits coolly bred people to gain power, but Jessica mated in a heat of passionate love for her man, who wanted a son. Paul is the super being that the Reverend Mother and her sisters have created, but he has the will and sense of unique destiny to defy them and provide the Fremen, the planet Dune, and the universe with what they need. And, in a like-mother-like-son conceit, Paul goes against Jessica's wishes by loving the earthy Fremen woman, Chani. Years before Barry Gifford wrote the phrase and Lynch made the film, Paul and Jessica resoundingly showed themselves to be wild at heart. In Lynch's art and life, the conflict between one's heart's desires and intuitions, and the rationalistic, calculating, controlling wills of other people, generates a resonant tension. Herbert has Jessica counsel Paul to "choose the course of happiness."[108]

Lynch, with his artist's love of free expression and his appreciation of marginal fringe-dwellers, is naturally drawn to the Fremen (free men), as are their spiritual kin, Paul and Jessica. The Emperor, the Harkonnens, and other powerful interests who've grown wealthy and fat mining the spice of Dune have seen the native Fremen as swarthy primitives fit only to be their machine operators and servants. However, the Fremen have potent secrets: Though scattered, there are many more of them than the Dune-occupiers suspect, they possess a shamanistic earth-wisdom that helps them master the harshest of living conditions, they are superb guerrilla warriors, and they have a dream. Living in dark desert caves, they don't covet the Emperor's obscenely gilded palace. They want to live in nature, a nature transformed by the rarest-of-rare touch of water, a place of sand-colored heat and sun-bleached light, but with the paradisiac addition of oasis green. Exiled to a bleak existence on their own world, they live generations in anticipation of a mystical leader who will come and help them regain their planet and transform it into a fertile garden. (The epic transition from desert to garden would mirror the transformation of Lynch's Los Angeles when William Mulholland brought water to the desert city in the 1920s.)

The impassioned drive to make a hellish existence heavenly is at the heart of Lynch's cinematic sensibility. We recall how, while shooting *Eraserhead*, he decided mid-film that Henry's unremitting nightmare should transmute into a happy dream. And eight years on from *Dune*, Lynch will make the ending of *Wild at Heart* considerably brighter than the one that source novelist Barry Gifford originally wrote. In *Dune*, the director's need to simplify his screenplay and, more primally, his belief in faith and sincerity as opposed to cynicism and irony, led him to alter one of Herbert's literary concepts. The book's Bene Gesserits, like master product marketers, have slyly planted fictional legends on various worlds that they can someday come and fulfill, thus swaying the gullible masses. Any idea that the foretelling of the Kwisatz Haderach was fabricated for the purposes of political manipulation is absent from Lynch's film. The potential coming of a chosen one is received as divine prophecy—both Bene Gesserits and Fremen believe it. In *Twin Peaks: Fire Walk With Me* (1992), high school girl Laura Palmer regularly abuses sex and drugs and is incestuously molested by her father. In misery, she stands before her bedroom picture of an angel guarding little children and wonders, "Is it true?" In Lynch's world, it is: The mystical and the preternatural are forever at hand.

Throughout *Dune*, Paul has had dreams of a water drop forming concentric circles, a moon floating in space, a human right hand aglow, and faces he's never seen before. When he and his mother link up with the Fremen, his visions achieve a critical mass of meaning which he can understand. When the Harkonnens attack the Atreides on Dune and kill the Duke, they drug Jessica and Paul and fly them out to the desert to be devoured by the monster worms. We've previously seen that Paul has mastered the masculine skills of self-defense and strategic logic, and on the Harkonnen ship he uses brute strength to overpower one of the pilots. But he also employs the Bene Gesserit Voice, which we have only seen women use. Paul's command of The Voice, along with his intuitive and prescient abilities, show that he has also developed the feminine aspects of his being, thus achieving a total integration of all possible human powers. Now he is ready to become superhuman.

Lynch, in his own life, has learned to wrestle with and surmount fears of going outside of his house, his school's regimentation, big cities, parenthood, family responsibilities, and artistic failure. He has coped with anger and depression by learning Eastern meditation, thus calming his mind and expanding its creative capacities. The director believes in the all-American idea of progress and the path of spiritual evolution, so it's not surprising that his films, beginning with *The Grandmother*, take us on a trip from hellish chaos to heavenly order, from a lower level to a higher one, out of the darkness and into the light.

For a man who has been educated more by life than books, it's rather touching that Lynch first presents Paul to us with the image of a young man studying a book, surely the only such introduction of an action hero in the cinema. But now, his father killed, the Harkonnens laying waste to the House of Atreides, his mother beside him facing the menacing, unknown wilderness of the desert, Paul must learn and adapt in the moment, not at leisure while contemplating written sentences. As Herbert puts it in his novel, "Paul felt that all his past, every experience before this night, had become sand curling in an hourglass."[109] The sand that Paul now faces is a trackless wasteland and it is up to him to find a path.

The first and, poignantly, last time we see Paul and his father share a moment alone together, they are standing at night on their home planet Caladan before leaving for Dune, looking out over the great waters that define their world. With soft voice and sensitive, shining eyes, Duke Leto tells Paul how proud he is that the family's royal trainers think the youth is their best student ever. Paul responds with a boyish splurge of love, "I *want* you to be proud of me." Then, as Leto says, "I'll miss the sea," Lynch gives us one of his favorite shots. The director doesn't show a close-up of Leto's face followed by a shot of the waves; he pictures the two men side by side, their backs to us, so that we watch their silhouetted black forms as they look at the horizon-filling green-black ocean beyond. We share these characters' real-time experience of the sea simultaneously with our awareness of its significance to their hearts and minds. We've seen similarly posed and framed images of human beings contemplating a portion of eternity in *The Grandmother* and *The Elephant Man*, and Kyle MacLachlan will step into this picture again in *Blue Velvet*; also, in 2002, Lynch's website shows a photo of him and his young son, Riley, from the back looking out at the Mediterranean Sea at the Cannes Film Festival.

Yes, Leto will miss the sea. "But a person needs new experiences. They jar something deep inside: the longing to grow. Without change, something sleeps inside us, and seldom awakens. The sleeper must awaken." These lines, some of the most eloquent in Lynch's screenplay, crystallize Frank Herbert's most deeply held philosophical principle. When Herbert was a boy, he learned an "ancient"[110] and "dangerous"[111] way of thinking: "It told me that the only valuable things were those I could hold unchanged."[112] As he matured, the author learned that this mindset "necessarily creates the conditions of crisis because it fails to deal with change; it does not square with a changing universe." We desperately grasp and hold tightly what is familiar and unchanging, thus maintaining peace of mind. But over-reliance on security systems can foster a moribund stasis: "Because the mind at ease is a dead mind."[113] Herbert came to believe that "one of the most beautiful things that we have going for us is surprise."[114] He feared that the human race would "tie ourselves into situations where we can't change our minds. It's a mistake to think about THE future, one future. We ought to plan for futures as an art form, for quality of life. We have as many futures as we can invent."[115] In Herbert's first novel, *Dragon in the Sea* (1956), written ten years before *Dune*, a sailor asks his captain, "What's your definition of sanity, Skipper?"[116] The man replies, "The ability to swim. That means the sane person has to understand *currents*, has to know what's required in different waters."[117] In *Dune*, Herbert not only maintains the continuity of this adaptability-celebrating concept, but also mirrors its form by referring to the desert's shifting sands with watery words—as when Paul "waded part way up the slope, kicking off sand rivulets, spurts of dust."[118] In this desert, the equivalent to carefully reading the nature of elemental forces and learning to swim with them is to ride the huge, deadly sandworms.

The Fremen know a profound secret, that the worms are the source of Dune's wealth, the makers of the spice that extends human life and helps visionaries see beyond the mysteries of time and space. The worms will also devour any animal, person, or machine that causes a rhythmic vibration to rustle the planet's sandy surface. The Fremen see the worms as spiritual agents of creation and destruction, and worship their power. The Fremen warriors in Herbert's book must all ritualistically bond with that power and prove their manly mettle by climbing onto one of the creatures and riding it. On the appointed day, the candidate calls a worm with a mechanical "thumper" driven into the sand, whereas on an average, survival-oriented day, the Fremen tread the sand in a purposefully random, nonrhythmic way to avoid attracting worms. Thus do the characters of *Dune*, like those of *Dragon in the Sea*, "know what's required in different waters."[119] Herbert details the artful technique with which the rider summons the worm, gauges its approach, climbs on, and gets the creature to roll just enough so the rider is standing tall on top. It's a process akin to a surfer catching a wave and riding *with* the flow of nature, knowing that any thought of taming the rushing water is futile and, if somehow possible, would destroy the surfer's delicious sense of hazard, of sliding in a barely controlled fall across the wave-face of chaos.

As noted earlier, Lynch has been criticized for being overly respectful of Frank Herbert's text, but with a single sentence, the director lays waste to Frank Herbert's literary ecology. For Paul, realizing the need for an ultimate gesture of bonding with his Fremen tribal brothers, will not just *ride* one of the sand-dwelling monsters: "I must conquer the worm" (the "ride"[120] of Lynch's script becomes the film's "conquer"). Conquest, with its connotation of subduing an adversary with force, of winning a victory, is far from Herbert's delicate, symbiotic man–worm balancing act. Yet Lynch's alteration is an example of the transmutation screenwriters perform on their source material in order to condense plot dynamics and heighten drama. Lynch having Paul set out to conquer the worm is akin to the director calling the Reverend Mother Mohiam "witch" early in the film and making her more of a sharply defined nemesis to Paul than she is in the book.

Lynch goes so far as to change the setting of Paul's Water of Life ritual from the book's cave interior to the open desert so that the worms can show him fealty. Lying on the sand and surrounded by his lover Chani (Sean Young) and his Fremen brothers, Paul sips the deadly poison and, like an alchemist of consciousness, transforms it into something golden. When Paul and Jessica first met the Fremen, and Paul saw the little glimpse-of-the-future fragments he'd envisioned months before start to coalesce into the reality he was now living, he said, "A dream unfolds"; he was entering that state of dream/reality interpenetration that's a primal mode of Lynch's storytelling and a key aspect of the way the director thinks about human consciousness and existence. When Paul has his Water of Life revelation, all the visionary bits and pieces that have tantalized his questing mind come together, and he sees that he can control the worms and spice production, defeat the Harkonnens and the Emperor, dictate terms to the Spacing Guild Navigators, avenge his father's killing, and help the Fremen create a paradisiacal world. As Paul has his vision and tells it to Chani and the Fremen, the great skyscraper-tall worms come and form a perimeter around the human beings. The creatures normally only open their mouths to attack, and their maws are now gaping wide, yet they don't disturb Paul's moment of revelation. In this awesome tableau, which isn't in the book, Lynch sums up the magnitude of Paul's now all-powerful physical and spiritual being: Even the worms know when they've met their master. Yet there's the sense that the Chosen One respects the worms as much as they do him. Paul may now be invincible, but he is a good man and will fight for justice and the freedom of those who are worthy of it. Invoking his spiritual link with his beneficent and beloved father, Paul cries out in a firm voice of resolution, "Father, the sleeper has awakened!" There's something very serene about the worms' presence in this image that conflates the awakened Paul, his lover, their friends, Paul's new desert home, his sense of galactic mission, and the memory of his father. Indeed, the image recalls American artist Edward Hicks's idealistic nineteenth-century folk painting *The Peaceable Kingdom*, in which Indians and white settlers, and lions and lambs, happily coexist in the bosom of nature. Paul will now fight so that the worm-revering Fremen will hold sway on Dune. Lynch may have had Paul speak of conquering the worms, but the director's images show that he has taken Herbert's message about ecological balance and adaptive flexibility to heart, for Paul knows when to ride the worms and when to let them run free. He will use his power over the worms as a political bargaining chip to help him banish evil and obtain the highest good for those who deserve it; he's not going to put the creatures in a zoo.

Each of the planets of *Dune* reflects an aspect of Lynch's sensibility. The Atreides' Caladan, with its eternally moist atmosphere and carpentered wood interiors, is like the Northwest of the director's youth, and the fictional settings of *Blue Velvet* and *Twin Peaks* to come. The Emperor's Kaitain is home to the prescient Reverend Mother Mohiam, and hosts the grotesquely mutated and deformed Third Stage Spacing Guild Navigator and his attendant transformational Navigators with their bursting skulls and body-piercing black tubes. Dune itself holds powerful secrets beneath its surface: the monster worms, the spice which gives people visions and lets them float from star to star, and the oppressed Fremen, the archetypal outsiders who are always Lynch's people. But it is Giedi Prime, home of the murderous, greedily scheming Harkonnens, that really struck Lynch's fancy. "I enjoyed filming Geidi Prime so much. That's sort of the imagery that appeals to me."[121] Imagery, and much more.

The Harkonnens' home world is a Lynchian Factory Fantasyland. The director has often spoken of his love for the look of heavy industry, the roiling black smoke, hissing white steam, shooting tongues of fire, and the massive curves and geometric forms of steel that hold these forces in check and shape them to man's bidding. Factories touch Lynch's soul, giving him intimations of cosmic workings and the organic-mechanistic plumbing hidden beneath our flesh, the fluid flowings and combustions that propel us through life. Artist that he is, Lynch is able to view real-life factories in a positive light, yet through his cinematic imagination, transform them into zones of terrible darkness.

On his impoverished *Eraserhead* budget, Lynch filmed bits and pieces of actual Los Angeles industrial sites and combined them with Alan Splet's chugging, pounding sound effects to create a palpably oppressive urban hellhole home for poor Henry. For *The Elephant Man*, with much more money to spend, Lynch crafted a thoroughly convincing reproduction of nineteenth-century London becoming engulfed by rampant industrial growth. And, as he did with *Eraserhead*, the director metaphorically intimated that polluted, machine-blackened skies and the eternal din of factories had the power to taint the human gene pool and deform our children. Now, in *Dune*, Lynch has the funds to fabricate every detail of Giedi Prime and, for the first time in his career, an inviting widescreen frame to fill and a full-spectrum color palette to play with.

Robert Henri, Lynch's early-twentieth-century aesthetic and spiritual mentor, writes in *The Art Spirit* (Lynch's "bible")[122] that in an artist's painting, "There is a color over all colors which unites them and which is more important than the individual colors."[123] Lynch's unifying color, the tone that underlies everything, is shadow. "I like something dark in the frame, so you can't see everything, then there's mystery."[124] The palette of *Dune*, like that of his paintings, has been dusted with shadow: rich, low-key shades of charcoal, jet black, and brown, with burnished highlights of subdued gold and red. In a room that glows brighter, like the Emperor's gold-leaf-layered Great Hall, all the many courtiers and visitors are clothed in night-sky black. We recall Lynch's unvarying fondness for black in his own wardrobe, and remember that in *The Grandmother*, *Eraserhead*, *The Elephant Man*, *Blue Velvet*, and *Twin Peaks*, there are black-suited Lynch-surrogate characters. In the realm of deeper meanings that Lynch loves, Jung envisions the hidden source of the psyche's unconscious wisdom as being black. In Lynch's films black can be both the cloak of menace and the unknown, and the fertile ground of imagination and creativity. It's no wonder that in many of his films, and even some song lyrics, we hear a certain phrase spoken literally or figuratively: "Now it's dark."

It is also, surprisingly, green, as Lynch violates his earth-toned *Dune* color scheme in two significant locations: the floor of the Emperor's gilt Hall, and everywhere on the Harkonnen's Giedi Prime. According to ancient color symbolism, green is naturally associated with vegetation and growth, but also with death and the lividness of bruised flesh. In film history, silent movie scenes of monsters and death were often hand-tinted in green hues; the 1950s brought an invasion of emerald-blooded space aliens who zapped earthlings with aquamarine rays. And we can't forget the pea-green face of the Wicked Witch in Lynch's favorite film, *The Wizard of Oz* (1939), and the pea-soup vomit of the *Exorcist*'s (1973) Satan-possessed girl; even the army of the dead in 2003's *Lord of the Rings: Return of the King* glow green. So it is devilishly appropriate that the homes of *Dune*'s villains should be tinged with green, and that the Harkonnens, in comparison to the Emperor, should be drowning in the sour shade of bile. Both the Emperor and the Harkonnens plot to destroy our heroes, but Shaddam behaves with sophisticated, courtly grace, while the Baron and his clan commit the cardinal Lynchian sin of being ravenously animalistic.

Smart with native intelligence, imagination, and intuition, Lynch fears the threat that raw, atavistic appetites pose to a carefully cultivated state of mind and spirit. From *The Grandmother* onward, the director cautions us to beware the beast in people: the human being who growls and roars and scratches the earth, who creeps bent low to the ground across a suburban living room, who wears a shiny leather black jacket like an insect's carapace, who feeds ravenously and messily on drugs, sex, and people's souls, eating until their brain is nothing but appetite, like a second mouth.

Frank Herbert's own human-versus-animal oppositional dynamic was a strong link between *Dune*'s author and director. We've already noted how the Reverend Mother Mohiam sneeringly states that Paul will be classed with the animals if he doesn't do well on the black-box pain test, and how the young man bristles with anger at this epithet. Throughout his book, Herbert brands the Harkonnens as being less than human. He has Paul's friend Gurney say of the Baron's nephew, Feyd: "He's no more than a beast you'd spurn with your foot and discard the shoe because it'd been contaminated."[125] And the words which the Baron speaks to his other nephew, Rabban, who's being sent to crush the desert planet into submission, could describe many villainous characters in Lynch's films. "You must be the carnivore. Show no mercy. Never stop. Mercy is a chimera. It can be defeated by the stomach rumbling its hunger, by the throat crying its thirst. You must always be hungry and thirsty. Like me."[126]

Lynch visualizes these words in some of *Dune*'s most striking scenes. If the Harkonnens are abuzz with appetite and dark power, so is their environment. Far from the large-scale, yet homey wooden interiors of the Atreides' Caladan home, the Harkonnens' huge "living room" looks like the impersonal lobby of a municipal building, fabricated of coldly gleaming green walls. Following Lynch's principle of disturbing our sense of secure familiarity, the room has no visible ceiling, like the interior of a box without a top. The walls just end, and we see that the space above is the sunless, eternal night of a planet-sized factory interior, punctuated by the random lightning-flashes of industrial fusions and the incessant roar of machines. The Baron has to yell out his orders over the din, but we know that he would shout even in the midst of a quiet meadow. In *Eraserhead*, poor Henry was dwarfed and oppressed by his industrial-zone milieu. But the Baron, who's so grossly gluttonous and overweight that he's encased in a pale, insect pupa-like suit with suspensor units that float him around the room, gets positively juiced up by the factory atmosphere. Spraying spittle, his face ruddy with pustules and diseased boils, he crows to Feyd and Rabban about his plan to crush the Atreides clan and claim Dune for himself. In an ecstasy of malevolent machination, he punches his suspensor control and floats aloft to the sound of an electrical droning, voluptuously letting dripping black oil from above spatter his face and chest. Then descending, his plump bare feet with their painted toenails obscenely pointed downward, the Baron swoops onto a terrified pubescent youth, and jerks out the boy's "heart plug," making a red arc of blood shoot from his chest. As the Baron caresses the boy's red-splashed face and flecks of blood dot the green wall, Feyd's eyes bulge with vicarious pleasure, Rabban cackles, and the head Harkonnen's inner voice concludes, "This is what I will do to Duke Leto and his family."

Beginning with *The Grandmother*'s Father character, who barked like a dog at his son and mashed the boy's face into his bed-wetted sheets, Lynch's villains have been larger-than-life. As an adult, the director has retained a child's ability to be awestruck by the intense expressions of good and evil in the world, and he has the visual and storytelling acumen to convey his impressions to an audience at full force. With the Baron and his Harkonnen nephews, Lynch gave a provocative new wrinkle to his screen malefactors: "They obviously enjoy their work."[127] They scheme devious strategies and annihilate people with gusto and glee. The Baron has planted a traitor close to Duke Leto, and when Feyd eagerly asks who it is, the grinning, obese head Harkonnen answers with teasing self-delight, "I'm not going to tell you," as though he were a four-year-old playing guessing games. Lynch's bad men aren't career criminals; they are the human psyche's ancient force of darkness walking on two legs, and a frolicsome, jocular manner only enhances their creepiness. As when a character in *Twin Peaks* recites a little ditty about the entity BOB, who possesses innocent people and makes them commit heinous acts: "He is BOB, eager for fun; he wears a smile—everybody run!" The perverse linkage of adult, worldly evil with childish playfulness evokes our childhood fears of schoolyard bullies and those scary strangers our parents said would do unspeakable things to us.

The unspeakable is David Lynch's second language. This man who, even in stifling heat, keeps his collar buttoned against the world, who is painstakingly guarded in interviews and is described by his close friends as "secretive,"[128] has an acute sense of his own physical and psychological freedom and the boundaries that guard it. Lynch has a pattern of trying to master his personal fears, as when he encountered an overwhelmingly urban New York City as a boy. He wanted to flee, but he kept progressing down into the dark tunnel and rode the train. And the director, though terrified of stepping in front of the cameras for anything more than a cameo shot, chose to play the male lead in Tina Rathborne's feature-length *Zelly and Me* (1988). A key fear that Lynch tries to exorcise in his art is the violation and penetration of the protective barriers that keep invading forces at bay. The artist who's fascinated by the inner workings of factories and reproductive plumbing and the dreaming neural networks in our heads shows us how terribly easy it is for the outside to get in. The heart plugs, with which Baron Harkonnen can spill a person's vital blood on a whim, are a Lynchian invention that do not appear in Herbert's book. Throughout recorded history, everyone from the ancient Egyptians to the European alchemists have seen the heart as the sacred center of the human being, the seat of the sun, eternity, and love. Lynch instinctively goes to the deepest sources, and when the Baron pops out the youth's plug, our viscera shudder.

Unfortunately, Lynch's aesthetically and dramatically expressive heart plug idea adds confusion to his narrative. At one point, in the director's script and film, the Baron says, "Everyone here is fitted with one," and indeed even a newly captured Atreides clansman already displays this deadly emblem of the Harkonnen tyrant's power of ultimate control. These small gateways to a person's insides are situated on the upper chest. The Baron's lower chest/big belly are often exposed, but his heart-plug region is covered, so we assume he has one too ("Everyone here"). Perhaps the Harkonnen leader sees his plug as a macho signifier: "See how tough I am; I can wear my vulnerability on my chest, and you still can't touch me as I grind you under my boot." Or, maybe the plug (which suggests a pierced nipple) and its site are an erogenous zone, an element of sex play for the Baron and his slave boys. The problem is that nephew Feyd clearly does *not* sport a plug, and we see Sting's sinewy, semi-nude physique often enough to be sure. Perhaps the De Laurenttis clan, not wanting to present a marred chest to Sting's millions of fans, made Lynch compromise on this point.

The landscape of the Baron's chest becomes important when Paul's little sister, Alia, kills him. Born with the synthesized knowledge of generations of Bene Gesserit Reverend Mothers, the five-year-old gives the Harkonnen a sisterhood slash with a gom jabbar needle, and lets him taste his own sadism by yanking out a wire that burrows into his chest flesh. This quick gesture goes by in a flash, but the action reads as though Alia has jerked out the Baron's heart plug. Yet there's no blood spurting. Previously, we've seen the Baron tap his chest to activate his suspensor system, which now goes haywire, sending him bobbing and spinning around the room until he's sucked out into the vortex of Paul's firestorm military attack, and is finally swallowed by a huge sandworm. The Baron's topsy-turvy flight around the room, as his life ebbs away, recalls *The Grandmother*'s title character's similar trajectory as she's propelled by the whistling air escaping from her lips. In Lynch's art, death is a significant, primal act, and aside from John Merrick's fact-based gentle demise in *The Elephant Man,* the director's characters leave this world emphatically.

Lynch's script says that Alia pulled out the Baron's "suspensor plug,"[129] but since this bit of chest equipment has not been introduced in the film, whereas the heart plugs have, we don't understand why Alia's attack on the Baron's chest doesn't yield blood—so maybe the tyrant and his family, including the pristine-chested Feyd, don't have heart plugs? Just more *Dune* details that add up to bewilderment for the viewer.

While he's still around, the Baron fits into another of Lynch's thematic patterns, the linkage of villainy with homosexuality. Herbert wrote the Harkonnen ruler as a seeker of the male touch, but Lynch stresses the Baron's incest-hinting lustful admiration of Feyd's stripped-down body. And Lynch invented the needle-wielding male technician who tends to the Baron's also-invented facial boils, and who passionately breathes into the Harkonnen's face: "Your skin, like love to me." (Dino De Laurentiis didn't like Lynch's idea of the Baron's diseased face, and the director had to lobby hard to get the livid visage on the screen.) Like an all-male insect colony that can somehow reproduce itself, the Harkonnen hive of Giedi Prime has no females. Lynch introduced a homoerotic shiver to the way *The Elephant Man*'s sideshow keeper Bytes treated his deformed "treasure," alternately caressing his hair and beating him senseless with a cane. In *Dune*, the director ventures deeper into this territory by having the Baron overtly force his attentions on a hapless youth and kill him in a single unholy embrace. The dark dance between villainy and homosexuality swirls through five of Lynch's nine major filmed projects (grouping the *Twin Peaks* TV series and movie as one). The director isn't making fun of gays or portraying stereotypical Hollywood-homosexual characters in his movies, nor saying that if you're gay, you're evil and should be quarantined on your own private island. In *Wild at Heart*, he even has his hero, Sailor, learn a harsh lesson in respecting "homosexuals" after he calls some street toughs "you faggots." Lynch is a man who identifies with misfits, deviants, and outcasts, and humanizes them in his work. But he is also a heterosexual male who loves women, fathers children, and was raised with, and still espouses, true-blue all-American values. The values and image of American security and happiness that he grew up with in the 1950s—Mom and Pop and Junior in their dear little house were direct descendants of (in rock 'n roller Little Richard's phrase) "Adam and Eve, not Adam and Steve."[130]

The United States is considered to be the most homophobic country on earth and it's the men who are most afraid. Raised on romanticized myths about tough, brave, stoical frontier-tamers, American boys try to measure up to the manly John Wayne ideal—and fall far short. Maybe, in their secret hearts, they would agree with writer Ray Bradbury: "We all have love affairs when we are children that are never equaled in our later days. You walk around, you look at clouds, you lie on hills, you hold hands, but you don't even know why you're holding hands—except this is your best pal."[131] As they grow, American males quickly learn that such feelings and expressions are not valued or even tolerated by most of their friends, neighbors, and institutions. So *they* learn not to tolerate their stirrings of tender love for other males, and banish them to the shadows of their psyches. They are he-men, not she-men; that shadow is the Other, not them and their studly fraternity brothers. They are not man-lovers, for you can see how vigorously they reject those who are.

The villains in Lynch's films are abstractions of his fears, multidimensional projections of life elements that haunt him. Though the director may have a touch of the old American garden-variety homophobia, it isn't really the sweet love of one man for another that spooks him, it's the threat of a rough man overpowering him sexually, the raping of his sovereign personal integrity and freedom. The menace of forced, invasive sex prowls through Lynch's world, a danger to both women and men. With his penchant for disturbing our comfortable sense of complacency, Lynch throws sexual threats at us from unexpected angles. In *Eraserhead* and *Wild at Heart*, men who are in love with women are the victims of aggressive sexual advances by their sweetheart's mothers. And in *Blue Velvet*, Frank Booth, whose main role in life is to sexually exploit and terrorize a woman, goes polymorphously perverse as he beats up the film's hero, then kisses him and sings him a soulful song ("in dreams, you're mine"). *Twin Peaks*' metaphysical entity BOB is a male spirit who feeds on women by occupying and animating a male human host perpetrator, but there's a homoerotic charge to the way he slips in and out of the man who unwillingly carries him around inside. Both Frank Booth and BOB are rapacious womanizers, not homosexuals. Their erotic aggression toward men is an assertion of their power over other males, like in a prison pecking order: "Your ass is mine."

Sleep researchers tell us that people in prison, far more than the general population, dream of being tortured. The sleep of the incarcerated is lashed by the inescapable knowledge that their lives are bounded by four walls, the ceiling, and the floor. They live with the certainty that their mobility, one of the key biological definitions of life, is monitored and controlled by the state. And whether or not they express remorse for their crimes by day, at night their dreams are mirrors of atrocity that reflect their own violence back upon them, allowing prisoners' predatory appetites to feed upon themselves.

Lynch often says that his films "allow me to dream."[132] The director doesn't appear to be in prison, but his acute concern over issues of personal freedom has, from the late 1960s onward, caused his film-dreams to focus on people imprisoned and tortured by life. And just when it seems they will never break loose, they find a means of solace and escape. Lynch even managed to fit the factual story of *The Elephant Man* into his tension-then-release pattern, but Frank Herbert's tale of *Dune* was another matter. As we've noted, Paul just doesn't seem to be trapped in his own story. The preordained nature of his course and the sense of optimistic discovery that informs his assumption of heroic stature keeps us from worrying about him. His culmination in triumph has been written in the stars and we've seen those stars all the way through *Dune*. The director's worshipful respect for Herbert's storyline kept him from entrapping Paul in a Lynchian living hell, but he still managed to work a dialogue of pain, a torturous dialectic between the powerful and the victimized, into his film.

In Lynch's world, torture inflicts agony on the mind and feelings as often as it pains the body. The victim is in an inferior position of enforced immobility, and is acted upon by superior forces. The *Grandmother*'s Boy sits at the dinner table, where he endures his parents' rage-filled, assaultive attempts to get him to eat. *Eraserhead*'s Henry sits on the X family's couch and at their dining table, a woebegone martyr to an evening of frozen conversation, a dinner that comes alive on his plate, the sexual hysteria and disturbingly crazy behavior of his jailer-like hosts. *The Elephant Man*'s John Merrick sits on a chair, having been stolen away from his perfumed London gentleman's life and thrust back into the animal stench of his former keeper

Bytes' freak show. Surrounded by paying customers, Bytes orders Merrick to stand up and exhibit himself to the gawkers, but he's too weak and sick of heart to try. Bytes will not be denied, and with club blows and furious commands, makes Merrick feebly rise to a position of physical misery and emotional degradation.

On Dune, after the Harkonnens attack and Duke Leto, Paul, and Jessica are at the Baron's mercy, Lynch again shows his appetite for screen violence and his ability to make us squirm by adding details that Herbert didn't write. All three family members lie drugged and unmoving on tabletops, the Duke being held in a separate chamber from his concubine and son. Lynch evokes our basic human fear of having our breathing stopped by having Feyd crouch over the supine Duke and alternately pinch shut his nostrils and mouth and release them as the captive writhes and gasps for air. The most repulsive torture is reserved for Jessica, who, as she groggily wakes from the bondage of an unwillingly drugged state, finds her limbs tethered and her Voice gagged. The first thing she sees on waking is an image of domineering, brutal male force: a pair of heavy black boots floating above her. The boots reveal themselves to be the Baron's, as he uses his suspensors to gain added height and advantage over her. Jessica is under extreme mental duress. She doesn't know how she got here or if the Duke and Paul are dead, or if she'll be killed in the next instant, especially when the Baron says, "Goodbye, Jessica." Then, to utterly debase his ancestral enemy, Duke Leto, by mortifying Leto's woman and the mother of his heir, the Baron says to Jessica, "I want to spit once on your head." Again Lynch focuses on the head, which in Jessica's case represents the female wisdom and power of the Bene Gesserit sisterhood. We see a gob of spittle dribble from the Baron's puffy lips, and Lynch cuts to Jessica's upturned, black-gagged face as the saliva spatters into the curve between her upper nose and eye. We viscerally register Jessica's involuntary shudder of revulsion, just as we did the jolt of the Baron pulling out the slave boy's heart plug. Can we imagine the perverse charge generated by the Baron's defiling of Jessica if she were actually his daughter? Well, in Herbert's book, she is.

The author shows how Paul's developing powers make him hyper-aware of the past as well as the future. The techniques and historical roster of the Bene Gesserit breeding plan are a sisterhood secret, but Paul is able to discern that, unbeknownst to his mother, the Baron is her father. Which makes Paul the blackguard's grandson and Alia, the Baron's eventual killer, his granddaughter. What irony that Paul, whose father and forefathers have sworn to vanquish the dreaded and reviled Harkonnens, is himself a Harkonnen. In the center of his book, Herbert quotes one of the *Sayings of Muad'Dib*: "What do you despise? By this are you truly known."[133] The idea that what we hate and fear and demonize in the outside world is actually our own shadow, an aspect of our own psyche, is seminal to Lynch's work. The awesome notion that "the Other is me" informs *The Grandmother*, *Eraserhead*, *The Elephant Man*, *Blue Velvet*, *Wild at Heart*, *Twin Peaks*, *Lost Highway*, and *INLAND EMPIRE*. The director's instinct for selecting the most psychologically disturbing viewpoint led him to have Laura Palmer's BOB-possessed father be her incestuous lover and murderer. So why didn't Lynch follow Herbert's lead and reap the added *frisson* of villainy that having the Baron spit on his own daughter and try to extinguish his own grandson would bring to the film?

Lynch, like Paul Atreides, knew the future. He had signed on to direct two *Dune* sequels, which he would adapt from Herbert's *Dune Messiah* (1970) and *Children of Dune* (1976), and was even working on the screenplay for *Dune II* while filming the first installment. He knew that there was plenty of screen time ahead in which to reveal Jessica, Paul, and Alia's connection to the dark Harkonnen bloodline and to show its evil influence on our heroes. Remembering the Herbertian concept that sparked *Dune* into being (beware the superhero and the easy solutions he appears to offer; think for yourself), we note that the author wrote some qualifications to Paul's Absolute Hero status. Herbert stressed Paul's discomfort with the proud and skilled Fremen's over-eagerness to turn off their own minds and let Messiah Muad'Dib chart their course for them. And the author showed that Paul has a taste for vengeful cruelty that he never could have inherited from the humane Duke Leto the Just.

The many viewers of *Dune* who found it clunky and chunky with plot-and-character-establishing information would scarcely believe that Lynch actually did some judicious streamlining of Herbert's opus. Lynch only emphasizes the Bene Gesserit sisters' mental and manipulative powers, highlights the adversarial relationship between Reverend Mother Mohiam and Paul, and doesn't visualize a religious cosmology for the sisters as he did with *The Elephant Man*'s John Merrick. The director also uses few key strokes to characterize the Fremen, stressing their tribal loyalty and the sacredness of water for their physical and spiritual being, and alluding to their worship of the great sandworms. Unfortunately, Lynch's simplification of the Fremen has these instinctively wary guerrillas welcome Paul to their tribe within an absurdly short moment of setting eyes on him. Their hasty acceptance of Paul is supposed to be a measure of their faith in his potentially messianic nature, but the scene rings false.

The primary element that Lynch simplifies in *Dune* is Paul. He is unambiguously good and true and pure of heart; his manifestation of the godhead eclipses any need to detail Bene Gesserit or Fremen spiritual belief systems. The open-palmed right hand that Lynch visualizes in Paul's dreams has become the hand of God: Paul's hand. He is the champion of all that is virtuous within us. *Dune*'s sequels can lead us into the shadows and let us feel the sickening measure of this fine man's fall from grace, the fulfilling of Frank Herbert's foreboding prophecy about the pitfalls of heroism. In the future *Dune* films, Lynch can introduce and embellish the theme of Paul's "terrible purpose,"[134] which Herbert wove into the first *Dune* book, but which the director chose to leave out of his picture. The film ends with Princess Irulan intoning about how "Muad'Dib will bring peace, love, and freedom to the people, and change the face of Dune." Yet readers of the *Dune* saga know that following Paul's deification ceremony he will torch the universe with the firestorm of a jihad, or holy war. Lynch chooses to present Paul with 100 percent positive sincerity, so he gives us no ironic foretaste of Paul's succumbing *"to the lure of the oracle,"*[135] his fixation—contrary to his father's advice about being adaptable to change—"upon a single-track life." A single track that establishes the doctrinaire "Muad'Dib's Pilgrim Church,"[136] brings ecological disaster to Dune, and duplicates the repressive governmental regime of the hated former Emperor Shaddam.

For the sake of brevity, Lynch limits the role of the Emperor's daughter, Princess Irulan, to being the film's beginning and ending narrator—whereas in the book, Paul takes her as his nominal wife out of a politically expedient need to "follow the forms"[137] and have the traditional Great Houses on his side. (Chani will remain the keeper of his heart and the mother of his children.) Setting aside *Eraserhead* Henry's one-night fling with the Beautiful Girl Across the Hall, *Dune* begins Lynch's portrayal of sustained, romantic, sexual love between couples. He shows us Jessica and Duke Leto's poignant head-and-naked shoulders embrace their last night at home before departing for Dune. And he visualizes Paul and Chani's coupling in a resonant image of their two heads together rippling as though reflected in dark water, alternating with wave after wave of sand dunes, the man from the world of water melding with the woman of the sand realm, with the additional connotation of Paul being the one who will bring water to Dune. In dramatic terms, how can a political marriage-of-convenience to Princess Irulan hold a candle to Lynch's belief in Paul and Chani's fires of true passion? A rule of thumb for Lynch's work: de-emphasize the political. "There's no winning in politics. It's something I don't even know a little bit about. Zip!"[138]

Frank Herbert begins and ends his book of *Dune* with the words of women. He traces a narrative arc from Princess Irulan's written *Manual of Muad'Dib* setup of story details to a conversational exchange between

Jessica and Chani. Herbert plays up the irony as Paul's mother tells Chani that though Princess Irulan may marry Paul and write his history, they are the ones who are intimately bound to Paul, the ones who have lived, and helped make, his history.

Lynch crafts no such meaningful linkage between his film's opening and closing moments, as he did with *The Elephant Man*'s mother-in-birth/mother-in-death (eternity) framing scenes. Like Herbert, the director begins with the Princess's introductory prologue, but in Lynch's film she's a semi-anonymous presence, she has no narrative weight, so there's no reason to reflect her in the film's conclusion. Paul's little sister, Alia, has the last words: "For he *is* the Kwisatz Haderach!" As if, for most of the film's long running time, we had any doubt that he was. Narratively, Alia's proclamation is the pay-off answer to all those inner-whispers of "*Is he the one?*" that have chorused throughout the film. Yet, as much as we like Paul, and in spite of all his exertions, it feels as though his triumph is unearned, as though he's just been riding the crosstown bus of destiny's time flow. What intriguing story and character complexities might have resulted if Paul had balked at his fate and fought against the genetic and cosmic mandate to be the Kwisatz Haderach? This Paul-as-rebel theme occurred to Lynch and he filmed Paul saying to his mother, "I curse the day you awakened what I am,"[139] but this defiant moment does not appear in any version of *Dune* that Universal Pictures released.

Visually, Lynch ends *The Grandmother*, *Eraserhead*, and *The Elephant Man* with images of abiding mystery, half-solving riddles of life, death, redemption, and transcendence, but leaving us with pictures that are haunting questions. Lynch often uses his characters' dreams and visions to create a mysterious and mystical mood, but Paul's views of his future seem too prosaic, like previews of coming attractions or reruns of past happenings that will impact his present life. We just don't get the usual Lynchian feeling of actually experiencing deep human and cosmic mysteries, hypnotically floating into precincts that are terrifying and wondrous all at once. If fear is the mind-killer, then *Dune*'s vast, superhuman scale is the extinguisher of Lynch's mesmerizing lyricism. Uncannily, Lynch can find the ineffable in the steam radiator of a confused little man's mundane apartment, a house trailer glowing in the gathering dusk, a red traffic light staining the night, an electric fan turning and turning in a small-town house, the stench of burnt motor oil in an antiseptic empty hospital corridor, the crackle of electricity in the neon light above a morgue examining table, the half-defined dark forms of roadside tumbleweeds as fleeing lovers drive through the night, and the lights coming on in a hotel room after a prolonged literal and spiritual blackout. Lynch brings unimpeachable pictorial beauty and a fine, grave nobility to Paul's story, but the director's deep-delving, neighborhood-scale talents are better suited to investigating the curious doings of that normal, sort-of-strange person across the street than to heralding the galaxy-wide legend of the Master of the Universe.

Lynch does take a poetic leap with the last thing he shows us in *Dune.* We've already seen that, as in the book, the Fremen have vast, secret underground caches of water that they've painstakingly extracted from every slightly moist puff of wind that's blown their way over the centuries. Now that Paul is their all-powerful leader and protector, they can bring the water to the surface, free at last to grow the green paradise they've dreamed of. So, as darkness deepens on the first night of Paul's supremacy, Lynch does something that none of the characters or their storylines really need. Something dear to the hearts of Northwesterners like Lynch and Frank Herbert and Kyle McLachlan. He makes it rain on the desert planet.

Surprisingly enough, Herbert did not appreciate Lynch's concluding rainfall. In his book, Herbert has a "great-grandmother of a storm"[140] accompany Paul and the Fremen's climactic battle with the Harkonnens, and before the fighting starts, Paul says, "It's my storm,"[141] metaphorically linking his burgeoning power with the aroused forces of nature. In his *Dune* script, Lynch has Paul mention the battle-storm, but not refer to it as his personal tempest. However, at the finale of his script, after the battle, Lynch takes Paul's "It's my storm" words literally: "Paul opens his mouth and issues an ever increasing wind,"[142] resulting in a downpour of rain. Realizing that onscreen the image of Paul puffing out a storm might look silly, Lynch filmed Paul slightly parting his lips to a soft wind sound. Then the director poetically links a shot of Paul's Fremen-blue eyes, a big blue wave he sees with his expanded inner vision, and rain cascading down on the Arakeen Palace. (*Dune*'s spice-enhanced blue eyes, a detail from Herbert's book, may have inspired Lynch's decades-long use of the color to signify esoteric, supernatural forces and states of being, from *Twin Peaks: Fire Walk With Me*'s "blue rose," to *Mulholland Drive*'s blue-lit Club Silencio, to a 2003 European Nissan car commercial in which disembodied glossy blue lips float and speak in the sky.) As the author's son, Brian Herbert, recounts, Lynch's Paul-induced rain was too much for Frank Herbert, who wanted Paul's "less godlike, more human qualities"[143] emphasized at the end of *Dune*: Paul should still be a man, not an "omnipotent"[144] being. Two-thirds of the way through *Dune*'s sequel, *Dune Messiah* (1969), Herbert does say that Paul, now the Emperor-god of Arrakis, "ordered"[145] rain to fall. For Herbert, Lynch's *Dune* precipitation was too much, too soon.

Lynch did film Herbert's book-concluding conversation between Jessica and Chani, but he didn't include it in the completed *Dune*. Just as Lynch, in *Twin Peaks: Fire Walk With Me*, disappointed fans of the TV show by leaving out charmingly familiar series elements and plunging into Laura Palmer's darkness, so the director disturbed Frank Herbert by letting his Lynchian muse shape his film's ending.

In Lynch's film, when Paul consumes the Water of Life and gains insight about his and the desert planet's destiny, the director unites Paul, his mother, and sister, in a stunning image. Though Paul is separated in space from Jessica and Alia, each of their bodies sheds a little blood (Paul from his closed eyes, his mother and sister from their mouths) at the same moment. This trinity of flowing red essence, which is not in Herbert's book, viscerally emphasizes the family bond between the three survivors of the House of Leto Atreides, the sharing of powerful esoteric knowledge, and suggests the sacrifice of their humanity as they gain more advanced capacities and sovereignty. It also stresses Paul's connection to the feminine, the wisdom and energies of those who bleed once a month.

Many of Lynch's films are more like cinematic paintings than literary constructs, canvases vibrant with an action-painter's abstract strokes of mood and atmosphere, bold splashes of surging grief, desire, fear, and love. The director was dedicated to the words of Herbert's book, but he was, as much as possible, making a David Lynch film, and the compass of his emotions pointed him toward a last scene that unites Paul, his mother, and sister, last seen apart from each other, leaking blood.

And Lynch, having himself sweated and toiled in the desert for what felt like half a lifetime, knew there was no more resonant concluding action than bringing cooling water to the desert planet. The dreams Lynch gives Paul all contain water, and the director seems to have been stirred by Herbert's passage in which Paul speaks to Stilgar: "My mother's sick with longing for a planet she may never see, where water falls from the sky."[146] In his film's ending, Lynch gives Lady Jessica what she wants. Paul's gift to the mother who gave him life and inner wisdom and power, and to the planet that is now their home, pours down in sheets, as Paul, Jessica, and Alia, together again, witness the wondrous event.

So Lynch got his visual-emphasizing ending and Herbert lost his wordy one. The last page of Lynch's script shows that he originally envisioned an even more personal conclusion that would reflect his devotion to Hindu spirituality. As the rain bathed Arrakis, the director would go to his favorite place: inside the head, deep within the human consciousness. In characteristic "as above, so below" fashion, Lynch would link the water falling from the skies with an ocean in Paul's mind, seen with Paul's inner eye. The scene is drenched in the director's mystical blueness: the word *blue* appears four times in the last five lines of his script.[147] The ocean Lynch sees inside Paul is a poetic, not a literal one, for a golden lotus blooms against the flowing blueness, the Hindu lotus connoting fertility, the realization of potentialities, and the birth of Brahma, creator of the world. In *Dune Messiah*, a Fremen legend speaks of their savior making a metaphoric flower blossom; Lynch makes it a lotus. Lynch's unproduced *Ronnie Rocket* script, which he began in the mid-1970s at the time he discovered Transcendental Meditation and Indian culture, contains another pointedly Hindu image: a "blue lady"[148] with four arms dancing on a lily pad, a progenitor of the Blue-haired Lady who will appear twenty-six years later in *Mulholland Drive*.

In the hectic post-production days of the *Dune* campaign, Lynch took a time-out to teach his daughter, Jennifer, to drive. She recalls, "I was behind the wheel, and he had me go down a peaceful residential side street parallel to a big busy four-lane thoroughfare. Going along, I was very nervous, scared of going on the big road. Before I know it, he has me turn onto it. I'm screaming, 'Dad, Dad!' he's grinning and saying, 'You're doing great, you're doing great'—and there I am, driving. He knew just the right moment to push me off the cliff."[149] Lynch didn't know it, but *Dune* was getting ready to push *him* off a cliff.

Prior to *Dune*'s December 1984 release, Waldenbooks sold an audiotape interview with "two magnificent artists of our time: David Lynch and Frank Herbert."[150] Herbert was "very pleased"[151] with the film Lynch had made of his book. "Some of David's scenes match my imagination precisely, some don't, some are better."[152] Lynch's mindset was decidedly more anxious: "You gotta be stupid or crazy to try this. I live in fear twenty-four hours a day."[153] For Lynch, this is a truly unguarded comment. Thinking about "the films I've loved,"[154] Lynch put his finger on their unique appeal. "They gave me an experience while watching that I never had before anywhere else, ever."[155] Then the man of the Art Life adds what, by implication, is the closest thing to a sales pitch he ever gave: "I would so gladly pay my five dollars to have that experience."[156] He ends his remarks on a positive note. "I hope that's what *Dune* will do. It's four different worlds and a trip through them that you can't experience anywhere else."[157] Lynch was eager to have more *Dune* movies occupy his future years, and Kyle MacLachlan, who would be Paul in all the sequels, changed his Seattle phone number to 547-DUNE.

Merchandisers went into high gear. Herbert's publisher, Berkeley/Putnam, reprinted all his books, and put out nine new titles relating to the film (*Dune Coloring Book*, *Dune Pop-Up Panorama Book*). Every box and piece of mail sent out by the publisher was stamped "The Year of *Dune*."[158] *Dune* toy action figures (including sandworms), T-shirts, posters, games, and record albums were available from coast to coast. School teachers were sent *The World of Dune* teaching kits, *Dune* fan clubs sprouted up, and the additional promotion costs swelled the film project's budget to a variously quoted $50 million to $68 million, an astronomical amount for the 1980s (Lynch says it was $75 million).

Two decades after Frank Herbert wrote *Dune*, its cinematic incarnation was ready to meet the world, but Universal Pictures seemed reluctant to let the media have an advanced peek at it. Rumors began to spread that Frank Price, chairman of MCA/Universal, had screened the film and gravely concluded that viewers were going to have a hard time understanding its complexities, and that it was going to be a major loser for his company. Then the grapevine started buzzing with the news of a screening for theater owners and managers, at which one of the attendees loudly accused Dino De Laurentiis of "making shit like this"[159] and wondered "when are you going to give us a picture we can play that will make some money? Are you trying to kill us?"[160] The negative advance word on *Dune* cast a pall over the film well before its release. In the public mind, *Dune* was damaged goods.

On December 4, 1984, Frank Herbert and Kyle MacLachlan attended a *Dune* screening in Washington, D.C., with President and Mrs. Reagan in attendance. When the lights came up after the final credits, the Reagans said they enjoyed the movie, and one woman ecstatically proclaimed, "Wow! Wow! O, wow!"[161]

A week later, at the Group Health Hospital in Seattle, Herbert took the stage and introduced the film to a full house. "This is for Bev,"[162] he said, and returned to his seat as a standing ovation roared around him. Herbert's wife, Beverly, who helped Frank shape his original *Dune* book, died of lung cancer just months before the film was released. One of her last requests was to have Frank coordinate a benefit advance screening of *Dune* for the hospital that she felt had extended her life. After the film, Herbert's son, Brian, remembers that Frank sat "staring at the screen, transfixed, eyes open wide. An empty popcorn box lay at his feet."[163] He and the audience had been thrilled by the film, and twenty years after *Dune*'s publication it topped the bestseller list ahead of books by Danielle Steele and Stephen King. *Forbes* magazine said that *Dune* might become the first movie to make $1 billion.

Mexican director Alejandro Jodorowsky, who wasn't able to fulfill his dream of turning Herbert's' book into a fourteen-hour movie ten years earlier, was nervous when he sat down to see an advance screening of Lynch's film, feeling that Lynch was the only director who could make a better *Dune* than he could. Jodorowsky was sweating and his stomach was in a knot as the film began, but as the movie progressed his nausea passed and he started to laugh: "I couldn't believe how bad it was. Oh, it was so terrible."[164]

Lynch was not only wearily "*Dune*-ed out"[165] by his three-and-a-half years of production travails, but he had to bear the pressure of the producers' expectation that the film which bore his name above the title was "supposed to make $100 million."[166]

In its first week of release, *Dune* made $6 million. *Beverly Hills Cop*, which came out at the same time, brought in just under $20 million in five days. After five weeks, *Beverly Hills Cop* had amassed over $122 million, while *Dune* had collected $27.4 million. *Beverly Hills Cop* would keep earning and packing in customers, but *Dune* had virtually run out of Americans who wanted to see it. A gargantuan mass of *Dune*-related merchandise was consigned to the remainder bins. The media eagerly enumerated the film's weaknesses. Science fiction fan and Pulitzer Prize–wining film critic Roger Ebert called *Dune* the worst film of the year.

Seven months after the embarrassingly speedy coming and going of *Dune* in America, the film was breaking box-office records in France, West Germany, Italy, Austria, and South Africa. After it had played for a couple of weeks in England, its business actually went up 39 percent, reflecting a surge of good word-of-mouth interest being spread by those who had seen the film.

Still, after all the revenues had been tallied, and all the reviews read, *Dune* was judged to be a disaster. A disaster that, Frank Herbert emphasized, was *created*, that did not have to happen. The author, whose interest in the effect of superheroes on masses of people had inspired *Dune*, was now qualified to write a treatise about how negative publicity and damning prejudgments could sink a major motion picture. Herbert also knew that the two-hours-plus theatrical release version of the film had been cut down from over four hours of original footage, and that those reels of film were under lock and key in the Universal vaults. In the Waldenbooks audio interview, both Herbert and Lynch had been understanding of the need to cut some scenes in order to keep the film "rolling like gangbusters,"[167] as the director put it, and of comparable length to other commercial-market pictures. Now Herbert wondered about how different the audience and critical response might have been if viewers had seen the longer version that he and Lynch had wanted to show them.

In 1988, American TV viewers got a chance to see fifty more minutes of *Dune* than had been screened in theaters, when MCA put together a longer version as a special "television event."[168] When Lynch, a card-carrying member of the Directors Guild of America, got a preview look at how MCA had assembled his footage, he lodged a formal complaint with the Guild. The director did not want to be identified with MCA's cut-and-paste job, and the Guild let him remove his name from it. So when the long version was broadcast, the director's credit read "Alan Smithee," the standard industry pseudonym for aggrieved directors. Lynch was allowed to be creative with the screenplay credit, taking his name out and putting in "Judas Booth," thus showing that he grouped those film-desecrators at MCA with the betrayer of Jesus Christ and the assassin of Abraham Lincoln.

Watching the opening moment of the MCA *Dune*, we can imagine how Lynch must have fumed. Princess Irulan floating in her field of vibrant stars and giving us her introduction has been replaced by a *painted* view of the cosmos, over which a man's voice narrates. The MCA prologue is considerably longer than Lynch's, some six minutes total. Though it is illustrated with a garishly-colored series of painted scenes that violate the film's more muted, elegant hues, the new lead-in does present a depth of information about the characters, locales, and institutions that better equips the viewer to understand the story they are about to witness than does Lynch's short introduction. Right off the bat, though, MCA's prologue also commits a gaffe, saying that it's the year 1092 before the Atreides family leaves for Dune (Lynch's Princess and Frank Herbert say 1091), and later informing us that the family landed on Dune in 1091. And the TV version blatantly insults its audience's observational powers by showing a Fremen character with his blue-within-blue eyes in one scene, and a few shots later presenting him without the blue effect. (After Raffaela De Laurentiis painfully experimented with dyeing her own eyes blue, it was decided that the Fremen's orbs would be tinted by special effects technicians, one frame at a time.)

The added footage of the MCA presentation definitely alters the tone of some sequences. On TV, the narration says nothing about the Bene Gesserit plan to breed a super being until eighteen minutes into the broadcast, unlike Lynch's version, which introduces the Chosen One concept in the first two minutes. Thus on TV, the Emperor's question, "Why does the Spacing Guild want the Duke's son killed?" and the Reverend Mother Mohiam's declaration, "We must investigate this Paul Atreides," which precede talk of a messiah, lend an air of true mystery to the first part of the presentation and delay our intuitive conclusion that Paul is the One. And added dialogue and affectionate gestures show Mohiam exhibiting some of Herbert's "kindness"[169] toward Jessica when she comes to test Paul with the pain box, a sentiment which Lynch edited out to heighten the Reverend Mother's contentious-nemesis status for Paul.

The MCA *Dune* shows us that Lynch left a tender love scene out of his version. The director's film has Jessica and Leto in bed with Jessica grieving about having to leave Caladan for the desert planet. The restored footage reveals that this is a wind-stormy night of special "influences," as Jessica reminds the Duke of her vision of a daughter "conceived in love at a time of parting." We realize that the child will be Alia, but first there has to be a verbal agreement. Full of whispered passion, their heads together on the pillow, Jessica says, "I must be sure that you want it," then entreats, "It has to be tonight." As he begins to kiss her neck, she pauses, listening without even breathing, and in a barely audible voice, ventures, "I didn't hear . . . you in the wind." With a wealth of gentleness, Leto quickly assures her, "I whispered 'yes.'" Then she adds, "And I whispered 'I love you.'" The heat and thoughtfulness of emotion exchanged by these mature lovers who have a grown son is remarkable, and a rebuke to those commentators who accuse Lynch of regressing to a teenage-crush level of romance in his work. This scene is also notable for portraying one of the director's recurring themes: disjointed communication. The young painter who grew up having trouble getting his thoughts across to people with words still feels that verbal communication is a compromise. As Lynch said in 1996 while making *Lost Highway*, "When you talk about things, unless you're a poet, a big thing gets smaller."[170] Not only can the director's beloved "abstractions"[171] of feeling and spirit lose some of their power when spoken, but people in his films have trouble getting each other's verbal messages. We recall *The Elephant Man*'s Dr. Treves hurling question after unanswered question at the silent enigma who wears a hood with a single eyehole. There are the mutating Spacing Guild Navigators in *Dune* who must speak through special microphones to be understood. And Lynch himself playing dual-hearing-aid-wearing Gordon Cole in *Twin Peaks*, thinking that a character talking about a bonsai plant is referring to a Kamikaze pilot in a World II movie saying "Bon-zai!" In the director's 1988 short *The Cowboy and the Frenchman*, a non-English-speaking French tourist wandering through the American West is assumed to be an "alien spy." Jessica and Leto's scene is actually an *allusion* to disjointed verbal communication, for though Jessica speaks of being unable to hear Leto because of the wind, he hadn't actually whispered "yes," nor she "I love you." The couple's actions speak loudly enough for them to understand each other, but the reassuring words are a sweet affirmation of their union. This is a case where, using Lynch's terminology, words made "a small thing get bigger." Maybe the visual artist is more of a verbal poet than he realizes.

If love is one of the throbbing life's-blood veins of Lynch's work, sex and violence are two others. The MCA *Dune* retains Baron Harkonnen's lustful ogling of his nephew Feyd, but eliminates the eroticized brutality of his heart-plug attack upon the hapless slave boy, as well as the Baron's dribbling of spit on Jessica's face. The added TV footage also reveals that Lynch had intended one particular scene, in which Feyd chokes off the drugged Duke Leto's breathing, to have more layers than the theatrical release showed. In theaters, we saw the Baron spit on Jessica, then float around the room in which she and Paul are held captive, then two shots of Feyd in another room smothering Leto and saying, "I wish this was Paul." Viewing the original footage, we see that Lynch intended to arc between the two torture rooms with a resonant, adroit cut from Jessica's close-up face plaintively wondering, "Leto, where *are* you?" to the Duke's unconscious, close-up head being roughly pushed from side to side by Feyd, who uses his captive's ear as a handle. Separated by space, Jessica and Leto's heads are subliminally joined for the edit's moment in time, poignantly recalling their tender pillow-talk positioning (she on the left, he on the right).

Then Dr. Yueh, the seemingly loyal Atreides physician who betrayed the Duke, is brought in to watch Feyd cut off Leto's breath. This is a moment of emotional complexity, for Yueh was of two minds about his dark deed, which has put the Duke into the Harkonnen's hands. He loves Leto and his family, but the Baron killed Yueh's wife. So by stunning the Duke with a drug, fitting him with a poison-gas-spewing tooth and telling him how and when to use it, Yueh has transformed Leto into a living weapon on a suicide mission who, by shooting the gas in the Baron's face, can both avenge Yueh's wife and strike a blow for the Atreides' ancient anti-Harkonnen vendetta. As Yueh watches Feyd sadistically smother Leto, he writhes with suspense (will Feyd kill Leto before the Baron can get within target range?) and remorseful anguish (My Duke, what have I done to you?). Lynch pumps up the drama by flashing his tableau with strobe-like bursts of electrical light (from lightning, in this case), a motif he often uses to jaggedly illuminate scenes of wild emotion and imminent death. The director shows his understanding of the cinematic power of sound as Feyd, enflamed with his sense of control over his captive, cuts off Leto's air. We are intensely aware of Feyd's almost-panting breathing, which is counterpointed against the silent Duke's excruciating lack of breath. Then Lynch mixes in Yueh's self-condemning sobs as Feyd demonically glares at him and the squirming traitor tries to avoid the villain's piercing look. Feyd's eyes beam out a message that will haunt other morally adulterated characters in Lynch's world: "You, too, dabble in darkness, my friend. You're just like me."

Feyd stops his physical torture of Leto by releasing his nose and mouth, but he amplifies Yueh's psychological suffering by tearing the Atreides insignia from the Duke's uniform and stuffing it in the doctor's weeping mouth. It's as though he's being made to eat and digest his own transgression against Leto, to cannibalistically consume his beloved Duke in an unholy communion. This perverse forcing of fabric into a victim's mouth, along with another tortured ear, will figure in *Blue Velvet*.

A black and white zigzag-patterned floor, which appears in Henry's *Eraserhead* apartment lobby and the other-dimensional Red Room of *Twin Peaks*, also shows up in *Dune*'s vault footage. The black-and-white signifies the charged interplay of primal opposites, and the zigzag design is a metaphor for lightning and the force of electricity, which Lynch finds mysterious and preternaturally powerful. Strange things happen at these sites, and *Dune*'s zigzag locus conjures up the sacrosanct spectacle of a young sandworm being sacrificed to yield its blue bile: the Water of Life that enables the Bene Gesserits and Paul Atreides to see the secrets of yesterday and tomorrow. Following the all-systems-are-connected design of Frank Herbert's fictional Dune ecology, the worms, having evolved on a planet where no rain falls, cannot survive in water. So the creatures, which produce the precious spice, are sacrificed in the Fremen's hoarded treasure, water, thus giving forth the metaphorical gold of the desert planet's alchemy, the Water of ultimate revelation.

Still more of Lynch's sensibility is evident in the long version. As when Stilgar the Fremen chief intones over the worm sacrifice, "Mystery of mysteries, the end and the beginning." The Reverend Mother Mohiam says of the mutated Third Stage Guild Navigator, "Their minds are so. . . . They move in strange ways." And Duke Leto, having just arrived on Dune, reads a welcoming message from the Fremen, "A column of smoke by day, a pillar of fire by night." The Duke's comrade responds, "Oh, boy." And Leto adds, "Obscure, at best." Lynch is, of course, the man who loves mysteries, who knows that the end is eternally the beginning, and that something wispy and insubstantial in daylight can burn with all-consuming power in the dark. And the director knows that the world often judges his dreamy creations to be "obscure, at best." Or maybe, as Paul says in Herbert's book, Lynch will someday find "my strangeness accepted as a familiar thing of high value."[172]

It still seems that Lynch is best at directing intimate, rather than mammoth-scale films, and better at discovering the infinite in a small room rather than deploying eight hundred men across a sand dune. But seeing more of the footage he originally shot gives rise to a paradox. For the theatrical cut of *Dune* seems at once too big and jammed with information, and not big enough. If only Lynch could have assembled the version he wanted, which would have explored more rich substrata like the worm sacrifice scene in tandem with telling Paul's story, he would have had an epic that gave the audience room to breathe. There would have been pauses and drifts of time in which the viewer could assimilate and fully appreciate the abundance and wealth of Herbert's—and Lynch's—teeming myths.

One of the things about Herbert's *Dune* that intrigued Lynch was doubles. There are two moons on Dune, Jessica has two children, the Baron has two nephews, Paul has two Fremen names, Jessica and Paul both drink the Water of Life, the Atreides have two homes (Caladan and Dune), the Duke's confidante, Duncan Idaho, pledges his allegiance to both the Atreides and the Fremen, and so it goes. But the director had to leave a couple of rather special twinnings out of the theatrical cut. Moviegoers see Paul kill Feyd in a knife fight, but they don't know that he also fought the Fremen Jamis to the death. The hot-headed Jamis had challenged Paul to test the young man's status as being the One from the messiah legend. Jamis was the first life that Paul had ever taken, and when he wept after his act, the Fremen were deeply moved, for they have trained themselves to not shed their own vital water in tears. Furthermore, Lynch had shot footage emphasizing that both Paul's and Chani's fathers had been killed by the Harkonnens, thus strengthening the bond between the soon-to-be lovers.

Another emotional connection that is augmented with extra footage is the camaraderie between Paul and his father. At an Atreides cabinet strategy meeting, Lynch shows Paul and Leto exchanging glances and smiles over a mutually apprehended moment of humor that no one in the scene verbally acknowledges. Like *The Grandmother's* Boy and his Granny and *Eraserhead's* Henry and his Lady in the Radiator, the Duke and Paul are a Lynchian loving pair who can communicate without a word. Lynch, whose own life is attuned to the ways chaos threatens the integrity of stable systems like individuals and homes and families, plays out this dynamic in his films. House Atreides is certainly another Lynchian home "where things can go wrong."[173] Having watched the extra scenes displaying the unsentimental warmth of affection between father and son, we feel Leto's death with a sharper pain and cheer on his proud, avenging heir with louder applause.

One scene that appears in both the theatrical release and TV version of *Dune* is David Lynch's feature-film debut as an actor. After arriving on the desert planet, Leto and Paul are flown out to observe a spice-mining operation. Seeing that the huge mining machine is about to be devoured by an approaching sandworm, the Duke radios the workers and says, "We'll pick you up; leave your posts immediately." The radio man is played by Lynch, who, with his most ardent, furrowed-browed look of concern, convincingly protests, "But Sire, we can't leave all this spice." And how could Lynch leave so much valuable footage out of his film?

One of the *Sayings of Muad'Dib* that Frank Herbert wrote in *Dune* was like a prophecy about the final shaping of the film: "Dune teaches the attitude of the knife—chopping off what's incomplete and saying: Now it's complete because it ended here."[174] Or is this a De Laurentiis family motto? During the latter editing stage of the film, Lynch said, "I've had this *fear*, the fear of being restricted—in every way."[175] The evidence of the director's art and life affirms this to be one of his cardinal principles. Yet, in the same time period, he maintained that

> I *like* being on a leash. A leash is nothing but a sense of restriction. Right now, I'm doing a very expensive picture. But, even if I was doing a movie on my own, a small picture, I'd still have restrictions. Restrictions are exciting. You need them. It's exciting trying to figure out how to make things work within certain boundaries. If you could just do *anything*, you might not be able to move. Restrictions are great to force you to think, to capture ideas. In that sense, this has been one of the most rewarding experiences I've ever had.[176]

The director sounds about as confused as Henry in *Eraserhead.* Seven years later, in 1991, Lynch had a more clear-eyed take on the theatrical cut of *Dune*: "I said that I liked the film. I convinced myself that I did. But I was a very sick person at the time. I was dying inside. And I didn't realize how much I'd fooled myself during that whole process. It was a terrible, terrible thing. *Dune* is definitely my least favorite film that I've made because I didn't have final cut."[177]

It almost sounds like Lynch had let *Twin Peaks'* demonic entity, BOB, slip inside his mind and make him behave against his will. When the director was growing up, "I would try to smooth things over. I really liked people. It was important to me to be liked."[178] On *Dune*, Lynch's natural tendency to be optimistic about his current project combined with his need for smooth interpersonal relations and the desire to please his bosses. He thought he was doing the right thing by going along with the De Laurentiises' perception of what constituted the complete version of *Dune*, the version that would please audiences. Lynch sadly came to realize that it wasn't just a cutting room problem, a situation in which the director had to shorten his vision of what *Dune* should be, leaving out passages of film that perfectly conveyed the look and mood that sprang from his heart and mind. The fundamental trouble was that so many components of the film, right down to many, many individual shots, were compromised.

> I think the people you are working with have a lot to do, in a subtle way, with the process—that the people you are bouncing ideas off of, the people who are in charge of the film, exert a force on you, and no matter how much you say, "This is my picture, I'm doing exactly what I want," everything is subtly altered a little bit by the people you are working with. They carry it a little bit further when you know that the picture is set up to be commercial. And so I had to almost edit myself before I opened my mouth, and once I opened my mouth, I realized that I was still far away from what their idea of the film was. I was in a strange sort of trap: I wasn't running on my instincts or intuitions. I was second-guessing everything. And I was making a different kind of picture. I was making a picture that I thought was safer. I didn't know I was doing that until a lot later, and, at the time I was doing it, I would take the attitude that if they didn't like a certain thing, I had the option of changing it and making them like it. But they always had to like it. And so that aced out a million possible options. [179]

As he finally concluded, "Dino's a businessman who doesn't want my ideas to interfere with his business."[180] When I recently asked Lynch if he would ever go into the Universal Pictures vault and assemble his definitive version of *Dune*, he indicated that he felt all the bits and pieces of the film were poisoned with compromise: "I'm afraid there isn't a better film there to be put together."[181]

Perhaps some of the director's suppressed resentments and frustrations gave birth to *The Angriest Dog in the World*, his comic strip that began in the *Dune* era and was published in the *L.A. Reader* until the early 1990s. How does David Lynch really feel about restrictions? In a high-contrast black-and-white suburban backyard with a house, lawn, tree, and picket fence, a black dog shaped like a horizontal teardrop is tethered. The house, and the stake that anchors the dog's leash, are on the right, the tree is on the left. Trying to do what comes naturally (urinate on the tree), the dog is at the end of its leash, straining forward as hard as it can. The cartoon balloon above its head is filled with "G r r r r r r r r."[182] To the left of the image is an introduction. "The dog who is so angry he cannot move. He cannot eat. He cannot sleep. He can just barely growl. Bound so tightly with tension and anger, he approaches the state of rigor mortis."[183] Three panels of the four-panel strip are white, daylight scenes of this tableau. The fourth is black with night, into which falls a fang-shaped blot of light from the house window. It's long after dark, but the dog still strains at his leash, his response to the world is still "G r r r r r r r r."[184] Week in and week out, except for a single variation, the panels remain unchanged. What makes each strip unique is the third daylight panel before the nightfall finale, in which a sentence or two balloons out from the house window. Spoken by the house's unseen occupants, the statements may address a lack of ideational consensus: "In this world, there seem to be several theories which differ from one another to a considerable extent."[185] Or an alienated sense of entropy: "It must be clear even to the non-mathematician that the things in this world just don't add up to beans."[186] They may portray an absurdist mini drama about a lack of human compassion: "What are you doing with that gun?" "I'm gonna load it and blow my brains out." "Man, you scared me. . . . For a second I thought you were going to use it on me."[187] Or show a marriage falling apart: "Go ahead and divorce me. You stupid, stinking idiot. I'd get a hell of a lot more out of you than I do now." "Oh yeah? Well?"[188]

The Angriest Dog in the World's dry, minimalist humor arises from the interplay between the weirdly unchanging continuum of the dog in the yard and the fresh pronouncements from within the house. In Lynch's world, houses often represent the head and the faculties of the mind. Here we have the head making intellectual observations and leashing up the body's base animal instincts, which strain to break free. The constrained cur can also be instinctive creator David Lynch, and the leash-holders the De Laurentiises. Lynch has said that he finds humor in human obsessions and the strip's dog certainly is locked in a stasis of emotional engulfment.

Lynch likes to say that after learning to meditate in 1972, the rage that he used to direct "towards those near and dear"[189] just "evaporated."[190] In 1992, he maintained that "the memory of anger is what creates *The Angriest Dog*, not the actual anger any more. I don't know where my anger came from and I don't know where it went, either."[191] The director is uniformly characterized by co-workers, friends, and journalists as being a calm, cool, patient, and empathetic man.

In the fall of 1991, I watched Lynch shoot a scene for *Twin Peaks: Fire Walk With Me* in the small town of Snoqualmie, Washington. This was an intense moment of confrontation between Laura Palmer and her evil-infested father, Leland. Driving in a convertible, they pulled into a gas station garage, stopped the car, and exchanged some highly emotional dialogue. Before the cameras rolled on each take, actress Sheryl Lee actually screamed a few times to work herself into the fever of feeling she was aiming for. Aside from the charged-up actors' speeches, everything else on the set was as quiet as could be. After a number of takes, the whole crew jumped as Lynch's loud nasal twang suddenly cut the air. Furious, he assailed a set dresser who hadn't noticed a certain license plate that was in the shot. "God *damnit!* Didn't you see this Texas plate? Don't you know this film is supposed to be taking place in *Washington State*, not Texas? You've just about ruined a whole fucking day of shooting!"

The Angriest Dog in the World may be lulled by the serene repetitions of Lynch's meditation mantra, but he hasn't quite fallen asleep yet.

During the *Dune* years, Lynch and his wife, Mary, welcomed a new life into the world: their son, Austin, who was born in 1982. A few more years of maturity and financial security seem to have banished the fears of fatherhood that so plagued Lynch in the late 1960s when Jennifer was born, and which fed the nightmarish blossoming of *Eraserhead*.

Lynch installed Mary and Austin in a pleasant country home near Charlottesville, Virginia, just down the road from his old Art Life pal (and Mary's brother) Jack Fisk and his wife, actress Sissy Spacek. Then the director took off for three-and-a-half years to make *Dune*, spending his time in Mexico or his small Westwood apartment in Los Angeles. As the *Dune* project was winding down, Lynch's wife of seven years said, "David makes an *unusual* husband. He's rarely here. What can I say? The guy's wanted to make films from day one, and I'm not going to be the person to stop him. But—he's still *real* interested in painting."[192] (Painting is an activity that Lynch wouldn't have to fly clear across the country to pursue.)

Once again, in Lynch's life there was an irreconcilable tension between his artistic needs and the bonds of caring and responsibility that joined him to his wife and child. The director's second try at marriage seemed tainted by the grievous conclusion to his *Dune* experience.

For the first time in his life, failure seemed to be David Lynch's middle name. The world had judged the *Dune* dream of Frank Herbert, Dino and Raffaella De Laurentiis, and Lynch to be a disastrous disappointment. Not only did the director feel that he had "sold out"[193] his creative muse to give the producers "their sort of film,"[194] but the producers' version of *Dune* had lost a planet-sized chunk of money. There would be no reason for Lynch to attend the Academy Awards this year, as there had been in the triumphant aftermath of *The Elephant Man*.

That Ladder of Success that Lynch had been steadily, confidently climbing seemed like a memory from somebody else's life. In the year following *Dune*'s demise, Lynch did a black-and-white pastel drawing of a man in a black suit falling through space. Having sustained a major wound, a large splash of the man's essence streams out behind him, stressing his plummeting velocity. In the air around him, but too far away to grab and too small to support him, are a few tiny ladders with broken rungs.

Lynch's faith in his filmmaking talents and instincts was deeply shaken. He felt devastated, down and out, dead. But through his pain and self-doubt, some part of his mind saw a small town neighborhood at night, a glowing light bulb, black shadows on a green lawn, a woman's red lips, and Bobby Vinton's song "Blue Velvet" playing far away.

5

NIGHT TOWN

1984–1986
(*Blue Velvet*)

David Lynch was lost. He fastened the top button of his white shirt every morning, but tendrils of panic and confusion snaked their way into his chest. How could his second attempt at sustaining a marriage be slowly withering? How could *Dune* turn out so bad? He couldn't understand how his thoughts and feelings, which he seemed to know so well, could be so at odds with each other, so scrambled. He experienced the way "you can play tricks on your mind, or your mind can play tricks on you, and it keeps you from seeing what's really happening. I don't know."[1]

Lynch continued to reside with Mary and Austin, but his soul needed to find a home. In *The Grandmother*, *Eraserhead*, and *The Elephant Man*, the director provided the flagging, downtrodden spirits of his heroes with a locus of solace and creative growth. Even Paul Atreides, who had to exchange his lush home world for a barren desert, found on Dune a place and people that nurtured and expanded his being. The director needed to go where, as Robert Frost said, "When you go there, they have to take you in."[2] A place where the voices of criticism and failure would fade into the silence of his inner peace. Where he could rediscover the ideas and reveries and sudden insights that had guided him to so much good work in the past, and know that he was following the true and only path of his art.

Lynch once said, "If you cut my father's leash, he'd run straight into the woods,"[3] where he had spent so much time communing with nature and studying the diseases that blighted healthy plants. Well, now the director was free of the leash that, if *Dune* had been successful, would have bound him to the task of making two mega-epic sequels. In his imagination, Lynch joined his father and headed for the trees. His mind dwelt in the Northwest lumbertown realm of his Spokane, Washington, and Sandpoint, Idaho, childhood, in the comforting innocence and security of the 1950s. Lynch didn't want to get on a jet and fly across the country to the actual towns of his youth, for if he saw the real locations "too clearly it would destroy the imaginary picture"[4] that had formed so evocatively in his head. And it would be Dino De Laurentiis, of all people, who would help him go home again.

The mogul had established his De Laurentiis Entertainment Group operation 200 miles south of Lynch, Mary, and Austin's Virginia home, in Wilmington, North Carolina. How perfect that the production family and the director of the calamitous *Dune* would shake hands on another deal in the treacherous hurricane country near Cape Fear. Lynch wasn't afraid to work with Dino again since he had comprehended the lesson of his three-and-a-half-year *Dune* ordeal: "The right of final cut is crucial."[5] Lynch would be getting a much-reduced director's fee and a production budget one-tenth the size of *Dune*'s. But for the first time since *Eraserhead*, he would be filming a story that sprang totally from his own subconscious; he would pick his own crew and actors and locations, and, as when he stood in front of one of his paintings, only he would know when the film was complete, and there it would end.

Lynch's *Dune* producer, Raffaella De Laurentiis (looking back from 2003), realized that due to the monstrous size of the production, the pressures of time and meeting budgets, "David had to give up his creative freedom."[6] (Lynch also had a problem with the way Raffaella, while working on *Dune*, was simultaneously producing Richard Fleischer's *Conan the Destroyer* on nearby Mexican soundstages. Once, when she left Lynch to visit Fleischer, David's face went white with anger.) She remembers that after *Dune* Lynch "said he'd never do another big movie, and he never has. He's been really happy doing smaller films: he's found his niche, the thing he loves doing."[7] *Blue Velvet* would begin (or reinstitute, á la *Eraserhead*) Lynch's felicitous outpouring of human-scale, deeply personal cinema.

Like *Eraserhead*, *Blue Velvet* would be synthesized from the substance of Lynch's life. The director's first feature film was built upon his experience of Philadelphia as an urban hell; his queasiness about procreation and fear of fatherhood and the freedom-restricting responsibilities of family life; his dealing with the fact of his own daughter, Jennifer, being born with clubfeet; and his belief in the powers of spirit and imagination to deliver us from earthly turmoil. *Blue Velvet* would portray the artist's base and lofty obsessions.

Having suffered the dilution and disintegration of his personal vision while toiling on *Dune*, Lynch sighed with relief as he returned to his primal first principles in *Blue Velvet.* The famous, iconic opening image of the film, in which the low-positioned camera looks up at red tulips bobbing against a white picket fence with blue sky beyond is, for former Spokane tyke Lynch, specifically "a child's view"[8] of an archetypal red-white-and-blue American tableau. Not only would Lynch's small-town roots be displayed in his new film, but this very private man would expose, and own up to, one of his own transgressive daydreams. "I always had this fantasy of sneaking into a girl's room, hiding, and observing her through the night."[9]

There have been secrets in the director's films from the earliest days: *The Grandmother*'s Granny hidden up in the attic, where she and the Boy share a clandestine life removed from his abusive parents; *Eraserhead* Henry's intimate bond with the Lady in the Radiator, a private treasure he keeps from his wife; *The Elephant Man*'s sweet and cultured soul, which is masked by the brutish monstrosity of his deformed flesh; and the concealed cosmic truth that *Dune*'s Paul Atreides *is* the prophesied messiah. Secrets aplenty, but, beginning with *Blue Velvet*, Lynch will forcefully make secrets and mysteries the declared subject of his work, something that his characters both live out and talk about. The elusive director, with unconscious self-revelatory humor, acknowledged his fascination with hidden verities in the year of *Blue Velvet.* When asked if he was secretive, the director responded, "That's a possibility, yeah."[10]

Lynch had carried around his fantasy of spying on a girl in her room at night since the early-1970s time of *Eraserhead.* Like a magnet, this story element attracted bits of the director's imagination over the years. Jeffrey, the young man who was the girl-watcher, would see a puzzle piece from a murder mystery in her room. In a field, he would find a severed ear that would take him to the police. He would become involved with the policeman's pure-hearted daughter, then also the darkness-tainted woman he had spied on. He would make a fearsome night journey from innocence to experience, discover that his tranquil town has a noxious underside, battle the forces of evil, and wonder if that evil stirs within his own heart.

Since the creation of *Blue Velvet*'s scenario was a gradual process, Lynch had plenty of time to talk about the project with his cinematographer friend, Fred Elmes. The two had met in 1971 when they attended classes at the American Film Institute's Center for Advanced Film Studies in Beverly Hills, and it was Elmes who had realized on film the evocatively dark-charcoal-and-ebony *Eraserhead* imagery that brooded within Lynch's mind. Lynch and Elmes's hours of *Blue Velvet* talk proceeded from the general to the specific.

What would the town look like? What do people do in this town? What's the feeling in Dorothy's strange apartment? What color makes it strange?

While determining the final shape of his story and its setting, Lynch set about casting *Blue Velvet*'s principal roles. Who better to portray Jeffrey Beaumont, an adventurous youth on the verge of manhood, than Paul Atreides himself: Kyle MacLachlan. *Dune* remained an emblem of negativity in Lynch's mind but the director greatly admired his lead actor's abilities. He felt MacLachlan possessed abundant mental and physical prowess, and projected both spiritual depth and innocence. He also knew that *Blue Velvet*, unlike *Dune*'s ponderous, magisterial narrative, had passages in which MacLachlan's boyish zeal and quirky playfulness could shine through.

The young actor wasn't feeling very frisky after *Dune* came out. The film's failure dissolved his six-picture contract with De Laurentiis, and he fell into a dark depression in which he questioned everything he was doing. Aside from sharing Lynch's post-*Dune* blues, MacLachlan agreed with his friend and director's post-mortem of the *Dune* problem: Given half a chance, studio bosses will fold, spindle, and mutilate your artistic vision. Oliver Stone offered MacLachlan a leading role in the much-anticipated production of *Platoon*, but the actor stayed on Lynch's wavelength and waited for *Blue Velvet* to gear up at its own proper time. The *Platoon* role turned out to be Charlie Sheen's breakout part, but MacLachlan felt that *Blue Velvet*'s Jeffrey made a far more fascinating journey than the comparatively undeveloped lead character of *Platoon*.

Sharing Jeffrey's journey is the immaculate Sandy, police detective's daughter and, for Lynch, "the most beautiful, popular girl in high school."[11] The director rhapsodizes in his inimitable way, "If you wanted to buy a bottle of innocence as a shampoo, you'd buy Sandy."[12] Sweet smelling and pure of heart, Sandy is nonetheless the one who facilitates Jeffrey's Walpurgis Night trip into a lethal small-town netherworld.

MacLachlan's film career was still in its fledgling stage, and he wanted his parents to be involved in the process he was going through, so he gave each of them a copy of Lynch's *Blue Velvet* script. "I wasn't too worried about my dad, but my mom was going through chemotherapy for ovarian cancer. She was very sensitive, very protective, and felt like her baby was getting into something that she was very concerned about. But I trusted David, and I finally said to her, 'You're going to have to be okay with this.' It was about being able to say to her, 'This is really important to me,' and her being okay with that. She died before the film came out, ironically."[13] So for both Jeffrey Beaumont and Kyle MacLachlan, *Blue Velvet* was a maturing, coming-of-age experience of independence from loving parents.

Lynch had talked to just about every young actress in Hollywood and still hadn't found his high school sweetheart. He was growing impatient and frustrated when in walked Laura Dern. Or rather, Dern was sitting on the hallway floor outside the director's office when Lynch dropped an earthy greeting as he hurriedly strode past her, "Hey, I gotta go pee. I'll be right back."[14] As Dern recalls, Lynch's job interview technique was casual as usual. "We talked about everything, from meditation to movies to clothing designers to lumber,"[15] and the director simply "decided he wanted me to be in the movie."[16] Lynch needed his new leading lady and leading man to get to know each other, so he initiated Dern and MacLachlan into one of his favorite rituals of creativity: lunch at Bob's Big Boy.

Sitting in his favorite restaurant, eating the burgers and fries and milkshakes he had loved as a kid in the 1950s, and dreaming about a film that would have the feel of that cherished era, Lynch felt his post-*Dune* malaise start to lift. For years, the artist had sat in this clean, well-lighted place, sketching images and jotting words onto paper napkins, doodlings that became paintings that hung in galleries and collectors' homes, and films that people throughout the world respected. As a boy, Lynch had loved "building forts"[17] with "lots and lots of friends."[18] Now, after being crushed underfoot by the relatively impersonal behemoth that was *Dune*, the artist would, as he did with *Eraserhead*, be building a deeply felt film with a human-scale circle of friends. The burger griddle was hot that day at Bob's, and Dern and MacLachlan sparked some warmth of their own, for their meeting generated a romance as well as one of the most notorious films of the 1980s.

So Lynch had found his Sandy, blonde angel of love and light, but where was Dorothy, the dark lady of pain and sorrow? In a serendipitous way, Dino DeLaurentiis would provide her. One night in New York, Lynch and a male friend were having dinner in Dino's restaurant, Allo Allo (the words the producer uses to answer the phone). Humphrey Bogart was not the nightspot's host, nor was Dooley Wilson playing "As Time Goes By" on the piano, but *Casablanca* was on Lynch's mind as he regarded an uncommonly beautiful woman across the room, who was dining with Dino's wife. "Would you look at her, she could be Ingrid Bergman's daughter,"[19] the awestruck director said to his friend. "You idiot, she *is* Ingrid Bergman's daughter"[20] was not only the reply, but also the answer to what Lynch needed—both as an artist and as a man.

Thirty-three-year-old Isabella Rossellini was indeed the daughter of actress Ingrid Bergman (1915–1982) and Italian film director Roberto Rossellini (1906–1977), whose union had caused one of Hollywood's most notorious scandals. In 1949, Bergman, at the height of her Hollywood success and near sanctification by adoring moviegoers, left America, and her husband and child, to make films with Rossellini in Italy. She divorced her spouse, married Rossellini after becoming pregnant by him, had three children with him (including Isabella), was vilified by the American media, and condemned in the halls of Congress. In the late 1950s, after divorcing Rossellini, Bergman was finally welcomed back by the American public and Hollywood moviemakers.

Isabella Rossellini—who, with her twin sister, Ingrid, was born in 1952—was insulated from the harsh winds of vilification that swirled around her mother. She enjoyed a happy childhood near Rome with lots of friends and pets and games. When it was time for the afternoon siesta she could never fall asleep, so she lay there quietly, daydreaming—sounds like a simpatico playmate for a younger David Lynch. Blessed with her mother's moon-faced beauty (she's been called one of the most lovely women in the history of the world), Isabella began modeling as a teenager, and she let loose her playful spirit performing on the *Saturday Night Live*–like Italian TV comedy *The Other Sunday*, for which she also filmed offbeat reports on notables such as Muhammad Ali and director Martin Scorsese. She was married to Scorsese for three years (1979–1982), acted in *A Matter of Time* (1976), *Il Prato* (1979), and *White Nights* (1985), and became the exclusive spokeswoman and representative image for Lancôme cosmetics. She had another short marriage, to filmmaker Jonathan Wiedemann, with whom she had a daughter, Elettra-Ingrid, in 1983.

Even before meeting Lynch, Rossellini had been swept away by his *Blue Velvet* screenplay. The script opened up "a world of deeper truths,"[21] and courageously portrayed "the reality of abused women, the many layers, the horrible twists, the unclear emotions."[22] The character of Dorothy was an actress's dream: a "beautiful broken doll,"[23] a tarnished-glamour façade that masked "shadings of desperation, helplessness, madness."[24]

Rossellini felt a kinship with the world of Lynch's art, and the director's intuition was quick to recognize her as *Blue Velvet*'s perfect Dorothy. She seemed to embody the very words of his script: the ripe, thirty-something sexuality of a woman who has borne a child, the "beautiful full figure, dark eyes, black thick wavy hair, full red lips."[25] The blooming, ruddy lips that had whispered *Blue Velvet* into being in Lynch's mind were now breathing and speaking before his eyes; Rossellini understood him so well. She saw Lynch as both "serene, happy, well-adjusted,"[26] and obsessed with "the dark side, the inexplicable, the mystery."[27] She marveled at his intuitive ability to tap into the "strange thoughts that we all have"[28] and blast them onto the screen with a "raw, emotional"[29] power.

Isabella would be Dorothy on screen. And, as the director acknowledges, Kyle MacLachlan would, to some degree, be Lynch's surrogate in the film. So while Dorothy leads the innocent Jeffrey into a realm of dark sensual experience, Lynch will find in Rossellini a kindred spirit and a lover who will crystallize his need to move beyond his second marriage.

Now who would Lynch choose to portray Frank Booth? Many Hollywood males, including Robert Loggia (*Prizzi's Honor*) and singer Bobby Vinton (whose "Blue Velvet" song helped inspire Lynch's film), dearly coveted the role. Just as children love to dress up as witches and monsters and devils on Halloween night, actors relish playing villains. Agents of the night, of tears, violence, and death, villains allow actors to express some of their own malevolent impulses, to unburden their souls in a safe, make-believe setting. In turn, members of the audience, in experiencing the actor's and dramatist's art, can recognize their own darkness in the villain's devilishness and then redemptively feel it vanquished and purged by the triumphant hero's killing stroke. Alfred Hitchcock often said that "the stronger, the more colorful the villain, the better the picture."[30] *Blue Velvet* would be powered by the hellish energy and twisted psyche of Frank Booth, a scary and fascinating monster who would stand alongside Norman Bates (Anthony Perkins) of Hitchcock's *Psycho* (1960) as one of the cinema's most unforgettable villains.

But there was a possible Frank Booth who Lynch was curious about, and more than a little afraid of. Dennis Hopper was celebrated as a gifted actor, painter, photographer, and director (*Easy Rider*, 1969), but he was also a notorious holy terror. Hopper had starred and became friends with James Dean in the archetypal teenage-angst film *Rebel Without a Cause* (1955), and he seemed born to live out the moody, sensitive, explosive persona that Dean acted for the cameras. Hopper tangled with director Henry Hathaway while shooting *From Hell to Texas* (1958), forcing Hathaway to shoot eighty-six takes of Hopper saying a few simple lines of dialogue. After fifteen ego-clashing hours, Hathaway yelled at Hopper, "You'll never work in this town again! I guarantee it!"[31]

A rebel for the cause of unbridled free expression, Hopper stormed through life wolfing down booze and drugs, and romancing every starlet he could get his hands on. Hopper's compulsion to maintain a militantly anti-establishment stance kept hurting his career: He couldn't resist alienating the very people who could help him. He wrote, "Jimmy Dean once pulled a switchblade and threatened to murder his director. I follow his style in art and life."[32] Hopper's former wife, Brooke Hayward, recalls, "We'd go to these parties where you'd have the crème de la crème of Hollywood, and he'd tell them that when he ran things heads were going to roll, they'd be in chains."[33]

Lynch calls the 1960s "the decade of change,"[34] an era in which America was divided against itself: young against old, those who hated the Vietnam War against those who supported it, the counterculture against the establishment. While Lynch was painting in his studio, Dennis Hopper was walking with the Reverend Martin Luther King Jr. in the Alabama Freedom March for African American civil rights and being spat on by southern bigots who called him "a nigger-loving Communist."[35]

Though Hopper's mind was engulfed in drugs, rage, and paranoia, the excess and chaos of his life spawned the landmark American film *Easy Rider*, which he directed, co-starred in, and co-wrote. Made for only $350,000, the movie tapped into the archetypal American myth of the promise of the open road, which had been sung by everyone from the first explorers and pioneers to Walt Whitman, Mark Twain, John Steinbeck, and Jack Kerouac. (In 1990, Lynch would join the freedom-loving road chorus with *Wild at Heart*.) Unlike Lynch's artwork, *Easy Rider* was consciously, overtly political, and it expressed the mindset of many baby boomer–generation youth who celebrated peace and free love and railed against the corporate warmongers who were napalming babies in the jungles of Vietnam. The film asks a wrenching question that haunts us today: How can each of us be free and make American the way *we* want it to be without hurting each other and trampling on each other's freedom?

Easy Rider made the brooding Hollywood outsider Dennis Hopper wealthy, famous, and instantly reclassified as "a creative genius."[36] His film changed the face of the movie business. Graying studio executives began catering to the "youth market" by hiring twenty-year-old "do-your-own-thing" filmmakers, and soon even the top-level-management ranks surged with younger blood. Hopper was given free reign to make his magnum opus, *The Last Movie*, a heavy-handed treatise against Hollywood/American imperialism presented in a boldly deconstructed narrative that turned off critics and audiences in droves. Hopper was once again exiled from Hollywood, and his professional and personal life spiraled down into drug addiction and psychotic hallucinations.

Hopper was absolutely out of control, and his friends stepped in and got him into a detoxification program. Actor Dean Stockwell, whose career had been revitalized after he played the traitorous Dr. Yueh in Lynch's *Dune*, was instrumental in helping his comrade stay clean and sober, one day at a time.

Lynch had put Hopper on his first list of possible actors to play Frank Booth, but the director figured that if even half the stories about the legendary rebel and crazy man were true, he'd best leave him alone. Still, he'd heard that Hopper had cleaned up his act in recent months, that his searing talent was no longer compromised by scrambled brain chemistry. One day, the director's phone rang, and Hopper's intense voice declared, "I've got to play this part, David, because I *am* Frank."[37] Impressed and shaken by the actor's unorthodox audition, Lynch said to the assembled cast and crew, "My God, he just told me that he *is* Frank. I don't know what he meant by that. Maybe he's right for the part, but how are we going to have lunch with him?"[38] They decided to risk it.

Once the world saw *Blue Velvet* and experienced the blast-furnace power, frightening, sadistic perversity, and commanding authenticity of Hopper's Frank Booth, word got around about the actor having said "I *am* Frank," and once again he had some explaining to do. "I understand Frank very well. I was known to abuse people when drunk or high, but not exactly in this way. I've also played a lot of sex games, but I'm more a masochist than a sadist."[39] For Brooke Hayward, Frank Booth's behavior was a portrait of "the way you would have seen Dennis behaving" in the 1960s.[40]

Whatever the origin and history of the ferocity that Hopper brought to Frank Booth, Lynch was thrilled to have captured it with his camera. And Hopper was excited to be playing "perhaps the most vicious person who has ever been on the screen."[41] The actor credited Lynch with helping him reach his peak of frenzy: "David kept me up really high, pushing all the time. He insisted I keep playing it at a high level. I love what I do in the film, and I love what David did with me."[42] Hopper admitted that just a few months earlier that he "would have taken cocaine"[43] to achieve his riveting acting effects, but now he was deeply gratified to be enjoying the sober life and drawing upon the pure, unadulterated streams of his talent. Lynch and company learned that having lunch with Dennis was no strain at all.

Hopper's old pal Dean Stockwell rounded out *Blue Velvet*'s cast as the flamingly suave drug dealer Ben, and Lynch completed his technical crew by bringing in his longtime friend and sound-design maestro Alan Splet. Isabella Rossellini's Dorothy would have to sing a couple of nightclub numbers, so the director hired composer Angelo Badalamenti to coach her vocal performances. Lynch had such a positive rapport with the genial, rotund music man that he engaged Badalamenti to score the entire film, thus beginning a creative "marriage" that has included the director's every movie, TV, and stage production through *Mulholland Drive*. Badalamenti wrote a beautiful melody to accompany Jeffrey and Sandy's falling-in-love scene, and Lynch was inspired to pen lyrics for it, thus opening up another avenue of self-expression that the director would pursue in the future. The resulting song, "Mysteries of Love," needed just the right person to sing it, and the ethereal-voiced Julee Cruise was given the job, initiating still another of Lynch's longtime artistic partnerships.

After *Dune*'s ultimately frustrating and dispiriting three-and-a-half years of inflated gigantism, making *Blue Velvet* felt like an intimate homecoming to Lynch. As with *Eraserhead*, the director was working with a smallish budget and an extended family of friends and collaborators, and he knew that the vision that reached the screen would be his alone. He was regaining his creative confidence after the *Dune* debacle, as Kyle MacLachlan recalls, "David was able to say, 'this *Blue Velvet* material comes from me; I'm going to trust that it's right.'"[44] Lynch's *Blue Velvet* dream was unique, but, as with Dennis Hopper's road-tripping *Easy Rider*, it tapped into a primal, potent American myth.

For the country's early, colonizing settlers, America was the frontier, a world of limitless space in which they could move about, build, worship as they pleased, and reap the bounty of their new land. Ordinary, common folks could chart their own course in this rural paradise, but as wave after wave of immigrants washed ashore and industrialized cities began to sprout, the frontier of wide-open promise and possibility kept elusively advancing westward. In 1890, newspapers from coat to coast delivered a traumatic shock to the American psyche: According to the latest census, the frontier was officially and forever closed. As more people jammed into cities, the urban areas expanded their boundaries and crowded out the wild, unsettled land. Cities pulsed to the oppressive beat of machines, and lived on a schedule of mechanized time, rather than the cycles of nature. An alfresco, neighbor-to-neighbor democracy was replaced by institutionalized government, blue skies became sooty gray, and the crime statistics worsened every year.

But there remained enclaves of rural hope and freedom, places that struck a perfect balance between the secure comforts of civilization and the spirited call of the wilderness. Small towns preserved the agrarian pursuits and free-ranging roots of the American experience. Sure, we've got cars and newfangled tractors and telephones, but in our hearts we know that the frontier starts right out where Maple Drive ends. The town grown-ups and kids all know each other, we leave our doors unlocked, and solve little problems in the front-porch twilight and tackle big ones at the town meetings. We jump right in to help in a crisis, but otherwise we let each other be. We're a tight community of ruggedly individualistic souls, not a cheek-by-jowl lonely crowd of strangers rat-racing after the almighty dollar in some skyscraper metropolis. Smelling fresh-cut wheat on the wind is more valuable than all the Mercedes-Benz exhaust fumes in the world.

In the American mind, there is a sun-dappled line of continuity that stretches from the earliest settlers' idealized New England image of a village in the seventeenth-century wilderness; to Sarah Orne Jewett's romanticized *Tales of New England* (1879); to Booth Tarkington's *The Gentleman from Indiana* (1899), whose town is "one, big, jolly family"[45]; to Thornton Wilder's *Our Town* (1938); to the Andy Hardy movies of the 1930s and 1940s; to William Saroyan's *The Human Comedy* (1943); to Norman Rockwell's *Saturday Evening Post* cover illustrations of the 1950s and 1960s; and to the wholesome TV and movie small-town fun of *The Andy Griffith Show, The Waltons, Happy Days, American Graffiti,* and *Back to the Future* of recent decades. The national imagination warms to the idea of small towns as repositories of tranquility, virtue, and bedrock democracy. However, for centuries, our psyches have also conjured dank and shivery forces of fear and evil waiting to seize us in shady, bucolic lanes.

The early Puritan settlers felt that they had found God's country in America, but they brought their Old World Devil with them. The sect had broken away from England's Anglican Church, an institution that, the Puritans believed, was woefully blind to the essentially corrupt nature of human beings and the Christ-ordained biblical manner in which fallen souls should properly worship. The benighted sinners could only attain the bliss of divine grace by strictly following God's written laws. The Puritans were masters at projecting their own dark psychic shadows onto convenient scapegoats. In 1692, Betty Parris, the daughter of sin-and-Satan-obsessed clergyman Samuel Parris, began to position her body in strange postures and speak words that no one could understand. Soon, five of Betty's girlfriends were suffering feverish fits in which it felt like insects were crawling beneath their skin, and seeing visions of wild animals with manlike faces (it seems Lynch's intuitive urge to portray insects and animalistic humans as agents of evil taps into an ancient archetype). The parson's daughter singled out Tituba, a black West Indian slave woman, as their tormentor. Tituba confessed to having made a pact with the Devil, whom she said was a tall man dressed in black who rode through the air on a stick. Witch-hunt hysteria gripped Salem, and the town locked up 150 bedeviled suspects, twenty of whom were put to death before the town's malignant mass-delusion passed.

It wasn't just the newly arrived European Americans who were seeing fearsome apparitions in the deep woods. The indigenous Native Americans, who the newcomers would tragically slaughter and displace from the lands that were the center of their universe, believed that mischievous and maligned spirits dwelled beyond the comforting glow of their cooking fires. In all cultures and eras, the ancient part of our psyches that fears being eaten by something bigger than us, that trembles at the seasonal death of the sun and the sudden, unaccountable deaths of our crops and our tribe-mates, stimulates our imaginations to produce images and scenarios of natural and supernatural predatory dangers. As a serpent slithered into Adam and Eve's garden, agents of darkness crept into even the most idyllic small settlements where human beings dwelled.

Some early European American settlers felt the Native Americans were void of humanity, and conjured up the image of the evil Indian, which the nineteenth-century's James Fenimore Cooper applied so forcefully in *The Last of the Mohicans* (and which he balanced against a host of beneficent and admirable Native Americans).

Caucasians were more than capable of haunting their own wilderness settlements, of course, and the souring of the pastoral dream began in earnest. Mark Twain detailed the emptiness of Mississippi village life in *Huckleberry Finn* (1885) and Edgar Lee Masters' *Spoon River Anthology* (1915) reveals people thwarted and wasted by the repressiveness and hypocrisy of their small-town home. Sherwood Anderson's *Winesburg, Ohio* (1919) examines the lives of misfits whose dreams and gifts are bigger than their narrow-minded little town. In Sinclair Lewis's *Main Street*, the town seems founded on the principle of "dullness made God"[46] and is a place lacking in "beauty and strangeness,"[47] qualities that Lynch sees everywhere. A town in the book (1940) and film (1942) *King's Row* was "a good place to raise your children,"[48] as well as for delving into insanity, murder, suicide, incest, euthanasia, unnecessary amputation, and embezzlement. In Alfred Hitchcock's *Shadow of a Doubt* (1943), chaos comes to sunny Santa Rosa, California, in the form of big-city Uncle Charlie, a killer of women, whose train pulls into the station spewing a monstrous black cloud of smoke as though, Hitchcock says, "the devil is coming to town."[49] So forces of darkness can come from the outside and invade a town, as also happens with the outer space–spawned seed pods of *Invasion of the Body Snatchers* (1956)—or the roots of malevolence can have been here forever, ancient as the roots of grass.

Blue Velvet's sense of lurking darkness is very close to that of Ray Bradbury's 1946 story *The Night*, in which a small-town boy approaches a dreaded ravine. "Here and now, down there in that pit of jungled blackness is suddenly all the evil you will ever know. Evil you will never understand.

All of the nameless things are there. Later, when you have grown you'll be given names to label them. Meaningless syllables to describe the waiting nothingness. Down there in the huddled shadow, among thick trees and trailed vines, lives the odor of decay. Here, at this spot, civilization ceases, reason ends, and a universal evil takes over."[50] Bradbury continues,

> There are a million small towns like this all over the world. Each as dark, as lonely, each as removed, as full of shuddering and wonder. The reedy playing of minor-key violins is the small town's music, with no lights but many shadows. Oh the vast swelling loneliness of them. The secret damp ravines of them. Life is a horror lived in them at night, when at all sides sanity, marriage, children, happiness, are threatened by an ogre called Death.[51]

We hear Bradbury's "reedy . . . minor-key violins"[52] in the sinuous Badalamenti music that accompanies Jeffrey's mystery-seeking night walks around Lumberton. Lynch's devouring insects hidden beneath a perfect lawn are "all the evil you will ever know,"[53] churning beneath giant grass blades as in "that pit of jungled blackness."[54] The nameless "disease" with which men poison Dorothy's psyche and make her want to die is the "meaningless syllables to describe the waiting nothingness."[55] And Jeffrey's town, like all the other towns, is full of "shuddering and wonder,"[56] so much fear and awe that his only response can be to exclaim, "It's a strange world."

In Ray Bradbury's 1920s Waukegan, Illinois, childhood, there was an actual spooky ravine. Visiting it as an adult with grown daughters, he found that this shadow zone was as deep, dark, and mysterious as ever. As Bradbury grew up, his indelible boyhood image of the ravine became the serpent in the small-town garden of his writing. David Lynch also carried with him a childhood image of paradise poisoned. The artist's childhood in the town of Spokane, Washington was

> "Good Times On Our Street." It was beautiful old houses, tree-lined streets, the milkman, building forts, lots and lots of friends. It was a dream world, those droning airplanes, blue skies, picket fences, green grass, cherry trees. Middle America the way it was supposed to be. But then on this cherry tree would be this pitch oozing out, some of it black, some of it yellow, and there were millions and millions of red ants racing all over the sticky pitch, all over the tree. So you see, there's this beautiful world and you just look a little bit closer and it's all red ants.[57]

The wounded tree has a special resonance for Lynch since his father was a research scientist who probed beneath tree bark seeking pockets of invasive disease to study. As the director once said of his daughter, Jennifer, who was launching her fledgling foray into surrealistic filmmaking: "The apple doesn't fall too far from the tree."[58] And like his father, Lynch digs beneath the surface of external appearances to explore deeper realities, the hidden life within all things. The diseased tree convinced young Lynch that "there is a goodness like those blue skies and flowers and stuff, but there is always a force, a sort of wild pain and decay, accompanying everything."[59] These childhood recollections show that the director's consciousness was working on *Blue Velvet* a long, long time before it became a typed script. The bleeding tree is Lynch's Bradbury ravine: that oozing bark, those *ants.*

At the height of *Twin Peaks* mania, *TV Guide* asked Lynch and some other celebrities "what was the most amazing thing that you've ever seen on television."[60] The director replied with scientific precision, "A bunch of tiny spider larvae hatching out of the body of a living fruit fly."[61] This is typical Lynchian thought: an invading predator living within—and living on the consumption of—another living being. The artist's fascination with bugs was born in his boyhood, when Lynch's father took him along on field trips into the deep woods. There, among the trees, young David saw a magical sight: a fully furnished office filled with wall-mounted glass cases containing hundred and hundreds of precisely mounted and labeled insect specimens. Lynch has loved sugary tastes all his life, and the first one he speaks of had eight legs attached to it. "I cooked a beetle on a candle once and ate it. It was very sweet. A lot of sugar in a beetle."[62] No wonder that, as an adult, Lynch would dream of filming Franz Kafka's *Metamorphosis*, the tale of a mild-mannered accountant who discovers that there's a hideous beetleishness stirring within him that wants to emerge and become him—and does. As a student at the American Film Institute, Lynch wrote an unproduced script called *Gardenback* (1970), in which a man's adulterous lust for a woman becomes "an insect"[63] that grows monstrous within the "attic"[64] of his head. The invading ants in the artist's 1990 painting *Ants In My House* are as big as the house. For Lynch, insects are emblems of chaos that ravenously attack his well-ordered world. Creeping and eating and breeding without need for rest, they can devour the timbers of your home, lay eggs in your food, suck your blood, give you diseases, get under your skin, crawl into your ear while you sleep. Insects will indeed assert themselves in *Blue Velvet*, but first Lynch has to get back to the 1950s.

The years in which young David Lynch so carefully observed those ants swarming on his small-town-backyard cherry tree were part of a golden decade. America had saved the free world from the Nazi and Japanese hordes, and the economy was booming. Young families with a single wage-earner could afford a house with all the newest appliances, a car, and vacations. The divorce rate barely registered on a graph, women were pregnant, and people felt no guilt about smoking cigarettes, eating cheese and charbroiled beef, and stomping on the gas pedals of their low-gas-mileage, high-horsepower, V8-powered cars, those big beautiful Detroit vehicles with voluptuous curves to rival Marilyn Monroe's. She and Elvis Presley were the iconic Queen and King of an era that gave birth to rock and roll music, drive-in movies, sleek modern houses, and a playful, future-imagining, optimistic sense of design and color. We weren't involved in any wars that were our fault, schoolkids respectfully minded their teachers, marijuana, cocaine, and heroin were the stuff of pulp fiction, not streetcorner business deals, and we learned our family values from Dr. Spock and TV's *The Adventures of Ozzie and Harriet*, *Leave It To Beaver*, and *Father Knows Best*. The possibility of realizing the age-old, land of plenty American Dream quickened hearts from coast to coast.

For the baby boomers, the largest generation in United States history, the golden dream of the 1950s was soured by the harsh realities of becoming adults in the 1960s. With a burgeoning sense of social conscience, young Americans saw their beloved President Kennedy gunned down and our military involvement in what seemed to be an immoral, genocidal war against Southeast Asians in Vietnam escalate. Carefree playtime was over: You could get drafted and die. Many young men didn't want to fight in a war they didn't believe in, a euphemized "conflict" that their father's generation of 1950s military-industrial, corporate empire-builders had blundered into and were perpetuating and lying about. The cadre of young folk was so big that it spawned its own youth culture, whose folkways were shaped as a reaction against the older generation's traditionalist establishment: To hell with those bland old 1950s, when the civil rights of African Americans and homosexuals were grievously ignored, when witch-hunting Senator Joe McCarthy imagined a Communist hiding under every bed, and people liked blond-wood furniture and pink and turquoise, for God's sake. We're going to stand Ozzie and Harriet on their ears. We're gonna grow our hair long and sleep in the park and ditch school and pop pills and live life instead of punching a time clock like those squares in suits. We're gonna fuck who we want when we want, we're gonna trash the dean's office until the university gives us the curriculum we want, we're gonna march until we stop the war, we're never gonna trust anybody over thirty.

In the 1970s, as the ignoble, soul-killing war finally ground to a halt, the counterculture and their semi-rebellious sympathizers gradually quieted down and were subsumed into mainstream life. The rift between generations narrowed and it became all right to relax and love America again, to embrace Mom and apple pie and hang up that Norman Rockwell print, though it was damnably hard to warmly welcome home the boys who had fought in the jungles. Having faced numerous national traumas in their early adulthoods, the grown-up baby boomers competed fiercely for jobs, realized that their standard of living was never going to even equal that of their parents, became walking definitions of the phrase "stressed out," and began to look back at the 1950s as though that time was a lost secret garden.

From the mid-1970s to the mid-1980s, filmmakers began to portray the 1950s and pre-Kennedy-assassination 1960s with a yearning, misty-eyed reverence: *American Graffiti* (1973), *Grease* (1978), *Back to the Future* (1985), *Peggy Sue Got Married* (1986). Rock musicians, who had stuck it to the establishment throughout the 1960s, now declared that "It's Hip to be Square."[65] Young Americans were being monogamous and having families again, buying cookbooks full of 1950s favorites like Pepsi-Cola cake, and plunking down big money for thirty-year-old blond coffee tables shaped like boomerangs.

Lynch's approach to the 1950s in *Blue Velvet* is very subtle; there are no artifacts in evidence, no wall-to-wall greatest hits soundtrack. He's not climbing aboard some retro-chic bandwagon, nor is he viewing earlier decades from a distanced, ironic, hipper-than-then stance, putting post-modernist quotation marks around the past. The flood of sweet imagery that flows in the film's opening seconds comes straight from Lynch's heart. The artist never repudiated the 1950s over the intervening decades; those weren't protest-song lyrics he was penning on Bob's Big Boy napkins, they were sketches of atomic-age furniture. The loyal Lynch lived by Beach Boy Brian Wilson's words, "Be true to your school,"[66] and he never stopped loving the decade that enveloped his idyllic Spokane, Washington, childhood. The director's earliest days are on his mind as he opens the film with his personal red tulip–white fence–blue sky American flag.

The director has said of his boyhood home life, "Yeah, it was like in the fifties."[67] And his experiences were so glowing that he recalls them in idealized images. "There were a lot of advertisements in magazines where you see a well-dressed woman bringing a pie out of an oven, and a certain smile on her face, or a couple smiling, walking together up to their house, with a picket fence. Those smiles were pretty much all I saw."[68]

In *Blue Velvet*, Lynch accomplishes the feat of suggesting the decade with his characters' attitudes and behavior, the sense of a kindly, mannerly social contract that binds neighbor to neighbor in a network of peace and safety. The director follows his flowers-fence-sky image with two more that show we're in a safe place for children: an old-fashioned fire truck, charming because it's small and coasts down a residential street, with the fireman smiling and waving in slow motion and a white-and-black Dalmatian sitting on the outside running board; and, in slow motion, a gray-haired woman stands in the street at a school crossing, a red stop sign in one hand and gesturing with the other for the parade of little ones to keep progressing across the intersection. Drifting by slowly and joined by gentle dissolves, these images are like dreamy memories of the director's, and our own, American past. Both shots are comforting, for they show us agents who strive to keep destructive forces from harming people, and we're painfully aware that menacing powers are at work in our and Lynch's world: a fire truck would really come in handy in *Wild at Heart* and *Twin Peaks*. There's even the sense that *Blue Velvet*'s toylike fire truck is protecting our childhood innocence and love of playful fun, for the Dalmatian on the running board subliminally reminds us of good ol' Uncle Walt Disney's *101 Dalmatians.* And, speaking of family, Lynch next shows us Mom sipping coffee and watching TV in the living room, and Dad wearing his sunglasses out on the lawn watering the garden with a hose. Everything is in its proper place and all is right with the world.

Looking at Lynch's *Blue Velvet* script, the tone he's attempting is evident in the words on page 1: "clean, sweet, clean, clean happy, safely, gorgeous, happy, sparkling, light."[69] Then things change: "SUDDENLY, dark, GETTING DARKER, ominous, black, LOUD HISSING."[70] The archetypal Lynchian struggle between light and darkness has begun. In his script, the director shows his gift for creating fraught imagery as he writes in a shot in which the lawn-watering man's neighborhood and its sheltering dome of blue sky are reflected in a close-up of his dark glasses, thus tainting the good and cherished world we've seen so far with shadow. However, this image isn't in the director's film: it was probably too technically difficult to get the effect of a whole neighborhood reflected in the dark glasses. Instead, Lynch begins his shift to a darker tone with the two-shot scene in which Mom is watching TV (the television set is one of those 1950s-style big, dark wooden boxes on four legs that stands in the middle of the living room). He cuts from Mom, relaxing on the sofa and lifting her coffee cup to her lips, to a shot of the TV, on which we see a black-and-white close-up of a hand holding a pistol and advancing from right to left (toward Mom) in the TV set frame. Lynch chooses and films the images in this opening montage with such care and precision that we pay rapt attention to the details that our eyes are drinking in. The pistol looms as a major signifier: danger is advancing on Mom; evil has entered the house of *Blue Velvet*. And the garden. Dad's enjoying his watering routine, but his green hose gets caught on a bush, putting a disruptive kink in the water flow. The soundtrack thus far has consisted of Bobby Vinton singing the favorite "Blue Velvet," in which the lead voice speaks of his intense love for a woman in blue velvet, and how their love blossomed, yet she left suddenly, leaving the man with his warm, melancholy memories and a vision of blue velvet seen through the veil of his tears. With the introduction of Dad, Lynch, with sound maestro Alan Splet, lightly mixes in the hissing of the watering hose and, when the kink is added, stresses an unsettling rumbling. Wayward water sprays from the unsound connection between hose and tap, and the rumbling intensifies as the kinked watering system is put under near-bursting pressure. Then, at the moment Bobby Vinton sings "like a flame burning brightly," referring to him and his Blue Lady's lost love, Dad slaps the back of his neck as though he's been bitten by an insect, and falls to the ground, making choking sounds as he's wracked by a massive seizure. Here's "a flame burning brightly" that the fire truck and its smiling fireman could never put out.

In this opening montage, Lynch does an almost subliminal manipulation of sound to further disquiet us. Beginning with the first shot of the tulips and fence, the director cuts to the next shot right on the beat of Bobby Vinton stressing a word or starting the next verse of his song. This harmonious pattern remains unbroken for eight shots/song passages, until the pressured throbbing of Dad's hose shatters the visual-aural rhythm that our senses, without our being consciously aware of it, have grown accustomed to. Once Dad is stricken, Lynch doesn't return to that regular rhythm that's been linked to the preceding happy times in this sequence.

Following Lynch's poetics, the TV gun pointing at Mom is Dad's imminent seizure, the throbbing water in the kinked hose is the blood beginning to burst the vessels in his head. A family and, metaphorically, a town, have been stricken with chaos. A few wooden stakes linked with string, which form the layout for some garden project, define a precisely right-angled, 90-degree-cornered grid pattern on Dad's lawn. Now the lawn's presumptive master lies writhing uncontrollably within the neat, schematic design he tried to impose upon nature.

The next shot in *Blue Velvet*'s opening sequence is one of the most amazing images in Lynch's entire body of work. Dad lies shuddering and gurgling on the ground, his hand rigidly gripping the hose and holding its nozzle near his groin, so it looks like he's peeing or ejaculating into the air. A small orange-and-white dog is standing with its front paws on Dad's thigh, growling and snapping at the water that spurts from the nozzle. With the horizontal man, hose, and dog large in the shot's foreground, a little toddler comes wobbling straight forward toward the incredible spectacle in front of him. With the groin shooting fluid, Lynch foreshadows the wildly unbounded sexual energies that will course through his film. The playful-ominous dog is the classic Lynchian nemesis, the embodiment of unleashed animalistic impulses. The child is, perhaps, the one who was looking up at those beautiful red tulips next to the white fence. Or maybe it's Lynch's memory of himself as a young watcher, taking in the phenomenon of the pained human being trembling on the ground, the beautiful spraying water, the frolicking dog, and learning that, as Jeffrey says later in the film, "It's a strange world."

The opening sequence ends with the famous camera's point-of-view shots of Dad's formerly aimed, now random, water spray falling onto the huge, close-up grass blades; diving through and beneath this jungle, and plunging into a glossy black pool of seething forms, beetles chattering and devouring until the end of time. In a passage of bravura filmmaking, Lynch has taken us from the innocent red tulips of small-town serenity to the hungry, gaping mouth of hell, in two minutes of screen time. And, true to his love of contrasting, balanced dualities, the trip has been exactly one minute light, one minute dark.

Jeffrey Beaumont is the young man who will bridge the worlds of sunshine and shadow, and discover that both realms compose the elemental core of his being. Whereas *Dune*'s Paul Atreides was pursuing a preordained path to self-knowledge which the viewer could surmise before Paul did, Jeffrey and the audience are on equal footing in a world of living mystery. Our minds and senses become as abuzz with alertness as Jeffrey's are. If external and internal Mystery is one of *Blue Velvet*'s key themes, then Family is the other. Lynch's opening montage has introduced us to another of his households with big problems.

Tom Beaumont (Jack Harvey), the lawn-watering man gravely stricken, is Jeffrey's father, and his hospitalization forces his son to leave his college studies and come home to run the small family hardware store. Jeffrey is now the man of the house that he shares with his mother (Priscilla Pointer) and chatty Aunt Barbara (Frances Bay). It's a lot of new responsibility for a youth not that many years past boyhood. And, walking through a vacant lot grass field to see his father after Tom's seizure, Jeffrey does a boyish thing, stopping to throw a rock at a distant shack and some debris. It's a warm spring day but Jeffrey wears what a grown-up male (and David Lynch) would wear, a black suit with an unbuttoned beige-gray shirt (which Lynch would button): his rock-tossing and attire emphasize his boy-man status. Before he heaves his rock, Jeffrey stands for a second with his back to us as he regards the tawny grassland, assuming a pose that Lynch's heroes have exhibited in *The Grandmother*, *The Elephant Man*, and *Dune*. The energy the watcher puts into his looking compels us to tip forward in our seats, as though the scene had a hidden message to tell us. This repeated image is the way Lynch the artist sees himself: a figure in black contemplating a murmuring world. Jeffrey's surroundings will have to speak to him, for his father cannot. At the hospital, Tom Beaumont lies in bed, his head immobilized within a torturous framework of metal rods. Pushing a button device at his throat, he tries to talk, but like many Lynchian characters (and, sometimes, the director himself), he can't get the words out. Father and son can only touch hands and shudder together on the verge of tears. Like all young children, Lynch had troubling thoughts of his parents getting gravely sick or dying, and *Blue Velvet*'s stricken-father theme may reflect an experience Lynch had when he was eight. Walking through his idyllic small-town Idaho neighborhood, Lynch "saw a boy my age sitting in the bushes crying. I didn't know this boy, but I asked him what was wrong, and he said his father died. It just killed me. I didn't know what to say, so I just sat with him for a while."[71]

Lynch continues his doubling ways and has Jeffrey pass by that grass field again. Needing to blow off his sadness, he stops and throws more rocks this time. Jeffrey's first field scene was accompanied by Angelo Badalamenti's low-key jazz music, but now Lynch subtly stresses the human hearing function by filling the soundtrack with the chirping and buzzing of birds and insects (the film's totemic symbols of, respectively, good and evil, innocence and experience). His ears absorbing the sounds of both light and dark forces, Jeffrey makes a discovery that tips his world toward shadowed realms. A human ear lies in the golden grass, as though it is an entryway leading down underground, where dark insect appetites pounce and devour. Lynch now fills our ears with a high insectoid singing as his camera studies this object that he has created with painterly care and detail. The pale ear, roughly severed from a living person, is smudged with a little dirt and some gray-green splotches of decay, a few blackhairs sprout from its top curve, and small brown ants crawl and feed near the central black hearing canal opening. The artist has spoken of the abstract beauty that he sees in objects that consensus reality deems to be repulsive, the way our preconceived associations about an object color our perception of it. "Take an old used Band-Aid in the street. It's got some dirt around the edges and the rubber part has formed some little black balls, and you see the stain of a little blood and some yellow on it, a little ointment. It's in the gutter next to some dirt and a rock and a little twig. If you were to see a photograph of that not knowing what it was, it would be unbelievably beautiful."[72]

Lynch himself no doubt finds the ear aesthetically pleasing, just as he loves rusty, old, moldering factories in real life but, as with the negative, threatening way he portrays heavy industry on the screen, he knows that most viewers will be shocked and frightened by the severed skin and he uses it for that effect. Jeffrey is fascinated by his find; he only winces slightly as he picks up the ear with his fingers and slips it into a paper bag. This is a bold meeting of live and dead flesh that eclipses Jeffrey's more self-protective approach in the script, where he uses a twig to push the ear into his sack. The young man has a need to touch the quick of death as well as life, and his journey has begun.

Lynch the artist knows that our alert senses can transport us into experiences of profound discovery. "If Jeffrey hadn't found the ear, he would have walked on home, and that would've been the end of it. But the ear is like an opening, a little egress into another place, a ticket to another world that he finds."[73] The director gives many of his heroes such tickets. *The Grandmother*'s Boy finds the bag of seeds that will grow his loving Granny, *Eraserhead*'s Henry enters his apartment's radiator and embraces Heavenly Love. When Dr. Treves meets *The Elephant Man*'s John Merrick, both of their lives change, and when Merrick rests his head on his pillow, he merges with his lost mother for eternity. For *Dune*'s Paul Atreides, a spaceship to the desert planet is the first step to becoming Master of the Known Universe. When Sailor and Lula blast off in *Wild at Heart*'s Thunderbird convertible, they begin a high-octane trip through Hell and Heaven. And Laura Palmer's plastic-wrapped corpse leads *Twin Peaks* into deep earthly and cosmic mysteries. Lynch adds that, in *Blue Velvet*, the ear "draws Jeffrey into something he needs to discover and work through."[74] The youth needs to become a man, to experience the hot, wet rawness of sex and violence and evil that's hidden within his chaste little town, to be fully conscious that he has the capacity for both light and darkness within his own soul, and to then resolutely choose the righteous path.

By day, the ear is a naturalistic object that Jeffrey dutifully takes to Detective Williams (George Dickerson) at the Lumberton Police Department, a clue that launches a careful combing of the grass field where Jeffrey found it. There, investigators lay out a gridwork of string lines like the one in the Beaumonts' garden where Jeffrey's father collapsed: human design again trying to put a frame around chaos. But by night, as Jeffrey walks dark neighborhood streets with rustling trees arching overhead, Lynch makes the ear a

A homey home in Lynch's life, and art.

passageway into the youth's primal psychosexual adventures. With his shirt now buttoned to the top like Lynch's, Jeffrey's form dissolves into a shot of the ear, which the camera approaches ever closer, dissolving through the archway of the hearing canal into the curving inner passageway of the organ as the soundtrack roars with a pressurized hissing. Lynch then dissolves this interior penetration into Jeffrey arriving at the arched doorway of Detective Williams' house, where he's welcomed in by Mrs. Williams (Hope Lange). The first thing we see inside the house is the arching, golden oval frame in which rests the cherished smiling photograph of the Williamses' golden daughter, Sandy. These five shots, subliminally joined by the echoing arched forms, are a hypnotic example of the way Lynch wants to "float"[75] us into the experience of his films, to carry us on a flow of imagery that feels like our own dream.

Like Lynch's father, Donald, Detective Williams has a homey inner-sanctum office, and he ushers Jeffrey in. Jeffrey may have gained access to Williams' private domain, but the policeman says he can't say anything more about the case until it's "sewed up." The youth literally twitches with curiosity and, carried away by his romantic view of crime fighting, says it must be "great" to be a defective, but the seasoned cop, who's actually seen the worst the world has to offer, somberly adds, "And horrible, too." The message to Jeffrey, courteously delivered: Leave this dirty business to the big boys.

Jeffrey, mannerly as any well-brought-up kid in a 1950s TV show, says goodnight to the Williamses and asks them to say "hi" to Sandy.

Once again, as in the grass field, Lynch puts Jeffrey in the position of "if he hadn't found the ear, he would have walked on home, and that would've been the end of it,"[76] but the severed flesh keeps echoing. As the youth leaves the Williamses' door and heads up the sidewalk, he hears the night speak to him in a disembodied female voice: "Are you the one who found the ear?" The voice is behind Jeffrey, and he turns toward it with the same motion that Henry in *Eraserhead* turned to find his love, the Lady in the Radiator, in a transcendent flood of light. Jeffrey sees only blackness and the hint of a weeping willow branch stirring upper left. Then, in one of Lynch's most gorgeous images, a faint, pale form materializes out of the dark, getting larger and taking on color as it approaches and becomes the teen angel, Sandy, golden hair falling down her long neck, bared collarbone framed by a pink dress, an unsmiling wisdom on her slightly parted lips. Lynch frames Sandy's approach from the waist up so that we don't see her walking; she truly does float into Jeffrey's life. The director has spoken of his admiration for the great American painter Edward Hopper (1882–1967), and the way that Lynch and his cinematographer Frederick Elmes make Sandy positively glow against the night reflects Hopper's technique of front-lighting objects and people that are standing before a looming darkness. Elmes's color photography for Lynch's films has occasionally been criticized by prosaic viewers for inconsistency: Some passages are super bright, others almost indiscernibly murky. The reason, of course, is that these shifting tonal moods create the atmosphere that the director is after. As Elmes once put it, "David and I spend a lot of time figuring out how dark is dark."[77]

Jeffrey answers Sandy's "Did you find the ear?" with a question of his own: "How did you know?" She continues to float in his mind as an agent of mystery as she replies, "I just know, that's all," and steps ahead on the sidewalk. Jeffrey, of course, follows her lead. They both acknowledge that her father said not to talk about the case, but the allure of the unknown makes them circumvent the rules. Lynch builds on the deadpan severed-ear humor that Detective Williams unconsciously expressed ("when the case is sewed up") by having Sandy say about the case, "I don't know much but bits and pieces; I hear things." Sandy, like lead characters in *The Grandmother*, *Eraserhead*, *The Elephant Man*, and *Twin Peaks*, has an upstairs bedroom. For most of these people, the house's upper regions, which symbolically correspond to the mind's higher consciousness, are places of deliverance from earthly trials, though *Twin Peaks'* Laura Palmer endures abusive terrors up under the eaves. Sandy's room gives her knowledge; it's situated above her father's office, so police-business details filter up through the floor. In Lynch's world, sometimes two people in a room can't make out each other's words, but on occasion the invisible can speak.

The communication between Sandy and Jeffrey is certainly flowing freely; there's an immediate bond of sympathy and trust between these two solitary nightwalkers who have found each other. She tells him that she keeps hearing her father mention a woman singer who lives in an apartment near Jeffrey's house and the field where he found the ear. To this moment, Jeffrey's equation of mystery had been simple and inert, with no place to go: It was just him and the ear. Suddenly, the beautiful woman at his side has given the equation a thrilling triangulation that vivifies it with open possibility; now it's Jeffrey, the ear, and this nameless singer. He is moved to sigh with the night wind, "It's a strange world, isn't it," and Sandy, his perfect complement, answers, "Yeah." As with a couple who's been together a long time, she anticipates his next thought: "You want to see the building where she lives, don't you?"

Reflecting the time-honored American myth that equates urban precincts with evil, Sandy and Jeffrey's night walk takes on an ominous air as they leave her tree-lined, homey street for the wide concrete boulevard downtown. He protectively takes her arm as a slinky black 1950s car cruises by and men leer from the windows, "Hey babe, hey." This is the seedy Lincoln neighborhood, the zone that Jeffrey's parents have warned him to stay away from all his life. Sandy points out the singer's forlorn, old brick apartment building and turns to go. "Come on," she admonishes, but Jeffrey stands transfixed, staring at the building for many moments as Lynch holds a traffic light on red in front of the dilapidated structure, a motif warning of infernal danger that he will memorably repeat in *Twin Peaks*. Sandy is intrigued by mysteries up to a point, but she knows when to pull back, her sense of self-preservation is strong. Jeffrey, on the other hand, is obsessed; like so many of Lynch's characters, he will risk his body and soul in order to learn the secrets that the night holds.

Back on home turf, heading toward the Williamses', Jeffrey lightens up, spouting a bit of Lynchian grotesquerie as he recalls "a kid I used to know who had the biggest tongue in the world." Sandy, who's in perfect synchrony with Jeffrey's moods, laughs. Then she turns solemn with him as he laments, "All my friends are gone," and we remember that this boy's father lies near death. Lynch has talked about a giddy feeling he's had while "saying goofy, corny things"[78] to a woman he's fond of late at night. Jeffrey suddenly asks, "Do you know the Chicken Walk?" and parades up and down the sidewalk with his knees bent low and his torso and head held unnaturally stiff. Sandy breaks up in laughter and Jeffrey touches her shoulder for a second in affection. Lynch ends his masterful night-walk sequence with a moody image worthy of an Edward Hopper painting. From far away we see the small forms of the boy dressed in black and white and the girl in pink strolling slowly under the canopy of dark trees, we hear their faint laughter on the wind, the spark of their shared joy clouded by the mournful low moan of a far-off foghorn.

Even in broad daylight, filling in for his father at their bright and clean family hardware store, Jeffrey finds mysteries. Working with him at the store are two older African American gentlemen who've been there forever. They radiate affection for Jeffrey and he just calls them Double Ed, since they always walk and stand together. One of the men is blind but he can tell you which shelf the overalls are on and correctly ring up cash register sales. When Jeffrey holds up four fingers and asks, "How many?," the blind man instantly answers, "Four." With an awestruck grin, the youth replies, "I still don't know how you do that!" In Lynch's script, there was just one Ed, who could see just fine. Aside from showing the director's love of twinning and doubling, the film's Double Ed scene projects his and Jeffrey's need for some mysteries to remain unsolved so that they retain their preternatural power. Like Lynch, Jeffrey wants to remain a little naive about some things; he seems to be willing himself not to guess Double Ed's secret. Even though we in the audience see the two men facing us from Jeffrey's point of view, it's pretty easy to realize that all sighted Ed (Leonard Watkins) has to do is tap blind Ed (Moses Gibson) four times on the back.

Jeffrey can cruise on past Double Ed's puzzle but he's compelled to burrow deeper into the ear. He plans to put on those store overalls, grab an insect-exterminating sprayer, tell the woman singer he's from pest control, jimmy a window in her place while he's spraying, and sneak back in at night to search for clues. On the surface, he seems to be an idealistic Hardy Boys–style junior crimefighter, but he isn't playing detective primarily to help Williams or impress Sandy: Subconsciously he's on a profoundly personal quest, an involved process that will make him a fully integrated human being.

Sandy is part of Jeffrey's plan, and he verbally pulls her away from her high school girlfriends and takes her to the local diner, Arline's (as she leaves with him, she tells her friends not to mention this trip to her boyfriend, Mike). Symmetrically left and right of Arline's front door are red drapes drawn back like theatrical curtains. These draped fabrics, which Lynch also features in *The Grandmother*, *Eraserhead*, *The Elephant Man*, and *Twin Peaks*, frame narrative details and concentrate the audience's focus. They also alert us to intermixtures of reality and illusion. Lynch echoes the entranceway's symmetry by placing Sandy on the left and Jeffrey on the right in a booth, each sipping a Coke. The stage is set for Jeffrey to convince Sandy to help him, and his words recall *Dune*'s Duke Leto's words to his son, Paul, which Lynch had screenwritten from Frank Herbert's novel. Lynch had Leto say, "But a person needs new experiences. They jar something deep inside: the longing to grow. Without change, something sleeps inside us, and seldom awakens. The sleeper must awaken."[79] Lynch pares this down for Jeffrey: "There are opportunities in life for gaining knowledge and experience. Sometimes it's necessary to take a risk." Jeffrey is gathering steam to take some major chances, and through them Lynch can live out hazardous fantasies through his art, as can we, the viewers, gaining some measure of Jeffrey's self-knowledge.

Lynch then has Jeffrey speak the director's own adolescent fantasy virtually verbatim. "I could learn a lot by getting into that woman's apartment. You know, sneak in, hide, and observe." Sandy shows how much she cares about Jeffrey by speaking right up when his notion violates her empathetic sense of his safety: "Are you crazy? This is too dangerous, she could be involved with murder!" But like an artist pursuing an alluring, dark muse, Jeffrey won't be deterred by mundane, cautionary worries. Lynch wants us to share Sandy's rational, common-sense concerns, but he, and we, are most interested in pursuing Jeffrey's imaginative scheme. Like *Dune*'s Bene Gesserit Reverend Mother Mohiam, Sandy's attempts to curb male initiative and enterprise will be overridden. The prevailing males in both films are played by Lynch's screen alter ego, Kyle MacLachlan, and there's the sense that we're witnessing some of the artist's uncensored psychodrama, his own obsessive pursuit of creative endeavors despite the curtailing entreaties of wives, friends, and business advisors. Perhaps Sandy is a version of Lynch's ideal woman, expressing her heartfelt feelings with spirit, then going along with his plan. Jeffrey wins Sandy over by saying, "No one will suspect us because no one would think two people like us would be crazy enough to do something like this." This awareness of their square, straight-arrow image in the community bespeaks Lynch's own understanding of the persona that the media have created for him: a friendly, grinning, Jimmy Stewart and Eagle Scout type who's secretly a crazed, far-out artist. Lynch is attuned to the multivalenced nature of things, the interplay between what is and what appears to be. We recall that Jeffrey told Detective Williams that he found the ear "behind Vista," referring to a street or neighborhood. The ear is the youth's mysterious ticket-to-ride, a portion of the secret world hidden behind the vista of Lumberton's wholesome facade, and Jeffrey wants to see the whole show.

Lynch, in his opening montage, symbolized the town's hidden world with the seething black insects and their ravenous, endless cycle of carnage and copulation. Jeffrey, dressed in his exterminating gear, enters the Deep River Apartments (deep waters being an ancient symbol for the human subconscious mind). Upon crossing the threshold, he hears the insectoid buzzing and humming of a "no vacancy" sign that's shorting out: This is indeed the entrance to the netherworld. The low-rent building's elevator is out of order, so he climbs seven flights of exterior stairs, as Lynch gives us the feeling that Jeffrey is beginning the exertions of an arduous quest.

Up the stairs, down the gloomy dark-gray hallway, Jeffrey travels deeper into the ear. The youth gets no response when he knocks on Dorothy's door, so that Lynch can build to her dramatic entrance into the film. The door suddenly cracks open the width of a safety chain, a vertical shaft of light falling on the ripe, red lips of the director's original *Blue Velvet* vision, and the anxious eyes of a woman teetering on the edge of fear. She spits out a foreign-accented challenge: "Yes, what do you want?," but Jeffrey's role-playing gets him past her defenses.

The exotic strangeness of Dorothy's accent is matched by the look of her living room, which is unlike anything Jeffrey has ever seen. It's as though his penetration of the ear canal has brought him deep inside a human body, or mind, where the walls and floor are dark red and the curve of an armless couch seems to have grown out of the wall like a fleshy organ. And, in contrast to the normal-looking plants that grow in the Beaumonts' garden, there are two green erections of frond foliage shooting up from unnaturally tiny pots against the red walls. These phallic plants reflect the surrealistically part-plant, part-animal growths that sprouted in Lynch's early animated film passages (*The Alphabet*, *The Grandmother*).

As the ants crawling on the newfound ear and the bug-like buzzing lobby sign indicate, Jeffrey's pursuit of the ear's mystery will lead him into the zone of raw animal impulses, a fearsome region that will both surround and inhabit him. As he sprays Dorothy's kitchen, he bends over at the waist, a creeping-animal posture that Lynch will assign to the feral BOB of *Twin*

Peaks. There's a knock at the door, which Jeffrey expects to be Sandy posing as a Jehovah's Witness to divert Dorothy's attention. But instead there's a big man in a canary-yellow sports coat, who takes a good, hard look at the youth. To explain Jeffrey's presence, Dorothy says, "It's only the bug man." This line wasn't in Lynch's original script, so the director must have decided during filming to add this phrase that describes Jeffrey's pretend occupation, his low-bending posture and dark, beetle-like jumpsuit that covers him from feet to Adam's apple, and his psychological metamorphosis into a darker self.

While Dorothy bids goodbye to the Yellow Man, Jeffrey spies her house key and pockets it. Back outside, Sandy apologizes to him for not coming to the door because she figured the Yellow Man did her diversionary job for her. That night, she lies to her boyfriend and father in order to be with Jeffrey as he plans his next step. At the Slow Club, Jeffrey, in true Lynchian food-and-beverage-appreciation style, rhapsodizes about the Heineken beer he's drinking. He and Sandy watch Dorothy Vallens sing two numbers, the stage set in what will be the standard for Lynch's performance scenes: red curtain backdrop with blue spotlighting. Indeed, the vertical folds in the Slow Club's curtains, and the white light behind them emphasizing the fabric's ruddy membranes, anticipate *Twin Peaks'* iconic Red Room. Starting out in what seemed to be the 1950s, the film has mixed in 1970s cars, 1980s computers, and now Dorothy sings into a 1930s art deco microphone. In *Blue Velvet*, Lynch is pioneering a subtle stylistic motif that other filmmakers will try to copy; he's giving us an evocative dream time, an ambiguous mix of various decade signifiers in which we float around, subtly disconnected from the waking realities of our own time-bound lives.

As Dorothy sings "Blue Velvet" on stage, we notice an incongruous talisman of bestial energies at her feet: the wicked six-foot-wide horns of a longhorn steer. Dorothy is not herself essentially animalistic, but she is a body in which bestial men deposit their impulses, debasing her emotions into a desperate sadness that's like an unsatisfied hunger. Sometimes Lynch's character's names are literal descriptions (The Man in the Planet, The Lady in the Radiator, The Blue-Haired Lady), but Dorothy's name at the Slow Club, The Blue Lady, refers more to her hidden bruised soul and midnight-stained grief than to her blue eyeshadow makeup and the light that bathes her on stage. She sings her last number, whose lyrics are Lynch's: "Shadows fall so blue; as lonely as a blue, blue star." The director then accomplishes another of his elegant, expressive scene transitions by taking the last musical note of Dorothy's lament and flowing into a progression of descending musical chords, which dissolve from the singer in shadow on stage to Sandy and Jeffrey driving into their nocturnal mission of mystery. The falling chords not only give a sinister gravity to the evening and Sandy's worried look, but the music's linkage to Dorothy is a prelude to her wish to end her miserable life by plunging from a great height. In his script, Lynch alludes to the possibility of Dorothy leaping from her apartment roof, but in the film he condenses her feeling of a panicky plunge into the abyss to a scream at street level: "I'm falling!"

In Lynch's aesthetic, the two primal modes of moving through space are floating and falling. Floating is the positive pole. The artist has spoken of how he "fishes"[80] for ideas and intuitions that "float"[81] by, and how he tries to transfix and float the viewer into his films and paintings and musical/song compositions. Floating figures are found in *Eraserhead*, *The Elephant Man*, *Dune*, *Wild at Heart*, *Industrial Symphony No. 1*, *Twin Peaks: Fire Walk With Me*, various paintings, drawings, photographs, and song lyrics ("You and I float in love and kiss forever,"[82] "We're floating as one"[83]). Falling is the negative pole. *The Grandmother*'s Boy falls over after his granny dies; *Industrial Symphony No. 1*'s bereft heroine, who floats singing 60 feet above the Brooklyn Academy of Music's stage, suddenly falls; figures plunge in drawings; the doomed Laura Palmer of *Fire Walk With Me* speaks of "falling forever until you burst into flame"; and song lyrics bemoan "Falling through this night alone."[84] Floating and falling are the physical equivalents of those heightened states of being and emotion that fascinate Lynch: times when our feet aren't firmly on the ground.

Sandy can feel the darkness pulling at Jeffrey, and she worries that he's going to fall. Parked in front of Dorothy's apartment, she regrets having told him the police-case details that got them to this moment, but she will help him by honking the car horn four times when Dorothy arrives, so Jeffrey will know she'll soon enter her flat. Just as Jeffrey's declaration, "It's a strange world," crystallizes the viewpoint of both *Blue Velvet* and the man who wrote and directed it, what Sandy now says to Jeffrey applies to both him and David Lynch. "I don't know if you're a detective or a pervert," she wonders, as Jeffrey heads up to hide in a strange woman's room.

Lynch's films delve deeply into disturbing realms of human emotion and behavior. The director is a detective scanning the psyche's netherworld for clues to the big mysteries of existence and death, but the fierce persistence of his fascination with the darkest veins of fear and desire seem sick and perverse to some viewers and critics. What really gets under our skin about Lynch's work, and causes some to demonize him, is the realization, if only subconsciously, that we ourselves might be capable of the thoughts and actions the director depicts so intensely. Even if we can't admit this, we like to watch.

We who view movies are voyeurs, we sit in the dark gazing at the often intimate behaviors of (albeit) fictional people who don't know we're looking at them. Of course, we're actually watching actors playing characters, but the aesthetic contract enforces the feeling that we're indulging the privilege of spying on other people's lives. While voyeurism is the subtext of the movie-viewing experience, some films consciously acknowledge the concept in notable scenes (*Psycho*) or extended thematic treatments (*Rear Window*, *Peeping Tom*). The watchers in these films are looking at sex and death, the twin aspects of human experience most guarded by societal taboos: Once again, the movies fulfill our secret desires, our urge to see all that human beings can do. Jeffrey wants to gather clues in Dorothy's apartment and help solve a crime, but, we're sure, he (and we) also want to see her naked. Perversion denotes abnormality, and the wish to see another's bared flesh is not unusual. It's the context of Jeffrey's viewing that will be transgressive: He's an uninvited, hidden spectator whose gaze will have power over the one that he's looking at.

To Sandy's "detective or pervert" musing, Jeffrey replies, "That's for me to know and you to find out." In Lynch's original script, we would already know of the youth's lascivious leanings by now. There was to be a scene early on in the film before Jeffrey was called home from college. Hiding in the shadows, the youth watched a male student "trying to rape his girlfriend. She is crying and telling him to stop but the boy keeps forcing her down toward the ground. . . . The boy is now hurting the girl."[85] Only when Jeffrey hears his off-camera friends calling for him does he (still concealed by the darkness) yell at the rapist: "Hey, shithead. Leave her alone. . . . Don't force girls!,"[86] at which point the boy releases the girl. Watching this scene, we would have noted that Jeffrey's fascination with what he was viewing allowed the crime to progress, and it was a reminder of outside social sanctions (his calling friends) that prompted his intervention. Without interruption, how long would he have watched? Though this is clearly a strong scene, Lynch chose to leave it out. So when we meet Jeffrey in the film, he's absolutely identified with the benign and wholesome small-town universe, against which his gradual descent into the ear's mystery and his own sexual and spiritual darkness will provide a more dramatically potent contrast.

Beginning with the wildly feeding beetles in *Blue Velvet*'s opening montage, Lynch has linked rampant animal appetites with primal evil, and as Jeffrey began to penetrate Lumberton's netherworld, he was called "the bug man" by one of this sinister realm's denizens, Dorothy, who ought to know one when she sees one. Now, as the youth breaks the law to enter her apartment, his appetites, and his penis, immediately get him in trouble. Because of all the Heineken beer he consumed at the Slow Club, Jeffrey is loudly peeing into Dorothy's toilet and flushing it when Sandy gives her warning beeps that the singer has entered the building. Jeffrey's cut off from Sandy's lifeline in this place; he doesn't hear her warning. The youth, in detective fashion, is starting to carefully examine Dorothy's dressing table for clues when she starts to open her front door. He dives for her living room closet where, hidden inside and peering out through its louvered doors, he looks more the pervert, recalling the image in *Psycho* where Anthony Perkins peeped through the wall hole at the undressing Janet Leigh. Lynch has realized his adolescent fantasy on film: His cinematic alter ego is secretly watching a woman in her room at night. Jeffrey provides a textbook example of the nefarious "male gaze" that feminist critics deplore. A man has written his visual sexual reverie into a film, shot by a male cinematographer, in which a man looks at an unpersonalized woman as a sexual object, and then a higher percentage of males than females watch the film. These are the facts in the case, but Lynch's truth is more complex and balanced than his detractors care to admit, or notice.

Lynch may be visualizing his teenage fantasy, but he presents Jeffrey's view of Dorothy stripping to her bra and panties and doffing her performance wig without a hint of erotic spark. She arouses no prurient interest as she has a desperate phone conversation with someone named Frank and, burdened with spiritual malaise, retreats to the bathroom where, far away from the camera, she quickly strips in rear view while standing straight up. Not only is the leering male viewpoint absent from this scene, but Lynch turns the traditional male power position topsy-turvy. For Dorothy hears (ears again) a rustle in her closet and, wearing her blue velvet robe, rousts out the frightened Jeffrey at the point of a butcher knife. Her surprisingly commanding voice is harsh and ragged: "Get on your knees. Do it!" Concealing his detective persona, Jeffrey takes refuge in a pervert's defense, saying he's the bug-spray man who "just wanted to see you." In a stunning reversal of Jeffrey's expectations for his spying session, Dorothy spits back, "Get undressed, I want to see you." The narrative surprise of this moment parallels the sudden revelation of the beetles churning beneath the Beaumonts' lawn, and it won't be the last rude shock that Jeffrey will endure as he ventures deeper into Lumberton's underworld. He's dealing with powerful, scary forces that he can't control. But like young David Lynch going down into that menacing New York subway tunnel, he can learn something about himself if he keeps riding into the darkness.

Lynch believes that both the malevolent and the benign aspects of life can teach us a thing or two, and Jeffrey's guides into the dark realms he doesn't yet know about will be Dorothy and Frank. The curriculum will let him experience the roles of both victim and sadistic perpetrator, the teaching tools will be sex and violence, and there will be minor electives in pain, weeping, degradation, and corruption. Homework will be inescapable; sleep-learning will consist of nightmares. Like the girl in *The Alphabet*, Jeffrey will be absorbing the horrors of learning. Lynch, aside from having Dorothy and Frank give Jeffrey life lessons in depravity, will use the pair as benighted, underground reflections of the youth's warm and loving aboveground parents. And the director won't shy away from pushing Oedipal logic to the nth degree. Dorothy makes Jeffrey take down his underpants, which are, naturally, all-American red plaid boxers. Kneeling in front of him, she invitingly asks, "What do you want?" He says, "I don't know," and she does what he wants, but won't speak, taking his penis into her mouth at an angle the camera can't quite see. Jeffrey gets a teasing few seconds of pleasure, but Dorothy is in control, holding her big knife a breath away from his genitals, and barking orders: "Don't move; don't look at me; don't touch me or I'll kill you." Dorothy is playing a sadistic game, but Jeffrey is no masochist, and tells her he doesn't like that threatening talk. They move to the fleshy couch that seems like an organic outgrowth of the wall, and enact one of the film's iconic tableaux of melded six and violence: Dorothy in her blue velvet robe straddling Jeffrey's pelvis and bending forward to kiss him, her ready blade glinting against the ruddy wall. She makes a potent dominatrix, but a sudden, thunderous pounding on her door announces the arrival of this underworld's alpha male predator, *the* power of Lumberton's darkness.

The Frank Booth that Lynch wrote and Dennis Hopper acts out is a phenomenal creation. If Jeffrey is trying on the role of bug man, Frank is the real thing. Wearing a stiff black leather coat like a beetle's carapace, sucking in nitrous oxide gas from a plastic inhaling mask that covers his nose and mouth and gives him a gleaming bug-like jawline, his eye popping, Frank is an insect ready to feed on flesh. And he's got a bug in his noggin: a buzzing sexual obsession with Dorothy, the Blue Velvet Lady. Like a demented artist of the libido, Frank has devised a theater-of-cruelty ritual that he enacts with Dorothy. As Jeffrey watches aghast and fascinated from his closet, he encounters a new mystery: Why does she put up with it?

Dorothy douses the electric lamp, lights a squat, white candle (like the ones at Laura Palmer's *Twin Peaks* murder site), and Frank intones the archetypal Lynchian incantation: "Now it's dark" (which isn't in the script).

Repeating an established pattern, Dorothy brings over a small chair and sits on it, and gives Frank a glass of bourbon. As in some perversion of a 1950s sitcom, Frank casts himself in the role of Daddy coming home, but Dorothy slips and calls him "Baby." An understandable mistake, for there's a maelstrom of Oedipal confusion in Frank's psyche. He next calls her "Mommy," and in a plaintive, childlike voice, declares, "Baby wants to fuck" and "Baby loves blue velvet." Then, as Lynch's script specifies, he gives commands to *himself*, which degrade into vocal self-abuse, "Get ready to fuck! You fuckers, fucker, you fucker." And when he throws Dorothy to the floor, jumps on top of her and, with all his clothes on, bounces up and down frantically for a few seconds before ejaculating, Frank is "Daddy" again, and keeps assuring us that "Daddy's coming home." (Many critics' theories about Frank being mad at the world because he's impotent—based on his staying zipped-up during his frenzy of sexual thrusting—are vaporized by a line in Lynch's script: "faster and faster, then he has a climax in his pants.")[87]

Whether Frank is seeing Dorothy as herself or his mother, he heaps abuse on her. His harrowing expression of sexuality is an act of rage against the world, women, and himself. Fueling his assaultive acting-out with hits of nitrous oxide gas, Frank attempts to hide his vile self-image by repeatedly yelling, "Don't you fucking look at me!" and striking Dorothy if she seems to disobey. To see himself in her eyes is more than he can bear. If Frank loathes himself, he also abhors Dorothy's femaleness. Before climbing on top of her, he roughly jams his fingers into her vagina, and after climaxing he looks at the hand that touched her, as if it wasn't part of him, and makes a splayed-finger throwing gesture like he's trying to rid himself of slime or the hand itself. No wonder Daddy chooses to come home in his pants.

Lynch stresses the brutal animalism of Frank's behavior by having Hopper growl and slaver vocalizations that aren't words. Frank's snarling sounds as he hovers over his victim recall *The Grandmother*'s Father barking and looming over his hapless Boy, and prefigures similar configurations of characters that will show up in the director's future works.

After Frank is finished with Dorothy, he stands above her supine form and cryptically says, "Stay alive, baby. Do it for Van Gogh." This data convinces the watching Jeffrey that Dorothy is suicidal, and adds to the youth's sense that Frank has kidnapped her little boy and husband, and has cut off her spouse's ear ("Van Gogh"). Frank then uses his control over Dorothy's loved ones to manipulate her any way he wants.

It now becomes clear that Dorothy's sadistic sexual bossing of Jeffrey is a pale reflection of the way Frank treats *her*, a way of coping with her hellish situation by taking on some characteristics of the man who has power over her (she commands Jeffrey using Frank's words, "Don't look at me"). Given Lynch's penchant for casting parents and parent-surrogates as potential and actual sexual abusers of young people (*The Grandmother, Eraserhead, Twin Peaks, Wild at Heart, Twin Peaks: Fire Walk With Me*), it's reasonable to surmise from the "Mommy loves you" and "Baby wants to fuck" of Frank's perverse sex ritual that the man has been traumatized by a past, perhaps incestuous, sexual experience. (Freud believed that a boy witnessing the primal scene of his father and mother having intercourse would develop a sadistic sexuality fixated on the power of the strong male dominating the weaker female. He also surmised that the last object a boy sees before he first glimpses his mother's genitals becomes fetishized: It wouldn't surprise us if little Frank Booth's mother wore a blue velvet robe.) Frank's victimization has compelled him to visit sexual violence upon Dorothy, who continues to cycle with Jeffrey. Foisting rough sex on Jeffrey may help Dorothy cope, but she's most deeply conditioned to express her erotic nature through victimhood. When Frank has left and she and Jeffrey are alone again, the youth gently comforts her and they both get aroused, and she implores him, "Hit me, hit me." He won't, so their first evening is over.

Or so Jeffrey may think as he's putting on his clothes. But walking away from Dorothy's building in the darkness, his black-clad form starts to glow with phosphorescence; then we see Jeffrey's father struggling in vain to speak, the guttering flame of Frank's white candle, Dorothy's face begging "Hit me," and a Dorothy's-eye-view of a grimacing Frank mashing his fist into our face to the sound of her scream. Then Jeffrey is in bed in the morning, his head reeling from a nightmare ("Man oh man"). Lynch has not only toyed with our sense of reality by slyly immersing us in what we now realize was a montage of Jeffrey's dream, but he's emphasized how profoundly the youth's consciousness has become immersed in the ear-mystery, and how dangerous his quest is. He's awake, his bad dream is over, he's in his own comforting bed. But on the wall above him is an animalistic rubber Halloween mask that's all devouring mouth and hungry teeth—a reminder of the metaphysical evil of the dark beetles gnawing beneath sunny lawns, Frank's brutal appetites, and the unsettling fact that the mask fits Jeffrey's face. As artist Vito Acconci says of Lynch's oeuvre, Lynch shows us that we are both "scared and scary"[88]: We are threatened by shadows from outside and inside.

Twenty-four hours after Jeffrey's dark introduction to Lumberton's underworld with Dorothy and Frank, the sober and sad young man sits in the Williamses' car with Sandy. Whenever Jeffrey drives, they go to the wrong side of the tracks. But when Sandy's at the wheel, they stop in front of a stone church with stained glass windows, in which we can hear an organist practicing a beautiful melody. Sandy, the agent of angelic goodness, would naturally guide them to this site. (We note that Jeffrey drives a convertible, signifying his dual nature as wholesome, upright youth and dabbler in darkness; *Twin Peaks'* Leland Palmer, Laura's demon-possessed father, also drives a convertible.) Gazing at Sandy's blonde loveliness, Jeffrey gathers himself to speak of the raven-haired Dorothy's inferno. He first said, "It's a strange world" to Sandy on their initial night stroll, when an amorphously defined forming mystery could be contemplated with innocent enthusiasm. Now, having gained some experience of the mystery's shape and lived some of the life its main characters lead, he says, "It's a strange world" with a melancholy whisper. Jeffrey has discovered a secret realm hidden within the world he thought he knew by heart, and it's tainted him. His account to Sandy keeps secrets from her: He makes no mention of the sexual activity of he and his two netherworld guides. Wanting to believe that people can be either all good or all bad, Jeffrey condenses the evil of the ear mystery into the form of Frank Booth, and passionately asks Sandy, "Why are there men like Frank? Why is there so much trouble in the world?" Sandy doesn't know the answer to this major mystery, but, given Lynch's love of opposing forces in contrast, she offers an antidote to the world's evil.

Sitting at the steering wheel, the church and its uplifting melody soft-focus in the background, Sandy says with sweet exultation, "I had a dream," words that are a Lynchian declaration of principles. "The world was dark because there weren't any robins, and the robins represented love. And for the longest time there was just this darkness. And all of a sudden, thousands of robins were set free. And they flew down and brought this blinding light of love, and it seemed like that love would be the only thing that would make any difference. And it did. So, I guess it means there is trouble 'till the robins come."

If Frank's sexual abuse of Dorothy is *Blue Velvet*'s most searing statement of malevolence, then Sandy and Jeffrey's car talk is its antithesis. And, as evidence that the powers of shadow and radiance are equally valuable to Lynch's sensibility, each scene runs about the same length of time. As Laura Dern has said, "David believes in the robins as much as in Frank Booth."[89] Some viewers, whose sense of wonder is dimmed by an overdeveloped need to find everything ironic, are convinced that Sandy's dewy-eyed dream description is a put-on, a way for Lynch to mock her corny credulity. But this artist who calls himself naive, who meditates on Eastern concepts of spiritual transcendence, values dream states, and in previous films has portrayed the ability of higher powers to deliver benighted souls, most certainly has his ears pricked for those robins' song.

Other than his creepy human animals, the critters that appear most in Lynch's work are insects and dogs, though there are a few other birds outside the precincts of *Blue Velvet*. The graceful, feathered creatures that can defy gravity have a positive connotation for the artist. There's the cheery robin on a fir branch in the *Twin Peaks* credits. The joyful feeling in Lynch's song "I Remember" that's "So happy, so warm / That sent seven little red birds up my spine / Singing."[90] The way the director compares a well-made film to the "perfect composition"[91] of a mallard duck's anatomy, the bird's eye having been positioned "in exactly the right spot." And there are Lynch's angel figures, one of whom, in *Twin Peaks: Fire Walk With Me*, has white-feathered wings.

Sandy's dream has the resonance of a prophecy but, unlike in *Dune*, where it's telegraphed ahead of time that Paul's visions will come true, *Blue Velvet* trades in true moment-to-moment existential mystery and revelation. (Every frame of this film shows how much more at home Lynch is here than in the imperial throne rooms of far-flung galaxies.) Sandy had her dream the night she met Jeffrey, so maybe he's the one who can make the robins come, though he seems more interested in debauchery than birds. Lynch cuts directly from Sandy and Jeffrey's sanctified scene in front of the church to Jeffrey on the prowl in night town, anxious for Dorothy to open her door, and more, to him.

There's something murky in him that responds to the dusky pull of her blood, and Jeffrey thrusts himself into Dorothy's desperate body. He can see that she's half crazy, looking for Jeffrey in her closet every night, scared of Frank and soul-sick over what he may do to her entrapped husband and little son. She's sunken so low in abuse that she keeps entreating Jeffrey, "I want you to hurt me." One night, when the youth says he'll tell the police of her predicament, she gets furious with him and literally starts to kick him out of bed. Up to this moment Jeffrey has maintained, "I want to help you, not hurt you" but, with relief, he yields to the darkness within him, and whacks her hard in the face with the back of his hand. (Following Freud's logic, Jeffrey, having psychically processed and absorbed the primal scene of his netherworld surrogate father and mother Frank and Dorothy having punishing sex, is now able to model Frank's sadistic erotic power-plays.) Like a visual reverberation of the blow, Lynch shows us a huge close-up of Dorothy's chipped front tooth, which dissolves in a gust of flames that becomes Jeffrey pouncing onto her in a sexual slow-motion embrace, over which we hear distorted animal roars and the sharp-end punctuation of a woman's scream. The scene goes to black and Dorothy says, "I have your disease in me now."

The question of the exact nature of this disease generated much discussion after *Blue Velvet* came out. In the mid-1980s, America and the world were still trying to comprehend and cope with the concept of AIDS, a horrendous, fatal plague spread from person to person primarily through sexual contact. A number of commentators thought that Dorothy's "disease" was AIDS and that Lynch was making a sociopolitical point about the Reagan administration's avoidance of this crisis-magnitude public health issue. Indeed, many hip viewers were sure that Lynch, by exposing the moral rot behind the sugar-sweet facade of smalltown USA, was subverting Reagan's Up With America ethos. Of course, these cognoscenti were shocked to learn that their radical-director hero was a supporter of the Gipper. Lynch wants his art to mean different things to different people, to speak to the individual viewer's needs and imagination: The connection between artwork and public is what matters, not the communication of a neatly formulated and circumscribed message from the author.

The "disease" in *Blue Velvet* is one of the director's beloved abstractions, which he wants us to interpret as we will, but his original script gives us some clues about his take on the concept. On the page, Dorothy ruminates, "You put your disease in me—your semen. It's hot and full of disease. Men are crazy. They put their craziness into me, then it makes me crazy—then they aren't so crazy for awhile. Then they put it in me again. . . . [*Starts Crying*] It's burning me!"[92] This from the supposedly male chauvinist director who lives to abuse women onscreen: These script words could have been written by Valerie Solanas, the woman who shot artist Andy Warhol and founded the Society for Cutting Up Men (SCUM). For Lynch, the disease is the evil that men do, which can invade another's personality and bring out their worst. Bad, twisted thoughts and actions can be contagious, and the director will further explore the question of whether evil is a possessing or an intrinsic force in *Twin Peaks*.

Lynch has said that *Blue Velvet* is "a trip into darkness, as close as you can get, and then a trip out. There's an innermost point, and from then on it pulls back."[93] Jeffrey makes his journey to the center of night in the hour after he struck Dorothy in bed. As he says goodnight to her, she makes plain her raw need for him and calls him "my special friend" (the next time MacLachlan works with Lynch, he'll be a special agent). While the youth and Dorothy talk, Lynch disconcerts us with an out-of-context shot looking down the apartment's staircase. Sixteen years earlier, in *The Grandmother*, the director surprised us with a shot looking *up* a staircase in the midst of a narrative about a parentally abused boy. The lad eventually discovered that the stairs led up to the nurturing world of his grandmother, while *Blue Velvet*'s harbinger steps will take Jeffrey down into purgatory. When he steps across Dorothy's threshold into the hallway, there are Frank and three of his depraved, cackling pals coming up. Previously, Jeffrey has only seen Frank from the relative safety of Dorothy's closet, and now he's face-to-face with the monster. Frank mixes a "Howdy, neighbor" mock joviality with his deep rage as he suggests a "joyride" to the trembling youth, who, with good manners, declines the invitation. But social niceties and personal boundaries are like dry fall leaves to the flaming furnace blast of Frank's will to power. He already holds Dorothy's family hostage, and now he spirits off her and Jeffrey in his roaring Dodge Charger, whose grille and headlights Lynch frames so that they look like a fierce animal's jaws and eyes devouring the night.

Along with Frank's three loony cohorts, they go to Ben's Pussy Heaven where, as did *Eraserhead*'s Henry, Jeffrey must endure a bizarre and punishing social evening. Pussy Heaven is a low-rent-district bordello stocked with fat women who sit silently aligned against a living room wall as though trapped in the numbing stasis of a Diane Arbus photograph. This blasphemous Heaven is presided over by the marvelously effete Ben (Dennis Hopper's pal Dean Stockwell) who, with his lip rouge and ruffled-front shirt, is, as Frank proclaims with deadpan Lynchian humor, "One suave fucker." Ben and his scarlet women hold Dorothy's little boy, Donny, behind a locked door. And when we hear her visiting him, it sounds like she's been accused of being an absentee parent, for she says, "No, no, Donny, Mommy still loves you!" Perhaps this moment is a guilty projection of Lynch's own sense of being, to some degree, an unavailable father to his children.

After Frank and Ben use Jeffrey as a punching bag and reveal their major-player role in Lumberton's clandestine drug-dealing network, Ben does a special performance at Frank's request, lip-synching to Frank's audiotape of Roy Orbison singing "In Dreams." This song and "Blue Velvet" are Frank's anthems; both speak of men weeping over lost loves. When Ben does his unforgettable pantomime, holding a construction-site electric lamp under his chin like a microphone so that the glaring light makes his pasty face glow, Frank is transported. He seems lulled as Orbison-Ben sings "Go to sleep, everything is all right," but his face stiffens with apprehension as the singer falls asleep "To dream my dreams of you," and he winces with pain when the narrator walks and talks with his now-vanished love. Many commentators simply characterize Frank as the Anti-Christ, an incarnation of abstract evil. He is certainly loathsome and terrifying, but Lynch as writer-director and Hopper as actor invest him with a wrenching pathos. We sense that Frank has grown monstrous because of some wounding loss or horrible abuse visited upon him. Frank and Dorothy, a sadist and his masochist partner, are ultimately both victims. Frank is possessed by some eros-perverting past trauma, as *Twin Peaks'* daughter-molesting Leland Palmer is possessed by the evil force of BOB. Both Lynch and Hopper say that Frank truly loves Dorothy, and when he watches her sing at the Slow Club, he weeps tortured tears, simultaneously grieving for her and himself.

Lynch understands the nuanced shadings of those who express themselves with malevolent behavior, just as he allows his upholders of righteousness to manifest a full human complexity. And once, years before *Blue Velvet*, he was surprised to learn that his daughter, Jennifer, was dwelling seriously on such matters. As she remembers, "I was very young, and I was fearless when it came to the grotesque. My father got upset with me when he found me reading my dog-eared copy of Vincent Bugliosi's *Helter Skelter*, which detailed Charles Manson's horrible crimes and how he was apprehended and brought to justice."[94] Just as Lynch, in his art, presents two characters with their heads almost touching when things get intense, "He leaned his head next to mine and said, 'This is beyond darkness, it is not the opposite of light, this is evil.'"[95] As though anticipating *Blue Velvet*'s "are-you-a-detective-or-a-pervert" dialectic, Jennifer replied, "But Dad, I'm not fascinated with Manson—what I like is the guy who caught him, the guy who figures everything out and captures him."[96] Still, Jennifer responded with humane empathy toward Manson: "Here's a soul tortured throughout his life, shunted from home to home, beaten, turned wrong by hatred and fear,"[97] just as her father sees Frank Booth as both a monster and "a man who's deeply in love but can't express it in a normal way."[98] Jennifer feels Frank "is a poignant character: I have a sadness and a pity for Frank. When he does his baby voice and his whimpering it's so revealing, the way he's violent to get what he needs."[99] She agrees with my thought that Frank was the victim of incestuous sexual abuse: "Yeah, all the Mommy/Daddy/Baby roles are fucked up in his head. My father puts such interesting details of humanity in *Blue Velvet*, it seems so absolutely real to me psychologically."[100] So the bestial Frank has a human side, the humane Jeffrey harbors animal impulses, and Roy Orbison will bring them face to face.

When Frank, Dorothy, Jeffrey, Frank's hoodlum trio, and one of Ben's fat whores drive off into the night, Jeffrey does something no one else in the film has had the courage to do: He defiantly glares into Frank's eyes after being ordered, "Don't look at me, fuck." Frank fires back a damning truth at the youth: "You're like me." And Jeffrey, as if to both acknowledge and defy Frank's insight, lashes out and punches him in the face. Jeffrey's shocking aggression inspires Frank the warped artist to pile out of the car and stage a perverse ritual comparable to his sadistic sexual theatrics with Dorothy.

While Frank's gang holds a knife to Jeffrey's throat, the fiend exhibits some of the homosexual leanings of Lynchian villains in *The Elephant Man*, *Dune*, and *Twin Peaks*. When Frank was ready to leave Ben's place he showed that his animalistic appetite encompassed all sexes (and perhaps species) as he declared," I'll fuck anything that moves!" (Frank's form then suddenly vanished from Ben's living room and was next seen driving down a highway. This split-second jump from one point in space to another could be Lynch's conscious or subconscious reference to *The Wizard of Oz*'s Dorothy's observation that in Oz, "People come and go so quickly here" [regarding the Witches' magical transports]. *Blue Velvet*'s Lumberton is far from the land of Oz, but near Twin Peaks on the map of Lynch's imagination, and the supernatural aura of Frank's uncanny mobility in this one instance prefigures BOB's [another evil force with a hunger for men and women] otherworldly coming and going every time he travels.) Frank calls Jeffrey "our pussy" and "pretty-pretty," and, after forcing the youth to feel his biceps, says, "You like that, huh." The villain then grabs Dorothy's lipstick, paints his mouth, and kisses Jeffrey repeatedly, smearing his face with red: a visual signifier of the dark erotic linkage between Jeffrey and his two netherworld guides, Dorothy and Frank, that makes all their mouths taste the same. Now Frank, his face harshly lit by a handheld electric light as Ben's was, does his own rendition of Roy Orbison's "In Dreams."

As the song plays, Frank exhibits a deranged intermingling of love and hate, sex and violence. First, he growls at Jeffrey that if the youth gets out of line, "I'll send you a love letter. Do you know what a love letter is? It's a bullet from a fuckin' gun, fucker. You receive a love letter from me, you're fucked forever." This passionately delivered physical threat is terrifying, but Frank's next mood swing is even more disturbing. Lynch stages arguably the most intense of his two-heads-in-confrontation clinch scenes, as Frank breathes into Jeffrey's face with the erotic ardor and cold malevolence that a predator holds for the victim he controls. In stunning close-up, his eyes burning cool blue, Frank intones with Roy Orbison, "In dreams, I walk with you. In dreams, I talk with you. In dreams, you're *mine*, all the time." Throughout the film, Dennis Hopper has given Frank expressive gestures: He always points with two aggressive fingers, like a child forming his hand into a revolver. As Frank says, "You're *mine*," he bunches his extended fingers together and holds them next to Jeffrey's head, as though he could reach in and own the young man's psyche. Because of the dark, mirror-image symbiotic bond between the two men, Jeffrey knows that Frank is capable of stealing his soul. Indeed, the youth may already have precious little of it left.

In Lynch's script, Jeffrey was to wake up lying on the ground after being beaten unconscious by Frank. His pants were to be pulled down and a lipstick "FUCK YOU" scribbled on his leg in the aftermath of a homosexual rape. Kyle MacLachlan pleaded with Lynch to delete the sexual violation details, and after giving the matter some thought, the director agreed. Lynch will sometimes acquiesce to his actors' strongly held opinions, as when he let Anthony Hopkins keep his beloved beard in *The Elephant Man* and, in *Twin Peaks*, he abandoned a certain romantic storyline for Agent Cooper that MacLachlan just didn't think was right.

Jeffrey has reached the heart of *Blue Velvet*'s darkness and seen it as the murky shading of his own psyche, and now it's time to start to pull back and journey toward the light. Lynch is interested in the full range of human emotions, and has said, "If you're a man, you can cry."[101] Jeffrey reaches his turning point sobbing in his room alone. But banishing Lumberton's darkness (and his own) isn't as easy as switching on a light. When he sits down to breakfast with Mom and Aunt Barbara, and Barbara starts to chatter about his beaten-up appearance, Jeffrey's answer sounds like Frank Booth: "I love you, but you're gonna get it."

The youth nurtures and strengthens his capacity for goodness by staying away from Dorothy, telling Detective Williams all he's learned about Frank's law-breaking activities (without mentioning Sandy's investigative help), and telling Sandy he loves her. She returns his feelings, and they dance and kiss to the music that accompanied her dream-of-the-robins narrative, the chorale-like melody which now has lyrics by Lynch sung by Julee Cruise: "Sometimes a wind blows / and the mysteries of love / come clear."[102]

Jeffrey is going straight and staying clean, but his choice to indulge his dark side has repercussions, as it always does in Lynch's world. The shadowy force that beetle-churned beneath the Beaumonts' lawn has spread all over town, and now it pops up in Jeffrey's living room. When Lynch and his brother were boys in a small Northwest town, they looked out their bedroom window one night and saw an unclothed woman walking in the street. Now, in the director's fiction, after Jeffrey and Sandy's dance, the achingly vulnerable, bruised, and naked Dorothy Vallens steps into those bastions of domestic propriety, the Beaumonts' front porch and the Williamses' living room. Once again, Lynch displays his gift for staging excruciating embarrassments and violating social niceties. As Jeffrey consoles the dazed Dorothy, hugging her exposed body against him, in front of Sandy and her mother, the clandestine sexual relationship that he's hidden from his golden angel comes gushing out. Dorothy calls him "my secret lover" and, looking directly at Mrs. Williams and Sandy, tells them, "He put his disease in me." Sandy and Jeffrey have not yet made love, but this grotesque revelation of his emotional unfaithfulness and untruthfulness causes her to break out in deep sobs, with the corners of her mouth curved down like the traditional Greek mask of tragedy. As with Sandy's narration of her robins-and-love dream, some viewers snicker at the extreme gestures of her weeping and think that Lynch is making fun of her. But, as Laura Dern has said more than once over the years, "that's how I cry."[103] True, her manner of weeping in other films resembles her *Blue Velvet* behavior, but her sadness seems most gut-wrenching under Lynch's direction.

Sandy and Jeffrey speak words to try to repair their rift, but the youth's actions are needed on the dark side of town, for Dorothy has called from a phone booth to say that they've hurt her husband, and entreated Jeffrey to "help him." Jeffrey first entered Dorothy's apartment to see what the police couldn't, and now he will be the one to precede the law and strike the decisive blow against the powers of night. As he approaches Dorothy's door, he knows he is in the realm of insect energy, for there's a buzzing from inside. A TV has been kicked in and a lamp is ready to short out. Like Jeffrey's father's hose caught on that bush, the natural pathways of electrical flow in this room have been kinked and disturbed. What Jeffrey next sees in the room defies the laws of gravity and mortality.

Earlier in the film, the youth discovered that the man in the yellow blazer who came to Dorothy's door is Detective Williams's partner, and also a partner to Frank's dope-dealing cabal. Now the Yellow Man, his head a travesty of oozing red, a police radio crackling in his pocket, *stands* frozen like a statue, not lying flat like a proper corpse should. Aside from Frank Booth's bizarre behavior, Lynch has exhibited plenty of evidence in *Blue Velvet* that would make Jeffrey declare "It's a strange world." One of the director's subtly disturbing motifs is to put people in places and postures that are a few degrees removed from normal. While Frank sang and punched "In Dreams" to Jeffrey, one of Ben's fat whores incongruously danced on the roof of Frank's car, and at Ben's, one of Frank's goons had stood on the arm of a sofa while Ben sang. Lynch once said, after viewing a music video of animated store-window mannequins, "Anything that looks human, but isn't, is frightening,"[104] and he creates this haunting quality in *Blue Velvet* by showing people who don't move. In an early establishing shot of the town, there's a large, immobile man positioned by a store for no explained reason. And when Jeffrey begins his first night walk to Detective Williams's house, there's an eerily inert man standing under the trees with a little dog on a leash. We're clearly not in Mr. Rogers' neighborhood.

Back in Dorothy's apartment, the seemingly dead standing Yellow Man scares Jeffrey and us when his hand twitches out and knocks over a lamp: Throughout his work, Lynch makes the boundary line between life and death ambiguous, a road that travels in twin directions. There's no question, however, that Dorothy's husband, Don, is dead. He sits bound in a chair, displaying the hole where his ear used to be, and in true Lynchian maximally disturbing fashion, littering his wife's kitchen countertop with the contents of his head. And where there is death, there is Frank's touch, for a length of blue velvet fabric spews out of Don's mouth like a frozen scream, recalling the attenuated animated scream line that flowed from *The Grandmother's* Boy's mouth. Lynch is adept at making pain palpably visible.

Jeffrey goes to leave this house of carnage, but he sees Frank coming up the stairs and Frank sees him. The youth must manfully face the responsibility of his decision to walk on the wild side of town, for there's no place to go but back into Dorothy's apartment. The first time Jeffrey laid eyes on Frank, the youth was invisible, hiding within Dorothy's closet. Following Lynch's characteristic scheme of balances and parallels, Jeffrey again takes refuge in the dark little room within a room. And if the hearing function got Jeffrey in trouble before (his toilet flush made him miss Sandy's warning car honks and get caught by Dorothy) it now benefits him. He calls Detective Williams for help on the Yellow Man's radio, and when he realizes that Frank can hear him on *his* radio, misleads the villain by telling Williams that he'll be hiding in Dorothy's bedroom. Jeffrey then grabs Yellow Man's pistol and dives into the closet just ahead of Frank's entrance. Now all of Dorothy's men are in attendance.

Lynch underscores his homosexual-villain subtext by having Frank call out, "I know where your cute little butt's hiding." Jeffrey's radio may be making noise in the bedroom, but the youth's not there. Frank yells "pretty-pretty," makes some animalistic grunts, and fires bullets into the empty room. Enraged and calling out, "Where are you?" like some wicked hide-and-go-seek player, Frank comes back to the living room. He is the maker of final deaths and when, in frustration, he pumps a bullet into Yellow Man, the standing canary figure must at last fall over and prostrate himself before the Lord of the Flies.

Through the slats in the closet door, Jeffrey has watched Frank commit brutal acts of sex and violence, and the youth has stepped through those doors to act out the parts of himself that are like Frank. Jeffrey is now fully aware of his capacity for good and evil, and that he can consciously choose which path to follow. In the next second or two he must use violence to save his own life, as well as to smite the predatory-animal powers that seethe in darkness a mighty blow. Frank throws open the closet door, and Jeffrey fires a single shot into his forehead. As the monster loses the back of his head, Lynch mixes the scream of a beast with the gunshot blast. If Dorothy and Frank have been Jeffrey's benighted parent figures, nurturing him in the ways of the netherworld, then the young man has now closed the Oedipal circle, having slept with his mother and killed the father who wanted her all for himself.

On this night, the police have closed in on Lumberton's web of criminals, and as Jeffrey and Sandy kiss in the apartment hallway, their true love is irradiated with white light, and outside we see light-flashing police cars descend on the building like robins pouncing on beetles.

Jeffrey has entered a severed ear and probed deep beneath the surface of his own and his town's consciousness, and now Lynch pulls out of a ruddy canal that is Jeffrey's sunlit ear, as he snoozes in the Beaumonts' backyard. When he opens his eyes, the first thing he sees is a plump red robin on a branch. As if to codify his status as the hero who has mastered darkness and light, Jeffrey wears black pants and a white shirt. Having destroyed his bad father, Frank, the young man's good father has been restored to him. In Lynch's favorite movie, *The Wizard of Oz*, far-traveling Dorothy concludes that "There's no place like home," and now Jeffrey enjoys the most wonderful of homecomings. For the first time in the film, the Beaumont and Williams families are conjoined, as if to bless Sandy and Jeffrey's union. Tom Beaumont is "feeling fine," and Detective Williams tends to the barbecue in the backyard. Sandy and Aunt Barbara are fixing lunch, and Jeffrey's and Sandy's moms can't wait to eat. Sandy's original involving of Jeffrey in the ear mystery, which she's regretted all along, has resulted in the vanquishment of evil. For there on the windowsill is her dream come true: that fat robin, a squirming black beetle in its powerful beak. Sandy looks at Jeffrey, recalling all the terrible and wonderful things they've shared, and there's only one way she can put it into words: "It's a strange world, isn't it."

The warm, sweet music of "Mysteries of Love" carries us to another homecoming. For the first time in the film, we see Dorothy Vallens in daylight, sitting on a park bench in the sun. Her little boy, Donny, now free as the wind, is enfolded in her smiling embrace. If any character in *Blue Velvet* has been as torturously entrapped as *The Grandmother*'s Boy, *Eraserhead*'s Henry, and *The Elephant Man*'s John Merrick, it is Dorothy. She evinces a shift in Lynch's sensibility toward a growing concern for the victimization of women. Each of the director's earlier characters escaped their bondage through the transcendent grace of love, and Dorothy also seems to have thrown off her web of darkness.

But Lynch knows how complex the world really is and he remains haunted by Dorothy's suffering. Her smile fades, and there's a tormented look in her eyes as we hear her voice sing the words that symbolize her unholy union with Frank: "And I still can see blue velvet through my tears." As Lynch pans up from her and Donny to a beautiful blue sky, we remember that Don and Frank, Dorothy's good and evil husbands, are both dead, and Jeffrey has chosen to stay on the side of the angels. But maybe some night the young man will again take a walk on the shadow side of town and Dorothy will find him in her closet. There are countless more hidden insects in the world than there are robins. The last thing we see in the film isn't the wide-open sky; it's a curtain of blue velvet that's being rhythmically moved, as though the darkness behind it would never stop breathing.

Lynch says he is able to visualize thoughts and behavior more horrific than anything he has put before our eyes. In an earlier conception of *Blue Velvet*, the director let Frank Booth's death-dealing perversity lunge out, violating the boundary of his own physical demise, and touch Dorothy one last time, making her, at this point in Lynch's career, the director's ultimate female victim. In a script-dialogue line not in the film, Lynch has Jeffrey say that Frank "had to have Dorothy cause her whole life was blue."[105] As the film ends now she's still the Blue Lady, but being reunited with her loving little Donny and the exultant atmosphere of a sunny afternoon have let some light into her life and dispelled some of her soul's gloom. Yet just as Lynch had initially planned for *Eraserhead*'s Henry to perish without the saving grace and love of his radiant Lady in the Radiator, Dorothy was originally to be swallowed by the ravenous black insects of darkness.

We would have seen the bloody body of little Donny, killed by Frank, found under Dorothy's bed, as though birthed into death by the twisted, violent sex his mother was at first forced to practice, then loved to practice, in this room. Then, looking up the towering facade of Dorothy's apartment building at night, we'd see a single red shoe fall toward us. Unlike Judy Garland in *The Wizard of Oz*, this poor Dorothy has no hope of finding Oz or getting back to Kansas, so she throws her unmagical ruby slipper into the abyss of night. Then her naked body, which we've previously seen stripped of protective clothes for sex and bruising, leaps from the rooftop toward us and past, into a final embrace with death, making literal her panicky words from earlier in the film that had summed up her plummeting spiritual state: "I'm falling!" Then her blue velvet robe drops toward us—can Lynch be providing a glimmer of redemption even in this darkest of endings?

The ruby slipper may not have gotten Dorothy where she wanted to go, but by throwing off the blue velvet robe that symbolizes her oppressive bondage to Frank, she has leapt into a transcendent freedom. (In *Sunset Boulevard*, which Lynch dearly loves, William Holden's character removes the expensive cuff links that symbolize Norma Desmond's oppressive hold on him before meeting his death.) As Lynch has said to me, he likes to "get people trapped in a hellhole"[106] and then he often shows us, or implies, that there is an escape route. For *Eraserhead*'s Henry Spencer and *The Elephant Man*'s John Merrick, the process of achieving a final release involves their own death, as it will for *Twin Peaks: Fire Walk With Me*'s Laura Palmer and *Mulholland Drive*'s Diane Selwyn. Perhaps, as death enabled John Merrick to merge with the spirit of his truest love, his dear mother, so Dorothy will unite with her husband and child who have passed on before her.

After Dorothy leaps to her death, her blue robe would have fallen into our faces and frozen there, filling the screen as Bobby Vinton's words "and I still can see blue velvet through my tears" hang in the air. Dorothy would be gone to some other place. We the living would be the ones still seeing blue velvet, still haunted.

David Lynch had found himself. He was home again, back from the dream-convolutions of *Eraserhead*'s mind, *The Elephant Man*'s nineteenth-century England, and *Dune*'s interplanetary future, to the small-town streets where America lives. *Blue Velvet* was just as he wanted it to be, for it sprang from his innermost feelings about a young man becoming sexually and psychically mature, the terrors and exhilarations of acquiring knowledge, and the sustaining potency of love and family. In Isabella Rossellini, Lynch had a passionate and devoted love of his own, and he would face the eruptive response to his film, both the veneration and vilification, with a renewed personal confidence. The lucid, reality-based style of *Blue Velvet* seemed to heighten the director's ability to convey resonant ideas, dream-like poetic associations, and complex states of being. Just like Jeffrey, Lynch was growing, learning, and maturing, but some things would always remain the same. There would be a beautiful cherry tree in a boy's backyard, and red ants swarming on it. Robins and bugs, blue skies and blue velvet, a curious young man and a severed ear, an FBI detective and a dead high school girl. Born amid Mount Sentinel and Mount Jumbo in Missoula, Montana, David Lynch would forever reside between twin peaks.

6

BUZZ SAW

1986–1990
(*Twin Peaks*, Season 1)

People couldn't stop talking about David Lynch. Never again, as with *Eraserhead*, would a small first-viewing audience stumble out of a Lynch film with nothing to say. In *Blue Velvet*, the director's maturing narrative skills enabled him to communicate his wrenching personal vision of "the things hidden within a young man's small town—and within himself"[1] in an evocatively dreamy, yet vividly accessible style that shook viewers to their core.

The film quickly became an international *cause célèbre*, a cultural phenomenon that sparked heated debate. Some thought Lynch was worshipping Reaganesque good-old-days and small-town values, others knew that he was subversively undermining retrograde village pieties and apple-cheeked wholesomeness. Some feminists deplored the director's male-gazing portrayal of violence against sex-object women and declared that an exploiter as "dangerous"[2] as Lynch should never be allowed to make another film. Other supporters of women's rights felt Lynch presented the theme of female victimization with uncommon insight and compassion and looked forward to his future insights into the state of womankind. *Newsweek* magazine wondered, "Is Black and Blue Beautiful?"[3] while *Christian Century* proclaimed, "The Best Film of 1986: Probing the Depths of Evil."[4] Some potential *Blue Velvet* viewers, hearing the furor about the film's disturbing nature, spent weeks preparing themselves mentally before venturing into the theater. After seeing the picture, a friend of brilliant film critic Pauline Kael told her, "This may sound sick, but I want to see that again,"[5] and

Woody Allen, who had made the highly praised *Hannah and Her Sisters* in 1986, declared that he hadn't seen a better film than *Blue Velvet* that year. Lynch, for the second time in a decade, was nominated by the Motion Picture Academy for the Best Director of the Year Oscar.

Many film industry observers were surprised that the conservative-leaning Academy would acknowledge the director of a disturbingly provocative picture like *Blue Velvet* by honoring him with a nomination. The Academy was more true-to-form in dealing with Dennis Hopper. Film critics almost unanimously felt that Hopper's Frank Booth was the supporting-actor performance of the year, but the Academy entered the actor's more palatable, less threatening turn as a reformed alcoholic basketball coach in *Hoosiers* into the Oscar sweepstakes. In the town where image is all, the powers that be gave the nod to the role that reflected Hopper's newly redeemed persona, rather than the hellion's ghost of his past.

Both Hopper and Lynch went home empty-handed from the Oscar ceremonies in the spring of 1987. Michael Caine won Best Supporting Actor for his solid work in *Hannah and Her Sisters*, and Vietnam veteran Oliver Stone was chosen Best Director for *Platoon*, the first film to truly capture the physical and psychological reality of America's descent into the moral chaos of the Vietnam War. The *Blue Velvet* boys, though un-awarded, were happy to have their work recognized by so many of their peers. In future years, they would see their lurid masterpiece canonized as one of the most extraordinary films not only of the 1980s but also in the history of the cinema, as well as a high point of both of their careers.

As Freud and almost everyone else says, love and work make the world go 'round, and in Lynch's post–*Blue Velvet* period, the artist made major growth spurts in both pursuits. On-set infatuations between directors and actresses are a commonplace in the history of cinema, but as with Roberto Rossellini's deep feelings for Ingrid Bergman, Lynch's love for Rossellini and Bergman's daughter was the real, abiding thing—and in tandem with Bergman's 1940s behavior, Lynch had to abandon his spouse and young child to be with his inamorata. He kept company with Isabella, who he sweetly called "Isa,"[6] for months before getting an amicable divorce from Mary Fisk. She and young Austin remained in Virginia, where the boy had started school, and Lynch made an effort to remain a fatherly presence in his son's growing life. But Lynch's most primal occupation, his Art Life, had to be situated in Hollywood, the movie capital of the world, so the director moved three thousand miles from Mary and Austin's doorstep.

In a supplemental segment of Lynch's 2005 *Eraserhead* DVD release, he speaks of the twenty minutes he cut from the film's original length in

1977. "I wish I had those scenes. I could have done a lot better job of taking care of things. Everyone has the experience when they need to move to another place: they find they can't take as much stuff with them as they would like and . . . so . . . later on they look back and they wish they'd taken a couple more things. And so . . . I've lost a lot of things from *Eraserhead* that I wish I'd kept."[7] When I talked to him about this subject in 1999, he'd been more forthcoming. Speaking about the whole of *Eraserhead*, not just the lost twenty minutes, he said, "I did a bad thing. I couldn't store my B negative, so I threw it away. I make myself sick thinking about it. Anyway, I kept a work print. And when I got divorced from Mary Fisk, half of that got thrown away."[8] We assume Mary did the throwing, since both Lynch's old friends Jack Fisk (Mary's brother) and Toby Keeler indicate Mary was angry with Lynch after their breakup. Talking to me about this most recently tossed-out *Eraserhead* material (jettisoned thirteen years earlier) aroused Lynch's against-all-odds optimism, as he enthusiastically enumerated, "I know where it was dumped. I know which garbage truck guy took it to the dump. I've contacted a garbologist—an archeologist who specializes in going into dumps—and a psychic, and we're going to try to find it."[9] As of today, Lynch's Lost Ark has not yet been unearthed.

Always sensitive to spaces and environments, houses and gardens, Lynch loved the bold statements of twentieth-century-modern design that dotted L.A.'s sprawling horizontal landscape. The artist had always believed in fate and luck and sudden thrilling surprises, so it seemed like a miracle, in the late 1980s, when he heard that a house designed by Lloyd Wright, the gifted son of modern-architecture god Frank Lloyd Wright, was for sale. Located in one of the Hollywood Hills canyons, the Johnson House (1963) was a pink-stucco wonder with expansive white interior walls, tall panoramic windows that looked east toward the center of Los Angeles, and wooden moldings fashioned from trees dear to Lynch and his father's Northwest hearts: Douglas fir. And as in the Northwest, the Southern Californian skies above the Johnson House would actually produce torrential rains, and the air year-round would be fifteen degrees cooler than in the simmering city below. Lynch signed on the dotted line.

For the first time in his life, Lynch had a substantial home that was 100 percent his and his alone. It had a threshold, but that didn't mean that he was going to carry Isabella across it. Not only had the pain of two failed marriages made him shy of the altar, but the lives Lynch and Rossellini led made them a separate-and-together couple. She was busy in New York with her Lançome Cosmetics and modeling pursuits, and making the outside-Hollywood films *Siesta* and *Tough Guys Don't Dance* (both 1987). Lynch enjoyed visiting Rossellini in the Big Apple and lazing around at her country house on Long Island Sound, where he kept a classic 1942 mahogany-decked Chris Craft speedboat. Ever the man to appreciate textural details, Lynch focused in on the shimmering-rainbow circles that oil and gas made in the water, and the pungently scented mixture of wetland and gasoline. Once again, the industrial and the organic met in Lynch's world.

In the year after *Blue Velvet*, Rossellini said of the man she loved, "I don't know what he does in Los Angeles."[10] Lynch had found the perfect relationship. Living alone, he could lose himself in solitary dreams and follow the promptings of the signs and voices he encountered there. He could draw and paint day and night, and conjure mind's eye images in concert with the eclectic range of music that blasted from his expensive, state-of-the-art Bang & Olufsen stereo system. He could spend hours studying the fantastical shapes of the hundreds of yucca and agave plants and aloe vera cacti that sprouted rampantly in his sunny back garden like the half-human plant forms in his early animated films. He could take the time to bury the almost weightless body of a hummingbird that had seen a patch of blue sky in the picture window of Lynch's living room and smashed to death against the cool glass. Without the pressure of a day-to-day state-sanctioned union, the obligation and expectation that he would be emotionally available seven days a week, Lynch gave his love and devotion freely. As his nineteen-year-old daughter, Jennifer, noted, "He always brightens and blossoms and becomes more funny when he's around Isabella."[11]

Back and forth across the country, like children playing house, they would fly into each other's arms. Accustomed to the cozy, lived-in hominess of her Manhattan duplex, Rossellini discovered that her amour was an exponent of the less-is-more school of interior design when she first set foot in his new house. Throughout the spacious place, the gleaming hardwood floors had no rugs and the high, white walls in this artist's abode displayed no pictures. There was an art deco sofa and two matching chairs upholstered in Frank Booth's favorite blue velvet in the living room, a bed in the bedroom, and a cappuccino machine in the kitchen. All of Lynch's other worldly possessions were hidden away in tall cupboards and closets. Some of the few visitors admitted to his sanctum have described it as "brutally spartan"[12] and "severe,"[13] stressing what is *not* there—the lack of traditional creature comforts. But Lynch, who is "thrilled by the way the Japanese live,"[14] is moved by the spare elements that *are* present.

Having been born in the Big Sky country of Montana and spent his childhood in the relatively unpopulated small towns of the 1950s Northwest, young Lynch was traumatized when he first experienced the blaring noise and surging, claustrophobic crowds of New York. This sensitive youth's nervous system was attuned to a sense of space, and when he discovered his "bible,"[15] *The Art Spirit* by turn-of-the-century artist-teacher Robert Henri, his thoughts and perceptions expanded with those of his spiritual guide. Henri noted that "We should not need to have a picture full of things. The Japanese can appreciate a simple proportion, but we are bred on excitement and thus do not appreciate a Japanese house. Most of our life in New York is directly opposed to the principle of simplicity."[16] Moreover, "The more simply you see, the more simply you will render. People see too much, scatteringly. It is not the barrenness of an empty room, or an empty life that we seek; rather, we would get rid of clutter, and thus get room for fullness."[17] Henri's words virtually define Lynch's sensibility: "There will be fewer things said and done, but each thing will be fuller and will receive fuller attention. By this means we will enter into the real mystery."[18]

In art and life, Lynch's credo can be summed up in the title of the cowboy song, "Don't Fence Me In"—don't encumber me with clutter. The artist craves the space in which to express himself freely, so he sloughs off many of the family and social responsibilities that encumber most other people. In his habitual practice of meditation, Lynch evades the din of his everyday, temporal interior monologue and expands his mind into the limitless reaches of spiritual space. He lives a continent's length away from his beloved in a large house with near-empty rooms, an abode from which he even bans cooking smells. In his drawings and paintings, Lynch surrounds lone figures and objects with plenty of space. From the time of his earliest films onward, he positions his actors against uniform, uncluttered, often dark backgrounds and surrounds them with silence or the absence of talk so that the essence of their fear or love, their sorrow or dreamy transcendence, can sing forth. Floating and falling in and through space become major elements in Lynch's metaphorical vocabulary. The bodies and spirits of his film characters are often oppressively entrapped, then set free in an expansive redemption. In "The World Spins," a song Lynch writes for Julee Cruise to record, he pens the words "Dust is dancing in the space."[19] Dust and space, form and void: the essence of everything, from wheeling galaxies to house interiors to a person's view of the world. Like all the rest of us, Lynch focuses much of his attention on the realm of manifest forms, but he has a special feeling for the fulsome presence of seemingly unoccupied air. In 1987, Lynch rode the currents of air to New York City, the place that had gripped him with fear as a child.

Now, as a grown-up who could negotiate the streets of the teeming metropolis without undue panic, Lynch, with Isabella at his side, made his way to the SoHo gallery of Leo Castelli, the most influential art dealer in America. Thanks to Rossellini, who had shown Lynch's pastels to her art-world friend Beatrice Monti della Corte, who then raved about them to Castelli, Lynch was granted an audience with the man who had brought Andy Warhol, Robert Rauschenberg, Jasper Johns, Frank Stella, and Roy Lichtenstein to international prominence. Since childhood, one of Lynch's primal responses to his life in the world had been the tracings of his hand upon paper. Now, those lines and white spaces and shadings were to be judged by one of the most formidable viewers imaginable. As Castelli slowly strolled back and forth along the row of assembled drawings, Lynch's senses were so clenched with nervousness that, for a second or two, he couldn't comprehend what the man was saying: "Good, David! Good! I like it! Now I want to see your earlier work too, because this is so totally professional that there must be some way you got to this point where you do it with such ease and perfection."[20]

The pastel images that Castelli was so impressed with evinced a number of Lynch's aesthetic preoccupations. Simple, anonymous, almost childlike human figures floated within the frames, surrounded by plenty of space. Many of the "characters,"[21] as the artist called them, were positioned horizontally, like Henry's dreaming form at the start of *Eraserhead*. Some were suspended between theatrically draped curtains, others were buoyed up by a beam of white light. One had little electrical wires sprouting from its chest, and a black cloud wafting near it. As he will do in many of his films, Lynch's drawings referred to the human capacity to receive jolts of power and, with the murky cloud, showed how a dark emotional state can smudge a person's perceptions so that he sees spiritual pollution in the world outside himself. The misty, monochrome hues of the artist's drawings had nothing to do with the sunny Southland city in which he crafted them; they were steeped in the subtle, soft gradations of the Northwest, where natives like Lynch have experienced countless, unnamed variations on the theme of *gray skies with water*. This man who doted on the idea of the world having hidden depths of meaning and strived to fill his films with "mood"[22] and "atmosphere"[23] illuminated his pastels with a pearlescent gray radiance that suggested a Northwest winter sun coolly burning behind layered veils of fog.

Castelli saw Lynch's light. As he muttered "*Molta bella*,"[24] the artist relaxed and, with boyish earnestness, made declarations that were keys to his sensibility. "You can't move or you won't float"[25] referred to his working method of sitting stock-still and letting ideas and intuitions waft into his consciousness. In his films, the director eschews flashy camera zooms and rapid-fire MTV editing; he gives his camera time and space in which to dwell on people and objects which, in not moving, manifest a hint of their cosmic mystery. And, just as Lynch sits quietly so that his mind can dream, his audience sits in rapt attention, letting their imaginations float forward into the artist's cinematic space.

For the first time in the history of film and fine art, a world-class motion picture director was given a one-man show by an international art potentate. For many in the New York art establishment, this occasion generated a less-than-positive resonance. Struggling artists were outraged to see a Hollywood guy, for Christ's sake, vault over their heads and land in the praise-bestowing, prestigious embrace of Leo Castelli. Though Lynch had painted steadily for twenty years, many art-world denizens saw him as a career-hopping dilettante. But the artist's pursuit of the visions of his inner eye remained steadfast. He kept painting, and chose to be represented on the West Coast by Santa Monica's James Corcoran Gallery, which Lynch, ever the one to take America's measure, described as being situated "two blocks from the edge of the United States."[26]

Isabella Rossellini had helped Lynch become established at the Leo Castelli–level of the art world, and now her sweetheart did something stupendous for her: He agreed to face down one of his biggest fears in life and act the lead male role in a feature-length motion picture.

Rossellini was set to star in fledgling theatrical feature film writer-director Tina Rathborne's *Zelly and Me* (1988), Rathborne's semi-autobiographical story of Phoebe (Alexandra Johnes), a lonely, orphaned, wealthy eight-year-old girl who suffers emotional abuse at the hands of her dictatorial, punishing grandmother, Coco (Glynis Johns). Phoebe takes refuge in the world of her imagination, interacting with her dolls and hero-worshipping Joan of Arc, who chose death as the price for listening to "the voices of her soul." Phoebe's loving friend and protector is her French governess, Joan (Rossellini), who in turn finds solace with her landed-gentry suitor, Willie, when Joan and Coco battle over the elder's mistreatment of the girl.

With a budget of only $1.5 million to spend, Rathborne was having an impossible time trying to find a forty-something actor with the requisite emotional stature and charisma she could afford. Lynch had read and admired *Zelly*'s (Phoebe's nickname for Rossellini's Mademoiselle Joan) script, and Lynch told Rathborne that, acting anxiety or not, he wanted to try out for the part of Willie. He came in and read some scenes for Rathborne, who was astonished to immediately see that he would be perfect for the role.

Sometimes when real-life couples act together on the screen their romantic chemistry is palpable (Humphrey Bogart and Lauren Bacall, Spencer Tracy and Katharine Hepburn), and sometimes it's not (Alec Baldwin and Kim Bassinger, Ted Danson and Mary Steenburgen). Watching *Zelly and Me* from today's viewpoint is a touching experience, for not only are Lynch and Rossellini so clearly and warmly in love but we know that they have now gone their separate ways.

For Rathborne, Rossellini, and Lynch, *Zelly and Me* was a nexus of entwined personal connections. Rathborne, like Phoebe, had lost her parents as a young girl and been sustained by an obsession with Joan of Arc's angel-touched grace-through-suffering. Rossellini also had a deep fascination for the martyred saint, and trimmed her hair in bangs in homage to her mother Ingrid Bergman's look in *Joan of Arc* (1948). And she felt that Phoebe was a thematic younger sister to her Dorothy Vallens in *Blue Velvet*: a female under the sway of a powerful evil who becomes convinced that her proper lot in life is to be punished and hurt. Lynch's affinity with *Zelly* extended from its 1950s time period to its setting in Virginia, where he had lived as a youth and where his son, Austin, and ex-wife Mary, and his close friends Jack Fisk and Sissy Spacek still resided. Furthermore, the film was driven by a narrative dynamic that was central to Lynch's own aesthetic: an abused, vulnerable person finds deliverance through spirituality and imagination. The film even had a line that summed up *Blue Velvet*: "All gardens have beetles." And, of course, he adored his co-star.

Watching Willie and Joan sit in a Lynch-style 1950s diner and talk about their concern for Phoebe and exchange sweet nothings, we feel like we're eavesdropping on Lynch and Rossellini's intimate talk. This sense of art imitating life comes, to a large degree, from the naturalness of Lynch's performance, for Willie's abiding patience, soft-spokenness, and air of gentle bemusement are artful modulations of Lynch's daily manner. And Willie's zesty exclamations ("Holy smokes!"; "You look great!") seem evidence of Lynch collaborating on his own dialogue. There's a wonderful moment of intertextual resonance when Joan says, "I got a new lipstick, Rapture Red; I never wore red before," and Willie responds "It *is* something," and we remember Rossellini's iconic red lips in *Blue Velvet*. As a director, Lynch often expresses his feelings of kinship with those whose bodies and psyches dwell outside society's definition of picture-perfect normal. Now that his own body is before the camera, Lynch the actor gives Willie a carefully not-overused stutter—which he employs to poignant effect when Joan speaks of going back to France and Willie says "What about Phoebe? What about . . . s-s-s-stay for me."

In true Lynchian fashion, Willie has a secret double life. He isn't actually the lord of the manor, but the master's manservant who, while his employer is traveling, plays squire so that he can impress Joan. She loves the man that Willie is, not his title, but he's enmired in the life he's leading and can't cast his fate to the winds and go with Joan to France. Sadly, she leaves him and Phoebe behind, but the girl now seems better able to cope with Coco, whose tyrannical ways mask a raw need for love. Willie and the girl are without their Zelly, yet traces of her spirit, like Joan of Arc's "voices," linger in their hearts.

And likewise, traces of the love between David Lynch and Isabella Rossellini will live forever in *Zelly and Me*: Lynch drinking in her face and wondering, "How in the world did you get so beautiful?"; the two touching their foreheads (and the minds that Lynch reveres) together; Lynch covering her face with whispers and little kisses. The public world knows Lynch as the hyper-self-controlled man in the buttoned-up white shirt, who expresses his thoughts and feelings through his art media, and even then somewhat obscurely. But in *Zelly* he seems naked, and in the company of his love onscreen, he does something extraordinary and unprecedented. He rises from the bed of Willie and Joan's one night spent together without his pajama top, baring his flesh, and his heart, for all to see. For someone with such an acutely self-protective sense of privacy, Lynch's chestbaring seems as daring and revealing as John Lennon and Yoko Ono standing naked on the cover of *Rolling Stone* magazine. Lynch's nakedness confirmed that he was Rossellini's romantic ideal, for as she says, "I like a 'lazy body' look in bed. An athletic body with muscles I could never love."[27] Because her film-director father liked to conserve his creative energy by not exerting himself and lazing in bed, Rossellini feels that the undeveloped muscles of someone who dwells inside their own head, rather than vigorously moving about, signal that they have "the kind of spiritual and intellectual wisdom my father possessed."[28]

Lynch definitely dwelled in realms of spirit, one of which Isabella was not eager to visit. He wanted her to practice Transcendental Meditation, the consciousness-expanding discipline to which he was devoted. As Rossellini told me in 2005, "Transcendental Meditation gave me a headache when I tried to do it. I was raised a Catholic, and my head was already too full of rules and regulations."[29] And she wryly noted that today the way Lynch, Mary Sweeney, and his whole office staff all meditate together is "a little extreme."[30]

If Rossellini made Lynch's love light shine in public, she also tickled his funny bone. As his daughter, Jennifer, noted, "David's wit sharpens around her. They smile constantly. I've never seen two people have more fun together."[31] No matter how unsettling, how physically and psychically violent

Lynch's films are, he considers that they all have comic elements. Certainly one response to the director's assaultive probing of the world's strangeness is to laugh. From *The Alphabet* through *Blue Velvet*, Lynch's humor stems from social embarrassment (*Eraserhead*'s dinner at the Xs' house), outrageous exaggeration (*Blue Velvet*'s Frank Booth responds to a polite beer request with "*Heineken*? Fuck that shit!"), bizarre juxtaposition (in *Dune* the mutant Guild Navigator, visiting the elegant Throne Room of the Master of the Known Universe, leaves a liquid trail that his minions energetically mop up), and a dry noting of absurdities (in *Blue Velvet* a person is said to have "the biggest tongue in the world"). These comic moments appear in films of decidedly serious tones. But now, in the years of *Zelly and Me* and Isabella, the grinning Lynch would attempt a task that has daunted many a storyteller over the centuries. He would spin a tale that was intended to be funny from start to finish, and both Americans and French people would be expected to laugh.

The impetus for Lynch's venture was the French magazine *Figaro* which, to celebrate its tenth anniversary, commissioned a number of renowned international filmmakers (Werner Herzog, Andrzej Wajda, Jean-Luc Godard, Luigi Comencini) to each shoot a short film on the theme of "France as seen by . . ."[32] Lynch was the only American invited to participate. The idea of a stereotypical cowboy meeting a stereotypical Frenchman popped into Lynch's brain, and he rounded up cinematographer pal Fred Elmes (*Eraserhead*, *Blue Velvet*) and his color camera, some actors, costumes, and Isabella, and headed for the hills of Southern California, where real cowpokes once roamed.

The Cowboy and the Frenchman (1987) not only celebrates transatlantic *fraternité*, it is also a comic parable driven by Lynchian difficulties of verbal communication. The superb character actor Harry Dean Stanton makes his first appearance in Lynch's cinematic universe as ranch foreman Slim, who's been "damn near stone-cold deaf" since a gun went off near his head as a boy. Now, as will Gordon Cole, the deaf character Lynch plays in *Twin Peaks*, Slim talks very loudly, and humorously misunderstands most of what is said to him. Lynch indulges his love of making behaviors take an abnormally long time, and of absurdist serial repetitions, as Slim stands by a corral fence and keeps looking into the distance and bellowing, "What the *hell* is that?" as the background violin playing "Red River Valley" continues to falter and start up again. The mysterious Other invading Slim's territory turns out to be a Frenchman (Frederic Golchan) dressed for the boulevard in black suit and beret. Slim and his fellow cowpokes (Jack Nance, Tracey

Walters) have never seen anything like him, and define the lost and confused Frenchman as a possible "goll-dang alien spy." Lynch has more fun with serial repetition as the ranch hands pull a parade of typically French items (wine, long phallic breads, stinky cheese, a plate of snails) out of the alien's valise, each of which the aghast and dumbfounded Slim greets with his "What the *hell*?" Lynch provides an American's viewpoint solution to this mystery of identity by having the boys find a plate of French fries in the traveler's bag and exclaim, "He must be a Frenchman!" Pop culinary culture bridges gaps in Lynch's world.

"Chow time at the old corral" brings everyone together in an extended Peaceable Kingdom finale that echoes the scene Lynch devised for *Dune* in which human beings and the monstrously huge desert sandworms shared a physical truce and a spiritual communion. First defined as an enemy, the Frenchman, Pierre, is now part of the group that aligns itself along the corral fence. And so is a local Indian (Michael Horse), a representative outsider/enemy/victim in terms of American history, who Lynch gives the poignant name of Broken Feather. Lynch further shows how he feels about the Indian question by having a ranch hand pay back a financial debt to Broken Feather with compounded interest. *The Cowboy and the Frenchman* is a testament to Lynch's democratic inclusiveness and sense of *bonhomie*, his gift for friendship. (Most of the film's cast and crew will work with him on future projects.) But one vital element is missing from Lynch's idyll of community: women.

Right on cue, three ranch gals with towering big hair drive up in Lynch's own beloved swept-wing-styled 1950s Packard Coupe. (Along with numerous images in his work, the shot of a space-age car entering a view of the Old West shows Lynch to be a cowboy who's kin to the French Surrealists: "I'm very happy to be a fellow traveler with any one of those guys."[33]) The women pass out the food and beer and, as night falls, Lynch presents a fantasia of Franco-American amalgamation. Images of western horses rearing up on two legs meld with can-can dancers kicking up dust. Slim gets friendly with some soigné Parisienne women, while Pierre sighs as two ranch gals ask him, "Voo-lay-vooz coo-shay avec mwah?" ("Do you want to sleep with me?"). Even the most difficult barrier, that of verbal misunderstanding, has fallen, for Pierre answers Slim's "Ooh-la-la" with a "Yipee ki-yi-yay."

The Cowboy and the Frenchman was the most sanguine work Lynch had made to date. Nowhere in it is there the usual literal or metaphorical sense that "Now it's dark." The director makes light of the American penchant for overkill violence by showing, in a nongraphic way, the ranch men reflexively shooting at any birds or snakes they see. And he has benign cosmic energy, in the form of three giant women in the sky, who occasionally lean in over the hills and corral to sing the harmony of life's continuity: "Nighttime fades to dawn, with the cheerful sound of the meadowlark." This is another of Lynch's birds of good tiding, which he must be particularly fond of, since he invokes "the happy sound of the meadowlark" five years later in a *Twin Peaks* episode introduction on Bravo TV. Or maybe he just likes the way *meadow* sounds, as in *Twin Peaks: Fire Walk With Me*'s Dear Meadow.

Unable to resist, the director tosses in a tart little fillip of mystery right at the last second. It's the morning after, and Broken Feather, Slim, Pierre, and the ranch hands sit on the ground, their backs against the corral fence. All are peaceful, quiet, and probably hungover. Suddenly, Slim yells "Damn!" like something bit him under the arm, and he grabs it and throws it into the dust. Lynch cuts to a big close-up of a black snail, its mucus secretions glistening as two flies plop onto it. This concluding raw touch of biology makes the viewer echo Slim's early dialogue: "What the *hell*?" Maybe the comparatively small price of consorting with French women is being beset by snails, rather that bearing mutant (*Eraserhead*) or malformed (*The Elephant Man*) children, or having to be neighborly with monster Frank Booth (*Blue Velvet*) after learning Dorothy Vallens' carnal knowledge. Lynch may also be toying with the idea of the shell as symbolic vagina, which French Surrealist filmmaker Germaine Dulac first visualized in *The Seashell and the Clergyman* (1928). The British Board of Film Censors' reaction to that film could double for some people's opinion of Lynch's *oeuvre*: "It is so cryptic as to have no apparent meaning. If there is a meaning, it is doubtless objectionable."[34]

The French certainly didn't object to *The Cowboy and the Frenchman* when it was shown on European television. Lynch had great fun making the film and exploring the comic mode of his sensibility, but didn't distribute it in the United States. Lynch let me show the picture at the Seattle Art Museum in 1996, and I sent him an audiotape of the responsive, overflow audience laughing at everything they were supposed to. The director eventually added the film to the DVD package of his short works that he released in 2002.

In 2004, Jennifer Lynch said, "My father really understands and appreciates the absurdities of life, and *The Cowboy and the Frenchman* gave him a big chance to show that. He's always had such a genuine sense of humor. All the serious talks we've had over the years have ended with both of us laughing."[35] Jennifer recalls a time when Lynch displayed his mastery of the humor of incongruity. David Lynch puts a lot of stock in his superior driving ability, and Jennifer was proud that her father (who taught her to drive) so appreciated her skill that he let her pilot the car when they went on a weekly dinner outing. Jennifer, who "can feather my starts and stops so you barely feel them,"[36] parallel parked perfectly and the two went in and sat at a small table with a lit candle on it. After ordering, without saying a word, David took some warm wax from the candle and formed it into a little ball, which he batted over to Jennifer. She batted it back, and father and daughter commenced a silent game of wax-ball table tennis. Back and forth, back and forth—then David suddenly said in his loud twang, "I've got to take the bull by the horns and call a policeman right *now*!"[37] In life and art, Lynch instinctively injects an unexpected strangeness into mundane environments and situations. When Jennifer told me this tale, she knew it was a perfect David Lynch story that didn't require another word, and certainly not an explanation of *why* Lynch needed a policeman. When I mentioned this story to Lynch and asked him if he wanted to add anything to it, he laughed gently and said, "No, it's fine."[38]

In 1987, something happened that brought no smiles to the faces of daughter and father. Jennifer was driving the blue Toyota Cressida that her father and Mary Fisk had given her when some people stepped into a crosswalk ahead of her. Slowing to a stop, she glanced in her rearview mirror and

> saw a Jaguar sedan coming towards me at forty miles-an-hour. I could see the driver bend down to get something off of the passenger seat, or the floor—he didn't see that I was stopped. I honked and made a waving motion to the people in the crosswalk, but they didn't understand the situation. The Jaguar hit me, and my car shot out into the intersection, missing the crosswalk people. The hood flew off my car, the battery sailed through the air. All this happened right in front of a cop. He rushed over and was stunned to see that I was alive.[39]

The doctors told Jennifer that "the impact had reversed the curves in my spine in three places."[40] Still, she, Lynch, and her mother, and those who loved her were happy to see her resume her normal lifestyle relatively quickly. "My father was relieved that I was healing well and wasn't afraid to drive after the accident, though the Cressida didn't handle too well after being smashed,"[41] she adds with a laugh. It would take fourteen years for her back injury to precipitate a dire health crisis that would deepen the three-way bond between she and her divorced parents.

Lynch's art manifests his thoughts, feelings, fantasies, and transmuted autobiography. When Jennifer staged a car accident in her 1993 film *Boxing*

Helena, her own crash was very much on her mind. The action required a vehicle "to come out of nowhere"[42] and strike a woman on foot, played by Sherilyn Fenn. To Jennifer, the accidents in other films were too much like "glossy ballets."[43] She wanted her movie's smash-up to have the feeling of her own collision: "stark images, like bad Polaroids. That's the way my brain photographed it: the car coming—a moment to think, 'Oh my God, I can't fucking move—oh my God, I can't—oh my God—it's gonna happen—here it comes—here it comes.'"[44] Jennifer perceived these horrendous moments with the sort of distorted, paradoxically two-way time sense that Lynch sometimes portrays in his work: "It took forever to happen, but it seemed sudden; it's a weird warp."[45]

Also in 1987, Lynch went through an unexpected, wonderful warp when he visited his love, Isabella Rossellini, in Italy. In addition to the French, Lynch felt a warm affinity for Italians. Lynch and the great maestro of Italian and world cinema, Federico Fellini (*La Strada*, *La Dolce Vita*, *8 1/2*), were both born on January 20. In addition to this fact, Lynch loved Fellini's films and was influenced by their imaginative blending of dream, reality, and memory, so he felt that he and the Italian master were, in a spiritual-aesthetic way, journeying through life together. Thanks to Isabella, whose renowned father, Roberto, had employed Fellini as a writer and actor in the pioneering glory days of post–World War II Italian filmmaking, Lynch got to literally walk the same path with Fellini.

Lynch was with Isabella near Rome, where she was working on a picture with Marcello Mastroianni, the esteemed actor and international star of *La Dolce Vita* and *8 1/2*, and Fellini's onscreen surrogate, as Kyle MacLachlan is for Lynch; and Silvana Mangano, wife of *Dune* and *Blue Velvet* producer Dino De Laurentiis and actress in *Dune*. Lynch recalls,

> I had the great pleasure of having dinner in an open-air restaurant. [*With emotion in his voice.*] This was, this was in the strangest, most beautiful area south of Rome. There were these great mansions—old, old houses—built into the hills, terraced. And we went to a restaurant one night that was open-air, and it was the height of the mushroom season, so the entire meal was several courses of different mushrooms, and the main course was a mushroom that was as thick as a steak, and Marcello Mastroianni was telling these fantastic stories, and these little lights were in the trees, and it was kind of incredible. And I mentioned to Marcello Mastroianni that I would love to meet Fellini.
>
> The next morning I came out of the front door of my hotel, and there at the curb was Marcello Mastroianni's car and driver waiting for me. They guy motored me into Cinecitta [Cinema City, the legendary Italian national film studio and archive that's as big as a town], and took me to Fellini's office,

> where everybody was waiting for me, and I got to spend the whole day watching Fellini shoot *Intervista* [1988].[46]

How appropriate that Lynch, whose own work often verifies Fellini's belief that there is "no dividing line between imaginational and reality,"[47] would witness the making of the Fellini film that melds more narrative layers than any other. Over the years, Fellini's art made a fascinating evolution from contributing to the screenplays of gritty, sociopolitically conscious neo-realist classics like Roberto Rossellini's *Rome, Open City* (1945) and *Paisan* (1946) to writing and directing audaciously personal, subjective films that intimately explored inner-consciousness (*8 1/2*, 1963; *Juliet of the Spirits*, 1965; *City of Women*, 1980). Fellini, Ingmar Bergman, and Luis Buñuel are often called the three great cinematic artists of the human psyche (a list to which Lynch can be properly added). Fellini fervently admired Franz Kafka's writing, and felt that the Czech author did in books what Fellini did onscreen: psychoanalyze and come to terms with his own life.

Intervista (*Interview*) was Fellini's homage to Cinecitta, Kafka, and the carnival that was Fellini's own life. It was a beautiful stroke of multiplied complexity that Lynch (born the same day as Fellini), who loved Kafka as much as the maestro, and was in love with the daughter of one of Fellini's best friends, would watch people make a film about a man making a film while he experienced dreams and memories of himself as a youth in which an actor played him, and fictional passages from his films in which an actor represented him.

Taking a break from these convolutions, Lynch recalls that "Fellini took me to lunch with a woman who was . . . *extremely* well-endowed in the uh, the uh, breast department."[48] (Large, bosomy women are an iconic part of Fellini's life story and often appear in his films and drawings. The female-respecting Lynch's description of the woman he had lunch with is as risqué as his locker-room talk ever gets.)

Lynch continues, "I got to come back with Isabella in the night, when Fellini was shooting in a subway station."[49] The scene showed people who were hoping to be extras in *Intervista*'s film-within-a-film arriving by subway train. A hefty woman says to her friend, "You see Elvis? It looks like he has a toothache." The two women are seen from the back, and when Fellini reverses the angle we realize the speaking woman is referring to the huge image of Elvis Presley adorning the front of her sweater, which is a bit worse-for-wear in the region of The King's pearly whites. Even Fellini honors a major avatar of Lynch's beloved 1950s American culture.

This would have been the last time Lynch saw Fellini, but in 1993, Lynch, after lionizing Elvis in his own film *Wild at Heart* (1990), was shooting a commercial in Rome. Word was circulating that Fellini was ill and sequestered somewhere up north. Then everyone said the maestro was being moved to a hospital in Rome. Lynch remembers,

> My cinematographer for the commercial was Tonino Delli Colli, who had shot *Intervista* and appeared in that film. I asked Tonino if I could go see Fellini, and he said, "I don't see why not, David."
>
> So on the day we finished shooting the commercial—it was a hot day, and in the late afternoon, in this beautiful warm light, we got to the hospital and were met outside by a lovely woman who was Fellini's cousin. She said, "Only Tonino and David can go in," so everyone else had to wait in the car, and they all understood. We went into the hospital, and she took us through corridors that were filled with people, and corridors that were empty—it was strange—and then we got to Fellini's door. The cousin went in, came out, and said, "Fellini will see you." Tonino and I went in, and there was another man in the room with Fellini, and Tonino knew that man, and Tonino went and talked . . . to that man, and I went and sat. Fellini was in a wheelchair between two beds, facing out into the room. I sat in a chair in front of him and held his hand, or he held my hand—*we* held hands [chuckles] for half an hour. He seemed to be in good shape, but he was sad, talking about the state of cinema in Italy, the way young people's take on cinema had changed—the sort of films they liked, and wanted to make, were so different from the ones Fellini and his friends had made over the years. Our talk came to a beautiful close, and I said to him, "Everyone's waiting for your next picture," and I thanked him for seeing me, and I left. Two days later, he went into a coma that he never came out of, and two weeks later he died. It was incredible being with him, and I'll treasure that for the rest of my life. [50]

Back in America with Isabella Rossellini after his first meeting with Fellini, Lynch was embarking on the most prolific period of his career thus far, and he was venturing forth with a business/creative partner at his side. Along the journey from his early days as a solitary artist, Lynch had learned that collaboration, like life itself, could be both a rewarding and a toxic experience. Always inclined toward optimism, Lynch listened seriously when his agent, Tony Krantz, said that there was a fellow who'd been writing TV scripts who David ought to link up with.

Seven years younger than Lynch, Mark Frost was raised in New York, Minneapolis, and Los Angeles by a family of actors. A born dramatist, Frost wrote his first play, for the renowned Guthrie Theatre, when he was fifteen. A few years later, while still in college, he was scripting TV episodes (*The*

Six Million Dollar Man) for mogul-in-the-making Steven Bochco. One of the pioneering writers for Bochco's acclaimed and influential police serial *Hill Street Blues*, Frost soon became the series' executive story editor.

Like Lynch, Frost has a sincere, low-key, down-to-earth manner, and the two got along harmoniously from the moment of their first handshake. Both men were fascinated by pop culture, the amusing absurdities of life, and secrets hidden and revealed. Frost would even say things that Lynch might have uttered. "There is a design behind the world that we are living in, which is veiled to most of us most of the time, but every once in awhile you catch a glimpse of it. To David Lynch, any film or television show should be life casting a shadow."[51]

The life that cast the shadow across Lynch and Frost's first screenplay was that of 1950s icon Marilyn Monroe. Marilyn and Elvis are the Queen and King of Lynch's 1950s fantasyland, and he will honor their spirits in his film version of Barry Gifford's novel *Wild at Heart*. Lynch is said to own the rippling piece of red velvet on which Monroe posed for her career-launching nude calendar photo, the cloth emanating the ruddy glow that suffused millions of lustful dreams. The connection in the director's mind between eroticism and velvet may have triggered *Blue Velvet* thoughts. And this Significant Red Cloth could be the archetype of the crimson curtains draped throughout his work.

Lynch and Frost wrote a script called *Venus Descending* (adapted from Anthony Summers's biography *Goddess: The Secret Lives of Marilyn Monroe*) which detailed the last months of Monroe's life. Her death had been officially ruled a suicide, but the screenwriters followed the conjectural romantic linkage of Monroe with John and Robert Kennedy, and posited that a conspiratorial assassination had snuffed out her life. Courting controversy, the scenarists were Oliver Stones before their time, and as Lynch recalls, "When we put in the script who we thought did her in, the studio bailed out real quick, for political reasons."[52] Lynch and Frost consciously or unconsciously honored the spirit of this abandoned project in *Twin Peaks*, for in both works an outsider-investigator enters a community to delve into the mysterious final days of a beautiful dead blonde female icon (the sleuths of both scripts use miniature tape recorders in their quests). And Marilyn's poignantly sad descent haunted Lynch for years: In 1990 he characterized her as "this movie actress who was *falling*,"[53] words that were like a blueprint for his protagonist Diane Selwyn in 2001's *Mulholland Drive*.

The writers next penned *The Lemurians*, a TV pilot that followed the exploits of two detectives tracking down extraterrestrial invaders long before anyone had dreamed up *Alien Nation*, *The X-Files*, or *Dark Skies*. A parallel story thread had Jacques Cousteau accidentally moving an undersea rock that releases the essence of the Lemurian continent, which, in mythological times, had been banished to the ocean depths because of its deeply rooted malevolence. Though not borne by insects this time, evil was again creeping into Lynch's world of goodness. NBC listened to Lynch/Frost's *Lemurians* pitch but didn't green light the show.

The partners' prospects seemed brighter with *One Saliva Bubble*, a comical science-fiction screenplay that Lynch planned to direct and which Steve Martin and Martin Short were eager to star in. A romp on the Lynchian theme of the fluid nature of personal identity, the script is set in motion when a lunkhead security guard at an experimental military lab blows a saliva bubble that floats into a computer console. This accidental joining of organic and inorganic matter causes a pulse to be sent to an orbiting satellite, which shoots a beam of energy back to Earth. This burst of cosmic power zaps a bunch of people in a small town, somehow shifting the personality of one person into the body of another. With a mental institution escapee now inhabiting a rocket scientist, a tough gangster dwelling within a hen-pecked husband, and Texans living inside Chinese acrobats, hilarious complications naturally ensue. *One Saliva Bubble* was a go at Dino De Laurentiis' empire when the mogul's financial bubble burst. The exasperated Lynch and Frost were two eager creators with their own company, and nothing to produce.

But once the pair took a seat in that fount of Lynchian inspiration, a 1950s coffee shop, would the muse not smile? The man to whom place is important remembers, "We were at Du Par's, at the corner of Laurel Canyon and Ventura, and all of a sudden, Mark Frost and I had this image of a woman's body wrapped in plastic washing up on the shore of a lake."[54] Once again, Lynch was feeling that haunting, cool wind from his northwoods boyhood home country. And Frost could feel a shiver of small-town darkness too, for as a child he and his family had summered in upstate New York, where the locals talked of secret love affairs, political intrigues, and ghostly women lurking in the trees.

Before Lynch and Frost finalized their *Twin Peaks* concept, they watched Mark Robson's 1957 film *Peyton Place*, which explored the emotional life and hidden secrets of a New England small town. The co-creators may not have been consciously influenced by *Peyton Place*, but there are a number of details in the film that remind us of the world of *Twin Peaks*. *Peyton Place*'s lead male character is a thoughtful, philosophical outsider figure who is introduced when driving his car toward the small town where he'll take on a new job. He stops his car at a burning red traffic light. *Peyton Place*'s major employer is a mill. There's a diner where characters gather that displays a prominent PIES sign. A man repeatedly forces himself sexually on his blonde high-school-age stepdaughter. There are good-girl, fast-girl, Doc, and girl-writer characters, businessmen cheat on their wives, there are clandestine romantic meetings, many characters harbor hidden fears and desires, one schoolgirl wears saddle shoes, a character is played by actor Russ Tamblyn. Much of the story centers on teenagers going to high school. Someone commits suicide by hanging himself. Some characters "want to dance in the dark," while others seek a blissful "season of love."

Doing something very Lynchian, putting their heads together, the partners brainstormed a two-hour TV movie that they could pitch to the networks. A tale set in motion by a dead girl, high school homecoming queen Laura Palmer, who'd had a secret passion for as much punishing sex and as many cocaine highs as she could find in her little town of Twin Peaks. Big-city FBI Special Agent Dale Cooper would come to town to investigate her murder, and he'd meet a cluster of quirky characters who had secret lives and hidden motivations of their own. Lynch and Frost would be producing this movie independently, they would own it, so they planned to push the boundaries of what constituted acceptable, profit-motivated TV fare. They wanted to drench the film in a moody downpour of grief, desire, and metaphysical dread. There would be plenty of time to contemplate the revelations and mysteries of silent human faces. Everything would be skewed off-center from waking reality. And, most importantly, Lynch and Frost would commit the audacious heresy of not identifying Laura's killer at the end of the two hours.

The creative clout of Lynch and Frost's track records, and their *Twin Peaks* proposal, intersected with adventurous ABC executive Robert Iger at an auspicious moment. Suddenly, within the hasty parameters of a TV production schedule, the partners had to make their north-woods dream come true.

As Mark Frost says in 2004, "the conglomerate, mainstream mentality hadn't totally taken over TV when David and I met in the late 1980s. There was a chance to fit into the network scheme of things and still do something truly new and different."[55] The partners tore into the project like a buzz saw, writing the pilot film, which contains thirty-eight interrelated characters, in nine days. *Blue Velvet*'s Lumberton was supposed to be a lumber town, but the film was mostly shot in Durham, North Carolina. Lynch added authentic timberland atmosphere with fully loaded logging trucks and a disc jockey's radio patter: "It's a sunny, woodsy day!

Let's get those chain saws going!" As previously noted, the feeling for small towns that Lynch projects in his films and paintings stems from his boyhood in Spokane, Washington, and the Boise area of Idaho. This time he would truly return to the source, for he and Frost set their storied Twin Peaks just up the way from Spokane toward the Canadian border, in the eastern half of Washington State where Kyle MacLachlan grew up. They chose to shoot their pilot film on the western side of the state, where *Dune*'s Frank Herbert had been raised and where the forests are deep and primeval. Situated 30 miles from Seattle, Snoqualmie, and North Bend, with their plunging waterfall, snowy mountains, rustic hotel, and 1950s diner in stone's throw proximity, would be the visual embodiment of the town Lynch and Frost had written.

The town would be populated by members of Lynch's cinematic family (Kyle MacLachlan, Jack Nance, Catherine Coulson, Charlotte Stewart, Everett McGill, Michael Horse) and Frost's actual family (his father, Warren Frost); seasoned pros like Piper Laurie, Ray Wise, and Michael Ontkean; rediscovered old-timers more potent than ever (*West Side Story*'s Richard Beymer and Russ Tamblyn, *The Mod Squad*'s Peggy Lipton); and dazzling newcomers like Lara Flynn Boyle, Dana Ashbrook, Madchen Amick, Sherilyn Fenn, James Marshall, Eric DaRe, Kimmy Robertson, and Joan Chen. And, most importantly, a lovely, effervescent young blonde Seattle actress named Sheryl Lee was hired to strip off her clothes in February, get wrapped in clear plastic, and be the cold corpse of Laura Palmer lying by a lake. As is usual in Lynch's world, death only brought her new life.

In the winter of 1989, Hollywood trekked up the coast to woo the spirit of the Northwest, and it proved to be a beautiful marriage. Lynch and Frost's *Twin Peaks* fiction fit seamlessly into the moody landscape that was home to the world's first flying saucer sighting; mystical painters Morris Graves and Mark Tobey; America's highest percentage of coffee guzzlers and serial killers; Native American spirit tales; Sasquatch the animal-man; edgy cartoonists Linda Barry, Matt Groening, and Gary Larson; and grunge rock's scream-pierced droning dirges of teen anger and anguish. Lynch's lifetime experience of television had been minimal; the last show he remembered watching was *Perry Mason*. The director had less than one-third the time of a normal feature-film production in which to shoot the *Twin Peaks* pilot, but he rose to the challenge, imbuing the film with his characteristic textured atmosphere and hypnotic, contemplative pacing. As cinematographer Ron Garcia appreciatively noted, "David's camera style is like drifting down a slow stream in a canoe."[56]

Lynch and Frost came in right on deadline and presented the *Twin Peaks* pilot to the ABC brass. The executives settled into their screening-room seats and experienced things they weren't used to seeing on TV. The pale-blue face of a dead girl presented like a religious icon, jewels of beach sand glistening on her forehead with its framing shroud of pale plastic. A deputy sheriff who bursts into tears over the corpse and a whole town that follows suit, giving more than twenty minutes of screen time to keening and wailing. A forensic investigator's tweezers probing beneath the body's fingernail for a clue, in close-up. An FBI man, the show's hero, who is both serious-minded and more than a little goofy. An undefined, yet eerily palpable sense of uncleanness and dread stirring like a wind in the fir trees. And no hint of who Laura's killer might be.

Mark Frost remembers that as the *Twin Peaks* creating/crafting process sprang forward, he expected the studio executives to put on the brakes, but they kept saying "Yes. What David and I were making was so foreign to the executives' experience that they couldn't presume to tell us how to do it any better or any different. They just said, 'Guys, you go make the series, and we'll be real anxious to see what it looks like.'"[57]

Lynch and Frost had their marching orders: ABC would premiere the pilot on April 8, 1990, and then run seven hour-long episodes, completing the first *Twin Peaks* season on May 23, 1990. Word of the series' artistic boldness spread throughout the Hollywood community, and the partners had an easy time recruiting top-flight independent directors (*Zelly and Me*'s Tina Rathborne, Tim Hunter, Lesli Linka Glatter, Caleb Deschanel) to stage the episodes that they themselves did not direct. Writers Harley Peyton and Robert Engels would help advance the storylines that Lynch and Frost began in the pilot episode.

Officially ensconced as the executive producers of *Twin Peaks*, Lynch and Frost met their scheduling responsibility: The pilot and seven installments would air in the spring of 1990. Then the big boys at ABC would judge the show's performance and decide if they would back the production of a second season. For now, the network was happy to show the nation's TV critics the *Twin Peaks* pilot some months before its premiere. This proved to be a masterfully wise move.

The men and women who criticize the nightly grind of formulaic programming *want* to like TV, and *Twin Peaks* gave them something to love. After seeing a preview of the two-hour pilot, everything else on the tube seemed instantly old-fashioned, and the grateful writers responded effusively. The day of the show's premiere, the Sunday *New York Times* ran a full-page ad that consisted of glowing quotes such as

"*Twin Peaks*, the series that will change TV."—*Connoisseur Magazine*
"Something of a miracle. The most hauntingly original work ever done for American TV."—*Time Magazine*
"*Twin Peaks* will change television history."—*Los Angeles Daily News*
"Unprecedented. *Twin Peaks* easily out-dazzles all the new network shows. This you gotta see."—Tom Shales, *The Washington Post*. [58]

And see it we did. In the cable-TV and home-video era in which the Big Three networks were losing more of their audience every year, more than one-third of America's viewers were glued to *Twin Peaks*' debut. The show obliterated everything else in its time slot and was the highest-rated TV movie of the year. Overnight, *Twin Peaks* had become *the* hot topic at work and school discussions. So while America wonders who killed Laura Palmer, let's ponder another haunting question: Who is the author of *Twin Peaks*? How much Frost is there in Lynch/Frost?

Frost had excelled at plotting the storylines of *Hill Street Blues* and writing a large ensemble of characters, and he contributed these gifts to *Twin Peaks*. He also disentangled the daily logjam of production problems and kept things flowing in as orderly a fashion as possible. He certainly developed the show's basic concept in tandem with Lynch and shared the director's view of life as a human comedy, which can be horrific, beautiful, bizarre, funny, sad, and absurd all at the same time. Then why does everything Lynch has ever written and filmed feel organically connected to *Twin Peaks*, while Mark Frost's non–*Twin Peaks*' projects do not? Frost may view the world from the same angle as Lynch, but he does not possess his partner's innate vision. As Kyle MacLachlan says, Lynch was "keeper of the flame,"[59] and series producer-writer Harley Peyton, who's a "diehard Mark Frost partisan,"[60] adds, "it was David's world and we were just living in it."[61] Throughout the run of *Twin Peaks*, there was the sense that Frost and the other writers and directors were the sorcerer's apprentices, that they were doing their interpretations of Lynch's primal sensibility. And we all know what mischief the apprentice can cause when the sorcerer is away. When Lynch returned from making and launching *Wild at Heart* (1990), he was truly dismayed to see the wayward paths the show began to follow while he'd been gone.

Part of what the TV critics cherished about the *Twin Peaks* pilot, and what contributed to its audience-grabbing power, was its cinematic look and tone, the sense of an idiosyncratic filmmaking *auteur* at work on Sunday-night television. Months before the pilot's TV debut, the Telluride Film Festival even showed the pilot episode as a self-contained motion picture.

Lynch saw the series as a grouping of individual *films* exhibited in a time sequence, whereas Frost stressed the value of week-to-week story continuity and carefully pre-planned action arcs. Everyone from actor Kyle MacLachlan to cinematographer Ron Garcia noted Lynch's penchant for disregarding the script to follow spontaneous creative urges. Garcia recalls, "Something will happen in the periphery of his vision and he'll take it as a sign: 'Maybe I should use that right *now*.'" Lynch's flashes of inspiration advanced his singular art, but what of the group effort? Director Tim Hunter (*River's Edge*, 1986) remembers that staging an episode that immediately followed one that Lynch directed was a formidable task of series-cohesion restoration.[62]

So was Lynch the true artist of the group, a frustrated creator who chafed against the constricting boundaries of weekly network television production and became depressed because he couldn't control every contour of *Twin Peaks'* shape? Or was he too much the artist, as perhaps he had been with various wives and children, prone, as Mark Frost put it, to "go off on his own thing and leave us hanging"?[63] As Special Agent Dale Cooper would say, "The truth wears more than one face." Welcome to *Twin Peaks*.

Watching the first few seconds of what will be more than thirty-three hours of *Twin Peaks* on TV and film, we see that we're already deep within Lynchland. The consistency of the director's imagery over the years is remarkable. He began and ended *Eraserhead* with a head floating in space, and showed us female eyes suspended in the cosmos at the start and finish of *The Elephant Man* and at the beginning of *Dune*. He opens *Wild at Heart* and *Lost Highway* (1997) with the fire of a striking match and a burning cigarette. Beyond the surface significance of these repeated visual elements, Lynch's vision resonates. For him, single things are double, vibrating with both temporal and spiritual/metaphysical/metaphorical meaning. The floating heads are a gateway to dreams, expanded consciousness, rebirth among the stars; the eyes are witnessing, nurturing, consoling cosmic forces; the flaring match and cigarette burn with the heat of human passion, violence, and psychic disturbance. A red robin heralded *Blue Velvet*'s close, and now it is the harbinger of *Twin Peaks*.

In *Blue Velvet*, the robins were the agents of love and light, who restored order to a chaotic world by eating up the black bugs of darkness and evil. The first thing we see in *Twin Peaks* is one of Lynch's plucky, cheery robin warriors perched on an evergreen tree bough. Then the director shows us double sawmill smokestacks with their white plumes of smoke rising in dreamy slow motion, then a slow-motion image of whirring abrasive wheels sharpening the wicked teeth of buzz saw blades. The contact between wheels and blades sprays fiery sparks, and at precisely the instant that double spark showers fill the frame, the evergreen title *Twin Peaks* is superimposed over the image.

Once again, concisely visualized in three images, we have Lynch's fierce, primal equation: "There is goodness and beauty, but there's also a force, a sort of wild pain and decay consuming everything."[64] The robins ended up commanding the balance of power in *Blue Velvet*, but here, forces that hunger for goodness are overwhelming. How can a tender robin survive when its home woods are being cut down and chewed up in a factory? How can a fearful high school girl and her town stand against a soul-harvesting entity's moaning buzz saw, his ravenous fires of damnation?

Flames will come later, for in the beginning (as in *The Grandmother*, *Eraserhead*, *Dune*, and *Blue Velvet*) there is water. Wanting to float us into his dream, Lynch bathes our senses with a progression of aqueous images: the falls by the Great Northern Hotel, a river, a lake shore. The waters flow hypnotically in a reverie of slow motion, stirring the deep currents of our subconscious. These opening moments signal that *Twin Peaks* will be awash in dreamy inner journeys, as well as in dualities. We've also progressed from two smokestacks to two showers of sparks, to two river flows joining in a single falling cascade to two ducks on a lakeshore, to two black ceramic greyhounds adorning a table lamp. In Lynch's world, objects and qualities that appear to be separate from each other can actually be conjoined on some hidden level; a singular-seeming phenomenon can mask and contain its opposite within. Reality is multivalenced.

As if to firmly embed this operating principle in our awareness of *Twin Peaks*, Lynch pans from the double-greyhounds lamp to the twinned image of a surpassingly beautiful Chinese woman (Joan Chen) looking at herself in an oval mirror. The first person that we see in *Twin Peaks*, she is an introductory mystery, a nameless woman lost in a reverie of unknown thoughts. But being good detectives, we see that she has two selves. And noting the prominent curve of the mirror's edge, we wonder if *Twin Peaks* is a place where reality doesn't proceed in a straight line from point A to point B, but arcs out into fierce and strange dimensions as it circles back upon itself. Aside from sketching the shape of *Twin Peaks'* cosmology, the scene with the woman and her mirror presents the show's primal color scheme: the warm glow of wood walls, the deep, inky black surrounding the radiant earth tones of the woman's face, the glistening red accent of her lips.

The colors of the pebbly lakeshore beach are gray and blue: It's a cold morning as Lynch gives his old friend Jack Nance the honor of discovering the plastic-wrapped corpse that will launch a TV sensation. Before Nance draws close enough to realize that a body is what he's found, the pale, lumpy plastic is just a shape on the beach, but it emanates an ominous charge like one of the bad-mood clouds accompanying a forlorn character in a Lynch painting. As the lawmen open the plastic cocoon and reveal the face of Laura Palmer (Sheryl Lee), Nance turns his body and face away from the sight, as he did in *Eraserhead* after causing a horror to be manifested by snipping into his baby with a pair of scissors.

The dead visage of Laura Palmer is one of *Twin Peaks*' iconic images. Lynch, the better to imprint her terrible beauty on our senses, gives us a huge close-up of the closed eyes, grey-ivory cheeks, chill blue lips, glistening grits of pale sand sprinkling her forehead and water-darkened blond hair. With her face-framing penumbra of water-beaded plastic, she's a Madonna of the Far Shore who will lure many travelers. Laura's image is creepy and scary, but given Lynch-the-artist's real-life ability to appreciate the aesthetics of wound-stained bandages, dissected dead cats, and display-bottled tumors, we're certain that he considers the dead woman's face to be a thing of beauty. For Lynch, an object, behavior, thought, or feeling can easily be both repellant and alluring.

One of the key methods Lynch uses to make the world of his films some dreamlike Other Place that's at least one step off-kilter from our familiar waking reality is the unnatural extension of time. We've noted how *The Grandmother*'s dying Grandmother keeps whistling and whistling and whistling before she finally expires. And in *Eraserhead* there are canyon-wide pauses within conversations, and a woman takes forever to pull a suitcase from beneath a bed. Lynch has already subtly confounded our expectations in the opening few seconds of *Twin Peaks* by having the first person we see on the screen be an exotic Chinese woman with a man's haircut and no defined social role, rather than a typical small-town-movie WASP housewife, and the director held her close-up so long that we clearly received a This-Woman-Is-Significant message. But the time Lynch takes to dwell on her face is like a dewdrop compared to the rain shower of grief he orchestrates to mark the passing of Laura Palmer.

The blade that took the life of Twin Peaks' favorite daughter has cut deep into the community's heart, and the town answers her shed blood with tears. Never before in a two-hour TV movie has so much screen time been devoted to active grieving. A sense of pain and loss and sadness is common in Lynch's work. Deep emotion is one of the driving forces of his art, and he firmly believes that "If you're a man, you can cry."[65] Still, the sight of a deputy sheriff—an icon of community security, who's no stranger to crime scenes—breaking down in sobs over Laura's corpse is a disturbing image, and one that indicates the uncommonly horrendous proportions of the evil that's loose in Twin Peaks.

Lynch stages the scenes of Laura's parents, Sarah (Grace Zabriskie) and Leland (Ray Wise), getting the terrible news of their only child's death with great dramatic force. The Palmer household is one of the director's most potent portrayals of the home as "a place where things can go wrong."[66] We see Sarah in her well-appointed kitchen, with the smiling face of the Quaker Oats man (a cereal-box image that's remained unchanged since the time of Lynch's childhood) seeming to anoint the scene with a blessing of domestic wholesomeness and health. But Sarah, for some reason phoning around town trying to locate her daughter on this typical school morning, is strangely tense with anxiety. As the series progresses, Sarah will be shown to have visionary powers, and on this morning she can feel the shape of something devastatingly wrong that she can't quite bring into her conscious mind. Sarah, and her community, will gradually come to realize that the horror haunting the Palmer home is the demonic entity BOB (Frank Silva), who has possessed Leland and made him have sex with his own daughter and then kill her.

The series will not reveal that Leland is Laura's slayer until the eighth episode, during *Twin Peaks'* second season, though Lynch and Frost knew from the beginning that he would be their perpetrator. Lynch says that "We tried to keep this knowledge out of our conscious minds, because it wouldn't come into the story for a long time."[67] But we know that Lynch's subconscious mind has a way of sneaking onto the screen, and this part of the pilot episode does allude to Leland's evil-stained state.

Pictorially to the right of Sarah as she frantically telephones in her kitchen is a bright window with a top fringe of curtain. This is one of Lynch's theater-stage-like tableaus to which we must pay close attention. *We* already know that Laura is dead, but Sarah hasn't gotten the bad news yet. In her state of fearful arousal about the whereabouts of her child, Sarah seems to project her *subconscious* knowledge of Laura's death onto the silhouetted windowsill still life that's visually right next to her head.

In the center of the tableau is a circular black wreath, below it on the left is a small bird figurine, and below it on the right is a small male figurine. These three elements compose Sarah's primal subconscious vision of her family. The wreath represents the dead Laura. The bird in the left, symbolically female, position is Sarah, her persona being related to the fabled avian qualities of a soul within a body winging to attain higher spheres of special, sometimes supernatural, knowledge. In the male position is Leland, the dark man whose figure appears to be wearing a tall, pointed hat like a sorcerer, a persona that is a symbolic personification of the Terrible Father. And, in concert with Lynch's fascination for what goes on within the human head, Leland needs a tall hat to accommodate BOB inside his cranium. The Leland figure is closer to the Laura wreath than the Sarah bird is, implying the unholy, secret father–daughter bond that lurks beneath Sarah's conscious awareness. The phallic shape of Leland's figure and the hole at the center of Laura's wreath clearly signify a sexual link.

With our knowledge of how Leland and Sarah Palmer's characters will develop over the course of *Twin Peaks*, it's easy to look back at the wreath and the bird and sorcerer figurines and see a symbolic tableau of family dysfunction and a death foretold. Did Lynch intend his still life to telegraph the idea that Leland should be feared and suspected? At the height of the series' popularity, when the whole country was wondering Who killed Laura Palmer?, some people did correctly predict that Leland was the murderer. No one who figured Laura's father as the culprit ever said they based their prognostication on the window tableau, but the signs and meanings evident in Sarah Palmer's kitchen could certainly have stimulated the viewer's subconscious doubts and misgivings about the Palmer patriarch.

In the *Twin Peaks* pilot, Lynch presents Leland as an overtly decent and untainted person, and the director stages the Palmers' devastating comprehension of their child's death in a way that the couple can poignantly be both together and apart. Situated in separate parts of town, they're talking to each other on the phone when Sheriff Truman drives up to Leland's location. Once again, Lynch emphasizes the human head as a target for trauma by posing Leland in front of a picture window, through which we see the sheriff with his news of Laura's death approaching in his police truck. As the truck comes roaring to a stop, it visually intersects with Leland's head, seeming to slam the bad news into his brain a few seconds before Truman actually speaks to him. As Truman walks toward him Leland lowers the phone receiver to his chest, and we hear Sarah's voice scream-sob "Laura!" over his heart. Leland, pierced by the knowledge of Laura's death, drops the phone, which falls to the floor with a crash. This focused moment of a household's and a family's tragic disruption parallels the point in *Blue Velvet* where Jeffrey's father, and hence his family, are stricken with a seizure of anguished hurt and loss. Lynch protracts Leland and Sarah's pain by slowly following Leland's phone cord down to the floor, where a mother's voice screams her lost daughter's name into the unanswering air. Lynch heightens the sadness of Sarah's and Leland's bad news by having them in separate locations when it strikes, and this lack of physical proximity subtly alludes to the later-episode-revealed fact that Leland has been living a second, hidden, separate life within his own house and family. Leland has killed his child but he doesn't yet consciously know it, though we note that he says "My daughter is dead" without Sheriff Truman ever verbalizing that fact. We've seen how Sarah began this morning in a state of aroused foreknowledge of Laura's doom, and Leland's ability to declare that she's dead without being told could be the result of his nonverbal clairvoyant phone link with his intuitive, visionary wife at the moment of Truman's approach. It's certainly possible that Leland's mind could process his wife's agitated concern about Laura, add in Sheriff Truman's solemn approach, and conclude that his daughter is dead. Indeed Lynch invokes his beloved sleuthing metaphor in stressing that "the mind, being a detective, pieces fragments together and comes to a conclusion."[68] Still, with Lynch's conscious mind trying hard to clamp down on the knowledge that Leland is Laura's killer, perhaps his subconscious let the truth flicker for a moment in the opening hour of *Twin Peaks*. In the days when the show was on the air before Leland had been officially revealed as the murderer, Lynch spoke of the "horror"[69] of trying to keep a secret and of the temptation to tell it.

A good example of Lynch's mind-as-detective concept comes as the news of Laura's death begins to spread. A high school class is commencing and the students are calling out their names as the teacher checks them off. (Surely the name Martha Grimes, alluding to the noted mystery novel author, is the contribution of detective-literature buff Mark Frost.) Once again, Lynch shows us how much powerful information can be communicated without words. Laura's best friend, Donna Hayward (Lara Flynn Boyle), sees a grim-faced policeman speak to the teacher, watches a screaming girl run past outside the window, and sees the teacher look at Laura's empty seat. Donna can read the silent writing on the wall and, whispering "Laura," she bursts into tears. In this beautiful little passage, Lynch shows us Donna's skills as an intuitive detective and links her with her future love, James (James Marshall), who's the only other student aroused to silent anguish before the bad news is announced. This sequence also initiates what will be a resonant linkage of Laura with the color red: the red of her secret dark passions, of metaphysical fire, her death blood, and the otherworldly Red Room she will inhabit. For in a classroom full of beige desk chairs, Laura's is the only one that is red.

Lynch stresses the apartness of Laura's parents as they receive the horrible news, but he emphasizes the togetherness of the victim's high school community as her grieving friends surround the central weeping figure of Donna, whose sob-contorted mouth recalls Laura Dern's anguished face of grief in *Blue Velvet*. The director has followed the town's gush of mourning from Deputy Andy's tears over Laura's corpse, to her stricken parents, to the school where she spent much of her daytime. Lynch climaxes his wrenching, beautiful, and exceedingly protracted progression of grief with the school principal (Troy Evans), alone in his office, asking over the public address system that links all classrooms for everyone to observe a moment of silence "for Laura and her dear memory." Then, having gamely fulfilled his duty, this big, physically imposing man breaks down in sobs. Finally, the town's river of tears floats Lynch's camera up to the high school trophy case in which we see a framed photograph of Laura and our first vision of what she looked like in life. True to Lynch's aesthetic of dynamic contrasts, the face that we've previously seen as a cold, grey-blue mask robbed of life is here a vibrant tawny gold, the eyes open and bright look toward a promising future, the parted lips smile warmly.

Lynch has done a masterful job of making us feel the pain of those who loved and lost Laura. The notably deep and lengthy outpouring of grief he has portrayed may have been inspired by his own "very bad"[70] experience when, as a seventeen-year-old high school senior, he heard that President John F. Kennedy, whose inauguration he had proudly attended as an Eagle Scout, had just been killed in Dallas. Just as in *Twin Peaks*, school officials made an announcement and closed down classes. Lynch's girlfriend, Judy Westerman, was a Catholic like Kennedy and "had a bond with this president like you couldn't *believe*! She was sobbing, so I took her home. She went into her room and didn't come out for four days. It was weird because TV coverage of big events happened before the assasination, but here was everybody sitting around in rooms looking at the same thing. Everybody saw Jack Ruby kill Oswald. It was called, 'Four Dark Days.'"[71] We recall that Lynch and Frost had written a screenplay about Marilyn Monroe's involvement with Kennedy, and note that his assassination will be mentioned in an early episode of *Twin Peaks*, and that the show's creators designed its narrative to cover the chronological succession of "Dark Days" immediately following Laura's death.

As with Kennedy, the light and dark aspects of Laura's legacy will live on, and the great mystery of her death and after-death will haunt the days and nights of her community. Jack Nance's Pete Martell said it straight and true: "She's dead." But, following Lynch's logic of paradox, the unhealed wound of her death, and the high-voltage emotion that coalesces around her absence, will imply her presence, so that, in a poetic sense, the director feels "she was in every scene."[72]

Laura's dead and gone, but her enigma moans in the wind and the owl's cry. Who can hope to fathom her secrets and confront the forces that took her, the evil whose appetite for Twin Peaks' townsfolk has only been whetted? Who can follow her into terrifying, unknown dimensions, ready to risk his own body and soul to bring her peace?

FBI Special Agent Dale Cooper (Kyle MacLachlan) enters the world of *Twin Peaks* riding inside one machine and talking to another one. We see a side view of his form as he drives his car toward town for the first time. Behind his head, the car window is like a movie screen showing an abstraction of the Northwest: an unbroken green rush of evergreen trees. Safely encapsulated within the car's steel skin, he's engaged by the trees as images seen beyond the boundary line of his sheltered space. But once he crosses the border into Twin Peaks his experience of the trees will deepen and grow: By the end of the pilot episode he will know their names (Douglas firs) and will have inhaled their moist, fragrant vapors on the night air. The pattern of evolving, expanding experience that Cooper lives out with the trees characterizes the narrative stream of *Twin Peaks*: the process of being drawn to something alluring and wondrously mysterious, discovering bits of information about it, and gaining full knowledge of it—only to realize that this "final certainty" is just a small part of a larger mystery. Lynch's presentation of a single phenomenon (the trees) as a visual, verbal, and olfactory experience alerts us to another of his characteristic perceptions: that reality is a multifarious state. Cooper will experience Laura Palmer as a dead body, a videotaped dancer, a breathing vision who whispers her darkest secrets in his ear, and each will be the real Laura. For Lynch, life vibrates where the emotional charge is hot, even if the flash point is a corpse. The border laws that separate life from death, videotape from live action, and movie watchers from the characters on the screen, were made to be broken.

The machine that Cooper speaks to as he drives is a tape recorder, which will enable his assistant, the forever unseen Diane, to process his observations on whatever case he's working on and hear his incidental remarks on everything from air temperature and weather to the place he had lunch (an agent of light and goodness, Cooper naturally ate at the Lamplighter Inn). In Lynch's world, the profound and mundane intermingle, so it's right and proper that a recitation about tuna sandwiches and cherry pie should have equal weight with the details of a murder case. As the series progresses, Cooper, like most of Lynch's heroes, will receive help, solace, love, and spiritual guidance and wisdom from prominent female characters, but the abiding female presence that he shares his life narrative with is the invisible Diane. In terms of *Twin Peaks'* narrative, Cooper's need to keep Diane abreast of everything allows him to speak aloud the kind of plot- and character-driving musings that *Dune*'s characters often whispered with their inner voices, much to the irritation of many viewers and critics. And by giving voice to his perspective on the world ("Diane, I am holding in my hand a box of small, chocolate bunnies"), Cooper shows us that he is a fictional detective like no other.

Twin Peaks' pilot episode presents Cooper as a man dedicated to chasing down evil and eliminating it from the world. Judging from the sharply focused energy he devotes to his quest, we sense that he is pursuing a deeply felt personal calling, rather than just punching an FBI time clock. He wants the world and its people to reveal themselves to him but it is not his job to return the favor. A serious man tightly held within himself, Cooper is obsessively preoccupied with the task at hand, yet every now and then a joyous flash of boyish zeal will burst forth, providing a surreal counterpoint to his somber mission. The game is grave and the stakes are high in Cooper's world, but the place is so permeated with wonder and absurdity that sometimes he just has to marvel and laugh.

These traits remind us of *Blue Velvet*'s Jeffery Beaumont, also played by Kyle MacLachlan, and evoke Lynch himself. Cooper's character suggests a Jeffery grown up, his youthful impulsiveness now channeled into a disciplined professionalism, his body more stiff and upright in carriage, his passionate appetites now restricted to comfort food and coffee. With his gleaming black hair slicked flat to his head, his body enclosed within the tightly buttoned armor of his black suit, white shirt, and black tie (like Lynch wears when he puts on a tie), Cooper is a virtuous warrior ready to battle America's enemies.

Judging from the pilot episode, Cooper's primary weapon is his keen intelligence. He seems to be able to deduce that A+B=C even when A and B are X factors. Laura's belligerent, juvenile delinquent-style boyfriend Bobby Brigs (Dana Ashbrook), who was cheating on her with Double R Diner waitress Shelley Johnson (Madchen Amick), is curiously not overcome with grief when he learns of her murder. And when Cooper and Sheriff Truman interrogate Bobby, he's bursting with scattershot rage and says that he never took drugs with Laura or killed her, and his overemphatic denials seem to signal that he's lying. Yet right in the middle of the questioning, Cooper passes a surprising message to Truman: "HE DID NOT DO IT."

Because Lynch never shows us how Cooper reaches his speedy (and, many episodes later, proven-to-be-correct) conclusion, the investigator's declaration seems uncanny, almost magical. Previous to this scene, we've mostly seen Cooper dictating to Diane and gushing about Douglas firs to Truman, so *Twin Peaks'* first stunning display of his analytical prowess has great power: This man is indeed a Special Agent. Later in the pilot episode, Cooper shows that he has the observational skills of a scientist, as he identifies the form of a Harley-Davidson motorcycle reflected in a videotaped close-up of the iris of Laura Palmer's eye the day she and Donna danced in the woods, and concludes that the man who shot the video was a biker. This time he shows us how he obtained his knowledge, but Cooper's process still strikes Sheriff Truman as being miraculous, and he responds with the very Lynchian "Holy smoke," which, this being the realm of doubles, is echoed by office receptionist Lucy's (Kimmy Roberts), "Holy smoke."

Cooper's clearly superior abilities make him seem almost otherworldly to Twin Peaks' law enforcement team but he's never condescending to them. In creating their Special Agent, Lynch, Frost, and MacLachlan wisely counterbalance Cooper's genius with his boyish enthusiasm for mysteries and the search for clues, his regular-guy love of lunch-counter food and simple, practical hotel rooms. Perhaps a similar sense of balance and intentionality informs the way Lynch presents himself to the world: the man with visionary gifts and extraordinary insights who seems at least one step beyond the rest of us, yet who makes us laugh with the almost childlike way he talks about himself; the man who is grinning, friendly, mannerly, and first in line at the coffee machine.

Cooper has shown us his powers of observation and deduction, and near the end of the pilot, he displays a very Lynchian capacity for simply sitting still until something meaningful happens, and having an intuitive hunch about it when it does. The FBI man and the sheriff want to question biker James Hurley (James Marshall), but he and Donna disappear into the night on James's Harley. Having lost the youngsters, Cooper and Truman sit in their vehicle by the roadside. Suddenly, James and Donna zoom into view, and Cooper says, "What goes around comes around." Just like Lynch sitting in his chair and waiting for ideas to surface in his brain, the lawmen's patience has paid off. And as anyone who has viewed the whole *Twin Peaks* series knows, Cooper's "What goes around comes around" is a prescient foretaste of the time-and-space-bending journeys that *Twin Peaks'* living and dead will traverse, and a summation of the transformative cycles that drive Lynch's fictions and his personal philosophy.

When the lawmen apprehend James and Donna, she declares, "He didn't do anything," and Cooper immediately turns to Truman, "She's probably right." Cooper's speedy intuition about James's innocence reminds us of his similar message to Truman about Bobby during the interrogation session, and we wonder if his conclusion about Bobby was partly based on a hunch, as well as spectacular powers of deduction.

Is Cooper a new breed of fictional detective? A sleuth for the twenty-first century, the new millennium, who incarnates a balance of yin and yang, mind and body, who harmonizes the aggressive masculine thrust of probing forensic science, the computation of gathered data, and the active pursuit of clues and suspects, with a receptive feminine sensitivity to currents of emotion and intuition: a lawman who carries a gun and listens to his dreams?

Detective fiction, pioneered by Edgar Allan Poe in the 1840s, is widely thought to have been inspired by the nineteenth century's belief in rational scientific inquiry. Men like Charles Darwin and, later, *The Elephant Man*'s Dr. Frederick Treves, were charting the mysteries of the human and animal body and bringing to light the previously hidden workings of the physical world. In Poe's *The Murders in the Rue Morgue*, the world's first storied detective, C. Auguste Dupin, reveres "the mind that *disentangles*,"[73] that solves a crime through the rigorous application of reason and logic. Sir Arthur Conan Doyle's Sherlock Holmes of the late nineteenth century and Frederic Dannay and Manfred B. Lee's Ellery Queen of the 1930s helped define and solidify the tradition of the cerebral sleuth, the man with an incredibly vast wealth of knowledge and razor-sharp deductive reasoning.

Writer Ronald Knox set forth some rules for proper detective stories in 1929. Supernatural or preternatural agencies were strictly forbidden, as were accidents that might help the detective by happenstance. On no account was the sleuth allowed to have an intuition that proved to be correct. One group of fictional detectives commonly broke these strictures: the female sleuths, who often used intuition and coincidental happenings to help solve their mysteries. Clearly, the detectives who have fought crime on our movie and TV screens for decades have been cerebrally focused types who play by Knox's rules. So, judging by the evidence of the *Twin Peaks* pilot, Cooper is indeed a new breed of investigator, a man who keeps his bearings and aids his cause by tapping into his subconscious, who knows that his calculating brain alone can't take him where he needs to go. And now that he has crossed the border into Twin Peaks, a realm whose symbol is two breast-like mountains, his sensitivity to womanly depths of perception can only grow. It is no coincidence that Cooper's modus operandi for pursuing mysteries also describes Lynch's method of producing his art and journeying through life.

So in what forms other than Cooper's persona does Lynch's sensibility manifest itself in the *Twin Peaks* pilot episode? The town of Twin Peaks, like *Blue Velvet*'s Lumberton, is a village engulfed in dread and desire. In terms of lurking menace, Lynch masterfully conjures an oppressive sense of familiar signifiers of safety and security being overcome by grief and fear: the tense, creepy feeling that something we can't see is watching us and waiting to snuff out all we hold dear. The magnitude of the menace that threatens Twin Peaks is measured by the way Deputy Andy, no stranger to crime scenes, is reduced to a flood of tears by the sight of an at-that-point-anonymous plastic wrapped female corpse. It is Andy who gives the first report of the abandoned train car where Laura was slain: "It's hoh-horrible, Goduhh, um ahh." Again and again, Lynch shows us the eloquence and power of communications that go beyond words, of emotions so devastating that they have no names. And Lynch imbues mundane objects like the counterclockwise-turning ceiling fan outside Laura Palmer's bedroom and the wind-swaying, nocturnal red town traffic light with an illogical, but palpable, connection to undefined evil forces. (In order to emphasize the harmony of Lynch and Frost's vision of *Twin Peaks* when they began their project, we note that the iconic red traffic light close-up, which we would reflexively recognize as a typically Lynchian touch, was the brainchild of Mark Frost—though Lynch did use a red traffic light for similar signification in *Blue Velvet*, two years earlier.)

The red light and its after-dark wind are the perfect coda to the shot that proceeded it, in which Agent Cooper, speaking to the assembled Twin Peaks community, links Laura's murder to a killing in another part of Washington State, and ominously reminds the group that "these crimes happen at night." In almost every film, Lynch acknowledges the night as a zone of heightened potential for evil, love, and special awareness. The black-painted interior walls of *The Alphabet* and *The Grandmother* set these films in a kind of permanent midnight, and in *Eraserhead* a living room lamp dramatically blowing out plunged the X family's living room into night and foretold Henry's dire future. *The Elephant Man*'s John Merrick resonantly declares that it's "Night-time," and *Blue Velvet*'s Frank Booth intones "Now it's dark."

In Lynch's world, creativity and eroticism certainly blossom at night, but his "Now it's dark" moments are usually steeped in menace. The words don't just tell us that the sun's gone down for the day, they announce an epoch, an ice age, an eternal metaphysical principal, an ineradicable component of human nature.

Lynch visualizes the abiding darkness in *Blue Velvet*'s Lumberton as an ebony convulsion of devouring beetles beneath the manicured green surface of a small-town lawn. The evil in Twin Peaks is more abstract; the town lawmen call it "Something dark in the woods that's always been there." *Blue Velvet*'s Frank Booth is overt and predictable in his villainy, whereas *Twin*

Peaks' BOB is an elusive shape-shifter. In *Blue Velvet*, young Jeffery Beaumont agonizes, "Why are there men like Frank, why is there so much evil in the world?" In the *Twin Peaks* pilot, we don't yet have a designated villain, but Lynch again projects the feeling of innocence devastated and fear triumphant, of something as amorphous as bad thoughts having devoured poor Laura. Using a motif similar to the disturbing black clouds that haunt some of his painted figures, Lynch visualizes Twin Peaks' ravenous darkness in an unlikely location.

The Sheriff's Office conference room where Cooper and Truman interrogate momentary suspect Bobby Briggs is dominated by a central table, and there's a large square blackboard on the far wall. On the end of the table near the chalkboard rests a TV monitor, on which Cooper shows Bobby images of Laura on the last afternoon of her life, cavorting and dancing with Donna near the woods. Even though Bobby's been cheating on Laura, she was still his girl, and Cooper taunts him with the knowledge that some unidentified male, first initial "J," shot this tape of her in a very happy state. Having expertly manipulated Bobby and aroused his anger and suspicion, Cooper lets him go, and the scene is over. But before the shot fades, Lynch imparts a potent nonverbal message. The chalkboard and the TV in front of it are the focal point of the shot, positioned at the far end of the room. The square TV picture of Laura's gay, smiling face is overshadowed by the much larger black square of the chalkboard, which seems about to swallow it and everything else in this well-lit, wood-paneled bastion of law and order. It's hard to imagine a more cogent condensation of *Twin Peaks'* ethos, yet Lynch adds more layers of meaning by having the TV image reflected upside-down in the shiny tabletop, implying the secret, double life of Laura and many of Twin Peaks' residents, as well as the general dualism rampant in this neck of the woods.

As noted in previous chapters, Lynch characteristically employs animalistic images, appetites, and behavior, as well as darkness, as signifiers of sinister forces. When Cooper and Truman visit the bank to examine the contents of Laura's safe-deposit box, they're led into a conference room with a big central table, on which rests the horizontally inclined head of a stuffed trophy deer. A deer head mounted on the wall would not be out of place in a small-town Northwestern bank, but the fact that it almost fills the sober table around which businessmen confer is surrealistically funny, as is the teller's matter-of-fact explanation: "It fell down." This dryly humorous, deadpan statement of the obvious recalls the dialogue Lynch wrote for *Blue Velvet*'s Detective Williams when Jeffrey brings him the severed ear he found in a field: "That's a human ear, alright." We laugh and marvel at the incongruous deer head, but there's something spooky about the image. The wooden mount that had held the head in its familiar upright position is still on the wall, so the deer's long neck now ends in a raw edge that looks severed. As a mounted trophy, the head would have been as commonplace as a piece of furniture, but in its weird, disruptively dominant position in the room, it seems to have transgressed some boundary of civilized law and introduced an element of bestial chaos.

When BOB (Frank Silva) enters the *Twin Peaks* narrative visibly, he will have an animalistic mane of hair, a subhuman way of crouching and creeping, hungering and feeding. Cooper will have many skirmishes with BOB, who will eventually have the power to evoke our hero's dark side and release it into the world. Many hours of screen time will pass before this terrible event occurs, but now, in the series pilot, Lynch positions Cooper behind the huge deer head, so that the beast's cruel, sharp antlers fall across his body and seem to pierce the vital region of his heart.

In the pilot episode, Bobby Briggs, Laura's two-timing boyfriend, who will eventually prove to be a dealer in drugs and murder, is locked in a jail cell opposite the cell holding biker James Hurley, who loved Laura and was seeing her behind Bobby's back. Glaring at James, Bobby vows, "When you least expect it," a form of verbal threat that Lynch has a character repeat virtually verbatim in *Lost Highway*, and which reinforces both films' atmosphere of free-floating menace. ("When you least expect it" could also be stated as "There's no place you can hide; you'll never feel safe": sentiments which recall the threatening dark cloud of oppressive fear that choked Lynch during his early days in Philadelphia.) Bobby's ferocious animus toward James then takes literal form as he begins to bark and yelp and wail at his rival, his teeth bared like a werewolf's between the framing cell bars. This scene recalls the caged monkeys screaming at the caged John Merrick in *The Elephant Man*, Frank Booth's guttural *Blue Velvet* growls, *The Grandmother's* Father terrorizing his Boy with barking, and the comic strip *The Angriest Dog in the World's* eternal "G-R-R-R-R-R." The nonverbal, animal-like vocal expression of hostility and aggression is certainly something that people do in real life, but in Lynch's world the behavior bears an unclean taint of bestial possession and connotes a sickening evolutionary regression down into the primordial muck of ungoverned impulses. Once again, a frenzy has invaded the rational mind.

As the *Twin Peaks* pilot draws to a close, Lynch shows us that in the first night following Laura's death a young man can howl with murder-lust, while others tremble with the chill of fear and grieving remembrance—but the director knows that the darkness can also generate warmth and light. Out in the deep woods, Lynch uses a camera setup that he returns to often over the years to show James and Donna joining heads. Their close-up-framed faces only inches apart, their cheeks softly glowing against the velvet blackness, these two who loved Laura so much find their intense feelings for her pulling them intimately together. This scene advances some plot points (both realize that Laura led a dark double life, Bobby Briggs probably "killed some guy," James feels guilty for not stopping Laura from fleeing to the forces that would snuff out her breath last night)—but the scene's most potent message is the transformation of grief into love, as their tear-stained, whispered words yield to shuddering breaths and a flurry of soft kisses.

In Lynch's own life, his love of art-making, women, and assorted comfort foods and beverages has delivered him from pain and fear, and in his fictions he's compelled to have his characters experience love's transformative power. In Lynch's world this golden gift doesn't just fall from trees like ripe fruit: It is won against all the odds and forces that could possibly extinguish it. The currents of *Twin Peaks* will course through Lynch's mind from the 1988-filmed TV pilot episode through the 1992 feature film, and he will eventually dream up a way for even Laura Palmer, a bruised icon of ultimate suffering and sorrow, to find peace and joy beyond death.

But now, on the Sunday evening of April 8, 1990, more than one-third of all American TV owners have enthusiastically received Laura's "ABC Movie of the Week" death certificate, and all that came with it. So much of the *Twin Peaks* pilot seemed refreshingly, and disturbingly, new to television: The multitude of neatly stacked donuts arrayed on a sheriff's conference table, the bikers' bar where intellectual Harley riders talk softly while a chanteuse delivers a dreamy love song, the Log Lady who carries a log around, the town where people cry and cry and cry, the FBI agent's forceps probing for a long, long time beneath a dead girl's fingernail, the detective's thrilled appreciation of trees and lunch-counter foods and beverages, and the beautiful, cold, blue girl on the beach.

As the end credits rolled at 11 p.m., even people who had never heard of David Lynch were phoning their friends to gush, "Can you believe that show was on TV—it was more like a real movie," or to wonder, "What was *that* all about?" In a single night, millions of television viewers who had never sought out a Lynch film at a theater were exposed to the director's deeper-and-edgier-than-mainstream sensibility, and the experience was as stimulating as a hot jolt of black coffee. The sad, unsolved mystery of Laura's death, the quirky characters, their secret power plays and romances, the absurdist humor and alluring air of menace, the enveloping enchantment of Angelo Badalamenti's music—this was heady stuff. Quite literally overnight, *Twin Peaks* had become a popular-culture phenomenon.

With eager anticipation and news of *Twin Peaks'* status as the highest-rated TV movie of 1990 on their minds, millions again turned in as the show settled into its regular Thursday night 9 p.m. timeslot.

Thursday's episode 1, written by Lynch and Frost and directed by the pilot episode and *Blue Velvet* editor Duwayne Dunham, had a decidedly different feel than our introduction to *Twin Peaks*. It didn't come stealing into our brains like a wisp of forest mist, the color images didn't seem printed on a base of saturated blackness. Aside from displaying a lighter-toned palette, the show did a journeyman's job of developing characters and themes that we met in the pilot, but without the pilot's sublime stylistic depth. Episode 1's Lynch-and Frost-supplied content was more interesting than its form: It was like looking at a photograph of Lynch's world, rather than totally inhabiting it.

In Lynch's personal life, numbers resonate with a special significance. Indeed, he used a private system of calculation to determine an auspicious date on which to release his 1997 film *Lost Highway* (we'll ponder the question of whether he chose well in a later chapter). In *Eraserhead*, the numbers of the X family's fateful house added up to an ominous thirteen. The numbers of Agent Cooper's hotel room total nine, which recalls Jimi Hendrix singing "If the six turns out to be nine, oh I don't mind,"[74] referring to the way six becomes nine when turned on its head. The capacity of six to flip down into nine is emphasized by the fact the Cooper himself is hanging upside-down when he dictates his room number into his tape recorder for Diane. Hendrix's lyric speaks of the way that expected certainties have a way of spinning 180 degrees into something altogether different. When waitress Shelley calls the Double R Diner's cherry pie "the best in the tri-counties," Cooper replies, "Nothing's a sure thing." Cooper senses that in taking on the mystery of Laura Palmer he's embarking on a journey that can't be mapped by the FBI procedural manual; his very survival may depend on his ability to navigate without solid, familiar signposts and to learn from points of view that turn methodical, rational analysis topsy-turvy.

As Cooper hangs head-down, the blood feeding his head, we note that the image of six becoming nine becoming six and so on also relates to the ancient Chinese yin-yang symbol, in which two forms (one black, one white) shaped like curving water drops, or sixes and nines, whirl in a circle head-to-tail through eternity. The image denotes the dynamic tension between all the universe's opposing dualities, which are primally reduced to matter and spirit, Earth and Heaven (the Chinese number for Earth being six, and for Heaven, nine). But if the universe can be reduced to two separate elements, how can the six become nine? Looking closely at the yin-yang symbol, we see that the black form contains a small inner circle of white, the white surrounds a measure of black, thus stating that each thing holds within it the seed of its opposite. Whether or not Lynch has studied the 1100 B.C. Chinese oracle the *I Ching* (*Book of Changes*), which is based on the yin-yang symbol, he insistently shows us the evil within goodness, light within darkness, life within death. The dynamic of mutability spins in his head, as does the understanding that multiplicity and oneness are not mutually exclusive.

Cooper's receptivity to esoteric systems of knowledge will grow as the series progresses, but for now, on his second morning in Twin Peaks, he sticks with his laser-beam powers of deduction and infers that Truman's been romancing sawmill owner Josie Packard (Joan Chen) just by seeing the two in proximity for a moment. The sheriff responds with one of Lynch's own pet phrases ("Jeez Louise") and Cooper concisely explains how he reached his correct conclusion: "Body language." To Truman (and the viewer), Cooper's deduction once again seems miraculous (we didn't see any give-away clues), but this time he tells us how he did it, thus duplicating a narrative pattern which Sherlock Holmes and Dr. Watson displayed in so many of their adventures. This literary linkage is made clear in another scene as Truman wryly observes, "I'm beginning to feel like Dr. Watson." These references to classic mystery fiction were inspired by Mark Frost's love and knowledge of the genre: In 1992, he would publish the novel *The List of Seven*, a Victorian adventure-puzzle whose protagonist is Sir Arthur Conan Doyle, himself, the author of the Holmes stories and the obvious prototype of Doyle's own fictional detective hero. Lynch conceives of Cooper as a unique, self-made, homegrown persona, while Frost seems to want him to be part of a pedigreed literary lineage. In the series' later episodes, it will be Frost who engineers Cooper's battles with the criminal-mastermind villain Windom Earle, thus invoking the figure of Dr. Moriarty from the Sherlock Holmes tales. As Lynch emphasized to me, "Windom Earle is all Mark Frost."[75]

As Cooper sits in the Double R, his head buzzing with cherry pie and coffee, he has his first encounter with one of Twin Peaks' primal sources of visionary wisdom, the Log Lady (played by Lynch's dear friend, Catherine Coulson). Having lost her husband in an arsonist's forest fire, Margaret Lanterman (a name probably in homage to Frank D. Lanterman, a Los Angeles assemblyman and philanthropist who pioneered legislation and community centers that aid the mentally ill and physically disabled), has a poignant understanding of the dangerous power of red flames. Now, in tune with Lynch's complex woodsy poetics, she carries a log that is both an emblem of the fuel that ignited to consume the man she loved, and a signifier of cherished life that is vulnerable to devouring forces. As if to emphasize the feminine nature of her sageness, she cradles the log like an infant. In contrast to inanimate objects like the red traffic light and the Palmers' ceiling fan, which radiate sinister vibrations, the log wants to be helpful. Lynch once said that human beings are like antennas that receive ideas and feelings emanated by the collective unconscious's Big Broadcast. In a similar fashion, the log tunes in to the mysteries of Twin Peaks and communicates its findings through Margaret, its oracular interpreter. Margaret, in a prickly and challenging manner, entreats Cooper to ask the log what it saw the night of Laura's murder, but he responds to her order with silence. Cooper's on the verge of being able to relax his hyper-logical brain cells and be more receptive to Twin Peaks' invisible warp and woof, but he's not quite there yet.

Episode 1 contains a humorous example of Lynch's life crossing over into his art. In one scene, Pete Martell (Jack Nance) serves eagerly awaited coffee to Cooper and Truman, and a moment later warns them not to drink a drop. He has a good reason: "There was a fish . . . in the percolator." Who put it there remains one of *Twin Peaks*' unsolved mysteries, but the incident was inspired by Lynch's memory of the time he chugged down some coffee and then found out that there was a bar of soap in the coffee maker: "The strange part was that I thought the coffee tasted pretty good."[76]

The coffee scene was written into the script well before it was shot, but episode 1 also showcases a major example of Lynch's capacity for spontaneous, on-set inspiration. Even as a teenage painter, Lynch was open to the new dimensions that an unplanned occurrence could bring to his work. His friend Jack Fisk recalls the time Lynch proudly showed him a painting of a wharf scene in which the thick oil paint was still wet. Suddenly, a moth fluttered into the paint, got stuck, and died, thus qualifying as the first insect to appear in a David Lynch artwork. The young artist, rather than getting angry about having to repaint his canvas, left the moth where it was and shifted his conception of the piece: "He thought it was great that way."[77] Lynch always admired the moment-to-moment inventiveness of 1950s and 1960s abstract painters like Jackson Pollock, who created out on the split-second existential edge of what Lynch calls "action and reaction,"[78] and welcomed surprising, happy accidents.

While filming the pilot episode, Lynch wanted to do a simple pan shot of Laura's bedroom to show us its layout and her possessions, and to provide an image that the grieving Sarah Palmer can think back on. Tall, long-gray-haired set dresser Frank Silva was preparing the room when Lynch got a sudden brain wave: "I was unsure about this idea, but something was happening."[79] He told Silva to crouch low at the foot of Laura's bed and peer through its wrought iron bars with a creepy I-am-watching-you expression. After filming the bedroom with Silva in it, Lynch shot a living room scene in which Sarah screams at some vision she's having. Silva was on hand to give Grace Zabriskie the already-lit cigarettes that Sarah prodigiously smokes. When the shot of Sarah screaming on the couch was completed, Lynch said, "*Beautiful!*,"[80] but the camera operator replied, "*Not* beautiful."[81] Alarmed, the director peered through the camera's eyepiece and saw that Silva had been reflected in a mirror hanging behind Sarah's couch. For some reason Lynch relaxed: "This is *perfect*!' But I still didn't know what the hell it meant."[82]

Lynch's modus operandi remains that of a painter, and his penchant for treating a film set like an unfinished canvas that he's still actively adding to and balancing resulted in the birth of BOB, one of the director's most horrific and memorable manifestations of evil. The artist's openness to intuition and experimentation with ethereal promptings seems to be contagious: just watch his alter ego Dale Cooper in the next installment.

Episode 2, directed by Lynch and written by he and Mark Frost, is one of the two or three most striking hours of the entire thirty-hour series. With Lynch at the helm, everything feels slightly and tantalizingly removed from reality. People and objects and landscapes seem charged with mystery and hidden meaning. It isn't just that people behave in a wonderfully strange way, it's the atmosphere itself, the air in rooms where no one's speaking or moving, the way we're in real time, but everything flows slowly like thick, black oil.

In the 1990s, ABC was the only network with a formal standards and practices office that reviewed show content, but Lynch and Frost were able to sneak some juicy sexual innuendos past their censorious eyes and ears. As Ben Horne ecstatically eats an odiferous Brie cheese sandwich, his face poised above the slit between bread slices, he cunnalingually declares he's reminded of a woman he once frolicked with. And at One-Eyed Jack's brothel (one-eyed-Jack being slang for the male member and a term Lynch uses again in his upcoming film *Wild at Heart*), Ben's tall, vertical form slowly thrusts into a passageway opening draped with vagina-formed petaloid red curtains as he follows his woman-for-the-night to her room.

Aside from once again showing Lynch's fascination for red curtains, the scenes at One-Eyed Jack's display one of his coded images for rampant animal appetites: The lobby lighting fixture is a horny tangle of elk antlers.

And the director uses a painting of an elk with antlers held erect to introduce us to scenes in the Palmer living room. As *Twin Peaks* progresses, the number of possible suspects mounts: Certainly the volcanically aggressive Leo Johnson, who was part of Laura's secret life, is a prime candidate, yet Lynch and Frost keep introducing details that make us question Laura's father, Leland's, innocence. Palmer's actions could just be reflecting his severe grief, but there's something subliminally disturbing about his behavior. In Lynch's pilot episode, the first time we see Leland at home after Laura's death, he's sitting on her bed holding her frilly-fringed, eroticized pillow over his genital region, and stroking it. From this position, he verbally resists Deputy Hawk's desire to open Laura's private diary. Now, in episode 2, having been introduced to the Palmer living room with that horned-elk image, we see the weeping, groaning Leland holding Laura's picture and dancing in a counterclockwise rotation. This motion away from clock-like orderliness into chaos mirrors the backwards-turning ceiling fan outside Laura's bedroom, which seems to spin evil vibrations into the world. In symbolic terms, a man dancing with a woman is a time-honored metaphor for marriage, and Sarah Palmer forcefully pulls her husband out of his incestuous roundelay with Laura, accidentally breaking the glass that covered her picture. Having cut his hand, Leland touches Laura's photographed face: It's the second time in four days that he's bloodied his daughter, though his conscious mind can't acknowledge this truth. Now Sarah screams all the built-up tension we've seen her exhibit so far into a question that codifies a key theme of Lynch's fictions: "What is going on in this house?"

Sharp as he is, Agent Cooper can't yet perceive Sarah's anguished call, but episode 2 reveals him to be a man of extraordinary vision, as well as intellect. Lynch has always identified himself as an artist first, a man fascinated by spiritual realms who's committed to expressing his inner life, rather than someone espousing an activist political agenda. Still, the artist did, not surprisingly, embrace the neo-1950s all-American Old-Hollywood aura of Ronald Reagan's ethos. But, in 1997, Lynch the devotee of Asian philosophical concepts spoke of the national need to "transcend"[83] the adversarial Democratic-Republican duality and focus on issues "that everybody can get behind."[84] Lynch is highly sensitive to personal and fictional invasions of one's spiritual house, and he was moved and angered when he met Tibet's Dalai Lama and learned of the holy man's forced exile since 1959, when the Chinese Communists swarmed into his country and began to obliterate one of the world's most ancient devout cultures. And so, in episode 2, Lynch, having become fired up about the plight of the Tibetan people, "added another layer to Cooper."[85]

First, our Special Agent assembles a chalkboard, table, and chairs among the trees, recalling the surreal scenes Lynch saw as a boy when he visited his tree-scientist father's office-in-the-woods. Cooper sits the members of the sheriff's department down and tells them of the Tibetans' sad story, and of his dream three years ago. In sleep, Cooper learned a decidedly un-Sherlock Holmesian Tibetan deductive technique based on physical action and intuition, rather than methodical logical analysis. So the FBI man thinks of various suspects in Laura's murder case while throwing stones at a milk bottle on a log, waiting to see if the universe will deliver a meaningful communication by breaking the bottle in synchrony with a certain person's name. (This oracular process is based on the ancient Chinese book the *I Ching*, which says that within the tao's eternal flux, the spinning cycles of yin and yang, of sixes becoming nines, a given moment in an ever-changing universe can be read and learned from by asking a question while tossing ritual sticks or coins.) The bottle tips over with psychiatrist Dr. Jacoby's (Russ Tamblyn) name and shatters with Leo Johnson's, both men having been intimately involved with Laura's sordid nether-life. We can only wonder what would have happened if Cooper had included Leland Palmer's name in his rocky ritual.

For all we know, the three-year-old Tibetan-technique dream that Cooper speaks of could have been a case of his own creative imagination inventing a new style of sleuthing, rather than a true spirit journey to the Himalayas. But for the last nine minutes of episode 2, Lynch certifies the agent's visionary status by *showing* us his current dream, which integrates things Laura Palmer has seen with places and beings that will become the extraordinary common ground of *Twin Peaks*' narrative in the future.

Lying in bed wearing blue pajamas and illuminated by a flash of blue lightning, Cooper enters his dream. Lynch, as he has in previous films, uses flashes of light and major discharges of electricity (like thought and emotion, a powerful invisible force) to heighten the drama of a narrative moment and to signal and facilitate a character's border-crossing into strange new dimensions of experience. We recall the momentous pilot episode morgue scene in which Cooper stood at the threshold of death and the blue-lipped mystery that is Laura Palmer, while the spectral azure light inside the room randomly flashed (Lynch himself was controlling the light switch). Back in Cooper's dream, there's a blue glow to Mike (Al Strobel), the former spirit-partner of the evil BOB. Mike intones a cryptic verse (which popped into Lynch's mind one day on the way to work): "In the darkness of future past / The magician longs to see. / One chants out between two worlds: / Fire-walk with me," the last phrase having been found at Laura's murder site.

We see BOB, wearing a sleeveless blue denim jacket, vow to "get you with my death bag" and promise that "I will kill again."

Then, as if to counterpoint all these blues, we are introduced to what will become *Twin Peaks'* most iconic space, the Red Room, which Lynch suddenly envisioned one evening in the L.A. twilight as he leaned the front of his body against the warm metal of a car. The room is composed of red-curtain walls that are evenly backlit, a black-and-white floor in a lightning-bolt-like zigzag pattern that mirrors the apartment lobby floor in *Eraserhead*, three sleek, darkly upholstered lounge chairs, two silver torchère lamps, and an ivory-colored life-sized nude statue of Venus, who chastely covers her breasts and genitalia.

Cooper, having grown much older, is sitting in one of the chairs watching a 3-foot-tall man in a red suit and shirt (The Man From Another Place: Michael J. Anderson) make a rustling sound by rubbing his hands together very fast, his body vibrating and trembling with the effort. Then Cooper notices someone sitting in the other chair, and with a startled thrill we gaze at a person we've only seen in photos and a videotape and dead on a beach: Laura Palmer, her red lips softly smiling, her eyes alert with intelligence. Lynch uses his unique audio-visual language to fuse a deep bond between Laura and Cooper. In *Eraserhead*, the director had Henry's dream-met loving soulmate, the Lady in the Radiator, offer all of her being to him in a silent gesture by extending her hands from her chest out into the air toward Henry. In Cooper's dream, Laura touches her face and extends her hand toward him, slightly opening her lips. Once again saying a lot without words, Lynch subliminally underscores the secret, enticing nature of Laura's communiqué by sonically melding it with a barely audible trill of birdsong (to hear this, one must turn the TV's volume way up).

They say that police homicide detectives love Otto Preminger's 1944 film noir *Laura*, in which sleuth Dana Andrews falls in love with the intangible essence of the dead woman whose murder he's investigating, because cops, in their secret hearts, have had a similar real-life experience. *Twin Peaks'* Laura is alive in some dimension of space and time that Cooper has access to, first in his subconscious sleep state, then later in waking life. Cooper knows that Teresa Banks was also killed in Washington State, but Laura is the one who speaks to him. Cooper is born to be a detective, and like *Blue Velvet*'s Jeffrey hiding in Dorothy's closet, and "the magician" in Mike's poem, he "longs to see," to shed light on the darkest secrets, and Laura, as the Red Room's Man From Another Place says, is "full of secrets." She is both Cooper's femme fatale and damsel in distress, his invitation to danger and love, his truly significant Other.

In Cooper's dream, his bond with Laura encompasses the realm of spirit (her nonverbal airborne message), touch (she softly kisses his lips), and words (she whispers the name of her killer in his ear). He wakes from his dream communion with a start, the hair on the left side of his head erect. When *Eraserhead*'s Henry transcended his life of pain and confusion to embrace his heavenly love for eternity, every hair on his head stood straight up. Only part of Cooper's hair is aroused because, even though he is a genius detective in the temporal world, he's still a fledgling dream-traveler who must develop his skills as an extra-dimensional explorer. It seems so straightforward and simple: She just told Cooper who murdered her. But the Red Room, being a David Lynch creation, erases certainties and sparks mysteries, and Cooper is far from being able to grasp its operating principles. He mistakenly thinks that he'll remember what Laura told him when morning comes.

Cooper's nine-minute dream was the most weirdly seductive, confounding slice of sustained surrealism that an American TV audience had ever digested, and, as with the pilot episode, viewers were buzzing late into the night about what they had just seen. Once again, an industrial-strength manifestation of Lynch's imagination had resonated with the psyches of his audience. Like *Eraserhead* Henry's live-wire hair, the Red Room would become a familiar emblem of Lynch's world, showing up in TV commercials, music videos, the popular animated family sitcom *The Simpsons*, and a fashion spread in the Sunday *New York Times Magazine* (1998).

Millions of TV watchers were gripped and fascinated by Lynch's prime-time visions, though one month into the series that group was considerably smaller that the horde that had seen the pilot episode. Mark Frost spoke of how America was now synchronized with Lynch's previously far-out sensibility, and evidence of the show's galvanizing effect on popular culture stretched from rapturous magazine cover stories to *Twin Peaks* viewing parties with pie, donuts, and damn fine coffee, to the halls of Washington, D.C., power, where conservative Republican Vice President Dan Quayle and liberal Democrat rising star George Stephanopoulos were both avid viewers. Angelo Badalamenti's hauntingly wistful, yet exultant *Twin Peaks* theme music resounded in elevators and supermarket aisles throughout the land, but there were also ominous rumblings in the wind.

Many average *Twin Peaks* viewers, as opposed to the core fans who would happily follow whatever convoluted, esoteric path Lynch and Frost presented, began to grow impatient with the unsolved status of the Laura Palmer case. They were not able to relax and flow along with Lynch and

Frost's grand design. Lynch felt that the murder mystery would eventually become the background story, with other plots taking precedence in various episodes, but he emphasized that they "weren't going to solve the murder for a long time."[86] Lynch's penchant for revealing secondary secrets (Laura was a cocaine addict and had sex with three men the night she was murdered) while preserving The Great Question of her killer's identity frustrated viewers accustomed to having TV mysteries arc from crime to solution in one or two episodes. Lynch and Frost had made Laura's death so emotionally, intellectually, and aesthetically compelling that viewers were desperate to discover Whodunit? As the weeks wore on and the answer wasn't forthcoming, millions turned off their TV sets. Still, a dedicated audience of ten million was so intoxicated by the mysteries and engaging storylines and bizarre charm of the *Twin Peaks* universe that they were, like Agent Cooper, ready to buy property and move in to stay.

As *Twin Peaks*' seven-week season approaches its conclusion, our fascination with Cooper's character grows like a sprouting forest mushroom. Kyle MacLachlan does an admirable job of maintaining Cooper's upright, businesslike demeanor and air of curious reserve even as he cordially interacts with the townsfolk. Via his dreams and intuitions, our detective is clearly receptive to female energies, but he can also be a bluntly aggressive male. When he and the lawmen visit the Log Lady's cabin, she rebuffs his impatient attempt to question her (and her log): He has to learn to slow down and synchronize with her rhythm of disclosure. It is with men that Cooper has discussions about the nature of the soul, and to whom he confides his own buried secret. Target shooting with the lawmen at the sheriff's office pistol range, he declares that "women were drawn from a different set of blueprints," and, gripped by a tragic memory, speaks of a lost love and "the pain of a broken heart" as he rapidly blasts six shots into the human-shaped target. And Cooper bonds with the Bookhouse Boys, the secret society that has for decades fulfilled the traditional masculine role of protecting the community from evil. (The Bookhouse Boys, who are composed of civilians as well as policemen, recall the western-lore archetype established by the real-life Sheriff Wyatt Earp, who would enlist friends and family in his battle against lawbreakers.) Cooper touchingly shows himself to be a fallible human being when he lets his friendship for Sheriff Truman short-circuit his valid doubts about Josie Packard's veracity: Truman says his lover is trustworthy, and that's good enough for Coop.

When it comes to luscious highschooler Audrey Horne, however, Cooper will not let his heart, or his loins, rule his head. A sensual young woman who speaks of her skin itching or feeling hot, she, like Leland after Laura's death, is a lone dancer who needs a partner, and Cooper's the one for her. Thanks to the power generated by her beautiful face and ripe body, and the fact that her father's the richest man in town, Audrey's used to getting what she wants, but Cooper literally won't tumble into bed for her. He cites her youth and the FBI professional code as the reasons he's holding back, but we sense that his past heartbreak is cooling his capacity for ardor. Audrey's feelings for Cooper run deep, and after agreeing to be "just friends" with him, she embarks on a plan to win his heart by secretly helping him solve the murder of Laura Palmer without telling him what she's up to, and then revealing her participation at a strategically advantageous moment. The art of detection is a pure expression of Cooper's being, whereas for the romantic, cunning Audrey it's an opportunistic means of snaring her man—but still, she's good at her appointed task. Images mean a lot in Lynch's world, and *Twin Peaks* puts Audrey in an iconic position that Cooper's fictional progenitor, *Blue Velvet*'s amateur sleuth, Jeffrey Beaumont, occupied: hiding in a closet and peering out to glean knowledge. Audrey is emotionally estranged from her father (she impishly thwarts one of his business schemes), so in dramatic terms, Cooper would be the prime candidate to help guide her dreamy, unruly impulses while he was also sharing love with her, and her saucy mischievousness would be a perfect foil for Cooper's button-up rectitude. Mark Frost and head writer Harley Peyton paid attention to the volume of viewer mail that spoke positively about a Cooper-Audrey romance and planned to make the budding alliance their storyline number one once the Laura Palmer murder was solved. So why was Harley Peyton, instead of David Lynch, charting *Twin Peaks*' future course with Mark Frost?

Collaboration is a tricky proposition for Lynch, whose youthful artistic nervous system was initially and for years attuned to the solitary act of applying his thoughts and feelings to canvas with a paintbrush. With *Eraserhead* and *Blue Velvet* he was able to bring his inner vision to the screen in a pure, unadulterated state, whereas his grand-scale conception of *Dune* suffered an assault of a thousand cuts perpetrated by many intervening minds and hands. In 1997, having made films both by himself and with thousands of helpers for twenty-nine years, Lynch said that collaboration is fine as long as it "doesn't inhibit free thinking."[87] Well and good, but how do two freethinkers meld their individual visions to create a product that is artistically satisfying to both? After the pain of his *Dune* experience, Lynch was hypersensitive about compromising his work and unwilling to walk down an artistic path that didn't seem "correct."[88] Embarking on the *Twin Peaks* project with Mark Frost felt like the right thing to do: pooling ideas with him was the opposite of compromise, it built something greater than either man could construct alone. But as the series progressed, the contributions of Frost and other producers, writers, and directors eclipsed Lynch's. Lynch needs to "fall in love"[89] with a project in order to feel inspired, and his artistic passion burned brightest in the episodes he personally wrote and directed. Otherwise, according to Frost and key members of the show's creative team, Lynch was relatively uninvolved in the series' day-to-day production. Frost and other writers would craft detailed story outlines to which Lynch would "occasionally respond with one or two comments."[90]

Frost had great respect for Lynch's ability to create moods and atmospheres that were so enthralling they "transcended story."[91] But for Frost, the master of plot construction and story arcs, Lynch's special skill made him a limited creator: "His failing is that he's not a strong storyteller. He doesn't have a strong interest in telling a story. He's not as interested in character as he is in fragments of personality."[92] Frost made similar comments in the *Twin Peaks*–production era, but he said these words a decade later, after *Mulholland Drive* came out. Looking at Lynch's career from *Eraserhead* onward, it is impossible to argue that Frost has created more resonant, culturally enduring stories and characters than Lynch. Today, Frost is fond of Lynch (though he doesn't keep in close touch) and can imagine working with him again. But some of his remarks about his former partner run the gamut from mildly disparaging to the absurd: "He doesn't work things out. He's not that good in logic. When people spend a lot of energy trying to figure out exactly what he meant by *Mulholland Drive*, I can assure you that he didn't know."[93] Frost continues, "He doesn't have a strong point of view. It's about sensation and feeling and arousing emotions."[94] One would think Lynch would have a hard time arousing emotions if he didn't have a strong point of view. A couple of years before Lynch and Frost amicably dissolved their partnership in the early 1990s, they clearly had varying approaches to the modus operandi of crafting *Twin Peaks* episodes. In an ABC promotional clip, a carefree-seeming Lynch made the production process sound like the joyful application of intuitive creativity, while Frost, looking a bit disgruntled, emphasized that doing the show was a lot of hard, day-to-day-grind work.

Harley Peyton says that Lynch "wouldn't really read the scripts (that some other director was going to film) until the night before they were to be shot,"[95] when it was too late to make changes. And besides, Peyton adds that Lynch didn't have "veto power"[96] over the "larger storytelling decisions."[97] It's no wonder that material was broadcast on the *Twin Peaks* airwaves that wasn't "correct"[98] for Lynch. An example is the way the ceiling and walls of the log cabin where Laura had sex, drugs, and torture on the night of her death are draped in red curtains, implying that a real-life location was the catalyst for Cooper's Red Room dream. Lynch, who conjured up Cooper's dream room in the first place, instinctively knew that the metaphysical space was a "nowhere place" that gained its poetic power from being absolutely outside and beyond any real-world compass points. When Lynch wrote and shot his 1992 theatrical feature *Twin Peaks: Fire Walk With Me*, the otherworldly Red Room was as magical as ever, and the ceiling and walls of the log cabin were just plain wood.

It wasn't that Lynch was bored with *Twin Peaks*. Long after the show had faded from TV screens and *Twin Peaks: Fire Walk With Me* had disappeared from theaters, he spoke of how much he still loved the fictional world that he and Mark Frost had created. Indeed, at the core of their Northwestern tale were Lynch's memories of being introduced to forest mysteries and beauties by his woodsman-scientist father, a fact which the director had planned to honor if he'd ever gotten to make a Television Academy Emmy Award acceptance speech.

Ironically, Lynch's sporadic, mercurial involvement with the ongoing *Twin Peaks* production, which so frustrated his collaborators, was a product of the same powers of white-hot inspiration that launched the show in the first place. Lynch's artistic fascination for border-crossings, transformations, and mutable realities is a metaphor for his need to change and grow and follow his passions as a human being. The primal sovereign he bears allegiance to is his imaginative intuition, and his uncommon ability to realize its promptings and visions makes him the unique artist that he is. Lynch is always on alert for a phone call from his muse, and when the bell rings, he's off and running, sometimes letting worldly responsibilities and complications fall where they may. With ill will toward no one, and pangs of guilt about his absence, he simply *must* go and hear what the woman floating in the stars has to tell him.

So, after embarking on his *Twin Peaks* journey with Mark Frost and company, Lynch took off on a simultaneous road trip that he just couldn't pass up. His friend Monty Montgomery, who was a co-producer of *Twin Peaks*, wanted Lynch to produce a film that Montgomery was going to direct. The picture would be an adaptation of author Barry Gifford's novel *Wild at Heart: The Story of Sailor and Lula* (1990), which Montgomery had enthusiastically optioned while it was still in pre-publication galley form. Lynch, knowing his own capacity for sudden, passionate inspiration, cautioned Montgomery that if he started reading the book and fell in love with it, it would drive him crazy if he couldn't be the one to direct it. Montgomery, who was fully aware of Lynch's preeminent directorial abilities, and who would never want to cause his friend to endure an episode of artistic coitus interruptus with a desired project, told Lynch he could have his way with *Wild at Heart* if he wanted to.

So, like a throbbing hunk of Detroit iron laying down scorching black-rubber tracks on Route 69, Lynch sped ahead into the new film after directing the *Twin Peaks* pilot episode. Sure, he enjoyed working with Mark Frost and the *Twin Peaks* family on their groundbreaking program, and he said he didn't mind staying within the constraints of ABC's standards and practices strictures regarding the show's content. But the pure oxygen of artistic freedom made Lynch's creative motor rev the hottest and strongest, and on *Wild at Heart* no one but him would write the screenplay and choose how to visualize it, and there would be no TV censors to restrain him from crafting extreme depictions of sex and violence.

The day before *Twin Peaks* concluded its debut season on May 23, 1990, word came that ABC would renew the show's lease on broadcast life and let Lynch and Frost beguile viewers with twenty-two new episodes beginning in September. At the time that Frost wrote and directed the first season's final installment, he had no idea whether the show would he renewed or not. So, like Sam Peckinpah's Wild Bunch going out in a last-stand blaze of honorable glory, he decided to make what could well be the last hour of *Twin Peaks* that anyone would ever see an ultimate cliffhanger.

The chutzpah of Frost's gesture is admirable, but the relatively frantic, hyper-plot-driven nature of the finale breaks the lulling, entrancing spell of the hours that have preceded it. The episode feels like the work of a prose writer on a spree, rather than the poetic conjuring of a dream-weaver. The first eight hours of *Twin Peaks* artfully alluded to soap opera conventions, whereas Frost's finale plunges straightforwardly into full-tilt melodrama. We can understand Frost's writerly impulse to put virtually every character in danger in this concluding episode, but the show, which is undeniably entertaining, plays like a formulaic gimmick. *Twin Peaks'* subtle moods and slowly unfolding mysteries are lost in a rush of hyperactivity: Nadine is committing suicide; Jacques is shot; Dr. Jacoby is conked on the head and has a seizure; Lucy is pregnant; James is accused of cocaine possession; Leo is shot; Leland smothers Jacques to death; Shelley, Catherine, and Pete are trapped in a burning mill; Ben Horne is about to unwittingly have sex with his daughter Audrey; and, with a nod to the famous 1980 *Dallas* cliffhanger, someone pumps three bullets into Dale Cooper's chest.

Across America, *Twin Peaks* fans gathered together in office and restaurant parties to watch the season finale. An especially large and enthusiastic group converged on Snoqualmie, Washington's Salish Lodge, where Lynch and company had filmed part of the enthralling pilot episode. Newly minted local celebrity Pat Cokewell, owner of the Mar T Café, which doubled as the show's Double R Diner, was there. In amazement, she said that since the series began her staff had barely been able to keep up with the public demand for the café's mouth-watering pies, and she recalled that during shooting David Lynch had gorged himself on the peanut butter chocolate cream variety.

The crowd at the Salish was digesting the last of the pie, donuts, and steaming coffee when those shots thudded into Cooper's chest. As the lights came up the room exploded with loud moans and groans, a sprinkle of applause, and some solid booing. One dismayed fan exclaimed, "It's a gip, it's a gip,"[99] and another added her disappointment, "I can't believe they did that to me—and they didn't tell me who killed Laura Palmer."[100] As a Seattle ABC station reporter taped a story on the gathering, the group chanted in the background: "We want to know, we want to know, we want to know."[101] Seattle, and woodsy Michigan, had the highest per-capita number *Twin Peaks* viewers, and when Seattle's KOMO TV presented the Salish Lodge viewing party story, they gave it a full one-fifth of their 11 p.m. airtime. During the half-hour newscast, the station conducted a phone-in poll about the *Twin Peaks* cliffhanger. Of the 1,320 viewers who called, 41 percent approved of the episode, while 59 percent hated or were confused by it. The series would return in September, but would the disgruntled viewers be too turned off to tune in? The station ran some footage of Lynch being asked about the show's unsolved puzzles and future course for the next season. Appearing poised and self-contained within his black suit and top-buttoned white shirt, Lynch sat with his hands folded in front of his chest on a table top; over his right shoulder stared a TV monitor churning with snowy blue electrical impulses. Looking to the left of our enquiring eyes, he softly smiled and said, "That's a good question."[102] On this day, like most every day, the keeper of mysteries was not giving anything away. Besides, Lynch had other things on his mind, for he was about to launch his fifth feature film, *Wild at Heart*.

But while TV viewers and Mark Frost and the *Twin Peaks* production team addressed themselves to the questions of Who Killed Laura Palmer?, and Who Shot Agent Cooper? in the chilly Northwest woods, Lynch's imagination breathed in Southern-fried air. Rather than being stuck in town, Lynch was roaring away, his accelerator to the floor, his eyes fixed on the speed-blurred horizon of a thrilling and deadly highway.

While America awaited the summer release of Lynch's new film, many TV viewers who were gripped by *Twin Peaks* fever chatted about some of the factors that made the show so special. After Lynch directed the pilot episode, six other directors helmed the remainder of the first season, yet the shows maintained a remarkable aesthetic consistency, thanks to the strong example Lynch had set. As in Lynch's feature films, *Twin Peaks'* images gained visual power through simplicity: The frames were uncluttered, so we could get lost in the beautiful shape and texture of a human face or a gleaming black telephone, or the purity of a steaming cup of coffee resting on a red countertop. As always, Lynch wanted to explore layers of reality, the exterior zones and interior realms of both environments and people (their surface and secret selves). To contrast with the shivery, gray, misty-green weather and forests of the Northwest, he mandated that rooms glow with the reddish wood hues he favors in his personal living spaces, and that characters' flesh tones be made warm as possible by filming them with coral-colored camera filters. Lynch was so concerned about maintaining the toasty look of interiors and faces that he sent a laboratory color consultant to ABC to make sure the correct tones he'd committed to film weren't lost or distorted when transmitted by television. In Lynch's mind, the warmly comforting rooms and visages were a perfect counterpoint to the characters' darkly anguished, unspoken feelings and hidden secrets. And when Lynch took us into the netherworld of shadow and night, we were immersed in the deepest blacks that had ever been seen on TV. *Twin Peaks* abandoned the bland, decades-old flat-lighting standard for TV lighting, and gloried in new dimensions of high-contrast and emotionally expressive shadings.

Lynch dreams up his art, and he wants our experience of it to be as dreamlike as possible. Today directors commonly move their cameras through space with operatic grandiosity or frantically fling them around as though they're mounted on a whiplash or a rollercoaster. And, thanks to the pernicious influence of MTV music videos, many directors take pride in chopping their footage into short little bits, so that the viewer is assaulted by a frenzied editing barrage of fragmented reality. Whether he's shooting for movies or TV, Lynch hardly ever moves his camera, and he films many scenes in long, unbroken takes (some single shots in *Twin Peaks* cover two whole pages of a forty-five-page script). Filming people talking in a room, he doesn't automatically fall into the typical rhythm of cutting back and forth between close-ups of characters' faces. Rather, he often films a tableau in which all the characters are visible, and has the ones who need to be emphasized come closer to the lens in turn. Lynch also violates standard directorial operating procedure by lingering on shots longer than normal. As Grace Zabriskie says, "The main thing David does is he uses the take. He doesn't edit your performance. He stays on you. I mean, he'll stay there until you're seeing what you're seeing and you *know* you're seeing what you're seeing."[103] His techniques don't call attention to themselves and distract the audience's concentration from the subtle moods and atmospheres he's conjuring. Many viewers felt that *Twin Peaks* was a dream *they* were having.

One of the viewers mesmerized by the show was writer-producer David Chase, whose show *The Sopranos* would attain *Twin Peaks'* TV-legend/cultural phenomenon status ten years in the future. Indeed, Lynch and Frost's series directly inspired Chase's mob-family/family drama: he thought of *The Sopranos* as "*Twin Peaks* in the New Jersey Meadowlands."[104] Chase's 2004 musings on the art of television sound like a summation of Lynch's style and substance in *Twin Peaks* and other works. "Television shows are usually full of talk. I think there should be strong visuals on a show, some sense of mystery to it, connections that don't add up. I think there should be dreams and music and dead air and stuff that goes nowhere. There should be, God forgive me, a little bit of poetry."[105]

Lynch has supreme confidence in his artistic instincts, and his intuitions about the correct way to precede made *Twin Peaks* a realm that felt like a stylized reflection of our familiar world. It was a place that seemed to be in the 1950s, 1960s, 1970s, and 1980s all at once; where mid-century idealism coexisted with rampant late-century greed, cynicism, and irony; where the expression of fear, rage, sorrow, guilt, and humor was pushed to extreme heights, yet eroticism and sex were implied and suggested. Psychological studies show that we tend to pay attention to things that are unexpected, that are outside the comfort zone of familiar occurrences. The enigma of Laura Palmer's death and life so permeates *Twin Peaks* that everything that happens in the town has an undercurrent of mystery. People seem to be thinking something other than what they are saying, and incongruous details, like a man fingering a domino during his parole hearing, or Christmas decorations stored at a shooting range, give the scenes we're watching a tantalizing aura of special, yet-to-be-discovered meaning. There's something else going on here—what can it be?

Lynch calls Twin Peaks "a desire town,"[106] and its citizens certainly exhibit a wide spectrum of cravings and yearnings. But the town itself is an object of desire for outsiders like us and Cooper, our surrogate explorer, our Special Agent, who, with his senses, intellect, and imagination fully aroused, is eager to be seduced. Speaking metaphorically, does Twin Peaks hold the sweet promise of true love, or the allure-veiled threat of a lethal femme fatale? As Sheriff Truman says to Cooper as they discuss the mystery of women, "the less I know, the more interested I get."

7

BURNING LOVE

1990
(*Wild at Heart*)

Lynch the rebel felt at home on the open road of *Wild at Heart*. Like Mark Frost, the man he had shared the most collaborative energy and time with, Lynch as a boy was the product of a stable nuclear family with wholesome, nurturing values: "middle America the way it was supposed to be."[1] He treasured his idyllic home life, but he also reacted against it, feeling deep embarrassment over his parents' square behavior and yearning for something wayward and disruptive to happen. When this intervening, sensed-but-not-realized force failed to materialize, Lynch created it in his mind and let it rage through his work, where stability and chaos achieve a dynamic, vibrant balance.

As a 1950s youth, Lynch wore striped T-shirts and plaid bathrobes like the boys in the happy-family sitcoms *The Adventures of Ozzie and Harriet*, *Leave It To Beaver*, and *Father Knows Best*, but he aspired to the fancy dark suits and racier style of his paternal grandfather, who sported engraved cowboy boots and tooled around town in a big, black car. Grandpa also practiced a behavior that reeked of worldliness and rebellion: He smoked like a furnace. The grown-up Lynch, who wears lots of black and consumes loads of nicotine, continually peoples his fictions with characters who look and act as though they're on the honky-tonk side of town, rather than in a PTA or Boy Scout meeting or in the pages of *Martha Stewart Living*. People who project the image and style of social transgression, who play loose with the law and live fast and low: the Boy's father and mother in *The*

Grandmother, *The Elephant Man*'s Bytes and Night Porter, *Twin Peaks'* Bobby Briggs, and, supremely, *Blue Velvet*'s Frank Booth. Frank is irrevocably a monster, but, like Lynch's beloved grandfather, he wears shiny black boots, a rakish dark suit, and drives a large black car. Lynch feels that the "suave"[2] Frank possesses "a certain kind of American cool,"[3] so the director must have thought he was entering a chilled-out deep freeze when he began to explore the world of writer Barry Gifford.

The author, who today makes public appearances wearing tight black T-shirts and pants, grew up in an alluring realm of colorful, dramatic events and exotic atmospheres that was the antithesis of Lynch's own staid, stable, homey-neighborhood youth. Gifford's parents were swingin'—not square. His father, Rudy, ran an all-night liquor store in Chicago, where Barry was born in 1946, the year of Lynch's birth. Barry's mother, Peggy, was a former Texas beauty queen and model who socialized with movie people, composers, and an exiled Russian count. After some years of marriage, Peggy grew tired of hobnobbing with Rudy's hoodlum friends at late-night drunken parties. The couple divorced, and Rudy died of natural causes when Barry was twelve.

When Rudy died, one of the obituaries said he was a cohort of "politicians, movie stars, high rollers, low rollers, no rollers, thieves, murderers, showgirls, junkies, bums, newspapermen, and every cop in the city,"[4] and that he was on a first-name basis with "the mayor, the governor, the Cardinal, and the Capones." Gifford discovered that his father had an FBI criminal record with four entries, and was a pal of mobster Bugsy Siegel. Rudy was at home in a tough-talking world where men made their own laws and wielded the power of life and death.

Gifford concluded his memoir, *The Phantom Father*, with a passage that shows his perfect compatibility with David Lynch's ethos. "I realized long ago that if forced to choose between revelation and mystery, I'll take mystery every time. Revelations solve very little; they serve only to preclude further thought, whereas mysteries continue to force speculation. The object, I concluded, is to encourage invention, not reduce possibilities."[5] And Gifford seemed to sum up the products of Lynch's mind and hand when he said, "Great art is always dangerous, daring the listener, viewer, or reader to go over the edge with the artist."

Just as Lynch's idyllic Northwest childhood and later rough years in toxic Philadelphia helped catalyze his art, Barry Gifford's early experiences fueled his writing. For hours, he would listen to the talk at his father's store. "I was always interested and I always listened to what they were saying, and what they really meant. So I had a real variety of voices to choose from, and that's where my ability to write dialogue comes from."[6] We hear that engaging multitude of voices in Gifford's fictions, which teem with vibrant, one-of-a-kind characters who often dwell on the low-down, night-side of life. Gifford's people may travel a mean and desperate road, but their journey is graced by the author's sharp satirical sense, which revels in bizarre, yet true-to-life extremes of behavior and circumstance. Gifford has said that "there are stranger things going on in the real world than I can invent."[7] And, a few years before he met Lynch, he noted that it "interests me that I can never imagine things as depraved as those that occur in *Blue Velvet*."[8] In Lynch, Gifford discovered a like-minded artist who could paint the world's twisted absurdities in colors more outrageous than his own. So what did Lynch discover when he got his hands on the pre-publication galleys of Gifford's *Wild at Heart*?

In forty-five short, concisely written chapters, Gifford told the story of Sailor and Lula, two North Carolina lovers in their early twenties who hit the road for points south and west in order to escape Lula's riled-up mother, Marietta. The two are also celebrating their reunion after Sailor's release from prison for killing one Bobby Ray Lemon in self-defense. Marietta had forbidden Lula from ever seeing Sailor again, and now that the unruly couple's on the run, she sends her paramour, detective Johnnie Farrugut, out to find them and bring Lula home. Mom is a determined woman, and she tries in vain to get Johnnie to kill Sailor, and talks about bringing hired killer Marcello Santos into the matter. (Surely the name Marcello Santos is an amalgamation of Carlos Marcello and Santos Trafficante, organized crime bosses of Barry Gifford's Gulf Coast and Florida home turf, who, some historians believe, masterminded the plot to assassinate President John F. Kennedy.) Johnnie has a balanced, rational view of Lula's flight: He sees that, as a grown-up woman, she's trying to break free of her hyper-possessive mother.

With a golden dream of California in their minds, Lula and Sailor pass through New Orleans and head into Texas, making love in the afternoons, staying up late, always talking about how strange and crazy the world is. As Marietta flies south to join Johnnie in pursuit, the young runaways stop off in the tiny town of Big Tuna, Texas. In this oppressively bleak and hot dump of a place, Lula tells Sailor that she's pregnant, and they meet a dark force named Bobby Peru, who has the power to snuff out all their bright tomorrows.

For Lynch, Barry Gifford's book was as enticing as the menu at Bob's Big Boy drive-in. So many of Gifford's preoccupations were mouth-wateringly similar to his own. Sailor and Lula's primal need to escape physical, emotional, and spiritual entrapment, and to freely seek their dreams, made them kin to many of Lynch's cinematic characters. When Sailor said these words to Lula, it sounded like Lynch talking to his muse: "We'll be all right, peanut, as long as we've got room to move."[9] As in Lynch's films, the odds against Sailor and Lula breaking free seemed hellishly high. And Gifford's runaways traveled in a zone that had fascinated Lynch for years, a realm of funky denizens and destinations that polite society would deem freakish and disreputable. Sailor and Lula's road was littered with grimy gas stations, seedy motels, juke joints that pour booze before noon, and people who are twelve different kinds of crazy, who mutter angrily to themselves in the street and pursue screwy and dangerous impulses with a vengeance. Gifford's fictional universe was, like Lynch's, funny, sad, scary, alluring, and repulsive all at once. In *Blue Velvet*, Lynch's alter ego sums up the situation by saying, "It's a strange world," and Gifford's people conclude, "The world is wild at heart and weird on top."[10] Like Lynch, Gifford stressed the head as the locus of creativity and imagination. As Sailor says, the way Lula's "head works is God's own private mystery,"[11] and anything "interestin' in the world come out of somebody's weird thoughts."[12] Lynch, the thought-traveler who in his work remains fascinated by communications that circumvent verbal language, must have nodded in sympathy with Lula's words: "I think somethin' and then later think I've said it out loud to someone?"[13] The piquant question marks that adorned many of Lula's declarative sentences were a trait of the Southern voices that Gifford heard while roaming around with his mother, and Lynch knew them too, having spent adolescent and grown-up time in Virginia and North Carolina. Lynch has always been sensitive to places; various locales have rooted and embedded themselves in his psyche over the years and inspired his art. The angst-ridden industrial grunge of Philadelphia has seeped into *Eraserhead* and parts of *The Elephant Man* and *Dune*, while a wholesome hominess and an ominous, chilling wind from the Northwest wafts through Lynch's paintings, *Blue Velvet*, and the *Twin Peaks* TV series and film. Making a film of *Wild at Heart* would allow him to explore some of the Southern roads of his Art Life.

In real and fictional Southern culture, interesting talk is the stuff of life. As Lula puts it, "Talkin's good. Long as you got the other"[14] (referring to a satisfying sex life). "I'm a big believer in talkin', case you ain't noticed."[15] Lula and Sailor don't censor their thoughts, they say what's on their minds, be it sweet words of endearment for each other or potentially shattering revelations about past traumas and misdeeds. Lynch was moved by these two people, each willful and strong within themselves, who shared hot sex and intimate secrets and a high respect for each other's unique being. He saw their free-ranging individuality, sizzling passion, and balanced equality as a thrilling archetype of "cool modern love."[16]

Barry Gifford, the product of a broken home who himself has enjoyed decades-long family life with his wife and children, had written *Wild at Heart* as a gritty paean to the binding power of love and its ability to overcome almost every obstacle. In the union of Sailor and Lula, Lynch saw a reflection of the freedom, happiness, and mutual respect that characterized the director's glowing relationship with Isabella Rossellini. Twice divorced, he had experienced the waxing and waning of longtime love and the sudden flash of new romance. In his fictions, Lynch had projected his idealized belief that love can break through any barrier, even transcending death in a cosmic consummation, flowing on and on as the 1950s songs said, until the end of time. *The Grandmother* and *The Elephant Man* showed a child's adoration of, respectively, his grandparent and mother, while *Eraserhead* was a valentine to the abstract purity of a young man's asexual love for his dream woman. In *Dune*, the interplanetary hero's lady love is a fellow freedom fighter who helps him fulfill his political destiny, while *Blue Velvet*'s Sandy is a classic high school sweetheart who first helps inspire, and then tries to curtail, her man's obsession with detecting dangerous mysteries. Thus far, the closest Lynch had come to portraying the less-than-dramatic, get up-have-breakfast-go-to-work love life that most of us lead was when he acted the role of Isabella Rossellini's lover in the film *Zelly and Me* (1988). Director Tina Rathborne had given him relaxed screen time in which he could cherish his real-life paramour with his caressing eyes and all the sweet words he could muster. In Barry Gifford's book, Sailor and Lula also exchanged tender terms of endearment, and though the author created a wild, threatening world for them to navigate, their passionate bond was a protective shelter for their hearts and bodies. Gifford had his couple do simple, mundane things like drive in a car and sit in bars and motel rooms. Yet these scenes were tuned to emanate the healthy hum of a romance in high gear. When Lynch signed on to make a film of *Wild at Heart* he realized that this would be his first opening-shot-to-end-credits love story.

Lynch was touched by the book's "heart," and its "wild" side gave his imagination a stimulating jolt. He had always coped with his fears by processing them through his work, manipulating his anxieties within an art-making context and thus lessening their power. Lynch felt an out-of-control craziness in the American air that Gifford captured in his book. The author wrote of Lula's father burning himself alive on purpose; the planet's protective ozone layer disappearing; a woman with a creepy, animalistic laugh; a girl who's afraid of letting the potatoes touch the meat on her dinner plate;

a young fellow who's convinced that men with metal hands are following him; beer made from polluted river water; a safecracking convict who's got his own church; a filthy hitchhiker who pulls raw liver from his grimy pocket and feeds it to a boxful of whimpering puppies; and a formerly violent man who reforms his life, stops taking drugs, becomes a celibate vegetarian who devoutly meditates daily, and is killed in a motorcycle crash.

Gifford's litany of rampant weirdness and psychosocial disintegration meshed with Lynch's sense of America's nihilistic devolution in the latter part of the twentieth century. The director sounds like a scared child who realizes that his previously omnipotent father can no longer protect him: "I used to think that the President of the United States had a handle on the future and had some sort of control over what happened in my neighborhood, but now we know that isn't true. We're in a time when you can picture these really tall, evil things running at night, just racing. The more freedom you give them, the more they come out and just race, and they're running in every direction now. Pretty soon there'll be so many of them that you can't stop them. It's really a critical time."[17]

The safe, sane, serene civilization that had nurtured Lynch's boyhood was being eaten alive by the animalistic law of the jungle. When, in Oliver Stone's 1987 film *Wall Street*, Michael Douglas's lizard-named (Gekko), soulless stock market insider-trader declared that "Greed is good," he seemed to be codifying the wisdom of the age. By looking out for number one and winning through intimidation, you could secure the latest badge of consumer-society honor: a pseudo-European house with a three-car garage, whose airtight insulated walls, kitchen cabinets, and carpets seeped carcinogenic vapors. People living on welfare or panhandling were inhumanely blamed for not being able to rise from their lowly status and were cut off from compassionate consideration. Ronald Reagan's policies shunted legions of people with troubled minds out of mental health institutions and onto the streets, where they babbled incoherently and acted out disturbing behaviors unsheltered. Cars with amplified music systems had become rolling, maximum-volume boom boxes that shattered the peace of quiet neighborhoods. People were suing each other over petty offences, shooting each other during driving confrontations, and killing their employers and co-workers when they felt victimized. Teenage punks who beat and raped people were said to be "wilding." Schoolchildren were becoming drug users, drug dealers, and drug-related killers, or just murdering kids of their own tender age for no good reason.

In Lynch's own Los Angeles, carjackings, gang warfare, drive-by shootings, and a rising tension between the city's many racial groups poisoned the air. The director knew that "dark things have always existed, but they used to be in a proper balance with the good."[18] He spoke of how fast-paced urban life fragments communities and puts people "right on the edge."[19] Now "the anxiety level of people is in the stratosphere,"[20] and he felt that the "mass media overloaded people with way more bad news than they could handle."[21] Lynch added that "with drugs people can get rich and whacked out and they've opened up a whole weird world,"[22] and concluded, "These things have created a new, modern kind of fear in America."[23] Lynch saw *Wild at Heart* as a chance to express his concern for the health of his cherished country and his belief in the saving grace of human connection. His sense of "modern fear"[24] and "modern love"[25] would power the road trip of Sailor and Lula.

Lynch was truly inspired by Gifford's book, and he took only a week to write his screenplay, which incorporated many of Sailor and Lula's character-defining dialogues. He clearly respected Gifford's text, but his mind started to supply ideas about how he could heighten the story's contrast quotient by making "the brighter things a little brighter and darker things a little darker."[26] Lynch made ominous characters more fearsome and actually murderous, and stoked up to volcanic temperatures Marietta's burning desire to regain control of her Lula and to wipe Sailor out of the picture. He added new evil and crazed characters, some reverential musical numbers, and made allusions to 1950s icons Elvis Presley and Marilyn Monroe, and to his favorite movie, that archetypal American road picture *The Wizard of Oz*.

Lynch knew where he was going, and who was going with him. When he first picked up Gifford's book and started to read, there were only two possible actors he pictured as Sailor and Lula: Nicolas Cage and Laura Dern.

Cage, the son of a California State University literature professor and a dancer-choreographer, grew up appreciating the arts and the value of make-believe. At the age of nine, he was constantly picked on by a school bully, but one day he got a bright idea. Putting on an atypical set of clothes, slicking back his hair, and donning sunglasses, he pretended to be his own older, exceedingly tough cousin. The power of Cage's performance forced his tormentor to swear he'd leave cousin Nicolas alone. Cage's parents divorced when Nicolas was twelve, and the boy, who was born with the last name of Coppola, spent a lot of time with his celebrated uncle, director Francis Ford Coppola (*The Godfather*, *Apocalypse Now*). Inspired by James Dean's sensitive-misfit performance in *East of Eden*, the fourteen-year-old Nicolas took an acting class in which he immediately excelled. Feeling that he had found his life's calling, he dropped out of high school and became a full-time actor at the age of sixteen. Nicolas was enthusiastically following his dream, but he still felt like an outsider on the set of *Fast Times at Ridgemont High* (1982) when his fellow players accused him of having an unfair advantage in getting roles because of his famous last name. Stung by his peers' incorrect assumption, Nicolas decided another transformation was in order. A lifelong comic book fan, he took the last name of Luke Cage, an African American magazine character who, having been unjustly framed and imprisoned, breaks free to become "Power Man, Hero for Hire."[27]

The newly christened Mr. Cage definitely got hired, but he was determined not to play heroes in the Sylvester Stallone–Arnold Schwarzenegger–Clint Eastwood mold. He wanted to portray characters who weren't invincible, who had vulnerabilities, faults, problems. These are the kind of fully human people who Lynch identifies with and presents in his work, and, in the 1980s, Cage performed a number of outstanding roles that would have caught the director's eye. He was an endearingly dopey punk rocker in *Valley Girl* (1983), a facially disfigured Vietnam veteran in *Birdy* (1984), and Kathleen Turner's oddball swain in *Peggy Sue Got Married* (1986). *Raising Arizona* (1987) showcased him as an ex-con who kidnaps a baby for his girlfriend, *Vampire's Kiss* (1989) saw him actually eat a writhing cockroach while playing a yuppie who thinks he's a vampire, and in *Moonstruck* (1987) he shatters a family's serenity and defies social convention as a morose one-handed baker who goes all-out to win the heart of the woman (Cher) who's about to marry his brother. Cage's *Moonstruck* performance alone, in which he makes a passionate speech about the all-consuming nature of love to his reluctant amore, would have been enough to convince Lynch that he'd found his Sailor.

Four years before *Wild at Heart*, Laura Dern had played *Blue Velvet*'s Sandy, a paragon of sweet teen innocence who wore pink sweaters, slept in a pink bedroom, and smooched with her boyfriend, Jeffrey (Kyle MacLachlan), while slow-dancing at a party. Dern had enjoyed a live-in romance with MacLachlan that broke up after four years, and she'd become a good friend of Lynch's, visiting the inner sanctum of his sparsely furnished home to sip coffee from his state-of-the-art espresso machine, listen to loud music on his high-tech stereo system, and talk of spiritual matters and ways to make the world a better place. The director knew that Lula, in contrast to Sandy, was a worldly woman who wore sexy outfits and bared her breasts, slept in sleazy motel rooms, and screwed her brains out with her man, Sailor. In *Blue Velvet*, Lynch had written a speech for Sandy about her dream of robins bringing the saving light of love flocking down to a dark, bedeviled world. The director felt that lust-kitten Lula had a similar core of idealistic purity and virtue, and he had seen Laura Dern's performance as a budding teenager trembling with her newly aroused sexuality in Joyce Chopra's *Smooth Talk* (1985), so he offered her the female lead role in *Wild at Heart*. Like Lynch, Dern practiced Transcendental Meditation and was interested in Eastern spirituality: she felt that things happen when they are supposed to, so she accepted her fate and told Lynch "Yes."[28] For Dern, Lula embodied her belief in spontaneous, uninhibited thought and behavior, and the role would tap into her strong feelings about female eroticism in the cinema. "One idea of sexuality is that the woman's the vixen, and there's Sandy in *Blue Velvet*, the Madonna you may want to marry but not sleep with. I've seen these two so much in films that it drives me nuts. I realized that Lula would give me the opportunity to be sexual yet pure at the same time. She's so turned on, but there's an innocence."[29]

Wild at Heart would also give Dern a chance to do something that was exceedingly rare in the history of motion pictures, for Lula's mother, Marietta—who's hell-bent on controlling her child's life and murderously destroying her daughter's bond with Sailor—would be played by actress Diane Ladd, the woman who gave birth to Laura Dern. Ladd and Laura's father, actor Bruce Dern, met while performing in the stage drama *Orpheus Descending*, by playwright Tennessee Williams, who was Ladd's cousin. Laura was conceived while Ladd and Dern were acting in their own road movie, Roger Corman's 1966 outlaw-biker flick *The Wild Angels*. The actors divorced when Laura was two, and she was raised by her mother and maternal grandmother. At the age of seven, Laura had a walk-on part in Martin Scorcese's *Alice Doesn't Live Here Anymore* (1974), in which Ladd played a supporting role to lead actress Ellen Burstyn. Laura's bit of stage business was to eat an ice cream cone, and as filming wore on, she had to swallow nine of them. Ladd commented, "She's going to get sick,"[30] but Scorcese declared, "No she's not. She's going to be an actress."[31] One of the gods of the cinema had spoken. Yet Ladd, who knew that Hollywood thrived on converting sensitive human beings into money-making commodities, tried to talk her daughter out of taking up the family profession. Ladd saw her opposition to Laura's acting interest as a test of her daughter's depth of commitment to her dream and her mother was most impressed when eleven-year-old Laura made an appointment to perform a monologue for a talent agent. Laura's initiative landed her a part in *Foxes* (1980), which starred Jodie Foster. At a screening of the film, director Adrian Lyne told Ladd that her daughter was "going to be a giant star."[32] Ladd became convinced of Laura's ability to play and win the show business game, and encouraged her to develop her talent by studying with Lee Strasberg and at London's Royal Academy of Dramatic Art.

Just as Ladd had spent early filmmaking time with rebellious Hollywood hipsters Peter Fonda, Jack Nicholson, Harry Dean Stanton, and Bruce Dern, so Laura got a taste of the fast and wild life when she played a punk-rock groupie in *Ladies and Gentlemen, The Fabulous Stains* (1981). Returning to high school, "where the rest of the kids were blushing over *The Diary of Anne Frank*,"[33] was a bit anticlimactic after hanging out with angry bad-boy rockers the Sex Pistols and the Clash. While Ann Frank, at age fifteen, had been sharing hot kisses with her boyfriend and worrying that her longing might make her "yield too soon,"[34] the sixteen-year-old Laura Dern was totally immersed in her first true love and was no longer a virgin. Young Laura was pursuing the profession and love life that she alone had chosen and acting out her need to break away from her mother and declare her womanhood: the daughter-mother dynamic that drove *Smooth Talk* was also central to Laura and Diane Ladd's private relationship in the mid-1980s. Dern was relieved that by the late 1980s she and Ladd had become close friends, but in *Wild at Heart* the pair would be reanimating their earlier child-parent conflict with a vengeance.

Laura Dern and Nicolas Cage would also have to interact at a high emotional temperature, and Lynch was happy to see that the two actors had an easy rapport with each other at the initial meeting. As if to symbolize the scorching cinema these three were cooking up at their first dinner together on L.A.'s Beverly Boulevard, the American Cinematheque movie house down the street caught on fire. The two actors truly bonded and got in the proper *Wild at Heart* mood by taking what Dern called "a Sailor-and-Lula road trip"[35] to Las Vegas. "Beef jerky and gambling and the baccarat room. At Caesar's Palace we got medallions from Caesar and his wife. I had made up a CARE package for us that included licorice, chewing gum, cigarettes, chocolate bars. It was really fun, and by the end of the trip, we had it down. We had the candy wrappers and the body odor."[36] Lynch was glad that his stars were out living in the spirit of his film, but he "didn't think they were ever coming back."[37]

Dern, who had been schooled at a private Catholic institution, may have thought she was ready to be Lula but during pre-filming rehearsals she displayed some inhibitions about portraying this torridly carnal creature. In her personal life Dern characteristically viewed the world with her intellect, but for *Wild at Heart* she had to access her body consciousness: "Lula *is* her body, and *everything* is sexy."[38] She felt secure with her trusted friend Lynch and let him break down her resistant barriers. Bubblegum was the key. Lynch says that "Laura caught Lula's character by saying her lines while chewing bubblegum. With the gum in her mouth she said the lines shower, and it created this real sexy mood, it made the pacing just right."[39] From that point on, the director of few words just said "bubblegum"[40] when he wanted to call forth the woman that he needed Dern to be.

While Dern was becoming Lula, Nicolas Cage worked out his conception of Sailor. He felt Sailor should possess more quiet inner strength than the manic, larger-than-life characters he usually portrayed. He wanted Sailor to be self-contained and super-cool to an almost absurd degree, and he wanted Sailor to radiate the Southern-gentlemanliness and endearing sincerity of the young Elvis Presley. "The way Elvis said 'sugar' or 'baby,' he really meant it. Like Elvis, Sailor isn't sexually innocent, but his love is innocent and simple. There's nothing tainted about it. He's an open book."[41]

The only reference to Elvis in Barry Gifford's book is when Sailor and Lula exchange a few words about the way some of the dead (1977) and buried rock and roll icon's devout fans believe that they've seen him alive and walking on today's green earth. The idea of blending Elvis's persona with Sailor's character was clearly Lynch's and Cage's invention. Gifford respected Lynch as an artist and was not disturbed by the director's intention to breath his personal obsessions into the author's book. And Lynch so valued Gifford's talent and trusted his judgment that he did something rare for a filmmaker, encouraging the author to visit the set during shooting and letting him watch the developed film reels at the end of the day. Lynch considered all of Gifford's suggestions, and for Gifford the film was a collaborative effort, though the resulting film was definitely "David Lynch's *Wild at Heart*."

When the completed film was chosen to be in competition at the prestigious Cannes Film Festival in the South of France, Lynch gave Gifford the honor of viewing a very exclusive first screening. Lynch personally brought the movie directly from the processing lab in L.A. to Cannes' 2,400-seat Grand Salon Lumiere, where he needed to check the print's optical and sound quality before it was publicly shown the next day. The director invited Isabella Rossellini, Barry Gifford, and film critic Gene Siskel and his wife along for the ride. At one-thirty in the morning the tiny, tired and excited group took their seats in the athletic field–sized theater and waited for the lights to dim. Lynch would be on edge for the next two hours, his tightly focused attention scanning for any visual or aural flaws, and as the picture started he whispered to Gifford, "When it's over I want you to tell me what you think of it in one word."[42] Midway through the film Siskel's wife, overcome with negative emotion, left her seat and never returned. As the house lights came up after 3:30 a.m., the director sighed: the print was in good shape. Siskel got up to go find his wife, and Gifford turned to Lynch and said, "Blowtorch."[43]

Lynch's film is born in flames. Out of blackness, the screen-filling bulbous, phallic head of a wooden match spurts slow-motion erect jets of fire, bringing light to the void as the director's acutely listening microphone picks up double hissing pops of dark air. In this, another of Lynch's twinned worlds, the two beats of sound herald a double view of fire, and the director cuts from the single match to a searing maelstrom composed of clouds within clouds of churning flame. The swelling, romantic orchestral strings of Angelo Badalamenti's Mahleresque main-theme music underscore the positive sense that the human-scale match-fire of sexual passion can explode into a self-transcending combustion of regenerative, spiritual love. But the roiling flame clouds, which recall the churning, devouring beetles undermining *Blue Velvet*'s serene lawnscapes, also signify fire's destructive aspect, its ravenous need to consume and annihilate in order to exist. This surely is the fire that *Twin Peaks*' evil entity BOB calls upon to walk with him. Some of the forces that fascinate Lynch can't be seen with the eye. *Wild at Heart*'s opening flame clouds are like fierce winds made visible, perhaps evoking the fire-fanning Santa Ana windstorms that annually scorch the hills and mountains of the director's Los Angeles home country.

In *Blue Velvet*, Lynch played up the contrast between his opening montage of sweet, safe, and sane small-town goodness and his exposition of the dark forces of moral and spiritual corruption that were attacking it from within. The film's youthful protagonist could have been Lynch himself, feeling shocked and afraid as the narcotic-inhaling murderous sexual sadist Frank Booth infected and assaulted Lynch's own memories of a golden small-town childhood. Lynch may have vanquished Frank and his evil animal energy on the screen, but, four years later at the time of *Wild at Heart*, the director knew that "really and truly, many, many, many things are wrong, and so many people are participating in strange and horrible things."[44] In his new film, the balance between light and darkness has shifted dangerously in the wrong direction, so Lynch's originally scripted opening montage for *Wild at Heart* was to be the shadow side of *Blue Velvet*'s. In the earlier film a kindly old woman helped children cross a street at the crosswalk, while the *Wild at Heart* screenplay showed a man speeding up a street on a motorcycle, ignoring a "KIDS PLAYING"[45] sign and crashing and skidding himself into a bloody mess. Instead of *Blue Velvet*'s idyllic balance between man and nature (the gorgeous close-up flowers, Mr.

Beaumont's carefully tended garden), Lynch envisioned rabid dogs "ripping each other's flesh"[46] and a group of "HARDENED CRIMINAL"[47] children "making animal noises of one sort or another"[48] attacking a wasp nest and stomping the insects as they landed on the sidewalk. The corrosive forces hidden beneath *Blue Velvet*'s wholesome green lawn would here be running rampant in the light of day.

Having established the malicious tone of *Wild at Heart*'s world with this parade of nasty images, Lynch's screenplay then introduced the film's primal Sailor and Lula–versus–Marietta conflict via a dialogue exchange in which Marietta wouldn't let her daughter talk to Sailor on the phone. But in the leap from script page to screen, a change occurred. Lynch felt the movie needed a stronger "kick-off,"[49] so he chose to begin *Wild at Heart* with a scene that Barry Gifford does not describe in his book: Sailor's killing of Bobby Ray Lemon. This change would let Lynch present his three main characters' heated conflict in the most immediate and dramatic way possible by showing a face-to-face confrontation between Sailor, Marietta, and Lula. Opening with this scene, which remains one of the most viscerally violent of the director's career, would also be a daring move. Lynch had originally planned to show us this disturbing passage as a flashback near the end of the film, as Sailor, who we've gotten to know and love over the last hour-and-a-half, gets ready to commit a new crime with the villainous Bobby Peru, and the director builds a narrative case for Sailor's inability to control his bad side being the cause of he and Lula parting. So how could Lynch expect Sailor to win our sympathy when he introduces us to the man as he repeatedly mashes a defenseless fellow's head against a marble floor with his bare hands?

Since Gifford's book provided no blueprint for the death of Bobby Ray Lemon, it is instructive to see what Lynch's imagination came up with. Freed from the constraints of *Twin Peaks*' TV censors, he pushes the outer limits of acceptable R-rated screen violence, while hewing to his personal guidelines of thematic fascination. Border crossings and transitions between various realities are a staple of Lynch's work, and when he shows us the grand public space of an elegant old hotel, a superimposed title not in Gifford's book adds that we're in Cape Fear, as a warm, festive place becomes chilled with dread. And it is on the hotel's huge staircase, midway between two levels that Sailor crosses a line and transforms himself from a law-abiding citizen into a red-handed killer. Lynch uses his principle of contrast to heighten the sequence's drama. He situates Sailor's horrendously messy, transgressive act in a highly civilized domain where well-dressed, politely mannered Southern folk have gathered for a night out dancing to big band music. And as Sailor lunges into action, Lynch silences the familiar, genteel strains of Glenn Miller's "In The Mood" with the aggressive, heavy-metal chords of Powermad's "Slaughterhouse," which pound like a butchering plant sledgehammer smashing a cow's head as Sailor splatters Bobby Ray's cranium across the marble floor. As usual in Lynch's world, the human head remains a fundamental focus and, like *Blue Velvet*'s Frank Booth, Bobby Ray Lemon has his head that is full of bad thoughts forcibly emptied out. (Lynch's concern for sound design makes this passage both a sonically and visually stunning experience.)

At the beginning of his opening sequence, before Sailor takes action, Lynch's title text announces that his characters are situated "somewhere" on a "border" zone, and he makes us experience a correspondingly disorientating transitional stretch of territory by first showing us unreadable geometric patterns and shapes that our brains gradually interpret as the hotel's high ceiling and walls as viewed from a strangely tilted angle. We see Lula standing beneath one of three 40-foot-tall archways, waiting for Sailor. Just as he did in *Blue Velvet*, Lynch introduces Laura Dern wearing a pink dress, though Lula's visible thigh-high black garter and dark choker necklace give her a spicy seasoned sexuality that Sandy could only dream of. Even Lula's coif is more vibrantly provocative than Sandy's straight hairdo, as it rises high on her head and cascades over her shoulders and back in energized wavelets. Lynch affectionately called Dern "tidbit"[50] during filming, and she is indeed a delectable morsel.

As Sailor joins Lula and they head down the stairs, Bobby Ray Lemon (Gregg Dandridge), a black man wearing a pale gray suit, catches up to them. His head close to Lula's body, he looks her up and down, seeming to sniff her like a lustful dog. Lula registers Bobby Ray's transgression with a look of disgust as the man goes to work on Sailor, saying Marietta told him that Sailor's "been trying to fuck her in the toilets for the past ten minutes," and that she gave Bobby Ray $1,000 to kill the "crazy fuckin' boy." We'll soon learn that Marietta, not Sailor, is the one who's seriously bad and crazy. But, provoked by this black man who's just called Lula a "cute little cunt" and whipped out a knife he means to use, Sailor gets a hormonal jolt from the dawn of masculine time. In Lynch's world, animal urges often pull people into darkness, and Sailor says "Uh-oh" as he feels a shadowy surge of ferocious energy galvanize his system. Breathing deeply like *Blue Velvet*'s Frank Booth inhaling his mayhem-augmenting gas mask, Sailor grins like *Dune*'s Baron Harkonen and *Twin Peaks*' BOB as they prepare to inflict a storm of pain upon a victim. All Sailor needs to do is disarm and overpower Bobby Ray and hold him until the police come—but he goes miles too far, finally soaking the lifeless shoulders of the knife-wielder's pale suit with blood, brains, and cranial fluid. Lynch, who could have envisioned Sailor's murderous act any way he wanted, once again chose to show a decent person yielding to the wild power of a bestial force within himself.

Lynch has shown us Sailor's crime in disgusting, horrifying detail, so how can we be willing to journey through the rest of the film in sympathy with this hot-blooded killer? Intellectually we understand that Sailor's act has saved himself and his lady love from harm, but our emotions are outraged: Why the hell did he have to go so out-of-control, ramming the gore-dripping pulp of his victim in our faces? Sailor's just bounced Bobby Ray off the mahogany-paneled wall with an animal grunt, and he stands over the body in a silent room as Lula, Marietta, and every aghast onlooker stares at him. In this highly dramatic, pregnant pause, Lynch throws in something that wasn't in his script: He has Sailor, his body spent, his eyes forlorn, pull out a cigarette and lighter and fire up a smoke. *Wild at Heart* viewers always laugh at this moment, both because it's unexpected and because it gives Sailor and the audience a shared, distancing, tension-relieving breather from the terrible experience they've just had. Lynch is also establishing a sex-and-violence linkage by evoking the cinematic convention of lovers smoking after the exertion of intercourse. (The director will accompany Sailor and Lula's lovemaking with the same "Slaughterhouse" music that powered Sailor's killing of Bobby Ray Lemon.)

Another key linkage in the film is the triangular relationship between Sailor, Lula, and mother Marietta, which Lynch reinforces with the triple arches at the head of the hotel staircase. As Sailor recovers from his seconds-old bestial killing rampage, the nicotine hits his system, his head clears, and Lynch delivers another of his powerful messages-without-words. Inflamed with a righteous passion beyond speaking, Sailor leans forward and points his bloody, accusing finger straight at Marietta, who flinches as though struck by an invisible hand and then bares her teeth in wicked defiance. At this point in the film we viewers have no idea that Marietta has just tried to seduce Sailor in the lavatory, rather than her accusatory vice versa, and that she's been involved in even more heinous past deeds. To us, Sailor is a man who's overreacted to a threat and committed murder, but the focused force of his pointing gesture is like a signpost entreating us to be detectives and delve beneath the surface story to discover dark, flaming truths. His aggressive stance toward Marietta implies that, despite his immoral act, she is the evil force in the room and that Sailor will challenge her malicious dominion. In a fallen world, Sailor's eloquent pointing gesture is like a battle cry for the greater good, and it wins our sympathy. (Part of the pointing's power may reside in its subliminal evocation of the gesture as frequently practiced by Elvis Presley while performing a song: It has a touch of the King's "If you're looking for trouble, just look right in my face.")[51] The axis point between Sailor and Marietta's warring animus is Lula, who Lynch positions midway down the stairs, with mama at the top and Sailor at the bottom. As her man tore into Bobby Ray, Lula screamed "Sailor," fearing for her lover's life, but also realizing that by going animal and pulverizing Bobby, Sailor has fallen into Marietta's trap. If he had just disarmed Bobby he'd be hailed as a hero, but now he's off to prison, branded as a killer, wrenched out of Lula's life. Marietta has won, she's in the superior position at the head of the stairs. Yet Lula, by figuratively choosing to descend to Sailor's level in opposition to her mother, will learn that in Lynch's world you have to sink hellishly low to reach heavenly heights.

We may be in Lynch's film, but Marietta rules it. In the movie's first *Wizard of Oz* reference, we see a huge, clawlike female hand with a ringed finger and long, blood-red nails gesture across the face of an opaque crystal ball like an omnipotent giant who can grasp and command the whole world. In *Oz*, the hand belonged to the powerfully evil Wicked Witch, who used her crystal orb to spy on the hapless souls who she wished to control and harm. A few shots after *Wild at Heart*'s hand-and-crystal image, we see a ring on Marietta's finger that identifies her as Lynch's Wicked Witch. Lynch saw Sailor and Lula's literal and emotional journey as a reflection of Dorothy of *Oz*'s odyssey: You have to leave home to find your home. So the director decided to have his couple verbally refer to *The Wizard of Oz* as the myth that guides their trip and serves as an allusive reference point for their fears and aspirations. *The Wizard of Oz*'s introduction dedicates the film to those who are "Young in Heart," and since Lynch retains his youthful ability to see the world with the childlike sense of innocent wonder that Dorothy exhibits in *Oz*, the director decided to bestow his gift upon his *Wild* protagonists. He saw Sailor and Lula as "the kind of people who could embrace that kind of fairytale and make it really cool."[52] Lynch's couple may speed down the yellow lines of an interstate highway in their convertible rather than walk a yellow brick road, but they "have this dream between them."[53] Sailor and Lula would be talking about *The Wizard of Oz*, but for Lynch words tell only part of the story; he would make the pictorial actuality of his lovers' dreams and visions part of *Wild at Heart*'s narrative landscape. Later in the film, Lula, in her mind's eye, sees an image of the fearsome Marietta in full witch's regalia riding a broomstick just like Margaret Hamilton's Wicked Witch does in *The Wizard of Oz*. This spooky sight is clearly Lula's vision, whereas the earlier clawlike hand-and-crystal image was not seen by any character in the film. The shot was an infusion of the supernatural, an omniscient abstraction from Lynch that cued us to Marietta's status as a witchy Bad Mother archetype.

In Sailor's flashback, we see him urinating in the hotel's elegant men's room before he's attacked on the staircase by Marietta's paid assassin, Bobby Ray Lemon. He's alone in this sacrosanct male space when around the corner slithers the drunken Marietta, who will violate any borderline of decency and morality to get what she wants. With a cutesy-pie edge of Southern belle seductiveness masking her rage, and knowing that he will soon be dead meat, she asks, "Sailor boy, how'd you like to fuck Lula's mama?" "No, ma'am," he politely declines, but she hotly persists, "Well Lula's mama wants to fuck you." Marietta's transgressive sexual approach to her daughter's lover recalls the moment in *Eraserhead* when Mrs. X assaults Henry with intimate questions ("Have you had sexual intercourse with my daughter?"), backs him into a corner, and nuzzles her head and lustful mouth up under his chin like a feeding vampire. Lynch has linked sex with violence throughout his work, from the Mother who forces a kiss on her Boy in *The Grandmother* to *Blue Velvet*'s Frank Booth and Jeffrey Beaumont's rough, face-slapping couplings with Dorothy and Frank's reference to bullets as "love letters"—but in *Wild at Heart* the director will go farther still in haunting some aspects of eroticism with the fetid stench of death.

Having made her indecent proposal to Sailor in the spacious public area of the men's room, Marietta pulls him into the claustrophobic, intimate confines of a toilet stall. As she spits angry words in his face, we see that both her sexual lust and bloodlust for Sailor are connected to a common G-spot: "I just wanted to kiss you goodbye." Lynch, who once described the act of giving birth as "pure meat and blood and hair,"[54] has a scientist's and an artist's fascination for the fundamental principles of biological processes and phenomena. Having worked sex, violence, and death into Marietta and Sailor's bathroom booth, the director adds excrement, as Lula's mama hisses, "You think I'd let my daughter hang around with a piece of shit like you, who belongs in one of these toilets?" Marietta is like a female spider who wants to mate and murder with a single embrace. Having sought to arouse Sailor's genitals, she now says, "Before I kill you I'm going to cut off your balls and feed them to you." At the end of his film, Lynch will give a positive meaning to the phrase "wild at heart," but 99 percent of the picture's wildness connotes chaotic craziness and volatile danger, and its name is Marietta.

Her and Sailor's bodies don't meet in the toilet stall, but their minds do. The emotional dynamic between them is reduced to a simple, dark understanding: "If you're going to keep me away from Lula, you're going to have to kill me"; "Oh don't worry, that can be arranged."

Marietta's attempt to erase Sailor from Lula's life fails when he kills her assassin Bobby Ray, but she has the satisfaction of watching her nemesis stagnate in prison for endless months while she gulps martinis in the middle of the day. And when Sailor phones from jail asking to speak to Lula, Marietta reasserts her dominance. She tells him, "If you ever think of seeing her, you're a dead man," and reminds Lula, "You're not going to see him ever—end of story." One of the motivating principles of Lynch's life is his opposition to forces that could constrain his artistic and personal freedom, an impetus that he fully expresses in *Wild at Heart*. The ultimate way to eradicate Sailor's cherished "room to move"[55] is to rub him out, a drastic step that Gifford's Marietta only talks about, but which Diane Ladd pursues with a vengeance in Lynch's film. Marietta is primarily a physical threat to Sailor, whereas for Lula (and Lynch) she is the Bad Mother: a fearsome and poisonous force that has invaded her daughter's psyche. There's a disturbing sense that Marietta represents more than a straightforward roadblock to Lula's coming-of-age separation from her mother. Lula's journey of emotional and sexual maturation with Sailor is haunted by something horrible hidden away in her subconscious—something that pierces her waking life with images of jagged broken glass and fire, and scary visions of the Wicked Witch with her mother's face, cackling on her broomstick in the night wind.

Marietta's witchy hand seems to hold Sailor and Lula in a strong, stifling grip, but in Lynch's world, surface appearances can be deceiving, and *Wild at Heart* explores two existential paradoxes: The more you try to control someone, the more elusive they become; and the freedom of the open road holds many traps. The phone in Marietta's house is located at the base of a curving stairway to the upper floor, on which Lula stands after Mama has rebuffed Sailor's attempt to talk to her daughter. Marietta says "end of story, you're not seeing him," but now Lula, in contrast to these two characters' spatial deployment at the hotel killing scene, is in the superior position, and she coldly replies, "Like hell." (When Lynch, Dern, and Ladd first tried this scene, the real-life mother and daughter burst out laughing, indicating that Lynch's art was touching on freedom/control issues that they had dealt with in their off-camera lives.) Wearing Lynch's favorite black-and-white, and pictorially merged with the white light from a background window, Lula, like *The Grandmother*'s Boy, *The Elephant Man*'s John Merrick, and *Blue Velvet*'s Sandy, is another Lynchian character who finds an aspect of enlightenment in the upper story of a dwelling. The domineering Marietta wishes the story was over, and that she and her daughter could live forever in their tastefully appointed house, where Mama keeps the curtains drawn. But Lula wants to follow the light out through the window and find her home speeding down the road with the man she loves.

A warm twilight glow ignites the faces of Lula and Sailor as we see them for the first time out-of-doors when she picks him up outside the prison gates. They're absolutely thrilled to see each other, and when she hands him his favorite mottled-gold snakeskin jacket to put on, he exclaims, "Oh, wow!" (This "wow," which isn't in Lynch's script, is an attitudinal expression that Nicolas Cage has worked into almost every one of his films: the word is the final, dying utterance of the actor's Oscar-winning *Leaving Las Vegas* [1996] performance.) After the "wow," Sailor adds that the jacket "is a symbol of my individuality and my belief in personal freedom." This jacket can be seen as Cage's homage to the archetypal 1950s rebel persona of Marlon Brando, who could radiate dangerous anger, a wounded heart, sexual heat, and an aching sensitivity just by walking into a room or gazing at a person. In *The Fugitive Kind* (Sidney Lumet, 1959), he played a smoldering, poetic musician-drifter whose trademark as an entertainer is a snakeskin jacket like Sailor's. Brando's jacket is not a personal signifier of "individuality and freedom": That role is filled by his beloved guitar. But this tragic, yet hopeful film is a paean to "something still wild in this country, something still free," and the sheen of that outsider spirit emanates from Sailor's garment. Aside from evoking Brando's *Fugitive Kind* aura, *Wild at Heart*'s snakeskin jacket honors a family lineage and legacy, for Lumet's film was written by playwright Tennessee Williams, who was Diane Ladd's cousin, and this was the stage drama in which she acted and met Bruce Dern, future father of Laura Dern. Some commentators are sure that Lynch borrowed the snakeskin jacket idea from *The Fugitive Kind*, but it actually came from Nicolas Cage, who called Lynch one day and asked if he could wear the snakeskin jacket he'd owned for some years. Lynch loved the idea and wrote it into the script, as he did the theme of having Cage sing Elvis Presley songs.

Watching *Wild at Heart*, we're charmed by Sailor's exuberance but, given Lynch's characteristic linkage of animalism with bestial deeds, we're also disquieted when Sailor clothes himself with animal skin. The snake is an ancient symbol of the primal cosmic force, which can be used for good and evil. Having splattered Bob Ray Lemon's brains, Sailor knows his capacity for acting out his inner darkness; his challenge on this journey will be to hew to the path of light.

Heat and ruddy light flush Sailor and Lula's faces as they make love in the Cape Fear Hotel. The couple's warm togetherness delineates their stand against Marietta's dictatorship and defines the moral center of their home-on-the-run, their fugitive community of two. In *Lost Highway*, Lynch will present longer, naturalistic real-time passages of people having intercourse, but in *Wild at Heart*, as with *Blue Velvet*'s couplings between Jeffrey and Dorothy, the director shows us a visual abstraction of the sex act that projects a particular emotional tone. In the earlier film, Jeffrey, after yielding to Dorothy's goading, masochistic passion, strikes her across the mouth and lunges his naked body on top of hers. More concerned with power than love, that scene shows Dorothy pushing Jeffrey to do what she wants, and he, against his verbal protestations, discovering the ugly thrill of expressing a violent side he didn't know he had. In a dark room, on bluish sheets, Jeffrey thrusts himself on top (though not inside) of Dorothy as Lynch goes into slow motion and mixes in the distorted sounds of animals roaring and a woman screaming as the couple fades to black. Prior to *Wild at Heart*, Lynch seemed more interested in portraying character's psyches penetrating one another, rather than their aroused bodies doing so. In *Eraserhead* and *Dune* lovers symbolically liquefied together. And *Blue Velvet*'s Frank Booth kept his pants zipped up while directing and acting out his theater of sexual perversion atop Dorothy's naked crotch.

Lynch has never been squeamish about showing sex on the screen: It's just that his imagination's gift for visualizing emotional states in abstract, unconventional ways has led him away from filming standard "the man and the woman have intercourse" scenes. In Gifford's book, Sailor and Lula express their love for each other through intimate conversation and love-making, so Lynch knew going in that *Wild at Heart* would require more sex scenes than any of his previous films. The directors' sense of aesthetic balance and proportion told him he should use a cinematic economy of means to convey his couple's ongoing, nearly constant sexual communion. For the first time in one of his films, Lynch shows us two naked bodies unequivocally (in an R-rated, simulated way, of course) joined in genital intercourse. Rather than lingering on a single sex act, the director presents short, impressionistic montages of Sailor and Lula in various positions (he's on top, she's on top, her leg's over his shoulder, he's mounting her from behind) throughout the film to indicate the frequency of their erotic embraces. Lynch bathes these passages in red and gold light to radiate the healthy heat of his couple's desire and passion for each other—a sharp contrast to the mood indigo of the sad, masochistic Dorothy's *Blue Velvet* bedroom. The director concludes one of *Wild at Heart*'s sexual montages with a lyrical flourish that evokes the 1950s culture he adores. As the sight and sound of Lula having a very vocal orgasm fades, we see Lynch's vision of the couple standing before a golden jukebox that's belting out a tune by 1950s rockabilly artist Gene Vincent. As Gene ardently sings "Be-Bop-a-Lula she's my baby," Sailor takes Lula's hand and puts it right on his heart. Sailor and Lula's couplings burn with a lustful fervency usually reserved for sudden cinematic seductions and one-night stands, and yet they've already been together for some years. For these two, sex and love burn with a single flame.

We've noted Lynch's fascination for the way that the boundary lines between beings can be penetrated and, for good or ill, one consciousness can get inside another's head. Sailor and Lula's souls, as well as their bodies and hearts, are intermingled. They both see *The Wizard of Oz* characters' adventures as a mythic narrative that resonates with their own journey toward their own personal Oz: the golden state of California, where they'll be free to live and love without anyone pushing them around. In Lynch's films, characters lying horizontally in bed often gain access to metaphysical knowledge and even realms of parallel, alternate reality. In the afterglow of sex, Sailor and Lula lie back, light cigarettes, and blow smoke, so that even the air between them is eroticized by bearing the caress of both their mouths. They are so profoundly bonded that Lula whispers, "You mark me the deepest," and speaks of a mystical, D. H. Lawrence–like communication between them: "It's like your sweet cock is talking to me when you're inside; it's got this little voice all it's own."

Barry Gifford's book, and Lynch's film, present Sailor and Lula's love as sexual, soulful, supportive, and steadfast: Their relationship spawns happy dreams and shields the couple against malicious Marietta and the maniacal, voodooed outer world. But Lynch knows that surface reality hides layers of subterranean experience and knowledge, and he adds this pet theme to Gifford's text, having Sailor declare, "We all got a secret side, baby."

Lula's first secret relates to her fecundity: Like Mary X in *Eraserhead*, she hasn't told her man that she is pregnant. In the first third of the film, Lula gladly tells Sailor that at thirteen she was raped by her Uncle Pooch. She says that Marietta didn't know about this occurrence, yet in Lula's flashback we see Mama bursting in just after Pooch finishes up, shrieking at him and hitting him with her purse as he flees. (Gifford's rapist was, according to Lula, "super gentle,"[56] and once he started, "it didn't seem all that terrible," whereas Lynch makes the rape a raging violation, with sobs pouring from Lula's bloodied mouth, the red-stained upper orifice a surrogate for the deflowered lower opening that we don't see.)

Over the years, viewers and writers have been puzzled about why Lula would lie to Sailor regarding mother's presence in her daughter's rape scene. Just before we see Lula's flashback, Lynch gives us another of his aesthetic dualities as Lula looks at herself in a mirror while she begins to tell Sailor the Marietta-less rape story. Lula has both the face that she presents to Sailor and the one she consciously keeps to herself. More disturbingly, she also carries the burden of a not-quite-realized awareness of her mother's shadow side. She doesn't make the connection between the image of Mama pounding on Uncle Pooch and the following shot of Pooch's car (with the dog man inside) rolling down a cliff in flames. Lula's conscious mind won't admit the terrible reality that links the intrusive images and sounds that trouble her: her father in flames, thrashing around their living room the night he died; a woman's shrieking laugh; the Wicked Witch with her mother's face.

Lula also does not tell Sailor that Uncle Pooch impregnated her and that Marietta then had to arrange an abortion for her, whereas in Gifford's book she readily informs him that she had an abortion after her uncle got her pregnant. In the film Lula has a private flashback about her abortion just as she gathers courage to let Sailor know that she's carrying his child, so it's natural at a big moment like this that she wouldn't want to mention her ugly previous pregnancy experience. There's also a sense that Lula's Pooch pregnancy is a link in a dark equation that she's trying to repress: Marietta's anger when she discovers Uncle has raped Lula, added to Mama's still greater fury when the violation produces a concrete emblem of the atrocity, a fetus, results in an abortion for Lula and a flaming car death for Uncle Pooch. Speaking of linkages, there's an interesting gestural correspondence that spans the fourteen years between *Eraserhead* and *Wild at Heart* and shows mothers trying to infantalize their daughters. In the earlier film, when Mary X is agitated, Mrs. X combs her long hair as though she were a little girl, and when Lula's lying on the abortionist's table (in footage that didn't make it into the final cut) Marietta tries to get Lula to lick a lollipop.

Lula's mother is too much with her, whereas Sailor experienced "a lack of parental guidance" growing up, and fell in with some bad company. Before he met Lula, he did some driving for Marcello Santos (J. E. Freeman), one of Lynch's suave, well-dressed villains, who gives us a dark thrill when his low, Southern-molasses voice intones, "I'm in a killin' mood." Not that Sailor ever heard Santos say such a thing. The youth wasn't apprenticing to become a hood, he just got a kick out of hanging around with the cool, rather shady Santos, who was some kind of operator in the North Carolina night world, and who didn't go around blabbing about his nefarious deeds, even to his young driver.

In Gifford's book, Lula's daddy, Clyde, went mad and killed himself by igniting his body with kerosene and a match. Lynch darkens the picture considerably in his film by having the fact that clandestine lovers Santos and Marietta murdered Clyde be the dark secret hidden at the center of his film. Before he quit working for Santos, Sailor sat in the car outside what he later would learn was Lula's house as it went up in flames, as Clyde, who'd been set on fire by Santos, ran from room to room, and Marietta laughed her high witchy laugh, Lula called for her daddy, and Santos snuck out Marietta's bedroom window. By creating this hellish night, Lynch gives Lula the fragments of memory and subconscious maternal suspicion that haunt her, provides Marietta with another reason to want Sailor rubbed out, and supplies Sailor with a secret to keep from Lula. Sailor didn't actually see what happened inside the house, but Marietta thinks he did, and this mistaken conclusion, combined with the way he spurned her sexual advances and ran off with her Lula, moves her, via Santos, to put out a contract on his life.

When Sailor finally tells Lula that he used to work for the notorious Santos and that he was outside her house the night her father died, she's wounded by the way he kept this information from her for so long, and sadly says, "It's shocking when things aren't the way you thought they were." Soon after revealing this secret to Lula, Sailor learns the full story of how, as Santos's cohort Perdita Durango (Isabella Rossellini) puts it, Lula's "mommy and Santos killed her daddy." Does our hero then contact the district attorney and help send to prison Perdita, Santos, Marietta, and the whole film noir–like web of interrelated criminals that Lynch added on to Gifford's novel? Of course not. Lynch's film is a passionate, messy romance powered by Sailor and Lula's relationship, not some formulaic, dryly logical, legal-eagles thriller with a courtroom climax. This artist doesn't paint by numbers, he draws the heart line that shapes poetic truth.

As Sailor and Lula drive across the sun-hammered, wasteland plains of Texas, she has a sensory-overload fit after hearing a litany of horrifying world news on the radio: "rape . . . severed . . . murder . . . mutilated . . . sex with the corpse . . . crocodiles devouring dead bodies. . . ." Unable to cope with this torrent of malevolence and depravity, Lula screams, stops the car, and leaps out. Sailor changes the station to some aggressive speed-metal rock music, and Lula kicks up dust, dancing away her fear and anger as the sun sets on the horizon. Sailor, who has spilled a man's blood while gripped by a bestial rage, is more understanding of the world's crazy, wicked ways, whereas Lula retains the raw vulnerability of a young woman still maturing and is not yet inured to devastating truths. Sailor will do whatever it takes to protect her from physical or psychological harm. And so, like a soldier falling on top of an exploding grenade to save his comrades, he chooses to contain within himself the terrible knowledge of Marietta's attempt to seduce him, her vow to kill him, and her part in the murder of Lula's beloved father. If Sailor were to tell Lula of Marietta's hidden machinations, she would feel instantly alienated from her mother. Instead, Lynch chooses to let Marietta's power over Lula flow at full force, undiluted by the revelation of Mama's evil secrets. The director will let Lula's relationship with her mother evolve at the daughter's own rate of discovery and understanding. And besides, Sailor's holding-in of all he knows about Marietta paradoxically gives him still another thing to share with Lula, for he too is now haunted by the scary vision of mama as the Wicked Witch.

Sailor and Lula's lips may withhold secrets from each other, but their hearts are true and loyal, and their unwavering love helps protect the couple from the many fragments of chaos that assault them. Much of that chaos is generated by Marietta's tumultuous thoughts and feelings. In Lynch's gallery of film characters, she is like a sister to *Blue Velvet*'s Frank Booth, as both try to ease the pain of their confused, erratic, and volcanically intense feelings by tightening a desperate grip of control around, respectively, Dorothy Vallens and daughter Lula. Marietta's obsessive focus is a bulwark against a horrifying abyss of aloneness and psychological implosion. The emotion that preoccupies and motivates her is her need to bend Lula's spirit to her will and possess it, but she also has a couple of men in her life.

Lynch, with his love of contrasting dualities, overtly plays out the rivalry between the good Johnnie Farragut and the bad Marcello Santos for the affections of Marietta, a dynamic that Gifford only alludes to in his book. Detective Johnnie, especially as played by the endearing Harry Dean Stanton, is a tremendously sympathetic character who presents a wise, rational view of Sailor and Lula to Marietta: Sailor has paid for his crime of killing Bob Ray Lemon, and besides, he was just defending Lula; and Lula is certainly now old enough to chart the course of her own romantic life. Johnnie is lovesick for Marietta and knows that she and Santos were once lovers, so she has power over the detective. Manipulating him with anger, tears, sweet talk, and threats of bringing Santos into the picture to rub out Sailor and potentially become her bedmate again, Marietta readily gets Johnnie to say he'll pursue the runaway couple and bring Lula back to mama. If poor Johnnie only knew Lynch's coded way of equating animalistic behavior with evil, he'd be seriously worried when Marietta, as part of her cajoling theatrics, playfully mimes the claws and growling jaws of a she-panther on the prowl.

Just as Sailor and Lula keep secrets from each other, Marietta hides a truth from loving Johnnie, but unlike the youngster's withheld information, Mama's shrouded news will have deadly consequences for her romantic partner. As soon as Johnnie has left town to track Sailor and Lula, she invites Santos over for drinks and presents herself in a seductive mode. (Unlike her daughter, Marietta is all show and no go in the bedroom department: She withholds sex from Johnnie in the present moment and seems to offer it as a future payoff for his satisfactory job performance.) Doing just what Johnnie wouldn't want her to do, she arranges for Santos to have Sailor killed. This being a Lynch film, the job will naturally involve head trauma: Sailor will be shot "in the brain," intones Santos, touching his forehead with the same two-fingered, gun-shaped gesture Frank Booth used in *Blue Velvet*.

A few years back, when Santos and Marietta had been lovers, they killed her husband, making it easier for them to be together and for Mama to have Lula all to herself. Given Marietta's penchant for pursuing spasmodic notions, it's easy to imagine her just dropping Santos for Johnnie at some past date. Now she only wants to conduct business with Santos, but he shows her, as has Lula, that it's damnable hard to control the idiosyncratic nature of other people. Santos wants Marietta to be his woman again and, against her shocked and fearful protestations, he says that he will snuff out Johnnie as well as Sailor.

Unlike Johnnie, Santos can't be talked out of his chosen course of action, and he sets in motion the criminal machine that will seal his rival's doom. Marietta then has an emotional explosion compounded with rage at having Santos thwart her will and her panicky guilt about inadvertently brokering Johnnie's death warrant. Lynch makes her inflamed feelings visible by having her, alone at home, mime self-destruction by tearing at her wrist with a blood-red lipstick. She then colors her entire face red, reflecting her capacity for generating murderous fire and bloodshed. It's as though that accusing, bloody finger that Sailor pointed at Marietta as he stood panting over the dead body of her paid assassin, Bob Ray Lemon, has finally touched and stained the head that launched a thousand of what Sailor calls "bad ideas."

Marietta makes another bad choice when she calls Johnnie, who's now in New Orleans. She knows that Santos is also in the big N.O. and is closing in on the detective, but she can't bring herself to tell Johnnie that, behind his back and against his wishes, she's brought Santos back into her life and set him on a planned (Sailor) and inadvertent (Johnnie) course of murder. But rather than risk losing Johnnie by confessing her errant ways, she keeps mum and joins him in New Orleans so they can pursue Lula together. Does she think that there's safety in numbers, that by being with Johnnie she can keep Santos from striking like a shadowy cobra?

Lynch often shows Marietta acting out extremes of negative emotion, for she is, after all, his larger-than-life Wicked Witch. (In the scene where she paints her face red she's even wearing witchy black slippers with curled-up toes.) But the director gives her a calm, naturalistic moment that poignantly hints at the fulfilling, psychologically healing life she might enjoy with the eminently sane, adoring Johnnie. After a fine restaurant meal, they kiss, say "I love you" to each other, and get ready to hit the road on Lula's trail. This is the couple's most sympathetic, warmly human scene together in the film—and for Lynch, the perfect moment to turn the lights out.

Happy and humming a little tune, Johnnie leaves Marietta to pack her luggage in her room and heads down the hall to get his things together. He pauses with an afterthought, something more he wanted to say to her, but he keeps on walking because he's got all the time in the world in which to tell her. In Lynch's universe, a radiant mood can lose its light in an instant, and as Johnnie steps into his well-lit room, someone hits him on the head and the chamber goes black: another of the director's portentous Now It's Dark moments.

When Johnnie doesn't meet Marietta in the hotel lobby as planned, she angrily thinks that he's chickened out of their romantic commitment and their mission to find Lula. She's wary when Santos appears, but when he says he hasn't hurt Johnnie she does a disturbing emotional about-face, quickly shifting her allegiance to Santos as he declares "You're my girl now." Marietta's feelings fluctuate in tune with her primal obsession, and Santos is the man who can both eliminate Sailor and bring Lula home. Sweet, sad Johnnie can haunt her mind some other time.

In Lynch's conception of *Wild at Heart*, if you play with the Wicked Witch, even if you don't know she's the Wicked Witch, you're going to get burned. Just as Lynch and Frost chose to maximize their *Twin Peaks* audience's psychological discomfort by having Laura Palmer's killer be her own father, so Lynch decides, in *Wild at Heart*, to rub out Johnnie, one of the most lovable, decent, and morally upright people in the film. In this out-of-control world, the good and the innocent are the first to go.

Since Johnnie is alive and well at the end of Gifford's book, Lynch was free to design the detective's murder any way he wanted to and, characteristically, he chose to make him suffer a psychological torment that's almost worse than death. Tied to a chair, his mouth taped shut, Johnnie is made the unwilling third partner in a death ritual that doubles as sex play for Santos' cohorts Juana (Grace Zabriske) and Reggie (Calvin Lockhart). Johnnie doesn't know these two work for Santos; he has no idea why they abducted him from his hotel and are now, frenzied by hot lust for each other and the thick, distorted words of a voodoo chant, preparing to blow his brains out. Like *Blue Velvet*'s Jeffrey with Frank Booth, Johnnie is kissed on the mouth by his tormentor, Juana the Cajun, who relishes his fear ("I smell yo shit now"). If Marietta personifies maternal energy perverted into ungovernable, dictatorial malevolence, then Juana is a shadow-zone image of female sexuality twisted into out-of-control bloodlust: Reggie consolingly says to Johnnie, "I can't stop her now." Like Frank Booth ("I'll fuck anything that moves"), Juana displays a polymorphously perverse, all-devouring sexual appetite as, thrusting her face into the camera, she waggles her tongue as though giving cunnilingus to the very air. Johnnie not only suffers the anguish of being the captive object of Juana and Reggie's unholy foreplay, but, just before Reggie blasts him, they show him Santos' ring, so that he wrongly thinks that an unfaithful Marietta has helped plot his death. As the final mean stroke, Reggie shoots Johnnie from behind, so that he suffers a final suspense over just which moment the thunder will explode his brain. Showing the saddest face of his life, Johnnie says his final words: "Oh God, Marietta honey. . . ." Juana screams "Fuck me now, Reggie" as her lover shoots. Then, with Johnnie gone, the two voodoo killers can, if they have not already, achieve their orgasm.

It's hard to imagine Lynch, who believes so strongly in the sanctity of his creative vision, altering his film because of a negative test screening, but that's exactly what happened with Johnnie's death scene. The original version protracted Johnnie's suffering and was more sexually and violently graphic. Twenty-two years before, in *The Grandmother*, the Boy and his grandparent had played a sweet touching game in which they lovingly communicated by repeatedly reaching out their hands to each others' faces, and over the years Lynch's kissing lovers touch their partner's faces, as the director continually emphasizes the head as the locus of personal identity. In the original *Wild at Heart* scene, Lynch had Juana set up a nightmarish perversion of these wholesome games that involved two separate soda bottles sitting on wooden stands (one stand a tree trunk, perhaps referencing Cooper's Tibetan deductive technique employing a pop bottle on a stump in *Twin Peaks*; the other a fence post—for *Blue Velvet*'s iconic picket fence?). Juana touches one bottle, then the second, then Johnnie's face, then she kisses Reggie, then she touches her genitals. She will repeat this pattern a number of times, but as her passion mounts, she will grow impatient and not touch the second bottle before touching Johnnie, signifying that the pistol shot will now come from behind his head, after which she and Reggie can culminate their death-dealing sex act. If one phallic bottle represents Reggie, and the other Johnnie, then when Juana withholds her vital, sexed-up touch from the detective's bottle, her hand on his actual face will be the mark of death. And, in a metaphor employing the forces of electricity that fascinate Lynch, Juana's repetitive touching pattern is an electrical circuit that, when broken, turns Johnnie's lights out forever.

Extending the amount of screen time in which the good-hearted Johnnie is tortured really bothered the film's test audience, but what absolutely repulsed them, and made, according to Lynch, "three-hundred out of maybe three-hundred-fifty"[57] get up and leave, occurred just after Reggie's gun blast. The shot severed Johnnie's head from his body, and the sex-crazed Juana obtained her orgasm by picking up the head and rubbing it between her legs. Aside from providing a sick-joke double meaning to the phrase "giving head," Juana's action was a logical conclusion to her sex-and-death touching game, an ultimate statement of her need to bend another person's sexuality to her controlling will that rhymed with Marietta's desire to both have sex with Sailor and kill him. Lynch is fascinated by the strange, paradoxical poetics of the transformative, fluid zone where life and love and death meet. The place where the death of *The Grandmother*'s Boy hybridizes new life; where the dying Henry in *Eraserhead* and John Merrick in *The Elephant Man* find fulfilling, cosmic love across the dark threshold; where Frank Booth in *Blue Velvet* calls a bullet a "love letter," and his own violent death brings light and love to a benighted town; where the murder of Laura Palmer is the vital spark that animates *Twin Peaks*; and where Juana's touch visits death upon Johnnie, whose lifeless touch in turn gives her the ecstatic aliveness of a sexual climax.

Lynch's imagination had generated this grotesque love scene between Juana and Johnnie's head, and he felt it had a proper place in his film which, after all, was about a world "coming unglued, going insane, with people gripped by brutality and mania, just like in real life." His fundamental artistic impulse, just like when he made a painting or crafted his earliest short films, was to accurately and forcefully portray his thoughts and feelings about a subject in visual form. Lynch's primal artistic dialogue was always with himself, but now millions of people around the world were interested in his creations. Since Lynch valued his chance to communicate with so many people, he was willing to alter "that one tiny bit"[58] of his film so as not to alienate his audience from the entire work. This compromise felt like it was part of his own intrinsic artistic process: Forced changes from outside were the ones that troubled his mind.

When darkness comes creeping in a Lynch film, it's almost impossible to stop it. The terrible night that swept Johnnie away isn't satisfied with just one victim: It must also engulf the journey of Sailor and Lula. While Johnnie is dying in New Orleans, the couple is driving through a mournfully unpopulated nocturnal wasteland of Texas highway. Accompanied by Chris Isaak's heartsick guitar playing "Wicked Game," an unfamiliar, troubling note of doubt enters their relationship as Sailor reveals that he's been keeping his presence at her father's death scene a secret. And, like a nightmare projection of Sailor and Lula's fears about the monstrously controlling Marietta, they come upon a delirious, dying car accident victim with a bleeding head wound (Sherilyn Fenn, *Twin Peak*'s Audrey Horne), who repeatedly babbles that "my mother's going to kill me" because she's lost her wallet and purse. This scene, which was actually shot in the California desert, makes expressive use of the sort of eerie, Joshua tree–studded landscape that the youthful Lynch had seen in 1950s science fiction films. We note that once again in a Lynch film someone (Fenn) is dying because something that shouldn't be there (an unspecified part of a big, black car) has invaded their head. For Lula, Fenn's talk of a sinister mother, and this intrusion of sudden, random death, are like a bad dream she can't wake from, a sinister omen that shadows the night—and things aren't much better in the morning.

Like a fish stranded in a desert, the shabby town of Big Tuna is full of people out of their element who are from, or on their way to, somewhere else. People low on money, hope, luck, and sanity, who hide from the heat in rat-trap motel rooms and come out at night when the sense of dislocation is sadly emphasized by colorful Christmas lights glowing in the humid summer air.

Sailor and Lula's warm relationship has been the rock-solid cornerstone of Lynch's film, but once the journey-battered couple limps into Big Tuna, the director builds in details that disturbingly foreshadow their potential dissolution. They don't make love anymore, and they're not together on the bed when they have an intimate conversation, nor do they smoke in tandem as before. Sailor says he's glad that Lula's pregnant, but she can't endorse his sentiment. To potently sum up their new, mournful sense of tension and alienation, Lynch invokes the language of the *Wizard of Oz* dream that he so reveres. Lula laments, "We broke down on that yellow brick road."

Still, the director strives to maintain a sense of togetherness between Sailor and Lula, even in a negative way, by having them both face a critical confrontation with bad man Bobby Peru (Willem Dafoe) (Gifford's book only had Sailor be tempted by this dark one). Lula calls Bobby "the Black

Angel," but he doesn't emanate an essence of ancient, mysterious, metaphysical evil like *Blue Velvet*'s Frank Booth and *Twin Peaks*' BOB do. He's understandable on a human level, as a guy who kills and steals for profit and who participated in a My Lai–style massacre of civilian natives during the Vietnam war. With his greased-back hair and breath-fouling, stumpy brown teeth, Bobby is a repulsive specimen. But Lynch, and Dafoe's fine performance, invest Bobby with that bad-ass swagger and black-leather-jacket cool that the director admires, and the villain's capacity for menace is blended with a crazed, grinning geniality: He seems to be a friendly guy. Asked if he's from Texas, Bobby replies, "I'm from all over." He has a world-wise sense of how to best lure each particular prey, and he tempts Lula with sex, and Sailor with easy money.

In *Wild at Heart*, Lynch's antipathy toward domineering people controlling the lives of innocent folk was so strong that he added Bobby Peru's name to Juana's as someone who toys with an unwilling person sexually in a scene that Barry Gifford did not conceive of in his book. Sailor's out, there's a knock on Lula's motel-room door. Wary when she sees it's Bobby, she only opens the door a few inches, but he slithers through the narrow opening as Lynch metaphorically insinuates the sexual nature of the coming encounter. Bobby has "gotta take a piss bad," and the former Marine uses military terminology when he asks to use the toilet. Anyone in a Lynch film should be on their guard when asked the double-meaning question, "Can I use your head?" Bobby's violation of Lula commences as he pees without closing the bathroom door, so the sound of his urine splashing into the bowl resounds throughout Lula's room—and of course he doesn't flush.

Lynch then orchestrates one of his highly dramatic clinch scenes in which two people seething with intense emotion confront each other, their faces only inches apart. With the stench of Lula's morning-sickness vomit, Bobby's rotten teeth, and the fearsome threat of his violence stifling the air, Bobby forcefully pulls Lula's body next to his. Standing together, she tries to push him away and tells him to go, but she doesn't scream for Sailor, who is outside the open window working on their car. Bobby orders her to "Say 'fuck me,' and I'll leave," and repeatedly whispers "fuck me" like a hypnotic love spell. When he slides his hand onto her genitals she does not try to push it away, and her breathing jumps with forbidden pleasure, her fingers splay out like they do when she and Sailor make love, and she does whisper "fuck me." Then, with the surrealistic incongruity of the absurdist, non-sequiter humor Lynch loves, Bobby suddenly jumps back from the quivering Lula and, with a big grin, says "Some day, honey, I will, but right now, I gotta get going." Bobby's domineering game is a cruel joke, for Lula is left in emotional devastation, both violated and sexually pleasured, weeping Sailor's name and clicking her red shoes together, as though that could transport her, like *The Wizard of Oz*'s Dorothy, home to some simple and innocent Kansas.

The sex that Lula enjoys with Sailor, which constitutes the hearth fire of their home-on-the-road, is straightforwardly sweet, loving, and soulful, whereas her encounter with Bobby is all mixed up with violence, degradation, humiliation, and guilt. Lula, like *Blue Velvet*'s Jeffrey, is developing her adult identity while separated from her parent, and like him, she tastes the shadow side of sexuality on her journey. Lynch, convinced that a measure of darkness dwells in us all, never shies from portraying the full spectrum of human desire and gratification. But for some viewers, Lynch's artistic forthrightness violated an emotional ideological boundary. A number of feminists saw the director's Bobby-and-Lula scene as a reprehensible example of the male-gazing fantasy in which the woman says no but means yes. Some aggrieved viewers declared that Lynch was a danger to women and should never be allowed to make another film. Yet many other women audience members found the scene to be admirably perceptive, provocative, and psychologically complex: They felt it revealed the hidden truth that some part of the psychosexual consciousness likes a man from the wrong side of the tracks, a statement Laura Dern said she believed.

Bad Bobby, having exploited Lula's vulnerabilities, works his will on Sailor by talking him into participating in a feed store robbery. It seems like the manipulator just wants to help out pregnant Lula and penniless Sailor. Lula's man is reluctant to commit even a nonviolent crime, but the extra $2,500 would help rekindle their primal dream of getting "a long way down that yellow brick road." Bobby and Sailor agree to do the hold-up the next day—so why does Lynch cover the image of their accord with Marietta's Wicked Witch crystal ball and her clawhand passing ominously over the scene? We learn that Marietta's wish to kill Sailor will be granted by the hand of Bobby, and that he will lethally and animalistically "strike like a cobra" during the robbery.

The night before the big day, Sailor and Lula lie in bed without touching, a great emotional distance between them. Lynch often evokes the fascination of untold secrets, but here he shows their danger, for if either would just speak to the other of their separate afternoon encounters with Bobby Peru, a grievous morning could be avoided. Left to his own inner counsel, Sailor, like many Lynch characters, has two realities warring in his head. As he waits for Bobby to pick him up for the robbery he says, "What am I doing here? I can't do this," but when Bobby pulls up Sailor puts one foot in front of the other and gets in the car. Just climbing into some car other than his and Lula's vehicle-of-love Thurderbird feels like a betrayal.

Lynch gives the feed store's town the mark of the beast, calling it Lobo (Spanish for "wolf") instead of Gifford's Iraq. And during the hold-up he shows that the forces of chaos can obliterate both Sailor's and Bobby's efforts to control the situation. Sailor has Bobby's word that no one will be hurt, but the Black Angel bloodily blasts the two attendants with his shotgun, then giggles "You're next." Sailor tries to fire at Bobby, but his gun has been loaded with blanks. He runs outside with Bobby in pursuit, then a policeman drives up and shoots Bobby, who falls forward on his own shotgun, which discharges. For Gifford, this was enough action to kill off his villain, but if Lynch sees a chance for head trauma he'll take it. In the film, Bobby's head is blasted off of his shoulders, bounces off the front of the feed store, and splatters noisily on the ground. In the director's original conception, this bad man losing his head would balance the good Johnnie Farragut losing his in the scene Lynch decided to delete after that highly negative test screening.

Sailor's face is in the dirt as the policeman arrests him, and Lynch makes his hero's anguish visible as clouds of charcoal-colored dust waft up next to his mouth as he sadly breathes Lula's name and says "I really let you down this time." The director also introduces Marietta back into Lula's life as a dark abstraction when her shadow materializes on the wall next to Lula's head just before Mama steps into the frame to claim her prized human possession. Lula protests that "Sailor's in deep trouble" here in Texas and she must stay with him, but Marietta's forward momentum cannot be derailed: Lula is coming home with Mama, period. And to ensure that Marietta's trap is steel tight, Santos steps into the frame and grabs and holds Lula securely in the guise of giving her "a friendly hug." This repulsive gesture of an evil older man enclosing a young, innocent female in an entrapping embrace recalls the nihilistic conclusion of Roman Polanski's *Chinatown* (1974), when the monstrous Noah Cross (John Houston) obliterates all the laws of God and man by hugging his granddaughter (and product-of-incest daughter) and pulling her into the shadows.

Lynch is very familiar with *Chinatown*. It's a movie he loves, so was he consciously emulating Polanski's scene? There are, indeed, echoes of other directors' work in Lynch's films: the absurdly stilted social interactions of Luis Bunuel's characters, the flickering domestic lights and eerie empty rooms of William Friendkin's *The Exorcist* (1973), the reference to "pie and coffee" in Werner Herzog's *Stroszek* (1977), the melding and exchanging of personalities between two people who pictorally put their heads together in Ingmar Bergman's *Persona* (1966), a villain who breaths an inhaler in Blake Edwards' *Experiment in Terror* (1962), and a man's discovery of, and immersion in, a hidden world of psycho-sexual darkness on a sunny residential street (Billy Wilder's *Sunset Boulevard*, 1950). There are also reflections of Lynch's themes and aesthetics in the films of, among others, the Coen Brothers, Oliver Stone, Quentin Tarrentino, Philip Ridley, Adam Rifkin, Sam Mendes, the Polish Brothers, the photography of Gregory Crewdson, the TV shows *The X-Files*, *Picket Fences*, *Carnivale*, *Lost*, and *Desperate Housewives* (ironically, ABC executives, who were impatient for Lynch to reveal who killed *Twin Peaks*' Laura Palmer, were anxious for Marc Cherry to delay solving *Desperate Housewives*' similar mystery).

For a film director, like any other artist, everything in the universe is a potential element for his or her cinematic picturemaking. In Lynch's case, he doesn't sit down with a piece of paper and calculate, "Let's see, I'll grab a bit of Scorsese, mix in some Kurosawa, add a touch of Kubrick, stir in some Fellini—and I'll have my movie." Lynch likes to work in an almost entranced state of instinctive, intuitive inspiration, in which he organically feels his way toward a balanced composition, letting his sense of the correct mood and degree of dramatic force tell him what to do next. As he says, "Ninety percent of the time I don't know what I'm doing, but sometimes I realize it later on."[59] And not always even then, for he has said to me as I've mentioned some specific detail of general theme or motivation in his work, "You would see that, but I wouldn't."

It is Lynch's way to take some of his characters (and us) deep into the dark abyss of fear, pain, sadness, and loss, but he is constitutionally unable to let them spiral downward forever. An uplifting grace is at hand, if they have the vision to see it and the courage to grasp it. The process of Lula's individuation from her mother has depended upon her being physically apart from Marietta, and on the maturing, nurturing fire of her relationship with Sailor. Now, with him in prison for six years, Lula must rely on the heat, drive, and spirit of the inner resources she's developed, and she does herself proud, investing her energies in the future rather than the past. Instead of having another abortion, like her mother wants, she gives birth to her and Sailor's boy, Pace (Glenn Walker Harris Jr.); sets up her own homey, welcoming household away from Marietta; and sends Sailor the flame of her love in many letters.

On the day that Sailor gets out of prison, Marietta, now an aging alcoholic, phones Lula and blusters herself into her Wicked Witch mode, screaming that her daughter must not go to meet her man. Lula, having rubbed up against the dark, bestial power of Bobby Peru, spits some of that wild force at her mother: "If you get in the way of me and Sailor's happiness, I'll fuckin' tear your arms out by the roots" (When Bobby was trying to get Lula to say "Fuck me," he had threatened, "I'll tear your fuckin' heart out, girl.") Earlier, in *Blue Velvet*, Lynch had shown his belief that we find parts of ourselves in evil characters when he had Jeffrey, after suffering a punishing night with the violently aggressive Frank Booth, say to his prying Aunt Barbara, "I love you, but you're going to get it."

At the beginning of the film, Lula's method of coping with Marietta was to race out of North Carolina with Sailor. Now, having lived through, and learned from, all of the wildness that the road can serve up, she has the strength to live independently and productively in her mother's community. Like *The Wizard of Oz*'s Dorothy, she's run away and circled back home; she's got her house and son, but the place needs Sailor to be truly over the rainbow. The trouble is, he doesn't feel he's worthy of being there with her.

Midway through Gifford's book, Sailor has a disturbing dream in which Lula, with small children around her, is unhappy and upset to see Sailor show up, so he leaves. And, in the book's conclusion, Sailor meets Lula and his son after getting out of prison, Lula weeps, Sailor says her fine life would be made tougher if he came back into it, he starts walking away, and she lets him go.

Instead of using Gifford's prophetic dream to cast a foreboding mood on Lula and Sailor's reunion, Lynch employs the car-accident motif which Lula had seen as a scary bad omen on her trip with Sailor. As Lula and Pace drive to meet Sailor, Lula almost smashes into one car, then immediately passes a freshly bloodied accident victim and a maimed and crazy survivor of a previous crash. (Filming in Los Angeles, Lynch shot this accident tableau in front of the concrete bridge that contains the gaping black aperture into which *Eraserhead*'s Henry Spencer stepped as he began his dark urban journey.) Then, remaining true to the book, Sailor meets his sweet, quiet son, Lula weeps, Sailor gives Pace the advice that when something doesn't feel right, you should take off before things get worse, and then walks out of their lives.

Lynch reacted strongly against this ending, given the heat of Sailor and Lula's feelings for each other, the way traveling with him helped her grow away from Marietta, and Lula's forgiveness of Sailor's past transgressions. The director felt Gifford's ending "didn't seem one *bit* real,"[60] and he told Sam Goldwyn, whose company would distribute the film, "I'm going to change it, *doggone it!*"[61] For Lynch, there must be life after death; and for Gifford too: He resurrected Sailor and Lula's relationship in future stories.

Sailor needs to get wise to the universal supremacy of love and resynchronize with Lula's and his *Wizard of Oz* dream, and Lynch uses both masculine violence and feminine wisdom to effect his hero's transformation. Sailor's heading in the wrong direction (away from Lula), so Lynch conjures up a street gang to turn him around. The Los Angeles riots would not erupt for a couple of more years, but Lynch, being a resident of the drive-by-shooting capital of the world, clearly had gangs on his mind. Yet, because the director was in a mood to end his road trip of madness and carnage with a flood of beneficence, his gang is composed of an idealized, harmonious racial mix of African American, White, Latino, and Asian men.

In Lynch's complex, multivalent world, giving way to aggressive impulses can both help Lula resist her mother's tyranny and get Sailor thrown in prison for manslaughter. And now, Sailor's pugnacity will send him over the rainbow. As though in a dream, the gang members materialize like shadows from the sides of buildings and telephone poles, and surround him. True to the aggressive side of his character, he calls the men faggots, and is beaten to the ground. Knocked out, with a swollen, bleeding broken nose, Sailor has a vision of *The Wizard of Oz*'s Good Witch. She floats inside her pink bubble, with her ballooning pink dress and magic wand, against an urban backdrop of run-down buildings, concrete bridges, and telephone wires, in a resonant Lynchian image that conflates the miraculous and the mundane. She is one of Lynch's delivering angels, his good women who float in the air, and she's played by Sheryl Lee, who the world knows as *Twin Peaks*' iconic corpse of Laura Palmer. Seeing her here attain heavenly heights hints that, when it comes to the dead high school girls, Lynch is in a resurrection frame of mind.

Six years after *Wild at Heart*, Lynch spoke of low points in his own life in terms that Sailor would recognize: "When you're *down*, when you've been kicked down the street, and then kicked a few more times till you're really bleeding and some teeth are out, then you really have only up to go."[62] The director's abiding optimism suffuses the final moments of his film, as the Good Witch brushes aside Sailor's wrong-headed notion that he's unworthy of enjoying happiness with Lula because he's a "robber and a manslaughter" and is "wild at heart." Both Gifford and Lynch have Lula use the words "wild at heart" to sum up and characterize all the pain, fear, madness, and danger that plague the world that her and Sailor, and all the rest of us, travel through. Lynch, not Gifford, is the one who has Sailor call himself wild at heart, and there could be no stronger form of self-condemnation than using his Lula's world-damning words against himself. Lynch's world is a realm of dualities and double meanings, where the same pounding music that accompanied a killing can also orchestrate a couple's lovemaking, where the hands that smashed Bob Ray Lemon's head can caress Lula, and where the Good Witch can reveal to Sailor that "if you're truly wild at heart, you'll fight for your dreams; don't turn away from love, Sailor, don't turn away from love."

When Sailor despairingly calls himself "a robber and a manslaughter" who's "wild at heart" he's letting Marietta's Wicked Witch point-of-view define him. But now, with the Good Witch's pronouncements, the essence of his being has been blessed by the high deity of Lula and his *Wizard of Oz* religion, and Lynch has again confirmed his radiant belief in the spirituality of the imaginations' dreams and visions. Using a gesture of airy communion that the director loves, the Good Witch and Sailor touch their faces and extend one hand out toward each other just before she floats away in her bubble.

Shifting back to street reality, Sailor thanks the gang of toughs for teaching him a valuable lesson and apologizes for "calling you gentlemen homosexuals." Then, screaming "Lula" and letting no obstacle stand in his way, he sprints past car wrecks, runs over the tops of an endless mass of traffic-jammed vehicles, and finally reaches Lula and Pace.

Before Lula defied her mother by going with Pace to meet Sailor, she threw a glass of water on Marietta's framed photograph. And now, to underscore the Good Witch's triumphant sovereignty, Lynch shows Marietta's photo image fading away in a puff of smoke just as actress Margaret Hamilton's Wicked Witch melted down when Dorothy doused her with water in *The Wizard of Oz*.

Wild at Heart's concluding sea of automotive chaos sums up the whole wild and crazy world that Lynch has shown us for the past two hours and that will keep churning after his camera stops. A robust man will still quack like a duck and brittle, stick-figure old men will haunt hotel lobbies; fires will wreak havoc; cars will suddenly crash into each other; men and women will bleed and die for no good reason; Sailor may never speak to Lula of Marietta lusting for him in the men's room; Santos and Juana will keep working their evil ways; and Lula may never achieve the conscious realization that her mother engineered her father's death, or tell Sailor about the darkly thrilling moments she spent in the grip of Bobby Peru. But still, no matter how wild the world is, and all that will be known and not known, Sailor surmounts the chaos of cars and pulls Lula up to join him on the hood of her Pontiac: the earthly position that's as close as they can get to heaven. Their bodies standing against the same blue sky in which Sailor saw the Good Witch floating, he tells Lula of his encounter with this goddess of love, thus reaffirming their mutual dream of Oz. Then he does what he earlier told her that he will only do for the woman who will be his wife, he sings "Love Me Tender" to her in his sweetly ardent Elvis voice. Looking up from the same awe-struck child's-view angle Lynch used to show us the serene flowers and picket fence in *Blue Velvet*, smiling little Pace gazes at his mom and dad against the sky: the coolest parents in the world. The embracing Sailor and Lula have prevailed over all the external and internal forces that might tear them apart—for the moment. They live in a threatening world of hazard and absurdity, so the trick is to make this moment go on and on. Though the concept might have confounded Einstein, Lynch believes, and Sailor sings, that he and Lula have the strength and faith to make love last "till the end of time."

The smiling faces of Sailor, Lula, and Pace are a diametrical contrast of the beleaguered, anxiety-ridden Henry, Mary, and their mutant baby in *Eraserhead*: *Wild at Heart*'s threesome remains the happiest nuclear family in Lynch's work. And making the film was like a joyous vacation for the director. Free from the restraints of *Twin Peaks*' TV censors and the compromises necessitated by working with too many collaborators, Lynch wandered more of his country than he'd ever put on film before, compiling a Walt Whitmanesque inventory of everything he feared and loved about America. And to top it all off, his love, Isabella Rossellini, was along for the on- and off-screen ride.

Lynch and Rossellini's *Wild at Heart* journey climaxed at the Cannes Film Festival, where their scorching movie generated more passionate response than works by Akira Kurosawa (*Dreams*), Fellini (*The Voice of the Moon*), Jean-Luc Godard (*Nouvelle Vague*), Clint Eastwood (*White Hunter, Black Heart*), and Zhang Yimou (*Ju Dou*). The French critics felt that Lynch was making a serious political statement against American violence, whereas the director said he was offering "some kind of strange cinema,"[63] a subjective, genre-melding portrait of his homeland that was part romance, road movie, musical, and comedy.

Whether viewers worshipped or despised the film, most everyone agreed that no other picture at the festival could match *Wild at Heart* for thematic audacity and cinematic verve, and at the awards banquet, jury president Bernardo Bertolucci (*The Conformist*, *Last Tango in Paris*, *The Last Emperor*) announced that the film had won top prize, the renowned Palm d'Or. Lynch, resplendent in his black-and-white tuxedo ensemble, and with his right shoelace untied for good luck, accepted the sculpted golden palm frond and beamed at the crowd, which responded with a cacophony of cheering and some booing, one of the major protestors being film critic Roger Ebert, his face ruddy with outrage.

For Lynch, this victory was as sweet as could be. The Cannes Festival wasn't just a French event, but the prestigious summit of the international film scene, the hallowed ground where artists Lynch esteemed, like Fellini and Ingmar Bergman, had walked. With Isabella to share his wondrous experience, Lynch, "with such a lightness in my heart,"[64] was charmed by everything he laid eyes on, from the "chalk-blue water and yellow ochre hills"[65] to the life-imitates-art sight of Nicolas Cage leaping up onto a formal dinner table and crooning "Love Me Tender" to the surprised wife of Cannes festival organizer Gilles Jacob.

As a younger man, Lynch had felt ill at ease and homesick in Europe, and cut short his stay to rush back to the United States. Now, at Cannes, he felt as though his comfort zone spanned the whole world. Still, even on the Côte d'Azur, there were signs of home that the director couldn't ignore. Each Thursday night during the festival, the American Pavilion threw a *Twin Peaks* party, serving pie and steaming black coffee to the hundreds who passed up festival film screenings so they could watch tapes of the latest *Peaks* episode on TV monitors.

As Lynch relaxed in the Mediterranean sunshine, a chill wind and the gloomy skies of a Washington State small town wafted into his mind, and he heard something in the air. A young woman, beautiful and dead, was calling to him, and he knew he must return to her.

8

OUR SCHOOLGIRL OF THE SORROWS

1990–1992
(*Twin Peaks*, Season 2 and *Twin Peaks: Fire Walk With Me*)

In the late spring, summer, and fall of 1990, everyone heard about David Lynch. All of America's TV viewers may not have been impatiently waiting to discover who killed Laura Palmer when *Twin Peaks* resumed in autumn, but anyone who came in contact with news and entertainment media felt like they were living in Lynch's world.

Wild at Heart's Cannes Film Festival win was trumpeted far and wide, and Lynch- and *Twin Peaks*–related articles appeared in, among others, *People*, *US*, *New York*, *M*, *Esquire*, *Arena*, *Rolling Stone*, *TV Guide*, *Entertainment Weekly*, *Egg*, *Video Watchdog*, *Radio Times*, and *Soap Opera Weekly*. Broadcast journalists Sam Donaldson and Diane Sawyer covered the *Twin Peaks* cultural phenomenon, and the hit daytime TV talk show king Phil Donahue devoted a whole show to *Twin Peaks*, CBS's series *Northern Exposure* parodied *Twin Peaks*, Kyle MacLachlan portrayed Agent Cooper when he hosted *Saturday Night Live*, and *Twin Peaks* received a stunning fourteen Emmy nominations. Lynch's daughter, Jennifer, published the bestselling *The Secret Diary of Laura Palmer*; the evocative strains of Angelo Badalamenti's *Twin Peaks* music haunted elevators and supermarkets aisles across the land; professional conservative William F. Buckley's magazine, *National Review*, featured a cover story called "David Lynch's Weird America"; and Lynch himself, his face half-lit with red and half with green, his eyes looking in two directions at once, adorned the cover of *Time* magazine and the feature story "Czar of Bizarre." And Lynch/*Twin Peaks* mania gripped foreign lands, especially Japan, where viewers were moved by the show's air of melancholy, and held mock funerals for Laura Palmer.

Lynch and his art had never before received so much attention, and he was gratified by all the recognition. But he also knew that, since the beginning of his career, a fair number of people would respond negatively to his work, so he tried to be ready for the "tearing down"[1] that would surely follow the "building up"[2] of his public image. With his formidable powers of mind, Lynch concentrated on "what you're supposed to be thinking about"[3]: the work that needs to be done.

Domineering Marietta may have melted out of Lula's life, but her meddling spirit was now trying to keep Lynch from being wild at heart. The Motion Picture Association of America, which assigns ratings to movies exhibited in the United States, would not let the Cannes Film Festival–winning version of the director's picture be shown here without an X (adults only) rating, which would severely curtail the film's earning potential: Some newspapers wouldn't even run ads for X-rated films. High-caliber directors like Martin Scorsese, Paul Veerhoeven, Phil Kaufman, Pedro Almodovar, and Peter Greenway were being told that they had to alter their films to secure a commercially viable R rating. Lynch says that it takes a lot of provocation to get him angry, but issues of artistic freedom really push his hot buttons, for his mission in life is to express his ideas with maximum power and feeling. Still, he knew that he was contractually obligated to provide an R-rated picture for the Samuel Goldwyn Company to distribute, so he artfully set out to do as little as possible to earn his film the stamp of approval.

The ratings board insisted that Lynch rework the scene in which Bobby Peru, twisting and falling from many bullet hits, accidentally lodges the barrel of his shotgun under his chin and blasts his own head off into the sky. The committee objected to the specific visual of Bobby's head tearing away from his shoulders, so Lynch simply added a puff of shotgun smoke to obscure the few milliseconds in which his villain's flesh is rent asunder. The image still explodes with the shocking surprise of what Lynch calls Bobby's "bad accident,"[4] but even without the smoke, it would be eclipsed for visceral impact by the censor-approved moment when Sailor takes Bobby Ray Lemon's battered head in his hands and smashes it again and again against the white marble floor. A moment which fully engages our kinesthetic senses through its use of hands performing a task, and which still, years after it was filmed, causes even some Lynch fans to moan and look away from the screen.

Wild at Heart generated a strongly mixed critical and audience response. Lynch's themes and aesthetics were becoming recognizable, familiar, and predictable, and since his characteristic fascinations and concerns were too unsettling for many viewers to cope with, he began to be blamed for being David Lynch. Millions celebrated the well-known artistic personalities of Alfred Hitchcock, Jane Austen, and Tom Clancy, but the dark, twisted vein of human psychology and behavior that Lynch tapped into was too disturbing to contemplate. Word began to spread that the film was a harrowingly sick and violent experience, so many moviegoers stayed away. Even some Lynch appreciators felt that the film's narrative was too fragmented, its characters and their actions too cartoonishly exaggerated: *Wild at Heart* didn't flow hypnotically and hint at deep, cosmic mysteries. But other viewers understood that Lynch intended his film to be an aggressively blaring recitation of lurid tabloid headlines, not a softly murmuring, half-hidden mystical text. They felt the director had painted a passionate, accurate portrait of American malaise, and were charmed and moved by Sailor and Lula's ability to, as Lynch put it, "find love in hell." Some filmmakers were clearly thrilled and inspired by the movie's fugitives-on-the-run road trip, it's lowlife atmosphere and raw-nerve violence and sex; *Wild at Heart* echoes in the work of Quentin Tarantino and Oliver Stone, and in films like *Keys to Tulsa*, *Things to Do in Denver When You're Dead*, *Truth or Consequences, N.M.*, *Love and a .45*, *American Strays*, and *A Life Less Ordinary*.

Some commentators, who'd been storing up negative feelings about Lynch's boundary-pushing art, launched their attacks after *Wild at Heart* came out. The director was accused of victimizing African Americans, as though it was inconceivable that the knife-wielding Bobby Ray Lemon could be a black man in this Southern tale. And those who could overlook the complex, partly erotic, partly violational nature of Lula and Bobby Peru's embrace, found it easy to brand Lynch as a cinematic perpetrator of violence against women. Those screaming "Misogynist!" found it best not to mention that, balanced against Lula's confrontation with Bobby, seven men were killed and an eighth fellow beaten up. And some damned Lynch for indulging himself with "gratuitous violence," ignoring the fact that the director's mayhem was integral to the plot, revealed character, and had meaningful consequences for those who practiced it.

Between *Wild at Heart*'s opening and the start of *Twin Peaks*' second season, people exchanged heated words about Lynch, the film brought in lukewarm revenues, and the director released a fifty-minute video called *Industrial Symphony No. 1: The Dream of the Broken Hearted*. In 1989, Lynch wrote the lyrics and composer Angelo Badalamenti (*Blue Velvet*, *Twin Peaks*, *Wild at Heart*) did the music for an album of songs performed by Julee Cruise, who, in the *Twin Peaks* pilot, had tenderly sung, "I long to see you, to touch you, to love you, forever more" as angry bikers and townies traded blows on the dance floor. When, in the autumn of 1990, New York's Brooklyn Academy of Music asked Lynch to stage a live performance piece for them, he called in his two musical collaborators and put on his thinking cap. With only two weeks in which to prepare something, Lynch had to "make stuff up real fast,"[5] and this exercise in spontaneous creativity stimulated him to merge aspects of his painting, music, film, and television work into a hybrid world.

As in one of Lynch's paintings, the structural stage-setting elements would remain unchanged throughout the performance, and the composition he created clearly evoked his canvases. Out of a rusty darkness emerged vertical factory towers left and right; a horizontal pipe, electrical wires, and a high-flying string of black bomber planes spanned the stage; steam and smoke filled the air; and blond Julee Cruise, suspended by a wire 60 feet above the stage, floated like one of the artist's pale oil-painting stick figures in the center of a murky space.

An echo of *Wild at Heart* is present in the form of Nicolas Cage (Heartbreaker) and Laura Dern (Heartbroken Woman), who have a painful phone conversation that ends their relationship, as though Lynch was visualizing the downbeat conclusion of Gifford's book that the director chose not to use in his film. After this sad introduction ("I can't do it no more, I gotta go"; "Please don't go, please, please") we experience the Heartbroken Woman's inner emotional turmoil as sung by Julee Cruise (Dreamself of the Heartbroken Woman) and enacted by stage performers.

Lynch's lyrics evoke the violent aspects of his films as the Heartbroken Woman sings "I fell for you baby like a bomb, now my love's gone up in flames"; "You should've shot me, baby, my life is done"; "I hear those sirens scream my name." As her anguish projects the pain of her lost romantic-sexual relationship, a bare-breasted woman wearing only black panties writhes within the prison-bar-like structure of the phallic stage-set tower, and she continues her tormented dance in that symbolic site of youthful American passion, the back seat of an old car.

Lynch is fascinated by darkness, as both a state of physical reality and a spiritual-moral condition, and he often announces its arrival through his characters' words or his cinematic mise-en-scène. Here the Brokenhearted Woman's "Now it's dark," whispered as she floats alone in the blackness high above the stage, signifies the depth of her grief and depression as she cries in song, "Where are you? Come back in my heart." In her world of pain, "Shadows fall so blue," recalling *Blue Velvet*'s shadowy Dorothy Vallens, the singer of melancholy nightclub songs who was known as "the Blue Lady." Lynch's *Blue Velvet* script emphasized that Dorothy wanted to kill herself and was terrified of "Falling . . . falling so low."[6] Now, suddenly, the Brokenhearted Woman plummets to the stage, as though acting on a suicidal impulse. Some men put her body in the car's trunk and close the lid ("My heart was stuffed in a trunk"). She has indeed fallen so low, but Lynch knows that light glimmers within darkness.

Interspersed with the Brokenhearted Woman's sad songs, the director has presented images of regeneration. Michael J. Anderson, who plays the red-suited little Man from Another Place, dancing and talking backward in *Twin Peaks*, here appears as a red-suited Lumberjack who saws and saws and saws on his log. Another example of surrealistic Lynchian time-stretching, the Lumberjack's focused concentration is a metaphor for an artist dedicated to his work. But, as Lynch has experienced in his own life, someone disrupts the Lumberjack's sawing and he retreats from his task, only to come back on stage with a single lit light bulb, showing that his resilient soul and inspiration still glow. And at another point in the performance, a dead deer, raw and red from having been skinned, is brought back to life when some men pass lights over its body, with the Lumberjack shining the biggest and brightest light of all.

The Brokenhearted Woman enjoys a hopeful rebirth to the light when the car trunk opens and she sings an up-tempo number ("I want you, Rockin' back inside my heart") accompanied by dancing debutantes and showgirls. And she recounts a happy memory of a woodsy day spent with her man that's right out of *Twin Peaks*, or Lynch's Northwest youth. The couple has a picnic by a lake, walks among the trees, builds a comforting fire at night, kisses and cuddles, feels a wind come up, and hears an owl call. The woman "thought our love would last forever," but in Lynch's world the wind can suddenly turn cold, and her song-and-dance number dissembles in panic as the bombers high above the stage start to drop their payload. This setback on the Brokenhearted Woman's road to recovery exemplifies Lynch's characteristic bad-things-happen-when-times-seem-good rhythm, and reflects the natural ebb and flow of the human grieving-healing process.

Always able to surprise us, Lynch has his planes drop not bombs, but an array of doll babies suspended on wires, their hair blond, their faces charred black. These infants are both the children that the woman and her departed lover will now never have, and the blonde woman's own disfigured and scattered sense of herself. But reintegration is still possible, for Lynch shows us one of the dolls with a clear, unscarred face as the woman begins her final song. This doll image appears on a TV monitor as the director once again stresses that there can be a number of simultaneous views of reality.

At the conclusion of *Industrial Symphony No. 1*, the Brokenhearted Woman's crisis of loss and sorrow is not over. She still yearns for her love to "Come back and stay, forever and ever," but she's able to see beyond the prison of her intimate pain: "The sun comes up and down each day, the river flows out to the sea." Working through her suffering in her dream, the woman is touched with sudden grace, for the air in which she floats, which once rained charred babies now fills with twinkling silver cosmic dust. Her immersion in this field of shimmering particles recalls Henry in his dust cloud at the end of *Eraserhead* and John Merrick's mother in her sea of stars in *The Elephant Man*, and affirms Lynch's belief in spiritual transcendence. Even a hell of hurt can pass away, for, as the Brokenhearted Woman sings in her final words, "The world spins."

The small-town boy from the Northwest who'd been scared of the New York subway had grown into an artist who explored a woman's emotional agonies on the New York stage. *Industrial Symphony No. 1* confirmed Lynch's commitment to the inner life of his characters: The original title of Arthur Miller's *The Death of a Salesman*, *Inside His Head*, would fit most of the director's fictions. And this time he made it perfectly clear which parts of his work were waking and dreaming reality (the lovers' break-up phone talk preceded the Brokenhearted Woman's dream). Lynch's first, and, so far, only stage production was well attended (Jodie Foster was in the house) and was received with varying measures of enthusiasm, respectful appreciation, skepticism, and repudiation. The director's daughter, Jennifer, was sitting in the audience, and heard someone say, "David Lynch should never show his face in public again!"[7]

Lynch did show his face at the Emmy Awards ceremony in September, and he had to make it a brave one, for *Twin Peaks* lost in twelve of its nominated writing, directing, and acting categories, picking up what felt like token statuettes for editing and costume design. During the evening Lynch gamely commented that since he always enjoyed the theater of the absurd, he felt right at home. Still, it was troubling that the industry which, a few months earlier, said it was eager to travel into Lynch's imaginative new realms was now content to celebrate programs of status-quo, formulaic mediocrity. Lynch's visage may have been staring out from the cover of every *Time* magazine in the land, but maybe masses of Americans were not in sync with the visionary auteur's unique sensibility.

One part of the country more than any other was on Lynch's wavelength and eagerly awaited *Twin Peaks*' second season return: the Northwest region centering on Seattle. Lynch and his Agent Cooper, Kyle MacLachlan, had both been raised in this upper-left corner of America, and the eerie, chilly wind that crept through the show's pilot episode and set the atmospheric tone for the series was filmed and recorded in the dark forests surrounding Seattle. Strange small-town characters brooded, and evil denizens lashed out, in this region where more serial killings went unsolved than anywhere else in the United States. And Lynch's almost religious love of coffee drinking was appreciated in Seattle, where one of its myriad coffeehouses is called The Church of Caffeine and sports a Coffee Saves (instead of Jesus Saves) neon sign. In the period that *Twin Peaks* rose to national prominence, Seattle's grunge music scene, with its roaring-chainsaw guitar sound, lumberjack flannel shirts, and screams of teenage anger, torment, and fear, sent waves of raw, evergreen energy thrashing through the pop-culture zeitgeist. At one point, there were more than a thousand rock bands playing in and around Seattle, and some of their names sounded like descriptions of Lynch's world: Screaming Trees, Malfunkshun, Room Nine, Dead Moon, Deranged Diction, Shadow, Dinette Set, The Throbbing Continum of Dirge, Love Battery, Mystery Machine.

One crisp fall day just before the start of *Twin Peaks*' second season, a sleek silver tour bus with no writing on it except for North Carolina plates glided into this Northwest bastion of shredded-metal rock and roll. The bus whispered to a stop in front of Seattle's Backstage, a funky little club in the blue-collar Scandinavian neighborhood of Ballard, and onto the sidewalk hopped Julee Cruise. Her T-shirt, jeans, and motorcycle jacket were well suited to the capital of grunge, but at her single-performance appearance that night she would be wrapped in David Lynch's imagination, and wear a pale-blue, angelic dress that perfectly matched her short, Kim Novak–esque platinum blonde 1950s haircut.

With her high, ethereal voice singing of gossamer melancholies, yearnings, and ecstasies, while her body was subdued in a trance of subtle gestures, Cruise's performance was the antitheses of grunge's explosively loud, semi-coherent yelp and frenzied stage presentation. And yet many of the young people who flocked in to see Cruise's show were dressed and groomed as though they were heading for a headbanger's ball. Cruise's concert was in no way connected to the ABC TV network, but the presence of the young and the hip in her audience showed that the *Twin Peaks* phenomenon was luring in exactly the demographic that the television executives were aiming for. Whether or not these eighteen-to-thirty-four-year-olds would buy the sponsors' products was an open question best left to the bean counters—what really mattered was that, in the six months since *Twin*

Peaks debuted, a cult had formed around the show and the world of David Lynch. So what if the series had lost all those Emmys and was not embraced by plodding mainstream viewers? Their rejection was a badge of honor worn proudly by that select, smart, and imaginative group who absorbed and interpreted *Twin Peaks'* most miniscule nuances and shared a sense of community based on their powers of observation and appreciation, and their collective special knowledge.

Julee Cruise's concert had the aura of a secularly religious ritual. Totemic steaming coffee urns and tall sacks of donuts provided the communion sacraments, and Cruise sang the beloved, familiar hymns of the Badalamenti-Lynch canon. To hear the ominous and rapturous notes of Badalamenti's music vibrate the air the audience breathed was a thrilling experience, and Cruise masterfully enacted the shifting moods of Lynch's lyrics. During the instrumental introduction to one of her sad ballads, some heretic male yelled out, "Hey Julee, why don't you set your dress on fire?" From the calm center of her being Cruise smiled slightly and said, "Maybe next time" in the slow cadence of the song she was about to launch. The silenced man was not excommunicated: *Twin Peaks* was a place that tolerated eccentric outbursts, and, lord knows, fire walked there.

Finally, after much anticipation, the opening, two-hour episode of *Twin Peaks'* second season aired on September 30, 1990. When Mark Frost had written and directed the first-season finale there was a good chance the show would not be renewed, so he made episode 8 an everyone's-in-jeopardy ultimate cliffhanger. Now, in episode 9, knowing that they have twenty-three hours to fill, Lynch and Frost begin to chart the course for their saga's future.

Fully aware that his audience is dying to know who killed Laura Palmer, Lynch begins his direction of episode 9 in a maddeningly perverse vein, with the shot-and-bleeding Agent Cooper, who's lying on the floor, having a full five minutes of dialogue exchange with the world's oldest, and slowest, bellhop (Hank Worden). As in a bad dream, the bellhop seems unable to register the fact that Cooper has three blood spots on his white shirt (which resemble the two eyes and gaping mouth of Lynch's drawing *Three Figures On A Stage* and his painting *I See Myself*). As the director once again stretches time out to absurd lengths, Cooper, though in dire straits, remains true to his character and politely signs the tab for the warm milk he ordered and exchanges the thumbs-up with the ancient man.

Just as Lynch had had visions of *Blue Velvet*'s standing, yellow-jacketed dead man and *Twin Peaks'* Log Lady well before he realized them onscreen, he had foreseen a giant interacting with Cooper, and the director has his Giant (Carel Struycken) appear to the wounded FBI man after the bellhop leaves. Along with the Log Lady's log, Sarah Palmer's visions, Cooper's Tibetan rock-throwing divination method and his dream of the Man Form Another Place and Laura in the Red Room, the Giant is another agent who will aid Cooper with knowledge from out beyond the boundaries of Aristotelian logic. Before vanishing, the Giant tells Cooper of three things that will come true: "There is a man in a smiling bag," "The owls are not what they seem," and "Without chemicals, he points."

In the movies, being shot even once in the stomach-chest area, let alone three times like Cooper, constitutes a certain death sentence. (Witness Bruce Willis in *The Sixth Sense*: his single gunshot wound is the strongest early clue that he's a ghostly presence for the remainder of the film.) Yet Cooper, citing the restorative powers of the will, gets operated on, taped up, and works on the Laura Palmer case for thirty-six hours without sleeping. (Because of Cooper's multiple middle-body wounds, some *Twin Peaks* analysts hypothesize that the rest of the series is the dream of the dead FBI man.) The agent's working-wounded zeal fits perfectly with Lynch and Frost's conception of Cooper as a man of extraordinary powers of mind who's a scholar of Asian cultures in which spiritually evolved people can control their own heart rate and blood pressure.

Cooper is, endearingly, both a semi-superman and a fellow who needs a giant's help, who makes some discoveries through blind luck and is fallible. The three bullets pierced his flesh because he rolled up his bulletproof vest to scratch his stomach. And, as the Giant tells him, "You forgot something." For one thing, Cooper didn't find Audrey's note about her going to the One-Eyed Jack's brothel, where's she's now entrapped, barely escaped having sex with her unknowing father (thanks to a hastily grabbed mask and feigned shyness), and is expected to be ready to service "everyone." Cooper couldn't forget the note he never found, but what has slipped his mind is the killer's name that Laura whispered in his ear in his dream.

Episode 9 underscores Cooper's harmony with, and affection for, the town's people and their caring, humane values, He takes the time to listen and give comfort to Ed Hurley (Everett McGill), who's distraught over his wife Nadine's suicide attempt. And he does his best to defend his new friends against the relentless sarcastic onslaughts of big-city cynic and forensics whiz Albert Rosenfeld (Miguel Ferrer), who feels that the townsfolk are at the barnyard level of the evolutionary scale.

As *Twin Peaks*' second season starts, Lynch and Frost keep Cooper true to form, but introduce changes for other characters. Laura's usually sunny and cheerful cousin Maddy shakes with terror when she envisions a red shape spreading across the Palmer's living room carpet, a foreboding abstraction of horrors to come that's like the dark cloud shape that drifts across Bill Pullman and Patricia Arquette's living room before *Lost Highway's* hell breaks loose. And Leland is a transformed man, his hair having turned white over night (a sign of encounters with the supernatural in *The Sixth Sense*) and his zeal for singing lighthearted songs has increased to manic proportions. Lynch and Frost, knowing that Leland (while he's playing host to the evil spirit BOB) is their killer, have him behave like a man possessed even in benign social situations. They cannily link Leland's debut as the white-haired living-room singer with Maddy's scary rug-stain vision, thus subliminally prefiguring a stunning future encounter between uncle and niece. And they introduce the theme of Leland's eventual redemption by having him sing "We're heading 'cross the river, wash your sins away in the tide, It's oh so peaceful, on the other side."

Lynch and Frost show how a powerful metaphysical aura can haunt a concrete object when the wholesome Donna Hayward puts on Laura's dark glasses and becomes an unsmiling, cigarette-smoking femme fatale type, who Sheriff's Office Receptionist Lucy barely recognizes when she comes to visit James Marshall in jail. Under the sway of Laura's darker, BOB-influenced shadow self, Donna exhibits a raw, uncharacteristically animal-like sexual appetite for James, hungrily kissing him through his cell bars and closing her teeth on his finger.

And usually belligerent bad boy Bobby Briggs and his upright, no-nonsense career-military father, Major Briggs, reveal surprising new depths as the father brings his son to the verge of tears when he tells him of his vision. In his mind's eye, the major had seen Bobby "living a life of harmony and joy," and by sharing this idyllic prophecy with his son, he is bestowing a loving gift, though the major touchingly remains true to his formal, military-man demeanor by ending the scene with a handshake rather than a hug. It's characteristic of Lynch's fictions that the verbal imagery of the major's happy-family vision is delineated in terms of a household and a homecoming.

In this episode, Lynch and Frost keep alive the poetic sense that the whole town of *Twin Peaks* is an empty home without Laura, and that her spirit has not settled down peacefully. As psychiatrist Dr. Jacoby surmises that Laura wanted to die, to let herself be killed (an idea that Lynch will fully explore in *Twin Peaks: Fire Walk With Me*), we see her dead, gray-blue face superimposed over his. And young Harriet Hayward (Jessica Wallenfels) recites a poem in which she's seen Laura off "in the dark woods."

Audrey, too, is far from home, and all her family clout and impish chutzpah can't help her escape from One-Eyed Jack's brothel. Trying to impress Cooper and aid his investigation, she's gone dangerously under-the-covers. Afraid, and confused as to why he hasn't come to rescue her (the note he didn't find), she poignantly prays to the deity she loves with all her high-school heart, "Special Agent, can you hear me Special Agent?"

Lynch and Frost conclude episode 9 in an atmosphere of free-floating distress and menace, a mood that is one of *Twin Peaks'* key characteristics. This afternoon, Cooper laid out a step-by-step overview of the known facts concerning Laura's murder, declaring that Leo Johnson and Jacques Renault were her partners in rough sex and drug use, but not her killers, and pointing toward a shadowy "third man" who took Ronette Polaski and Laura to the abandoned train car, where Ronette escaped and Laura bled her life away. Now the midnight hour is dark with something more than night: Audrey prays for deliverance from her flesh-world trap, the Giant troublingly tells the sleeping Cooper that he forgot something, and at the hospital a terrifying vision invades Ronette's coma.

Anyone needing to be convinced of Lynch's powers as a filmmaker should take a look at the final moments of episode 9. The director shows us different dread-inducing shots of empty hospital corridors, with no comforting doctors or nurses in sight. Each hallway image has its own distinct, low-level humming sound, and as Lynch's camera starts to move down one of the corridors and pick up speed, the tone becomes higher, as though the point of view of an unstoppable, space-penetrating force was going into overdrive. This incoming-force viewpoint then glides up to Ronette's bed and slips into her mind, where she dwells in a house of horror: the ugly black derelict train car in which Laura is being killed.

During the ten hours of *Twin Peaks* that have led up to this moment we have both longed to see and been afraid to watch the scene of Laura's murder. When it comes, it has a great impact, for it seems to answer the call of all the sad emotion poured out over her loss at the beginning of the series. The subjective viewpoint of the hallway-penetrating force, which has been *our* view, becomes BOB racing toward us in slow motion, as Lynch implies that there's a bit of BOB in all of us. His long hair flaps back from his ears like gray bird wings ("The owls are not what they seem"), and his grimacing-grinning mouth bares the teeth of his bestial appetite. Lynch presents Laura's murder as a nonexploitive, though definitely harrowing, abstraction. In blackness illuminated by lightning-like flashes, we see short, chaotically random-feeling bursts of imagery: Laura's ruddy face screaming, BOB raising his joined hands high and plunging them down to strike the body that we can't see below the frame line. Laura's now-pale face lying still, the "FIRE WALK WITH ME" note written in blood, BOB tossing back his head to scream-growl three times above his victim, emitting a chilling sound that mixes an animal's roar of bloodlust satisfied with the pained voices of multiple souls in torment. While we experience Ronette's nightmarish vision we see her thrashing and screaming in her hospital bed, one of the long line of Lynch's characters who's tormented in bed (or in a horizontal position) that stretches back to 1968's *The Alphabet*.

By showing us the privileged sight of Laura's murder, (something that Agent Cooper will never see), Lynch and Frost underscore the savagery of the evil that's loose in *Twin Peaks*, and sensitize us to be more afraid than ever of anything to do with BOB. They may not have tied the Laura Palmer case up in a neat bow in the first episode of season 2, but they have shown us her killer—or at least one of his forms. But *is* BOB such a bad guy? The challenging sport of interpreting *Twin Peaks* was very popular as the second year debuted, and seasoned *Los Angeles Times* TV critic Howard Rosenberg insisted that BOB was trying to resuscitate Laura by pounding on her chest.

The following week's episode 10, directed by Lynch and written by Robert Engels (the two would combine talents on *Twin Peaks: Fire Walk With Me*), is a solid effort, though it does not present any of the inspired set-pieces that highlight each of the other installments the director personally guided. Still, even an "average" Lynch episode has its rewards. As Cooper enjoys his breakfast at the Great Northern Hotel, he speaks of the former rulers of Tibet, known as "the happy generations," while a cheery barbershop quartet serenades the diners. The FBI man, and Lynch, understand the age-old threat of malevolent forces that would supplant joyful Tibetan rulers and shatter their culture, as the Chinese Communists did, or would endanger the pleasant scene of breakfasters relishing good food and music, as does something in the dark woods of *Twin Peaks*. Indeed, Cooper's mood shifts toward concern and fear as he learns that his former partner, Windom Earle, has escaped from an asylum. And Cooper is surprised by the pang of emotion he feels when he's told that Audrey is missing (we know that she's being held against her will at One-Eyed Jack's). The agent's tendency to "dwell on the contents of her smile" is the beginning of the storyline that would have developed a romance between Cooper and the high schooler, a relationship which Kyle MacLachlan found unseemly and talked Lynch into abandoning. Episode 10 also launched the connection between the doings in *Twin Peaks* and extraterrestrial activity, as Major Briggs tells Cooper that the agent's name and the phrase "The owls are not what they seem" are linked in recorded radio signals ("COOPER") from outer space. The further development of this extraterrestrial plotline, which Lynch did not endorse, showed the director that the world of *Twin Peaks* that he loved so much was not as subject to his control as he would like. As this episode scans the communicative skies, it also may have inspired future *X-Files* creator Chris Carter, especially as Major Briggs declares, "Any bureaucracy that functions in secret inevitably lends itself to corruption."

Laura's best friend, Donna Hayward, is interested in secrets, especially the ones that would shed light on her best friend's murder. In her girl-detective mode, Donna takes on Laura's former Meals-on-Wheels duties, hoping to gain information while visiting homebound town residents. At the home of old bedridden Mrs. Tremond (Frances Bay), Donna has an entertaining experience. While chatting with the woman and her young grandson, who's studying magic, the creamed corn on Mrs. Tremond's plate vanishes, then appears cupped in the boy's hands, then dematerializes completely. Donna appreciatively responds as though she's witnesses a well-done trick, but we, who have beheld more of the town's paranormal space-time properties than she has, know that the magic is real, a visual manifestation of the multidimensional currents that course through *Twin Peaks*. The grandson is played by Lynch's eight-year-old son, Austin, who was named after the director's beloved grandfather. The boy has the face, hair, speaking style, mannerliness, and black suit and white shirt of his father. It's a telling point that Lynch chooses to have his own flesh and blood portray a magician. In the Lynch-authored poem Cooper hears in his earlier dream, "The magician longs to see," the FBI agent, with his uncanny deductive abilities, is that magician—as is Lynch, who wants to see things that are hidden and, through his artistic conjuring, show them to us. For Lynch, one who makes magic is a metaphor for one who makes art. Both tap into powers of spirit and pull a tangible conclusion out of the air that wasn't there before: As Cooper says to Harry Truman at a puzzling crime scene, "Sheriff, a picture is forming." Cooper's abilities may seem like magic to his fellow mortals, but he, in turn, is mystified by the deeper necromancy of the Giant, the Man From Another Place, the Red Room, and BOB, and it will be his ultimate test to try to fathom its methods and meanings.

It is indeed a black art that enables BOB to inhabit the uncomprehending Leland and make him kill his own daughter. Episode 10 is the first to overtly link the two males, as Leland recognizes BOB's face on a police poster and remembers him as a boyhood neighbor.

Cooper is both challenged by *Twin Peaks'* mysteries and soothed by the town's old-fashioned, kinder, and gentler way of life, which reflects

Lynch's idealization of the 1950s. Sensitive biker boy James, equipped with his electric guitar and two microphones, and his girlfriend Donna and Laura's cousin Maddy aren't out in the garage stoned senseless, screaming anarchic punk anthems. They're safely and soberly ensconced in Donna's living room, with good old Doc Hayward upstairs, singing a slow song that could have come out in 1955, in which Lynch's simple lyrics say it all: "Just you, and I; just you, and I; together, forever; in love." The song is soulful, so they aren't smiling, but they seem to embody that Tibetan "happy generation" spirit Cooper referred to. Lynch's artistic intuition tells him, of course, that this is the perfect time to add emotional discord and fear to the scene. There's a reverb echo in James's sound system, so he's singing with two voices. And, as he faces toward his love, Donna, and Maddy, who looks so uncannily like his lost love, Laura, it's like he's singing to multiple women. Seeing the eye contact between him and Maddy, Donna is upset and breaks off the song, and James goes to comfort and reassure her. Alone in the living room, Maddy feels the comfy space become charged with menace as Lynch mixes a breathing sound into the soundtrack and BOB enters. Moving directly toward Maddy (and us), he creeps bent over like an animal, stepping over the barriers of the sofa and coffee table and lunging his face into ours. He vanishes as quickly as he came, but we have the terrible feeling that Maddy has a demon suitor who lusts to tell her, "Just you and I, together, forever."

The next episode that Lynch directed, number 15, does indeed consummate Maddy's terrifyingly unwished-for relationship with BOB. This outstanding installment, written by Mark Frost, conveys the same all-consuming dread and sadness that the co-creators brought to their series' pilot episode. In this episode, Lynch revisits one of the fundamental dynamics of his artistic sensibility: a perfect home world invaded by contagion. For Leland and Sarah Palmer, niece Maddy, who looks just like their dear Laura, has been a consoling presence who's helped fill the void left by their daughter's tragic death and eased their period of traumatized grieving. Lynch positions Maddy snuggly between Sarah and Leland as Louie Armstrong sings "What a Wonderful World," his words evoking the idyllic, before-the-fall town in *Blue Velvet* and the imagery of Lynch's own childhood memories: "trees of green, red roses too, clouds of white, skies of blue." As the three sip after-breakfast coffee, Maddy announces that she's going to head back to Missoula, Montana (Lynch's birthplace), to resume her own home life. Leland reacts with avuncular understanding, which surprises the women. But we, the viewer-detectives, note that Leland's "I'm happy, everything's fine" demeanor often seems to mask more agitated and disturbing subterranean feelings.

The vinyl surface of the "Wonderful World" record glows white with the same reflected morning light that bathes Maddy's, Leland's, and Sarah's loving-family tableau. That night, however, the living room is empty, and the now-shadowed record clicks and clicks endlessly long after the song is over. No longer broadcasting love and goodness, the dark, unstoppable spiral of the spinning record is like a black vortex waiting to suck in souls. The endlessly circling disc and its sound recall the incessant, oppressive mechanical poundings of other Lynch films, and it foreshadows a primal theme of Stephen King's 1998 miniseries *Storm of the Century*: "Hell is repetition."[8]

Across town, at the Road House bar, Cooper has a vision of Julee Cruise singing on stage being replaced by the Giant, who gravely tells him, "It is happening again." Everything that the Giant has previously told the agent has come true, so Cooper ponders the full weight of his spiritual helper's ominous words. But what could be happening, now that Cooper's got Laura's killer, Ben Horne, locked up in jail? Horne may have violated his marriage vows and any number of society's moral codes, but he didn't murder Laura, who he had been sleeping with. How can it be that Cooper has made such a big mistake? The agent has demonstrated his keen ability to discern meaningful patterns within clusters of seemingly random events. As a police detective in Lynch's 1997 film *Lost Highway* says, "There's no such thing as a bad coincidence," but Lynch and Frost know that this isn't always true. In a world where Absolute Knowledge is hidden behind a fog of uncertainty, it's comforting to believe that we can combine the small glimmers of truth we see into an approximation of the everlasting Light that will illuminate our correct path of action. This practice has stood Cooper well in the past, as it has his creator Lynch, whose life's work is built upon synthesizing thoughts and feelings that occur together into expressive artistic structures. Lynch likes to let his mind drift into that childlike, dreamy state in which the associations, coincidences, and correspondences the world sends him have magical significance; but he also knows that, of the four times he's presented a movie at the Cannes Film Festival, the fact that his left shoe was untied has only won him one Palm D'Or.

All the signs that Cooper's read have told him that Ben Horne is the killer, so having the unscrupulous tycoon behind bars should put our FBI man at ease, but instead he's edgy and hyper-alert as he sits in the Road House. It's as though a kind of atmospheric disturbance generated by the Palmer house's rotating ceiling fan and spiraling record turntable, and the horror about to be unleashed there, have galvanized the air all over town.

Before passing out, the drug-groggy Sarah Palmer sees a white horse, a traditional symbol of death, in her living room. In an ancient Chinese legend, the Yellow Emperor used magic to imprison the cosmic forces of chaos within mirrors, but it was known that someday the spell would weaken and our human world would suffer a terrible invasion. Now, as Leland admires his image in a living room mirror, Lynch and Frost give us the payoff we've waited months and hours for: Reflected back at the smiling patriarch is the lasciviously grimacing BOB. Even if we've suspected that Leland had sex with and killed his own daughter, this moment of revelation is stunning, as is the realization that Leland, as BOB's unwilling human host, has been a victim along with Laura.

While we're off-balance from receiving this dramatic news, Lynch hits us with one of the most disturbingly violent sequences ever shown on non-cable television. Maddy, smelling the stench of burnt motor oil that emanates from BOB's murderous frenzy, and fearing there's a fire in the house, runs into the living room and right into Leland's attack. Wearing white surgical gloves, he bloodies her face with a single hard punch and, as she babbles and cries in a delirium of pain and terror, he pulls her slumping, gasping body against his chest and spins her in a ghastly dance. Leland alternately weeps and calls Maddy Laura as though she's his dying daughter, and manifests as BOB, who with guttural animal sounds hungrily nuzzles her throat. Then, enraged that Maddy, his consoling surrogate-Laura, wants to leave him, Leland yells, "You're going home to Missoula, Montana," and fatally smashes her head into a photo of a serene mountain lake. Another Lynchian character with a will to stifle others' freedom, BOB-as-Leland has shown Maddy that he is the ultimate controller of her comings and goings. But if he had been getting what he wanted from Laura, by enjoying her sexually for years, why did he kill her? Lynch will delve into this mystery in his *Twin Peaks* feature film.

For now, the director makes us register the full impact of a dear young life extinguished. Maddy may have wanted to be like her fast-living, darkness-dabbling cousin Laura, but she wasn't, and Lynch saturates the final moments of episode 15 with a poignant mood of innocence snuffed out. The harsh white light that has supernaturally linked the hellish doings at the Palmer house with Cooper and the Giant in the Road House fades, as does the Giant, but both locations remain awash in sadness. We now know the tragedy that the BOB-possessed Leland has been living, and at the Road House, Donna feels responsible for the suicide of recluse Harold Smith, and toughie Bobby Briggs realizes that his scheme to enjoy domestic bliss with Shelley, that's subsidized by Leo's comatose condition, isn't going to work. Donna and Bobby have their own problems, but as agitation and pain distort their faces, they seem poetically to be responding to Maddy's death. And the old bellhop from the hotel who stood interminably above Cooper after he'd been shot comes over and tells the FBI man "I'm so sorry," as though the agent has lost a member of his own family. Cooper doesn't know that Maddy's dead. He doesn't know that Leland kills young women. Try as he might to read the vibrations in the room, he doesn't know what has just happened. Lynch has spoken of his characters and he himself being "lost in confusion," and for a person of Cooper's abilities to be in such a state indicates the magnitude of the mysteries he is facing. It is a sad night, ruled by evil and loss and indecipherable happenings, but our hero does not bow his head and slink away in defeat. Lynch leaves us with one of his archetypal headshots, and one of *Twin Peaks*' most iconic close-ups, as Cooper's alert, pale face, tilted upwards, scans the air for signs and meanings. Behind him, red curtains materialize, and his head slowly fades into them: The Red Room will be his ultimate destination and challenge.

Episode 15 aired on November 10, 1990, and Cooper won't set foot in the red Room until June 10, 1991, in the Lynch-directed second-season finale. During these twenty-eight weeks, ABC consigned *Twin Peaks* to the death-zone slot of Saturday night, put it on hiatus for two months, and saw its viewership decline to only 10 percent of TV-owning households. Laura's murdered body was found in the April 8, 1990, pilot episode, and her case wasn't wrapped up until episode 17, shown on December 1. In the time frame of the town, only eighteen days passed, while viewers had to wait eight months for the mystery's resolution. Fans of the show were happy to absorb the narrative at Lynch and Frost's slow-for-TV pace, while less-committed viewers felt frustrated, angry, and exploited. Without the emotional dynamo of the Laura Palmer case to drive the series, and since Kyle MacLachlan was unwilling to let his Dale Cooper fall in love with teenage Audrey (some say MacLachlan's jealous lover, Lara Flynn Boyle, who plays Donna, influenced his decision), *Twin Peaks*' various writers launched a number of lower-voltage subplots that weren't able to sustain a mass audience's interest. It seemed that *Twin Peaks* couldn't win: Viewers deserted the show both because Laura's murder wasn't being solved, and because it finally was resolved. Also, since the show presented such a complex and voluminous intertwining of plot threads, quirky characters, unfamiliar cosmologies, and paranormal happenings, it was dauntingly difficult for a casual viewer to drop into *Twin Peaks* in mid-stream and understand what was going on. The show was indeed "TV like you've never seen it," but also TV that was too different, challenging, and provocative for many to want to see.

Most commentators agree that *Twin Peaks'* second season scattered its creative energy all over the landscape while trying in vain to regain the intense, inspired focus of season 1. Still, even though it was firing on less than eight cylinders, the show provided enough engaging material to keep its loyal followers watching. They witnessed a Mark Frost–written passage where Agent Cooper tenderly guides the dying, head-wounded Leland into a redemptive spiritual light in which his beloved Laura dwelled. They saw scheming land-grabber Ben Horne, (deliciously played by Richard Beymer) descend into madness, recover his psychological bearings by elaborately acting out tableaus of the South winning the Civil War (reverse the flow of history, reverse the course of your life) and emerge as a zealous environmentalist who chomps carrots instead of his usual foot-long cigars. And writers Mark Frost and Harley Peyton paid due respect to the multitude of impulses warring within Ben by having him declare, "Sometimes the urge to do bad is nearly overwhelming." Since daughter Audrey doesn't get to consort and cavort with Cooper, and probably be prime victim material for BOB, she does enjoy an emotionally closer, full-fledged-adult relationship with her father. *Twin Peaks* is rife with family dysfunction and upheaval: Even the stable and secure Hayward household is about to be rocked as Donna discovers that nefarious Ben, not good old Doc Hayward, is her real father. So it's gratifying that there's a new warmth and mutual respect between Ben and Audrey, but how can we not miss the Audrey who cut a swath through town with impish attitudes and pranks, rather than grown-up behavior? Still, even though she wears gray power suits and takes high-level meetings in Seattle, she's able to give us a major surprise, for this schoolgirl with a gale-force air of sexual knowingess, whose tongue can massage a cherry stem into a blissed-out knot, is still a virgin.

While Audrey is discovering sex and love with the preternaturally pretty Billy Zane, Cooper, with the biggest smile we've seen on his face, is falling for diner waitress Annie Blackburn (Heather Graham), who's fresh from a convent where she'd sought solace from an unhappy relationship that drove her to slash her wrists. Good guy Cooper sees Annie as a beautiful young woman who he can rescue from sadness, but he's also drawn to her for a very Lynchian reason. Because she's been cloistered away from the wide, wide world, she now sees things the way a child does, the way Lynch likes to. For Annie the world is new and amazing, and mundane occurrences have a wondrous significance: "music and people, the way they talk and laugh, the way some of them are so clearly in love." And she has a Lynchian sense of the balance between known and unknown worlds: "It's like a foreign language to me; I know just enough of the words to realize how much

I don't understand." Drawn to Annie's innocent, life-discovering viewpoint, Cooper feels that by embracing her they can each start afresh on the road to love and redeem their own personal romantic tragedies.

Cooper had been in love and having an affair with Caroline, the wife of his psychotic former FBI mentor and partner, Windom Earle (Kenneth Welsh), who stabbed Caroline to death and is now lurking in the woods of *Twin Peaks* waiting to destroy our hero. If BOB, who says little but terrifies much as he evokes the timeless primal power of animalistic evil, is a Lynchian villain, then the brainy, verbose, multiple-disguise-wearing, chess and social game-playing Windom Earle is a Mark Frost malefactor. (As Lynch says, "Windom Earle is all Mark Frost."[9]) Earle is like a mastermind villain out of the Sherlock Holmes books, whose cerebral malevolence is spiked with a wicked sense of humor and who relishes the theatrical flair he employs to stay at least one step ahead of Cooper. If Earle is an earthly spark of evil adept at destroying human flesh, then BOB is a roaring fire who spans worlds as he devours the very marrow of human souls. This is the "incomprehensible" power source that Earle covets, and which his scholarship has told him resides in the Black Lodge, a spectral dimension which relates to Major Briggs' extraterrestrial monitoring and which is the source of the town legend's ancient darkness. Earle's mission is to gain access to the Lodge and obliterate Cooper in the process, which brings us to the second-season finale, scripted by Mark Frost and chief writers Harley Peyton and Robert Engels, and directed by Lynch.

Lynch's working procedure when making one of his own films centers on the actors and technicians "tuning in"[10] and harmonizing with his fundamental conception of the project. He considers others' suggestions and sudden intuitions as part of the process, but he hews to the core of his original inspiration. Working on a weekly TV series with a multitude of collaborators frustrated his natural modus operandi: "There are other directors, other writers, other things that come in. It may be fine, but it's not what you would do."[11] And whatever he wants to do is the motivating principle of Lynch's art. The director felt that "Cooper is real close to me; he says a lot of the things I say,"[12] and earlier in the series Lynch felt that Frost and some of the other writers weren't striking the proper Cooperesque note of awestruck terseness in the agent's speeches. It's more than a casual remark when Lynch, playing FBI boss Gordon Cole, tells Cooper to lose those colorful, open-collared plaid flannel shirts and get back into his crisp, black Federal Bureau of Investigation suit.

Peggy Lipton, who played Norma Jennings, notes that as the second season progressed Lynch was "no longer as involved as he had been,"[13] and "tensions and dissentions began to divide the *Twin Peaks* family."[14] It is a measure of Lynch's distance from the day-to-day shaping of the show that, when we total up the entire two seasons of *Twin Peaks*, he has four writing credits, while Frost, Peyton, and Engels together have thirty-two. When it came time to direct what turned out to be the final hour of *Twin Peaks* that would ever be broadcast, Lynch could not abide the all-important conclusion of the script that his colleagues handed him: "It was completely and totally wrong."[15] Lynch and Frost had conceived and launched the show in a perfect synchrony of creative energy but, in Lynch's judgment, *Twin Peaks* had wandered off course, bogging down in a swamp of conventional soap-opera plotting and cerebral, prosaic, rationalistic philosophy. Knowing that his relative lack of hands-on participation had contributed to this sorry state of affairs, he dipped into his rich pool of inner vision, determined to give *Twin Peaks* a final jolt of magic and poetry.

First, he gave his old friends, *Eraserhead* colleagues, and former husband and wife Jack Nance (Pete Martel) and Catherine Coulson (the Log Lady) their only face-to-face scene of the series. Then, after filming written plot elements in which benign Doc Hayward brutally attacks Ben Horne for announcing that he is Donna's real father, and Audrey is in danger when a bank blows up, Lynch threw away the script and spontaneously created a heartfelt fantasia on what he considered to be the key *Twin Peaks* themes.

Throughout the series, Cooper's masculine, heroic quest has been aided by the feminine intelligence, courage, wisdom, and vision of the Log Lady, Sarah Palmer, Audrey, Donna, Ronette Pulaski, and Laura, who finally makes sure he remembers her whisper about Leland being her killer. And now the Log Lady, with her news about the scorched motor oil being "an opening to a gateway," helps Cooper slip through the forest's red curtains into the Black Lodge.

Windom Earle, with the kidnapped Annie in tow, has proceeded Cooper, certain that the agent will come to rescue his love, and thereby fall victim to Earle's Black Lodge–enhanced evil power. Frost, Peyton, and Engle's script had the season's final confrontations occurring in an abstracted black-and-white location that melded a doctor's office with a throne room, but Lynch knew that he must return to that ultimate seat of mystery, the Red Room.

Cooper has visited this Lynch-imagined place in dreams, but now he's really there, breathing the air contained by the red-curtained walls as his polished black shoes click on the zig-zag-power-field-patterned floor. As the poem has it, Cooper has been the seeker who "longs to see," and here he's met by a vocalist (the legendary Jimmy Scott) who seems to personify the

Black Lodge's secrets as he soulfully sings, "And I'll see you, and you'll see me," implying that all will be revealed. The singer also ominously intones, "I'll see you in the trees," recalling the way that Josie Packard's spirit, thanks to the gloating BOB, ended up imprisoned within a wooden drawer knob: The Black Lodge is a place charged with great danger as well as potential knowledge.

In the last thirty minutes of *Twin Peaks*, Lynch gives us a profound gift by making the red-curtained rooms and corridors of the Black Lodge a place beyond Cooper's and our absolute comprehension. At first we're able to keep track of which room the agent is in by noting the placement of a white marble Venus statue in the corridor outside, but then the signpost statue is gone, and it's impossible to know which way is backwards or forwards, and Cooper is able to enter the same room from different directions. After disorienting Cooper's familiar sense of space, Lynch brings time into the mix by having the agent receive a cup of coffee that, within a few seconds, turns from liquid to solid to a viscous sludge that oozes slowly from the cup like one of Salvador Dali's melting watches. Further confusion is added when the Man From Another Place (the dancing, backward-talking dwarf) tells Cooper that the Great Northern Hotel's old bellhop and the Giant are "one and the same," or is it the Giant and the man From Another Place that are the same—or all three?

The little man also says that the Red Room contains the doppelgangers, or shadow-selves, of people Cooper is familiar with, and as the agent traverses corridors and rooms, he has some scary and mystifying encounters. The doppelgangers have creepy white eyes, and Cooper meets a pale-pupiled Laura, who screams at him; Leland in his sly "I didn't do anything wrong" mode; and Caroline, Cooper's former love who was slain by her cuckolded husband, Windom Earle. Then Annie and Caroline seem to interchange places, evoking Cooper's guilt and pain over his adulterous part in Caroline's death and linking it with his anguish over the way his love for Annie has made her a potential victim of Earle and the Black Lodge. Has Windom Earle absorbed enough of the Lodge's power to be able to torment Cooper by manipulating these images of Caroline and Annie trading places, or is some higher authority trying to break down our hero's stalwart sense of righteous self-possession?

Earle thinks the force is with him and bossily tells Cooper he'll let Annie live if the agent will give up his own soul, which Cooper agrees to do. However, BOB, and probably Lynch as well, is tired of wordy windbag Earle trying to usurp the Black Lodge's power, and the demonic entity growls "Be quiet" in his face. Asserting his dominance, BOB tells Cooper that

Earle had no right to make such a bargain. And, facing the terrified Earle, tears his soul out, which Lynch visualizes as a flame shooting up out of the villain's head. Flaming souls feed the fire that walks with BOB, as does fear. Cooper is usually cool under pressure, but his psyche has just received two major blows: He's been wracked with guilt over the perverse way that his love for both Caroline and Annie has put them in harm's way, and, in darkness whipsawed with white-hot flashes of malevolent electricity, he's seen BOB's ferocious, soul-stealing power close up.

Cooper's face remains calm, but inside he's beside himself with agitation. Lynch has said that the Red Room reflects the mindset of the person experiencing it. When Cooper first visited the Room in his dream shortly after arriving in Twin Peaks, he was falling in love with the young, beautiful, murdered Laura, so his encounters were pleasantly mysterious. It was a place of "good news" with "music in the air," where the Man From Another Place smiles sweetly, as did Laura, who kissed Cooper and told him her biggest secret. And now that Cooper's actually in the Red Room, and has, for the past weeks been immersed in the dark side of Laura, Leland, and the whole town, and has been reminded of some of his own profound mistakes and failures, the Room has become a head-splitting locus of disorientation and fear. Our intrepid, resolute, single-minded hero has lost his way, and the Black Lodge is able to pounce on his vulnerability, splitting him in two, so that a shadow-shelf Cooper cackles with BOB and chases the terrified good Cooper down the red corridors.

And yet, behold: An unconscious Cooper and Annie materialize back in the real-world woods, where good old Sheriff Truman has been keeping a vigil all night. Again and again in his work, Lynch projects a sense of home disrupted and then reconstituted. A feeling of homecoming and reunion permeates the endings of *Eraserhead*, *The Elephant Man*, *Dune*, *Blue Velvet*, and *Wild at Heart*, and now, Cooper wakes in his familiar bed, surrounded by Doc Hayward and Truman. This tableau makes the world of *Twin Peaks* seem once again safe and secure, as Lynch evokes the ending scene of his beloved *The Wizard of Oz*, in which far-traveling Dorothy awakens to find family and friends at her bedside. Cooper's first words are "How's Annie?," and Truman reassures him that she's doing fine in the hospital. As if to certify the restoration of order over chaos, creature-of-habit Cooper gets up to enact one of the simple ritualistic pleasures he (and Lynch) so appreciates, and that keep his life centered.

Alone in the bathroom standing before the sink and mirror, Cooper picks up his toothbrush and paste and starts to squeeze the tube. But, with the significance of a cosmic disruption, he's gripped by an uncivilized, animal impulse, and empties the whole tube in the sink. Then, to our horror, he smashes his head into the mirror, causing two trickles of blood to stain his forehead, for now Cooper, like the rest of Twin Peaks, is marked by doubleness. Then, to end the season and the series, we see the most dreadful sight Lynch could imagine: the feral face of BOB leering in the mirror back at Cooper, just as the evil one reflected back at Leland. The last thing we hear is our normally sincere and caring hero mocking his own recent words of loving concern ("How's Annie?") with a sneer and laughing and laughing like a man possessed.

There weren't many *Twin Peaks* viewers left to witness Cooper's sad and tragic last moments on the air. The series' premiere had attracted an audience of thirty-five million, while its finale only managed to scrape together six million. The show finished a distant third in its time period, beaten by sitcom reruns and a rerun of *Northern Exposure*, a much less challenging and daring Northwest small-town show with quirky characters and occasionally surreal storylines that some called "*Twin Peaks* for beginners." When the first season ended the year before, so many fans wanted to watch the finale in the series' spiritual home, the Snoqualmie Valley of Washington State, that they filled the big dining room of the Salish Lodge (*Twin Peaks*' Great Northern Hotel) to overflowing. This year, there were barely enough supporters to fill the booths at the little Mar T Café (the show's Double R Diner). As that last, disturbing image of Cooper faded into the eleven o'clock news, the fans' reactions were mixed; "The show started off plain and simple and then really went off into the bizarre"[16]; "How could David Lynch do that to Agent Cooper—it just really hurt"[17]; "It's the evil that I really like"[18]; "They kept leaving more strings untied—there better be more to come"[19]; and "To show that even Cooper could succumb to BOB was a perfect way to end."[20]

Today, Lynch looks back at *Twin Peaks* with frustration and regret over "the many clues and threads that we never got to follow."[21] Frost is more calmly philosophical about the show's demise. "That three-year period was great from start to finish. It would have been much better to see *Twin Peaks* continue for another year or two. But sometimes the best experiences aren't the longest running, and in a way that makes them sweeter. As the years go by I think of the show with great fondness. It was a very happy experience, something really special and meaningful in all our lives and in our work—a very rare combination."[22]

Twin Peaks is a glowing memory for Frost: He ranks it at the top of his list of distinguished creative accomplishments. But he also honorably takes responsibility for production decisions that caused the show's downfall:

> I left to make *Storyville* during the second half of the second season, after we finished the storyline of Leland Palmer being his daughter's killer. I regret my decision to not be there. That's where we dropped the ball. Once the central Laura Palmer–Leland Palmer story was resolved, we were at a deficit in coming up with a story that was as compelling. And frankly, we didn't. The Windom Earle thread took too long to develop, it didn't start off with a bang. Selecting that story and allowing it to get too leisurely paced really hurt us.[23]

Mark Frost and writer-producer Harley Peyton assumed that the show would follow the stunning death of Leland Palmer with a radiance of love. The smoldering longings of Audrey and Cooper for each other would flame into overt romance: The series' two most charismatic surviving characters would share their hearts and bodies, and because we cared about them so much, they'd be prime candidates for exciting plot lines that would put them in jeopardy.

Stacks of letters from eager viewers reinforced Frost and Peyton's conviction that the Cooper-Audrey union would bring robust life to post-Leland Palmer *Twin Peaks*. But Cooper, rather than offering Audrey an invitation, was an impediment to love. As Frost recalls, "even though we made a point of stressing that Audrey was eighteen, Kyle MacLachlan felt strongly that Cooper, with his steadfast moral and ethical compass, would never engage in that relationship. He may well have been right."[24] Frost half-seriously jokes that "we should have revealed that Audrey had flunked high school for three years and was actually twenty-one—that might have satisfied Kyle."[25] So since Cooper and Audrey couldn't face love and danger together, "we introduced the Annie Blackburn character for him, which was too little too late. And the Windom Earle storyline got pushed to the launching pad before it was ready to go, which was a big problem."[26]

Everyone from Harley Peyton to directors Tina Rathborne and Lesli Linka Glatter to actors Kyle MacLachlan, Catherine Coulson, Kimmy Robertson, and Jack Nance felt that the show had lost its focus and initial high level of inspiration: The quality of the material just wasn't up to the rarified level to which they'd become accustomed. Some of the actors entreated Lynch to step in and somehow make things like they used to be when the series was fresh and magical. But Frost was jumping at the chance, made possible by the notoriety of *Twin Peaks*, to go and direct a film, and Lynch felt stymied and frustrated by his other collaborators doing "not what you would do."[27] His heart wasn't absolutely devoted to the show any more; it was no longer the center of his Art Life: "you don't have enough time to get in there and do what you're supposed to do."[28]

Aside from a unified Lynch-Frost energy not being engaged with the latter stages of *Twin Peaks*, the ABC executives made what Frost calls "the bonehead move"[29] of shifting the show to the TV graveyard of Saturday at 10 p.m. And President Bush the first was culpable. Frost stresses that "the Gulf War was an under-appreciated element in the show not making it over the hump. We were pre-empted for six out of eight weeks, and we didn't have a chance to come back from that. Too much time had gone by when we resumed. Viewers couldn't sustain their concentration over the gap. We'd laid out so many threads that it was very difficult for even dedicated fans to keep track of them."[30]

Frost had some definite threads in mind for season 3, a series of episodes which he felt would far surpass the second year in quality. Audrey and Pete would survive the bomb blast at the bank, Ben Horne would be back, the good Cooper would be trapped in the Black Lodge for a long time, while the bad Cooper menaced Annie and other townsfolk. Frost recalls that during the second season, Joan Chen, who played Josie, asked to leave the series to make a film. To accommodate her, the writers stuck Josie in a wooden drawer pull for safe keeping, so that she could be retrieved for a comeback. But there would be no season 3, so *Twin Peaks* fans were left with the mystery of flesh melded with wood grain, and the sorry spectacle of an evil, cackling Cooper loosed on an unsuspecting world.

Because the script for *Twin Peaks: Fire Walk With Me* mentions creamed corn, and since the film's co-writer Robert Engels has spoken a number of times of a cosmology in which one-armed Mike, BOB, and the Man From Another Place all come from a "place of corn,"[31] many people assumed that Engels originated the corn concept. Actually, it's another of Lynch's spontaneous inspirations, which struck two years earlier during the first third of the TV series' production. In 2003, Mark Frost told me that "David always loved the process of discovery, of finding something in a scene or a performance or in life that would take things in a completely unexpected turnaround. He had the confidence to see and sense that something was happening, and to make the most of it, to not rely completely on Plan A."[32] Frost always insisted on discussing changes before they were shot, so one of Lynch's alterations of Plan A "threw me for a loop."[33] Looking at the rushes of the day's shooting, Frost watched a scene in episode 10 in which Donna brings a Meals-on-Wheels to the bed-ridden old Mrs. Tremond. There was no creamed corn mentioned in Harley Peyton's script, but here was Mrs. Tremond stressing that she didn't like the stuff, and then Frost saw the corn on her plate vanish, only to materialize across the room in the cupped hand's of David Lynch's son. Young Austin, playing Tremond's magician grandson, and dressed and groomed to look just like his dad, held the golden corn in his hands, then made it vanish into thin air. After viewing the footage, Frost tracked down Lynch and asked him what the deal was. Lynch replied, "I was eating creamed corn at lunch; it looked so fantastic, I just had to do something with it."[34] So the corn component of the *Twin Peaks* mythos was born because David Lynch had lunch at the ABC commissary on a certain day.

The folks watching the final episode at the Mar T Café in Washington State may have had divided opinions on the series' conclusion, but they voiced a unanimous sentiment as they stepped into the rainy June night to go home: "I hear they might make a *Twin Peaks* movie—wouldn't that be great!"[35]

Twelve hundred miles to the south, David Lynch shared their sentiment. "At the end of the series, I felt sad. I couldn't get myself to leave the world of *Twin Peaks*. I was in love with the character of Laura Palmer and her contradictions: radiant on the surface but dying inside. I wanted to see her live, move, and talk. I was in love with that world and I hadn't finished with it."[36] Rather than brood over the loss of the TV series, Lynch poured his creative energy into writing a feature film screenplay with the series' head creative script consultant Robert Engels. There would be no UFO references, no Miss Twin Peaks Contest or Civil War reenactments, no double-crossing business schemes, no arch and clever Windom Earle, and no plaid shirts for Agent Cooper. Series co-creator Mark Frost amicably declined to be part of the film project, citing his belief that the audience hungered for the story to move forward and tie up loose ends. Whereas Lynch wanted to return to the broken heart and endangered soul of *Twin Peaks*: the final seven days of Laura's life, so that "we could actually see things we had only heard about"[37] on the TV show from those who had survived the town's favorite daughter. And Lynch would conduct his mission to reclaim the authentic essence of *Twin Peaks* up north where he'd shot the pilot episode, where "a certain wind"[38] blows through the woods and small towns of Washington State.

Lynch chose cinematographer Ron Garcia, who'd shot the pilot episode in the sunless, overcast February of 1989, to lens the feature film, which would be called *Twin Peaks: Fire Walk With Me*. Assuming they would again be working with a palette of chilly grays and earthen browns, Garcia and Lynch were shocked to find Seattle and the Snoqualmie valley bathed in eighty-five-degree Indian summer sunshine in September 1991. Rather than being thrown off course aesthetically by the unexpected weather, the pair decided to, according to Garcia, "exploit the contrast, with these golds and greens and blue skies against which these horrible things were happening to Laura Palmer."[39] Once again, Lynch let happenstance help determine the "correct" form of his art.[40]

It was chance that let me witness some of Lynch's art-making process. Being the director of the Seattle Art Museum's film program, I often work late and don't watch the local eleven o'clock news. But one night I saw that Lynch and company had arrived to begin filming at a dilapidated Snoqualmie trailer park. By early afternoon the next day, I was on the case. Lynch, who loves to delve into hidden secrets in his work, wanted the plot details of his film to remain a mystery until it hit the screen, so the news cameraman had only been allowed to catch a glimpse of the closed trailer park set through a knot hole in a cedar fence. Lynch wanted absolutely no media coverage of the production, and I later learned that a friend of mine who wrote for *Entertainment Weekly* magazine out of New York was told to "not even think about catching a plane to Washington State." I didn't want to photograph or write about the production or have fire walk with me, but I did want to *see*. I was fascinated by the way that Lynch's fictional neighborhood intersected with the touchstones of my own physical and imaginative life. My Swedish-immigrant father had been a young pre-chainsaw lumberjack in the woods just outside Twin Peaks, I'd gotten my first driver's license a stone's throw from the Double R Diner and graduated from high school in a nearby salmon-hatchery town, and as a boy the surrounding rivers, forests, and mountains had been the dwelling places of Huckleberry Finn and Rip van Winkle. And at night the deep black sky and its sparkling stars, at full force so far from city lights, held the promise of stories and possibilities without end.

As I approached the trailer park near Meadowbroook Street in Snoqualmie, I was stopped by a roadblock that was backed up with numerous police cars and local law enforcement officers. Parking a few blocks away, I approached the police blockade on foot, trying to look purposeful and busy, like the movie crew members who swarmed back and forth within the cordoned-off area. Expecting to be challenged at any second, I strode past the policemen, picked up my pace, rounded a corner, and almost smacked right into Dale Cooper. What an arresting sensation, suddenly sharing three feet of sidewalk with a fictional character, his double-breasted overcoat, monumental ivory chin, and slicked-back black patent-leather hair as perfect as they were on my TV at home. The illusion passed in a second, as Kyle MacLachlan's natural, looser-than-Cooper body posture and grinning demeanor asserted themselves, and I marveled at the transformative power of the actor's art.

I found the fence that the TV news crew had peeked through, and an unexpected gap through which the crew was moving equipment, so I slipped into the film's Fat Trout Trailer Park. And, right behind me, stepped David Lynch. He was wearing baggy tan khakis, a white shirt with its collar button closed, a rumpled black blazer with holes at the elbows, and a charcoal, long-billed cap. A toothpick, like a little splinter of divining rod, jutted from his lips. The furrow between his eyebrows gave him an earnest, concerned look that opened easily into amusement and amazement. For eight years (in *Dune*, *Blue Velvet*, and *Twin Peaks*), MacLachlan had tracked clues and read dreams as Lynch's truth-questing alter-ego, and the two men—who both spent their early years in Washington State—began work on their new collaboration with a firm handshake.

First up is a scene in the town of Deer Meadow, where young Teresa Banks (Pamela Gidley) has been found murdered and wrapped in plastic. FBI boss Gordon Cole (David Lynch) has sent agents Chet Desmond (Chris Isaak) and Sam Stanley (Keifer Sutherland) to investigate, and Desmond has mysteriously disappeared. This is one of Cole's "blue rose cases," referring to the botanical impossibility of a blue rose and thus coding the mystery as one that violates the borders of rational scientific investigation and delves into paranormal dimensions. This is Cooper's territory, so Cole sends him out to see where Desmond went one year before. Once in the field, Cooper hears about a place called Twin Peaks and a girl named Laura.

The last place Desmond had been seen was the Fat Trout Trailer Park, and I watch Lynch set up scenes in which Cooper talks to scruffy, haggard park manager Carl Rodd (Harry Dean Stanton) and they look around the lot. Rodd points Cooper toward a certain trailer and then, exasperated, sees the agent, who seems almost in a trance of aroused intuition, wander off in another direction. For a number of rehearsals and takes I savor Stanton bellowing, "Why the *hell* are you going up that way?" Lynch speaks only a few quiet words of direction, but on one take says "Okay, Harry Dean, let's get that anger up there" before calling "Action!" through his amplified megaphone. As the Gordon Cole–volume twang of his voice cuts the still Snoqualmie air over the course of the afternoon, I notice that he calls actors by their real names, but refers to MacLachlan as "Cooper."

With the scenes involving Stanton and MacLachlan in the can, Lynch thanks them for their "doggone good job." A teenage girl crosses the shooting area and joins two friends near me. One asks, "Could you see a lot over there?" The girl looks wistfully at MacLachlan and sighs, "All I know is, there *he* is." But in a blink, *he* isn't there anymore, nor are Lynch and Stanton.

I follow a dirt path arcing left through the trailers to the lazy Snoqualmie River. On the grassy banks, kids skip stones across the green water that flows from here to the double smokestacks of the Weyerhaeuser sawmill (the Packard Mill in the series' opening credits), on to the Salish Lodge (the Great Northern Hotel), and over the 217-foot Snoqualmie Falls (Whitetail Falls) that local Native Americans still worship. Hearing an occasional soft murmur of voices, I look over my shoulder and see Lynch and his two actors sitting on the narrow porch of Stanton's character's trailer. After taking a silent pause to gaze at the river, Lynch gets up and spends a lot of time playing with a hose and some dirt. His fascination with the interface between industrial and organic textures is fully evident as he alternately floats dust and mists water onto the weathered steel of a 1970s car. Finally, the car looks like it hasn't been driven or touched in months—except that it's got "Let's rock" written across its windshield in hot pink.

Speaking of rock, this evening the MTV Music Awards are being handed out three hours ahead in New York, and they've sent a crew here to beam a live message to the viewers from popular singer-actor Chris Isaak. Wearing his Chet Desmond FBI overcoat, he sits down with the river in the background for a short on-camera interview. While Isaak is earnestly answering questions, Kyle MacLachlan exhibits an un-Cooperesque sense of mischief. Grabbing a small tray and a cup of coffee, and wearing his own FBI overcoat, he intrudes on the interview. Like a butler, he holds out the tray, saying, "Your coffee, sir." Isaak throws him a curve: "I didn't order any coffee," to which MacLachlan responds with BOB-like intensity "You *must take* this coffee!"

As the afternoon spends itself in golden splendor, a little group of production-watchers gathers. The cast and crew cheerfully mingle with trailer park residents, town locals, and tourists from New York, England, and Sugarland, Texas. There's a feeling that we're all Twin Peaks dwellers in spirit, and it seems perfectly natural that when Lynch has to stop a take around 4:30 p.m. ("We've got a bad siren"), a Snoqualmie resident calls out, "That's the Packard Mill changing shifts."

As twilight adds an eerie aura to the meandering rows of ramshackle old trailers, Lynch sets up a shot in which Isaak will walk between them looking for clues. The director reveals his eagle eye, and part of his conception of *Twin Peaks*, when he spots a 1990 trailer license tab the size of a postage stamp in the far corner of his camera frame. A production assistant, responding to Lynch's "We gotta lose that ninety," covers it with tape, thus keeping the director's fictional world running on expansive dreamtime rather than constrictive calendar chronology.

Lynch and his work bespeak his feeling of kinship with those who are physically and socially outside the consumer-culture-imaged mainstream. The director next readies for a scene in which Isaak and Stanton are interrupted by an old woman with a sunken chin and permanently stiff arms ending in curled hands. "Where's my goddam hot water? Where's my goddam hot water? Where *is* my goddam hot water?," she importunes Stanton. The woman, a local, speaks at the wrong moment. This is the last natural-light shot of the day and there are precious few minutes left to get it. Lynch stops the take and patiently tells the woman how he wants her to enter the action. They take the shot three times, and she demands a lot of hot water in perfect form. After the final "Cut!" he walks straight past Isaak and Stanton and puts his long arm around the woman's stooped shoulders: "That was very, very good, Margaret."

Night gathers around the trailer park, which is illuminated into hyper-reality by all the movie lights, and a sense of camaraderie and happily shared experience bathes the scene. Lynch, with his hand on an electrical switch, experiments with various ways to get a flash of bright light to flood through the window of a trailer when someone opens its door. He calls this "a beautiful day," and grins when Mar T Café owner Pat Cokewell arrives with a steaming bowl of special-order chili for Harry Dean. Chris Isaak signs autographs and Keifer Sutherland, who plays his FBI cohort Sam Stanley, shows up with a bag of burgers from the 1950s-vintage Burgermaster drive-in. He's accompanied by two large, loving golden dogs that have traveled with him from L.A. And if you think that anyone's going to mention the fact that the *Pretty Woman*, the *Runaway Bride* herself, Julia Roberts, just called off her and Sutherland's romance and wedding a few days ago, you've been out in the woods too long.

Watching the production at work was an addictive experience, so as the strangely unshrouded Northwest sun beat down on a balmy September and October, I tracked the filmmakers all over the territory. Since they adamantly did not want any plot details leaking out, I realized that my anonymous six-foot-two presence could be challenged at any moment. Sure enough, as I stood at Lynch's elbow while he watched a scene rehearsal of Laura Palmer (Sheryl Lee) and Donna Hayward (Moira Kelly) walking to school, assistant director Bill Jennings gently pulled me aside and asked, "Are you with us?" If I said yes, he would want to know in what capacity, so, reluctantly, I replied "Not really" and retreated to a respectful distance. Over the weeks Bill's gatekeeper stance relaxed, and I huddled with him in the deep night woods watching moths flame out as they batted into hot movie lights, while I listened to this African American who so wanted to be in the film industry speak movingly of his mentorship with independent director John Korty (*Crazy Quilt*, 1966). The crew got used to seeing me around, and I developed a chatting relationship with Lynch assistant/publicist Gaye Pope and location scout Julie Duvic, started using actor's trailers for bathroom breaks, and heard Dana Ashbrook's (bad-boy Bobby Briggs) enthusiastic rendition of a dirty joke involving a hunter who enjoyed getting blowjobs from a grizzly bear. Still, no matter how at-home I felt with the production, I knew that Lynch could instantly eject me, so I diligently tried to avoid catching his eye.

In this film all eyes would be on Sheryl Lee, the young Seattle actress who became world famous playing the corpse of Laura palmer in the *Twin Peaks* pilot, and did a solid job of portraying Laura's unworldly cousin Maddy. For *Fire Walk with Me* she would have to carry the full, harrowing emotional weight of Laura's tormented existence but, like Lynch, she was eager to return to the character: "Laura always had a tremendous amount of life, because for two seasons everybody talked about her—yet I didn't get to do those things and *be* her."[41] But being Laura was an emotionally draining ordeal, in which Lee felt she was "living a lifetime in just two short months."[42] Desperation, fear, pain, and weeping were her constant companions, and above all, "Everyday I felt an incredible loneliness that was very hard to bear."[43] We know that Lynch and his protagonists love the thrill of pursuing and revealing dark, hidden secrets. But in *Fire Walk With Me* the director is exploring the "horror of secrets"[44]: the torturous burden that the one keeping the secrets must bear. Lee had to inhabit the terrible truth that though Laura's community sees her as its golden girl, she's actually whoring and drug-sniffing her way through life. And, at the root of everything, there's BOB, the scary entity with long gray hair who's been forcing sex on her for years and who is also, somehow, her father Leland. And there's BOB's voice hissing from the ceiling fan that he wants to *be* her or he'll kill her. Believing that she's contaminated by some virulent spiritual contagion and is beyond saving, she doesn't reach out to those who might help her, but rather strives to contain her "disease" and not infect those who love her. Lee felt all the isolation and psychic tension of Laura's double life: "There were days when I didn't know how I was going to go another minute."[45] Lynch fully understood and appreciated the anguish Lee was experiencing for the sake of his art, and he tenderly guided her through Laura's journey. "Thank God for David. I had to go to a deep place to play Laura, a place I didn't think I could reach, but he helped me get there and survive it all."[46]

I first witnessed Sheryl Lee's awe-inspiring incarnation of Laura as Lynch filmed a traffic-jam scene in which Leland and daughter are accosted by one-armed Mike (Al Strobel), BOB's former familiar in malevolence who's now out to stop his partner's evil. While Laura and Leland are stuck in traffic, Mike raves at them, concluding, "It's your father," meaning that Leland is BOB's incest-committing host. While Mike yells, Leland simultaneously holds one foot on the brakes and races the engine with the other, a motif that Lynch employs in his unproduced screenplay of *One Saliva Bubble* and the 1999 film *The Straight Story*. In the context of *Fire Walk With Me*, this gesture mirrors the conflicting impulses warring within Leland, who is both Laura's loving, protective father (brakes) and her slavering, BOB-inspired molester (accelerator).

Mike drives off and Leland roars the Palmer convertible into a gas station, where he and Laura have an intensely emotional scene while sitting in the car. Mixed feelings boil in close-up shots. Even though Leland isn't consciously aware that BOB sometimes uses his body to do bad things, the BOB-part of his psyche is severely disturbed by the threat Mike poses, leaving the surface Leland confused and angry. Intercut with this scene in the finished film will be footage detailing Leland's extramarital sex with Teresa Banks (who "looks just like my Laura") and the time Teresa lined up an extra girl to party with, who turned out to be his daughter (unbeknownst to Laura, he fled when he realized it was her). So, back in the car, there's a component of BOB-inflamed suspicion and sexual jealousy to Leland's inner turmoil (So, *my* girl is ready to screw an anonymous man for money!).

Filming Leland's subtly shifting, distraught face without any dialogue, crouching just outside camera range, Lynch calls for "absolute silence" and, as he and Ray Wise focus intently, the director intones: "Look at her . . . now back forward . . . change slightly, settle into it . . . steal a look . . . a little more devious, more frightening . . . and cut. That was *beautiful* Ray."

In this scene, Laura's emotional storm has to even exceed Leland's. She has to react to Mike's raging, denouncing words, her father's extreme reaction to Mike, and his weird stomping on the accelerator while they're stopped, plus, in the midst of her fear and trembling, she must project an accusatory, angry tone toward Leland as she speaks of the day she first realized he and BOB may be one and the same. In order to reach the emotional heights she needs, Lee surprises us all by screaming loudly a few times just before the first take rolls. Lynch seems thrilled by her heartfelt participation in his project. He began his odyssey with her by carefully arranging sand grains on her forehead as she lay wrapped in plastic on a freezing Washington beach. And now, almost two years later, he speaks softly to her between takes and gives her a little kiss on her blond bangs. Her arduous day over, Lee strolls toward her trailer, smiling down at the waist-high Snoqualmie kids who encircle her and say, "Goodbye, Laura, goodbye."

A few nights later Lynch demonstrated both his affectionate bond with his leading lady and his embrace of spontaneous happenings. The film production was occupying a large section of land in the center of the town of Fall City, just downriver from Snoqualmie Falls. This huge set encompassed the parking lot and exterior of the Roadhouse and the exterior of the Log Lady's (Catherine Couslon) cabin. So on a Friday night, lots of unusual lights and activity were evident right next to the town's only bridge across the Snoqualmie River, and a crowd of hundreds had gathered to watch the moviemakers. Dana Ashbrook was there just to hang out, and Coulson arrived cradling her log and wearing her hiking boots, long tweed coat, and glasses for the upcoming scene. As Lynch talked camera moves with Ron Garcia, Sheryl Lee arrived dressed in Laura's all-black, short-skirted night-prowling ensemble, her long blonde locks pulled up away from her face by large pink hairpins. The director stepped over to her end and, as they put their arms around each other's waists and he kissed her on the cheek, the segment of the watching crowd nearest to them went "Awhhh."

In the scene, Laura, with her hair down, will drive her yellow '56 Buick into the dirt lot, park, and walk to the Roadhouse entrance, where the Log Lady will intercept her and give her some words of advice. Everything goes fine in rehearsal, and Lynch gets ready to roll his camera. During the preparation period, the crowd has been in a festive mood, eating snacks, drinking beer, keeping track of their children, and shooing away a big white dog that's been cruising for handouts and occasionally trying to hump the backs of various crowd members who are sitting on the ground. Just to be safe, assistant director Bill Jennings grabs the canine and plants it firmly on the sidelines, where it is content to sit.

Lynch calls "Action!" through his megaphone, and Lee pulls up, stops her car, gets out, and starts across the puddled parking lot. At this point the dog stands up and strides straight into the shot, almost clipping Lee as she walks, and then keeps right on going off into the night at a diagonal angle from Lee's trajectory. Lee completes her walk, meeting the Log Lady, and Lynch yells "Cut!"—and then for all our benefit, "Perfect!" He's got a grin on his face, and his crew and the watching hundreds erupt in laughter, cheers, and applause.

On another night, without spectators, the director and his crew shot what would have been the largest-scale scene in the film, but it didn't make the final cut. At a forested place appropriately called Ravendale, we see on the right a ramshackle low building that will be the truckstop bar where Laura and Donna spend a debauched evening with lustful loggers Buck (Victor Rivers) and Tommy (Chris Pedersen). Left of the structure is a long dirt lot with a tall metal post supporting a sign that says, with Special Agent resonance, "Cooper Tires." Lynch positions his camera near the bar looking back into the lot, with the paved forest road beyond. To round out his composition, the director has placed a long line of parked logging trucks on the paved road that will dwindle to the vanishing point in the background of the shot, and behind the trucks, in the woods, he's put an atmospheric light source that shines spectrally through the trees. In the midst of all these hectic preparations, which take hours, property master Daniel Kuttner brings over a tarnished old silver metal ice chest with a red Coca-Cola logo on it for Lynch to approve. The director's ability to disengage from the commotion around him and focus on the object was positively Dale Cooper–like. He silently stared at the chest for what seemed like two minutes, and simply concluded, "That's a beautiful thing."

Around 10 p.m. everyone's ready to realize on film these few lines from the script: "EXTERIOR, BORDER TRUCK STOP—NIGHT. Establish. Tommy takes the car like a rocket into the parking lot and does a complete three-sixty before rocking to a stop."[47] The scene will not use stunt people. Chris Pedersen will be driving, with Moira Kelly at his side and Sheryl Lee and Victor Rivers in the back seat, and they'll all be grasping beer bottles. They rehearse the action at half-speed and then, after workers sweep the dirt lot smooth, they're ready for what everyone hopes will be a one-take shot.

With the camera rolling, the car's headlights appear way down the road and quickly grow larger as the vehicle roars along the line of logging trucks. Without slacking its speed, the car veers off the pavement into the truck-stop lot, heading straight toward the camera. If it kept coming for a second or two more it would wipe out Lynch and many of his crew, but Pedersen expertly jerks the steering wheel, sending the car into a perfect donut spin around the Cooper Tires signpost. Almost up on its two inside wheels, the sliding car spews dust and sprays a wave of gravel in its wake. The car skids to a stop after circling the signpost, and the driver and his three passengers climb out on wobbly legs as the camera cuts. All eyes but two are on the intrepid riders as Lynch and his crew crowd in with cheers and congratulations. I notice that the bill of Lynch's cap is pointing straight up and follow his gaze in time to see a round beige cloud of dust rising into a twinkling star field. I am sure that if he could have grabbed a camera fast enough he would have tried to film this poetic exhalation of his car-action scene.

I spent my final night watching the production miles above North Bend's Mar T Café in the lower Cascade Mountains. I turned off the highway, drove down a secondary road, parked, and trekked in to the encampment. Up here, night is night, and in a sweeping, murky panorama of forest, mountains, and black sky, the only light and heat emanated from the moviemakers' electrical generators.

There was definitely enough illumination for the prop men to see what they were doing as they stuffed the head of a mannequin that resembled actor Rick Aiello (Deputy Sheriff Cliff Howard) with raw hamburger and explosive blood packs: it looks like Cliff isn't going to make it through the night. Like drivers who can't resist looking at a car crash, a group of crew workers and actors eating dinner from paper plates gathered to watch the gory head-shot preparations, knowing their stomachs were going to turn flip-flops. But at least they got to emote in histrionic disgust, "Oooooh, yuk!," and one wag added, "Hey, spoon some of that onto *my* plate."

After eating, the crew, using flashlights to see with, carries the mannequin and all the necessary equipment a half-mile down a narrow dirt path deep into the evergreen forest. Setting up camp at the base of a huge old-growth cedar tree trunk, Lynch takes hours to film the sequence in which Laura and Bobby, high on cocaine, meet with Deputy Cliff Howard to score more of the drug. Laura and Bobby arrive before Cliff, and Lynch illuminates their scenes with just their flashlights, which play only on their faces and a few spooky trees, so that the darkness truly envelops them.

Laura, giddy and goofy with cocaine, gigglingly points out some of the natural attractions to her escort ("Bobby, I found a leaf; Bobby, I found a twig") in a drug-induced perversion of Lynch and Cooper's wonderstruck way of seeing the world. In the next scene, when Cliff shows up with the snow, he pulls out a gun and looks as though he's going to plug Bobby, so Bobby shoots first. Even though Dana Ashbrook's gun is loaded with blanks, a concussion and some black powder will still shoot out of the barrel, so the actor does some test firings against a white sheet to gauge the safe distance he should stand from Rick Aiello. With a very high percentage of assurance that he will be safe, Aiello takes his "bullets" like a man and dies a good movie death. Still, I am on edge watching this scene. We've all seen thousands of gun killings on the screen, but to witness firsthand someone pulling out a revolver and shooting a person a few feet away from them is a viscerally shocking experience. In a few seconds the illusion of violence is committed to film and vanishes from our world, with Ashbrook and Aiello both laughing as the killer helps his victim to his feet. My composure is just returning to normal when, out of the corner of my eye in the dim light, I realize that the man standing next to me has a long narrow face and shoulder-length gray hair brushing his black leather jacket. It is BOB himself, standing in the middle of the night woods, and I have to concentrate to transform his grinning face into that of the friendly, jocular Frank Silva. It's slightly reassuring to realize that I'm a bit taller than one of the creepiest essences of evil ever put on film, the fiend who has haunted some of my friends' dreams and attics. Lynch concludes the first stage of this evening's work by splattering the Cliff Howard mannequin's meaty brains and blood across the forest's green vegetation. And he lingers on the incongruously smiling face of Laura, who feels her own life is so devalued that she reflexively laughs and laughs above the lawman's steaming corpse. She gets the joke of just how close her own death is to her.

This evening's stage two begins around ten o'clock as Lynch and company penetrate still deeper into the woods and set up their camera on the narrow path looking back in the direction they've come from. And in the scene they're preparing, Laura and biker James (James Marshall), her truest love, pause on the metaphorical abyss-edge of Laura's coming dive into death and poignantly sum up their relationship. This will be one of those visually uncluttered, emotionally complex two-person scenes that Lynch does so well.

As Lynch's characters often do, Laura and James emerge out of darkness, the tiny far-off flicker of his Harley's headlight growing larger and larger as James, with Laura clinging to his waist, rumbles up the forest path and stops in front of the camera. Lynch wants to make the lighting even more atmospheric, so he has his crew rig a translucent window shade over a big light, and they practice the new setup a few times. As the motorcycle couple rides up near the camera, Lynch hand-signals "Now!," and two crew members raise the windowshade, seamlessly bathing James and Laura in extra illumination, so that her golden hair and ivory skin glow against the rich, deep, forest black.

Sheryl Lee and James Marshall rehearse their most intense moments together in the film, as she does a bravura job of inhabiting Laura's sadly fluctuating feelings. No single way of being brings her peace, so she wavers desperately between emotions, alternately kissing him with lust, mocking him with words and a slap, declaring her love and saying "Let's get lost together," then coolly withdrawing and telling him to take her home. Laura was drugging and boozing before he picked her up so, in addition to portraying Laura's fragmented emotions with breathtaking conviction in her forest scene with James, Lee makes a wonderfully subtle transition from a woozy, sexy, slurred manner to a chilly, alienated lucidity.

Because the dense woods comes right down to the narrow path Laura and James are on, Lynch and about ten of us are just outside the camera's frameline as Sheryl Lee slaps James Marshall and they whisper and weep and cling to each other for dear life. If I tripped and fell forward I'd be in the shot so, standing on a spongy carpet of fallen twigs and leaves, I try to freeze my muscles and scarcely breath during the long-duration takes. Lynch is very subdued and soft-spoken with Lee and Marshall, and during filming only he and a few of the crew look directly at them. These are actors pretending to be other people, and yet when they share their intimate moments, most of us can't bear to intrude with our eyes, so we look down at the ground.

By now, it's after midnight, and I've got to be at work later this morning. So when everyone takes a breather before finishing the scene, a couple of crewmembers head back down the path toward the filmmakers' main encampment, and I go with them. It takes a while for me to walk all the way back out to my car in the total darkness, but my key finds the lock and I look back toward the production area. In the horizon-to-horizon blackness, a bright spot of light emanates from the trees, giving the stone bases of the surrounding mountains an eerie sheen. Lynch is beginning the shots in which Laura gets an unexpected jolt of terror and seems to see something in the woods beyond James' shoulder—but nothing's there. Suddenly, far off, yet weirdly close in the still air, I can hear Laura scream.

Back in Los Angeles, she most certainly screamed again on Halloween night, when Lynch finished shooting the film with the train-car-interior scene of her murder by the BOB-possessed Leland. Out of respect for the arduous emotional journey Sheryl Lee was taking with Laura's life cycle, the director chose to have her enact the death scene in sequence at the end of the production process. Even though BOB was wielding the power in the scene, the night was disturbing and "scary"[48] for Frank Silva, and it gave Sheryl Lee nightmares. But the dark, death-of-Laura vibrations generated on that October 31 were somewhat mitigated by the fact that after shooting the harrowing scene everyone celebrated Frank's Halloween birthday.

Lynch told his old friend Catherine Coulson (The Log Lady) that on *Fire Walk With Me* "he's never been happier shooting a movie,"[49] but the May 1992 Cannes Film Festival did not help him sustain a well-pleased mood. The film was poorly received by the audience and Lynch, reacting to all the "hostility, upset, and anger"[50] in the air, fell ill during the night and had to call a doctor to his hotel room. When he walked into his press conference, "feeling like I was made of broken glass,"[51] some critics actually hissed and booed. Surrounded by a cadre of friends (composer Angelo Badalamenti, co-writer Robert Engels, actor Michael Anderson, producer Jean-Claude Fleury), Lynch kept his cool and politely fielded many questions. He maintained his familiar positions, saying that just because his films contain drug use and savage violence it doesn't mean that he condones such activities, and emphasizing that his works have definite meanings for him, but that he doesn't want to color the viewer's personal interpretation by talking about his own private conception. Lynch summed up his remarks by restating the core of his worldview: that studying the details of a phenomenon like the life and death of Laura Palmer, and receiving some answers from it, will not dissipate its essential mystery.

From the international media's point of view, Lynch himself was a walking mystery as he strolled the sun-bleached promenades of Cannes, for two years earlier he had kissed Isabella Rossellini on the lips before a mass of flashing cameras, and now he was holding hands with an anonymous, and very pregnant, woman in black. England's *The Daily Mail*, after interviewing Rossellini, reported that she had, in the paper's words, "severed all romantic ties"[52] with Lynch, having found his "individualism, eccentricity, and whacky idiosyncracies tiresome and irksome."[53] But later Rossellini said, "I had thought David had finally relaxed and had believed after so many years that we could finally, officially, be a couple."[54] Lynch doesn't like to talk about his romantic relationships, but Jennifer Lynch told me that "there was a time near the end of his five years with Isabella when she wanted more than he felt he could safely give. What man doesn't want to be everything for a woman like that? But he realized you can be everything you are and still not be everything the woman is looking for. Things end in relationships for him for what may at the time seem really brutal or sad reasons, but they all seem appropriate."[55] Rossellini must have felt like the Heartbroken Woman in Lynch's *Industrial Symphony No. 1*, but like that suffering character who found a glimmer of hope in a shower of sparkling space dust, Rossellini, as Lynch does, believed that "there is always some light in every situation."[56] After some time passed she achieved a state of equanimity in which she spoke of Lynch's talent with warm respect, said that she would love to work with him again, and declared that of all the men she has had relationships with, including Martin Scorsese, Lynch was the most supportive of her creative endeavors. In 2004, Jennifer Lynch added that "my father and Isabella are very close to this day."[57]

The media covering the 1992 Cannes Film Festival learned that the pregnant woman accompanying Lynch was his new "girlfriend," as he said in his 1950s-adolescent way. Mary Sweeney, a graduate of the prestigious New York University cinema studies program, was a painter and film editor who had helped Lynch piece together *Blue Velvet*, *Industrial Symphony No. 1*, *Wild at Heart*, and part of *Twin Peaks*. Lynch had been drawn to the black-haired, sweet, laughing woman who sat with him in Los Angeles and put as much energy and care into poring over every frame of his films as he did. She was already sharing the rhythms of his work, and Lynch found it natural and wonderful to embrace her into the flow of his life. What a perfect situation for an artist, to have one's professional collaborator and romantic partner be the same person. Lynch felt so at home with Mary that he allowed her to move into his artist-bachelor's Hollywood Hills lair and fill the architectural work of art with cooking smells. Leaving their disappointing *Twin Peaks: Fire walk With Me* experience behind them in the South of France, Lynch and Sweeney stopped off in Paris on their way back to Los Angeles. Lynch has spoken of how, when you look in the mirror, one becomes two. And now, in the City of Light, two became three as Sweeney gave birth to Riley, Lynch's third child and second son.

In August, Lynch and Sweeney broke away from their bundle of joy for twenty-four hours and flew up to Washington's Snoqualmie Valley for the American premiere of the film, which had already been playing to big crowds in Japan. A local Washington group, headed by Snoqualmie's Vicki Curnutt, thought it would be great to have a summer festival honoring *Twin Peaks* and its fans. Combining efforts with New Line Cinema, the film's distributor, the group presented "Twin Peaks Fest 92" on the weekend of August 14–16. New Line flew in actors Sheryl Lee, Ray Wise, Moira Kelly, Catherine Coulson, Al Strobel, and Jonathan Lepell for the event. The esteemed visitors amiably mingled with the ten thousand fans who gathered from around the world to talk about the show, buy *Peaks*-related souvenirs, and sample a number of activities such as a celebrity look-alike contest, tours of filming locations, a cherry pie-eating contest, a climb up Mt. Si (one of *Twin Peaks*' peaks), the Log Lady Relay Race, and a raffle of the old gray sedan in which Agent Cooper first drove into Twin Peaks. There were also several soldout events which allowed smaller gatherings of fans to have "Dinner With the Stars" and "Breakfast With the Stars," all leading up to the big film showing in the funky old North Bend Theatre just across from the Mar T Café. This would be an unusually racy, R-rated evening for the movie house, which normally showed Disney and other family-oriented fare. The whole weekend had a mildly subversive air about it, as the church-going, flag-waving towns of North Bend and Snoqualmie were swarmed by people obsessed with a fiction that centered on sex, drugs, incest, and child-murder.

Lynch had been scheduled to appear at earlier festival events, but he kept his participation under tight control, flying in late on Sunday afternoon, talking to no media representatives, and, with Mary and the actors, only showing up a few minutes before the film screening at 8:00 p.m. The premiere was long-ago soldout, but throngs of people crowded the sidewalk outside the theater hoping for a spare seat and at least a glimpse of the celebrities as they pulled up in long black limousines, with the mountains of Twin Peaks filling the twilight background.

Lynch stepped out of the car, waved to the cheering crowd, and stepped into the sweltering, non-air-conditioned theater, his hand outstretching to whoever would first take it, that person being a local boy who tore tickets on the weekends. The director said "Glad to meet you" to his impromptu greeter and, with Mary, took a seat in the far right back section of the auditorium, on the aisle. The director, Sweeney, Sheryl Lee, Moira Kelly, Catherine Coulson, Al Strobel, and Jonathon Lepell were each dressed in formal black (no tie for Lynch), but Ray Wise, perhaps to counteract all the darkness he portrays in the film, wore a white suit and tieless shirt. In contrast to Lynch, the actors sat halfway down toward the screen, surrounded by adoring fans, who included Pat Cokewell, owner of the Mar T Café and maker of those heavenly pies.

The seats filled quickly, and as everyone exclaimed about how bloody hot the room was, Lynch said a few words before the film. A tall dark figure against the white screen, he stood onstage and, with a wide smile, acknowledging the standing ovation. He spoke with confidence to the large group, and his natural humor bobbed to the surface. "Thank you guys very much. This really reminds me of a theater in Los Angeles called the NuArt, where I once stood in front of a packed theater and talked a little bit about *Eraserhead*. You've got a great theater here. [*Audience laughter, assuming he's being sarcastic.*] No, I'm not kidding you—this is, ah—it smells—and it—it's definitely the real thing." [*Much crowd laughter.*] Then he treated the group to a classic Lynchian non sequitur, beginning a convoluted story that went on and on and led up to the reason he and Mark Frost originally decided to shoot *Twin Peaks* in the Snoqualmie Valley: "'I'm still not sure where we're going to shoot it, Mark.' So I said, 'Call me,' and he said 'Okay'—now before the film, I want to introduce some members of the cast." [*Audience laughter over another abrupt Lynchian swerve away from revealing information.*]

Lynch introduced his actors and had them join him on stage, as the crowd whooped and applauded, and he acknowledged, "in the back, my girlfriend, Mary Sweeney, the editor of the film." He closed by thanking all the Washington communities that had helped make the film possible and said, "the cast, Mary, and I are all very happy to be here and we truly hope that you love *Twin Peaks: Fire Walk With Me*." The Lynchian paradox was palpable:

This well-mannered, funny, and endearing master of ceremonies was proudly ready to plunge us into his carefully wrought creation, which many critics would characterize as a depressing miasma of moral degradation.

However, thanks to the complexity of human nature, the audience jammed into the North Bend Theatre was ready and eager to take the dive with Laura. The buzz of voices faded as the auditorium grew dim—but then a woman's voice called, "Lights! Turn on the lights!" As though in a Norman Rockwell *Saturday Evening Post* cover depicting a small-town community project goof-up, Twin Peaks Fest organizer Vicki Curnutt took the stage to do two things she'd forgotten. After directing a round of applause at the festival's many volunteers, she called Lynch back to the stage. Since he hadn't been around to attend that afternoon's Celebrity Awards Ceremony, she handed him his trophy: a varnished wooden plaque with a rope hangman's noose attached to it. He chuckled along with the crowd's laughter and applause, and added, "Things were a little slow at Cannes this year, so this really hits the spot."

At last, it was night in the room, and Lynch's darkness would flow. The director could not have handpicked a more receptive audience for his work. They were thrilled to be the first in the country to see the film, and, especially to have key cast members and Lynch himself in the auditorium with them breathing the same hothouse air. As the film opened, the crowd cheered and clapped for every actor's name and technical credit name, and when each actor first came on the screen, no matter how far into the movie it was, they exploded again. Lynch was sharing less of this experience with the crowd than they thought, however. Like parents who have tucked their audience in bed so it can have a dream of Laura Palmer, Lynch and Sweeney tiptoed out the back after the first few minutes unreeled, so they could hasten back south to their dear little Riley.

The first thing we see is one of Lynch's visual abstractions signifying mood and emotion, like a black smudge of malaise that haunts an oppressed character in one of the artist's drawings. Here the screen is filled with a vibrating blue storm of electrical particles that roil within the frame of a TV set like the churning black insects beneath the idyllic lawnscape of *Blue Velvet*. In the earlier film Lynch used insects to represent the evil hiding within our environment and our own psyches, and in *Fire walk With Me*, electrical energy, the wires that transport it, and the Palmer's humming ceiling fan, allow malevolent forces to invade our world and wreak havoc. A moment after watching the angry swarm of blue energy we hear a woman scream "Nooo" for the last time in her life, and then the ugly thud of a death blow. Filtering his feelings about electricity through the childlike-wonder part of his sensibility, Lynch restores a sense of primal magic and menace to the invisible force that hums within galaxies and the neurons in our heads, flows into our homes to heat us and cook our food, and which can kill us if we're not careful.

Michael J. Anderson remembers a moment during the filming that illustrates Lynch's mystical feeling about electrical vibrations. They were shooting a scene in the Red Room where The Man From Another Place holds a ring up to the camera.

> The generator blew out in this scene. So they plugged in another generator and tried to run the scene again. And it blew the generator again. So they plugged in a third generator and this time Lynch made some changes: "Well, this time say this part first and then this part, and instead of being over here, stand over there and point this way." Now, he didn't change the power requirements, he did not adjust the lights or the camera or anything. He merely moved the pieces of the scene around a little bit. When we hooked up the third generator it ran, and kept on running. I heard David say, "Yep, I thought that might have been it."[58]

In 1997, Lynch spoke about how the massive concentration of electrical lines can cause tumors to grow in the heads of people living near the wires. "Just because you can't see it doesn't mean it's not, you know, whacking you."[59] (The workers who strung the original power lines of Thomas Edison's pioneering electrical company said they were afraid of "the devils in the wires."[60]) The director's first major fictional linkage of electricity with danger and evil occurs in his unproduced screenplay for *Ronnie Rocket*, which he began in the mid-1970s. Inspired by the concept of alternating electrical current, Lynch imagined a story in which a villain reverses the flow of power so that he can control a large city by zapping people with "bad electricity."[61] This terrible rain of negative power makes people confused, dizzy, and unable to talk straight, and when the rain becomes a deluge, some start to eat their own hands and feet, and others burst into flames. Like the motif of a man simultaneously braking and accelerating a car in his earlier unproduced *One Saliva Bubble*, which Lynch eventually utilized in *Fire Walk With Me*, the director uses the *Ronnie Rocket* idea of bad electricity in his *Twin Peaks* movie, though in a more subtle way. In *Ronnie Rocket*, the villain overtly employs the electricity as a weapon, while in *Fire Walk With Me* it is a darkly poetic signifier of evil's intrusion into our world, a warning of disturbance in the air when BOB's dimension hungrily invades the one we live in.

The blue-electricity TV screen that opens the film is linked to the murder of Teresa Banks (Pamela Gidley), which FBI agents Chet Desmond (Chris

Isaak), Sam Stanley (Keifer Sutherland), and, later Dale Cooper (Kyle MacLachlan), come to investigate in Washington State. Lynch uses this first, thirty-minute portion of his film, before he takes up Laura's story, to show us the depth of the mystery that his detectives are confronting and to indicate the limitations of their investigative skills.

In a fanciful, yet straightforward way, Lynch spells out, through his character of FBI boss Gordon Cole, his sense of the correct proportion between phenomena we can decipher and happenings that are beyond our understanding. Enacting the same artist-to-audience relationship that Lynch has with his viewers, Lynch as Gordon Cole presents Desmond and Stanley with a performance-art piece for them to decipher. This puzzle is Lil (Kimberly Ann Cole), a gawky, pinch-faced woman in a red dress who makes odd, dance-like motions. The seasoned Desmond helps Stanley read her messages: They'll have trouble with the local authorities on the Teresa Banks case, the sheriff is hiding something, there'll be lots of legwork, the case involves drugs. But, Stanley wonders, what about the blue rose pinned to Lil's lapel? Desmond replies, "I can't tell you about that." What a succinct summation of Lynch's ethos: By paying close attention we can comprehend much that we encounter in life, but the more we learn, the more we realize we don't know. That botanically impossible blue rose, that bit of the Beyond that remains a mystery, will forever tantalize us and arouse our questing souls.

Desmond and Stanley enact a condensed version of the investigative process that *Twin Peaks*' TV lawmen played out over many episodes. The two make careful observations, perform forensic science, and talk to witnesses, but they're nowhere near a solution to Teresa Banks' murder. Then Desmond follows his intuition into blue rose territory, revisiting the trailer where the victim lived, getting an eerie vibration from the number six electrical pole, and, at dusk, finding Teresa's lost ring beneath a strangely shining silver trailer. Having plugged into some ineffable energy circuit, Desmond vanishes from the film.

After Lynch gives us a patriotic Eagle Scout image of the Liberty Bell, he shows that more mysteries are gathering at Philadelphia's FBI headquarters. For the audience members who viewed the whole *Twin Peaks* TV series, the experience of watching *Fire Walk With Me* creates the almost subliminal sensation that we're simultaneously seeing things that happened both before and after the TV show. And this feeling perfectly synchronizes with the fluid, dimension-interpenetrating sense of space and time that permeates Lynch's film. So when we see Agent Cooper crisply stride into Gordon Cole's office, it's as though he's snapped out of some of the sartorial and touchy-feely emotional excesses that Lynch didn't like about Copper's second-TV season presentation, those character modifications that happened while Lynch was disengaged from the production. Cooper is hyper-alert this morning because of a troubling dream about February 16, and his nocturnal subconscious agitation takes daytime substance in the form of long-lost agent Phillip Jeffries (David Bowie), who unexpectedly shows up at the FBI building.

Jeffries comes in via a veritable Blue Rose Highway, whipping out of the elevator through a blue archway and striding down an azure carpet into Gordon Cole's office. When he enters the room, it becomes charged with metaphysical turbulence. We've never seen Cole and Cooper so unsettled, and as the deeply shaken Jeffries spews out fragmentary impressions of the things he's witnessed, a strange reality takes over Cole's office and fills the screen. The agent mentions someone named Judy that he's not going to talk about (more blue rose material) and says "we live inside a dream" (a truly Lynchian sentiment) as we see what he saw at "one of their meetings" above a convenience store. Assembled in the dilapidated space are *Twin Peaks'* extra-dimensional BOB and The Man From Another Place, sitting at a table covered with pans of creamed corn, which they call "garmonbozia." Across many cultures, corn has been seen as a sacred food since ancient times. It is a vegetable composed entirely of edible seeds, so when we eat it we are literally and poetically consuming the kernel of life, gobbling up the future in the present moment. In ancient Mexican and South American lore, corn symbolizes death as well as life, and is linked with blood sacrifice. BOB may dine on garmonbozia, but his primary occupation is consuming the lives, souls, and futures of human beings; and at the end of the film the corn takes on the connotation of "pain and sorrow." *Twin Peaks* is also concerned with the point at which life and death meet and change places, and *Fire Walk With Me* is a journey leading to Laura's blood sacrifice—and beyond. It was Lynch's intention to imbue the creamed corn with sacramental power, and Michael J. Anderson (The Man From Another Place) says that Lynch "got quite upset"[62] when the actor spilled some of it. "He didn't get angry, but it was like a big concern came up and he got down and talked to me, and he goes, 'Now you don't want to spill this at all. Not even a little bit. It's like gold.' And then he just stood there like, 'Do you get it? Can you grasp what I am telling you?' He was very serious. It wasn't a joke."[63]

Among those present at the convenience store gathering Jeffries witnessed are Mrs. Tremond (Frances Bay) and her grandson (Jonathan Leppell), the pair who Donna encounters on TV in her Meals-on-Wheels route. The boy, who's a clairvoyant magician, wears Lynch's favorite black-suit-and-white-shirt outfit, and was played by the director's son, Austin, in the series. The film's grandson wears a white plaster mask that lifts momentarily to reveal a shadowed monkey's face. The mask and what it hides are another statement of Lynch's belief in a multifarious reality, in deep truths concealed by facades. Looking underneath the detestable surface behavior of Elephant Man–exploiter Bytes, *Blue Velvet*'s Frank Booth, and Marietta of *Wild at Heart*, Lynch finds love—a quality of primal grace and goodness—that's been twisted and perverted into evil. Most often, however, the director delves into the darkness hidden beneath benign surfaces, thus projecting the balance he sees in the world around him. The monkey behind the mask signifies Lynch's characteristic linkage of animalism with evil, and is a metaphor for monkey man BOB's dwelling within Leland. Jutting out from the mask's "third eye" position on its forehead is a crooked stick of wood, indicating that the BOB-possessed Leland's spirituality is earthbound and blocked. Only when he is released from BOB in death is Leland able to "go into the light," where he sees his beautiful, shining Laura. In her poem, young Harriet Hayward had also seen Laura glowing after death. For *Fire Walk With Me*, Lynch reshot the iconic image of Laura's dead blue face being unwrapped from its plastic cocoon and, as he did two years earlier on a cold Washington beach, he carefully placed a glimmering grain of sand in the region of her third eye. Leland tragically succumbed to BOB's domination, while Laura heroically defied it, and thus her forehead's spiritual eye is ready for an illuminated divine vision.

Jeffries' remembered experience with this otherworldly crew seems to bleed through the reality of Gordon Cole's office in a cloud of blue static like the film's opening TV screen. As the spent and screaming agent finishes his narration, Lynch stresses his notion of electrical-atmospherical disturbance being a sign of transport between dimensions by having Jeffries vanish amidst more blue static and a shot of power lines against blue sky. In the *Fire Walk With Me* script, Lynch specifies that Jeffries is standing in a Buenos Aires hotel one moment, and the next he's in Gordon Cole's office, and then suddenly back in Argentina. In the film, the director pumps up the mystery quotient by having Jeffries materialize from nowhere and everywhere. It's interesting to note that the numerals in Jeffries' hotel room number add up to nine, as do Cooper's at the Great Northern Hotel, and to recall our discussion of the cosmic, circling, yin-yang energy that impels nine to become six: the universal constant of dualistic poles trading places and realities transforming. With his white tropical suit and burnt-out, shell-shocked manner, Jeffries is like one of novelist Graham Greene's or Joseph Conrad's northern men whose life falls apart in southern climes. Lynch wants his characters, and us, to hit the road, delve into mysteries, learn all we can, and gain enlightenment from the experience. But he also knows that this path is fraught with dangers, and he makes Jeffries a man who bears the psychic wounds of too much traveling. Earlier, Fat Trout Trailer Park manager Carl Rodd sounded a cautionary note about voyaging when he talked with agents Desmond and Stanley. Lynch juxtaposed a shot of eerily twittering power lines against blue sky with the haggard, bandaged face of Rodd, who spoke like a haunted man: "I've already been places. I just want to stay where I am."

When Cooper travels to Washington State to investigate agent Desmond's disappearance, he visits Carl Rodd's trailer corral and is drawn to what looks like an unremarkable patch of earth where a trailer was once parked. We know what Cooper doesn't, that this is where Desmond touched the ring and was lost to sight, that the trailer belonged to two members of *Twin Peaks'* otherworldly cosmology, and that the "Let's rock" written in red on the windshield of Desmond's car is a phrase the little Man From Another Place will say to Cooper in a dream twelve months from now. Cooper, the magician who longs to see, can recognize investigational elements that give him "a strange feeling," but he can't perceive what they mean. This state of mind mirrors Lynch's comments about how his own process of art-making proceeds in a "strange, abstract way,"[64] in which he lets his feelings guide his creating hand and only later sees how the assembled elements coalesce into intellectual meaning.

Agent Chester Desmond: vanished. Agent Phillip Jeffries: vanished. The murder of Teresa Banks: unsolved. Even Cooper, the detective's detective, must concede that the FBI's quest has reached "a dead end." In *The Wizard of Oz*, which Lynch loves so much, Dorothy and her three male companions reach a roadblock on their odyssey to Oz when they're told that they can't enter the city that they've been striving so hard to reach, and which holds the Wizard's special knowledge that they seek. But, when the officials see that Dorothy is wearing ruby slippers, the doors are opened. And, likewise in Lynch's world, there is often a means of entry, a gateway to deeper mysteries, that is waiting to be recognized. The investigating men can take us no further into the dark wonders of *Fire Walk With Me*. To proceed all the way to the end of the night, we must walk and die with Laura Palmer, the saddest schoolgirl in the world.

As Lynch opens Laura's story, he presents images that make a quick transition from sunny innocence to dark experience, as he did at the start of *Blue Velvet*. Teenage Laura and her best friend, Donna, wearing their 1950s-echoing plaids and sweaters, walk to school down the same sidewalk they've trod for years and years together. At school they link pinkie fingers to say goodbye—and then Laura's snorting cocaine into her brain and weeping and saying, "I'm gone, long gone" as James, one of her boyfriends, touches her naked breast. In *Blue Velvet*, a shadowy, insectoid force churning beneath an idyllic small town invaded the daylight world when, like a bug bite to the neck, Jeffrey's father was stricken with a seizure. In *Fire Walk With Me*, the darkness seems to have already been gnawing at Laura for some time; she must have been doing some harrowing traveling to feel so "long gone" at such a young age.

It is a measure of Lynch's commitment to his artistic vision that, in *Fire Walk With Me*, he strips away all the user-friendly, trademark *Twin Peaks*-on-TV elements that viewers love (detectives, pie and coffee, humorously quirky characters) and focuses the world through Laura's pained, sad, and desperate consciousness. The second law of thermodynamics states that everything in the universe will eventually run down, wear out, fade away, melt; that unless new energy is introduced from an outside source, things will devolve from order to chaos. Lynch has spoken of his poignant feeling that there's an underlying "wild pain and decay"[65] gnawing at the world, of how even bright new buildings and bridges carry the seeds of their own dissolution. The director says that "it's the scariest thing"[66] to see the forces of entropy consuming a human being, especially one as beautiful, gifted, and loved as Laura. She's the community's golden girl, but Lynch shows us that this radiant seventeen-year-old is "dying on the inside."[67]

Since age twelve, BOB has been a plague on her body and mind, creeping through her bedroom window in flashes of blue light and thrusting himself between her legs as she moans with eyes closed like a troubled dreamer. She sees BOB as the animalistic man with long gray hair, whereas most people viewing the film, because of their experience of the TV show, already know that her sexual partner is her BOB-possessed father, Leland. Part of *Fire Walk With Me*'s drama hinges on Laura coming to this shattering realization late in the film. For now, BOB is not content to feed on her sexuality, he also wants her soul, her personhood, and much of the film is devoted to Laura's attempt to cope with this threat. Enthralled beneath the ceiling fan outside her bedroom, which whirls infernal energies into her life, Laura hears BOB hiss, "I want to taste with your mouth." She lives with BOB using her sexually, but she fights against his hunger to penetrate and own her soul. Lynch, in his screenplays for *Blue Velvet* and *Wild at Heart*, uses the verb "open" to denote one person having transgressive sexual access to another (Bobby Peru leers at Lula, "I'll open you like a Christmas present."[68]) In the *Twin Peaks* TV series, when Leland lies dying, the terrible knowledge that he killed his own daughter and was possessed by BOB finally comes flooding into his conscious mind. Even though the young Leland had invited BOB in to play his wicked games, the dying adult's language of recollection connotes a homosexual rape: "He opened me and he came inside me." By implication, BOB joins a list of Lynch's villains (*The Elephant Man*'s Bytes, *Dune*'s Baron Harkonen, *Blue Velvet*'s Frank Booth) with homoerotic appetites, for if *Fire Walk With Me*'s evil entity gains possession of Laura, he will be having sex with the men she beds.

Those who perform dark deeds in Lynch's work often do so with an ecstatic glee that embodies the Marquis de Sade's idea that "crime is an enchanting affair, for, in truth, from the flames by which it licks us is kindled the torch of our lust. Only crime is sufficient, it alone inflames us, and only crime can ravish pleasure through all degrees of our sensibility."[69] Hearing this idea, BOB would certainly grimace and grunt his agreement, but Laura would burst into tears. She is sexually promiscuous, sells her body for money, has a major cocaine addiction, and laughs when Bobby blows Deputy Howard's head open, yet her night prowling brings her no pleasure or solace. So, as her friend Donna entreats, "*Why* do you do it?"

In Jennifer Lynch's book, *The Secret Diary of Laura Palmer*, young Laura often hears BOB's disembodied voice like her own private cult leader giving her affirmations from hell. "I'VE BEEN HERE FOR YEARS AND YEARS, YOUR BELIEF DOESN'T MEAN A THING. YOUR OPINION IS NOTHING. THINNK ABOUT IT. LOOK AT YOUR LIFE. YOU GO FUCKING AROUND WITH PEOPLE. DRUGS ALL THE TIME. YOU'LL BE SIXTEEN SOON. YOUR LIFE IS SHIT AND YOU'RE NOT EVEN SIXTEEN YET. LOOK IN THE MIRROR AND SEE FOR YOURSELF. YOU ARE NOTHING."[70] Ironically, Laura has devolved into this degraded state by trying to elude BOB, reasoning that it was her sweet innocence that first attracted the long-haired invader through her bedroom window, so if she acts like a depraved slut, he will leave her alone. To her despair and horror, she learns that she can't loosen his grip on her no matter what she does, and that the manipulative BOB thrives on toying with her autonomous sense of self and personal volition as "an experiment."[71]

In his film, Lynch characteristically avoids the detailed verbal sparring matches between BOB and Laura that Jennifer Lynch includes in her book, preferring to keep his villain and heroine's minimal exchanges on the primal level of an animalistic predator stalking his prey: "He wants to be me or he'll kill me." By not spelling out the motivation for Laura's bad-girl behavior, Lynch frees us to hypothesize that BOB's intrusion into her life at a crucial stage of her psycho-sexual development has twisted her sense of identity so that she feels unworthy of leading a normal, wholesome life, and that the dark, shadow side of her nature is her true self. She can be kind and giving and loving to those around her, but she feels she doesn't deserve the same in return and she uses her sexuality to manipulate and gain power over others. If BOB wants to be her, then she must already be BOB-like. She feels that her angels have all gone away at the same time that she has turned away from them. The girl who feels "long gone" parties until dawn with a fellow night-denizen who calls himself "The Great Went," as in Go all the way to death; a fellow whose motto is "There's no tomorrow."

As nihilism and despair make Laura's world a permanent midnight, she becomes fictional kin to *Blue Velvet*'s Dorothy, another victim of deeply wounding sexual-emotional abuse. In the earlier film Kyle MacLachlan's Jeffrey strove to keep Dorothy from embracing death, and in *Fire Walk With Me* his Agent Cooper, appearing in Laura's dream, warns her not to take the ring that's linked to Teresa Banks' murder and Agent Chet Desmond's disappearance. Lynch, through his alter ego MacLachlan, again shows his urge to protect victimized women. And he again illustrates the fluid nature of space and time in *Twin Peaks*, for the Cooper that Laura sees is from the future, the "good Dale" who's trapped in the Red Room, while his dark self provides the TV series with its final, chilling images (BOB grinning back at him in the mirror). Jeffrey was able to prevent Dorothy from losing her mortal life, but Cooper can't stop Laura's death. Lynch as he did with Henry in *Eraserhead* and *The Elephant Man*'s John Merrick, has a higher destination in mind for Laura, a rewarding realm beyond our temporal world that she, like Henry and Merrick, can only reach through the portal of death. In her dream, Laura quakes with fear when the ring pops into her hand for a moment, but her journey toward spiritual fulfillment has already begun.

Hungry BOB, with his ability to get inside your head and poison your house, is the force of willful control that Lynch fears, and that some of the director's characters resist unto death. Poor Leland Palmer has yielded his psyche to BOB, and actor Ray Wise shows the inhabiting entity's shadowy presence creeping into Leland's pleasant face with superb subtly. One afternoon Laura encounters BOB in her bedroom tampering with her diary, and then sees Leland emerge from the Palmer house. Her conscious mind panics and tries to deny the thought that BOB and her father are one and the same, but her being begins to absorb this terrible possibility. Laura at this moment is an interesting contrast to *Wild at Heart*'s Lula, who never gained the conscious realization that her mother killed her father. Like Agent Cooper, Laura's soul moves her to want to see and to know, and when BOB next comes through her window at night, she focuses her mind while he has intercourse with her and furiously demands, "Who *are* you?" And, as BOB's grunting face fleetingly transforms into Leland's, her most devastating suspicion is confirmed. Lynch includes a few precious moments of loving tenderness between Leland and Laura in the film, thus poignantly giving us a measure of how much emotional treasure BOB has stolen from the Palmer family. Ray Wise and Sheryl Lee deserve surpassing praise for their rich, complex, and emotionally draining incarnations of Leland and Laura. Every moment of their relationship is heartfelt, and indeed Wise for months carried Lee's photograph in his wallet with the pictures of his own family.

The don't-fence-me-in dynamic of *Wild at Heart* propelled Lula away from her dictatorial mother and out onto the road, where she found her maturing sense of self, sexuality, and love while traveling with Sailor. Laura tries to define her identity apart from her father by seeking the solace of friends, lovers, and drugs, but Leland is also BOB, and BOB is everywhere. Taking a road trip away from Twin Peaks would only bring her to the same dead end. Like *Eraserhead*'s Henry and *The Elephant Man*'s John Merrick, she must find physical escape and spiritual deliverance close to home.

A true friend with a heroic sense of loyalty, Laura does her utmost to keep the darkness that's engulfing her from tainting and endangering those she loves, such as Donna, James, and Harold Smith, the keeper of her secret diary. Lynch has—either consciously or not—put Laura in a position that, with poetic resonance, echoes the mythic stance of Tibetan Buddhist nuns who, in ancient tales, personally engaged and grappled with devouring demons in order to keep the world safe from harm. However, Laura is not a sacrificial lamb with a martyr complex. Her primal need is to save herself from BOB, and to do so she must die. Like Henry, she must follow a trail of subconscious promptings, reading her dreams and the clues in the wind, and finally committing an act that obliterates her temporal self. Henry picked up scissors and killed his baby, and Laura slides that fateful ring onto her finger.

A derelict train car that no longer travels is Laura's point of departure for her journey beyond death. As the air crackles with blue electricity, the bound Ronette Pulaski is freed when she prays for deliverance and her guardian angel appears. Laura feels she's in an abject state that's unworthy of prayerful help: she's seen her guardian angel vanish from her bedroom picture, and the angelic figure of roadhouse singer Julee Cruise asks in her song, "Why did you turn away from me?" Laura has fought to keep BOB from invading her psyche, and in the train car she glimpses what it would be like if she lost the battle when she sees the fiend glowering back at her from a mirror. This horrifying vision gives her the final jolt of courage she needs to leap into the unknown, and she slips on the ring.

Lynch, rather than simply having Leland be BOB's unwitting pawn at this climatic moment, makes him tragically semi-conscious of the horror he is about to perpetrate, as he matches his daughter's screams with one of his own: "Don't make me do this!" Lynch visualizes Laura's murder as an abstraction in which we see short-duration images separated by flashes of light and blackness: Leland thrusting a knife, BOB thrusting a knife, a passage of various views of Laura's pale face spurting blood from her mouth, her golden broken-heart necklace, her face finally not moving. This last shot, which Lynch frames upside-down, with her forehead at the bottom of the frame and chin at the top, recalls a shot he composed for his 1968 film *The Alphabet*. In that student work, he had positioned a woman's face in the same topsy-turvy way and added a false nose on her chin to make it look like the bottom of her face was actually the top, as if to say, "Appearances can be deceiving." In the twenty-four years sine *The Alphabet*, Lynch had not composed a close-up of an inverted face until he filmed Laura, whose dead face paradoxically hides the truth of her deathlessness.

After killing Laura, BOB propels Leland into the extra-dimensional realm of the Red Room, where he's confronted by the only entity he fears: Mike, his former partner in crime. After moving Leland's body to bow respectively to Mike, then emerges from his host and the two stand facing Mike and the little Man From Another Place. When Mike had decided to spurn BOB and live on the side of good, he took off his arm, which was tattooed with the powerfully evil symbol that's still inscribed on BOB's arm and which adorns the ring that Laura chose to wear. Mike's discarded arm was transformed into the Man From Another Place, who can still exhibit a malevolent streak. But now Mike and his "arm" speak in unison, demanding that BOB give back the sacramental corn ("garmonbozia") he stole. Garmonbozia also means "pain and suffering," some of BOB's choicest food, so giving it up is true punishment for the demonic entity. BOB accomplishes Mike's demand by touching Leland's shirt, which is stained red from the bloody murder-scene towels he stuffed inside it. BOB then pivots his hand away from Leland and, with a throwing-away gesture, splatters Laura's blood onto the zig-zag-patterned floor.

BOB, one of the scariest fictional manifestations of evil to be portrayed in late-twentieth-century culture, has been, at least for the moment, subdued—though he's certainly back at full power to wreak havoc in the TV series that's still to come in some alternate time stream. Still, in our time frame, this movie comes after the series, and its conclusion allows us to depart the world of *Twin Peaks* in a glow of exaltation. In counterpoint to the hours of fear, pain, sadness, and dread we have lived through in the *Twin Peaks* experience, Lynch leaves us with the feeling that a hard-won measure of justice had been attained. As the Man From Another Place, following the proper ritualistic protocol of his realm, lovingly sucks up the golden garmonbozia corn between his full lips, we see the face of the monkey that was hiding behind the mask in Philip Jeffries' recollection-vision of his harrowing encounter with the extra-dimensional denizens. The mask is now gone, and the simian face smiles slightly and softly says, "Judy." Throughout his career Lynch has linked animalism with evil, and in the Middle Ages the monkey was a symbol of the devil, heresy, lust, vice, and paganism. The simian was related to the Fall of Man and represented a distorted, debased aspect of humankind. And in Lynch's dear *The Wizard of Oz*, menacing flying monkeys abducted Dorothy and her friends and delivered them to the Wicked Witch. In Jeffries' vision, the monkey behind the mask suggested BOB, with his ravenous animal appetites, hiding within Leland. But now the garmonbozia has been returned and consumed, Laura's burden of pain and sorrow has been lifted, and the face of animalistic energy wears a benign expression and speaks the name ("Judy") of she who is perhaps the ultimate authority/spiritual figure in this dimension. Is BOB a bad boy who eternally disobeys a maternal goddess? Or is it just that Lynch knows that when, in his beloved *The Wizard of Oz*, one of the little Munchkin women comes up to Dorothy (Judy Garland), she looks at Garland and says, "Judy" by mistake.

Lynch maximizes the evocative power of his *Twin Peaks* lore by not spelling out its details too clearly. Fantasist writer-director Clive Barker has emphasized that in his *Hellraiser* films he doesn't tell the audience where the monstrous villains, the Cenobites, come from: There's a mythology, a cosmos, that we only glimpse. As Lynch says, "it leaves you room to dream."[72]

At any rate, BOB will soon be back in potently evil form, riding the black wind of night, manipulating Leland like a puppet, making him kill Maddy, then making Leland smash his own head to death, extracting Windom Earle's soul, and guiding the dark aspect of Agent Cooper into an unsuspecting world. But Laura will not be his. As the Roman philosopher Seneca (4 B.C. –65 A.D.) said, "He who learns how to die unlearns slavery."[73] Defying the forces that would control her soul, Laura had courageously chosen her own spiritual path—but where does it lead?

The iconic image of the plastic wrapping being pulled aside to reveal Laura's cold, dead blue face with its glittering grain of sand in the "third eye" position of the forehead melds with a familiar zigzag-patterned floor and ruddy curtains, and we find ourselves in the Red Room, where a more grown-up-looking Laura wearing a long black dress sits in a comfortable chair. Standing beside her, his hand on her shoulder, is Dale Cooper the Good. She has a blank, lost look, but as blue-white light illuminates her face and draws her gaze, a smile begins to form, mirroring Cooper's beneficent smile. With a childlike expression of wonder, Laura receives all the grace and love of the universe, and she sees the white-winged guardian angel that had faded from her bedroom picture now, magnificently, floating in the dark air above her. Throughout the film, she has wept with shame, loneliness, fear, and despair, but now, for the first time, she cries tears of joy and laughs as though she would laugh forever.

The felicitous meeting of Laura and Cooper in the Red Room has a beautiful poetic resonance. The abject victim/courageous heroine and the questing detective, both longing to *see*, have followed their dreams, intuitions, and deeply felt impulses and reached this point together. The translucent walls of the Red Room are like the enclosing membranes of a heart, and in this ruddy chamber Laura sees both Cooper, her loving protector, and her winged female angel, and Cooper watches Laura his dark muse and dream lover finally find the light. Will they gaze on until the next heartbeat, or as long as the world spins? These are Blue Rose questions.

This moment, which gloriously culminates David Lynch's *Twin Peaks* saga and perfectly balances his craving for both knowledge and mystery, is one of the director's most magnificent achievements. Surely, he felt, fans of the series would empathize with their dear Laura's last seven days of degradation and abuse and glory in her well-earned spiritual triumph. And *Twin Peaks* novices would be intrigued by this in-depth psychological exploration of an incest-infested home and be swept up in the romance of all the lowdown nightlife, the evocative dream sequences, the surreal Red Room, and the one who lurks in the dark woods and behind the eyes of Leland Palmer. How much more wrong could David Lynch be?

9

HEAD LIKE A HOUSE ON FIRE

1992–1997
(*Lost Highway*)

In mid-to-late 1990, when *Twin Peaks* had the world fascinated and David Lynch appeared on the cover of *Time* magazine as the "Czar of Bizarre,"[1] his creative partner, Mark Frost, observed that the rest of us had finally caught up with Lynch's quirky sensibility and were in sync with it. However, the hostile and indifferent responses to the director's 1992 film *Twin Peaks: Fire Walk With Me* showed just how quickly the majority of Lynch watchers could change direction and revile and reject his deeply felt artistry.

In our flavor-of-the-month culture, home of the incredibly shrinking attention span, our ears are filled with blaring sound bites, our eyes and brains made dizzy by assaultive images edited at quantum speed. We build up celebrities, worship them, then reject them in record time. By the summer of 1992, Lynch was no longer "a hot topic" in the public mind, but it was nonetheless shocking that *Time*, *Newsweek*, and the popular TV film-review show *Siskel and Ebert at the Movies* did not deign to say one word about Lynch's new film.

Some critics, however, did have plenty to say, the majority of which was resoundingly negative. Roger Ebert, writing about *Fire Walk With Me* after seeing it at Cannes, called it a "shockingly bad film, simple-minded and scornful of the audience."[2] *People* magazine's Tom Gliatto characterized it as "a nauseating bucket of slop."[3] *Interview* viewed it as "an ill-structured, lurid, shock-crazy prequel to a once-popular saga. This is torture."[4] *Entertainment Weekly*'s Owen Gleiberman judged the movie to be "a true folly—almost nothing in it adds up."[5] And the esteemed Vincent Canby of the *New York Times* added it up thusly: "It's not the worst movie ever made; it just seems to be."[6] Some reviewers, such as David Baron of New Orleans' *The Times-Picayune*, attacked Lynch as fervently as they did his film: "This is the latest lurid monstrosity by the nation's most repellant director. It is as gratuitous as it is ugly,"[7] containing "sophomoric insights"[8] that reveal only "the banality of Lynch's vision."[9]

Al Strobel, who plays BOB's one-armed former consort, Mike, has an eloquent response to the attack-dog critics. "*Twin Peaks: Fire Walk With Me* is hard to look at if you're not prepared to look at a work of art. It's like going to a gallery and seeing extremely expressionistic paintings when you were expecting English landscapes. This was more a piece of art than a movie. The juxtaposition of horror and beauty has an elevating sense that brings out things in your mind and in your heart and in your soul like a very fine piece of art does. The critics didn't see that, and that makes me angry."[10]

No one in our Christian-majority society even gave Lynch credit for having a biblical angel figure prominently in his film, as he presciently anticipated the angel-adoring pop-culture trend that culminated in the Broadway hit *Angels in America*, TV's *Touched By An Angel*, and millions of white-winged commercial items. Lynch's Presbyterian roots still influence his art, despite his chapter-and-verse embrace of Hinduism and the Hinduistic endings of his original *Dune* script and unproduced *Ronnie Rocket* screenplay. Like many baby boomers, Lynch takes spiritual nourishment from both Western and Eastern traditions.

Compared to the dearth of TV coverage that has greeted Lynch's post–*Twin Peaks: Fire Walk With Me* films, it's amazing to see the *hours* that *Entertainment Tonight*, CNN, and MTV devoted to *Fire* just before it was released. Lynch, Dana Ashbrook, Sheryl Lee, and James Marshall went on TV talk shows separately to generate positive buzz for the film, and Lynch and Kyle MacLachlan were interviewed together on *Good Morning America*. This joint appearance of the director and his cinematic alter ego made Lynch fans buzz, because MacLachlan's strangely minimal participation in the movie spawned the idea that there was some creative discord, even a rift, between the two old friendly collaborators. But everything seemed harmonious as Lynch and MacLachlan sat side-by-side in a Hollywood café having pie and coffee and fielding *Good Morning America*'s questions, beaming their *Twin Peaks*-is-still-cool message out to as many million viewers as used to see their show. The interviewer, a blonde woman named Chantal, noted that there was a lot of coffee and pie in the world of *Twin Peaks*. Lynch replied in classic, deadly serious form: "In the Northwest where I grew up, coffee is extremely important. And pie is extremely important. And people have pie and coffee, sometimes together."[11] After chuckling at Lynch's furrowed-brow earnestness, Chantal asked if he was ready to take a lot of heat for the sexual violence in his film, and he replied, "I live in an oven, that's how much heat I'm going to take,"[12] to which MacLachlan responded with a sympathetic laugh. As she concluded the interview, Chantal noted that "You two have such a great relationship: do you finish each other's sentences?"[13] Lynch and MacLachlan looked into each other's eyes, and the quick-witted Lynch said, "Yes . . ."[14] expecting MacLachlan to complete the sentence with "we do." But MacLachlan didn't get it, and said, "I think we did from the start."[15] Lynch prompted him again, "Yes we."[16] MacLachlan still didn't supply the "do," and Lynch said, "He's rusty; I haven't seen him in awhile."[17]

Eight years later MacLachlan spoke about why he'd been relatively absent from Lynch's world in the early 1990s. Like others in the *Twin Peaks* TV-cast family, MacLachlan felt "abandoned"[18] when Lynch didn't participate as fully in the second season of the show as he did in the first. "So I was fairly resentful when the film, *Twin Peaks: Fire Walk With Me*, came around. I wanted to have a meaningful discussion about some of the scenes, and David was unwilling to do that, so I was not in those scenes; Chris Isaak was in there instead of me."[19] And today MacLachlan's assessment of the film is less than glowing: "It was very violent and disturbing in a way that the show hadn't been. I was, 'Oh, can't we go back to the way it was when the show started,' but David wanted to take things further, and I was resisting that. It was just too in-your-face."[20] MacLachlan has said he "really abused"[21] his relationship with Lynch, but the director still feels the actor, who has contributed so much to some of Lynch's best work, is "a really great person"[22] and has welcomed him to his home. And in June 2004, MacLachlan, his hair now as gray as Agent Cooper's in *Twin Peaks'* "twenty-five-years-later" passages, grinned and waved as he drove past the small Washington State villages where the show originated, on his way to his Yakima hometown to surprise his dad on Father's Day.

Bad reviews can't sink a film that moviegoers want to see, but even *Twin Peaks* fans didn't flock to *Fire Walk With Me*, except in Japan and France, where it was a minor hit for a short time, though not long enough to make much money. An in-depth exploration of Laura Palmer's darkness was not the movie that the world was waiting for or wanting to see. *Twin Peaks: Fire Walk With Me* generated as much negative energy as *Dune* did, and Lynch had to face the fact that with this film viewers were rejecting his pure vision, not a *Dune* that was another writer's original idea and which had been grievously compromised and shortened by the De Laurentiis family.

In the summer of 1992, Lynch received a second critical and audience drubbing for his and Mark Frost's ABC TV series *On the Air*. Premiering in June, this was a comedy that chronicled, according to Lynch, the wacky trials and tribulations of "a fourth- or fifth-rate"[23] 1950s New York TV network (Zoblotnick Broadcasting Company) trying to put on a weekly variety program, *The Lester Guy Show*. Since the 1950s was the age of live TV broadcasting, many unexpected, absurdly humorous happenings foil the best-laid plans of ZBC president Buddy Budwaller (Miguel Ferrer, *Twin Peaks*' acid-tongued FBI forensics wizard, Albert Rosenfield). He must cope with nervous, ineffectual producer McGonigle (Marvin Kaplan) and bumbling director Gochktck (David L. Lander), nephew of ZBC owner Zoblotnick (Sydney Lassick), who, with his uncle, speaks with a barely intelligible eastern European accent ("scream" sounds like "scram") that has to be translated and subtitled. Crossing over from the world of *Twin Peaks* to join the new Lynch/Frost production were writers Robert Engels and Scott Frost and directors Lesli Linka Glatter and Jonathan Sanger (producer of *The Elephant Man*). Lynch also brought in his longtime friend, and early painting buddy, set designer, director, and former brother-in-law, Jack Fisk. Fisk filmed episodes 3 and 7 of *On the Air*, but viewers only got to see 3, since ABC shifted the series from Wednesday night to Saturday (the graveyard evening that helped kill *Twin Peaks*) and only broadcast three episodes (1, 3, and 5) of the seven installments that Lynch/Frost filmed.

As with *Twin Peaks*, ABC lost faith in the latest Lynch/Frost product after an initial burst of high enthusiasm, though with *On the Air* the network's attitude shift happened at relatively lightning speed.

ABC committed to *On the Air* at the moment of the *Twin Peaks* cycle in which the zeitgeist was buzzing about the enchanting, groundbreaking show and its mastermind creators. The network was happy to give Lynch and Frost a new stage on which to enact their imaginative and profitable visions. But by the time *On the Air* was ready to hit the air the *Twin Peaks* craze was dead, the show had been cancelled, and the advance word from the May 1992 Cannes Film Festival was that Lynch's *Twin Peaks: Fire Walk With Me* was a stillborn atrocity.

Nonetheless, buoyed by positive reviews from *TV Guide* and *Variety*, ABC debuted *On the Air* with an episode written by Lynch and Frost and directed by Lynch. In a half hour dense with frenetic events and slapstick behavior, the director explored some familiar themes in a comic context. In his own life, Lynch the longtime visual artist warmed up gradually to the process of communicating verbally, and in his fictions he often portrays the difficulty people have in understanding each other and correctly comprehending information. There is a flurry of words in the air at the Zoblotnick Broadcasting Company, but much confusion. Most people in the studio can't follow what the thickly accented director Gochktck says, and sweet, slow-on-the-uptake Betty (Marla Rubinoff), Lester Guy's co-star, speaks non sequiturs as her brain grasps only fragments of concepts while she strains to see the whole picture.

In past works, Lynch has often shown chaos intruding into a person's home and head, and as *The Lester Guy Show* enacts a domestic scene for the live cameras, it happens again. The little play is supposed to show Betty, playing a married woman, ironing clothes in her kitchen, and the then greeting her secret lover, played by Lester Guy (Ian Buchanan, *Twin Peaks'* haberdasher Dick Tremayne), at the window. They are surprised by Betty's enraged husband, who bursts into the room and shoots Guy, who then dies at Betty's feet while she mourns, "Oh, I loved him so!" In episode 1, Lynch employs the same narrative dynamic he used at the beginning of *Blue Velvet*, in which he first showed us a perfect world and then revealed everything that could go wrong with it. *The Lester Guy Show*'s domestic scene played smoothly in rehearsal, but when the future of the underdog network depends on it and the show is being performed live, everything falls apart.

Framing the opening, show-within-the-show image with the theatrical curtains he loves, Lynch shows us smiling Betty in her all-white kitchen, recalling the smiling-housewife homey tableaus that Lynch saw in 1950s magazine as a child, and in his own family's kitchen. Young Lynch had longed for some force or occurrence to disrupt the wholesome sameness of his domestic life, and in *On the Air*, as he's done in most of his fictions, he introduces such an element. Beyond foregrounded Betty, deep in the scene, we see an older man who shouldn't be there, squatting with his back against the kitchen cabinets. We laugh, because the man is an unexpected, incongruous factor juxtaposed with the unsuspecting Betty, who's blithely smiling to the cameras and doesn't know the man is behind her. The image yields humor, but it is also disturbingly Lynchian: The man, a distressed look on his face, his aged body frozen in a strange position, his purpose a mystery, contributes a suspended moment of disquieting surrealism.

The fellow turns out to be a prop man whose suspenders are caught in a cabinet door, and when he tries to run out of the scene the rubberband-like straps stretch and spring him through the air like a cartoon character.

This action causes a fluffy white dog to fly through the air and Lester Guy, for some reason hanging upside-down from a rope tied around his ankles, to suddenly swing into the center of the tableau instead of appearing at the window to talk to Betty. Swaying back and forth in his inverted position, Guy dispiritedly mouths his lines ("Our brief moment of happiness is over") as the audio engineer miscues a cacophony of discordant sounds. This is all hilariously funny, but as half the stage lights go out and the upside-down Lester Guy becomes an eerie black shape and Betty's husband fires his gun again and again, Lynch gives the tableau a sinister edge that blends Dadaist theater of the absurd with film noir. Earlier the director had evoked the atmospherics of noir as Guy opened his show playing the role of a lonely nocturnal stroller traversing a night-city backdrop accompanied by the midnight-saxophone sound of an Angelo Badalamenti theme. This poetic-mood moment is a touch of pure Lynchness, as is the first thing we see in *On the Air's* opening credits: a neon sign representing flashing lightning bolts of electricity pulsing against the deep darkness of a cosmic star field.

Another Lynchian passage occurs early in the kitchen scene when the timing's all wrong and poor Betty is left with minutes of dead air to fill. Grown-up Betty has the kind of childlike sensitivity and capacity for wonder that Lynch admires; her sweetness of soul reminds us of John Merrick in *The Elephant Man*. Director Gochktck, faced with the prospect of dim-bulb Betty having to wing it, pronounces the situation "A nightmare." But she, like other of Lynch's angelic women, faces adversity with grace and wisdom. Invoking her mother, as Merrick did, she pulls out her good-luck music box and sings a schoolyard-simple song that recalls the little ditty of beneficence and happy promise that the Lady in the Radiator sang to beleaguered Henry in *Eraserhead*. As Betty's music box tinkles and her words ring out ("The bird in the tree / It sings merrily / With a tweedle dee for you / A tweedle dee for me"), Lynch links her song with the lighting bolt sign flashing against the night sky, the red lights on the ZBC phone bank happily lighting up, and old grannies at home smiling dearly, as though a benign force was making the whole world hum. Of course, a few seconds later, Lester Guy swings into the scene upside down and chaos continues to reign at the ZBC studio. Everyone, from the network president to the producer and director, to the soundman and Lester Guy himself, thinks the show was an absolute disaster. Their willful attempts to control reality and shape it to their liking have failed miserably; they are defeated and depressed. But Betty, with her pure, childlike vision, her ability to follow her intuition and ride the wild wave of spontaneous occurrence, sees the evening differently: "That was fun!" This is certainly the view of Lynch and Frost and also, it turns out, that of ZBC owner Zoblotnick, whose necessarily subtitled words are piped through the studio, and end episode 1: "WE HAVE A HIT!"

The ZBC may have inadvertently created a crowd-pleaser, but ABC, alarmed by the underwhelming ratings performance of *On the Air*'s first episode, decided to show less than half of the installments that Lynch/Frost had produced. Thankfully, all seven episodes are available on tape and disc, and show the program following the perfect-rehearsal/disastrous-broadcast dynamic set up in episode 1. The emotional-dramatic thread linking the weekly explosions of physical comedy is Lester Guy's jealousy of Betty, who becomes America's TV sweetheart overnight. Guy, an effete, egotistical, washed-up, minor movie star who pompously puts on grand airs, resents the fact that Betty is showered with love and acclaim for just being her own simple self. Surely, it is unfair, unjust, that his protean talents and sophisticated charm are not recognized and celebrated. Guy is English, so once again in American fiction, an elitist foreigner has been trumped by a homegrown innocent. But Guy is a trouper, and he mounts various schemes to sabotage Betty's rise to stardom and remain the sovereign monarch of his own show. However, in the moralistic world of *On the Air*, Guy is born to lose, and his plans (infiltrating Betty's dinner with Mr. Zoblotnick, rigging a quiz show on which she appears, ruining her singing with a Voice Disintegrator) suffer humorous reversals of fortune that cast him as the fall guy.

The universe of *On the Air* is a cartoonish, make-believe place, where a stagehand can fall from a high platform, dust himself off, and continue his business, and where one answered phone makes a quacking sound and another, which has an angry boss on the other end of the line, shoots flames. The burning air bursting from the receiver has no metaphysical *Fire Walk With Me* significance, just as the show's characters naturally lack the resonant depths of Agent Cooper, Laura, Leland, and BOB. Still, the power of Lynch's aesthetic is so strong and transferable that seeing Miguel Ferrer as Buddy Budwaller (whose verbally abusive manner easily reminds us of Ferrer's Albert Rosenfield on *Twin Peaks*) holding a phone that's flaming makes part of our brain think, "Oh my god! BOB's calling!"

Throughout the seven installments of *On the Air*, no matter who wrote or directed them, there are flashes of Lynch's sensibility. Characters on the show love (and sometimes nervously spill) coffee, and chew Chiclets gum (perhaps this is the gum that *Twin Peaks*' Man From Another Place tells Cooper is going to "come back in style"). A woman traumatized by being on TV has a seizure in which she repeats "I forgot my purse; I forgot my purse," recalling dying car accident victim Sherilyn Fenn in *Wild at Heart* ("My purse is gone; my purse is gone"). Fenn, like a number of Lynch's female victims, had blood in and around her mouth; as *The Lester Guy Show*'s jittery makeup man tries to apply Betty's lipstick before the big premiere, he gives her mouth area a similar red-stained look. The lipstick that crazily strays beyond its proper bounds also reminds us of madwoman Marietta's lipstick face-painting fit in *Wild at Heart*. In one episode Betty, carrying a cloth sack, walks among a group of white ducks and says, "Who wants corn?," recalling us of the corn manna that *Fire Walk With Me*'s entities BOB and Mike revere. And, also recalling Lynch's *Twin Peaks* film, we see Betty wearing a white-winged angel costume, which underscores her role as a secular agent of goodness. Episode 6 finds Budwaller making a disparaging remark about guest magician the Great Presidio, whose grasp on reality seems tenuous, and whose words would fit perfectly in a film Lynch hadn't even written yet (1997's *Lost Highway*): "As far as I can ascertain, he thinks he's an auto mechanic." Presidio makes us think of BOB when he voices his fear of "a shadow walking the earth" and "the dog of transformation." Presidio appears to be a charlatan, but to everyone's surprise, he's a true wizard who makes Lester Guy vanish and reappear in Akron, Ohio, where the episode ends with the repeating industrial-pounding sound of *Eraserhead*.

Episode 7, co-written by Lynch with Robert Engels, is the most thematically interesting of the series, and gives *On the Air* a felicitous conclusion. By now, we know that Lynch loves the 1950s (specifically, he would like to live in 1956) and that he's attracted by the decade's melding of two polar qualities: the square and the hip, Eisenhower and Elvis, Norman Rockwell and Jackson Pollack, the Eagle Scout and the Northwest Surrealist. We recall the artist's 1950s childhood when, nestled within a safe and nurturing family and a reassuringly stable sense of the world at large, he yearned for a counterbalancing power of disruptive wildness to manifest itself. Experiencing a broader spectrum of life as he grew up, Lynch learned that forces of transformation, disintegration, violence, and pain do dwell inside places and people. A tension between a secure status quo and the impulse to violate boundaries and limitations vitalizes Lynch's creative expressions and shapes the way he likes to live: relaxed, yet alert within a supporting framework of ritualized habits and controlled occurrences, from which he can launch his consciousness to the farthest reaches of imagination and subconscious inspiration.

The Surrealists of the early twentieth century opened up this fertile artistic territory, listening to their inner voices and seeing with their mind's eye. In episode 7 of *On the Air* Lynch reverently evokes the names Man Ray and Marcel Duchamp, avant-gardists with whom he is "very happy to be a fellow traveler."[24] There's plenty of chaos-producing transgressive energy coursing through the series' first six episodes, but it's all generated by the establishment culture of which *The Lester Guy Show* and the ZBC network are a part. *On the Air*'s last installment brings in something new: a beatnik counterculture element that introduces the spirit of art—and being—without limits.

Into the studio comes a personification of Lynchian mystery dressed in a black leotard, the Woman With No Name (surely she is full of secrets). In her clothing of seamless night, she is clearly a member of 1950s Beat culture, but she also evokes the image of Irma Vep, the feline nocturnal criminal in French director Louis Feuillade's landmark serial *Les Vampires* (1915–1916), who, with her black tights and brazen villainy, thrilled and inspired the young Surrealists.

The Woman With No Name performs her uninhibited free-form dance to the untamed squawks and wails of the jazz group The Void, who are like abstract expressionist artists aggressively applying sounds instead of paint. Especially frenzied is the playing of the saxophonist, who, along with that earlier episode reference to an auto mechanic, foreshadows two of *Lost Highway*'s (1997) main characters.

This installment of *On the Air* is the only one with a strain of true darkness, and contains the sole passage of sinister music that Badalamenti wrote for the show, which accompanies the inventor of the Voice Disintegrator's boast that his machine could "start World War III in a matter of hours" by scrambling communications at the United Nations building. Lester Guy, of course, plans to use the infernal machine to obliterate Betty's sweet singing and shoot down her rising star. (We note that in a 1966 episode of TV's *Batman*, a show familiar to *On the Air*'s baby boomer creators, Catwoman wreaks havoc with her "Voice Eraser"[25] machine.) This episode also reveals that hard-to-understand director Gochktck has a shoe fetish, and he thinks that the "beatnik" woman dancer is actually a "bootmaker," so he falls head-over-heels for her. The menacing Voice Disintegrator and Gochtck's kinky sexuality establish a decidedly Lynchian tone, to which the director adds a coffee ritual (a white and an African American technician keep calling each other "my good friend" as they obsess over their java: "It's very fresh!"), some wood (Lester Guy hides a microphone in a wooden planing tool to record Betty's voice), and an anxious and despondent heroine (Betty is distressed because she can't remember her mother's first name).

Present in every episode, and introduced on the premiere that Lynch directed and co-wrote, is a character that personifies Lynch's fascination for altered states of perception and consciousness. Blinky (Tracey Walters) the soundman has a condition called Bozeman's Simplex that makes his visual field 25.62 times wider than ours. In our realm, he's virtually blind and he navigates by touch and the help of his friends. But, beginning with episode 1, Lynch set the precedent of giving us a momentary peek at the world through Blinky's extraordinary eyes. What we saw were a toy Santa Claus figure, a fuzzy toy dog, and a female doll. Blinky is an adult studio technician, not a toy salesman, so these images indicate the childlike innocence of his inner nature. The Santa Claus image reminds us of *Wild at Heart* Lula's disturbed cousin Dell (Crispin Glover), who we saw wearing a Santa suit all year round and bemoaning the fact that "trust and the spirit of Christmas" are being destroyed by aliens from outer space. For Lynch, trust, love, the Christmas spirit, and the sincere goodness of a child's viewpoint, are defenses against devouring forces outside and within us.

The impoverished art student who playfully dangled paper clips and colored bits of paper over his daughter Jennifer's crib matured into an artist who reveres the freshness and wonder of the child's world. Lynch began *Blue Velvet* with the viewpoint of a little person with young eyes looking up at swaying flowers and a white picket fence, in *Lost Highway* twenty-year-old Pete gazes over his backyard fence at a child's wading pool and rubber duck, and *The Straight Story*'s (1999) middle-aged Rose regards a child's pale rubber ball rolling down the sidewalk outside her window as night falls. The "child things"[26] in Lynch's work don't always project a sunny mood, but usually they connote a sense of joy and unpolluted promise, as does the ten seconds of stop-motion animation the director crafted for a 1991 Japanese TV program about *Twin Peaks*. This snippet of film, which has never been shown in the United States, marks Lynch's first return to animation since the days of *Six Figures Getting Sick* (1967; moving drawings), *The Alphabet* (1968; drawings and live action), and *Eraserhead*'s (1976) perky live-action worm. The Japanese segment shows familiar *Twin Peaks* touchstones (a piece of pie, a cup of coffee, a donut, two pine cones, Cooper's mini tape recorder) happily circling around on a Double R Diner table top, while red and green Christmas ball ornaments dangle and dance above, with the parade of objects being accompanied by an orchestration of *Twin Peaks* music that includes jingling sleigh bells. The playful spirit of benevolent fellowship that informs Lynch's gesture toward his Japanese fans also infuses his conclusion of *On the Air*.

Viewing the show's first six episodes, we've laughed at the characters' vanities, egomaniacal rants, venal schemes, general foibles, shortcomings, and penchant for making big mistakes, and have recognized them as our own. As he did in *Wild at Heart*, Lynch is showing the mass of humanity to be an unruly, messy, and confused lot, but human nonetheless. He has spoken of the way art-making helps one shape the chaos of life into a manageable form, and he illustrates his point in the finale of *On the Air*. As usual when *The Lester Guy Show* is broadcasting live, pandemonium reigns. Lester and Betty are dressed in 1920s flapper-era beach costumes for their big number, which fell apart when he tried to use the Voice Disintegrator on her and ended up reducing his own song to a croaking warble. Discombobulated Betty, still plagued by the fact that she can't recall her mother's name, stumbles onto the stage where The Woman With No Name is gyrating to wild saxophone sounds. Betty incongruously starts to sing her 1920s song, which involves the words "the good ship Queen Mary"—and she suddenly remembers that Mary is her mother's name. Betty's art has led her to the truth she's been seeking, and it's allowed Lynch to dramatically highlight the name of his lady love, Mary Sweeney, on national TV.

Betty and the beatnik (the square and the hip, the old-fashioned flapper-style entertainer and the cutting-edge performer) have shared Lynch's *On the Air* stage, and now he makes room for Gochktck to express his erotic fixation. *The Lester Guy Show* director, joined by ZBC owner Zoblotnick himself, zealously deposits armloads of shoes at the feet of the Woman With No Name as though bringing offerings to a goddess. Then, after Lynch thoroughly emphasizes Gotchtck and Zoblotnick's obsessive passion for footwear, Gotchktck declares his love for the "beatnik" ("bootmaker"). Then, while perennial loser Lester Guy is being consoled by his loving assistant and Betty is off calling her mother, Lynch leaves us with an egalitarian, everyone is included, Peaceable Kingdom finale. Labor and management, technicians and performers, all crowd onto *The Lester Guy Show* stage. Like children playing with their parents' over-sized footwear, they put their hands inside shoes and raise them high overhead, swaying in unison with the Woman With No Name's dance as the saxophone plays on into the night. Gochktck, his heart overflowing, signs off with a final, double-meaning pronouncement: "There's no business like shoe business!"

In *On the Air*, as he did with *Wild at Heart*, Lynch shows us how messy and unpredictable life can be, though here he conveys the message with goofy humor rather than torture, murder, sexual power plays, and fatal accidents. The show is a decidedly good-natured work that corrals the darkness of human nature within a comic context, and it once again allows Lynch to express his respect for feminine wisdom. When everything's going wrong in episode 1, golden-haired Betty saves the day with her sunny, a-song-can-solve-any problem philosophy, which recalls *Twin Peaks*' Gordon Cole's (played by Lynch) credo, "Let a smile be your umbrella." Betty's tradition-revering character is also linked to hearth, home, and family-loving values. The concluding episode's black-tressed Woman With No name incarnates the lunar feminine aspect, the undomesticated wild woman who, through the spontaneous movements of her body, expresses the flow of what she feels in the night air. Betty sang *On the Air*'s first love song, the Woman With No name leads its final dance, and so Lynch again honors both squaresville and the avant-garde, the twin poles of his worldview.

However, it seemed as though there were not that many people still interested in having David Lynch show them the world as he saw it. When ABC only broadcasted three, out-of-sequence episodes of *On the Air* and hastily ended the series, there was no protest movement calling for its return. Whereas when the network shifted *Twin Peaks*' schedule back and forth and put the show on hiatus for a time, they were flooded with angry phone calls, faxes, and letters. In the summer and fall of 1992, Lynch learned that the populace didn't care much for his TV show or his film (*Twin Peaks: Fire Walk With Me*), which was in theaters for just barely six weeks and lost an average of 60 percent more business each successive week of its release. The picture made just more than $4 million, which was less than its production cost and roughly equivalent to what a highly successful film would take in for a portion of a day's ticket sales on its opening weekend.

The general climate of Lynch's underappreciation spread still wider when, in his birthday month of January 1993, the pay-TV cable network HBO presented *Hotel Room*, the fledgling effort of Lynch's own production company, Asymmetrical. This three-story, ninety-minute omnibus was executive-produced by Lynch and his friend Monty Montgomery, who helped produce *Twin Peaks*, *Wild at Heart*, and *Industrial Symphony No. 1*. Lynch directed episodes 1 (*Tricks*) and 3 (*Blackout*), both written by *Wild at Heart* novelist Barry Gifford, while director James Signorelli staged author Jay McInerney's (*Bright Lights, Big City*) episode 2 story, *Getting Rid of Robert*. Each of the tales takes place in the same room of New York's Railroad Hotel during a different decade. *Hotel Room*'s introduction, narrated by Lynch's voice, defines the show's concept in mystical-poetic terms. Mankind "captured" the "space for the hotel room" from the undefined flow of time, "gave it shape, and passed through." And in passing through, people sometimes "found themselves brushing up against the secret names of truth." Lynch, in his art and life, believes that there are abstract, hidden truths that can be easier sensed and felt than verbally named. And if verities are too glaringly obvious, he will use the eraser of his imagination to keep them floating, powerful, magical: something you inhale from the air rather than read as a computer printout.

Tricks, set in 1969, is a challenging piece that requires that the viewer be an intuitive detective, as Lynch's works often do. Gifford's tale, in which Moe (Harry Dean Stanton) brings a prostitute (Glenne Headly) to the room, where he is later surprised by the arrival of his acquaintance Lou (Freddie Jones), fits perfectly with Lynch's characteristic preoccupations. From 1968's *The Alphabet* onward, the artist has shown a fascination for shifting realities and a fluid, boundary-crossing sense of human identity, the idea that *this* can also be *that*, that surface seeing can be misleading. In *The Alphabet* a voice tells us to "remember, you are dealing with the human form," while we read an image of a face (a mouth beneath a nose) that is actually a face upside-down, with a false nose positioned on its chin: Lynch addresses the human form by shaping it with his art. *The Grandmother*'s Boy sprouts a strange botanical form from his shoulders and, in *Eraserhead*, Henry's head pops off and is replaced by the wailing head of his burdensome mutant baby. *The Elephant Man*'s John Merrick is perceived to be a monstrous sideshow freak and a refined English gentleman, while his benefactor, Dr. Treves, sees himself as both a good and a bad man. *Dune*'s Paul Atreides feels himself to be a normal young man, but he is nonetheless inexorably becoming the messiah of an ancient prophecy. *Blue Velvet*'s Sandy isn't sure if Jeffrey is "a detective or a pervert" as the wholesome youth starts living life on the dark side of town. *Wild at Heart*'s Sailor and Lula hide their shadow sides from each other, and in *Industrial Symphony No. 1* a lovelorn woman (Laura Dern) grieves in a song cycle performed by her Dream Self (Julee Cruise). *Twin Peaks* shows masked identities, secret lives, and intruding supernatural dimensions to be as plentiful as fir trees. And in Lynch and Mark Frost's unproduced script *One Saliva Bubble*, four main characters and thirty-five Texans and Chinese acrobats find that their identities have accidentally taken up residence in each other's bodies. Lynch's hotel room signals that it too will be a place where one's self and sense of reality change and transform, for its number 603, which numerically adds up to nine—the nine that becomes six that becomes nine in the symbolic, eternal yin-yang cycle.

Tricks is the first project Lynch staged that he did not write or co-write, but since he co-executive produced and directed it, and hence endorsed every word that is spoken, I will refer to him as the one guiding our experience of the piece.

From the first moment that Moe and the prostitute Darlene walk into room 603, Lynch establishes the theme of doubled reality and identity. Moe calls her Arlene instead of Darlene, and he says things twice ("Okay, okay," "Right, right,"; "You, you need to use the bathroom?") He turns on a lamp with a two-stage motion, reaches for the room-service phone twice, and is disappointed that the room has single beds instead of a double.

Moe and Darlene are rather wan and grey characters, whose life force is at low ebb. Lynch has brilliantly visualized them and room 603 (with its grey walls, carpets, and bedspreads, and sparse, outmoded furniture) to evoke the mood of melancholy and inertia that permeates the paintings of American artist Edward Hopper (1883–1967), whom the director greatly admires. Hopper portrayed transient lives momentarily frozen in interiors and landscapes that connoted a lonely stasis, a spiritual limbo. The name "Railroad Hotel" is probably an homage to Hopper's famous painting *House by the Railroad*, and we note that room 603 displays photographs of speeding streamlined locomotives that comment ironically on the lives of hotel visitors who are going nowhere. We recall that Lynch, in *Eraserhead* and *Twin Peaks: Fire Walk With Me*, used the sound of a passing train to symbolize an elusive freedom for both Henry and Laura Palmer, who are trapped in a hellish existence.

Moe and Darlene are half-heartedly going through the motions of a john and a hooker about to transact business when a vital burst of energy knocks on the door. It's Moe's acquaintance Lou, whose arrival agitates and angers Moe, as he indicates in his double-speak way: "What's Lou doing here, doing here now?" Lou, looking like a vibrant, lascivious Santa Claus with his bushy white hair and beard, takes control of the room and walks all over Moe, drinking his bourbon and fucking the woman he's paid for, as Lynch focuses on Moe's woebegone face and we hear Lou's grunts of sexual exertion. A palpable tension between the two men remains in the air, but the balance of power shifts back and forth as they talk about Lou's late wife, Felicia, and Moe brings up the Hollywood star Martine Mustique who, in this multiple-identity matrix, was really named Rema De Duguide, and who played the role of the Great Voukovara.

We learn that Moe, Lou, and Darlene are vulnerable human beings who have each suffered losses, but the exact nature of Moe and Lou's decades-long antagonistic-yet-companionable relationship, with its strong half-defined emotions, remains tantalizingly mysterious. Everything the men say to each other seems to have an undefined double meaning, and Darlene says that they're playing some strange kind of game she's never seen before. Her notion that what Moe and Lou are engaged in is less than serious enrages Moe, and suddenly an unspoken threat of violence, even death, hangs over Darlene, who manages to slip out of the room when the maid comes to the door. Back inside the room, the men fraternally share the bottle of bourbon and say, "That was close," and "It could have happened," meaning, we almost got caught; we might have killed her. While Moe tells a story about the single occurrence of good luck in his life, Lou clandestinely slips a wallet into Moe's coat. Then, saying "Are you coming? . . . Don't wait too long," Lou departs. Lynch fades in on a shot of Moe sleeping on one of the beds and being woken by a pounding on the door. It's the police, who find Lou's identification cards in the wallet, but with Moe's picture on them. As the police get ready to haul him off to jail for the murder of Felicia, the bewildered and anguished Moe repeats himself: "No, no, I don't understand, I don't understand."

In Lynch's work vivid worlds full of places, people, situations, and engaging, compelling emotions exist within the human mind. *Eraserhead*'s Henry can have encounters with the woman of his dreams that thrill both him and us while lying on his bed. For Lynch, dreams, visions, and intuitions can communicate at least as much truth as waking reality, and our intuition tells us that Moe and Lou are one and the same person. Moe is a cautious man with a heart condition who has nonetheless murdered his wife, Felicia, and perhaps Martine Mustique, who was found dead in her bathtub. Moe's mind is unable to accept the fact that he perpetrated dark deeds, so it creates Lou, who mocks Moe's heart trouble, goes about lustfully indulging his appetites and has the unrealistic, superhuman ability to intuit all the details of Darlene's downward slide in life without ever having met her. The scenes we've seen with Moe, Darlene, and Lou have been a psychodrama that Moe has been living out while sleeping a boozy sleep in room 603. Perhaps earlier he did have a session with a prostitute, just him and her, but he experienced it as a situation in which the Lou part of his nature was a major player. The state of being in which Moe was interacting with a despised part of himself that was still him accounts for the curious, knowing looks between the two men and their edgy, yet comradely exchanges, and it explains why Moe angrily tells Darlene "Felicia was *my* wife" while Lou's in the bathroom: Moe's inner drama sees Felicia as wife to both the good and bad aspects of himself.

Lynch gives us a visual clue that Lou is an imaginary part of Moe's psyche when he shows Moe and Darlene, who are talking to Lou, reflected in a mirror in which Lou does not appear. Lynch being Lynch however, he suspends us in a moment of perfect ambiguity, for the shot is angled so that if Lou *was* in the room he might be just barely too far to the left to be reflected. Lynch and writer Barry Gifford are intently focused on drawing the viewer's imagination and intellect into their tricky cinematic puzzle box, and this twenty-six-minute episode of *Hotel Room*, as we shall see, introduces a particular identity-mixing dynamic that the two creators will explore at feature-length in 1997's *Lost Highway*.

One of Lynch's artistic objectives is to probe the psychological depths of his characters, so it's understandable that he would leave the direction of *Hotel Room*'s second episode, *Getting Rid of Robert*, to someone else (James Signorelli). This story, penned by Jay McInerney, the celebrated chronicler of Manhattan yuppiedom, inhabits an urbane world of social-climbing golddiggers, catty comments, and cutting ironies that is foreign to Lynch's sensibility. Set in 1992, this episode brings together bitchy Sasha (Deborah Unger) and self-absorbed Robert (Griffin Dunne) for a tryst in room 603. Before they arrive, we learn that they've both been cheating on each other. Director Signorelli, in order to herald the battle of the sexes that's about to commence, cuts to a close-up of a bronze sculpture of two wrestlers grappling. It's hard to imagine Lynch including such an obvious this-is-a-symbol moment in his own work. Sasha fully intends to initiate a break up with Robert, but he surprises her by saying he's through with her and her egomaniacal emotional terrorism. This sudden power shift in the room throws Sasha off balance, and, rather than being cast as the loser, she tells Robert she'll change her behavior in order to keep him. But his mind's made up, he's leaving, and to keep him from walking out the door, Sasha picks up a fireplace poker and smashes in the back of his head (cut to a still larger close-up of the sculpted wrestlers). In a dark variation on the classic screwball comedy theme of a couple's verbal and physical combat actually being an expression of their affection for each other, Sasha says "You really hurt me," Robert apologizes, and they start to kiss passionately. The only problem is that the contents of his head just won't stop seeping out onto the tasteful beige carpet. This, their final, perverse embrace is the closest thing to love one can find in the mean-spirited world of *Getting Rid of Robert*, which serves as a black-comedy social-satire interlude before Lynch concludes *Hotel Room* with the masterful *Blackout*.

Lynch's direction of Barry Gifford's story, like *Getting Rid of Robert*, also presents a couple under emotional duress, but unlike the Jay MacInerney–James Signorelli entry, *Blackout* employs a hypnotic stylistic simplicity that gently reveals the deep-rooted cause of its lovers' disquietude.

It's a hot, muggy night in 1936, and all the lights are out in New York City. Danny (Crispin Glover), a young man from a small Oklahoma town, brings Chinese food back to room 603, where his wife, Diane (Alicia Witt), waits for his return with just a few candles glimmering in the black air surrounding her. Beyond this tale's literal darkness, *Blackout* explores the primarily Lynchian theme of the absence of light in the human soul. When we first see Diane, she's holding her hand over her eyes to shield them from Danny's bright flashlight beam, but she's also trying to keep a past horror from registering and being retained in her mind's eye. It's immediately clear to us that something is not right with Diane; her grasp of reality is tenuous as she muddles the time scheme of events in her and Danny's seventeen married years and wonders if he's been speaking Chinese and if it's a Chinese doctor she'll be seeing tomorrow, to which her patient husband replies, "The only thing Chinese is this food."

Danny speaks slowly, carefully choosing his words as he talks to Diane, as though he's speaking to a child; and with her almost plump, smooth, fleshy face and full lips, she suggests a very young, innocent person new to the grown-up world, yet her wide, unblinking eyes are haunted by too much experience. In the eerie darkness, Danny looks at his wife as he talks to her, but her gaze trails off into her own inner reality: She's one of Lynch's living mysteries who commands our attention as we try to understand and soothe her. The first nine minutes of the half-hour *Blackout* are a textbook example of the director's ability to create a floating, mesmerizing journey for the viewer. We're entranced by the two people speaking softly, cryptically in the blackened room, their words almost subliminally supported by Angelo Badalamenti's spellbound musical tones. We're gripped by the ancient power of storytelling as Diane speaks of walking by the black waters of a nocturnal lake (Did this really happen; is it a dream she had?). Then, after pausing for a rapt sixteen seconds, she says, "I saw you on the other side of the lake,"—and suddenly screams out, "And I shouted, *Danny, Danny*, but it wasn't you." Diane's panicky outburst shows the severity of her psychological torment, and we feel the terror of a woman wandering like a lost child within her own mind. But Lynch, by having Diane suddenly half-rise from the stable sitting position she's established, and lurch toward Danny as she screams his name, makes us fear Diane herself: She becomes a startling presence of true Otherness. The fearsome spectacle of Diane's mental anguish gives a full measure of the burden Danny gladly, but wearily bears in living with and trying to help this woman he loves so much. Like a detective, he tries to decipher the clues of dislocated sentences and strange images she presents so that he can map a pattern of cogent narrative that will help guide her home.

One of Lynch's "special people"[27] with an extraordinary consciousness, Diane has visions that are at once mystical, poetic, and reality based. She speaks of a Chinese fish that jumped up from the black waters of a lake and spoke to her of Danny and their "five perfect girls." We, like Danny, see that the Chinese fish comes from their earlier talk about Chinese food, and the nighttime lake setting recalls the many evenings they spent at Lake Osage back home. But what of the five girls, for Diane insists, "Danny, these are our children; don't you recognize them?" Gently, he leads her back to the terrible truth she's trying so hard to separate herself from through dissociative denial and fantasy. The couple once had a child, a baby boy they nicknamed Danbug, who drowned in Lake Osage while they were preoccupied making love on the shore. What tragedy, to have the loving act of intimacy that produced their child also metaphorically snuff out its present and future. This trauma was compounded by the pitiless attitude of townsfolk who said Diane wasn't responsible enough to mother children, and the medical fact that she could never have any more. So, her vision of her and Danny's five girls was both a healthy rebuke to their neighbors' condemnatory stance and a sad defiance of her physical inability to conceive again.

Diane felt that the whole unspeakable mess "stuck in my brain like a knife" (still another Lynchian head trauma), thus distorting her rational thought process. Pain, sorrow, and shame are her constant companions, even though she tries to bury them beneath her conscious mind, and Lynch stages a beautiful poetic association between the thought of Diane and Danny's drowned baby and the blackness-reflecting mirror in Room 603 which, framed left and right by two burning white candles, is like an altar to their loss. Barry Gifford's spare writing, Lynch's economical, unshowy direction, and the subdued performances of Crispin Glover and Alicia Witt present this highly emotional material in an unsentimental, Midwestern-dry idiom that gives certain dramatic moments great force—as when the almost otherworldly Diane jerks her hand out to touch Danny's shoulder and says, "I couldn't live without you, Danny, I . . . I really couldn't."

The couple can never produce another child, but Danny labors day and night to achieve the rebirth of his wife, to bring the mind and body he loves into a healthy balance and restore Diane to herself and to him. He's tried as hard as he can to find the bright side of their travails, but he feels desperate and "useless." He's afraid that part of her wants to keep wandering in the dark, for she says of their blacked-out hotel room, "I could get used to this." Danny knows that she already has. Still, maybe the New York doctor can work miracles.

Like so many of the people in Lynch's work, Diane and Danny are in danger of being overwhelmed by a world of trouble and confusion: They are in need of deliverance and grace. Now, on top of everything else, Diane has a burning fever, but she wants Danny to kiss her anyway as she lies on the bed. He hasn't been afraid to confront the dis-ease of her mind, and he doesn't shy away from her body, leaning down to touch his lips to hers. Their kiss signifies the reestablishment of the erotic circuit between them that was sundered by the death of their love's child—and at this moment, the lights come on. Even the bed headboard's carved art-nouveau plant forms, which are now illuminated, herald growth and renewal. Like tender shoots turning toward the nurturing light, Danny pulls Diane off her sickbed and to the window, where their faces glow with reflected brilliance. He says, "Look, Di, the whole city's lit up," and, her smile mirroring his, she says the word that has brought light to her world like a benediction: "Danny!"

This ending, in which rays of transcendent love brighten benighted lives with an exaltation of hope, is spiritual kin to the conclusion of *The Grandmother*, *Eraserhead*, *The Elephant Man*, *Dune*, *Blue Velvet*, *Wild at Heart*, *Twin Peaks: Fire Walk With Me*, and *On the Air*, and speaks to Lynch's optimistic belief in the intervening power of goodness. Danny and Diane's illumination especially recalls the moment in *Blue Velvet* when Jeffrey, having extinguished Frank Booth's evil energy with a bullet, pauses with his loving Sandy in an apartment hallway. Like Danny and Diane, they kiss beneath the glow of a regular ceiling-mounted light source, but as Lynch fades the scenes in both films, he bathes his lovers in a supernaturally bright, poetic light that comes from all directions at once.

Hotel Room displayed Lynch's ability to compellingly direct material bounded by the parameters of a single stage set, as in one of those special stage-curtained areas within his other films and artworks, where certain moments and dramas are given special attention. The HBO program also found Lynch exploring favorite, primal themes like the fluidity of human identity and the conjunction between anxiety, eroticism, and death. Lynch and his co-producer, Monty Montgomery, conceived *Hotel Room* as an ongoing series, but HBO confined it to the one, low-rated installment. In a period of just seven months, Lynch had to cope with the fact that *Twin Peaks: Fire Walk With Me*, *On the Air*, and *Hotel Room* were deemed to be critical and financial failures. Naturally, it was painful to have work he put so much of himself into rejected by the masses who had celebrated him not so long ago. But, following the lead of many of his fictions, he philosophically concluded that rebirth follows death, and set about bringing himself back to creative life. Instead of feeling trapped and blocked, he realized that he had the freedom and the expressive talent to travel some avenues other than feature films and television shows.

In the five years between *Twin Peaks: Fire Walk With Me* (1992) and *Lost Highway* (1997), Lynch felt honored to exhibit his paintings, drawings, and photographs in solo shows at galleries, museums, and city halls in Valencia, Spain; Paris; twice in Los Angeles; and in four Japanese cities including Tokyo. Despite his meager performance in the film-revenue-grosses department, his reputation as a cinematic artist remained high. Prestigious international firms sought him out to shoot their commercials, which helped maintain a positive cash flow for Lynch, Mary Sweeney, and little Riley, and kept Asymmetrical Productions, housed in a compact former home next to his own Hollywood Hills abode, busy.

It's fascinating to see how the director's advertisements bear the brand of Lynch as well as the name of the particular product. In "Opium" for Yves Saint Laurent, he emphasizes the dreamy interior of a private sensual experience by gliding his camera into the black opening of a perfume bottle and dissolving through a wavy dark curtain of Asian plum blossoms, to focus in close-up on a woman titling her head back with eyes closed and touching her perfumed fingers to her throat as Angelo Badalamenti's music climaxes. For Calvin Klein's Obsession perfume, Lynch interpreted four short, romance-themed quotes from the fictions of F. Scott Fitzgerald, Ernest Hemingway, D. H. Lawrence, and Gustave Flaubert, and he managed to work *Twin Peaks* actors Heather Graham, Lara Flynn Boyle, and James Marshall into his mix. A couple kisses against a field of stars, a pining lover's eye fills with a huge tear as lightning flashes, we hear a wind of mystery, and, as we've seen so often in Lynch's work, lovers touch and hold each other's faces as they kiss (D. H. Lawrence: "To gather him in by touch").[28] The artist's love of Southern California's modern architecture is even in evidence, as we note the Mayan brick walls of a Los Angeles Frank Lloyd Wright house behind the Obsession bottle.

Mystery and revelation permeate Lynch's work, and in "Reveal," for the American Cancer Society, a pleasant-looking sixty-year-old woman with a neutral expression strips to her brassiere to encourage older women to have mammograms, her blouse's mother-of-pearls buttons reflecting the brilliant blue of her eyes. "The Wall" for Adidas athletic shoes shows a male runner's head distorting as he strains at his task and, via a close-up of his ear, we go inside to see his red-pink cells laboring hard. Lynch dives his camera down the man's screaming throat, where fires burn and, after the runner bursts through a literal wall, he serenely strides along in the clouds. Another Lynchian character has persevered and gone from hell to heaven. A young woman's head floats in the clouds after "breaking free"[29] from her cold, thanks to Alka-Seltzer Plus. And in "Sun, Moon, Stars" (for Karl Lagerfeld's new perfume), Darryl Hannah is in two places at once, both dreamily wishing while looking skyward, and floating among the stars, her pale hair and dress streaming in a gorgeous flow of celestial images that dissolve from one to the next. Lynch employs earthier motifs in "Instinct of Life," which heralds Jil Sanders' masculine eau de toilette fragrance. We see the director's favorite red curtains, a candle blowing out in a Now-It's-Dark moment, and the linkage of human and bestial energy as a man and a black panther race through the night.

The extended, sixty-second commercial Lynch filmed for Giorgio Armani's perfume Gio is the director's personal favorite, and it contains this apolitical artist's most blatant political statement. Lynch has lived in Los Angeles since 1970, and he dearly loves his adopted hometown, but his acute perceptions can't help but notice its troubling fault lines. In the late 1980s and early 1990s, fear and animosity clouded the air as racial tensions approached the flash point. Gang warfare and drive-by shootings were commonplace; many Asians, African Americans, and whites regarded each other with mistrust. The police beating of black motorist Rodney King reinforced prejudices on both sides of the color line, and the trial of the officers who wielded the clubs galvanized intense emotions. It was during this time of charged racial feelings that Lynch shot the Armani commercial (in black and white), which is driven by the question "Who is Gio?"

Another Lynchian woman of mystery, she moves in a social circle of wealth and taste, turning heads wherever she goes, being photographed by the paparazzi, and kissing various men. Universally adored, she seems to have it all, but her moody eyes often gaze right or left out beyond her immediate environment, looking for something more to complete her life, or perhaps seeing something she's trying to forget. She often wears a subdued expression, but she really comes alive in an extended music club sequence in which, as Lynch says, "all races and religions are getting along so fantastically."[30] Gio and a huge multiethnic group of musicians, dancers, and photographers all swing and sway to a hot salsa beat in a production number of harmonized opposites that recalls *On the Air*'s big beatnik-shoe-dance-number finale that unified the disparate factions of the Zoblotnick Broadcasting Company. Ironically, Lynch shot his Gio dance scene, which anticipates the spirit of Rodney King's famous and haunting question, "Can't we all just get along?," on the very night that the L.A. riots broke out. Earlier in the day, the California judicial system dismissed the men who beat King with a slap on the wrist, and by nightfall there was rampant looting and property destruction in the ghettos of the South Central neighborhoods. What Lynch calls "the strangeness"[31] quickly spread around town and soon "they were setting fire to Hollywood Boulevard"[32] and there were "five thousand fires burning."[33] The artist has spoken of how he found the "drastically out of control"[34] feeling of the L.A. unrest "very unnerving."[35] Lynch's art tells us how deeply he understands the human capacity for physical and emotional violence, but to see so many people acting out their darkest impulses was a very scary and saddening sight. In the middle of his commercial's happy dance, Lynch cast a brooding shadow over the scene, as Angelo Badalamenti's synthesizer strikes a somber note and Gio's wistful gaze, for the first time, looks right at us. When evoking Gio's melancholy, Lynch may have had the real-life supermodel Gia Carangi (1960–1986), at one time a $10,000-a-day *Vogue* model, in mind. An international fashion- and party-world sensation, Gia was wracked with emotional pain, slid into heroin addiction, and was one of the first American women to die of AIDS.

Lynch revisited the world of *Twin Peaks* in four thirty-second commercials for Japan's popular Georgia Coffee. Only shown in Japan, each segment works as an independent episode in which Agent Cooper enthusiastically endorses pop-top cans of Georgia Coffee and gives a hearty thumbs-up gesture. Taken together, the four segments tell a story about Cooper's efforts to locate Isami, a missing young Japanese woman, and reunite her with her boyfriend, Ken. Cooper's investigation is aided by the TV series' Officer Hawk, Deputy Andy, receptionist Lucy, and the Log Lady, and the segments include familiar motifs such as cherry pie, Cooper saying "Damn fine coffee," a taxidermy deer head on a conference table, and the Log Lady switching the lights on and off. Lynch was concerned that portraying the *Twin Peaks* realm in a light-hearted vein might destroy its somber, hypnotic magic, but Cooper manages to give us a dark thrill when, surrounded by a nocturnal forest, he soberly intones, "The Black Lodge is not in this world."[36]

In the world of 1993, Lynch's daughter, Jennifer, was getting ready to launch her debut feature film, *Boxing Helena*. Her father had been making movies all her life (her crying voice enlivens *The Alphabet*, made in 1968, the year of her birth), and some of her earliest happy memories were of being surrounded by the actors and technicians making *Eraserhead* in the first years of the 1970s. While growing up, Jennifer helped out on the sets of some of her father's films, and had been entrusted to write *The Secret Diary of Laura Palmer*, the bestselling book which created details of Laura's character, and story elements, seminal to the evolving shape of *Twin Peaks* and *Twin Peaks: Fire Walk With Me* (Sheryl Lee told Jennifer that she "studied the diary like a bible" while making the film).

After the *Twin Peaks* cycle ended, Jennifer wrote a screenplay from a story she developed with Philippe Caland. It's a story that David Lynch said was "sick"[37] and that he would never film himself; and a story that, when Jennifer's mother, Peggy, described it to her friends, they said, "Why would any viewers want to submit themselves to *that*?"[38] *Boxing Helena* tells the tale of a surgeon who's crazy about a woman who despises him, and after she's in a car crash he amputates her arms and legs and keeps her captive in his house, enshrined on a throne-like box.

Madonna, at a time in her career when she was interested in exploring daring, taboo themes, was interested in playing Helena, but she backed out before the start of production. Then Kim Basinger got cold feet after she said she would be Helena on screen. Jennifer, believing in a "Screw me once, it's your fault; screw me twice, it's my fault"[39] philosophy, joined with her producers in bringing legal action against Basinger, and won her case, forcing the actress to pay $7.4 million for breach of contract.

As Jennifer says, Madonna and Basinger had been "vocal about their bravery and how little the role frightened them. People aren't real big on recognizing that one of the bravest things you can say is that you are afraid. I owe Madonna and Kim for showing me some colors of people I didn't know existed."[40]

Jennifer offered the part to Sherilyn Fenn, whose alluring, vixenish charm had made *Twin Peaks*' Audrey Horne's journey from mischievous highschool girl to fledgling woman so compelling. Jennifer knew Fenn was right for the role when Fenn "came up to me and said, 'I'm terrified of it—and that's why I want to do it.' I strongly felt she could execute the material with honesty."[41]

With Fenn on board as Helena, and Julian Sands eager to play the surgeon, Jennifer and cinematographer Frank Byers, who shot all of TV's *Twin Peaks* (except the pilot), began filming scenes. When David Lynch saw the finished movie he said to Jennifer, "How did you learn how to do that?,"[42] knowing that he and Peggy had had a profound effect on their daughter's sensibility and ability to design and build an arduous project. Peggy visited the production while the film was being made, and was "stunned that Jennifer was so calm and commanding; it was like she was born to do it."[43]

In 1993, Lynch and Peggy found themselves in a position that David's parents, Sunny and Donald, had been in in 1970: watching a film (*Boxing Helena*) that their child had made, in which a mother and father were portrayed in a scathingly negative light. As Lynch says, his mom and dad were "very upset"[44] by *The Grandmother*'s Mother and Father, who made life hell for their Boy: Sunny and Donald "wondered where all this stuff came from."[45] In *The Grandmother* Lynch wasn't saying that his parents, like those in the film, victimized him with emotional, verbal, physical, and sexual violence. But in his fiction he *was* forcefully communicating core dynamics of his psychological self: *I'm sensitive*; *I have extraordinary perceptions that inspire me to make things*; *Don't fence me in—let me be free to hear and respond to my muse's call*. Lynch and his parents had been acting out this psychodrama in the years before *The Grandmother*, generating family tension while going back and forth about David's obsessional need to be an artist. Even if it was not Lynch's conscious intention to jolt his parents, he made *The Grandmother* an anti-authoritarian cry for independence.

Even when Lynch and his parents were having their differences, they all loved each other, and even though Jennifer's parents separated and divorced, and David didn't live in her house anymore, she never doubted his love for her. But she still ached with the pain of her playful and imaginative father not being as available as he had been during the first six years of her life.

It's hard to read the first scene of Jennifer's film as not being a portrait of David Lynch. Lynch has said he'd have enjoyed being a doctor, and we see a little boy, Nick Cavanaugh, approach his doctor father's study door, which has a Lynchian red curtain. The boy pokes his head in and softly says, "Daddy." We only see the back of the father's head—he doesn't turn to face his son, and bluntly says, "Not now, I'm working." In Lynch's work, his art, he explores deep within the human interior, and Nick's father is poring over an X-ray of someone's insides.

After seeing *Boxing Helena* Lynch said, "The apple doesn't fall far from the tree,"[46] and Jennifer's film dwells on a theme that's central to almost every Lynch picture: "The home is a place where things can go bad."[47] If Nick's father is too busy to spare a moment for his son, his mother is aggressively rejecting, striking him, not telling people that she has a child, and not minding that Nick knows she's cheating on daddy. Sensitive young Nick is perfectly situated to grow up with a warped psychosexual nature. His father shows him how to be remote and unavailable, and his mother, who's sometimes nude while she berates him, links eroticism with being shunned in the boy's mind.

So where does Nick turn for emotional connection and sustenance? In the world of the Lynches, to art, of course. A focal point within the Cavanaughs' opulent mansion is a white Venus de Milo statue (reminding us of the one in *Twin Peaks*' Red Room), to which Nick is obsessionally attached. For Jennifer the statue is significant because, unlike Nick's parents, it looks lovingly at Nick and doesn't move away from him or strike him. After Nick grows into manhood (Julian Sands) and assumes his father's position as a master surgeon, he's able to love people, but only in the twisted way he learned at home. As Nick's father was with him, he's lukewarm and evasive toward Anne (Betsy Clark), who really cares for him, while he's desperate to win the affection of the unattainable Helena (Sherilyn Fenn), who, like his mother, is sensual, hostile toward him, and would rather spend time with her lovers.

In Lynch's *Blue Velvet*, a young man hides in a woman's closet and watches her have sex with Ray, a psychotically domineering man, and Jennifer has Nick climb a tree outside Helena's apartment and watch her have sex with a possessive macho stud (there's a ruddy David Lynch–style curtain on the window). Jennifer emphasizes the intensity of Nick's Helena-fixation by having him spy on her while he's neglecting Anne, who fixed dinner for him at his house hours ago.

Nick's parents have died, but he chooses to live in the big old house of his tormented youth, alone with his dear Venus de Milo statue. Nick once had a one-night-stand with Helena, but now she wants nothing to do with him. He lies to her and uses manipulative tactics to get her to his house, where he offers her food and passionate Puccini opera music. Like David Lynch and many of his fictional characters, Nick is a romantic who believes in the supremacy of love's healing power. Jennifer Lynch and Julian Sands sympathetically portray Nick as a pubescent boy in an adult's body, a man whose emotional-erotic development has been stunted through no fault of his own. His perceptions seem blinded by his overwhelming need for Helena to be the object of all the unexpressed love he's stored up over the years, for she's clearly a shallow, mean-spirited, vindictive woman—or does Nick feel his ardor can call forth a warmly amorous, caring aspect of her nature that she doesn't even know she has?

Before the film presents a major dramatic development it establishes Nick as a Lynchworld guy who's wild at heart and follows his dreams, but who's dangerously close to being a pathetic stalker (*Blue Velvet*: "Are you a detective or a pervert?"). After Nick lures Helena to his house, she explodes with anger, and while running away is hit by a truck, thus galvanizing Nick into acting out his light and dark emotions in extreme forms.

Helena's legs are crushed by the truck, and instead of taking her to the hospital, Nick keeps her in his house and operates on her, removing her ruined limbs (we see none of this). Nick cuts himself off from the world outside, centering his life on Helena, who's his unwilling prisoner. The Venus de Milo is still visually prominent in his house, and for Jennifer, Nick is an artist "moulding Helena into something that doesn't make him afraid and doesn't go away,"[48] like the statue he's always worshipped. And to be exactly like Nick's statue, Helena's arms have to come off. Jennifer's mother, Peggy, grew up looking daily at *her* mother's Venus de Milo statue, and in adolescence found the figure titillating: "Because she had no arms, she couldn't cover her breasts; she couldn't stop someone from touching them."[49] But Nick isn't interested in forcing himself on Helena—he wants her to love him.

Now, at last, Nick, the adoring, perverse artist, has completed his creation: beautiful in a dress as white as the Venus's marble, armless, legless, and never in physical pain, Helena sits as the centerpiece of Nick's idealized composition, a devotional altar surrounded by white flowers. Nick's parents never wanted or needed him, and Helena certainly doesn't want him, but now she must depend on him to provide everything she needs to stay alive. It's interesting to note that David Lynch, who grew up in an intact, undivided family unit that came to feel "claustrophobic"[50] to him, made early films about characters who feel trapped by their families and need to escape the physical presence, dependencies, and demands of others. While Jennifer, an unplanned child who's the product of a broken home, made a film whose main character finds bliss being cocooned with a person who needs him every hour of every day and night. (A few years after creating *Boxing Helena*, Jennifer had a daughter to whom she is an attentive, devoted mother.)

Like her father, Jennifer is adept at burrowing beneath surfaces. Nick may have sculpted Helena into his living Venus de Milo goddess, but this is a flesh and blood woman with a mind of her own who angrily engaged Nick in dialogues that tear at the roots of his psychosexual dysfunction. Her clear-sighted rage sees and speaks aloud his fear of "women, me, yourself, everything." It would take Helena craving his tender touch on her aroused body to complete his growing-up process. Nick doesn't say this but the tension of his primal need agitates the air. Helena senses it and returns it; she wants to "feel like a woman again," and she kisses him with awakened desire. Yes, everything we've seen after Helena got hit by the truck has been Nick's dream. He visits Helena's hospital room and finds her sleeping peacefully, with all her limbs intact.

The film's conclusion takes a final measure of Nick's psychosexual health. He wakes with a woman, presumably Anne, sleeping next to him. It seems Nick's psychodrama sessions with Helena in dreamland have purged his painful, toxic feelings for his mother by letting him act them out with mother-surrogate Helena, thus freeing him from being emotionally stuck in childhood. He's truly a grown-up now, who knows he's worthy of healthy love and able to give it, so he can accept Anne, the one who's consistently loved him, as his appropriate partner.

But Helena's pre-accident lover, Ray, bursts in and attacks Nick, and just as the Venus statue is falling to crush Nick, he hears Helena say, "I need you; I love you"—and then he wakes up, in the hospital.

Blue Velvet is one of Jennifer Lynch's favorites of her father's films, in which the light and dark aspects of its male protagonist's (Jeffrey) psyche are stimulated by, respectively, Sandy and Dorothy. *Boxing Helena*'s Nick, like Jeffrey, takes a trip into a netherworld, experiences his own capacity to act out transgressive impulses, and learns to choose the path of light. At the end of *Blue Velvet* Jeffrey is resolutely with Sandy, but, given Lynch's understanding of human complexity, might he not still be tempted by Dorothy? In *Blue Velvet*'s final shot, we see Dorothy, the film's battered Dark Mother figure, for the first time in daylight, reunited with her kidnapped son and looking peaceful, yet on the soundtrack her voice hauntingly sings, "I still can see blue velvet through my tears." Jennifer beautifully evokes this complex, "yes . . . but" mood of conscious/subconscious dissonance in *Boxing Helena*'s final shot. Nick, having left Anne sleeping in bed, goes to the Venus de Milo statue and touches his forehead to the marble woman's forehead (the intimate closeness of two heads is a David Lynch trademark), as his inner voice shows that Helena is still deeply on his mind: "I'm still haunted by my love for her. Those dreams. . . ."

After *Boxing Helena* came out, Jennifer Lynch seemed to have a target on her back. No matter which way she turned, she was vilified. Some accused her of not having the courage of her convictions by having Nick's physical reshaping and imprisonment of Helena be just a dream, hence trivializing and negating half of her film. While others felt that even treating Helena's mutilation in a dream was a misogynistic sin that set the women's movement back decades. Jennifer responded that "the only way I would make this film is if it were a dream: I want no part of a movie that condones the act of removing a woman's arms and legs as the way to get her to love you."[51] As David Lynch discovered in *The Grandmother* when he portrayed the imaginary act of the Boy killing his abusive parents in an animated vision, Jennifer knew that she could best confront the raw, gruesomely intense psychological and physical issues that intrigued her in passages that were one step removed from cinema-verité naturalism. Her father's films had taught her that onscreen all states of consciousness (waking reality, dreams, fantasies, memories) are capable of communicating resonant, meaningful emotions to the viewer. The woman and man who brought Jennifer into the world were artists who venerated the inner life, and Jennifer says,

> I was raised to base a tremendous amount of value on my dreams. Dreams aren't just little things you have at night; they're what's going on inside you. The fact that people may or may not feel that I copped out at the end of the film has everything to do with how much respect they have for their subconscious. If you're not paying attention to the voice inside you, there's some kind of denial happening there. I don't consider my dreams prophecies, but I don't ignore them. It was a tremendous gift for me, as a child, that nobody put fences around my imagination.[52]

This last sentence echoes Lynch's praise of his parents for giving him art-making materials and not forcing him to stay inside the lines when he was drawing on a piece of paper as a boy. Some critics wondered if *Boxing Helena*'s bitter portrayal of Nick's parents as rejecting and unavailable was Jennifer's way of sending a message to David and Peggy. If, on some level, she was expressing animus toward her parents, as her father may have been doing toward his folks in *The Grandmother*, it shows the value of art as a pressure-release valve for calming and dissipating the artist's negative emotions, albeit in a public way.

Lynch's response to Jennifer's film was warm and supportive. He turned to Catherine Coulson, who'd been part of Jennifer's extended family ever since the *Eraserhead* production days twenty years earlier, and voiced his fatherly pride and praise in artistic terms: "Cath, she's round as a ball."[53] Jennifer was thrilled that "he totally digs my movie."[54]

No matter how the world reacted to *Boxing Helena*, Jennifer knew, as her father does, that realizing your vision the way you want to is the true reward of making art. The film's story was a personal one for Jennifer, allowing her to express her adult feelings about voyeurism, intimacy, sex, love, emotional freedom, and dependence. She began working on her *Boxing Helena* concept six years before making the film, at age nineteen, but the story also touched the vulnerable little girl within her. For as a child, wearing braces on both legs because of being born with clubbed feet, she had gazed lovingly at the Venus de Milo statue in her maternal grandmother's house. Like Jennifer, the marble figure's limbs were "not perfect, but she was still so, so beautiful."[55]

In the months following *Boxing Helena*'s release, denunciation, and burial, David Lynch finally felt that his book, *Images* (for which he began to compile materials in 1991), was ready for publication. Composed of scenes from his films and *Twin Peaks*, and some of his paintings, drawings, and photographs, the 192 pages contain rare examples of his non-screenplay writing. The book's cover is primal Lynch: a color photo of a couch in front of flowered curtains, a mundane domestic tableau into which intrudes a ghostly mystery—a vertical cloud of white smoke that floats above the furniture. A sourceless something that shouldn't be in the house nonetheless occupies its space.

Opening the book, *Blue Velvet*'s Jeffrey Beaumont peering through the louvered slits of Isabella Rossellini's closet door leads us to the control room of *Dune*'s evil Baron Harkonen, then on to Laura Palmer and Cooper in *Twin Peaks*: *Fire walk With Me*'s Red Room, to a big close-up of Isabella

Rossellini in *Wild at Heart* and, finally, to the two-page-filling icon of Laura Palmer's dead face with its plastic shroud. Lynch has compelled our attention with his mysterious cover, and then Kyle MacLachlan, *Twin Peaks'* magician who longs to see and Lynch's surrogate who, in *Blue Velvet* acts out the director's personal closet-hiding voyeuristic fantasy, leads us into successively intimate rooms, and progresses to the deep enigma of life, death, and secrets coded in Laura's cold face. Lynch has designed his book as a journey that, like his films, shows us images and ideas that move him, and then concludes with a mystery undiminished in power: the white smoke from the book's cover still floating in the living room of his mind.

Before Lynch takes us back through his film and TV career, from most recent to earliest, he shows us his self-portrait, a pale, simple clay figure with arms and legs that dwindle down to no hands and feet. The image displays a modest genital bulge and has a huge, almost torso-sized, faceless head that is half-eaten by black ants. Insects: those troubles, confusions, and bad thoughts that can plague the head can also eat away at the house, the supposed sanctum of safety and sanity, as Lynch's 1990 painting *Ants in My House* indicates. The title of a 1992 drawing done the year *Twin Peaks: Fire Walk With Me* was released could sum up the desperate state of Laura Palmer's head and homelife: *Bugs Are in Every Room—Are You My Friend*? (In the film a sobbing, traumatized Laura, who's beginning to believe that her father and BOB are one, asks Donna, "Are you my best friend?")

Always a man who likes to get down to first principles, Lynch groups some of his black-and-white photographs in Industrial and Organic categories. The Industrial shots focus on the factories he loves, the powerful machines that keep our familiar world humming along (a number of the shots relate to electrical energy). Rather than showing us clean, bright, new machines, Lynch exercises his fascination for textured surfaces by presenting aged equipment in dimly lit spaces where the entropic forces of rust, dirt, gravity, and corrosive liquids are at work. Decay and dissolution are built into the world Lynch sees, and he records their beauty. Even his Organic section includes mostly subjects that are not alive: a weathered cat corpse almost indistinguishable from the earth, an oyster shell, the fake bloody head that pops off Henry's shoulders in *Eraserhead*, a medical specimen jar containing an amputated foot.

And speaking of severed body parts, we finally get to see Lynch's fabled *Fish Kit* and *Chicken Kit*, which are photographs of messily dissected dead animals that are arranged and labeled on white paper bearing instructions for their assembly ("Place finished fish in water, Feed your fish, Watch your fish swim, Clean and scrub your room"[56]; "If assembled properly your chicken will either lay eggs or automatically wake you very early in the morning").[57] The grisliness of these torn-apart-animal photos is mediated by their being monochromatic, but they can still be an off-putting aesthetic experience: when Laura Dern was working with Lynch, her father, hip actor Bruce Dern, was appalled when the director gave him a *Chicken Kit* image as a gift. We can only imagine the public outrage that would result if Lynch had used a dog or cat as his subject.

For Lynch, the glistening internal organs, wings, fins, tails, beaks, and bodily fluids arranged on white paper are intriguing visual abstractions, and the process of segmenting the wholeness of nature and examining it with great care evokes the scientific methods of his tree-researching father. Like author Mary Wollstonecraft Shelley who, in *Frankenstein* (1818), wrote of a man piecing together human body parts to make a living being, Lynch is fascinated by the primal force that gives animal tissue life: the spark of electricity.

An invisible flow of electrons enables us to think and move, it pulses within plants and animals and sings in the stars. It's possible to learn specifically how and why electricity is such a universal motivating factor, but Lynch chooses to see it as a mysterious force, a poetic principle that he allies with both dark (*Ronnie Rocket*, *Twin Peaks: Fire Walk With Me*) and luminous (the *Blackout* episode of *Hotel Room*) aspects of human nature. He devotes ten pages of his book to close-up black-and-white photographs of spark plugs and their component parts, which are accompanied by text detailing the interrelationship of electrodes, insulators, and spark gaps. The words are scientifically precise (the gap between two wires must be .015 to .025 inches), yet the overall impression of this section is mystical. In Lynch's pictures, the spark plugs and their parts are held by human hands, thus imaging the linkage of inorganic and organic energy. And because the spark plug material is presented in the context of an artist's book, the gleaming wires, ceramic rods, steel circle, and triangular gap-adjuster seem like esoteric tribal power implements which, when combined under the proper spell, enable 3,000 pound metal living rooms on wheels to transport people down wondrous highways.

Lingering in the realm of electrical fascination, Lynch devotes two pages to photographs of car-engine distributor caps, black plastic domes pierced by nine holes through which wires carry the igniting charge to the spark plugs. The distributor is another vital component that facilitates the mysterious invisible flow of electrical energy, but it may also intrigue Lynch with its form and numerical message: eight symmetrically arrayed holes in a circle surrounding a central ninth. This mundane plastic product bears the pattern of a mandala, the ancient circular symbol that unites all opposing dualities in a transcendent universal wholeness. It also signifies the number nine, which Lynch has placed in *Twin Peaks*, *Wild at Heart*, and *Hotel Room*, and which symbolically represents ultimate truth, for no matter what other number you multiply it by, you always get nine (by numerological mystic addition):

9 × 247 = 2,223 (2+2+2+3 = 9);
9 × 248 = 2,232 (2+2+3+2 = 9);
9 × 12,345 = 111,105 (1+1+1+1+5 = 9).

Aside from the textbook-like spark-plug dissertation, Lynch's prose contributions to *Images* consist of lightly humorous character dialogues that introduce the distributor and spark-plug topics ("Pete Wants To Speak To Bob,"[58] "Old Doug Talks To Billy"[59]) and a 900-word paragraph called "Meaningless Conversations."[60] Having the feel of a stream-of-consciousness notation dense with ideas that poured out too fast for normal punctuation, this section mentions familiar Lynchian preoccupations: "several abstract somewhat hidden emotional tendencies . . . positive and negative forces . . . a vital link between the subconscious and superconscious minds . . . the much argued over proposition that one cannot tolerate the existence of two or more intensely opposing ideas at one point in time . . . knowledge of the truths behind the all-pervading essence which is unending . . . the long journey toward understanding,"[61] "abstractions associated with the laws of nature,"[62] and "the dark and evil forces which would have us living forever in confusion."[63] This philosophical declamation segues into passages of imagistic brilliance: "Sometimes in the evening a feeling of the type which haunts young children in the forest will come in on a dark wind and all the light will fade leaving a low sound penetrating the eyes which follow the dark shapes running for safe nests just out of reach of small white teeth."[64] A foresty, haunting wind, an animalistic threat accompanied by a low droning sound—we are clearly in Lynch territory. Next, he provides an autobiographical-sounding section: "the home which will remind us of the red cookie jar and the smiles dancing around it in the golden afternoon while the pipe puffs out clouds of smoke from the mouth of the father with an axe to cut wood growing on the tall mountains."[65] What's surprising about Lynch's writing is not the vivid simplicity of these descriptions, but the convincingly academic-speak tone of the material that surrounds them: "which therefore can only be considered as actual structures with two separate and distinctly different qualities as we have seen when one or more intensely varying energies become associated with the higher levels of perceptible phenomena."[66] Could you run that by me again? In Lynch's fictions, sonic barriers and distortions can curtail human communication, and here he shows us that even clearly rendered words can diminish meaning and understanding. He concludes his book's prose section with an archetypal image of head-invasion, in which dental disease can "fester and transfer negative energies to the once quiet and peaceful mind giving it over to strange and unproductive thinking."[67] Along with "people trying to find love in hell,"[68] these words constitute the most concise summation of his themes that Lynch has voiced.

Senseless confusion and chaos threaten the precious human mind in Lynch's book, but the artist counters their entropic power with properly installed automobile distributors, fresh spark plugs, proper dental care, and Ricky Boards. We've previously noted Lynch's appreciation of the serenity-inducing sparseness of Japanese domestic interiors, and how he keeps his own home meticulously clean and uncluttered. And he's spoken of how symbolically manipulating the elements of life through art gives the artist an illusory, but nonetheless sanity-preserving, sense of control. Ricky Boards and Bee Boards are Lynch's notion of how a Japanese artist might organize the maddening swirl and swarm of existence into neat four-by-five rows of collected dead flies and bees (some real, some drawn) with individual name tags (Ricky, Ronnie, Chuck, Sid) mounted on white paper or wood. Out in the world, as in *Blue Velvet*, brutal insectoid energy may gnaw at the roots of beautiful gardens, but in the artist's studio, Lynch is their whimsical master. The image of mounted bugs also contains a loving echo of Lynch's childhood, when his scientist father took him into the magical woods and showed him trees and insects that he had labeled.

There is much darkness and some light in Lynch's work, and often a complex, ambiguous blending of the two. *Images*' fourteen pages of black-and-white dental hygiene photographs, if viewed without their reassuring captions ("Next the hygienist uses the tools to scrape the plaque off all the teeth"[69]), look as torturous as they are therapeutic. (Lynch doesn't state this in *Images*, but he had "soft, bad teeth as a kid,"[70] and spent a lot of time in the dentist's chair; his dental hygiene photos can be seen as his homage to Dr. Chin of Santa Monica, "the greatest dentist in the world." [71])

In general, the photographs in *Images* make a stronger impression than Lynch's paintings. (Catherine Coulson's beautiful black-and-whites of the years-long *Eraserhead* production are outstanding, and among other wonders, show us the white Nair foam mound with a black mouse tail protruding from it that indicates the Lynch-legend stripping of hair from a dead rodent is in progress.) The paintings, which in person have a great deal of surface interest and texture, lose impact when reproduced on the page: three 42" x 48" canvases are reduced to 2 1/2" x 2 1/2" squares, thus hampering Lynch's intention to open up "a huge, big world"[72] of viewer-participating interpretation. In general, the paintings show large blackish or grayish color fields in which recognizable forms (a human figure, a head, fish, cloud, building, tower, rectangles, triangles, biomorphic shapes) are rendered semi-legible by bold brush strokes. We can admire Lynch's compositions, which feel like undesigned, intuitive outpourings, and appreciate the paintings' subtle color modulations, and get a hint of the works' surface detail and layered depth, but the book format in which the paintings are presented keeps us from dreamily floating into these particular worlds of the artist's imagination.

Lynch's drawing, being much smaller (11" x 14") than his paintings in their original state, fare better in book form. Consisting of a few black ink lines and strokes on a white paper background, the drawings have a free, loose, naïve feeling that suggests a child's work. Amidst the seemingly casually applied lines, blots, and smudges we recognize the rough, primitively rendered shapes of a house, rectangle, dog, fish, gun, and electrical outlet that are like fragments of a world that's deconstructed or not put together yet. With his Ricky Boards and Bee Boards, Lynch organized chaos by giving individual names to particular insects from the swarm of an anonymous crowd. (He's spoken of feeling disquieted because many people in the world know a lot about his life while they remain nameless, unknown quantities to him.) Various words (Pin Dog Wind, Wood Fly Ammo, Fish Hot Bandaid, Monkey), rendered in a coarse, unrefined printing style, are also part of his drawings' picture plane, but since they don't match up with any recognizable images, there's a sense of dislocated reality as though a child were trying to figure out which words match parts of the world he sees. This feeling of dissociation also projects Lynch's belief that there are unclassifiable realities beyond words.

Lynch's *Images* book is an engaging sampler of his themes and aesthetics that shows the wide range of his creative expressions, though the best way to become immersed in the flow of his unique mind is to watch and listen to his moving images on a movie or TV screen.

During the artist's 1992–1997 cinematic dry spell, Americans had a chance to revisit or discover *Twin Peaks* when the Bravo cable network broadcast the entire series starting on Halloween night, 1993. Bravo obviously reached fewer homes than ABC, but they were pleased with the audience response to the show and have rebroadcast it a number of times over the years. Lynch showed his abiding love for the series' imaginative world by shooting some short introductory prologues for Bravo that featured his dear friend Catherine Coulson as the Log lady: she of the fire-killed husband and the oracular log, conduit of visions and messages from beyond our immediate sensory sphere. Margaret Lanterman sits before her boarded-up fireplace, cradling her log and speaking words that Lynch wrote, short philosophical-poetic passages that shun the dense verbal convolutions of *Images*' "Meaningless Conversations." "Where there was once one, there are now two. Or were there always two? What is a reflection? A chance to see two. Where there are chances for reflection there will always be two or more. Only when we are everywhere will there be just one." In the series' final episode, the Red Room shows us that the singular Laura, Leland, and Cooper indeed do have two aspects. And if we had truly enlightened powers of sight we would see that all manifestations of being, even seemingly opposing entities like Cooper and BOB, are each part of the universe's single primal consciousness: the One masquerading as the world's manifold forms, most of which aren't wised up enough to realize they're all the same being. The Hindu-based teachings of the Maharishi Mahesh Yogi's Transcendental Meditation movement, which Lynch has practiced since 1973, certainly struck a resonant, long-lasting chord in the artist: In December 1999, he said that the Maharishi was the most important man of the twentieth century.

As the 1990s approached their finale, Lynch tried to launch a new film project. *Dream of the Bovine*, according to co-writer Robert Engels (*Twin Peaks*, *Twin Peaks: Fire Walk With Me*), concerned "three guys who used to be cows. They're living in Van Nuys, trying to assimilate their lives. Trying to live with us. They look like people, but they're cows. They do cowlike behavior. They like to watch cars drive by the house and stuff."[73] Since the early 1990s, Lynch had a three-picture deal with French industrial magnate Francis Bouygues' company CiBy 2000, which financed *Twin Peaks: Fire Walk With Me*. Lynch thought his agreement with CiBy meant that it would automatically fund whatever project he proposed, but, perhaps gun shy over *Fire Walk With Me*'s abysmal performance, the company passed on *Dream of the Bovine* and nixed a couple of the director's other movie ideas. Lynch's lawyers eventually pointed out to him that a "play or pay" clause had been violated and that this was an actionable offense. The court ruled in Lynch's favor, so one afternoon he found himself $6.5 million richer. As usual, Lynch used this money to further his Art Life and pay the salaries of his professional associates, rather than to indulge in the Hollywood high life.

Lynch kept his hand in the film game by lending his name to Terry Zwigoff's 1994 documentary *Crumb* ("A David Lynch presentation"). Robert Crumb, who now lives in France, was America's most brilliant and notorious underground comic book artist of the 1960s and 1970s, who used his artistic gifts to satirize uptight, militaristic, corporate-suburban American society and to portray the full-tilt counterculture boogie of cross-racial kinship, rampant drug use, and polymorphous sexual expression. Lynch was happy to endorse Crumb's obsession with artistic freedom ("he doesn't have any responsibility to paint pretty pictures of people!" [74]). And he was fascinated by Crumb's two brothers, whose emotional and behavioral extremity, their social-outsider strangeness and quirky humanity, are qualities that Lynch of the Norman Rockwell childhood has always been attracted to, and which propel his fictions.

Lynch and his love, Mary Sweeney, produced Michael Almereyda's 1995 independent feature *Nadja*, in which Dracula's daughter (Elin Lowensohn) stalks the nocturnal streets of contemporary Manhattan. Lynch appears in a cameo as a tousle-haired, unsmiling morgue attendant who is suspicious when Lowensohn comes calling.

In *Nadja*, Lynch dwelt in the realm of the dead and undead, and in the 1992–1997 period of his real life, he suffered the loss of three members of his professional family. Prop man Frank Silva who, thanks to a flash of Lynch's intuition, had been catapulted from film crew anonymity to international fame for his chilling portrayal of BOB in *Twin Peaks* and *Twin Peaks: Fire Walk With Me*, was living with his girlfriend in the greater Seattle area in the mid-1990s. He had fallen in love with the Northwest, and was occasionally hired to meet with thrilled *Twin Peaks* tour groups of often-Japanese travelers. He would grimace and growl like BOB and then become his naturally warm, good-humored, and outgoing self, posing for pictures, signing autographs, and telling behind-the-scenes stories for hours. During the August 1995 *Twin Peaks* Festival, actor Michael J. Anderson (The Man From Another Place) and some fans drove to Frank's apartment and tried to get him to join in the weekend's fun, but he begged off, saying he wasn't feeling too well. On September 13, this lean and physically active man died of a heart attack, and was buried in his Northern California hometown. Frank's incarnation of BOB's otherness and ravenous evil was so convincing that he scared even seasoned viewers of movie and TV horror. It is a measure of the mystery and art of acting that Frank always maintained he didn't recognize BOB as being part of himself. "During the series I had a rough time watching it. It really disturbed me. And it still disturbs me when I see it, but I also know that that's not me."[75]

Lynch also lost Francis Bouygues, the Parisian industrialist who had championed and financed his cinematic vision, and who had visited the *Fire Walk With Me* production at the Mar T Café in rural North Bend, Washington, gamely and elegantly wearing an ascot around his neck and a tweed jacket in the Indian Summer heat. In the period after Bouygues' death, his company affirmed their intention to maintain their late leader's financial-backing deal with Lynch.

For Lynch the hardest death to accept was the tragic slaying of his friend Jack Nance, the man who labored for six years to brilliantly incarnate the character of Henry Spencer in *Eraserhead* (1976), hence giving cinematic shape to the raw fears and moody ruminations of Lynch's own psyche. Nance, also, was not a stranger to darkness in his off-screen life. Before meeting Lynch in 1970, he had performed for eight years with the prestigious American Conservatory Theater, toured in children's theater, and starred in the acclaimed, politically radical West Coast production of *Tom Paine*. With his quizzical, impish, intense expressions, his warm grin, and drawling speech that gave words an emphatic stretching, he was a gifted actor and a lovable human being. But Nance had a tendency to be as dedicated to the bottle as he was to his craft. As a young man beginning his acting career in Dallas, Nance thought, "This is not half bad. I can drink, and I'll never have to get a job!"[76] In the seven years after *Eraserhead*, Nance did more drinking than working. His marriage to Catherine Coulson broke up, and he scraped by doing menial odd jobs, slept in rented rooms as bleak as Henry Spencer's, and even lived on the street for two years. More than once Lynch pulled his friend up out of the gutter, and Nance credited the Eagle Scout with saving his life, as Lynch had previously done for the illness-stricken Catherine Coulson.

Lynch found good, small parts for Nance to play in *Dune* (1984), *Blue Velvet* (1986), *The Cowboy and the Frenchman* (1987), *Wild at Heart* (1990), *Twin Peaks: Fire Walk With Me* (1992, cut out of the released version), and *Lost Highway* (1997), and gave him the memorable, continuing role of Pete Martell in TV's *Twin Peaks* (1989–1991). Nance also did solid work for directors Dennis Hopper, Ken Russell, and Wim Wenders, and appeared in low-budget genre films.

In the spring of 1991, when *Twin Peaks'* TV run was drawing to a close, Nance took a chance on love and married Kelly Van Dyke, the spirited daughter of TV funnyman Jerry Van Dyke (brother of Dick), who was also, like Nance, a recovering alcoholic. During the course of their marriage, Nance discovered that Kelly was still abusing booze and tranquilizers, and during one of Nance and Kelly's high-volume fights she told him that she'd secretly been staring in X-rated sex films. With the happy prospect of his new marriage soured, Nance told friends that he and Kelly were going to divorce.

While on a movie location in a remote part of California, Nance was on the telephone with Kelly when she threatened to kill herself. Their frantic conversation was cut off when a big storm knocked out the phone lines, and Nance was terrified that Kelly might think he'd purposefully hung up on her. Sure enough, Kelly was found dead, dangling at the end of a nylon cord tied to a ceiling plant hanger. So now not only was Nance's wife tragically dead, but he had to live with the possibility that she might have been pushed over the edge by believing that he didn't care enough to talk to her anymore.

Lynch was always there to listen if his old friend wanted to share his troubles or elations, but oftentimes Nance preferred to be alone with his thoughts, out where the vibrant blue of Pacific ocean and sky merged, piloting a little sailboat with "nobody around to complain when I light up a cigar."[77]

Once Lynch and Nance went on an archeological expedition and found, in the industrial part of Los Angeles, the mammoth concrete wall with the gaping square aperture into which Nance as Henry Spencer had disappeared in the beginning of *Eraserhead*. Revisiting the site that launched them both into the cinematic history books, the actor and his director retraced Henry's steps, walking into the shadowy mouth, pausing to feel the chilling darkness, and emerging back into the bright sunlight.

When Nance attended the 1995 Twin Peaks Festival in Seattle, he was lit up with the high spirits of being appreciated for all his good work and the simple fact of being his own unique self. As usual, I presented the festival's film night at the Seattle Art Museum, and when I first shook hands with Nance he excitedly said, "I hear you're going to show *The Grandmother*." When Nance first met Lynch and the director tried to interest him in playing the lead role in *Eraserhead*, Nance was confused by the unorthodox project's "weird world and strange characters."[78] Lynch, not wanting to lose the man who he knew would make a perfect Henry Spencer, projected a 16mm print of *The Grandmother* for Nance to show him what his cinematic style looked like on the screen, rather than the printed script page. Nance, jolted by the film's fierce, dark poetry, said watching it was "like sitting in the electric chair for thirty-four minutes!"[79] Awestruck by the artistry of Lynch's fictional universe, Nance felt that "suddenly there was nothing more in the world I wanted to do than *Eraserhead*."[80]

I was proud to be the one providing Nance with his second viewing of *The Grandmother* since Lynch showed it to him twenty-five years earlier, and before the lights went down in the packed auditorium, he gave me a big wink. Nance and the audience had a good time with the film, but during the feature presentation of *Twin Peaks: Fire Walk With Me* I passed through the museum's cavernous lobby and saw Jack sitting by himself on a bench. "Taking a breather?" I asked. The film was heading into the harrowing passages in which Laura Palmer tries to numb the pain of her torn heart and endangered soul with a steady diet of illicit drugs, promiscuous sex, and a conclusive choice of death. Perhaps Jack's late wife's own descent into similar abuse that ended in death was heavy on his mind as he replied, "I just can't stand to watch her go."

Before Nance showed up in 1997's *Lost Highway*, he joined Lynch, his former wife, Catherine Coulson, and Charlotte Stewart (Mary X) for an *Eraserhead* reunion that was filmed by Lynch's boyhood friend Toby Keeler and included in Keeler's excellent *Lost Highway*/world-of-Lynch documentary, *Pretty as a Picture*. As the four reminisced on the grounds of Beverly Hills' Greystone Mansion, where they'd toiled six years for the sake of art in the early 1970s, each showed the signs of passing years, but Nance seemed truly wizened: pale, white-haired, and walking with a cane after having suffered two strokes. At age fifty-three, he was only three years older than Lynch, but he looked like he was in his late sixties. Still, Nance's dry humor was as alive as ever as he reminded his laughing comrades of the days when the *Eraserhead* makers had grown their own crop of potatoes to help keep body and soul together. "When we harvested them they were the size of little pinto beans. Little bitty 'pea-taters,' we called them. They were small, but there was a bunch of them, and we made little bitty French fries."[81]

As twenty-somethings, Lynch and Nance, with meager financial resources and a surfeit of talent and imagination, had crafted a film that made them both pop-cultural icons, and *Pretty as a Picture* showed the two now-middle-aged men repeating an idiosyncratic gesture of mutual respect and love that spanned thirty years. As Lynch said "Great to see you, Jack,"[82] the two stood side by side, each with a hand on the small of the other's back, and made a fast patting motion. Many many pats on the back from one to the other, in the fast rhythm of the beating of a small animal's heart.

In the mid-1990s, Nance was living alone in a South Pasadena apartment. On December 29, 1996, he told a friend that he got what he deserved when two young Latino men beat him up after he "mouthed off"[83] to them at a Winchell's Donut House. When Nance's friend checked on him the next morning, he found the actor dead. The investigating detective recognized Nance and said, "Jack left me with a mystery. He'd probably appreciate the shit out of that."[84] And a mystery it remains, for Nance's death is still unsolved.

MEMORIAL SERVICE

January 21, 1997
11:00 AM

First Church of the Nazarene
Pasadena, CA

Marvin John (Jack) Nance – Actor

Born
December 21, 1943
Boston, MA

Passed Away
December 30, 1996
Pasadena, CA

A saddened Lynch said, "Sometimes people irritated Jack, so he'd be verbally abusive."[85] He added that Nance was in poor physical shape and "always said he wouldn't be too hard to kill."[86] Lynch concluded that he acutely felt the loss of his friend, who had "been like part of my family for twenty-five years,"[87] and would miss "his absurdist humor and all the great characters he didn't get to play."[88]

When I was talking to Lynch four years after Nance's death and mentioned the actor's name in relation to a topic we were discussing, he paused in the conversation and softly said, "Bless his heart."[89]

Lynch regretted that he hadn't seen Nance as often as usual in what turned out to be his last days, but his old friend remained such an active part of Lynch's psychic life that he came to him in a waking dream, a very Lynchian dream: black-and-white, cloudy day, a wind weighted with unhappy music. Nance and Lynch walk down a deserted road in a rundown industrial zone, telephone wires hanging overhead. The place looks like the 1950s. It's a city with no name and Lynch has never been here before. He and Nance share the sort of emotional communion Lynch often portrays in his fictions and enjoys in life: no words necessary.

The friends encounter things that make Jack nervous: the gaping mouth of a car trunk, an abnormally tiny baby, and one of Lynch's familiar agents of darkness, an insect. Feeling threatened, Jack lags behind, but Lynch needs to penetrate the mystery and presses forward. Nance, as others in Lynch's world do, becomes the thing he most fears: the insect turns into Jack, who says, "I'm done, I'm done."[90]

Lynch and so many of his characters "long to see," so, in his Jack Nance dream, did Lynch's detective-like urge to keep examining strange phenomena somehow cause his friend's death? Lynch doesn't speculate on any unresolved guilts or emotional issues that his subconscious may have mixed into his dream scenario. The cold fact is that not even his dream can make Jack breathe again.

In 1995, the 100th anniversary year of Auguste and Louis Lumiere's public demonstration of the world's first motion picture camera and projection system, Lynch participated in a project that honored the French cinematic pioneers. The Lumieres' short films of people performing mundane actions like feeding a baby or watering a garden charmed and thrilled late-nineteenth-century spectators: This was technology so advanced that it seemed magical. And it was dramatic, for when a big locomotive came chugging toward the audience, viewers bolted from their seats in panic. Over the next century, the moving strip of film became a fundamental way for the world to convey its ideas and emotions, and in the mid 1990s Paris' *Figaro* magazine decided to honor the Lumiere Brothers' contribution by inviting forty top-flight international directors to take a turn with the Lumieres' original handwound camera. After being cranked up, the camera would run for fifty-eight seconds, and each director would have only this little time to work in. Lynch was proud to be one of those chosen to participate and, unlike his contemporaries, who followed the Lumieres' documentary-style lead and photographed naturalistic views of people and places, he decided to make a stylized, self-contained little narrative episode. It doesn't seem possible for Lynch to keep his unique artistic personality out of any work he does: His surrealistic spirit, more than the Lumieres' naturalism, animates his fifty-eight seconds. The result is stunningly Lynchian, but it also shows his ability to harmoniously orchestrate the efforts of many helpers, for this mini-production is a tour de force of coordinated action and split-second timing.

The antique camera's slight flicker and soft focus float us into a dark dream on a sunny day. Three background policemen walk in unison toward the camera and the horizontal foreground from a dead boy. Blackness. A woman in a house, who we intuitively know is the dead child's mother, looks with apprehension out beyond the right side of the frame. Blackness. Three young women lounge in a backyard settee, then one stands up with a look of concern as the image starts to flare or flame with an intrusive burst of energy, which transitions directly to a peek into hell. In some infernal factory, a naked woman with splayed arms and legs floats motionlessly under the water contained within a big glass cylinder, which has a thick electrical cord or water-supplying hose attached to it. Scary men in black and white, with bald, somehow distorted heads enter from the left. One pounds on the woman's cylinder with a heavy hammer, another carries a smoking frying pan (is torture or dinner in the offing?) Lynch pans left to right across this hellish scene to a black scrim that burns and splits like curtains parting to reveal the domestic interior where the mother we saw before sits with her husband. (The evil factory, the burning scrim, and the house interior are all contained within a single, traveling-camera shot—there are no cuts.) The man and woman rise from their chairs and cross to the right, for there's a policeman holding his hat in his hands at the door, and bad, bad news has once again invaded a pleasant home in Lynchland. There's a window in this living room tableau, and just before the director leaves the sunny interior and stops his film we see silhouetted on the window shade a dark, human-seeming shadow.

Lynch called his mini-movie *Premonitions Following an Evil Deed*, alerting us to the fact that the director is presenting two narrative streams in his fifty-eight seconds: (1) the dead boy; the mother with a premonition; the horrible realization that her feeling of foreboding is true. (Did Lynch uncharacteristically make the victim a boy because he now had a young son in his life?), and (2) the young woman enjoying a pleasant afternoon with two friends suddenly stands up, looking anxious; a young woman is trapped in a water tank surrounded by monstrous men. The lounging woman's presentiment could mean that she is the victim in the water, or that some absent woman friend is. The latter possibility recalls the *Twin Peaks* moment when Laura Palmer's friend Donna, seeing Laura's empty chair in class, gets a godawful feeling. And later in the series Lynch clouds the Roadhouse with disturbing foreshadowing while Maddy is about to be/is being killed across town. In his personal life, Lynch believes in paying attention to the feeling that "something's in the air."[91] The shadow at the window only appears in the dead boy/mother gets bad news story arc, yet it feels like a Lynchian abstraction of evil darkness that haunts his whole film, his other films, and the world that exists after the camera stops turning.

Lumiere and Company played the film festival circuit in this country and was released on video and disc. Whenever the project was reviewed or commented on, Lynch's episode was singled out for high praise. His fifty-eight-second effort showed that his imaginative and filmmaking skills were as potent as ever, and it made his admirers still hungrier for a full-length movie. And, in addition to *Lumiere and Company*, 1995 brought the news that their patience would be rewarded, for the director announced that he would soon shoot a screenplay called *Lost Highway* that he and Barry Gifford had written.

Lynch had previously adapted and augmented Gifford's novel *Wild at Heart* for the screen, and Gifford had penned the HBO *Hotel Room* segments that Lynch had directed. Lynch loved Gifford's noirish, hip, cool characters and their sparse dialogue, and he was thrilled by the phrase "lost highway"[92] in Gifford's novel *Night People* (he later learned of Hank Williams' "Lost Highway" song). Just as the words *eraserhead* and *elephant man* had sparked something in Lynch's brain, so *lost highway* sent him speeding down a creative road.

Gifford recalls that he and Lynch first built on the director's question, "What if one person woke up one day and was another person?"[93] As we've noted, Lynch is drawn to fictional situations of distorted, dual, and transformed identity in his own work, and has long admired Franz Kafka's seminal *Metamorphosis*, in which an average man wakes up and realizes that he's become an insect. For *Lost Highway* Gifford and Lynch melded the shifting-identity theme with a scary thought that the director and Mary Sweeney had talked about late one night driving home from the L.A. shooting on *Twin Peaks: Fire Walk With Me*. What would you do if anonymous videotapes were left at your door, tapes that showed you sleeping in the middle of the night? What if someone had, for some unholy reason, invaded the sanctuary of your house without you knowing it? Lynch often conceives of the house as a metaphor for the head, and a dark force that haunts the heads of Angelenos like Lynch and Mary is the inescapable reality of Charles Manson and his murderous family. The year before Lynch started school at the American Film Institute, young people under the sway of Manson, the satanic hippie cult leader, would, on some nights, "creepy crawly"[94] in and out of posh L.A. homes without waking a soul; while on other nights they would rouse the householders, only to put them to sleep forever, slit open and drenched in their own blood and screams.

The screenwriters then added in Lynch's long-held concept of the Mystery Man, a character who "seems supernatural: both real and not real,"[95] and they shaped the space and time of their creation in the form of a Mobius strip. Picture a length of cut ribbon, white on one side, black on the other. Give a single twist to the ribbon and tape its ends together. Then put your finger on the white side and run it along the ribbon's surface, until you realize that you've traveled from top to bottom, white to black, on one continuous highway.

As the opening credits fly into our faces out of blackness, David Bowie's voice sums up the fundamental theme of the coming two hours and fifteen minutes: "I'm deranged." The camera's point of view roars down a highway at night, with the road's yellow broken centerline positioned in the middle of the frame, showing that the vehicle we're in has violated the boundaries of safe driving. Traveling supernaturally fast, the black asphalt melts into the black night, and the centerline's yellow blips become rounded, biomorphic, like a stream of organic bullets shooting bad thoughts directly at us, into the brain.

In *Lost Highway*, Lynch, more than with any of his protagonists since *Eraserhead*'s Henry, dwells within the troubled mind of a central character. The black night of the speeding highway fades into another darkness, the head of Fred Madison (Bill Pullman), which is dimly delineated from the shadows when he lights a cigarette. It's a bright, sunny day in the steep, canyoned streets of the Hollywood Hills, but inside the slit-windowed house of the jazz saxophonist and his wife, Renee (Patricia Arquette), an obscuring gloom prevails. Alone with his thoughts, Fred hears only his own ragged, sighing breath—and then a male voice on the front-door intercom says,

"Dick Laurent is dead" (as Lynch swears an anonymous intercom voice once said to him). Fred crosses to his house's single large, full-size window (located in the dwelling's southeast corner, as is the only big front window in Lynch's house, which is literally just up the street) and looks down. No one's there.

Nor is anyone visible up or down the street when the anonymous videotapes start showing up on Fred and Renee's front steps. Inside the modest-sized house as well, it's hard to be sure who's there and not there. At various times, both husband (in a dream) and wife (late at night after a party) can't find their spouses. Lynch films the living room, bedroom, Fred's music room, and various corridors and hallways in such a way that we're not sure how they all connect spacially. The house's interior sense of murky dislocation reflects the emotional state of its occupants. Joy and vitality have been leached from Fred and Renee's marriage; they seem drugged with emotional fatigue and enervation. The unacknowledged tension between them is like an atmospheric pressure in the room that slows their movements and reduces their talk to bare-minimum, bland verbal exchanges. A pressure is building in Fred, and when he plays his sax at the club all his suppressed rage, sorrow, and fear come wailing out (Lynch, when directing Fred's playing, fervently said, "It's got to be insane."[96]). The laughter has left Fred and Renee's relationship, and Renee reminds him that she "likes to laugh." Fred worries that she's getting her jollies elsewhere, and remembers seeing her sneak out of the club with some slinky, thin-mustached guy. And when she says she's going to stay in and read while he goes to work, and he calls home to check on her, she's not there. Her sexual passion certainly doesn't stream in their marital bed anymore, for when Fred makes love to her she contributes no motion of her own and lies there looking up at him with icy eyes. Frustrated by her lack of participation in their act of intimacy, Fred comes with a sigh of frustration and humiliation, and then Renee adds insult to his hurt by patting him on the back and whispering, "It's okay," as though she's comforting a little boy who's peed his pants.

Fred's psyche is seething with doubt, suspicion, and animus toward Renee, but he doesn't attempt a healthy, direct resolution of his inner crisis by talking to her about his troubled mind. Even playing music wild and loud doesn't relieve the pressure steaming within him, so some part of his brain, like an unexplored corner of his house, starts to show and tell him things. In Fred's dream, when he can't locate Renee, Lynch's camera shows us Fred's point of view as it glides down the corridor to their bedroom past red curtains (which reference *Twin Peaks*' Red Room and code this as a zone where reality is in a fluid state). Rounding the corner into the room, Fred sees "someone who looks like" Renee but isn't her (she looks like Renee to us) lying on their bed, and the Fred's POV camera dives down toward her as she screams in terror. The dark, amorphous, secret life Fred is sure Renee is leading on the sly makes her not the woman he married, so his dream portrays her as the Other. In what seems to be the base reality of the film, Fred is narrating his dream to Renee after their cold-hearted lovemaking session. They're lying in bed, and just after telling her she seemed like someone else in his dream, he looks over at her and momentarily sees the pale visage of a strange man (Robert Blake) where his wife's face should be. Fred's inner turmoil has reached a point where, dreaming or awake, his wife's identity is in flux: He can't be sure of her.

When Fred and Renee attend a party at the gaudy, nouveau riche Hollywood mansion of a guy named Andy (Michael Massee), Fred's obsessive suspicion that his wife's leading a dirty, secret life nears the boiling point, for he recognizes sleazy Andy as the fellow Renee snuck out of the jazz club with that night. At the party, Renee treats Fred like a lackey, spending her time with Andy and sending her husband off to get a drink for her. As usual, no anger is visible on Fred's surface, but as he goes to fulfill Renee's drink order, the party-mix soundtrack segues into The Classic Five's "Spooky," and he meets the pale-faced man he had momentarily seen replace his wife's image the other night in bed.

With his Kabuki theater–like pallor and dark lips, the Mystery Man (Robert Blake) is a strikingly unusual presence, but Lynch directed the party crowd to view him as nothing out of the ordinary, thus indicating that he is a special entity for Fred alone. And indeed, the party's clamor fades away and the Mystery Man speaks, most intimately, just to Fred. With a sneering grin frozen on his face, the man tells Fred they've met before, at Fred's house. Fred says that this just isn't so, but the man insists, saying that he's at the house right now. He hands Fred a cell phone, and when he calls the house the Mystery Man answers. Somehow, this fellow can be at two places at once, and Fred asks how he got "inside my house?" The man responds, "You invited me, for it is not my custom to go where I'm not wanted." Fred, shaken by this invasive stranger's power, demands to know "Who are you?" From the man right in front of him, who is also in his house, comes a double rumble of deep laughter, and the fellow departs, saying, "It's been a pleasure talking to you."

Lynch subtly lights this creepy encounter so that Fred's eyes are shadowed and lifeless, while the Mystery Man, who never blinks, beams out a hot, reflected light from his black pupils. Fred may be exhausted from trying to grasp and hold onto his cold, slippery, wayward wife, but some deep part of his brain, projected and personified as the Mystery Man, has come to life and is ready to act out dark, malevolent impulses. In *Twin Peaks*, BOB was both an extra-dimensional entity and an abstraction of "the evil that men do" who was invited by the weak and vulnerable part of Leland Palmer's psyche to live within him. And likewise, Fred has unconsciously invited the Mystery Man into his house, which, with its soft-textured ruddy interior walls, we see as a metaphor for his soft head. In Fred's house, where the intruder alarm keeps going off for no visible reason, Fred is the only one who casts looming shadows onto walls, and when he goes to the house front's single big right-corner window and looks out, it's like a head with one eye that can only see half of what's going on.

When Fred and Renee return home after the party, Lynch immerses them in one of his most resonant "Now it's dark" passages. Husband and wife don't speak to each other, and she, her voluptuous body wrapped in a gleaming black robe, removes her makeup in front of the large bathroom mirror. Fred, in the bedroom around the corner, hears a disturbing echoing sound and slowly walks into one of his house's mysterious corridors, his black-T-shirted back gradually being swallowed by a deeper blackness, in which he dimly sees himself in a mirror, his face reflecting some of the Mystery Man's pallor. Cutting back to Renee, she's startled and a little afraid to see that Fred isn't in the bedroom. Standing tremulously at the gaping mouth of Fred's corridor, she calls his name, but the black abyss of danger and unreason is mute. She withdraws, and we see two amorphous shadows pass through the living room. Then Fred emerges toward us out of the corridor, coming forward until his head blackens out the frame. The darkness of his head then becomes the blackness of the TV screen in Fred and Renee's living room. Lynch, with this sublimely composed poem of echoing shadow tints, shows us the unbridgeable distance between Fred and Renee, and Fred's frightening susceptibility to the call of the night, and, with its mirror-doublings of husband and wife, it prefigures the character multiples that will drive the film's second half.

Lynch's linkage of Fred's head with the TV screen is one of the keys to *Lost Highway*. After videotapes showing an uninvited tour of the Madisons' house interior start mysteriously arriving, two plainclothes police detectives come to check things out. When the cops ask if they own a video camera, Renee says, "Fred hates them," and Fred adds, "I like to remember things my own way—the way I remember them, not necessarily the way they happened." Fred may say he doesn't like video cameras, but the trajectory of the mystery tape's point of view virtually duplicates the view his eyes have shown us when he walks down the corridor toward the bedroom in both waking life and his dream. The dream had ended as Fred's viewpoint swooped down on a screaming Renee, as though his subconscious was showing him a pathway that would relieve his long-suppressed rage toward her. The urge to perform an act far more meaningful and conclusive than just wailing his pain and anger into his saxophone has been stirred in Fred's psyche, and with a grim inevitability, Fred sits down alone to watch the final mystery tape.

The black-and-white tape image travels down a corridor into Fred and Renee's bedroom. This time, they are not sleeping. On the floor, Renee's pale body has been cut in two at the waist: there's a sickening gap of dark carpet between her torso and hips, her right leg is missing below her thigh, one of her hands is on the bed. Fred, his hands, arms and chest stained with her black blood, kneels amid the sundered parts of his wife. Fred, in his living room watching the tape in horror, calls out "Renee!" and there is no answer.

The sectioning of Renee's body seems to be Lynch's homage to a real-life case of L.A. noir: the notorious, still-unsolved 1947 slaying of Elizabeth Short, the Black Dahlia of police files and crime-novel pages. Both Short and Renee had long, brunette hair and were found in a similarly dismembered state. Lynch once discussed Short's case with one of its original investigators over dinner. The director often projects the thoughts, moods, emotions, and dreams that are inside his characters' heads out into the tangible world, so it seems perversely logical that Fred, in his madness, would want to look inside the woman he loves and hates. As author James Ellroy (*L.A. Confidential*) says of the uncaught man who killed Elizabeth Short, "he cut the Dahlia open to see what made women different from men."[97]

After we see Fred watch the tape and call for his wife, the police rough him up and accuse him of her murder. (Since Fred's dissociated minds naturally thought some intruder killed her, he must have called the cops.) Fred "likes to remember things my own way, not necessarily the way they happened," and he's not sure what occurred: He desperately entreats his interrogators, "Tell me I didn't kill her!" From the *Lost Highway* viewer's vantage point, it seems logical that Fred has snuffed out the one person he loves madly and yet is unable to possess. And Lynch has given us a visual clue, for while Fred is watching the black-and-white tape image of himself with Renee's corpse, the director throws in a subliminal few frames of bloody color with no tape grain, which reads as a scary flashback burst of Fred's actual experience. The tape makes him remember, and quickly suppress, the memory of being bathed in the red fluid that flowed from the wife he tore open.

Fred is quickly convicted and sentenced to die in the electric chair (more Lynch electrophilia). As Fred sits in his cell, which is a solid steel room with no bars, Lynch emphasizes the condemned man's head more than he has any other characters in his work. Fred complains of piercing headaches that won't go away, has a doctor examine his noggin, and at one point even screams out, "My head!" Fred's brain is wrenched by contradictory forces: he killed Renee—no, someone killed Renee—no, he killed Renee. In *Eraserhead*, when Henry looked into his room's steel radiator, he saw in his mind's eye the lighted theatrical stage that would ultimately provide an answer and an escape from his entrapped, painful state. And as Fred stares at the locked door of his cell, its charcoal-hued surface parts like stage curtains to reveal a riveting image. Surrounded by darkness, a shack-like cabin burns in reverse, like something materializing out of Hell and taking solid form in Fred's world. At the party, the Mystery Man said that Fred had invited him into his house/mind, and this windowless cabin is the deeply interior sanctum where the Man dwells. The pale-faced fellow steps out of his front door, seems to look at Fred, then goes inside, leaving the door open as though he's waiting for a visit.

Earlier, when the two plainclothes cops came to Fred and Renee's house in response to their distress call about the disturbing videotapes, Lynch linked a sense of strangeness-within-the-ordinary to Fred's viewpoint. Fred stays inside while the men go outside with Renee to look around. As he watches his wife and a cop walk by a window, their lips moving without sound, Fred seems dissociated from reality, as though he's seeing alien beings pass by. And when he hears weird bumps on the roof and looks up, light brightening his face, he sees the other cop through the ceiling skylight like some powerful abstract force making itself felt. Then, when Fred, again alone in his living room, views the tape showing his wife's bloody body and yells out, "Renee!," he again looks up, and this time his face is illuminated by a blue-white lightening flash like in one of the electrical-disturbance moments from *Twin Peaks* that signaled the presence of unnatural forces. Lynch, with a time-and-space-bridging flash from one shot to the next, then leaps from Fred's upturned, lightening-lit face to the cop he's previously seen through the skylight slugging him in the face and calling him Renee's killer. In a single edit linking two shots, the director has established the transportive power of an image: when Fred looks up, his face flashed with light, he ends up somewhere else.

In his cell, Fred again looks up, his face reflecting the strongest electrical flashes we've seen yet as Lynch launches his protagonist on a major journey. We glimpse the opening-credit-sequence night highway with its streaming yellow line and see a young man we don't know standing at the roadside. The director turns Fred's small steel room into a flashing factory of transformation as, through smoke, we see Fred thrashing his head from side to side, recalling the similar motion of the *Grandmother*'s Boy just before his head sprouted into a human/botanical hybrid form. Lynch makes a poetic abstraction of Fred's transfiguration, as we see darkness, quick flashes of bone, cartilage, blood, and a long look at a blobby, out-of-focus head that is the director's homage to the painted heads-in-flux of Francis Bacon, whose work he so admires. When the guards check Fred's cell, he is not there, but the shadowy young man from the roadside is.

Pete Dayton (Balthazar Getty), nursing a bump on his forehead, has no idea how he got in a cell on death row, nor do the guards and prison warden who, in silent embarrassment, hands Pete over to his parents (Gary Busey, Lucy Butler). Surely, this groovy mom and dad, who enter the warden's office wearing pale blue jeans, black leather jackets and sunglasses, are the ones young 1950s Lynch longed for when he grew weary of his own parents' wholesome squareness.

Back home in the San Fernando Valley suburbs, Pete seems dazed, as though he's gradually feeling his way back into his own life. Or is it Fred who's getting used to a change of scene and identity? When Lynch was "two or three"[98] in Spokane, Washington, he "lived on a little chaise lounge,"[99] and he shows us Pete lying on a chaise in his backyard and rising to look over a wall into the neighboring backyard. The director's autobiographical reverence for a child's perspective permeates the scene Pete sees: green grass, a plastic wading pool, a ball and toy sailing ship bobbing on its waters, and (referencing the child's eye opening of *Blue Velvet*) a garden hose and small white dog. The world seems safe and fresh and full of possibilities, but as Pete rests his chin on the brick wall, a comforting soft-focus wash of sunlit trees gently undulating behind him, we note that Lynch has positioned his face directly above a dividing line between two bricks, connoting fracture, splitting, doubleness.

Back in the swing of things, Pete hangs out with his quasi-delinquent pals and dances with his loving girlfriend, Sheila (Natasha Gregson Wagner). Our first glimpse of her, slow-dancing with Pete in dim light, provides a delicious *frisson*, for Natasha Gregson Wagner seems to be her tragically drowned mother, Natalie Wood (1938–1981), come to life. Gregson Wagner's physical resemblance to her lost mother is striking, and the moment has added resonance thanks to Lynch and Gifford's screenplay, which earlier mentioned "the observatory."[100] The structure referred to, the Griffith Park Observatory, is iconic in terms of both the topography of Los Angeles and the history of cinema, for it was here that director Nicholas Ray staged the death-dealing climax of his teen-angst masterpiece *Rebel Without a Cause* (1955), which featured Natalie Wood as a tender high schooler trembling on the verge of womanhood. In the film, Wood loved archetypal young misfit James Dean, who is remembered with a bronze plaque near the observatory (it was Sal Mineo who died in *Rebel*). A road-burning driver in real life, Dean was killed in a car crash before *Rebel Without a Cause* hit the theaters, his racing Porsche scattered all over a California desert highway, which is the landscape Lynch's road trip is moving toward.

Sheila's words to Pete show that there's been some distance between the couple: He's been "acting strange," like "the other night" when she last saw him. But now their bond seems firmly reestablished, though when they make love in the back seat of Pete's car he seems to be indulging in a familiar habit rather than expressing the love of his life.

Pete's an auto mechanic, and when he goes back to work at Arnie's Garage, some odd things happen. The screaming saxophone solo we heard Fred Madison play early in the film comes on the radio and Pete, as though pierced with pain, touches his head and heart. Desperate to stop the sound, he turns off the radio, much to the displeasure of fellow grease monkey Phil (Jack Nance favors us with another inimitable line reading: "I *like* that"—meaning the loud, jazzy music).

Fred and Renee had their two investigating cops (John Roselius, Lou Eppolito), and Pete has his (Carl Sundstrom, John Solari), who've been clandestinely keeping an eye on him since he showed up in Fred's prison cell. When gangster Mr. Eddy (Robert Loggia) cruises into the garage to have Pete check his big black Mercedes sedan, the detectives recognize the elegant hoodlum by another name, Dick Laurent, recalling the "Dick Laurent is dead" message anonymously left on Fred Madison's intercom.

And later, when Mr. Eddy brings in his other car, there's a gorgeous woman in the front seat who looks just like Renee, except her hair is white-hot blonde. This is Alice Wakefield, and if Fred *Mad*ison is mad, then Alice could easily wake a field—wake the dead, and perhaps, in her own case, she has. Played by Patricia Arquette, as was Renee, Alice is Mr. Eddy's girlfriend, but before his tough henchmen safely seal her up within the reflective fortress of the black Mercedes, she and Pete exchange some soul-searching eye contact. Lynch emphasizes Alice and Pete's instantaneous connection with a series of dreamy back-and-forth close-ups that feel like a sexual exchange, and he crystallizes their aroused emotions with a classic 1950s love song. It is indeed "This Magic Moment," but the mood-darkening edge of irony in Lou Reed's deadpan voice makes us wonder if the magic isn't voodoo.

Has Fred supernaturally become Pete, and Renee Alice? Is Fred dreaming all this? Is Alice Renee's avenging ghost? Has Lynch finally overwhelmed our ability to penetrate his layers of mystery?

Beginning with his earliest short films, Lynch has made the inner thoughts and feelings of his characters visible to us. Sometimes, as when *The Grandmother*'s Boy fantasizes guillotining and squashing his abusive parents, we know we're seeing a mental event inside his head. But in the notoriously hard-to-read *Eraserhead*, Henry's psychological turmoil permeates both his waking and dream life to such an extent that one viewer will swear that everything that happens after Henry's wife leaves him is a psychic happening, while others insist that the entire movie is a dream. In striving to communicate his characters' depths, their psychological reality, Lynch often merges their inner and outer worlds into a seamless flow of subjective consciousness. Speaking of *Lost Highway*, he said, "We all have an inner knowing and feeling that responds to human things like jealousy and fear and love, even if they're presented in an abstract way and not articulated in words."[101] This is indeed the complex landscape of Fred Madison's inner being that Lynch visualizes in *Lost Highway*, but whether the average linear-storyline-appreciating audience could "feel" the underlying meaning of this puzzling road trip is questionable. Carl Jung, the great student of the inner and outer realities of human behavior once said that it's a mistake to assume that another person's psychology is the same as your own. Lynch may be overestimating the interpretive ability and goodwill of many viewers when he says "in a lot of ways, it's a straight-ahead story"[102] and that everyone "can relate to almost any kind of human behavior, no matter how bizarre."[103] Unfortunately, many who saw *Lost Highway* could glean nothing of value from Lynch and Gifford's darkly beautiful artistry.

In common parlance, the phrase "it was only a dream" connotes disappointment and derogation: the material witnessed was just the product of randomly firing neurons, a will-o'-the-wisp that can't be seen or touched in the real world of waking reality. Lynch, who's "sure I'll be surprised when I learn what reality is,"[104] so values the states and productions of his own mind that he invests Fred Madison's head trips with a vibrant emotional and sensual immediacy. Fred's body may be lying on his bed in his death-row cell during the two hours and fifteen minutes *Lost Highway* plays out, but he is, moment-to-moment, living a high-stakes drama that Lynch makes compellingly real for both Fred and us.

Fred's troubled mind can't accept the fact that he slaughtered the woman he loved and is trapped in a cell waiting to be fried for his crime, so his brain gives him an escape route: He forgets all about Fred and Renee and lives

Pete's life, with a new house, parents, job, and girlfriend. But stray bits of his Fred self, such as that saxophone music on the garage radio, slip into his Pete reality and give him a headache. Fred may have wiped Renee's body out of his life, but she remains a major character in his psychic drama, and materializes as Alice in Pete's world. And, wonderfully, as it always should have been, Alice is as eager to love Pete as he is to embrace her.

In contrast to Fred and Renee's cold and distant interactions, Pete and Alice seem to communicate through the heat of their lovemaking, and Lynch makes their passion for each other compress time by leaping from their first night together, through the next day's sunset, and into bed again. This passage glories in the mood of L.A. noir: the smoky, scorched-orange sunset, the lovers' motel framed by black palm tree trunks, Alice's red lips huge in the frame purring "Meow-meow" into a black phone receiver.

In *Lost Highway*, Lynch and Gifford work variations on some classic film noir themes. We have the amnesiac protagonist who's not sure if he's done something very, very bad melding with the innocent (part of Fred thinks so) guy who's wrongfully imprisoned and sends his loyal secretary out into the night to track down the real culprit. By discovering a mental way to get outside his cell, Fred not only gets to enjoy intimacy with a responsive Renee (as Alice), but he has a chance to, as actor Bill Pullman (Fred) says, find out "who is at the source of the crime."[105] Also in the vein of film noir is the fact that, by cheating on a powerful and violent man (Mr. Eddy) with Pete, Alice has put both their young lives in mortal danger. And there's Alice herself, a classic femme fatale with a sordid double life who professes her love for Pete while manipulating him to help her get rich quick so she can fly away from Mr. Eddy.

Before Fred killed Renee, he was tortured by the suspicion that she was having sex with someone else, so in his life as Pete he gets to steal another man's woman. Fred's mind may have given him this ego-gratifying chance to right the scales of emotional justice, but Renee and Alice won't let him have a happy ending. She was a wrong one for Fred and she is a wrong one for Pete. Alice's naked body and musky smell are a drug in Pete's blood, and when he can't be with her he gets the heebie-jeebies like an addict desperate for a fix. Having neglected the good and truly loving Sheila, he watches her storm out of his life hurt and angry.

Pete's need for Alice and the threat of Mr. Eddy finding out about it are solid realities in his life, but he's also preoccupied with an intangible mystery. Both Sheila's and Pete's teary-eyed parents have questions about something momentous and strange that happened to Pete "that night," and the police would like to know about it too. This must be the night that he supernaturally vanished from his usual routine so that he could show up in Fred Madison's prison cell. Fred's mind, horrified by his crime and cell-bound, created all the details of Pete's life and escaped into it. Like a screenwriter, Fred gave Pete a backstory, a stretch of time and life events that existed before the Fred-as-Pete present tense we've been witnessing. *Lost Highway*'s continuum of time, space, and identity evokes the eternal existential question of how we got here. Like others who believe in reincarnation, Lynch wonders where we were before we arrived in this life.

True to Lynch's love of narrative doubling, Pete's blind spot about what happened "that night" echoes Fred's inability, or unwillingness, to remember killing Renee. As Pete ponders the mysterious block of time that's lost from his memory we see a quick flash of the bloody head bones that signaled Fred's transformation into Pete, and a view of Renee dead on the carpet. These momentary, intrusive images show us that Fred is the one sending the signal that we're watching: His mind is manufacturing Pete and his world. There's also the sense that Fred is trying to put the blame for his crime onto Pete, and that the young man sees Renee on the floor because he put her there.

Lynch expands this notion later in the film, after Alice has immersed Pete in her toxic secret life. Evoking the very real and deadly threat of Mr. Eddy's retribution for her and Pete's affair, Alice makes the kind of proposal to her young lover that has driven hundreds of film noirs: "If we could just get some money we could go away together." Alice's plan is so simple and foolproof: She'll go to Andy, her rich pornographer friend, and distract him with her body while Pete sneaks in downstairs. At 11 p.m. she'll send Andy to get her a drink, Pete will conk him on the head, then she and Pete will gather up Andy's valuables and take them to a middle man who will give them cash in exchange. Sounds easy, but in film noir people and their carefully engineered crimes were made to go bad.

Since the movie we're watching is the one that Fred Madison is playing in his own head, Pete's story, as its dramatic tension grows, begins to include more elements from Fred's psychodrama with Renee. Andy turns out to be the mustached man Fred saw Renee slip out of the jazz club with one night, and the guy who hosted the party where Fred encountered the Mystery Man. As Pete sneaks into the house where Fred partied, he sees confirmation of Fred's worst suspicions about Renee, for projected on a big screen is a 16mm film of Alice/Renee being screwed from behind by a huge black man, and loving every inch of it. (Lynch subtly cued us for this shocking verification of Fred's fears by having Renee, early in *Lost Highway*, seem slightly edgy and nervous when that first anonymous tape showed up at their house and she and Fred were sitting down to watch it, as though the tape might reveal her sexcapades.) Anyone who still believes that Lynch routinely exploits women in sex scenes should note the contrast of emotional tone between the bluish, grainy 16mm image of Alice and her doggy-style/anal penetrator and *Wild at Heart*'s Lula and Sailor in the same sexual position. Alice's film portrays an exercise of power, domination, and whorish enjoyment, whereas Lula and Sailor's ruddy-faced exertions pump love and a deep passionate sharing into every frame of their scene.

The life-as-Pete that Fred's mind constructed for himself was rewarding at first: a fresh beginning as a virile, younger man who got to love and be loved by someone who had the look and allure of Renee. But Renee generates so much negative energy in Fred's psyche that even as Alice, she poisons his (as Pete's) days and nights. As in a classic film noir, things start to go so bad they can never be fixed.

Pete's nauseated by the filmed evidence of Alice's debased moral state, but she's got her hooks in him deep, and when Andy pads downstairs to get the drink, Pete follows Alice's plan and knocks him out. Andy regains consciousness and launches himself at Pete, only to land forehead-first on the sharp glass end of a table. Another head-piercing moment in Lynch's oeuvre (he meticulously orchestrated the corpse's barely audible "dry skull cracks")[106] and no doubt the only death-by-coffee-table in cinema history. (Actor William Holden, the male lead in one of the films Lynch loves most, *Sunset Boulevard*, perished when he fell, struck his head on the edge of a table, and bled to death.) When Alice joins Pete downstairs, she's cold-hearted and scary, stripping the jewelry off of Andy's impaled body, "playfully" pointing a big pistol at Pete, and stressing that "you," not "we," killed him. Andy's death was an accident, but Fred's mind inside Pete's world is starting to paint the young man as the fall guy. When the cops who arrested Fred for Renee's murder investigate Andy's death scene, they see a photo of Renee, find Pete's fingerprints all over the place, and conclude, "There's no such thing as a bad coincidence," implying that Pete may well have rubbed out Renee as well as Andy, thus making Fred an innocent man.

With a big pillowcase full of Andy's loot, Alice and Pete steal their victim's car and head into the nocturnal desert, where the burning-backward-into-materiality cabin Fred envisioned in his cell constructs itself to meet them. This is where the fence will give them cash for the stolen goods—but no one's there when they arrive. While they wait, Lynch crafts an iconic image of Southwest noir, as Alice and Pete make love on the dusty desert floor. Lit by the car's headlight beams, Alice is (naturally) in the superior position on top of Pete: naked, surrounded by black velvet darkness and wind puffs of pale dust, the almost overexposed image of her flesh mirrors the white-hot hue of her swaying platinum hair.

Lynch uses the same musical theme to link Fred's sexual-emotional frustration over Renee's unresponsive iciness in bed to Alice hissing to Pete in the desert, "You'll never have me." As Alice and Pete's affair has progressed, and he's gradually discovered her sordid side, she has asked, almost tauntingly, "Do you still want me, Pete?" Even now, knowing she's as bad as they come, he has a bottomless yearning for her. But, just as Fred reached a point where he felt Renee could never be his the way he needed her to be, Pete realizes that Alice has slammed the door in his face. As Lynch says, "Pete can't go any further with Alice,"[107] so she vanishes from the film, as does Pete.

Thus far, Lynch has shown us Fred and Renee's world, Fred alone in his cell, and Pete's world, which Fred has created in his mind. Now the director intermingles Fred's psychic spaces by having him emerge in Pete's realm, in the desert with the fence's cabin and Andy's car. Lynch gives a darkly humorous clue to the Mystery Man's role in Fred's drama by having the pale-faced fellow pop up behind the driver's seat in the car, in the position of a backseat voice that tells the driver what to do. Like *Eraserhead*'s Man in the Planet pulling Henry's levers and *Twin Peaks*' BOB making Leland kill, the Mystery Man is another of Lynch's powerful inhabiting presences who steers the course of the protagonist's life. Early in the film, Fred said that he hated the impersonal, objectively recording eye of a video camera and preferred his own, remembered version of events. Now, wanting to show Fred some harsh truths about his life, the Mystery Man points his video camera at him, and Fred runs to the car in panic and flees into the desert night.

Next, we see Fred arriving at the desolate, nocturnal desert Lost Highway Hotel where Lynch, without giving any indication that he's showing us a flashback, dips into the timestream of Fred's life when Renee was still alive and enthusiastically cheating on her husband with gangster Dick Laurent (Robert Loggia) in one of the hotel rooms. After Renee departs, Fred jumps Laurent and takes him into the desert at gunpoint. Full of fight, Laurent surprises Fred and pummels him down to the ground. The Mystery Man shoots Laurent with a pistol (yes, in the head) and vanishes, leaving Fred standing over the dead Laurent with the gun.

The Mystery Man's shack, the Lost Highway Hotel, and the endless road Fred drives are situated in the nocturnal desert east of Los Angeles, some scenes, most appropriately, being shot in Death Valley. Lynch's use of these locales resonates with the way, as author Barry Hoskyns notes, "Los Angeles has always been haunted by the desert that surrounds it—by its emptiness, its inhospitality to life, and the way it provides a refuge for freaks, cultists, and killers. As everyone from Aldous Huxley to Jim Morrison to Gram Parsons has understood, the desert lends itself to apocalyptic fantasy."[108] Film director Michaelangelo Antonioni and songwriter/murderous visionary Charles Manson were other artists who saw the arid, elemental American desert landscape as a stage setting for explosive violence and sudden death.

Before Fred and the Mystery Man killed Laurent, they showed him why he was sentenced to die. On a small, handheld TV screen, Laurent watched one of the Mystery Man's videotapes showing him and Renee getting aroused while watching a movie that was part sexual pornography, part snuff film. How can the man who's capable of inflaming Renee's passion be allowed to live? The Mystery Man is both a projection of Fred's shadow side, the part of him with a raging will to punish those who hurt him, and the witness and recorder of deep, ugly truths. The videotapes that arrived at Fred and Renee's weren't left by some outsider, they were shot by the Mystery Man part of Fred's brain and showed the progression of a murderous thought into the house, down the hallway, and into the bedroom of Fred and Renee's final, bloody bedroom encounter. The tapes don't exist in the world of Fred's murder trial, sentencing judge, and prison cell. The reading of *Lost Highway* that answers most of its mysteries locates the film's base reality with Fred lying on his prison bed, living in mental worlds of desire and anger, love and revenge. The first section of the film detailing Fred and Renee's interactions is as much a creation of Fred's imprisoned, streaming mind as are the passages showing Pete and Alice and later Fred executing Dick Laurent. Fred wasn't convicted on the evidence of the tapes except within his own self-judging mind. In Fred's mental movie, Renee's growing fear as more tapes kept arriving was a displacement of her rising apprehension about Fred's animus toward her, and her knowledge that he had good reason to suspect and be mad at her. In his mind, Fred played out a scenario in which his bad thoughts were concretized as the tapes, which he could blame on the Mystery Man's camera, and which brought the police to the house to investigate. In real life, Fred, having blacked out the fact that he killed his wife, called them to report her death.

True to the time-bending capacity of Fred's mind, *Lost Highway*'s final portion, in which Fred kills Laurent for sleeping with Renee, and the Mystery Man is established as official videographer, actually precedes the film's beginning. For, leaving Laurent's corpse in the desert, Fred drives to his own house and says, "Dick Laurent is dead" into the intercom: the message and voice Fred hears over the intercom from inside the house as the film opens. And before the Mystery Man (Fred's dark self) departs the scene of

Laurent's killing, he whispers in Fred's ear, perhaps saying, "What about Renee? She too must die" and setting Fred in motion on the path that will lead down the hall and into the bloody bedroom of Renee's dismemberment.

From the convoluted evidence that Lynch has shown us, we surmise that Fred has killed his wife and Dick Laurent and that Fred can only occasionally realize this truth as bits and pieces of psychic narrative flit through his consciousness. Part of Fred's mind knows that he's transgressed horribly and deserves to be punished, so the movie his head is producing (and *Lost Highway* itself) ends with a line of police cars chasing his speeding vehicle into the desert. Again, we see a primal Lynchian dynamic at work: external forces seeking to control and curtail the forward progress of a freedom-seeking individual, though both sides of the equation are part of Fred's psyche. Fred is at war with himself, lost in Lynch's "darkness and confusion,"[109] unable to become fully aware of his capacity for evil and choose the road of light and love in spite of it, as many of the director's characters have done. As the yellow highway markings fly into Fred's face and the police sirens and flashing lights gain on him from the rear, his head flails from side to side and supernatural light flashes as when Fred transformed into Pete. As the film ends, Fred's mind is ready to vault him into some fresh scenario, where he can again try to break free from his cycle of desire and pain. But for now he dwells within a closed system: the end only becomes the beginning of an endless night.

Most of Lynch's protagonists manage to take off-ramps from their lost highways, they break free from their personal hells. But Fred's irresistible urge to always choose Renee keeps his inferno torturously burning.

When ABC canceled *Twin Peaks*, we left Agent Cooper under the sway of BOB's evil, but surely if the series had continued Lynch and Frost would have devised a way to free their hero's good self from the prison of the Red Room. An ABC management decision left Cooper in dire straits, whereas in *Lost Highway* the director, most atypically, deliberately chooses to leave his protagonist in an unenlightened state. But Lynch's boundary-crossing consciousness easily flows out beyond the ending credits of his film. He feels that "there's perfect justice in the world, which is hard to believe when a guy like O. J. walks free. The only way it makes sense is through reincarnation."[110] Lynch believes that our souls live out "a continuing story"[111] over many lifetimes (no wonder he wanted to take his time in revealing who killed Laura Palmer), and that "there's no escaping your good actions and there's no escaping your bad actions."[112] He feels that "eventually, maybe not in this lifetime, the good things come back and visit you and the bad come back and visit you."[113] So if O. J. Simpson, as Lynch says, "sliced up two people"[114] and, like Fred Madison, repressed the truth of his crime beneath his conscious mind, he will pay for his transgression in the fullness of time. Applying Lynch's forever-after justice system to his fiction, we see that *Eraserhead*'s Henry, despite having killed his offspring, gets to bask in heavenly radiance with his grace-filled Lady in the Radiator angel, and hence is more spiritually evolved than Fred.

The highway ahead of Fred's speeding car is as black and long as when his film began, but he's still moving forward, the horizon remains open, and the cops haven't caught him yet: Maybe there is morning at the far-off end of night.

Lost Highway fully explores Lynch's fascination with double identities, the emotional and physical violence people visit on each other, and the mind's ability to create and dwell within multiple realities, yet the film feels less personal than masterworks like *Eraserhead*, *Blue Velvet*, and *Twin Peaks*. The director crafts some visually ravishing and intellectually challenging variations on the conventional characters, situations, and atmosphere of film noir, but the presence of so many noir elements received from popular culture makes the film less uniquely Lynchian. The aesthetic convolutions of Fred's inner roadtrip are brilliant and stunning, and Bill Pullman, Patricia Arquette, and Balthazar Getty do an admirable job of acting out Fred's journey, yet their cool demeanor and tamped-down affect keep them from engaging us on the visceral, heart-and-soul level where Lynch's most resonant characters live.

Lost Highway's resemblance to classic film noir may have sprung from Barry Gifford's sensibility. In his searing 1988 book on noir, *The Devil Thumbs a Ride* (*Lost Highway* would have been an apt alternate title), Gifford analyzed Edgar G. Ulmer's 1945 film *Detour*, a movie that may have been on Gifford's conscious or unconscious mind as he wrote the *Lost Highway* screenplay with Lynch.

In Gifford's words, *Detour* is about "fate, about bad luck and trouble, and death around the corner."[115] The film's protagonist is "an unhappy nightclub musician"[116] who loves a woman so desperately that "he can't live without her."[117] When she splits for another state he "suffers the tortures of the road"[118] trying to get to her. In the process, through bizarre circumstances, he takes on the trappings of another man's life, wearing his clothes, carrying his identity papers, driving his car. The musician's life spirals downward: "Now he's really a killer, and he takes to the road again."[119]

Gifford's book also describes parallels between Ulmer's fictional musician/killer and the real-life drama of the man who played him on the screen, actor Tom Neal. And there are echoes of Neal's situation in *Lost Highway*. Like Fred Madison, Neal loved a woman who was drawn to another man, a fellow who Neal beat up (Fred kills his male rival). Then, as in Fred's wish-fulfilling fantasy where, as Pete, he gets another chance with Renee, Neal's woman left the other guy and returned to him. Lethal violence entered Neal's love scene later, when he married another woman, murdered her, and sat in prison contemplating the road-to-hell trajectory of his life.

Lost Highway can also be seen as an acting out of lines from The Eagles' 1977 song "Hotel California" (penned by Don Felder, Don Henley, and Glenn Frey), a dystopic L.A. anthem that's been part of pop culture since Lynch debuted *Eraserhead*. The song's narrator, like Fred Madison, drives in the desert on a nocturnal, lonely road and sees a gleaming light up ahead, as when Fred eyes the upcoming flashing vortex that will transport him into Pete's life. The man encounters a Significant Woman (like Pete's Alcie Wakefield), and finds himself in a situation that could be positive or negative. Like those in "Hotel California," Fred is trying to keep something out of his mind: his horrendous crime. But try as he might to escape into Pete's life, he remains, like the song's denizens, trapped by his own actions. The song's narrator desperately needs to find a way back to where he was earlier (we picture Pete and Fred mired in sexual betrayal and murder in the corridors of the desert-situated Lost Highway Hotel). When Fred's existence as Pete turns to nightmare he does get back to where he's been before, he becomes Fred again. But he can't outrun his sin, his bad karma: in the Hotel California it seems easy to leave when you want, but can never quite get away.[126]

Film critics and fans were excited about Lynch's return to the big screen after such a long absence, and a number of Comeback Kid articles preceded *Lost Highway*'s February 1997 release. Unlike *Twin Peaks: Fire Walk With Me* (1992), which barely got reviewed, Lynch's new film was critiqued by more than forty notable newspapers and magazines: Once again people seemed ready to take a trip into the director's singular sensibility. Some writers rightly applauded Lynch's artistic heroism, his uncompromising plunge into emotional and spiritual darkness and his faith in the viewer's intuitive ability to glean meaning from a complex narrative that plays havoc with the standard linear presentation of time and space, and that erases the expected firm delineation between a character's inner reality and the world outside his head. Many reviewers, however, just scratched their heads, unwilling or unable to puzzle their way through the labyrinthine roadmap discernable beneath *Lost Highway*'s dazzling surface. Even critic Gene Siskel, who habitually defended Lynch's films from the heated animus of his partner, Roger Ebert, confessed, "I can't make heads or tails of this material."[127]

Lynch, in consultation with October Films and his personal brand of numerology, ascertained what he felt was the most auspicious time to release *Lost Highway*, though the magic held for only a short time. The initial audience turnout was solid, for an independent production with a relatively small advertising budget, and in some markets, especially Japan and Europe, the film opened in the top ten on its first weekend. But generally negative reviews and condemnatory word-of-mouth quickly took their toll. Most viewers couldn't understand that Pete suddenly appeared in Fred's cell to give Fred another chance at life and Renee, and they reacted with confusion and irritation. Lynch had believed people would be intrigued by *Lost Highway*'s mysterious surface and intuitively grasp the emotional truths living within its flux of human identities.

Sadly, for Lynch's status in the film industry marketplace, and the generally unresponsive state of the public imagination, most of *Lost Highway*'s viewers felt they shared Fred Madison's predicament all too intimately: bewitched, bothered, bewildered. These are states of mind common to Lynch's characters and intimately familiar to their creator, but not eagerly sought by your average ticket-buying moviegoer. People didn't want the Mystery Man messing with their heads, but in 2001 millions of people became fascinated by the doings of the actor who played him.

As a child performer, Robert Blake (born 1933) acted in numerous *Our Gang* and *Red Ryder* films, and he won international acclaim for his sympathetic portrayal of a killer in *In Cold Blood* (1967). From 1975 to 1978 he endeared himself to TV viewers as the title character on "Baretta," the tough-talking, anti-establishment police detective with a pet cockatoo, who'd say, "Don't do the crime if you can't do the time"[128] as he pounced on villains. There were fewer roles for Blake in the 1980s and 1990s, and he was thrilled to be asked to be part of a David Lynch project. Blake responded to Lynch as a fellow maverick creator dedicated to preserving a personal vision, and during the shooting of *Lost Highway* said, "It's nice to feel like an artist and to be around artists and work on that level."[129]

In *Lost Highway*, Blake, his pale face emerging from darkness, brought a riveting intensity to his portrayal of the Mystery Man, the animalistic aspect of Fred Madison's psyche who enabled Fred to unleash his repressed fury and slaughter the wife who enraged him. In May 2001, some wondered if a part of Robert Blake's brain had given him permission to violently act out his anger and make *his* wife stone cold forever.

Bonnie Lee Bakely, Blake's wife of six months and mother of their daughter, Rosie, was shot twice in the head and killed outside Blake's favorite Italian restaurant in Los Angeles. Blake was inside the eatery when the killing took place, but L.A. prosecutors maintained that they can prove that he solicited the help of others who did the job for him.

Blake has said that he received little love and much abuse from his parents. His feisty, pugnacious manner always telegraphed the message that he was quick to get angry when someone did him wrong. And for a long time Bonnie Lee Bakely had behaved in ways that enraged many a man.

For years, Bonnie placed want ads and lewd photos of herself in porno publications, like *Twin Peaks*' Laura Palmer did in *Flesh World* magazine. Hinting at sensual favors to be granted in the future, she swindled money from lonely letter-writing men (authorities found approximately 7,500 letters in her possession). One of her pen pals who she met in person was an eighty-two-year-old grandfather, who she stayed married to for a week before running off with his $80,000.

Moving to Hollywood, she met Robert Blake. They married and seemed happy with each other until Bonnie violated their agreement that she would not get pregnant, and then would not abort the child. Blake, feeling trapped and manipulated, was furious, but he fell in love with Rosie the moment she was born. So the prosecutors believe Blake killed to rid himself of the aggravating Bonnie and have his cherished daughter to himself.

Not only did Bonnie initially not tell Blake about her pregnancy, but she, like Fred Madison's wife, was leading a double sexual life, sleeping with Marlon Brando's son Christian, who'd been convicted of killing his sister's boyfriend in 1992. So Blake had another reason to be infuriated with his morally corrupt wife, and Brando was angry that she was pregnant with Blake's child. There are court references to a phone-call recording in which Brando tells Bonnie she's lucky someone hasn't killed her yet.

In 2004, the jury for Blake's murder trial found that there was reasonable doubt as to whether the actor had had Bonnie killed, so he was set free. However, in 2005, as the result of a civil case brought by Bonnie Lee Bakeley's family, Blake was judged guilty and ordered to pay Bonnie's kin $30 million.

After the earlier, not-guilty verdict, some said that Blake the expert performer had acted his way out of being convicted. But during his second trial, the jury foreman says Blake was "his own worst enemy,"[130] fuming with anger and calling the prosecutor "junior"[131] and "sonny."[132]

So *Lost Highway*'s Mystery Man is the star of his own mystery. A victim of past crimes of the heart, only he knows if he has also committed one.

There were none of Lynch's penetrating, truth-revealing cameras allowed in the courtroom of his mind. Austrian composer Olga Neuwirth, who adapted *Lost Highway* into an opera in 2003, could be speaking of both Fred Madison and Robert Blake when she says, "This is the horrible thing. You remain a prisoner of your body and mind. You can't escape from yourself, your fears, your inner life."[133]

10

AN AUTUMN AFTERNOON

1997–2000
(*The Straight Story*)

As the twentieth century approached its end, David Lynch was, gauging by actuarial projections, more than half way through his life. Now in his early fifties, the still-full shock of hair on the crown of his head was graying, his face looked heavier, more fleshy, the bags beneath his eyes more prominent, the furrow between his eyebrows deeper. With the treadmill he bought for exercise gathering dust in his garage, he had to watch his weight. Abstaining from the milkshakes and pies he'd obsessively enjoyed for years, he shifted his food fixation to the "hunter-gatherer" diet his daughter Jennifer devised, eating a big salad of greens, tomatoes, tuna, feta cheese, and balsamic vinegar every day. He savored red wine and, still considering coffee to be a vital part of his creative process, downed steaming cups (not always black) from morning to night. Having stopped smoking as a younger man, he had, against the protestations of his old friend Toby Keeler, taken it up again, blitzing his neurotransmitters with as much nicotine as caffeine in a twenty-four-hour span. The Eagle Scout who'd voted for Ronald Reagan and deeply loved his country smoked American Spirit cigarettes, the "organic" brand whose logo was a proud Indian chief, and he chose the packs that were turquoise, an iconic hue of his beloved 1950s. Ronald Reagan was now seventy-six years old, and the current president of the United States (Bill Clinton) was Lynch's age.

In 1968, Jim Morrison of The Doors had declared, "We want the world and we want it now,"[1] and, by the late 1990s, members of Lynch's baby boom generation had become major players in the arenas of international politics, medicine, business, science, technology development, and the arts. A member of what has alternatively been called the rock and roll, Vietnam, and film generation, Lynch made moving image works that were nowhere near as widely popular and financially profitable as those of fellow fifty-ish directors Steven Spielberg, George Lucas, Ron Howard, Francis Ford Coppola, and Martin Scorsese. These men had the kind of industry track records that would garner them mega-million-dollar budgets for their new projects, while Lynch still couldn't afford the special effects necessary to film his long-contemplated version of Franz Kafka's *The Metamorphosis*, in which a fellow wakes up to discover that he's become a man-sized insect. The careers of Lynch's generation of filmmakers all had their ups and downs, but Lynch's films, even when they didn't lose money, made the level of total international profit that others' movies would realize in half a day in America.

Lynch had been putting his thoughts and feelings on film for thirty-one of his fifty-two years, and the response of his fellow human beings was most often mixed. In the late 1990s, he seemed to be traveling his own lost highway, trapped by a closed system in which his last two films, each shaped by his deeply felt emotions and intuitions, connected with only a relative handful of the viewing public. The response to his work, or its lack, could be frustrating and depressing, but Lynch knew that his life was a process of art-making, not just filmmaking. His ability to express his perceptive, imaginative mind through many mediums gave balance and perspective to a world that couldn't always properly see his filmic visions. The free-flowing, nonverbal world of painting was an abiding joy and refuge for the artist, and now he was becoming intrigued by the idea of making prints and exploring the creative possibilities of cyberspace.

When Lynch first became a painter as a young man in the 1960s, his view of the Art Life stipulated vast amounts of time spent alone, communing with his mind and then representing the contours of his inner being with the tools of canvas and paint. Relationships with people came second, at best. Thirty years of learning which existential factors helped or hindered his art-making, and enabled him to grow as a human being, had expanded his sense of the Art Life. If, as the director says, Fred Madison's problem was that he was "walking with the wrong woman"[2] in *Lost Highway*, then Lynch, in his own life, was certainly walking with the right one. Mary Sweeney, herself a gifted artist whose dreamy editing rhythms helped Lynch's images float all the more beautifully, had a passionate respect and love for her man and what he was doing with his life. In the year 2000, Lynch spoke of how important it is to "have a good setup so that the creative process can flow."[3] Being able to collaborate with Mary professionally and have her act as a buffer between him and the outside world's clamor, to share his love and dreams with her and their son Riley, contributed immensely to the happy state of Lynch's current setup. He was being a more fully present intimate partner and father than ever before. In earlier years, few people were allowed inside the artist's Lloyd Wright house and no food was cooked there. Now Lynch shares his days and nights with others, cooking smells settle on his pristine 1950s-modern furniture, and there are children's toys in the backyard.

Mary is decidedly more athletic than Lynch, and in the late 1990s he put in a swimming pool on the slope above his house more for her benefit than his own. Always concerned with aesthetic integrity and consistency, Lynch had Lloyd Wright's son (Frank Lloyd Wright's grandson), architect Eric Lloyd Wright, design a pool and pool house that perfectly matched the blocky horizontal form and lilac-pink hue of Lynch's Lloyd Wright house. The builders discovered a way to construct the massive Lloyd Wright chevron forms that adorn Lynch's house in lightweight resin instead of the original concrete. Even though both chevrons look the same, Lynch naturally opted for the original building material that Lloyd Wright used. After the job was done, the workers started picking up a few stray nails that dotted the pale gray floor stones bordering the pool, but Lynch stopped them: "No, no, no, when the nails rust they'll make a beautiful pattern."[4] He also tossed down chunks of cigar that he hoped would produce additional "organic stains."[5] Thanks to Lynch's largess, two more members of his clan were soon on the premises, for his daughter, Jennifer, and his towheaded granddaughter, Sydney, who looks a lot like Jennifer did when she was a girl, lived for awhile in the completed pool house. Today, in their own house, Jennifer and Sydney enjoy two of the Lloyd Wright chevrons, proudly displayed like sculptures on their fireplace hearth.

When Lynch first joined his life to Mary's he discovered another Significant Place to add to the touchstone environments of his life's journey (the Pacific Northwest, Philadelphia, the Mexico of *Dune*, and Los Angeles). Mary was a down-to-earth, soulful Midwestern woman who'd been raised in Madison, Wisconsin, and still had close ties to relatives in the area. Visiting the Madison region with Mary in 1991, Lynch enjoyed taking a breather from L.A.'s usually blissed-out weather, and he reveled in Wisconsin's rain and snow and was moved by the deep stands of evergreens that brought back memories of youthful times in the Northwest woods with his now-retired forest-researcher father. A world away from Hollywood's trendy, status-worshipping wheeler-dealers, Lynch felt right at home with Wisconsin's idiosyncratic, yet warm-hearted, kindly, straight-talking folk, who reminded him of the small-town people he grew up with, though at first "they were so gentle I thought they were kidding me."[6] Lynch, Mary, and Riley were spending so much time in Wisconsin that they bought a 1950s modern home-away-from-California on Lake Mendota outside Madison. Lynch chuckles when he remembers a UCLA film student's shocked reaction when the young man encountered Lynch at a Midwestern baseball game.

Lynch characterizes his artistic lifestyle as "always busy,"[7] so he didn't just eat cheese and stare at grain silos and cows while in Wisconsin. Pretty soon the state's agricultural landscape showed up in his photographs (did the cornfields remind him of the idea that *Twin Peaks'* BOB and Mike came from a planet of corn?), and the cows became characters in his and Robert Engels' screenplay *Dream of the Bovine*, which CiBy 2000 chose not to produce. (Cows first entered Lynch's fiction in his early 1970s *Eraserhead* script, where Henry envisioned bovines grazing in the "landscape"[8] of his pillowcase folds.) In December 1997, a Madison printmaking studio, Tandem Press, which was affiliated with the University of Wisconsin, invited Lynch to be their visiting artist. Always interested in trying his hand at new mediums of expression, he eagerly accepted their offer.

The staff at Tandem Press, which is curated by Tim Rooney, were so eager to accommodate Lynch that they lifted their strict ban on smoking so that their visitor could go into action in his favorite nicotine-and-caffeine-fueled state. Working for nine days straight, the artist created more than forty images, which were printed as limited-edition monoprints and collographs. Lynch has always been fascinated by the myriad physical textures of the world he moves in, paints, draws, films, and photographs, and at Tandem he loved the way the factory-like hydraulic machines pressed his images into sheets of dense, fluffy handmade white paper. Working primarily in shades of black and gray, he mixed extra-thick pigments that, when printed, made the image stand out from the picture plane as in the protruding surfaces of his paintings. Some of the prints featured a few simple pictorial elements floating against a white background, while others were more "atmospheric"[9] and placed the subject in a field that the artist had stroked vertically, giving a darker, wood-grain feeling to the composition.

Some of the images Lynch chose to print were derived from his other art forms. An unnaturally huge ant filling the outlined shape of a dwelling recalls his 1990 painting *Ants in My House*, and *Ricky Fly Board* evokes his earlier *Ricky Board* collages in which he mounted dead flies in neat rows. A series of black suit–wearing male figures with asymmetrically misshapen, blobby black heads suggests John Merrick in *The Elephant Man* (as well as Francis Bacon's heads-in-flux portraits), and the naked woman submerged in a glass cylinder from Lynch's short Lumière film makes an appearance. A simple round head form with an anguished mouth hole emitting a red vapor echoes *The Grandmother*'s Boy orally spurting out a red cloud of pain and anger. Lynch's preoccupation with the head continues as he prints a wiener dog's body with a human noggin on its shoulders, and a head that's just had a bullet blast through it. In his prints, the artist finds new forms for themes that have obsessed him for decades: intrusive animal energies invading a domestic sanctuary, a melding of human and animal qualities, a woman torturously entrapped, an interior, negative emotional state expressed tangibly (the red cloud from the mouth) in the outer world, heads contorted and deformed (by external pressures or bad thoughts), and traumatic suffering.

The stylized shapes in Lynch's print images are powerful in their straightforward simplicity, and the artist often completes his compositions by including the print's title spelled out in letters that look like a child might have cut them out of heavy black paper. In addition to the printed images that evoke his full body of artwork, Lynch produced studies of a female torso, two birds joined in flight (mating?), and a fish in a stream. As a boy, Lynch observed many fish in their natural habitat and he presents his printed one through the lens of the watery optical effect in which ripples seem to displace the fish's head from its body. Again he has shown us that surface reality can distort and hide a deeper truth beneath its surface.

Lynch even manages to work one of his favorite states of mind, a sense of mystery, into some of his printed images. A pistol, a stain, a question mark, and the words "billy's problem"[10] conjure up haunting possibilities, and he presents a labyrinth form in which black, right-angle shapes enclose white space. Perhaps this is an abstraction of Lynch's twenty-five-year-long practice of meditation, depicting a spiritual journey inward between dark walls of confusion that lead to a central chamber of illumination. The realities of Lynch's fictions are often presented in terms of dualities, and the path in his monoprint naturally flows in two directions, suggesting the way many of his characters journey into darkness, then turn around and come out into the light. This print enters the mystery of Lynch's personal mythology, for it is keyed to the number nine, which shows up in everything from the population of Twin Peaks to hotel room numbers to his close-up photograph of a car's electrical distributor cap. Tracing our way into his labyrinth print, it takes nine right-angle turns to reach the center, and nine to come back out. Nine plus nine equals eighteen and, by numerological addition: 18 is 1 + 8, which equals 9.

Lynch's Wisconsin art project gave him something he wasn't accustomed to: financial success as well as artistic satisfaction. The images from two printmaking sessions with Tandem Press sold solidly at exhibits in Chicago and New York.

While Lynch was crafting prints, his partner, Mary Sweeney, was contemplating a creative Wisconsin saga of her own. In 1994, she was touched and charmed by a *New York Times* article on the epic journey of Iowa's Alvin Straight. A proud and independent-minded man in his seventies, with failing eyesight, emphysema, sluggish circulation, and arthritic hips so painful he had to walk with two canes, Alvin was moved to action when he heard that his brother, Lyle, from whom he'd been estranged for ten years, had suffered a severe stroke. Wanting to see Lyle and make peace, Alvin, who couldn't qualify for a driver's license, rigged up a 1966 John Deere riding lawnmower and set off for his brother's Wisconsin cabin, traveling 350 miles at the rate of four miles per hour. Sweeney admired Straight's inventiveness, courage, plucky sense of dignity, and "age-be-damned attitude"[11]—and she knew the makings of a good movie when she saw them. Straight, a widowed former farmer with seven adult children, passed away in 1996, while Sweeney was trying to obtain the rights to film his story. She discovered that producer Ray Stark had beaten her to the punch, obtaining Straight's tale as a vehicle for Paul Newman that Larry Gelbart (TV's *M*A*S*H*) would script. But Sweeney remained vigilant, and when the rights to the property became available again in February 1998, she quickly bought it.

Mary Sweeney is a sophisticated woman of the world with a master's degree from the prestigious New York University Film School, who has worked at the A-list level (Warren Beatty's *Reds*) of Hollywood production, yet she sprouted from humble roots. Her ancestors worked a dairy farm in Wisconsin, and her heart holds a love and reverence for people whose lives are "wise, not ignorant, in their simplicity."[12] Sweeney felt such a personal connection to Alvin Straight's story that she *had* to be the one to write it for the screen, something she'd never done before. She enlisted the help of film and video producer John Roach (*The Sports Writer* on TV), who she'd been friends with since first grade, and who shared her warm feelings for the Midwestern land and its people. Sweeney and Roach decided that if they wanted to do justice to Straight's journey in a screenplay, they should travel his route themselves.

Cruising along from Straight's little house in Laurens, Iowa, to his brother's place in Mt. Zion, Wisconsin, Sweeney and Roach were struck by the wonder and humor of the fact that Alvin had driven these same roads on a lawnmower at an excruciatingly slow pace. It was also clear that, given Straight's old age and infirmities, his journey was a dangerous and heroic adventure. The two researchers talked with six of Straight's seven children, and listened to stories told by folks who had encountered Alvin as he traveled, getting a lot of flavorful material from a family who had let him camp in their yard for a whole week when his mower broke down. Sweeney and Roach now had enough detail to flesh out Straight's character in their screenplay, and Sweeney began to see their story about a particular old man as a reflection of the human condition in which we all travel along receiving what we need from others and giving back to them, coping with problems that arise, and trying to face the inevitability of death with a measure of grace.

While Sweeney and Roach worked on their script for *The Straight Story*, Lynch was supportive of film editor and producer Mary's venture into writing, but he wasn't intrigued enough by the surface idea of Alvin's mower ride to even think about directing the story. Mary, however, spent a lot of time considering that very possibility. Like everyone close to Lynch, she knew that "Dave,"[13] as she sometimes calls him, has "a tenderhearted, sweet side"[14] that's often obscured or overwhelmed by his works' raging tide of warped psyches, lost souls, toxic families, hot sex, violence, sorrow, and pain. For a long time she'd been on the lookout for a project that would allow her man's humane, spiritual qualities to glow like a long-burning campfire, rather than as a single, precarious flame surrounded by predatory darkness.

Sweeney and Roach finished their screenplay in the summer of 1998, and Mary nervously presented it to Lynch. "It was something we both faced with some trepidation. We have a very nice working relationship—we've been working together much longer than we've been living together. I didn't think he was going to decide to make the film."[15] Lynch was "apprehensive to read the script because I didn't know what I was going to say if I didn't like it."[16] But, to his and Mary's relief, "the screenplay turned me around. I loved it. I was so moved by the screenplay that pretty soon I found myself in Iowa."[17] Lynch also likes to feel that fate and higher forces play a part in the course of his life: "This story comes along at this moment, it jives with something in the air, and you're going, that's it, you're boogying."[18]

Lynch decided to shoot Straight's journey in sequence so he could capture the same gradual change of seasons that Alvin encountered. And retracing Straight's path exactly as he experienced it would feel like an homage to the intrepid rider. With his impeccable sense of narrative-aesthetic correctness, Lynch knew that this story wasn't like his usual projects. It shouldn't be told in a surreal way, with poetic obscurity; it was more simple with fewer elements that needed to be presented in a straight, linear way. For years, Lynch has experimented with heightening the mood and emotion of shots and scenes by stretching their duration, and, with his long Transcendental Meditation habit of viewing the world with contemplative eyes, the director was guided by Alvin Straight's lack of speed. "We're always in a hurry, days fly by, and by dinnertime you can't remember what you did in the morning. The film will show how Alvin comprehends space in his own way—by slowness. This changes the whole world, you can make out more details, and the sky gets a totally different dimension. It becomes a meditation image that's changing real slow. If you move slowly, you'll see more."[19] Lynch's ethos of slowness was born when, as a small child, he cruised around in a shiny black Buick with his "very cool"[20] paternal grandfather. "He drove really slow, which I loved, and to this day I hate riding fast."[21]

As usual, the director had a firm idea of how he wanted to proceed with a project, though settling on an actor to play Alvin took a fair amount of position shifting. Gregory Peck passed on playing the role, as did Richard Farnsworth, who cited ill health. Word came out that John Hurt, who incarnated John Merrick in Lynch's *The Elephant Man*, would portray Straight, but then the official, final announcement said Farnsworth would do the honors. This seemed like poetic justice, for Farnsworth's own seventy-nine-year life was illuminated by the pioneering spirit. He had learned to ride a horse at ten and, after befriending Hollywood's "Singing Cowboy," Gene Autry, he plunged into the movie business with both feet in the stirrups, doing breathtaking stunts for the likes of Cecil B. DeMille, John Ford, Howard Hawks, and Stanley Kubrick. Farnsworth worked his way into speaking roles, and was Oscar-nominated for playing a gentle old cowboy in *Comes a Horseman* (1978). And his portrayal (at age sixty-two) of a courtly, soft-spoken train-robber in *The Grey Fox* (1982) won him Canada's Genie Award for Best Actor and set female hearts aflutter onscreen and in the audience. After injecting some needed life into *The Getaway* (1994), Farnsworth became a real-life cowboy, raising Longhorn steers on his remote New Mexico ranch.

The cowpoke considered himself to be retired, and he'd never heard of David Lynch, but he responded enthusiastically to the *Straight Story* screenplay. "I identified with this old character, and I fell in love with the story. Alvin is an example of fortitude and a lot of guts."[22] Lynch felt "Richard Farnsworth was born to play Alvin Straight. He has the ability to make things real; he feels things deeply and it comes through every part of him. It was the emotion coming out of these characters that got me."[23] Like

Straight, Farnsworth was in need of hip replacement surgery and moved painfully with a cane. Still, Alvin Straight was a role that Farnsworth could feel in the accumulated wisdom and courage of his being, let alone his aching bones, so that when Lynch assured the actor that they'd make him a special cushioned lawnmower seat, he signed on for the ride.

Lynch then filled up his *Straight Story* roster with three old friends. Actress Sissy Spacek, who had given Lynch money to help him complete *Eraserhead* in the early 1970s, would play Alvin's daughter, Rose, whose character became a major player in Sweeney and Roach's screenplay after they met Alvin's real-life daughter Diane, on whom Rose is based. And Spacek's husband, Jack Fisk, Lynch's painting buddy from the 1960s who acted in *Eraserhead* and directed two episodes of *On The Air*, would design the production. British cinematographer Freddie Francis (himself in his eighties), who had done such magnificent work on *The Elephant Man* and *Dune*, was chosen to capture the burnished tones of the autumnal heartland on film. The Midwest at harvest time would certainly be a major element in the picture, but Lynch chose to begin in a realm that existed before human beings walked on Earth.

Since childhood, this artist has sensed the presence of cosmic, primal forces at work in the world, and he has manifested their power in his work. In a multitude of Lynch's art forms, various anonymous figures, Henry Spencer, John Merrick's mother, Princess Irulan, The Good Witch, The Dreamself of the Heartbroken Woman, Laura Palmer's angel, and Darryl Hannah (for Karl Lagerfeld's Sun Moon Stars perfume), have floated in the stars, the sky, the air. They have been metaphysical seekers; bearers of solace, knowledge, and wisdom; and finders of eternal consolation, joy, and dreams come true.

In *The Straight Story*, Lynch presents a naturalistic view of the world: People don't have visions and float in the sky. The star field he opens with has the familiar beauty of the one we see when we look out our window at night. It could be some footage from a *National Geographic* educational TV program, but Lynch imbues it with a poetic resonance, a deeper reality, for it makes a sound. The pulsing tones of insects meld with the faint singing sound of the stars' energy as Lynch's camera moves slowly forward into the night sky's mystery. This is the primal space from which life emerged, and the stars dissolve into a whorl of golden light as the camera curves in over an amber field of grain being harvested by a big-wheeled machine puffing out white clouds like the cosmic dust that billows in a number of Lynch's films.

Lynch stresses the unswerving ethos of his film by dissolving from the parallel golden crop rows to the straight-ahead lines of small-town residential and downtown streets, which lead us to a green patch of grass between two simple white houses. A large woman sunning herself on the lawn completes Lynch's montage of pastoral-village beneficence and serenity. Then, as the woman leaves the scene to get more snacks, the air seems charged with expectation, and as the camera approaches the side window of the house on the left, we hear a sickening thud from within. It's fascinating to see Lynch returning to the introductory narrative rhythms of *Blue Velvet* and *Twin Peaks*, in which he established a safe and benign small-town world and then invaded it with chaotic forces (Mr. Beaumont's seizure and the devouring insects in *Blue Velvet*, the discovery of Laura Palmer's dead body in *Twin Peaks*.) The director's internal sense of correct timing is so strong that, even though different people edited the three projects, the disordering energies enter each of the three films a little over two minutes after the picture starts.

We quickly learn that the painful thump from inside the house was poor Alvin hitting his kitchen floor when his worn-out hips failed him. He's still lying prone at the feet of two concerned neighbors when his adult daughter, Rose, comes home from shopping. Rose, struck by this catastrophic tableau, says, with an odd speech rhythm, "What have you . . . done to my Dad?" Of course it's just old age that has struck Alvin a mean blow, and we note an exceptional occurrence: This is the only one of Lynch's feature films in which we don't witness a person doing violence to another. No wonder the director says, "This may be my most experimental film."[24]

Before Alvin is dragged off to see the doctor, we absorb some details of him and his world. His grizzled white beard can't hide the weathered wrinkles of his face, earned by working thousands of hours in the sun. He still wears the blue jeans and plaid shirt of the farmhand he once was and his cream-colored (good guy) cowboy hat and boots evoke an independent, rough-and-ready Western spirit. Alvin's wallet is chained to his belt, and we gather there probably aren't many greenbacks in it. Demographic tables would place him and his neighbors on the low end of the economic and formal education scale, but Sweeney, Roach, and Lynch show that these Midwesterners are blessed with love and concern for each other and a will to accommodate, and see the humor in, each other's quirks and foibles. It's poignant and painful to see Alvin unable to get up from his kitchen fall, but we have to laugh when Dorothy (Jane Galloway Heitz) the rotund lawn-lounger grabs the phone and frantically says, "What's the number for 911?" And old Bud (Joseph A. Carpenter) seems most worried that now Alvin won't be able to keep their date at Davmar's tavern. (Is the name "Davmar's" an homage to Dave and Mary?)

There's also humor to be found as Bud drives Alvin to the doctor, and simultaneously races the car's motor and brakes as they approach their destination, a motif that Lynch first wrote into his unproduced *One Saliva Bubble* script (1987) and initially realized on film, in a much darker vein, as Leland Palmer drove daughter Laura one morning in *Twin Peaks: Fire Walk With Me* (1992). This braking-while-accelerating passage is not in Sweeney and Roach's screenplay: throughout the film Lynch will instinctively inject his own artistic sensibility into the mix.

Recalling his 1974 videotape *The Amputee*, in which Lynch played a doctor doing grisly things to Catherine Coulson's leg stumps, the director makes *The Straight Story*'s doctor's office a place of foreboding for Alvin. A chart of human innards, metal medical tools, and a biohazard sign make it look like he's going to undergo a torturous inquisition rather than a healing session. But, in counterpoint to these fearsome elements, there's a picture of a shepherdess tending her flock that echoes the female guardian pictures we've previously seen in John Merrick's and Laura Palmer's bedrooms. Still, the news for Alvin isn't good: Most of his major bodily systems are suffering from extreme wear and tear, and the doctor criticizes his smoking and all-meat diet. Straight takes the harsh news and remains steadfast: no tests, no operations, no aluminum walker to keep him from falling. Conceding that he'll use a second cane, he heads home.

Like *Wild at Heart*'s Sailor Ripley (with his treasured snakeskin jacket), and Lynch himself, Alvin values his individuality and personal freedom, and as he sits at his kitchen table he defiantly fires up a Swisher Sweet cigar. Rose looks fretfully at her father and asks, "What did the doctor say?" Thoughtful Alvin, wanting to shield his daughter from fear, cheerfully replies, "Said I'm going to live to be a hundred," but Lynch holds tight on Alvin's brooding eyes, which register the full weight of the knowledge that he's already close to knocking on heaven's door. From the youthful days when he herded cows on horseback, Alvin has been a man of action, an archetypal rider, and, shaking off depressing thoughts of mortality, he gets up from the kitchen table and announces, "I'm going to mow the lawn" on his old riding machine.

An estranged brother crippled by a stroke, a frail old man near the end of his life, a fortyish daughter with a speech impediment and a simple, child-like mind still living with him who doesn't want to see him go: Sweeney and Roach realized that this material contained potential pitfalls of sentimentality. Lynch was deeply moved by *The Straight Story*'s characters, but he knew it was very important for him to maintain, in his direction, the dry, restrained tone that Mary and John Roach had established in their script. The people in his films often exaggerate and distort normal, everyday behavior for heightened emotional and stylistic effect, but the director also knows the power of things left unsaid, of deep thoughts and feelings reflected in a facial expression and an eloquent glance.

Like the ailing machine of his own body, Alvin's mower won't start properly. We've already seen him act gruff and bossy with two characters who want to help him earlier in the film, and now he displays some of the anger that's kept the bitter split between him and Lyle alive, as he smashes his cane down on the offendingly silent mower. Later, enraged at the machine again, he will blast it into fiery oblivion with a shotgun. The filmmakers heat up the drama of their tale by not simply portraying Alvin as a lovably sympathetic old curmudgeon: They give us a searing look at the demons that he wrestles with and strives to overcome.

Anger and pride have poisoned Alvin's relationship with his brother, but the way he treats his daughter, Rose, must certainly buy him credit in heaven. Rose is one of Lynch's "very special people"[25] whose physical and/or mental difference-from-the-norm the director often, and reverently, includes in the spectrum of humanity he portrays. This middle-aged woman's brain retains all sorts of facts and figures, but the unguarded, emphatic emotionality of her expressions and her halting-speech impediment give her a childlike air, as when she proudly shows Alvin the birdhouse she's made: "It has a . . . red roof. I want to paint the . . . next roof . . . blue." The way that Rose seems to mentally grope for words and then blurt them out interspersed with pauses gives her utterances the forceful condensation and rhythm of poetry. It's easy to see why Alvin loves and feels protective of Rose, who stares out the window in some sad twilight reverie as she watches a little boy play on the sidewalk. (The filmmakers pay off the mystery of Rose's sorrowful mood later when Alvin tells a pregnant, runaway hitchhiker that when one of Rose's four children, a boy, was burned in a fire that was not Rose's fault, the state judged her to be "a little slow" in the head, an incompetent mother, and took away her kids.) Alvin has helped his daughter hold her life together, making her feel genuinely useful around their small home and encouraging her crafting of wooden dwellings for little birds, an activity which, though Lynch doesn't emphasize the point, is a poignant expression of Rose's maternal instinct. The character Rose is one of *The Straight Story*'s treasures, and if Mary Sweeney and John Roach hadn't met Alvin's daughter Diane on whom Rose is based, she wouldn't be a vital part of the film's emotional design. Lynch, carefully shaping his words into a kindly, respectful understatement, told me, "that is the way that Diane talks."[26]

Lynch's parents met while on a nature hike and his father worked in the forest; as a boy David loved to play outside, and today he thrives on gardening and painting in his studio that's open to the Southern California sunshine and canyon breezes. *The Straight Story* allowed him to portray a family that lives closer to nature than any other in his work. We see no TV or books in Alvin and Rose's home, but they get plenty of entertainment sitting together at the window watching a ferocious lightning storm. Their position near the glass is a measure of the Straight family's independent, rebellious spirit, for the Weather Bureau has warned people to stay away from windows. The side-by-side positioning of Alvin and Rose recalls a favorite visual-thematic motif of the master Japanese director Yasujiro Ozu (1903–1963), who often showed two people sitting together as they contemplate a scene in nature or a tableau connoting the primal *is*ness of life. And Ozu, like *The Straight Story*'s filmmakers, frequently told stories of old men coming to terms with the inevitability of change, loss, and disappointment.

Lynch's tendency to see double meanings in a single reality surfaces in his use of the lightning motif. Previously in his work, flashing discharges of electricity have always signaled a moral/metaphysical disturbance, an invasion by dark forces. In *The Straight Story*, the lightning reflects something new: the warm bond between Alvin and Rose ("I love a lightning storm;" "Me . . . too Dad"). But, when the bad news about Lyle's stroke comes calling, Lynch underscores its arrival with a thunderous bolt of sky fire. Later, during Alvin's journey, Lynch restores a positive connotation to lightning as the old man finds shelter from a downpour, fires up a cigar, and contentedly watches the dark clouds flash.

The news of Lyle's stroke causes Alvin to ponder the gulf of bad feeling between him and his brother, how each of them has helped maintain the estrangement by keeping silent, and that every day there's less time left for both of them. The only possible conclusion forms in Alvin's mind, and he announces to Rose that he's "going back on the road" to see Lyle, though he doesn't know how. He listens to Rose vent her objections: his eyes are bad, Wisconsin's so far away, his hips are old ("You were born when Calvin Coolidge was President of America"). Alvin knows this is all true, and he's touched by her concern, but at this stage of his existence the equation is pretty simple: "Rosie, darlin', I'm not dead yet."

Lynch, whose own life centers on the creative process, lovingly shows Alvin solving the problem of how to get to Lyle. Combining a steel frame, wheels, and some old plywood panels, Alvin crafts himself a rolling wooden box in which he can sleep and carry supplies. Like Lynch as a young man, Alvin is a shed-builder, and the director films the steadfast flame of

Straight's welding torch and the silver ball of a trailer hitch glistening with lubricant as though they were sanctified elements in a reverent ritual.

Alvin hasn't told Rose what he's working on (another Lynch character with secrets), but she gets the picture when he backs his ancient Rehds riding mower up to the big wooden box-on-wheels. Agitated and worried, she voices some more reasonable objections to her father's crazy venture. Alvin listens patiently, but like an artist who's wild at heart, he's moved by an inner vision that he must single-mindedly strive to realize in the tangible world. The loving force of his simple declaration ("I got to go see Lyle; I got to make this trip on my own") kindles her understanding.

When the "Lyle's had a stroke" phone call that sparked Alvin's journey came, he and Rose had been sitting together watching a lightning storm. Now, on the night before Straight leaves, Lynch again positions father and daughter side-by-side as they contemplate nature. Out in the yard, Alvin urges Rose to look up, and her worries about him are calmed by a deep black sky full of stars. He looks at her with adoration as she regards the universe with wonder, and Lynch subtly tugs at our emotions by evoking the Dad-shows-daughter-the-world pattern that Alvin and Rose have repeated ever since her earliest days and nights. And we remember that Lynch, too, is a father, who, in the early Philadelphia days when money was scarce, used his ingenuity instead of costly toys to stimulate little Jennifer's interest and delight in the world around her.

Connoting a sense of blessing and heavenly guidance, Lynch dissolves from Alvin and Rose's star field to a sunny morning as Alvin slowly drives his mower and trailer on a straight track out of town. The rider heads down Main Street, past the Ace Hardware where his fellow seventy-something cronies pass their time. This store, whose interior reminds us of the tool emporium where Jeffrey works in *Blue Velvet*, is one of Lynch's timeless places, like his diners, bars, coffee counters, cheap motels, and auto mechanics' shops, which could have come directly from the 1950s. Earlier, when Alvin had come to the hardware store and bought supplies and lots of gasoline, he'd maintained his David Lynch–like close-mouthed secretiveness and kept mum about his endeavor. And when Alvin purchased a simple grabbing device (a wooden shaft with an opening and closing C-shaped pincer), the director emphasized his own reverence for tools and the humble tone of his film by giving the gadget a loving close-up. Seemingly without effort, Lynch has immersed us in a world where a truly heroic quest can be launched by a tottering old man with precious little money, but who's rich with inspiration, inventiveness, and spirit. In contrast, Alvin's same-age hardware store comrades are crabby stay-at-homes who voice their fears rather than giving him an optimistic send-off. But no matter: All Alvin needs to hear is his inner guiding voice. He is silent and proud as he leaves the nay-saying men (who seem so much older than him) behind and heads out onto the open road.

As though following Lynch's Law of Contrast, Alvin has left the predictable sameness of his town life behind him and put himself in a position where potential hazard and discovery flood his consciousness. Exhilarated by the free and open air of adventure's road, he beams and waves at a Norman Rockwell–like tableau of a blond farm mother, towheaded son, and golden dog in a yard he passes. Lynch adds levity to this warm tone by showing the yellow highway centerline that in *Blue Velvet*, *Wild at Heart*, and *Lost Highway* flew past the camera in a blur, passing beneath Alvin's mower at walking speed. And he stresses the long, drawn-out nature of Straight's trek by panning up from the slow-going mower to a sky luminous with clouds, pausing for awhile, and then tilting back to earth to see that Alvin is only *slightly* further down the road.

We've noted how Lynch likes to establish a mood of carefree security (the beautiful tree of his boyhood backyard), and then shock us with the revelation of a chaotic threat (the disease-bearing insects he discovered within the tree). Alvin feels like he's on top of the world as he putts along munching one of his beloved raw wieners; the moment even seems blessed by a sign heralding the upcoming religious roadside attraction, the Grotto. Lynch instinctively knows that this is the time to strike, so he introduces an ominous, quickly intensifying roaring sound that becomes a tall, twenty-five ton, eighteen-wheel truck rig that just misses Alvin's mower as it growls past in a demonic cloud of dust. In real life, since the truck was going in the same direction as Alvin, it would blow Alvin's cowboy hat off in a forward-flying whoosh. But Lynch emphasizes a sense of setback by having Straight's Stetson sail back toward the town he's courageously ventured forth from. Wincing with pain and moving slowly, Alvin dismounts, retrieves his hat, and climbs back on his steed—only to have it fail to start. Mad and frustrated, he accepts a ride on a tour bus, as the filmmakers again contrast Alvin with others his own age. The coach is full of dear old women whose husbands have died, who ride in air-conditioned comfort, while Alvin, who has survived his wife, forges along at the mercy of weather and all other drivers on the road. Still, the silently smiling Straight (and real-life ladies' man Farnsworth) seems happy to be nestled in a bushel of admiring female company.

When Alvin and his mower rig are hauled back into town in seeming defeat, Lynch underscores the sympathetic sensibility at the core of his film's world by having the previously carping Ace Hardware crew say "Poor Alvin," rather than "I told you so." Lynch is always alert to the way that human beings, and fictional characters, can often be read two ways (or more), and so some of his gruff Midwestern men betray warm hearts. Straight has too much gumption to quit his quest, so, after buying a thirty-year-old John Deere riding mower (sold to him by salt-of-the-earth Everett McGill, who played *Twin Peaks'* Big Ed), he hits the road again. In the screenplay, Rose did some more argumentative worrying about Alvin resuming his journey. But Lynch pares the emotion of Straight's second leave-taking down to a single poignant image of Rose, standing in their green yard, not waving or smiling, growing smaller and smaller as Alvin pulls away.

Regarding *Lost Highway*, Lynch has said that by "walking with the wrong woman"[27] (Renee/Alice), Fred Madison damned himself to a hellish existence. And now that Alvin Straight has rejected his old unfaithful red Rehds mower and embraced his new green John Deere, it's as though his journey has been green-lighted. Now his hat doesn't blow off when behemoth trucks roar by, and currents of sympathetic magic seem to link his forward-moving vehicle with the energetic, green-growth-colored harvesting machines working the fields he passes. When Alvin had first set out in his Rehds, the hardware boys had said, "you'll never make it past the Grotto," and he didn't. Now, he glides past the dark, yet sparkling and crucifix-crowned construction of rock and crystal, which a Catholic parish pastor began in 1912 and labored at for the remaining thirty-two years of his life. Obviously, Alvin's trip to see Lyle is but one small phase of his long life, but Lynch will strive to show us the Grotto-sized shelter of spirit and wisdom that Alvin has built over the years. Lynch cuts from Alvin rolling past the Grotto to a shot without Alvin in it. It's the road ahead: no vehicles, just a gray concrete strip, green countryside, and the motion of cloud shadows passing over the earth, as though they were blessing a pilgrim's progress.

Throughout the film Lynch communicates Alvin's (and his own) love of nature in gorgeous montage passages in which his traveler almost seems to merge with golden stands of trees wreathed in white mist, the sinuous whorls and eddies of grain field patterns, and green farm machines reaping the harvest. These sequences also give us a palpable sense of the extended duration of Straight's trip. However, the filmmakers devote most of their screen time to illuminating their hero's character and observing the nature of human beings.

Lynch strikes a humorous note as a car whizzes past a female hitchhiker up ahead, and as Alvin putts by her at a snail's pace, she (Anastasia Webb) gives him a disdainful look. In her mid-teens and wearing torn jeans and a plaid flannel shirt, she has the look of a Seattle grungester and the air of a tough customer. In the screenplay, the girl is named (Crystal) and is shown noticing Alvin's nighttime campfire and approaching it. Lynch chooses to leave her anonymous and have her reappear at night out of the dark trees as an eerie surprise to Alvin and us, a moody moment he underscores with the only ominous notes of Angelo Badalamenti's music in the film. It doesn't seem like the girl plans to rob or hurt Alvin, but she's both sullen and surly, scorning his food of choice ("Wieners?") and his mower and trailer ("What a hunk of junk"). Her ornery manner arouses his gruffness, and he bossily shuts her up: "Eat your dinner, missy."

As the campfire crackles and wieners are eaten in silence, the two wary, guarded souls start to let down their defenses. The girl, who began their standoff with her dirty look at Alvin when he passed her on the highway, offers the first peace feeler ("How long you been out on the road?"). And Alvin, perhaps bearing in mind that he's on a mission to make amends with his brother, accepts her offer ("I've traveled just about all my life"). He goes on to tell her about his wife being dead, his rift with Lyle, and the sad story of how the state took away Rose's kids when her boy got burned accidentally. Alvin senses that the wistful young hitchhiker is carrying a heavy emotional burden and, becoming the Agent Cooper–like kind of detective who can ascertain people's romantic secrets, correctly intuits that his dinner guest is a pregnant runaway. She adds that her parents and boyfriend don't know she's going to have a baby.

Alvin has suffered the pain of intimate loss and sundered family ties, and his long life has taught him the supreme value of love sustained and, he hopes, rekindled with Lyle. Lynch, Farnsworth, and the screenwriters maintain an impeccably unsentimental, yet warm and compassionate tone as Alvin tells the runaway about a game he used to play with his kids. He'd give each child a stick, which they could easily break. Then he'd have them join sticks together in a bundle, which they were not able to split. Using a hands-on metaphor, Alvin had concretized the idea of family cohesiveness and strength for his children, and the hitchhiker also absorbs his message. He's respected her intelligence and her freedom of choice by giving her something to think about, rather than a lecture. A small bond of appreciation and understanding has been forged between these two disparate travelers, a connection which the filmmakers stress by having the girl say she likes to do something we've seen Alvin and his daughter enjoy: thinking while looking up at the stars. Once again, Lynch links the human head with the cosmos.

When Alvin wakes the next morning, he sees that the young traveler has moved on, but she's left him something that shows she's another of Lynch's characters who communicates without words. On the ground outside Alvin's trailer is a bundle of sticks tied together with one of her shoelaces: a kindly, practical gift for an old man who can barely bend down to gather kindling, but also an emotional, eloquent indicator of the hitchhiker's homeward-bound direction of travel. In the scenes with the runaway, Lynch unconsciously links *The Straight Story* with his beloved *The Wizard of Oz*, for in both films an old man (respectively, Alvin Straight; Professor Marvel) advises a young woman (pregnant hitchhiker; Dorothy Gale) to return home to her family.

Lynch often speaks of how there's "something in the air that you pick up on,"[28] and his bunch of sticks is one-half of a remarkable synchronicity. Daniel Myrick and Eduardo Sanchez's *The Blair Witch Project* (1999) also has a character camping out who wakes to find a tied bundle of sticks outside their tent, though neither set of filmmakers could have known about the other's use of the motif. *The Blair Witch Project*'s dreadful gathering of sticks shows just how far Lynch is from his usual shadowland realm, for *Blair*'s bundle contains bloody body parts, whereas *The Straight Story*'s sticks are a benign talisman of love's power. The coincidental double manifestation of the bundled-sticks motif itself seems Lynchian: the universal polarities of good and evil reflected in wood.

Lynch introduces Alvin's next encounter with his fellow road-travelers in a sequence that, thanks to Mary Sweeney's film cutting and Lynch's sound design, is an award-caliber example of editing. With a cornfield on his right and the concrete highway on his left, Alvin is tooling along—when an abstract blur of color seems to materialize out of the hot air and zip past his left ear with a buoyant sound that's part mechanical whir, part wind, part whizzing insect. Beaming a "What the heck?" grin of dazzled wonderment, Alvin looks back over his shoulder, then whip-pans his view left to right as a colorful biketour rider shoots past, then another and another, until the highway is full to the horizon with happy cyclists. Embodying the concept of freedom of the road, the bicycle riders use the full width of the two-lane highway, and as Alvin says "Doin' good" in answer to a cheery greeting, Lynch's camera floats skyward on a warm updraft of euphoria. The director and his editor-writer end their sequence with a God's-eye view looking down on fertile fields and a road brimming with travelers, many young and one very old, as the gentle buzz of insects in the corn becomes the eternal hum of universal being. Young Riley is not the only beautiful offspring that Sweeney and Lynch have produced.

The cyclists naturally move much faster than Alvin, so they've already set up their camps at a park by the time he joins them. In keeping with the film's benevolent tone, the young bicyclists are presented as health-conscious, friendly folk who literally applaud Alvin's physical effort when he pulls into their midst, and then thoughtfully listen to his wise summations of a lifetime's worth of experience. He knows that getting old is the last thing on these carefree youths' minds, but he assures them that climbing through the decades clarifies one's sense of direction: "You've seen most everything life has to dish out and can separate the wheat from the chaff. You know to let the small stuff fall away." Alvin's sharply focused mission to see Lyle exemplifies his words, yet the white-bearded philosopher is not wholly at peace, for he adds that the "worst thing about being old is remembering when you were young." We get the sense that not only does Alvin poignantly feel the gap between his present enfeebled state and the vitality of youth, but that he has done things he wishes he could forget.

The Straight Story has established a narrative pattern of Alvin being moved to speak, and having someone listen to him, but his next encounter leaves him speechless. The Deer Woman episode is one of the most typically Lynchian passages in the film, and we wonder if part of Mary Sweeney's motivation in writing it was to entice her man into directing the film.

Since this low-budget picture was filmed in sequence on Alvin Straight's actual route, Lynch had to accept circumstances of weather, lighting, and landscape as he found them: He couldn't afford to go into the post-production computer graphics studio and reshape the images Freddie Francis had filmed on the road. So he was thrilled when he found the natural conditions "a bit surreal"[29] while filming the Deer Woman scenes.

The skies are bright as Alvin happily motors along the roadside, but as he rolls past a No Passing Zone sign, the clouds turn dark, an event which in Lynch's world has the magnitude of an ominous metaphysical shift. The director has added the cautionary road sign to the script, so that when a black sedan swerves out around Alvin's rig and roars past, the motion has the force of a transgression. Straight's face registers some terrible sight as we hear screaming brakes and a heavy thud. Alvin slowly dismounts and approaches the car that passed him, its dark front end smashed in because it's hit and killed a big eight-point deer, which lies showing its left profile in front of the car. There can be no puddle of blood or torn flesh in a G-rated Disney movie, and the fact that the dead animal's form is pristine and dry adds an uncanny air to the scene.

The Deer Woman's (Barbara Robertson) expressive face is twisted with sadness, anger, and fear, recalling Laura Dern's intense *Blue Velvet* facial reaction when she discovers that her boyfriend's been sleeping with Isabella Rossellini. Alvin is silent as the woman wails and rants about how she has to drive this road every day, and has killed thirteen deer (an animal she loves) in seven weeks. (Is this her *Lost Highway* on which she's paying off a debt of bad karma?) Lynch's own voice gets emotional when he says that while filming the woman's tirade "a beautiful wind"[30] came out of nowhere to animate her long hair and clothing, as though the very air was alive with her agitation. And there's a note of Lynchian mystery as she wonders, "Where do they come from?" as the director scans a landscape that's unlike any other in the film: a flat, eerie plain of pale, dead grass punctuated by a black, barren tree. This may be a Disney film, but we're a long way from Bambi's lush, cozy forest. Lynch concludes this sequence with a tableau steeped in his sensibility of strange, disturbing dislocation. The woman has driven off, leaving an old man supported by two canes standing in the middle of a gray strip of road under a heavy gray sky. On the concrete next to him are a dead animal and a black stain from the woman's car, an abstract dark form like those in the artist's paintings, drawings, and prints that in this case signifies a violation of the natural order.

The hurrying woman who works in an office killed the deer, but slow-moving Alvin, who lives closer to the earth, knows how to honor the creature. Like a Native American who respects the animal's life he takes so that he may live, Alvin cooks and enjoys the deer's flesh and mounts its proud antlers on his trailer. All well and good, but Lynch makes the moment more emotionally complex by giving Straight "a visual pang of guilt."[31] For as Alvin munches on his meat, he glances warily over his shoulder at a number of life-sized deer statues positioned behind him in the tall grass. Lynch says that these concrete figures are an example of "the strange places" one encounters in the rural Midwest. And he laughs in appreciation of his viewers' imaginations when I tell him that some people think that the figures are part of a memorial cemetery that the Deer Woman erected.

Lynch's thematic fascination with one reality merging into another extends to the aesthetics of his often-beautiful scene transitions, and in *The Straight Story* we see a flame-colored stand of autumn trees become the close-up texture of a house on fire. In his previous work, Lynch has used the elements of fire and invaded houses to connote dangerous, evil forces on the loose, and here he links the flaming structure to the action of Alvin losing control of his home-on-wheels. A drive belt has broken in the mower, the transmission is gone, and Alvin comes careening down a steep hill as Lynch and Sweeney blitz us with shaky views of the flaming house, Alvin's desperate hands trying to steer as the ground flies by beneath his bucking steed, Alvin's panic-stricken eyes, and the screaming whine of machinery stressed to the breaking point.

Disturbance and unease are the usual status quo in Lynch's fictions, but in *The Straight Story* they are the exception, and as Alvin skids to a stop and onlookers rush in to help him, we feel the divine angels of mercy that Lynch earnestly believes in reasserting their dominion. Thanks to Richard Farnsworth's masterful acting, Alvin has never seemed so weak and time-worn as when, just after his harrowing ride, he's quietly gasping for breath, trying to slow his racing heart and compose an "I'm alright, I can handle it" expression on his stricken face. Many viewers assume this scene is a jolt of melodrama the screenwriters added for effect, but Lynch stresses that the incident was a "100 percent authentic part of Alvin's real journey."[32]

People are present to calm and assist Alvin because the flaming house is a controlled-burn fire department project that's being enjoyed by spectators having a late-autumn picnic. The first words out of Danny Riordan's (James Cada) mouth are "Mister, are you okay?," then he and his wife, Darla (Sally Wingert), and their chums walk Alvin and his rig over to the Riordan's backyard, where they let him camp until his mower's roadworthy again. Full of curiosity, Alvin's new friends incorrectly guess that he's traveled only a few miles on his mower. It is white-haired Verlyn (Wiley Harker), who's seen as many years as Alvin and is a Lynchian reader of wavelengths, who intuitively knows the truth that "You've come a long way, haven't you?"

One mile at a time, hour after hour, Alvin has been on the road for five weeks, slowly approaching his goal. At his advanced age, time is more precious than gold, and he sure wasn't planning to waste days of it twiddling his thumbs waiting for his ailing motor to get fixed. Still, Alvin's done enough traveling to know that he can't fight the twists and turns the road takes, and that he'll be happy enough if his eyes open tomorrow morning. Lynch conveys a comforting sense that everything's right with the world as Alvin watches the lights wink out in the Riordan's house and then looks up at the stars that cast down their light forever.

Alvin wakes up alive the next day, and wants to give daughter Rose a call, reversing the conventional absent-child-phones-parents-to-reassure-them dynamic. Of course, Alvin is not your usual septuagenarian, and he proudly refuses Riordan's repeated invitations to come inside and phone, preferring to stay outdoors with a portable unit and leave a few dollars to cover the long distance charge. His old-fashioned American sense of economy won't let him accept a free ride: He must give back for what he receives from life. It's wonderful to have Rose's unique, halting voice reintroduced to the film, as she and her father show the robust state of their emotional exchange rate with words that aren't in the screenplay: "I love you Rosie"; "I love you . . . Dad."

We have no trouble hearing what Alvin and his daughter say to each other, but at various times during the film Lynch does a curious thing, dropping the sound level by half so that we only catch a stray word here and there. The director combines the reduced audibility with outdoor scenes that are distanced from his camera, giving us a full, expansive sense of the air and trees that surround people in a landscape. The small size of figures within the frame reflects the proportions of Lynch's paintings, and the diminished audio echoes his "love of hearing sound through a little wind and not being able to really understand it."[33] For Lynch—who, when he's present for a screening of one of his films has the volume played at ear-melting levels—this softened-sound technique seems radically experimental, and very effective. It gives us the dreamy feeling of life heard and glimpsed at a slight remove, like everyday occurrences just up the block that will never happen exactly the same way again. Lynch makes us feel the sweet richness of simple moments as they dissolve in the river of time.

The director's faraway scenes celebrate human beneficence, as Danny and Darla Riordan help Alvin erect a lean-to shelter in their backyard, and later, after the Riordans' friend Janet has given Alvin a plate of brownies, he shares them with Verlyn, who in turn invites Alvin to go into town for a beer. As the two white-haired men sit side-by-side at the bar, Lynch deepens the bond of elderly male kinship he established earlier when Verlyn recognized, without being told, that Alvin was a far-traveler. (Lynch was pleased that octogenarians Richard Farnsworth and cinematographer Freddie Francis bonded during the film: "It helps Freddie to look over and see Richard, and it helps Richard to look over and see Freddie. If Richard Looks over and sees a thirty-five-year-old hotshot director of photography, it's different."[34])

Thus far, Lynch has been bound by the surface, albeit engaging, facts of Straight's true-life story, but now he delves into his favorite artistic territory: the hidden, emotional-spiritual landscape of the inmost self. By now we're familiar with Alvin's independent, dryly amiable, sometimes temperamental persona, but as he sips a glass of milk and Verlyn enjoys a beer, we meet his demons. While fighting in France during World War II, Alvin developed "a mournful taste for liquor," which made him mean and angry, rather than happy. Back in the United States, he kept hitting the booze to try and ease his horrendous visions of combat experiences, until a preacher helped separate Alvin from the bottle by talking him through his traumatic memories. There's a lot of time and distance between the European wartime inferno of the mid-1940s and the bucolic 1990s Midwest, but Alvin and Verlyn are haunted still. Lynch invades the quiet bar with the sounds of bomb blasts and machinegun fire as Verlyn speaks of the terrible day when he and his buddies were waiting for their first hot meal in ten days. A Nazi plane materialized out of the treetops, dropped an incendiary bomb, and Verlyn watched all his friends burn alive. Alvin also suffers the guilt of a combat survivor who has seen his comrades die, as he adds that "the more years I have, the more they lost." And he regrets the Germans, the "moonfaced boys," who they killed.

Alvin's deepest wound of sorrow and remorse was inflicted by his own hand. Because of his farm boy upbringing, young man Alvin was a good shooter, and he became a combat sniper, on the alert for stirrings of enemy movement in the woods. (Even in the context of this true-life film, Lynch links menace with Verlyn's "treetops" and Alvin's "woods.") One night, doing his duty and concentrating hard, Alvin fired at a movement, and killed Kotz, the reconnaissance scout for his own company. Everyone thought that a German bullet (a head shot) had stolen Kotz's life, but Alvin, to his undying horror and shame, knew that he was the sinning killer. Over the years, Alvin learned that booze couldn't cleanse his bloodstained conscience and that guilt would be his companion for the rest of his life. Since the war, Alvin and Verlyn have done an admirable job of soldiering on with their lives, trying to be loving and to forgive themselves and others for the darkness within us all. Still, so many lives and spirits have been killed and wounded, and Lynch concludes this sequence on a somber note. The two mournful old men sit silently at the bar with their backs to us, while behind the bar, facing us on the far left, a young man who blessedly has not had to go to war stands with his head bowed, quietly absorbing what the men have said. More than one commentator noted that this dramatically restrained, hushed moment communicates more soulful reverence for those who fought and died in World War II than anything in Steven Spielberg's mega-million-dollar, pyrotechnically grandiose *Saving Private Ryan* (1998).

This night Alvin sits alone in the Riordans' back yard, not smoking his usual Swisher Sweet cigar. The pain of his wartime guilt clouds his face, but as he looks up at the stars, the ever-burning light that seems to forgive the misdeeds of men, his burden seems a shade easier to shoulder.

Before Alvin can resume his journey to see Lyle, he has to settle up with the Olsen brothers (John and Kevin Farley), who've been fixing his mower. These two are the kind of offbeat characters we expect in a Lynch film: Both wearing bib overalls and red caps, their faces smudged with industrial grease, these are biological twins who don't look quite alike, and one sports a huge lump of a bandage on his cheek. Alvin rightly surmises that much of the Olsens' working time was devoted to petty, one-upmanship bickering with each other. Speaking of his estrangement from Lyle, and conveying how much it means to him to overcome it, Alvin concludes, "A brother is a brother," as he gives the twins a pointed look. Lynch has championed the bonds of family and love in other works, but never in such an overt, Hallmark-greeting-card sort of way. Or if he has made a strong verbal thrust of beneficence, as in Sandy's *Blue Velvet* speech about the robins of love and light flocking to earth, it seems properly balanced by opposing forces of toxic darkens. Compared to Lynch's usual territory, the world of *The Straight Story* is so thoroughly benign that Alvin's Western Union message about brotherly love seems glaring and blatant and gives us something the rest of the film scrupulously does not: more than is necessary.

Thankfully, any preachy sentiments have been banished from the film by the time Alvin and Danny Riordan say goodbye. Danny's wife, Darla, has given Alvin warm hospitality, hanging a cheery, red wooden fish she made on his lean-to, but Danny's the one who's spent a lot of time with their backyard guest. (The married life of these two middle-agers, in which Danny casually launches a topic while sipping a beer in the kitchen as Darla half-listens while doing some baking and playfully shoos away his attempt to nuzzle her from behind, is the most homey, "normal"-seeming love relationship Lynch has ever put on the screen.) Danny has shared smokes and coffee with Alvin (a Lynchian bond of nicotine and caffeine), given him moral support as he argued the Olsen twins' mower-repair fee down to a reasonable rate, voiced his concerns about the dangers of Alvin continuing his trip, and offered to drive him to Lyle's place. Alvin has engaged Danny's emotions. Like an adult son, Danny worries about an aging parent figure, but as a John Deere company man who's retired on a comfortable pension, he respects and admires this independent old cuss with just a few bucks in his jeans who's living a moment-to-moment adventure out on life's open road.

In *Wild at Heart*, Sailor and Lula hit the asphalt to flee Marietta, who was hellbent on destroying their love; and *Lost Highway*'s Fred Madison was being chased by both his own capacity for murder and those who would punish his crimes. Lynch's third road trip is one humble man's mission of personal and family redemption, and Danny can sense Alvin's sacred dedication to his quest. On their final night together, Alvin rises to his feet, wincing from the pain in his hips, and faces Danny like an old-school gentleman raised with proper manners (paying for long-distance phone calls, saying goodbye the right way). With gentle voices, the two men speak their last words to each other: "I want to thank you for your kindness to a stranger"; "It has been a genuine pleasure having you here, Alvin." Then, no soupy hugs, just a fond look in each others' eyes and a firm Lynchian handshake that would make Agent Cooper and Gordon Cole proud. The director and his actor perfectly gauge the emotional tone of this scene, and we reap the reward of deep, organic feeling, rather than script-written sentiment. Unbeknownst to Alvin, Danny stands at his window for a long time the next morning, watching silently until Alvin is out of sight.

In John Roach and Mary Sweeney's script, the sequence of Alvin crossing the Mississippi River on a bridge between Iowa and Wisconsin is a time for human interaction and humor, as Alvin's slow bridge-crossing causes a huge traffic backup that pours into the town of Prairie de Chien. Two police cars intervene, escorting pokey Alvin over to side streets, where the whole affair is greeted by the locals as an impromptu parade, with Alvin as the hand-waving grand marshal.

Lynch chooses to jettison these Norman Rockwell/Frank Capra–like scenes of small town communality and make Alvin's river crossing a solitary experience illuminated by one soul's sense of wonder and accomplishment. Alvin gawks and grins at the river's almost immeasurable width and length, at the criss-crossed steel bridge structure gliding by overhead, and at the bridge's glinting metal surface passing beneath his mower. The Mississippi is both a major milestone of Alvin's trip and a resonant link with the voyaging spirit of America's storied and real-life past, with Tom Sawyer and Huckleberry Finn and explorers Father Jacques Marquette and Louis Jolliet. Lynch emphasizes the sense of present time evoking the past by skipping over a number of script pages to join a panoramic shot of Alvin's bridge-crossing with an image of him camping for the night in a historic graveyard. Achieving another of his beautiful scene transitions, the director rides the droning horn sound of a Mississippi barge into the nocturnal cemetery, where the river sound becomes the far-off wail of a passing train. Alvin has come more than three hundred miles to see his brother, and tonight he's camped on ground that's the final resting place of men who, more than three hundred years earlier, ventured forth with Marquette and Jolliet to determine if the Mississippi flowed all the way down to the Gulf of Mexico. (The remaining explorers, fearing capture by Spanish colonists, eventually turned back, but correctly surmised that the Mississippi did empty into salty southern waters.)

Marquette and Jolliet's quest was aided by a number of Native American tribes, and Alvin has likewise enjoyed the helpful kindness of the people he's encountered. There's a little church attached to the cemetery Alvin's camping in, and a young priest (John Lordan) comes into the night with a plate of dinner for the traveler. The scenes of the two men talking allow the filmmakers to heighten the drama by detailing the now-severed childhood bond between Alvin and Lyle on the eve of Alvin's discovering whether he can repair it or not. The two "grew up close as brothers could be," helping their parents try to make a meager farm productive. The boys devised games to help make their chores seem less arduous, and at night they'd look up at the stars and wonder about life on other planets. They kept up a dialogue that "made our trials seem smaller; we pretty much talked each other through growin' up." But there's been no talk for ten years, which makes Alvin feel like he hasn't had a brother for a decade. He blames anger and vanity, mixed with liquor, and knows that "it'll be a hard swallow of my pride" to make peace. But, just as he told the young bicyclists that age teaches you how to separate the wheat from the chaff, Alvin has let "whatever made me and Lyle so mad" blow away in the chill autumn wind. His being is attuned to restoring harmony, his goal is simply to "sit with Lyle and look up at the stars again." Hearing this, and remembering the night that Alvin and Rose looked heavenward in their backyard, we see that for Alvin the stars provide not only a feeling of cosmic connection and consolation, but the solace of a cherished family ritual.

Besides summing up the film's central emotional dynamic, this long scene with the priest is notable for the fact that the man of God looks and sounds like Mark Frost. Lynch has said that *The Straight Story* "taught me the lesson of forgiveness and making things right."[35] After partnering for five years and having some creative differences, the two men who dreamed up *Twin Peaks* chose to go their separate ways. Could the conciliatory spirit of Alvin Straight's story have subconsciously moved Lynch to include a Mark Frost figure in his film?

The cold gravestones in the blackness surrounding Alvin's campfire are pale as bones, and the old man is near enough to death that any night could claim him, let alone one in which he sleeps in a field of fallen voyagers. But he's still around to see the sunrise on his big day. To celebrate, focus his courage, and reinforce his sense of self-mastery, Alvin stops at a roadside tavern and lets himself have his first drink in years: one, and only one, glass of Miller Lite beer. Alvin's been so long away from Lyle that he can't remember how to find his place, so the elderly barkeep gives directions, concluding with the troubling words "if he's there."

The lane that leads to Lyle's place is called Weed, and as its name implies, it is nothing more than a humble dirt road, yet it sings with the kind of commonplace beauty celebrated by everyone from Walt Whitman to John Updike to Japanese filmmaker Yasujiro Ozu. The dusty road, the scrubby, dust-and-copper-colored trees, a leaf falling through the golden air: Alvin's heightened-with-anticipation senses drink in every detail—and then his mower conks out. The steady droning hum of Alvin's mower has become second nature to us, like a mechanical representation of the life force, so it's shocking when the sound stops. Dejected, and afraid to try to start the engine, Alvin sits and sits, as morning becomes afternoon. Lynch knows how to subtly disturb us even with a quiet scene like this, for he films Alvin from a distance doing something we've never seen him do: sitting on his mower in a landscape, but not moving forward.

Over the years, Lynch has presented guiding angel figures in the form of an aged woman (*The Grandmother*, 1970), a young woman living in a radiator (*Eraserhead*, 1976), a deceased mother (*The Elephant Man*, 1980), a golden teenage girl (*Blue Velvet*), a female bar singer and a traditional divine, white-winged woman (*Twin Peaks: Fire Walk With Me*, 1992), and a *Wizard of Oz*–like Good Witch (*Wild at Heart*, 1990). In *The Straight Story*, he introduces an old guy riding a big John Deere Tractor that towers like a Supreme Being above Alvin's pint-sized mower. Lynch stages the beautifully simple encounter between the two old men as the third, and most eloquent, of his faraway, reduced-sound scenes. Mixed with the tree-murmur of the autumn air, we barely hear the tractor man urge Alvin to "try it again," and hear Alvin reply, "I guess I lost my faith." Then, almost like a miracle, his mower roars back to life. Alvin's words reinforce the spiritual context of his journey, and we note a Lynchian twinning as the two old men on their green John Deeres chug down the road together, until Alvin's guide points out Lyle's road and Alvin turns in. Ozu often presented passages in which two people in a frame, sitting or moving together, feel themselves in harmony with each other, their surroundings, and all of being. There was another touching moment of twinning before the scene of Alvin and his angel was shot. Lynch and his oldest friend, Jack Fisk, who had for decades lived the Art Life they chose to pursue as teenagers, stood together on Alvin's autumn road, working the dusty dirt and fallen leaves with brooms to get just the right texture.

Ever since Lynch had a personal spiritual experience in the early 1970s at the Los Angeles County Museum of Art, in which white light beamed from an ancient Indian Buddha figure into his eyes, the director has often used a radiance of pure, pearly light in his moving-image work to mark concluding moments of exaltation. While making *The Straight Story*, as Alvin slowly and painfully dismounted from his mower and started walking up the incline toward Lyle's little house, an unscripted opportunity for a flood of illumination presented itself. Lynch wanted to do a single panning shot that would cover Alvin advancing from his mower on the right, brushing near the camera, and continuing left, where the lens would pick up Lyle's house. Given the lay of the land, there was just one camera position that would capture all the necessary angles in one shot, and the director realized that "for less than twelve minutes"[36] a bright sun flare of light would perfectly coincide with Alvin's close-up position in the center of the shot. Everyone made haste and the shot turned out perfectly, as a white radiance suffuses the final steps of Alvin's pilgrimage, blessing the moment and once again adding a spiritual grace note to a David Lynch film. Call it a happy coincidence or, as the director sees it, "a beautiful . . . fate kind of thing."[37] The sun flare truly is serendipitous, for it rhymes with a small wood carving mounted to the right of Lyle's front door, which depicts the sun's orb radiating beams of light. Covered with peeling asphalt shingles, Lyle's old house is weathered and worn, and so is its occupant. Alvin is clearly the older brother, but Lyle's (Harry Dean Stanton) grizzled cheeks and sunken eyes, and the way he painfully grips an aluminum walker as he drags his stroke-frozen right side onto the porch convinces us that both brothers' remaining time on Earth is dwindling fast.

The filmmakers' decision to be reticent about the expression of emotion pays off beautifully as Alvin sits to the left of Lyle's open front door and Lyle slumps into a chair to the right of the aperture. Lynch stresses how concrete the gap between them is by not showing both brothers in the same frame, and cutting back and forth between separate shots of Alvin and Lyle. Alvin has had the will and fortitude to engineer and complete his journey to Lyle, and Lyle has what it takes to bridge the abyss of their estrangement by acknowledging his brother's physical effort and the message of emotional reconciliation it proclaims. Lyle already knows the answer to the question he poses to Alvin; it's just his way of giving voice to his love: "Did you ride that thing all the way here to see me?" And "I did, Lyle" is the love returned. No more words need to be said. The brothers don't break into beaming smiles, but there are tears welling in Lyle's eloquent eyes and a sudden catch of breath in Alvin's throat as both men tip their heads back and look heavenward. Lynch has wept over Alvin uttering that little half-sob: The brothers communing without words echoes the deep love David felt for his paternal grandfather as a small child, when they drove for miles, slowly, without speaking.

Each brother is still in his individual shot, but Lynch dissolves from their separate faces to a single image of a night sky full of stars, as duality merges into unity, the one behind the many. The stars that Alvin has looked up at previously in the film have been stationary in the firmament, but the ones that he and Lyle see, and which close the film, move past left and right past their (and our) point of view as we penetrate space. As *The Straight Story* ends, Alvin is far from his house, but his spirit is home. As boys Alvin and Lyle saw the stars as faithful, consoling companions, and as catalysts for their imaginations, prompting them to wonder if "there might be people like us" living out there in the universe somewhere. Now, as the aged brothers, who are only lightly attached to the earth, look up, they are not merely repeating a cherished childhood ritual, they are heading back to the source, into the mystery, moving forward into the next stage of the journey that never ends. This concluding sense of Alvin and Lyle being absorbed into the stars, back home to the cosmic ground of being, echoes the ending of John Huston's *The Misfits* (1960), starring Clark Gable and Marilyn Monroe. Both Gable and Monroe would die before making another film, and in *The Misfits'* last scene the two are driving through a roadless desert at night. Monroe asks, "How do you find your way back in the dark?" Gable, playing an old cowpoke reminiscent of Richard Farnsworth, sounds almost like Alvin Straight: "Just head for that big star straight on."

Like Lynch himself, Agent Cooper, and many of the director's characters, Alvin and Lyle long to see. And like Lynch's conception of *Twin Peaks*, and his belief in the flowing stream of life and death and new life, the brothers are part of a "continuing story."[38] And likewise, for those who truly see Lynch's art, the works are part of a continuum of thought and feeling that streams through our heads and hearts. *The Straight Story* moved Lynch to contemplate his own continuing story and the people who are close to him on the go-round of this particular lifetime incarnation. "In the editing room I cried like mad. When I chose the pieces of music for the scenes, the emotions returned, and every time I watch the film I've got a lump in my throat. I don't tend to cry easily, but this story touches a sore point in me."[39] Lynch saw Alvin Straight and the folks he interacted with on his adventure, whether they were kin or strangers, as being "like a big family, and you have to rely on one another. Family has never been important to me. It took me a long time to realize that it determines our behavior and our entire life."[40] Lynch's sensitivity to Straight's story of courageous independent voyaging, and kindly cooperation and sharing, of brothers and daughters and fathers, is fully understandable. Lynch always speaks admiringly of his younger brother John, but Peggy Reavey has said that David has experienced some of the natural sense of rivalry that an older brother feels toward a younger one. Not only did David and John look up at the starts together like young, and old, Alvin and Lyle, but Lynch told me that while making the film his grandfather and father were often on his mind. When I visited Lynch's parents, Donald, with his love of cowboys and the West, his white hair and beard and gentle manner, easily made me think of Richard Farnsworth. And, watching footage of Lynch tenderly giving Farnsworth some advice about a scene and, after the final shot with the two brothers looking skyward was finished, walking away from his film's last camera setup with his arm around Farnsworth's shoulder at the actor's slow pace, it's easy to imagine Lynch communing with his own father. In what the Lynch family calls the Western Room, with its cowboy art and memorabilia, I noticed a recent photograph of Donald. Sunny playfully commented that Donald was displaying a bit more belly than she liked. What struck me was that he was wearing a Western-style wheat-colored straw hat that would do Richard Farnsworth, and Alvin Straight, proud. Unlike with his darker films, Lynch's father and mother attended *The Straight Story*'s premiere, and when Donald chatted with Richard Farnsworth, the two old-timers discovered that they knew some of the same people from long-ago days in Montana.

Many people around the world felt at home in *The Straight Story*, and it earned more than twice its production costs in pre-video revenue, a rare feat for a Lynch film. The early positive buzz for the picture started at the spring 1999 Cannes Film Festival where, as the movie concluded in the huge Grande Palais, the overflow audience rose to its feet in a cheering ovation that included even the usual Lynch-detractor film critic Roger Ebert. Lynch and Mary Sweeney came to France without a distributor for their film, but left with the Sleeping Beauty Castle logo of Walt Disney's Magic Kingdom affixed to *The Straight Story*'s opening credits.

"What an incongruous combination!" the media world proclaimed when word spread that the apostolic, family-friendly Disney corporation would be proudly promoting a film by David Lynch, who some consider to be an anti-Christ of the black arts. In his time, Disney (1901–1966) was called "the world's most honored citizen"[41] and celebrated as the creator of "enlightened, wholesome and educational entertainment,"[42] a "benefactor of the whole human race"[43] who brings pleasure to a world that needs "the healing power of laughter and beauty."[44] In the mainstream view, this was everything that the subversive, fear-sex-violence-dysfunction-perversion-deformity-pain-and-nightmare-obsessed Lynch was not. However, those on intimate terms with Lynch and his work knew that the director valued the same positive values and behaviors that Disney championed, though he frequently chose to present a more probing exploration of the dark forces that threatened them. A happy ending to a Disney film seemed to be part of the American Bill of Rights, a golden clause in the social contract you sealed when you bought your ticket. Felicity did shine at the conclusion of some Lynch works, though characters, and even some viewers, had to suffer some psychic damage and live through hell to attain it. Disney's world, once put right, might stay that way forever, while Lynch's planet could tip nauseatingly out of control again before sundown. But in *The Straight Story* the director was listening to a different muse: the voice of his love Mary Sweeney and of gritty old Alvin, and the call of his own capacity for gentle warmth and radiant beneficence. Disney's organization was drawn to this light, and by distributing the film brought Lynch the largest number of glowing reviews since *The Elephant Man*. Maybe the surreal marriage of the ear mutilator and the Magic Kingdom of Mouse Ears was ordained in the heavens, for Walt Disney, a rapt appreciator of the night sky like Alvin Straight, used to sum up his ethos with the phrase, "When you wish upon a star."

As though supporting the fact that Lynch was resolutely siding with the angels in *The Straight Story*, a broader demographic spectrum of viewers saw his film. Sunday afternoon matinee screenings were attended by young families with small children and a higher-than-usual percentage of white-haired oldsters, who had the unique pleasure of watching one of their own star in an American movie. Lynch says that his love and respect for his own paternal grandfather's independent style are "definitely in the film,"[45] and the picture provided a chance for younger viewers to discover and venerate the spirit, courage, determination, intelligence, and wit of the oldest among us. Mary Sweeney was especially gratified by the positive response to her and Lynch's creative offspring, for the film showed that her man's nature was warm, kindly, fully human, and humane—and that he could bring his formidable filmmaking powers to bear on a benignly mainstream project that some were calling the best G-rated film since the all-ages-admitted G designation was instituted in the 1960s. Sweeney concludes, "I'm very proud of my script, but David took it to a whole other level and made it like a prayer."[46]

Finally, *The Straight Story* silenced those hip Lynch appreciators who always assumed that the director was being subversive and mockingly ironic when, in the context of his darker works, he sang the praises of good-hearted common folk and sweetly innocent sentiments. Lynch's Eagle Scout sincerity rang forth from every frame of the film, and Disney executives said they'd like to sign Lynch up for future projects. Intriguingly, Walt Disney made some philosophical statements in the 1950s that endorsed Lynch's deepest beliefs: "Fantasy and reality often overlap,"[47] and "The screen has too long been confined to what we can see and hear, what the camera can show, things which reveal not the half of a man's life and his most intense interests, the emotions, the impulses of the mind."[48] This is certainly Lynch's home turf, but his passionate need to explore its most lurid and fearsome shadow zones would certainly disqualify him from receiving Disney studio underwriting for his most transgressive films. Indeed, in the time of *The Straight Story* the Disney organization, in the form of the ABC TV network, squelched a Lynch project that the director cared about dearly.

Lynch and Mark Frost first envisioned *Mulholland Drive*, a multicharacter interweaving of stories evoking both the romantic legend of Hollywood and the malevolent power plays of the film industry, while Lynch worked on *Twin Peaks* in 1990. As Frost recalls, "we talked about *Mulholland Drive* as a spin-off show for the Audrey Horne character. We were going to take her to California and plunk her down in the middle of the Hollywood film scene."[49]

The history and lore of Los Angeles beats with a divided heart, a sound that always captures Lynch's attention. Even before Portuguese navigator Juan Rodrigues Cabrillo first set foot (1542) on the land we know as Southern California, a Spanish novel characterized the region as a literally golden territory, an earthly paradise. And the City of Angels of 1769, with its encircling mountain ranges, caressingly warm, amber-tinged air (there was a natural haze centuries before smog), peacock-blue sea, and spring-green and wildflower-rainbowed hillsides, was clearly a blessed locale. For someone like Lynch, raised in the rainy, cool, gloomy, and sleepily provincial Northwest, coming to Los Angeles can seem like stepping into a heaven of economic health, multicultural artistic excitement, eternal sunshine, Christmastime drifts of magenta-flowering bougainvillea and hibiscus, and banana palms heavy with fruit right outside the front door. But these lush paradisiacal trees (which pattern the exterior and the wallpaper of the archetypally elegant Beverly Hills Hotel) can hide big black rats in their fronds, as Lynch, who traps the vermin with a nonkilling homemade device, well knows. This city that was built on dreams, and promised physical rejuvenation and spiritual and creative free expression, constructed itself with the involuntary labor of enslaved Native Americans, and diverted its precious-as-gold water supply from the once-verdant agricultural community of the Owens Valley far to the north, leaving it a parched rural wasteland as the price of rapacious urban growth and the Southland blossoming of a million turquoise swimming pools.

The "beautiful animals"[50] that Lynch snares with his "humane rat trap"[51] (which, no surprise, is built of wood and electrical circuits), he takes up the hill behind his house to Mulholland Drive, where he releases them into the wilderness zones that coexist with luxurious residential enclaves. Mulholland is the legendary road that snakes for fifty miles from the Hollywood Bowl west to the Pacific Ocean along the roof-of-the-world Santa Monica Mountains, from which you can see a panorama spanning a hundred miles stretching from the snowy, 5,700-foot San Gabriel peaks on the right, across the broad San Fernando Valley, over the Santa Monicas, down into the largest metropolis west of New York, and out to the shimmering blue promise of Santa Catalina Island.

This fabled route, which connects high civilization with ancient wildness, lovers' lanes with the shallow graves of crime victims, is named for William Mulholland (1855–1935), the city water commissioner who, after viewing the bountiful Owens Valley River, said to his Angeleno constituents back home, of the Valley's endlessly flowing water, "There it is—Take it."[52] Mulholland engineered the massive pipeline that drained the Owens Valley and enabled the Southland desert to bloom as the long-dreamed-of heaven on earth. A heroic pioneer of L.A.'s boom times, Mulholland was honored in 1924 with the beautiful road that commemorates his name. But time has tarnished his image and associated his name with shady, unscrupulous men who didn't let laws curtail their hunger for land and power. Soon the sickly scent of overripe municipal corruption clung to the frayed palm trees, blood-stained the sunsets, and fanned the Santa Ana winds of human evil in the L.A. noir novels of Horace McCoy, Raymond Chandler, James M. Cain, Nathaniel West, and James Ellroy. Screenwriter Robert Towne noted the aura of conspiracy that haunted Mulholland's "water miracle"[53] and fictionalized it, and him, in the milestone Los Angeles elegy *Chinatown* (1974).

Artist Ed Ruscha, whose CinemaScope frame-shaped paintings have for decades portrayed L.A.'s thrusting horizontality, charred-orange sunsets, and iconic images (gas stations, the Hollywood sign), perfectly captures the city's sunshine/noir dichotomy in *WOLVES, EXPLOSIONS…, 1980*. This large canvas is like an illustration of Lynch's worldview: A curved line fills the frame, the comforting word HOME on one end of the continuum, and the threatening WOLVES, EXPLOSIONS, DISEASE, POISONS on the other. Both Ruscha's painting and Lynch's fictions are powered by the oppositional tension and interplay between zones and forces of safety and danger, light and darkness. These days we tend to see wolves as benign creatures which should be protected and allowed to thrive in their natural habitat, just as lions, bears, and alligators do. Ruscha gives WOLVES the more archetypal connotation of bestial evil, a meaning that animalism has in Lynch's work. Certainly a wolf loose in the suburbs of L.A. would be a fearsome, though unlikely, prospect. More commonly encountered are the surprisingly ubiquitous coyotes, who hunger to devour prey larger than Lynch's coyote-victim dog, Pepito. When diminutive Michael J. Anderson leaves parties late at night where coyotes are near, he has friends escort him to his car.

Lynch, with his lifelong sensitivity to contrasts between physical and spiritual darkness and light, worked L.A.'s sunshine and noir moods into his personal take on *Mulholland Drive*. Lynch has had mixed experiences with his television projects (*Twin Peaks*, *On the Air*, *Hotel Room*), in terms of having his personal art satisfactorily expressed by other writers, producers, and directors; the way audiences have, or have not, responded to the finished product; and the necessity of network businesspeople having a big say in the marketing and scheduling of his work. In the early 1990s, after every show he'd ever launched on TV had been canceled, he declared that the medium was "a joke"[54] and swore he'd never work in it again. Yet here he was in 1998, having co-written a *Mulholland Drive* pilot with Joyce Eliason and pitched it to ABC, the network that had mishandled and canceled *Twin Peaks*. The characters and plot lines of that singular series may have stopped short in the world of weekly broadcasts and corporate bottom lines, but they continued to live and evolve in Lynch's mind. Like the director's personal belief in souls reborn and living lives in cycle after cycle, *Twin Peaks* was still "part of a continuing story"[55] in Lynch's mind, but it was a tale that could no longer feasibly expand on TV or movie screens. Yet *Mulholland Drive*, another multicharacter saga with diverging and intersecting stories well might thrive, for the current ABC decision makers, Ms. Jamie Tarses and Steve Tao, were mesmerized and excited by the carefully chosen story details that Lynch divulged in his pitch-presentation.

The opening passages of *The Straight Story* showed Alvin's world bathed in golden light, whereas the *Mulholland Drive* screenplay plunges us deep into the Hollywood night: another of Lynch's primal "Now it's dark" moments. In contrast to the civilized concrete strip of road, headlights illuminate encroaching wild-growing patches of poison-leafed oleander, as well as eucalyptus foliage. In an instant, the road becomes the stage setting for a riot of human and mechanical violence. Lynch uses his favorite "floating"[56] mode of exposition to glide us into chaos. A black Cadillac limousine drifts majestically along the twisting nocturnal road, as a dark-haired woman in the back seat looks out the window, lost in thought. Her dreamy expression shatters in terror as the car stops suddenly and one of the men in the front seat comes after her with a pistol. In this suspended moment, another reality intrudes: two cars racing each other, each filled with "crazed teenagers"[57] and "flying with psychotic speed,"[58] come roaring around a bend, and the car in which two girls are standing up through the open sunroof, "screaming as their long hair is whipped straight back,"[59] smashes into the stopped limousine with its two men and the dark-haired woman. In a Lynchian conflation of eroticism and violence, the colliding cars couple with each other, shudder in an orgasmic explosion, and "become one in death."[60] The offspring of this traumatic coition is the dark-haired woman, who's reborn as a person with an external head wound and no internal sense of who she is: no memories, no imagined future, no name. Another of Lynch's head cases who's suffered a psychic injury, she stands with a tranced, vacant look on her face, clutching her purse, and recalling *Wild at Heart*'s car accident victim Sherilyn Fenn, who was also head-wounded, and babbled desperately because she couldn't find her purse.

The *Mullholland Drive* woman may have her handbag, but she's one of Lynch's displaced, disoriented people, and vulnerable to predatory animal energies, as a coyote attacks her. She may be a lost soul, but she has the gumption to escape the coyote's jaws, as Lynch once again contrasts fearsome danger with great beauty by showing the glowing lights of Los Angeles below, shimmering in the inky blackness like a celestial city. Drawn by the promise of these lights, like millions before her, she stumbles down from the Hollywood Hills with no map of destination and personhood to guide her. Wandering in a realm that is wholly mysterious and new, she personifies two Lynchian modes of being: a childlike innocent discovering the world, and a detective figure. She's full of questions without answers, but they'll have to wait, because now the only thing on her mind is shelter, a place to sleep and pray that someone she recognizes as herself will eventually come knocking at her door.

In *Blue Velvet*, the inner chambers of an ear, which dissolved into the front door of a beautiful high school girl's house, were the entryway to adventures of self-discovery for a Lynchian hero, and in *Mulholland Drive* the open, unattended door of a Hollywood apartment is a similar gateway for our anonymous accident survivor. She burrows deep into the dwelling and falls asleep, only to be discovered by Betty, a young woman hoping to realize her dream of becoming a great actress. Betty, whose name recalls the sweet and lovable heroine of *On the Air*, is blond, Midwestern, optimistic, and sincere, a golden harvest of wholesome family values who we first meet in the radiant California sunshine. The raven-haired accident survivor, who takes the name Rita from a femme fatale image of a Rita Hayworth poster in Betty's apartment, is a creature of the night, who, even as a victim, seems part of a power-wielding world of big black sedans and sudden death. So we have a good and cheerful young woman pursuing her art, and one who's dazed and maybe a little bit bad who's searching for her identity at the same time that the police, and the men who wanted her dead, are chasing after her—all set against the backdrop of numerous intriguing characters and an insider's view of the movie-making game. What's not to love, thought the ABC executives as Lynch paused in his pitch. Then the director made a gutsy move that showed his confidence in his mood-conjuring storytelling skills. He said that in order to hear what happens next, they'd have to literally buy the pilot. Tarses, Tao, and ABC Entertainment Television co-chairman Stu Bloomberg eagerly said yes and committed an unusually large sum of $4.5 million to producing a two-hour TV movie of *Mulholland Drive*, which could then grow into a weekly series. The project's forward momentum also pulled in Disney's Touchstone Television, who added more money to the effort, raising the pilot's total budget to an amazing $7 million.

Lynch has said, "it's possible that there are aliens on earth, and they work in television."[61] The director is fascinated by strange behavior and absurd situations, but the shape-shifting attitudes of the ABC brass surprised and dismayed him. They had digested every word of his pilot script and enthusiastically embraced it; they had heard a roomful of advertising salespeople gasp with excitement when they announced that David Lynch was returning to TV. They wanted what Lynch was eager to give them, but, as they started watching and worrying about the footage he was shooting, they also wanted *Mulholland Drive* to reflect their mounting concerns. Once again, Lynch was facing the worst-case nightmare he so often fictionalized in his work: control-crazed outside forces invading the sovereign, sacred sanctum of his uniquely creative mind. After suffering the severe truncation of his *Dune* vision at the hands of the De Laurentiis Group and seeing the pure black coffee of his beloved *Twin Peaks* diluted by too many collaborators, Lynch was hypersensitive about others trying to shape and manipulate his art: "You want your creations to come out of *you*, and be distinctive."[62]

The network captains, however, were painfully aware that their once-captive audiences were gradually defecting to myriad other enticements: cable TV channels, video games, DVDs, the Internet. Paralyzed by paranoia, they simultaneously wanted the cachet of being allied with a maverick creative genius and feared (remembering how *Twin Peaks*' initially huge audience soon scattered to the winds) doing anything that might alienate viewers or sponsors. Like Fred Madison endlessly driving his lost highway, they were stuck in the tired old formula of talking about adventurous risk-taking while agonizing over and over-analyzing the minutest details of what they thought people would want to see. They were happy to have Lynch on board, but they ultimately wanted Lynch as filtered through ABC. (No wonder the heroine of the director's 1968 film *The Alphabet* suffered when she learned her letters.) Lynch has explored the theme of an individual's hallowed sense of integrity being assaulted in many forms over the years and, in his *Mulholland Drive* screenplay, he ironically stages it in almost autobiographical terms.

Adam Kesher is a fictional young film director whose vision is manipulated and violated by executives—a position Lynch has occupied more than once in his career, and which he was sadly fleshing out again in regard to the project in which Adam appears. The language that the studio directs at Adam ("there are some suggestions to be brought forward") is a carbon copy of what Lynch was hearing from the ABC brass. When Adam balks at being told that a certain actress *must* play the heroine of his film, he becomes the victim of the ultimate power play: "It is no longer your film."[63] (*Mulholland Drive*'s dictators in suits are Italian, and are perhaps surrogates for the De Laurentiis family, which shaped Lynch's *Dune* to *their* liking.) When Lynch has had to endure such abuse of his artistic integrity he's behaved in an outwardly gentlemanly manner, so there's a feeling of pent-up animus finding sweet physical release as he has Adam take a seven-iron golf club and smash the perfect black surface of his tormentors' fine car. No, not a nine-iron, for in recent years Lynch's favored personal number has become seven (in one of the introductions to the Bravo cable network rebroadcast of the *Twin Peaks* series, he has the Log Lady say, "Balance is the key; the word 'balance' has seven letters.") Lynch is sensitive to occurrences of synchronicity in the world. When I told him that my Seattle Art Museum key—which I was given by chance, out of a possible choice of hundreds, and which opens most of the doors in our huge, five-story building—is seven, he said, "See, there you go."[64] So, instead of the nines prominent in his earlier work, most of *Mulholland Drive*'s hotel, motel, office, and audition room numbers add up to seven.

The theme of an artist's, or a person's, creative sovereignty being threatened, which is common to Lynch's life and fiction, perhaps came to his early attention in *Sunset Boulevard*, where the hero's vision and personal freedom are compromised by both the Hollywood studios and the monstrous, pitiful Norma Desmond. The *Mulholland Drive* screenplay exhibits a number of other familiar Lynchian preoccupations. There's a central mystery (who is Rita, and why does someone want her dead?), which the script links to a web of disparate people, from lowlifes to wealthy power brokers. And there are secondary mysteries: the way that gaining knowledge reveals still more unknowns, the human capacity for visualizing something that can't be put into words, the question of what occupies the mind of someone who can't remember anything, the supernatural mobility of a person in time and space, and the mystery of love—the way that two characters who don't know each other (as in *Eraserhead*, *Dune*, *Blue Velvet*, *Twin Peaks*, and *Lost Highway*) "feel the thunderbolt"[65] of sudden mutual attraction. Also, as in *The Grandmother* and *Twin Peaks*, there is an uncommon boy (perhaps a reflection of Lynch's son, Riley) who possesses an air of wisdom and mental power well beyond his years. And, echoing *Twin Peaks: Fire Walk With Me*'s enigmatic "blue rose" FBI cases, there's a puzzling, emblematic "BLUE KEY" (the key to the case?) in Rita's purse which, for some reason, strikes fear in her heart.

If mystery is present in a Lynch work, then visions are sure to follow, and *Mulholland Drive* presents a dream so dark and troubling that it kills the one who dreams it. The dream also contains a potentially supernatural mystery man (as in *Twin Peaks* and *Lost Highway*), who here appears in the form of a Bum who lurks behind a Denny's restaurant, his face charred, his eyes burning red. In Lynch's fictional world, violence always has consequences, and his screenplay carries this concept to blackly absurd lengths, as one of the director's 1950s juvenile delinquent–style bad guys, after rubbing out his target (head shot, of course), has to dispatch a number of unplanned-for witnesses in record time. Also recognizably Lynchian is an oracle figure (like *Twin Peaks'* Log Lady, Giant, and Man From Another Place) who provides a character with some pieces of the puzzle, and people who act on their intuitions, or have a "possessed"[66] look, or who start to look like someone else. There is cool saxophone music, folks with French names, those who crave particular foods, and a dark light bulb that sparks into life. There's an artist who gets a creative boost by yielding to a spontaneous, direction-changing inspiration, as Lynch often has. There's a concern for biological functions and organic textures (two shots of dog turds on a sidewalk), and something new to Lynch's work: a cornucopia of loving references to the romantic spirit of Los Angeles and Hollywood's heritage.

Lost Highway was matter-of-factly set in L.A., but the director's warm feelings for his home of thirty years permeate *Mulholland Drive*. His screenplay evokes actual streets (Fountain, Havenhurst), the scent of jasmine, Pink's Hot Dog Stand, purple-blooming jacaranda trees, vintage cream-colored stucco apartments, the Hollywood sign and the panoramic lightscape of nighttime L.A., and the legacy of the early days that's carried in the minds of those who lived them. The director has Betty approach the iconic gates of Paramount Studios just as William Holden did in *Sunset Boulevard*. And Rita says "Mulholland Drive" with all the poetic resonance of a character uttering the almost metaphysically fraught word "Chinatown" in that seminal L.A. film.

The *Mulholland Drive* pilot has much to entice and hold an audience and make them eager to learn what happens next—so why didn't ABC put it on the air? The networks executives had loved the pilot on paper, but they had a number of issues with the pilot footage beyond the obvious no-no of the close-up dog feces. The hypnotic, floating opening, which introduced Rita and followed her from the hills into town, was too slow. There were many characters who smoked cigarettes. The chain-reaction gun-violence scene was too gory and constituted a political danger zone in the wake of the April 1999 shooting rampage at Colorado's Columbine High School (the popular TV series *Buffy, the Vampire Slayer* postponed its season finale, which dealt with a supernatural war at a high school, for months). Betty was too much the corny, wide-eyed innocent, Rita the sleepwalking zombie. The Bum's eyes weren't glowing red because Lynch secretly planned to launch *Mulholland Drive* (à la *Twin Peaks*) into unfathomable realms of weirdness that would alienate viewers, were they?

Lynch tried to calm ABC's fears, reminding them that it was the slow-for-TV, entrancingly paced first twenty minutes of *Twin Peaks* and the opening installment's provocatively unanswered questions that hooked one of the biggest television audiences of 1990. He tried to be diplomatic, but did they want his unique artistry, or did they not? To be fair to the executives, Lynch's previous experience with television production should have taught him that networks are primarily interested in securing big ratings and raking in dollars, and that some measure of compromise might rightly be expected from him in helping to achieve that goal. Lynch's desire to do things his way even extended to the notion that ABC should broadcast his pilot at an unheard-of two-and-a-half-hour length. The network put its foot down: Lynch simply *had* to cut his footage down to an eighty-eight-minute standard-pilot length.

With a knot in his stomach, the director bit the bullet and, with Mary Sweeney, stayed up all night and made the cuts ABC requested (dog turds smaller in the frame, less blood and brains in the shootings), ending up with the requisite eighty-eight-minute "butchered version"[67] that was "like an accident" (that is, like a tragic crash). Sadly, Lynch wasn't through hurting, for, just as he was leaving to attend the Cannes Film Festival screening of *The Straight Story*, he was told that "ABC doesn't want *Mulholland Drive* for the fall, they don't want it for the midseason. They don't want it."[68] Mark Frost, Lynch's *Twin Peaks*–era partner and TV industry veteran, told me

> David was deeply disappointed when the *Mulholland Drive* pilot failed. The real stupidity of the whole enterprise was for ABC to hire him and then be surprised when he turned out to be exactly the person that they hired, doing the work that is characteristic of him. This was perfectly emblematic of how short-sighted and ignorant networks can be. I wish I'd been able to work on the pilot with David, because I think we probably could have shaped it in a way that it would have gotten past the first hurdle and onto the air.[69]

Even with the concessions Lynch had made, the network's enthusiasm for the project was gone with the wind, and they scheduled the teenage drama *Wasteland* (created by Kenneth Williamson, writer of the phenomenally popular *Scream* movies and TV's *Dawson's Creek*) into the Thursday night slot *Mulholland Drive* was to have occupied. There must have been laughter that spanned the spectrum from ironic to gloating in the Lynch camp when ABC cancelled *Wasteland* after only two shows due to abysmal ratings.

As *The Straight Story* made its way through the world, charming critics and audiences, Lynch's business associates talked to the FOX TV network (of *X-Files* fame) about a *Mulholland Drive* miniseries, but negotiations broke down. Lynch fans hoped that one of the cable networks with an imaginative programming agenda, like HBO (*The Sopranos*), might pick up the project, but no such luck. For Lynch, *Mulholland Drive* "was over,"[70] and he repeated the declaration he'd made years before: no more TV, because "feature films are what I should be doing; I don't want to do anything with people who aren't enthusiastic."[71]

The director was happy to see *The Straight Story* placing high on a number of critics' ten-best lists for 1999. Disney, who had done little to promote the film, got on the bandwagon and strategically positioned ads in the entertainment industry trade papers suggesting that Lynch's masterful direction and Richard Farnsworth's outstanding performance be considered for accolades in the Spring 2000 awards season. And sure enough, Farnsworth harvested well-deserved Best Actor nominations from the Golden Globes and the Academy Awards. Before these ceremonies were held, he was voted Best Actor by the prestigious New York Film Critics Circle, he received the Grace Prize for Most Inspirational Performance from the Christian Film and Television Commission, and *The Straight Story* was chosen Best Non-European Film at Berlin's European Film Awards. However, the Best Actor Golden Globe went to Denzel Washington (*The Hurricane*), and Kevin Spacey took home the Oscar for his fine work in *American Beauty*.

But Richard Farnsworth and Alvin Straight's don't-fence-me-in ethos was rewarded at the Independent Spirit Awards, where Farnsworth crowned a well-spent Hollywood life by accepting the Best Male Lead prize. Sponsored by the Independent Film Project and held in a big tent on a Santa Monica Beach afternoon, the Independent Spirit Awards are decidedly more freewheeling and raucous than the establishment prize fests. Spectators and nominees sit at tables eating, drinking, and, in Lynch's case, smoking cigarettes, during the ceremonies, and some of the award presenters wear untucked shirts or T-shirts (Lynch naturally wore a black suit with his white shirt). When the camera caught candid views of Lynch, who was sitting next to Mary Sweeney, he looked gray, grim, and rather disengaged from the proceedings. But he cracked a big grin and took a drink of red wine as Farnsworth triumphantly took the stage, walking slowly with a cane just like Alvin Straight. The old cowboy gentleman took off his white Stetson hat and, looking more like Lynch's beloved grandfather than ever in his Western-tailored gray suit, accepted his award from actress Julianne Moore and actor Jeff Bridges and basked in a whooping standing ovation. He thanked Mary Sweeney and John Roach for their story, said he'd been "tickled to death"[72] to be directed by Lynch, and assured everyone that he'd be "thinking of you all after I get my hip replacement and I'm riding my horse out on the ranch."[73] Richard Farnsworth, onscreen and off, will ride tall until the end of his days.

Lynch was nominated for Best Director, but young Alexander Payne stepped up to receive the award for crafting the excellent, hipper-than-*The Straight Story* film *Election*. The first words out of Payne's mouth were, "Look, I'm not a better director than David Lynch."

When Lynch made his first animated film in 1968 at age twenty-three because he wanted to see his paintings move, he looked up to older cinematic masters like Alfred Hitchcock, Billy Wilder, Federico Fellini, Ingmar Bergman, and Stanley Kubrick. Now, in his mid-fifties as the second millennium dawns, Lynch has become one of the legends who fledgling filmmakers admire. He is an inspiring example of an artist who's absolutely devoted to his vision, who looks at the world with a naked eye both innocent and darkly experienced and responds with deeply personal feelings, dreams, intuitions, and subconscious surprises that he lets pour out of himself uncensored. Lynch has created a vibrant record of his being in the world.

A man who investigates the innermost mysteries of his own psyche, Lynch, in his work, exalts those who quest to uncover and learn the truths hidden within human desire, fear, longing, sadness, and pain; the process of birth-death-rebirth; and the single cosmic mind that is all. Lynch seeks to organize his life so that he can often be in an optimal state in which there's a smooth circuit of energy flowing from his eye to his mind to his artist's hand. Looking with what Surrealist pioneer Andre Breton called "the savage, wild eye,"[74] Lynch sees the connection between darkness and light, the inner and the outer, the brain and the universe, the terrifying and the marvelous, cherry pie and black coffee, the commonplace and the infinite. Lynch explores and expresses realms of thought, emotion, and spirit *not* because he wants to emulate his artistic elders, reap more profits and awards than Steven Spielberg, or be a shining role model of genius-level talent, single-minded drive, and creative integrity for beginning artists. He puts his mark on paintings, drawings, photographs, films, videos, TV shows, comic strips, song lyrics and music, architecture, furniture and interior design, and cyberspace simply because he must. Retaining a sensitive child's ability to feel what's in the air and listen to what the world and his innermost voice are telling him, Lynch has always understood that his way of existing was to be the Art Life. Following his inner calling, pleasing his eye and mind with his creations, helping himself stay sane by artistically processing intense personal forces and fierce perceptions, and presenting them to the world, Lynch shows us ourselves in all our strange, monstrous glory.

Like a detective reading clues and stray thoughts and musing, I've been pursuing the mystery of David Lynch since I saw *The Grandmother* at the age of twenty-five in 1970. This thinker and artist who is like no other, who inhabits the mundane world we all share, yet who's able to combine its elements in previously undreamed of ways that seem organic and perfectly natural, yet which bear an uncanny charge of metaphysical poetry. This is a man who can steal your sleep with nightmare visions of human depravity and evil that are too intimate and disturbingly familiar. Yet he can, at the same time, make your soul sing with the dark, wild beauty of pain and tears and then exalt in the pure white light that erases suffering and transcends death. He is a creator whose work is feared and damned and celebrated to the point of worship, who is characterized as being the epitome of both weirdness and morality. A person described as a reclusive agoraphobic, who's fully aware of all the fearful, threatening forces loose in the world, yet who travels the globe and often describes a vast range of the phenomena he encounters as "a beautiful thing."[75]

I have expressed my active interest in Lynch's work and life, and the worldwide cultural response to his artistic and personal persona by publishing articles, observing him anonymously while he filmed *Twin Peaks: Fire Walk With Me*, meeting and having phone conversations with those who have known him over the years, writing these pages, and corresponding and having phone talks with Lynch. In one of our conversations, he spoke of the period in 1970 just after he'd arrived in Los Angeles. Inspired by his love for Billy Wilder's classic film noir *Sunset Boulevard*, Lynch had driven in vain for hours trying to find a certain driveway featured early in the film. An opening, an entranceway in the curb and thick foliage into which Joe Gillis (William Holden), who's being chased by car-repossession men, swerves his car when it has a blowout, and accidentally begins his ensnarement in Norma Desmond's (Gloria Swanson) entrapping web of warped love and monstrous neediness. By chance, I had been reading an *Architectural Digest* about the locations used in the film. Lynch had already heard that the exterior of Norma Desmond's mansion had actually been on Wilshire, not Sunset Boulevard, was the property of the Getty family, and was now the headquarters of Getty Oil. But he didn't know that the fabled driveway, as *Architectural Digest* put it, "led to the first house that Vincente Minnelli and Judy Garland had lived in after their 1945 marriage."[76] Lynch responded with a touching note of awe and reverence in his voice as he said, "Judy Garland," for the forces of synchronicity had just linked Sunset Boulevard with the world of his other favorite film, *The Wizard of Oz*. I jokingly said he could go into his detective mode and find a homes-of-the-stars maps from the 1940s and locate the address that way—and left it at that.

Over the next few days that driveway stayed on my mind, and after doing some research in Minnelli's autobiography and the Internet (Judy Garland fan clubs), I came up with the street (Evanview) and the number. The situation was tantalizingly complicated by the fact that Minnelli and Garland's *second* L.A. home *was* on Sunset, and very near where Lynch had been searching.

Knowing that I was coming to Los Angeles in the summer of 2000, I got the idea that I could help Lynch complete his decades-long quest and we could go find Norma Desmond's driveway together. I also knew that this artistic workaholic was busier than ever, hoping to resolve the question of whether France's Canal Plus company might buy the rights to *Mulholland Drive* from ABC so that he could complete it as a self-contained feature film; that he had fallen behind schedule in building his website, davidlynch.com, and generally did not often leave his house. When I proposed the excursion over the phone, he paused, then said, "Well, yeah, maybe we *could* do that." I told him I would scout the two locations after I hit town, and call him with a report. "Cool enough. Swingin'."

Arriving in L.A. on a Sunday afternoon, I located Minnelli and Garland's residence on Evanview, which is many roads removed from Sunset. The simple, modern structure presented a windowless white wall to a narrow hillside street: there wasn't a hint of Billy Wilder's film to be seen. Dropping down to Sunset, I found the home Minnelli and Garland occupied from 1948 to 1951, or rather, saw the palatial gate and landscaping which hid it from the street. Then, a bit further west on Sunset, I saw the curve opening onto a straightaway, the cuts in the curb, the light post on the right, the driveway into which a car could make a right turn: even without the aid of Billy Wilder's dramatic camera angles, this was clearly it. Then I saw why Lynch had thought this wasn't it: a tall, white wall that fenced this part of the property back in the 1970s cut across the driveway at a point that would have prevented Holden's car from proceeding far up the drive like it had in the film. Sunset Boulevard is like a four-lane highway with a lower speed limit: You can't stop on it and there are no sidewalks. I parked on a side street and followed the wall back to the driveway so I could take a picture of the scene. I studied the disparate ages of the driveway and wall and concluded that the barrier had been erected well after *Sunset Boulevard* had been filmed. So, decades earlier, Lynch *had* reached his goal without realizing it; his original pathfinding instincts had been correct. He'd be happy to hear this, but I was disappointed that now we wouldn't be doing our exploratory jaunt together. Maybe I'll get to meet him in some other lifetime.

I was going to be in L.A. through Friday, and during the week, I couldn't even get Lynch on the phone. I just missed him twice, and one day his assistant conveyed the artist's simple tantalizing message to me: "I'm up to my neck in foam." By chance, *Sunset Boulevard* was on TV Thursday night, and I thought how a tenant of the Aldo Nido apartments, where William Holden's character lived in the film, could be watching the movie in Holden's very room as Wilder's camera approached the window to enter Holden's life.

I took a final shot at calling Lynch at Friday noon, and got him. In his mind, synchronicity was doing its usual, expected thing, for his first words were "*Sunset Boulevard* was on TV last night!" I told him that he *had* found the right driveway back in 1970, and he said he'd been overwhelmed with work, trying, as a favor for a friend, to complete a project that he's known about for two months, is due in a few days, and he's just started. "It's pedal-to-the-metal time," but then a surprise: "Hey man, why don't you come over."

In the upper reaches of the Hollywood Hills, Lynch's property line stretches for hundreds of feet along a precipitous, twisting street, where houses cling at various levels to a steep bank crowned by Mulholland Drive. In a descending arc from left to right I see the pale-gray concrete *Lost Highway* house, a darker, smaller central office structure, and, nestled in a low, green curve of pines and spiky agaves, the horizontal mass of Lynch's Lloyd Wright house, blooming lavender-pink in the summer light.

Climbing the *Lost Highway* stairs where Renee found the mysterious videotapes, I press the intercom button like Fred Madison did and am told by an associate where to find Lynch. Huffing and puffing up a nearly vertical, handrail-less staircase that ascends the hill, I hear Lynch's loud twang ring out "That must be Greg" before I emerge onto a top-of-the-world wooden platform. The first thing I see is a life-size white fiberglass cow, the stump of its severed neck smeared red. Lynch's smiling, tanned face squints into the hot, bright sunshine as he gives me a solid Gordon Cole/FBI handshake. He's unshaven, the thick topknot of hair is silvered, there's sweat on his brow, red lines in the whites surrounding his brilliant blue eyes, a flash of gold fillings in his mouth, and splatters of red "blood" on his pricey, untucked, top-buttoned French white shirt ("This was a good shirt—I got carried away.")

I'm introduced to Lynch's eighteen-year-old son, Austin, a tall, lanky, quiet, and mannerly fellow who's visiting his father for the summer. Named after Lynch's beloved paternal grandfather, Austin played a boy magician on *Twin Peaks*, looking very much like his father, with black-and-white clothes and a tall stack of sandy hair. His hair's now short and black, and he drinks English Earl Grey tea instead of dipping into his father's river of black coffee.

The three of us contemplate Lynch's white cow, one of four given to selected L.A. artists to do with as they choose, the resulting artworks to be used for a paint company's promotional campaign. Lynch is doing this project as a favor for a chum and former employee, and aside from the satisfaction of doing a good, Eagle Scout–like friendly deed, he'll receive "a bunch of free paint" in compensation. I silently wonder how a commercial firm is going to reap advertising gold from Lynch's grisly, victimized bovine. He's hollowed out a cavity in the cow's back and top-left flank and half-buried the animal's bloodied head within it. I only just got here and already I see a being's (the cow's) normally interior region bared to the outside air, and a prominent, traumatized head: this must be Lynchland, all right. The artist has oozed big cream-colored dollops of some industrial foam product around the head and body cavity, as though the insides of the head and body are spilling out. The tarp beneath the cow is a Jackson Pollock abstraction of foam-and-red-paint splatters, punctuated by many stained pairs of pale rubber surgical gloves.

For Lynch this project isn't an act of animal desecration, but a visceral examination of organic systems, a surrealistic rearrangement of fleshly elements like his *Fish Kit* and *Chicken Kit*, a high school science project carried to shocking, absurd lengths. He's playing with polymers and pigments, but he sounds like an earnest biological scientist, talking about how the sun heats the head, the cavity, the foam, and the action of gravity adds the force that makes the work a living process that moves by itself. He wants me to touch the warm innards, which I do.

We take refuge from the cow-cooking sun in a small picture-windowed pavilion next to Lynch's open-air work platform. This is the only space that he lives in that is cluttered, a mélange of canned and spilled paint, well-used brushes, various tools, a storage cabinet, a worn desk, and mismatched 1950s flea market chairs. As in many of the spaces we will enter, there's a turquoise carton of American Spirit cigarette packages at the ready. Through the fine cotton of his shirt, I can see the muted turquoise glow of an open pack in his breast pocket, like a politically incorrect badge of honor over his heart.

A soft, cool breeze disturbs the cloud of smoke rising over Lynch's head as, backlit by the west-moving sun, he talks about whatever pops into his head. He chuckles when I say I'm a sacrilegious Seattleite who doesn't drink coffee, and he lets me get away with swigging bottled water. He seems very relaxed for a deadline-driven artist, leaning back in his chair sipping hot coffee, but that characteristic hyper-concerned, brow-furrowing look occasionally tightens his face, even when he's talking about something pleasant. When he gestures, his right hand splays open, sometimes quivering, seeming to feel invisible currents in the air.

I'm intrigued to hear him spontaneously verbalize themes that permeate his work. He's just bought an undeveloped lot still higher up the hill, so now his holdings encompass a vertical city block, climbing from the street way below where my car's parked clear up to Mulholland Drive. His fascination for what goes on beneath the surface is irrepressible. He speaks of the concrete pilings and hidden superstructure sunken into the hillside to anchor his compound, and the geological substrata that are virtually earthquake-proof (he knocks on his wooden desk for luck). I picture his forest-scientist father boring into tree trunks when Lynch, with great excitement, talks about wanting to drill down into his new property to discover what's underground. Like a pioneer of the early California days he romanticizes that he wants to "drill for treasure—I don't care if it's water, gold, or oil." However, this thrilling possibility becomes clouded by thoughts of having to deal with environmental laws and authorities, which prompts a concise statement of a core Lynchian value: "I won't have other people telling me what to do, or what I can't do." These words, bespeaking the dynamic tension between freedom-seeking and controlling forces, resonate throughout the saga of the artist's work and life. When I jokingly suggest he should look into the air rights for the space above his property, he gets seriously interested.

After dwelling on the reasons he feels safe on his rock-solid hillside, Lynch, as he's done so often in his films and TV shows, veers into the realm of terrible danger. The earth grading down from Mulholland above our heads appears firm and secure, but it's actually "light and loose" and hides an occasional huge boulder. Years ago, one of these heavy brutes, freed by the erosive force of a rain storm, "thundered down the hillside like an earthquake" and stopped just short of the house across the street only because it landed in a frontyard pool. So the dark energies Lynch first sensed in his idyllic boyhood backyard, and which haunt his art, now threaten his safe and snug hillside kingdom.

In *The Straight Story*, Lynch and Mary Sweeney resoundingly showed how close family ties can help us weather the vicissitudes of life, and currents of family connection flowed through Lynch's art studio pavilion the day I visited. The artist's private domain is a wired world: There's a wall phone with nine lines (yes, nine again) by the toilet, and intercoms everywhere, so that every now and then invisible people speak to him out of the air. Austin is content to sit listening while us oldsters chatter on, but when his half-sister (Lynch's daughter, Jennifer) rings in, he takes the phone and does his own talking. Lynch tells me that his parents, Donald and Sunny, are both alive and well, wintering in Riverside, California, and enjoying woodsy summers in Montana, the state of David's birth.

Over the years Lynch has gratefully acknowledged the love and support his scientist father and teacher-homemaker mother have given him—he who, compared to his electrical-engineer brother and financial-planner sister, chose an unconventional path through life. The artist traces his own reverence for wood and the music of the forest to formative boyhood times in the trees with his father. Though retired, Donald keeps up with developments in the forestry profession and, using wood David has bought for him, handcrafts violins. Using words he's often used about himself, Lynch proudly stresses that his father's "always been a builder." The wood that he's supplied his father is special indeed: shipwrecked Canadian timber that's lain for a century on the bottom of Lake Superior. The wood's color and grain are especially beautiful, but it takes a long time to dry out and produce the final sound-tone quality of the instrument. "It takes ten years to dry, and Dad's eighty-four. . . ." For a split second I think of my own woodsman father, who's been gone for thirty-five years. "Here's hoping," I add. "Yeah."

Talking of family must have made Lynch see double, for he suddenly stares intently at me and says, "You look just like my cousin—his name is Mike—are you a runner?" Surprised and flattered by this rush of declaration, I say, "No, but I like to take walks at night," thinking that his "runner" question exemplifies his natural tendency to seek expanding degrees of correspondence and synchronicity: Mike must be a runner.

For twenty years, Lynch has dreamed of having his own sound studio, and he's eager to show me his new baby. I follow him on a narrow path through green, low-growing ground cover that rises and dips along the hillside. He pauses on the trail, speaking of a set he's built further up the hill, a tableau he wants to film that needs one more element to complete the picture: a live coyote. He's been trying to lure one of the wild animals into his artwork, and mentions that actor Gary Oldman, who lives nearby, has had two dogs eaten by the feral predators. And Lynch remembers Pepino, the dog which Isabella Rossellini gave him, that suffered a similar fate. Some coincidences are best left unacknowledged, so I don't call attention to the fact that Lynch and Oldman, in addition to losing dogs to coyotes, have both been intimate with Ms. Rossellini.

We enter the uppermost level of the *Lost Highway* house and walk into the kitchen Lynch designed right down to the last cabinet knob. This elegant study in black counters, glowing orange-amber wood, stainless steel, and gleaming chrome coffee makers, is, like many of the rooms in this dwelling, an asymmetrical space. Gentle curves and corners which expand beyond the standard right-angled ninety degrees give the chambers the feeling of having been patterned on nature's forms, rather than a schematic, mechanistic grid.

We proceed to a large room with a partition wall that rises to the high ceiling, but which has spaces to the left and right of it through which one can walk. There's an unadorned, off-center fireplace niche in this partition, and the wall tips more severely toward the right side of the room than the left. The floors and walls throughout the house are formed of a plasticized concrete with a tonal spectrum of light-to-dark gray, and random-seeming textural variations that suggest natural rocks and Northwest fogs. Lynch sums up the effect with an artist's pride: "It's organic."

Back behind the fireplace wall a conference table is nestled in the house's upper corner where two windows meet, the aperture, I realize, from which Fred Madison apprehensively looked down to the street after someone buzzed his intercom with an eerie message in the opening of *Lost Highway*. From the window, Lynch points down to a point where strange forces have again injected chaos into a serene setting. Next to his across-the-street neighbor's driveway, I see a massively tall tree trunk that has had its huge limbs removed. Lynch points out the reddish, now-exposed diseased wound that had secretly weakened the largest, heaviest limb until (he makes an explosion gesture with both hands) it crashed down "like a ton of two by fours," splitting a car wide open.

Back on the other side of the partition wall, Lynch uses the large, living-room-like concrete space as a storage area for his paintings, several of which lean against the walls on both sides of the room. The approximately 5x7-foot canvases are lighter in hue than his pervious paintings, displaying a tan-umber colorfield background instead of the usual charcoal/black dominant color. His earlier works employed color in a hyperminimal way, with small dabs or smears of red, gold, or white standing out from the dark backgrounds. The newest paintings display larger and brighter color areas which, combined with the earthy backgrounds, give the works a warmer, more buoyant mood. Familiar from previous canvases are words and phrases (which, in this case, detail the doings of "another Bob," not the *Twin Peaks'* villain), an animal body part or two (the hooved foot of some small critter has been painted and worked into the surface of one painting), and an oozing, lumpy, thickly built-up surface texture composed of pigment mixed with glue. In some ways, this artist with a healthy bank account retains the mind-set of a struggling art student: He's thankful that he can get quantities of the sticky stuff "real cheap." One painting shows something Lynch has never portrayed on canvas before, a blue male and a red female figure engaged in a sexual coupling. Surprised by this subject matter, a little laugh pops out of my mouth, and I start to explain that I'm not laughing *at* the painting. Lynch chuckles and, with a small, wry smile, says, "I know what you're laughing at."

Having seen the outdoor work area where Lynch puts his visual ideas and feelings on canvas—and a cow—I now step into his sound laboratory, the studio in which his creations enter the audience's brain through the ears. This windowless, hushed space is truly impressive. Done in black and the warm, terra cotta, orange-wood tone Lynch favors, there are fourteen (seven doubled) tiered theater seats on the left, and, in the center, a state-of-the-art electronic-digital console at which the artist can record sound effects, record and mix music, and mix film and video. The righthand end wall of the room is composed of a luminous white movie screen, approximately 12 feet high by 24 feet wide, that floats at eye level. Beneath the screen, standing vertically in their holders, cream, gold, white and red-wine-colored electric guitars gleam beneath the soft sunken ceiling lighting. In a glass-fronted room to the right of the screen sits a gold-and-white drum set.

On the opposite wall, to the screen's left, hang the crimson folds of a curtain that could have come from *Twin Peaks*' Red Room.

At the high-tech console, wearing a Hawaiian shirt, sits the quietly amiable John Neff, master guitarist, singer, and sound engineer, who surveys a computer screen and myriad knobs and levers that control the most minute of adjustments. Lynch, the visual artist who probes the biological world and the human psyche like a scientist, sees this room as a locus of "experimentation," where he likes to play an electric guitar "upside down and backwards" and seeks sounds no one's ever heard before. And, working with Neff and, respectively, singer-violinist Jocelyn Montgomery and longtime collaborator Angelo Badalamenti, Lynch has crafted beautiful sounds we *have* heard. Montgomery's album of twelfth-century visionary abbess Hildegard von Bingen's songs and Badalamenti's music for *The Straight Story* were recorded and fine-tuned in this room.

Lynch, who is sitting smoking in the upper theater seats above me, wants to play something for me. "Rebekah?" he wonders, looking over to Neff, who nods. Directing the experience as he would a movie scene, Lynch slowly dims the ceiling lights and dramatically fades in floor-mounted, up-pointing lights that softly illuminate the hulking shapes of three gigantic black, tall-as-the-screen speakers hidden behind the screen's white skin. In a previous conversation, I'd asked Lynch which artistic medium most readily produced the "floating" experience he likes to provide for his audience. Without hesitation, he said, "Sound." I was ready to be swept away into a "Now it's dark" moment, but I was also apprehensive, having attended a *Lost Highway* screening where Lynch personally cranked up the volume so high that even the twenty-somethings around me were frantically stuffing Kleenex and anything that would fit into their ears.

Thankfully, the sound is full enough to fill my chest and head, but not so loud that it blasts away the magic. Rebekah's voice is strong and heart-rending as, against a background of reverberating 1950s slow-ballad electric guitars, she sings Lynch's poetically simple lyrics of her finding an intense love that's linked to the stars in the night sky. (Again, a field of stars illuminates Lynch's art.) Riding the love-borne exaltation of Rebekah's voice, I feel blessed to be in this particular spot of the universe, watching the music pulse on the sound console's computer screen and sitting with the man who first pulled it out of the air. A breeze of old California wafts into the song and makes it more romantic as Rebekah repeats the lyrics in Spanish. Then, as often happens in the world of Lynch's art, the mood quickly shifts and darkens, for Rebekah loses her love, and for her the stars are now dead. Over and over, sometimes in Spanish, sometimes almost in a speaking-whispering voice, she laments, "no stars, no stars, no stars," her sorrow flowing almost to the end of time, and drowning in a wash of slowing, finally stopping, guitar chords. Hearing this beautiful, long, slow song in the dark is an emotional, transportive experience, and as Lynch raises the lights it takes a moment for the three of us to recompose ourselves into sociable people. With a catch of aroused emotion in his voice, Lynch softly says, "I think the ending is a hair too long." I respond, "Well, I've only heard it once, but it seemed dreamy and wonderful at this length," to which Neff playfully says in Lynch's direction, "*See*," indicating that this is a point of debate between the collaborators.

Lynch's fascination with what goes on beneath the visible surface of things is evident as he explains how the room we're in is enclosed within an outer room we can't see, and that the floor beneath us "floats" atop a hidden space so that absolutely no sound from outside can penetrate. With a grin I ask him if there's "a strange room behind those red curtains?," referring to *Twin Peaks'* Red Room. A slight smile breaks through his deadpan reply, "No, there isn't." "Have any weird people come through those curtains?" "No, they have not."

There is the loving spirit of a dead person in the room, however. Alan Splet, Lynch's dear friend and sound wizard who helped him craft the otherworldly soundscapes of *The Grandmother* (1970), *Eraserhead* (1976), *The Elephant Man* (1980), *Dune* (1984), and *Blue Velvet* (1986), died of cancer in the mid-1990s. The director was given "one third of his ashes," and reverently buried them beneath his sound studio's console.

Lynch explains how the studio, which appears to have square corners, is actually asymmetrical, and is carefully designed so that sounds recorded here are sonically neutral and convey no intrusive sense of room presence to the listener. I ask him if he ever comes in here alone and sits in the rarified hush. He says he does, but that the total lack of sound "can be eerie."

From Lynch's hillside painting platform above the house, to his kitchen, living room/painting storage room, conference room, and sound studio, we've been working our way downward deeper and deeper into his house of art.

Now he opens the door to his inner sanctum, the gray concrete, cavelike office which, in terms of square footage, would occupy only a small corner of the spacious sound studio. In one of our previous talks, I had spoken of the psychological effects of prisoners being confined to small, enclosed spaces, of "living in an 8-foot-by-8-foot world," and Lynch completed the thought: "But your mind can soar." The air in his intimate office is scented with something slightly sweet—incense, he explains, which his friend and sometime collaborator, producer Deepak Nayar, brings from India. This all-permeating fragrance, which can be sensed but not seen, seems the perfect atmosphere for a man who contemplates spiritual evolution in his life and work, for symbolically incense represents the ascendant soul. And this artist who's obsessed with the head as a repository of good and evil, and a conduit to the cosmos, would certainly understand why the ancient Mayans called incense "the brain of the heavens." There's a magazine about Hindu spiritual practices called *Enlightenment* on a table and, opposite Lynch's black 1950s lounge chair, an aperture that's a source of pure light more than a view-providing window. So this is the ground zero where Lynch sits quietly and casts his mind down into the cold, savage reptile brain, and out into the warm, loving glow of the stars, the seat where he tries to mull over the problems and tribulations of his life with a detached serenity, and waits for the ideas that he thrives on, the thoughts that no one else has, to swim into his head.

During the day, white light illuminates Lynch's small room, and at night he can contemplate another primal force in his cosmology: fire, for there's a simple wall-niche, mantleless fireplace near his chair. Opposite the fire aperture, near the entrance door, is a window to Lynch's past and future; a huge Apple computer screen shaped like the wide, horizontal CinemaScope screen in his sound studio.

If Lynch sits in his chair, he has fire on his left, white light in front of him and, on his right, the fruits of his meditations. Arranged in rows on his computer screen, like the flies on his Ricky Boards, are a staggering number of visual icons, not filed away, but all ever-present: his artistic legacy displayed in schematic form. He can scan this visual field and decide which direction he wants to pursue at this particular moment, then his large right hand can access everything from a 1960s art school project to his new Flash-animated *Dumbland* cartoons, which he's laboring over in preparation for launching his website, www.davidlynch.com. The computer screen is a living map of where he's been and where's he's going, a visual summation of the creative process that is Lynch's way of manifesting the universe's energy. We've noted how Lynch believes that the progress of a soul through time, and lifetimes, is "a continuing story" which flows freely beyond borders and forces that would seem to contain and stop it. Lynch has expressed himself in every possible artistic medium (he has handbuilt Douglas fir tables in his office, and he has choreographed dancers, and actors in dancing motions). He has marked this world and touched on the next, in as many ways as he can. And, as technology continues to evolve a thousand times faster than human biology and culture, even the sky's not the limit.

With his access to his deep inner being and myriad ways of art-making, the cherished personal and professional bond with Mary Sweeney, the love and respect of their young Riley and his older children, and that of his ex-wives, and all the actors, technicians, and artists he works with, the appreciation of bright, imaginative people around the world, David Lynch has what he's always wanted: "a pretty good setup." He also understands that the world is not a static place. He's lived through enough ups and downs to know that flux and change animate his own continuing story. This man who believes in ongoing spiritual evolution through multiple lifetimes has spoken of how even the smallest subatomic particles within something as solid-seeming as a steel girder are in motion. During the afternoon I spent with him, Lynch often mentioned the process of change, growth, transformation: the way the art materials he used on his cow sculptures were still moving and "will never be dry in time" for his deadline; the way he pushed on the thick, pigment-glue of a completed painting and said, "See, you can still move this," and knew that his sound studio would always be "a work in progress" that will discard and embrace technologies as his needs and interests shape-shift. The little towheaded kid who loved to play in Montana puddles and "work the mud" now has an art factory on one of the more expensive hillsides on Earth, a safe and elegant place where his mind, heart, and head sense and shape the forces of creation and destruction into forms that have deep meaning for people all over the world. Lynch's Art Life shows us the full, vibrant spectrum of all our lives.

Maybe, soon, even in Seattle. From top to bottom, Lynch and I have penetrated to the deepest zones of Lynch's house-that-art-built, and now say some final words inside the closed front door. Knowing that none of his paintings, drawings, prints, or three-dimensional artworks have been shown in my hometown, I offer to help him accomplish that goal. Jolted with boyish enthusiasm, his face lights up: "Gee, thanks, man."

He's also thrilled to hear that the Los Angeles County Museum of Art just opened a major exhibit on L.A. design pioneers Charles and Ray Eames (his wife), who dreamed up some of the futuristic 1950s furniture Lynch loves and owns and, like Lynch, expressed themselves in film and many art forms. Perhaps Lynch sees himself, or himself and Mary Sweeney, as following in the Eames' Renaissance Person footsteps. Knowing that the Eames show is on for four more months, and that Lynch has recently spoken of still being somewhat agoraphobic, I urge him to attend the exhibit and stress that "the crowds will probably get smaller after the first months." One of the last things he says to me after a solid parting handshake is, "I don't like to go out of the house very much."

He stood in the open doorway, and I gave him a wave over my shoulder as I descended the steps Fred and Renee Madison had trod, and stepped into the street. The burnished late-afternoon sunshine illuminated his golden domain, his red-splattered white shirt, his smile. But there was a shadow I couldn't see somewhere inside his head, and he had both feet firmly planted inside the threshold.

Driving away from the *Lost Highway* house, I remember the moment in the film when, after being terrified by the anonymous videotape showing Renee and Fred sleeping, she calls the police and gives them directions to the house: "We're near the observatory," referring to the Griffith Park Planetarium. Lynch's house isn't actually that near the observatory, so maybe the reference was poetically emphasizing the act of looking and trying to see what's real, the subjective relativity of truth. Or maybe the director was (also?) making a personal homage to Man Ray, onetime Philadelphian and one of the surrealist artists Lynch admires. Ray's most famous painting, *Observatory Time—the Lovers*, shows a planetarium dome small in the frame, dwarfed by a huge pair of red lips that fill the sky above it: the cool rationality of scientific observation overwhelmed by the wild power of desire and passionate feeling, just as Fred Madison's mind is taken over by lust, jealousy, and murderous anger.

The Griffith Park Observatory is one of Los Angeles' iconic locations: its triple, white-and-black, art-deco domes perched on a high hilltop like a temple for sky-worshippers. At night, the structure provides a view of twin marvels: the starry, expanding universe of constellations and galaxies above, and the twinkling, golden grid pattern of lights in the Los Angeles basin below, which stretch farther than the eye can see. Like Lynch, I was raised at a time when the far, unknown reaches of space were the cinematic spawning ground of monsters, and then the romantic, thrilling setting for the first manned space flights and moon landing. Schooled on the wonder of the heavens, I always find visiting the observatory in Griffith Park to be a moving experience. As I drove up the twisting approach road around 9:30 the night before I made contact with Lynch, there was a special electricity in the air.

The town was abuzz with the possibility that the Los Angeles Lakers would win their first National Basketball Association championship in twelve years by defeating the scrappy, formidable Indiana Pacers on this night. Most of those who weren't jammed into the new, mammoth Staples Center downtown to see the game firsthand were watching it on TV: The traffic was noticeably lighter driving toward Griffith Park. But still, the observatory parking lot was overflowing, and just as I crested the park's hilltop, I heard on the radio that the Lakers had won.

There was no celebratory horn-honking audible within the precincts of the park, just the soft bustle of people eager to look skyward through the telescope and down onto the panorama of city lights. In the distant, dark air above the Staples Center, I saw twinkles and flashes of light—no doubt fireworks giving a festive salute to the Lakers' triumph.

The observatory was teeming with visitors on this summer-vacation night, and I was struck by how many high-school-age couples there were. Kids crowding around science exhibits, and patiently standing in a long line listening to the guide's patter, waiting for a chance to peer through the telescope for a few seconds at twin stars whose light had taken seventy-four light years to reach their teenage eyes. Who needed booze and drugs? The awesome majesty of the universe, and maybe a smooch overlooking the lights of L.A., were intoxicating enough. The observatory seems like a model of racial accord for a community that's been torn and torched by violent factionalism. Whites, Asians, African Americans, and Latinos were mixed in every possible combination as they chattered happily and enjoy the evening with tourists from Japan and the Middle East.

As I dropped down the hillside toward my hotel, I looked up at the observatory's white domes glowing against the black sky, and saw it as a locus of high civilization, full of people in harmony, who, if just for a moment, had shed their earthbound egos and let their senses, minds, and spirits float in star fields of wonder. Descending from these rarified heights, I heard horns honk as I left Griffith Park, and remembered that L.A. had occasion to celebrate athletic bodies as well as far-traveling minds. A driver shot past me, hanging half out his window, roaring like a grizzly bear and pointing a "We're Number One" index finger to the skies. The bumper-to-bumper traffic froze into dead-stopped gridlock on the Sunset Strip. Young men with bare chests lurched from black SUVs, spilling beer and roaring-dancing the Lakers' victory under the green traffic light of an intersection. A group of thirty to forty young white men who'd been whooping and drinking on the sidewalk jumped from the curb to help commandeer the street. I'm all for kids letting off steam, and I was happy for the city I consider to by my second home, but the feeling of wild animal energy in the air was disturbing and made me remember hellish images of the 1992 riots. I turned out of the traffic line onto a side street and took the long way back to my hotel.

In Lynch's world, where his art often reflects his view of life, we're reminded that surface appearances can be deceiving. When I turned on the late TV news I saw that those light flashes in the darkness above the Staples center weren't happy-time fireworks, they were the lights from police and news helicopters circling above a riot. Transfixed until I went to bed at 1:30 in the morning, I flipped from channel to channel as news crews followed groups of mostly white young men rampaging outside the site of the Lakers' triumph, moving in random motion like wild fire steered by shifting winds. A decapitated fire hydrant flooded a street and spewed the precious water (that makes this desert bloom) thirty feet skyward in a wasteful fountain. Looters broke into stores and stole other people's property. A group of men rocked a van back and forth until it tipped over; another bunch smashed up a TV station's van. The authorities, fearing for the safety of the team L.A. had defeated, barricaded the Pacers inside the Staples Center and wouldn't let them leave. An image that the TV stations kept repeating showed men tearing the young limbs from trees that had only been planted six months earlier, setting the limbs on fire, waving them like torches as they ran pell-mell through the streets, and finally setting a police truck on fire and yelling and hooting until it was a charred wreck.

So here was the shadow side of human nature, the animalistic slippage into raw, impulsive aggression, the exaltation of destruction that provided the opposing, balancing polarity to the communion of starlight, the joy of mental voyaging and sweet wonder that I'd been part of at the observatory.

So why would people who are winners, whose flashy L.A. tribe had just symbolically pounded those farm boys from the Midwest back into the dirt, want to trash and burn their own turf? When I saw Lynch, who's pondered trees and fires, angels and man-shaped monsters, I asked him about this eternal human paradox. Fourteen years earlier, in *Blue Velvet*, Lynch's alter ego, Jeffrey Beaumont, was tormented by the idea and fact that evil, and bad people, were part of his idyllic small town. Seeking to see and know, he journeys down secret passages of shadow and light, encountering malevolence and mercy, tender innocence and world-weary pain, and discovers his own capacity for being a dirty boy who hurts others—yet he ends up saving his community's collective soul. Mysterious questions, surprising answers: What else could Jeffrey conclude but that "It's a strange world"?

Lynch speaks of both coyotes hungry for blood and gentle families of deer visiting his house, and I ask him if it's still a strange world. His face both quizzical and amused, apprehensive and smiling, he answers without hesitation. "Absolutely." And, after a pause, "It's a beautiful thing."

11

ROAD TO DREAMSVILLE

2000–2001
(*Mulholland Drive*)

In his art and life, David Lynch likes to stay at home. Over a span of decades, the climaxes of many of his short films, features, and TV shows take place in bedrooms; only *Wild at Heart* and *The Straight Story* end with the main characters outdoors. For Lynch, his home is a locus of creativity, a place where he has the tools to shape art of myriad forms and materials, and where he can generate and catch vital new ideas, safe from a dangerous world that can steal his time and hurt him in unimaginable ways.

Even a life-sized fiberglass cow can find the world outside Lynch's sanctuary and art factory to be an inhospitable, threatening place. From what Lynch had said, I thought the purpose of his bloody bovine was to advertise Somalier paints while displaying his artistry, but its intended role turned out to be participating in New York's CowParade. This family-friendly public art exhibit (that is held in cities worldwide) amassed six hundred cows, some decorated by school children as well as artists, and placed them throughout five New York boroughs and parts of Connecticut and New Jersey. Lynch's violence-victim animal would have been right at home in *The Sopranos'* crime-spattered Jersey, but it didn't pass muster in the Big Apple of Mayor Rudy Giuliani (famous for being a cultural reactionary before becoming a 9/11 hero), who was on a holy mission to sanitize the city's traditionally sleazy enclaves and banish edgy, visceral art from public view. He had even promised that the CowParade would present "complete cows, not cut-up and stuff like that."[1]

Lynch's bovine which was indeed "cut-up"[2] and oozing "stuff,"[3] was set before the public with a politically correct herd of candy-colored, pastel-hued, sweetly whimsical creatures that would have been right at home, if miniaturized, in a child's toy box. Lynch's cow made kids scream and cry, though some little ones exhibited the same simultaneous revulsion and fascination for the artist's work that millions of adult movie watchers do. Such an awestruck response is certainly on Lynch's personal wavelength, for, at various times in his life, he has viewed everything from the city of Philadelphia to sex, parenthood, violence, and death with a passionate, complex mixture of repulsion and attraction.

New York Parks Commissioner Henry Stern's reaction to Lynch's cow was decidedly unambiguous. After being before the public eye for only two-and-a-half hours, the artist's animal was jerked from the cow lineup by Stern, who had said he thought the creature had been made by "Charles Manson,"[4] that "David Lynch should stick to his day job, making movies,"[5] and emphasized to CowParade officials, "If you can't stop Lynch's cow, you can't stop any cow."[6]

The creature, thus defined as the epitome of undesirability, had had two embellishments added since I'd seen it in Lynch's backyard. His final touch had been to stab a bristling array of chrome knives and forks into the animal's upper hindquarters above the tail, and emblazon the words "Eat My Fear" across the cow's side from its chopped-off neck to its hind leg. The words weren't applied in a wide, soft-edged line, as though finger- or brush-painted: they were sharp, as though carved into the bovine's hide. The simple, printed words combined upper- and lower-case letters randomly, as thought a child had written them, thus, by poetic association, stressing the sense of an innocent, defenseless creature having been mutilated and killed. By adding "Eat My Fear" to his bloodied cow, Lynch, the visual artist who's often been leery of the way words can diminish the power of a work, has codified a message of unjust victimization and made his first artistic political statement. "I'm not a vegetarian—I had a burger last night—but I know where meat comes from. One can imagine that the cow experiences tremendous fear in line at the slaughterhouse. Picture that enormous pumping cow heart with all that adrenaline—fear—soaking the meat."[7]

Once again, Lynch has probed beneath the surface of a seemingly benign all-American institution (beef-eating) and revealed raw, disturbing truths. "Eat My Fear" isn't exactly "Don't Eat Meat," but it's still the most overt political statement Lynch's art has spoken. And "Eat My Fear" sums up the social contract Lynch has with those who consume his art. But in this case, the public didn't get a chance to digest his aesthetic and conceptual ideas.

With a sad sense of familiarity, Lynch saw that the clear stream of creative energy that flowed from his mind, to his hand, to the viewer had again been muddied and diverted by restrictive meddlers. "Don't you think when people tell you you're allowed to do what you want, as long as it's not sexually X-rated, they should stand behind their word and show your cow?"[8] He felt that it's "the beginning of the end"[9] when censors "describe what's best for society. You should be free to hate my cow for yourself."[10]

In 2002, Lynch's best friend, Jack Fisk, told me that "David's life is centered on his creative drive; more than anyone I know, he selfishly protects his time so that he can keep working."[11] In Lynch's earliest days of art-making, this meant painting alone in a room for hours and hours. But over the years, his work in the moving-image arts of film and TV have necessitated his becoming more engaged in the world beyond his studio. His pure art life has transformed into the life of an artist-citizen. After saying that he voted for Ronald Reagan in the 1980s, Lynch entered a period in which he characterized himself as being apolitical, yet in 2000 he brought his cinematic skills to bear on that year's presidential election.

Out of *The Straight Story*'s Iowa heartland came Natural Law Party presidential candidate John Hagelin. A scientist (like Lynch's father), Hagelin is a renowned quantum physicist who believes that government should be run in harmony with the carefully studied laws of nature. Lynch, who feels that his art manifests the laws of nature (action and reaction, the balancing of "fast"[12] and "slow"[13] elements, the presentation of sharply contrasting polarities that are revealed to share an underlying unity), immediately saw Hagelin as a kindred spirit. Lynch was eager to support a candidate endorsed by the Natural Law Party, since the group was the political wing of the Maharishi's Transcendental Meditation movement.

Lynch filmed a twenty-seven-minute infomercial for Hagelin in which the strikingly intelligent, amiable, down-to-earth candidate stands before a gold curtain (not the usual Lynchian red) and speaks his views. He's for gun control, abortion rights, the separation of church and state, the rehabilitation of criminals, preventive medicine, organic agriculture, renewable energy sources, a low flat income tax, and against the mega corporations and monied special interest groups that have stolen democracy and sovereign free choice from average Americans.

Hagelin pictured an America that Lynch wanted to see, and his film helped the Natural Law Party pull in 1.4 million votes in the November election. The contest between George W. Bush and Al Gore was the closest in U.S. history, and siphoned more votes from Hagelin and other third-party candidates than was expected.

So Lynch's candidate lost, the CowParade condemned and excluded his bovine, and he was sad and furious over ABC's response to his *Mulholland Drive* pilot: "They saw it, hated, and killed it. And they never told me why they rejected it."[14] As he had done more than once before, he declared, "I'm through with TV."[15]

Still, he couldn't get *Mulholland Drive* out of his head: "It makes an injury if you don't finish something, and part of your mind is always going back to it."[16] Attempts were made to interest FOX (*The X-Files*), and HBO (*The Sopranos, Sex and the City*), two of the more imaginative and adventurous TV networks, in putting *Mulholland Drive* on their airwaves, but both passed on the project.

Over the months since ABC's rejection of *Mulholland Drive*, some of the pilot-episode crew and several of the actors had a sustaining intuition that the project was not dead. And once again, French Lynch-appreciators stepped in to further the cause of his art.

After participating in months of negotiations and reading reams of mostly incomprehensible legal language "like you wouldn't believe,"[17] Lynch learned that ABC TV had sold the rights to *Mulholland Drive* to France's Canal Plus company. This corporate giant, which has seemingly helped fund every French film made in recent years (as well as Lynch's *The Straight Story*), would give the director enough money to shoot ten days and nights worth of new film, which he could then combine with the pre-chop-job ABC pilot footage to create a feature picture. There was talk of having the feature film spawn a subsequent TV series, à la *M*A*S*H*, but Lynch told me it was "people around me,"[18] not him, who were interested in this possibility.

Lynch realized it would be a tall challenge to take a TV pilot which was intended to launch "all these threads going out into the infinite"[19] and round it off into a two-and-a-half-hour film with its own solid artistic integrity. But, he knew that he had steered a decades-long creative course through an abstraction of Philadelphia (*Eraserhead*), Victorian London (*The Elephant Man*), outer space (*Dune*), various small lumber towns (*Blue Velvet, Twin Peaks, Twin Peaks: Fire Walk With Me*), the Gothic South (*Wild at Heart*), New York City (*On the Air, Hotel Room*), twenty-first-century Los Angeles (*Lost Highway*), and the rural Midwest (*The Straight Story*). Under usual creative conditions, Lynch had as much time as he wanted to develop his ideas, an organic gestation period that sometimes took years. But, with the film green-lighted, he had to come up with a completed story *now*, and this would require some real mental gymnastics, a paradigm shift in his *Mulholland Drive* thinking process.

Lynch was gripped by the panic of performance anxiety. He needed new, intriguing ideas, but he didn't have any—or so he thought with his conscious mind. But one night, in his office inner sanctum, he sat in his favorite 1950s modern armchair meditating, and, without any mental strain, Lynch's previously open-ended *Mulholland Drive* concept linked up with a perfect conclusion. The stimulus of having to view *Mulholland Drive* from a different angle had enabled him to productively "play a trick on my mind,"[20] a process similar to the way Lynch's beloved Surrealists would suddenly rearrange the elements and change the direction of a project they'd been working on for a long time. Lynch trusted that his subconscious, imagination, and intuition would guide him in the right direction. So in the fall of 2000, Lynch's Hollywood Hills art factory hummed with the happy buzz of freshly shot film being viewed, and pictures and sounds being turned over again and again in the artist's mind and combined in ways no one had ever thought of. Then Richard Farnsworth, *The Straight Story*'s Alvin Straight, shot himself to death.

Lynch, Sweeney, Spacek, and everyone who worked with Farnsworth on *The Straight Story* production in 1999 knew that the seventy-nine-year-old actor, like the character he played, suffered severe pain from arthritic hips. In interviews, and when he received his Independent Spirit Award for Best Male Lead, the sweet, courtly, weathered old man would grin and say that, unlike Alvin Straight, he would soon be having hip replacement surgery. Farnsworth left his audience with the image of his post-operation self, the movie and real-life cowboy back in the saddle again and "riding my horse out on my New Mexico ranch."[21] Stoically, he hid the truth that he had terminal bone cancer, and that nothing medical science could do would ease his pain and restore him to the active life he'd always loved. In *Come a Horseman* (1978), Farnsworth played an aging ranch hand who, after suffering a nasty fall, resolutely concluded, "My ridin' and ropin' days are through." In what turned out to be Farnsworth's last days of real-life ranching, the adventurous scope of his existence was poignantly reduced to feeding his animals and watching TV all day. After working with Farnsworth on *The Straight Story*, actor Everett McGill, who played Big Ed in *Twin Peaks* and Stilgar the Fremen leader in *Dune*, said, "I can't think of anyone more prepared to go than Richard."[22]

Like Lynch himself, and many of the director's fictional characters, Farnsworth was an all-American champion of personal freedom, and on October 6, 2000, he committed the ultimate act of self-determination. Lynch knew that Farnsworth had lived a well-spent life. The actor had told him that the role of Alvin Straight was "the best work I've gotten to do."[23] Lynch had helped make the last chapter of Farnsworth's life a golden time, and he respected the old cowboy's right to make that big final choice, and understood that "he didn't want to be a burden"[24] to his middle-aged children, grandchildren, and fiancée. But nonetheless, Lynch was sad, and uneasy.

Lynch's first wife, Peggy Reavey, told me that, in the early 1970s when David first learned the Transcendental Meditation technique he still practices daily, he immersed himself in books on Hinduism and Eastern religious philosophy and spent hours pondering spiritual matters. He came to believe that sitting in meditation helps position one near the center of a cosmic stream that flows into the heart of universal being. Reading Paramahansa Yogananda's *Autobiography of a Yogi*, he learned that by enduring earthly "whips of pain, man is driven at last into the Infinite Presence,"[25] that living with suffering brings one closer to divinity. Lynch concluded that in opting out early by taking one's own life, the soul was condemned to many reincarnations until some harsh lessons were learned. As Peggy says, "David felt that suicide receives horrifying punishment in the next world."[26] Jennifer Lynch has been practicing Transcendental Meditation for as long as her father (all but six years of her whole life), and has often pondered the workings of karma.

> I think Dad worries about what's next for Richard Farnsworth. My father's had back problems, so he knows how severe pain can get, but still, to take your own life. Beyond the sadness of losing someone so precious, how do you figure that one out? How do you make that okay in your heart? Where do you send the prayers? Can you reverse the negativity of his taking his own life? Maybe Richard's karma was balanced out by the good life he led, and all the joy he brought to so many people. Pain can bring us to great personal transformations and realizations, but it can also become so dark that it becomes evil in a way because it can make someone like Richard choose not to be here anymore. It's not just an issue of him relieving himself and sending himself to maybe a worse place. What about everybody who's left here who loved him? His personal pain is transmitted to a bigger, wider form, it's spread out over a wider area. Instead of there being hope for him from all the people around him, there's devastation.[27]

Lynch coped with Farnsworth's death by immersing himself in his work. *Mulholland Drive* had no U.S. distributor, so the director felt he could take lots of time to fine-tune his film. The pilot version that he'd presented to ABC had a complete Angelo Badalamenti music score, which complemented his images with moody shadings of synthesizer and organ tones. But now, as with *Lost Highway* two years earlier, the director and his longtime musical collaborator wanted to give some of *Mulholland Drive*'s passages that special orchestral Eastern European edge that the Film Symphony of Prague could provide. So, as Christmas-season decorations glittered in L.A.'s sixty-five-degree sunshine, Lynch took off for the gloomy thirty-eight degrees of Kafka's city of birth.

When the director returned to his California compound with a satchel full of gorgeous new music tracks for his film, he didn't just concentrate on the *Mulholland* project. The term *multitasking* might have been invented to describe what Lynch has been doing for years: expressing the energy flow of his imagination in as many forms as he can think of, all the time. In the first months of 2001 he produced episodes of *Dumbland* (his Flash animation cartoon series set to air on the Shockwave website), worked on his do-it-yourself backyard live-action TV show, *Rabbits*, and made a surrealistic commercial for Sony's PlayStation 2.

Unlike the majority of Lynch's work, his PlayStation 2 game console commercial presents a benign view of a human-animal melding. For sixty seconds we proceed through a labyrinth of Lynchian themes and motifs visualized in black and white, thus signifying the bifurcation of the world into two polarities. A man in a black suit and white shirt encounters eerie passageways, sudden flames, barren trees, factory smoke, a woman who won't speak her secrets, a wounded figure wrapped in bandages. The man meets his own double, and a man with a duck's head. A sourceless voice asks, "Where are we?" The dualistic duck-man, who synthesizes animal instinct and human learning, knows: "Welcome to the third place."

Once again, Lynch has given artful form to a primal dynamic of his worldview, which sees that "we live in a world of opposites. It's that way here for a reason, but we have a hard time grasping what that reason is. In struggling to understand the reason, we learn about balance, and there's a mysterious door right at that balance point. We can go through that door any time we get it together."[28] As William Blake shows in his illustration for *The Marriage of Heaven and Hell*, life, the "Infant Joy,"[29] springs into being in the calm space between any two contrasting, opposing elements, states, or forces. Lynch seeks to "get it together"[30] through art-making and by practicing meditation. His commercial implies that by performing another technique that integrates mind and body, playing games with your PlayStation 2, you can have a transportive experience, achieving a fulfilling self-unification, a blissful oneness of consciousness.

Lynch's own consciousness was a bit frazzled as the spring of 2001 approached. Every feature film he'd made since 1990's Cannes Film Festival

Palme D'Or–winning *Wild at Heart* had been accepted for screening at the renowned French event that lights up the Riviera nights every May. The Festival, which had been running annually for only one year less than the fifty-five-year-old director, had his highest respect "because they love film so much, they worship the cinema."[31] Beyond being a great honor, screening *Mulholland Drive* at Cannes would be a good business move, since the film needed a U.S. distributor, and *The Straight Story* had picked one up even before it was shown there in 1999. French and American magazines were already assuming that the noirish, hence more characteristically Lynchian than *The Straight Story, Mulholland Drive* would be welcomed by the Cannes programmers. The trouble was, those who choose the films hadn't seen it yet, nor had the cast and crew that made it.

Mulholland Drive is the first Lynch feature film to employ some computer-generated imagery, and working with that technology, and other last-minute details, kept the director toiling in numerous Hollywood film labs until all hours. (Maybe working up to the last minute is a good omen and a subconscious strategy, for he was in the same harried mode with *Wild at Heart* before it won top prize). Eleventh-hour news came that Lynch had made the deadline: the Cannes programmers had seen the final, two-and-a-half-hour cut of *Mulholland Drive* and would include it (out of 854 features submitted) with twenty-two others in Festival competition.

I spoke to Lynch before he headed off to Cannes, saying, "You must be relieved to have completed the film in time to have it accepted for competition." He just had his morning coffee, but he seemed more pragmatic and sober than hopped up with optimism: "We've got a long way still to go."[32] Leaving home, coping with tidal-wave-scale crowds, meeting the press, and trying to sell a film that no U.S. distributor wanted to buy were not some of the director's favorite things.

His mood brightened a bit when I told him I'd just seen a film (*Good Men, Good Women*) by Taiwanese director Hou Hsiao-Hsien (who would be one of his competitors at Cannes) that reminded me of Lynch's fictional world. A young woman sleeping on a couch is awakened by the bell on her fax machine. As she crosses the room to read the fax that's just arrived, we see a large poster for *Blue Velvet* leaning against the wall. (This detail moved Lynch to exclaim, "I'll be darned.")[33] The fax turns out to be a page from her diary, which has been stolen by someone unknown. Over the course of the film more pages arrive, which describe her and her lover's sex games and his eventual gangland murder. She never learns who's sending her the faxes. Sometimes her phone rings, and no one's on the other end of the line, though she proceeds to speak confessionally into the receiver.

I said I thought the woman was sending the pages to herself, that the film was her interior journey, her subconscious processing of her intense feelings of love and loss. I said, "maybe the whole thing's a dream, because when we first see her. . . ." Lynch finished my thought with "she's asleep on the couch,"[34] but he didn't say another word as to whether this was the key to his own head, the strategy by which he manipulates time and space, memory and fantasy, worldly and interior experience. He excitedly asked if this film would be shown at Cannes, but I told him it was one of Hsiao-Hsien's earlier (1995) works.

I knew Lynch had a lot to do before he would have the thrilling and harrowing experience of showing his new baby to 2,500 people in the Grand Palais. I told him to "break a leg in Cannes." In *Twin Peaks*, the character that Lynch plays, FBI boss Gordon Cole, counsels, "Let a smile be your umbrella." And in *Mulholland Drive*, the young director character says, "I believe that a man's attitude goes a long way towards determining how his life will be." Lynch signed off with, "Hold a good thought, bud."[35]

That I did, and so must a lot of other people. On a balmy night in May, Jodie Foster, wearing a robin's-egg blue Armani gown, stepped to the microphone and addressed, in perfect French, the 4,000 international film lovers gathered in Cannes' Lumière Auditorium. Foster had originally been tapped to head the film-judging jury, but had to drop out because of a tight shooting schedule, and she'd flown in especially for this moment. She told the crowd some unusual news: two filmmakers had been chosen Best Director. The first, Joel Coen for *The Man Who Wasn't Here*, wasn't there, and his producer accepted the award. The second was David Lynch, who, dressed in a traditional tuxedo with a black bow tie, smiled at the applauding audience and said, "Hello,"[36] followed by a little chuckle. Jury president Liv Ullmann and her jurors sat to Lynch's left on stage. Lynch, always an appreciator of womankind, looked at Ullmann with a warm smile and said, "To the beautiful Liv Ullmann and the rest of her jury, thank you very much for this honor at the world's greatest film festival. Thank you."[37] Roger Ebert (famous for leading a chorus of boos when the director won the 1990 Palme d'Or for *Wild at Heart*), who did like *The Straight Story* and *Mulholland Drive*, remarked, "David Lynch makes the weirdest movies, but when he speaks he sounds like a very polite Rotary Club member."[38] (The Rotarians are an international organization devoted to community service and the advance of world peace.)

Back in Los Angeles, Lynch began organizing a cast-and-crew screening of *Mulholland Drive*, and I was flattered when he invited me to fly down from Seattle to attend. In recent months, illegal, black-market video copies of the 88-minute *Mulholland Drive* TV pilot had been circulating, a fact that infuriated Lynch, who hated the idea that some people would now know which parts of the feature film were composed of old and newly shot footage. For the purpose of writing this book, I very much wanted to see how Lynch solved the creative problem of melding the year-and-a-half-old pilot with the new scenes, to understand exactly what he meant when he said, regarding the process of extending the story from pilot to feature, that "the beginning led to the middle and the end."[39] I had obtained a bootleg copy of the pilot from a guy in Hollywood who was so paranoid about being caught with it that he kept the unmarked cassette hidden inside a box for the horror film *Leprechaun* (*Twin Peaks*' receptionist Lucy [Kimmy Robertson] was in *Leprechaun 2*).

Despite the poor quality of the tape (people's heads looked like blobs of glowing phosphorous), the pilot episode was absolutely engrossing, and I could tell that the feature film version would be a work of considerable complexity. I talked to Lynch a few days before flying to L.A. and asked if it would be possible to see *Mulholland Drive* a second time in addition to the cast-and-crew screening. He said that a second viewing opportunity probably wouldn't be possible given the short duration of my stay.

Feeling foolhardy, I said, "You're probably going to kill me, but I've seen a tape of the pilot, so I have some idea of what part of the film will be like, and. . . ." Lynch's voice, cranked up to Gordon Cole volume, cut me off: "*No*, you don't know what it's like *at all*—this is going to *putrify* your experience of the film."[40] While I savored his flavorful use of the word "putrify" I realized that I was going to have to think of the right thing to say, in a heartbeat (I flashed to Lynch's first wife, Peggy, telling me, "David can drop people just like snapping his fingers."[41]) Thinking "Transcendental Meditation, Asian spirituality, serene consciousness," I said, "I'm going to come to *Mulholland Drive* with a pure mind." We both took a few breaths, and he said, "Well good, that's good. But you know, I wish I could burn every one of those goddamn tapes and slap around whoever made them."[42] As we signed off, his positivity and enthusiasm returned full-force, and I learned that I had a new nickname: "Okay, hotshot, I'll see you front row and center."[43]

Thirty-six hours later I located the Directors' Guild of America building, perfect for a Lynchian evening, as it was situated on Sunset Boulevard. Once inside the copper-colored contemporary structure of reflective glass, I made my way to the large auditorium and saw that "front row and center" was already packed with people. The room had three sections of seats separated by wide aisles, and I grabbed an open spot on the right aisle halfway to the screen. Stylistically the audience ran the gamut from denim and sneakers to tailored Italian suits. I couldn't see Lynch anywhere, but as I got out my notebook and pen, I glanced left and realized that Ann Miller, who plays apartment manager Coco, was sitting across the aisle from me. This perky eighty-two-year-old, who in the span of her sixty-four-year career has worked with Milton Berle, Jimmy Stewart, Jean Arthur, Katharine Hepburn, Lucille Ball, Ginger Rogers, Frank Sinatra, Judy Garland, Fred Astaire, and Louis Armstrong, among others, looked lovely with her gleaming black hair, ivory skin, and bright green silk dress. Due to L.A.'s often horrendous traffic, events often start late, but it was definitely time to get the show on the road. I looked over at Ann Miller again and saw Lynch striding down the aisle making a beeline for her. Dressed in an impeccable black suit, his white shirt top-buttoned, he squatted down to position his head at Ann's level, and I heard his knee joints pop. He spoke a few soft, hurried words to her, then hustled down to the front third of the center seats, where he climbed over people to the middle of the row, where he plopped into the seat Mary Sweeney had been saving for him. Most everyone in the room probably knew that Lynch is no fan of public speaking, but after sitting for a moment, he stood up, crawled across those sitting to his left, and walked down the left aisle to the stage.

Lynch climbed the stairs to the left side of the stage, and stood facing us without a smile on his face, thus forming a tableau that could have come from one of his films: a sullen figure behind a chrome microphone stand, a red curtain behind him, just like Isabella Rossellini in *Blue Velvet* and Julee Cruise in *Twin Peaks* and *Twin Peaks: Fire Walk With Me*. Pulling out a cassette audio recorder like the one Agent Cooper often spoke into in *Twin Peaks*, and holding it next to his deadpan face before the microphone stand, Lynch, tall and imposing in his back-and-white clothes, silvery hair rising high from his head, assumed the attitude of a performance artist. He switched on the recorder, and we heard an orchestra play a fanfare, then he turned off the machine. A beat of silence, then he said, "Good evening." Then the machine on (fanfare), off, "Welcome to the cast and crew screening of," machine fanfare on, off, "*Mulholland Drive*," more recorded fanfare on, off, "Thank you all for being here." As Lynch quickly left the stage and took his seat next to Mary the crowd laughed and applauded their clever master of ceremonies as though they'd just witnessed a comedy club routine. Lynch's impassive, unsmiling face had made his presentation funny, but beyond evoking laughter, his performance had planted a metaphor for his movie in our brains.

For thirty years, a current of intermingled reality and illusion has flowed through Lynch's films. As if to remind us of the way he feels the world to be, he's shown us something (if we closed our eyes) that we'd perceive to be real and present in the room (musicians blowing a fanfare), but which is actually a sonic illusion. ("Is it real or is it Memorex?," as the ads for audio tape used to say.) And he's shown us something real: himself speaking into the microphone. Or does he want us to question whether he's real too, and on how many planes of being at once?

With *Mulholland Drive*'s two-image prologue, Lynch returns to the first principles of his worldview and shows us that we're in for an evening of surprise and mystery, aesthetic pleasure and brain-twisting challenge.

The initial image shows the director, for the first time in a feature film, using computer-generated imagery to create one of his visual-conceptual abstractions. To the bouncy beat of 1950s swing music, we see smiling young couples dancing all over the screen. Lynch isn't showing us a typical real-life shot of people moving around on a floor in a room somewhere. He uses the dancers as stylized visual elements against a superimposed lavender-lilac-colored background (some couples are close-up, some faraway; some bob at the bottom of the frame, some float near the top), as though a two-dimensional collage of springtime blossoming and ebullience has come to life. Lynch adds another layer of reality as a white blob of light glides into the plane of the dancers and becomes the beaming face of a blonde woman who's as happy as she can be. (The wafting motion of her introduction makes her kin to the many women who float in Lynch's frames.) The swing music abruptly stops cold as the director cuts to a dimly lit bedroom, in which the curtains are unnaturally, depressingly, closed in the middle of the day. The faded mauve-red sheets and agitation-rumpled pillow we see mirror the color of Dorothy Vallens' apartment in *Blue Velvet*, which was a chamber of human interiority, roiling with desires and fears deep inside the ruddy heart and brain. We hear the breathing of someone in the grip of a powerful dream, breaths that sound like the whimpering sighs of the saddest person in the world. Lynch uses intuition to form his thoughts and feelings into narratives, and our own intuition helps us find meaning in his tales. It won't be announced until later in the film that its main character (Naomi Watts) once won a jitterbug dancing contest, and then saw her hopes and dreams die a tormented death, but somehow we know that the pained viewpoint we're inhabiting, as her eyes (our camera lens) burrow into the shadowed pillow, is that of the formerly smiling blonde, and that Lynch is once again about to delineate the eternal interplay between light and darkness.

Lynch's introductory images (the memory of dancing and winning; the real-time despair of the dancer fallen low), conjoined in a position of prominence before the opening credits, alert us to the form the director's storytelling will take. For the next two-and-a-half hours, Lynch, who's obsessed with what goes on inside people's heads, will obliterate the boundaries between reality, waking fantasy, dream, and memory in a narrative that seems to be happening to a number of people, but which is actually the interior psychodrama of the Naomi Watts character's consciousness, the projection of her subjectivity. Lynch feels that mystery is good for his, and our souls, so he doesn't give us a linear roadmap to his evocative cinematic terrain. Jolts of confusion and wonder keep our reasoning abilities, imaginations, and intuitions alert; no matter if what we're witnessing is real or the mind's eye vision of an anguished woman, Lynch's streaming images ripple with powerful emotional truths that give meaning to our experience.

Aside from encapsulating the triumph-to-tragedy trajectory of his main character's life, Lynch's brilliant two-shot prologue shows him living by his personal artistic credo. Since his earliest painting days as a youngster, he's believed that "contrast is super important,"[44] and there couldn't be greater difference in mood and motion between the gregarious, jitterbugging winner and the depressed woman hiding from the world beneath her pillow (as usual in Lynch's domain, a person living in dreams is positioned horizontally, even when awake). And the two shots (respectively) exemplify the Lynchian qualities of being "fast"[45] or "slow,"[46] which the nineteen-year-old artist spoke of to Peggy Lentz, his young wife-to-be, at art school in Philadelphia. Comparable to *Eraserhead* and *Lost Highway* as a nonlinear narrative, *Mulholland Drive* is like a painting composition that Lynch is balancing as he goes along, making it "correct" by following his urges to add a busy, blaring section up here, a serene, quiet passage down there; a splash of red passion now, and later, blue, in the night.

The credit sequence that follows the prologue is permeated with the nocturnal romanticism of one of Lynch's "Now it's dark" moments. As in the TV pilot version, a limousine, like a glistening shadow, floats through the night with a dreamy slowness, with its passenger an ebony-tressed woman in black (Laura Elena Harring), silently gazing outward and inward: In an instant, she seems full of secrets, like *Twin Peaks'* Laura Palmer and other Lynchian women who live their lives on the far other side of day. The shimmering light-grid of Hollywood gliding below is magical (we who are watching the film at the Director's Guild on Sunset Boulevard are, at this moment, sitting in the field of lights that's portrayed on the screen), but the woman's reverie is invaded by terror as the driver stops the car and points a gun at her. As in the TV pilot, she's saved by an accident, when a speeding car full of screaming-banshee teenagers smashes head-on into the limousine. The sureness of Lynch's touch as a filmmaker is beautiful to behold. He stages the crash like a nightmarish abstraction, as the screaming white glare of imminent-impact headlights progressively brightens the limousine woman's horrified face, and the seconds following the smash-up are strangely quiet, as pale smoke swirls, obscuring the scene, and a soft puff of flame blossoms from twisted black steel.

Marked with an emblematic Lynchian head wound, and clutching her purse, the woman staggers down toward the entrancing, almost otherworldly, pattern of twinkling lights below. (Stephen Spielberg got the inspiration for his light-grid-encrusted mother ship in *Close Encounters of the Third Kind* from gazing down at the lights from Mulholland Drive while standing on his head.) Lynch doesn't just use the lights as a stunning visual, he emotes over them. More than just a film he has made, *Mulholland Drive* is imbued with his love for Los Angeles, his home for thirty years, and for the resonant ambience of Old Hollywood, the glimmers and echoes of landscape, architecture, and community that evoke the romantic tradition of making movies, crafting dreams, in an earthly paradise.

Lynch first experienced Hollywood, the place and the state of mind, when he saw Billy Wilder's *Sunset Boulevard* (1950) as a young man. As *Mulholland Drive* draws to a close, the director will reveal that his film is a major homage to the daring narrative strategy of Wilder's picture, but even early in Lynch's movie we see reverent references to the classic film noir. The typography style of the *Mulholland Drive* title road sign (a stylization, not an actual street marker) has the same square-cut letter curves as Wilder's opening logo. And as the accident-surviving woman makes her way down from Mulholland's wilderness to Hollywood's residential blocks, Lynch prominently features signs for Franklin Avenue (a cross-street of William Holden's *Sunset Boulevard* apartment), and Sunset itself. Perhaps due to budgetary constraints regarding the acquisition of music from one movie to be used in another, Lynch's picture does not contain the momentary sampling of *Sunset Boulevard*'s urgent orchestral score that accompanies the Sunset Boulevard sign in *Mulholland Drive*'s TV pilot version. At this point Lynch's film does retain a visual reminder of Wilder's movie, as a siren-wailing police car roars up Sunset (racing to the car crash scene on Mulholland?), just like one did to investigate a dead man floating in Nora Desmond's swimming pool in 1950.

The plot of *Sunset Boulevard* gets rolling when the tire of William Holden's car blows out while he's speeding down Sunset, trying to lose two men in a car who want to trap him. This happenstance brings him to a seminal dwelling place and puts him face-to-face with Miss Desmond (Gloria Swanson), thus establishing the key emotional pairing of Wilder's film. Driving down a parallel track, the *Mulholland Drive* woman's accident allows her to escape her two male assailants, find her way to a classic Spanish Colonial courtyard apartment that will be a locus of intense feelings, and introduce her to her primal partner in Lynch's tale.

We first see Betty when she arrives at LAX airport, enchanted by the "Welcome to Los Angeles" sign and every sweet whiff of flower bloom and dream-realizing potential that the City of Angels has to offer, just as Lynch did when he hit town in 1970. ("When I came out here I arrived at night. And when I got up the next morning and I went outside. I had never experienced light that bright, and it thrilled me. It was like happiness coming into me. It was beautiful."[47]) Betty's beaming face and blonde hair radiate even more golden light than the sunshine glowing in the clear blue sky. She's from the midwest of Canada, and her name and sunny manner recall the wholesome Betty of Lynch's *On the Air* TV series, as well as the good-neighborly world of *The Straight Story*'s American Midwest, and the serene, benevolent communities Lynch has shown us in *Blue Velvet* and *Twin Peaks*, which must suffer the intrusion of dark forces. Betty is from the town of Deep River, thus evoking the sad figure of Isabella Rossellini's *Blue Velvet* character, Dorothy Vallens (who writhed in spiritual torment at the Deep River Apartments), and giving us a subtle foretaste of the story arc Lynch has planned for Betty.

Lynch has his little miss sunshine arrive at the airport with an angelic, grandmotherly travel companion (Jeanne Bates), who blesses Betty's first moments in Los Angeles with her goodwill, warmly saying she'll look for the aspiring young actress up on the big silver screen. After saying goodbye to the elderly woman and her equally sweet husband, who's come to pick her up, Betty gets into (naturally) a bright yellow taxi that would be right at home in a buoyant 1950s Technicolor musical. Her heart set on a happy future, Betty gives the driver a Havenhurst address and heads off. Havenhurst is a real Los Angeles street: throughout his L.A. story (as he did not do in the Southland-located *Lost Highway*), Lynch will saturate *Mulholland Drive* with cherished local color.

To this day Lynch remains bitter about the way ABC spurned *Mulholland Drive* "without telling me why, or who made the decision."[48] Still, even in the months immediately following his work's crushing rejection, and realizing that if he moved to Europe he'd have a much easier time launching projects and receiving kudos from audiences and critics, Lynch said he loves, and would stay, in Los Angeles. What made him passionate about the industry town that could often see little, or nothing, of value in his best efforts? "The light . . . and the feeling in the air . . . the feeling of optimism."[49] Betty's Los Angeles saga, this journey within her consciousness, will manifest both Lynch's ebullient affection for his hometown and his fear that malevolent, unnamed local forces are making big decisions about the course his life will take against his will. As in Lynch's real-life domain and his fictional worlds, *Mulholland Drive*'s Los Angeles will be a composition in darkness and light.

Just as Lynch and Mark Frost made the most psychologically disturbing character (*Twin Peaks*' Laura Palmer's town-paragon father, Leland) an agent of evil energy who is her sexual violator and murderer, so the director casts Betty's sweet, grandmotherly airport traveling companion (and her grandfatherly mate [Dan Birnbaum], who meets her at LAX) as hosts of shadowy impulses. For after Betty heads for town in her sunshine-colored taxi, the dear couple drives off in a midnight-hued limousine just like the one the dark-haired woman crashed in on Mulholland, and the oldsters chuckle and grin as though they have diabolical plans for Betty. (The elderly woman emanates an extra, subliminal aura of menace for those who have seen *Eraserhead*, for she's played by the woman who portrayed the Henry-threatening Mrs. X.) The elderly pair's sudden shift from kindliness to some undefined, yet palpably devilish, intent moved the person sitting behind me to say, "That's Lynch for you." When I related this to Lynch the next day, he laughed and laughed.

This shot not only abruptly darkens the emotional tone of the grandparently couple, it looks different (more washed-out-blue and grainy) than the warm, saturated palette of Betty's L.A. adventure. It's as though this shot is intruding from some alternate-universe narrative stream, as when, in *Twin Peaks: Fire Walk With Me*, the angry, storming pattern of blue TV static spews monstrous urges into a beneficent community.

Lynch doesn't just link *Betty* to agents of wicked intent. At Winkie's fast food restaurant on Sunset (in a sequence Lynch cut out of his TV pilot while trying to please ABC), a nervous young man named Dan (Patrick Fischler) tells his friend, Herb (Michael Cooke), "I had a dream about this place." Herb, crystallizing the response of numerous viewers of Lynch's dream-drenched art, replies, "Oh boy," as if to say, "Here we go again." *Mulholland Drive*, like many of the director's fictions, will be an echo chamber of doublings, so, naturally, this is the second time Dan has had his dream, and it's a nightmare. He has envisioned a creepy, bedraggled man living behind the back wall of Winkie's. More than being just a community eyesore, the Bum is an embodiment of metaphysical darkness, like *Twin Peak*'s BOB and *Lost Highway*'s Mystery Man: the one who's "causing all the fear," like "the beast"[50] that can't be killed in the Eagles' song "Hotel California." In *Dune*, Paul Atreides says, "Fear is the mind-killer." Just as the young Lynch confronted his subterranean urban terror by going through with a New York subway ride, Dan wants to exorcise his "god-awful feeling" by taking a look out behind the restaurant. After his subway fright, Lynch lived on to experience other trepidations and anxieties. But when Dan rounds the back wall of Winkie's and stares into the black-fungus-covered face and long scraggly hair of his dream man, he drops dead. (Lynch has added a subliminal sense of added strangeness and dislocation to this shocking visage, for the mystery man is played by a female.) A man who's actually a woman; an enticing, entrancing city whose true essence may be toxic and haunted. In *Twin Peaks*, the Log Lady sagely counsels that "the owls are not what they seem," and in *Mulholland Drive* Lynch will show us the pervasiveness of illusion and the dangers of being misled by appearances. When Dan walks along the Winkie's building on the way to encountering his worst fear, we notice a sign taped to the structure that shows the word "entrance" accompanied by a hand-drawn arrow pointing away from the word. The way to get inside and get what you want may seem to be here, but it's actually somewhere else. The temporal, phenomenological world before our eyes may seem to hold the answers we seek, but the real truths are located in a dimension beyond.

We the audience have seen Lynch hover dark forces near Betty (the sweet grandparently couple reveals a sinister aspect as they drive off), and across town we've watched a man drop dead at the sight of a weird blackened face, but so far our blonde Hollywood hopeful hasn't experienced malevolence directly. We suspect it's only a matter of time.

Betty's Aunt Ruth (Maya Bond), one of *Mulholland Drive*'s female angel figures, is an actress who's gone to Canada to work on a film. Ruth has lovingly paved the way for Betty's dream factory debut by arranging an audition with seasoned, influential industry professionals and by letting her niece stay in her gorgeous courtyard apartment. Lynch's favorite passage in *Sunset Boulevard* occurs when William Holden's character makes his first, entranced approach to the courtyard of Norma Desmond's Spanish-Mediterranean mansion, and Lynch conjures Betty's first, floating-camera, entrance to the apartment's Spanish-Mediterranean courtyard an evocative "penetration into an inner space of secrets and desires."[51] Betty is welcomed to her posh new digs by apartment manager Coco, who is a compendium of the Old Hollywood history and atmosphere that Lynch reveres. She's a jovial, zesty gatekeeper who introduces Betty to the place that will be the young woman's seminal location. For Lynch, Norma Desmond's moulderingly opulent, decadent *Sunset Boulevard* mansion is "an avenue into another world"[52] for William Holden's character. For small-town Midwesterner Betty, her aunt's homey, yet luxurious apartment is a wonderland, an embodiment of the Hollywood she aspires to. Betty sees herself as an artist whose medium of expression is acting. She's not here to reap material wealth, but the apartment's sun-tanned golden walls, vintage movie posters, oil paintings, books, fireplace, flowers, and big chestnut-brown leather couch cast a spell on her. After the dark-haired woman had her accident, Lynch showed her walking in a trance-like state as she approached the lights of Hollywood. Now, after the cheery Coco leaves, Betty is lost in reverie as she passes through rounded Spanish archways and almost floats down some of those Lynchian hallways that always lead to transformative realms. (*Mulholland Drive* has more traveling-through-spaces shots and subjective, camera's-eye-view passages than any other Lynch film, thus reinforcing the sense of a journeying consciousness experiencing places, people, and events.)

Lynch is a master at conjuring sublime moods that turn ominous, and as Betty ecstatically gazes at herself in the circular bathroom mirror, no doubt imagining getting made up for a stellar acting role, she hears something move in the room. (Building suspense rather than settling for prosaic surprise, Lynch has previously shown *us* the dazed, traumatized dark-haired accident victim sneaking into the apartment and falling asleep, and we've wondered if, and when, Betty is going to come upon her—or maybe the woman has left.) In a shot that shows the cinema's power to convey multiple levels of meaning in a split second, we see two Bettys: the back of her head, and her face reflected in the mirror, and both heads suddenly turn with alarm when she hears the stir of a presence in the room. Lynch composes this image so that, at the precise moment Betty is gripped by fear, the horizontal line of tiles that decorates the room (which look like sharp white shark teeth, or inverted white fence pickets, against a black background) visually intersects with her neck. The bright Hollywood future she can see in her mirror is invaded by a vector of predatory menace: She could lose her head in this town. And not only does Lynch hint at his film's overall narrative design by doubling Betty's identity in the mirror, he presents the visually coded idea of her head cut loose from her body and floating freely, observing and containing the entire universe of *Mulholland Drive*.

When Betty first sees the dark-haired woman, the accident victim is standing naked inside a translucent shower stall: her body softly diffused by the misty glass, she's like an image on a screen, an emotion-laden fantasy figure projected by Betty's mind. At this point in the film, we don't consciously know that everything we're seeing is taking place inside the blonde woman's head, but ninety minutes from now we'll realize that Lynch has carefully and subtly prefigured the revelation of this truth throughout his narrative.

After her shower, the woman tells Betty, "My name is Rita." She may be wrapped in a towel instead of plastic, but like *Twin Peaks'* Laura Palmer, she is a Lynchian woman of mystery, whose presently evident personhood is only half the story. Why did those men in the car want to kill her? Why, unbeknownst to Betty, is she using the name she saw on the Rita Hayworth poster in the bathroom? The true nature of her life has yet to be revealed—even to herself. The accident has stricken her with one of Lynch's deepest fears: the erasure of selfhood, in this case due to car-crash-induced amnesia. Her unique personality and memories are gone, and the deep terror of her loss burns in her dark, frantic eyes.

Betty, with her kind-hearted Midwestern enthusiasm, begins to help her new, lost, friend solve herself. Lynch makes the game intriguing as Rita, having no idea why they're in her purse, pulls thick bundle after thick bundle of hundred-dollar bills out of her black bag. This extended activity, another example of Lynch making a mundane task take an absurdly long time, pulls a laugh from the audience. (An earlier moment of Lynchian humor sparked when a young man, who was helping Betty's aunt load her luggage into a waiting taxi, himself tipped over into the trunk as he shoved in a supernaturally heavy suitcase). The director intuitively knows how to make the simplest, most everyday occurrences wondrous and strange.

Curious also is the blue key that Rita finds in her purse. Not just a flat piece of stamped-out steel, the key, which has a hefty three-dimensionality, looks like it's made of some precious metal that's been sculpted into a design. The key form itself, and the crescent moon and triangle inscribed on it, comprise a gestalt of mythic and symbolic significance. In ancient lore these shapes relate to ultimate mystery, the gates of the afterlife, the female pubic triangle, the spectrum of being from appearance to disappearance, the journey from death to reincarnation, and the stage of endeavor prior to finding something dearly sought after.

As *Mulholland Drive* plays out, we'll learn that the blue key unlocks a particular blue box. A key fitting into a lock is an overt sexual metaphor, but in old stories, the box is the hiding place of the feminine subconscious, especially in its unexpected, excessive, and destructive phases. It's an open question as to whether Lynch pored over moldering old texts of the world's myths and fables before designing his blue key, but it's certain that the time-honored denotation and connotations of the key, box, triangle, and moon crescent are germane to his *Mulholland Drive* tale.

A pile of one-hundred-dollar bills and a blue key: what a mystery. With the Betty character, who plunges into amateur detective work with youthful zeal and wants to psychologically rescue the traumatized Rita, Lynch is revisiting a primal dynamic of *Blue Velvet*. In that 1986 film, young Jeffery becomes an impassioned, tenacious sleuth who's trying to save another of Lynch's emotionally and physically battered black-haired women. Of course, in *Blue Velvet* the helpful detective's investigations uncovered a disturbing hunger for darkness within his own heart; time will show us if Betty's trail of clues will lead her into her own inner zone of shadows.

For now, Rita's the one in the dark, and Betty wants to help illuminate and dispel the fears that torment her from that unknown time before her accident. The blue key chills Rita's heart—but why? When Betty says, "I wonder where you were going that night," two words float to the surface of Rita's confused mind. Lynch heightens the dramatic resonance of Rita's utterance by studying her rapt face for a few moments before she speaks: "Mulholland Drive." Lynch loves Roman Polanski's masterful 1974 L.A. film noir *Chinatown*, and feels that it's ending, which, in a kind of verbal code, sums up a world of pain and tragic loss with the words "Forget it Jake, it's Chinatown," "is just perfect."[53] Just as the word "Chinatown" has a metaphorical depth and richness, so "Mulholland Drive" conjures a night-world that shimmers with an alluring, undefined promise that can become lethally dangerous in a heartbeat. As Lynch says, "there are lots of hairpin curves—you can be dead in a split second."[54]

The director speaks of Mulholland Drive as a poetic inspiration: "It's all by itself on the crest of mountains, and it overlooks many dark things at night. It gives you a feeling; it's a dream road."[55] It is a Lynchian place that unites contrasts: a bridge between enchanting Hollywood and the prosaic San Fernando Valley; a matrix of "danger and romance,"[56] of gentle deer and ravenous coyotes, and of lovers' trysts and the shallow graves of crime victims. The highway evokes the memory of William Mulholland, the man who heroically brought in water to make Los Angeles bloom and later suffered a tarnished reputation as an associate of greedy empire builders who committed ecological rape and jerked the entire San Fernando Valley out from under unsuspecting farm families. *Chinatown* fictionalizes the power-hungry historical figures whose schemes and manipulations made it possible for them to own L.A.'s future; men who are "capable of anything" to get what they want. Lynch's fictions document his personal fear of those predatory forces and people who violate and steal the soul-territory of others, and this theme will soon shape *Mulholland Drive*'s narrative.

When Rita intones "Mulholland Drive," Betty's detective's mind gets a bright idea. They'll go to a pay phone, call the police, and ask if there was an accident last night on the legendary road. Excited by the pursuit of knowledge, Betty makes a statement that codifies Lynch's worldview, for it reflects an overt reality and presently hidden, yet-to-be-revealed, deeper meaning. For when Betty speaks to Rita about calling the police and says, "It'll be just like in the movies; we'll pretend to be someone else," she is precisely summing up the film we're watching. It will be some time before Lynch directly shows us who The Pretender is, but he gives us a subtle hint about a certain person's mysteries of identity when the police sergeant on the other end of the line asks for Betty's name: she answers with silence and abruptly hangs up. This moment lays groundwork for the eventual arc of Betty's story, but the director craftily camouflages it within the plot pattern of Rita's mystery, for she, after all, is the one who doesn't know her real name.

After the phone call, the two women have coffee (what else?) at the Winkie's diner where we earlier saw the man recount, and die from, his fearsome dream. Betty is still in her full-on sleuthing mode: The police may have confirmed that there was a smash-up on Mulholland last night, but she scans the *L.A. Times* in vain for any mention of the accident. With her protectiveness toward Rita and her will to guide this lost soul to psychological wholeness, Betty is a radiant blonde angel to the benighted crash victim. Even her Midwestern politeness is helpful, for when she notices and reads the waitress's (Melissa Crider) nametag and says, "Thank you . . . Diane," a spark of recognition brightens Rita's solemn face.

In Lynch's world, the name Diane has warm, consoling connotations. For in *Twin Peaks* Diane was the never-seen, witnessing FBI angel to whom Agent Cooper sent countless tape recordings of his musings on everything from forensic reports, crime suspect motivations, the mysteries of life and death, and the minute details of what he had for lunch. Even though she couldn't be seen, Cooper's Diane was a companionable presence in his psyche, a validation of his ongoing life story. Aside from using this significant *Twin Peaks* name in *Mulholland Drive*, Lynch (and his loving editor, Mary Sweeney) includes the new Diane in a narrative/editing trope that recalls an exasperating moment in *Twin Peaks*. When Cooper first dreamed of the otherworldly Red Room, and had the experience of Laura Palmer whispering the name of her killer in his ear (we couldn't hear her), he immediately woke up and called Sheriff Truman. Telling Truman he knew the murderer's identity, he concluded, "I'll tell you in the morning," and hung up. Fade to end of episode. At the beginning of next week's show Cooper maddeningly couldn't remember the information that millions of viewers were anxious to hear. In *Mulholland Drive*, after Betty says the waitress's name, Rita gets a thrilled look and says, "I remember something." Then, naturally, Lynch fades to black. In the TV pilot, commercials were to be inserted at this point, but even in the film version the director holds the secret suspended in the air until the women get back to the apartment and Rita speaks a name that has a significance for her that she can't fathom: "Diane Selwyn."

Rita thinks this may be her own name, and detective Betty, after looking up Selwyn's telephone number, picks up the phone and dials. The calling device is a cell phone, which *Lost Highway*'s eerie Mystery Man used to striking effect. Standing beside Fred Madison at a party, the Mystery Man had Fred dial his own home, and then laughed menacingly when the Mystery Man (who was also, somehow, at Fred's place) picked up the phone there and laughed back at himself and Fred standing at the party. As Betty phones Diane Selwyn's apartment Lynch again plays with the ideas of there being multiple selves and the possibility of occupying two separate places at the same time, for Betty says, "Strange to be calling yourself." Betty means that Rita may be Diane, and hence would be calling herself, but Betty's the one who's actually dialing when she says this. Once again, beneath the surface of his "Who is Rita?" story, Lynch is gently starting to guide our awareness toward the thematic question, "Who is Betty?"

No one answers at Diane Selwyn's place, but Betty finds the address of Selwyn's Sierra Bonita Apartments on the map and proposes to the reluctant Rita that tomorrow they go investigate the place in person. Mystery-pursuing Betty and wary, resistant Rita recall the character dynamic exhibited by *Blue Velvet*'s sleuthing Jeffrey and cautious Sandy, though Sandy was motivated by concern for Jeffrey's safety, whereas Rita fears that dangerous, undefined forces will be roused to attack her as a result of Betty's quest for knowledge.

Lynch believes we live in a "learning world,"[57] and is fascinated by the duality of opposites and the balancing point between them. Two of the most ancient polar pairings that thinkers and storytellers have pondered is the relationship between knowing and not knowing. The human mind has the biological capacity and the psychological need to process more and more data, but it can never learn everything—and sometimes knowledge can be dangerous. In Greek mythology, the demigod Prometheus stole fire from Zeus, the father of the gods, and gave it to mankind, symbolizing the acquisition of deep wisdom and scientific and artistic learning. But in retaliation Zeus sent Pandora into the world. Lusting for knowledge, she opened her forbidden box, thus loosing toil, trouble, grief, and evil upon us all. And when Adam and Eve defied God and tasted the Tree of Knowledge's fruit, they were forced to leave Paradise. Desire versus constraint, liberation versus imposed limits: The whirl of opposing energies spins forever.

St. Augustine called the appetite for knowing "the lust of the eyes,"[58] since vision helps us accomplish so much of our learning. Lynch has spent his life expressing his unfettered thoughts and feelings in visual forms, and the freedom of his naked eye is the cardinal sacred principle of his personal Bill of Rights. He has watched (as a boy) a naked woman walk down a residential street, seen the bloody form of his newborn daughter emerge from the body of his wife, and examined the insides of cut-up animals. And the passionate desire to see is a driving force of his fictions. Dr. Treves, and hordes of his fellow Londoners, want to gaze at the fabled Elephant Man. *Blue Velvet*'s Jeffrey wants to hide in a woman's closet at night and watch her (a teenage fantasy of Lynch's) and disturbingly sees more than he bargained for. The idea that *Wild at Heart*'s Sailor may have seen someone burn someone else alive makes him a man marked for premature death. In *Eraserhead*, Henry Spencer wants to look beneath his deformed baby's bandages, and experiences horrific, yet rewarding consequences. *Lost Highway*'s Fred Madison watches videotapes from the dark side of his own psyche, which show him having severed the body of his loved and hated wife. In *Twin Peaks*, "The Magician longs to see." Both heroic Agent Cooper and his nemesis, Windom Earle, want to look behind the curtains of the extra-dimensional Red Room. Earle, striving to usurp the power of forces he doesn't understand, loses his soul, while Cooper suffers a splitting of self which releases a sinister aspect of his persona into an unsuspecting world. *Twin Peaks*' Laura Palmer, who endured trials of pain and sorrow and committed countless sins, wants to see her delivering angel, and she does. And *The Straight Story*'s Alvin goes on an arduous quest motivated by his wish to reconcile with his estranged brother and "sit with him again and look up at the stars," a gazing activity that Lynch and his brother, John, enjoyed as boys.

Crossing the boundaries of politically correct good taste and Boy Scout mannerliness, Lynch enables us to look at extremes of transgressive behavior and warped thinking that are nonetheless recognizably human, and thus mirror some of our own half-hidden desires and fears. Shimmering on the edge of taboo, simultaneously both alluring and repulsive, many of Lynch's images of sex, physical and mental torture, and death are aggressive and harshly vivid, while others are subtle, lyrical, poetic. Lynch shows us what he knows of the world in spatters of blood and brains, as well as drifts of steam and the unspoken whisperings of love. Seeing reality straight on helps us learn about the way things are, but truths also abide in oblique views and sensed presences. Lynch knows that sometimes, as French Symbolist poet Paul Valery (1871–1945) said, "To see a thing clearly is to forget its name."[59] German philosopher Friedrich Nietzsche (1844–1900) crystallized a key aspect of Lynch's sensibility when he declared that "every living thing needs a surrounding atmosphere, a shrouding vapor of mystery."[60]

A mystery in a shroud comes calling on Betty and Rita the night they contemplate the map to Diane Selwyn's place: The women are startled by a heavy knocking on the door just as Rita's finger, tracing the route to Diane Selwyn's on the map, passes the Hollywood Memorial Cemetery. In the cut-down pilot version of *Mulholland Drive* we see a subjective, camera's-eye point-of-view shot come swooping up to Betty's doorstep like an approaching denizen of the night. Then we cut to the women inside with their map. In the film version, Lynch restores the passage as he originally intended it, following the approach shot with the arrival of an eerie female figure. (In *Twin Peaks: Fire Walk With Me*, the director used this same floating-approach point of view followed by the arrival of a strange woman, who mutely trembled at a trailer doorstep as the FBI investigated the death of a young woman.)

Betty answers the door and sees a seventyish woman, her head cloaked in a dark blue shawl, staring into her face. Once again, we encounter an archetypal Lynchian image: a person standing on a threshold. A boundary line, a passageway, between this zone or world and another, the realms of inside and outside and multiple realities, and the ability to pass from one to another. Whether serving as transitional gateways to a new level of life for a character, the stage setting for rites of passage, or functioning like the director's often-seen theatrical curtains that focus dramatic emphasis, Lynch's thresholds span three decades of his work.

A threshold is where *The Grandmother*'s Boy first contemplates the room that will spawn his loving grandparent; Dr. Treves gains access to the "No Entry" world of the Elephant Man; *Blue Velvet*'s Jeffrey meets (on separate occasions) Dorothy and Frank, his netherworld surrogate parents; *Dune*'s Lady Jessica opens a gate and lets in the vengeful Reverend Mother Mohiam, who will haunt the life path of her beloved family; *Wild at Heart*'s Sailor is told by Perdita that no one is trying to kill him, when the opposite is true; *Twin Peaks*' Agent Cooper enters the metaphysically and emotionally labyrinthine Red Room; *Twin Peaks: Fire Walk With Me*'s Laura Palmer passes into the dream that is also her life; and *Lost Highway*'s Renee, in her familiar bedroom, stands on the abyss edge of her husband's shadowed psyche and her own benighted future. As his characters move through hallways, thresholds, doorways, or rock-formation portals (*Dune*), Lynch emphasizes a sense of journeying and transition: In *Dune*, with its motifs of outer- and inner-space voyaging, the director puts his cast members in the hallway/doorway/threshold position an amazing average of every three minutes in his 137-minute film.

The fables of Asian cultures often contain threshold spirits who serve a protective and warning function, and the shrouded old woman on Betty's doorstep is one of these. (As was the Log Lady in *Twin Peaks: Fire Walk With Me*, who stood on a doorstep with Laura Palmer and metaphorically cautioned her against the falling-in-flames trajectory she was pursuing.) The old woman confronting Betty is the former actress Louise Bonner (Lee Grant), who's confused because she expected to have Betty's Aunt Ruth open the door to Ruth's apartment. Instead, she sees a young blonde woman (and in the living room, a black-haired one) who she doesn't recognize. She's understandably mixed up, but she exhibits a preternatural degree of emotional agitation that makes her words chilling: "Something bad's happening. Someone is in trouble." Almost tranced in her confusion, Louise seems to possess some special insight, and Rita shudders, knowing that she's the one who must fear this omen. Still, Betty is the one who's speaking with Louise, and Lynch slips in a fleeting, disquieting moment that will ultimately resonate at the core of his narrative. For when the young blonde says, "My name is Betty," the old woman replies, "No, it isn't."

Earlier, when Betty was trying to convince Rita that they should call the police from a pay phone to inquire about the accident on Mulholland Drive, she'd said with the fervor of a born actress, "We can pretend to be someone else." When the call was placed, it was Betty who did the pretending, but now, on the morning of her studio audition, Lynch lays groundwork for the ultimate destination of his narrative by showing that Rita is also adept at taking another's identity.

Standing in Aunt Ruth's kitchen in their bathrobes, Betty and Rita speak passionate words of love and anger to each other, which we soon realize are the lines of Betty's scene, with Rita standing in for the part of Betty's character's older male lover. Like a classic sultry femme fatale, Betty's character says to Rita's male, "This will be the end of everything . . . get out before I kill you." Then Betty says her character "cries and cries and cries, and then I say with big emotion, 'I hate you . . . I hate us both.'" Amused by the overheated speeches, the women's thespian composure dissolves into laughter.

In the *Mulholland Drive* TV pilot, this kitchen line-reading scene plays like a pleasant, light-hearted diversion from the mainline mysteries of the plot, and it has the same tone in the movie version. But, faced with the creative problem of making an open-ended TV show that might have run for years into a two-and-a-half-hour film, Lynch devised a story strategy in which the *literal* reality of the women's kitchen line readings eventually plays a primal part.

Betty's studio audition finds Lynch evoking the Old Hollywood (and *Sunset Boulevard*) he loves, and providing wry social commentary on some of the movie industry absurdities he's intimately familiar with. He begins his sequence with a shot of the Paramount gate, the one William Holden walked toward in Billy Wilder's film (and another portal for Betty to pass through on her journey). We see the huge, graceful ivory stucco archway, the delicate black tracery of the wrought-iron gate, and beyond it is parked an elegant open-topped automobile that's older than faded former star Norma Desmond. This car, which recalls the one Norma drove to the studio buoyed by hopes of returning to the screen, is Lynch's homage to both *Sunset Boulevard* and the FBI-boss Gordon Cole character he played in *Twin Peaks*. In Wilder's film Gordon Cole was a character we never saw, but who played a pivotal role in Norma Desmond's tragedy. For Cole was the studio assistant whose phone calls to Desmond made her think Cecil B. DeMille himself wanted to launch her movie comeback, while Cole was only interested in renting Norma's old car for use as an atmospheric prop. Cole was trying to do a good job for his employer, but he precipitated a major confusion about what was real and what wasn't. No wonder Lynch took Cole's name when he wanted to pretend he was someone else.

Betty's angel of an aunt has arranged for her to audition for Ruth's old friend, producer Wally Brown. Lynch paints the occupants of Brown's wood-paneled office as an amalgamation of old and new Hollywood culture. White-haired, venerable old-school gentleman Wally wears an argyle-patterned sweater that might have come from the 1940s; fifty-something director Bob Brooker's short-sleeved sport shirt is tieless; casting director Linny and her oh-so-coolly-unsmiling assistant, Nicki, have hipsters' de rigueur black outfits. Sixtyish silver fox Woody Katz, the actor who will play the scene with Betty, is resplendent in a dark three-piece suit and tie.

Betty's nervous as she joins Woody for her big moment; she didn't realize she'd be performing in front of seven (Lynch's favorite number again) people in such a relatively small space. Lynch pokes fun at the sort of pretentious, arty psychobabble some directors spout as Bob gives Betty and Woody some peculiar last-minute advice: "It's not a contest, see, the two of them with themselves, so don't play it for real until it gets real." After an unspoken reaction of "Huh?" passes around the room in the wake of Bob's pronouncement, it's showtime for Betty.

Woody says he wants to play the scene close, like he did with an unnamed "black-haired" actress, subtly advancing Lynch's approach to a surprising future plot point. Betty is flustered as Woody pulls her to him so their pelvises and breaths touch. This forced familiarity isn't what Betty was expecting, but it's a recognizable posture to viewers who've seen a number of Lynch's films and TV shows. One of the director's signature ways of raising emotional intensity to the boiling point is to have a predatory character pull their unwilling victim into a tight clinch. Heads almost touching, feeling the heat of each other's exhalations, one character invades the other's sovereign physical space and claims the sacrosanct territory of their mind and volition. The scene Betty and Woody enact charts the quick-shifting emotional currents between a young woman and her older, clandestine lover, who happens to be her father's best friend (the scene takes places at her unsuspecting parents' house—and Mom and Dad are only a flight of stairs away from their daughter's tête-a-tête). This fictional scene positioned within the base reality of *Mulholland Drive* is typically Lynchian in centering on a secret: the May-December couple's love affair. And the emotions Betty herself (not the character she's playing in the scene) feels while in Woody's grip recalls *Wild at Heart*'s Lula's harrowing embrace with the villainous Bobby Peru. While her boyfriend was absent, Bobby had grabbed Lula, held her close, and with the imminence of violence and rape hanging in the humid air, ordered her to "Say 'fuck me'" over and over again. Bobby was the scummy, repulsive antithesis of a man Lula would even want to talk to, let alone get lusty with. But still, against her will, as his foul hands roamed over her body, she became sexually aroused, much to her self-disgust.

Bobby was like an atavistic personification of the ravenous male id, with his leering gutter talk and caveman behavior, rotten-swamp breath, and black leather jacket. Woody, on the other hand, is impeccably tailored, groomed, and urbane, and looks to be at the opposite end of the masculine species from Bobby. Yet Lynch's script specifies that he have "a big lecherous smile,"[61] and when he pulls the resistant Betty up next to his body he lasciviously says, "Dad's best friend goes to work." No wonder Lynch changed the marauding character's name from the earlier-script-draft Jimmy to the final film's Woody (a slang term for a male erection). Woody wields much power at this moment. He's an established actor with a steady job, whereas Betty is a novice hoping for a break, so why not feast on her nubile presence for the short time they have together? *Isn't that one of the perks of being a big movie star? This blonde—what's her name?—Betty, sure as hell isn't going to blow her chance by stopping the scene if I slide my hand down toward her hip*. This rude bit of business certainly wasn't on the script page Betty memorized, but she surprises herself by guiding Woody's exploring hand to touch her below the waist. By reinforcing and participating in Woody's lustful move, Betty isn't just being a resourceful actress by spontaneously adapting to the changing flow of the scene. Like *Wild at Heart*'s Lula, she is entrapped in a man's embrace that she did not invite, yet she finds an aroused passion rising within her. Betty's sultry body heat contributes beautifully to the scene, as Woody responds (once again, Lynch's "action and reaction")[62] and the two cling together. Like a classic film noir femme fatale, Betty, pretending to hold a knife in her right hand, pulls him into a deep kiss with that hand. Then, with the blade behind Woody's head, she threatens to kill him. This image of a woman with a knife in her right hand recalls the moment in *Blue Velvet* (1986) when Dorothy Vallens enacted another knife-wielding tableau of female power by poising a blade above Jeffrey Beaumont while she sat on his chest. (The blade, with its ability to penetrate the body, is a primal phallic symbol, which Lynch lets both his male [*Twin Peaks*' Leland Palmer, *Lost Highway*'s Fred Madison] and female characters [Dorothy Vallens, Betty] control).

Even though Betty is holding the knife, she doesn't feel empowered by her actorly dance with Woody. As she did when she was practicing with Rita, she ends the scene with the words "I hate you . . . I hate us both," but this time she cries real tears. In Lynch's world, profane, base animal urges can be dangerous, possessing forces, and need to be carefully controlled: We don't want to become savage devourers like *Blue Velvet*'s Frank Booth or *Twin Peaks*' BOB. Both Betty and *Wild at Heart*'s Lula suffer the humiliation of having their bodies respond to invasive men without having their hearts go along for the ride. As Lynch says in his *Mulholland Drive* script, Betty cries "because she's ashamed of how the sex of the scene took her over."[63]

Everyone in the audition room may have silently chuckled when Bob the director spoke of playing the "scene for real when it gets real," but that's exactly what Betty has done. Lynch shows his abiding fascination for shifting states of mind by having Betty pause for a moment as she disengages from the trance of her performance and regains her self-consciousness and awareness of the people in Wally's office watching her. Almost shyly she says, "Well, there it is." Indeed, and as the room full of seasoned moviemakers regains their composure they reward Betty's first professional Hollywood effort with beaming faces and awestruck applause.

Everyone watching Betty's audition is impressed and thrilled with her performance, but director Bob qualifies his response in his own unique way: "It was forced, but still . . . humanistic." (The Director's Guild Theater audience I'm watching *Mulholland Drive* with are film industry folk, and they laugh uproariously at Bob's comment, no doubt being overly familiar with authority figures who make "profound," wrong-headed, snap judgments.) Betty thanks everyone profusely like a good Midwestern girl should and leaves the room with Linny the casting director. Linny, with her eyes on the freshly minted prize that is Betty, wants to vault over Wally's senior-citizen, ever-diminishing industry status and link the actress up with Hollywood's hot young movers and shakers. Rising director Adam Kesher (Justin Theroux) is the man Betty *has* to meet.

Relatively speaking, Lynch is closer to Wally's age than Adam's, but Lynch expresses his identification with the young director in almost autobiographical terms. As with Lynch, Adam's hair is short on the sides and stands up on top, he wears the same black, heavy-rimmed, 1950s-style glasses Lynch sometimes sports, owns an expensive German car, and lives with his love in a mid-century-modern home on a Hollywood hilltop. Aside from these surface correspondences, Adam is presented as being in the position Lynch detests the most: People are messing around with his business.

When Lynch first viewed *Sunset Boulevard*, he saw William Holden's screenwriter character's story idea get twisted and mutilated by an overbearing producer. Then, when Lynch wrote and directed the gargantuan, multimillion-dollar *Dune* project in 1984, he found himself living out Holden's scenario. He had envisioned *Dune* as a "poetic, symphonic epic,"[64] but to him it emerged lifeless and inert, with none of his beloved abstractions and no "room to dream."[65] Producer Dino De Laurentiis and his daughter, Rafaela, wanted the Lynch who had made the relatively straightforward, literal-minded *The Elephant Man*, not the man who had let his uncensored subconscious flow into the enigmatic, fantasy-drenched *Eraserhead*. Prevented from wholeheartedly pursuing his artistic intuitions, Lynch died the death of a thousand compromises, and the *Dune* experience became a nightmare that the traumatized director will still barely talk about to this day. Folklore maintains that if only he could go back and add in all the extra *Dune* footage he had to cut out to achieve the studio's idea of what a reasonable theatrical running time should be, the film would be revealed as a masterpiece. But Lynch had to truncate and modify so many of his ideas all along the way that he has sadly told me, "I'm just not sure there's a better film there to be found."[66] He blames himself for not fighting harder to get his vision onto the screen, and he says he doesn't hate the De Laurentiis clan. But clearly, their actions created the most anguishing experience of Lynch's professional life. The director may not have consciously chosen to reference the Italian De Laurentiises in *Mulholland Drive*, but the two family members who willfully change the shape of Adam Kesher's film project are also Italian: the Castiglianes.

Wanting to stage Adam's first meeting with the Castiglianes as a familiar social occasion that becomes an entrapping ordeal, Lynch takes inspiration from 1976's *Eraserhead*, in which the unspoken tension between Henry and the X family expressionistically erupted in the commonplace act of serving a chicken dinner, as the cooked bird flopped around on the plate and oozed disgusting fluids.

When Adam meets the Castiglianes, Lynch substitutes a business-world conference table for the X's dinner table, as in *Eraserhead*'s dinner scene, long, emotionally fraught conversational pauses hang heavy in the air as Adam and the Castiglianes stare at each other. And when Luigi Castigliani (Angelo Badalamenti) tastes his espresso, he forces it out of his mouth into a white napkin in repulsive surges of black, gummy liquid, which recall the icky fluids flowing from the X family's chicken.

In Lynch's world, satisfying the primal urges to eat and drink (especially coffee) are affirmations of the Life Force, so it takes a truly chaotic Bad Vibration in the air to shatter a chicken dinner or a sip of espresso. Lynch hates having to meet with the men in expensive suits who have the power to recast the shape of his art projects, and the Castiglianes visit Lynch's fear and resentment upon poor Adam. They insist that the lead actress in Adam's film be one Camilla Rhodes, rather than someone Adam thought he had been free to choose. And in conclusion they speak the blackest words of all: "It is no longer your film."

Adam is furious as he leaves the meeting, as Lynch must have been on similar occasions. But since Adam is Lynch's fictional surrogate, he can act out the rage and frustration Lynch has had to keep clenched and hidden beneath his Eagle Scout good manners. So before Adam zooms off in his silver Porsche, he takes his seven-iron golf club (Lynch's lucky number) and smashes the windshield and headlights of the Castiglianes' limousine and beats dents in its perfect black surface.

As Adam's day progresses, he learns just how fast his world can fall apart. His film project is shut down, and when he seeks the solace of home, as Lynch's characters often do, he finds that it's a Lynchian "place where things can go bad."[67] Adam's wife (Lori Heuring) is in bed with the pool-cleaning man (country singer Billy Ray Cyrus), and the brawny hunk pounds Adam into the ground.

Adam beats a hasty retreat in his Porsche and holes up in a cheap hotel, where his sense of the world slipping out of his control only increases. Cookie (Geno Silva), the hotel manager, comes to Adam's doorstep (another Lynchian threshold scene with major significance for a character) and tells him that two men from Adam's bank came by and said that his account is overdrawn and his credit account has been canceled. Lynch has said that the disturbing thing about celebrity is realizing that many people whom he doesn't know know everything about *him*. In the *Mulholland Drive* script Adam's scene goes no further, but in the film, Cookie ominously adds, "The people you're hiding from . . . they know where you are."

One of Lynch's gifts as an artist is his ability to conjure a shiver of menace in the wind, the sense of our bodies and minds being vulnerable to forces lurking just beyond our direct perception; to shape a dark poetry that builds small rhymes of disquiet into full-blown dread. Scenes and moments in *Mulholland Drive* begin to form a sinister gestalt, like wicked sparks igniting here and there along an unseen power grid of Bad Electricity (Lynch's term for the evil dynamo that bedevils the characters of his unproduced script *Ronnie Rocket*). Betty's grandparently couple with their nasty cackling, the man who dropped dead from his scary dream at Winkie's, the old woman full of foreboding who came to Betty's door, and Adam's twelve hours of incredibly unlucky happenings seem like strands of a vast night web that blankets the City of Angels.

Earlier evidence has shown us that flesh-and-blood people are spying on Adam and manipulating his world: the powerful, wheelchair-bound Mr. Roque, played by *Twin Peaks*' little dancing man, Michael J. Anderson, encased within a big-person's suit, had listened in by microphone on Adam's confrontational meeting with the Castigliane brothers. Then Roque ordered, using the fewest words possible (as, throughout history, most powerful people have always done), that Adam's production shall be shut down. Roque is a *human being* in a mysteriously unspecified position of vast authority, but because he's portrayed by the actor who was *Twin Peaks*' extra-dimensional Man From Another Place, and since Roque's office is eerily unusual (a huge, black-shadow space defined by smaller scallop shapes of white light), he emanates an otherworldly aura. Another being who can exude a preternatural air of formidable, concealed knowledge is David Lynch. It's no accident that the few, sometimes enigmatic, words that his fictional authority figures use to express themselves echo his own minimalist style of directing actors and meeting the press, and presenting himself to the world. In the fifteenth century, another artist, Leonardo Da Vinci, spoke of the sad and sorry fate awaiting "him who opens his mouth too much and thereby puts himself at the mercy of the listener."[68]

If fear and menace are never far away in Lynch's fictions, neither is his reflexive focus on the doubleness of things. Perhaps in homage to the two men in a car who pursued William Holden in *Sunset Boulevard*, there are two limousine men who threaten Rita before her crash, two men in a car who strike terror in her later in the film, two Castigliane brothers who plague Adam, and "two men from the bank" who come to what Adam had thought was his secret-hideout hotel. As Adam talks on the phone to his assistant, Cynthia (Katherine Towne), from his dark pit of misery, Lynch once again touches on his pet, paradoxical theme of two opposing realities existing at once. Speaking about the news that his bank accounts have been emptied, Adam says, "But I'm not broke," and Cynthia replies, "I know, but you're broke."

One of Lynch's angel figures, the independent-minded Cynthia is a voice of reason and emotional solace for the troubled Adam, and tries to guide him toward a path that will ease his suffering. When Adam speaks to her from his hotel room there's an image of the Virgin of Guadalupe (another manifestation of Lynch's L.A.-centric *Mulholland Drive* vision) on the wall by his head, which, combined with Cynthia's soothing voice, evokes the sense of a benevolent femaleness watching over him. (Can anyone still believe that Lynch doesn't absolutely adore women?) Cynthia represents the possibility of romantic love for Adam, but his life being complicated enough, he declines her offer to stay at her place. (Could dark-haired Cynthia be a fictional version of the dark-haired, sweet, and helpful Holly, Lynch's assistant who offered him coffee and counsel at the time he wrote *Mulholland Drive*?)

Cynthia feels Adam should talk to someone named the Cowboy. Rare for a character Lynch has written, Adam has an ironic, sarcastic streak, but he reins in any possible wiseacre quips and follows Cynthia's advice.

Lynch's mood-setting powers are operating at full force as Adam drives at night up to the top of a dark canyon road, passing the unmarked boundary between manicured residential blocks and wild country studded with unkempt brush and blowing dust. Like Lynch-surrogate characters in a number of the director's films, Adam stands with his back to us, contemplating a field of space that's fraught with potentiality. (In *The Grandmother* and *Blue Velvet*, the space was a grass field; *The Elephant Man*, a wall of sideshow whirligigs; *Dune* the surging sea at night). We, along with Adam, regard the flat, dusty ground of a circular corral, waiting to hear the essence of this space talk to us, to see what Lynch the artist/filmmaker chooses to paint/project on this canvas/screen.

For Lynch, electricity is one of the mysterious, primal forces of the universe, and almost every one of his moving-image works acknowledges its presence. In *Twin Peaks: Fire Walk With Me*, buzzing-twittering power lines and blue TV static injected an otherworldly evil into human hearts and minds. Earlier in *Mulholland Drive*, a string of telephone calls (which

Lynch realized in a crisp, short montage that cannily indicated the socio-economic status of each caller/call recipient just by showing the various phone instruments) linked, like a humming, malevolent night web, those who are manipulating Adam's film production with the nameless ones who want Rita dead. Lynch loves to stress the power of electricity by flashing it on and off in a strobing effect, which simultaneously emphasizes his own power, since his hand is always on the effect-controlling light switch. As Adam stands in the dark corral, a single bulb hanging from a wooden-pole archway flutters and crackles into a solid flood of illumination.

With the light comes the Cowboy, who strolls into the corral's circle wearing a plaid-saddle-blanket-fabric coat, white Stetson hat, and a red bandana around his neck. This singular figure (played by Lynch's friend, Monty Montgomery, who co-produced *Wild at Heart* and is married to ethereal-voiced singer Jocelyn Montgomery, whose record *Lux Vivens* Lynch produced) evokes Lynch's love of Old California and recalls his appreciation of Ronald Reagan as "a cowboy and a brush-clearer,"[69] actor Richard Farnsworth (*The Straight Story*) as an authentic Man of the West, and Lynch's own beloved, Stetson-wearing grandfather. Lynch says he devised the Cowboy scene, which was filmed on ground where ranches once stood and cattle grazed, "purely on instinct. I like to imagine the old cowboys living somewhere high up in the canyons of Hollywood, singing songs around a campfire with their horses near."[70]

With a mild manner and voice, the Cowboy says, "Howdy. Beautiful night." As opposed to Adam's impatient, ironic, smart-alecky verbalizations, the Cowboy, like Lynch himself, offers straight-talking sincerity. Expressing profound concepts with just a few words, he crystallizes one of Lynch's key beliefs: "A man's attitude goes a long way toward determining how his life will be." Adam says he agrees with this statement, so he's taken aback when the Cowboy concludes, "I guess you're a person who doesn't care about the good life." Somehow, the Cowboy has an uncannily thorough knowledge of the terrible downturn Adam's life has taken today.

Adam's way of squandering his vital energy in confrontational, aggressive behavior has gotten him pummeled physically and psychologically. Like a Taoist master with a soft, Gene Autry drawl, the Cowboy counsels Adam to go with the flow: "So let's say I'm drivin' this buggy, and you fix your attitude, you can ride along with me." As Jesus Christ advised in Matthew 5:38–41, "And whosoever shall compel thee to go a mile with him, go with him twain."[71] Blend with your opponent's movements; give way to an opposing force in order to remain unscathed. In the days of the collaborative project *Dune*, Lynch rode many a mile in the buggy the De Laurentiises were driving, suffering from having to thwart his own need to be the driver, but knowing that they held the reins of ultimate power. By not spewing out his frustration and emotional pain in angry, relationship-rending outbursts, and remaining cordial and friendly with the De Laurentiises, he was able to enjoy their financial help in making and launching his intensely personal masterpiece *Blue Velvet*. Adam's worn himself out trying to fight 'em, so he can at least try joining 'em, while remaining alert for any advantages or benefits that come his way. As a young man, Lynch learned that channeling his anger into his art, rather than acting it out, brought a new depth and authenticity to his work and added serenity to his being. Both *Wild at Heart*'s Sailor and *The Straight Story*'s Alvin discovered that cooling their rage brought them closer to a state Lynch calls "divine mind,"[72] in which they were more receptive to the power of love.

By harmonizing his efforts with the Cowboy's design, Adam will get to go back to work tomorrow and direct his film, with the one condition that he choose Camilla Rhodes, the actress the Castiglianes insisted on at the meeting, as the movie's female lead. Lynch sets up suspense for the future by having Adam respond to the Cowboy's order with silence, rather than saying, "Okay, I will," or "No, I won't."

In Lynch's script, the Cowboy not only has a supernatural knowledge of all of Adam's previous comings and goings, he seems to be one of the director's mystery men who can bend our familiar laws of time and space. For after saying goodnight to Adam in the corral, he disappears, only to be waiting by Adam's car for more words when the young man walks back to his Porsche. In the *Mulholland Drive* film, Lynch makes this exiting passage more evocative by tightening it up. One moment the Cowboy is with Adam in the corral, the next moment he's gone. The hanging lightbulb goes out. Now it's dark.

For decades, Lynch has read and thought about Hindu spirituality, and he's concluded that there are individuals with highly evolved consciousnesses who have "realized the truth of life."[73] In *Twin Peaks* and *Twin Peaks: Fire Walk With Me*, The Man From Another Place, the Giant, and the Log Lady were characters who had an expansive overview of knowledge that others did not, and who spoke signpost words of guidance to Agent Cooper and Laura Palmer. The Cowboy serves a similar function for Adam Kesher.

The Man From Another Place could be both helpful and malevolent. Similarly, the Cowboy seems part spiritual advisor and guide, part benign dictator, but his message has an ominous edge, for he says, "You'll see me one more time if you do good, two more times if you do bad." He appears to have a positive, stabilizing effect on Adam's life. However, remembering how Betty's grandparently couple revealed sinister shadow-selves in a split second, we suspect that the Cowboy may reside on the night side of sunny California. Like the Cowboy with Adam Kesher, film director David Lynch chooses just how much of the Big Picture, the overall design, he will reveal to his audience at any one time. Loving to probe the unknown and trace mysterious connections in his own mind, Lynch suspends us in a state of alert cerebral and emotional anticipation. Knowing that our brains seek to recognize patterns, he's given us hints and clues that are forming a brooding, dark L.A. gestalt. Lynch's effort is imbued with the poetry of suggestiveness, for we're not sure how everything links up, but there seems to be something wrong in the vibrant, golden air.

In an earlier passage, Lynch emphasized that, beyond manipulating Adam's career, *Mulholland Drive*'s hidden power plays can make you dead. In a seedy building, two low-life criminals (Joe and Ed) linked to the car-crash-disrupted hit on Rita ("an accident like that . . . who coulda foreseen that") pose and chat in Ed's seedy office. Hungry for Ed's little black book ("the history of the world in phone numbers"), Joe pulls out a silenced pistol and reams a bullet through Ed's brain. Lynch wants his movies to be potent, visceral experiences for viewers, and when he first started making films in the late 1960s, he—like other cineastes of that socially and culturally adventurous era—experimented with and explored the new cinematic vocabulary of violence. With the awestruck curiosity of a half-afraid, half-fascinated child and the steady gaze of a scientist, Lynch has for decades presented scenes of torture, maiming, murder, and lethal accidents, and pored over the textures of severed flesh, vomit, the fluids of sex, birth, and death, and the spilled contents of various people's heads. With the passion of a poet and a painter, Lynch wants to get inside where the secrets are, past the barriers of taboos and standards of polite taste, to burrow into behavior and tissue, to shock and enlighten himself with the searing image of the soul in flesh.

An acknowledged master of screen violence, Lynch employs it with the purest of artistic intentions. However, in recent years, he's come to think that since carnage has become so commonplace in popular culture (movies, TV, video games, music lyrics, and even chic, decadent fashion magazine photospreads), its force as an element of dramatic expression has been diminished. For now, at least in *Mulholland Drive*, the bloodletting is minimal and discretely portrayed. Lynch says that "your work can be cooler when you don't do the standard, expected thing."[74] So, instead of the brains and blood we would expect to see littering the just-shot Ed's desk, the director shows us an arresting image we've never seen before. Ed has long, greasy black hair, and the force of the bullet coming out of the side of his head has whipped a twist of his hair out into the air, where it projects like a frozen stream of smoke.

In some of Lynch's drawings, paintings, and early animated films, tendrils, unspecified filaments, or wires have linked human bodies to forces and dimensions either visible or not pictured. In *The Grandmother* a red cloud issuing from the Boy, and in *Blue Velvet* a long strip of cloth flowing from a dead man's mouth, are both visual manifestations of the abstract qualities of pain and suffering. The ancient alchemists believed that smoke symbolized the soul leaving the body at death, and the smoke-like hair wafting away from Ed's head certainly fits with this meaning. And the way Lynch links smoke with a death bed later in the film also conveys the sense of a human essence floating free of its spent earthly shell. As Lynch is wont to say: "Holy smoke!"

Lynch brings an air of cosmic poetry to his lethal violence in *Mulholland Drive*, as well as a touch of his characteristic absurdist humor. For as Joe positions his pistol in Ed's hand to make the killing look like a suicide, he accidentally triggers a shot through the wall, hitting an overweight woman in the adjoining office, who thinks she's been nipped by one of Lynch's bedeviling insects ("Something bit me *bad*"). Frustrated because his own mistake has just made his job twice as big, Joe is in a disgusted funk, which Lynch characterizes with the script notation, "the sense of 'just more stuff I got to do.'"[75] Lynch often feels put-upon having to go to meetings and live up to the social obligations that go with launching various artistic projects into the outside world. We note that he expressed Joe's irritated state of mind in virtually the same words eight years earlier in *Twin Peaks: Fire Walk With Me*, when fed-up trailer park manager Harry Dean Stanton said, "more shit I got to do."

Anyone still claiming that Lynch exploits females in his fictions will be silenced by *Mulholland Drive*, for it is a poignantly sympathetic journey within a woman's sensibility and consciousness (as he has told me, "I love the female psyche"[76]). Because he has portrayed victimized women on screen doesn't mean he has a victimizer's mentality. Females in *Dune*, *Blue Velvet*, *Twin Peaks*, and *Twin Peaks: Fire Walk With Me* have fiercely resisted having their bodies and minds manhandled. The large woman Joe accidentally shoots joins this sisterhood as she crunches him with her weight and pummels his face but he finally stops her cold with a bullet.

Lynch escalates Joe's travails into gallows-humor absurdity, as the shooter has to blast both a too-observant janitor and the man's screaming vacuum cleaner, which blows electrical circuits and sets off the fire alarm. But the killer escapes with his black book of numbers.

With Joe's disastrous day, Lynch has shown us that life is cheap in L.A., and he's further extended the web of career manipulation, lethal danger, and nameless dread that blankets the City of Angels. But Lynch's life has taught him, and his art of balanced contrasts proclaims, that there are other days that not only go the way you hope they might, but ascend further to unplanned heights.

Betty's audition has propelled her onto the Hollywood fast track to success quicker than she could have imagined. This is as good as it gets—and then it gets better. As Betty and Linny the casting director make small talk walking down a hall, Lynch treats his characters and us to one of his art's most gorgeous passages of the mundane transforming into the marvelous. With the voice of a pink bubblegum teen angel, blonde 1950s songbird Connie Stevens sings "Sixteen Reasons (Why I Love You)," and the music floats Betty and Linny into the large soundstage studio where Adam Kesher is testing actresses for the lead in his film. However, Lynch doesn't cut directly from the hallway to the studio, he gets us there via a multilayered illusion.

The music starts while the women are in the hall, then we cut to a view of a woman who looks like Connie Francis (another, black-haired, 1950s songstress from Lynch's teen era), not Connie Stevens, singing into a microphone. As the camera pulls back we see that she's in a 1950s recording studio and is flanked by two backup-singing couples, each composed of a black and a white man and woman, as Lynch adds racial harmony to his love-is-in-the-air pop symphony: one level of reality established. Lynch's camera keeps pulling back, and we see that the recording studio is a set which Adam and his crew are filming: second level of reality. As the shot pulls all the way out, revealing that the far-off walls of the huge studio space display backdrops from other movies (a city skyline, the familiar range of soft-curved mountains that surround Los Angeles), we see that Lynch had done something unprecedented with this continuous, unbroken zoom that lasts longer than a minute. With this flow of imagery that's not disrupted by edits, Lynch crystallizes the idea that the cinema/art/the imagination can transform reality, and gives us a metaphor for his personal and philosophical-spiritual way of contemplating the world. The space-penetrating, observing camera is the human consciousness journeying through life (or cycles of life-death-new life), experiencing a reality that becomes layered realities as our perspective broadens and deepens over time, so that we finally see the Big Picture. In Lynch's *Mulholland Drive* script, Coco the apartment manager says, "you don't know half of it"[77] when Betty observes, "I guess I've come to quite a place."[78] And later, the Cowboy says to Adam, "you're probably thinkin' I don't know the half of it."[79] Lynch approaches the world with a learner's mind, knowing that there's always something more to discover and explore. In the director's long zoom shot, right at the moment we realize the singers are in a pretend recording studio that's inside a film studio whose walls are the backdrops of other movies, Connie Stevens sings, "that's just half of sixteen reasons why I love you."

One reason for this studio sequence is to show Adam presumably heading for a more stress-free future by choosing Camilla Rhodes for the lead in his film, like the Castiglianes and the Cowboy want him to. But the main reason is to have Betty and Adam exchange significant eye contact. Lynch's first wife, Peggy Reavey, has told me about Lynch's lifelong belief in the possibility of an electric spark of sudden love arcing between two people who've just laid eyes on each other for the first time. Lynch is a romantic man who's been smitten a number of times in his personal life, and he adds musical accompaniment to the moments of eroticized eye contact in his films. When *Twin Peaks*' James, while singing and strumming his guitar, locks orbs with Laura's cousin Maddy, his girlfriend, Donna, is sitting right beside them. And in *Lost Highway*, Pete's sizzling eye exchange with Alice occurs in the presence of her gangster lover, Mr. Eddy. These gazing embraces are fraught with potential conflict and, in Pete's case, deadly danger, which Lynch ironically underscores by having Lou Reed's flat-toned, edgy voice sing "This Magic Moment."

Connie Stevens' sincere "Sixteen Reasons" delivery, by contrast, is all hearts and flowers, for there are no impediments to Betty and Adam making a love connection. Not only is Adam in the same emotionally bereft position as *Eraserhead*'s Henry (having been spurned by his wife), but he mirrors Henry's action when he, somehow knowing that his new blonde love was behind him, turned and saw her standing there. Lynch is a master at constructing narrative-aesthetic linkages that reinforce the mood he's building, as when Bobby Vinton's sung words "like a fire burning brightly" coincide with Jeffrey's father being stricken in *Blue Velvet* (the director will further reinforce his pleasure-pain conflation when Frank defines "love letter" as "a bullet from a fucking gun"). In *Mulholland Drive*, at the precise point when Adam senses something life-changing behind him, turns, and first locks eyes with Betty, Connie Stevens is singing "they way you thrill my heart." This glowing moment, which combines Lynch's passion for 1950s culture (Stevens' song, the retro singing group and recording studio) and expresses his devotion to the jolting power of love, is a high point of his onscreen romanticism.

In his films, Lynch likes to extend the duration of certain actions and occasions to absurd lengths for emphasis, but he also understands the power of narrative compression and brevity to heighten drama. When *Eraserhead*'s beleaguered Henry finally finds his soulmate, the Lady in the Radiator, and embraces her, the director cuts away while the ecstatic moment is playing at full force. And just when currents of loving attraction are flowing at flood tide between Betty and Adam, she has to, as Lynch's script says, "run from the soundstage like Cinderella"[80] without getting within thirty feet of him or speaking a word (again Lynch shows us the potency of nonverbal communication). Her potential romance and career-building are going to have to wait, because this is the appointed hour in which Betty promised Rita that they'd plunge into the mystery of Diane Selwyn. Afterall, Rita is the first person in the film that Betty made big-close-up eye contact with.

Betty's caring concern for Rita is the warm, touching heart of *Mulholland Drive*. Just as Lynch's parents helped their terrified young David go down into that shadowy New York subway tunnel and complete the journey they'd set out on, so does Betty try to allay Rita's fears as they taxi toward the eerily dark-at-midday interior of Diane's apartment.

With Rita teetering on the edge of panic, Betty knocks at number 12, and a middle-aged-woman opens the door. Breaking eye contact with Betty and Rita, as though she's hiding something, the woman tells them that she and Diane switched apartments, and that Diane "still has some of my stuff." Lynch introduces the sense of a lesbian love affair gone sour as he pays off a motif he set up early in the film. At Winkie's diner, where the man died when his scary dream came true, there was a sign showing that what seemed to be the entrance to the restaurant wasn't really the way in; and now Betty and Rita have to reorient themselves toward number 17, the actual portal to Diane's world. Over the course of *Mulholland Drive*'s two-and-a-half-hours, how many times will *we* have to recalibrate our idea of just where the film's essential truth can be found?

The mystery woman doesn't answer her door, but Betty won't be deterred, while Rita cowers as though all the plagues of Pandora's Box are about to be let loose. Betty sneaks in through a side window and opens the door for Rita.

The exterior of Aunt Ruth's apartment has a sunny, Mediterranean-tropical ambience, while Diane's doorstep, with its heavy, black Northern-European style timbers, makes it look like a fairy tale witch's cottage or the gloomy houses that populate Universal and Hammer horror films. The Gothic atmosphere perfectly fits the action Lynch has designed for this location, for the way Betty and Rita cover their noses and mouths telegraphs the probability that Diane is home, but hasn't drawn a breath in some time. So how will Lynch, who "loves his blood shots,"[81] as his longtime location manager, Julie Duvic, once told me, present Diane's body?

When Betty took her first, awestruck exploratory stroll though her aunt's lovely apartment, Lynch established a spatial continuity so that Betty (and we) knew how the various interior spaces and features related to each other. But in Diane's dark apartment Lynch presents Betty with spaces shattered into fragments (a cheerless room corner here, a disconnected staircase there) as he did inside Fred and Renee's *Lost Highway* house, thus creating a queasy feeling of dislocation and dread.

Betty and Rita find Diane dead on her bed. She's wearing a gray dress and lying on her left side. Congruent with the unusually discreet way Lynch visualized hitman Joe killing Ed, the large woman, and the janitor, Diane's body is not blown open or blood-spattered. Instead, Lynch has dreamed up a new way to portray dead flesh on screen, for Diane's gray face seems slightly liquefied, its skin beginning to melt away from firm, lifelike contours, and its features eerily indistinct, as the ghost of painter Francis Bacon nods in approval.

Rita knows that this could be *her* death, the death those two men in the limousine planned for her on Mulholland, or the death the two men she and Betty passed on their taxi ride to Diane's are eager to administer. (These menacing double men in cars are another of Lynch's hommages to *Sunset Boulevard*.) Rita feels the night webs closing in and choking her in Diane's bedroom, and as she and Betty burst into the daylight on Diane's doorstep, they are literally beside themselves with fear, their stricken faces a flutter of multiplied faces, their selfhood shaken and sundered in terror.

Lynch, a true Romantic and Expressionist, has always been moved by "the beauty of torment,"[82] and his fictions feature ecstatic, transportive passages of tortured feeling. In *Twin Peaks: Fire Walk With Me*, when Laura Palmer discovers that the man having sex with her is her father, possessed by the demonic entity BOB, Lynch transitions her screams into an image of the most disgusting-looking bowl of breakfast cereal in the world, a symbol of her repugnant domestic situation. In *Mulholland Drive*, the director lets Badalamenti's synthesizer music scream for Rita, as Lynch dissolves her fear-contorted face into a shot of her sobbing head jammed into the bathroom sink of Aunt Ruth's apartment, as she wildly snips at her long, beautiful black hair with scissors. The frantic Rita knows she can't appear as herself in public anymore, she has to look different so the men who want to hurt her won't recognize her.

For years, Lynch has played out his fascination with transformations of identity. In *The Grandmother*, a seed becomes a grandparent and the Boy becomes a half-botanical being; *Eraserhead*'s Henry's body grows the head of his mutant baby; the monstrous *Elephant Man* becomes a Victorian gentleman; *Dune*'s young Paul Atreides becomes the Kwisatz Haderach, the messiah for the ages; *Blue Velvet*'s Jeffrey starts feeling and acting like Frank Booth; *Twin Peaks*' Leland Palmer and Agent Cooper are literally moved by BOB's evil spirit; *Industrial Symphony No. 1*'s Heartbroken Woman (Laura Dern) becomes the Dreamself of the Heartbroken Woman (Julee Cruise); *Hotel Room*'s Mo has a visible alter ego, Lou; and *Lost Highway*'s Fred and Renee morph into Pete and Alice. Since boyhood, Lynch has seen the world with an artist's eyes, so the process of transforming reality is second nature to him. Taking in the raw phenomenological materials that surround him, Lynch transmutes them with his inner vision and shaping hand. In his own life, Lynch has gone through some major metamorphoses: the small-town kid becomes an international celebrity, the nonverbal youth becomes a published author, the remote, live-alone artist turns into an engaged family man—and his spiritual studies and practices have shown him that *this* can also be *that*.

Betty and Rita stand reflected in the bathroom mirror. Both have jaw-length blonde hair. Betty characterizes the surface reality: "You look like someone else." But, as Lynch will soon reveal, she could also be saying this about her own reflection, as well as Rita's. And we will see that there is a key significance in the fact that Betty designed and executed Rita's new look, much as someone making movies creates his, or in this case, her, own vision.

[For Lynch, blue, his favorite color, is the shade of the unknown, the beyond, of mystery itself. It's the hue of *Twin Peaks*' FBI chief Gordon Cole's (played by Lynch) Blue Rose (botanically impossible) Cases, invasive blue-TV-static forces, unholy supernatural crimes, dimension-bridging flashes of electricity, and, in accordance with *The Tibetan Book of the Dead*, the sourceless light of the afterlife. In his work, Lynch, like the European Symbolist artists, dwells in secret inner realms of desire, obsession, and dream, and he would no doubt second French poet Stephane Mallarmé's words: "I am haunted! The Azure! The Azure! The Azure! The Azure!"[83] In *Mulholland Drive*, disparate touches of blue (a blue key, a blue box, the blue-lit creepy old couple, the blue fringe on the hood the foreboding woman who comes to Betty's door wears—"something bad is happening") generate an atmosphere of otherworldliness, menace, and dread. Lynch intends that a small part of our brain should notice that when Betty pulls the hair-lopping scissors from Rita's desperate hand, she sets them down on a blue book. It's only onscreen long enough for us to absorb the title *TOUT PARIS* and the fact that it's written by a French author. For thirty years, Lynch has lived in one of the world's most multicultural cities, but his all-American, 1950s' kid sensibility still regards foreign people and places with wonder—hence the exotic auras of Isabella Rossellini, Joan Chen, and Frederic Golchan in his, respectively, *Blue Velvet*, *Wild at Heart*, *Twin Peaks*, and *The Cowboy and the Frenchman* small-town USA/Western-frontier visions. Later in *Mulholland Drive*, the director will use the French and Spanish languages as mysterious veils of layered reality. In general, his use of French character names is an homage to the Gallic penchant for funding his films and appreciating them both with audiences' francs and Cannes Film Festival awards. In *Mulholland Drive*, Coco is also referred to as Mrs. Lanois. Lynch puts a lot of stock in double meanings and the open interpretability of the way things sound, as opposed to the way they read. We know that Lynch dwells in realms of blue, but La-nois evokes another place he's right at home: the noir of film noir, black hearts, shadow souls.]

The *Mulholland Drive* TV pilot episode ended as the twin blondes, Betty and Rita, contemplated their double selves in the mirror. So this is the point where Lynch, coming back to the project a year and a half after finishing the pilot, faced the daunting challenge of shaping the existing narrative, "which is open-ended, with all these threads going out into the infinite"[84] into a self-contained feature film. His solution took him somewhere he couldn't have gone on ABC TV, a place where even he, the transgressor of boundaries, had never gone before.

It is the night of Betty and Rita's big day, the day Betty triumphed at her audition, and she and Rita together lived through the horror of finding Diane Selwyn's dead body (psychologists say that experiencing a major fright with another person is a powerful bonding stimulus). Previously Rita has slept on the living room couch, but tonight Betty invites her to get a more comfortable sleep by joining her in Aunt Ruth's big bed. Naked, the voluptuous Rita nestles in beside Betty, saying "Sweet Betty, thank you for everything, you're so good to me." Rita's little thank-you kiss enflames something in both of them, and soon they're kissing with deep passion as Betty whispers again and again, "I'm in love with you." This passage, which is one of the most beautiful and emotional scenes of sexual love in Lynch's work, lets us witness the very moment of erotic awakening in the hearts, minds, and bodies of two people. And, thanks to Naomi Watts and Laura Elena Harring's superb performances, Lynch's and cinematographer Peter

Demings' intimate half-light, and composer Angelo Badalamenti's yearning strings, Betty and Rita's discovery of each other feels absolutely spontaneous, inevitable, and right. And Lynch adds a tension-relieving moment of perfectly judged humor that's grounded in his character's personas. Betty the detective wonders, "Have you ever done this before?" And Rita the amnesiac replies, "I don't know."

Most American men are queasy about male homosexuality, fearing unwanted sexual approaches and perhaps their own suppressed homoerotic impulses, as well as the potential threat that free-roaming gay males pose to the sacrosanct ideal of the American mom-pop-and-kids nuclear family. But these same homophobes don't feel threatened by romantic love between women, and may even find it titillating. In *The Elephant Man*, *Dune*, *Blue Velvet*, *Twin Peaks*, and *Twin Peaks: Fire Walk With Me*, Lynch portrayed the eroticisation of one male's power over another as a dark, menacing force. The director considered filming Barry Gifford's 1992 novel *Night People*, about two lesbian lovers (one of whom is named Betty, and one of whom Lynch's daughter, Jennifer, wanted to play) who go on a man-killing spree, but Lynch rejected the project because of its need to center on graphic violence. Lynch does not shy from showing people hurting each other, and thematic violence is at the heart of his art, but he felt that the balance in *Night People* was too heavily weighted on the savage side of the love/death equation.

In *Mulholland Drive*, Lynch has already shown Betty and Adam, as his script says, "feeling the thunderbolt"[85] of mutual attraction. But just as the sign on Winkie's diner indicates, the entrance that seems to be *here* is actually over there. Betty and Adam may have exchanged glances across a span of empty air, but she and Rita have tasted each other's bodies. At Betty's audition, Bob the director had advised, "Don't play it for real until it gets real," and the real, hot-burning, primal love of Lynch's tale is clearly Betty's passion for Rita. The women's loving communion, which Lynch tastefully cuts away from before the climax, initiates the string of surprising and strange occurrences that show us how Lynch chose to conclude his saga. Looking back over the pilot footage, we see that, beyond strongly establishing Betty's heated emotional involvement with helping and taking care of Rita, Lynch was laying down a subtle pathway that leads us to the women's physical romance. In earlier scenes, Betty often touches Rita, at one point holding her hand suspended just above the towel-clad woman's naked thigh. When Rita sleeps, she's covered with Aunt Ruth's dark-maroonish velvet robe (no, it's not blue), which has a note pinned to it for Betty referring to the robe and the whole apartment ("Dear Bitsie, Enjoy!, Aunt Ruth"), and which also seems to refer to the scrumptious female package snoozing within the robe. And when, after they've discovered Diane's body, Rita knows she has to change her identity, Betty caresses her face with her hand (something lovers do to each other in Lynchland) and coos "Let me do it, let me do it." "It" seems to denote "let me groom you and change your hair color," but it connotes, "let me touch you all over."

In *Wild at Heart*, Lynch moved beyond his previously characteristic linkage of homosexuality with villainy when Sailor, having called a group of street toughs "faggots," gets beaten up by them, has a beatific vision of loving goodness, and graciously apologizes to the "homosexuals." Nine years later, in *Mulholland Drive*, Lynch's personal and artistic conception of love has grown more expansive, so why shouldn't Betty and Rita discover and explore each other in Aunt Ruth's bed? (Peggy Reavey has told me that Lynch has lost friends to AIDS in the last ten years, and he has broken his all-black-and-white-attire rule at public gatherings by wearing a red AIDS-awareness ribbon over his heart).

Lynch's spiritual pursuits have taught him that wisdom is gained "through knowledge and experience of combined opposites,"[86] and he plays on the visual polarities of Betty and Rita as they lie in bed after making love. Rita has taken off the blond wig that she'll wear to mask herself in the outside world. She presents herself to blond Betty (Miss Sunshine) as the black-haired woman of shadow and mystery that she is. Lynch films their horizontal visages from a certain angle, so that their two faces seem to from a single face: the woman of light and the woman of darkness conjoined in love. Beyond conveying the Lynchian reconciliation-of-opposites meaning, this image is an homage to Ingmar Bergman's *Persona* (1966), one of Lynch's favorite films. In *Persona*, the faces of actresses Liv Ullmann and Bibi Andersson merged into one, signifying a psychic melding between a psychiatric nurse (Andersson) and her emotionally disturbed patient (Ullmann). (What poetic justice: Ullmann was president of the Cannes Film Festival jury that awarded Lynch the Best Director award for *Mulholland Drive*.) Like Andersson's character, Betty is a caregiver for a woman of mystery (Ullmann's character, an actress, has lost the will to speak [*silencio*], and is full of secrets like the amnesiac Rita). Andersson and Ullmann's merging has a scary edge of combative animosity, whereas Betty and Rita are united in love—at least in the narrative we're presently witnessing.

Lynch says that *Mulholland Drive* "is both optimistic and pessimistic."[87] So far, things have been going as well as Betty could have hoped. Her intelligence, acting talent, and loving attitude toward Rita and the world have shone like the Southland sun. Outside her range of knowledge, people have dropped dead, been shot, discovered that their wives were cheating on them, lost control of their film projects due to the machinations of some powerful, obscurely connected cabal—but this darkness, which seems condensed to form the blackened, shaggy man lurking behind Winkie's diner, has not touched Betty directly. Now, however, the night wind she breathes will be threatening, her smile tinged with panic and rage, her bright sense of promise turned to cold ash, her loving heart lusting only for the kiss of death.

Betty will now find herself in the archetypal Lynchian situation, as her secure life is invaded by chaos and *things go bad* within the house of her selfhood. Lynch accompanies Betty's fall with a shift in his narrative style from the linear exposition of the pilot footage to his unique, abstract way of telling a story through dream-logic poetic associations. He makes us share Betty's bewilderment about the downward, and multidimensional, turns her life begins to take.

Lying at peace next to the woman she loves, in the city that's making her dreams come true, Betty is disturbed when Rita, seemingly entranced, starts urgently repeating "Silencio" and mumbling some Spanish words. This is not your usual post-coital behavior. Once again, Lynch has presented us with a stunning non sequitur, a disruptive intrusion of strangeness that does not rationally fit into a context of serene domestic equanimity (the couple's satisfied slumber after having sex). Jolted by this disjunction, we are alert for whatever will come next. This is a pivotal moment of transition in the film. Lynch, having established the opposite polarities that are Betty (blonde, active, nurturing, self-aware, a gifted, celebrated actress) and Rita (black hair, passive, needy, amnesiac, an unsung actress of minimal talent, as evidenced by her flat kitchen line-readings with Betty), and having had them join together in Aunt Ruth's bed, will now have them switch polarities, with each taking on many qualities of the other. Thus far, the independent Betty has virtually been Rita's life force, gently but firmly instigating every step of the search for the dependent Rita's identity and past. But now the dark-haired one will become vital, motivated, glowing with purpose, while the blonde will diminish to a pathetic, reactive position of following the other's lead. Lynch will show us that Betty is the one with a forgotten, hidden identity. And starting now, Rita sets the agenda: a journey into the realm of Special Knowledge. Fully awake, Rita says to Betty, "Come with me, I want to take you somewhere."

Lynch evokes the atmosphere of a dream as he shows the two blondes (Rita's wearing her wig) taxi across town past distorted-looking side streets and glides his point-of-view camera across an empty parking lot rustling with windblown paper scraps and up to and into a blue-light portal in a wall emblazoned with "Silencio" in blue neon. Like a metaphysical ritual he performs again and again, Lynch (acting out his karmic inheritance for this lifetime?) must penetrate an exterior reality. He glides us through a wash of supernatural-signifying blue light, and into the House of Mystery, where we take our seats in the Theater of the Mind. Betty and Rita's twin blonde heads face a stage with a red curtain (by now an almost reassuring staple of Lynch's universe) and a gleaming chrome microphone in the foreground. Julee Cruise doesn't step up to sing; rather, a black-suited, white-shirted Magician (Richard Green) welcomes his guests to Club Silencio. The Magician and his stage are a metaphor for Lynch and his movie screen, and as the conjurer performs, Lynch reveals the primal dynamic of this film and the cornerstone of his spiritual philosophy.

Repeating the Spanish words that Rita said in bed, the Magician emphatically tells us, translating into English, that there is no band playing, but yet we hear music. He echoes his message in French, underscoring Lynch's idea that we may be able to understand part (through one language), of what life, his art, and the cosmos, are telling us. So, no musicians are visible, yet, if we want to hear a clarinet, a trombone, we hear them (and we do). *The explanation?* The music is on tape: "It's an illusion." Someone behind the curtain (we assume), like the trickster Wizard of Oz in Lynch's favorite movie, has been fooling us by using a hidden machine to produce a magical show-business effect for the audience. The Magician is stating directly the principle that Lynch personally demonstrated in a more enigmatic, shorthand form in his introduction to the Director's Guild *Mulholland Drive* screening, when he stood at the microphone and turned a tape-recorded orchestral fanfare on and off and on and off. Lynch's and the stage Magician's performances illustrate the core truth of the Hindu philosophy that Lynch has studied for years: our everyday world is an illusion (maya) of duality and multiplicity from which we need to wake up (*Dune*: "The sleeper must awaken") in order to perceive the one, undifferentiated absolute reality (Brahman). In *Twin Peaks: Fire Walk With Me* a character codified a concept that's never far from Lynch's mind: "We live inside a dream," which recalls one of Asian-philosophy exponent Alan Watts' pet phrases: "The world is God's dream."[88]

In *Mulholland Drive* Lynch is also touching on the idea that film directors like Adam Kesher, and himself, are themselves primal creators of illusion, and are hence metaphors for the process of universal becoming and being. Paramahansa Yogananda's book *The Autobiography of a Yogi*, which Lynch took to heart as a young man, spoke of the world of illusion we occupy as "the cosmic motion picture."[89] Decades later, in the mid-1990s,

Lynch again saw this idea expressed in print when he read Richard Hallas's classic 1938 pulp novel *You Play the Black and the Red Comes Up*, which he was thinking of adapting for the screen. In the book, a film director character speaks of a state of consciousness in which "there'd be no world left, only a movie of the world."[90] When Lynch writes and shoots a movie, he likes to follow the lead of his moment-to-moment intuitions, embracing ideas that "feel correct"[91] as they flash into his brain. It's only later that he sometimes grasps the overall pattern of his process. Michael J. Anderson, *Twin Peaks*' Man From Another Place and *Mulholland Drive*'s Mr. Roque, once overheard Lynch, while he was editing *Twin Peaks* footage with Mary Sweeny, say, "So that's what I was thinking."[92] After I've referred to some recurring motif or theme in his work, or expressed my sense of a conscious design behind some certain detail, Lynch has said to me, "You would see that, but I wouldn't."[93] And he has more than once ruefully spoken about gaps in his middle-aged memory. Still it's impossible not to conclude that *You Play the Black and the Red Comes Up*'s particular way of expressing the idea of illusory realities wasn't at least on Lynch's subconscious mind when he filmed the scene in which Adam Kesher was screen-testing actresses for the lead in his film. When the first woman sings "Sixteen Reasons," the illusion of a 1950s recording studio is seamless. But when Camilla Rhodes sings "Why I Haven't Told You," we see, at the right edge of the frame, a small glimpse of a backdrop of mountains from some other movie which destroys the seamless recording-studio-setting illusion that the "Sixteen Reasons" performance enjoyed. We also notice that there's a two-by-four propping up the "recording studio." It's very characteristic of Lynch to have a piece of wood supporting an artist-created world, and also typical of Richard Hallas, for in *You Play the Black and the Red Comes Up* he writes: "We only think they're there. And they're not. It's just a movie set. If you go round the other side of that mountain, you'll see nothing but two-by-fours that hold up the canvas."[94]

Lynch has shown us that tape-recorded music and painted landscapes can be mere shadows of a more vivid and hard-to-perceive reality. Now, as Betty and Rita are riveted by his Theater of Philosophy stage show, the director dramatizes life-and-death itself. A woman named Rebekah steps to the microphone and starts to sing. (This is the same Rebekah whose gorgeous vocalizing "no stars, no stars, no stars, *no* stars" Lynch had played for me a year earlier.) With black hair swept back and an emblematic, sparkling tear on her cheek (Lynch's homage to a famous photograph by fellow surrealist and ex-Philadelphian, Man Ray), Rebekah begins to sing a beautifully full-voiced, heart-rending version of Roy Orbison's "Crying" in

Spanish (*Llorondo*). The raw, unguarded emotion conveyed by Orbison's (1936–1988) soaring, octaves-spanning voice was one of the wonders of rock and roll. "Crying" was a painful slice of Orbison's own life. Three years after breaking up with a woman, he saw her by chance on the street one day and had the urge to try to rekindle their romance, but, stubborn and proud, he didn't speak to her and let the moment slip away. He was pierced with sadness and self-recrimination: He thought he'd been doing fine without her, but now his eyes and his heart couldn't stop crying.

Rita certainly has reason to cry: She was in a horrible car wreck, she doesn't know who she is, unknown forces want to take her life, she has to disguise herself to appear in public. Her woundedness and vulnerability put her in a weeping state, and she's also linked to Rebekah the Spanish-"Crying" Latina singer by Rita's entranced Spanish verbalizations to Betty in bed, and her own Latina beauty. Part of the magic of a song like "Crying" and a galvanizing performer like Rebekah is that she expresses and evokes the sorrows of all who witness her. So Betty joins Rita in one of Lynch's intimate frames, their blonde heads together, trembling and shedding tears in all their love and sadness, just as their heads had visually merged in their serene, after-lovemaking repose. As we know, Lynch is fascinated by doubleness and twinning, and he's put a lot of narrative-aesthetic energy into conjoining Betty and Rita in a simpatico bond of helpful kindness, shared fears and concerns, and mutual passion and love. But now, as he rounds off his originally open-ended *Mulholland Drive* pilot into a self-contained film, and reverses the polarities of Betty and Rita's characters, he will make their bond a psychologically obsessive union.

Before Rebekah started singing, when the Magician said that what seems to be real (a band playing music) is actually on tape, is just an illusion, Betty's body shook as she watched, as though some chilling, buried truth was trying to intrude into her conscious mind. As the Magician vanished in blue-flashing smoke, the blue light reflected on the distressed Betty, recalling the bluish imposition of the wickedly smiling-cackling grandparently couple into the narrative of Betty's sunny L.A. arrival. Some dark realization is trying to invade Betty's world, and Lynch gives it two metaphorical shapes.

At the point where Rebekah's/Orbison's song is reaching its mournful, stunning climax, Rebekah's head tips oddly away from the microphone, and she falls to the stage and doesn't move anymore. Lynch doesn't need close-ups or slow-motion flourishes to intensify this shocking occurrence. He just springs it on us from a medium distance: One moment Rebekah is alive and vibrant, the next she appears to be dead. As her body is carried offstage, the Magician's/Lynch's earlier point is again illustrated, for her voice continues to sing "Crying" even though she's gone. A tape is being played: Rebekah was an illusion of life. As Betty and Rita watch Rebekah's collapse, they weep as though their own warm hearts are being touched by a cold hand, and their own deaths foretold. In a single box seat high to the right of the stage, a woman with blue hair looks down on both the stage and Betty and Rita. Unspeaking, and with an inscrutable expression on her face, she is the Spirit of Silencio herself, the ultimate Lynchian woman full of secrets, who we will see again.

Another summation of Lynch's *Mulholland Drive* ideas is the shiny, square blue box Betty finds in her purse when she reaches for Kleenex to stop her crying. The director loves asymmetry (it's the name of his production company), but the symmetry of his *Mulholland Drive* narrative design is beautiful: a mysterious blue key in Rita's purse, a strange blue box in Betty's bag; Rita and Betty are conjoined lovers and investigators of secrets, and inserting the key in the box's lock will reveal the deepest hidden truths, staining their lives with blue, and blood.

Back in the apartment bedroom where they'd made love a few hours earlier, the now-more-active-Rita gets the blue key, turns to face Betty and the blue box—and sees that Betty's gone. Just as when the Cowboy vanished, leaving Adam alone in the corral, Betty's just not there anymore. After Rita takes the box in her hand and opens it, Lynch's camera penetrates the black aperture of its interior, and it drops to the floor. Then we see Aunt Ruth casually look around the corner into her bedroom. We see the bed neatly made, with no evidence of Betty and Rita ever having been there. When Rita and Betty first discovered the blue key in Rita's purse, it made Rita afraid for some reason she couldn't grasp. But now the blue key and the box it opens have been linked to *Betty* vanishing, and she has not gone to a good place.

Hindu philosophy speaks of states of being in this temporal world and in the other, eternal world of Brahman beyond, and of intermediate zones in which the self can see both realms. Since the early 1970s, when Lynch embraced Hindu spirituality and practices, he has manifested, sometimes fleetingly, the region of coexistent realities in his fictions. For an instant in *Mulholland Drive*, he holds the reality of two rooms in his frame, as though they're both existing in a common matrix: Aunt Ruth's bedroom and a space we half-recognize (master sound designer that he is, Lynch gives the second space a different room-presence tone than Ruth's room). The director's camera moves fully into the second space, and we see where

Betty's gone—or been all along. She's asleep in Diane Selwyn's bedroom, lying in the same position Diane's corpse was when Betty and Rita found it. As our brains race to assimilate and try to make sense of this confounding information, the Cowboy leans into the room and says, "Time to wake up, pretty girl." Lynch emphasizes the conflation of Betty's live body and Diane's dead one by momentarily alternating back and forth between them with the speed of an eye blink.

Lynch often presents a character's living space as a metaphor for their head, their inner life, and he frequently portrays the invasion of domestic havens by unwanted and/or threatening forces since he fears such assaults on his inner spaces so much in his own life. Early in our stay within the blonde woman's living quarters, Lynch establishes the motif of an unwanted, toxic knocking on her door. Standing on the threshold looking irritated is the middle-aged woman who Betty and Rita had encountered when they'd come to find Diane Selwyn's apartment, the one who'd said she's switched apartments with Diane and that "Diane's still got some of my stuff." Well now she's here to collect it, and we realize that the blonde we've known as Betty is Diane Selwyn, and that everything we've seen up to the point of Diane just now waking up in bed has been her dream.

Following his rule of contrasts, Lynch shows us that Diane is the antithesis of the pink-cheeked, bouncy, chipper, optimistic Betty. Diane's unsmiling face is sallow-ashen, her hair unwashed, her manner bitter and annoyed as she bickers with her former roommate over which of them owns certain flea-market-value trinkets. Alone now, wrapped in a mousy old dust-colored bathrobe, her mental state matches the blue-gray walls of her disturbingly under-decorated rooms. In a beautiful, sad image, Lynch's camera stares for a long time over Diane's left shoulder as she stands at the kitchen sink, frozen in misery. Seemingly able to convey emotion with the back of her unmoving head, Naomi Watts shows Diane lost in depression, the kitchen windows (the windows of her soul) before her clouded with dust and flyspecks, her gaze turned deep within her tortured mind. For the first time in his work, Lynch presents the ritual of coffee-making and drinking as joyless drudgery: Even his personal universal elixir and tonic can't brighten Diane's mood. Noting the mauve-red sheets on her bed, we realize that hers was the bed of beleaguered breathing and broken-hearted sighs Lynch showed us immediately after his prologue shot of happy, jitterbug dancers.

Faced with the challenge of making his *Mulholland Drive* pilot into a film, Lynch followed the pathway established by certain small details in his existing footage (Betty hangs up when the police ask her name; she says, "Strange to be calling yourself" when she rings Diane's number; the old woman Louise Bonner says, "Who are you?" when she comes to her friend Ruth's door and Betty opens it) and he decided to have Betty be Diane. In the pilot the director also had Betty say to Rita, when she had her blond wig on, "You look like someone else." So, who is that someone? Who is Rita in Diane's waking, as opposed to dreaming, life? A truism of the dramatic arts is that by presenting your audience with something they don't expect, you keep them in their seats, in which case this section of *Mulholland Drive* should have viewers absolutely mesmerized. For Rita's still the woman Diane's mad about, but her name is Camilla Rhodes.

In the last third of his film, Lynch shows us that Betty was Diane's fantasy idealization of herself, her career, and her love life with Camilla, who became Rita in Diane's mind's-eye movie. Diane did not wow her audience when she had her big audition, and she watched Camilla become the overnight star who is universally adored and gets all the biggest and best roles to play. Betty gave loving support to the fearful, vulnerable Rita and helped her make her way in the world. But in another reversal, Camilla now uses her influence to get Diane small bit parts in her films. Like Rita, Camilla has shared love with Diane, but she's also broken the poor girl's heart and led a double life. A character who's cherished by individuals and her community, who's involved in dark, secret doings—sounds like *Twin Peaks'* Laura Palmer, but in Lynch's canon Camilla most closely resembles *Lost Highway's* Alice Wakefield, as we'll soon see. Traumatized by emotional pain, Diane has memories that have the immediacy and vividness of hallucinations. Moping around her dingy apartment, she remembers when Camilla came back to her after a hurtful absence, and bare-breasted, prepared to make love on her couch. Diane was on top, but Camilla had all the power in the room. She said, "We shouldn't do this any more," sounding frighteningly casual about her depth of emotional involvement with Diane, while Diane, feeling her beloved pulling away from her, responded with sudden fury, "It's him, isn't it."

In her wish-fulfilling dream as Betty, Diane was primed to have a romance with Adam Kesher, but in reality Camilla withdraws her affections from Diane to entwine with the celebrated young director. Thus Camilla gains love and professional advancement in one neat package: She's happy to let her career agenda steer her romantic choices. Diane dreamed herself, as Betty, sharing a mutual attraction with Adam, but she ran from his soundstage before she could meet him and potentially become his love and lead actress because she wanted to keep an appointment with Rita. Diane/Betty will choose Camilla/Rita over Adam, but Camilla/Rita will not reciprocate. Naomi Watts has spoken to me about Diane being a heterosexual woman who's overwhelmed by her feelings for Camilla: This is probably the only time the character's fallen in love with a female. And part of that love is kindled by the way that Camilla represents all the Hollywood success that Diane yearns to achieve, but figures she will never have: Maybe some of the dark screen goddess's good fortune will rub off on the blonde girl.

In real life, Camilla shatters Diane's world by choosing to be with Adam. So Diane, the dream artist, transforms this ugly truth into a scenario in which the only thing that could keep Adam from choosing Diane (as Betty) for his professional and personal mate is the shadowy machinations of the Castigliane brothers and other power brokers, who force the young director to accept a blonde "Camilla Rhodes" as the lead actress in his film.

Diane's need to reshape a poisonous, self-damaging truth into fantasy makes her close kin to another of Lynch's fictional characters: Fred Madison of *Lost Highway*. A true Lynchian who relies on intuition and imagination, Fred doesn't like video cameras, preferring to remember things "the way I want to remember them." Wanting to escape a horrible situation (he's killed his cold, untrustworthy wife, Renee; he's sitting on death row waiting to be executed), Fred makes a psychic leap into a new persona (Pete), who lives life in a world removed from Fred's backstory, in which Fred, as Pete, gets a second chance with Renee, who's now in the form of Alice, a torrid, receptive woman. In *Lost Highway*, Fred's dark story came first, and then he tried to escape into Pete's more optimistic scenario. In the *Mulholland Drive* film, Lynch, needing to match the conclusion of his narrative with all the pilot footage he'd already shot (which would comprise at least two-thirds of the finished picture), chose to first present Diane's fantasized, more hopeful retelling of her Hollywood story, and then show us the noxious realm she needs to escape from.

Lost Highway's Renee seems born to torment the paranoid, delusional Fred. Feeling he doesn't really posses her as he should, he kills her. But she haunts his mind so unrelentingly that he has to lose himself in a new-identity scenario, in which she becomes first his welcoming lover, and then a malevolent femme fatale. After using him for what she can get out of him, she declares with a slippery serpent's hiss, "You'll never have me, now and forever." In *Mulholland Drive*, Lynch confines overt femme fatale behavior to the Camilla side of the Camilla/Rita bifurcation. She doesn't reject Diane with the vicious bluntness of Alice's words to Pete, though her more socially decorous, drawn-out approach is equally torturous and cruel.

On the set of Adam Kesher's film, which stars Camilla, she and the director share a deep kiss while rehearsing a scene. Standing a few feet away, Diane, with a devastated look of hurt, watches her lover enjoy herself with

Adam. Lynch stresses the status difference between the two women by costuming Diane in a lowly waitress's uniform, while Camilla-the-star sports an elegant black dress. Camilla, as if to say, "Hey girl, look at me, I'm in the catbird's seat; I own the lead role and the director!," flashes a wicked, close-up glance at Diane that pierces her heart. Earlier, in Diane's dream, when Betty and Adam first saw each other as "Sixteen Reasons" played, Lynch portrayed their emotional exchange of glances with huge alternating close-ups of their eyes. But the first time he showed close-up eyes intimately dancing with each other, they belonged to Betty (Diane) and Rita (Camilla), thus prefiguring the fact that Camilla will be Diane's primal love interest. Now, as Diane looks at Camilla and Adam sitting in the convertible, Lynch's ability to convey the nuances of evolving feelings in aesthetic terms makes a close-up eye-exchange between Camilla and Diane a bond of animus and sadness.

In Diane's dream, Adam's soundstage displayed expansive painted backdrops of the beautiful mountains and open skies surrounding Los Angeles, which soared as high as her aspirations. But in reality, as Diane watches Camilla and Adam kiss in the car, she's hemmed in by a backdrop of looming, soot-smudged, low-rent-district buildings which reflect Lynch's early Philadelphia-as-urban-hell experiences. Adam, wanting to shut out the watching world (as represented by Diane) and fall into a deeper intimacy with Camilla, exercises his God-like directorial control, saying, "Kill the lights," which a stagehand does. Now, it's dark once again in a Lynch film, and a truly black moment for Diane, which Naomi Watts etches on Diane's pained, fierce face as the light fades.

When Diane and Camilla were half-naked on the couch and Camilla said she wanted to break off what for her was a dalliance, but which was a deep love on Diane's part, a spasm of fury electrified Diane. Her lip curled as if to snarl like an animal, her hand shot down (off camera) between Camilla's thighs and roughly tried to arouse her and blot out her spurning words. Camilla asked her to stop, so Diane's hand-thrusting was a sexual violation, and played as a polar opposite to the gentle, first-time unfolding of their sexual passion we saw earlier in Aunt Ruth's bed.

Diane, screaming "this isn't easy for me, so I'm not going to make it easy for you," had shoved Camilla, who wanted to be civil about their breakup, out over the threshold and slammed the door. Since the floating stedicam of Diane's/Betty's consciousness/dream has smoothly glided us through so many passageways and doorways, the abrupt whamming-shut of Diane's front door, closing out the woman she loves, had great kinesthetic-dramatic force.

Lynch fractures his film's time sense to reflect Diane's shattered psychological state. So, after the Camilla-rejects-Diane scene on the couch, we see Diane watching Camilla and Adam in the soundstage convertible, as Camilla wickedly rubs Diane's nose in Camilla's blossoming love for Adam. Then we're back in Diane's apartment, just after Camilla's rejected her on the couch and been kicked out. (When I told Lynch that what matters in *Mulholland Drive* is its powerful through-line of emotional truth, which consolidates whatever we're seeing, be it reality or illusion, dream or memory, in life or in the afterlife, he said, "Fantastic, Greg.")

Emotionally overwrought, Diane goes back to the couch, lies down, and masturbates. The only other masturbation scene in Lynch's work occurs in *Wild at Heart*, when a woman, Juana, rubs between her legs as part of a sex-torture-execution ritual with her male lover, which involves blowing a second man's brains out. Juana touches herself for pleasure, albeit a sexual thrill conflated with the spilling of a fellow human being's blood. Diane, in contrast, masturbates alone, because Camilla isn't there, and never will be again. She rubs herself desperately, trying to escape her anguish, to keep her so-alone self from imploding into madness: She's like the young, nightmare-haunted man at Winkie's diner, who wanted "to get rid of this god-awful feeling."

Just as Lynch presents his beloved, bliss-yielding ritual of coffee-drinking as a sad, unfulfilling activity for Diane, so her masturbation is a bitter measure of her suffering. Sweating, her reddened face weeping, Diane seems to be plunging the anger she feels toward Camilla into her own being, as she brutally and assaultively fingers the sweet parts between her thighs that she's offered to Camilla with all her heart. This is a brilliant, emotionally nuanced, courageous moment for actress Naomi Watts, and the only instance so far in which a Lynchian character has engaged in both sex *and* violence with a single, empty, hand. As Aerosmith's Steven Tyler sings, "that kind of love was the killing kind."[95]

Watts spoke to me at length about the challenge, and ordeal, of filming this scene.

> I knew that I was doing the best work of my life in this film. I trusted David completely, and I was in a frame of mind where I wanted to be pushed hard, at the risk of hurting myself emotionally. David wanted me angry in the scene: Diane's trying to get back the warm feeling of love with Camilla, but she can't get there, the feelings have been poisoned; she's in a depraved state of being. David reduced the crew to the minimum number needed to get the scene, but it required a lot of focus changes, so we did take after take with these technicians hanging close above me. I'm shy, I get stage fright, and I was in a bad

> state. I couldn't stop crying. I was in absolute panic like a threatened animal. I had to keep getting up to go to the bathroom. We were burning up hundreds of feet of film, but at one point I just couldn't go on. I said, "David, I can't do this, I can't." I was ready to stop and go home and let him be satisfied with what he'd already shot. He knew what he was putting me through, and he was there for me all the way, but he still had to get what he needed as an artist. He said, "Don't worry, Naomi, we'll take our time; we'll wait for you." I was so reassured by his voice, his understanding of my torment. I calmed down a bit, and we finished the scene. It's so good as an actress to have the opportunity to play those moments that are deeply human, but deeply dark. Seeing the scene on the screen is not as bad as how I felt that day.[96]

Lynch has often shown us how closely linked are the impulses toward sex and violence, as though both expressions of human nature are powered by a common stream of emotional energy. Characters in *The Elephant Man*, *Dune*, *Blue Velvet*, *Twin Peaks*, and *Twin Peaks: Fire Walk With Me* all have sex with/love and batter/kill the objects of their affection. In *Wild at Heart*, the same music accompanies the hero's killing rage and his lovemaking with the heroine, a man's torture and murder has an aphrodisiac effect on the couple assaulting him, and the hero's name goes on a hit list after he refuses to have sex with his girlfriend's mother. Lynch is fascinated by the way that a control-mad will to power, a paranoid fear, can infest the sexual/loving urge, twisting it into a killing stroke. When *Lost Highway*'s Fred Madison feels his cherished wife, Renee, starting to withdraw her love from him, he stops her dead before she can go any further—but she does. Fred's tortured mind, retreating from the horror of his murderous action, creates a tangible new world in which he, as Pete, gets to enjoy hot embraces with Renee (as Alice). But then she, along with pursuing forces born of Fred's own guilt, brings him down. Lynch is following a similar narrative strategy in *Mulholland Drive*, so what can he devise to push Diane's psychic pain to Fred Madison extremes?

If Camilla's romantic soundstage tête-à-tête with Adam was rude and hurtful to Diane, then her wanton femme fatale behavior at a later dinner party scene is virtually lethal. Despite evidence to the contrary, Diane keeps hoping, and fantasizing, that Camilla will come back to her, so she's thrilled when Camilla calls, tells her to put on her party dress, and get in the big, black car when it comes to get her. This will be the night—again their pounding hearts will flame together as one.

Lynch gives us one of his most beautiful realizations of his fascination with doubleness and twinning as we see, just as in the film's opening, a black limousine majestically serpentining along Mulholland Drive, floating on the hypnotic strains of Angelo Badalamenti's night music. Riding exactly the same editing rhythms of the earlier limousine trip, Lynch cuts to the car's interior, and we see a close-up of the blonde, pensive Diane, instead of the black-haired Rita Diane envisioned for us in her opening dream. The exact duplication of this passage, this time with Diane instead of Rita, concretizes which parts of Lynch's narrative are real, and which are fantasy. We have our bearings, at least for now.

In Diane's dream, Rita was threatened by the limo driver and then struck by the horrible car crash. In reality, the car, as in the dream, makes an unscheduled stop, but here there's nothing to fear, and Diane's door, like a magic portal, opens onto the prospect of an enchanted evening. Her beloved Camilla steps out of the night, takes Diane's hand and coos sweet words to her as they climb up through lush trees and foliage to a Hollywood hilltop, as Lynch emphasizes the romantic promise of their vertical progression by wedding it to the yearning strains of Badalamenti's *Love Theme*. The women's climb up through looming trees recall's *Dune*'s Paul Atreides and Lady Jessica's ascent through rock formations to their first encounter with the Fremen, and hence a major chapter in Paul's prophesized destiny. And in Lynch's *Mulholland Drive* pilot script there's a scene in which Betty and Rita climb steps to the roof of Aunt Ruth's apartment at night. With smiling anticipation and optimism in their faces, they gaze out across Hollywood, hoping to catch a glimpse of a bright future in the shimmering nest of light before them. This buoyant, expectant mood grips Diane as Lynch's floating camera and Badalamenti's music waft her up through the trees to the hilltop with Camilla: This will be the night their love blossoms anew. This evocative, uplifting passage feels more like a wish-fulfilling sequence in Betty's fantasyland, rather than an actual life event of the depressed loser Diane, so there is still hope in the real world. The intensely romantic Lynch not only dreamed up this scene, but when he was rehearsing it with his actresses, Laura Elena Harring asked, "Is it working the way you want it?"[97] to which he replied, "The only problem is my heart."[98]

In Lynch's fictions, moving vertically, being in an upper/higher position, often brings you closer to heaven. *The Grandmother*'s Boy, *Eraserhead*'s Henry, and *The Elephant Man*'s John Merrick all commune with their loving soulmates in upstairs bedrooms, and in her second-story room *Blue Velvet*'s Sandy gains knowledge that will help purge her town of a hidden evil. Sometimes, however, Lynch's characters who are elevated above street level learn harsh lessons and pay a heavy price. In the bedroom of *Twin Peaks: Fire Walk With Me*'s Laura Palmer, she has years of intercourse with a marauder named BOB, then discovers that he is an entity possessing the sexually thrusting body of her own father. Diane, with her lover, Camilla, may have climbed up from Mulholland Drive to the top of the Hollywood Hills, but she's moving in a hellish direction.

Diane realizes that Camilla (who promised her "a surprise") has not brought her to a private relationship-renewing tryst, but set her up for a public fall into bottomless despair. At the top of the hill is Adam Kesher's house, where Diane's lowly role, so far beneath the romantic reunion with Camilla she had hoped for, is to be Camilla's tag-along friend at a dinner party. A gathering where Adam and Camilla, talented, fawned over, and in love, are to be figuratively crowned king and queen of Hollywood. Diane, embarrassed and humiliated about having to talk about her less-than-stellar career, recounts how she may have won a jitterbug contest, but, unlike in her self-fulfilling dream as Betty, she just didn't have the talent to shine in the Hollywood system. Remembering, in Diane's dream, director Bob's hedging response to Betty's audition, we hear that the real director Bob "didn't think that much of me." (Naomi Watts has told me how she produced Betty's buoyant, happy voice up near the front of her mouth, and found Diane's sullen, depressed tones at the back of her throat.) While people at the table praise Camilla's fabulous starring performances, Diane says that she had to settle for small bit parts that Camilla used her influence to set up.

In *Eraserhead*, when Henry came to dinner at the Xs' house, the tension-filled social occasion assaulted him with life-changing news he didn't want to hear: He was, unexpectedly, the father of a mutant baby. With *Mulholland Drive*'s dinner party, Lynch again reveals a toxic essence buried beneath the positive surface connotations of a social occasion. He also uses the gathering to show where Diane, the artist who rearranges life the way she wants it to be in her mind's-eye movies, gets her cast of characters. Coco, the guiding-angel apartment manager from Betty's dream, turns out to be Adam's testy and inhospitable mother, who nonetheless gives Diane a sympathetic look and pat on the hand after she tells about not making the grade in Hollywood. We see the fellow who was the Cowboy wander through the background, as well as the large man who became gangster Luigi Castigliane in Betty's fantasy.

As the dinner continues, Lynch makes things as bad as they can be for poor Diane. Not only has she had to publicly affirm her lowly professional status and sit staring at Camilla and Adam, who are obviously deeply in love, but then the beautiful blonde Camilla Rhodes in Diane's dream of Betty's world sashays up to the real Camilla and kisses her lingeringly on the mouth. Whispering words about meeting her later on, the blonde departs, showing Diane that Camilla, in addition to leaving her for Adam, has been carrying on with another woman. (Again the cheating theme rears its head in Lynch's world, and like Renee/Alice in *Lost Highway*, Camilla bedevils the film's protagonist by having more than one extracurricular partner.) Once more in *Mulholland Drive*, we get the sense that in real life Diane doesn't care about Adam romantically: Camilla is her one love. So, in her dream as Betty, her attraction to both Camilla and Adam, which was reciprocated by both, was a way of exclusively monopolizing the affections of the alpha female and male in her sphere, a fantasized way of keeping her Camilla from falling for Adam.

In sadness and horror, Diane looks across the elegantly appointed dinner table as Camilla and Adam repeatedly kiss with open mouths: another example of Lynch's sensitivity to raw, animalistic forces invading a normally well-mannered and civilized domestic setting, as when *Eraserhead*'s Mrs. X had an eroticized fit while a chicken served for dinner oozed dark, viscous fluids.

Lynch believes in angels and prayer, and that sometimes wishing for something can make it so, but even Diane's fiction-conjuring mind can't transform the grievous reality that's staring her in the face. Lynch has often extended a torturous moment for devastating effect, and as Adam and Camilla kiss, the young man slowly begins to speak words that whipsaw Diane's heart. With unnaturally drawn-out pauses, he says, "So I guess we've saved the best for the last. . . . You've probably already guessed it. . . . Camilla and I are going to be. . . ." For a screen-time eternity of eight seconds, Diane gathers strength to hear the inevitable "married," but it never comes, because she can't face it and violently turns her head away from the scene like she's been slapped, as though she's condensing Lynch's mistrust and fear of words into a single stunning gesture of abhorrence. This is another superb moment for actress Naomi Watts, and once the shot was concluded she bowed her head and shed real tears.

Directing this scene, Lynch, suspended in the silence following Adam's "Camilla and I are going to be . . . ," waited for the moment that felt right and, when he wanted Diane to lash her head away from the social certification of her loss of Camilla, he shouted "CRASH!"[99] through his bullhorn. In the director's mind, Diane, just as much as Rita on Mulholland Drive, has now had her car crash. Her dreams of Hollywood success and fulfilling love have been smashed to smithereens.

Over the years, Lynch has characterized himself as suffering in fear, pain, and confusion, and many of his fictional people are plagued by these torments. Lynch has said that the anger which flamed within him as a youth has cooled, though some who've known him for years speak of his present-day capacity for temperamental outbursts. Suffering permeates the director's fictions and virtually saps the life force of many of his characters, but sometimes they retain enough vital energy to direct righteous anger at their tormentors. The fury burns white-hot when the person lacerating your emotions is the one to whom you've given your heart and soul. *Lost Highway*'s Fred Madison was moved, below the level of his conscious mind, to murder his wife when she withheld her essence from him. Diane, too, has reached the point where she wants to erase the one she loves. In a breathtaking scene transition, Lynch melds the motion of Diane whipping her head away from Camilla's dinner-party engagement announcement to Diane tossing her head to the side when, behind her back, a waitress drops a tray at Winkie's diner. With a grim, tense look on her face, Diane's got good reason to be jumpy: She's just plopped down a photo of Camilla in front of a hitman. By linking Diane's dinner-party head-jerk to the one at Winkie's, Lynch shows her frantic party pain and revulsion becoming a calculated killing scheme in a single gestural spasm of emotion.

As Diane makes her deal with the assassin (the man who was Ed, the triple-killer in her dream), she glances at a blonde waitress (who had the nametag "Diane" in her dream; in real life she's "Betty"), and sees a fellow standing at the cash register (the man who dropped dead from seeing the scary dark Bum in her fantasy). Seeing all these details (Camilla, Adam, Coco, the Cowboy, the blonde "Camilla Rhodes," the hitman, the waitress, the dream-haunted man, the bag of money) that are the raw materials from which Diane fashioned her dream, we're satisfied that we haven't missed a beat of Lynch's narrative juggling act. But as we follow the scene-by-scene progression of the story, a nagging question arises: What is the base reality from which all these elements are being experienced by Diane? Her dream began the film, progressed from point A to point B to point C, then she woke up—and then she started to encounter, for the first time, some of the component parts that made up her dream. We need to gather a bit more information before we can determine what point of view can logically encompass the various episodic time frames Lynch is showing us. Like Rita in Diane's dream, Diane has a purse full of money, which she gives to the hitman. At the dinner party, Diane had mentioned that she inherited some money when her Aunt Ruth died, so she could be spending her legacy to rub out Camilla, thus emphasizing how much she's willing to give up to put her lover in the ground. But, whenever possible, Lynch likes to have it two ways, so he also earlier dropped the detail that two detectives were looking for Diane, implying her connection to conceivably lucrative criminal doings. In Diane's dream, there appeared a skanky prostitute with Diane-length blonde hair: Has Diane been earning extra bucks for her kill-Camilla fund by working the streets?

The hitman asks Diane, "Are you sure you really want this?" With steely resolve, she answers, "More than anything in the world." Diane is an immensely sympathetic character: certainly most of us have dreamed big and lost large. Betty may be a preternaturally sweet version of Diane, but she's still an aspect of Diane's psyche, an idealization of capacities Diane possesses, and, sadly, is not able to realize in the real world. Betty is a reminder, a measure, of how much Diane could have achieved, and of how much she's lost. For, in terms of film noir iconography, Diane is now more of a femme fatale than Camilla could ever imagine being. As *Lost Highway*'s gangster Mr. Eddy might say, Diane "really out-uglied them sons of bitches." She has become, as Fred Madison did in *Lost Highway*, the sort of person Lynch typically abhors in his fictions: the one who seeks to impose their totalitarian control on another, whose will to power transgresses boundaries of decency and the law. Like Norma Desmond in *Sunset Boulevard*, Diane will stop the person she loves from escaping her with a hail of .45-caliber forget-me-nots.

The hitman says he'll send Diane a blue key as a sign that Camilla has been snuffed out. When Diane asks what the key opens, the assassin, like Lynch being asked to explain the mysteries of his fictions, just laughs. At this point, we remember that we first saw the hitman's blue key (a simple hardware-store-bought item that becomes the one-of-a-kind, sculpted object in Diane's dream) on Diane's coffee table after she'd awakened from her dream. So we realize the while we've been watching the dream and seen Diane moping around her apartment in her mousy robe, her mind has been processing the knowledge that she's killed Camilla. And we understand that the post-dream passages in which Diane and Camilla are together (half-naked on the couch, on-set with Adam and the convertible, at the dinner party) are Diane's flashbacks. In Diane's dream, when Betty and Rita go to Club Silencio, they're enjoying the first night of their new-born love: the music that accompanies them should be encouraging and celebratory. Instead, Diane's mind tells the truth, and we see Rebekah the teary-eyed singer drop dead from "Crying," after Roy Orbison's words describe the actual state of Diane's relationship with Camilla: "But darling, what can I do?/For you don't love me/and I'll always be/Crying over you."[100]

Now we see why, in Diane's dream, Camilla as Rita feared the blue key: It was a signifier of her death. And we understand that, in the dream, when Rita opened the blue box, it dropped to the floor because she wasn't there to hold it any more: The black abyss inside the box, into which Lynch plunged his camera, was the darkness of her death. Rita vanished from Diane's dream because Camilla just died, but why did Diane's dream-self, Betty, disappear—was it just because Diane was starting to wake up, or is she sleeping the big sleep that lasts forever?

Witnessing Diane's dream, we literally experience her second thoughts about having killed Camilla. Lynch knows that the opposites and dualities that surround us can also inhabit our psyches, and that the line between love and hate can disconcertingly shift within our hearts. In *Blue Velvet*, the polymorphously perverse Frank Booth lusts for both sex and violence with Dorothy and Jeffrey. Gripped by a fury that's also a twisted expression of his impulse to love, Frank says he'll "send a love letter" to Jeffrey, a communication which he defines as "a bullet from a fucking gun." In *Wild at Heart* a couple's foreplay consists of torturing and shooting a man, and another couple's lovemaking is accompanied by music that earlier orchestrated a brutal slaying. And *Twin Peaks*' evil entity BOB brings tastes of pleasure as well as pain to the victims he possess. Diane loves Camilla so much that she feels her world crumble when Camilla withdraws from her. Diane feels dead inside and she wants Camilla to feel dead forever. For Diane, the depth of her love for Camilla becomes the measure of how far she wants Camilla to fall. *Lost Highway*'s Fred Madison disposed of his unfaithful mate with his own hands, whereas Diane hires a man to do her killing, as did *Wild at Heart*'s Marietta. Lynch, due to his love of 1950s culture and social norms, perhaps has a traditional sense of propriety about what women should and shouldn't do with their hands. Women just don't directly kill people in Lynch's fictions, except in *Dune*, since certain females were cast as killers in Frank Herbert's source novel. Aside from Lynch's predilection for women not to be hands-on slayers, having Joe the hitman do the deed for Diane in the new *Mulholland Drive* footage lets the director retain the Joe-offs-three-people sequence he'd already shot for the pilot. The pilot killing sequence became Diane's dream vision, which showed what a thorough worker Joe is, using his gun to silence each new witness to his first murder, while Diane's real-life interaction with Joe consists of her hiring him at Winkie's.

Diane doesn't verbally express remorse for having rubbed out Camilla's life, but her subconscious, as manifested in her dream, is drenched in guilt and remorse. In her mind's movie, Diane makes Camilla (as Rita), in that black limousine on Mulholland Drive, escape death by pistol and car crash. Diane casts Camilla as a woeful amnesiac she can help, befriend, and fall in love with. Diane, as sweet Betty, can show herself what a good person she is, and since Rita (Camilla) can't remember her own past, she doesn't know that Diane's responsible for her death. In Diane's tortured mind, still wounded by Camilla's rejection of her, it seems that the only way that Camilla (as Rita) can fall in love with Diane (as Betty) is if she doesn't remember who she is. Diane's dream enables her to sublimate her guilt by being an angelic nurturer and guide for Camilla (Rita), and as a reward she gets to dazzle Hollywood with her talent and enjoy the ascendant social position that Camilla occupied in real life. But as with *Lost Highway*'s Fred Madison, who mentally creates an alternate identity and world in which he tries to escape the truth that he killed his loved one, Diane's mind injects veiled reminders of her sadness and dark deed into her wishful fantasy. And the real-life hitman's blue key becomes the mysterious blue key of Diane's dream, which strikes terror in Rita (Camilla) and eventually unlocks her death, as she releases the blackness inside the blue box and vanishes as the box falls to the floor. In *Lost Highway* Fred the murderer, living inside his hopeful vision, is punished by never getting to possess the woman he yearns for, while Diane, as Betty in her sunny Hollywood dream, is haunted by the old couple from the airport, who invade her rosy fantasy and reveal their malevolent aspect. As Lynch builds toward his finale, the oldsters and the creepy homeless Bum who made the young fellow at Winkie's die of fright combine efforts to render karmic justice on Diane.

All his life, Lynch has sought to discover and reveal the "sense of wild pain and decay"[101] hiding beneath the membrane shell of surface appearances. In *Twin Peaks: Fire Walk With Me*, BOB, the extra-dimensional purveyor of fear and devourer of souls, was referred to as "the man behind the mask," the mask being the cheery, solid-citizen face of Leland Palmer, behind which he hid. In *Mulholland Drive*, out back behind the happy façade of Winkie's diner, on the far side of the wall Lynch's crew built just to conceal him, dwells "the one who's causing all the fear." The homeless person charred by hellfire, the Dark One who invaded a man's dreams, then his life, killing him in the process. Just like the poor man victimized by his potent dream (which was a scenario Diane was dreaming), Diane, now awake, finds the Dark One generating her downfall.

In the night, behind Winkie's, the Dark One who is homeless (like BOB, he can be everywhere) turns the blue box that signified Camilla's death over and over in his hands, like a necromancer performing a ritual, then he puts it in a rumpled paper bag. Is this shaggy creature a supernatural being bedeviling hapless Angelenos with fear and death, who's now retiring his black-magic blue box to his bag of tricks? Or is this some mortal guy living on the streets who happened to find the box and thinks maybe he can trade it for some dough? In which case, is the box the lost property of some ultrapowerful, mysterious, otherworldly owner we never see (like the enigmatic "Judy" who's referred to in *Twin Peaks: Fire Walk with Me*)? If the box was a *Blue Velvet*–style lethal "love letter" from Diane (like "a bullet from a fucking gun"), that caused Camilla's erasure, it now visits the same fate upon Diane.

For Lynch, who, with his belief in a Hindu cosmology, feels we're living in the most debased, dangerous time period (the Kali Yuga) of the cyclic spiritual calendar, the Winkie's Dark One may represent the goddess Kali, the blood-thirsty destroyer always portrayed with a blackened face. As the box rests in the homeless man's bag, inch-tall versions of the cackling old couple creep out of it, then slither under Diane's front door and invade her home. The transgressive crossing of the boundary between outside and inside, the violative entry of malevolent forces into someone's private territory, are key dynamics of Lynch's vision. The realm that's invaded, as he overtly stated in his unproduced *Gardenback* script, is the human mind: "the house"[102] of a male character, which is taken over by a monstrous insect, "is like his head."[103] In his professional and personal life, Lynch is hypersensitive about having sovereign control over both the wonders his psyche produces and the admission of visitors to his Hollywood Hills domain. When *Eraserhead*'s Henry gives in to a violent impulse and kills his little mutant baby, the creature's head seems to fill Henry's room, as, metaphorically, Henry's foul deed fills the space where he lives (and we all live in our heads). And in, respectively, *Twin Peaks* and *Lost Highway*, BOB and the Mystery Man poison the psychic abodes of Leland Palmer and Fred Madison.

In the beginning of the *Mulholland Drive* film, two detectives investigated Rita's car crash, then never appeared again, whereas in the pilot script and episode, we saw them do more sleuthing. For his final conception of the film, Lynch chose to make pairs of males menacing (the Castigliane brothers, Mr. Roque and his silent assistant, the two guys cruising by Aunt Ruth's apartment, the pair parked near Diane's apartment), thus subliminally echoing the original detectives who (since all this narrative takes place in Diane's mind), are the ones Diane believes are tracking her for killing Camilla, the ones the woman she traded apartments with mentioned: "those two detectives were looking for you." (The two men in cars are also Lynch's homage to the ones who hounded the hero of *Sunset Boulevard*). After Lynch has informed us that Diane is responsible for Camilla's death, and that her psyche is wrenched and fractured by that guilty knowledge, he periodically adds a sonic element that disturbs the inner peace of her living space: an insistent pounding on her front door. So at the end of a sad and hellish day spent reliving flashbacks and hallucinating that Camilla's come back to her, Diane sits in the night contemplating the hitman's blue-key signifier of Camilla's death. (She's wearing the mousy robe that Lynch uses to establish a temporal base-line continuity for her experiences: After she wakes up from her Betty-and-Rita dream, everything we see takes place during her morning-to-night bathrobe-wearing day.) She feels an overwhelming need to be punished, so all the dark forces she unleashed on Camilla come slavering after her. When the night-pounding batters her door, it's not two flesh-and-blood detectives (who we never see) trying to get in, it's the monsters of her mind, the blue box's yawning abyss, the Dark One from behind Winkie's, the tiny menacing old couple, who, feeding on Diane's screams, horrifyingly grow larger as her fear increases.

Echoing Diane's screams back at her, the oldsters chase Diane to the door of her bedroom. Throughout the film, Lynch has glided his camera and characters across thresholds, through portals, and down passageways, emphasizing the fluid, free-floating nature of Diane's consciousness, which is producing the narrative we see. One of the key portals was the entrance to Club Silencio, which glowed with Lynch's metaphysical/otherworldly blue light. This entranceway admitted Betty and Rita to a stage representation of the illusion of life and the certainty of death, a tableau which moved both women to tears, as though they were being shown that their own personal extinction would come much sooner than they expected. Camilla (as Rita) was the one who insisted they come see this presentation, as if to say that if she and Diane (Betty) kept pursuing the path they were walking down together, they'd both end up dead. And, indeed, Camilla (Rita) died and vanished from Diane's dream, but Diane (Betty) also disappeared—and now we see why.

Diane's mind had used its dream-vision movie-making ability to sugar-coat the nightmare of her life, but the raw, horrific truths still assault her consciousness. Lynch, who since youth has seen himself first and foremost as an artist, and whose art-making has often delivered him from depression and psychic pain, has to sadly concede that even Diane's artful mind can't save her. Indeed, having retreated to the deepest, darkest reaches of her psyche, she finds her weeping, burnt-out life and her guilt over killing Camilla glaring her in the face. Lynch has spent years, through meditation and silent contemplation, dwelling within his thoughts and feelings. And he's dedicated decades of his life to showing us images and sounds of his inner journeys, the patterns of his fears and desires. A fluid shifting between inner and outer states of being is his stock-in-trade and, in his fictions, his characters sometimes manifest their mental/emotional core in the external world around them. Naomi Watts has emphasized to me that "our minds create everything the we dream; everything that's in our dreams is us,"[104] and so Diane's sorrowful, remorseful, self-condemning subconscious conjures up the agents of her own destruction. So, after worming their way into her living room (her head), the miniscule malevolent old couple becomes bigger than life, engulfing her consciousness as they chase her to her bedroom door.

The blue-lit entrance to Club Silencio admitted Diane (as Betty) to a space in which she metaphorically saw her own death racing toward her. Now Lynch, with almost subliminal subtlety, lets us fleetingly register that the portal to Diane's bedroom is glowing with the same blue. As Bob the director said at Betty's audition, "Don't play it for real until it gets real"; now Diane's room will be the chamber of her true death. Screaming in her inner sanctum, frantic on her bed of dreams, she finds the key that will let her escape her pain and guilt and unlock her future: a loaded gun.

Lynch presents Diane's suicide with an aesthetic restraint that makes it all the more devastating. Instead of the blood and torn flesh with which he splattered the gun deaths in his earlier films, the director spiritualizes Diane's act by instantly dropping the light level in her bedroom as we hear the shot and see steamy clouds of smoke gush into the air around her bed, as her temporal world dissolves and her essence wafts beyond life into whatever comes next (Lynch says "Our world is a smoke screen"[105]). Like a metaphysical weather system, the clouds fill the room and blue lightning flashes. Then we see, in a dark, blue light, the Club Silencio curtain, the chrome microphone, and an empty stage. No one is there to perform. Above the stage in her box seats sits the blue-haired woman, an eternal, mysterious, Mona Lisa–like expression on her face. She, and Lynch, have the final word: "Silencio."

We've experienced the buoyant Betty's Hollywood dream and immersion in her love of Rita, as well as Diane's depressing professional decline and the wrenching nightmare of Camilla spurning her love. Thanks to the requirements of Lynch's TV-pilot-converted-to-feature-film narrative, and Naomi Watts' talent, we've seen this blonde woman, in the form of two women, express the full spectrum of human emotion. (Watts has spoken of "the gift David Lynch gave me of letting me act out my dark side,"[106] since "there's so much pressure in Hollywood to be sweet and charming and gushing with smiles all the time."[107]) Even though she's responsible for Camilla's killing, Diane is an immensely sympathetic and affecting character, and we're shocked and pained when she pulls out that bedside gun we didn't know she had (with mountains of respect for Alfred Hitchcock, sometimes surprise, rather than suspense, is most dramatically effective). In a beautiful abstract passage, Lynch emphasizes what we've lost in Diane by showing smiling Betty arriving in Los Angeles, her heart brimming with hope. Then, to the poignant, yearning chords of the romantic Badalamenti music that accompanied Betty's approach to her triumphant audition, her first lovemaking with Rita, and Diane and Camilla's hand-in-hand climb up through nocturnal trees to a hilltop, we see white-hot images of the couple's smiling faces, like the dual, reigning queens of Hollywood, superimposed over the movie capital's downtown lights. Without a drop of sentiment, Lynch, in a few seconds of poetic condensation, makes us feel the full weight of what could have been: the love and artistic achievement and fulfillment these two women might have shared. The director makes the tone of this moment complex and sublime by melding sadness with the sheer beauty of the movie town's panoramic nightscape, as the red neon-sign beacon of the grand old El Capitan theater beams out Lynch's abiding love for Hollywood's true, and cheating, heart.

This is a natural place to conclude *Mulholland Drive*, conflating Diane's particular death with the lights Hollywood's illumination, which, though beautiful and alluring, can be seen as a warning light to nameless young women who end up bought and sold, their starry aspirations buried six feet under. Naomi Watts feels that at this point Diane's narrative stops: Her story's over—but is it?

Club Silencio's singer, Rebekah, who lives in Diane's dream, is a personification of the grieving Diane, just as, in Lynch's *Industrial Symphony No. 1*, singer Julee Cruise portrays the dream-self of the heartsick Laura Dern character, whose love, like Diane's, has been spurned by the person she cares about most in the world. Literally floating above Lynch's staged vision of violent, wrenching loss and sadness, Cruise receives a quasi-divine benediction, as a silver shower of space dust shimmers in the air around her and she sings hopefully of the world spinning on in spite of the universal suffering it encompasses. Cruise's character is an innocent who deserves a blessing, whereas Diane, who we care about and who has been wronged, is nonetheless responsible for Camilla's death, and must pay the price. So, in her dream, she trembles and weeps when Rebekah, in midsong, "dies" away from the microphone and falls to the stage: this is to be, or already has been, Diane's fate.

When Rebekah dies on stage, her song, on tape, keeps singing. Lynch believes that the individual soul, its essence and energy, passes beyond the body's death, journeying further along its own unique path of birth-death-rebirth, experiencing the tribulations and rewards it has earned in its previous lives. *Lost Highway*'s Fred Madison, who, like Diane, has killed the one he loves, is punished by losing her again, by hearing her say, "You'll never have me." Then, like an American Indian warrior who dies without honor and must restlessly wander between the winds, Fred is condemned, at least for now, to relive his primal psychodrama as a repeating tape loop, driving cursed down a Mobius ribbon of desert highway. Lynch says that, following the spiritual laws by which souls, over sometimes-vast stretches of reincarnation, pay off their karmic debt, Fred may yet experience redemption, it's just that "the movie ends here."[108]

Mulholland Drive ends with the blue-haired lady in her box seat looking down on an empty stage, a single word on her lips: "Silencio." Lynch, in his tale of actors portraying personas and people living illusory lives, has reached a finale that recalls Shakespeare's "Life's but a walking shadow, a poor player/That struts and frets his hour upon the stage/And then is heard no more"[109] (*Macbeth*, Act V, Sc. 5, line 19). And the blue-haired lady's concluding word is a Hispanicized condensation of the dying Hamlet's last words: "The rest is silence"[110] (*Hamlet*, Act V, Sc. 2, line 372).

For now, silence, yes, but Lynch knows that Diane's essence, like Rebekah's song, plays on. Unlike hellbent Fred Madison, roaring down his lost highway, Lynch doesn't show us where Diane has gone. She isn't united with her loved one like characters in *Eraserhead*, *The Elephant Man*, *Dune*, *Blue Velvet*, *Wild at Heart*, *Hotel Room*, *The Straight Story*; she isn't watched over by her guardian angel like Laura Palmer in *Twin Peaks: Fire Walk With Me*. The Cowboy told Adam Kesher he'd "see me two more times if you do bad," but Diane is the one who sees the Stetson-wearing authority figure twice. The Internet trailer for *Mulholland Drive*, which did not play in theaters or on TV, includes the sentence, "Will Betty and Rita survive, or end up again on Mulholland Drive?"[111] Lynch the reincarnationist believes that Diane has some repeating lessons to learn, but their form is for the all-witnessing Blue Lady to know, and for us to wonder about. Judging by Lynch's Hindu beliefs, Diane has two strikes against her. Speaking generally, and before this film was made, Lynch has said, "there's perfect justice in the world, because whatever wrongs you commit will visit you in exactly the same form."[112] This is fierce, eye-for-an-eye adjudication: "Imagine having killed somebody really brutally, then realizing that you're going to have to go through that exact same thing."[113] So will a hired shooter snuff out Diane's next life, as she had done to Camilla? And then there's the fact that Diane killed herself, which according to Hindu philosophy, condemns one who caused their own unnatural death through the act of suicide to more pain and suffering than they would have experienced had they remained alive. So, we are left with no hopeful vision of Diane receiving angelic consolation or enjoying a cosmic merging with her loved one. Lynch's all-purpose, one-sentence summation of *Mulholland Drive* is "a love story in the city of dreams."[114] But in a British publication he added that the film is in segments, which he poetically characterized as: "she found herself inside a perfect mystery/a sad illusion/love."[115] The mystery is Rita the amnesiac night creature, the sad illusion is Diane's certainty that Camilla loves her, and the love is Diane's burning ardor, which darkens into a perverse passion that devours both Camilla and herself.

Lynch's final image returns us to a state of perfect mystery, which is presided over by the Blue Lady. Like an archetypal sphinx figure, she is a wise watcher, an embodiment of enigma, a knower of some ultimate meaning that is beyond human understanding, at least on this side of the grave. From her box seat, she can observe both this world and the next, and, being neither devil nor angel, she does not judge humankind's acts of creation and destruction. She is one of the still points Lynch speaks of, where opposites are in perfect balance. Mirroring a pose that singer Julee Cruise assumed in a 1991 photograph Lynch took of her, the Blue Lady's hands are together across her chest, the fingers entwined in a gesture that to the ancient alchemists symbolized the reconciliation of the forces of black and white magic.

After seeing *Mulholland Drive*, I said to Lynch that some of the scenes that had musical accompaniment in the pilot, such as Diane's first exploration of Aunt Ruth's apartment, are now silent in the film. He tersely replied, "There are three silent parts,"[116] as though divulging a clue to one of the aesthetic-structural strategies he used in converting the TV show into a film. There are actually more than three silent passages in *Mulholland Drive*, but the Big Three relate to Diane and add resonance to her story. The first quiet stretch occurs when Diane (as Betty), wonderstruck at finally being in the magic kingdom of Hollywood, walks through Aunt Ruth's gorgeous apartment, building her golden dream of success as she passes from room to room. This silence enhances Betty's sense of entranced reverie, and is the perfect neutral sonic space into which Lynch can intrude the sound of Rita in the shower, which Betty hears before she sees Rita. Rita's audio introduction is a shock and surprise to Betty, who thought she was alone in the apartment, and is a suspense payoff for us, since we had seen Rita sneak into Aunt Ruth's place before Betty arrived, and have wondered when Betty might discover her presence. The second silence is the sonic gloom of Diane alone in her drab, psychologically chilling apartment, which is the polar opposite of Aunt Ruth's warm, comforting nest. The silence of Diane's sad coffee-making ritual is an abysmal open space into which her despair, fury, and dislocation from reality can expand like a malignant growth. The final hush is the Blue Lady's silence of death, of whatever lies beyond life, of secrets kept and knowledge not spoken.

Scientists and storytellers say that there was a sound when matter first emerged from the void of nonmatter. Silence is the space between musical notes, and hence a vital part of a composer's creative process. The Blue Lady's silence may be the quiet stretch between the musical note of a soul's Diane-reincarnation, some of which we've witnessed, and the next, still-to-come note of this soul's progression. Silence is a crucial part of Lynch's search for ideas, for out of it, as he quietly sits with an open mind, come the conceptual building blocks that structure his films. And after the films finish running through the projector, there is silence again.

Before the Blue Lady says her final "Silencio," we see the stage where Rebekah "died" in midsong, thus foretelling the deaths of Rita and Betty, who were watching her performance. When Lynch shows us the empty stage at the end of his film, we're looking at it from the same position the two women viewed it from. The shadow play that is life will end for us too, as it will for David Lynch. And even if there is no reincarnation, if the possibility of multiple lifetimes is just a comforting thought that helps him get through his Hollywood days and nights, Lynch will live on through his art works: sure promises of life after death, that break the silence.

Movies can keep those who made them and appear in them alive, and sometimes the stories they tell override the laws of life and death. Lynch learned this magical lesson decades ago when he first saw *Sunset Boulevard*, which is a tale narrated by a dead man. Naomi Watts believes that Diane's consciousness, her story, ends with her suicide gunshot. But the Blue Lady, who exists after Diane's death, was part of the dream Diane had twenty-four hours before she pulled the trigger on herself, and is hence part of Diane's after-death consciousness, which is telling us the film's story. Lynch knows that Joe Gillis floating facedown in Norma Desmond's *Sunset Boulevard* swimming pool isn't the only dead person who can tell a classic tale of the Hollywood night. When I told Mark Frost about my dead-Diane-as-narrator theory, he said, "Yeah, I agree."[117]

On Sunset Boulevard, inside the Director's Guild Theater, the packed house watching the cast and crew screening of *Mulholland Drive* applauded loud and long as the final credits rolled and the lights came up. As though rousing themselves from a spell, people rose slowly from their seats and began to buzz excitedly as they gradually filed up the aisles into the lobby. I saw Lynch across the room in the aisle opposite mine, grinning, shaking a few hands, and speaking to two or three people in his immediate vicinity.

The lobby was elbow-to-elbow with people, but I'm tall and knew I could spot Lynch and deliver my congratulations when he emerged from the auditorium door. Bill Pullman (*Lost Highway*), Michael J. Anderson (*Twin Peaks*, *Twin Peaks: Fire Walk With Me*, *Industrial Symphony No. 1*), Laura Elena Harring (Rita/Camilla), and Jack Fisk, Lynch's old pal, former brother-in-law, and collaborator (*Twin Peaks*, *On the Air*, *The Straight Story*, *Mulholland Drive*), who'd flown in from Virginia for the screening, were among those waiting to give the man of the evening a good word.

Shouldn't everyone who'd been in the auditorium have made it to the lobby by now? Someone opened the door leading to the aisle Lynch was walking up a moment ago. The big room contained only air and rows of seats. The red-carpeted stage was as empty as that of Club Silencio. The artist who'd just shared his heart and mind with us for two-and-a-half hours was once again the Mystery Man. David Lynch was on the loose.

12

MAN OF THE WORLD

2001–2007
(DavidLynch.com, *INLAND EMPIRE*)

In both his art and life, David Lynch tries to keep a tight control over what is revealed and what is hidden. Naomi Watts says, "Our minds create everything that's in our dreams, from a table leg to the texture of someone's coat; we are our dream."[1] With Lynch, a deep-delving, intuitive, resolutely personal artist, he is all the extreme rage and consuming love, physical pleasure and pain, hellish entrapment and euphoric spiritual transcendence that fills his films, TV shows, paintings, and songs. Always sensitive to dualities, Lynch knows that he lives a double life: His essence is in his art, but it also dwells with the body he moves toward his meditation chair, through his son's bedroom, and into press conferences in Los Angeles, California. His artist's mind, manifested in his work, is here and there for everyone to experience; its passion and inventiveness are both his bliss and our gift. But his public persona constitutes a genial, well-mannered barrier that hides his motivations and intentions about his work, and the detailed, day-to-day life process that generates them. Lynch's head is his most precious, sovereign territory, and he will decide who, where, and when anyone else can have access to it, and for how long. In one of his late-2001 thirty-second Sony PlayStation 2 commercials, an artistic-type man wearing dark sunglasses is being interviewed by an insistent off-screen voice, which keeps requesting that the man remove the glasses so we can see his eyes. As many times as the interviewer makes the request, the arty man says, "No, I can't do that,"[2] clearly reflecting Lynch's own guarded attitude about self-revelation.

Two months after Lynch shared *Mulholland Drive* with us at the Director's Guild screening and then vanished from the room, Julee Cruise appeared in Seattle, where she performed and talked to me about some troubling truths that have been hidden behind the public perception of her and Lynch's heavenly collaboration.

Cruise, the child of alcoholic parents who's suffered physical illness and feels she's "led a tragic life,"[3] has a habit of "latching onto men who are brilliant and who inspire me,"[4] and who give her the extra measure of approval she needs. Lynch certainly seemed capable of meeting all these qualifications. But as they began to work together, in the mid-1980s, he treated her "as though I was a nobody, naïve and moldable,"[5] even though she had "many awards and accolades"[6] to her name and a substantial professional track record. Characteristically, Lynch knew what he wanted, and single-mindedly strove to transform Cruise, who considered herself "a Broadway belter,"[7] into a thirty-something teen angel whose ethereal voice could channel the music of the spheres. Before meeting Lynch, Cruise, who feels she's "incredibly angry and aggressive,"[8] had been rewarded for letting those harsh emotions power her work (she had done a knockout portrayal of 1960s rock queen Janis Joplin). Just as Lynch sensed that *Mulholland Drive*'s Naomi Watts was capable of playing Diane's darkness as well as Betty's sunshine, he felt that Cruise had a "soft, sad side"[9] that could rain down in songs of tender yearning and aching loss. "He's intuitive; he understood that I was damaged."[10] Cruise says Lynch knew she was the perfect "musical actress"[11] to be the tear-stained song-voice of his films, TV shows, and records.

Cruise had known Angelo Badalamenti before she met Lynch, and feels the composer, who had been a Nashville tunesmith before settling in the Northeast, "has the best ear in the music business."[12] When the three began to collaborate (Lynch writing lyrics; Badalamenti, music), Cruise says Badalamenti was "seeking technical perfection, while David was after more abstract qualities: beauty and emotion."[13] The song "Falling," the trio's most gorgeous and resonant song (as the theme of *Twin Peaks*), hides a secret that even David Lynch doesn't suspect. "David wanted me to sing about love, but I didn't love people. He never knew what my internal process was—he didn't want to know. I sing 'Falling' to my cocker spaniel, Rudy, who died. He was my true love. People would wonder where the tears, the emotion of that song came from. They came from my dog."[14] Rudy may have been in Cruise's heart when she sang "Falling," but she feels Isabella Rossellini was in Lynch's. "He adored her, he used to call her 'Bellini'; I think all those songs were about her."[15]

Harmonious, tender feelings may have inspired Lynch's lyrics, but sometimes, while trying to record his songs, more discordant emotions flared. "Once he made me sing a phrase eighty fuckin' times, and I lost it and blew up at him."[16] Lynch's gift for humorous understatement came to the fore as he strolled over to Cruise and calmly said, "Julee, I don't like your energy."[17]

Lynch had shaped Cruise's talent as a singer and actor into a persona that was like a work of art he had created: the musical soul of *Twin Peaks*, the romantic woman singer whose, pure, fragile, high-as-heaven voice sang the ecstasies and tragedies of love and loss. She was like something he had dreamed into being, so he had a hard time dealing with Cruise's real-world assertions of her own creative needs and desires. She told Lynch that the rock-pop singing group The B-52s had asked her to go on tour with them, and said she wanted to accept their offer. "He said, 'No,' and I said, 'Bye.' I just wasn't part of his loyal corps of people. I love Catherine Coulson dearly, but I was not going to be shut in a box with the Log Lady."[18]

Cruise broke out of Lynch's box, hopping around the country with The B-52s, belting out loud, fast, up-tempo rock songs that were the antithesis of the muted, slow, mournful laments that Lynch and Badalamenti had carefully groomed her to sing.

> I came off the road with The B-52s and I'd been making $5,000 per show for eight months. David and Angelo did not help me financially at the beginning, and I question that. I was waiting tables when I got the call to go on *Saturday Night Live* and sing "Falling." I told David that with The B-52s I'd been living a different life—with respect. I said, "You and Angelo did not respect me," and he said, "You have to earn respect." He was right about that, but I sure thought I'd paid my dues with him by then.[19]

Despite the tension simmering between them, Cruise and Lynch (with Badalamenti) started to work on a new record project (*Julee Cruise: The Voice of Love*). "On the second album, unlike the first, they didn't include me in the creative process; they had me come in and read sheet music—that's why we split. They mixed the record without me and then played me the mix, and I said, 'This is crap.' The project had my name on it, but it wasn't my record. David got so mad he had to go out in the hall to collect himself. He is just as insecure as I am, his ego is just as big as mine. I hurt his feelings by saying I didn't want to work with him anymore. That would hurt, coming from someone he'd given so much to. He said, 'I gave you a gift,' and that's true: It's this voice I never knew I had before he and I discovered it together, and the way that voice expressed parts of myself that

I'd never tapped into in a creative way. And he got me a record deal and taught me so much, about recoding and how to approach my songs like an actress. But still, it was over. I couldn't go on. He had no idea I could get out of my contract, but I did, I fucked the shark."[20] After they split, Cruise sent Lynch a card, from one dog lover to another. "I had said some awful, horrible things to David. The card showed a snarling German shepherd wearing a tiara—he'd understand that this was me—and inside I wrote, 'I'm sorry I was such an asshole.'"[21]

Today, Cruise still has strong, complex feelings about Lynch and Badalamenti. "They treated me like shit"[22]; "They really loved me, and I loved them."[23] As closely as she worked with Lynch in the late 1980s and early 1990s, she feels that "he's a mystery; he's not going to show you who he is."[24] But one time, "I saw a glimpse inside, just a glimpse. He told me about back when he was in grade school. There was a girl who was the least pretty girl in class, and a lot of the kids would make fun of her. One day the girl came to class wearing a beautiful string of pearls around her neck. David said that this just broke his heart."[25]

Cruise felt broken herself after her creative divorce from Lynch. "I don't have children. Music and performing are my whole life, and my life stopped. My agency, William Morris, dropped me. The phone didn't ring. No one wanted to hire the ethereal voice that David Lynch made famous all around the world. I get real depressed and angry when I don't work. This went on for four years, and I had a nervous breakdown; I didn't realize that show business could do that to you."[26] Rather than drowning in fear, rage, and self-pity, Cruise, whose father was a doctor, began to integrate her fascination with medical science and criminology into the process of songwriting. Now *she* would be the one dreaming up and crafting the songs, as well as singing them. "I discovered the joyful feeling you get when you create something, and to perform what you've created is really fun."[27]

Today Cruise calls herself a "Techno-jazz-diva,"[28] and collaborates, makes records, and performs with the musician Khan. In demand from the United States to Paris to Moscow, and sharing the stage with the likes of Bobby McFerrin and John Cale, she says with a throaty laugh, "I want to hit my peak when I'm sixty-five!"[29]

Cruise has discovered that she can create her own good music, not just sing other artists' compositions, and she knows that her hellish, and heavenly, time with Lynch was a vital part of her journey. "I'd be doing bad dinner theater somewhere if I hadn't had my experience with David and Angelo. Looking back, I wouldn't change a thing. I wouldn't change fate. I don't regret it one bit."[30] Speaking of their first album, *Floating Into the*

Night, she says, "I'm so grateful we made a goddamn masterpiece. David molded my voice into a masterpiece. I think ultimately we were meant to work on one project. It was worth everything for that."[31]

When Cruise performs today she sings her and Kahn's music, but she closes with "Falling," the anthem of *Twin Peaks* and her time with Lynch, the song that best shows off the angelic, high voice he found within her. "People cry over 'Falling.' They come up to me and weep. One guy got down on he knees the other day when he saw me going into St. Vincent's. It's because of that record."[32]

Cruise has found her personal and creative balance in recent years and has reached the point where "I finally wanted to tell the truth about everything."[33] Still, the beautiful range of deep emotion in her songs and voice flows from the woman's own essence, and when I thanked her for talking with me and asked if I might follow up with a couple of questions some time, she said no. "This has been really hard for me to go back over all this. It still hurts."[34]

Like everyone in Lynch's orbit, she knew that he'd quit smoking in the early 1970s, but since she hadn't seen him in years, she was "sad to hear he's smoking again. When he got me the record deal to do our first album, he helped me get off cigarettes, so my voice wouldn't sound gravely."[35]

As Cruise and I said goodbye, I asked her if there was anything she might like to have me say to Lynch for her. "Tell him I'm grateful for everything. And that I'm smoking again too."[36]

In Lynch's art, smoky dark clouds are abstractions of evil, and a few days after Julee Cruise's Seattle appearance, black clouds over New York shattered America. On September 11, 2001, Islamic-fundamentalist terrorists hijacked four U.S. commercial jet flights and crashed them into New York's World Trade Center and Washington, D.C.'s Pentagon, destroying the Twin Towers and killing more than 3,000 people.

For the first time in history, the "friendly skies" above the United States became an ominously silent zone in which no commercial or private planes flew. Panicked by the probability of more attacks, Americans feared that every ordinary activity and place was now threatened. All shopping malls closed; Disneyland shut down; for the first time since World War II, organized baseball cancelled all games; for the first time since World War I, American financial markets closed. Churches were full of weeping people. The mournful sound of Samuel Barber's "Adagio for Strings," which Lynch graced *The Elephant Man*'s sad story, emanated from radios and televisions. On the TV screen we saw, as though in a nightmare loop, the networks repeating the images of the planes exploding into the towers again and again, as horrified onlookers in the streets below raised their hands in the air as though they might stop the tallest buildings in the United States from falling. A well-dressed businessman, his face contorted with rage, yelled, "We should be bombing somebody now—I want to kill somebody *now*!" A man and a woman, standing tall in the Manhattan sky as the tower burned beneath them, held hands and jumped to their deaths.

Like all Americans, Lynch reacted with shock, terror, anger, and sadness to the literal and symbolic devastation that the United States suffered on September 11. Naomi Watts told me that she, Lynch, Laura Elena Harring, and the *Mulholland Drive* team were doing press interviews for the Toronto Film Festival when the south tower of the World Trade Center was struck by a jet plane. "We were each in separate rooms doing our interviews. The TV was on, and it seemed like a horrible accident. How could this happen? We all passed each other in the hall going to our next interviews, and when the second plane struck the second tower we realized this was something far worse than an accident. The interviews stopped. We all gathered in one room in front of the TV. There was a lot of crying."[37]

Before the tragedy struck, Lynch had agreed to meet more press in New York, but all arrangements were forgotten. Scared and grief-stricken, Lynch and his friends just wanted to get home to Los Angeles. David is queasy about flying even in the best of times, so even when planes started flying again, taking a bus back across the country seemed the best way to go. Lynch consumes massive amounts of nicotine even when feeling hunky-dory, so we can only imagine the depth of his need to smoke in the wake of September 11. In this day and age, bus riding and smoking are mutually exclusive, so Lynch rented a car, drove as far as Colorado, then caught a flight to L.A. in what felt like the safer skies of the western half of American.

In the 1980s, Lynch supported President Ronald Reagan, the man who called the Soviet Union "the Evil Empire," and at the time Jennifer Lynch said her father "has strong feelings about the enemies of America."[38] In his fictions, Lynch often deals harshly with perpetrators of evil, and he no doubt will continue to do so, but in recent years his attitude about how to address real-world international mayhem has evolved. Back home in the Hollywood Hills, Lynch told his ex-wife, Peggy Reavey, that "it's a changed world, Peg."[39] His recurrent fictional dynamic of a zone of domestic safety being invaded and harmed by dark forces had just been enacted with unprecedented horror and destruction within the sacrosanct boundaries of his beloved homeland. America's post–World War II sense of national-borders security and economic optimism, which had been Lynch's baby-boomer birthright, had vaporized in the dust of granite, steel, and human beings that was the only remnant of the World Trade Center. I thought Lynch might be ready to pilot a retaliatory B-52 bomber over terrorist-harboring Afghanistan single-handedly, but the program of spiritual growth and purification that has motivated him to give up his cherished red wine and adhere to a strict Ayurvedic eating regimen has erased any vengeful feelings toward America's attackers. More than ever, his philosophy was *accentuate the positive*. "Don't throw fuel on the fire: wrong actions bring more suffering. We get caught in a vicious cycle like Fred Madison at the end of *Lost Highway*. Don't worry about analyzing how we got to the point where September 11 happened. It's so complicated to figure out, and we need simplicity. Negativity is so wrapped around this planet. We've got to stop this thing of an eye for an eye and a tooth for a tooth. Don't worry about the darkness, don't try to figure it out—just simply turn on the light, and darkness automatically flees."[40]

The idea of the microcosm affecting the macrocosm, of the individual's consciousness influencing the global consciousness, has been part of Lynch's mindset for decades. In the late 1970s, he said that "we all have our own little thoughts, and those thoughts go out into the air. If you could see a picture of all the little thoughts, you'd have a picture of the world. And the only way you can change the world is to change each person's thoughts."[41] This concept fits perfectly with the Maharishi's idea that the individual's spiritual practice can "influence the whole world consciousness towards positivity, towards harmony, towards higher intelligence."[42]

Spiritual beliefs, from Christianity to Hinduism to Voodoo, rely on the practitioner's faith that a certain philosophy is true. The Transcendental Meditation movement bolsters its philosophy with scientific, statistical studies, which show that rates of crime and violence decline in communities where people meditate. Since practicing TM is such a positive experience, we assume that a relatively unvarying number of people practice it daily worldwide, sending a constant quantity of healing vibrations into the atmosphere. How then do we explain the monumental difference between the comparatively placid weeks in Manhattan preceding September 11, and the horrific day itself?

Lynch, a believer in reincarnation and karma, has told me that "there's a perfect justice in the world,"[43] since the wrongs you commit "will visit you in exactly the same form in this life or future lives."[44] Victims are victims because, due to their "karmic debt,"[45] they've got it coming. As the Maharishi says, "Everyone has to go sometime or another, and the basic principle about going or surviving is that no one—now listen to me!—no one is responsible for giving any difficulty or any pleasure to anyone. Problems or successes, they are all the result of our own actions, our karma."[46] So does this mean that 3,000 people, each who had killed someone in this or a previous life, were fated to gather in the World Trade Center on September 11 to pay their karmic debts by violently losing their lives?

When CNN TV interviewer Larry King asked the Maharishi about September 11 in May 2002, he said, "I have no time to look back. I have always looked forward, forward, forward."[47] When I asked Lynch about the karma of those who died when the towers came down, he immediately answered, "No, there's no way. . . . They say it's so complicated that you don't even want to go there. It's a terrible thing. It happened, and it puts all of us who are here into another whole mode, and that mode can continue the problem or accelerate it, or it can once and for all make a good, lasting result. It's always the same. It's always the same throughout history that people react by wanting revenge, but now we should take a look at the correct step."[48] I tried again: "What I meant was, was it an accident, a horrible happenstance that those particular people were in the towers that day, or were they fated to be there?" Lynch tersely replied, "I'm telling you, you know, you can't even talk about it. It doesn't matter. What matters is that we're where we are right now this minute, and what are we going to do?"[49]

Even the horrors of September 11 couldn't stop the forward momentum of *Mulholland Drive*, for on the evening of September 24, 2001, Betty Elmes/Diane Selwyn and Club Silencio's Magician stepped out of the fog and entered my place of business.

As film curator for the Seattle Art Museum, I sometimes have the privilege of hosting the premiere Seattle screenings of new films in advance of their commercial release (everything from *Moulin Rouge* to *Girl With a Pearl Earring*). I don't put in requests to try to get certain films; they just come to me via an unexpected phone call. So, thanks to what David Lynch would call fate, I was offered *Mulholland Drive*, accompanied by Naomi Watts. I instantly agreed, and made a call of my own to the film's Magician, Richard Green, who'd become a friend since I presented the U.S. premiere of Chris Leavens' beautifully sad, funny, touching Jack Nance documentary *I Don't Know Jack*, which Richard co-produced with Donna Dubain. As soon as I knew Naomi was coming to the museum, I envisioned Richard, with his Magician's cane in hand, introducing her on our stage before the film. With his warm, mellow, melting-butter voice in top form, Richard said, "I'll be there."

Plans for the screening were finalized in mid-August while the museum was presenting the annual Twin Peaks/David Lynch Festival's film night, so I was able to tell Lynchophiles from all across the country about the *Mulholland Drive* screening. The showing would be free, but tickets were issued to assure that seats would be waiting for attendees.

Unlike in late September 1991, when Lynch and his cinematographer Ron Garcia were surprised by sunny, warm Seattle weather and had to adjust the look of *Twin Peaks: Fire Walk With Me* accordingly, September 24, 2001, was perfectly *Twin Peaks*y with its pale oyster-shell light and clinging, chill mist.

Richard and Naomi had been doing publicity interviews for *Mulholland Drive* from the early morning on, and an afternoon phone call from the Seattle publicity woman representing the film emphasized to me that Naomi was "shy and not comfortable" with the idea of doing a formal question-and-answer session in front of a large group of people at the museum. I said that Naomi could size up the situation when she arrived and do whatever she did feel comfortable with.

Thirteen days after September 11, a fear of flying paralyzed the North American continent, but intrepid Lynch fans from Canada, the American East Coast and Midwest, California, and Oregon joined Northwest devotees to form an overflow crowd that jammed into the museum auditorium.

Richard arrived first—warm, outgoing, and good-humored as ever, his arched eyebrows and Van Dyke beard perfect for his Magician persona. On his gray suit, he sported a dark blue enameled *Mulholland Drive* road-sign lapel pin that the film's team wore at the Cannes Film Festival in May. He told me he'd be with Naomi for the question-and-answer session after the film, which would put her at ease.

Naomi, surrounded by her L.A. publicists, arrived after the audience had filed into the auditorium, and approached Richard and me, who were standing with a few others in the lobby. From my 6'2" height she was a truly diminutive woman, with long blond hair (darker than Betty's), wearing a black cocktail party dress with a demure neck and hemline and black high-heeled shoes with vine-like tendrils that twined up toward her calves. She broke away from her escorts and stepped forward to me. Her salmon-pink lips parted reveling two perfect white front teeth as she smiled, shook my hand, and said, "David said to be sure to say hello to Greg." To which I replied, "And after that he probably said, 'Tell him to play the movie *loud*.'" She laughed and said, "Yeah, he does have rather strong feelings about that." She struck me as being very bright, down-to-earth, and modest about her beauty and talent.

Earlier in the evening, Richard told me that when he introduced Naomi he was going to say something that probably was going to embarrass her.

When he took the stage (without his Magician's cane), he declared to the crowd that "You're about to see what I think is one of the best female performances in the history of the cinema." Then, in his mellowest vocal tones, he asked her to join him. At the back of the auditorium, Naomi straightened her dress, took a swig from her Arrowhead water bottle, cleared her throat, and walked up to the stage. Thanking Richard for his effusive words and the crowd for their warm welcome, she hoped we would all enjoy the film and promised she'd have more to say after the screening.

Richard, Naomi, and her handlers went out for dinner while the movie played, and returned just after Diane blasted her life away and we saw the sad, fading images of her and Camilla, the lost lovers, smiling together in happier times. In the dim light, as the end credits rolled, Naomi came up to me and asked, "What did you think of the film?" Wanting to both be funny and compliment her on her deeply stirring performance, I said, "I'm still drying my eyes," to which she responded, "Awww."

Richard stepped onto the stage, pulled his black cane out of thin air, gestured with it portentously, and introduced Naomi again, this time to an ovation that went on and on. The two of them sat on the edge of the stage and asked if there were any questions. Due to the stunning effect the film had on the audience, only a few people raised their hands.

They both spoke of how easy it had been to tune into Lynch's creative wavelength, and how they'd each done their best-ever work for and with him, how they had a strong sense of collaborating with a true artist. They stressed that David had never told them a single word about his own interpretation of the film, either in terms of its overall meaning or the significance of individual scenes, and how the director didn't want anyone to know which parts were shot for the ABC TV pilot, and which were new footage.

Naomi offered her *Mulholland Drive* interpretation, feeling that the earlier parts with Betty are Diane's fantasy of how she wished things were—a sunny view, whereas actually her world is dark and crumbling around her—the whole film is what's flashing through her mind as she reached for the gun. Richard chuckled and said, "That's exactly how I see it." They both hoped this film would help them get better parts in the future, and knocked on the wooden stage for luck. They said they'd had a great time and thanked everyone for coming.

The pair had been talking about the film since early this morning, and it was now after midnight, but in the museum lobby they signed autographs and graciously stayed for as long as fans wanted to chat. Feeling like Santa Claus, I handed out the *Mulholland Drive* posters, key chains, and matchboxes that Universal Studios had sent. Naomi got to see the *Film Comment* magazine featuring *Mulholland Drive* for the first time and, sounding like an excited child on Christmas morning, was thrilled by the photos and glowing coverage of the film.

The genial Richard disappeared into the night, promising me a dinner "anywhere you want in L.A." Naomi was interested in my book project and agreed to talk with me in the future about working with Lynch. She was about to give me her L.A. phone number when her publicity representative stepped between us and said all contact with Naomi would have to go through her business office. As we parted Naomi, sounding full of secrets, said, "I've got a lot to say about David Lynch."

Over the next months, first in a formal interview and then (thanks to the phone numbers Naomi did give me) in casual conversations (once while she was doing her Sunday afternoon laundry), she was forthright, thoughtful, and humorous about her involvement in Lynch's world.

She said *Mulholland Drive* was the most fun she'd ever had in her fifteen-year career. "David's spirit, charm, and humor infect all of us who work with him: he's a great energy. He chooses like-minded people to work with, intuitively knowing that we can be a conduit for his art and properly express his messages, story, and emotions."[50]

Although it's not directly stated, a number of people who watch *Mulholland Drive* get the feeling that Naomi's Diane and the Woman in #12 (Joanna Stein) had had a lesbian relationship. Naomi said she was so focused on Diane's truth and perspective that she didn't extrapolate about that possible backstory, and Lynch didn't give her any hints about a woman-woman sexual experience for Diane prior to her involvement with Camilla.

> David never divulges what's going on in his head, but I think he intended to emphasize the uniqueness of Diane embracing Camilla: "I want to do this with *you*." Diane is in a precarious emotional situation. Camilla is the one person who lifts Diane's spirits. So much of what Camilla has in her life Diane lacks, so she becomes totally dependent on her. Diane is so broken and vulnerable that she falls into a bad and dark place. In Diane, David created the most incredible character an actor could hope for. You could spend a whole career looking for a role like this, which gave me a chance to express the spectrum of emotions from Betty to Diane. What David said to me about this was, "These are two extreme people juxtaposed." He loves to explore all sorts of contrasts. He was brave enough to address the way we all have light and darkness within us, inner battles, forces inside that we both fight and yield to. When we're too good or too bad we don't like ourselves. Sometimes it feels good to be bad and bad to be good. There's always a striving for balance. It's not interesting

> enough or creative enough when we're too pure. We don't want to admit this about ourselves. I love this about David's work, that it is courageous and confronting. I think that sometimes artists need to offend people, especially in these conservative times when much of society feels it's ugly to explore deep truths like Lynch does.[51]

Lynch the intuitive seer realized that there were some deep truths hidden within Watts. As she says,

> I think he sees things other people don't see. I was at a very low point when I met David. I'd been in some films, but I was spending my time auditioning for shit parts I didn't care about or believe one word of—and not getting hired. I'm shy, and I felt I had to pretend to be happy and perky with everyone in the industry. I was afraid of offending people, that they would think I'm strange. There were things in me that I spend a lot of energy trying to hide, and this affected my confidence, my career, my life, my sense of myself. You dilute your personality so much that there's nothing left.[52]

As much of her post–*Mulholland Drive* career (*21 Grams*, *We Don't Live Here Anymore*, *The Painted Veil*, *Funny Games*) has shown, she has a supreme gift for expressing every wrenching nuance of human pain, anger, grief, and existential darkness. A talent that Lynch realized was begging to be released, and which contributed a golden dividend to his and her art, and gave sweet relief to her psyche. Betty and Diane showed the world a full portrait of Naomi Watts, and the world embraced it. "David *loves* women, and not just in the obvious way. He creates some of the best, fully complex female characters: They're three-dimensional and true to life, and reality is sometimes violent and ugly. He was like my horse whisperer. He really got something out of me, in a subtle way. It felt like we were in this created world together and he was speaking a language with his hands; we were having an unspoken dialogue."[53]

Lynch's way of not spelling out plot details for his audience, and his artistic collaborators, stimulated Naomi to come up with some interesting *Mulholland Drive* interpretations. She feels that the two men in Winkie's diner, the fellow listening to his friend telling of his scary dream, are a psychiatrist and his patient. And for her the blue box "is Diane's mind. The box is opened, and out comes all the horrible darkness of her psychosis. She can't face this part of herself, so that's why her dream self, pure sweet Betty with everything wonderful, disappears from the room before the box opens."[54] Naomi says, "Sometimes I wonder if Diane is the Bum at the end. To me the Bum represents darkness, the depths to which you can sink."[55] Naomi was very much in tune with Lynch's narrative-aesthetic method of having people, things, and event express a character's state of mind and emotions. "They say that in your dreams you are everything and every person, the leg of every table, the textures of the fabrics that people wear. All the energy that goes into your dream comes from your subconscious, and *Mulholland Drive* is composed of Diane's outer and inner stories."[56]

Lynch and Watts may have communicated with almost telepathic ease, but when it came to one of the film's major scenes, there was confusion in the air. It was time to film the climax, when Diane, wracked with guilt and fear, is chased by the old couple and, as Naomi says,

> You hear a gun shot. I said to David, "Wait a minute. Is this me shooting them or am I shooting myself? Or is the couple shooting Diane? I'm not sure what it means." There was a long pause. He scratched his head. I'd posed a question he really had to think about. Usually when you question him he has everything already worked out, and he smiles cause he knows what he's doing and he's not going to give it away. This time it struck him that perhaps he was creating more mystery for the viewer than even he was comfortable with, throwing things off-balance. We shot the scene various ways. Once I just scrambled for the gun. Then I said, "How about if I do this?" I picked up the gun and put it in my mouth. He saw that image, and I think he liked it. It's such an image of self-loathing, as raw as you can get. So we filmed it that way too. When you see the finished film, there's so much smoke in the room that it makes you wonder what's happening. But I feel it's definitely Diane shooting herself. That is the end of the story of Diane's life.[57]

And the Blue-Haired Lady—does she exist beyond/outside of Diane's story? Naomi feels that's "a really good question. I saw the Blue-Haired Lady and 'Silencio' as something metaphysical, symbolic, representational. Everything's silent now. Diane can be quiet now. All the shit going around her no longer exists. She kills herself because she couldn't cope, couldn't function in her life. She needed that silence."[58]

Regarding the idea that *Mulholland Drive* is Lynch's most L.A.-centric film, Naomi said, "I've always been shocked and surprised by how much David loves Los Angeles. Most people have mixed feelings about the place. Though he doesn't leave his house much, so he's not exposed to the everyday goings on in the city. He holds on to how Hollywood was, how he remembers it from movies and things he's read: He taps into the old mythology he loves."[59]

Despite Lynch's reputation for being a stay-at-home type, Naomi invited him to her birthday party. "Everyone said he wouldn't come, but he did."[60] Aside from being forever grateful to him on a professional level ("I'm spoiled for working with other directors now; he's a hard act to follow" [61]), Naomi enjoys a friendship with him and treasures the advice he gives her. Though he doesn't like to be thought of as a father-figure to her: "he'd prefer 'uncle.'"[62] Sometimes she gives him helpful hints. Lynch has had a lot of back trouble, and one day when he was hurting she said, "You should wear a magnet. They say it changes the electro-magnetic balance in your system. I knew someone with chronic back pain who got better with magnets. He got excited: 'Oh, really, really?' Then he paused, his eyes narrowed, and he said, 'I don't know about that, Naomi. It might take away my ideas.'"[63]

In addition to living inside Diane's emotional torment, Naomi suffered some physical pain of her own while making *Mulholland Drive*. Lynch set up the scene where Betty and Rita return from Club Silencio and are in the bedroom together. "David said to me as Betty, 'You have to disappear, to suddenly not be here.' I said to myself, 'Why?' I didn't know, and David didn't say."[64] In order to maximize the mystery of Betty's departure, he wanted to film this occurrence in a single unbroken take, with no camera tricks or edits. Given the small space in which they were filming, Naomi had only one escape route that the camera wouldn't see. "I had to do a backwards somersault over the bed. I tried it three times and everything was fine. But the fourth time I put my neck out of whack, and had to wear a brace for awhile."[65]

Despite all her travails, Naomi says,

> I burn to play this complex a role again. David is a sensitive artist. He feels everything in an extreme way and that's why he's so good at what he does, why his work produces a visceral response in the viewer. His outlook on life is that of a creative person, so he hates to be controlled or stifled. He wants to get ideas, to build and grow, search, and explore. He delves into darkness to find humor, sexuality, and the seat of creativity. And he knows that some of the best things in life are things that can't be explained. There's nothing literal and linear about many of his films, including *Mulholland Drive*. It's an expression of the whole human psyche. We who work with him are conduits sending out messages from David's mind, his truth. Diane is like a symbol of the absolutely darkest place.
>
> Like all of us, David likes praise. If there's a positive reaction at a screening, he lights up. He's like the little kid who gets the ice cream he wanted. But I think what gratifies him most is that his films are alive, first for him, then for others. People interpret them, argue about them, think about them. They live on. That's his whole endeavor.[66]

I stayed in touch with Naomi, chatting with her when she was up in the Northwest shooting *The Ring* and being buffeted by some of the worst No-

Naomi Watts overlooks Seattle, September 2001.

vember-December weather we'd ever had (none of the film's gloomy skies and downpours were created by computers). One late afternoon I caught her as she bobbed around in a small boat on thrashing Puget Sound waters, being lashed with rain and wind. With a plucky laugh she said, "I can take it. I'm English."[67] Then her other, Australian, homeland came to mind and she added, "But I can't wait to immerse myself in the ocean"[68]: The warm Tasman Sea of Sydney was her Christmas destination. And she'd get to be with her family and best pal, Nicole Kidman. Kidman has known Naomi since they were teenagers and has given her stalwart support and encouragement through the worst of personal and professional times, always recognizing her talent and telling her "all you need is one big break."[69] Naomi is modest, and it embarrasses her to talk about how good an actress she is. But once she said that, "Nicole visited the *Mulholland Drive* set one day and watched us shoot some scenes. After we were done, she came up to me and said, 'You are *so* Betty. You take my breath away.'"[70]

Mulholland Drive brought Lynch some of the best reviews of his career; the film and Watts' acting, placed high on many critics' best-of-the-year lists. In January 2002, Naomi called me, nervous about the fact that she'd been tapped by the National Society of Film Critics to present David with their Best Film award at an exclusive dinner ceremony in New York. Her task involved making a short introductory speech, and she wondered what I thought would be some good points to touch on. I told her to think of the speech as some work she was doing for David, just like being in the film. To see it as a part of her journey, like portraying the arc of a character she was playing. I faxed her some thoughts about Lynch's career, and off she flew to the east. Later, on TV, I saw a shot of her and Lynch emerging from the award soiree in New York. They were both smiling and carrying prizes (Naomi was voted Best Actress). When I asked Lynch how Naomi's speech had gone, his words seemed to sum up everything she meant to him as a collaborator and friend: "She did a beautiful job."[71]

Naomi Watts' performance as Betty and Diane was universally celebrated, garnering much Oscar buzz, but she ended up not being nominated (her pal Nicole Kidman was nominated for *Moulin Rouge*). Among the accolades she did win was the Sappho Award for Best Actress from the lesbian-culture magazine *Girlfriends*. Though Watts had been acting for years, she seemed newly minted, her complex performance unprecedented in revealing depths and nuances of female psychology. Once again, Lynch heard professional commentators and average moviegoers summing up his work with the same words they'd used for thirty years: "I've never seen anything like it."

Lynch is indeed a trailblazer, an auteur with a unique vision, but like any artist curious about, and enthralled by, the world around him, he processes the work of other painters, writers, musicians, and filmmakers through his brain, if only subconsciously. Lynchian folklore incorrectly maintains that he doesn't read books or see other directors' films: He may not consume massive quantities of cinema and reading matter like Quentin Tarantino, but he's no stranger to DVD players and printed pages. Lynch's first wife, Peggy, has told me that when her husband was an early 1970s American Film Institute student he would come home after film screenings and tell her about the movies in great detail, thus sharpening his sensitivity to story structure, dramatic balance, imagery, and visual narrative. (Ironically, a film that Lynch loved to talk about in the period when he was unfaithful to Peggy was Claude Chabrol's 1969 *La Femme Infidele*.)

Early in his career, everyone said Lynch *must* have been influenced by the great Spanish surrealist director Luis Buñuel (1900–1983), but at that time he hadn't seen any of the master's films. And I've often wondered if Lynch viewed the films of pioneering American avant-gardist Maya Deren (1917–1961), whose lyrically subjective, consciousness-manifesting pictures alter time and space and intermix dream and reality as hypnotically as Lynch's do. When I asked him in 2004 if he had experienced Deren's work, or even heard of her, he said, "No."[72] Of course, it's possible for two artists to independently explore similar territory fifty years apart from each other.

Deren's *Meshes of the Afternoon* (1943), like *Mulholland Drive*, is the inner emotional journey of a dead Hollywood woman, and features a metal key as a signifier of violent death.

Lynch's reverence for artistic independence and integrity prompts him to say that consciously taking another person's ideas would be "like eating somebody else's food."[73] Lynch prides himself on being able to generate his own thematic and aesthetic concepts, but he understands that sometimes his preoccupations parallel or echo those of another artist, and he speaks of "identifying with someone else's ideas"[74] and how "thoughts and ideas come during the filmmaking process, and it doesn't matter where they originated."[75] Lynch loves the feverish spontaneity of art-making, and when a sudden inspiration grips him, he doesn't analyze it and comb through the Internet and a list of footnotes to find out where it came from. Because "ninety percent of the time while I'm making a film I don't know what I'm doing,"[76] Lynch feels that, subconsciously, he *thinks* he's been influenced by other artists. The vagaries of human memory are also a factor in maintaining Lynch's foggy view of his creative process, for I've discovered in conversations that he doesn't always recall the details of films he's seen and liked in the past. When Lynch was in production on the DVD for *Blue Velvet*, he viewed slides of scenes that had been deleted from the release version of the film, and he realized that he'd forgotten having shot some of them.

Director Steven Soderbergh (*sex, lies, and videotape*; *Kafka*; *Out of Sight*; *Ocean's 11*) says he suffers from anxiety about being influenced by other directors. This is one fear that does not plague Lynch. The great Warner Brothers cartoon animator-director Chuck Jones (*Bugs Bunny*, *Daffy Duck*, *Wile E. Coyote*, *Roadrunner*) consciously knew that he based some of his characters and their actions on Charlie Chaplin, Douglas Fairbanks, and Zsa Zsa Gabor. Animator Matt Groening realizes that Chuck Jones' *The Three Bears* was a thematic source for Groening's *The Simpsons*. But Lynch, with absolute sincerity, does not remember most of the likely influences on his films.

The way Lynch presented Renee Madison's corpse in *Lost Highway* seems to be inspired by the photographs of nude, segmented murder victim Elizabeth Short ("The Black Dahlia") in Kenneth Anger's book *Hollywood Babylon II*. The darker aspects of *Mulholland Drive* echo Anger's Hollywood-dream-gone-sour tone in *Hollywood Babylon II* and *Hollywood Babylon*. Anger quotes early horror-film actor Lionel Atwill speaking words that encapsulate Lynch's fascination with the duality of human nature. "*See*—one side of my face is gentle and kind, incapable of anything but love. The other side, the other profile, is cruel and predatory and evil, incapable of anything but lusts and dark passions. It all depends on which side of my face is turned toward you—*or the camera*."[77] (Atwill was voicing his personal beliefs, not talking as one of the characters he played.) Anger's chapter title "Two Faces of Tinseltown"[78] could be *Mulholland Drive*'s subtitle. Anger chronicles various Hollywood lesbian relationships and names another chapter "The Magic of Self Murder."[79] Anger devoted a two-page spread to the Black Dahlia's body parts, and he gives similar large-scale coverage to an image that could have inspired the second shot of *Mulholland Drive*. Anger's photograph of the bed Marilyn Monroe committed suicide in, with its lumpy pillow and lonely, disheveled sheets, could easily be the archetype for Lynch's shot of future suicide Diane Selwyn's empty bed, which was accompanied by the mournful sound of her depressed, sighing breathing.

Anger quotes some dialogue from the 1934 musical *Moulin Rouge* that sounds like a blueprint for the bubbly-Betty-to-anguished-Diane arc of *Mulholland Drive*. A young woman laments: "Oh, I guess it's an old story. . . . There was a beauty contest in Little Rock. I won it."[80] (As Betty won her dance contest.) "Came to Hollywood to win fame. Instead—I'm on Hollywood Boulevard at two in the morning. And no place to go (sob). I thought Hollywood was a boulevard of beautiful dazzling dreams."[81] Dick Powell responds, "But I'm afraid you're *dead* wrong!," and then sings: "I walk along the street of sorrow/The Boulevard of Broken Dreams."[82] Elsewhere Anger characterizes the double reality of Hollywood: "It was *Dreamland*" (we recall Betty's "I'm in this *dream* place"), and also a place of "ever present thrilling-erotic *fear* that the bottom could drop out of the gilded dream at any time."[83]

The final resonant correspondence between Anger's books and Lynch's film is a photo of a dead woman lying on rumpled sheets and pillow. This is Marie Prevost, a fading silent screen star who drank herself to death and was found stone cold in "her seedy apartment,"[84] as was Diane Selwyn. Also like Lynch's fictional Diane, Marie hailed from Ontario, Canada. Lynch may have first become aware of both the Black Dahlia and Marie Prevost when these victims of Hollywood were mentioned in *Sunset Boulevard*, and later incorporated them into his work, just as Billy Wilder may have chosen to have *Sunset Boulevard*'s Joe Gillis reside in the Aldo Nido Apartments before moving to the site of his murder, after hearing that Elizabeth Short, the Black Dahlia, lived there a few years before Wilder shot his film.

The archetypal fiction chronicling the absurd gulf between Hollywood's soaring dreams and sordid actualities is Nathaniel West's (1903–1940) *The Day of the Locust* (1939). When a French journalist told Lynch that

Mulholland Drive reminded him of West's legendary novel, the director accepted the compliment with pride and said he loved West's book. West's portrayal of Hollywood as a town dedicated to gossamer make-believe and cold, hard cash, a soul-killing place that disregards the high human cost of frantically chasing success, is certainly in the spirit of Lynch's film.

Lynch, who is galvanized by synchronicity, felt *The Day of the Locust* speaking to him beginning with page one, for the book's protagonist (Tod Hackett), like Lynch, is a painter. And both Tod and Lynch are drawn to subject matter festering on the fringes of polite society: lonely figures with thwarted dreams, people nurtured on bitterness and suppressed fury, victims and perpetrators of crimes of the heart, those who can't control sudden spasms of sex and violence.

Tod incorporates the vacant-eyed, resentful, silently raging people he sees on the margins of Hollywood society into an apocalyptic painting called *The Burning of Los Angeles*. Like Lynch, he cathartically transforms his fears and dark thoughts into art "to escape tormenting myself."[85] West's vision of Hollywood is unrelentingly corrosive and despairing, whereas Lynch expresses his love for "the city of dreams" in *Mulholland Drive*, as well as his skepticism and animus.

A major parallel between *The Day of the Locust* and *Mulholland Drive* is the focus on an actress character who's positioning herself for a fast climb to the top. At one point *The Day of the Locust*'s Faye Greener seems to sum up the trajectory of *Mulholland Drive*'s Diane Selwyn in two sentences: "I'm going to be a star some day"[86]; "If I'm not, I'll commit suicide."[87] Like Camilla Rhodes, Faye both enthralls people with her beauty, sensuality, and charm, and plans to give her love to someone who can advance her career. If you're not Mr. Big (as Adam Kesher is for Camilla), watch out, because falling for Faye can be dangerous: "Her invitation wasn't to pleasure, but to struggle, hard and sharp, closer to murder than to love."[88] This sentence certainly characterized the dynamic of Camilla and Diane's souring relationship. And as Faye becomes bored and wants to move onward and upward beyond someone who loves her but can't hold onto her, she, as Camilla does to Diane, sadistically flaunts her attraction to someone new right in the loser's face. When Faye has trouble making ends meet, she falls back on her back, prostituting herself to help her get what she ultimately wants, as do (Lynch implies) Diane and Camilla.

Like *Mulholland Drive*, *The Day of the Locust* presents a cowpoke of the canyons above Hollywood Boulevard who behaves in a formal manner, though he's not a supernatural oracle like Lynch's Cowboy. *Mulholland Drive*'s Cowboy has the power, the potential, to dish out trouble, whereas

Nathaniel West's Earle Shoop serves it up raw, lashing out at a man who's been teasing him. Tod Hackett finds "the seriousness of his violence"[89] funny, just as Lynch couldn't stop himself from laughing when a grave and intensely fervent Dennis Hopper (*Blue Velvet*) sexually assaulted Isabella Rossellini. In Lynch's world all-consuming love easily becomes dangerously obsessive (as it does for *Lost Highway's* Fred Madison), and in *The Day of the Locust* West speaks of passion's power to destroy. Fred is bedeviled by his possessive desire for his wife: his head is hot with jealousy and rage, which Lynch visualizes as a house burning down. While in *The Day of the Locust* West compares a man being swept away by out-of-control feelings for a woman to "dropping a spark into a barn full of hay."[90]

Aside from correspondences with *Mulholland Drive*, *The Day of the Locust* displays other similarities to Lynch's world. There are red curtains, a railroad hotel (*Hotel Room*), a person has "a whole set of personalities, one inside the other,"[91] two young women become prostitutes for a madam (like Laura Palmer and Ronette Polaski at *Twin Peaks'* One-Eyed Jack's), a backstage world of props, scenery, and costumed people is a surrealistic jumble of mismatched landscapes, time periods, and cultures, as is *On the Air's* TV-production realm. A man wants to tear another man's ear off (*Blue Velvet*), people possessed by a "demonic"[92] force are likened to animals, a man feeling confused and emotionally "washed out"[93] sits on the edge of his bed staring into space like Henry in *Eraserhead*.

Lynch was clearly dwelling within a *Sunset Boulevard/Hollywood Babylon*/L.A. noir mindset when he was creating his *Mulholland Drive* TV pilot and film. It isn't likely that he happened to see a low-budget 1975 picture called *Gemini Affair*, but if he did, it could have had a subconscious influence on *Mulholland Drive* twenty-six years later. Both films begin with an aspiring blonde actress from the Midwest coming to Hollywood hoping to realize her dreams. Both have two blonde women living in the same abode, which is available because its owner is traveling. In each film the actress seems to be warmly appreciated by film industry authority figures, then rejected. In *Mulholland Drive* the actress performs in a steamy audition scene with a silver-haired man named Woody; in *Gemini Affair* the actress, trying the lifestyle of her call-girl housemate, turns a trick with a silver-haired man named Woody. Both films' actress characters have sex with their female bedmates, though this doesn't begin a love affair in *Gemini Affair*, as it does in Lynch's film. *Gemini Affair's* actress character is disturbed by this tryst and confused about her sexuality. After an emotional outburst on the subject, she apologizes for "acting like Camille," referring to author Alexandre Dumas' tragic heroine who was famously portrayed by Greta Garbo in a 1937 film. (It's a short drive from "Camille" to *Mulholland Drive*'s "Camilla"). The survival sense of *Gemini Affair*'s actress is stronger than that of *Mulholland Drive*'s Diane Selwyn: she sours on the Hollywood life and heads back to her small-town home.

Mulholland Drive also shows the possible influence of Herk Harvey's intriguing low-budget 1962-horror film *Carnival of Souls*. Lynch's film, like Harvey's begins with a car full of teenagers practicing dangerous driving and crashing. *Carnival of Souls*' vehicle falls into a river, and three hours later a young woman who'd been in the car emerges from the water, to the amazement of the assembled townsfolk and police who've been searching for bodies. The woman's name is Mary Henry, a conflation of *Eraserhead*'s lead characters' names that Lynch would have seen as an enticing synchronicity. Like *Mulholland Drive*'s Rita, Mary "doesn't remember" what happened. Like *Mulholland Drive*'s Betty, Mary is a gifted artist (a master organ player) who travels west to perform her art professionally.

In the last seconds of *Carnival of Souls* we realize that Mary, like *Mulholland Drive*'s Diane, has been dead all along, and that her trip to Salt Lake City and activity there have been a mental construct of her dying or after-death consciousness. Screenwriter John Clifford has Mary speak some double-meaning dialogue that refers to her dual alive/dead status before the viewer learns of it. Confronting a wooden gate, Mary says, "It would be easy to step around this barrier," just as, unbeknownst to us, she has stepped around the barrier of a fatal car to enact the narrative we're seeing. And Mary's "I want to satisfy myself that this place is nothing more than it seems to be" hints at the multiplicity of reality and the hidden nature of truth that's at the core of *Carnival of Souls*, and is the heart of Lynch's view of life and art.

In Salt Lake City, Mary stays in an apartment with a friendly landlady, like Betty does in *Mulholland Drive*. And, just as Betty thrills her potential employers with a knockout audition, Mary's organ playing greatly impresses the church minister. Mary's doings, like Betty's, are the psychic scenario of a dead person, and as both women experience "life," they get disquieting, scary reminders that something's not right, that there's some hidden, threatening reality behind their situations that they're not fully conscious of. A grandparently couple friendly to Betty begins to cackle with sinister intent, Betty trembles with fear when a performer appears to die onstage, and a supernatural Dark One, the Bum, infests the city with evil and makes young people drop dead. Mary has disturbing episodes in which she talks to people and they don't answer, and look right through her as though she's not there. (In Lynch's *Lost Highway* script, when Fred is living his fantasy life as Pete, there are moments when other characters can't see him.) When Mary is practicing a devotional organ piece at the church her hands seem possessed, and play eerie tones that the minister calls "blasphemous." And like Betty, Mary's psychodrama is haunted by a Dark One, a pasty-white-faced man whose presence terrifies her (this figure seems to be kin of *Lost Highway*'s white-faced Mystery Man). And, just as *Mulholland Drive*'s Bum and grandparently couple eventually push Diane through death's door, so does Mary's *Carnival of Souls* cadaverous phantom "prevent me from living,"

Experiencing the world we all live in with an artist's sensibility, Lynch lets his intuition ("that's thinking and feeling combined"[94]) focus on the elements "that feel correct, that talk to me,"[95] and then links and shapes them into works of art that no one's ever seen before. Throughout his career Lynch has not calculatingly pored over other director's films. Thinking, "Let's see, I'll throw in a dollop of *Persona*, sprinkle in a bit of *La Strada*, and warm with some *Lolita* heat." When Lynch is actively creating, he likes to be in a mode of spontaneous discovery. "My reasoning mind doesn't say, 'What the hell am I doing?' Making films is a subconscious thing. Words get in the way. Rational thinking gets in the way. It can stop you cold. Film has a great way of giving shape to the subconscious, when it comes out in a clear stream, from some other place."[96]

It does not diminish Lynch's unique artistry to note some correspondences between his images and themes and those of films, and a book, we know he's seen and appreciated.

Lynch had his first movie experience in 1952 at age six, when he saw *Wait Till the Sun Shines, Nellie* (Henry King, 1952) with his family. We can easily predict which two scenes he remembers to this day: a little girl accidentally swallows a button, her father panics, her little brother screams and yells, and the dog adds its continuous barking to the cacophony; and a man reclining in a barber's chair for a relaxing shave is killed by machine gun fire that suddenly comes blasting through the shop's front window. Situations in which a realm of safety is invaded by chaos have fascinated Lynch throughout his life, and he still responds to them in other directors' films. In 2002, he excitedly told me about a scene in Gregory Nava's *Selena* (1997), the biography of the twenty-four-year-old Tejano superstar singer who was shot to death by her female fan club president. The moments that captivate Lynch occur at Selena's (Jennifer Lopez) huge outdoor concert in Mexico. The singer, her guitar-playing boyfriend, and her overflow audience are bubbling with joy as she performs her most popular song, spinning and prancing back and forth. But in the next second the plywood stage is splitting and lurching beneath her feet, the crowd pressing forward, pinning a woman beneath the stage front as the happy music stops and screams fill the air.

Lynch consciously recalls the scary parts of *Wait Till the Sun Shines, Nellie*, but the film contains other details that relate to his work. The picture, which takes place in the late-1800s Midwest, is a small-town, neighborhood story (*Blue Velvet*, *Twin Peaks*, *The Straight Story*). The starfield of a night sky is emphasized (*Eraserhead*, *The Elephant Man*, *Industrial Symphony No. 1*, *Sun Moon Stars* commercial, *The Straight Story*). A man is nervous and agitated about his wife having a baby (Lynch's own life, *Eraserhead*). Lynch has emphasized the color blue throughout his career, and *Nellie* features a woman wearing a brilliantly blue dress who stands up at a party and whistles bird song in a moment of small-town surrealism. Another key Lynchian color, especially in his films, is red, which he often iconically relates to women in the forms of lipstick and/or blood, and *Nellie* has a woman prominently applying red lip rouge. *Nellie*'s central emotional dynamic, in which one person's freedom and aspirations are curtailed and squelched by a powerful, dominating individual, is certainly familiar to Lynch-watchers, and as in *Eraserhead* and *Twin Peaks: Fire Walk With Me*, the sound of a far-off night train whistle has the ring of potential escape to an entrapped soul.

As in most of Lynch's fictions, two of *Wait Till the Sun Shines, Nellie*'s characters are having a secret emotional relationship behind the back of someone who trusts them. The film, like *Blue Velvet*, features a young-adult son character who's drawn into a netherworld of morally suspect behavior. *Nellie* first showed Lynch the image of a stage with draped curtains, a church at night with its windows lit up (as in *Blue Velvet*), and a flaming wooden structure being tended by firefighters (*The Straight Story*). Like *Blue Velvet*, *Nellie* ends with a sense of darkness banished and wholesome small-town values reaffirmed, though a woman paid a terrible price in the process.

The children's book *Good Times on Our Street* (Gates, Huber, Peardon, Salisbury, 1945), which Lynch says he cherished "about a hundred years ago,"[97] is a compendium of the benign spirit and imagery of his boyhood life, and a key to themes and motifs in his adult artwork.

On the first page, we find a tree-lined street of a small town that's surrounded by woods: the archetypal setting for many "neighborhood stories"[98] to come. Naturally, the welcoming front yards are bounded by white picket fences, against which brightly colored flowers bloom. The boy protagonist (wearing a horizontal-striped T-shirt like young Lynch did) always has a girl companion, with whom he experiences exciting adventures, at his side.

The book's town is full of appealing little shops like the hardware stores in *Blue Velvet* and *The Straight Story*, and blue-collar workplaces like *Twin Peaks'* gas station and *Lost Highway*'s car repair shop. The presence of smiling firemen and child guardians recalls the opening and closing of *Blue Velvet*. The book's way of calling characters The Little Boy, The Grocery Man, The Bread Man, and The Farmer's Wife probably inspired Lynch's method of giving some of his characters names (The Boy, The Man From Another Place, Curious Woman, Little Girl) that have the evocative resonance of archetypes.

An episode in the book is a forerunner of the scenes in Lynch's fictions (especially *Blue Velvet*'s ending) where people get together, the human and natural worlds are in harmonious balance, and all is right with the world. At the conclusion of one *Good Times on Our Street* story, characters gather on the grass to share food and radiate their love for each other. The similar concluding backyard communion in *Blue Velvet* is preceded by a huge close-up of a robin on a branch, the bird signifying the triumph of light and love over darkness and evil (malevolence symbolized by the black insect in the bird's beak). After showing the close view of the robin, Lynch has his young hero and heroine gaze out the window at it in wonder. The director's use of this robin motif is a prime example of the way a long-buried, forgotten memory "can be released into your conscious mind, and it seems like a new idea."[99] For as a six-year-old, looking at *Good Times on Our Street*, Lynch saw a full-page illustration of a robin on a branch. On the next page, the book's boy and girl peer at it from their window with enchanted looks on their faces. The book speaks of the robins' springtime return as a breath of fresh air, the end of the dark season, the flourishing of new life. In Lynch's film the birds are first spoken of regarding the heroine's dream of long-absent robins returning like a blessing to their benighted town. The birds in *Good Times on Our Street* hold no devilish bugs in their beaks, but in the book's only instance of violence and pain, a boy is repeatedly stung by insects.

Remaining in the animal kingdom, the book presents a twenty-page story about elephants, which contains a picture of a pachyderm looking angry and scary, like the nightmarish elephant that menaced Mrs. Merrick in *The Elephant Man*. And did *Good Times on Our Street*'s trickster monkey and the frequently mentioned name of the book's leading female character ("Judy")[100] combine in Lynch's subconscious to produce *Twin Peaks: Fire Walk With Me*'s mysterious monkey whispering, "Judy"?

The kids in the book have plenty of playtime, but *Good Times on Our Street* also emphasizes that work can be fun, especially when you pursue your heart's desire. Like Lynch's father did with David, the book's Father shows the main boy character, Jim, how to organize and carry out a project using wood and tools. Jim and young Lynch both want to devote themselves to making things with their minds and hands.

The Wizard of Oz (Victor Fleming, 1939), which Lynch has seen many times from boyhood on, maps major portions of his artistic territory. With its opening-credit cloudy sky and evocative wind sounds, the film vividly conveys the enthralling, transportive power of cinema, a force that director Lynch, with the help of some of that same whooshing wind, communicates so well. And, in *Oz*'s sepia-toned opening moments, as Dorothy walks down a desolate-seeming, farm-country dirt road, Lynch felt the quiet magic of "America's nowhere places"[101] touch him, and he absorbed the sense of film, and life, as being a road trip, a journey, a quest. The rounded shapes of brown earth that flank Dorothy's road and form humps in her aunt and uncle's farmyard seem to answer Lynch's lifelong question of where his "love of mounds of dirt"[102] comes from. The barren, denuded trees that adorn Lynch's drawings and paintings, animations (drawn and computer-generated), and films also populate the landscape of Dorothy's Kansas. If we note the gaunt, leafless tree sprouting from the earth mounded over the Gales' storm cellar, we see a prototype of *Eraserhead* Henry's bedside earth-mound-with-bare-tree-branch, which today Lynch displays like a sculpture in his home.

Lynch took to heart *The Wizard of Oz*'s narrative dynamic of having a sympathetic character overwhelmed by darkness, assaulted and trapped by forces more powerful than her, and in desperate need of a way out. Like Lynch and so many of his characters, Dorothy is a dreamer, and she showed young David that having the imagination to envision a brighter tomorrow, and the courage to go out and find it, can transform the mundane and threatening world into a charmed and rewarding place. The possibility of a magical deliverance from trouble and pain thrilled Lynch as he first watched *The Wizard of Oz*, as did the idea that the means of attaining it was mysterious: "you can't get there by a boat or plane; it's far away beyond the moon, beyond the rain." After Dorothy sings her reverie of yearned-for escape ("Somewhere, Over the Rainbow"), we hear birdsong and see glowing shafts of light break through dark clouds, a passage which could easily have inspired *Blue Velvet*'s Sandy's recitation about robins and the pure light of love banishing the evil of her small town.

One of the most influential concepts Lynch absorbed from *The Wizard of Oz* was the idea that Dorothy's vivid, super-detailed adventures in the

Land of Oz take place within her own mind, yet are as real as life—they *are* her life. The emotional authenticity and dramatic validity of Dorothy's dream journey showed Lynch the wondrous way that film scenarios can externalize a character's psychic conflicts and interior narrative: the portal to the greatest storyland of exploration and discovery is the human head. In Lynch's cranial-centric cinema characters often receive head wounds, and Dorothy's trip begins with a bump on her noggin. Throughout his career, Lynch has been fascinated by the idea of multiple selfhood, which *The Wizard of Oz* visualizes with Dorothy's single face becoming many as she slips into dreamland. (Lynch has Betty's and Rita's faces flutter multitudinously in *Mulholland Drive*.)

The Wizard of Oz is a resonant parable about a child learning to grow up and cope with a world that's both "not very nice" and "beautiful," and Lynch reflects its core dynamic in *Blue Velvet* as Jeffrey comes to see that life can be "horrible" as well as "great." Dorothy's surrogate parents are weak and unable to keep evil at bay (like Jeffrey's folks), so she has to take action. In her dream she confronts the Wicked Witch, which represents her own capacity for darkness (as does *Blue Velvet*'s Frank Booth for Jeffrey), and destroys her nemesis (as Jeffrey does), thus affirming her ability to choose goodness. In her dream, Dorothy's self-perceived lack of a smart-thinking brain, a feeling heart, and courage to act for what's right are externalized as the needy Scarecrow, Tin Man, and Cowardly Lion. At story's end she's fully integrated, realizing that she already possesses, and has exercised, the inner-resource qualities she needs to get home: The house of her psyche is resoundingly in order and able to withstand the most wicked Kansas twister.

Secrets and revelations drive Lynch's fictions, and a key Lynchian moment occurs in *The Wizard of Oz* when the great and powerful Wizard is discovered to be not a fearsome giant head surrounded by fire and smoke, but a non-supernatural man hiding behind a curtain, pulling levers. This showman who creates illusions is a metaphor for what Lynch does with his life: dreaming up realities and using technology (movie cameras, paint brushes) to project them onto screens and canvases. The way that the Oz Show director is hidden behind a masking curtain reinforced Lynch's sense that there are veiled realities working behind/beneath the obvious ones we perceive, concealed forces pulling the strings of our lives. *Eraserhead*'s lever-pulling Man in the Planet, *Twin Peaks*' Leland-possessing BOB, and *Lost Highway*'s Mystery Man are certainly kin to *The Wizard of Oz*'s man behind the curtain.

Other *Wizard of Oz* elements are reflected in Lynch's work. Dorothy asks a seminal question: "Are you a good witch or a bad witch?" just as *The*

Elephant Man's Treves wonders, "Am I a good man or a bad man?" and *Blue Velvet*'s Sandy ponders whether Jeffrey is "a detective or pervert?" As Dorothy proceeds into the Land of Oz she has to learn the place's special physical and metaphysical properties, its games and rules, and the balance of its powers, just as do many of Lynch's stranger-in-a-strange-land protagonists. As in Lynchland, there are dark forests with creepy trees (complete with a spooky owl), threatening fires in various forms, and menacing animalism (in the Wicked Witch's subhuman flying monkeys.) In *The Wizard of Oz*, a sudden snowfall, provided by angel figure Glinda the Good Witch, saves Dorothy and her friends, just as an unexpected rainfall blesses the ending of *Dune*, and showers of space dust do in *Eraserhead* and *Industrial Symphony No. 1*. Glinda's snow drifted down after the suffering characters entreated the skies for help, just as, in *Twin Peaks: Fire Walk With Me*, Ronette Pulaski is released from a dire predicament after praying to her angel for help.

There's a harbinger of Lynch's characteristic emphasis on the colors blue and red in an iconic close-up of Dorothy's blue ankle socks and ruby-red slippers. And the lightning-shaped sparks that the slippers emit, beyond showing Lynch the power hidden within objects, have zapped the air in a number of the director's films and TV shows, lent their form to the patterns of floors, and leapt from the electric guitar Lynch plays in his website *Thank You Judge* music video. The Wicked Witch, like *Dune*'s Baron Harkonnen, *Blue Velvet*'s Frank Booth, and *Twin Peaks*' BOB, is a villain who fiendishly enjoys her evil work. In the *Wizard of Oz*, she speaks words that could sum up the world as Lynch often sees it, with one pole of reality hidden inside another: "something with poison in it, but attractive to the eye."

The Wizard of Oz showed Lynch how affecting a happy ending based on a literal or metaphorical homecoming could be, and exemplified the dramatic power of a story that centered on the dark and light aspects of womankind.

Lynch admired *It's a Gift* (Norman Z. McLeod, 1934), one of grumpy funnyman W. C. Fields' best pictures, for its long, drawn-out comedy sequences that highlight the absurd interactions of people with each other, with objects, and the environments that surround them. Lynch has cited the film as an influence on his and Mark Frost's wacky TV series *On the Air* (1991–1992). The film also showed Lynch the importance of sound in a story, as Fields keeps mistaking the squeaking of a clothesline pulley for the squeaking of a mouse. As for specific correspondences between *It's a Gift* and Lynch's work, Fields' film contains a scene of a blind man and a sighted man entering a store. Just as when, in *Blue Velvet*, the two men (one blind) who comprise Double Ed come into Beaumont's hardware store, the two fellows in *It's a Gift* are side-by-side, shoulders touching, with the blind man bobbing his cane left-and-right as they advance toward us. With shades of Gordon Cole, the FBI character Lynch plays in *Twin Peaks*, the Fields film's blind man is severely deaf—and a detective.

One of Lynch's, and America's favorite movies, the Christmas tradition *It's a Wonderful Life* (Frank Capra, 1947), makes a very Lynchian revelation of darkness lurking within a sunny-seeming small town. And within protagonist George Bailey, played by America's' favorite cinematic son, the folksy, affable, modest James Stewart, to whom Lynch has often been compared.

Parallels between Capra's film and some of Lynch's movies also abound. In both *It's a Wonderful Life* and *Blue Velvet*, the young-man protagonist must forgo his dreams and college career and stay in his hometown to support his family after his father is removed from the picture. But by staying put George and Jeffrey have harrowing adventures and find loving, nurturing romantic partners, and in both films (thirty-nine years apart from each other), the men stroll tree-lined nocturnal sidewalks with the women who will eventually be their mates.

Both George and Jeffrey are products of loving, wholesome homes who discover toxic energies at work that threaten not only them but their entire town. *It's a Wonderful Life*'s Mr. Potter's hunger to control and monstrous web of hidden machinations are reflected in the dark, secret doings of *Blue Velvet*'s Frank Booth and his criminal cohorts; *Twin Peaks*' BOB, Ben Horne, and various co-conspirators, as well as in *Mulholland Drive*'s Bum, Mr. Roque, and the Castigliane brothers.

It's a Wonderful Life's George is a good-hearted, optimistic, cheerful person, but as his story develops, he reveals depths of regret, anger, and despair that make him choose suicide as the only way out. His stunning transition from radiance to shadow could well have influenced the similar character progressions of *Twin Peaks*' Agent Cooper and *Mulholland Drive*'s Betty Elms as they are assaulted by fear and guilt.

It's a Wonderful Life lets us see how bad things can be in its seemingly benign town when Clarence, an angel needing to earn his wings, enables the suicidal George to experience the scary film noir version of his town that would have existed if he had not been there to help hold back the night. *Blue Velvet*'s Jeffrey has no supernatural angel from Heaven to show him the proper path, but he *is* guided by the angelic Sandy, who gives Jeffrey a vision of potential redemption for their town that parallels angel Clarence showing George a hellish town future. The large amount of screen time devoted to George's visionary episode convinced Lynch that a character's experiences removed from normal reality could be gripping and dramatically valid, and could effectively portray the character's story and state of mind maybe even more powerfully than naturalistic narrative. Many Lynch films other than *Blue Velvet* show that he learned this lesson well.

When George Bailey is shown the vision of his town's sorry fate without his intervening presence, he's in an existential state that signifies ultimate terror in Lynch's world: "You have no identity." In *It's a Wonderful Life* both earthly and heavenly authority figures proclaim, "It's against the law to commit suicide," which is one of Lynch's strongest beliefs. And the film's belief in guardian angels and its portrayal of Heaven as a dark sky full of stars echoes throughout Lynch's work.

When George gets his life back, he's in an ecstasy of appreciation: Even the cut on his mouth and the freezing, snowy night seem like miracles. Watching *It's a Wonderful Life* as a young person, Lynch saw his way of perceiving the world as brimming with oversized fear, awe, and joy reflected in George Bailey's concluding attitude. For Lynch, years before he discovered Transcendental Meditation and Hinduism, a Hollywood movie gave him a model of the state of being enlightened.

Lynch has long been fascinated by Edward D. Wood Jr.'s *Glen or Glenda* (1953), a documentary-like meditation on the theme of men who clandestinely wear women's clothing—transvestism being the secret passion of Wood's own, heterosexual, life. Bearing in mind that Lynch, in his own films, often portrays people who live a second, hidden emotional-sexual life that those nearest to them don't know about, it's understandable that he would be drawn to *Glen or Glenda*.

The film opens with elements that would become seminal Lynchian motifs: flashes of light/lightning bolts and wind sounds. Wood's friend, actor Bela Lugosi (*Dracula*, 1931) plays a character who could easily be the inspiration for *Eraserhead*'s Man in the Planet: a powerful, cosmically controlling figure who mixes liquids in a beaker and says, "pull the string; a new life is begun," as we hear the wail of a newborn baby. This scene immediately reminds us of the Man in the Planet pulling leavers, thus plopping the rudimentary elements of a new human life into a liquid-mixing pool, which spawns Henry's crying mutant baby. Also rhyming with Lynch's film is a shot in which Glenda (who is Glen dressed up as his female self), wearing a big blond wig, silently gestures to his beloved by holding his hands out to her, then drawing them in to his chest and heart, as the blond Lady in the Radiator does to Henry in *Eraserhead*.

A key scene in Lynch's *The Elephant Man* (which is not in Dr. Frederick Treves' historical Elephant Man account or Bernard Pomerance's "The Elephant Man" play) evokes a dramatic moment in *Glen or Glenda*. Hounded by a taunting crowd leering at him, John Merrick is backed into a corner, but he courageously asserts his true essence ("I am not an animal! I am a human being!"). While in Wood's film, Glen, attired and groomed as Glenda, has a nightmare in which a harassing group backs him up against a wall, then retreats as he triumphantly advances toward the camera.

Lynch, with his sympathy for and identification with outsiders and misfits, naturally responded to *Glen or Glenda*'s plea for social tolerance and the right for consenting adults to express their particular psychosexual orientation in peace. But he couldn't help but crack a grin over the film's crazed tone, as a super-serious narrator's voice speaks about the tragedy of "a tough electrical factory worker having to conceal the fact the he's wearing pink satin undies." The film mirrors Lynch's preoccupation with the complexity of human identity, the way that one person can have multiple selves. In Lynch's world, one can actually be two, just as what seems to be two can really be one. In the final episode of *Twin Peaks*, Lynch has the Man From Another Place sum up this paradox with words spoken in *Glen or Glenda*: "one and the same." As Lynch well knows, and says in *Blue Velvet*, "It's a strange world," or, as Ed Wood says in *Glen or Glenda*, "The world is a strange place to live in."

Along with *The Wizard of Oz* and *Sunset Boulevard*, Alfred Hitchcock's *Rear Window* (1954) is high on Lynch's list of most loved films. The picture centers on James Stewart playing a photographer confined to his small Manhattan apartment and a wheelchair because of a broken leg. Stewart's neighbors keep their doors and windows open, providing a constant spectacle of human interaction for him to look at. His window, and all the others, face onto a large inner courtyard. This massive film set is not actually outdoors, yet rain falls, the sun shines, and the light changes from early morning to sunset to night; grass, trees, and flowers grow in the courtyard, dogs run around, and there are pigeons, and their droppings, on rooftops. Like the other movies lynch most reveres, *Rear Window* creates a world on film, which is always Lynch's highest goal in his own work. Hitchcock's artistry in *Rear Window* is especially close to Lynch's, because it presents a detailed reality that we recognize as commonplace, yet which tantalizes us with the feeling that it is, at the same time, unreal. Like the townscapes/cityscapes of *Blue Velvet*, *Twin Peaks* and *Twin Peaks: Fire Walk With Me*, *Lost Highway*, and *Mulholland Drive*, *Rear Window*, in its meticulous stylization, *evokes* reality and arouses a part of our consciousness receptive to dream and poetry.

Stewart, like Lynch and many fictional Lynch surrogates, is an artist-detective. Peering out his window, Stewart gathers evidence (the observed fragmentary views of other people's doings), and composes narrative surmises about the life paths his "characters" (neighbors) are following. Spying on the joys, loneliness, frustrations, and family strife of others keeps him interested day and night, but Stewart really gets focused when true darkness creeps into the picture.

There's been a disturbing change in the life-story of two "characters" Stewart's been observing. Through Stewart we've become familiar with the way salesman Thorwald (Raymond Burr) and his invalid wife (Irene Winston) argue and fight—and now Mrs. Thorwald's not there anymore.

Hitchcock, as Lynch loves to do, has engaged us with a recognizable, flavorful neighborhood that's maintaining a moral balance, and then served up a dizzying mystery, creating a need for someone to unearth hidden truths and restore order to the community. The person best positioned to challenge and vanquish evil forces is the one who's been spying on everyone. It's not surprising that *Rear Window* reminds us of *Blue Velvet*, for the two films share a number of intriguing parallels. Hitchcock's detective figure is named Jeffries, Lynch's is Jeffrey. In addition, Jeffrey, becoming involved in a mystery while peering out of a closet he's hiding in at a villain figure, is akin to Jeffries gazing out his apartment window at his villain (Jeffries pulls back into the shadows while watching, as though he's hiding).

Jeffrey's obsessional need to watch and follow the doings of certain individuals who are in trouble is seen as morally suspect by his blonde girlfriend (Sandy), who asks him, "Are you a detective or a pervert?" And Jeffries' blonde girlfriend, Lisa (Grace Kelly) tells him, "What you're doing is diseased" (in *Blue Velvet* Lynch also has a female character emphasize the word "disease" in reference to unsavory aspects of male psychology and behavior). Another friend of Jeffries could be talking about the universe of *Blue Velvet* when he says, "That's a secret, private world you're looking at; people do a lot of things they couldn't explain in public." Jeffrey, after finding a severed ear in a field, is thrilled to be "seeing things that were always hidden," as is Jeffries, who's now viewing a realm that was hidden from him until his broken leg made him stay indoors. *Blue Velvet*'s severed ear and *Rear Window*'s courtyard panorama are tickets to voyages of discovery for both films' protagonists, who solve their mysteries and gain self-knowledge about their sexual/emotional desires and needs.

Rear Window, which takes place in the pre-women's movement and pre-New Age movement 1950s, features a male police detective friend of Jeffries matter-of-factly saying, "That female intuition stuff's been overrated; it's a fairy tale." But Hitchcock, whose screenplays and artistic decisions were influenced for decades by his wife, Alma, knows better. It takes Lisa's hunches, along with Jeffries' empirical deductions, to solve *Rear Window*'s crime, a fact which may have influenced Lynch to combine intuitive skills and scientific inquiry in the character of *Twin Peaks*' Special Agent Dale Cooper.

The only TV show Lynch watched weekly while growing up was *Perry Mason*, in which hefty Raymond Burr played the iconic lawyer who defended truth, justice, and the American way. Seeing Burr transform from the familiar wholesome, dark-haired Perry Mason to *Rear Window*'s white-haired wife-murderer greatly impressed Lynch, and may have inspired *Twin Peaks*' good-then-evil Leland Palmer's hair-transition from dark to white.

Another aspect of Raymond Burr's presence in *Rear Window* may have influenced Lynch's art. Hitchcock's film presents narrative events that add up to a mystery: What happened to Burr's wife? This is, so to speak, the prose exposition that delineates an enigma, whereas a certain specific image in the film is pure poetry, is itself a mystery. The CinemaScope-shaped rectangle of Burr's window is dark, but we can make out shapes that compose a typical living room: a table, a lamp, a couch. Then, into this familiar tableau, from the bottom of the window frame, floats some thick, cloud-like masses of white smoke. In a few seconds, our rational brains tell us, *Oh, I see. Burr must be reclining below the window frame and smoking.* But before we realize this, the image is drenched in eeriness and dread, as though the wife-killer's malevolent spirit is haunting the room. Surely, this *Rear Window* smoke is the first puff of the sourceless pale smoke that wafts above a living-room couch on the cover of Lynch's book *Images* and floats disturbingly inside the house of Fred Madison's recounted dream in *Lost Highway*.

Federico Fellini's *La Strada* (1954), which chronicles the road trip of Gelsomina (Giulietta Masina), a sweet, simple-minded woman who travels the countryside performing, is, like *The Wizard of Oz*, a film that taught Lynch how compelling a story that takes the viewer on a journey can be. Fellini the master stylist entranced Lynch with the gritty poetry of desolate locations and decaying textures, and the breeze of mystery and wonder that wafts through a discarded, dilapidated world. (As in almost every one of Lynch's favorite films, wind sounds grace the audio track of *La Strada*.)

Gelsomina beautifully enacts Lynch's favored way of looking at the world with the eyes of a childlike innocent. Masina's artistry creates magical, poetic moments. Like a character from *Twin Peaks*, she stares into a nocturnal campfire and says, "Flame that sparkles, flame that shines, rise to the night sky, over the pines." And she carefully looks at a dusty little roadside garden plot as if she'd never seen plants growing before, then puts her ear up to a wooden utility pole, as though she can hear the hum of its electricity—the force that for Lynch is the pulse beat of the universe.

In a lyrical scene that grabbed Lynch's attention, Gelsomina encounters a boy with a hood over his larger-than-normal head. *Is his cranium devoid of sense, brimming with divine wisdom, full of something dangerous, fearsome?* Gelsomina and the boy stare into each other's faces for a moment of suspended mystery—then the nuns who are his caretakers shoo her out of the room, as though she's seen something forbidden. Awestruck, Gelsomina recounts her experience to Zampano with words that could have come from, or laid the groundwork for, Lynchland: "Such a head . . . hidden!"

There are motifs and moments in *La Strada* that seem to echo in Lynch's films. Lynch's penchant for signifying a character's villainy and evil through their animalistic behavior began with *The Grandmother*, when the Boy's domineering, insensitive parents vocalized like barking dogs: in Fellini's film, it is said of the beastly Zampano that "he's like a dog—a dog looks at you, wants to talk, but only barks." Gelsomina, with her broad face and fleshy cheeks framed by puffy blonde hair and forehead bangs, strikingly resembles *Eraserhead*'s Lady in the Radiator, especially when she gives a little shoulder-shrug of pleasure, just as the Radiator Lady does when stomping spermatozoid fetus forms underfoot. Odd gestures are favored by both Lynch (his *Twin Peaks: Fire Walk With Me* character, Gordon Cole, puts his hand on top of his head so that his fingers crown his forehead) and Fellini (Gelsomina pets her own shoulders, arms, and forehead bangs). The form and heartsick mood of a shot in which Gelsomina says goodbye to a friendly nun and heads off down the road with the gruff Zampano, the nun's centered figure shrinking as the camera pulls away, is mirrored in *The Straight Story* where Alvin Straight's daughter, full of worry about her father's journey, stands on their home lawn and fades in the distance as he drives off. Also, just as in *Twin Peaks*, *La Strada* is an affecting tale of a woman victimized by animalistic wildness, a woman accompanied by a sad and beautiful signature tune.

Stanley Kubrick's *Lolita* (1962), which Lynch calls "a perfect film,"[103] seems to have had a lasting influence on his work. The backdrop for *Lolita*'s credit sequence is a curtain with folds, which could have inspired the many curtains in Lynch's images. Lynch often speaks of wanting to "float"[104] the viewer into a mysterious, space-penetrating narrative experience, and *Lolita*'s first shot qualifies as an archetype of hypnotic drift, as the camera's point of view glides on and on down a road to who-knows-where, shrouded with white fog and dark trees.

Lolita contains such Lynchland standards as a white small-town picket fence; an eroticized reference to cherry pie; a man desired by both mother and daughter; a person trapped in an intolerable domestic relationship; people leading secret emotional lives; everyday activities (like answering a ringing phone) that take a long, long time; and an intense romantic obsession ("I want you to live with me and die with me and everything with me"). There's a mid-century-cool, dancing bohemian woman with black bangs who looks like the beatnik dancer in Lynch's *On the Air*, and a play titled "The Lady Who Loved Lightning"—certainly a woman after Lynch's heart. One character speaks of another's "twofold nature"; another has "an Oriental philosophy of life" and convincingly pretends to be a number of other people.

In *Lolita*, a man in a spiffy blazer has an encounter with a stuffed weasel, much as *Twin Peaks*' dandy Dick Tremayne confronts a pine weasel. When Leland Palmer has lost his teenage blonde daughter in *Twin Peaks*, he sits on her bed, weeps, and puts her pillow in his lap, recalling how *Lolita*'s Humbert Humbert, having lost his blonde teenage daughter-by-marriage, sits on her bed, weeps, and buries his face in her pillow. Of course, both Leland and Humbert harbor more than fatherly affection for their budding girls.

Federico Fellini's masterpiece *8 1/2* (1963) not only contains elements that repeatedly show up in Lynch's films, it mirrors Lynch's professional life more than any of his other favorite movies. *8 1/2* opens with a stunning condensation of the trapped-character-breaks-free dynamic that Lynch often plays out in his films. A man is in his car, which is stuck in an unmoving sea of cars that surrounds him on all sides. He can't get out of the jam or his car, the windows are fogging up, he can't breathe—then somehow he's floating above the quagmire, and up into the clouds. Guido (Marcello Mastroianni) is a famous film director overwhelmed by endless personal and professional problems and conflicts, and this opening sequence is clearly his fantasy of escape. In *8 1/2* Lynch saw how seamlessly a master filmmaker could integrate passages of dream, fantasy, and memory into the flow of a character's waking life, and how all the character's shifting aspects of consciousness comprise the person's essential truth, the full spectrum of their reality.

Lynch recognized Fellini as a kindred spirit, for the maestro believed that "everything is realistic. I see no dividing line between imagination and reality. I see a great deal of reality in imagination."[105] Like Lynch, Fellini seeks to explore "all that there is within a character, not just social reality, but spiritual reality, metaphysical reality."[106]

Lynch is famous for taking a long time to choose his film projects, while his public and associates wish he'd hurry up. Guido is in just such a state of indecision—intensified to the nth degree. The more people pester him with questions, the less he has to say, and when he speaks, he voices attitudes synonymous with Lynch's. An actress wants a dissertation on her character's motivation, and Guido answers, "You know more about that than I do," just as, Naomi Watts has told me, Lynch will tell an actor to "figure out"[107] the specifics of their character's essence. And when Guido's collaborators and the press hound him about plot details and how they add up to some ultimate meaning, he replies, "You don't have to know a thing."

The criticisms fired at Guido are the ones Lynch receives: "Your film is just a series of senseless episodes; their ambiguity is, perhaps, amusing, but what is your intention? To make us think? To frighten us?" Guido's producer understands that "you want the film to show the confusion and ambiguity man has inside himself." But he adds, "Just make sure that what interests you interests everybody. Remember, the audience has to understand the film!" Lynch feels that what captivates him does excite his fellow human beings, and that their capacity for "inner knowing"[108] allows them to comprehend what he's showing them, though it seems only a relatively small percentage of moviegoers are able to get and appreciate his message, and are even willing to buy a ticket for the chance to do so. *8 1/2* proclaims that Fellini's deepest concern is art-making, not money-grubbing: Having the courage to pursue and realize one's visions is of primary importance. In his 1963 film, he has a character speak words that Lynch, if he was more bombastic in his public pronouncements, could rightly say today: "I've been in this business for thirty years, and I've made pictures none of you have the guts to try!"

The film that everyone wants Guido to hurry up and proceed with is autobiographical, and since his personal life is in undecided disarray, he doesn't have the resolute sense of direction and focused energy that he needs to be creative. As Lynch has said of *Eraserhead*'s Henry (and himself): "he's lost in darkness and confusion."[109] Guido's shadowed with chaos, but Fellini gives him a vision of "order, purity, sincerity, innocence" in the form of a beautiful woman wearing a pale dress and bathed in white light. This stunning agent of redemption, hope, and love could well have inspired

Eraserhead's Lady in the Radiator (who brings solace and deliverance to Henry) and all the other female angel figures who grace Lynch's films.

Lost Highway's Fred's declaration that he likes to remember events his way, not necessarily the way they happened, recalls someone in *8 1/2* saying of Guido, "You show what suits you; the truth is another matter." Fellini is philosophical kin to Lynch, proclaiming in *8 1/2* that "we're already suffocated by words." And Fellini may have paid a visit to the Club Silencio of *Mulholland Drive* and communed with the Blue Lady, for an associate of Guido says, "An artist should swear an oath: 'Dedication to silence.'" Still, there is a time to speak. As *8 1/2* ends, Guido realizes he is a seeker who can live with the fact that he doesn't know all the answers, which is just the sort of character Lynch populates his fictions with. Guido's personal and creative energies are stirring again, and he is finally ready to fully engage with all the characters who fill his dreams and realities. It's time to start the show, so he picks up his bullhorn and calls "Action." The first sight that greets a visitor to the offices of Lynch's Asymmetrical Productions is a giant poster for *8 1/2*. Loving the film as he does, it's no wonder that Lynch uses a bullhorn to set in motion his imaginary/real scenes.

Swedish writer-director Ingmar Bergman, who Fellini called "a great artist,"[110] is another European master of cinema whose dreamlike narratives impressed Lynch. In *The Silence* (1963), a boy (Jorgen Lindstrom), his earthy, extroverted mother (Gunnel Lindblom), and her cerebral, introverted sister (Ingrid Thlin) arrive in an unnamed city where people speak a language they don't understand. The inadequacy of verbal communication is a major Lynchian theme, but there are many more elements in *The Silence* that can also be found in his world.

Balancing sharply defined polarities is a key aspect of Lynch's artistic process in all his mediums of expression, and Bergman's film centers on such a dynamic. Today Lynch says he doesn't remember details of *The Silence*, but seeing it decades ago he would have been struck by the feeling that Bergman's two very different women seem like two aspects of the same psyche, and indeed Bergman's original idea was to have both characters played by the same actress. *The Silence* could well have inspired Lynch's career-long fascination with presenting the full spectrum of human thought, emotion, and behavior through two characters who seem to be opposites but are truly, in a poetic sense, "one and the same." In *Lost Highway* Lynch did have one actress (Patricia Arquette) play two women (Renee and Alice).

The Silence's boy explores empty hotel corridors, which, like so many Lynchian passageways, seem fraught with Otherness—and at the end of one of them, he sees a dwarf in a suit walking to some unknown destination. Since childhood Lynch has been enthralled by the wonders and terrors that his eyes have shown his brain, and in his films he often emphasizes the act of visual discovery by peering through/passing through an aperture or portal. He may have developed this motif without outside influence or absorbed it from the films that he admires. In *Sunset Boulevard*, there's a striking moment where William Holden's character (viewed from the back) opens a door and gazes into Norma Desmond's phantasmic bedroom as though it were another world. This shot could be the inspiration for an image Lynch has repeatedly shown us, in which we see a figure from the back who's looking at some entrancing sight.

In *The Silence*, the boy peers through a hotel room doorway and sees dwarf men—some sitting, some standing, one smoking a cigar, others playing cards, another fiddling with a musical instrument. The immediate impact of this scene is a potent strangeness, and the undefined relationship of these men to each other and the unknown reason for them doing what they're doing are echoed in *Twin Peaks: Fire Walk With Me*, as we see David Bowie's character's flashback of a room above a convenience store, in which a bizarre group of extra-dimensional denizens are mysteriously passing time together.

The Silence flirts with the transgressive sort of sexuality Lynch often portrays. The little men turn out to be stage performers, and they invite the boy into their room and dress him up as a girl. This excites the men, and one of them, wearing a monkey mask, hops up and down on a bed, reminding us that the indulgence of animalistic appetites is a fundamental component of Lynchian darkness. The dwarf's simian face recalls the evil monkeys in *The Wizard of Oz*, and the monkey face that enigmatically says "Judy" at the end of *Twin Peaks: Fire Walk With Me*, as though referring to some formidable, undefined entity in that film's universe. In *Twin Peaks: Fire Walk With Me* we learn something about the balance of power between those who inhabit the Red Room, and in *The Silence*, a dwarf we haven't seen before enters the hotel room, calms the ruckus, takes the dress off the boy, and sends him on his way. Lynch's work centers on the tension between people carrying varying charges of power, and sometimes the balance is tipped by the incursion of dark energies that can't be seen. In *The Silence*, the boy's aunt, feeling that hope and optimism have been drained from the world, speaks words that many of Lynch's characters might say: "The forces are too strong. I mean the forces . . . the horrible ones."

Like the final episode of *Twin Peaks* (Cooper entrapped and possessed) and the endings of *Lost Highway* and *Mulholland Drive*, Stanley Kubrick's

Barry Lyndon (1975), set in eighteenth-century Britain, arcs from optimistic beginnings to a harrowing downfall that leaves its protagonist unredeemed. A devolved wildness often erupts in Lynch's world, as domestic stability is invaded by chaotic energies. *Barry Lyndon* showed Lynch a stunning staging of this theme as Barry, who's eager to gain entrance to the rarified ranks of high society, entertains a roomful of rich and elegant folk—but he can't control the beast within him, and suddenly pounces on his stepson and beats him with savage force.

A key *Mulholland Drive* moment mirrors a scene in Kubrick's film. In both pictures the protagonists (respectively, *Mulholland Drive*'s Diane Selwyn, Barry Lyndon), sitting across a dinner table from their true loves, hear a glass tapped to call the group to attention, and are lacerated by the unanticipated news that their amours are going to marry someone else—a fact emphasized by the newly engaged couples kissing at the table.

Lynch is clearly in harmony with Kubrick's cinematic universe, but with his belief in karmic progression beyond death and the playing out of moral consequences over many lifetimes, he couldn't agree with *Barry Lyndon*'s last words: "Good or bad, they are all equal now" (in the grave).

The ending of Kubrick's *2001: A Space Odyssey* (1968), on the other hand, echoes Lynch's personal and artistic sense of metaphysics and spirituality. As Kubrick says, astronaut Bowman, swept away by a mystical force, enters a room that's "drawn out of his dreams and imagination."[111] As in *Twin Peaks*' Red Room and so many Lynchian environments, characters experience the conflicts, blisses, and terrors generated inside their own heads as externalized encounters. Going a quantum leap beyond Lynch in explaining the ending of one of his films, Kubrick shows that *2001: A Space Odyssey* could be a blueprint for many Lynchian film conclusions. After death, Bowman "is reborn, an enhanced being, a star child, an angel, and returns to earth prepared for the next leap forward in man's evolutionary destiny."[112] Lynch suffuses the endings of most of his fictions with an optimistic glow, and *The Grandmother*, *Eraserhead*, *The Elephant Man*, and *Twin Peaks: Fire Walk With Me* specifically posit a hopeful, rewarding evolutionary journey after death.

Today *2001: A Space Odyssey* is hailed as a masterpiece, but when it came out it had as many detractors as appreciators. Kubrick's space epic has to be the most-seen film with an enigmatic, ambiguous ending in film history. So not only are Kubrick and Lynch both eager to probe the depths of inner space, but each has earned the artistic merit badge of having infuriated audiences with their uncompromising visions.

Jack Torrance (Jack Nicholson), the protagonist of Stanley Kubrick's *The Shining* (1980), knows he's a first-time visitor to the isolated Hotel Overlook and is to be its winter caretaker, but is he also possessed by the evil spirit of the place, or is he a soul who's resided there for lifetimes—or both?

Like Lynch's villains in *Dune*, *Blue Velvet*, *Twin Peaks*, and *Lost Highway*, being bad seems to be the natural expression of Jack's life force, as he spews mayhem with an intense, grinning zeal. His angry resentments toward his wife and child become murderous attacks under the influence of Lloyd the bartender, just as, in Lynch's *Twin Peaks*, and *Lost Highway* (respectively), a father's sexual attraction to his daughter, and a husband's suspicion of his wife's unfaithfulness, are transmuted into evil behavior, thanks to the possessing, motivating inspiration of BOB and the Mystery Man. In *The Shining* Lynch saw an echo of his favorite theme of domestic security or a person's consciousness/selfhood being threatened by dark energies, as a character speaks of shoring up the Hotel Overlook's structural integrity, "so elements can't get a foothold." Sinister elements have definitely moved into Jack's cranium, subsuming him in a sinister presence that has haunted the woods "for as long as anyone can remember," a repeating, closed circle of malevolence. Jack's artistic output consists of the same sentence typed thousands of times, while on TV a cartoon character, speaking of Wile E. Coyote, says, "If he catches you, you're through" over and over. Years after seeing Kubrick's film, Lynch introduced this sense of repeating metaphysical cycle of evil into *Twin Peaks* (a phonograph needle at the end of a record clicks and clicks like a metronome accompaniment to a ghastly murder; an oracular character in another part of town intones, "it is happening again") and *Lost Highway* (a man who's killed his wife can't find an exit from the hellish, endless road he's speeding down). *The Shining* reinforced Lynch's fondness for portraying villains as animalistic brutes (begun in 1970's *The Grandmother*), for in Kubrick's film Jack consciously evokes the Big Bad Wolf as he chases the little piggies (his wife and son) with an ax. We note that both Jack and *Twin Peaks*' BOB wear blue jeans and waist-length denim jackets, have long hair, grizzled beards, and a snarling verbal delivery, and move crouching low to the ground.

Jack Torrance is a monster. Yet Lynch, who as a young man just wanted to live an Art Life unencumbered by family responsibilities, and forcefully portrayed this theme in *Eraserhead*, had to have a smidgen of fellow feeling for Jack Torrance the artist, who's just trying to get his work done, but is hindered and suffocated by his wife and child. Jack is kin to Lynchian artists of darkness like Baron Harkonnen (*Dune*), Frank Booth (*Blue Velvet*), BOB (*Twin Peaks*), Bobby Peru (*Wild at Heart*), and the Mystery Man

(*Lost Highway*), who devote their energy and creativity to shaping toxic narratives of damage and mayhem.

Lynch reveres Kubrick's imaginative worlds, and something in Kubrick's soul was moved by *Eraserhead*, which he often praised and screened at his Elstree, England, home retreat. In addition to feeling a spiritual kinship with Kubrick, Lynch may have been inspired by the expatriate American's lifestyle: living to dream and work inside a large, self-controlled and self-realizing studio compound that he didn't often leave, and dealing with the outside world via electronic devices as much as possible, on his own terms.

Both Kubrick and Lynch are renowned for the individuality of their vision and style, yet each has been influenced by the work of other artists and has more (Kubrick) and less (Lynch) consciously put their unique stamp on images, ideas, atmospheres, and sounds that other filmmakers have shown them. (Kubrick would knowingly take souvenirs from the films of Fritz Lang, G. W. Pabst, Vsevelod Pudovkin, Jean Renoir, Vittorio De Sica, and Max Ophuls.)

Throughout evolutionary history, it has been a human trait to observe, and learn from, each other. The French painter Delacroix (1798–1863) saw the world as a dictionary from which the artist metaphorically composes his or her sentences. Charles Baudelaire (1821–1867), the French poet and critic who was one of the architects of modernist thought (who was himself influenced by Vermeer and Goya, and who influenced Cezanne, Matisse, and Robert Motherwell), felt that his sensibility, though composed of all the art and literature he'd experienced, was yet profoundly original. This characterization, and Baudelaire's concept of naiveté, by which an artist unconsciously absorbs some aspect of another's artwork, perfectly defines Lynch's relationship to the sources that have influenced him over the years. As Fellini said, "But how can we remember all the books that helped us grow up, revealing ourselves to us?"[113]

As a teenager first yearning to become an artist, Lynch read Robert Henri's thoughts on the idea of one creator influencing another in *The Art Spirit*. Henri admonished the art student not "to be afraid to do as any other artist."[114] He added that "from the antique cast there should be no work done if it is not to translate your impression of the beauty the sculptor has expressed."[115] Surveying the vast field of visual elements which are potential building blocks of a composition, and which include other artists' work, the artist selects "the traits that best express you."[116]

If Lynch doesn't comb the world formulaically choosing the raw materials for his art with his rational, calculating mind, then by what alchemical process does he forge his visions? True to form, he delves deep inside himself, letting his unconscious be his guide, embracing elements and linking them with a thrill of fresh discovery "because they make me dream."[117] As a teenager, *The Art Spirit*, which Lynch called "my bible,"[118] inspired the course his life would take. But at an even younger age he was set to dreaming by some of the most widely read tales in human history—the Holy Bible's Revelation of St. John. Lynch's inclination, even as a youth, to see the world as rife with portents, mysteries, and veiled wonders was certainly reinforced by his reading of divine writ. But is there anything more specific than the Bible's general high contrast between the forces of good and evil that has found its way into Lynch's art?

Lynch's favorite number, seven, which is overtly and covertly represented in his art and which guides some of his life choices, is abundantly present in the book of Revelation like a holy unit of measure: "As for the mystery of the seven stars which you saw in my right hand, and the seven golden lampstands, the seven stars are the angels of the seven churches and the seven lampstands are the seven churches."[119]

In Revelation's awesomely universe-spanning, phantasmagoric battle between good and evil, the flashing illumination of lightning, smoke, and fire become metaphorical elements, just as Lynch gives them a supernatural charge. The Bible's "legs like pillars of fire"[120] could have inspired *Twin Peaks'* "Fire Walk With Me," and in both Revelation and Lynchland, fire represents an ultimate danger and punishment. Such Lynchian themes and motifs as demons possessing people, a pale horse representing death (*Twin Peaks*), and insects bedeviling human beings are proclaimed in St. John's seven visions. Lynch's intuition, his unconscious memory of Revelation's "a woman clothed with the sun, with the moon under her feet, and on her head a crown of twelve stars,"[121] may have prompted him to accept the job of creating the commercial for Karl Lagerfeld's perfume Sun Moon Stars.

Revelation's woman "on whose forehead was written a name of mystery"[122] could be the archetype for all the Lynchian females who are "full of secrets." And words in Revelation bear a striking correspondence to the essential mystery of *Mulholland Drive*, as though the Blue-haired Lady, the overseer of this world and the next, was speaking to Diane Selwyn: "I know your works"[123] (the dream you have created), "you have the name of being alive"[124] (Betty), "and you are dead"[125] (Diane).

The conflict between darkness and light keeps Lynch's fictions spinning, with good or evil alternately having the upper hand to one degree or another, for each powerful force contains the seed of the other. As a youth, Lynch's experiments with drawing and painting, and the written guidance of Robert Henri's *The Art Spirit*, showed him the dramatic value that contrast could bring to his pictures. But perhaps his first lesson in balancing opposing energies came from the Bible, for Revelation portrays an eternal conflict between "the Lord God, who is and who was and who is to come"[126] and "the beast who was and is not and is to come."[127] Revelation's many references to evil as bestial, and the mystical, physics-defying sense of simultaneous states of reality (is/was/is to come) seem to have had a formative effect on Lynch. Lynch finds that the impulses to create and destroy persist in the world, and he often portrays the urges to do good and evil as warring within a single person. And how seamlessly his adult belief in Hindu karmic justice ("whatever wrongs you commit will visit you in exactly the same form")[128] melds with the Revelation verses he read as a youth: "if any one slays with the sword, with the sword must be slain."[129]

As a boy and a man, Lynch looks for signs of Otherness, and of himself, in the world around him. He says that "the biggest influence in my whole life was the city of Philadelphia,"[130] where he had his first independent, unique thoughts, fell in love, fathered a child, made his first film, and was enthralled by the terrors and thrills waiting for him around every corner. We can imagine that he felt he was exactly where he was meant to be, doing what he was meant to do, when he read these words in Revelation: "And to the angel of the church in Philadelphia write: 'The words of the holy one, who has the key of David, who opens and no one shall shut, who shuts and no one shall open.'"[131]

Despite his years of calming meditation, Lynch still has the capacity to flare with anger in reaction to a specific situation of the moment, but he doesn't voice criticisms of others. As Naomi Watts told me, "David sees a sweetness in people that I don't see; he just doesn't speak ill of people or their work."[132] Indeed, Lynch habitually only mentions other directors' films that he likes. But once, when asked his definition of an immoral film, he responded, "An immoral film is one that glorifies negativity, like *Saturday Night Fever*."[133] He had named one of the most critically and commercially successful films of the 1970s, the tale (directed by John Badham in 1977) of a Brooklyn young man (John Travolta) stuck in a dead-end blue-collar job and oppressed by his toxic family, who finds emotional release and a sense of meaning dancing at the neighborhood disco club. It's surprising that Lynch did not appreciate *Saturday Night Fever*, for its story parallels his own: the uninspiring early jobs, the family tension over the youth's need and desire to pursue his passion (painting, in Lynch's case), the exhilaration of immersing himself in his art (they don't call Travolta's character "Nureyev" for nothing—he's a supreme artist of the dance floor). And *Saturday Night*

Fever's narrative dynamic mirrors the dramatic strategy of Lynch's fictions, which he has succinctly described to me as "a character reaches a point where they're tired of suffering, and they look for a way out."[134]

Lynch was especially disturbed by an early passage in *Saturday Night Fever*: "That family scene that took place at the dinner table was one of the most horrible things I've ever seen."[135] As Travolta, his grandmother, mother, father, and siblings eat, every conceivable expression of dysfunction erupts: yelling, sarcastic criticism, sullen silences, swearing, and slaps to the face and head are exchanged by many characters. When Lynch saw *Saturday Night Fever*, he had already made *The Grandmother* and *Eraserhead*, which contain comparably intense dinner-table episodes of emotional and physical violence. Perhaps only subconsciously, these corrosive, fictional family scenes are a heightened exaggeration, an emblem, of Lynch's feeling about the family tensions he had endured in his own life in relatively recent history. Psychologists tell us that we tend to criticize others who manifest qualities of our own dark shadow side, so maybe for Lynch, *Saturday Night Fever*'s polluted atmosphere of domestic discord was too much like the air he used to breathe, so he spoke out against it.

We must also remember that Lynch had his youthful subway-panic experience in Brooklyn, and *Saturday Night Fever* portrays the place as a raw, gritty, inhospitable zone that would seem threatening to a Boy Scout from the idyllic Northwest. Four-letter words and racial slurs filled the air; youths have sex, sometimes rape, in curbside cars in public view; willful ignorance and macho posing are celebrated; women are second-class citizens at best; and overkill violence settles disputes between street tribes of youngsters.

Yet Badham's film, as Lynch's work often does, features an angelic female character who represents the hope of spiritual expansion and rewarding transformation for the male protagonist. The sense of a loving community moving as one that Tony experiences on the dance floor is intoxicatingly redemptive. Still, all Lynch focuses on when he speaks of *Saturday Night Fever* is that rancorous dinner table gathering. It seems Badham's "negativity"[136] has gotten under Lynch's skin just as Lynch's dark tales disturb many of his viewers.

Lynch's first ex-wife, Peggy, remarried in 1979 and stayed in friendly touch with David, and his sensibility. When she got excited about a short novel she read, she passed it along to him as a possible film subject. *Mrs. Caliban* (1983), by Rachel Ingalls, does indeed teem with Lynchian potential.

The story centers on a Southern California couple, Fred and Dorothy, whose marriage has been drained of life and love (did this Fred suggest the enervated Fred of *Lost Highway*'s estranged Fred and Renee?). Like so many of Lynch's characters, Dorothy is languishing in dark and troubling times, shell-shocked from the loss, through illness, then miscarriage, of her young son and unborn child. One day, the voice on the radio advertising cake mix says, in a "dreamlike"[137] way, "It's all right, Dorothy. It's going to be alright."[138] As in Lynch's work, the miraculous inhabits the mundane. As do Lynch's fictions, *Mrs. Caliban* engages our minds with questions of what is real and what is not. Is Dorothy imagining the consoling voice on the radio, or is it really there?

Next, the radio warns of an escaped "six-foot-seven-inch frog-like creature"[139] that has killed the scientists who found it on a South American expedition. One night, the creature barges into Dorothy's kitchen. Lynch's works counsel us to look beneath the surface of outward appearances to discover deeper truths. The introduction of the frogman fits the form of a primal Lynchian theme: the intrusion of menacing bestial energy into a previously safe and secure abode. Indeed the outside world describes the creature as a "highly dangerous animal"[140] with an "alien intelligence."[141] Yet on closer inspection, the frogman turns out to be a Lynch-style, extraordinary angel figure who provides Dorothy with a release from her torment. Author Ingalls echoes Lynch's fascination for linking the fabulous and the commonplace, for the creature's name is Larry.

Lynch's characters often lead double emotional/romantic lives, and, unbeknownst to Fred, Dorothy and the frogman make love, talk, listen to music, and eat (he loves avocado salads) together. This situation is deliciously absurd, but Ingalls, like Lynch, is a master of tonal complexity, and we feel the full emotional gravity of a wounded woman finding and clinging to what she desperately needs in life. (When Lynch first spoke to Peggy after reading the novel, he said, "It's about grieving."[142])

Larry evokes *The Elephant Man*'s John Merrick, *Twin Peak*'s Agent Cooper, and Lynch himself in his sensitive, childlike response to the wonders that surround him. For the frogman, certain foods, television shows, and the scent of Southern Californian gardens at night, are ecstatic experiences. Just as Lynch and his thrilled-by-life characters inspire us to appreciate our world more, Larry's exaltations reinvigorate Dorothy's capacity to experience "holiness and beauty and love."[143]

Larry is a tender being who loves Dorothy with a true heart. Dorothy is on cloud nine and voices her happiness in an ecstatic passage: "A lovely, warm night, full of promise and romance as she had dreamed about in her teens and as the advertisements had promised and still promised, for her and for everyone else too."[144] These words evoke Lynch's personal sense of surging romanticism, the teen-dream aspects of his work, and his warm memories of the 1950s advertisements that were like snapshots of the paradisiacal life he led as a youth.

Having Larry with her is perfect for Dorothy and wonderful for him, but he pines for his real home; she cares for him so much that she hatches a plan to sneak him down across the Mexican border. Then, she receives a piercing reminder that her loving beastie is still a beast. Larry tells her that when he was out by himself, smelling the perfume of the night, he was attacked by five teenage boys—and he slaughtered them all. At this point, we learn that Larry is not Dorothy's imaginary love, for one of the victims is the son of Dorothy's best friend, Estelle.

From his earliest days as a painter, Lynch has spoken of carefully balancing fast and slow elements of a composition, and his films exhibit a deft sense of contrapuntal rhythm, orchestrating alternating passages of entrancing languor and frenzied action. Reading *Mrs. Caliban*, Lynch was galvanized by Ingalls' acceleration into stunning eventfulness in the book's last pages. In breathtaking succession, Dorothy's friend Estelle and Dorothy's husband Fred both betray her, and key characters die in a flaming car crash.

Earlier in this night of shattering revelations, Dorothy had kissed Larry goodbye as they agreed to meet later at the beach. Now each evening she waits at the water's edge, "But he never came."[145]

Mrs. Caliban's exploration of a woman's subjective consciousness, her loneliness, longing, and aroused desire, seemed like prime material for a Lynch film. But, as much as he believed in the barrier-bridging power of love, Lynch feared that physically portraying the romance between the woman and the amphibian could provoke mood-killing audience laughter: "after all, Larry would have to be green."[146]

Lynch, with his "learner's mind"[147] attitude, has often been *green* himself, in the sense of being untrained and inexperienced when he approaches various mediums of artistic expression. He had taken no classes in drawing, painting, filmmaking, printmaking, furniture-making, song-writing, cartooning, or guitar-playing before trying his hand at these disciplines, and distinguishing himself in each. In 2000 and 2001, Lynch learned new computer and digital-technology skills and prepared to take a crack at the newest, freshest art medium going: the Internet.

For years, Lynch has decried television's poor-quality image and sound as compared to film, but he has nonetheless worked in TV because the medium let him indulge his passion for "continuing stories,"[148] though those long tales have always been cut short by the network. The images and sounds we receive on our computers are exponentially worse than TV's, so why has Lynch embraced the Internet?

In his early painting days, Lynch became intrigued by the evocative power of fragments of figures and objects, and has contemplated the mind's need and ability to make sense of seemingly unrelated puzzle-piece bits of information, to make a legible whole out of broken, incomplete elements. Our dreams are often composed of half-formed scenes and snatches of dislocated images and emotions that are fragments, but that add up to portray our psychic selves.

Lynch sees his website as a home for short artistic "fragments and experiments"[149] that he wouldn't express elsewhere, or which might inspire further development in longer narratives. It is a way to try out ideas using Photoshop, Flash animation, After Effects, and DV cameras, instead of big 35mm cameras and a full movie crew. The Internet puts Lynch happily back in the position of his early Art Life, staying at home and working mostly by himself, mainlining his pure-vision thoughts, feelings, and images without any outside interference. Decades ago, the results of his efforts would reach a handful of people at an art gallery or experimental-film festival, but now thousands can access his just-completed work in an instant. Lynch, with characteristic depth of thought, sees the Internet as much more than a wall to hang his pictures on. He has a romantic, mystical feeling about the medium: the way it manifested itself in his lifetime; its pioneering nature and open-ended future; the way people all over the planet, day and night, seven days a week, can have the same simultaneous experience. The Internet is humming electricity and creative thoughts and good-vibe dreams of peace flowing out of his Hollywood Hills art factory and uniting the world in a glowing, blissful circuit of positive energy, just as the worldwide practice of Transcendental Meditation does. It's art and life, together again, and for always.

So what are some of these "fragments that wouldn't fit anywhere else"[150] that Lynch presents on his website?

Lynch, a self-described "funaholic,"[151] welcomes us to his Internet world with a declaration of his credo, "Let's Have Some Fun."[152] Some of the "experiments"[153] that amuse Lynch exhibit his characteristic love of nature and organic processes divorced from ideas of beauty and ugliness: We see bees happily swarming on a bush and ants merrily devouring the flesh of a dead rat. An eerie segment illustrates Lynch's key concept of domestic security being invaded by a dangerous animalistic energy. The director shows us a static shot of a living room: two chairs, a table with glowing lamp, a black window confirming that it is night. We watch this unchanging image for minutes on end. Then there's a slight stirring in the shadows at the edge of the room, and a large coyote emerges into the light, prowling and hungry in a place it shouldn't be. (This disturbing, barrier-violating confluence of inside and outside was filmed in Lynch's very large backyard. It took many nights to lure the animal into the open-air stage set, and some of the director's neighbors complained bitterly about the bright lighting needed to get the effect Lynch wanted.)

Lynch permeates his website with his sense of life's absurdity. Against the backdrop of a landscape with a horse trailer, two characters whose heads are white medical gloves blown up like balloons make squalling-child sounds until one drops out of the frame. In a segment called *Out Yonder*, Lynch and his adult son, Austin, wearing stocking caps pulled low on their foreheads, sit on a sunny porch like country folk. They speak in a curious verb tense that exists only in the mind of David Lynch: "It bein' hot. It bees like that some days. It bees hard to figure. Is that bein' the door bell?"[154] Their goofy conversation is interrupted when the neighbor boy, who happens to be a giant ("He bees bein' a monster")[155] stops by to borrow some milk. (Lynch inventively introduces the not-directly-seen-giant's presence by having his huge shadow fall on the porch scene of father and son talking.) Also absurd, but nonetheless an aspect of life we can empathize with, is the sight of a man sitting surrounded by a mechanical apparatus that regularly pounds him on the head with a hammer. Trapped and tortured by existence, he is unable, or unwilling, to get up, move away, and end the pain.

Pain of a more specific, autobiographical sort (the divorce of Lynch's sound engineer-musical collaborator John Neff) flows amusingly in the website's *Thank You Judge* video. The segment's music is by Blue Bob, the Lynch-Neff duo that takes inspiration from the "pounding machines of smokestack industry and the raw amplified birth of rock 'n' roll: fire, smoke, and electricity."[156] Lynch asked Neff to list everything that the judge ordered him to give to his ex-wife when they divorced, and thus a song was born. With a blues singer's gravelly voice and stinging guitar, Neff rattles of a humorously long catalog (stuffed deer head, VCR, .38 gun, favorite rug, stash of beer, and so on), while Lynch, playing an electric guitar upside down, accompanies him with droning, distorted chords. Lynch's guitar sounds are in the spirit of The Who's master songwriter-guitarist Pete Townshend, who refined the art of blasting out buzz saw–sounding power chords that hang in the air like sculpted electricity (in the video Lynch's thunderstorm of noise is visualized as animated jagged golden lightning bolts). Lynch also acts in the video, wearing an unchanging rubber mask while playing three different characters, as though illustrating his Hindu belief in a single soul incarnating as many manifestations.

More Blue Bob music is available on DavidLynch.com, but the site's prime offering is the *Dumbland* series of short animations. These were originally supposed to go on the Shockwave site along with work by other notable directors like Tim Burton. But, as Lynch says, "*Dumbland* didn't test too well with them, and then their business fell with the stock market."[157] Lynch told me about the agonizing, unbelievable amount of time it took him to master the Flash animation technique and get *Dumbland* on the computer screen, compared to the traditional hand-drawn animation he began his film career with thirty years earlier. Because of technical strictures, *Dumbland* was crude, minimalist, and black-and-white, whereas *The Grandmother* (1970) was sophisticated, detailed, and in color.

Given the technical-aesthetic constraints of Flash animation, Lynch wisely came up with a subject perfectly matched to his limited palette. *Dumbland* taps into familiar aspects of Lynch's artistic personality: goofball, dumb-guy humor; emotional and physical violence and pain; seedy lowlifes; neighborhood stories; and anger, but he manifests them in a simplified, shorthand form comparable to his 1983–1992 *L.A. Reader* comic strip *The Angriest Dog in the World*.

Evoking the serial sameness of a newspaper comic title panel, each episode of *Dumbland* shows the word (looking like it was printed by a naïve child or a minimally educated person) suspended over a street crammed with dangerously speeding cars. In the foreground is an iconic Lynchian white picket fence, showing that the roaring cars are right outside someone's front yard. This place isn't a sylvan small-town paradise, it's one of the director's "hellholes"[158] like *Eraserhead*'s Philadelphia or *Wild at Heart*'s Big Tuna, Texas; the very surface of the film seems gritty and fly-specked.

In *The Angriest Dog in the World*, the title canine was always seen in the yard, frozen with unexpressed fury, as though he was a collecting vessel for the human tensions and conflicts that emanated from the house of his unseen owners in cartoon-balloon dialogue exchanges. In *Dumbland*, the householders are on full display. The volcanic agent of anger is an anonymous Man who's an archetypal slob: undershirt-wearing, fat and bald, with only three teeth in his mouth, a mouth which Lynch renders (as he has in other art forms) as a black circle, connoting a malicious hunger and a capacity for spewing emotional poison.

The Man, like many Lynchian villains, lives to exert his will over others and indulge his base impulses. Given the short amount of time the director has to characterize the Man, he eschews any plot complexities and subtle machinations and just lets the guy rip pinto the world around him. With his patriarchal tyranny and animalistic grossness and rage, he's close kin to *The Grandmother*'s Father. Sloshing beer into his mouth with the sound of a beast lapping liquid, watching two football players butt heads on TV, the Man is irritated by the sound of his wife's treadmill. Screaming, "Stop your fucking exercising,"[159] he swats her off the machine, sending her crashing into the next room. In *Dumbland*, the usual result of the Man interacting with his spouse is for her to have a terrorized-victim screaming fit. One afternoon he pulls down her backyard clothesline, bellowing, "What if I had to take a shit at night—I could slice my fucking head off"[160] (by running into the line with his throat). As his wife screams, he takes her head in his huge hands and crunches it into a little blob.

The toxic reach of the Man's power extends beyond abusing his wife. The hurricane-force farts that blast from his pants (Lynch confesses that "these are homemade sound effects")[161] bend trees over, various objects he tosses over his picket fence cause car and truck crashes, he reduces a man with a stick caught in his mouth to a bloody pulp, and agrees with his friend who hunts deer, sheep, fish, horses, dogs, cats, and pigs: "I like to kill things."[162] The outrageous intensity of the Man's behavior makes him funny, and Lynch tosses in some cornball jokes (the Man tells the mailman, "I got some letters for you: F.U.")[163] But the director is making some serious points about the unrestrained exercising of a male power that's comparable to BOB's "evil that men do" in *Twin Peaks* and the almost metaphysical "disease" that men put in *Blue Velvet*'s Dorothy.

Domineering, malevolent male energy most often chills the shadows in Lynch's artistic world. His natural tendency is to portray women as muses, lovers, wise guides, guardians, and victims. But the director sometimes shows us women of darkness who thrive on tyranny, degradation, and death, and we meet one in a *Dumbland* episode.

Occupying a mother-in-law role, as did *Eraserhead*'s Mrs. X to Henry and *Wild at Heart*'s Marietta does to Sailor, the *Dumbland* Man's wife's mother is the one force that lords it over him. Disrespecting the Man (she calls him "dickhead"),[164] the mother-in-law threatens his masculinity on a primal level ("I'll cut your nuts off.")[165] This declaration echoes Marietta's words to Sailor ("I'll cut your balls off and feed them to you") and projects Lynch's fear of having his free will chopped off. Following Lynch's belief in karmic justice, the Man, whose familiar role is to terrorize his household, is himself intimidated by his mother-in-law, and hides in a tree until she's gone.

Commentators say that one reason HBO's series *The Sopranos*—which details the black comedy and high drama of a suburban family that's part of New Jersey's crime family—mesmerizes massive audiences and virtually all TV critics is that it lets us identify with men who reap illicit money, and indulge in extramarital sex and vengeful violence, within the socially sanctioned framework of a supportive guys-only organization. As the twenty-first century dawns in the United States, some feel that, in boosting the professional status of women and self-esteem of schoolgirls and culturally valuing politically correct sensitivity, cooperation, and the sharing of feelings, traditional male behaviors and attitudes are being stigmatized, thwarted, and socially conditioned out of the American human race. Naturally, in our world of action and reaction, some men fight back and try to reassert their cultural potency by producing aggressive, unmannerly, dumb-ass movies, TV shows, video games, and websites about goofball, gross-out, teen guys in heat, or middle-aged slobs like the star of Lynch's *Dumbland*. Lynch has looked me in the eye and, as though summing up all his life's passion in one sentence, said, "I love the female psyche." Indeed, and without a doubt. In his work and life, he supports and celebrates women's temporal and spiritual being, now and forever—but he's also a guy. Lynch worships a 1950s, pre–women's movement, "it's a man's world" period of American life; he's an artist who rebels against being dictated to and pushed around, and his antennae vibrate when there's "something in the air"[166] of the zeitgeist around him. The result is Oprah Winfrey Nation vs. *Dumbland*.

Lynch's aroused testosterone flows freely in *Dumbland*'s absurdly extreme political incorrectness. In *Rabbits*, his site's other outstanding effort, his absurdist territory of choice is the existential mystery of daily domesticity. In a high-ceilinged living room set, furnished with a couch right out of *Twin Peaks*' Red Room and a torchère lamp familiar from other Lynch productions, male and female characters perform mundane actions that are made strangely funny and sublime by being isolated and emphasized. From *The Grandmother* on, Lynch has shown his ability to make household objects and behavior we've all seen and done thousands of times seem charged with hidden meaning and portent. And here Lynch adds a jolt of surreal humor by presenting home-making characters with live-action human bodies and voices—and fuzzy gray-brown rabbit heads with big tall ears that cast vertical shadows onto the walls. (The rabbits, Jane, Suzie, and Jack, are played by Laura Elena Harring, Naomi Watts, and Scott Coffey, who all acted in *Mulholland Drive*.)

Many resonant passages in Lynch's moving-image works illustrate his abiding love of "going down into"[167] the depths of a place, a person, an emotion. The *Rabbits* episodes hark back to his youthful desire to see the elements in one of his paintings move, for we always experience Jane, Suzie, and Jack's living room from the same unchanging, unmoving angle. Every time, we see the same left and right walls, the same floor and back wall: we're looking at a tableau, and we never go in for a close-up. As the characters sit on the couch, iron clothes, answer the phone, go in and out of the front door, they talk. They verbally share information that seems meaningful to them, but we the viewers perceive them as practicing another Lynchian variation of fragmented, incomplete, non sequitur communication. A typical exchange between Suzie, Jane, and Jack goes like this (each comes from a new speaker): "I have misplaced it. I am sure of it now."[168] "All day."[169] "It was a man in a green suit."[170] "Why?"[171] "It may even be later."[172] "I am going to get them."[173] "Where was I?"[174] "I only wish that they would go somewhere."[175] "I almost forgot."[176] "Were you blonde? Suzie?"[177] Maybe Lynch figured that since rabbits hop from place to place, their conversation should randomly jump from subject to subject. Or is the progression random? Being detectives, we trace one of the character's speeches over many episodes to see if there's a logical through-line to their utterances. This analysis yields Jack saying: "Were there any calls?"[178] "I have the secret."[179] "I am not sure."[180] "A coincidence."[181] "I hear someone."[182] "It must be seven p.m."[183] "I will bet you are both wondering."[184] These words certainly don't add up to a typical mainstream-entertainment story flow, but they do form a characteristic Lynchian narrative in which the viewer must piece together clues to attain meaning. Given the Internet freedom of not having to sell his product to millions of paying customers, Lynch experiments with presenting story information in an extremely abstract way. He gives us a strong sense of the *feeling* in the rabbits' room, and will let the plot coalesce in its own sweet time. Or maybe not, given his *Twin Peaks* passion to delay the revelation of Laura Palmer's killer perhaps forever, a desire overridden by his collaborators and ABC executives, none of whom have a thing to say about what he does with *Rabbits*.

The sight of people with human voices and rabbit heads following the mundane routines of their lives in a sober, deadpan manner is inherently funny, but Lynch gives his domestic scene a sinister edge. With typical care, Lynch orchestrates a resonant soundscape of ominous, sustained Badalamenti synthesizer chords, the sound of endlessly falling rain, and distant foghorns or industrial horns (previously heard in *Eraserhead* and *Blue Velvet*) that oppressively dampen the sitcom laugh-and-applause-track noise that bursts forth at strangely random moments. Just as Jack, Jane, and Suzie's words don't follow from what was just said before they speak, the appreciative-response sounds of an invisible audience are disturbingly haphazard and out of synch with what we're responding to.

The progressing episodes of *Rabbits* generate a palpable mood of anxiety and fear that pierces the absurdist surface of the characters' living room life. These fuzzy creatures who would look at home on a Saturday morning children's show recite creepy phrases ("dark smiling teeth,"[185] "the socket drips . . . disease,"[186] "tearing scraping black oil blood,"[187] "yellow saliva"[188]). As we often find in Lynch's art realm, there's a dreadful feeling that "something's wrong,"[189] that some malevolent force or alien energy hungers to invade this one-room domestic haven. There are footsteps outside the door; the phone rings and rings, and when answered emits an eerie electric hum. A huge matchhead flames up on the wall, as though it's been thrust into the space. The lights go out, and a disembodied, guttural voice says words made all the more scary by being impossible to understand. The rabbits seem suspended in the certainty that something terrible is going to happen, gripped by troubling anticipation over the longest, rainiest nights in the world.

DavidLynch.com received hundreds of thousands of hits after launching on December 10, 2001. But, as Lynch says, there was "a little hurdle"[190] for those interested in experiencing all the site's goodies: they had to pay for that pleasure. It took sixty hours of Lynch's time to create the visuals for just one short *Dumbland* episode, and the site needed expensive hardware, software, and the paid participation of a group of consultants, programmers, and sound engineer John Neff to function. As Lynch told me, "without financial support this thing will fold like a cheap tent."[191] Site membership cost just less than $10 per month, and thousands signed up and enjoyed what it offered, which included a store selling Lynch DVDs, T-shirts, and coffee mugs. For many, DavidLynch.com's most attractive feature was the chance to talk to Lynch himself in the site's chat rooms, and Lynch quickly came to treasure his almost daily interaction with his ardent admirers, a relationship of constant support that none of his other art endeavors had brought him.

Lynch took a break from working on his site (and savoring positive DavidLynch.com magazine reviews) to attend the inaugural event of Hollywood's Kodak Theater, the Academy Awards ceremony's new, permanent home. In the spring of 2002, one would think Lynch was green with envy as he watched Ron Howard take the stage to accept the Best Director Oscar for *A Beautiful Mind*, but no. His biggest complaint about the evening was that it was a long, long way from his seat to the smoking-allowed zone. Capping the numerous critics' accolades and awards Lynch received for *Mulholland Drive*, he had been nominated for the Best Director Oscar along with Robert Altman for *Gosford Park*. The fifty-six-year-old Lynch told me that he and seventy-seven-year-old Altman "had bonded after running into each other a number of times before Oscar night. He's really a cool guy in my book."[192] As Ron Howard's name was announced and the huge crowd rose in a standing ovation, Lynch strolled down the aisle and put his arm around Altman's shoulder. The two film industry mavericks stood together as everyone applauded Howard the Hollywood insider, and just as the camera cut away, Altman whispered something in Lynch's ear. When I asked Lynch what Altman's message was, he responded, "He said, 'It's better this way,'"[193] like a proud declaration of independence for both of them.

The words *shut* and *open* characterize Lynch's alternating modes of addressing himself to the world that's outside himself. As he put it to me, "Sometimes it feels right to go inward, and other times to go outward."[194] In 2002, he'd been in a decidedly outgoing frame of mind: as his daughter, Jennifer, says, "I've never seen him be in a more communicative mood."[195] Via his website chatrooms, he was having conversations with people all over the world, exchanging views about everything from how much the human soul weighs to how to make a screen door. And, on the day Billy Wilder died, he was wishing that everyone would go out and rent *Sunset Boulevard*. Still, all this social interaction was taking place within the controlled environment of Lynch's concrete studio compound. But in May 2002, he would take a major step out into the public eye, for he had agreed to be president of the jury of the 55th Cannes Film Festival 6,000 miles from the familiar security of his own front door.

When I spoke to Lynch before he took off for his three-week stint in France, he said that he was apprehensive and nervous, and that being jury president was "a horrible job."[196] Knowing how much of his "heart and mind and soul"[197] go into his own films, and feeling that "every film is special,"[198] he felt queasy about passing judgment on other artists' work, creating losers in the process of choosing winners. But, counterbalancing Lynch's trepidations was his respect for the larger idea of the Cannes Film Festival as the ultimate celebration of cinema—with movie lovers from the four corners of the earth reveling in intellectual discussions, boozy parties, business deal–making, and fleeting romantic infatuations in a ten-block carnival by the sparkling blue Mediterranean Sea. Lynch believed in the mission and the mystique of Cannes, and his memory of the first of his four previous trips there was like the recollection of a first love. "I had always wanted to go to the Festival, and when I got there I enjoyed every minute, and, on top of that, I won the Palme d'Or for *Wild at Heart*."[199]

After some lean years competing in Cannes with *Twin Peaks: Fire Walk With Me*, *The Straight Story*, and *Lost Highway*, Lynch was rewarded with the Best Director Prize for *Mulholland Drive* in 2001. When passionate French cinema-worshipper Gilles Jacob, who's been president of the Cannes Festival since 1977, called in January 2002 and asked Lynch to be jury president, David hesitated. Still, with his respect for Jacob, and knowing he could bring his love Mary and young Riley, and a supportive small entourage with him, and that he could manage the jury like an American democracy ("I'll have one vote, just like every other jury member—I'm not going to try to influence people and play games"[200]), Lynch "had to say yes."[201] He would do his duty for the cause of world cinema, try to enjoy the crowded socializing, and, by bringing his website collaborators with him, practice his personal art amid the public whirl.

Once in Cannes, Lynch's anxiety about his major responsibility of being jury president abated somewhat as he realized he was, in the space of a few "glad to meet you" moments, in warm fellowship with people who were devoted to the cinema as much as he was. This would be a team effort of individuals with a common purpose, just like working on a movie shoot.

To say that the French are proud of their culture and language is an understatement, and though many of them already regarded Lynch as an artistic demigod, he charmed their deepest hearts by speaking a French salutation at the Festival's opening press conference. His suit was black, his shirt was white and buttoned to the top as always, but throughout the Festival Lynch went to lengths of formality he didn't even display at his own film premieres: He wore a black necktie. Lynch sat in the center of a long table surrounded by his jury: Malaysian actress Michelle Yeoh, Indonesian actress-producer Christine Hakim, French director Claude Miller, French director Régis Warnier, Chilean director Raoul Ruiz, Danish director Billie August, and Brazilian director Walter Salles. To Lynch's left was an empty seat. The chair was to be filled by American actress Sharon Stone, who in the past year had suffered a cardiovascular seizure in her brain, but was, judging from her glowing appearance at the Academy Awards in March, back in top form. So where was she now? On the eve of departing California for Cannes, she had felt a sharp head pain and rushed to the hospital. Thankfully, her doctor felt her headache was nothing out of the ordinary, so she jetted off to join the jury a bit late. When she entered the pressroom, acknowledged the group's warm, welcoming applause with a "Bonjour!"[202] and sat next to Lynch, he created a curious little *what does it mean?* moment right out of one of his films. As Stone settled into her chair with a radiant smile on her face, Lynch, with that serious, earnest look of his, rummaged through the pockets of his suit. He spoke not a word, but you could feel him thinking, "Was it here? No. How about here? No." Finally, he produced a white handkerchief, which he slowly spread out flat on the tabletop and slid over toward Stone. Was this the way the chief magician of the jury welcomed his second in command? Or did gentleman Lynch, sitting within inches of Stone's face, detect a tear of joy the cameras were too far away to notice? When I asked him about this months later, he said, "I don't remember."[203]

For Lynch, one of the rewarding by-products of being an artist is getting to interact with many beautiful women. Photos from the Festival's first day showed a genuinely shell-shocked-looking Woody Allen, whose *Hollywood Ending* opened the event, being simultaneously kissed on his left and right cheeks by his actresses Debra Messing and Tiffany Thiesen, and Lynch grinning like a school boy, appearing to be in his element as Sharon Stone leaned into his shoulder and patted his stomach. The unidentified hand on Lynch's other arm probably belonged to an understanding Mary Sweeney. And as the Festival progressed we saw images of Lynch happily escorting Michelle Yeoh to a screening and smiling at an AIDS benefit where he was nestled among supermodel Naomi Campbell, Elizabeth Taylor, Sharon Stone, and to Stone's right, Elton John.

During the Festival's twelve days, Lynch enjoyed the camaraderie of film folk of all genders, savored some magnificent meals, and drank the wine he'd recently been denying himself at home as part of his spirit-purifying practice. Such were the pleasant fringe benefits of being in Cannes this year, but his primary dedication was to the prestigious and serious duty he'd been entrusted with, and many of the films Lynch and his jury were viewing spread a solemn tone over the proceedings.

In 1990, the year Lynch won the Palme d'Or for *Wild at Heart*, the outside world intruded on the self-contained realm of the Festival in the joyful form of two *Twin Peaks* episodes (the first season was then running in the United States) that a fan of the show presented to huge crowds at the American Pavilion. In 2002, the Festival was lacerated daily by news reports of more Palestinian suicide bombers blowing themselves and innocent Israelis to shreds, of heightened post–September 11 terrorism warnings in America, and the world-encompassing threat posed by the possibility that India and Pakistan might start lobbing nuclear missiles at each other at any moment. As though responding to the sorry state of the world, this year's international roster of Cannes films were dripping with pessimism, psychological and moral confusion, and abundant jolts of political and personal violence. Lynch's perennial artistic inspiration, the dark side of the human psyche, was everywhere to be seen. Michael Moore's documentary *Bowling for Columbine* explored America's sickening, worshipful obsession with guns. Roman Polanski's *The Pianist* portrayed a Warsaw family that did not anticipate the oncoming horror of the Holocaust. Atom Egoyan's *Ararat* grimly chronicled the killing of Armenians in 1915 Turkey. In David Cronenberg's *Spider*, a mental patient plunged into his inner world of childhood traumas, and Gaspar Noe's *Irreversible* centered on the erotic savagery of a rape that spawns murder.

After watching a number of films each day for almost two weeks and being sequestered to make their final selections, the jury emerged into the sunlight just hours before the award ceremony was to begin. As attendees and jurors alike made their way up the red-carpeted steps to the Grand Palais' entrance, Sharon Stone, with Lynch and juror Walter Salles, paused to speak to James Lipton, whose interview show *Inside the Actors Studio* runs on the Bravo TV network. Stone kept up a constant, charming patter as she introduced the men to Lipton. Lynch was characteristically a man of few words, saying nothing until Lipton asked what it was like working with this jury. Lynch allowed that "It was heaven"[204] before a female handler grabbed him from behind by the shoulders and hustled him, Stone, and Salles inside.

The audience in the huge auditorium was treated to some Côte d'Azur-blue-tinted film footage of 1890s children and grown-ups frolicking on the beach at Cannes, which gave the feeling of an impressionist painting come to life. Then the mistress of ceremonies, willowy French actress Virginie Ledoyen, took her position at a podium on the left side of the stage, where she welcomed the applauding audience. Next, speaking in French, she introduced the short-film-competition jury, presided over by Martin Scorsese, who emerged from a door on the right side of the stage and took their seats in a row. Then came the feature film jury, the last person coming through the door being "Le President, Dahveed Leench."[205] As his jury mates took their seats in a row in front of the short-film jury row, Lynch remained standing and picking up a black wireless microphone. Rather than holding it down beneath his mouth, he held it in front of his face, like a big cigar he was getting ready to puff. At the Festival-opening press conference, he had impressed the audience by speaking a bit of French, but now he was in his dedicated-professional mode, and he needed his native tongue to precisely voice his thoughts.

Characteristically insecure about his ability to express himself verbally, Lynch had, a few days earlier, joked that "my English isn't much better than my French."[206] But now, with the eyes of the world on him, he plunged ahead, pausing for Régis Warnier to translate each sentence: "Even though the world it reflects is in trouble, the world cinema here at Cannes is alive and well. It has been an honor and a privilege to serve with this magnificent jury. There are not enough prizes available to reflect all our desires. Yet we as a jury feel very good about our final choices."[207] Then, with much warmth in voice, "Merci beaucoup."[208]

The applause for Lynch's words became the crowd's loud welcome for one of the director's best actresses, *Mulholland Drive*'s Naomi Watts, who smiled toward Lynch and announced the awarding of a special 55th Festival anniversary prize. Sounding Lynchian-cryptic, she said, "It didn't exist last year. And next year if won't be here either."[209] Lynch looked a little mystified himself. His face reflected concern and momentary confusion as his lips silently asked, "Say right now?"[210] Virginie Ledoyen cleared things up: "Dear President, what is the prize of the 55th anniversary?"[211] Lynch stood and bellowed out, Gordon Cole style, "*Bowling for Columbine* by Michael Moore."[212] The hefty, usually scruffy Moore looked svelte in his tuxedo as he acknowledged the crowd's enthusiastic response. Moore chuckled that since U.S. President George W. Bush had just landed in France, perhaps the Festival could show him Moore's film which, "in the wake of September 11 exposes America's culture of violence and fear, and shows where that comes from and where that leads. It's a powerful statement for the French to honor this message. Merci beaucoup."[213]

A year before Bush embarked on a self-proclaimed God-inspired mission to bring freedom to Iraq by raining bombs on it, the 55th Cannes Film Festival projected a the-world-versus-Bush sensibility. Lynch didn't applaud when Moore received his award, for the Eagle Scout, patriotic-yet-peace-loving jury president probably had mixed feelings. Lynch certainly appreciated a compelling film decrying gun violence in America, but that didn't mean he endorsed taking away gun owners' freedoms. He once said, "This country is in pretty bad shape when human scum can walk across your lawn, and they put *you* in jail if you shoot 'em."[214] And when I mentioned an upcoming national mothers' march against guns, he said, "I'm not so sure about that."[215]

Lynch did clap for Jury Prize–winner Palestinian director Elia Suleiman (*Divine Intervention*) and appreciated the man's acknowledgement of a producer all filmmakers should be so lucky to have: "the only pressure I got from my producer was to prevent me from censoring myself."[216]

Virginie Ledoyen asked "Dear Dahveed"[217] to announce the Best Screenplay prize, and Lynch obliged with "Paul Laverty for Ken Loach's *Sweet Sixteen*."[218] Scotsman Laverty contributed to the rather anti-American tone of the evening's political expressions as he said, "I want to thank the French for their defense of diversity. That's really important t these days. I don't think that the voices of young people from Scotland, or Korea, or Senegal, or Mexico, or France, or anywhere else are any less important than the predominantly white, rich faces and voices that swamp our screen."[219] After the clapping died down, Laverty continued, "I should give my prize to George W. Bush, because when you hear some of the things he's said, like, 'most of our exports come from overseas,' and 'I know something about small-business growth, I used to be one,' you have to admit that those are much better lines than any screenwriter could have come up with."[220] A burst of applause filled the huge hall, Sharon Stone's mouth fell open in laughter, and Lynch begrudgingly offered the slightest of grins.

The Spanish director Pedro Almodóvar provided a moment of levity as he strolled onstage with two prizes for Best Director. Talk about your Lynchian doublings: Lynch (*Mulholland Drive*) and the Coen Brothers (*The Man Who Wasn't There*) had both won the award the previous year, and now Lynch and Almodóvar, who had won for *Talk to Her*, were staring at each other. The audience laughed and applauded as Almodóvar said, "David, if you tell me the names, I have here two prizes,"[221] and Lynch replied, "Two,"[222] and Almodóvar said, "Two—you and I but, you know, somebody else."[223] This spontaneous comic pause seemed to relax Lynch, and he flashed his biggest, warm-eyed smile of the evening.

Cannes 2002's Best Directors were South Korea's Im Kwon-Toek for *Chihwasean* and America's Paul Thomas Anderson for *Punch-Drunk Love*. Im Kwon-Toek summed up the harmonizing, boundary-bridging spirit of Cannes ("this prize goes not just to South Korea, but to the two Koreas")[224] and the Asian, unified-field philosophy Lynch believes in ("here's to life in its totality"[225]). In conclusion he spoke for Lynch and countless independent-minded film artists: "thanks to my producer for making films that don't necessarily make money." Paul Thomas Anderson's bubbling boyish American enthusiasm ("thank you very, very, very, very much"[226]) was a sweet contrast to Im Kwon-Toek's more formal, self-composed presentation, and he spoke words Lynch might have said: "When you grow up loving movies, you always want the French to like your movies."[227]

Lynch and Finnish director Aki Kaurismaki produced a little moment of mystery when the latter's name was announced as his *The Man Without a Past* won Grand Prize. Before heading to the podium, Kaurismaki walked up to the standing Lynch and, like a scene in a Lynch film, touched his head to Lynch's and gripped him like a dance partner. As they stood in a motionless embrace, Lynch's eye roved from side to side as he intently listened to whatever it was that the Finn was whispering in his ear.

Kaurismaki then took the podium and delivered the best, most succinct acceptance speech in award show history: "First of all I would like to thank myself. Secondly, the jury. Thanks."[228] Like a Zen arrow to the heart of truth, Kaurismaki celebrated the primal fact that without his original vision, not even God, Kaurismaki's parents, his patient and supportive wife and kids, and all the producers, actors, and technicians in the world could have made *The Man Without a Past* a living reality. The huge audience applauded the beautifully condensed wisdom and courage of Kaurismaki's few words, and no one clapped more enthusiastically than Lynch, who's intimately aware of how an individual's unique, personal inspiration generates art.

Actress Juliette Binoche stood at the podium to set the stage for the awarding of the Palme d'Or, and as if to remind us that Cannes is a rarified realm far removed from the comparatively crass and prosaic Oscar ceremonies, she spoke her own fey, poetic summation of this evening, "Life is movement. Plants are growing. Animals are moving. We humans are giving. So tonight it is for me to give to the one who gave, and is going to receive."[229] Ah, the French.

Ah, the expatriate Poles who once resided in America but are now exiled to living in Paris. The evening's most coveted award went to Roman Polanski (for *The Pianist*), a cinematic master whose psychologically probing work has, as one commentator said, "influenced so many of this year's films at Cannes."[230] The man who made *Repulsion*, *Rosemary's Baby*, and *Chinatown*, who's mother died at Auschwitz and who was forced to flee his homeland during World War II, who's wife was killed by Charles Manson's family, and who was shunned by many Americans when he jumped bail and fled the charge of having sex with a fourteen-year-old girl, acknowledged the Cannes crowd's long, standing ovation. As though closing, and perhaps exorcising, a circle of torment that curves back to the land of his birth, he said, "I am honored and moved to receive this prize for a film that represents Poland."[231] Polanski would still be arrested if he set foot in America, but what matters tonight in Cannes is that everyone in this huge room knows that after turning out half-hearted, mediocre films during his exile, Polanski has crafted a new picture that radiates all the cinematic power and emotional conviction of his best work. Polanski's brooding, darkly humorous sensibility has always attracted Lynch, and *Chinatown* is one of his favorite films. Holding his Palme d'Or, Polanski nods to Lynch, who's standing and clapping with everyone else, and Lynch nods back.

David Lynch, the kid from the small-town Northwest who wanted to be a painter, and then wanted to make movies so he could see his paintings move, has grown up to be a respected member of the worldwide family of elite filmmakers, and a peer of the artists he reveres.

Before the awards ceremony began, Lynch spent a quiet moment alone looking at the neatly stacked red-ribbon-tied rolls of thick, creamy paper, which were the certificates that all prizewinners would receive. Now, forty-five minutes later, these certificates, the fruits of his and his jury's labors, have been bestowed upon the winners, and as the ceremony concludes, Lynch stands with his fellow judges and the award recipients in a happy, buzzing racially and internationally diverse group that fills the wide Grand Palais stage. The language of cinema is indeed universal.

As usual with Lynch, there is more than one layer to reality. Behind the scenes of his TV-and-newspaper-reported Festival experience, Lynch's website crew was filming a more intimate *Cannes Diary*, which only paying members of DavidLynch.com could view in constantly updated installments.

In 1992, after *Twin Peaks: Fire Walk With Me* had been scorned at the Cannes Film festival, Lynch and the very pregnant Mary Sweeney took the trail north to Paris, where Mary gave birth to their son, Riley. Now, ten years later, Lynch and his family have returned to Paris, and David and Mary enjoyed showing young Riley the magnificent city in which he first drew breath. Then they took the train south to Lyon and Marseilles and down the coast to Cannes to attend the Festival.

As Lynch steps off the train in Cannes, we get an instantaneous impression of what a major cultural event the Cannes Festival is for Europeans, for he and Mary are immediately surrounded by journalists, fans, and photographers with video and still cameras. Lynch is in an amiable mood as he faces this crush of attention, and it takes just a few minutes for us to sense two major themes of this Cannes sojourn. First, David Lynch is hugely popular in France: A well-dressed man seems to sum up a group sentiment when he says, "I love your heart, Dahveed,"[232] to which Lynch replies, "Thank you very much."[233] Second, food and drink are central to Lynch's legend: We hear the first pronouncement of what will become a litany over the coming weeks, as he declares his passion for "café au lait, pain du chocolate, baguettes avec fromage, fois gras, and vin rouge."[234] Clearly, as he predicted to me before his trip, his spiritual practice, Ayurvedic, no-wine diet plan has been thrown out the window while he's in Europe.

Like characters in one of his own fictions, Lynch and his family have made a journey from darkness into light, for Paris's gray and rainy skies have given way to the sun-dazzled Côte d'Azur. Lynch exhibits his sensitivity to environments as he recalls that this year's train was an hour faster than last year's, so as they approached the legendary Carlton Hotel (the "queen of the Croisette,"[235] where Cary Grant and Grace Kelly filmed *To Catch a Thief*) in 2002, they were not bathed in the "golden light"[236] he remembered. Still, and no doubt, the sky, the sea, the beach, the palm-tree-studded Croisette promenade, and the ivory-hued hotels were "just beautiful."[237]

One of Lynch's favorite filmmakers, the comic genius Jacques Tati (1908–1982) is to be honored with a retrospective tribute at this year's Festival. Aside from being influenced by Tati's method of eloquently structuring soundtracks, Lynch's personality is kin to the Frenchman's amiable, bemused manner, and both men are sensitive to the dry, poetic absurdity that life just happens to serve up. Surely, Tati's spirit gave a grin over a little scene Lynch, Mary, and their driver spontaneously produced as their Renault pulled into Cannes. The French driver responds to Lynch's "beautiful"[238] with a cheery "Nize deh,"[239] to which the French-fluent Mary replies, "Qu'est qu'il fait beau"[240] ("It certainly is beautiful"). Lynch doesn't speak French, but would like to be able to say some French words when he addresses the Festival audience for the first time. His pronunciation skills could use some work, so he rises to the challenge, and he and Mary engage in a humorous back-and-forth.

Mary: "Qu'est qu'il fait beau."[241]
David: "Qu'est que skay beau."[242]
Mary: "Qu'est qu'il fait beau."[243]
David: "Qu'est que ee fait beau."[244]
Mary: "Qu'est qu'il fait beau."[245]
David: "ee fait, ee."[246]
Mary: "il, il fait."[247]
David: Qu'est que il fait beau."[248]
Mary: "Qu'il fait."[249]
David: "Qu'est qu'il fait."[250]
Mary: "Qu'est qu'il fait beau."[251]
David: "Qu'est qu'il fait beau."[252]

Lynch goes silent and turns his head back to looking out the window as Mary's gentle laugh puts the final punctuation on another unique moment of life with David.

Lynch's sensibility is attuned to signs and portents, and the mural-sized poster arching over the entrance to the Grand Palais seemed to bestow a Lynchian blessing. The poster was touched with the happy-ending grace and imagery of his fictional universe, and it bespoke his beneficent view of the cosmos: A female angel held the hand of a boy/man, and both figures' arms were spread wide as they flew into a blue starfield.

During the Festival's twelve days and nights, Lynch enjoys the camaraderie of film folk and roamed around town making *Cannes Diary* segments about whatever caught his interest. Not surprisingly, subjects of fascination include fois gras ("I'm not even sure what it is"),[253] vin rouge (David is amused to discover the appellation Chateau Lynch Bages), and lengths of wood sawed according to European measurement standards ("It's fantastic, actually, the proportions of the lumber here"[254]).

Lynch's boyish excitement bursts out as he conjures a vivid image: "We're getting ready to go see the 70mm restoration of Jacques Tati's *Playtime*. I've heard, only heard, that we'll be driving a small red car up the Croisette, and when we get to the red carpet, many many many small dogs will be released and they'll go happily up the steps to the Grand Palais, so this will be the beginning of the show."[255] Lynch has both the ability to picture such a scene in his mind and the charming capacity to revel in its reality to the nth degree. Throughout their trip, he and Mary have done an admirable job of keeping ten-year-old Riley out of the media glare, but we catch a glimpse of the slender, dark-haired lad as he and his parents get into a little Renault (blue, as it turns out) and join the small-car parade. Riley sits in the front seat, his parents in back, and they're all laughing like kids on holiday.

Tati's antic spirit reigns at the entrance to the Grand Palais. The red carpet is patterned with big, random yellow and blue dots, and as Lynch expected, a motley group of funny little dogs is scampering pell-mell all over the carpet, just like the canines who roam the streets of Paris in Lynch's favorite Tati film, *Mon Oncle*. And, as in that picture, one dog pees where it's not supposed to—in this case on an elegant potted palm tree. In Lynch's work and mind, the dead are not, in essence, dead, and though Tati passed away in 1982, here he is with his familiar beige raincoat and umbrella, walking up to Lynch. Face to face, the two directors bow, shake hands, and applaud each other.

After a good movie, only one thing hits the spot: In reverent tones Lynch says, "Let's go get a coffee."[256] The world has never seen Lynch more blissed out than when he sits with a "French cappuccino"[257] in his hand. Slowly he raises the steaming cup to his lips, sips, and with soft, whispery emotion says, "Whew, this is *so* good; this is *very* tasty."[258] In *Twin Peaks*, Sheriff Truman counseled Cooper (and all of us) to "give yourself a present every day": Lynch has just followed the sheriff's orders. The importance of java in Lynch's life cannot be overestimated. He talks about how "Coffee is made differently all over the world, so sometimes I have to say, 'Oh no, I don't go there—the coffee is terrible.'"[259]

Lynch is dedicated to his website members, and when he has a spare moment at Cannes he chats with them. Who else but Lynch would have Web-talk pals named Maladroit, Shoebox, Crying Out Loud, Little Man, Jungle of Whispers? Topics of conversation include everything from squirrels ("I haven't seen any in Cannes, but I'm sure there are squirrels in France"[260]) to Roman Polanski being banned from the United States ("It's, uhm, because of certain, uhm, things involving, ah, the law and, uhm, law enforcement"[261]) to homesickness ("Where you are, you are *there*, so you're always with yourself; you are there and not thinking about the past or home or someplace else; you're just thinking about the work today"[262]). Of course it's easier to feel at home when your personal and professional families are with you, and hard to have wandering thoughts when you're "getting up early and going to screenings all the time."[263] Lynch's sense of equanimity and contentment reflect the happy balance of his current emotional situation: At other times in his life, he has felt lost and afraid both at home and away from it.

In the period when Lynch and Isabella Rossellini were real-life lovers, he played her fictional paramour and displayed physical affection in the 1987 film *Zelly and Me*. When being filmed for the documentary *Pretty As a Picture* he hugged Jack Nance, but now, late at night in *Cannes Diary*, he does the most intimate things he's ever done on camera. He looks left and says, "Come here, bud, and give me a hug,"[264] and his son Riley leans into the frame, nestles his head under Lynch's chin, and puts his right arm around his neck. Father and son hold each other for a moment, pat each other on the back, and as Riley pulls back and stands up straight, he faces the camera and flashes a big grin. With a proud, gentle, loving laugh, Lynch says, "All right then, goodnight from Cannes. All along the Croisette they go. We'll see you next time for some more answers to some more great questions."[265] Lynch has a satisfied, sleepy, end-of-a-perfect-day smile on his face—but it may not last long.

Lynch's films are often dreamlike, and Lynch has always valued sleep, being unable to get up early as a young man and angry with those who would wake him. Staying at the ritziest hotel in Cannes, Lynch found himself in a situation that "absolutely guarantees no sleep. There's a drum corps that plays outside from eight at night 'till two in the morning, at 100 to 115 decibels. The hotel has double-pane windows, but it sounds like the drummers are in the room. Someone has the idea that this is something that people would want to hear at this hour, which is an indication of the trouble the world is in."[266] So that dark, creeping sense of "wild pain and decay"[267] that Lynch has been sensitive to since boyhood is alive and thriving and drumming outside his window at Cannes.

Sleep-deprived or not, Lynch feels part of a grand tradition: "There's a feeling wafting here of the golden age of cinema."[268] Lynch has made good on his youthful, modest hope that "I might create a little cinematic magic"[269] in his lifetime. Even though he's told me he doesn't ponder his professional or personal legacy, he's proud that his children and granddaughter are all artistically gifted.

Not only has Lynch, in past years, won the Cannes Film Festival's two highest awards, (the Palme d'Or and Best Director), but by accepting the honor of helping to choose the 2002 prize winners, he's joined the esteemed ranks of past jurors, which include: Jean Cocteau, Fritz Lang, Luis Buñuel, Otto Preminger, Henry Miller, François Truffaut, Michael Powell, Jeanne Moreau, Olivia de Havilland, Vincente Minnelli, Gabriel Garcia-Marquez, Georges Simenon, Françoise Sagan, Ingrid Bergman and Roberto Rossellini (both parents of his former love Isabella), Gene Kelly, Charles Aznavour, Arthur Schlesinger Jr., Pauline Kael, Stanley Donen, Carlos Fuentes, Andre Bazin, George Stevens, Rene Clair, Peter Ustinov, Anthony Burgess, Alain Robbe-Grillet, Louis Malle, Sophia Loren, Luchino Visconti, Yves Montand, and Tennessee Williams.

Just before he left for France, "this tune came in one night,"[270] and he wrote a simple, charming, pleasantly wistful melody that was like a theme song; he called it "Cannes Memory." With John Neff's keyboard backing his trumpet, Lynch recorded the song and produced 1,000 CDs. Once in France, Lynch and company distributed the tune around town. So the clear, brassy sound of Lynch's music, as well as his jury stewardship and bemused, beneficent presence, was absorbed into the ongoing Cannes Film Festival legend.

David Lynch has become part of the cultural history of the modern era and, as if to certify that fact, he was inducted into the prestigious French Legion of Honor. In keeping with Lynch's neighborhood-guy sensibility, the ceremony took place after a little snack in a book-lined room that recalled *Twin Peaks'* Bookhouse Boys retreat. Rather than being surrounded by a Grand Palais–sized audience, Lynch chose to have Mary, Riley, Cannes Festival President Gilles Jacob, and Lynch's friends from his jury witness his big moment. A statement expressing French President Jacques Chirac's "gratitude and admiration"[271] for Lynch was read, and a red-ribbon-and-gold-sunburst medal pinned on his black suit over his heart. Lynch, beaming and shaking his head from side to side in awe and disbelief, kissed the officiating male dignitaries on both cheeks and then turned to Mary and Riley with a loving look and touched them both on the shoulder as everyone in the room applauded. With thankfulness and tenderness in his voice, he said "Merci . . . beaucoup"[272] and declared how honored he was to be appreciated by, and in kinship with, "the French, who are the greatest lovers of art and protectors of art in the world."[273] Yes, David Lynch is now *un chevalier*, but we're sure he doesn't want to be called "Sir David." (There are five levels of Legion of Honor status, and Lynch received a higher-rank award in late 2007.)

With the Legion of Honor badge gleaming on his chest, Lynch had joined an august fraternity that includes, yes, Jerry Lewis, and the legendary Jacques Tati. Lynch was now part of the French cultural elite, but when he attended a night screening of Tati's *Mr. Hulot's Holiday* (1953) on the beach, the only attitude he displayed was his natural humbleness. He spoke of Tati's "unsurpassed comic genius and extraordinary understanding of human nature,"[274] then added, "*but* it is Jacques Tati's tender heart, at work in every frame, that makes us fall in love with his films."[275]

Lynch stood on the beach with hundreds of French movie lovers and laughed with them as Tati's alter ego, Monsieur Hulot, revealed the comically absurd poetry that spices the salt air of a seaside resort. Watching the film, Lynch saw some of his own soul and art reflected back at him. Hulot, like *Eraserhead*'s Henry, and Lynch himself, projects a childlike innocence as he sees the world with fresh eyes and seems to be forever learning about the laws that govern physical phenomena and human interactions. In Tati's film, Lynch heard, as in his work, a wind stream into a room like an invisible force. He saw a man spill the beer he's holding when the fellow turns his wrist to check his watch, as a character in *Twin Peaks: Fire Walk With Me* spills coffee when he checks his watch, and heard an outdoor water tap with a hose attached throb *Blue Velvet*–style when Hulot turns it on. A man in Tati's picture is in a position Lynch and his fictional characters detest: being ordered around and forced to bend to the will of someone other than themselves. And as Hulot accidentally sets off a bunch of fireworks outside at night, Lynch watched a Lynch-like scene of a dark interior that was illuminated by lightning-like flashes—and the light bursts added up to his lucky number, seven.

As the film ended and Lynch looked up into the blue-black sky sparked with stars that was like the starfield he and his brother had gazed at as kids, and which *The Straight Story*'s Alvin and his brother had contemplated, it was easy to feel at one with the continuum of art and life and the universe, now, then, and forever.

Lowering his gaze to the horizon, the Croisette spotlights shooting into the night looked like the Statue of Liberty's up-angled crown points transformed into blue fire; soon he would be heading home to America.

The evening was over, and the people on the beach weren't just a crowd, they were a community celebrating two art-makers: Tati and Lynch. As David's footprints blended with everyone else's in the lumpy sand, he could feel himself stepping into legend. As he walked slowly toward the car waiting for him, he stopped to sign autographs and shake outstretched hands as people shouted, "Dahveed, Dahveed."[276] He kissed women and men on both cheeks, posed for photos as folks put their arms around him, and paused to say a few words to a young boy standing with his father and gazing up at him with a star-struck look. Inside the car, his voice soft with emotion, Lynch said to Mary, "That little kid, his dad was showing him. . . ."[277] Lynch's modesty stopped him from saying his own name, but Mary completed the sentence: "David Lynch."[278] This affecting moment inspired Lynch to add another element to the evening's mood of all-inclusive, loving continuity. "It makes my heart break, cause my granddad took my father, got down on his knees in Fort Benton, Montana, and pointed across the road and said, 'Donny, that's Charles Russell, one of the greatest Western painters in the world right there—don't ever forget you saw him.' My dad was five, and he never forgot it."[279]

Just as Lynch and his art are part of the world culture's immediate experience and replayable heritage, the 55th Cannes Film Festival was now part of David Lynch's life stream. The tents along the Croisette were folding, the red carpets rolling up: As Lynch says with metaphysical humor, "It's time to get in the car and go over to Los Angeles,"[280] as though he could really bend time and space as he does in his fictions.

Watching Lynch at Cannes, he seems to be the happiest man in the world, living a stage of his life best summed up by one of his favorite phrases: "a beautiful thing."[281] He's banished fears about leaving home, performed his duties, even made speeches, like a rock-solid professional; received and returned the respect and affection of worldwide cinema lovers and art appreciators, enjoyed delectable food and drink, spent quality time with his extended website-family, and experienced it all with the woman and son he loves. Sure, it means a lot to receive the Legion of Honor, but the value of his grinning verbal byplay with Mary, and the moment when Riley hugs him around the neck, nestling his head next to his, cannot be measured.

It's been rewarding and fun to take bows on the world stage, but something's calling David Lynch. In spite of all the fulfilling bounty the Cannes experience has provided, and even though he's had his family, both personal and professional, with him, something's been missing. There were no messy cans of industrial paint, worn paintbrushes, or big empty canvases sitting on a wood platform in the Hollywood Hills sunshine. A series of new paintings was exciting Lynch's mind, and he couldn't wait to burrow back into his California hillside, shut the front door, and pursue the passion that first made him an artist as a youth.

Lynch had art-making on his mind when he got home from Cannes in the summer of 2002, but there were more urgent matters of the heart to attend to. His dear daughter, Jennifer, now in her mid-thirties, had suffered from back trouble for years due to a car accident. After recent surgery, she initially felt better, but had suffered a relapse, and was now flat on her back in her mother's (Peggy Reavey) house south of Los Angeles. Once when I called Peggy to chat she said, her voice filled with emotion, "that was just David on the phone—we're trying to figure out what to do about Jennifer."[282] And what to do about Jennifer's little daughter, Sydney, since mom was in no condition to care for her five-year-old's domestic needs, let alone get her to school.

Jennifer was enduring the most horrible period of her life. Her physical condition was dire: Aside from being in

> excruciating pain, the doctors told me I might never walk again, and that if I moved, I could lose my bladder, bowel, and sexual functions. When you lose mobility it's amazing how fast the mind goes. Physical pain and emotional pain can promote each other, and I started thinking that I was being pushed out of the world for some reason, like I was being punished for something. I meditated on these feelings and received an answer: Be quiet and still. I'd been in emotional pain for so long and I'd been ignoring it. I'd always thought the only way to go forward was to continue moving, when in fact it was to stop and take a break and just get quiet. I was handed that opportunity—very significantly [*laughs*]. I thought and meditated and realized I'd screwed myself up into tiny little knots. So I worked on all my resentments and said to myself, "I don't want to hold onto anything I'm angry about, I want to forgive myself and forgive others; I'm just going to whoo [*makes a blowing-wind sound*]—clear the space."[283]

Jennifer can now make that *whoo* sound with more gusto than she could before her painful year spent flat on her back, for the ordeal prompted her to quit smoking for the rest of her life.

"Here I was living in a bed in my mother's house. I had to get completely humble. I had to let my parents be my parents again, and let the three of us be as frightened as we really were. I'm so grateful to them; they took all the things that were terrifying me off my shoulders. They took Sydney wherever she needed to go and kept her in school."[284]

So, the family of David, Peggy, and Jennifer, the family Lynch didn't originally want and which was severed by divorce when Jennifer was nine, was together again twenty-five years later. Both David and Peggy have fulfilling relationships with their own romantic partners, but the intense feelings that accompanied the reconstituting of their original family for the sake of their suffering child had a healing effect on dad, mom, and daughter.[285] When I talked to Jennifer before her bedridden ordeal, she would usually refer to her father as "David," and in a 1991 interview she said, "It was easier for David to handle having a child that could be his buddy rather than a responsibility; we're far more best friends than father and daughter." Over the hours I've spent talking to her since her incapacitation, she's never once called him David. "My father really got the opportunity—with all his new wisdom and serenity—to be my dad. My parents and I have a neat new thing going on now. All of us are getting to reboot the whole thing [*laughs*]."[286]

Jennifer may not have been able to take Sydney for a walk or to school and doctor's appointments, but she did some wonderful mothering in the intimate world defined by her inability to be mobile. When Jennifer was tiny, new father Lynch, unable to afford fancy toys for her, made little mobiles out of colored paper and string that he dangled before his daughter's face to stimulate her senses. Now mother Jennifer, using inexpensive materials at hand (pictures, words, and letters cut from magazines, plus paper sheets and tape) made books with her little Sydney. "We spent hours cutting stuff up, making our own books and reading books, and Sydney's teacher marveled at what an advanced reader she was. I'm so glad I was able to give her the gift of my time."[287] Jennifer, who had felt "freakish"[288] as a schoolgirl because of her clubfoot-surgery-scarred legs and orthopedic shoes, understood that for Sydney to have a mother who was never able to be with her at school and social functions was hard on her daughter. So, she told her, "It's nothing to be ashamed of; it's just the way things are right now,"[289] and was gratified to overhear Sydney saying to her little friends, "That's the way things are right now."[290]

As time passed, and when it was meant to be, things were a different way: Jennifer got better. "Every morning when I stand up I am so happy. Just performing that act makes everything special—it's like being born again. How many people get the chance to realize how much they really want to live at the age of thirty-four? Boy do I want to live, and walk around [*laughs*]."[291] Over the years, David Lynch has taught Jennifer "to see crises as the birth of something new, of new opportunities: the universe has provided this for me; there is something in it for me."[292] Immobilized in bed for over a year, she found herself in the position of many of Lynch's characters: horizontal and living inside their heads. "I had to rely so much on my mind for sustenance, and that was so valuable to me. When I was bedridden at my mom's—I was down for two Christmases—I used my imagination to move around. Hope makes its nest in movement, and since I didn't know what the streets were like outside mom's place, and where the trees were, I created streets in my mind that I would walk in. I would daydream about just walking around the corner."[293] Like the favored of Lynch's fictional people, Jennifer has made the soul-wrenching journey from darkness to beneficent light. She has faced intense fear, calmed seething resentments and angers, and basked in the accepting and bestowing of love. "As my father says, 'It's a world of lessons.' I've received so much from this experience, and I make sure I'm giving back."[294]

After recovering from her ordeal, Jennifer is

> in this huge hurry to pay back my parents financially and emotionally, like I have to redeem myself somehow. Maybe the biggest gift they've given me is that they keep reminding me to just take it slowly, that their repayment is my physical comfort and well-being. When I think of my relationship to my daughter, of course that makes sense; that would be my attitude too. But when I think of me to my parents, I get manic and I think, "But God, I just want to *do* something for you." Anyway, they've helped me see that I shouldn't sweat the stuff I can't do right now, and that what's most rewarding for all of us is for me to enjoy my life, to do everything I love, everything I can do each day.[295]

To do what you love as often as possible has certainly been David Lynch's credo over the years. Sometimes the pursuit of his Art Life bliss had left little time, energy, and will to meet the needs and wishes of others. Of their earliest period as parent and child, Jennifer has said, "I don't think he was ready to teach anything to anyone."[296] But now, looking back over the decades, she speaks glowingly of the life principles that she's learned from her father:

> Our family values hold that we're not on this planet to crap on everything. We have to improve the space we're in and make the world better for those who come after us. My father is someone I forever look to for growth and new wisdom. I'm so fortunate to have him as an example because he's an incredible artist and an incredible man. He's taught me that life is not about sideways

> motion and getting something that someone else has. It's about rising and discovering your own path upwards. He sees the exceptional beauty in what other people call the ordinary; the word *ugly* is not in his vocabulary.[297]
>
> It's really inspiring to see my father take such joy in what he does. Sure, if he had Spielberg's money he could do things differently, but having that high level of wealth isn't all of the permission to create: The permission is something he grants himself. My father's got so much respect for what he's putting out there. He doesn't do things for everybody else, he does them because of something inside him that he has to express. What an amazing thing that he chose to be an artist at such a young age. He knew that it would be a difficult path—but why would that stop him? He's shown me that difficult things can be more fun, because you feel so rewarded by accomplishing them. My father and I don't shy away from hard work, but we avoid what's unnecessary.[298]

Lynch has spoken of how his mother "saved my imagination"[299] by encouraging him to draw on paper free of restricting lines, and he has passed this gift along to Jennifer. "I was raised to place such a tremendous amount of value on my dreams and imagination; there was no fence around my head."[300] She is moved, and guided, by the way Lynch "shows us things with the intensity of a child's view, as if we were seeing them for the first time. He comes from innocence, curiosity, and being open to the absolute potential of the smallest thing. I really think that's how we redeem ourselves, by seeing our lives through the eyes of a child. They're absolutely willing to take in anything. Everything is new and precious to them."[301] The Lynchian visionary sense, which centers on the mystery and wonder of existence, is something Jennifer will strive to pass along to her daughter. Thanks to the example her father set for her, Jennifer is able to treasure gifts of perception and spirit that little Sydney spontaneously passes along. "The other day Sydney stopped at the base of a big tree. She touched it, stared up into its branches, and said, 'Are you sure this started as a seed?'"[302]

Jennifer is a no-nonsense, streetwise, outspoken L.A. woman who can boss teamsters around and argue and win a multimillion-dollar lawsuit. Like her father, she's a fully functioning adult who can survive and grow in the often-toxic atmosphere of the American entertainment industry. But also like Lynch, she's ever ready to be an amazed youngster. In an instant, she'll interrupt a deep-dish conversation about the nature of the human soul to exclaim, "Wow—a mother skunk and five babies are walking across the lawn! Mary Sweeney and my dad call me Saint Francis, because no matter where I go, animals come to me."[303] She tells me about the huge, timid raccoon "with a damaged, deformed front leg"[304] that became accustomed to her leaving water out for it. And she speaks excitedly of her litter of just-born kittens: "It's like a nativity scene; I'm a proud grandmother! There's nothing like waking up in the middle of the night with a little kitten on your head to put a smile on your face."[305] The kittens were born a few days before Jennifer's birthday, the anniversary of the day she entered the world with two severely clubbed feet that had to be operated on. She seems to take a special pleasure in saying, "I'm so glad they were all born so healthy."[306] Jennifer's beloved cat, Fiction, which had been part of her life from the sixteen years since her original, back-injuring car accident, had just died. She's decided to find good homes for the newborn kittens, and raise one herself to "keep the cycle going."[307]

Cycles, passages, transformations, death, and rebirth: It sounds like a David Lynch movie, and the movie of Lynch's life. The small-town boy whose world was defined by the street where he lived has become a renowned artist who is known around the globe. He has suffered setbacks, losses, and emotional wounds, but has always mustered the fortitude to keep moving forward on his chosen path. His belief in evolution and growth, both for himself and his fellow creatures, has given his work and his relationships a deepening maturity and a more expansive sense of humanity. As Jennifer says, "When my father finds himself presented with something to learn from, he does it. He'll do it in his own time, but he learns. Now he has more faith and trust that it is an abundant universe in which we're all provided for. He's calmed down; he has fewer fears in his life."[308] Fewer, yes, but strong fears still plague him. Lynch strives to control his work and his world as much as possible, so just the idea of getting on a plane and putting his life in someone else's hands fills him with, as Jennifer says, "tremendous anxiety."[309] Still, he will force himself to fly if he can define it as being a necessary part of his artistic process. Late in 2002, he and his sound engineer and musician, John Neff, took off for Paris, where the two played music from their *Blue Bob* CD in front of concert audiences. They and their electric guitars did a fine job of conveying *Blue Bob*'s industrial heavy metal, pounding-factory sounds, but Lynch felt very uncomfortable performing before a live crowd, as opposed to playing nestled within the safe confines of his home studio. A French photographer named Sophie who saw the show noted that Lynch's mood went from "more nervous"[310] to "freaked-out."[311] As Jennifer says, "He's got to put on some kind of mental armor in a situation like that. He's afraid of things coming at him, rather than him being able to observe *them*."[312]

Lynch was leery of the *Blue Bob* European concert concept well before he experienced it. But, also in 2003, he contemplated another transcontinental trip with eager anticipation. He learned that for a large sum of money he could, with a few other lucky Transcendental Meditation devotees, spend days and nights with his spiritual leader, the Maharishi Mahesh Yogi, at the sage's retreat in Vlodrop, Holland. So he wrote out the check, made his plane reservation, and flew off into the scary skies. As Peggy Reavey told me, Lynch's deep meditations with the Maharishi "took him into dark areas as well as joyful ones,"[313] and Mary Sweeney received some long-distance calls from her troubled partner late at night. Still, Lynch remembered that years ago his deep Philadelphia fears had eventually lifted, and soon so did his Vlodrop ones. Coming from menacing Philadelphia to California for the first time in 1970, Lynch experienced the soft, warm, golden-bright Los Angeles air as an anxiety-evaporating, restorative, stimulating balm to his mind and senses, just as his character Betty Elms does in *Mulholland Drive*. Back in his Hollywood Hills sanctuary, he regarded his time with the Maharishi as a "wonderful experience,"[314] even though he had one major disagreement with his spiritual teacher. "The Maharishi said, 'David, I wish that you would stop smoking,' and I said, 'I'm not going to do that.'"[315]

The Beatles' 1967–1968 championing of Transcendental Meditation inspired the world's interest in the Marharishi and his spiritual practices and teachings. The Fab Four were also the first to raise some doubts about the white-bearded wise man from the East. When they and other Western-culture notables, including actress Mia Farrow, visited the Maharishi's ashram in India for meditation and teaching sessions, a member of the Beatles' retinue claimed that the Maharishi, who never claimed that he was celibate, was using his exalted position to gain sexual favors from at least one of the female meditators. And Mia Farrow interpreted the Maharishi touching her after a private meditation session as a romantic advance.

Angry and disappointed, the Beatles and Farrow went home early in a huff, and John Lennon wrote the song "Sexy Sadie" as a veiled mockery of the Maharishi and said he no longer believed in the guru. The Maharishi has never been given a chance to deny or explain these sexual allegations, and no corroborating witnesses ever came forward, so the truth remains ambiguous.

John, Paul, and Ringo may have lost faith in the Maharishi, but George Harrison remained a devoted TM practitioner and Maharishi supporter until his death in 2001. Today there are more people practicing TM around the world than ever before, and no one believes more in the Maharishi and his ethos than David Lynch.

Another longtime Transcendental Meditator is singer-actress Julee Cruise, whose lost-angel, high heavenly voice, wedded for eternity to Angelo Badalamenti's music, was the achingly emotional aural soul of *Twin Peaks*. August 2002 marked the tenth anniversary of the U.S. premiere of *Twin Peaks: Fire Walk With Me* in North Bend, Washington, where part of the picture was filmed. Lynch and the whole cast weren't here for the anniversary as they had been for the debut, but Julee Cruise was. As film curator for the Twin Peaks Festivals each summer, I'd long dreamed of having Julee sing the gorgeously melancholy "Questions in a World of Blue," which provides a thematically potent passage in *Twin Peaks: Fire Walk With Me*, before showing the film. On August 17, 2002, my dream came true.

In a small-town movie house kitty corner from the Double R Diner (Mar T Café), and packed with Lynch fans, Julee stepped from behind a red curtain, her expression sad, her tranced movements slow, and sang the song without any musical accompaniment. It was her artistic choice to deliver the song with only her voice, and the effect was stunning, as she sang at a slowed-down tempo, as though drugged with wounding dreams, filling every word with poignant feeling, and with every heart-breath audible. Lynch's lyrics, which perfectly expressed Laura Palmer's mournful turning away from light and love, were written at a time when he and Cruise shared a happy musical partnership. Knowing that they were now estranged, and having heard respectful, yet acrimonious accounts of their split from both sides, Cruise's 2002 performance of the song seemed to me to speak of her and Lynch's sundered state: "Why did you go? Why did you turn away from me? When all the world seemed to sing. Why, why did you go? Was it me? Was it you? Questions in a world of blue."[316]

When I thanked Julee for her stunning performance, she spoke excitedly of her high hopes for the Broadway show she was about the launch. The project would showcase her acting talent as well as her singing, for she would play eight parts, including Andy Warhol. Sadly, perhaps due to a particularly negative review (Julee says the drama critic had a personal vendetta against her project's director), the show never gained audience momentum, and closed quickly. This professional setback, coupled with the death of her beloved dog, put Julee in a world of blue. But, knowing that performing an optimistic act is the best thing to do when you're feeling the worst, she spontaneously grabbed the phone and called David Lynch.

Lynch's 1990 stage production *Industrial Symphony No. 1*, in which Julee sang the role of a rejected lover writhing in emotional pain, began with Nicolas Cage and Laura Dern on opposite ends of a phone line as Cage extinguished their love and broke Dern's heart. Cruise and Lynch's 2002 phone talk was the antithesis of Cage and Dern's. Cruise's Christian faith and Lynch's Hindu beliefs met on a beneficent plane of past hurts forgiven and love rekindled, and they spoke warmly of once again making beautiful music together.

Grief and loss, as well as joyful reconciliation, filled Lynch's life in recent times. Gaye Pope, his longtime assistant, died suddenly from an illness she didn't know she had: Again Lynch saw that "force of wild pain and decay"[317] hidden beneath the surface of things manifest itself. I first met Gaye in 1991 when she challenged me about taking notes on the set of *Twin Peaks: Fire Walk With Me*; over the years she became a great friend of my book project. In addition to keeping Lynch's hectic Asymmetrical Productions office running smoothly, managing publicity for his projects, and giving him professional advice, Gaye was the one who typed the words Lynch spoke as his mind produced ideas and sentences that became the screenplays of many of his works, including *Mulholland Drive*. She was devoted to Lynch's art, and even after she amicably departed from Asymmetrical and formed a production company with Neil Edelstein, she would come to Lynch's house to take dictation. Again and again in his fictions Lynch portrays the theme of domestic invasion, of a safe, tranquil abode, or a mind, being pierced by dark, destructive forces. One day, in the hushed, familiar solitude of his Hollywood Hills compound, Lynch was speaking words that Gaye wrote down, as he had hundreds and hundreds of times before. Pausing, he asked her to read back what he'd just said, and she replied, "I can't see the words; something's happening."[318]

For thirty-three years Lynch's Hindu philosophy has helped him deal with sorrow and loss and joy and everything in between, and today his spiritual beliefs shape his life more than ever. He knows that, in addition to living in the beginning of the twenty-first century, we are also, more importantly, experiencing the cyclic Hindu cosmology's Kali Yuga ("age of strife"),[319] a dangerous time (lasting 432,000 years) that reinforces his decades-long perception of the world as a "fearful place filled with darkness and confusion."[320] He still eats an occasional burger or drinks a glass of red wine, but otherwise he strictly adheres to a diet in harmony with India's ancient Ayurvedic ("life knowledge") health system. Hindus see the cow as the seat of many gods, and the substances the animal produces as imparting spiritual purity to those who consume them. Lynch eats a lot of ghee (clarified butter), along with vegetables, salad greens, some chicken, the spices cumin and turmeric, and, for breakfast, stewed pears. He promotes Transcendental Meditation during his DavidLynch.com chatroom sessions, displays official TM information and news from the Maharishi's media network on his website, and takes dips in "the ocean of oneness,"[321] meditating with his office staff in the soundproof studio where, at other times, he blasts rock and roll music and screens his fierce, soul-searing films.

The actual measurable threat to a given American on a given day, even after September 11, is low. Yet all his life, Lynch, due to his sensitive nature, which helps make him so artistically gifted, has sought to protect himself from the fearsome chaos he perceives in the world by adhering to reassuringly regularized patterns of eating and drinking, sleeping and waking, working and meditating. These repeating habits give his soaring imagination a secure grounding and a sense of control over his life. In recent years, his spiritual pursuits have become a unifying motivator that has influenced more of his thinking and behavior. Peggy Reavey tells me that Lynch—who voted for arch-Republican Ronald Reagan and was a committed political hawk—"can't stand George W. Bush"[322] with his preemptive, God-ordained, dubiously justified war against Iraq; his belligerent, gauche manner and fumbling speaking style; his disdain for international consensus, science, and fact-based reality; and his pushing for establishment of the Patriot Act, which endangers the civil liberties that Lynch the Eagle Scout grew up pledging his allegiance to. "David's become a total peacenik,"[323] with a strong personal belief in nonviolence that Peggy has urged him to express in his films, citing the inspiring example of Martin Luther King Jr. (who in turn was inspired by the Hindu political-spiritual leader Mahatma Gandhi). It's hard to imagine Lynch ever abandoning his artistic obsession with the dark recesses of the human psyche, but these days he has a growing desire to spread the hopeful radiance, which has also always been present in his work out beyond movie screens, gallery walls, and chatrooms.

Lynch's guide for proclaiming the good news of spiritual awakening is, of course, the Maharishi Mahesh Yogi. The core of the Maharishi's message is derived from Patanjali's *Yoga Sutras*, written two centuries before Christ's birth. The *Sutras*' 194 aphorisms proclaim that the sins of greed, delusion, and anger can be counteracted by practicing the virtues of truth, love, and nonviolence, thus helping the individual attain peace of mind, the effect of which radiates outward, influencing others to live in harmony. The well-being of one was said to increase the well-being of all; the effect of peace-grounded individuals would be so strong that even wild animals would become tame. As the Maharishi put it in 1977, his Year of Ideal Society, "Individuals meditate—Individual life improves—Society as a whole improves."[324] The Maharishi, John Hagelin (the Natural Law Party's 2000 presidential candidate who Lynch supported), Lynch himself, and the multitudes who practice Transcendental Meditation in more that fifty nations believe this passionately. But, as when I talked to Lynch about the

September 11 tragedy, a logical question arises: If the number of people meditating on a given day is constant throughout the world, producing a uniform protective mantel of beneficent security, how do sudden eruptions of massive violence, and natural and economic disasters occur?

All his life Lynch has been sensitive to the battle between forces of light and darkness, good and evil, and has portrayed it in his work with a rare balance of elegant beauty, raw-nerve power, brain-twisting complexity, and shadowland poetry. In *Blue Velvet*, Lynch's surrogate, Kyle MacLachlan, his brow furrowed like Lynch's, fervently asks, "Why is there so much trouble in the world?" The film viscerally shows us that there are indeed sadistic sex and mutilation, suicidal despair, catastrophic illness, endless tears, violent death, and an eternal devouring darkness in the world. But there is also a blond angel with a dream of deliverance and redemption, a dream that comes true. In *Twin Peaks: Fire Walk With Me*, Laura Palmer, Lynch's most poignant victim of the night, looks at a picture of an angel watching over vulnerable young children and wonders, "Is it true?" In his heart and soul, Lynch knows that it is. So does the Maharishi, who also knows that the present level of pure-minded Hindu spiritual practice cannot completely counteract negative influences from "our own society, other countries, other cultures, even sun, moon, stars, galaxies—influences, so many, many influences from all over the world, make the mind of a person, make their intellect to decide this, and this, and this."[325] Thus, terrorists with poisoned minds are able to fly hijacked jet planes toward the two tallest buildings in New York.

Lynch, entranced in his art-making, or meditating, or enjoying a good meal, talking to Mary, playing with Riley, feeling free and energized in whatever he does, knows that being in a blissful state is not only possible, but is the natural birthright of humankind. And by making it possible, through Transcendental Meditation, for more and more people to feel this way, to attain this spiritual realization, Lynch's world, and our world, will be brighter, safer, and happier.

Lynch contemplates a universe that is mostly composed of unknown dark matter, in a world where human beings share more than 90 percent of their genetic makeup with apes. Where some people get sexual pleasure from eating and excreting the heads of Barbie dolls, or squishing small live animals with their bare feet. Where thieves use computers to steal people's identities, creating an "evil twin" with your identification numbers who spends money you don't have. Where a policewoman wakes in the night and instead of reaching for her asthma inhaler, grabs her pistol and blows a hole in her cheek; and a man who gets overcharged at McDonald's smashes his SUV through the restaurant's front window and demolishes the counter and cash register. A place where frog populations are becoming deformed and whales are swimming onto beaches and dying, and where a group of people poison themselves to death in order to join their spiritual masters, who they believe are waiting for them behind the Hale-Bopp Comet. Where preachers sin and condemned serial killers find God, and the incidence of political torture and Alzheimer's disease and AIDS climbs ever higher, and drug-resistant bacteria attack our bodies, computer viruses gnaw at the information age, and government policies and the corporate state devour our personal privacy and freedom. The world is as crazy and scary as ever: We are indeed living in the Kali Yuga, the age of strife. According to Lynch, we're 5,000 years into it, with 427,000 to go. But there will be a momentary respite, a blink of the eye in the vast cycle of world time: "a tiny golden age of less than 2,000 years—something to look forward to."[326] In the deepest shadows, Lynch will always find an aperture of illumination, a doorway he can best see by dwelling in the dark. Then the Kali Yuga will continue to its conclusion, in which the universe will be destroyed by fire, then be reconstituted in a vast golden age that will eventually devolve into the next Kali Yuga, and thus, forever.

Lynch knows his proper place in this huge scheme of things. He's right where he's supposed to be, manifesting the thoughts and feelings and intuitions that hum through his being, expressing his unique humanness that reflects all our humanity, from the mud to the stars. His evolving spirit tells him that what he deeply needs to do with his life is what the world needs him to do.

In the following months, Lynch committed to being an official ambassador for the Transcendental Meditation movement, and planned to give lectures at some of the Maharishi's Peace Universities to be built in Moscow, St. Petersburg, and other international locations. He also accepted a Lifetime Achievement Award from the Stockholm Film Festival in Sweden. Animator-director Mike Judge (*Beavis and Butt-head, King of the Hill, Office Space*) told me that Lynch had been the greatest influence on his art, and Lynch-protégé Eli Roth's horror film *Cabin Fever* was well received by critics and audiences. England's *Guardian* newspaper, working with an esteemed group of international film critics, selected a list of "the world's forty best directors,"[327] and David Lynch was number one. Among those chosen were Martin Scorsese, Joel and Ethan Coen, Terence Malick, Abbas Kiarostami, David Cronenberg, Wong Kar-Wai, Quentin Tarantino, Paul Thomas Anderson, Ang Lee, and Lars von Trier. The directors were judged on the substance, look, craft, originality, and intelligence of their work, and Lynch was the only one to score a nineteen out of a possible twenty for originality. The jurors felt that "David Lynch is the most important filmmaker of the current era,"[328] and that "no one makes films like him."[329] They concluded, "We wouldn't want to live in the places he takes us. Somehow, we suspect, we do."[330]

Lynch mourned the deaths of California's golden cowboy (and Lynch's candidate for president) Ronald Reagan, and *Mulholland Drive*'s Coco, Ann Miller, who Lynch called "a straight shooter, a kind, honest person"[331] who was "down-to-earth *and* in the upper echelons—a great human being and a great star."[332] He saw that the International Film Critics Society ranked *Blue Velvet*'s Frank Booth number five on their list of The World's Top 100 Villains, noted that the Library of Congress added *Eraserhead* to their archive of the greatest American films, and heard Dino De Laurentiis say that *Blue Velvet* was the best film the mogul ever made. These days, thanks to video, Lynch sees more movies than when he was younger. Naturally, he enjoys some (*The Terminator* series, *The Bourne Identity*, *Face/Off*, *The Hours*—especially Julianne Moore as a quietly depressed and desperate 1950s housewife) more than others (*Magnolia*, *Adaptation*).

Meanwhile Lynch was at work on his latest unique artistic place: *Snootworld*. This film would return him to animation, the medium in which he first made his images move, though this time they would be computer-generated and cavort on the screen for feature length instead of a few minutes. Eschewing the raw and nasty content of his *Dumbland* website cartoons, *Snootworld* would be family friendly and have a companion book: Peggy Reavey said it "would be David's *Harry Potter*."[333] Lynch typically wouldn't divulge any story details, but Michael J. Anderson, remembering tidbits Lynch mentioned years earlier, thinks *Snootworld* is "a place where all the men have the same first name, and all the women have the same first name."[334]

Financing for *Snootworld* was not materializing in the spring of 2004, so Lynch made some TM-related appearances in Eastern Europe and attended a Polish film festival. Some close to him surmised that while in Europe he was location-scouting old factories with the idea of finally doing *Ronnie Rocket*.

Back home, Lynch's summer of 2004 was proceeding routinely: He'd shoot a big commercial for L'Oreal hair-color products starring 2004 Best Actress Oscar–winner Charlize Theron to help pay the bills and then head to Wisconsin with Mary (who was trying harder than ever to get him to stop smoking), Riley, daughter Jennifer, and granddaughter Sydney. Wisconsin, the heartland where Mary's family is rooted, and where Lynch was flooded with thoughts and feelings about brothers and parents and children, the journeys and passages of life, when he filmed *The Straight Story*. June was going good—but then how could *this* be?

Lynch's parents, Donald and Sunny, both approaching ninety years of age, are Southern California residents who summer in the cooler, Big Sky breezes of Donald's native Montana. They were driving in the Whitefish area where they live in a log home surrounded by the retired woodsman's favorite Ponderosa Pines. Pulling from a side farm road onto a highway at a forty-five-degree angle, their view of the road hemmed in by big trees, they were struck by a fast-moving truck. The truck hit Donald's driver's side, breaking his leg. Sunny, his wife of fifty-nine years, died instantly. The terrible news traveled fast in the Lynch family. Over the phone, David kept saying in disbelief, "My mother's dead. My mother's been killed."[335]

Donald was in a Montana hospital, and David and his sister, Martha (both in California), and brother, John (in Washington State), flew to his bedside. Donald didn't know yet that Sunny was dead, and the pastor of Donald and Sunny's church, after discussing the situation with their children, told him that his wife was gone. David and his siblings decided that Dad should not live alone, and would decide which of them would welcome Donald to their home for the rest of his life. They also worried that their father would blame himself for Sunny's death. When I was honored to spend time with Donald and Sunny a few years earlier, they (in addition to being warm, gracious, good-humored, and proud of their children) seemed the picture of vital resilience, as they beamed and declared that they'd lived through eight decades. After the car crash, Peggy Reavey told me that Sunny was a strong person, a survivor, whereas Donald was a more vulnerable soul.

From youth onward, Lynch's mind has dwelled on the beautiful backyard cherry tree which, he suddenly sees, has a seeping wound in which red ants swarm; the idyllic small town or household or human psyche where, when you least expect it, "things can go bad."[336] Bachelor Henry in *Eraserhead* discovers that he's the father of an unplanned, monstrous baby; *The Elephant Man*'s John Merrick is abducted from his hospital heaven into freak-show slavery; *Blue Velvet*'s Sandy comprehends that her Jeffrey's been sleeping with shadow-zone denizen Dorothy; *Twin Peaks*' Sarah and Leland Palmer learn that their daughter's been murdered; *Wild at Heart*'s ideal lovers Sailor and Lula find out they're each capable of betrayal; and *Lost Highway*'s Fred and *Mulholland Drive*'s Diane see that their rosy dreams of a better life mask nightmares that they can't escape. But Lynch also sees, and shows us, dark pathways flooded with beatific light, bonds of love renewed and strengthened by enduring harrowing trials, and rebirths as the inevitable outcome of deaths.

Fifty-one years ago, when Lynch was seven and playing with other kids in the forested twilight of Idaho, he and the grown-ups had heard a strange, spooky moaning from the trees. Everyone stopped, listened, and they heard it again. Lynch's mother, wanting to banish her and everyone's fear said, "I hope those are friendly sounds."[337] Lynch's life and art have been rich with fear and friendliness: all the dire, destructive, death-dealing, hopeful, creative, life-affirming aspects of the human condition.

Peggy Reavey recalls that Sunny Lynch was "smart as a whip"[338] and that her ready humor could be tart at times. She and her husband were the best of friends, and she had high standards for her children. Peggy says David "definitely felt pressure to measure up."[339] He feels his mother set him on an artistic course as a child, when she gave him drawing paper without lines on it, metaphorically opening up the whole wide world for his aesthetic exploration. She didn't like it when her teenaged artist son said he was going to his studio to paint instead of attending his high school classes, but she let him go.[340]

Sunny wasn't always charmed by her son's work. *Eraserhead* prompted her to say, "I hope I never have a dream like that,"[341] and right after she saw *Blue Velvet*, Lynch says, "she had open-heart surgery."[342] She suffered from heart trouble for years, but got to live a long, full life, rich with education, family, and friends. She presided over an extended Lynch clan that included three successful adult children, nine blossoming grandchildren, a great grandchild, and even a son's ex-wife, Peggy. Many times in the past, she might have succumbed to health problems, but she didn't. Still, David Lynch's mother was dead. She would never again hug him or scold him or give him an extra helping of turkey and gravy on Thanksgiving. She wouldn't be there to help resolve any lingering mother-son issues, or hear a goodbye "I love you."

In speaking, Lynch sometimes uses the phrase "car crash"[343] to denote a very bad happening, and in his films car crashes are more than colliding vehicles: they are chaos unleashed, the hungry jaws of death itself. Lynch is especially sensitive to the lethal power of automobiles (Jennifer says as the years go by he's become a slower, "more tentative" driver),[344] and now that power has taken away the woman who delivered him into the world. This is tragic—but for someone like Lynch who believes in the workings of fate and karma and the certainty of reincarnation into new worlds of life, this is also the way things happen: what *is*. She is on her way.

The Northwest where Lynch grew up, and especially the region in which he imagined and realized his *Twin Peaks* saga, is permeated with the spirit of nineteenth-century Native American Chief Seattle. This Suquamish leader spoke eloquently of the here and the hereafter: "Our dead never forget this beautiful world that gave them being. They still love its winding rivers, its great mountains, and its sequestered vales, and they ever yearn in tenderest affection over the lonely-hearted living, and often return to visit, guide, and comfort them."[345]

Lynch's Hindu beliefs consoled him, the certainty that he and his mother were forever inseparable aspects of "the unified field of consciousness, the self of us all."[346]

As the months rolled by, Jennifer Lynch prepared to make her film *Surveillance* and attended the Twin Peaks Festival in the Northwest, where she had a ball and "was treated like a god."[347] Donald Lynch's recovery proceeded slowly; he wasn't up to attending his wife's funeral, but his children told him that Sunny, the former naval officer, had been given a twenty-one-gun salute. David Lynch's name was mentioned by the media more often for his Transcendental Meditation connection than for his artistic pursuits. He established the David Lynch Foundation, which sought donations to enable those who couldn't afford the $2,500 TM program to learn the technique for free. Talking to his former love Isabella Rossellini on the phone, he chuckled and asked, "Do you know anyone with a billion dollars?"[348] Stay-at-home, afraid-to-fly, crowd-shy Lynch embarked on a college tour of eastern, middle, and western America in the fall of 2005, appearing with TM luminary John Hagelin and testifying to the blissful effect the spiritual discipline has had on his personal and professional life. Lynch himself accepted no money for this grueling tour; it was a labor of love, and hundreds of people had to be turned away from each overflow-crowd venue.

Lynch knew that those who came to his one-night-only appearances were more interested in his art than his promotion of Transcendental Meditation, and he had news regarding both of his occupations to share. True to his view of the world, big things had been going on hidden beneath the surface, for Lynch had been secretly shooting a new feature film, *INLAND EMPIRE*, for two years. The film's focus will be the theme of all his work: a person, in this case a woman, "who's in trouble, and who gets involved in a mystery."[349] Lynch said nothing publicly about his film beyond this succinct summation. But he knew that the empire inland was the inner life of his heroine (Laura Dern), that there would be an ominous curse and identities in flux, secret romantic/sexual relationships, characters having to prostitute their bodies and/or their ideals and integrity; and he would blend some of his website's

Rabbits and a Polish circus into the mix. More than ever, he would express his spiritual beliefs in his art, for *INLAND EMPIRE*'s organizing principle would be reincarnation and past lives, and a recurring karmic reminder would proclaim, "There's a bill that must be paid."

Peggy Reavey has always felt that "David would be an effective guru for Transcendental Meditation."[350] And when he gave his TM presentation at my alma mater, Seattle's University of Washington, it was clear that the man speaking of *INLAND EMPIRE*'s troubled soul was himself radiating intense happiness. The massive audience listened raptly as Lynch's passion for world peace filled the room and he conjured one of his unique images: "Meditation makes the suffocating rubber clown suit of negativity start dissolving."[351] He concluded with the kind of nonverbal communication that abounds in his work: He silently offered the crowd the peace sign—and they rose in a long, standing ovation.

Backstage I shook Lynch's hand and he eagerly asked, "How did you like it?" He squeezed my hand a little tighter when I said, "You always bring the light."

Lynch maintains that "negativity can't live in the light of" the positive, peaceful vibrations that meditators radiate out into society, but in our world of dualities, some people disagree. Master filmmaker Werner Herzog proclaimed in his stunning film *Grizzly Man* that "the common denominator of the universe is not harmony, but chaos, hostility, and murder." Herzog feels that "we cannot sit all the time turning our consciousness inward. We must be looking outward and be active, not passive, so that we can detect evil and fight it." Some commentators wonder—given that the Maharishi and his organization, which includes key participant David Lynch, all believe that increasing the number of Transcendental Meditators will bring world peace—why do they charge $2,500 per person to learn TM? Why don't they just show everyone how to do the technique for free, thus achieving universal bliss *now*, instead of at some never-quite-arrived-at future time?

Lynch was blissed in the now as he contemplated his father's ninetieth-birthday cake at a family gathering at the end of 2005. The confection was like a family sacrament, decorated with a golden sun for his departed mother, Sunny, and evergreen trees for Donald, the woodsman.

Lynch grinned as he, his love Mary, son Riley, daughter Jennifer, granddaughter Sydney, son Austin, sister Martha, brother John, and some of Donald Lynch's old Forest Service pals celebrated Donald's big day. The cake was shared, a beaming Donald was showered with loving appreciation, four generations of Lynches chatted happily, and David's young son scooted around the room taking pictures of everyone; like his father, turning the world into images.

A love of images first brought art school students David Lynch and Peggy Lentz (now Reavey) together. For more than forty years, whether married or divorced, they have been intimately part of each other's lives. As Peggy says, "We're soul mates who can't live together."[352] For the thirty-three years that Lynch has been a Transcendental Meditation devotee he's urged Peggy to embrace his chosen spiritual practice. She never has. But in the fall of 2005 she'd been doing her own form of spiritual house cleaning, and she phoned David and came over to his studio for lunch.

As Peggy began to enjoy the salad Lynch made for her, she watched David concoct his curious lunch. "He poured some green goop with seaweed in it into a glass, and had a bowl of raisins, peanuts, and M&Ms."[353] They chatted about *INLAND EMPIRE*, Francis Bacon, the painter they both love, and the mystery of why, after not smoking for twenty years, he's inhaled cigarettes nonstop for the past fourteen years. Lynch explained with characteristic simplicity, "All that time I wasn't smoking I realized how much I loved it, so I started again."[354] Even Lynch's TM guru, the Maharishi, couldn't get him to quit. Ironically, Peggy says, "I think David feels that his involvement with Transcendental Meditation balances anything damaging he does to himself, or to others."[355]

But Peggy was here with David to do some major spiritual damage control of her own, to "make amends."[356] Knowing well Lynch's capacity for anger, she spoke of something she did to him decades ago, which has given her a heavy burden of shame, guilt, and remorse. Lynch smiled at her and said, "No, no. I deserved that; I needed to feel that at the time. It wasn't bad for you to do that."[357]

Doing what we need and want always affects other people. Three years earlier, Lynch began doing photographic studies of a young woman he'd met. He learned that Emily Stofle had acting experience, and cast her in *INLAND EMPIRE*. Shooting a scene for the film, Lynch operated the digital video camera himself, literally kneeling at the woman's feet in a reverie of aesthetic adoration. Lynch the romantic artist and man had a new muse. He was in love with this woman, who was dark-haired like Lynch's major loves Peggy Reavey, Mary Fisk, Isabella Rossellini, and Mary Sweeney. Mary endured Lynch's divided affections for months, then moved out with their son Riley, in the spring of 2006. For personal reasons, Lynch and Mary married for a month in June, then divorced over "irreconcilable differences."[358]

Some close to Lynch were dismayed, feeling he was letting his heart overrule his head, saying that Mary Sweeney was the glue that had held his art factory and business enterprise together. But Lynch trusted his inner sense that a new chapter of his life was beginning.

And sometimes old chapters are expanded. In August 2006, father, mother, and daughter, David, Peggy, and Jennifer, had a special get-together at Lynch's studio. Like *Eraserhead* (which Lynch had made when Jennifer was a little girl and he and Peggy were still married), *INLAND EMPIRE* was an independent production, and Lynch, free from any constraints imposed by co-creators or corporate bosses, shot hour and hours of footage at leisure. But now he was in a frenzy of "editing, editing, editing!"[359] by himself, since Mary Sweeney, his editor for twenty years, was out of his art-making life. And Lynch had a drop-deal deadline: the Venice Film Festival would give him their prestigious Golden Lion Award for Career Achievement achievement award on September 6, and *INLAND EMPIRE* had to be ready to show on that date.

Lynch screened his rough cut for Peggy and Jennifer, who he loved so much and whose intelligence and artistic acuity he valued and trusted. And they lovingly told him what was fabulous and confusing, too long or too short, beautiful, mysterious, funny, and scary about his new work. Father, mother, and daughter were touched by a feeling of creative and family communion. Jennifer says the gathering was "one of the best days I ever had."[360] It was an Art Life afternoon.

Lynch heard what Peggy and Jennifer said about the film needing more recognizable signposts, which would help that audience navigate the *INLAND EMPIRE* labyrinth. Peggy felt that "no matter how much more understandable reality you add, you can never extinguish the film's mystery."[361] Lynch acted on some of their suggestions, but at the Venice Film Festival, where he received the award, *INLAND EMPIRE*'s dreamy mystifications were deemed drearily incomprehensible by many viewers. And the film's low-end-video look, its murk and graininess, garnered few devotees.

A number of Lynch's films that were greeted with catcalls and bewilderment upon release have grown into classic stature, but the process has always taken years. Within a few months after *INLAND EMPIRE*'s Venice premiere, in late 2006 and early 2007, an excited, more-positive buzz about the film spread from fan blogs to print reviews to ten-best-films lists. Articles in the *Sunday New York Times* and *Time* magazine celebrated Lynch as an indy-cinema cultural hero in this era of mega-corporate filmmaking: a man who made his film his way, promoted it himself (with the participation of a live cow on Hollywood Boulevard), and distributed it (with the help of the human-scale company 518 Media) without big-studio backing.

Lynch expressed his can-do pioneering spirit and far-reaching imagination many times before he discovered Transcendental Meditation at age twenty-seven, but he now sees the practice as the bedrock of his creative process. In the past year, Lynch condensed his thoughts on the link between TM and his Art Life into a book, *Catching the Big Fish*. As the winter of 2007 gripped America, Lynch embarked on a book tour, which, in some cities, was combined with a premiere screening of *INLAND EMPIRE*.

I was proud to host the first Northwest presentation of the film at Seattle's 1960s-retro-mod Cinerama Theater, where I had first seen the mind-bending classics *2001: A Space Odyssey* and *The Shining*. After I introduced Lynch to the huge overflow crowd, he had the gifted Seattle musician Paul Rucker play a visceral, spirit-stirring improvisation on his cello to "set a mood." Lynch spoke of how our lives are like dreams, and then the movie began. *INLAND EMPIRE* is Lynch's most complex cinematic dream, and like *Eraserhead*, it's a "dream of dark and troubling things."[362] Over the three years of making the film, Lynch did not give Laura Dern an overview of her character, but before she first saw the assembled footage she wrote down her interpretation, and Lynch says it "was amazingly accurate."[363]

Before filming began, the first thing Lynch wrote was a long monologue for Dern: seventy electrifying minutes that the director, manning the camera himself, was able to film in just two long takes, thanks to has newly beloved digital technology (a long take on film can only last a few minutes). The extended flow of filming allowed Dern to lose herself in her Battered Woman character, with her bruised mouth and spirit. When Lynch and I did the question-and-answer session after *INLAND EMPIRE* screened at the Cinerama, a viewer asked what the film means, and Lynch replied, "It's on the poster," referring to his official summation: "A woman in trouble."[364] And here's Dern's "amazingly accurate"[365] interpretation: "It was about a woman in trouble, a woman who is dismantling, and her emotional and abstract journey back to herself."[366]

This primary key to the film, which sounds so simple and straightforward that any viewer must readily perceive it while watching *INLAND EMPIRE*, is veiled within shifting realities, each brimming with mysterious information. For Lynch, the organizing principle, the core, generating idea for a film, is like a fish he catches, and this fish is mighty slippery.

Indeed, Dern's Battered Woman monologue doesn't occur until we're far into the film, after we've become immersed in the stories of the *other* women Dern is playing. We're introduced to her as Nikki, a Hollywood actress who wins the coveted lead role in a new film, *On High in Blue Tomorrows*. Her costar will be Devon (Justin Theroux) and the production will be directed by Kingsley (Jeremy Irons). Their film centers on two sophisticated Southerners, Sue and Billy, who fall in love, despite being married to other people. The two stars and their director are ebullient about embarking on their creative venture, so David Lynch, Mr. Contrast, adds a disturbing, eerie note. During rehearsal of a scene, Kingsley's assistant (Harry Dean Stanton) sees someone watching them from the shadows. Devon investigates and finds no one, and "nowhere for anyone to have disappeared to." Tension mounts as Nikki's husband tells Devon there will be dire consequences if Devon starts craving Nikki the way Billy does Sue. Lynch deftly establishes a milieu that presents the themes of people making believe (filmmaking), a phantom presence, the threat of a loving relationship being betrayed, and the certainty of you-reap-what-you-sow punishment for transgressive behavior. The air may be thick with foreboding, but we're still in the world as we know it. Then things get strange.

One day, while acting a scene in which Sue starts to fall for Billy's charms, Sue says, "Damn, this sounds like dialogue from our script!" Kingsley yells "Cut," and asks Nikki "What's going on?" As Lynch casts his spell, Dern, and the viewer, need to ask this question with every scene he shows us. The fictional drama of adultery that Nikki's acting for the camera begins to merge with her own life, and as she and Devon make love in a dim room the shadowy figure of her husband silently peers at them from around a corner. Under the covers, she tells Devon that she had a strange experience yesterday while shooting a scene in which her character Sue had bought groceries for the Billy character and was returning to her car alone in an alley. As she talks, she frantically tries to keep her identity grounded: "It's me, Nikki, look at me, Devon." When she was in the alley, she was drawn to odd markings by a dark doorway, and entered. Groping her way down a murky passageway, she came upon a scene that terrified her. It was the earlier moment in her life when she and Devon were rehearsing with Kingsley and his assistant, and the assistant saw a mysterious presence and Devon went to investigate. Her eyes clouded with fear, she looks at herself sitting with the three men, then flees as Devon, seeing nothing, comes toward her. Is she not real?

Earlier, when Devon pursued whoever was watching them, he approached the set of a small house that would be in their film. In the half light, he peered in the house's front window, and saw only emptiness. Now Nikki, immersed in her scary experience of being pursued by Devon, takes refuge in the house, and as he approaches and squints at the window, she screams "Billy! Billy!," but he hears nothing. Later in the film, she and her husband sit down to dinner—but they're sitting in the cramped little house, not the grand mansion we've previously seen them living in. Sometimes Dern sees a man in a green coat, who looks like her husband, creeping around corners. Or she sees the living room of the little house full of young lounging prostitutes who naively think that their "tits and ass" will get them through life, and who jump up and dance and sing "The Loco-Motion," but disappear in mid-song. Or, in one of the most stunningly surreal passages of Lynch's career, Dern and the women emerge from the small 2006 California house into the nocturnal, snow-covered streets of Poland in the 1930s, as Lynch's voice sings of how strange it is, what love can make you do.

So if Lynch feels Dern's monologue-delivering Battered Woman character is the key to the film, what shelter can her words provide from the storm of disorienting sights we've seen? Her face is weary and bitter, and her voice quavers with sadness and fury, which are emblemized in a ruddy bruise from having been struck on the mouth. At various times in his life, Lynch has felt the corrosive poison of anger flaming in his veins, and the Battered Woman tells a silent confessor figure, "When I get mad, I get *really* mad." When people try to control us by inflicting pain and fear we respond by either fleeing or fighting, and the Battered Woman is a fighter. At age fifteen, a man tried to rape her, and she gouged out his eye and "clawed his nuts." She says that "men reveal themselves over time," and in her experience they are fearsome, destructive creatures. She speaks of a creepy man called The Phantom, a dark figure who can mess with people's minds and disappear at will. Her scary composite portrait of maleness recalls *Twin Peaks'* BOB—who could be both an actual man (Leland Palmer, who commits incest with his daughter and kills her) and an extra-dimensional supernatural entity—who's summed up as "the evil that men do." It isn't just bad men who make the Battered Woman's world "a big ball of shit." She speaks of toxic pollution making people crazy, and a little girl having a vision of the world: "All fire and smoke and blood rain." (The Battered Woman's long monologue brims with Lynch's dark poetry.)

The Battered Woman's fear and anger are steeped in sadness; she's living blue tomorrows like the title of Nikki and Devon's film. After her young son died, she went into "a bad time" in which her sense of self started unraveling (once again Lynch's fear of depersonalization drives his art). She doesn't know "what was before or after" in her life, she feels numb and isolated as vibrant, healthy life goes on all around her, she's "in a dark theater, and they haven't brought the lights up yet." (We recall the theaters in *Eraserhead* and *Mulholland Drive* in which Henry and Diane watched their psychic dramas play out.) Lynch's art has always centered on the battle and the dance between darkness and light, but the Battered Woman's dark theater before the light comes up has a spiritual meaning: It is the benighted soul suffering before the illumination of enlightenment. The film began with a beam of white light penetrating blackness and making the title *INLAND EMPIRE* glow. The empire inland is the Battered Woman's subjective consciousness, her shattered psyche needing to be made whole. She tells the confessor, "I figure one day I'll wake up and see what yesterday was all about." By making everything in the film part of the Battered Woman's fragmented mind, Lynch is able to provide a unifying context for three years' worth of intuitively, spontaneously inspired filming done without an overall blueprint.

Before the lights went down for *INLAND EMPIRE* to begin, Lynch read some lines from the Hindu scripture *The Upanishads*: "We are like the dreamer who dreams and then lives in the dream." *INLAND EMPIRE* is the Battered Woman living within her broken psyche's multifaceted dream, and as a Hollywood TV announcer says, "dreams make stars." In *Mulholland Drive* terms, the Battered Woman, with her sad world of loss, pain, and violence, is like the later, dark aspect of Diane Selwyn, while movie star Nikki is like the early, optimistic, creative, life-is-wonderful Betty Elms aspect of Diane. The Nikki persona is the Battered Woman's escape route from her hellish, intolerable real life. But as we know, self-erected barriers are often violated in Lynch's world, and just as Diane and Fred Madison's safe, rewarding psychic compartments are pierced by strange, disturbing forces, so is the Battered Woman's inner I'm-movie-star-Nikki scenario.

Nikki's invader is her "new neighbor" (the ever-fabulous Grace Zabriskie), a smiling, pleasant woman who comes calling to introduce herself. When Lynch read the *Upanishad* line about living within a dream that we create, he alluded to the film's key concept that the Battered Woman's psyche is generating everything we experience in the film. A second *Upanishad* line Lynch read likened us to "the spider: we weave our life and then move along in it." This refers to reincarnation, the film's other organizing principle (and one of Lynch's deepest spiritual beliefs), for in karmic terms we currently live in the web we've created for ourselves with our past good and bad actions. Repeating in the Battered Woman's mind, spoken by various characters throughout the film, the words "actions have consequences" and "you reap what you sow" echo like mantras.

Lynch is always concerned with the deepest realities hidden behind facades and beneath surfaces, and he has Zabriske speak to Nikki of "the alleyway behind the marketplace," where there is "an unpaid bill" that must be dealt with, and she adds, "This isn't something you remember." The bill that needs paying is a karmic debt, something you did in a past life that must be atoned for in this life, so that you suffer in the same way that you made someone else suffer in an earlier time that you, as a reincarnated soul, do not recall. What can Zabriske's ominous words have to do with Nikki's sunny, happy life?

Zabriskie's character speaks with a thick European accent. She's from the old country and she alludes to the oldest story in the world: You love someone, they cheat on you, you get mad enough to kill. At the beginning of the film, we see a needle on a revolving phonograph record, which points us in the direction of the past in our digital-technology age. The spinning record connotes circularity, repetition, the playing out of a groove pattern that is predetermined: It's a potent abstraction of cycling multiple lifetimes and the inescapability of fate. We hear the crackling sound the old record makes, and a voice speaking of "the longest-running radio play in the Balkan region." Throughout *INLAND EMPIRE* the crackling sound accompanies sepia-toned images from a 1930s Balkan city, in which an unnamed husband, wife, and lover enact "the longest-running" story of love, betrayal, and revenge. The film's various levels of reality echo each other. The movie Nikki and Devon are making is about characters who cheat on their spouses, and Nikki and Devon cheat on *their* spouses (despite Nikki's husband's deadly threats) and they learn that their film project is a remake of an earlier film abandoned because its adulterous male and female lead actors were brutally murdered. And in the passage where one moment Nikki is standing in sunny L.A., and the next she's on a nocturnal, sepia-toned, snowy 1930s Balkan street, Lynch forges a direct thematic link.

In the Balkans seventy years ago, on a 2006 Hollywood movie set, in the lives of the movie's actors, and in a small house in Southern California's east-of-L.A. Inland Empire region, people hurt their mates by falling in love with new people, sparking violent reactions, and the weapon of vengeance is a screwdriver. Lynch has structured *INLAND EMPIRE* so that it is both a display of the Battered Woman's mind and a reincarnation-karmic justice tale. In footage that Lynch didn't include in the film's final cut, we hear the Battered Woman's voice say she found herself in "some other place" as we see Dern enter and explore a blue-collar woman's little Inland Empire house, and then we're in movie star Nikki's mansion as Dern comes down a grand staircase. In her mind the Battered Woman *is* these other personas; from the clues Lynch presents, we infer that in her "real" life her physically abusive husband can't father children, but she gets pregnant from an affair. When her son dies, she loses her grip on sanity, descending into despair and prostitution, becoming the Battered Woman who delivers the monologue. At the beginning of the film we heard Grace Zabriskie talk about reincarnation and emphasize that "actions have consequences," and we've seen a 1930s Balkan wife kill her husband's lover with a screwdriver—so it's easy to make the leap of thinking that the Balkan screwdriver-murderess's soul has been reincarnated as the adulterous Battered Woman, who gets murdered with a screwdriver by her lover's wife, while cruising for tricks on Hollywood Boulevard.

The Battered Woman's death scene is one of the most stunning Lynch has ever created. In the ultimate Hollywood noir image, Dern, having been stabbed in the stomach, vomits blood on the golden stars set in the sidewalk of the street of dreams. She lies down prone up against a building between two sitting homeless women, an older African American woman on her left, a younger Japanese woman on her right. Dern's eyes are open, she doesn't speak, there's a look of pain and puzzlement on her face. The left woman, her head next to Dern's, is tenderly matter-of-fact: "It's okay, you dyin' is all." Then, in moments that mix pathos with the absurdity of real life, the left and right women start talking across Dern's long horizontal form about whether or not you can catch a bus to Pomona from where they are now. ("Pomona" alludes to California's Inland Empire region, as well as Lynch's beloved *Sunset Boulevard*. Billy Wilder's film is also reflected in Grace Zabriskie's Norma Desmond–like bulging eyes and dramatic head tilts, and in a direct quote of one of Desmond's speeches: "Cast out this wicked dream from my heart.") The Battered Woman's wicked dream has been her propensity for fury and violence, but in the last seconds of her life she's comforted by the African American woman, who holds a lit cigarette lighter before her eyes, just as *Twin Peaks'* Agent Cooper eased the dying Leland Palmer "into the light." The woman tells Dern, "The flame burns forever," and as Dern's eyes close forever, "You on high now, love." Lynch, with his knowledge of art history, frames a moving pieta (pity) of the dead woman and her sidewalk attendants, then floats his camera up and up into a God's-eye view of the scene. God may be the ultimate viewer of *INLAND EMPIRE*, for just as *Mulholland Drive* is a tale told by a dead woman, *INLAND EMPIRE*'s narrative may be passing before the dying Dern's eyes as she looks skyward into Lynch's camera. Film directors are like gods creating worlds, and as Lynch's camera rises to its highest point it passes *another* camera filming Dern's death scene. This moment, which makes filmmaking a metaphor for Hindu spirituality, reflects the "cosmic motion picture"[367] concept Lynch read in *Autobiography of a Yogi* as a young man. Our seemingly solid world is really an illusory movie of shifting light and shadow, God's dream.

The dream persists, for the Battered Woman, as Nikki, gets up from the sidewalk and is complemented by director Devon. The astonishing revelation that the death we've witnessed is a movie being filmed echoes another book Lynch read and that he referenced in *Mulholland Drive*. In *You Play the Black and the Red Comes Up* (which Lynch wanted to film at one point), a character says, "Wherever I go the world won't be itself. It becomes a movie set the moment I get there."[368] Movie or dream, before death or in the afterlife, the Battered Woman's quest for psychological wholeness is mesmerizing and compelling. When Peggy Reavey and Jennifer Lynch watched the end of *INLAND EMPIRE* before Lynch took the film to the Venice Film Festival, it reminded Peggy of the *Bhagavad Gita*. This seminal Hindu text speaks of spiritual seekers being freed from delusion and attaining "the bright worlds of those whose actions have been meritorious."[369] At various times during the film a glowing light source has flared, but it hasn't been the conclusive, sustaining illumination that will brighten that "dark theater" the Battered Woman feels trapped in in her mind.

Now, as Nikki, with a gun in her hand, she confronts The Phantom. Earlier, when we saw the Battered Woman's husband pummel her, he said, "I'm not who I appear to be," implying that he is The Phantom in disguise. The monster/angel duality of human nature has fascinated Lynch throughout his career, and the husband's words recall Grace Zabriskie's words about a reflection, an evil twin being born when a male enters the world. Among the many character pairs in Lynch's work, the husband reminds us of Leland Palmer possessed by BOB, who's the personification of "the evil that men do." For the Battered Woman, The Phantom is all the men who ever shamed her, lied to her, hurt her with poisonous words or their fists or their whoremaster's cocks. The Phantom is everything she fears, and she is courageously facing it, but she needs to learn one final lesson. (We hear the crackling record-playing sound, reminding us that this is an old, old, universal story.) The Battered Woman has been a victim all her life, but, enraged, she has victimized others, feeding and perpetuating the cycle of pain and suffering. Yielding to her familiar impulse to angrily strike back, she fires her gun at The Phantom—and is surprised by a horrifying image: her own dying face superimposed on The Phantom's dying face. This wrenching, beautiful, Francis Bacon–like double visage carries the message home: Don't create bad karma for yourself; you kill someone with a gun, you will be killed with a gun. (This moment rhymes with the way the woman who stabbed the Battered Woman with a screwdriver later stabbed herself with it.)

At the beginning of *INLAND EMPIRE* we saw a scene from Lynch's *Rabbits* Web series, in which humans with rabbit heads spoke non sequiturs to each other: Their words didn't add up to an understandable meaning (in Hinduism souls at a lower karmic level can be reincarnated as animals). Now the Battered Woman goes through door 47, showing that she's conquered her Fear (*47* was the name of the cursed film that Nikki and Devon are remaking. The number also subliminally reinforces the idea that this ancient tale is repeating again and again, 24/7, with a varying cast of souls). The Battered Woman is now alone on the *Rabbits* stage set, standing in the bright light that doesn't fade away, taking the unseen audience's (the witnessing Hindu gods?) applause. The end of the *Bhagavad Gita* says, "I have remembered myself."[370] For three hours, we've seen the many selves with whom the Battered Woman has peopled her inner scenarios, and those who are good are reaping rewards. The weeping woman who's been watching the film's narrative on TV now smiles as she's reunited with her husband and son. And Nikki the movie star sits with serene, quiet joy on her couch, the literal and spiritual embodiment of her last name, Grace.

With her long blond hair and sky blue dress, Dern reminds us of Alice in Walt Disney's *Alice in Wonderland*. And there are other parallels between Lynch's and Disney's films. Both *Wonderland* and *INLAND EMPIRE* are fictional names for the dream world of the subconscious, where both heroines encounter confusing distortions of reality as they try to get back home to an integrated sense of self. In their inner-self quests, both see large talking rabbits and feel like outsiders in a place where "Who are you?" and "Who am I?" are profound existential questions. Both films have doubled characters, puzzling non sequiturs and riddles that seem to have no answer, and make great emphasis of what time it is. And *Alice in Wonderland* and *INLAND EMPIRE* exist in a time-space matrix in which *this* can also be *that*. When characters sing in Disney's movie, they could be characterizing both films: "Forward, backward, inward, outward. Here we go again."

Many of Lynch's films, and *Alice in Wonderland*, portray an alienated person's view of a confusing world populated by mysterious, menacing authority figures, a kindred sensibility that the young Lynch recognized in Franz Kafka's writings. Indeed, the key *INLAND EMPIRE* scenes in which Dern, after climbing a punishingly high, dark staircase, sits in a dim, grimy room and tells her most intimate thoughts and feelings to a grim, affectless confessor, are worthy of the master Czech writer. The unnamed Balkan city Lynch shows us in *INLAND EMPIRE* is actually Lodz, Poland, where over the years he has befriended a group of artists and actors. Kafka's home was Prague, Czechoslavakia, where Lynch has visited to record music with the Prague Symphony. In *INLAND EMPIRE*, Lodz provides the ancient, dank stone streets, labyrinthine passageways, and eerily empty architectural spaces that Kafka conjured into the artistic archetype of haunted Eastern Europeaness. It's said that the past is present, and as Dern experiences selves and events that have gone before, she personifies the title of Kafka's autobiography: *I Am a Memory Come Alive*.

With *INLAND EMPIRE* Lynch has broken free from the restrictions of 35mm filmmaking, traditional cinematic narrative, studio intervention, and status quo distribution and publicity methods, just as he's tried to shape his entire life in the way his intuition says it should be. As the lights come up in Seattle's Cinerama Theater, the audience's thundering applause is like a blessing of his art and life. It's after midnight, and Lynch has an early flight home to L.A., where' he's getting ready for a massive exhibition of his paintings in Paris. Lynch steps through the theater's back door and turns for a second, illuminated against the freezing darkness by an overhead light, and waves goodbye.

The mystery of the way time speeds up as we age was on Lynch's mind as the next year sped by. He contemplated adding a third movie to *Mulholland Drive* and *INLAND EMPIRE* to form a trilogy of films about Hollywood. He produced a rave-reviewed *INLAND EMPIRE* DVD with supplemental extra footage that reinforced the idea that the film's multiple Laura Dern personas emanate from her Battered Woman character. His romance with Emily Stofle simmered nicely; the French government upgraded his Legion of Honor status; he was given the largest exhibition of his paintings, drawings, and photographs in years at Paris's Cartier Foundation; and he shot a perfume commercial for Gucci in the City of Light.

Lynch's worldwide Transcendental Meditation promotion suffered a sociopolitical setback at a Berlin lecture where his German-speaking colleague Emanuel Schiffgens spoke about plans for a new TM University. Pumped up with zeal for his mission, Schiffgens spoke of how the expansion of individual consciousness through TM practice can make his whole country spiritually powerful and invulnerable. But he summed up this concept with the German phrase for "Invincible Germany,"[371]which he repeated again and again. The audience was instantly outraged, feeling these were words Adolf Hitler would have chanted. Schiffgens further enflamed the situation when, responding to a man who shouted, "That's what Hitler wanted!,"[372] he said, "Yes, but Hitler did not succeed!"[373] When a translator helped Lynch understand the emotional explosion taking place he remained impressively calm, stepped to the microphone, and tried to steer the chaotic energy in the room "toward a bright and shining future."[374] But Protestant groups and Berlin politicians vowed to investigate Lynch's university project.

Back home, Lynch held a damage-control meeting at his Hollywood Hills compound and, near year's end, proudly saw media critics give best-of-2007 awards to his full-series *Twin Peaks* DVD box set, davidlynch.com, and his *INLAND EMPIRE* DVD.

Then, weeks before Christmas, Lynch was spending time in California's Inland Empire, where his beloved father, Donald, was about to leave this world at the age of ninety-two. Donald, who Lynch calls "a woodsman,"[375] first introduced his son to the mysteries of the Northwest forests and showed him how to build things with his hands and mind. Lynch's mother had died in a car crash, but David and his father had time to speak their love and goodbyes before Donald passed away.

Then, early in February, Lynch's spiritual father, the Maharishi Mahesh Yogi, died at the age of ninety-one.

Thoughts of death and after-death, reincarnation and the journey of consciousness have permeated Lynch's sensibility for decades. In the artist's work characters attain a blessed state of floating, free of gravity's restraints and life's travails, in bright light, uplifted by love. And the only way to get there is through the beautiful dark.

In spring 2008, the director made a heavenly film for just two people and himself. Before Jennifer Lynch flew to the Cannes Film Festival to premiere her film *Surveillance*, her father gave her a fortieth-birthday present: a carefully crafted compilation of home movies from *The Grandmother* era, when Jennifer was a baby and her parents newly married. Lynch shed tears while working on Jennifer's surprise present, and eyes were misty when he sat down with Jennifer and Peggy to watch it.

On screen, a smiling Peggy bathes a smiling towheaded Jennifer, while outside on the mean streets of Philadelphia a white cop hassles African American youths, an image that Lynch pairs with the sound of Martin Luther King Jr.'s "I have a dream" speech. The happy mother and daughter laugh and lounge on the black-painted *Grandmother* set and Jennifer peeks into the white "SEEDS" bag. Images of domestic harmony and joy dance with songs like "Jennifer Juniper" and "Strawberry Fields Forever," and the film seems to glimpse a lost paradise, yet the warm feelings depicted are alive and well forty years later.

There's a shot that could come from any recent Lynch film, in which he slowly floats his camera up to a pensive Peggy's face at night until her so-close head blurs, and he can almost see his wife's mind. Lynch's film makes a redemptive 2008 declaration to Peggy and Jennifer as, at age twenty-four, he looks into the camera while the song track speaks of one who can seem to be mad and bad and not always an angel, but whose intentions are good, and who needs to be understood. Finally, only one word can say it all: a glowing white "LOVE" against a black background.

David Lynch is feeling good. Revved up on coffee and cigarettes, he stands alone on his outdoor art-making platform. A warm, golden light is breaking through the haze, bathing the pure white canvas before him. He stares at the untouched surface for a while, then picks up a brush, and dips it in black.

NOTES

CHAPTER 1

1. Tim Curtis, author interview (AI).
2. Consultation with the Fort Missoula Museum.
3. Donald Lynch, AI.
4. Ibid.
5. Ibid.
6. Ibid.
7. Kristine McKenna: "David Lynch, a Conversation," *Los Angeles Reader*, September 1986, 12.
8. Ibid.
9. Mark A. Altman: *Twin Peaks Behind the Scenes* (Pioneer Books, 1990).
10. Christopher Domino: *Francis Bacon, Painter of a Dark Vision* (Harry N. Abrams, Inc., 1994).
11. David Lynch, AI.
12. Kristine McKenna: "An Interview With David Lynch," *David Lynch* (Sala Parpallo/Vei, 1992).
13. Kristine McKenna: "Dreamer of Dark and Troubling Things," *Los Angeles Reader*, October 8, 1982.
14. David Breskin: *Inner Views* (Faber and Faber, 1992).
15. Mark Cousins (presenter): *Scene by Scene with David Lynch*, BBC Television, 1987.
16. Altman: *Twin Peaks Behind the Scenes*.
17. Ibid.
18. Altman: *Twin Peaks Behind the Scenes*.
19. Breskin: *Inner Views*.
20. David Lynch, AI.
21. Ibid.
22. Jennifer Lynch, AI.
23. David Lynch, AI.
24. Ibid.
25. Altman: *Twin Peaks Behind the Scenes*.
26. George Wingfield Digby: *Symbol and Image in William Blake* (Oxford University Press, 1957).
27. Breskin: *Inner Views*.
28. Ibid.
29. Donald Lynch, AI.
30. Ibid.
31. Ibid.
32. James Verniere: "David Lynch, American Primitive," *Twilight Zone*, October 1988.
33. John Sutherland Bonnell: "What Is a Presbyterian?" *A Guide to the Religions of America*, edited by Leo Rosten (Simon & Schuster, 1955).

34. Ibid.
35. David Lynch, AI.
36. Bonnell: "What Is a Presbyterian?"
37. Alister McGrath: *A Life of John Calvin* (Basil Blackwell, 1990).
38. Bonnell: "What Is a Presbyterian?"
39. Breskin: *Inner Views*.
40. Chris Rodley (editor): *Lynch on Lynch* (Faber and Faber, 2005).
41. Breskin: *Inner Views*.
42. Ibid.
43. Ibid.
44. Ibid.
45. Ibid.
46. Ibid.
47. "Lynch-Time": *Vogue*, February 1990, www.davidlynch.de/Vogue.
48. Ibid.
49. Ibid.
50. Richard B. Woodward: "A Dark Lens on America," *New York Times Magazine*, January 14, 1990.
51. Breskin: *Inner Views*.
52. Donald Lynch, AI.
53. Rodley: *Lynch on Lynch*.
54. Ibid.
55. Bushnell Keeler, AI.
56. Ibid.
57. Ibid.
58. Ibid.
59. David Lynch, AI.
60. Ibid.
61. Ibid.
62. Robert Henri: *The Art Spirit* (Icon, Harper and Row, 1984).
63. David Lynch, AI.
64. Ibid.
65. Ibid.
66. Breskin: *Inner Views*.
67. Ibid.
68. Henri: *The Art Spirit*.
69. Altman: *Twin Peaks Behind the Scenes*.
70. Ibid.
71. Ibid.
72. David Lynch, AI.
73. Ibid.
74. Richard Corliss: "Czar of Bizarre," *Time*, October 1, 1990.
75. Ibid.
76. Jerry Leiber, Mike Stoller: *Trouble*, RCA, 1958, www.lyrics.astraweb.com.
77. David Lynch, AI.
78. Bushnell Keeler, AI.
79. David Lynch, AI.
80. Bushnell Keeler, AI.
81. Ibid.
82. Ibid.
83. Ibid.
84. Donald Lynch, AI.
85. Busnell Keller, AI.
86. Ibid.
87. Ibid.
88. Donald Lynch, AI.
89. David Lynch, AI.
90. Peggy Reavey, AI.
91. Donald Lynch, AI.
92. David Lynch, AI.
93. Bushnell Keeler, AI.
94. Toby Keeler, AI.
95. Ibid.
96. Ibid.
97. Ibid.
98. Ibid.
99. Ibid.
100. André Breton, www.thinkexist.com.
101. David Lynch, AI.
102. Ibid.
103. Domino: *Francis Bacon*.
104. Anthony Blunt: *The Art of William Blake* (Columbia University Press, 1959).
105. Ibid.
106. Bushnell Keeler, AI.
107. Ibid.
108. Ibid.
109. Ibid.
110. Ibid.
111. Ibid.
112. Altman: *Twin Peaks Behind the Scenes*.
113. David Lynch, AI.
114. Klaus Albrecht Schroder, Johann Winkler (editors): *Oskar Kokoschka* (Prestel-Verlag, 1991).
115. Ibid.
116. Ibid.
117. Ibid.
118. Jack Fisk, AI.
119. Ibid.
120. Ibid.

121. Ibid.
122. Ibid.
123. Ibid.
124. Ibid.
125. Ibid.
126. Ibid.
127. Altman: *Twin Peaks Behind the Scenes*.
128. Ibid.
129. Bushnell Keeler, AI.
130. Ibid.
131. Altman: *Twin Peaks Behind the Scenes*.
132. Jack Fisk, AI.
133. Bushnell Keeler, AI.
134. Ibid.
135. Ibid.
136. Ibid.
137. Ibid.
138. Ibid.
139. Ibid.
140. Ibid.
141. Ibid.
142. Ibid.
143. Ibid.
144. Ibid.
145. David Lynch, AI.
146. Altman: *Twin Peaks Behind the Scenes*.
147. Henri: *The Art Spirit*.
148. David Lynch, AI.
149. Altman: *Twin Peaks Behind the Scenes*.
150. Ibid.
151. Henry Bromell: "Visionary From Fringeland," *Rolling Stone*, November 13, 1980.
152. Ibid.
153. Ibid.
154. David Lynch, AI.
155. Ibid.
156. Kenneth C. Kaleta: *David Lynch* (Twayne Publishers, 1993).
157. David Lynch, AI.
158. Kaleta; *David Lynch*.
159. Altman: *Twin Peaks Behind the Scenes*.
160. Ibid.
161. Breskin: *Inner Views*.
162. Toby Thompson: "Alien," *Esquire*, January 1985.
163. Toby Keeler, AI.
164. Breskin: *Inner Views*.
165. George Hickenlooper (editor): *Reel Conversations* (Citadel Press, 1991).
166. Peggy Reavey, AI.
167. David Lynch: *The Short Films of David Lynch*, DVD comments, Absurda, 2005.
168. Peggy Reavey, AI.
169. Ibid.
170. Ibid.
171. Ibid.
172. Ibid.
173. Ibid.
174. Ibid.
175. Ibid.
176. Ibid.
177. Ibid.
178. Ibid.
179. Rudy Martinez: *96 Tears*, Cameo, 1966, www.lyrics.astraweb.com.
180. Peggy Reavey, AI.
181. Jennifer Lynch, AI.
182. Breskin: *Inner Views*.
183. Jim Jerome: "David Lynch," *People*, September 3, 1990.
184. Breskin: *Inner Views*.
185. David Lynch, AI.
186. Ibid.
187. Ibid.
188. Breskin: *Inner Views*.
189. Ibid.
190. Ibid.
191. Ibid.
192. Peggy Reavey, AI.
193. Ibid.
194. Ibid.
195. David Lynch, AI.
196. Ibid.
197. David Lynch: *The Short Films of David Lynch*, DVD comments.
198. Altman: *Twin Peaks Behind the Scenes*.
199. David Lynch, AI.
200. Hans Biedermann: *The Wordsworth Dictionary of Symbolism* (Wordsworth Editions, Ltd., 1996).
201. Henri: *The Art Spirit*.
202. David Lynch, AI.
203. Lynch: *The Short Films of David Lynch*.
204. Ibid.
205. Ibid.
206. Peggy Reavey, AI.

207. Ibid.
208. Rodley: *Lynch on Lynch*.
209. Peggy Reavey, AI.
210. David Hughes: *The Complete Lynch* (Virgin Publishing Ltd., 2001).
211. David Lynch, AI.
212. Henri: *The Art Spirit*.
213. Ibid.
214. Ibid.
215. Ibid.
216. David Lynch, AI.
217. Ibid.
218. Breskin: *Inner Views*.
219. David Lynch, AI.
220. K. George Godwin: "Eraserhead," *Cinefantastique*, September 1984.
221. Ibid.
222. Lynch: *The Short Films of David Lynch*.
223. Godwin: "Eraserhead."
224. David Lynch, AI.
225. Peggy Reavey, AI.
226. Ibid.
227. Toby Keeler: *Pretty as a Picture: The Art of David Lynch* DVD, 1997.
228. Godwin: "Eraserhead."
229. Ibid.
230. David Lynch, AI.
231. Ibid.
232. David Lynch (presenter): *Ruth, Roses, and Revolvers*, BBC Television, 1987.
233. David Lynch, AI.
234. Jennifer Lynch, AI.
235. Patricia Highsmith: "The Terrors of Basket-Weaving," *The Black House* (Penzler Books, 1981).
236. Ibid.
237. Ibid.
238. Ibid.
239. David Lynch, AI.
240. Henry David Thoreau: *Faith in a Seed: The Dispersation of Seeds and Other Late Natural History Writings* (Island Press/Shearwater Books, 1993).
241. *Chandogya Upanishad* quoted in *Heaven's Banquet: Vegetarian Cooking for Lifelong Health the Ayurvedic Way*, by Miriam Kasin Hospodar (Dutton, 1999).
242. Karl Krogstad: *Surrealism* DVD, 1993.
243. Hughes: *The Complete Lynch*.
244. David Lynch: *Bellevue Film Festival Program Notes*, July 1970.
245. Henri: *The Art Spirit*.
246. David V. Erdman (editor): *The Complete Poetry and Prose of William Blake* (University of California Press, 1982).
247. Ibid.
248. Sheldon Renan: *Bellevue Film Festival Program Notes*, July 1970.
249. Ibid.
250. Chris Rodley: "David Lynch," *ICON*, March/April 1997.
251. Bromell: "Visionary From Fringeland."
252. J. Hoberman, Jonathan Rosenbaum: *Midnight Movies* (Da Capo Press, 1983).
253. David Lynch, AI.

CHAPTER 2

1. David Lynch, AI.
2. Toby Thompson: "Alien," *Esquire*, January 1985.
3. Richard B. Woodward: "A Dark Lens on America," *New York Times Magazine*, January 14, 1990.
4. David Magarshack: introduction to *The Overcoat and Other Tales of Good and Evil* (Robert Bentley, Inc., 1957).
5. Nikolai Gogol: "The Nose," *The Overcoat and Other Tales*.
6. Ibid.
7. Ibid.
8. Ibid.
9. Ibid.
10. Ibid.
11. Ibid.
12. Ibid.
13. Ibid.
14. Ibid.
15. Ibid.
16. Ibid.
17. Peggy Reavey, AI.
18. David Lynch, AI.
19. Peggy Reavey, AI.
20. David Lynch, AI.
21. K. George Godwin: "Eraserhead," *Cinefantastique*, September 1984.

22. David Lynch, AI.
23. Benedict Spinoza in *Familiar Quotations by John Bartlett* (Little, Brown, 1967).
24. Godwin: "Eraserhead."
25. Otis Blackwell, Elvis Presley: *All Shook Up*, RCA, 1957, www.lyrics.astraweb.com.
26. Peggy Reavey, AI.
27. Mark A. Altman: *Twin Peaks Behind the Scenes* (Pioneer Books, 1990).
28. Peggy Reavey, AI.
29. David Lynch, AI.
30. Peggy Reavey, AI.
31. Chris Rodley, AI.
32. David Hughes: *The Complete Lynch* (Virgin Publishing Ltd., 2001).
33. David Lynch: *Eraserhead*, DVD comments, Absurda, 2005.
34. Ibid.
35. Altman: *Twin Peaks Behind the Scenes*.
36. David Lynch, AI.
37. Ibid.
38. Ibid.
39. Ibid.
40. Christine McKenna: "Dreamer of Dark and Troubling Things," *L.A. Reader*, October 8, 1982.
41. David Lynch, AI.
42. Ibid.
43. Mark Kermode: *The Exorcist* (British Film Institute, 1998).
44. David Lynch, AI.
45. David Lynch, Angelo Badalamenti: *Into the Night*, Warner Brothers, 1989, www.lyrics.astraweb.com.
46. David Lynch, AI.
47. Walter Donaldson, George Whiting: *My Blue Heaven*, Imperial, 1957, www.lyrics.astraweb.com.
48. David Lynch, AI.
49. Marie Pohl: "David Lynch on Meditation," *Sueddeutsche Zeitung*, May 13–14, 2006.
50. Godwin: "Eraserhead."
51. Jack Nance, AI.
52. Pohl: "David Lynch on Meditation."
53. Peggy Reavey, AI.
54. Martha Lynch, AI.
55. Ibid.
56. David Lynch, AI.
57. Catherine Coulson, AI.
58. Robert Henri: *The Art Spirit* (Icon, Harper and Row, 1984).
59. David Lynch, AI.
60. George Hickenlooper (editor): *Reel Conversations* (Citadel Press, 1991).
61. Christine McKenna: "An Interview With David Lynch," *David Lynch* (Sala Parpallo/Vei, 1992).
62. Ibid.
63. Ibid.
64. Ibid.
65. Catherine Coulson, AI.
66. Godwin: "Eraserhead."
67. Ibid.
68. Peggy Reavey, AI.
69. Ibid.
70. Ibid.
71. Ibid.
72. Ibid.
73. Ibid.
74. Ibid.
75. Ibid.
76. Ibid.
77. Ibid.
78. David Lynch: *Eraserhead*, DVD Comments.
79. Walt Whitman: *The Complete Writings of Walt Whitman* (G.P. Putnam's Sons, 1902).
80. David Breskin: *Inner Views* (Faber and Faber, 1992).
81. Ibid.
82. Ibid.
83. Whitman: *The Complete Writings*.
84. Ibid.
85. Peggy Reavey, AI.
86. Godwin: "Eraserhead."
87. Whitman: *The Complete Writings*.
88. Ibid.
89. Altman: *Twin Peaks Behind the Scenes*.
90. Joscelyn Godwin: *Mystery Religions of the Ancient World* (Harper and Row, 1981).
91. Ibid.
92. McKenna: "A Conversation With David Lynch."

93. Jennifer Lynch, AI.
94. Ibid.
95. David Lynch, AI.
96. Jerry Leiber, Mike Stoller: *I Want to be Free*, FCA, 1957, www.lyrics.astraweb.com.
97. Doc Pomus, Mort Shuman: *Turn Me Loose*, Chancellor, 1959, www.lyrics.astraweb.com.
98. Jennifer Lynch, AI.
99. *All About Twin Peaks*, Japanese TV documentary, 1990, courtesy of Catherine Coulson Collection.
100. Ibid.
101. Ibid.
102. David Lynch, AI.
103. Ibid.
104. Ibid.
105. Ibid.
106. Jennifer Lynch, AI.
107. David Lynch, AI.
108. Ibid.
109. Ibid.
110. Jennifer Lynch, AI.
111. David Lynch, AI.
112. Godwin, "Eraserhead."
113. David Lynch: *Eraserhead* script, unpublished, undated.
114. Ibid.
115. Godwin: "Eraserhead."
116. Ibid.
117. Ibid.
118. Ibid.
119. David Lynch: *Eraserhead* script.
120. Peggy Reavey. AI.
121. Catherine Coulson, AI.
122. Ibid.
123. Ibid.
124. Ibid.
125. Ibid.
126. Ibid.
127. Mark Frost, AI.
128. Catherine Coulson, AI.
129. Conversation with Matt Marshall.
130. Godwin: "Eraserhead."
131. Ibid.
132. Paul A. Woods: *Weirdsville USA* (Plexus, 1997).
133. Godwin: "Eraserhead."
134. Catherine Coulson, AI.
135. Godwin: "Eraserhead."
136. David Lynch, AI.
137. William Grimes: "Adventure Returns for David Lynch," *New York Times*, May 31, 1995.
138. Glenn O' Brien: "Fenn-Tastic!," *Playboy*, December 1990.

CHAPTER 3

1. Mark A. Altman: *Twin Peaks Behind the Scenes* (Pioneer Books, 1990).
2. Kristine McKenna: "A Conversation With David Lynch," *The Prints of David Lynch* (Tandem Press, 2000).
3. Stephen Saban and Sarah Longacre: "Eraserhead: Is There Life After Birth?," *Soho Weekly News*, October 20, 1978.
4. Ibid.
5. Peggy Reavey, AI.
6. Jennifer Lynch, AI.
7. David Lynch, AI.
8. "*Twin Peaks: Fire Walk With Me* Cannes Press Conference," *Cinema Papers*, August 1992.
9. *The American College Dictionary* (Random House, 1957).
10. Gordon Godwin: "Eraserhead," *Cinefantastique*, September 1984.
11. Terry Gross (presenter): "David Lynch," *Fresh Air* (National Public Radio, December 15, 1995).
12. Ashley Montagu: *The Elephant Man, A Study in Human Dignity* (E.P. Dutton, 1979).
13. Ibid.
14. Ibid.
15. Ibid.
16. Ibid.
17. Ibid.
18. Ibid.
19. Ibid.
20. Ibid.
21. Ibid.
22. Bernard Pomerance: *The Elephant Man, A Play* (Grove Press, 1970).

23. Altman: *Twin Peaks Behind the Scenes*.
24. Godwin:"Eraserhead."
25. Chris Rodley (editor): *Lynch on Lynch* (Faber and Faber, 2005).
26. Jennifer Lynch, AI.
27. David Lynch, AI.
28. Ibid.
29. Gross: "David Lynch."
30. Altman: *Twin Peaks Behind the Scenes*.
31. Kathleen Raine: *William Blake* (Praeger Publishers, 1971).
32. David Lynch (presenter): *The Elephant Man*, TNT Television, August 3, 1995.
33. Jennifer Lynch, AI.
34. Ibid.
35. Ibid.
36. Ibid.
37. Ibid.
38. Ibid.
39. Ibid.
40. Quentin Falk: *The Authorized Biography of Anthony Hopkins* (Interlink Books, 1993).
41. David Lynch, AI.
42. Gross: "David Lynch."
43. George Hickenlooper (editor): *Reel Conversations* (Citadel Press, 1991).
44. Henry Bromell: "Visionary From Fringeland," *Rolling Stone*, November 13, 1980.
45. David Lynch: *The Elephant Man*.
46. Ibid.
47. Ibid.
48. Gross: "David Lynch."
49. Falk: *The Authorized Biography of Anthony Hopkins*.
50. Michael Feeney Callan: *Anthony Hopkins: The Unauthorized Biography* (Charles Scribner's Sons, 1994).
51. Falk: *The Authorized Biography of Anthony Hopkins*.
52. Ibid.
53. Ibid.
54. Ibid.
55. Ibid.
56. Gross: "David Lynch."
57. Callan: *Anthony Hopkins: The Unauthorized Biography*.
58. Bromell: "Visionary From Fringeland."
59. David Lynch, AI.
60. Ibid.
61. Ibid.
62. Leslie Fielder: *Freaks: Myths and Images of the Secret Self* (Doubleday, 1993).
63. David Lynch: *Ronnie Rocket* script, unpublished, undated.
64. David V. Erdman (editor): *The Complete Poetry and Prose of William Blake* (University of California Press, 1982).
65. McKenna: "An Interview."
66. David Lynch, AI.
67. Ibid.
68. Richard Corliss: "Czar of Bizarre," *Time*, October 1, 1990.
69. Gross: "David Lynch."
70. Ibid.
71. Christopher De Vore, Eric Bergren, David Lynch: *The Elephant Man* script, undated.
72. Corliss: "Czar of Bizarre."
73. David Macey: *The Lives of Michel Foucault, A Biography* (Pantheon Books, 1993).
74. Montagu: *The Elephant Man*.
75. Ibid.
76. Pomerance: *The Elephant Man*.
77. Ibid.
78. David Lynch, AI.
79. Ibid.
80. David Lynch, AI.
81. Bromell: "Visionary From Fringeland."
82. Ibid.
83. John Leonard: "The Quirky Allure of *Twin Peaks*," *New York*, May 7, 1990.
84. David Lynch, AI.
85. Montagu: *The Elephant Man*.
86. Ibid.
87. Pomerance: *The Elephant Man*.
88. William Blake: *The Marriage of Heaven and Hell* (University of Miami Press, 1970).
89. J. R. R. Tolkien: "Tree and Leaf," *The Tolkien Reader* (Ballantine Books, 1966).
90. Ibid.
91. Ibid.
92. Ibid.

93. Robert Henri: *The Art Spirit* (Icon, Harper and Row, 1984).
94. Tolkien: "Tree and Leaf."
95. Jolande Jacobi, R. F. C. Hull (editors): *C. G. Jung: Psychological Reflections* (Princeton University Press, 1973).
96. David Lynch, AI.
97. Swami Prabhavananda and Christopher Isherwood (translators): *The Song of God: Bhagavad-Gita* (Mentor Books, 1962).
98. Kathleen Raine: *William Blake* (Praeger Publishers, 1971).
99. David Lynch, Angelo Badalametni: "The World Spins," *Floating Into the Night*, Warner Brothers, 1989, www.lyrics.astraweb.com.
100. Walt Whitman: *The Complete Writings of Walt Whitman* (G.P. Putnam's Sons, 1902).
101. Hickenlooper: *Reel Conversations*.
102. Ibid.
103. Ibid.
104. David Breskin: *Inner Views* (Faber and Faber, 1992).
105. Isabella Rossellini, AI.
106. Breskin: *Inner Views*.
107. Jennifer Lynch, AI.
108. Johnny Carson: *The 53rd Academy Awards*, NBC Television, March 31, 1981.

CHAPTER 4

1. David Hughes: *The Complete Lynch* (Virgin Publishing Ltd., 2001).
2. Jennifer Lynch, AI.
3. David Lynch, AI.
4. Chris Rodley: "Introduction," *Lost Highway*, by David Lynch and Barry Gifford (Faber and Faber, 1997).
5. David Lynch, AI.
6. Paul M. Sammon: "David Lynch's Dune," *Cinefantastique*, September 1984.
7. Frank Herbert in *The Maker of Dune: Insights of a Master of Science Fiction*, edited by Tim O'Reilly (Berkley Books, 1984).
8. Ibid.
9. Ed Naha: *The Making of Dune* (Berkley Books, 1984).
10. Ibid.
11. Ibid.
12. Ibid.
13. Ibid.
14. Chris Hodenfield: "Daring Dune," *Rolling Stone*, December 6, 1984.
15. Ibid.
16. Ibid.
17. Hal Calbom: "Frank Herbert Goes to the Movies: The Wrapping of Dune," *Pacific Northwest*, June 1984.
18. Ibid.
19. Ibid.
20. Ibid.
21. Ibid.
22. Brian Herbert: *Dreamer of Dune: The Biography of Frank Herbert* (Tor/Tom Dougherty Associates, 2003).
23. Ibid.
24. Ibid.
25. Ibid.
26. Ibid.
27. Naha: *The Making of Dune*.
28. Hodenfield: "Daring Dune."
29. Naha: *The Making of Dune*.
30. Ibid.
31. Ibid.
32. Frank Herbert: *Dune* (Chilton Book Company, 1965).
33. Ibid.
34. David Lynch, AI.
35. Ibid.
36. Herbert: *Dune*.
37. David Lynch, AI.
38. Herbert: *Dune*.
39. Ibid.
40. Ibid.
41. Ibid.
42. David Lynch, AI.
43. Ibid.
44. Ibid.
45. Ibid.
46. Herbert: *Dune*.
47. Ibid.
48. Ibid.
49. Ibid.

50. Ibid.
51. Ibid.
52. Ibid.
53. Kristine McKenna: "A Conversation with David Lynch," *The Prints of David Lynch* (Tandem Press, 2000).
54. Herbert: *Dune*.
55. Calbom: "Frank Herbert Goes to the Movies."
56. Ibid.
57. Ibid.
58. Naha: *The Making of Dune*.
59. Ibid.
60. Ibid.
61. Ibid.
62. Ibid.
63. Sammon: "David Lynch's Dune."
64. Ibid.
65. Ibid.
66. Ibid.
67. Naha: *The Making of Dune*.
68. Ibid.
69. Ibid.
70. Sammon: "David Lynch's Dune."
71. *All About Twin Peaks*, Japanese TV documentary, 1990, courtesy of Catherine Coulson Collection.
72. Ibid.
73. Ibid.
74. Ibid.
75. Ibid.
76. *The Making of Dune*: Universal, 1984, broadcast on *Night Flight* TV show, courtesy of Sean Axmaker Collection.
77. Randy and Jean-Marc Lofficier: "Dean Stockwell: The Traitor of Dune," *Starlog*, January 1985.
78. Naha: *The Making of Dune*.
79. Ibid.
80. Ibid.
81. Ibid.
82. Ibid.
83. Catherine Coulson, AI.
84. Ibid.
85. Naha: *The Making of Dune*.
86. Ibid.
87. Ibid.
88. Ibid.
89. Ibid.
90. Ibid.
91. Ibid.
92. Ibid.
93. Ibid.
94. Hodenfield: "Daring Dune."
95. Ibid.
96. Ibid.
97. Ibid.
98. Herbert: *Dune*.
99. Ibid.
100. David Lynch, AI.
101. Harlan Ellison: *Harlan Ellison's Watching* (Underwood-Miller, 1989).
102. Ibid.
103. Herbert: *Dune*.
104. Ibid.
105. François Truffaut: *Hitchcock* (Simon and Schuster, 1967).
106. Frank Herbert: *Dune*.
107. Ibid.
108. Ibid.
109. Ibid.
110. Herbert in *The Maker of Dune*.
111. Ibid.
112. Ibid.
113. Ibid.
114. Ibid.
115. Ibid.
116. Frank Herbert: *Dragon in the Sea* (Doubleday, 1956).
117. Ibid.
118. Herbert: *Dune*.
119. Herbert: *Dragon in the Sea*.
120. David Lynch: *Dune* script, December 9, 1983, unpublished.
121. Naha: *The Making of Dune*.
122. David Lynch, AI.
123. Robert Henri: *The Art Spirit* (Icon, Harper and Row, 1984).
124. David Lynch, AI.
125. Herbert: *Dune*.
126. Ibid.
127. David Lynch, AI.
128. Jack Fisk, AI.
129. Lynch: *Dune* script.
130. Little Richard, quoted from many TV talk show appearances.
131. Wayne L. Johnson: *Ray Bradbury* (Frederick Ungar, 1980).

132. David Lynch, AI.
133. Herbert: *Dune*.
134. Ibid.
135. Ibid.
136. Ibid.
137. Ibid.
138. David Breskin: *Inner Views* (Faber and Faber, 1992).
139. David Lynch, AI.
140. Herbert: *Dune*.
141. Breskin: *Inner Views*.
142. Lynch: *Dune* script.
143. Herbert: *Dreamer of Dune*.
144. Ibid.
145. Frank Herbert: *Dune Messiah* (Ace Books, 1969).
146. Herbert: *Dune*.
147. Lynch: *Dune* script.
148. David Lynch: *Ronnie Rocket* script, unpublished, undated.
149. Jennifer Lynch, AI.
150. *Frank Herbert and David Lynch on Dune*, Waldenbooks audiotape, 1984.
151. Ibid.
152. Ibid.
153. Ibid.
154. Ibid.
155. Ibid.
156. Ibid.
157. Ibid.
158. Paul M. Sammon, AI.
159. Ibid.
160. Ibid.
161. Herbert: *Dreamer of Dune*.
162. Ibid.
163. Ibid.
164. Norman Hill, AI.
165. David Lynch, AI.
166. Ibid.
167. *Frank Herbert and David Lynch on Dune*.
168. TV ad for *Dune* broadcast 1988.
169. Herbert: *Dune*.
170. Chris Rodley: "Introduction," *Lost Highway* by David Lynch and Barry Gifford (Faber and Faber, 1997).
171. David Lynch, AI.
172. Herbert: *Dune*.
173. David Lynch, AI.
174. Herbert: *Dune*.
175. Naha: *The Making of Dune*.
176. Ibid.
177. George Hickenlooper (editor): *Reel Conversations* (Citadel Press, 1991).
178. Breskin: *Inner Views*.
179. Mark Rosin: "The Wild Heart of David Lynch," *Montage*, September 1989.
180. Herman Weigel: "Director David Lynch," *Tip Filmjahrbuch*, Nr. 1, 1985.
181. David Lynch, AI.
182. Corliss: "Czar of Bizarre."
183. Ibid.
184. Ibid.
185. Ibid.
186. Ibid.
187. Ibid.
188. Ibid.
189. Breskin: *Inner Views*.
190. Ibid.
191. Ibid.
192. Toby Thompson: "Alien," *Esquire*, January 1985.
193. David Lynch, AI.
194. Ibid.

CHAPTER 5

1. Richard B. Woodward: "A Dark Lens on America," *New York Times Magazine*, January 14, 1990.
2. *Collected Poems of Robert Frost* (Henry Holt and Company, 1941).
3. Toby Thompson: "Alien," *Esquire*, January 1985.
4. David Breskin: *Inner Views* (Faber and Faber, 1992).
5. David Lynch, AI.
6. Raffaella De Laurentiis: *Dune*, DVD comments, Sanctuary Records Group Ltd., 2003.
7. Ibid.
8. David Lynch, AI.
9. Ibid.
10. Breskin: *Inner Views*.
11. David Lynch, AI.
12. "Gary Indiana Interviews Laura Dern," *Interview*, September 1990.

13. Libby Brooks: *The Guardian*, July 2002.
14. Ralph Rugoff: "Wild at Heart," *Premiere*, September 1990.
15. Ibid.
16. Ibid.
17. Mark A. Altman: *Twin Peaks Behind the Scenes* (Pioneer Books, 1990).
18. Ibid.
19. Isabella Rossellini, AI.
20. Ibid.
21. Isabella Rossellini: *Some of Me* (Random House, 1997).
22. Ibid.
23. Ibid.
24. Ibid.
25. David Lynch: *Blue Velvet*, DVD commentary, MGM, 2002.
26. Rossellini: *Some of Me*.
27. Ibid.
28. Ibid.
29. Ibid.
30. Pat Hitchcock, AI.
31. Elena Rodriguez: *Dennis Hopper* (St. Martin's Press, 1988).
32. Ibid.
33. Ron Rosenbaum: "Riding High: Dennis Hopper Bikes Back," *Vanity Fair*, April 1987.
34. David Lynch, AI.
35. Rodriguez: *Dennis Hopper*.
36. Ibid.
37. Ibid.
38. Ibid.
39. Ibid.
40. Rosenbaum: "Riding High."
41. Rodriguez: *Dennis Hopper*.
42. Ibid.
43. Ibid.
44. Kyle MacLachlan: *Blue Velvet*, DVD comments, MGM, 2002.
45. Booth Tarkington: *The Gentleman from Indiana* (Doubleday and McClure Co., 1899).
46. Sinclair Lewis: *Main Street* (Harcourt, Brace & World, 1948).
47. Ibid.
48. Henry Bellamann: *King's Row* (Simon & Schuster, 1942).
49. François Truffaut: *Hitchcock* (Simon & Schuster, 1967).
50. Ray Bradbury: "The Night," *The Stories of Ray Bradbury* (Alfred A. Knopf, 1981).
51. Ibid.
52. Ibid.
53. Ibid.
54. Ibid.
55. Ibid.
56. Ibid.
57. Altman: *Twin Peaks Behind the Scenes*.
58. Catherine Coulson, AI.
59. Altman: *Twin Peaks Behind the Scenes*.
60. *TV Guide*: 1990–1991.
61. Ibid.
62. James Verniere: "David Lynch, American Primitive," *Twilight Zone*, October 1988.
63. K. George Godwin: "Eraserhead," *Cinefantastique*, September 1984.
64. Ibid.
65. Bill Gibson, Sean Hopper, Huey Lewis: *Hip to be Square* (Chrysalis Records, 1986), www.lyrics.astraweb.com.
66. Brian Wilson, Mike Love: *Be True to Your School* (Capitol Records, 1963), www.lyrics.astraweb.com.
67. Breskin: *Inner Views*.
68. Ibid.
69. David Lynch: *Blue Velvet* script, unpublished, August 24, 1984.
70. Ibid.
71. Kristine McKenna: "A Conversation with David Lynch," *The Prints of David Lynch* (Tandem Press, 2000).
72. Kristine McKenna: "An Interview with David Lynch," *David Lynch* (Sala Parpallo/Vei, 1992).
73. Terry Gross (presenter): "An Interview with David Lynch," *Fresh Air* (National Public Radio, December 15, 1995).
74. Ibid.
75. David Lynch, AI.
76. Gross: "An Interview with David Lynch."
77. Catherine Coulson, AI.
78. George Hickenlooper (editor): *Reel Conversations* (Citadel Press, 1991).

79. David Lynch: *Dune* script, December 9, 1983, unpublished.
80. David Lynch, AI.
81. Ibid.
82. David Lynch, Angelo Badalamenti: "Mysteries of Love," *Floating Into the Night*, Warner Brothers, 1989, www.lyrics.astraweb.com.
83. David Lynch, Angelo Badalamenti: "Floating," *Floating Into the Night*, Warner Brothers, 1989, www.lyrics.astraweb.com.
84. David Lynch, Angelo Badalamenti: "The World Spins," *Floating Into the Night*, Warner Brothers, 1989, www.lyrics.astraweb.com.
85. Lynch:, *Blue Velvet* script.
86. Ibid.
87. Ibid.
88. "(Why) Is David Lynch Important," *Parkett*, No. 28, 1991.
89. Woodward: "A Dark Lens on America."
90. David Lynch, Angelo Badalamenti: "I Remember," *Floating Into the Night*, Warner Brothers, 1989, www.lyrics.astraweb.com.
91. David Lynch, AI.
92. Lynch: *Blue Velvet* script.
93. Gross: "An Interview with David Lynch."
94. Jennifer Lynch, AI.
95. Ibid.
96. Ibid.
97. Ibid.
98. Ibid.
99. Ibid.
100. Ibid.
101. Virginia Campbell: "Something Really Wild," *Movieline*, September 1990.
102. Lynch and Badalamenti: "Mysteries of Love."
103. Mark Rowland, "Wild Innocent," *American Film*, July 1991.
104. David Lynch (presenter): *Ruth, Roses, and Revolvers*, BBC Television, 1987.
105. Lynch: *Blue Velvet* script.
106. David Lynch, AI.

CHAPTER 6

1. David Lynch, AI.
2. KING AM Seattle talk-radio discussion, October 1986.
3. David Ansen: "Is Black and Blue Beautiful?," *Newsweek*, September 15, 1986.
4. J. M. Wall: "The Best Film of 1986: Probing the Depths of Evil," *Christian Century*, January 7–14, 1987.
5. David Hughes: *The Complete Lynch* (Virgin Publishing Ltd., 2001).
6. Jennifer Lynch, AI.
7. David Lynch: *Eraserhead*, DVD comments, Absurda, 2005.
8. David Lynch, AI.
9. Ibid.
10. Stephen Schiff: "The Weird Dreams of David Lynch," *Vanity Fair*, March 1987.
11. Jennifer Lynch, AI.
12. Ibid.
13. Ibid.
14. David Lynch, AI.
15. Ibid.
16. Robert Henri: *The Art Spirit* (Icon, Harper and Row, 1984).
17. Ibid.
18. Ibid.
19. David Lynch, Angelo Badalamenti: "The World Spins," *Floating Into the Night*, Warner Brothers, 1989, www.lyrics.astraweb.com.
20. Schiff: "The Weird Dreams of David Lynch."
21. Ibid.
22. David Lynch, AI.
23. Ibid.
24. Schiff: "The Weird Dreams of David Lynch."
25. Ibid.
26. David Lynch, AI.
27. Isabella Rossellini: *Some of Me* (Random House, 1997).
28. Ibid.
29. Isabella Rossellini, AI.
30. Ibid.
31. Jim Jerome: "David Lynch," *People*,

September 3, 1990.
32. David Lynch, AI.
33. David Lynch (presenter): *Ruth, Roses, and Revolvers*, BBC Television, 1987.
34. Georges Sadoul: *Dictionary of Films* (University of California Press, 1972).
35. Jennifer Lynch, AI.
36. Ibid.
37. Ibid.
38. David Lynch, AI.
39. Jennifer Lynch, AI.
40. Ibid.
41. Ibid.
42. Ibid.
43. Ibid.
44. Ibid.
45. Ibid.
46. David Lynch, AI.
47. Peter Bondanella: *The Cinema of Federico Fellini* (Princeton University Press, 1992).
48. David Lynch, AI.
49. Ibid.
50. Ibid.
51. Mark Altman: *Twin Peaks Behind the Scenes* (Pioneer Books, 1990).
52. David Breskin: *Inner Views* (Faber and Faber, 1992).
53. Ibid.
54. *All About Twin Peaks*, Japanese TV documentary, 1990, courtesy of Catherine Coulson Collection.
55. Mark Frost, AI.
56. Stephen Pizzello: "Twin Peaks: Fire Walk With Me," *American Cinematographer*, September 1992.
57. John Leonard: "The Quirky Allure of Twin Peaks," *New York*, May 7, 1990.
58. All quotes from single page ad on the day of *Twin Peaks'* premiere, *New York Times*, April 8, 1990.
59. Altman: *Twin Peaks Behind the Scenes*.
60. Harley Peyton's letter to the editor, *Wrapped in Plastic*, No. 54, August 2001.
61. Ibid.
62. Pizzello: "Twin Peaks: Fire Walk With Me."
63. Craig Miller and John Thorne: "The Mark Frost Interview," *Wrapped in Plastic*, No. 9, February 1994.
64. Chris Rodley: "Introduction," *Lost Highway* by David Lynch and Barry Gifford (Faber and Faber, 1997).
65. Virginia Campbell: "Something Really Wild," *Movieline*, September 1990.
66. David Lynch, AI.
67. Ibid.
68. Ibid.
69. Breskin: *Inner Views*.
70. Chris Rodley (editor): *Lynch on Lynch* (Faber and Faber, 2005).
71. Ibid.
72. David Lynch, AI.
73. David Lavery (editor): *Full of Secrets* (Wayne State University Press, 1995).
74. Jimi Hendrix: *If 6 Was 9*, MCA, 1968, www.lyrics.astraweb.com. **[song]**
75. David Lynch, AI.
76. Toby Keeler: *Pretty as a Picture: The Art of David Lynch* DVD, 1997.
77. Ibid.
78. David Lynch, AI.
79. Rodley (editor): *Lynch on Lynch*.
80. Ibid.
81. Ibid.
82. Ibid.
83. Ibid.
84. Ibid.
85. Ibid.
86. David Lynch, AI.
87. Ibid.
88. Ibid.
89. Ibid.
90. Craig Miller and John Thorne: "Peyton's Place: Harley Peyton Interview," *Wrapped in Plastic*, No. 17, June 1995.
91. Luke Ford: "Mark Frost Interview," www.lukeford.net/profiles/profiles/mark_frost.htm.
92. Ibid.
93. Ibid.
94. Ibid.
95. Miller and Thorne: "Peyton's Place."
96. Ibid.
97. Ibid.
98. David Lynch, AI.

99. KOMO, ABC Television, Seattle, May 23, 1990.
100. Ibid.
101. Ibid.
102. Ibid.
103. *Twin Peaks* DVD comments.
104. Virginia Heffernan: "The Real Boss of 'The Sopranos,'" *New York Times*, February 29, 2004.
105. Ibid.
106. David Lynch, AI.

CHAPTER 7

1. Mark Altman: *Twin Peaks Behind the Scenes* (Pioneer Books, 1990).
2. David Lynch, AI.
3. Ibid.
4. Barry Gifford: *The Phantom Father* (Harcourt Brace and Company, 1997).
5. Ibid.
6. Ibid.
7. Barry Gifford: on *Today*, NBC Television, June 29, 1994.
8. Barry Gifford: *The Devil Thumbs a Ride* (Grove Press, 1988).
9. Barry Gifford: *Wild at Heart* (Vintage Contemporaries, 1990).
10. Ibid.
11. Ibid.
12. Ibid.
13. Ibid.
14. Ibid.
15. Ibid.
16. David Lynch, AI.
17. Kristine McKenna: "An Interview With David Lynch," *David Lynch* (Sala Parpallo/Vei, 1992).
18. Ibid.
19. Ibid.
20. Ibid.
21. Ibid.
22. Ibid.
23. Ibid.
24. Ibid.
25. Ibid.
26. Ibid.
27. Virginia Campbell: "Something Really Wild," *Movieline*, September 1990.
28. Ibid.
29. Ibid.
30. Phoebe Hoban: "Childhood's End," *Premiere*, September 1990.
31. Ibid.
32. Ibid.
33. Ibid.
34. Anne Frank: *The Diary of a Young Girl* (Bantam Books, 1997).
35. Hoban: "Childhood's End."
36. Ibid.
37. Ibid.
38. Ibid.
39. David Lynch, AI.
40. Ibid.
41. Campbell: "Something Really Wild."
42. Barry Gifford: comments at *Wild at Heart* screening, Pacific Film Archive, Berkeley, September 1990.
43. Ibid.
44. David Breskin: *Inner Views* (Faber and Faber, 1992).
45. David Lynch: *Wild at Heart* script, unpublished, August 2, 1989.
46. Ibid.
47. Ibid.
48. Ibid.
49. David Lynch, AI.
50. Ibid.
51. Jerry Leiber, Mike Stoller: *Trouble*, RCA, 1958, www.lyrics.astraweb.com.
52. Chris Rodley (editor): *Lynch on Lynch* (Faber and Faber, 2005).
53. Ibid.
54. Breskin: *Inner Views*.
55. Gifford: *Wild at Heart*.
56. Ibid.
57. David Lynch, AI.
58. Ibid.
59. Ibid.
60. Breskin: *Inner Views*.
61. Ibid.
62. Chris Rodley: "David Lynch," *ICON*, March/April 1997.
63. Campbell: "Something Really Wild."
64. Rodley: *Lynch on Lynch*.
65. Ibid.

CHAPTER 8

1. David Lynch, AI.
2. Ibid.
3. Ibid.
4. Ibid.
5. David Lynch, AI.
6. David Lynch: *Blue Velvet* script, unpublished, August 24, 1984.
7. Chris Rodley (editor): *Lynch on Lynch* (Faber and Faber, 2005).
8. Stephen King: *Storm of the Century* (Pocket Books, 1999).
9. David Lynch, AI.
10. Ibid.
11. Rodley: *Lynch on Lynch.*
12. Ibid.
13. Peggy Lipton: *Breathing Out* (St. Martin's Press, 2005).
14. Ibid.
15. Rodley: *Lynch on Lynch.*
16. KOMO TV, Seattle, June 10, 1991.
17. Ibid.
18. Ibid.
19. Ibid.
20. Ibid.
21. Tory Patterson and Jeff Jensen: "Our Town," *Entertainment Weekly*, No. 540, Spring 2000.
22. Mark Frost, AI.
23. Ibid.
24. Ibid.
25. Ibid.
26. Ibid.
27. Rodley (editor): *Lynch on Lynch.*
28. Ibid.
29. Mark Frost, AI.
30. Ibid.
31. Craig Miller and John Thorne: "We're Going to Talk about Judy—and a Whole Lot More!: An Interview with Robert Engels," *Wrapped in Plastic*, No. 58, April 2002.
32. Mark Frost, AI.
33. Ibid.
34. Ibid.
35. KOMO TV, Seattle, June 10, 1991.
36. Rodley: *Lynch on Lynch.*
37. Ibid.
38. Ibid.
39. Stephen Pizzello: "Twin Peaks: Fire Walk With Me," *American Cinematographer*, September 1992.
40. David Lynch, AI.
41. Craig Miller and John Thorne: "Sheryl Lee: Actress Enrapt," *Wrapped in Plastic*, No. 16, April 1995.
42. Ibid.
43. Ibid.
44. David Breskin: *Inner Views* (Faber and Faber, 1992).
45. Miller and Thorne: "Sheryl Lee."
46. Ibid.
47. David Lynch and Robert Engels: *Twin Peaks: Fire Walk With Me* script, unpublished, August 8, 1991.
48. Craig Miller and John Thorne: "'Killer Bob' Speaks!," *Wrapped in Plastic*, No. 8, December 1993.
49. Catherine Coulson, AI.
50. Rodley: *Lynch on Lynch.*
51. Ibid.
52. Paul Kerton: "Revealing All: Rossellini's Revolution," *The Daily Mail On Sunday* at geocities.com/Hollywood/2092/intrelrosell.
53. Ibid.
54. Ibid.
55. Jennifer Lynch, AI.
56. Isabella Rossellini: *Some of Me* (Random House, 1997).
57. Jennifer Lynch, AI.
58. Conversation with Matt Marshall.
59. Rodley: *Lynch on Lynch.*
60. Public Broadcasting System Television documentary on Thomas Edison.
61. David Lynch: *Ronnie Rocket* script, unpublished, undated.
62. Conversation with Matt Marshall.
63. Ibid.
64. David Lynch, AI.
65. Chris Rodley: "Introduction," *Lost Highway* by David Lynch and Barry Gifford (Faber and Faber, 1997).
66. David Lynch, AI.
67. David Lynch: *Blue Velvet* script, unpublished, August 24, 1984.
68. David Lynch: *Wild at Heart* script, un-

published, August 2, 1989.
69. The Marquis de Sade: "Juliette," *Surrealism* by Julien Levy (Da Capo Press, 1995).
70. Jennifer Lynch: *The Secret Diary of Laura Palmer* (Pocket Books, 1990).
71. Ibid.
72. David Lynch, AI.
73. Lucius Annaeus Seneca: *Seneca in Ten Volumes* (Harvard University Press, 1928–1972).

CHAPTER 9

1. Richard Corliss: "Czar of Bizarre," *Time*, October 1, 1990.
2. Roger Ebert: *Chicago Sun Times*, May 1992.
3. Tom Gliatto: *People*, September 1992.
4. Unknown author: *Interview*, September 1992.
5. Owen Gleiberman: *Entertainment Weekly*, September 1992.
6. Vincent Canby: *New York Times*, September 1992.
7. David Baron: *The Times-Picayune*, September 1992.
8. Ibid.
9. Ibid.
10. *Twin Peaks: Fire Walk With Me* DVD comments, New Line, 2002.
11. *Good Morning America*, ABC Television, September 1992, tape courtesy of Chris Matthews Collection.
12. Ibid.
13. Ibid.
14. Ibid.
15. Ibid.
16. Ibid.
17. Ibid.
18. David Hughes: *The Complete Lynch* (Virgin Publishing Ltd., 2001).
19. Kyle MacLachlan: *Twin Peaks: Fire Walk With Me* DVD comments.
20. Ibid.
21. Hughes: *The Complete Lynch*.
22. Ibid.
23. Ibid.
24. David Lynch (presenter): "Ruth, Roses, and Revolvers," BBC Television, 1987.
25. Joel Eisner: *The Official Batman Batbook* (Contemporary Books, Inc., 1986).
26. David Lynch, AI.
27. Ibid.
28. David Lynch: *Commercial Reel*, courtesy of Asymmetrical Productions, 1997.
29. Ibid.
30. David Lynch, AI.
31. Chris Rodley (editor): *Lynch on Lynch* (Faber and Faber, 2005).
32. Ibid.
33. Ibid.
34. Ibid.
35. Ibid.
36. Lynch: *Commercial Reel*.
37. Jennifer Lynch, AI.
38. Peggy Reavey, AI.
39. Jennifer Lynch, AI.
40. Shari Roman and Dean Lamanna: "Limbless Love," *Film Threat*, No. 10, June 1993.
41. Ibid.
42. Peggy Reavey, AI.
43. Ibid.
44. K. George Godwin: "Eraserhead," *Cinefantastique*, September 1984.
45. Ibid.
46. Jennifer Lynch, AI.
47. David Lynch, AI.
48. Jennifer Lynch, AI.
49. Peggy Reavey, AI.
50. David Lynch, AI.
51. Roman and Lamanna: "Limbless Love."
52. Ibid.
53. Catherine Coulson, AI.
54. Roman and Lamanna: "Limbless Love."
55. Jennifer Lynch, AI.
56. David Lynch: *Images* (Hyperion, 1994).
57. Ibid.
58. Ibid.

59. Ibid.
60. Ibid.
61. Ibid.
62. Ibid.
63. Ibid.
64. Ibid.
65. Ibid.
66. Ibid.
67. Ibid.
68. David Lynch, AI.
69. Lynch, *Images*.
70. David Lynch, AI.
71. Lynch: *Images*.
72. Ibid.
73. Hughes: *The Complete Lynch*.
74. Michael Sragow: "The Man Behind the Man in 'Crumb,'" *New York Times*, 1994.
75. Craig Miller and John Thorne: "'Killer Bob' Speaks!," *Wrapped in Plastic*, No. 8, December 1993.
76. Craig Miller and John Thorne: "The Jack Nance Interview," *Wrapped in Plastic*, No. 27, February 1997.
77. Ibid.
78. Ibid.
79. Ibid.
80. Ibid.
81. Toby Keeler: *Pretty as a Picture: The Art of David Lynch* DVD, 1997.
82. Ibid.
83. Maximillian Potter: "Dark Journey," *Premiere*, UK Edition, September 1997.
84. Ibid.
85. Ken Ellingwood: "Star of 'Eraserhead' Found Dead After Fight," *New York Times*, January 4, 1997.
86. Ibid.
87. Ibid.
88. Ibid.
89. David Lynch, AI.
90. Ronald Reng (editor): "I Have a Dream," *Die Zeit*, Nr. 509, December 1999.
91. David Lynch, AI.
92. Barry Gifford: *Night People* (Grove Press, 1992).
93. Steve Biodrowski: "'Lost Highway': The Solution," *Cinefantastique*, April 1997.
94. Barney Hoskyns: *Waiting for the Sun* (St. Martin's Press, 1996).
95. David Lynch, AI.
96. Keeler: *Pretty as a Picture*.
97. James Ellroy: *My Dark Places* (Vintage Books, 1997).
98. Rodley: *Lynch on Lynch*.
99. Ibid.
100. David Lynch and Barry Gifford: *Lost Highway* (Faber and Faber, 1997).
101. David Lynch, AI.
102. Lynch and Gifford: *Lost Highway*.
103. Ibid.
104. Ibid.
105. Matt Marshall, AI.
106. Keeler: *Pretty as a Picture*.
107. David Lynch, AI.
108. Hoskyns: *Waiting for the Sun*.
109. David Lynch, AI.
110. Ibid.
111. Ibid.
112. Ibid.
113. Ibid.
114. Ibid.
115. Barry Gifford: *The Devil Thumbs a Ride* (Grove Press, 1988).
116. Ibid.
117. Ibid.
118. Ibid.
119. Ibid.
120. Don Felder, Don Henley, Glenn Frey: "Hotel California" (Long Run Music, Fingers Music, WB Music Corp., 1976), www.lyrics.astraweb.com.
121. Ibid.
122. Ibid.
123. Ibid.
124. Ibid.
125. Ibid.
126. Ibid.
127. Gene Siskel: *At the Movies*, KOMO Television, Seattle, February 1997.
128. David Bianculli: *Dictionary of Teleliteracy* (Continuum Publishing Company, 1996).
129. Keeler: *Pretty as a Picture*.
130. Greg Risling: "Jury Says Blake Behind Slaying," *The Associated Press*, November 19, 2005.

131. Ibid.
132. Ibid.
133. Robert Hilferty: "How to Make an Opera a Riddle: Adapt David Lynch," *New York Times*, November 2, 2003.

CHAPTER 10

1. Jim Morrison, Ray Manzarek, Robbie Krieger, John Densmore: *When the Music's Over*, Elektra, 1967, www.lyrics.astraweb.com.
2. David Lynch, AI.
3. Ibid.
4. Peggy Reavey, AI.
5. Ibid.
6. www.davidlynch.de/99spiegel.
7. David Lynch, AI.
8. David Lynch: *Eraserhead* script, unpublished, undated.
9. David Lynch, AI.
10. *The Prints of David Lynch* (Tandem Press, 2000).
11. *The Straight Story* Electronic Press Kit, Walt Disney Pictures, 1999.
12. Ibid.
13. Amy Wallace: "David Lynch, Mild at Heart," *Los Angeles Times*, September 12, 1999.
14. Ibid.
15. Ibid.
16. Ibid.
17. Ibid.
18. Michael Sragow: "I Want a Dream When I Go to a Film," *Salon Magazine*, October 28, 1999.
19. Ibid.
20. Ibid.
21. Ibid.
22. *The Straight Story* Electronic Press Kit.
23. Ibid.
24. David Lynch, AI.
25. Ibid.
26. Ibid.
27. Ibid.
28. Ibid.
29. Ibid.
30. Ibid.
31. Ibid.
32. Ibid.
33. Ibid.
34. *The Straight Story* Electronic Press Kit.
35. David Lynch, AI.
36. Ibid.
37. Ibid.
38. Ibid.
39. Margret Kohler: "David Lynch: 'In the editing room I cried like mad,'" *Cinemaxx Filmtips*, December 1999.
40. Ibid.
41. Walt Disney: "From the Wisdom of Walt Disney," *Wisdom Magazine*, October 1, 1959.
42. Ibid.
43. Ibid.
44. Ibid.
45. David Lynch, AI.
46. Mary Sweeney, AI.
47. Disney: "From the Wisdom of Walt Disney."
48. Ibid.
49. Mark Frost, AI.
50. David Lynch, AI.
51. Ibid.
52. Margaret Leslie Davis: *Rivers in the Desert* (HarperCollins, 1993).
53. Ibid.
54. David Lynch, AI.
55. Ibid.
56. Ibid.
57. David Lynch: *Mulholland Drive* pilot script, unpublished, January 5, 1998.
58. Ibid.
59. Ibid.
60. Ibid.
61. Tad Friend: "Creative Differences," *The New Yorker*, September 6, 1999.
62. Ibid.
63. Lynch: *Mulholland Drive* pilot script.
64. David Lynch, AI.
65. Ibid.
66. Lynch: *Mulholland Drive Pilot* script.
67. Friend:"Creative Differences."
68. Jeffrey Lantos: "The ABC of Going from the Big Screen to the Small,"

Movieline, August 1999.
69. Mark Frost, AI.
70. Friend: "Creative Differences."
71. Ibid.
72. *Independent Spirit Awards*, Independent Film Channel Television, March 2000.
73. Ibid.
74. Richard Leslie: *Surrealism* (Smithmark, 1997).
75. David Lynch, AI.
76. Gavin Lambert: "Origins of the *Sunset Boulevard* Mansion," *Architectural Digest*, April 1998.

CHAPTER 11

1. *New York Times*, August 3, 2000.
2. Ibid.
3. Ibid.
4. Ibid.
5. Ibid.
6. Ibid.
7. Tad Friend: "Kidnapped? A Painted Cow Goes Missing," *The New Yorker*, August 21, 2000.
8. Jack Fisk, AI.
9. Ibid.
10. Ibid.
11. Jack Fisk, AI.
12. David Lynch, AI.
13. Ibid.
14. David Hughes: *The Complete Lynch* (Virgin Publishing Ltd., 2001).
15. Ibid.
16. Ibid.
17. Ibid.
18. Ibid.
19. Hughes: *The Complete Lynch*.
20. David Lynch, AI.
21. *Independent Spirit Awards*, Independent Film Channel Television, March 2000.
22. Craig Miller and John Thorne: "From Dune to Earth," *Wrapped in Plastic*, No. 44, December 1999.
23. David Lynch, AI.
24. Ibid.
25. Paramahansa Yogananda: *The Autobiography of a Yogi* (Self-Realization Fellowship, 1999).
26. Peggy Reavey, AI.
27. Jennifer Lynch, AI.
28. Kristine McKenna: "An Interview With David Lynch," *The Prints of David Lynch* (Tandem Press, 2000).
29. William Blake: *The Marriage of Heaven and Hell* (University of Miami Press, 1970).
30. David Lynch, AI.
31. Ibid.
32. Ibid.
33. Ibid.
34. Ibid.
35. Ibid.
36. *2001 Cannes Film Festival Closing Night*, Independent Film Channel Television, May 20, 2001.
37. Ibid.
38. Ibid.
39. David Lynch, AI.
40. Ibid.
41. Peggy Reavey, AI.
42. David Lynch, AI.
43. Ibid.
44. Ibid.
45. Peggy Reavey, AI.
46. Ibid.
47. Kristin Hohenadel: "Real L.A., The One That's Lived in," *New York Times Magazine*, October 7, 2001.
48. Tad Friend: "Creative Differences," *The New Yorker*, September 6, 1999.
49. Jeffrey Lantos: "The ABC of Going from the Big Screen to the Small," *Movieline*, August 1999.
50. Don Felder, Don Henley, Glenn Frey: "Hotel California," www.lyrics.astraweb.com.
51. David Lynch: *Mulholland Drive* DVD comments.
52. David Lynch, AI.
53. Ibid.
54. Lynch: *Mulholland Drive* DVD comments.
55. Ibid.
56. Ibid.

57. David Lynch, AI.
58. Whitney J. Oates (editor): *The Basic Writings of St. Augustine* (Random House, 1948).
59. Roger Shattuck: *Forbidden Knowledge* (St. Martin's Press, 1996).
60. Ibid.
61. David Lynch: *Mulholland Drive* pilot script, unpublished, January 5, 1999.
62. David Lynch, AI.
63. Lynch: *Mulholland Drive* pilot script.
64. David Lynch, AI.
65. Ibid.
66. Ibid.
67. Ibid.
68. Robert Greene and Joost Elffers: *The 48 Laws of Power* (Viking, 1998).
69. David Breskin: *Inner Views* (Faber and Faber, 1992).
70. Lynch: *Mulholland Drive* DVD comments.
71. *The Holy Bible* (The World Publishing Company, 1962).
72. David Lynch, AI.
73. Kristine McKenna: "A Conversation With David Lynch," *The Prints of David Lynch* (Tandem Press, 2000).
74. David Lynch, AI.
75. Lynch: *Mulholland Drive* Pilot script.
76. David Lynch, AI.
77. Lynch: *Mulholland Drive* Pilot script.
78. Ibid.
79. Ibid.
80. Ibid.
81. Julie Duvic, AI.
82. David Lynch, AI.
83. Philippe Jullian: *Dreamers of Decadence* (Praeger Publishers, Inc., 1971).
84. Lantos: "The ABC of Going from the Big Screen to the Small."
85. Lynch: *Mulholland Drive* script.
86. McKenna: "A Conversation With David Lynch."
87. David Lynch, AI.
88. Alan Watts: *Eastern Asian Wisdom and Modern Life*, PBS Television, 1965.
89. Yogananda: *The Autobiography of a Yogi*.
90. Richard Hallas: *You Play the Black and the Red Comes Up* (Gregg Press, 1980).
91. David Lynch, AI.
92. Matt Marshall, AI.
93. David Lynch, AI.
94. Hallas: *You Play the Black and the Red Comes Up*.
95. Steven Tyler, Joe Perry, Taylor Rhodes: "Cryin'" (Geffen Records, 1993), www.lyrics.astraweb.com.
96. Naomi Watts, AI.
97. David Lynch: *Mulholland Drive* DVD Special Features, Universal Pictures, 2002.
98. Ibid.
99. Naomi Watts, AI.
100. Roy Orbison, Joe Melson: "Crying" (Monument Records, 1961), www.lyrics.astraweb.com.
101. Mark A. Altman: *Twin Peaks Behind the Scenes* (Pioneer Books, 1990).
102. K. George Godwin: "Eraserhead," *Cinefantastique*, September 1984.
103. Ibid.
104. Naomi Watts, AI.
105. David Lynch, AI.
106. Naomi Watts, AI.
107. Ibid.
108. David Lynch, AI.
109. William Shakespeare: *Four Great Tragedies* (Penguin Group, 1987).
110. Ibid.
111. www.mulhollanddrive.com.
112. McKenna: "A Conversation With David Lynch."
113. Ibid.
114. David Lynch, AI.
115. Chris Roberts: "Wild at Art," *Uncut*, February 2002.
116. David Lynch, AI.
117. Mark Frost, AI.

CHAPTER 12

1. Naomi Watts, AI.
2. Website with this commercial has been withdrawn.
3. Julee Cruise, AI.

4. Ibid.
5. Ibid.
6. Ibid.
7. Ibid.
8. Ibid.
9. Ibid.
10. Ibid.
11. Ibid.
12. Ibid.
13. Ibid.
14. Ibid.
15. Ibid.
16. Ibid.
17. Ibid.
18. Ibid.
19. Ibid.
20. Ibid.
21. Ibid.
22. Ibid.
23. Ibid.
24. Ibid.
25. Ibid.
26. Ibid.
27. Ibid.
28. Ibid.
29. Ibid.
30. Ibid.
31. Ibid.
32. Ibid.
33. Ibid.
34. Ibid.
35. Ibid.
36. Ibid.
37. Naomi Watts, AI.
38. Jennifer Lynch, AI.
39. Peggy Reavey, AI.
40. David Lynch, AI.
41. Kristine McKenna: "Dreamer of Dark and Troubling Things," *L.A. Reader*, October 8, 1982.
42. Larry King (interviewer): "Maharishi Mahesh Yogi," *Larry King Weekend*, CNN Television, May 12, 2002.
43. David Lynch, AI.
44. Ibid.
45. Ibid.
46. King: "Maharishi Mahesh Yogi."
47. Ibid.
48. David Lynch, AI.
49. Ibid.
50. Naomi Watts, AI.
51. Ibid.
52. Ibid.
53. Ibid.
54. Ibid.
55. Ibid.
56. Ibid.
57. Ibid.
58. Ibid.
59. Ibid.
60. Ibid.
61. Ibid.
62. Ibid.
63. Ibid.
64. Ibid.
65. Ibid.
66. Ibid.
67. Ibid.
68. Ibid.
69. Ibid.
70. Ibid.
71. David Lynch, AI.
72. Ibid.
73. Brian Libby: "David Lynch," salon.com, November 11, 2001.
74. Ibid.
75. Ibid.
76. David Lynch, AI.
77. Kenneth Anger: *Hollywood Babylon II* (New American Library, 1985).
78. Ibid.
79. Ibid.
80. Kenneth Anger: *Hollywood Babylon* (Bell Publishing, 1981).
81. Ibid.
82. Ibid.
83. Ibid.
84. Ibid.
85. Nathaniel West: *Novels and Other Writings* (Penguin Books, 1997).
86. Ibid.
87. Ibid.
88. Ibid.
89. Ibid.
90. Ibid.
91. Ibid.
92. Ibid.
93. Ibid.

94. David Lynch, AI.
95. Ibid.
96. Ibid.
97. Mark Cousins (presenter): *Scene by Scene with David Lynch*, BBC Television, 1987.
98. David Lynch, AI.
99. Ibid.
100. Gates, Huber, Peardon, Salisbury: *Good Times on Our Street* (The Macmillan Company, 1945).
101. David Lynch, AI.
102. Ibid.
103. Ibid.
104. Ibid.
105. Anna Keel and Christian Strich (editors): *Fellini on Fellini* (Eyre Methuen, 1976).
106. Ibid.
107. Naomi Watts, AI.
108. David Lynch, AI.
109. Ibid.
110. Costanzo Costantini (editor): *Conversations with Fellini* (Harcourt Brace & Company, 1995).
111. Thomas Allen Nelson: *Kubrick* (Indiana University Press, 1982).
112. Ibid.
113. Giovanni Grazzini (editor): *Federico Fellini: Comments on Film* (The Press at California State University, Fresno, 1988).
114. Robert Henri: *The Art Spirit* (Icon, Harper and Row, 1984).
115. Ibid.
116. Ibid.
117. David Lynch, AI.
118. Ibid.
119. The Holy Bible.
120. Ibid.
121. Ibid.
122. Ibid.
123. Ibid.
124. Ibid.
125. Ibid.
126. Ibid.
127. Ibid.
128. David Lynch, AI.
129. The Holy Bible.
130. David Lynch, AI.
131. The Holy Bible.
132. Naomi Watts, AI.
133. McKenna: "Dreamer of Dark and Troubling Things."
134. David Lynch, AI.
135. McKenna: "Dreamer of Dark and Troubling Things."
136. Ibid.
137. Rachel Ingalls: *Mrs. Caliban* (Dell Publishing Co., Inc., 1983).
138. Ibid.
139. Ibid.
140. Ibid.
141. Ibid.
142. Peggy Reavey, AI.
143. Ingalls: *Mrs. Caliban*.
144. Ibid.
145. Ibid.
146. Peggy Reavey, AI.
147. David Lynch, AI.
148. Ibid.
149. Ibid.
150. Ibid.
151. Ibid.
152. www.davidlynch.com.
153. David Lynch, AI.
154. www.davidlynch.com.
155. Ibid.
156. Ibid.
157. David Lynch, AI.
158. Ibid.
159. www.davidlynch.com.
160. Ibid.
161. David Lynch, AI.
162. www.davidlynch.com.
163. Ibid.
164. Ibid.
165. Ibid.
166. David Lynch, AI.
167. Ibid.
168. www.davidlynch.com.
169. Ibid.
170. Ibid.
171. Ibid.
172. Ibid.
173. Ibid.
174. Ibid.
175. Ibid.

176. Ibid.
177. Ibid.
178. Ibid.
179. Ibid.
180. Ibid.
181. Ibid.
182. Ibid.
183. Ibid.
184. Ibid.
185. Ibid.
186. Ibid.
187. Ibid.
188. Ibid.
189. Ibid.
190. David Lynch, AI.
191. Ibid.
192. Ibid.
193. Ibid.
194. Ibid.
195. Jennifer Lynch, AI.
196. David Lynch, AI.
197. Ibid.
198. Ibid.
199. Ibid.
200. Ibid.
201. Ibid.
202. "55th Cannes Film Festival," Independent Film Channel, May, 2002.
203. David Lynch, AI.
204. "55th Cannes Film Festival."
205. Ibid.
206. Ibid.
207. Ibid.
208. Ibid.
209. Ibid.
210. Ibid.
211. Ibid.
212. Ibid.
213. Ibid.
214. John Powers: "Getting Lost Is Beautiful," *L.A. Weekly*, October 19, 2001.
215. David Lynch, AI.
216. "55th Cannes Film Festival."
217. Ibid.
218. Ibid.
219. Ibid.
220. Ibid.
221. Ibid.
222. Ibid.
223. Ibid.
224. Ibid.
225. Ibid.
226. Ibid.
227. Ibid.
228. Ibid.
229. Ibid.
230. Ibid.
231. Ibid.
232. www.davidlynch.com.
233. Ibid.
234. Ibid.
235. Cari Beauchamp and Henri Behar: *Hollywood on the Riviera* (William Morrow and Company, Inc., 1992).
236. www.davidlynch.com.
237. Ibid.
238. Ibid.
239. Ibid.
240. Ibid.
241. Ibid.
242. Ibid.
243. Ibid.
244. Ibid.
245. Ibid.
246. Ibid.
247. Ibid.
248. Ibid.
249. Ibid.
250. Ibid.
251. Ibid.
252. Ibid.
253. Ibid.
254. Ibid.
255. Ibid.
256. Ibid.
257. Ibid.
258. Ibid.
259. Ibid.
260. Ibid.
261. Ibid.
262. Ibid.
263. Ibid.
264. Ibid.
265. Ibid.
266. Ibid.
267. Mark A. Altman: *Twin Peaks Behind the Scenes* (Pioneer Books, 1990).
268. www.davidlynch.com.

269. Ibid.
270. Ibid.
271. Ibid.
272. Ibid.
273. Ibid.
274. Ibid.
275. Ibid.
276. Ibid.
277. Ibid.
278. Ibid.
279. Ibid.
280. Ibid.
281. David Lynch, AI.
282. Peggy Reavey, AI.
283. Jennifer Lynch, AI.
284. Ibid.
285. Jim Jerome: "David Lynch," *People*, September 3, 1990.
286. Jennifer Lynch, AI.
287. Ibid.
288. Ibid.
289. Ibid.
290. Ibid.
291. Ibid.
292. Ibid.
293. Ibid.
294. Ibid.
295. Ibid.
296. Ibid.
297. Ibid.
298. Ibid.
299. David Lynch, AI.
300. Shari Roman and Dean Lamanna: "Limbless Love," *Film Threat*, No. 10, June 1993.
301. Jennifer Lynch, AI.
302. Ibid.
303. Ibid.
304. Ibid.
305. Ibid.
306. Ibid.
307. Ibid.
308. Ibid.
309. Ibid.
310. Sophie May: "Blue Bob," chez.com.
311. Ibid.
312. Jennifer Lynch, AI.
313. Peggy Reavey, AI.
314. Ibid.
315. Ibid.
316. David Lynch, Angelo Badalamenti: "Questions in a World of Blue," *Twin Peaks: Fire Walk With Me*, Warner Brothers, 1992, www.lyrics.astraweb.com.
317. Altman: *Twin Peaks Behind the Scenes*.
318. Peggy Reavey, AI.
319. Kristine McKenna: "A Conversation With David Lynch," *The Prints of David Lynch* (Tandem Press, 2000).
320. Ibid.
321. David Lynch, AI.
322. Peggy Reavey, AI.
323. Ibid.
324. Maharishi Mahesh Yogi: *Science of Being and Art of Living* (Penguin Books USA, Inc., 1995).
325. King: "Maharishi Mahesh Yogi."
326. McKenna: "A Conversation With David Lynch."
327. www.filmguardian.co.uk: "Cut and Print: The 40 Best Directors."
328. Ibid.
329. Ibid.
330. Ibid.
331. Craig Miller and John Thorne: "The World Spins," *Wrapped in Plastic*, No. 74, June 2005.
332. Ibid.
333. Peggy Reavey, AI.
334. Matt Marshall, AI.
335. Peggy Reavey, AI.
336. David Lynch, AI.
337. Tim Curtis, AI.
338. Peggy Reavey, AI.
339. Ibid.
340. David Lynch, AI.
341. Gerald L'Ecuyer: "Out of Bounds: David Lynch," *Interview*, 1987, thecityofabsurdity.com.
342. "CBC David Lynch Interview, 1990," thecityofabsurdity.com.
343. David Lynch, AI.
344. Jennifer Lynch, AI.
345. Chief Seattle: "Treaty Oration, 1854," *Four Wagons West*, Roberta Frye Watt (Binsford & Mort, 1934).
346. David Lynch, AI.

347. Peggy Reavey, AI.
348. Isabella Rossellini, AI.
349. David Lynch: "Consciousness, Creativity, and the Brain," University of Washington, Seattle, November 7, 2005.
350. Peggy Reavey, AI.
351. Lynch: "Consciousness, Creativity, and the Brain."
352. Peggy Reavey, AI.
353. Ibid.
354. Ibid.
355. Ibid.
356. Natalie Finn: "A Lynchian Divorce," www.eonline.com.
357. Peggy Reavey, AI.
358. Ibid.
359. Ibid.
360. Peggy Reavey, AI.
361. Ibid.
362. David Lynch, AI.
363. Daniel Nemet-Nejat: "David Lynch's Empire," *Moviemaker*, Winter 2007.
364. Lynch: "Consciousness, Creativity, and the Brain."
365. Nemet-Nejat: "David Lynch's Empire."
366. Ibid.
367. Paramahansa Yogananda, *The Autobiography of a Yogi* (Self-Realization Fellowship, 1999).
368. Richard Hallas, *You Play the Black and the Red Comes Up* (Gregg Press, 1980).
369. W. J. Johnson (translator): *The Bhagavad Vita* (Oxford University Press, 1994).
370. Ibid.
371. "David Gets Lynched over 'Invincible Germany' Meditation Plan," no author credited, spiegel.de/intermational/zeitgeist, November 20, 2007.
372. Ibid.
373. Ibid.
374. Ibid.
375. David Lynch, AI.

BIBLIOGRAPHY

55th Cannes Film Festival, Independent Film Channel, May 2002.

All About Twin Peaks, Japanese TV documentary, 1990, courtesy of Catherine Coulson Collection.

The American College Dictionary. New York: Random House, 1957.

Altman, Mark A. *Twin Peaks Behind the Scenes*. Las Vegas: Pioneer Books, 1990.

Anger, Kenneth. *Hollywood Babylon*. New York: Bell Publishing Co., 1981.

———. *Hollywood Babylon II*. New York: New American Library, 1985.

Ansen, David. "Is Black and Blue Beautiful?" *Newsweek*, September 15, 1986.

Baron, David. *The Times-Picayune*, September 4, 1992.

Barron, James. "'Gruesome' Cow Gets the Axe," *New York Times*, August 3, 2000.

Beauchamp, Cari and Henri Behar. *Hollywood on the Riviera: The Inside Story of the Cannes Film Festival*. New York: William Morrow and Company, Inc., 1992.

Bellamann, Henry. *King's Row*. New York: Simon & Schuster, 1940.

Bianculli, David. *Dictionary of Teleliteracy: Television's 500 Biggest Hits, Misses, and Events*. New York: Continuum, 1996.

Biedermann, Hans. *The Wordsworth Dictionary of Symbolism*. New York: Wordsworth Editions, Ltd., 1996.

Biodrowski, Steve. "'Lost Highway': The Solution," *Cinefantastique* (April 1997).

Blackwell, Otis and Elvis Presley. "All Shook Up," *All Shook Up*, 1957, RCA, http://lyrics.astraweb.com/display/256elvispresley..all_shook_up.

Blake, William. *The Marriage of Heaven and Hell*. Coral Gables: University of Miami Press, 1963.

Blunt, Anthony. *The Art of William Blake*. New York: Columbia University Press, 1959.

Bondanella, Peter. *The Cinema of Federico Fellini*. Princeton: Princeton University Press, 1992.

Bonnell, John Sutherland. "What Is a Presbyterian?" In *A Guide to the Religions of America*, edited by Leo Rosten. New York: Simon & Schuster, 1955.

Bradbury, Ray. "The Night." In *The Stories of Ray Bradbury*. New York: Knopf, 1980.
Breskin, David. *Inner Views: Filmmakers in Conversation*. Boston: Faber and Faber, 1992.
Breton, André. "Beauty will be convulsive, or not at all." http://thinkexist.com/quotes/Andre_Breton/.
Bromell, Henry. "Visionary From Fringeland," *Rolling Stone*, November 13, 1980.
Brooks, Libby. "Hitting New Peaks." *The Guardian*, July 24, 2002.
Calbom, Hal. "Frank Herbert Goes to the Movies: The Wrapping of Dune," *Pacific Northwest* (June 1984).
Callan, Michael Feeney. *Anthony Hopkins: The Unauthorized Biography*. New York: Scribner, 1994.
Campbell, Virginia. "Something Really Wild," *Movieline* (September 1990).
Canby, Vincent. *New York Times*, September 1992.
Carson, Johnny. *The 53rd Academy Awards, NBC Television*, March 31, 1981.
"CBC David Lynch Interview, 1990," http://thecityofabsurdity.com/intcbc.
Chandogya Upanishad quoted in *Heaven's Banquet: Vegetarian Cooking for Lifelong Health the Ayurvedic Way*, by Miriam Kasin Hospodar. New York: Dutton, 1999.
Chief Seattle: "Treaty Oration, 1854," *Four Wagons West: The Story of Seattle*, by Roberta Frye Watt. Portland: Metropolitan Press, [not after 1937].
Collected Poems of Robert Frost. New York: H. Holt, 1939.
Corliss, Richard. "Czar of Bizarre," *Time*, October 1, 1990.
Costantini, Costanzo (editor). *Conversations with Fellini*. San Diego: Harcourt Brace, 1995.
Cousins, Mark (presenter). *Scene by Scene With David Lynch*, BBC Television, 1987.
Mabel Msonthi, site manager. "Cut and Print: The 40 Best Directors," http://www.filmguardian.co.uk.
Davis, Margaret Leslie. *Rivers in the Desert*. New York: HarperCollins Publishers, 1993.
DeLaurentiis, Raffaella. DVD comments, *Dune*, Sanctuary Records Group Ltd., 2003.
De Vore, Christopher, Eric Bergren, and David Lynch. *The Elephant Man* script. Hollywood: Script City, undated.
Disney, Walt. "From the Wisdom of Walt Disney," *Wisdom Magazine*, October 1, 1959.
Domino, Christophe. *Francis Bacon: Painter of a Dark Vision*. New York: Harry N. Abrams, Inc., 1997.
Donaldson, Walter and George Whiting. "My Blue Heaven," *Still Rockin'*, 1957, Imperial, http://herkolson.com/names_f/fats_domino_songs/my_blue_heaven_lyrics.
The Eagles. "Hotel California," *Hotel California*, 1976, Asylum Records.
Ebert, Roger. *Chicago Sun Times*, May 18, 1992.
Eisner, Joel. *The Official Batman Batbook*. Chicago: Contemporary Books, 1986.
Ellingwood, Ken. "Star of 'Eraserhead' Found Dead After Fight," *New York Times*, January 4, 1997.
Ellison, Harlan. *Harlan Ellison's Watching*. Los Angeles: Underwood-Miller, 1989.
Ellroy, James. *My Dark Places*. New York: Knopf, 1996.
Erdman, David V. (editor). *The Complete Poetry and Prose of William Blake*. Berkeley: University of California Press, 1982.
Falk, Quentin. *The Authorized Biography of Anthony Hopkins*. New York: Interlink Books, 1993.
Felder, Don, Don Henley, Glenn Frey, "Hotel California," 1976, (Long Run Music, Fingers Music, WB Music Corp.).
Fielder, Leslie A. *Freaks: Myths and Images of the Secret Self*. New York: Anchor Books, 1993.

www.filmguardian.co.uk: "Cut and Print: The 40 Best Directors."

Finn, Natalie. "A Lynchian Divorce," http://www.eonline.com/news/article/index.jsp?uuid=cad5aee1-8243-4828-b2c5-8fa210f7e2b8.

Ford, Luke. "Mark Frost Interview," http://www.lukeford.net/profiles/profiles/mark_frost.htm.

Frank, Anne. *The Diary of a Young Girl: The Definitive Edition*. New York: Doubleday, 1995.

Friend, Tad. "Creative Differences," *The New Yorker*, September 6, 1999.

———. "Kidnapped? A Painted Cow Goes Missing," *The New Yorker*, August 21, 2000.

"Gary Indiana Interviews Laura Dern," *Interview*, September, 1990.

Gates, Huber, Peardon, and Salisbury. *Good Times on Our Street*. The Macmillan Company, 1945.

Gertsch, Franz and Thomas Ruff. "(Why) Is David Lynch Important," *Parkett*, No. 28, 1991.

Gibson, Bill, Sean Hopper, and Huey Lewis. "Hip to be Square." *Fore!*, 1986, Chrysalis Records, http://lyrics.astraweb.com/display/709/huey_lewis_and_the_news..fore..hip_to_be_square.

Gifford, Barry. *The Devil Thumbs a Ride and Other Unforgettable Films*. New York: Grove Press, 1988.

———. *Night People*. New York: Grove Press, 1992.

———. *The Phantom Father*. New York: Harcourt Brace, 1997.

———. on *Today*, NBC Television, June 29, 1994.

———. *Wild at Heart: The Story of Sailor and Lula*. New York: Grove Weidenfeld, 1990.

———, comments at *Wild at Heart* screening, Pacific Film Archive, Berkeley, September 1990.

Gleiberman, Owen. *Entertainment Weekly*, September 18, 1992.

Gliatto, Tom. *Twin Peaks: Fire Walk with Me* review, *People*, September 4, 1992.

Godwin, Joscelyn. *Mystery Religions in the Ancient World*. London: Thames and Hudson, 1981.

Godwin, K. George. "Eraserhead," *Cinefantastique* (September 1984).

Gogol, Nikolai. "The Nose," *The Overcoat and Other Tales of Good and Evil*. Cambridge: R. Bentley, 1957.

Good Morning America, ABC Television, tape courtesy of Chris Matthews Collection. September 1992.

Grazzini, Giovanni (editor). *Federico Fellini: Comments on Film*. Fresno: The Press at California State University, Fresno, 1988.

Greene, Robert and Joost Elffers. *The 48 Laws of Power*. New York: Viking, 1998.

Grimes, William. "Adventure Returns For David Lynch," *New York Times*, May 31, 1995.

Gross, Terry (presenter). "David Lynch," *Fresh* Air. National Public Radio, December 15, 1995.

Hallas, Richard. *You Play the Black and the Red Comes Up*. Boston: Gregg Press, 1980.

Heffernan, Virginia. "The Real Boss of 'The Sopranos,'" *New York Times*, February 29, 2004.

Hendrix, Jimi. "If 6 Was 9," *Axis: Bold as Love*, 1968 MCA, http://lyrics.astraweb.com/display/145/jimi_hendrix..axis_bold_as_love..if_6_was_9.html.

Henri, Robert. *The Art Spirit*. New York: Harper & Row, 1984.

Herbert, Brian. *Dreamer of Dune: The Biography of Frank Herbert*. New York: Tor, 2003.

Herbert, Frank. *Dragon in the Sea*. Garden City, NY: Doubleday, 1956.

———. *Dune*. Philadelphia: Chilton Books, 1965.

———. *Dune Messiah*. New York: Putnam, 1969.

———. in *The Maker of Dune: Insights of a Master of Science Fiction*, edited by Tim O'Reilly. New York: Berkley Books, 1987.

Frank Herbert and David Lynch on Dune. Ann Arbor: Waldenbooks audiotape, 1984.

Hickenlooper, George (editor). *Reel Conversations*. Seacaucus, NJ: Carol Pub. Group, 1991.

Highsmith, Patricia. "The Terrors of Basket-Weaving," *The Black House*. New York: Penzler Books, 1981.

Hilferty, Robert. "How to Make an Opera A Riddle: Adapt David Lynch," *New York Times*, November 2, 2003.

Hoban, Phoebe. "Childhood's End," *Premiere*, September 1990.

Hoberman, J. and Jonathan Rosenbaum. *Midnight Movies*. New York: Harper & Row, 1983.

Hodenfield, Chris. "Daring Dune," *Rolling Stone*, December 6, 1984.

Hohenadel, Kristin. "Real L.A., The One That's Lived In," *New York Times Magazine*, October 7, 2001.

The Holy Bible. Cleveland, OH: The World Publishing Company, 1962.

Hoskyns, Barney. *Waiting for the Sun: Strange Days, Weird Scenes, and the Sound of Los Angeles*. New York: St. Martin's Press, 1996.

Hughes, David. *The Complete Lynch*. London: Virgin Publishing Ltd., 2001.

Independent Spirit Awards, Independent Film Channel Television, March 25, 2000.

Ingalls, Rachel. *Mrs. Caliban*. Ipswich, MA Gambit, 1983.

Jacobi, Jolande and R. F. C. Hull (editors): *C. G. Jung: Psychological Reflections*. Princeton: Princeton University Press, 1973.

Jerome, Jim. "David Lynch," *People*, September 3, 1990.

Johnson, Wayne L. *Ray Bradbury*. New York: F. Unger Pub. Co., 1980.

Jullian, Philippe. *Dreamers of Decadence*. New York: Praeger, 1971.

Kaleta, Kenneth C. *David Lynch*. New York: Twayne, 1993.

Keel, Anna and Christian Strich (editors). *Fellini on Fellini*. London: Methuen, 1976.

Keeler, Toby. *Pretty as a Picture: The Art of David Lynch* DVD, 1997.

Kermode, Mark. *The Exorcist*. London: British Film Institute, 1998.

Kerton, Paul. "Revealing All: Rossellini's Revolution," *The Daily Mail On Sunday* at http://www.thecityofabsurdity/intrelrosell.

King, Larry (interviewer). "Maharishi Mahesh Yogi," *Larry King Weekend*, CNN Television, May 12, 2002.

King, Stephen. *Storm of the Century*. New York: Pocket Books, 1999.

KING AM Seattle. Chris Brecher Show, talk-radio discussion, October 1986.

Kohler, Margret. "David Lynch: 'In the editing room I cried like mad,'" *Cinemaxx Filmtips*, December 1999.

KOMO, ABC Television, Seattle, May 23, 1990.

KOMO, ABC Television, Seattle, June 10, 1991.

Krogstad, Karl. *Surrealism* DVD, 1993.

Lambert, Gavin. "Origins of the *Sunset Boulevard* Mansion," *Architectural Digest* (April 1998).

Lantos, Jeffrey. "The ABC of Going From the Big Screen to the Small," *Movieline* (August 1999).

Lavery, David (editor). *Full of Secrets*. Detroit: Wayne State University Press, 1995.

L'Ecuyer, Gerald. "Out of Bounds: David Lynch," *Interview*, 1987, http://www.thecityofabsurdity.com.

Leiber, Jerry and Mike Stoller. "I Want to Be Free," *Vol. 1—First Moves*, 1957, RCA, http://lyrics.astraweb.com/display/6/elvis_presley..vol_1first_moves..i_want_to_be_free.html.

———. "Trouble," *Elvis Elvis Elvis: The King & His Movies*, 1958, RCA, http://lyrics.astraweb.com/display/249/elvis_presley..elvis_elvis_elvis_the_king_his_movies..trouble.html.
Leonard, John. "The Quirky Allure of Twin Peaks," *New York*, May 7, 1990.
Leslie, Richard. *Surrealism*. New York: Smithmark Publishers, 1997.
Lewis, Sinclair. *Main Street*. San Diego: Harcourt Brace Jovanovich, 1948.
Libby, Brian. "David Lynch," http://www.archive.salon.com/people/bc/2001/11/06/lynch, November 11, 2001.
Lipton, Peggy. *Breathing Out*. New York: St. Martin's Press, 2005.
Little Richard, quoted from many TV talk show appearances over the years.
Lofficier, Randy and Jean-Marc. "Dean Stockwell: The Traitor of Dune," *Starlog* (January 1985).
Lynch, David. "The Angriest Dog in the World," *L.A. Reader*, 1990.
———. *Bellevue Film Festival Program Notes*, July 1970.
———. *Blue Velvet* script, unpublished, August 24, 1984.
———. *Commercial Reel*, courtesy of Asymmetrical Productions, 1997.
———. "Consciousness, Creativity, and the Brain," University of Washington, Seattle, November 7, 2005.
———. *Dune* script, unpublished, December 9, 1983.
———. *Eraserhead*, DVD comments, Absurda, 2005.
———. *Eraserhead* script, unpublished, undated.
——— (presenter). *The Elephant Man*, TNT Television, August 3, 1995.
———. *Images*. New York: Hyperion, 1994.
———. *Mulholland Drive Pilot* script, unpublished, January 5, 1999.
———. *Ronnie Rocket* script, unpublished, undated.
——— (presenter). *Ruth, Roses, and Revolvers*, BBC Television, 1987.
———. *The Short Films of David Lynch*, DVD comments, Absurda, 2005.
———. *Wild at Heart* script, unpublished, August 2, 1989.
———. "I Remember," *Floating Into the Night*, Warner Brothers, 1989, http://www.lyrics.astraweb.com/display/912/julee_cruise_floating_into_the_night..i_remember.
———. "Mysteries of Love," *Floating Into the Night*, Warner Brothers, 1989, http://www.lyrics.astraweb.com/display/694/julee_cruise_floating_into_the_night..mysteries_of_love.html.
———. "Questions in a World of Blue," *Twin Peaks: Fire Walk With Me*, Warner Brothers, 1992, geocities.com/HollywoodGuild/2057/lynch/blue.
———. "The World Spins," *Floating Into the Night*, Warner Brothers, 1989, http://www.lyrics.astraweb.com/display/476/julee_cruise..floating_into_the_night..the_world_spins.
Lynch, David and Angelo Badalamenti. "Floating," *Floating Into the Night*, Warner Brothers, 1989, http://www.lyrics.astraweb.com/display/717/julee_cruise..floating_into_the_night..floating.
Lynch, David and Barry Gifford. *Lost Highway*. London: Faber and Faber, 1997.
Lynch, David and Robert Engels. *Twin Peaks: Fire Walk With Me* script, unpublished, August 8, 1991. www.davidlynch.de/99spiegel/trans.
Lynch, Jennifer. *The Secret Diary of Laura Palmer*. New York: Pocket Books, 1990.
"Lynch-Time," *Vogue* (February 1990): http://www.davidlynch.de/Vogue.
Macey, David. *The Lives of Michel Foucault: A Biography*. New York: Pantheon Books, 1993.
MacLachlan, Kyle. *Blue Velvet* DVD comments, MGM, 2002.
Magarshack, David. Introduction to *The Overcoat and Other Tales of Good and Evil*. Cambridge: R. Bentley, Inc., 1957.

The Making of Dune, Universal, 1984, broadcast on *Night Flight* TV show, courtesy of Sean Axmaker Collection.
Marshall, Matt. "Interview with Bill Pullman," February 8, 2000, courtesy of Matt Marshall.
———. "Interview with Charlotte Stewart," August 15, 1999.
———. "Interview with Michael J. Anderson."
Martinez, Rudy. *96 Tears*, Cameo, 1966, http://www.lyrics.astraweb.com.
May, Sophie. "Blue Bob," http://www.chez.com.
McGrath, Alister E. *A Life of John Calvin: A Study in the Shaping of Western Culture*. Cambridge: B. Blackwell, 1990.
McKenna, Kristine. "A Conversation with David Lynch," *The Prints of David Lynch*. Madion: Tandem Press, 2000.
———. "An Interview with David Lynch," *David Lynch*. Valencia: Sala Parpallo/Vei, 1992.
———. "David Lynch, A Conversation," *Los Angeles Reader*, September 1986, 12.
———. "Dreamer of Dark and Troubling Things," *L.A. Reader*, October 8, 1982.
Miller, Craig and John Thorne. "From Dune to Earth," *Wrapped in Plastic*, No. 44, December 1999.
———. "The Jack Nance Interview," *Wrapped in Plastic*, No. 27, February 1997.
———. "Killer Bob Speaks!," *Wrapped in Plastic*, No. 8, December 1993.
———. "The Mark Frost Interview," *Wrapped in Plastic*, No. 9, February 1994.
———. "Peyton's Place: Harley Peyton Interview," *Wrapped in Plastic*, No. 17, June 1995.
———. "Sheryl Lee: Actress Enrapt," *Wrapped in Plastic*, No. 16, April 1995.
———. "We're Going to Talk About Judy—And a Whole Lot More!: An Interview With Robert Engels," *Wrapped in Plastic*, No. 58, April 2002.
———. "The World Spins," *Wrapped in Plastic*, No. 74, June 2005.
Montagu, Ashley. *The Elephant Man: A Study in Human Dignity*. New York: E.P. Dutton, 1979.
Morrison, Jim, Ray Manzarek, Robbie Krieger, John Densmore. "When the Music's Over," *Strange Days*, 1967, Elektra Records http://lyrics.astraweb.com/display/543/doors_the..strange_days..when_the_musics_over.html..
Mulholland Drive DVD Special Features, Universal Pictures, 2002.
www.mulhollanddrive.com
Naha, Ed. *The Making of Dune*. New York: Berkley Books, 1984.
Nelson, Thomas Allen. *Kubrick*. Bloomington: Indiana University Press, 1982.
Nemet-Nejat, Daniel. "David Lynch's Empire," *Moviemaker*, 2007.
New York Times, August 3, 2000.
Oates, Whitney Jennings (editor). *The Basic Writings of St. Augustine*. New York: Random House, 1948.
O'Brien, Glenn. "Fenn-Tastic!," *Playboy* (December 1990).
Orbison, Roy and Joe Melson. "Crying," *Crying*, 1961, Monument Records.
Panczenko, Paula McCarthy. *The Prints of David Lynch*. Madison, WI: Tandem Press, 2000.
Patterson, Tory and Jeff Jensen. "Our Town," *Entertainment Weekly*, No. 540, 2000.
Pizzello, Stephen. "Twin Peaks: Fire Walk With Me," *American Cinematographer* (September 1992).
Pohl, Marie. "David Lynch on Meditation," *Sueddeutsche Zeitung*, May 13–14, 2006.
Pomerance, Bernard. *The Elephant Man: A Play*. New York: Grove Press, 1979.
Pomus, Doc and Mort Shuman. "Turn Me Loose," Chancellor, 1959, http://www.lyrics.astraweb.com.
Potter, Maximillian. "Dark Journey," *Premiere*, UK Edition, September 1997.
Powers, John. "Getting Lost Is Beautiful," *L.A. Weekly*, October 19, 2001.

Prabhavananda, Swami and Christopher Isherwood (translators). *The Song of God: Bhagavad-Gita*. London: Dent, 1976.
Public Broadcasting System Television documentary on Thomas Edison.
Raine, Kathleen. *William Blake*. New York: Praeger, 1971.
Renan, Sheldon. *Bellevue Film Festival Program Notes*, July 23, 1970.
Reng, Ronald (editor). "I Have a Dream," *Die Zeit*, Nr. 509, December 1999.
Risling, Greg. "Jury Says Blake Behind Slaying," *The Associated Press*, November 19, 2005.
Roberts, Chris. "Wild at Art," *Uncut* (February 2002).
Rodley, Chris. "David Lynch," *ICON* (March/April 1997).
———. "Introduction," *Lost Highway*, by David Lynch and Barry Gifford. London: Faber and Faber, 1997.
———. (editor). *Lynch on Lynch*. New York: Faber and Faber, 2005.
Rodriguez, Elena. *Dennis Hopper*. New York: St. Martin's Press, 1988.
Roman, Shari and Dean Lamanna. "Limbless Love," *Film Threat*, No. 10 (June 1993).
Rosenbaum, Ron. "Riding High: Dennis Hopper Bikes Back," *Vanity Fair* (April 1987).
Rosin, Mark. "The Wild Heart of David Lynch," *Montage* (September 1989).
Rossellini, Isabella. *Some of Me*. New York: Random House, 1997.
Rowland, Mark. "Wild Innocent," *American Film* (July 1991).
Rugoff, Ralph. "Wild at Heart," *Premiere* (September 1990).
Saban, Stephen and Sarah Longacre. "Eraserhead: Is There Life After Birth?," *Soho Weekly News*, October 20, 1978.
Sade, Marquis de. "Juliette." In *Surrealism*, by Julien Levy. New York: Da Capo Press, 1995.
Sadoul, Georges. *Dictionary of Films*. Berkeley: University of California Press, 1972.
Sammon, Paul M. "David Lynch's Dune," *Cinefantastique* (September 1984).
Schiff, Stephen. "The Weird Dreams of David Lynch," *Vanity Fair* (March 1987).
Seneca, Lucius Annaeus. *Seneca in Ten Volumes*. Cambridge, MA: Harvard University Press, 1928–1972.
Schroder, Klaus Albrecht and Johann Winkler (editors). *Oskar Kokoschka*. Munich: Prestel, 1991.
Shakespeare, William. *Four Great Tragedies*. New York: Penguin Group, 1987.
Shattuck, Roger. *Forbidden Knowledge*. New York: St. Martin's Press, 1996.
Siskel, Gene. *At the Movies*, KOMO Television, Seattle, February 1997.
Spinoza, Benedict. In *Familiar Quotations by John Bartlett*. Boston: Little, Brown, 1967.
Sragow, Michael. "I Want a Dream When I Go to a Film," *Salon Magazine*, October 28, 1999.
———. "The Man Behind the Man in 'Crumb'," *New York Times*, April 23, 1994.
The Straight Story Electronic Press Kit, Walt Disney Pictures, 1999.
Tarkington, Booth. *The Gentleman from Indiana*. New York: Doubleday and McClure, 1899.
Thompson, Toby. "Alien," *Esquire* (January 1985).
Thoreau, Henry David. *Faith in a Seed: The Dispersation of Seeds and Other Late Natural History Writings*. Washington, DC: Island Press/Shearwater Books, 1993.
Tolkien, J. R. R. "Tree and Leaf," *The Tolkien Reader*. New York: Ballantine Books, 1966.
Truffaut, François. *Hitchcock*. New York: Simon & Schuster, 1967.
TV ad for *Dune* broadcast, 1988.
TV Guide, 1990–1991.
Twin Peaks DVD comments.
Twin Peaks' premiere ad page, *New York Times*, April 8, 1990.

Twin Peaks: Fire Walk With Me DVD commentary, New Line, 2002.
"Twin Peaks: Fire Walk With Me Cannes Press Conference," *Cinema Papers* (August 1992).
2001 Cannes Film Festival Closing Night, Independent Film Channel Television, May 20, 2001
Tyler, Steven, Joe Perry and Taylor Rhodes. *Cryin'*, 1993, Geffen Records.
Tzu, Lao. "The Way of Life." In *The Natural Mind*, by Andrew Weil. Boston: Houghton Mifflin, 1986.
Verniere, James. "David Lynch, American Primitive," *Twilight Zone* (October 1988).
Wall, J. M. "The Best Film of 1986: Probing the Depths of Evil," *Christian Century*, January 7–14, 1987.
Wallace, Amy. "David Lynch, Mild at Heart," *Los Angeles Times*, September 12, 1999.
Watts, Alan. *Eastern Wisdom and Modern Life*, KQED Television, 1960.
Weigel Herman. "Director David Lynch," *Tip Filmjahrbuch*, Nr. 1, 1985.
West, Nathaniel. *Novels and Other Writings*. New York: Penguin Books, 1997.
Whitman, Walt. *The Complete Writings of Walt Whitman*. New York: G.P. Putnam's Sons, 1902.
Wilson, Brian and Mike Love. "Be True to Your School," 1963, Capitol Records.
Digby, Wingfield and George Frederick. *Symbol and Image in William Blake*. Oxford: Clarendon Press, 1957.
Woods, Paul A. *Weirdsville USA*. London: Plexus, 1997.
Woodward, Richard B. "A Dark Lens on America," *New York Times Magazine*, January 14, 1990.
Yogananda, Paramahansa. *The Autobiography of a Yogi*. Los Angeles: Self-Realization Fellowship, 1997.
Yogi, Maharishi Mahesh. *Science of Being and Art of Living*. New York: Meridian, 1995.

INDEX

ABC TV, 94, 269, 285, 289, 298–300, 335, 347, 357, 366, 398, 401, 406, 428, 451, 488, 490, 492–93, 495–96, 499, 518, 520, 529, 530, 556, 594, 635
Academy Awards, 140, 141, 147, 200, 496, 636, 638
Aiello, Rick, 375
Alexandria, Virginia, 2, 10, 19
Almereyda, Michael, 429
Aloca, Michelangelo (Mike), 22, 24
The Alphabet, 35–40, 44, 45, 48, 49, 60–62, 66, 67, 113, 126, 229, 234, 258, 282, 352, 391, 404, 407, 416, 493; appearances are deceiving, 37; childlike view, 35; Cubism, 37; dream and reality, 35; fear of learning, 35; Peggy Lentz inspires and acts in, 35; Jennifer Lynch's voice in, 38; wins American Film Institute grant, 40
American Film Institute, 35, 39, 51, 54, 76, 95, 205, 216, 437, 600
Amick, Madchen, 268, 279
The Amputee, 92–93
Anderson, Michael J., 146, 292, 345, 377, 382, 384, 429, 490, 545, 561, 584, 662
Anger, Kenneth, 601
Annis, Francesca, 158
Antonioni, Michaelangelo, 450
Arbus, Diane, 240
Arquette, Patricia, 350, 437, 444, 452, 620
Ashbrook, Dana, 268, 279, 371, 373, 375, 396

Bacon, Francis, 3, 18, 443, 461, 554, 667, 675
Badalamenti, Angelo, 211, 222, 286, 293, 314, 341, 343, 377, 400
Bakely, Bonnie Lee, 455
Bancroft, Anne, 109, 119
Barenholtz, Ben, 95–96, 140
Barker, Clive, 392
Barrie, J. M., 133
Bates, Jeanne, 63, 529
Bay, Frances, 221, 353, 384

Beatles, The, 17, 29, 69, 656
Bellevue Film Festival, 50, 51
Bergman, Ingmar, 147, 158, 335, 340, 558, 620
Bergman, Ingrid, 207–8
Bergren, Eric, 102, 106, 113, 149
Beymer, Richard, 268, 358
Bhagavad Gita, 136, 675, 676
Blake, Robert, 439, 454–56
Blake, William, 6, 50, 88, 107, 117, 134, 136, 521
Blue Bob, 631, 632, 655
Blue Velvet, 201–50 (primary reference); aesthetics of decay, 222–23; angel figure, 225, 237; autobiographical, 205; Angelo Badalamenti enters Lynch's life, 211; beneficent dreams, 237, 246; bestial energies, 230; birds, 238; creepy stillness, 244–45; Julee Cruise enters Lynch's life, 212; detectives, 224–25; disease, 239; domestic security threatened, 219–20; doubling, 222, 226; evil possession, 242–43; falling, 231, 248; family, 221; female gaze, 233; first ending, more negative, 247–48; floating, 224, 225, 231; Freud's primal scene in, 238–39; homosexual evil, 242–43, 245; Dennis Hopper considered for villain's role, 209–10; humor in, 225–26, 226–27; incest, 236, 241; Lynch on his background, 215–16; Lynch reflects on inner darkness, 231–32; Jennifer Lynch on Frank, 241; Kyle MacLachlan as Lynch's alter ego, 228–29; male gaze, 233; maleness as a disease in, 239; masterful opening sequence of, 219–21; nightmares, 236; 1950s essence in, 216-219; "Now it's dark," 234; order restored, darkness persists in, 247; Oscar nomination, 250; as pure, unadulterated Lynch, 204, 249; red curtains, 228; related to *Eraserhead*, 204; restores Lynch's artistic confidence, 212; secrets and mysteries, 205; and small-town America tradition, 212–15; strange postures, 244; stricken father, 222; strong public reaction to, 249–50; threatening insects, 216, 229–30, 232–33, 234; trangressive sex, 235; upstairs bedroom, 226; urban evil, 226; voyeurism, 232; we watch someone watching, 222
"Blue Velvet" (song), 201, 209, 220, 230, 240
Bond, Maya, 531
Bouygues, Francis, 428, 430
Bowie, David, 384, 437, 621
Boxing Helena (film), 416–22
Boyle, Laura Flynn, 268, 276, 357, 414
Bradbury, Ray, 26, 181, 214–16
Brando, Christian, 455
Brando, Marlon, 321, 455
Breton, André, 19, 498
Briggs, Nancy, 21
Brooks, Mel, 106–7, 113, 138
Buchanan, Ian, 399
Buñuel, Luis, 57, 263, 334, 600
Burke, Edmund, 19
Busey, Gary, 443
Butler, Lucy, 443

The Cabinet of Dr. Caligari, 49
Cada, James, 477
Cage, Nicolas, 66, 309–13, 321, 340, 344, 657
Caland, Philippe, 416
Calvin, John, 7
Cannes Film Festival, 8, 172, 313, 339, 341–42, 355, 377, 378, 398, 486, 495, 521, 556, 558
Capra, Frank, 481, 612

Carroll, Lewis, 133
Castelli, Leo, 254–55
Chadwick, Robert, 40
Chase, David, 301
Chen, Joan, 268, 272, 287, 365, 556
Chief Seattle, 665
Children of Dune, 184
Chinatown, 334, 489, 495, 534, 643
Cokewell, Pat, 299, 370, 380
Comencini, Luigi, 258
Cook, Michael, 530
Coppola, Francis Ford, 96, 143, 309, 458
Cornfield, Stuart, 102, 105–6
Coulson, Catherine, 69, 72, 91–94, 95, 159–60, 268, 287, 360, 364, 373, 377, 379, 380, 422, 426, 428, 430, 432, 467, 587; Lynch saves her life, 93
The Cowboy and the Frenchman, 49, 193, 258–60, 430, 556; American gun culture satirized, 259; difficulty of communicating, 258; feminine presence in, 259–60; Lynch invited to contribute short film, 258; peaceable kingdom, 259; Surrealism in, 259; invading Other, 258–59
CowParade, 515–17
Creature from the Black Lagoon, 8
Cruise, Julee, 66, 212, 243, 253, 344, 347–48, 355, 390, 407, 525, 555, 560, 580, 582, 586–89, 656–57, 665; on "Falling" (song), 586; and Lynch, 588–89, 657–58; Seattle performance on eve of *Twin Peaks* season two, 347–48; singer at Twin Peaks Festival (2002), 657; "soft sad side" of and Lynch, 586; tours with B-52 against Lynch's wishes, 587;
Cumutt, Vicki, 379, 381
Cyrus, Billy ray, 544

Dafoe, William, 331
Daniel, Frank, 54, 59
DavidLynch.com, 630–36; *Cannes Diary*, 644–50; *Dream of the Bovine*, 428, 460; *Dumbland*, 632–34; *Out Yonder*, 631
Rabbits, 634–36; *Thank you, Judge*, 631–34
David Lynch Foundation, 665
Dean, James, 209, 309, 444
De Laurentiis, Dino, 147, 148, 149, 150, 151, 158, 180, 190, 198, 200, 204, 207, 262, 266, 543, 662
De Laurentiis, Raffaella, 147, 149, 150–51, 156, 158, 159–160, 192, 200, 204
Del Rio, Rebekah, 507, 561–63, 574, 580, 583
Deren, Maya, *Mieshes of the Afternoon* (film), 600–1
Dern, Bruce, 311–12, 321, 424
Dern, Laura, 100, 207, 237, 244, 276, 309, 310–13, 316, 320, 321, 333, 344, 407, 424, 475, 555, 580, 657, 665, 669–71, 673–74, 676–77
Deschanel, Caleb, 269
De Vore, Christopher, 102, 105, 106, 113, 149
Dickens, Charles, 133
Dickerson, George, 223
Disney, Walt, 219, 486–87, 676
The Dream of the Bovine (unproduced film), 460
Dubain, Donna, 592
Dulac, Germaine, 260
Dune (book), 147–268
Dune (film), 147–207 (primary reference), 20–623 (passim); animalism, 168; animalistic evil, 177; battle of the sexes, 167; black and white floor, 195; box-office performance is poor, 191; Joseph Campbell's hero myth and, 166, 167; color blue in, 187, 189; color green in, 176–77; contrasts between longer

TV version and theatrical version, 192–93; control versus freedom, 170–71; a deluge of information, 161, 162; Dino De Laurentiis and, 147; Raffaella De Laurentiis and, 147, 149; detectives, 167; doubling, 196; earlier *Dune* attempts, 147–48; erotic violence, 168; factories, 175–76; father and son, 196; fear kills the mind, 168; floating, 161; headcentric, 164–65; Hell becomes Heaven, 171; Frank Herbert, 151–52, 173, 187; hero blends male and female power, 171–72; Alejandro Jodorowsky and, 147, 190–91; longer TV version contrasts with theatrical version, 192–93; love of mystery, 195; Lynch has depressing experience, 200; Lynch deviates from Herbert's book, 163, 174–75, 184–85; Lynch fears/embraces restrictions while making, 197; Lynch and Herbert, 149–50, 153–55; Lynch more prosaic than poetic in, 186–87; Lynch's sensibility reflected in each planet, 175; Lynch writes screenplay by himself, 150; Kyle MacLachlan and, 156–58; merchandising of, 189–90; "Now it's dark," 176; the Other is me, 183; Paul as rebel in, 186; the peaceable kingdom, 175; each planet reflects part of Lynch's sensibility, 175; Ridley Scott and, 148–49; screening honors Herbert's late wife, 190; *Star Wars* related to book, 150; suspense, or its lack, 165–66; torture, 182–83; villains who enjoy their work, 178–79; villainy and homosexuality, 180–82; a visual, not verbal ending for, 188–89; we watch people watching, 172; "You're like me," 195

Dune Messiah (book), 184, 187, 189

Dunham, Duwayne, 286

Dunn, Griffin, 410

Duvic, Julie, 371

Easy Rider, 86, 209–10, 212

Ebert, Roger, 191, 340, 395, 454, 486, 523

The Elephant Man (film), 102–42 (primary reference), 43–663 (passim); abstraction, 128; animalistic evil, 129, 131; balance between free expression and control, 131; black and white cinematography in, 107; Mel Brooks and, 106; Christianity, 135; consoling happy endings, 134; darkness within good people, 123–24; depersonalization, 115–16; doubling, 120, 132; as fairytale, 133–34; and Freudian psychology, 126–27; headcentric, 122; the historical Elephant Man (John Merrick), 102–105; home invasion, 130; homosexuality, 122; humor, 138–39; infectious evil, 123; Lynch fails to create Elephant Man makeup, 109–10; Lynch responds to London atmosphere, 107; Lynch wants to be commercially and artistically successful, 113; Lynch works with John Gielgud, 110–11; Lynch works with Anthony Hopkins, 111-113; Lynch works with John Hurt, 111; Jennifer Lynch moved by Merrick's story, 109; John Merrick, 116–27; nightmare, 128–30; "Now it's dark," 128; opening abstract sequence of, 113–15; original sin, 137–38; physical and social outsiders, 132; related to Jean Renoir's *The River*, 137; social class, 139; starfields, 136; Tantra, 135; transgressive sexual behavior, 115; transcendent rapture, 121–22; watching and seeing, 116–17; we watch someone watching, 115

The Elephant Man (play), 105, 614
The Elephant Man: A Study in Human Dignity (book), 106
Eliason, Joyce, 490
Ellison, Harlan, 162–63
Elmes, Fred, 92–93, 94, 95, 97, 145, 205, 225, 258
Elphinck, Michale, 125
Emerson, Ralph Waldo, 70
Engels, Robert, 269, 365, 366, 377, 398, 402, 428, 460
Eppolito, Lou, 444
Eraserhead, 53–98 (primary reference), 42–671 (passim); adultery as freedom, 78; abstraction, 6; angel figure, 76–77; autobiographical for Lynch, 61–62, 87; blood sacrifice, 83–84; boundary violation, 65, 66; catalyst image for, 59; difficulty of communicating, 62, 63; electricity, 65, 81; environment reflects psychic states, 65; erasure equals rebirth, 80, 83; Gnosticism, 84–85; headcentric, 79; Lynch buys back ownership of, 97; Lynch creates world of, 60; Lynch on parts that are missing, 251; Lynch's spiritual growth mirrored, 87–88, 90; Lynch view of, 60; Jennifer Lynch on, 85–86, 87; magical thinking, 63; mental and emotional confusion, 62; the metaphysical in the mundane, 62–63; midnight movie phenomenon, 96; non sequiturs, 64; "Now it's dark," 65; numerology, 63; original darker ending for, 88–90; poetic logic of, 74; sound in, 61; subliminal signs, 63; surreal/grotesque imagery, 64; unplanned fatherhood, 75; violence has consequences, 81
E.T. The Extraterrestrial, 42, 156, 164
Evans, Troy, 277
Farley, John and Kevin, 479
Farnsworth, Richard, 464–65, 471, 473, 477, 478, 485, 486, 496–97, 519–20, 547; award for *The Straight Story*, 496–97; David Lynch on Farnsworth's suicide, 520; Jennifer Lynch on Farnsworth's suicide, 520;
Fellini, Federico, 147, 262–64, 335, 339, 340, 497, 616–20, 624
Fenn, Sherilyn, 94, 97, 262, 268, 331, 401, 417, 418, 491
Ferrer, Jose, 158, 163
Ferrer, Miguel, 349, 398, 401
Fisk, Jack, 13, 17, 18, 20, 23, 24, 29, 51, 90, 94, 100, 142, 200, 251, 256, 288, 398, 465, 483, 517, 584, 682, 693, 707
Fisk, Mary, 203, 204, 250, 251, 261, 667. *See also* Lynch, Mary
Fiskler, Patrick, 530
The Fly, 8, 57
Foster, Jodie, 140–41, 311, 346, 523
Foucault, Michel, 127
Francis, Connie, 551
Francis, Freddie, 107, 155, 465, 475, 478
Freeman, J. E., 324
Freud, Sigmund, 46, 50, 70, 126–28, 135, 236, 238, 250
Frost, Mark, 91, 94, 264–71, 274, 276, 277, 280, 282, 286, 287, 289, 290, 293–94, 295–96, 297–98, 299, 301, 303, 328, 348, 349–52, 354, 355, 356, 357, 358, 359–60, 363–66, 380, 395, 398, 400–1, 407, 451, 482, 488, 495–96, 530, 583, 611
Frost, Robert, 203
Frost, Scott, 398
Frost, Warren, 268

Garcia, Ron, 268, 271, 366, 373
Gardenback (unproduced script), 56–58, 78, 88–90, 117, 216, 577;

adultery, 57; house as metaphor for head, 57; insects, 57–58
Garland, Judy, 247, 392, 499, 525
Getty, Balthazar, 443, 452
Gidley, Pamela, 368, 382
Gielgud, John, 109–10
Gifford, Barry, 13, 170, 171, 265, 297, 304–8, 309, 313–14, 315, 320, 323, 324, 325, 326, 331–32, 336, 337, 344, 406–7, 409, 410, 412, 436, 443, 445, 446, 452, 557; pre-Lynch life of, 304–5; sensibility like Lynch's, 304–5
Glatter, Lesli Linka, 269, 364, 368
Glover, Crispin, 404, 410, 412
Godard, Jean-Luc, 258, 339
Godwin, Jocelyn, 84
Gogol, Nikolai, 54–56
Golchan, Frederic, 258, 556
Gordon, Hannah, 118
Graham, Heather, 358, 414
The Grandmother, 40–51 (primary reference), 56–634 (passim); animalistic evil, 40–42, 45; autobiographical for Lynch, 47; barren trees, 42; depersonalization fear, 46; dualities synthesize third state, 40; elongation of time, 44; Hinduism, 48; Lynch interprets his own work, 50; Lynch's parents react to, 45; narrative ambiguity, 50; otherness, 45; power figure forces intimacy, 41; the power of love, 43; secret double life/cheating on relationship, 42–44; stage setting, 43; starfields, 40; toxic family life, 40; unrestrained appetite, 45; violence, 42; we watch someone watching, 44
Grant, Lee, 539
Green, Richard, 560, 592
Grizzly Man (film), 666

Hallas, Richard, 561
Hagelin, John 517
Happy Birthday Jen-O, 678
Harker, Wiley, 477
Harring, Laura Elena, 527, 556, 570, 584, 590, 634
Harris, Glenn Walker, Jr., 335
Harvey, Jack, 221
HBO program, 406; *Blackout*, 410–13; *Getting Rid of Robert*, 410; *Tricks*, 407–9
Headly, Glenne, 407
Henri, Robert, 10, 11, 26, 33, 35, 71, 134, 176, 253, 624, 626
Herbert, Frank, 147–55, 156–57, 161–62, 163, 165, 168, 170, 171, 172, 173–74, 175, 177, 179, 180, 182–86, 187–88, 189–92, 195–96, 197, 200, 268, 575
Herzog, Werner, 258, 334, 666
Heuring, Lori, 544
Highsmith, Patricia, 46
Hiller, Wendy, 109, 121
Hinduism, 6, 33, 48, 50, 69, 70, 88, 135, 136, 145, 188, 396, 428, 520, 523, 548, 560, 563, 577, 581, 591, 613, 626, 632, 657, 658, 659, 660, 665, 672, 674–76
Hitchcock, Alfred, 165–66, 209, 214, 343, 497, 579, 614, 615, 616; Hoffmann, E. T. A., 49–50
homosexuality, 411, 414, 416, 473, 507, 520, 544, 557, 570, 586
Hopkins, Anthony, 109, 111–13, 125, 160, 243
Hopper, Dennis, 46, 65, 86, 138, 209–12, 234–35, 240–42, 250, 430, 604; on working with Lynch, 211; pre-Lynch life of, 210–11
Hopper, Edward, 225, 227, 408
Horse, Michael, 259, 268
Hunt, Linda, 158
Hunter, Tim, 269, 271
Hurt, John, 109, 111–12, 121, 140–42, 464

I Don't Know Jack (film), 592
Industrial Symphony No. 1: The Dream of the Broken Hearted (stage production), 231, 343, 346, 378, 406, 407, 555, 580, 584; Michael J. Anderson in, 345; Nicolas Cage in, 344; Laura Dern in, 344; emotional pain, 344; factories, 344; falling, 345; Lynch collaborates with Angelo Badalamenti and Julee Cruise on, 343–44; "Now it's dark," 344; project melds many arts, 344; spiritual transcendence, 346; woodsiness, 345
Ingalls, Rachel, 627–29
INLAND EMPIRE, 184, 665–78 (primary reference); actions have consequences, 672–73; Battered Woman, 669–70, 672, 673–74; cheating on a relationship in, 673; colors, 670; dreamed up while it was being shot, 672; fear and anger, 671; identity and spatial dislocation in, 670–71; karmic justice, 673, 675; Lynch announces project on college tour, 665; Lynch screens film for Peggy Reavey and Jennifer Lynch, 668; male menace, 671; prostitution, 674; reincarnation, 673; related to *Alice in Wonderland*, 676; related to *Bhagavad Gita*, 675–76; related to Franz Kafka's world, 676–77; transcendent grace, 676
Intervista (film), 263–64
Irons, Jeremy, 670
Isaak, Chris, 331, 368, 369, 370, 397

Jesus Christ, 192, 547
Jennings, Bill, 370, 373
Jodorowsky, Alejandro, 147, 190
Johns, Glynis, 255
Jones, Alexandra, 255
Jones, Chuck, 601
Jones, Freddie, 120, 158, 407
Joseph, Allen, 64
Jung, Carl, 46, 70, 77, 135, 176, 445

Kafka, Franz, 3, 54–55, 57, 216, 263, 436, 458, 521, 676, 677
Kaplan, Marvin, 398
Keeler, Bushnell, 11, 13, 14, 19, 23, 24, 680, 681, 682
Keeler, Toby, 10, 16, 17, 27, 251, 432, 457, 681, 682, 684, 698, 704; Kelly, Moira, 370, 374, 379, 380
Kennedy, John F., 17, 141, 148, 277, 305
King, Martin Luther, Jr., 210, 678
King, Rodney, 415
King, Stephen, 190, 355
Kingsley, Charles, 133
Kline, Franz, 31
Kokoschka, Oscar, 20, 22, 107
Kubrick, Stanley, 96, 335, 464, 497, 617, 621–24

Ladd, Diane, 66, 311, 312, 320, 321
Lander, David L., 398
Lange, Hope, 224
Lange, Jean, 64
La Pelle, Roger, 33, 39–40, 68
Lassick, Sydney, 398
The Last Movie (film), 210
Laughton, Charles, 136
Laurie, Piper, 268
Lawrence, D. H., 323, 414
Lear, Edward, 133
Leavens, Chris, 592
Lee, Sheryl, 199, 268, 273, 337, 370–71, 373–74, 376, 377, 379–80, 390, 396, 416, 429
Leno, Jay, 3
Lentz, Peggy, 27, 100, 527, 667. *See also* Reavey, Peggy
LePell, Jonathan, 379
The List of Seven (book), 287
Lockhart, Calvin, 329

Loggia, Robert, 209, 444, 449

Los Angeles, 53–656 (passim); Griffith Park Observatory, 511–12; L.A. Lakers win championship, 512–13

Lost Highway, 436-56 (primary reference), 24–663 (passim); Robert Blake's real-life murder case, 454-56; doubling, 444; evocation of Lynch's childhood in, 443; femme fatale, 444, 449; as more film noir–conventional than personal Lynch film, 452; headcentric, 437; home invasion, 437; house as head, 438, 440; Lynch collaborates with Barry Gifford, 436; Lynch films hard to read, 445, 453–54; Mobius strip concept in, 437; Mystery Man in, 437, 439–40; made into opera, 456; "Now it's dark," 440; powerful controlling figure, 449; reincarnation, 447–48; related to the Black Dahlia, 441; related to classic film noir, 446–47; related to *Detour*, 452–53; related to *Hotel California*, 453; related to O. J. Simpson case, 451–52; sexuality, 447–48; shifting identity, 436–37, 439; summary explanation of, 450–51; visions, 442

Lucas, George, 96, 143, 150, 458

Lumiere, Auguste, 434–35

Lumiere, Louis, 434–35

Lumiere and Company, 436. *See also Premonitions Following an Evil Deed*

Lynch, Austin (Lynch's grandfather), 11

Lynch, Austin (Lynch's son), 200, 203, 204, 250, 256, 353, 365, 384, 501, 503, 631, 666

Lynch, David, art: 4, 9, 11, 13, 24, 26, 27, 51, 71, 83, 106, 189, 200, 250, 306, 364, 428, 458, 483, 498, 510, 623, 630, 653, 668, 669; artists influence each other, 334–35; artists influence Lynch, 600–1; art world of, 3; at American Film Institute, 54; buys first movie camera, 34; Cannes Film Festival, 2002, 638–39, 640–44; childhood, 1, 3, 5, 9; the color blue, 555–56; collages, 3, 460; comic strips, 198–99, 632; and composition, 38–39; and CowParade cow, 501–2, 515–17; *Crumb* documentary, 429; definition of, 11; and Walt Disney think alike, 487–88; early artwork, 15–16; exhibits drawings at Leo Castelli Gallery, 254–55; exhibits paintings, drawings, photographs, 413; film subject (possible) *Mrs. Caliban* (book), 627–29; films as dreams/trances, 48–49; films infomercial for Natural Law Party presidential candidate, 517; his house of art, 505–10; humor in his work, 138, 257–58; and Bushnell Keeler, 10, 13-14, 16, 19, 23–25; and Toby Keeler, 10, 17; and *The Lemurians* project, 265–66; and Peggy Lentz (short films), 34–35; love of creating artistic worlds, 73; Lynchian names, 230; and Marilyn Monroe, 265; negative reaction to *Saturday Night Fever*, 626–29; parents' support, 9; print (*Ant in My House*), 57; printmaking, 460–62; red curtains in his work, 265, 292; Venice Film Festival Golden Lion Career Achievement Award, 668; world's best director award, 661–62. *See also* DavidLynch.com; David Lynch Foundation; *films by title*; *Industrial Symphony No. 1*; Lynch, David, books; Lynch, David, commercials; Lynch, David, drawings; Lynch, David, inspirations and influences of; Lynch, David, paintings; Lynch, David, personal;

Lynch, David, photos/assemblages; Lynch, David, possible influences on; Lynch, David, TV
Lynch, David, books: *Catching the Big Fish: Meditation, Consciousness, and Creativity*, 669; *Images*, 9, 422-27; *Fish Kit and Chicken Kit*, 423–24, 425–26, 427; Lynch, David, commercials: *Georgia Coffee*, 416; *Instinct of Life*, 414–15; *Opium*, 414; *PlayStation 2*, 521; *Reveal*, 414; *Sun, Moon, Stars*, 414; *The Wall*, 414; *Who is Gio?*, 415–16
Lynch, David, drawings: *Bugs Are in Every Room—Are You My Friend?*, 423; *Crucifixion*, 6, 15; *Friendship Fire Department Founded in 1774 by George Washington*, 15; *Resurrection*, 15, 615; *Three Figures on a Stage*, 348
Lynch, David, inspirations and influences of: Europe, 26–27; humor, 257–58; law of contrast, 5; *The Nose* (Gogol), 54–56; value of accidents, 28–29, 39; interest in Internet, 629–30; interpretation of work, 75; interpreting his work is challenge, 75; Lynch, David, paintings: *I See Myself*, 348; *Oww, God, Mom, the Dog He Bited Me*, 11; *Shadow of a Twisted Hand Across My House*, 5
Lynch, David, personal: Accidents valued, 28–29, 39; and American gun culture, 641; attire of, 2; belief in fate, 10; beneath the surface viewpoint of, 502; birth of in Montana, 1; George W. Bush, dislike of, 659; and Frank Daniel, 54, 59–60; and Norma Desmond's driveway, 499–500; earliest memory of, 2; family and friends move to Hollywood, 51; family time spent in Wisconsin, 459–60; fascinated by concept of power, 101; and father, 14, 503–4, 666–67, 678; favorite things, 53; fears of, 4, 26, 29–30; and Federico Fellini, 262–64; first trip to Europe doesn't inspire, 26–27; and Jack Fisk, 13, 17, 18, 20–22; and Mary Fisk, 100–1, 250-51; and Mark Frost, 264–65; habits (likes security of regular habits), 99–100; and Robert Henri, 10–11; Hindu philosophy and diet of, 658–59, 661; home life of, 252–53; influence of individual consciousness on global consciousness, 591; and John F. Kennedy inauguration and assassination, 17–18; and Peggy Lentz/Lynch, 27, 29, 91; likes to stay home, 515; lurking danger viewpoint of, 503; and Jennifer Lynch, 29, 189; life in 2007–2008, 677–678; and Los Angeles, 53; and Maharishi Mahesh Yogi, 656, 678; meets Marcello Mastroiani, 262–64; mother's death, 663–65; need to feel in control, 4–5; needs freedom in relationships, 101; and the 1950s, 6; as nonverbal, 110; parents and siblings of, 2, 6; patriotism of, 8; and personal freedom, 502; Gaye Pope death and, 662; post-*Dune* depression, 203; Presbyterianism, 6–7; and Elvis Presley, 13; prints, 460–62; son Austin Lynch born, 200; Ronald Reagan death and, 662; Peggy Reavey emotional relationship with, 667; and self-revelation, 585; and Isabella Rossellini, 207, 251–52, 262; and smoking, 502; spiritual crisis of, 68–69; and squares and hipsters, 12–13; Emily Stofle relationship with, 667; strange world viewpoint of, 513;

and *Sunset Boulevard*, 53; and Mary Sweeney, 667; and Transcendental Meditation, 69–71, 72; value of intuitive inspiration to, 297; and Vietnam War draft, 23; virginity (loss of), 27; visionary experience of, 71; world peace advocacy of, 659–60, 661; Lloyd Wright house, 251; youthful rebellion of, 8–9, 13

Lynch, David, photos/assemblages: *Chicken Kit*, 24, 423, 502; *Fish Kit*, 24, 423, 502

Lynch, David, possible influences on: *2001: A Space Odyssey* (film), 622; *8 1/2* (film), 618–20; *Barry Lyndon* (film) 621–22; *Carnival of Souls* (film), 605–6; *The Day of the Locust* (book), 602–4; *The Gemini Affair* (film), 604–5; *Glen or Glenda* (film), 613–14; *Good Times on Our Street* (book), 607–9; *Hollywood Babylon, Hollywood Babylon II* (books), 601–2; *The Holy Bible* (book), 625–26; *It's a Gift* (film), 611–12; *It's a Wonderful Life* (film), 612–13; *La Strada* (film), 616–17; *Lolita* (film), 617–18; *Rear Window* (film), 614–15; *The Shining* (film), 623–24; *The Silence* (film), 620–21; *Wait Till the Sun Shines, Nellie* (film), 606–7; *The Wizard of Oz* (film), 609–11

Lynch, David, TV: *Hotel Room*, 406–13 (primary reference), 158, 406, 409, 410, 413, 424, 425, 436, 490, 518, 555, 581; *The Lemurians* (unproduced TV pilot), 265. *See also* HBO program; *individual TV shows*

Lynch, Donald, 2, 3, 6, 8, 9, 13, 14, 15, 18, 47, 224, 417, 486, 503, 504, 663, 665, 666, 678, 679, 680, 681, 720

Lynch, Edwina (Sunny), 1, 2, 14, 15, 47, 95, 417, 486, 503, 663, 664, 666

Lynch, Jennifer, 5, 29, 30, 38, 46, 51, 71, 85, 86, 87, 88, 90, 91, 101, 107, 108, 109, 141, 145, 189, 200, 204, 215, 241, 252, 257, 260, 261, 262, 341, 346, 378, 388, 404, 416, 417, 418, 419, 420, 421, 422, 459, 470, 503, 520, 557, 590, 606, 637, 651, 652, 653, 654, 655, 663, 664, 665, 666, 668; *Boxing Helena* (film), 91, 416–22; car accident of, 261–62; on experiences with her father, 108; on father's fears, 655; and father's wisdom, 653–54; on her father and Isabella Rossellini's relationship, 257; on her father's need for freedom in relationships, 101; on her parents' breakup, 107–8; in London with father, 108–9; on Lynch family values, 653–54; new appreciation of life, 652–53, 654–55; reads about Charles Manson, 241; *Oddio* (radio show), 108; rebonding with parents, 651, 652; *The Secret Diary of Laura Palmer* (book), 46, 91, 341, 388, 416

Lynch, John, 2, 86, 485, 537, 663, 666

Lynch, Martha, 2, 69, 143, 663, 666 686

Lynch, Mary, on David's career, 200. *See also* Fisk, Mary

Lynch, Riley, 172, 379, 381, 414, 459, 460, 474, 494, 510, 638, 644, 646, 647, 648, 649, 650, 660, 663, 666, 667

Lynch-Peterson, Sydney, 459, 651, 652, 654, 663, 666

MacDonald, George, 133

MacLachlan, Kyle, 8, 44, 47, 153, 154, 156–58, 162, 168, 172, 189, 190 206–7, 209, 212, 228, 239, 243, 262, 268, 270, 271, 278–80, 294, 310, 341, 347, 352, 357, 364, 367–69, 383, 389, 396–97, 423, 660

Madonna, 417
Mahesh, Maharishi, 69–70, 88, 428, 517, 591–92, 656, 658–61, 666, 667
Maitland, Virginia, 40
Mangano, Silvana, 150, 158, 262
Manson, Charles, 65, 241, 437, 450, 643
Marshall, James, 268, 276, 280, 350, 376, 396, 414
Mar T Café, 299, 363, 366, 370, 374, 379, 380, 430, 657
Massee, Michale, 439
Masters, Tony, 155
McGill, Everett, 158, 268, 349, 472, 519
McGinnis, Dorothy, 42
McInerney, 406, 410
McMillan, Kenneth, 158
Merrick, John, 102–5, 111, 112, 114, 120
Metamorphosis (book), 54–55, 57, 216, 436, 458
Miller, Ann, 525, 662
Miller, Arthur, 346
Minnelli, Vincente, 499, 648
Missoula, Montana, 8, 248, 356
Monroe, Marilyn, 217, 265, 277, 309, 485, 602
Montagu, Ashley, 106
Montgomery, Jocelyn, 547
Montgomery, Monty, 297, 406, 413, 547
Morrison, Jim, 450, 457
Mulholland Drive (film), 488–96, 518–84 (primary references), 3–679 (passim); angel figure, 546; Best Director award at Cannes Film Festival, 523; blue key in, 574–75; cast and crew screening of, 524, 530, 542, 583–84; cheating in relationship, 571, 572; coffee, 564; colors, 533, 555–56; contrast, 527; cowboys, 547; desire to see and know, 537; detective, 534; doubling, 532, 569–70; electricity, 546–47; evil entity in, 530–31; floating, 526, 531; go with the flow, 548–49; head trauma, 528; identity, 535, 536, 539, 555, 559; inside/outside, 538; layered reality in, 551; lesbian love in, 553, 556–58; light and dark, 526; Los Angeles in, 529–30; Lynch's alter-ego Adam, 543; Lynch's introduction to reality and illusion, 525–26; Lynch on three segments of, 582; Lynchian romanticism in, 552, 570; masturbation in, 568–69; narrative clues in, 532–33; nightmare, 530; 1950s, 551; "Now it's dark," 527; oracle figure, 539, 547; Oscar nomination for Best Director, 636–37; the power of few words, 545; reincarnation, 581–82; related to *Industrial Symphony No. 1*, 580; screening in Seattle, 592–95; sex and violence linkage, 569; silence, 582–83; smoke, 550; threshold/passageway, 538–39; TV pilot made into film, 518–19; vertical motion, 570–71; violence, 549
Mulholland Drive (TV pilot): ABC rejects pilot of, 495; a childlike view, 491–92; colors, 494; creative sovereignty threatened, 493; detectives, 491; dream/nightmare, 494; ending related to film, 556; floating, 491–92; Mark Frost on pilot's rejection, 496; headcentric, 491; Hollywood aspirations in, 491; identity confusion, 493; L.A. as character in, 488–90, 494–95; light and dark, 491–92; Lynch alter-ego in, 493; Lynch and Mark Frost first envision, 488; Lynch pitches project to ABC, 492; Lynch violently

opposed to bootlegs of, 524; Lynch writes pilot screenplay with Joyce Eliason, 490; mystery, 493–94; oracle, 494; related to *Chinatown*, 534; related to Pandora's Box, 536–37; related to *Sunset Boulevard*, 528–29; relationship to *Lost Highway*, 566; relationship to *Persona*, 558; sinister gestalt forms in, 545; spiritual suicide in, 579; transition to film, 564–65, 575; and Naomi Watts, 595–600; woman fights back in, 550; the world as illusion in, 560–61, 562–63

Mystery Religions of the Ancient World, 84

"Mysteries of Love" (song), 243

Nadja, 429; Nance, Jack, 61, 69, 85, 89, 91, 93, 94, 95, 108, 158, 159, 258, 268, 272–73, 277, 288, 360, 364, 430–44, 592, 647; death of, 430, 434; *Eraserhead* reunion attended, 432; marries Kelly Van Dyke, 430–31; pre-Lynch life of, 430; Twin Peaks Festival (1995) attended, 431–32

Near, Laurel, 76

9/11 tragedy: Lynch reacts to, 590–91, 592; Naomi Watts reacts to, 590; Maharishi Mahesh Yogi on, 660; Neff, John, 507, 631, 636, 648, 655

Neuwirth, Olga, 456

Night of the Hunter, 136

Night People (book), 557

North Bend, Washington, 268, 374, 379, 381, 430, 657

On the Air, 17, 94, 398–406, 413, 415, 465, 490, 491, 518, 529, 584, 604, 611, 618; ABC shows only few episodes of, 401; bad timing of show launch, 398; Christmas spirit, 404; difficulty of communicating, 399; electicity, 400; funny/sinister mood in, 399–400; hip and square, 406; invading darkness, 403; Lynch and Frost do comedy, 398; Lynch and Surrealists, 402–3; Lynch's playful spirit in, 404; Lynch's sensibility in episode seven, 402–3; 1950s, 399; related to other Lynch works, 401–402; starfield, 400; summation of, 405–6; surreal imagery in, 399; transcendent (beneficent moment in), 400

One Saliva Bubble (unproduced script), 266, 372, 382, 407, 467

Ontkean, Michael, 268

Orbison, Roy, 240, 241, 242, 561–62, 574

Ozu, Yasujiro, 469, 482

The Peaceable Kingdom (painting by Hicks), 175

Pederson, Chris, 373

Peyton, Harley, 269, 270, 295, 296, 352, 358, 359, 364, 365

Peyton Place (film), 266–67

The Phantom Father, 304

Philadelphia, Pennsylvania, 24–27, 30, 284, 304, 306, 383, 459, 470, 511, 516, 518, 527, 561, 567, 626, 632, 656

Phillips, Sian, 158

Pointer, Priscilla, 221

Pollock, Jackson, 31, 288, 402, 501

Pomerance, Bernard, 105, 106, 121, 127, 134, 614

Pope, Gaye, 371, 658

Premonitions Following an Evil Deed, 435-36. *See also Lumiere and Company*

Presley, Elvis, 13, 57, 86, 217, 234, 263, 264, 265, 309, 313, 318, 321, 339, 685, 719

Pretty as a Picture (film), 432
Prochnow, Jurgen, 158
Pullman, Bill, 350, 437, 446, 452, 584

"Questions in a World of Blue" (song), 657

Rathborne, Tina, 179, 255, 269, 307, 364
Reagan, Ronald, 8, 140–42, 190, 239, 249, 290, 308, 457, 517, 547, 590, 659, 662
Reavey, Peggy, 42, 56, 58, 69, 71, 76, 87, 88, 89, 101, 485, 520, 552, 558, 590, 651, 656, 659, 662, 663, 666, 667, 675, 681, 683, 675; breaking with Lynch, 73. *See also* Lentz, Peggy
Reavey, Tom, 101
Rebel Without a Cause (film), 209, 444
Reed, Lou, 444, 552
Renen, Sheldon, 51
Renoir, Jean, 137, 623
The River, 137
Rivers, Victor, 373
Roach, John, 462
Roberts, Judith Anne, 77
Robertson, Barbara, 475
Robertson, Kimmy, 268, 364, 524
Robie, Wendy, 132
Rockwell, Norman, 32, 213, 218, 381, 402, 429,471, 481
Ronnie Rocket (unproduced script), 50, 101–2, 117, 143–46, 189, 382, 396, 424, 545, 662; Rooney, Tim, 460
Reselius, John, 444
Rossellini, Isabella, 138–39, 207–8, 211, 248, 255, 257, 262, 264, 307, 313, 325, 339, 378, 422, 475, 505, 525, 529, 556, 586, 604, 647, 665, 667; break-up with Lynch, 378; on Lynch's sensibility, 208-209; pre-Lynch life of, 207-208; on Transcendental Meditation, 257
Rossellini, Roberto, 147, 207, 250, 263, 648
Rossetti, Christina, 133
Rubinoff, Marla, 399
Rucker, Paul, 669
Ruscha, Ed, 489
Ruskin, John, 133

Sands, Julian, 417–19
Sanger, Jonathan, 105–6, 107, 112, 398
Saturday Night Fever, 626–27
The Seashell and the Clergyman, 260
Seattle Art Museum, 260, 367, 431, 493, 592
Scorsese, Martin, 96, 140, 141, 208, 342, 378, 458, 640, 661
Shakespeare, William, 157, 581
Signorelli, James, 406, 410
Silva, Frank, 46, 274, 284, 289, 375, 377, 429
Silva, Gino, 544
Simpson, O. J., 451–52
Siskel, Gene, 313, 453
Six Figures Getting Sick, 32–34, 404
Smith, Paul, 158
Snootworld (unproduced film), 662
Snoqualmie, Washington, 199, 268, 299, 363, 366, 367–69, 372, 373, 379, 380
Solari, John, 444
The Sopranos, 301, 496, 515, 518, 633
Spacek, Sissy, 90, 100, 141–42, 200, 256, 465, 519
Spielberg, Stephen, 42, 96, 156, 458, 479, 498, 528, 654
Splet, Alan, 35, 48, 51, 73, 94, 97, 155, 176, 211, 220, 508
Stanton, Harry Dean, 358, 312, 326 368–69, 370, 407, 484, 550, 670
Stevens, Connie, 551, 552
Stewart, Charlotte, 61, 94, 268, 432
Stewart, Patrick, 158, 160
Sting, 144, 158–59, 160, 179

Stockwell, Dean, 158, 210, 211, 240
Stofle, Emily, 667, 677
The Storm of the Century, 355
Storyville, 364
The Straight Story, 15, 372, 404, 462–88 (primary reference), 490, 495, 497, 503, 507, 515, 517–19, 522–23, 529, 537, 547, 548, 581; absence of violence in, 466; actor resembles Mark Frost in, 482; angel figure, 483; anger and pride in, 468; beneficent helpers in, 477; celebration of old age in, 478; cosmic connections in, 485; cowboys, 466; creativity, 469–70; Deer Woman, 475–76; a Disney Corporation film, 485–86; doubling, 489–90; estrangement in, 480–82; Richard Farnsworth as Alvin, 464–65, 496–97; fate in making film, 484; film editing, 474; fire, 476–77; happy accident in, 483–84; heeding inner voice in, 471; humor in, 466–67; intuition, 477; living close to nature, 469; Lynch diverges from script, 481; Lynch drops sound level, 478; Lynch family feeling, 485–86; Lynch on the wisdom of going slow, 464; Lynch third road film, 480; personal freedom, 467; related to *Blair Witch Project*, 474; related to films of Ozu, 469, 482–83; restrained emotion in, 467–68; serenity masks danger, 471; sound of the universe in, 465; starfield, 465, 470, 484–85; Alvin Straight, 473, 475, 478–79; Rose Straight, 468–70; Mary Sweeney, 462–63, 474; and *Wizard of Oz*, 474; wordless communication, 473; World War II mourning and forgiving in, 479
Strobel, Al, 291, 371, 379, 380, 396
Struycken, Carel, 349
Summers, Anthony, 265
Sundstrom, Carl, 444
Sunset Boulevard, 53, 54, 96, 248, 335, 448, 493, 494, 499, 500, 528–29, 531–32, 540, 543, 545, 554, 574, 577, 602, 604, 614, 621, 637, 674
Surveillance (film), 665, 678
Sweeney, Mary, 257, 378–81, 405, 414, 429, 437, 458–60, 462–63, 465, 466, 467, 468, 474, 475, 476, 481, 486, 487, 495, 497, 503, 510, 519, 525, 535, 638, 639, 644–46, 648–50, 654, 656, 660, 662–63, 666, 667–68, 706

Tamblyn, Russ, 267, 291
Tati, Jacques, 146, 645, 646, 649
The Terrors of Basket-Weaving, 46
Thackeray, William Makepeace, 133
Theroux, Justin, 543, 670
The Thing, 8
Thoreau, Henry David, 48
Tolkien, J. R. R., 134
Towne, Katherine, 546
Transcendental Meditation, 50, 69, 72, 88, 90, 145, 189, 257, 311, 428, 464, 517, 520, 524, 591, 613, 630, 656, 658-61, 665–67, 669, 677
Treves, Sir Frederick, 106
Tucker, Chris, 109, 110, 112
Twin Peaks (TV): ABC greenlights, 269; animalism, 283–84; atmospheric disturbance, 355; balance of known/unknown, 358–59; Bravo channel broadcasts series, 427–28; changes for characters in, 349–50; colors, 272, 276, 282, 291–92; complete series, 8–678 (passim); doubling, 272, 283, 354–57; dread and desire, 281–72; dreams, 291–93; electricity, 291; Emmy awards token win, 346; episode one different from pilot episode, 286; extended community extreme grieving in, 273–74;

extraterrestrial activity in, 352–53; extreme violence for network TV in, 356; favors number seven, 493; fire, 272, 348; Mark Frost on abandoned storyline of, 364; Mark Frost and creation in Windom Earle, 359; Mark Frost on legacy of, 363–64; Mark Frost literary leanings, 287; Mark Frost on Lynch, 296, 365–66; Mark Frost on potential third season plot threads, 365; Mark Frost on season-ending cliffhanger, 298; galvanizes popular culture, 293; genesis of, 267–68; hellish repetition, 355; history of detective fiction in, 281; humor in, 283–84; infectious evil, 350; lurking menace, 351; Lynch collaboration 295–96, 359; Lynch ends season/series his way, 360; Lynch and Frost envision first image of, 266; Lynch and Frost's contributions to who is author, 270–71; Lynch known to millions worldwide, 341; Lynch leaves to make *Wild at Heart*, 298; Lynch on legacy of, 363; Lynch's sensibility experienced by millions of TV viewers, 285–86; Lynch's son, Austin, in, 353; Lynch's state of world at millennium, 458–59, 497–98; Lynch's sympathy for Tibet's plight in, 290, 352; Lynchian opening images of, 271–72; the magician longs to see in, 353; Northwest milieu of, 268; Northwest viewers respond to series, 298–99; "Now it's dark," 282; numerology, 286; oracle figure, 287–88, 348–49; Harley Peyton on Lynch's series participation, 296–97; pre-launch critical ecstasy over, 270; reality as circle, 272; related to film *Peyton Place*, 266–67; season one, 266–301 (primary reference); season two, 348–66 (primary reference); and the Seattle/Northwest zeitgeist, 346–47; secrets, 276; sexual innuendo in, 289–90; specialness of, 300–1; time and space are slippery, 361; time stretching, 273, 348; viewers, 357, 363; visions, 350; water, 272; yin-yang, 286-87

Twin Peaks: Fire Walk With Me, 366–98 (primary reference), 33–660 (passim); angels, 393; author encounters BOB in the flesh, 375–76; beneath the surface, 385; blue rose cases in, 368, 383, 393; box office (poor), 397–98; coded knowledge, 383; colors, 381–82; critics attack film and Lynch, 395–96; detectives, 386; electricity, 381–82; filming big scene that didn't make final cut, 373–74; filming Bobby and Laura high in the woods, 375–76; filming Laura and James's last emotional scene, 376-77; filming road house night scene, 373; garmonbozia in, 384, 391; homosexual evil, 388; ill-received at Cannes Film Festival, 378–79; incest, 387; intensely emotional scene in, 371–72; Jeffries' convenience store vision, 384; Sheryl Lee screams before camera rolls in, 372; Sheryl Lee on playing Laura in, 371; Lynch and company return to Northwest to shoot film, 366–67; Lynch directs Ray Wise in, 372; Lynch erases 1990 from, 369; Lynch films trailer park scene of, 368; Lynch incorporates local woman into, 370; Lynch gives entertaining introduction at premiere, 380–81; Lynch returns to core *Twin Peaks* story, 366; Lynch and Mary Sweeney, 378–80;

Kyle MacLachlan's participation in, 396–97; Kyle MacLachlan and Lynch distancing over, 397; Laura Palmer, 385, 388–89, 390, 391; as prequel and sequel, 383–84; production comraderie, 370; related to *Wizard of Oz*, 392; *Secret Diary of Laura Palmer*, 46, 91, 341, 388, 389, 390, 416; series cancelled, but Lynch inspired to make film of, 366; Al Strobel defends film, 396; the third eye, 385; time and space are slippery, 383–84; visions, 384; yin-yang, 385
Twin Peaks Festival, 370, 429, 431, 657, 665
Tworkov, Jack, 31

Ullmann, Liv, 523, 558
Ulmer, Edgar G., 452
Unger, Deborah, 410
The Upanishads, 672
Updike, John, 482

Van Dyke, Jerry, 430
Van Dyke, Kelly, 430–31
van Gogh, Vincent, 16, 235
Venus Descending (unproduced film), 265
Vietnam, 23, 51, 65, 210, 217, 250, 310, 332, 458
Vinton, Bobby, 201, 209, 220, 248, 552
von Sydow, Max, 158, 160

Wagner, Natasha Gregson, 443
Wajda, Andrzej, 258
Walters, Tracey, 258–59, 403
Warhol, Andy, 86, 239, 254, 657
Wasserman, H. Barton, 33–34, 35, 39
Watts, Naomi, 526–27, 556, 564, 565, 567–69, 571–72, 578–80, 583, 585, 586, 590, 592–600, 619, 626, 634, 641
Wayne, John, 181
Webb, Anastasia, 472
Westerman, Judy, 17
White, Richard, 41, 47
Whitman, Walt, 70, 74, 75, 79, 137, 210, 339, 482
Wiene, Robert, 49
Wild at Heart (book), 305–9
Wild at Heart (film), 299–343 (primary reference), 5–663 (passim); authoritarian control, 320; and American society's devolution, 308–9; attacks on, 343; bad mother, 319; balance of light and dark, 314; book on Lynch's wavelength, 305–6; book reflects amusing/dangerous American craziness, 307–8; book summary, 305; border violation, 319; Cage relates his Sailor to Elvis Presley, 313, 339; wins Cannes Film Festival Palm d'Or, 339–40; circuit, 330; Laura Dern's *Wild at Heart* and *Blue Velvet* characters compared, 310–11; Laura Dern responds to Lula's sexy innocence, 311, 312; Laura Dern acts with her mother in, 311; dualities, 326; freedom of the road in, 320, 321; Barry Gifford responds to Lynch's film, 313–14; head invasion, 331; headcentric, 316, 327, 330; homosexuality, 337; influences on other directors' films, 343; Lynch book's ending changed, 336–37; Lynch and cool, hip style, 303–304; Lynch death scene not in book added, 334; Lynch film opens with scene not in book, 315; Lynch Johnny's death in, 328–29; Lynch scene altered because of test-audience reaction, 329–30; Lynch scene reworked to get R rating, 315–16, 342; "Now it's dark," 328;

painting with sex, 322–23; generates strong positive and negative reaction, 342–43; Bobby Peru in, 331–32; the power of love, 338–39; related to *Chinatown*, 334; related to *Wizard of Oz*, 318–19, 323, 337, 338; secret of, 325; sex, 317, 319, 323, 328–29, 330; snakeskin jacket in, 321; a key triangle in, 317–18; violence, 315–16, 317
Wilder, Billy, 53, 213, 335, 497, 499–500, 528–29, 540, 602, 637, 674
Wilder, Thornton, 213
Williams, Tennessee, 311, 321, 648
Wingert, Sally, 477
Wise, Ray, 268, 274
Witt, Alicia, 158, 410, 412
Wood, Natalie, 443, 444
Worden, Hank, 348
"The World Spins" (song), 137, 253, 346
Wright, Lloyd, 459

Yogananda, Paramahansa, 520, 560
Young, Sean, 158, 174
You Play the Black and the Red Comes Up (book), 561, 675

Zabriske, Grace, 274, 289, 300, 329, 672, 674–75
Zane, Billy, 358
Zelly and Me (film), 255–58
Zwigoff, Terry, 429

ABOUT THE AUTHOR

Greg Olson is the film curator of the Seattle Art Museum. He has written on film for several publications including *The Seattle Times, Moviemaker, Premiere*, and *Film Comment*. He has contributed to the books *Vietnam War Films* and *Contemporary Literary Criticism*. He is a board member of the Film Noir Foundation and a juror for the American Film Institute's annual *100 Years . . . 100 Movies* television programs.